PRIVATE JUSTICE: THE LAW OF ALTERNATIVE DISPUTE RESOLUTION

by

KATHERINE V.W. STONE
Professor of Law
Cornell Law School

NEW YORK, NEW YORK
FOUNDATION PRESS
2000

 TEXT IS PRINTED ON 10% POST
CONSUMER RECYCLED PAPER

PREFACE

Alternative dispute resolution has become a dynamic area of legal practice. Individuals and institutions are increasingly using arbitration, mediation, and other alternative mechanisms to resolve disputes that grow out of private transactions. Arbitration clauses now appear in many residential leases, medical informed consent forms, banking and credit card agreements, attorney-client fee agreements, health maintenance organization agreements, and residential housing association charters. Similarly, many consumer, commercial, employment and family law disputes are routinely submitted to mediation in lieu of litigation. And many states have amended their rules of civil procedure to impose court-ordered arbitration and/or mediation as a mandatory step in civil litigation.

The increased use of alternative dispute resolution ("ADR") has given rise to a multitude of controversies. In the past decade, countless cases have been brought in federal and state courts concerning the Federal Arbitration Act, mediation, ombudsmen, and other forms of ADR. In addition, state bar associations and professional organizations of ADR providers have promulgated new ethical standards and codes of conduct for mediators and arbitrators. Several state bar associations have ethical rules that require attorneys to inform their clients about the possibilities of alternative dispute resolution when they give legal advice. At the same time, private mediation, arbitration, mini-trials, third-party evaluation and other such techniques have become necessary staples in the toolbox of practicing litigators. Knowledge about the law of alternative dispute resolution is quickly becoming indispensable to legal practice in the fields of commercial law, securities law, antitrust, labor and employment law, family law, real estate, medical malpractice, insurance law, and international business transactions. Any student preparing for a career in civil litigation needs to understand the legal rules governing the use of private mechanisms for resolving disputes both because they are implicated directly in many civil lawsuits today, and because they delineate the possibilities and limits of utilizing ADR when structuring transactions.

This book addresses the legal issues posed by the growing use of ADR within the legal system. Despite the recent expansion of the role of ADR in the practice of law, the legal issues concerning ADR are often neglected in standard ADR courses and, indeed, in the rest of the law school curriculum. Most casebooks in the ADR field are tailored to courses that teach the techniques and goals of mediation or arbitration, rather than the legal issues that frame the practice of ADR. *Private Justice: Alternative Dispute Resolution and the Law* fills this void in the law school curriculum. It focuses on the legal rules that govern each type of alternative dispute resolution mechanism and that define how each fits into our legal system.

Taken together, the legal doctrines that pertain to the use of ADR within the civil justice system define the boundary between the public judicial system—a system which attempts to implement societal norms of due process—and private judicial systems—systems which attempt to effectuate the parties' consent. That boundary is in constant flux. Doctrines that govern such issues as the enforceability of agreements to arbitration, the standard of review for arbitration awards, the extent to which mediators enjoy a privilege from testifying and immunity from liability, the right of a party to cross examine a third party fact-finder, and a host of others map the scope for private judicial systems within our legal system. They define the extent to which private parties can exempt themselves from the legal system and the extent to which public norms are brought into the world of private dispute resolution. The precise location of this boundary and the ways in which it fluctuates are matters of great practical importance to many fields of practice. The boundary is also intensely political—it delineates the extent to which public norms of fairness shall govern transactions and disputes between private parties.

This book is the product of a seven year effort to which many people have contributed. I am particularly indebted to two former students, Alex Colvin and Phil Hostak, who have been deeply involved at every stage, providing suggestions, insights, and perspectives that have enriched the project immeasurably. My law students at Cornell Law School and Stanford Law School have provided a laboratory in which to try out the materials and experiment with approaches. Several remarkably skillful research assistants have worked with me, including Walter Buble, Audrey Ellis, Robert Fisher, Jennifer Illingsworth, Christopher McRorie, Jared Nagley, and Alan Story. In addition, I am grateful to my colleagues Greg Alexander, Kevin Clermont, Ted Eisenberg, Martha Fineman, Bob Hillman, Susan Koniak, Judith Meyer, Bill Simon, Charles Wolfram, and numerous others who have served as sounding boards, gentle critics, and sources of inspiration. I want to extend special thanks to my assistant, Jack Glezen, who helped in the arduous and tedious task of preparing the manuscript, always with great diligence, professionalism, and good spirit. I am also grateful to Cornell Law School for generously providing me with the resources and time I needed to complete this project. And finally and most importantly, I thank my husband, Matthew Drennan, who has given me love, support, encouragement, and advice at every step of the way.

November, 1999

ACKNOWLEDGEMENTS

Foundation Press and the author gratefully acknowledge the authors and publishers that permitted us to reprint excerpts of copyrighted works. They are:

Abel, Richard L., *The Contradictions of Informal Justice, in* 1 THE POLITICS OF INFORMAL JUSTICE 267 (1982). Permission granted by Academic Press, Inc.; Richard L. Abel, University of California at Los Angeles School of Law.

American Arbitration Association, *Commercial Arbitration Rules.* Permission granted by the American Arbitration A ssociation.

Auerbach, Jerold S., JUSTICE WITHOUT LAW? (1983), pages 4-6. Permission granted by Oxford University Press.

Bernstein, Lisa, *Understanding the Limits of Court-Connected ADR: A Critique of Federal Court-Annexed Arbitration Programs,* 141 U. Pa. L. Rev. 2169 (1993). Permission granted by Lisa E. Bernstein, University of Chicago Law School.

Bryan, Penelope E., *Killing Us Softly: Divorce Mediation and the Politics of Power,* 40 Buff. L.Rev. 443 (1992). Permission granted by Buffalo Law Review.

Robert A. Baruch Bush, *Efficiency and Protection, or Empowerment and Recognition? The Mediator's Role and Ethical Standards in Mediation,* 41 Florida L. Rev. 253 (1989). Permission granted by Robert A. Baruch Bush, Hofstra Univ. School of Law.

Coffee, John C., Jr., *The Corruption of the Class Action: The New Technology of Collusion,* 80 Cornell L. Rev. 851 (1995). Permission granted by Cornell Law Review.

Edwards, Harry T., *Alternative Dispute Resolution: Panacea or Anathema,* 99 Harv. L. Rev. 668 (1986). Permission granted by Hon. Harry T. Edwards, United States Court of Appeals for the District of Columbia Circuit; Harvard Law Review.

Fineman, Martha, *Dominant Discourse, Professional Language, and Legal Change in Child Custody Desisionmaking,* 101 Harv. L. Rev. 727 (1988). Permission granted by Martha Fineman, Cornell Law School.

Fiss, Owen M., *Against Settlement*, 93 Yale L.J. 1073-1090 (1984). Reprinted by permission of The Yale Law Journal Company and Fred B. Rothman & Company.

Fiss, Owen M., *Out of Eden*, 94 Yale L.J. 1669-1673 (1985). Reprinted by permission of the Yale Law Journal and Fred B. Rothman & Company.

Fuller, Lon L., *Mediation—Its Forms and Functions*, 44 S. Cal L. Rev. 305 (1971). Permission granted by Southern California Law Review.

Galanter, Marc S., *Reading the Landscape of Disputes: What We Know and Don't Know (and Think We Know) About Our Allegedly Contentious and Litigious Society*, 31 UCLA L. Rev 4 (1983). Permission granted by Marc S. Galanter, University of Wisconsin School of Law.

Galanter, Marc S., *Why the "Haves" Come Out Ahead: Speculations on the Limits of Legal Change*, 1974 Law & Soc. Rev. 95 (1974). Permission granted by Marc S. Galanter, Univ. of Wisconsin School of Law.

Grillo, Trina, *The Mediation Alternative: Process Dangers for Women*, 100 Yale L. J. 1545 (1991). Reprinted by permission of The Yale Law Journal Company and Fred B. Rothman & Company.

Kanowitz, Leo, ALTERNATIVE DISPUTE RESOLUTION (CASES AND MATERIALS), (West, 1985). Permission granted by West Group.

Korhauser, Lewis, *Bargaining in the Shadow of Law*, 88 Yale L.J. 950 (1979). Reprinted by permission of The Yale Law Journal Company and Fred B. Rothman & Company.

Kovach, Kimberlee K., *Dissection of the Mediation Press*, MEDIATION: PRINCIPLES AND PRACTICE (West, 1994). Permission granted by West Group.

McThenia, Andrew W., *For Reconciliation*, 94 Yale L.J. 1660-1668 (1985), Reprinted by permission of The Yale Law Journal Company and Fred B. Rothman & Company.

Menkel–Meadow, Carrie, *For and Against Settlement: Uses and Abuses of the Mandatory Settlement Conference*, 33 UCLA L. Rev. 485 (1985). Reprinted by permission of Carrie Menkel–Meadow, Georgetown Law School.

Mnookin, Robert H., *Bargaining in the Shadow of Law*, 88 Yale L.J. 950-997 (1979). Reprinted by permission of The Yale Law Journal Company and Fred B. Rothman & Company.

Nader, Laura, *Controlling Processes in the Practice of Law: Hierarchy and Pacification in the Movement to Re-Form Dispute Ideology*, 9 Ohio St. J. on Disp. Resol. 1 (1993). Permission granted by Laura Nader, Dept. of Anthropology, Univ. of California, Berkeley.

National Institute for Dispute Resolution, *Report of the Ad Hoc Panel on Dispute Resolution and Public Policy* (1983). Permission granted by National Institute for Dispute Resolution.

Resnik, Judith, *Managerial Judges*, 96 Harv. L. Rev. 374 (1982). Permission granted by Professor Judith Resnik, Yale Law School; Harvard Law Review.

Resnik, Judith, *Many Doors? Closing Doors? Alternative Dispute Resolution and Adjudication*, 10 Ohio St. J. on Disp. Resol. 211 (1995). Permission granted by Judith Resnik, Yale Law School.

Shaffer, Thomas, *For Reconciliation*, 94 Yale L.J. 1660-1668 (1985). Reprinted by permission of The Yale Law Journal Company and Fred B. Rothman & Company.

Singer, Linda A., *The Ombudsman*, in Settling Disputes (Westview Press, 1990). Permission granted by Perseus Books Group.

Sochynsky, Yaroslav, *Mediation: A Guide for Practitioners*, in California ADR Practice Guide (The American Law Institute, 1996). Permission granted by Lexis Publishing Co.

*

SUMMARY OF CONTENTS

PREFACE iii

ACKNOWLEDGEMENTS v

TABLE OF CASES xxi

CHAPTER ONE. Introduction to Alternative Dispute Resolution 1

1. The Critique of the Legal System and the Growth of ADR 2
2. Description of Alternative Dispute Resolution 5
3. History of Alternative Dispute Resolution in the United States 10
4. The Definition of Disputes 12
5. The Role of ADR in Redefining Disputes 19
6. Critical Perspectives on Alternative Dispute Resolution 21
7. Questions 32

CHAPTER TWO. Mediation 33

1. Introduction to Mediation 33
2. Legal Effect of an Agreement to Mediate 50
3. Confidentiality in Mediation 59
4. Compelling Mediators to Testify 83
5. Mediator Liability for Negligence 97
6. Professional Responsibility Issues in Mediation 112
7. Critical Perspectives on Mediation in Family Law 129

CHAPTER THREE. Third Party Evaluation, Fact–Finding, and Ombudsmen 144

1. Introduction 144
2. Legal Effect of Agreement to Utilize Third–Party Evaluator 147
3. Legal Status of Fact–Finding Report 152
4. Right to Cross–Examine a Third Party Evaluator 159
5. Ombudsmen and Privilege 165

CHAPTER FOUR. Settlement 176

1. Introduction 176
2. Perspectives on Settlement 176
3. Interpreting Settlement Agreements 191
4. The Public Stake in Settlement Agreements 197
5. Settling Class Actions 204

CHAPTER FIVE. Arbitration I: The Agreement to Arbitrate 303

1. Introduction 303
2. State Versus Federal Law 325

3. Enforceability of Agreements to Arbitrate ----------------------------- 378
4. Arbitration Under the Labor Management Relations Act—An
   Alternative Statutory Framework ----------------------------- 456

CHAPTER SIX. Arbitration II: Defenses to Arbitration ------- 482

1. Arbitrability --- 484
2. Fraud in the Inducement -- 505
3. Adhesion Contracts, Duress and Unconscionability --------------------- 516
4. State Consumer Protection Law -- 545
5. Public Interest -- 563
6. Contracts of Employment --- 570
7. Successors and Assigns --- 597

**CHAPTER SEVEN. Arbitration III: Due Process, Remedies,
   and Judicial Review** --- 602

1. Introduction -- 602
2. Notice, Ex Parte Hearings, and Default ------------------------------- 603
3. Right to an Evidentiary Hearing -------------------------------------- 616
4. Right to Counsel -- 625
5. Provisional Remedies -- 629
6. Discovery --- 651
7. Evidence -- 672
8. Confidentiality of Arbitral Transcripts ----------------------------- 687
9. Arbitral Bias and Misconduct -- 689
10. Arbitrator Immunity and Testimony ---------------------------------- 715
11. Standard of Review of Arbitral Awards ------------------------------ 727
12. Remedies in Arbitration -- 774
13. Arbitral Awards and Claim Preclusion ------------------------------ 790

**CHAPTER EIGHT. Alternative Dispute Resolution Within
   the State and Federal Courts** --------------------------------------- 799

1. Introduction -- 799
2. Small Claims Courts --- 800
3. Court–Annexed Arbitration -- 819
4. Court–Ordered Mediation -- 855
5. Perspectives on Court–Ordered Mediation ----------------------------- 865
6. Court–Induced Settlement --- 871
7. Perspectives on Settlement Conferences ------------------------------ 890
8. Summary Jury Trials --- 898
9. Perspectives on the Role of Court–Connected ADR in Civil Litigation --- 909

APPENDICES --- 913
INDEX --- 955

TABLE OF CONTENTS

PREFACE... iii
ACKNOWLEDGEMENTS v
TABLE OF CASES xxi

CHAPTER ONE.   Introduction to Alternative Dispute Resolution. 1

1. The Critique of the Legal System and the Growth of ADR............. 2
2. Description of Alternative Dispute Resolution 5
   Report of the Ad Hoc Panel on Dispute Resolution and Public
      Policy, Appendix 2 5
   *Many Doors? Closing Doors? Alternative Dispute Resolution and
      Adjudication* by Judith Resnik 9
3. History of Alternative Dispute Resolution in the United States..... 10
   JUSTICE WITHOUT LAW? by Jerold S. Auerbach 10
4. The Definition of Disputes.. 12
   *Reading the Landscape of Disputes: What We Know and Don't
      Know (And Think We Know) about Our Allegedly Contentious
      and Litigious Society* by Marc S. Galanter 13
5. The Role of ADR in Redefining Disputes................................. 19
   *Efficiency and Protection, or Empowerment and Recognition? The
      Mediator's Role and Ethical Standards in Mediation* by Robert
      A. Baruch Bush.. 20
6. Critical Perspectives on Alternative Dispute Resolution 21
   Alternative Dispute Resolution: Panacea or Anathema? by Harry
      T. Edwards... 22
   The Contradictions of Informal Justice by Rick Abel................. 25
   *Controlling Processes in the Practice of Law: Hierarchy and
      Pacification in the Movement to Re-form Dispute Ideology* by
      Laura Nader.. 28
7. Questions... 32

CHAPTER TWO. Mediation. 33

1. Introduction to Mediation.. 33
   A.   Description of Mediation 33
   B.   The Mediation Process.. 35
        Dissection of the Mediation Process by Kimberlee K. Kovach 35
        Mediation—A Guide for Practitioners by Yaroslav Sochyn-
           sky, Esq. 37
   C.   The Role of the Mediator... 41
        The Role of the Mediator by Yaroslav Sochynsky, Esq. 41
   D.   Two Views of Disputes and How They Are Resolved............... 44
   E.   The Distinctive Advantages of Mediation........................... 46
        Mediation—Its Forms and Functions by Lon L. Fuller.......... 46
   F.   Questions.. 49

2. Legal Effect of an Agreement to Mediate -------------------- 50
    DeValk Lincoln Mercury, Inc. v. Ford Motor Company ----------- 50
    Questions-- 57
    Kirschenman v. Superior Court of Contra Costa County --------- 57
    Questions-- 59
3. Confidentiality in Mediation -------------------------------- 59
    A.   Confidentiality by Contract ---------------------------- 60
         Questions--- 62
    B.   Confidentiality under the Rules of Evidence------------- 63
    C.   A Mediation Privilege --------------------------------- 64
         Harry H. Hudson v. Gloria P. Hudson------------------- 66
         John R. McKinlay v. Louise R. McKinlay --------------- 68
         Questions--- 73
         Note on *Folb v. Motion Picture Industry Pension & Health
            Plans* --- 73
         Question-- 75
         Snyder–Falkinham v. Stockburger---------------------- 75
         Questions--- 82
4. Compelling Mediators to Testify----------------------------- 83
    State of Florida v. Castellano ----------------------------- 83
    The People of the State of New York v. George Snyder -------- 84
    Andrew L. Smith v. Clayton J. Smith, et al. ---------------- 87
    Questions-- 97
5. Mediator Liability for Negligence--------------------------- 97
    Elizabeth P. Lange v. Richard M. Marshall ------------------ 97
    Questions--- 100
    Vickie Howard v. Robin Drapkin --------------------------- 101
    Questions--- 111
6. Professional Responsibility Issues in Mediation ------------- 112
    A.   Unauthorized Practice of Law-------------------------- 112
         Michael Werle d/b/a Werle Consultants Family Mediation
            Center v. Rhode Island Bar Association-------------- 112
         New Jersey Ethics Opinion, Number 676 Alternative Dis-
            pute Resolution ----------------------------------- 117
         Questions--- 121
    B.   Conflict of Interest --------------------------------- 121
         McKenzie Construction v. St. Croix Storage Corporation ------ 121
         Questions--- 128
7. Critical Perspectives on Mediation in Family Law ------------ 129
    A.   Mediation in Divorce Negotiations--------------------- 129
         *Killing Us Softly: Divorce Mediation and the Politics of
            Power* by Penelope E. Bryan ----------------------- 129
    B.   Mediation in Child Custody Disputes ------------------ 133
         *Dominant Discourse, Professional Language, and Legal
            Change in Child Custody Decisionmaking* by Martha Fine-
            man -- 133

**CHAPTER THREE.   Third Party Evaluation, Fact–Finding,
    and Ombudsmen.** -------------------------------------- 144

1. Introduction -- 144
    Factfinding by Leo Kanowitz ----------------------------- 144

The Ombudsman by Linda Singer --- 146
2. Legal Effect of Agreement to Utilize Third–Party Evaluator --------- 147
   AMF Incorporated v. Brunswick Corporation ----------------------- 147
   Questions -- 152
3. Legal Status of Fact–Finding Report ------------------------------- 152
   Jeffery v. Weintraub -- 152
   Questions -- 158
4. Right to Cross–Examine a Third Party Evaluator ------------------- 159
   McLaughlin v. Superior Court of the County of San Mateo --------- 159
   Questions -- 165
5. Ombudsmen and Privilege --- 165
   Garstang v. Superior Court of Los Angeles County and California
      Institute of Technology --------------------------------------- 165
   Carman v. McDonnell Douglas Corporation ----------------------- 172
   Questions -- 175

CHAPTER FOUR. Settlement. ----------------------------------- 176

1. Introduction -- 176
2. Perspectives on Settlement --------------------------------------- 176
   A. Fiss on *Against Settlement* ------------------------------------ 176
   B. McThenia and Shaffer on *For Reconciliation* ----------------- 183
   C. Fiss Responds --- 185
   D. The Debate Revisited -- 187
   E. Settlement in the Shadow of the Law ------------------------- 188
       Questions -- 191
3. Interpreting Settlement Agreements ------------------------------ 191
   Press Machinery Corporation v. Smith R.P.M. Corporation --------- 191
   Questions -- 195
4. The Public Stake in Settlement Agreements ----------------------- 197
   United States v. Bechtel Corporation ------------------------------ 197
   Questions -- 203
5. Settling Class Actions -- 204
   A. Fairness and Adequacy of Review ----------------------------- 206
       Parker v. Anderson -- 206
       Questions --- 214
       J.A. Shults, et al. v. Champion Int'l Corp. ------------------ 215
       Questions --- 220
   B. Claim Preclusion --- 220
       Martin v. Wilks -- 220
       Questions --- 227
   C. Special Problems of Settlement Classes --------------------- 228
       In re Baldwin–United Corporation --------------------------- 228
       Questions --- 238
       In re Silicone Gel Breast Implant Products Liability Litiga-
          tion --- 238
       Questions --- 253
       Amchem Products, Inc., et al. v. Windsor, et al. ----------- 255
       Manual for Complex Litigation, Third ----------------------- 280
       *The Corruption of the Class Action: The New Technology of
          Collusion* by John C. Coffee ---------------------------- 285

Questions -- 289
Note on *Ortiz v. Fibreboard Corp.* and Limited Fund Class
    Actions -- 291
Questions -- 294
Stacey A. Williams, et al. v. General Electric Capital Auto
    Lease, Inc. -- 295
Questions -- 301

CHAPTER FIVE. Arbitration I: The Agreement to Arbitrate. -- 303

1. Introduction -- 303
   A.   Historical Background ------------------------------------ 305
     Tobey v. County of Bristol ------------------------------------ 306
     Questions -- 308
   B.   The New York Arbitration Act of 1920 --------------- 308
     Justice Without Law by Jerold S. Auerbach ------------ 309
     Questions -- 312
   C.   The Federal Arbitration Act of 1925 ------------------ 312
     Questions -- 315
     Kulukundis Shipping Co., S/A v. Amtorg Trading Corporation -- 316
     Questions -- 324
2. State Versus Federal Law -- 325
   Bernhardt v. Polygraphic Company of America, Inc. ---------- 325
   Questions -- 332
   Southland Corporation v. Keating ---------------------------------- 332
   Questions -- 348
   Note on *Perry v. Thomas* --------------------------------------- 349
   Questions -- 351
   Volt Information Sciences, Inc. v. Board of Trustees of Stanford
     University -- 351
   Questions -- 361
   Allied–Bruce Terminix Companies, Inc., et. al. v. G. Michael
     Dobson, et. al. -- 362
   Note on *United States v. Lopez* -------------------------------- 376
   Questions -- 377
3. Enforceability of Agreements to Arbitrate ----------------------- 378
   Wilko v. Swan -- 379
   Questions -- 384
   Dean Witter Reynolds, Inc. v. Byrd ------------------------------ 385
   Questions -- 391
   Scherk v. Alberto–Culver Co. -------------------------------------- 392
   Questions -- 400
   Mitsubishi Motors Corp. v. Soler Chrysler–Plymouth, Inc. ---- 401
   Questions -- 419
   Shearson/American Express, Inc. v. McMahon ------------------ 420
   Questions -- 438
   Rodriguez De Quijas v. Shearson/American Express, Inc. ---- 438
   Questions -- 443
   Gilmer v. Interstate/Johnson Lane Corp. -------------------------- 443
   Questions -- 455

4. Arbitration Under the Labor Management Relations Act—An
    Alternative Statutory Framework 456
    Textile Workers Union of America v. Lincoln Mills of Alabama 457
    Questions 465
    Note on *Local 174, Teamsters v. Lucas Flour Company* 466
    Questions 468
    United Steelworkers of America v. American Manufacturing Co. 469
    Questions 471
    United Steelworkers of America v. Warrior and Gulf Navigation
    Co. 472
    Questions 480

CHAPTER SIX. Arbitration II: Defenses to Arbitration. 482

1. Arbitrability 484
    Country Mutual Insurance Company v. Kosmos 484
    Questions 485
    John V. Bowmer v. Dorothy B. Bowmer 486
    Questions 492
    Moses H. Cone Memorial Hospital v. Mercury Construction Corp. .. 493
    Questions 498
    First Options of Chicago, Inc. v. Kaplan 499
    Questions 505
2. Fraud in the Inducement 505
    Ericksen v. 100 Oak Street 505
    Note on *Prima Paint v. Flood & Conklin* 514
    Questions 516
3. Adhesion Contracts, Duress and Unconscionability 516
    Graham v. Scissor–Tail, Inc. 516
    Questions 528
    Hope v. Superior Court of the County of Santa Clara 528
    Questions 533
    Broemmer v. Abortion Services of Phoenix, Ltd. 533
    Questions 542
    Note on Consent in Consumer Arbitration 542
4. State Consumer Protection Law 545
    Casarotto v. Lombardi and Doctor's Associates, Inc. 545
    Questions 558
    Doctor's Associates, Inc. v. Casarotto 558
    Questions 563
5. Public Interest 563
    Faherty v. Faherty 563
    Questions 569
6. Contracts of Employment 570
    Tenney Engineering, Inc. v. United Electrical Radio & Machine
    Workers of America, (U.E.) Local 437 570
    Questions 576
    Craft v. Campbell Soup Company 577
    Question 585
    Note on Employment Arbitration 585
    Prudential Insurance Co. of America v. Lai 585
    Questions 590

Pony Express Courier Corp. v. Morris ------------------------------ 590
Questions --- 593
Note on Unconscionability in Employment Arbitration Agreements --- 594
Questions --- 597
7. Successors and Assigns -- 597
Kaufman v. William Iselin & Co. --------------------------------- 597
Questions --- 600
Note on Assignment of Obligation to Arbitrate ------------------- 600
Question -- 601

CHAPTER SEVEN. Arbitration III: Due Process, Remedies, and Judicial Review. --- 602

1. Introduction --- 602
2. Notice, Ex Parte Hearings, and Default ----------------------- 603
Gingiss International, Inc. v. Norman E. Bormet ------------------ 603
Amalgamated Cotton Garment & Allied Industries Fund v. J.B.C. Company of Madera, Inc. -- 607
Questions --- 611
Waterspring, S.A. and Trans Marketing Houston Inc. ------------- 611
Questions --- 616
3. Right to an Evidentiary Hearing ------------------------------ 616
Federal Deposit Insurance Corporation v. Air Florida System, Inc. 616
Casualty Indemnity Exchange v. Jack Yother ---------------------- 619
Questions --- 624
4. Right to Counsel --- 625
Mikel v. Scharf --- 625
Outdoor Services, Inc. v. Pabagold, Inc. ------------------------ 626
Questions --- 629
5. Provisional Remedies --- 629
Merrill Lynch, Pierce, Fenner & Smith, Inc. v. Hovey ------------ 629
Merrill Lynch, Pierce, Fenner & Smith, Inc. v. Bradley ---------- 634
Note on Criteria for Imposing Provisional Remedies Pending Arbitration --- 639
Performance Unlimited, Inc. v. Questar Publishers, Inc. --------- 640
Questions --- 650
6. Discovery -- 651
Mississippi Power Company v. Peabody Coal Company --------------- 651
Recognition Equipment, Inc. v. NCR Corporation ----------------- 656
Questions --- 660
Meadows Indemnity Company, Ltd. v. Nutmeg Insurance Co. -------- 660
Integrity Insurance Co. v. American Centennial Insurance Co. ---- 663
Questions --- 668
Golub v. Spivey --- 668
Questions --- 672
7. Evidence --- 672
Totem Marine Tug & Barge, Inc. v. North American Towing, Inc. -- 672
Questions --- 676
Michael and Mary Smaligo, Administrators of the Estate of Elizabeth Smaligo, Deceased v. Fireman's Fund Insurance Company 676
Questions --- 680

Note on *Robins v. Day* ---- 680
Bonar v. Dean Witter Reynolds, Inc. ---- 681
Questions ---- 687
8. Confidentiality of Arbitral Transcripts ---- 687
Industrotech Constructors, Inc. v. Duke University ---- 687
Questions ---- 689
9. Arbitral Bias and Misconduct ---- 689
Commonwealth Coatings Corp. v. Continental Casualty Co. ---- 689
Questions ---- 694
Merit Insurance Company v. Leatherby Insurance Company ---- 695
Questions ---- 704
Morris v. Metriyakool ---- 705
Questions ---- 714
10. Arbitrator Immunity and Testimony ---- 715
Corey v. New York Stock Exchange ---- 715
Note on *Baar v. Tigerman* ---- 721
Questions ---- 723
Legion Insurance Company v. Insurance General Agency, Inc. ---- 723
Questions ---- 726
11. Standard of Review of Arbitral Awards ---- 727
    A.   Judicial Review Under Section 301 of the Labor Management Relations Act ---- 727
        United Steelworkers of America v. Enterprise Wheel and Car Corp. ---- 727
        Questions ---- 729
        United Paperworkers International Union v. Misco, Inc. ---- 730
        Questions ---- 735
    B.   Judicial Review Under the Federal Arbitration Act ---- 735
        Sobel v. Hertz, Warner & Co. ---- 735
        Questions ---- 740
        Swift Industries, Inc. v. Botany Industries, Inc. ---- 741
        Questions ---- 748
        Quick & Reilly, Inc. v. Jacobson ---- 749
        Questions ---- 753
        Moncharsh v. Heily & Blase ---- 753
        Questions ---- 770
        Note on Modification of Arbitral Awards and the Doctrine of *Functus Officio* ---- 771
        Questions ---- 773
12. Remedies in Arbitration ---- 774
Garrity v. Lyle Stuart, Inc. ---- 774
Antonio Mastrobuono and Diana G. Mastrobuono v. Shearson Lehman Hutton, Inc. ---- 780
Questions ---- 789
13. Arbitral Awards and Claim Preclusion ---- 790
Vazquez v. Aetna Casualty & Surety Company ---- 790
Note on *McDonald v. City of West Branch* ---- 796
Questions ---- 798

CHAPTER EIGHT. Alternative Dispute Resolution Within the State and Federal Courts. -- 799

1. Introduction --- 799
2. Small Claims Courts -- 800
   City and County of San Francisco v. Small Claims Court ------------- 803
   Questions --- 809
   Bruno v. Superior Court of the City and County of San Francisco; Gridley, Real Party in Interest ----------------------------------- 810
   Houghtaling v. Superior Court for the County of San Bernardino; Rossi, Real Party in Interest -- 813
   Questions --- 819
3. Court–Annexed Arbitration -- 819
   A. Description of Court–Annexed Arbitration ----------------------- 819
      Understanding the Limits of Court–Connected ADR: A Critique of Federal Court–Annexed Arbitration Programs by Lisa Bernstein --- 819
   B. Constitutionality -- 822
      Firelock, Inc. v. District Court in the State of Colorado -------- 822
      Questions -- 833
   C. Good Faith Participation -- 835
      Employer's Consortium, Inc. v. Aaron --------------------------- 835
      Questions -- 839
      State Farm Insurance Co. v. Kazakova -------------------------- 840
      Questions -- 843
   D. Finality of Awards --- 843
      Flynn v. Gorton --- 843
      Question --- 847
      Habick v. Liberty Mutual Fire Insurance Co. ------------------- 847
      Questions -- 854
4. Court–Ordered Mediation --- 855
   Decker v. Lindsay --- 855
   Questions --- 858
   Raad v. Wal–Mart Stores, Inc. -------------------------------------- 859
   Questions --- 864
5. Perspectives on Court–Ordered Mediation ------------------------------- 865
   The Mediation Alternative: Process Dangers for Women by Trino Grillo. -- 865
   Question -- 871
6. Court–Induced Settlement -- 871
   G. Heileman Brewing Co., Inc. v. Joseph Oat Corporation ---------- 871
   Questions --- 889
7. Perspectives on Settlement Conferences -------------------------------- 890
   Managerial Judges by Judith Resnik ------------------------------- 890
   For and Against Settlement: Uses and Abuses of the Mandatory Settlement Conference by Carrie Menkel–Meadow ------------------ 893
   Questions --- 896
   Note on *Conolly v. National School Bus Service* ------------------ 896
   Question -- 898
8. Summary Jury Trials -- 898
   Strandell v. Jackson County, Illinois -------------------------------- 898
   Federal Reserve Bank of Minneapolis v. Carey–Canada, Inc. ------- 903
   Questions --- 909
9. Perspectives on the Role of Court–Connected ADR in Civil Litigation -- 909

Question -- 911
Appendix A. The Federal Arbitration Act --------------------------------- 913
Appendix B. The Labor Management Relations Act, § 301(a) ------- 919
Appendix C. American Arbitration Association Commercial Arbi-
    tration Rules -- 920
Appendix D. Model Standards of Conduct for Mediators ------------- 935
Appendix E. Standards of Practice for Lawyer Mediations in
    Family Disputes -- 941
Appendix F. Proposed Standards for Lawyers Who Conduct Di-
    vorce and Family Mediation -- 946

Index -- 955

*

TABLE OF CASES

Principal cases are in bold type. Non-principal cases are in roman type. References are to pages.

Action Orthopedics, Inc. v. Techmedica, Inc., 775 F.Supp. 390 (M.D.Fla.1991), 835

Agent Orange Product Liability Litigation, In re, 611 F.Supp. 1223 (E.D.N.Y.1985), 255

Agent Orange Product Liability Litigation, In re, 597 F.Supp. 740 (E.D.N.Y.1984), 254

Alliance Bond Fund, Inc. v. Grupo Mexicano de Desarrollo, S.A., 143 F.3d 688 (2nd Cir.1998), 640

Allied–Bruce Terminix Companies, Inc. v. Dobson, 513 U.S. 265, 115 S.Ct. 834, 130 L.Ed.2d 753 (1995), **362,** 376, 377, 378, 558, 790

All Points Traders, Inc. v. Barrington Associates, 211 Cal.App.3d 723, 259 Cal.Rptr. 780 (Cal.App. 2 Dist.1989), 770

Allstate Ins. Co. v. Avelares, 295 Ill.App.3d 950, 230 Ill.Dec. 482, 693 N.E.2d 1233 (Ill.App. 1 Dist.1998), 834

Amalgamated Cotton Garment & Allied Industries Fund v. J.B.C. Co. of Madera, Inc., 608 F.Supp. 158 (W.D.Pa. 1984), **607**

Amchem Products, Inc. v. Windsor, 521 U.S. 591, 117 S.Ct. 2231, 138 L.Ed.2d 689 (1997), **255,** 289, 290, 291, 292, 293, 294, 295, 301

American Airlines, Inc. v. Louisville and Jefferson County Air Bd., 269 F.2d 811 (6th Cir.1959), 514

American Safety Equipment Corp. v. J. P. Maguire & Co., 391 F.2d 821 (2nd Cir. 1968), 420

AMF Inc. v. Brunswick Corp., 621 F.Supp. 456 (S.D.N.Y.1985), **147,** 152

Amoco Oil Co. v. M. T. Mary Ellen, 529 F.Supp. 227 (S.D.N.Y.1981), 543

Application of (see name of party)

Astoria Medical Group v. Health Ins. Plan of Greater New York, 227 N.Y.S.2d 401, 182 N.E.2d 85 (N.Y.1962), 722

Baar v. Tigerman, 140 Cal.App.3d 979, 211 Cal.Rptr. 426 (Cal.App. 2 Dist.1983), 721, 723

Baldwin–United Corp., In re, 105 F.R.D. 475 (S.D.N.Y.1984), **228,** 238

Barazzotto v. Intelligent Systems, Inc., 40 Ohio App.3d 117, 532 N.E.2d 148 (Ohio App. 2 Dist.1987), 834

Bechtel Corp., United States v., 648 F.2d 660 (9th Cir.1981), **197**

Bernhardt v. Polygraphic Co. of America, 350 U.S. 198, 76 S.Ct. 273, 100 L.Ed. 199 (1956), **325,** 332, 348, 577

Bonar v. Dean Witter Reynolds, Inc., 835 F.2d 1378 (11th Cir.1988), **681,** 687

Bowmer v. Bowmer, 428 N.Y.S.2d 902, 406 N.E.2d 760 (N.Y.1980), **486,** 493, 498

Bridges v. City of Troy, 112 Misc.2d 384, 447 N.Y.S.2d 124 (N.Y.Sup.1982), 835

Broemmer v. Abortion Services of Phoenix, Ltd., 173 Ariz. 148, 840 P.2d 1013 (Ariz.1992), **533,** 695

Bruno v. Superior Court, 219 Cal.App.3d 1359, 269 Cal.Rptr. 142 (Cal.App. 1 Dist. 1990), **810,** 819

Carman v. McDonnell Douglas Corp., 114 F.3d 790 (8th Cir.1997), **172**

Casarotto v. Lombardi, 268 Mont. 369, 886 P.2d 931 (Mont.1994), **545**

Casino Properties, Inc. v. Andrews, 112 Nev. 132, 911 P.2d 1181 (Nev.1996), 834

Castellano, State v., 460 So.2d 480 (Fla. App. 2 Dist.1984), **83**

Casualty Indem. Exchange v. Yother, 439 So.2d 77 (Ala.1983), **619,** 625

C. Itoh & Co. (America) Inc. v. Jordan Intern. Co., 552 F.2d 1228 (7th Cir.1977), 543

City and County of (see name of city)

Clarendon Nat. Ins. Co. v. TIG Reinsurance Co., 183 F.R.D. 112 (S.D.N.Y.1998), 773, 774

Cole v. Burns Intern. Sec. Services, 105 F.3d 1465, 323 U.S.App.D.C. 133 (D.C.Cir. 1997), 594

Colonial Penn Ins. Co. v. Omaha Indem. Co., 943 F.2d 327 (3rd Cir.1991), 772, 774

Commonwealth Coatings Corp. v. Continental Cas. Co., 393 U.S. 145, 89 S.Ct. 337, 21 L.Ed.2d 301 (1968), **689,** 695

Connolly v. National School Bus Service, Inc., 177 F.3d 593 (7th Cir.1999), 896

Cook Chocolate Co. v. Salomon, Inc., 684 F.Supp. 1177 (S.D.N.Y.1988), 544

Corey v. New York Stock Exchange, 691 F.2d 1205 (6th Cir.1982), **715,** 722, 723

Country Mut. Ins. Co. v. Kosmos, 116 Ill.App.3d 914, 72 Ill.Dec. 294, 452 N.E.2d 547 (Ill.App. 1 Dist.1983), **484,** 486

Coventry v. United States Steel Corp., 856 F.2d 514 (3rd Cir.1988), 204

Craft v. Campbell Soup Co., 177 F.3d 1083 (9th Cir.1999), **577,** 585

Dean Witter Reynolds, Inc. v. Byrd, 470 U.S. 213, 105 S.Ct. 1238, 84 L.Ed.2d 158 (1985), **385,** 391

Decker v. Lindsay, 824 S.W.2d 247 (Tex. App.-Hous. (1 Dist.) 1992), **855,** 858

DeValk Lincoln Mercury, Inc. v. Ford Motor Co., 811 F.2d 326 (7th Cir.1987), **50,** 57, 59

Doctor's Associates, Inc. v. Casarotto, 517 U.S. 681, 116 S.Ct. 1652, 134 L.Ed.2d 902 (1996), **558,** 715

Doughboy Industries, Inc., Application of, 17 A.D.2d 216, 233 N.Y.S.2d 488 (N.Y.A.D. 1 Dept.1962), 543

Drans v. Providence College, 119 R.I. 845, 383 A.2d 1033 (R.I.1978), 543

Duncan v. Black, 324 S.W.2d 483 (Mo.App. 1959), 197

Employer's Consortium, Inc. v. Aaron, 298 Ill.App.3d 187, 232 Ill.Dec. 351, 698 N.E.2d 189 (Ill.App. 2 Dist.1998), **835,** 839, 843

Equitable Lumber Corp. v. IPA Land Development Corp., 381 N.Y.S.2d 459, 344 N.E.2d 391 (N.Y.1976), 779

Ericksen v. 100 Oak Street, 197 Cal.Rptr. 581, 673 P.2d 251 (Cal.1983), **505,** 514, 516

Erie R. Co. v. Tompkins, 304 U.S. 64, 58 S.Ct. 817, 82 L.Ed. 1188 (1938), 325, 332, 348

Faherty v. Faherty, 97 N.J. 99, 477 A.2d 1257 (N.J.1984), **563**

Federal Deposit Ins. Corp. v. Air Florida System, Inc., 822 F.2d 833 (9th Cir. 1987), **616**

Federal Reserve Bank of Minneapolis v. Carey–Canada, Inc., 123 F.R.D. 603 (D.Minn.1988), **903,** 909

Firelock Inc. v. District Court In and For Colorado, 776 P.2d 1090 (Colo. 1989), **822,** 833

First Options of Chicago, Inc. v. Kaplan, 514 U.S. 938, 115 S.Ct. 1920, 131 L.Ed.2d 985 (1995), **499,** 505, 516, 790

Flynn v. Gorton, 207 Cal.App.3d 1550, 255 Cal.Rptr. 768 (Cal.App. 4 Dist.1989), **843,** 854

Folb v. Motion Picture Industry Pension & Health Plans, 16 F.Supp.2d 1164 (C.D.Cal.1998), 73, 97

Garrity v. Lyle Stuart, Inc., 386 N.Y.S.2d 831, 353 N.E.2d 793 (N.Y.1976), **774**

Garstang v. Superior Court, 46 Cal. Rptr.2d 84 (Cal.App. 2 Dist.1995), **165,** 175

General Elec. Co. v. United Elec. Workers, 353 U.S. 547, 77 S.Ct. 921, 1 L.Ed.2d 1028 (1957), 582

General Motors Corp. Pick–Up Truck Fuel Tank Products Liability Litigation, In re, 55 F.3d 768 (3rd Cir.1995), 290

Georgine v. Amchem Products, Inc., 83 F.3d 610 (3rd Cir.1996), 289, 290

G. Heileman Brewing Co., Inc. v. Joseph Oat Corp., 871 F.2d 648 (7th Cir.1989), **871,** 889, 890

Gibson v. Berryhill, 411 U.S. 564, 93 S.Ct. 1689, 36 L.Ed.2d 488 (1973), 714

Gilmer v. Interstate/Johnson Lane Corp., 500 U.S. 20, 111 S.Ct. 1647, 114 L.Ed.2d 26 (1991), **443,** 455, 456, 533, 570, 577, 585

Gingiss Intern., Inc. v. Bormet, 58 F.3d 328 (7th Cir.1995), **603**

Golub v. Spivey, 70 Md.App. 147, 520 A.2d 394 (Md.App.1987), **668,** 672

Graham v. Scissor–Tail, Inc., 171 Cal. Rptr. 604, 623 P.2d 165 (Cal.1981), **516,** 528, 533

Gruntal & Co., Inc. v. Steinberg, 854 F.Supp. 324 (D.N.J.1994), 600, 601

Habick v. Liberty Mut. Fire Ins. Co., 320 N.J.Super. 244, 727 A.2d 51 (N.J.Super.A.D.1999), **847,** 854

Henningsen v. Bloomfield Motors, Inc., 32 N.J. 358, 161 A.2d 69 (N.J.1960), 543

Hooters of America, Inc. v. Phillips, 173 F.3d 933 (4th Cir.1999), 595

Hope v. Superior Court, 122 Cal.App.3d 147, 175 Cal.Rptr. 851 (Cal.App. 1 Dist. 1981), **528,** 533

Houghtaling v. Superior Court, 21 Cal. Rptr.2d 855 (Cal.App. 4 Dist.1993), **813,** 819

Howard v. Drapkin, 222 Cal.App.3d 843, 271 Cal.Rptr. 893 (Cal.App. 2 Dist.1990), **101,** 111

Hudson v. Hudson, 600 So.2d 7 (Fla.App. 4 Dist.1992), **66**

Industrotech Constructors, Inc. v. Duke University, 67 N.C.App. 741, 314 S.E.2d 272 (N.C.App.1984), **687,** 689

In re (see name of party)

Insurance Co. of New York v. Morse, 87 U.S. 445, 22 L.Ed. 365 (1874), 305

Integrity Ins. Co. v. American Centennial Ins. Co., 885 F.Supp. 69 (S.D.N.Y. 1995), **663**

Jackson Dairy, Inc. v. H. P. Hood & Sons, Inc., 596 F.2d 70 (2nd Cir.1979), 640

Jeffery v. Weintraub, 32 Wash.App. 536, 648 P.2d 914 (Wash.App. Div. 1 1982), **152,** 158, 165

John Wiley & Sons, Inc. v. Livingston, 376 U.S. 543, 84 S.Ct. 909, 11 L.Ed.2d 898 (1964), 499

Kaufman v. William Iselin & Co., 272 A.D. 578, 74 N.Y.S.2d 23 (N.Y.A.D. 1 Dept.1947), **597,** 600

Kirschenman v. Superior Court, 36 Cal. Rptr.2d 166 (Cal.App. 1 Dist.1994), **57,** 59

Kulukundis Shipping Co., S/A v. Amtorg Trading Corporation, 126 F.2d 978 (2nd Cir.1942), 305, **316,** 324, 514

Lange v. Marshall, 622 S.W.2d 237 (Mo. App. E.D.1981), **97,** 100

Legion Ins. Co. v. Insurance General Agency, Inc., 822 F.2d 541 (5th Cir. 1987), 695, **723**

Lindsey v. Dow Corning Corp., 1994 WL 578353 (N.D.Ala.1994), **238**

Local 174, Teamsters, Chauffeurs, Warehousemen and Helpers of America v. Lucas Flour Co., 369 U.S. 95, 82 S.Ct. 571, 7 L.Ed.2d 593 (1962), 466, 468, 469

Lopez, United States v., 514 U.S. 549, 115 S.Ct. 1624, 131 L.Ed.2d 626 (1995), 376, 377, 378

Loving & Evans v. Blick, 33 Cal.2d 603, 204 P.2d 23 (Cal.1949), 770

Ludwig Honold Mfg. Co. v. Fletcher, 405 F.2d 1123 (3rd Cir.1969), 748, 749

Marathon Oil Co. v. Ruhrgas, A.G., 115 F.3d 315 (5th Cir.1997), 600

Martin v. Wilks, 490 U.S. 755, 109 S.Ct. 2180, 104 L.Ed.2d 835 (1989), **220,** 227, 253

Mastrobuono v. Shearson Lehman Hutton, Inc., 514 U.S. 52, 115 S.Ct. 1212, 131 L.Ed.2d 76 (1995), **780,** 789, 790

Maui Land & Pineapple Co. v. Occidental Chemical Corp., 1998 WL 758422 (D.Hawai'i 1998), 639

McDonald v. City of West Branch, Mich., 466 U.S. 284, 104 S.Ct. 1799, 80 L.Ed.2d 302 (1984), 796, 798

McKenzie Const. v. St. Croix Storage Corp., 961 F.Supp. 857 (D.Virgin Islands 1997), **121,** 128

McKinlay v. McKinlay, 648 So.2d 806 (Fla. App. 1 Dist.1995), **68,** 73

McLaughlin v. Superior Court, 140 Cal. App.3d 473, 189 Cal.Rptr. 479 (Cal.App. 1 Dist.1983), **159,** 165

Meadows Indem. Co. Ltd. v. Nutmeg Ins. Co., 157 F.R.D. 42 (M.D.Tenn.1994), **660**

Medical Development Corp. v. Industrial Molding Corp., 479 F.2d 345 (10th Cir. 1973), 543

Merit Ins. Co. v. Leatherby Ins. Co., 714 F.2d 673 (7th Cir.1983), **695,** 704

Merrill Lynch, Pierce, Fenner & Smith, Inc. v. Bradley, 756 F.2d 1048 (4th Cir. 1985), **634,** 639

Merrill Lynch, Pierce, Fenner & Smith, Inc. v. Hovey, 726 F.2d 1286 (8th Cir. 1984), **629**

Merrill Lynch, Pierce, Fenner & Smith, Inc. v. Ware, 414 U.S. 117, 94 S.Ct. 383, 38 L.Ed.2d 348 (1973), 349

Middleton v. Baskin, 618 A.2d 1263 (R.I. 1992), 834

Mikel v. Scharf, 85 A.D.2d 604, 444 N.Y.S.2d 690 (N.Y.A.D. 2 Dept.1981), **625**

Mississippi Power Co. v. Peabody Coal Co., 69 F.R.D. 558 (S.D.Miss.1976), **651**

Mitsubishi Motors Corp. v. Soler Chrysler–Plymouth, Inc., 473 U.S. 614, 105 S.Ct. 3346, 87 L.Ed.2d 444 (1985), **401,** 419, 443, 486, 590, 740

Moncharsh v. Heily & Blase, 10 Cal. Rptr.2d 183, 832 P.2d 899 (Cal.1992), **753,** 770, 771

Morris v. Metriyakool, 418 Mich. 423, 344 N.W.2d 736 (Mich.1984), **705**

Moses H. Cone Memorial Hosp. v. Mercury Const. Corp., 460 U.S. 1, 103 S.Ct. 927, 74 L.Ed.2d 765 (1983), 348, **493,** 498, 505

NLO, Inc., In re, 3 F.3d 153 (6th Cir.1993), 898

N.L.R.B. v. Jones & Laughlin Steel Corp., 301 U.S. 1, 57 S.Ct. 615, 81 L.Ed. 893 (1937), 377, 576

N.L.R.B. v. Joseph Macaluso, Inc., 618 F.2d 51 (9th Cir.1980), 74

Ortiz v. Fibreboard Corp., ___ U.S. ___, 119 S.Ct. 2295 (1999), 291, 292, 293, 294, 295

Ottley v. Schwartzberg, 819 F.2d 373 (2nd Cir.1987), 771

Outdoor Services, Inc. v. Pabagold, Inc., 185 Cal.App.3d 676, 230 Cal.Rptr. 73 (Cal. App. 1 Dist.1986), **626**

Parker v. Anderson, 667 F.2d 1204 (5th Cir.1982), **206,** 214, 215

People v. _____ (see opposing party)

Performance Unlimited, Inc. v. Questar Publishers, Inc., 52 F.3d 1373 (6th Cir. 1995), **640**

Perry v. Thomas, 482 U.S. 483, 107 S.Ct. 2520, 96 L.Ed.2d 426 (1987), 349, 351, 361, 376, 483, 544, 558, 601, 798

Pony Exp. Courier Corp. v. Morris, 921 S.W.2d 817 (Tex.App.-San Antonio 1996), **590,** 593

Press Machinery Corp. v. Smith R.P.M. Corp., 727 F.2d 781 (8th Cir.1984), **191,** 220

Prima Paint Corp. v. Flood & Conklin Mfg. Co., 388 U.S. 395, 87 S.Ct. 1801, 18 L.Ed.2d 1270 (1967), 348, 514, 516

Progressive Cas. Ins. Co. v. C.A. Reaseguradora Nacional De Venezuela, 991 F.2d 42 (2nd Cir.1993), 544

Provident Tradesmens Bank & Trust Co. v. Patterson, 390 U.S. 102, 88 S.Ct. 733, 19 L.Ed.2d 936 (1968), 224

Prudential Ins. Co. of America v. Lai, 42 F.3d 1299 (9th Cir.1994), **585**

Pryner v. Tractor Supply Co., 109 F.3d 354 (7th Cir.1997), 456

Quick & Reilly, Inc. v. Jacobson, 126 F.R.D. 24 (S.D.N.Y.1989), **749**, 753

Raad v. Wal–Mart Stores, Inc., 1998 WL 272879 (D.Neb.1998), **859**, 864

Recognition Equipment, Inc. v. NCR Corp., 532 F.Supp. 271 (N.D.Tex.1981), **656**, 660

Riverdale Fabrics Corporation v. Tillinghast–Stiles Co., 306 N.Y. 288, 118 N.E.2d 104 (N.Y.1954), 543, 544

Robbins v. Day, 954 F.2d 679 (11th Cir.1992), 680

Robert Lawrence Company v. Devonshire Fabrics, Inc., 271 F.2d 402 (2nd Cir.1959), 514, 515

Rodriguez de Quijas v. Shearson/American Exp., Inc., 490 U.S. 477, 109 S.Ct. 1917, 104 L.Ed.2d 526 (1989), **438**, 443, 533

Rosenberg v. Merrill Lynch, Pierce, Fenner & Smith Inc., 163 F.3d 53 (1st Cir.1998), 544

San Francisco, City and County of v. Small Claims Court, 141 Cal.App.3d 470, 190 Cal.Rptr. 340 (Cal.App. 1 Dist. 1983), **803**

Sanko S.S. Co., Ltd. v. Cook Industries, Inc., 495 F.2d 1260 (2nd Cir.1973), 695

Scherk v. Alberto–Culver Co., 417 U.S. 506, 94 S.Ct. 2449, 41 L.Ed.2d 270 (1974), **392**, 400, 443

Shearson/American Exp., Inc. v. McMahon, 482 U.S. 220, 107 S.Ct. 2332, 96 L.Ed.2d 185 (1987), **420**, 438, 443, 533

Shults v. Champion Intern. Corp., 821 F.Supp. 520 (E.D.Tenn.1993), **215**, 220, 302

Silicone Gel Breast Implant Products Liability Litigation, In re, 1994 WL 578353 (N.D.Ala.1994), **238**, 253

Simrin v. Simrin, 233 Cal.App.2d 90, 43 Cal. Rptr. 376 (Cal.App. 5 Dist.1965), 61, 62

Smaligo v. Fireman's Fund Ins. Co., 432 Pa. 133, 247 A.2d 577 (Pa.1968), **676**, 680

Smith v. Smith, 154 F.R.D. 661 (N.D.Tex. 1994), **87**, 97

Snyder, People v., 129 Misc.2d 137, 492 N.Y.S.2d 890 (N.Y.Sup.1985), **84**

Snyder–Falkinham v. Stockburger, 249 Va. 376, 457 S.E.2d 36 (Va.1995), **75**, 82

Sobel v. Hertz, Warner & Co., 469 F.2d 1211 (2nd Cir.1972), **735**, 740

Southland Corp. v. Keating, 465 U.S. 1, 104 S.Ct. 852, 79 L.Ed.2d 1 (1984), **332**, 348, 351, 361, 438, 486, 715, 798

State v. _____ (see opposing party)

State Farm Ins. Co. v. Kazakova, 299 Ill.App.3d 1028, 234 Ill.Dec. 88, 702 N.E.2d 254 (Ill.App. 1 Dist.1998), **840**, 843

Stirlen v. Supercuts, Inc., 60 Cal.Rptr.2d 138 (Cal.App. 1 Dist.1997), 594

Strandell v. Jackson County, Ill., 838 F.2d 884 (7th Cir.1987), **898**, 909

Sunbeam Products, Inc. v. West Bend Co., 123 F.3d 246 (5th Cir.1997), 639

Swift Industries, Inc. v. Botany Industries, Inc., 466 F.2d 1125 (3rd Cir.1972), **741**, 748, 753

Tenney Engineering, Inc. v. United Elec. Radio & Mach. Workers of America, (U.E.) Local 437, 207 F.2d 450 (3rd Cir. 1953), **570**, 576, 577, 585

Textile Workers Union of America v. Lincoln Mills of Alabama, 353 U.S. 448, 77 S.Ct. 912, 1 L.Ed.2d 972 (1957), 456, **457**, 466, 469, 582

Tobey v. County of Bristol, 23 F.Cas. 1313 (C.C.D.Mass.1845), 305, **306**, 308, 316, 324, 325

Totem Marine Tug & Barge, Inc. v. North American Towing, Inc., 607 F.2d 649 (5th Cir.1979), 616, **672**, 676, 695

United Paperworkers Intern. Union, AFL–CIO v. Misco, Inc., 484 U.S. 29, 108 S.Ct. 364, 98 L.Ed.2d 286 (1987), **730**, 741, 771

United States v. _____ (see opposing party)

United States Asphalt Refining Co. v. Trinidad Lake Petroleum Co., 222 F. 1006 (S.D.N.Y.1915), 311

United Steelworkers of America v. American Mfg. Co., 363 U.S. 564, 80 S.Ct. 1343, 4 L.Ed.2d 1403 (1960), **469**, 471

United Steelworkers of America v. Enterprise Wheel & Car Corp., 363 U.S. 593, 80 S.Ct. 1358, 4 L.Ed.2d 1424 (1960), **727**, 729, 730, 735, 740

United Steelworkers of America v. Warrior & Gulf Nav. Co., 363 U.S. 574, 80 S.Ct. 1347, 4 L.Ed.2d 1409 (1960), **472**, 481

Valler v. Lee, 190 Ariz. 391, 949 P.2d 51 (Ariz.App. Div. 2 1997), 834, 835

Vazquez v. Aetna Cas. & Sur. Co., 112 Misc.2d 125, 446 N.Y.S.2d 176 (N.Y.City Civ.Ct.1982), **790,** 798

Vernon v. Acton, 693 N.E.2d 1345 (Ind.App. 1998), 82

Volt Information Sciences, Inc. v. Board of Trustees of Stanford University, 489 U.S. 468, 109 S.Ct. 1248, 103 L.Ed.2d 488 (1989), **351,** 361, 468, 483, 558, 563, 789

Walker v. Sheldon, 223 N.Y.S.2d 488, 179 N.E.2d 497 (N.Y.1961), 778

Waterspring, S.A. and Trans Marketing Houston Inc., 717 F.Supp. 181 (S.D.N.Y. 1989), **611,** 616

Watkins v. K-Mart Corp., 1997 WL 597913 (E.D.Pa.1997), 835

Werle v. Rhode Island Bar Ass'n, 755 F.2d 195 (1st Cir.1985), **112,** 121

West Bend Mut. Ins. Co. v. Herrera, 292 Ill.App.3d 669, 226 Ill.Dec. 862, 686 N.E.2d 645 (Ill.App. 1 Dist.1997), 835

Wilko v. Swan, 346 U.S. 427, 74 S.Ct. 182, 98 L.Ed. 168 (1953), **379,** 391, 400, 438, 443, 729, 740, 745

Williams v. Cigna Financial Advisors, Inc., 1999 WL 1101178 (5th Cir.1999), 770

Williams v. Dorsey, 273 Ill.App.3d 893, 210 Ill.Dec. 310, 652 N.E.2d 1286 (Ill.App. 1 Dist.1995), 834

Williams v. General Elec. Capital Auto Lease, Inc., 159 F.3d 266 (7th Cir.1998), **295,** 301, 302

Williams v. Walker–Thomas Furniture Co., 350 F.2d 445, 121 U.S.App.D.C. 315 (D.C.Cir.1965), 543

Wright v. Central Du Page Hospital Ass'n, 63 Ill.2d 313, 347 N.E.2d 736 (Ill.1976), 833

*

PRIVATE JUSTICE: THE LAW OF ALTERNATIVE DISPUTE RESOLUTION

*

CHAPTER ONE

INTRODUCTION TO ALTERNATIVE DISPUTE RESOLUTION

Modern legal education concentrates almost exclusively on the study of the public judicial system. Law students study the criminal, civil, and administrative law systems with the aim of understanding and mastering the substantive rules that govern, the procedures that pertain, and the values that animate them. Yet while understanding these public legal systems are of vital importance to the students' future professional life as lawyers, there are other legal systems that also deserve serious attention and study. These are the legal systems of alternative dispute resolution, the systems that comprise the growing world of private justice.

Alternative dispute resolution ("ADR") has become a major feature of legal practice. Arbitration, mediation, and other alternative dispute resolution mechanisms are commonly utilized today in such disparate fields as securities regulation, commercial law, employment law, family law, labor law, medical malpractice, construction law, insurance and international private law. Parties and their lawyers increasingly seek means to resolve their differences without resorting to litigation, and thus they increasingly turn to alternative mechanisms. In fact, it is difficult to practice law in any area today without encountering contractual provisions or institutional arrangements that mandate the use of alternative dispute resolution.

When parties choose to use alternative dispute resolution rather than judicial resolution for their claims, lawyers are not banished from the scene. Contrary to popular belief, lawyers are in great demand in the world of private justice. Lawyers draft the agreements pursuant to which parties utilize alternative dispute resolution mechanisms in lieu of litigation. Lawyers are also called upon to enforce these agreements by obtaining judicial decrees to compel parties to honor their promises to arbitrate or to mediate. If there is a dispute about the meaning or scope of an agreement to utilize ADR, lawyers are the ones who advocate their client's position. Lawyers also raise defenses and claim exceptions to the enforcement of such agreements in order to assist parties who want to avoid having their cases decided in alternative fora. Lawyers frequently participate in ADR proceedings directly, either by presenting cases or advising from the sidelines. Also, on occasion, lawyers are required to enforce the awards or the settlement agreements that result from ADR mechanisms. Thus lawyers need to know what procedures apply, what evidentiary rules will be invoked, what discovery is possible, what remedies might be forthcoming, and what is the standard of judicial review in the various ADR tribunals.

In recent years, the Supreme Court has expanded the reach of ADR agreements to apply not only to issues of contract formation, performance and breach that may arise between contracting parties, but also to disputes concerning statutory rights. The Court has held that civil disputes concerning alleged violations of the antitrust laws, the securities laws, and the anti-discrimination laws, are within the scope of parties' arbitration promises. As a result, these and many other statutes are now interpreted and applied by arbitrators in private tribunals rather than by judges in courtrooms. Thus, in order for practitioners to understand the developments in regulatory laws, it is necessary that they understand how such laws are applied in arbitral settings.

This book focuses on the evolving law of alternative dispute resolution. The cases and materials that follow explore the legal issues posed by the growing use of ADR mechanisms. Together, the cases and materials map the interface between the privatized justice of alternative dispute resolution and the public world of justice embodied in our substantive laws. It is an interface that is constantly changing. Alternative dispute resolution is the partial privatization of justice—law is always at the boundaries defining the scope and role of ADR within the legal order. This book addresses the extent to which law is being privatized, and the extent to which judicial oversight is reasserting itself in order to ensure that our society continues to operate under a public rule of law.

1. THE CRITIQUE OF THE LEGAL SYSTEM AND THE GROWTH OF ADR

The recent popularity and proliferation of alternative dispute resolution is to a large extent a response to widespread dissatisfaction with the judicial system. Many critics have claimed there is a crisis in the civil justice system, a crisis caused by the excessive delay, expense, inflexibility, and technicality of the courts. These factors, it is claimed, undermine the ability of the legal system to provide justice, and instead offer parties a judicial process that is too little, too late, at too much expense. For example, it is claimed that court congestion and expansive discovery rules make litigation time-consuming, arduous and expensive for the parties. Furthermore, litigation involves a high degree of technicality, so that law is relegated to experts and it is impossible for ordinary citizens to know their rights or to order their affairs. The high cost of litigation, due to discovery and high lawyer fees, makes the judicial system inaccessible to the poor. It is also claimed that the legal process dehumanizes participants, terminates human relationships instead of affirming them, and therefore destroys families and undermines communities.

Critics of the civil justice system further contend that the legal system imposes excessive costs on society. They claim that court congestion and docket-crowding mean that litigation consumes too much judicial resources—i.e., that it is too expensive for society.

The concern that our courts are over-burdened is related to a concern that the populace is overly-litigious. In 1982, Chief Justice Warren Burger warned that our society was experiencing a "litigation explosion." Rapidly expanding case filings and swelling judicial caseloads, he contended, were indicia of a trend toward burgeoning civil litigation that was harming society, distracting individuals from their normal pursuits and diverting businesses from productive activities.[1] Since then, many others have expressed the view that our society is overly litigious. They point to the vast private resources that are spent on lawyers and vast public resources that are spent on judges, clerks, stenographers, jurors, and the other personnel who staff the burgeoning "lawsuit industry." These critics see ADR as a way for courts to reduce their dockets. Both private and court-mandated ADR take cases away from judges and place them before alternate decision-makers. If ADR expands and we are able to de-legalize many of our disputes, it is claimed, all of society would be better off.

In 1976, Chief Justice Warren Burger convened the National Conference on the Causes of Popular Dissatisfaction with the Administration of Justice to develop proposals for judicial reform.[2] The conference, known as the Pound Conference, was timed to commemorate the 70th anniversary of Roscoe Pound's 1906 speech to the American Bar Association in which Pound made a powerful plea for judicial reform. In his Keynote Address, Chief Justice Burger discussed the problems with the judicial system, particularly the problems of delay, high costs, and unnecessarily technicality. He said, "Inefficient courts cause delay and expenses, and diminish the value of the judgment. Small litigants, who cannot manipulate the system, are often exploited . . . by the litigant 'with the longest purse.' . . . Inefficiency drains the value of even a just result either by delay or excessive cost, or both."[3] The Chief Justice made several suggestions for reform, including giving a greater role to ADR. For minor disputes involving consumer complaints and the like, he suggested:

> "[W]e could consider the value of a tribunal consisting of three representative citizens, or two nonlawyer citizens and one specially trained lawyer or paralegal, and vest in them final unreviewable authority to decide certain kinds of minor claims. Flexibility and informality should be the keynote in such tribunals and they should be available at a neighborhood or community level and during some evening hours."[4]

For larger cases, Chief Justice Burger urged that we "divert litigation to other channels," particularly the channel of arbitration.[5] He also recommended that we devise an expedited system similar to the worker' compensation system to deal with accident and injury claims.[6]

The other speakers echoed the Chief Justice's call for increased use of alternative dispute resolution mechanisms to resolve legal disputes. Har-

---

1. W. Burger, *Isn't There A Better Way?* ANNUAL REPORT ON THE STATE OF THE JUDICIARY (1982).

2. The papers from the Pound Conference are reported at 70 F.R.D. 79 (1976).

3. Warren E. Burger, Agenda for 2000 A.D.—A Need for Systemic Anticipation, 70 F.R.D. 83, 92 (1976).

4. Id. At 93–94.

5. Id. At 94.

6. Id. At 95.

vard Law Professor Frank E. A. Sander proposed that courts be transformed into "Dispute Resolution Centers," in which "the grievant would first be channeled through a screening clerk who would then direct him to the process (or sequence of processes) most appropriate to his type of case."[7] The proposed Dispute Resolution Centers would have the following room directory posted in the lobby:

Screening Clerk	Room 1
Mediation	Room 2
Arbitration	Room 3
Fact Finding	Room 4
Malpractice Screening Panel	Room 5
Superior Court	Room 6
Ombudsman	Room 7

Sander contended that his proposal for a "multi-door courthouse" would inject greater flexibility, efficiency and fairness into our legal system.

The Pound Conference signified the beginning of the modern ADR movement.[8] In its immediate aftermath, the American Bar Association Committee on Dispute Resolution recommended that three jurisdictions set up pilot multi-door courthouse programs. These have since been expanded so that over 100 state and federal courthouses now offer multi-door options. In addition, since the 1970s, many state and federal courts began to experiment with court-annexed arbitration systems in which litigants were offered, or in some cases required, to take their claims to an arbitrator before getting a hearing before a judge. The practice quickly spread, so that as of 1998, one-quarter of the 94 federal district courts and one-half of all state courts have either mandatory or voluntary arbitration programs as part of their judicial process. In addition, 51 federal district courts have court-annexed mediation, and 48 report that they offer summary jury trials as an ADR option. And 14 federal districts have early neutral evaluation programs. In all, three-quarters of federal district courts now authorize one or more forms of ADR, as compared to a small handful in the late 1970s.

The use of ADR has also grown dramatically in the private domain. The American Arbitration Association had 92,000 arbitration requests filed in 1998, an increase of 21% over those filed in 1994. The Center for Public Resources, an organization formed by the general counsels of 500 major corporations and law firms to promote the use of alternative dispute resolution, obtained pledges from 4000 corporations to explore ADR options before resorting to litigation. JAMS, a for-profit ADR provider that utilizes primarily retired judges to hear arbitration cases, has offices in 30 cities and handled over 20,000 cases in 1996. The use of industry-specific arbitration systems and international arbitration systems has also expanded dramatically. For smaller disputes, over 350 neighborhood justice centers

---

7. Frank E. A. Sander, *Varieties of Dispute Processing*, 70 F.R.D. 111, 131 (1976).

8. See Carrie Menkel–Meadow, *What Will We Do When Adjudication Ends? A Brief Intellectual History of ADR*, 44 UCLA L. REV. 1613 (1997).

have been established to offer mediation services for such matters as landlord-tenant, consumer-merchant or neighbor-neighbor disputes.

In 1990, Congress enacted the Administrative Dispute Resolution Act, which requires federal agencies to consider ADR in settling disputes. As a result, numerous federal and state agencies now utilize ADR procedures to handle their caseloads. The Equal Employment Opportunity Commission, the U.S. Department of Labor, state human rights departments, and local consumer protection departments are some of the government agencies that have begun to utilize mediation and arbitration to resolve claims.

2. DESCRIPTION OF ALTERNATIVE DISPUTE RESOLUTION

The term "alternative dispute resolution" refers to a large variety of dispute resolution mechanisms or techniques that share one essential characteristic: They all differ from the dispute mechanism of litigation in a federal or a state court. Thus the term alternative dispute resolution, or ADR, includes many sorts of processes, some familiar and some less familiar, such as:

mediation

private arbitration

mediation-arbitration ("med-arb")

third party evaluation

appraisals

fact-finding panels

mini-trials

court-mandated settlement conferences

court-mandated arbitration

court-mandated mediation

summary jury trials

small claims courts

federal magistrates and special masters

speciality courts like housing courts or patent courts

The most common forms of ADR are defined in the following Report of the National Institute for Dispute Resolution, as follows:

Report of the Ad Hoc Panel on Dispute Resolution and Public Policy, Appendix 2[9]

"*Arbitration*, widely used in commercial and labor-management disagreements, involves the submission of the dispute to a third party who

---

9. National Institute for Dispute Resolution, Report of the Ad Hoc Panel on Dispute Resolution and Public Policy, Appendix 2 (1983). Reprinted with permission.

renders a decision after hearing arguments and reviewing evidence. It is less formal and less complex and often can be concluded more quickly than court proceedings. In its most common form, Binding Arbitration, the parties select the arbitrator and are bound by the decision, either by prior agreement or by statute. In Last Offer Arbitration, the arbitrator is required to choose between the final positions of the two parties. In labor-management disputes, Grievance Arbitration has traditionally been used to resolve grievances under the provisions of labor contracts. More recently, Interest Arbitration has been used when collective bargaining breaks down in the public sector, where strikes may be unlawful.

"*Court–Annexed Arbitration* is a newer development. Judges refer civil suits to arbitrators who render prompt, non-binding decisions. If a party does not accept an arbitrated award, some systems require they better their position at trial by some fixed percentage or court costs are assessed against them. Even when these decisions are not accepted, they sometimes lead to further negotiations and pretrial settlement.

"*Conciliation* is an informal process in which the third party tries to bring the parties to agreement by lowering tensions, improving communications, interpreting issues, providing technical assistance, exploring potential solutions and bringing about a negotiated settlement, either informally or, in a subsequent step, through formal mediation. Conciliation is frequently used in volatile conflicts and in disputes where the parties are unable, unwilling or unprepared to come to the table to negotiate their differences.

"*Facilitation* is a collaborative process used to help a group of individuals or parties with divergent views reach a goal or complete a task to the mutual satisfaction of the participants. The facilitator functions as a neutral process expert and avoids making substantive contributions. The facilitator's task is to help bring the parties to consensus on a number of complex issues.

"*Fact Finding* is a process used from time to time primarily in public sector collective bargaining. The Fact Finder, drawing on both information provided by the parties and additional research, recommends a resolution of each outstanding issue. It is typically non-binding and paves the way for further negotiations and mediation.

"*Mandated Settlements and Negotiated Settlements*. Alternative dispute resolution techniques involving the use of neutrals are often divided into two categories: (1) settlements negotiated by the disputants and (2) settlements mandated by a third party. A more recent development has been the merging of the two; if the parties are unable to resolve their differences voluntarily, the third-party is authorized to dictate the terms of the settlements (see Med–Arb below).

"*Med–Arb* is an innovation in dispute resolution under which the med-arbiter is authorized by the parties to serve first as a mediator and, secondly, as an arbitrator empowered to decide any issues not resolved through mediation.

"*Mediation* is a structured process in which the mediator assists the disputants to reach a negotiated settlement of their differences. Mediation is usually a voluntary process that results in a signed agreement which defines the future behavior of the parties. The mediator uses a variety of skills and techniques to help the parties reach a settlement but is not empowered to render a decision.

"The *Mini-Trial* is a privately-developed method of helping to bring about a negotiated settlement in lieu of corporate litigation. A typical mini-trial might entail a period of limited discovery after which attorneys present their best case before managers with authority to settle and, most often, a neutral advisor who may be a retired judge or other lawyer. The managers then enter settlement negotiations. They may call on the neutral advisor if they wish to obtain an opinion on how a court might decide the matter.

"The *Multi-Door Center* (or Multi–Door Court House) is a proposal to offer a variety of dispute resolution services in one place with a single intake desk which would screen clients. Under one model, a screening clerk would refer cases for mediation, arbitration, fact-finding, ombudsman or adjudication. The American Bar Association plans to experiment with multi-door centers in three cities in 1983.

"*Negotiated Investment Strategy* is a mediation process which has been used on a limited basis to bring together federal, state and local officials and community members to resolve differences, disputes and problems related to the allocation and use of public resources.

"*Neighborhood Justice Center* (NJC) was the title given to the three local dispute resolution centers (Atlanta, Kansas City and Los Angeles) funded by the Department of Justice in an experimental alternative dispute resolution program in the mid 1970's. That experiment contributed to the start of about 180 local centers now operating throughout the country under the sponsorship of local or state governments, bar associations and foundations. NJC's deal primarily with disputes between individuals with ongoing relationships (landlord-tenant, domestic, back-yard conflicts, etc.) Many draw their caseloads from referrals from police, local courts or prosecutors' offices with which they affiliated. The dispute resolution techniques most often offered by the centers are mediation and conciliation. Some centers employ med-arb. Referrals to other agencies are a common feature. Many centers earn some income providing training and technical assistance services. They are also known as Community Mediation Centers, Citizen Dispute Centers, etc. (See ABA's Dispute Resolution Program Directory)

"*An Ombudsman* is a third party who receives and investigates complaints or grievances aimed at an institution by its constituents, clients or employees. The Ombudsman may take actions such as bringing an apparent injustice to the attention of high-level officials, advising the complainant of available options and recourses, proposing a settlement of the dispute or proposing systemic changes in the institution. The Ombudsman is often employed in a staff position in the institution or by a branch or agency of government with responsibility for the institution's performance. Many newspapers and radio and television stations have initiated ombudsman-like services under such names as Action Line or Seven on Your Side.

"Public Policy Dialogue and Negotiations is aimed at bringing together affected representatives of business, public interest groups and government to explore regulatory matters. The dialogue is intended to identify areas of agreement, narrow areas of disagreement and identify general areas and specific topics for negotiation. A facilitator guides the process.

"Rent-a-Judge is the popular name given to a procedure, presently authorized by legislation in six states, in which the court, on stipulation of the parties, can refer a pending lawsuit to a private neutral party for trial with the same effect as though the case were tried in the courtroom before a judge. The verdict can be appealed through the regular court appellate system."

* * *

The many ADR mechanisms vary in many respects. Some operate within the current litigation system, and are public tribunals that have added non-judge-centered means to resolve what is otherwise an ordinary litigation. Others involve a wholly privatized form of dispute resolution that takes parties out of judicial purview altogether. Indeed, alternative dispute resolution processes can be seen as existing along a continuum according to how far they move parties away from the legal and judicial system into a world of privatized justice.

One can also distinguish the various ADR mechanisms according to the degree of formality they employ in their procedures. Some utilize formal rules of evidence, discovery, motion practice, and the like, while others entirely dispense with procedural formality and encourage participants to simply "tell their stories." Similarly, some involve decision-makers who are constrained by legalistic notions of precedent and stare decisis, while others permit decisions simply on the facts and equities of each case.

Alternatively, one can distinguish ADR mechanisms on the basis of whether they culminate in a consensual resolution of a dispute or whether ultimately a settlement is imposed. Mediation and other settlement-enhancing processes result, if successful, in a consensual settlement of the dispute. On the other hand, arbitration and some of the other processes result in a third party decision, comparable to a judgment by a court.

Another way to distinguish ADR mechanisms is to characterize them according to the roles that third parties play. Professor Judith Resnick divides ADR mechanisms into three basic types, a quasi-adjudicatory mode, an outside evaluation mode, and a persuasion/consent mode. She writes:

Many Doors? Closing Doors? Alternative Dispute Resolution and Adjudication by Judith Resnik[10]

"While the current vocabulary of ADR could enable a lengthy discussion of distinctions among processes now called arbitration, court-annexed arbitration, mediation, med-arb, mini-trial, summary jury trial, early neutral evaluation, and judicial settlement conferences, all of these forms involve the state's introduction to the disputants of a third party, who is called upon to do something. Therefore, I will group the various methods into modes that are delineated by the nature of the work of that third party.

"A first mode is quasi-adjudicatory; this form of ADR offers a truncated, abbreviated fact-finding process that yields an outcome, decided by a third party, in the hopes that with that result, the parties will conclude their dispute. Both private contractual and court-annexed arbitration fit this mode. The difference is that under contractual arbitration, individuals or entities have an agreement, predating a dispute, to arbitrate, and that agreement also specifies the mechanism for selection of arbitrators. In contrast, under many court-annexed arbitration programs, litigants are sent to arbitration without such prior agreements and have varying amounts of control over the selection of arbitrators. Court-annexed arbitration typically permits parties to reject the arbitrator's decision and litigate, albeit sometimes with penalties and disincentives. However, if the parties do not object, the judgment of the arbitrator functions as a judgment of the court.

"Under both court-annexed and contractual arbitration, the assumption is that information, provided to an outsider, will enable that outsider to render a fair outcome. What makes this process not adjudication is that the proceeding is not conducted by a state-employed individual who bears the title 'judge,' formal evidentiary rules do not apply, and opinions are often not written. It is, however, important to keep in mind that this process shares with adjudication a commitment to a case-specific outcome made by a third party and predicated upon an inquiry into the claims of fact made by disputants.

"A second mode of ADR also relies upon some third party intervention but for a different purpose. A third party is introduced not to make a decision, but rather to inform the disputants of how outsiders view the dispute and how these outsiders would decide, were they asked to do so. The hope is that with such information, the disputants themselves will obviate the need for third party intervention by settling their differences. That settlement, however, is presumed to have been shaped in light of the views of the outsiders. The views of those outsiders, in turn, are presumed to have been shaped by the information that the parties' provided in a

---

10. Judith Resnik, *Many Doors? Closing Doors? Alternative Dispute Resolution and Adjudication,* 10 Ohio St. J. On Disp. Resol. 211, 218–220 (1995). (Citations omitted).

format akin to adjudication. In both 'summary jury trials' and 'minitrials,' information comes either from witnesses or with arguments by lawyers or litigants.

"A third form of ADR moves further away from formal modes of information development. Conversation (sometimes called mediation, sometimes called a conference, sometimes called evaluation) is employed to elicit agreement by the parties. Judge-run settlement conferences are an example of this genre of ADR, as are 'early neutral evaluations' ('ENE'). In this form of ADR, the relationship between information and outcome may be obscure, in part by virtue of the absence of formal articulation by the third party of its views of the respective positions of the disputants. Reaching agreement is one goal, as is the narrowing of the dispute, should further proceedings or adjudication be needed. When settlements take place, it is because of parties' consent, which may or may not track their legal rights."

* * *

Each form of ADR has distinctive benefits and is valuable in resolving certain types of disputes. One of the most pressing, and also most controversial, issues for the multi-door approach to dispute resolution is to develop a typology to determine which type of ADR mechanisms are best suited to which types of disputes. In this book, we will study most of the prevalent forms of ADR. We will attend to the particular advantages each one provides as well as to the legal issues and potential problems that each one presents.

3. HISTORY OF ALTERNATIVE DISPUTE RESOLUTION IN THE UNITED STATES

While the current trends are toward increasing use of ADR to resolve disputes of all types, ADR is not a new feature of American society. Since colonial times, many religious groups, voluntary associations and other small sub-communities have rejected the formal judicial system and established their own dispute resolution mechanisms to resolve disputes between members. In the following passage, Jerold Auerback gives a picture of the prevalence and function of alternative dispute resolution in earlier periods in American history.

JUSTICE WITHOUT LAW? by Jerold S. Auerbach[11]

"In many and varied communities, over the entire sweep of American history, the rule of law was explicitly rejected in favor of alternative means for ordering human relations and for resolving the inevitable disputes that arose between individuals. The success of non-legal dispute settlement has

---

11. Jerold S. Auerbach, JUSTICE WITHOUT LAW? (1983) (Reprinted with permission).

always depended upon a coherent community vision. How to resolve conflict, inversely stated, is how (or whether) to preserve community.

"Historically, arbitration and mediation were the preferred alternatives. They expressed an ideology of communitarian justice without formal law, an equitable process based on reciprocal access and trust among community members. They flourished as indigenous forms of community self-government. Communities that rejected legalized dispute settlement were variously defined: by geography, ideology, piety, ethnicity, and commercial pursuit. Yet their singleness of vision is remarkable. Despite their diversity they used identical processes because they shared a common commitment to the essence of communal existence: mutual access, responsibility, and trust. The founders of Dedham (a seventeenth-century Christian utopian community in Massachusetts), Quaker elders of Philadelphia, followers of John Humphrey Noyes at Oneida (a nineteenth-century utopian commune), the Chinese in San Francisco and Scandinavians in Minnesota, and even Chamber of Commerce businessmen easily could have collaborated on a common blueprint for dispute settlement. Sharing a suspicion of law and lawyers, they developed patterns of conflict resolution that reflected their common striving for social harmony beyond individual conflict, for justice without law.

". . . For centuries merchants and businessmen have been among the most outspoken proponents of non-legal dispute settlement. At each crucial stage in the development of commercial arbitration, it represented the effort of businessmen to elude lawyers and courts and to retain control over their disagreements. The familiar patterns of commercial custom were (and remain) vastly preferable to the alien procedures, frustrating delays, and high costs of litigation. Even in the modern era, when business interests have used non-legal dispute settlement to escape the strictures of government regulation, they have expressed a tenacious commitment to communitarian values (in their case, a community of profit). Secular and selfish to the core, they nonetheless have emerged among the most persistent American defenders of alternative dispute settlement. Buried in that irony lies a revealing example of the commercialization of the community impulse in modern America.

"Among the most committed practitioners of non-legal dispute settlement were immigrant ethnic groups. From the Dutch in New Amsterdam to the Jews of the Lower East Side of Manhattan, in a wide geographical arc that encompassed Scandinavians in the Midwest and Chinese on the West Coast, some newcomers from other cultures and traditions tried to place their disputes as far beyond the reach of American law as possible. Aliens in a hostile land, they encountered a society whose legal institutions often were overtly biased against them or, at best, indifferent to their distinctive values. Their own indigenous forms of dispute settlement, centuries old in some instances, shielded them from outside scrutiny and enabled them to inculcate and preserve their traditional norms. Ethnic-group dispute settlement often demonstrated a strong preference for community justice over legal due process, which was significantly less benevolent for new immigrants than government officials and legal professionals proclaimed.

"Yet for immigrants, as for religious utopians and businessmen, there was persistent tension between courts and their alternatives. The legal system, which ultimately was the arm of the state, discouraged autonomous pockets of resistance to its processes. Law was one of the primary instruments of acculturation; its rapid extension to immigrant communities was a national imperative. This made law appealing to some ethnic groups, as a vehicle to hasten their absorption into American society. But it threatened others, who feared loss more than they anticipated gain. If some immigrant groups (the Chinese, for example) retained their own dispute-settlement institutions to preserve cultural distinctiveness, so others (Jews in New York) modified theirs to facilitate acculturation. The pattern was as intricate as the American ethnic mosaic itself."

* * *

Jerold Auerbach's historical perspective demonstrates that every method of dispute resolution expresses the values and norms of a community. Thus we could attribute the current turn to, or return to, ADR as a reflection of the rebirth of community in modern life. We could identify ADR as one aspect of the rich and multi-dimensional associational life in which we participate, expressing not merely our commitment to these associations but our desire to be governed by their own, self-generating, norms. However, while the expression and construction of community can partially explain the recent expansion in the use of ADR, it cannot fully account for the phenomena. As we shall see in the materials that follow, there is a widespread and growing interest in ADR amongst all sectors of American society and all positions on the political spectrum, not merely amongst members of a shared community, but also in arms length dealings between strangers. Judges and policy-makers increasingly advocate expanding the use of ADR to be used in disputes between parties who do not share a normative community and are not using it to invoke shared values.

4. THE DEFINITION OF DISPUTES

Any consideration of the relative merits of different forms of dispute resolution must at some point address the question, what is a dispute? In the following excerpt, Marc Galanter poses that question and by doing so, challenges the empirical foundations of the alleged "litigation explosion." Galanter creates a pyramid-shaped typology of disputes, in which the many perceived grievances and injustices of everyday life are at the bottom and litigation is at the top. He uses this typology to argue that we may not have a litigation explosion at all. Galanter's typology is useful not merely for addressing the issue of the existence *vel non* of a litigation explosion, but also in explicating the variety of disputes that are amenable to resolution, whether through alternative techniques or conventional ones.

Reading the Landscape of Disputes: What We Know and Don't Know (And Think We Know) about Our Allegedly Contentious and Litigious Society by Marc S. Galanter[12]

"Whether or not America has experienced a 'litigation explosion,' or is suffering from 'legal pollution,' or is in thrall to an 'imperial judiciary,'" there has surely been an explosion of concern about the legal health of American society. A battery of observers has concluded that American society is over-legalized. According to these commentators, government, at our urging, tries to use law to regulate too much and in too much detail. Our courts, overwhelmed by a flood of litigation, are incapable of giving timely, inexpensive and effective relief, yet simultaneously extend their reach into areas beyond both their competence and legitimacy. A citizenry of unparalleled contentiousness exercises a hair trigger readiness to invoke the law, asking courts to address both trifles unworthy of them and social problems beyond their grasp. In short, these observers would have us believe that we suffer from too much law, too many lawyers, courts that take on too much—and an excessive readiness to utilize all of them....

"Typically the evidence cited for the litigation explosion consists of:

1.   The growth in filings in federal courts;

2.   The growth in size of the legal profession;

3.   Accounts of monster cases (such as the AT&T and IBM antitrust cases) and the vast amounts of resources consumed in such litigation;

4.   Atrocity stories—that is, citation of cases that seem grotesque, petty or extravagant: A half-million dollar suit is filed by a woman against community officials because they forbid her to breast-feed her child at the community pool; a child sues his parents for 'mal-parenting'"; a disappointed suitor brings suit for being stood up on a date, rejected mistresses sue their former paramours; sports fans sue officials and management; and Indians claim vast tracts of land; and

5.   War stories—that is, accounts of personal experience by business and other managers about how litigation impinges on their institutions, ties their hands, impairs efficiency, runs up costs, etc.

"Even if these statistics and accounts establish that we have a great deal of litigation, how do we know it is too much? This evidence draws its polemical power from the implicit comparison to some better past or some more favored place. Pervading these reports is a fond recollection of a time when it wasn't so—federal courts had fewer cases, there were fewer lawyers, people with outlandish claims were properly inhibited or chastened by upright lawyers, and managers could carry out their duties without fear of being sued. In this golden pre-litigious era, problems which were not solved by sturdy self-reliance or stoic endurance were addressed by vigorous community institutions. Not only was our own past more favored but, it is often noted, other societies of comparable advancement and amenity have fewer lawyers and less litigation. Japan, in particular, is viewed as exemplary. Its few lawyers and scarce litigation are thought to betoken a state of social harmony conducive to high productivity and prosperity...."

The Dispute Pyramid

1. The Lower Layers: The Construction of Disputes

"We can visualize litigation as the arrival at courts of disputes which arose at other locations in society. Counting the number of cases that arrive turns out to involve some tricky questions, but in theory, we can imagine measuring the amount of litigation by this method. Disputes, however, are even more difficult to chart. They are not some elemental particles of social life that can be counted and measured. Disputes are not discrete events like births or deaths; they are more like such constructs as illnesses and friendships, composed in part of the perceptions and understandings of those who participate in and observe them.

"Disputes are drawn from a vast sea of events, encounters, collisions, rivalries, disappointments, discomforts and injuries. The span and composition of that sea depend on the broad contours of social life. For example, the introduction of machinery brings increases in non-intentional injuries; higher population densities and cash crops bring raised expectations and rivalry for scarce land; advances in knowledge enlarge possibilities of control and expectations of care. Some things in this sea of 'proto-disputes' become disputes through a process in which injuries are perceived, persons or institutions responsible for remedying them are identified, forums for presenting these claims are located and approached, claims are formulated acceptably to the forum, appropriate resources are invested, and attempts at diversion resisted. The disputes that arrive at courts can be seen as the survivors of a long and exhausting process.

"In this view, the arrival of matters at the doors of lawyers and courts is a late stage in an extended process by which the dispute has crystallized out of the sea of proto-disputes. As part of a larger system of disputing, the institution of litigation is shaped by this process of construction and selection that provides it with cases. Litigation, in turn, profoundly affects what happens at earlier stages by providing cues, symbols, and bargaining counters which the actors use in constructing (and dismantling) disputes. In order to understand what lawyers and courts do, we need to know about the ' "earlier" ' stages of this process.

"We can visualize the early stages of the process as the successive layers of a vast and uneven pyramid. Only recently has there been any attempt to examine systematically the lower layers of the pyramid ... We begin, in effect, with all human experience which might be identified as injurious. This should alert us to the subjective and unstable character of the process, for what is injurious depends on current and ever-changing estimations of what enhances or impairs health, happiness, character and other desired states. Knowledge and ideology constantly send new currents through this vast ocean.

"Some experiences will be perceived as injurious.... Among these perceived injurious experiences, some may be seen as deserved punishment, some as the result of assumed risk or fickle fate; but a subset is viewed as violations of some right or entitlement caused by a human agent (individual or collective) and susceptible of remedy. These, ... are grievances. Again, characterization of an event as a grievance will depend on the cognitive repertoire with which society supplies the injured person and his idiosyncratic adaptation of it. He may, for example, be liberally supplied with ideological lenses to focus blame or to diffuse it.

"When such grievances are voiced to the offending party they become claims. Many will be granted. Those claims not granted become disputes. That is, '[a] dispute exists when a claim based on a grievance is rejected in whole or in part.'" [citation omitted] Using this terminology lets us attempt a crude sketch of the lower layers of the pyramid.

"First, a very large number of injuries go unperceived. Breaches of product warranties and professional malpractice may be difficult to recognize and go undiscovered. Even if the injury is discovered, the injured may not perceive that he has an entitlement that has been violated, the identity of the responsible party, or the presence of the remedy to be pursued.

"The perception of grievances requires cognitive resources. Thus Best and Andreasen found that both higher income and white households perceive more problems with the goods they buy and complain more both to sellers and to third parties than do poor or black households. [citation]

"Even where injuries are perceived, a common response is resignation, that is, 'lumping it.' In the most comprehensive study available, Miller and Sarat report that over one-quarter of those with reported 'middle range' (i.e., involving the equivalent of $1,000 or more) grievances did not pursue the matter by making a claim. This proportion was fairly uniform across subject matters (with the striking exception of discrimination problems; almost three quarters did not move from grievance to claim). Of course this figure is not a precise measure of the phenomena of 'lumping it' because it may include individuals who took other forms of unilateral action—like exit, avoidance or self-help....

"Exit and avoidance—withdrawal from a situation or relationship by moving, resigning, severing relations, etc.—are common responses to many kinds of troubles. Like 'lumping it,' exit is an alternative to invoking any kind of organized remedy system, although its presence as a sanction may support the working of other remedies. The use of 'exit' options depends on a number of factors: on the availability of alternative opportunities or partners and information about them; on bearable costs of withdrawal, transfer, relocation, and development of new relationships; on the pull of loyalty to previous arrangements; and on the availability and cost of other remedies.

"Disputes are also pursued by various kinds of self-help such as physical retaliation, seizure of property, or removal of offending objects.

The amount of self-help in contemporary industrial societies has not been mapped, but it evidently occurs very frequently....

"The most typical response to grievances, at least to sizable ones, is to make a claim to the 'other party'—the merchant, the other driver or his insurer, the ex-spouse who has not paid support, etc.... Some claims may be granted outright, but a large number are contested in whole or part. It is this contest that Felstiner, et al. label a dispute. [citation] Miller and Sarat found that about two-thirds of claims lead to disputes. A large portion of disputes are resolved by negotiation between the parties.... 'Negotiation' ranges from that which is indistinguishable from the everyday adjustments that constitute the relationship to that which is 'bracketed' as a disruption or emergency.

"Some disputes are abandoned by their initiators. Ladinsky and Susmilch, who coined the term 'clumpit' for those who make a claim but don't persist, found that more than one-quarter of all consumers with problems abandoned their claims. [citation] Similarly, a study of medical malpractice claims found that 43% were dropped without receiving any payment. [citation]

"Other disputes are heard by the school principal, the shop steward or the administrator—i.e., in forums that are part of the social setting within which the dispute arose. Such 'embedded forums' range from those which are hardly distinguishable from the everyday decision making within an institution ('I'd like to see the manager') to those which are specially constituted to handle disputes which cannot be resolved by everyday processes.

"We know that such forums process a tremendous number of disputes. We have no count of them, but we do have some idea of the conditions under which they flourish. Resort to embedded forums is encouraged where there are continuing relations between the disputants. Continuing relations raise the cost of exit, they increase the likelihood of some shared norms, and they supply opportunities for application of sanctions—e.g., by direct withdrawal of beneficial relations or by damage to reputation that reduces prospects for other beneficial relations.

2. *The Upper Layers: Lawyers and Courts*

"The pyramid imagery imparts to the process of dispute construction and transformation a stability and a solidity that are illusory. Changes in perceptions of harm, in attributions of responsibility, in expectations of redress, in readiness to be assertive—all of these affect the number of grievances, claims and disputes....

"As we trace the movement of disputes up the pyramid and laterally from one forum to another, it is useful to recall that the dispute does not remain unchanged in the process. The disputes that come to courts originate elsewhere and may undergo considerable change in the course of entering and proceeding through the courts. Disputes must be reformulated in applicable legal categories. Such reformulation may restrict their scope.

Diffuse disputes may become more focused in time and space, narrowed down to a set of discrete incidents involving specified individuals. Or, conversely, the original dispute may expand, becoming the vehicle for consideration of a larger set of events or relationships. The list of parties may grow or shrink; the range of normative claims may be narrowed or expanded; the remedy sought may change; the goals and audiences of the parties may alter. In short the dispute that emerges in the court process may differ significantly from the dispute that arrived there, as well as from 'similar' disputes that proceed through other settings.

"Lawyers are often viewed as important agents of this transformation process. They help translate clients' disputes to fit into applicable legal categories. But lawyers may also act as gatekeepers, screening out claims that they are disinclined to pursue. Macaulay, in studying the dissemination of consumer law to Wisconsin lawyers, found that lawyers tended to defuse consumer claims, diverting them into mediative channels rather than translating them into adversary claims. [citation] . . .

"Those disputes that are not resolved by negotiation or in some embedded forum may be taken to a champion or a forum external to the situation. Recourse to any such third party is relatively infrequent across the whole range of disputes. . . .

3. *The Litigation Process: Attrition, Routine Processing, Bargaining and Settlement*

"Of those disputes which are taken to court, the vast majority are disposed of by abandonment, withdrawal, or settlement, without full-blown adjudication and often without any authoritative disposition by the court. In fact, of those cases that do reach a full authoritative disposition by a court, a large portion do not involve a contest. They are uncontested either because the dispute has been resolved, as in divorce, or because only one party appears. Over 30% of cases in American courts of general jurisdiction are not formally contested. This predominance of uncontested matters in American courts is long-standing.

"Many cases are withdrawn or abandoned because the mere invocation of the court served the initiator's purpose of harassment, warning or delay. Police may make an arrest or file charges for purposes of control with no intention of pursuing prosecution. Similarly, Merry reports that it is the issuance of the complaint and holding of the preliminary hearing that are the crucial goals of court use among residents in a poor neighborhood. [citation] The invocation of official adjudicatory institutions does not necessarily express either a preference or an intention to pursue the dispute in official forums, to secure the application of official rules, or to obtain an adjudicated outcome. The official system may be invoked, or invocation may be threatened, in order to punish or harass, to demonstrate prowess, to force an opponent to settle, or to secure compliance with the decision of another forum. . . .

"[M]ost civil cases in American courts are settled. That is, they terminate in an outcome agreed upon by the parties, sometimes formally ratified by the court, sometimes only noted as settled, and sometimes, from the court's viewpoint, abandoned. The settlement process may begin even before the suit is filed. For example, a great majority of automobile injury claims are settled before filing. Of those claims that become lawsuits, settlement is the prevalent mode of disposition. Of the cases in ten courts studied by the Civil Litigation Research Project, about 88% were settled; only 9% went to trial. . . .

CONCLUSION

" . . . [C]ontemporary patterns of disputing [are] an adaptive (but not necessarily optimal) response to a set of changing conditions. There have been great changes in the social production of injuries as a result of, among other things, the increased power and range of injury-producing machinery and substances. There has been a great increase in social knowledge about the causation of injuries and of technologies for preventing them; there has been a wide dissemination of awareness of this knowledge to an increasingly educated public. There is an enhanced sense that harmful and confining conditions could be remedied. At the same time more of the interactions in the lives of many are with remote entities over which there are few direct controls. Government is used more to regulate these remote sources of harm and to assuage previously unremedied harms. Legal remedies become available to large segments of the population who earlier had little occasion to use the law. It may be easier to mobilize social support for disputing. In the light of all these changes, the pattern of use is conservative, departing relatively little from earlier patterns.

"But overshadowing the change in actual disputing patterns are changes in the symbolic aspects of the system. There is more law, and our experience of most of it is increasingly indirect and mediated. Even while most disputing leads to mediation or bargaining, rather than authoritative disposition by the courts, the courts occupy a larger portion of the symbolic universe and litigation seems omnipresent.

"Is more and more visible litigation the sign and agent of the demise of community? This view of litigation as a destructive force, undermining other social institutions, strikes me as misleadingly one-sided. If litigation marks the assertion of individual will, it is also a reaching out for communal help and affirmation. If some litigation challenges accepted practice, it is an instrument for testing the quality of present consensus. It provides a forum for moving issues from the realm of unilateral power into a realm of public accountability. By permitting older clusters of practice to be challenged and new ones tested and incorporated into the constellation it helps to 'create a new paradigm for the establishment of stable community life.' If we relinquish the notion of community as some unchanging and all-encompassing gemeinschaft in favor of the multiple, partial and emergent community that we experience in contemporary urban life, we need not regard litigation as an antagonist of community."

* * *

Professor Galanter's typology of disputes illustrates that the term "dispute" is socially constructed and highly variable. He concludes from the fact that few "disputes" are actually litigated, there may not be a litigation explosion in relation to the number of actual disputes. In part, Galanter relied upon data assembled by the Wisconsin Civil Litigation Research Project, which studied some 1500 organizations and 1650 legal cases in the early 1980s. That study concluded that very few disputes end up as lawsuits, and of those, even fewer are litigated.[13] The study supports the view that the so-called litigation explosion is highly exaggerated, if not utterly mythical. If the litigation explosion does not exist, or at least does not take the form of a crisis, then one is left to wonder whether those courts and commentators who advocate increased use of ADR have some other goals in addition to reducing the number of litigated cases. Here Auerbach's historical perspective is helpful. As he suggests, whether or not there is a litigation explosion, the rhetoric of excessive litigation plays a powerful symbolic role in the world of ADR because it suggests an imagined world of self-regulating communities and shared communal values.

5. THE ROLE OF ADR IN REDEFINING DISPUTES

Thus far, we have considered alternative dispute resolution as a set of *techniques and procedures* that are different from the techniques and procedures available in a state or and federal court. In this view, ADR is a proxy for litigation, a change in forum that does not affect the outcome. However, there is a view of ADR in which it is not merely an alternative forum, a more efficient version of the civil justice system. Some commentators claim that the alternative processes differ from courts not only in terms of the procedures followed, but also in terms of the substantive norms to be applied. It is claimed that alternative dispute resolution involves, and should involve, the application of different rules and different norms than a court would apply in the resolution of a dispute. For example, historically arbitration tribunals permit decision-makers to apply customary or community norms of justice rather than legal rules of decision in deciding disputes. This practice is justified, indeed extolled, on the grounds that the norms of the community are better suited to the specific parties' dispute than an impersonal, one-size-fits-all legal rule. For this reason, some commentators advocate ADR not only as cheaper justice or expedited justice, but as better justice.

In addition, some commentators favor alternative dispute resolution for its ability to provide different remedies than law courts can. For example, through mediation and other ADR mechanisms, parties can devise compromise solutions rather than winner-take-all damage awards. Thus, it is claimed, ADR can preserve on-going relationships even in the face of disruptive disputes.

13. D. Trubek, et. al., CIVIL LITIGATION RESEARCH PROJECT: FINAL REPORT, VOL. I: STUDY- ING THE CIVIL LITIGATION PROCESS, 1–78 et. seq. (1983).

Some advocates of alternative dispute resolution make an even stronger claim. They suggest that ADR is a method, not of resolving, but of redefining disputes. In the informal settings which ADR provides, it is claimed, disputing parties need not lock into rigid adversarial positions. They need not be aggressive nor do they need to deploy aggressive lawyers on their behalf. Because dispute mechanisms are less concerned with formal rights and more concerned with the psychological aspects of disputes, disputing parties can affirm the positive side of their relationships while acknowledging and attempting to resolve conflict. As Carol J. King writes, "The alternative dispute resolution movement can ... be interpreted to represent a rebalancing of social values towards a more cooperative orientation, away from the focus on individual rights characteristic of the 1960s."[14]

Reflecting the way disputes are redefined by an ADR framework, the vocabulary of alternative dispute settlement is peppered with psychological terms such as needs, motivations, perceptions, and understandings, rather than more familiar legal terms such as entitlements, duties, performance, and breach. Similarly, in ADR settings, third-parties are not considered judges who have been brought in to decide cases and award remedies; rather they are neutrals brought in to mediate, to facilitate, to reconcile.

The psychological perspective on dispute resolution is particularly evident in the discussions about mediation. Mediators, some claim, are superior to judges precisely because they deal with the psychological rather than the confrontational aspects of disputes. They are less interested in blame than in reconciliation. Thus, they can foster healing and preserve relationships while resolving current disputes. Professor Robert Bush describes the distinctive virtues of mediation in the following excerpt:

Efficiency and Protection, or Empowerment and Recognition? The Mediator's Role and Ethical Standards in Mediation by Robert A. Baruch Bush[15]

"Thoughtful mediation theorists and practitioners have given much consideration to identifying mediation's unique powers. In their comments, two points consistently are expressed regarding the capacities of the mediation process.

"The first special power of mediation, and what some call '[t]he overriding feature and ... value of mediation,' is that 'it is a consensual process that seeks self-determined resolutions.' Mediation places the substantive outcome of the dispute within the control and determination of the parties themselves; it frees them from relying on or being subjected to the opinions and standards of outside 'higher authorities,' legal or otherwise.

14. Carol J. King, *Are Justice and Harmony Mutually Exclusive: A Response to Professor Nader*, 10 OHIO STATE J. OF DISPUTE RESOLUTION 65, 72 (1994).

15. Robert A. Baruch Bush, *Efficiency and Protection, or Empowerment and Recognition?: The Mediator's Role and Ethical Standards in Mediation*, 41 Florida L. Rev. 253 (1989). Reprinted with permission.

Further, mediation not only allows the parties to set their own standards for an acceptable solution, it also requires them to search for solutions that are within their own capacity to effectuate. In other words, the parties themselves set the standards, and the parties themselves marshall the actual resources to resolve the dispute. When agreement is reached, the parties have designed and implemented their own solution to the problem. Even when the parties do not reach an agreement, they experience the concrete possibility, to be more fully realized in other situations, that they can control their own circumstances. They discover that they need not be wholly dependent on outside institutions, legal or otherwise, to solve their problems. I call this the empowerment function of mediation: its capacity to encourage the parties to exercise autonomy, choice, and self-determination. . . .

"The second special power of mediation was described classically by Professor Lon Fuller: 'The central quality of mediation [is] its capacity to reorient the parties to each other . . . by helping them to achieve a new and shared perception of their relationship, a perception that will redirect their attitudes and dispositions toward one another.' What Fuller describes here is not just a technique to produce agreements, but an inherently valuable accomplishment uniquely attainable through mediation. Fuller sees mediation as evoking in each party recognition and acknowledgment of, and some degree of understanding and empathy for, the other party's situation, even though their interests and positions may remain opposed. Of course, such mutual recognition often will help produce concrete accommodations and an ultimate agreement. But even when it does not, evoking recognition is itself an accomplishment of enormous value: the value of escaping our alienated isolation and rediscovering our common humanity, even in the midst of bitter division. Professor Riskin observes accordingly that one of the great values of mediation is that it can 'encourage the kind of dialogue that would help . . . [the disputants experience] a perspective of caring and interconnection.' Others also have stressed this special power of mediation to 'humanize' us to one another, to translate between us, and to help us recognize each other as fellows even when we are in conflict. I call this the recognition function of mediation."

* * *

The psychological perspective on dispute resolution has been a subject of lively debate, with fervent defenders as well as critics. The pros and cons of this viewpoint will be explored more fully in the cases and materials on mediation, in Chapter 2, below.

---

6.   CRITICAL PERSPECTIVES ON ALTERNATIVE DISPUTE RESOLUTION

Decisions about how much scope to give to ADR and how much courts should police and constrict its use are informed by one's views of the values and advantages ADR offers. There are many perspectives about the advantages of different dispute resolution mechanisms and the role each one can and should play in resolving disputes. Thus, along with the rise of ADR within our legal system, there have arisen skeptics who question whether alternative dispute resolution provides better justice than the civil justice system. Some of the writings of the leading ADR skeptics are excerpted below, and others are reprinted, by topic, throughout the casebook. The issues raised by the skeptics are often echoed in the debates between the majority and dissenting judges in the controversial legal issues that surround the use of ADR as a substitute for litigation.

* * *

Alternative Dispute Resolution: Panacea or Anathema? by Harry T. Edwards[16]

In *Alternative Dispute Resolution: Panacea or Anathema?*, Judge Harry T. Edwards warns that public law disputes—which he defines as disputes over constitutional issues or other issues of great public concern—are not appropriate for a form of ADR that does not operate within the purview of the courts. He writes:

"The Alternative Dispute Resolution (ADR) movement has seen an extraordinary transformation in the last ten years. Little more than a decade ago, only a handful of scholars and attorneys perceived the need for alternatives to litigation. The ADR idea was seen as nothing more than a hobbyhorse for a few offbeat scholars. Today, with the rise of public complaints about the inefficiencies and injustices of our traditional court systems, the ADR movement has attracted a bandwagon following of adherents. ADR is no longer shackled with the reputation of a cult movement. . . .

"Popularity and public interest are not sure signs of a quality endeavor. This is certainly true of ADR, because the movement is ill-defined and the motives of some ADR adherents are questionable. It appears that some people have joined the ADR bandwagon, without regard for its purposes or consequences, because they see it as a fast (and sometimes interesting) way to make a buck. It has also been suggested that some of those people who promote ADR as a means to serve the poor and oppressed in society are in fact principally motivated by a desire to limit the work of the courts in areas affecting minority interests, civil rights, and civil liberties. And it is sometimes claimed that there are those who subscribe to the ADR movement because they view efficient and inexpensive dispute resolution as an important societal goal, without regard for the substantive results reached. If the ADR movement prominently reflects such thinking then it is unclear whether the movement is a panacea for, or is anathema to, the perceived problems in our traditional court systems. . . .

16. Harry T. Edwards, *Alternative Dispute Resolution: Panacea or Anathema?*, 99 Harv. L. Rev. 668 (1986). Reprinted with permission.

"It is clear, however, that a number of ADR proponents have a far more ambitious vision of ADR than [simply a substitute for litigation]. Some, such as Jerold Auerbach, seem to favor community resolution of disputes using community values instead of the rule of law. Others, such as the Chief Justice, complain that 'there is some form of mass neurosis that leads many people to think courts were created to solve all the problems of mankind,' and believe that ADR must be used to curb the 'flood' of 'new kinds of conflicts' (such as 'welfare ... claims under the Equal Protection Clause') that have purportedly overwhelmed the judicial system. In either case, these ADR advocates propose a truly revolutionary step—the resolution of cases through ADR mechanisms free from any judicial monitoring or control.

"If we can assume that it is possible to finance and administer truly efficient systems of dispute resolution, then there would appear to be no significant objections to the use of even wholly independent ADR mechanisms to resolve private disputes that do not implicate important public values. For instance, settling minor grievances between neighbors according to local mores or resolving simple contract disputes by commercial norms may lead to the disposition of more disputes and the greater satisfaction of the participants. In strictly private disputes, ADR mechanisms such as arbitration often are superior to adjudication. Disputes can be resolved by neutrals with substantive expertise, preferably chosen by the parties, and the substance of disputes can be examined without issue-obscuring procedural rules. Tens of thousands of cases are resolved this way each year by labor and commercial arbitration, and even more private disputes undoubtedly could be better resolved through ADR than by adjudication.

"However, if ADR is extended to resolve difficult issues of constitutional or public law—making use of nonlegal values to resolve important social issues or allowing those the law seeks to regulate to delimit public rights and duties—there is real reason for concern. An oft-forgotten virtue of adjudication is that it ensures the proper resolution and application of public values. In our rush to embrace alternatives to litigation, we must be careful not to endanger what law has accomplished or to destroy this important function of formal adjudication. As Professor Fiss notes:

> Adjudication uses public resources, and employs not strangers chosen by the parties but public officials chosen by a process in which the public participates. These officials, like members of the legislative and executive branches, possess a power that has been defined and conferred by public law, not by private agreement. Their job is not to maximize the ends of private parties, not simply to secure the peace, but to explicate and give force to the values embodied in authoritative texts such as the Constitution and statutes: to interpret those values and to bring reality in accord with them. [quoting Fiss, Against Settlement, 93 Yale L. J. 1073, 1085 (1984)].

"The concern here is that ADR will replace the rule of law with nonlegal values. J. Anthony Lucas' masterful study of Boston during the busing crisis highlights the critical point that often our nation's most basic values—such as equal justice under the law—conflict with local nonlegal mores. This was true in Boston during the school desegregation battle, and it was true in the South during the civil rights battles of the sixties. This conflict, however, between national public values reflected in rules of law and nonlegal values that might be embraced in alternative dispute resolution, exists in even more mundane public issues.

"For example, many environmental disputes are now settled by negotiation and mediation instead of adjudication. Indeed, as my colleague Judge Wald recently observed, there is little hope that Superfund legislation can solve our nation's toxic waste problem unless the vast bulk of toxic waste disputes are resolved through negotiation, rather than litigation. Yet, as necessary as environmental negotiation may be, it is still troubling. When Congress or a government agency has enacted strict environmental protection standards, negotiations that compromise these strict standards with weaker standards result in the application of values that are simply inconsistent with the rule of law. Furthermore, environmental mediation and negotiation present the danger that environmental standards will be set by private groups without the democratic checks of governmental institutions . . .

"We must also be concerned lest ADR becomes a tool for diminishing the judicial development of legal rights for the disadvantaged. Professor Tony Amsterdam has aptly observed that ADR may result in the reduction of possibilities for legal redress of wrongs suffered by the poor and underprivileged, 'in the name of increased access to justice and judicial efficiency.' Inexpensive, expeditious, and informal adjudication is not always synonymous with fair and just adjudication. The decision makers may not understand the values at stake and parties to disputes do not always possess equal power and resources. Sometimes because of this inequality and sometimes because of deficiencies in informal processes lacking procedural protections, the use of alternative mechanisms will produce nothing more than inexpensive and ill-informed decisions. And these decisions may merely legitimate decisions made by the existing power structure within society. Additionally, by diverting particular types of cases away from adjudication, we may stifle the development of law in certain disfavored areas of law. Imagine, for example, the impoverished nature of civil rights law that would have resulted had all race discrimination cases in the sixties and seventies been mediated rather than adjudicated. The wholesale diversion of cases involving the legal rights of the poor may result in the definition of these rights by the powerful in our society rather than by the application of fundamental societal values reflected in the rule of law.

"Family law offers one example of this concern that ADR will lead to 'second-class justice.' In the last ten years, women have belatedly gained many new rights, including new laws to protect battered women and new mechanisms to ensure the enforcement of child-support awards. There is a real danger, however, that these new rights will become simply a mirage if all 'family law' disputes are blindly pushed into mediation. The issues presented extend beyond questions of unequal bargaining power. For example, battered women often need the batterer ordered out of the home or arrested—goals fundamentally inconsistent with mediation. . . .

"Finally, there are some disputes in which community values—coupled with the rule of law—may be a rich source of justice. Mediation of disputes between parents and schools about special education programs for handicapped children has been very successful. A majority of disputes have been settled by mediation, and parents are generally positive about both the outcome and the process. At issue in these mediations is the appropriate education for a child, a matter best resolved by parents and educators—not courts. Similarly, many landlord-tenant disputes can ultimately be resolved only by negotiation. Most tenant 'rights' are merely procedural rather than substantive. Yet tenants desire substantive improvement in housing conditions or assurances that they will not be evicted. Mediation of landlord-tenant disputes, therefore, can be very successful—often more successful than adjudication—because both parties have much to gain by agreement.

"In both of these examples, however, the option of ultimate resort to adjudication is essential. It is only because handicapped children have a statutory right to education that parent-school mediation is successful. It is only because tenants have procedural rights that landlords will bargain at all.

"ADR can thus play a vital role in constructing a judicial system that is both more manageable and more responsive to the needs of our citizens. It is essential—as the foregoing examples illustrate—that this role of ADR be strictly limited to prevent the resolution of important constitutional and public law issues by ADR mechanisms that are independent of our courts. Fortunately, few ADR programs have attempted to remove public law issues from the courts. Although this may merely reflect the relative youth of the ADR movement, it may also manifest an awareness of the danger of public law resolution in nonjudicial fora."

* * *

The Contradictions of Informal Justice by Rick Abel[17]

In the following selection, Professor Richard Abel argues that informal procedures actually disempower people by individualizing disputes and rendering them invisible. He also argues, along with other critics, such as Professors Martha Fineman, Trina Grillo, and others whose writings appear in later sections of the book, that informal mechanisms deny litigants the due process protection of a court, protection that can equalize power relations between wildly unequal parties. Thus he claims, the poor and disadvantaged members of society will lose in informal settings because in

17. Richard L. Abel, *"The Contradictions of Informal Justice,"* in Richard L. Abel, ed., THE POLITICS OF INFORMAL JUSTICE, vol. 1 at 267, 267–296 (1982) (citations omitted). Reprinted with permission.

such settings their lack of power or resources amplifies their disadvantage and therefore exacerbates problems of inequality. Professor Abel writes:

"Informal institutions neutralize conflict by denying its existence, by simulating a society in which conflict is less frequent and less threatening, and by choosing to recognize and handle only those forms of conflict that do not challenge basic structures. Informal processes moderate the antagonistic adversarial posture of the parties. This is a difficult task because people involved in conflict usually want to win; they seek vindication. For the same reason, they prefer to represent themselves; failing that, they invoke the support of an ally or advocate; and as a last resort they appeal to an authority they believe will be sympathetic. But informal justice prohibits many forms of aggression, isolates disputants from allies, and refuses to be partisan.

"[W]hereas violent conflict is waged by groups and legal conflict by individuals, informal justice renders conflict *intraindividual*—an expression of the personal problems *within* each party. The slogan that mediation offers to disputants was best stated by Pogo: 'We have met the enemy, and he is us.' The mediator is trained in counseling skills, and *she* (for there are many more women mediators than women judges) seeks to help the parties accommodate. . . .

"If informal justice denies the existence of conflict, its advocates simultaneously (if inconsistently) insist that there is too much controversy. Chief Justice Burger has perhaps been most eloquent on this theme, condemning 'our vicious legal spiral,' 'the inherently litigious nature of Americans,' and 'excessive contentiousness,' but many other legal notables have seconded his view, urging (with heavy irony) 'let's everybody litigate' or decrying the legal 'explosion,' 'California's colossal legal appetite,' 'legal pollution,' our 'Litigious Society,' or 'hyperlexis: our national disease.' Formal legal conflict has replaced the 'outside agitator' as the serpent in the garden. This attitude sounds reasonable and value-neutral; after all, most of us would prefer peace to conflict. But it obscures the fact that conflict is necessarily the act of *two* parties, one making a demand and another resisting it. The proponents of informalism seek to reduce conflict by curtailing demands, never acknowledging that just as much conflict would be eliminated if those to whom the demands are addressed would accede—cease discriminating, polluting, exploiting, oppressing.

"Advocates of informalism suggest the unreasonableness of the demands of oppressed groups by extolling social settings where those demands would never be made: small towns, nineteenth-century America, the patriarchal family, tribal societies, Far Eastern cultures. . . . [T]hese disparate environments were united by their respect for authority. The necessary concomitant of such respect is an acceptance of place, the subordination of women to men, young to old, nonwhites to whites, religious minorities to the majority, consumers to sellers, workers to capitalists. Furthermore, most of those societies were far more homogeneous than contemporary America. Our greater heterogeneity produces not only increased conflict but also conflict that is subversive, rather than supportive, of the social order. Whereas conflict in homogeneous societies reinforces shared norms by creating occasions on which they may collectively be asserted; conflict in heterogeneous societies threatens norms by highlighting incompatibility and decencies.

"One of the most powerful ways in which informal (and formal) legal institutions neutralize conflict is by individualizing grievances. ... The individual grievant must appear alone before the informal institution, deprived of the support of such natural allies as family, friends, work mates, even neighbors. ... In one respect, informal institutions actually excel their formal counter-parts in individualizing conflict: They operate in total privacy. Although this guarantee of confidentiality is justified in the name of process, its effect is to isolate grievants from one another and from the community, inhibiting the perception of common grievances. Without the possibility of aggregation, of some greater impact, even the most committed grievant will burn out and 'lump' the complaint.

"Informal institutions ... tend to be antinormative: The complainant who protests a normative violation may find himself criticized for making the complaint; the intermediary who is too judgmental may be instructed to relax his standards. This hostility to norms is consistent with an ideology that elevates the market over politics and individual choice over collective decision making, and with a pop psychology that urges: 'if it feels good, do it.'

"[I]nformalism is simply the latest in a long line of reforms that seek to realize the promises of liberalism. Consistent with liberal ideals, they do so by concentrating on *process* not *outcome*. ... Yet as Marc Galanter has persuasively argued, ... changes in process will not alter outcomes as long as the structure of the adversaries remains constant. Labor arbitration works (when it works) because capital is opposed by organized labor, not by individual workers; if the process is transposed to conflict between slumlords and unorganized tenants, for instance, it will inevitably favor the former. Informalism can respond to such criticism only by trying to evade it, by stressing process to the neglect of outcome, pretending that no one wins or loses, advancing the satisfaction of individual disputants as the only appropriate criterion. Mediators can conclude that they are extraordinarily successful, and government and private notables (including the chief justice and attorney general of the United States and the president of the American Bar Association) can lavish uncritical praise on institutions we know to be virtually ineffective.

"[I]nformalism may ensure that more claimants get *some* redress, but the relief is almost always less adequate—that is certainly the history of workers' compensation, no-fault divorce, and no-fault compensation for automobile accidents. Laws designed to protect and benefit the disadvantaged, such as those protecting the consumer, are ignored in informal tribunals. We can see the differential resources conferred by formal and informal institutions if we look at a particular disadvantaged category—

women—and note that informal institutions offer them less protection against spousal violence and worsen their chances of obtaining custody after divorce.... [T]he claim that informal institutions are speedier than their formal counterparts is often based on a false comparison with full-scale trials; if informal processes are compared, instead, with the abbreviated proceedings by which the vast majority of cases are disposed in formal courts, they are no quicker and may even be slower.... [I]nformal institutions are ineffective in ensuring the performance of agreed outcomes. Unrepresented individual plaintiffs have much more difficulty executing judgments than do unrepresented corporate plaintiffs. Given all this, evidence, that individual grievants are 'satisfied' hardly proves that they are benefited by informal institutions, especially since those grievants appear to be just as 'satisfied' when the informal institution *fails* to hold a hearing and even when the institution itself labels the dispute as 'unresolved.' By the time the informal institution measures satisfaction, it has so depressed the expectations and shaped the wishes of the grievant that any outcome will be satisfactory. Indeed, even the advocates of informalism acknowledge that it is ineffective in redressing the grievances of individuals against powerful entities. This inefficacy is neither accidental nor rectifiable but is rather essential to another function that informal institutions share with the other legal institutions of liberal capitalism—legitimating that social system by publicly declaring rights and remedies while simultaneously ensuring that they are systematically unenforced or underenforced."

* * *

Controlling Processes in the Practice of Law: Hierarchy and Pacification in the Movement to Re-form Dispute Ideology by **Laura Nader**[18]

Professor Laura Nader, a Professor of Anthropology at the University of California at Berkeley, argues that the rapid rise of the ADR movement in the United States marks the ascendency of an ideology of "coercive harmony." She describes how harmony ideology leads dispute resolution professionals to reshape disputes over rights, values and interests into "communications problems." Once disputes are so recharacterized, Nader contends, issues of power, coercion and injustice become irrelevant. She writes:

"Over the past twenty years lawyers and judges in the United States have been pummeled in the popular media and in dispute resolution journals by an accelerating wave of antagonism toward litigation and the adversarial process. During the same period, enthusiasm for alternative dispute resolution (ADR) has promoted these mechanisms as being efficient, as providing access to resolution, and as exalting harmony rather than rights. The intensity was striking and so was the impact. So successful

---

18. Laura Nader, *Controlling Processes in the Practice of Law: Hierarchy and Pacification in the Movement to Re-form Dispute* *Ideology*, 9 Ohio St. J. on Disp. Resol. 1 (1993). Reprinted with permission.

has the movement against litigation and the adversary process been, that there has been widespread acceptance of a legal harmony model of law as an answer to the concerns of how to deliver justice to the many.

"The movement was not about theory. It was directed towards practice. ADR was on the agenda of legal practitioners. Trial lawyers met to ponder their complicitous part as promulgators of anger and the adversary process. Federal judges bought into the reframing of what is wrong with our legal system, and often indiscriminately accepted the ADR analysis. Even stranger were the 1960's activist lawyers, who are now born-again mediators who accept ADR forums and use them to erase issues of class, gender, and race, to 'treat people equally.' By 1993, ADR has become a major industry, which includes social workers, mental health professionals, lawyers, behavioral scientists, and dozens of journals where ADR is formalized.

"The ADR rhetoric of the past two decades was a response to the law reform discourse of the 1960s, a discourse concerned with justice and root causes, and with debates over right and wrong. In the early 1970s, when the justice talk of the various rights movements (civil rights, consumer rights, environmental rights, etc.) was replaced by talk of harmony and efficiency, the public debate was over the question of 'too much litigation.' A change in the manner of thinking about rights and justice was shaped through a new discourse, and by means of this discourse produced a movement against the contentious or adversarial qualities of American law. In some ways, it was a rebellion against law and lawyers—often by lawyers themselves. A movement to control litigation was being constructed to replace justice and rights talk with what I call harmony ideology, the belief that harmony in the guise of compromise or agreement is ipso facto better than an adversary posture.

"In any period of history, harmony ideology is accompanied by an intolerance for conflict. The intention to prevent the expression of discord rather than to deal with its cause takes on prominence. The rationalization for ADR was from the outset articulated as protecting the courts from the 'garbage cases,' such as gender, environmental, and consumer cases, as well as protecting the courts from overload. The Harvard Law School was in the lead, and soon a plethora of new courses and journals began to appear in law schools around the country, all of which included training in alternative dispute resolution. After I summarize the components that became the centerpiece of the ADR movement, I will focus on the questions: Why have so many people in the legal profession fallen prey to ADR rhetoric? Why did members of the legal elite accept this ideological takeover of their profession with such placidity? I argue that harmony ideology—manifested in the reluctance of many lawyers to defend their profession against this ADR onslaught—finds fertile ground through mechanisms of hierarchy and coercive harmony. . . .

"For my research, the turning point was 1976, the year of the bicentennial celebration of the United States. During that year, the Roscoe Pound Conference, 'Perspectives on Justice in the Future,' was held in St.

Paul, Minnesota, where Roscoe Pound delivered his long-remembered 1906 talk to the American Bar Association on 'The Causes of Popular Dissatisfaction with the Administration of Justice.' The Pound Conference brought together judges and staff from all of our fifty states in what became a key social drama, the beginning of a serious attack on the adversary process. The Conference was described as serving 'to arouse a new spirit . . . a new optimism about the possibility of creative innovation in the administration of justice.' The presenters were law-trained, and their messages covered the common theme of procedural reform from adversarial to alternative dispute resolution.

"I examine the presentations and give specific attention to the discourse because the Pound Conference was rich with a rhetoric designed to accomplish what Burke called 'the manipulation of men's beliefs for political ends.' The rhetoric of ADR builds on the ideology of consent, hiding relations of force behind the notions of persuasion and mutual accord. The drama set the stage for the alternative dispute resolution movement. Each man in turn spoke about some version of the following complaints: The courts are crowded; American lawyers are too adversarial and the American people too litigious; new tribunals are needed to divert cases generated by the regulated welfare state; 'cumulative tinkering' should be adopted as a strategy, a way of creeping in with reform. Furthermore, alternative dispute agencies were portrayed as agencies of settlement or reconciliation, peace rather than war.

"In the years following the Pound Conference, the public was immersed in alternative dispute resolution rhetoric, which by the end of the decade had the quality of discursive cement. Chief Justice Warren Burger had set the tone for a change. In his work he was aided by members of the American judiciary, leaders of the American Bar Association, and the growing group of alternative dispute resolution professionals. The rhetoric was restricted and formulaic, and its users were assertive and repetitive. They made broad generalizations, invoked authority and danger, and presented values as facts. The Chief Justice warned that adversarial modes of conflict resolution were tearing the country apart, and that there had to be a better way. . . . Pointing to the early uses of arbitration, he said lawyers should serve as healers, rather than warriors, procurers, or hired guns. He also repeated that Americans were the most litigious people on the globe. During his time as Chief Justice, Burger continued to speak about lawyers as healers, and plaintiffs as patients needing treatment; there was little talk of rights, remedies, injustice, prevention, or unequal power.

"The framework of a harmony law model took hold. Justice Burger was quoted as saying that 'the nation was plagued 'with an almost irrational focus—virtually a mania—on litigation as a way to solve all problems.' Although there was common sense in Burger's speeches, the fact that many of his declarations were not supportable did not seem to matter. There was a momentum building. The ideology of harmony began to be believed and to be institutionalized. By the late 1980s, the newspapers, the major political speeches, the evangelical radio stations, the latest insurance copy, all had some comment on the litigation explosion and anti-litigation. The rhetoric was part of the formula central to building a movement that would implement a harmony ideology of legal reform. It did not hurt that there was a close fit between the rhetoric, the ethic of Christian harmony, the interests of corporations in cutting legal fees, psychologists and other therapists, the woman's movement, and a myriad of vested interests. The harmony law model was for some anti-law, anti-confrontation, anti-anger, and for many a response to the 'too many rights' movement. Furthermore, the ADR movement was being spearheaded by the Chief Justice of the U.S. Supreme Court....

"Critics of the alternative reform movement since the mid 1970s are abundant, many of them seeking to separate myth and rhetoric from substantiated evidence. [The author then summarized some of the leading critiques of ADR].

"In addition, a series of studies began looking at ADR practice. Judy Rothschild studied a neighborhood justice center in San Francisco and wrote about the ideology of mediation. She noted that the ideology depends upon a negative evaluation of the traditional legal system and that it does not pursue the substantive aspects of conflict, nor identify standards of justice. Disputants are trained to associate litigation with alienation, hostility, and high cost. On the other hand, the same neighborhood justice center portrayed mediation as a process that 'encourages civic and community responsibility for dispute resolution,' a defense against state law. Rothschild observed that disputes are reshaped in the intake process so that value conflicts or interest conflicts become 'communication problems.' Facts about disputes and legal rights become disputes about feelings and relationships. The model Rothschild describes is in good part a therapeutic model. The difference between confrontations and violence is blurred, and in harmony ideology anger appears to be inherently violent.

"When mediation becomes a process of communication, justice is measured by implicit standards of conformity, and as we will see, issues of what is just become irrelevant. The potential plaintiff becomes the victim (or the patient), and the ethic of treatment prevails. Furthermore, treatment by means of mediation fictionalizes the conflict...."

"The hard sell stage was initiated to overcome public hesitancy and resistance to using ADR. ADR became mandatory in many states, and its ideology spread into the schools, therapy, business organizations, hospitals, and every level of American life from the living room to the board rooms, and even into the White House (where observers regularly praise presidents for harmonious or mediating styles, rather than for assertive leadership). Professors in universities are negatively measured on their level of contentiousness, as are workers in white collar jobs, irrespective of work performance. Both style and organizational changes are imbued with conformist ideology, intolerant of dissent, what I have called coercive harmony."

* * *

7.   QUESTIONS

As you read the cases and materials that follow, consider how the themes from this Introduction arise in the context of actual cases and are reflected in the legal doctrines that have developed. At the same time, consider the following general questions about the role of ADR within our legal order.

1.   Does the type of forum and the type of procedure utilized to resolve a dispute affect the substantive rights of the parties in particular cases? Do they affect outcomes in particular cases?

2.   Does the type of forum and procedure utilized in dispute resolution affect the content of the rules of decision, and thus shape underlying social norms and values?

3.   Does the type of forum and procedure utilized in dispute resolution have a consistent and systemic effect on different social groups, and thus affect the distribution of wealth and power in society?

4.   To what extent do the different forms of ADR address the psychological aspects of disputes? Which forms are more suited to this task?

5.   Who wins and who loses when disputes are characterized in psychological terms, such as misunderstandings, rather than as causes of action? Who benefits when the disputes are resolved rather than decided?

6.   Which types of ADR are best suited to redressing power imbalances between parties to disputes? Which types are most advantageous to parties who lack access to a lawyer?

7.   Is alternative dispute resolution a superior form of justice or is it second-class justice?

CHAPTER TWO

MEDIATION

1. INTRODUCTION TO MEDIATION

A. DESCRIPTION OF MEDIATION

Mediation is a procedure in which a neutral third party facilitates communications and negotiations among parties to a dispute in an effort to achieve resolution by agreement of the parties. Mediation is non-binding. The mediator cannot impose a resolution on the parties. However, there is a paradox involved in mediation: While the mediation process is consensual and the mediator does not have the authority to impose a settlement on the parties, the procedure frequently leads to a binding resolution. This is because once an agreement is reached, it is generally reduced to writing and signed by the parties. At this point, the mediation settlement becomes an enforceable contract.

For a mediation to succeed, the parties must be willing to discuss their positions, interests, fears and goals frankly and openly with the mediator. Only then can the mediator work with both parties to attempt to achieve a compromise. If one side perceives the mediator to be biased against her or as favoring the other, then compromise becomes impossible to achieve. Thus one of the essential features of mediation is the neutrality of the mediator. Without neutrality and the attendant trust of the parties, a mediator cannot succeed in resolving a dispute.

Mediation can be distinguished from arbitration in that the mediator has no power to impose a settlement on the parties. Rather, the mediator's role is facilitative, to help the parties reach their own settlement. *Facilitative mediation* is defined as, "A procedure in which a neutral third party facilitates communication and negotiations among the parties to seek resolution of issues between the parties. Mediation is non-binding and does not, unless otherwise agreed to by the parties, authorize the third party neutral to evaluate, decide or otherwise offer a judgment on the issues between the parties."[1]

While the mediator facilitates communication and party negotiation, in some forms of mediation, the mediator may also engage in evaluative tasks by helping parties and their counsel assess likely outcomes and inquiring into the legal and factual strengths and weaknesses of the problems presented. This latter form of mediation is known as *evaluative mediation*, and is distinguished from *facilitative mediation*. In evaluative mediation

---

1. CPR–Georgetown Commission on ethics and Standards in ADR (Draft for Comment, April 1999).

"the third party neutral may engage in evaluative tasks or be called upon as a discovery master, or to perform other third party neutral roles."[2] Unless the parties agree otherwise, a mediator usually plays a facilitative rather than evaluative role.

Recently some mediators have become critical of the distinction between facilitative and evaluative roles and assert that the distinction is meaningless in practice. One mediator writes:

> "[I]t is hard to divide facilitative from evaluative in any absolute way. Even a classically facilitative mediator, by the very questions he asks and the way he phrases those questions, is going to impart an impression of evaluation to the parties. To think otherwise is naive. Only if you define an evaluative mediator as one who says 'your case is worth $xxx', or 'you will win (or lose) at trial,' can you truly divide the facilitative from the evaluative. The more I practice the more evaluative I not only become, but the more evaluative the parties seem to want me to be.... I do couch evaluation in the Socratic method so that by posing a series of questions, a party comes to its own determination or resolution of its case. It is not quite so manipulative as it sounds, but it is hardly just a facilitative approach in which the mediator is simply an active listener."[3]

Another mediator has proposed that the evaluative-facilitative distinction be dropped altogether and the term "Facilitative Evaluation" be used instead. Under this proposal, Facilitative Evaluation would be defined as a process in which a neutral helps the parties evaluate their dispute.

Voluntary mediation occurs as a result of agreement between the parties. An agreement to mediate can arise in two ways. Parties might agree at the outset of their relationship to mediate any disputes that might arise out of their future anticipated dealings. In this case, the commitment to mediate is made prior to the emergence of a dispute. Alternatively, disputants might decide to utilize mediation after a dispute arises. In this case, mediation is an attempt to resolve an existing dispute, often as part of efforts to settle and avoid litigation. Whether an agreement to mediate arises pre-dispute or post-dispute, the mediation process is the same.

In recent years, mediation has been used increasingly in settings in which it is not the result of a voluntary agreement between two disputing parties but rather imposed by law or by a court. Some courts have adopted local rules requiring parties to attempt to mediate certain categories of disputes before they can have their dispute placed on a trial calendar. Also, some states have enacted laws requiring that all disputes of a certain type be mediated before they can be heard in court. For example, California sends all matrimonial disputes to mediation before they can be heard by a court. Florida has gone further, and requires that all civil actions be submitted to court-ordered mediation prior to court action. These types of "mandatory mediation" pose some special issues that will be reserved for

2. Id.

3. Judith P. Meyer, Esq., correspondence with author (June 3, 1999).

Chapter 8. However, many issues involved in mediation are the same, regardless of the source of the obligation to mediate.

B. THE MEDIATION PROCESS

Two descriptions of the mediation process follow. While each one emphasizes different features of the process, the are similar in their account of the structure that the arbitrator imposes on the process.

Dissection of the Mediation Process by Kimberlee K. Kovach[4]

"[A] variety of authors and trainers have enumerated the stages or segments of mediation. These many range from a four or five stage model to one with ten or more stages. The majority of these set forth the same basic concepts, and recognize the inherent fluidity of the process.

"For education purposes, the process can be separated into nine stages, all of which should be present in nearly every mediation. In addition, there are four components of the process which are considered optional. While these stages are often part of the mediation process, they frequently occur as part of another stage. Resolution may also be reached without involvement of these steps. The optional stages are listed in parentheses, close to where, if used, they would occur. Employment of these optional stages will depend upon the parties, the nature of the matter, and the mediator's style. The basic model is as follows:

> Preliminary Arrangements
>
> Mediator's Introduction
>
> Opening Statements by Parties
>
> (Ventilation)
>
> Information Gathering
>
> Issue Identification
>
> (Agenda Setting)
>
> (Caucus)
>
> Option Generation
>
> (Reality Testing)
>
> Bargaining and Negotiation
>
> Agreement
>
> Closure

"The preliminary arrangement stage encompasses everything that happens prior to beginning the actual mediation session. This includes matters of referral, getting to the mediation table, selection of the mediator, the determination of who should attend, issues of fees, settlement

---

4. Kimberlee K. Kovach, *Dissection of the Mediation Process*, MEDIATION: PRINCIPLES AND PRACTICE (West, 1994). Reprinted with permission.

authority issues, timing and court orders. Moreover, from the standpoint of the mediator, this stage also includes items such as gathering or gaining information from the parties or their attorneys, as well as dissemination of information about the mediator and mediation process to the parties. Selection of the location, the room or rooms to be used, and arrangement of furniture are also part of the preliminary arrangements stage of the process. Because it is the first stage, initial decisions about the process are made as part of preliminary arrangements. The impact on the process is considerable, and the importance of preliminary matters should not be overlooked.

"The mediator's introduction, is just that. The mediator introduces himself, the parties, and their representatives; describes the process; and sets out any ground rules that will be followed. By doing this, the mediator provides time for the parties to become comfortable. Goals and objectives from the mediator's standpoint may be set out here, as well as any housekeeping details. This introduction sets the stage for the remainder of the mediation.

"In the opening statements, the parties and/or their representatives are invited to make an uninterrupted presentation of their view of the case or dispute. It is important that each side be given this opportunity, and not be interrupted by either the other party or the mediator. The opening statement stage is the time for parties to fully express and explain to the mediator, and more importantly, to each other, in their own words, how they view the dispute. Ideally, there should be little restriction placed on the opening statements. However, in complex, multi-party cases, it may be necessary to establish time limits.

"If the parties' opening statements do not provide a clear or complete picture of what the dispute is about, as often they do not, the mediator will engage the parties in an information gathering process. In most instances additional information is necessary, and the mediator should ask open-ended questions. During either the opening statements or during the information gathering process, the disputing parties may need to express their feelings. This is termed venting or ventilation. It is important to afford individuals an opportunity to ventilate their frustration, anger, and emotions. Often, if such emotions are not expressed, the dispute cannot be resolved.

"Once it appears that sufficient information about the case has been exchanged, the mediator will attempt to identify exactly what issues are in dispute. This may or may not be similar to identifying the underlying interests of the parties.[5] Once the mediator has the issues identified, he will move the parties toward generating ideas, options or alternatives which might resolve the case. It is usually during these two stages (identifying issues and underlying interests and option generation) that the mediator may meet privately with each party. This is also termed caucusing. It is

---

5. Identifying the interests is at the core of *Principled Negotiation*, as set forth by Roger Fisher and William Ury, Getting to Yes (1981).

advisable, however, that some attempt at issue identification take place while the parties are together so that there is an agreement between the disputing parties and the mediator as to the actual issues in dispute. In complex cases, the mediator may also want to set an agenda, that is, determine which issues will be dealt with in a specific order. There are a variety of strategies with regard to agenda setting.

"Once the potential options or alternatives for settlement have been identified by the parties and the mediator, the negotiation process begins. This is the 'give and take' part of the mediation, where the mediator assists the parties in their bargaining. As part of this process, the mediator may also engage in 'reality testing', that is, checking out with each side the realistic possibility of attaining what he or she is hoping for. If the parties are in a purely positional bargaining approach, this will also help to move them off of unrealistic positions.

"If the negotiations result in an agreement, the mediator will restate it and in many instances, draft either the complete agreement or a memorandum of settlement. If no agreement is reached, the mediator will restate where the parties are, noting any progress made in the process. The final stage of the process is closure, although in some models there is subsequent action on the part of the mediator.

"While the process usually consists of these stages, it is designed to be flexible, and often there is a variation in the occurrence of one or more of the stages. Some of the stages may overlap; and many times the mediator must revisit one or more of the stages."

* * *

Mediation—A Guide for Practitioners by Yaroslav Sochynsky, Esq.[6]

§ 12.05 General Format of a Mediation

"[T]here is no set format for a mediation. Indeed, one of the appealing aspects of mediation is that the parties can adopt whatever structure they agree is best for their particular dispute. But there are some basic elements that are present in most mediations.

"Many mediators expect the parties to present a short written summary of their positions prior to the actual mediation. This provides the mediator an opportunity to become aware of the legal and factual issues involved in the dispute. Most mediation sessions begin with introductions and a brief statement by the mediator, the purpose of which is to put the parties at ease and to build their confidence in the mediator and the process. After these preliminaries, each party is given the opportunity to make a brief oral presentation of its position in the presence of the other

---

6. Yaroslav Sochynsky, Esq., *Mediation—A Guide for Practitioners*, CALIFORNIA ADR PRACTICE GUIDE, ch. 12 (American Law Institute). Reprinted with permission.

party. Although these opening statements are typically made by the attorneys, experienced mediators will encourage the representatives of the parties to speak their minds at this stage as well. This phase is important because it gives each side a chance to hear the other side's position in an unfiltered form.

"After the opening statements, most mediators will meet with each side in private sessions that have come to be known as caucuses. In these caucuses the mediator explores in a confidential setting the interests, objectives, and real positions of the parties in an effort to find the heart of the dispute. A good mediator will be very careful in what he or she reveals to the other side to make sure no confidences are breached. Eventually, through a series of caucuses, a negotiating process will ensue with the mediator acting as the broker or emissary between the parties. Agreement may initially be reached on only some of the issues, but eventually a momentum can develop in the negotiations which hopefully leads to a settlement.

"Experienced mediators will endeavor at the conclusion of the mediation to have the parties sign a memorandum setting forth the essential terms of the settlement and which contemplates (but is not expressly conditioned upon) the preparation of a more comprehensive settlement agreement. The intent is to make the memorandum an enforceable settlement contract.

"The foregoing is a very general outline of a typical format for a mediation in a legal dispute. However, limited only by reasonableness and common sense, parties and mediators are free to devise whatever structure is best suited for their particular matter. There is no single correct method for conducting a mediation. As the following discussion will demonstrate, mediation is a flexible process and each step of the mediation process may be varied to adapt to the particular, unique circumstances of your case."

§ 12.09   Preliminary Conference

"[I]n complex or multi-party cases, it may be desirable for the parties to meet with the mediator in advance of the actual mediation to cover format and ground rules, and to air any procedural or housekeeping matters that would otherwise have to be dealt with at the start of the mediation. A preliminary meeting can also serve as an opportunity for the parties to observe the mediator and to make sure they are comfortable with the individual they have selected. At the preliminary conference the parties can also address the schedule for the mediation, requests for the exchange of pertinent information such as expert reports or damage studies, and requests for any informal discovery. If appropriate, the mediator can help the parties devise a discovery plan for the mediation which might, for example, limit discovery to the exchange of documents and depositions of a few key witnesses or experts. . . .

§ 12.11   Mediation Statements

"It is customary, although not essential, to provide the mediator and the other side with a brief mediation statement outlining your client's legal

and factual position and identifying the key documentary evidence supporting your case. Such a statement should include a summary of the relevant
facts, and should anticipate any legal issues that the other side can be
expected to raise. It is not uncommon for such a statement to include a
damage analysis and experts' reports. Nor would it be inappropriate to
include key deposition testimony on an important issue. It is also of
interest to the mediator what prior settlement negotiations have occurred,
and this is an appropriate subject to cover in the mediation statement. The
complexity of the case will dictate the length of the presentation, but the
most effective mediation statements are brief and to the point. Typically,
mediation statements are presented simultaneously at a predetermined
time before the mediation, and not in the 'opposition' and 'reply' sequence
common in motion practice.

"Although most mediators would encourage the parties to serve their
mediation statement on the other side, some parties may be concerned
about disclosing certain aspects of their position to the other side prior to
the mediation. There is nothing in the rules of mediation or professional
conduct to preclude a party from providing a confidential communication to
the mediator in advance of the mediation. Some mediators will encourage
the parties to serve formal mediation statements on the other side, but will
also allow 'side letters' in which they can communicate matters to the
mediator confidentially. Although at first glance this kind of ex parte
communication might seem unfair or unprofessional, it is entirely consistent with the practice of confidential caucuses discussed below. . . .

§ 12.13   Opening Statements

"Following the introductory stage, each party is given the opportunity
to make a brief opening statement. Although both sides will usually have
submitted written mediation statements, this oral presentation is useful to
highlight the important issues and, perhaps more importantly, to allow
each side to hear the other side's position first hand. In the normal
litigation process, where everything is handled through attorneys, this kind
of exchange usually does not happen until trial. Mediation gives the client
on each side a much earlier opportunity to hear and evaluate the effectiveness of the other side's presentation and to evaluate how the other side's
case will come across to a judge or jury. Opening statements should be brief
and to the point, and not overly adversarial.

"Some mediators may interrupt the presentations and ask clarifying
questions, or perhaps focus on weak points as a judge might on oral
argument. This will vary according to the style of the particular mediator.
Lawyers should anticipate such questions and be prepared to address
obvious weaknesses in their position.

"After the opening statement, some mediators will recite back in
condensed form the party's position as just stated. This technique serves a
dual purpose. First, it confirms to the delivering party that their position
has been heard and understood by the mediator. Second, the other side

may hear and consider their adversary's arguments differently, and perhaps more objectively, when they are stated again by a neutral third party.

"The mediator may well invite the parties themselves to make statements. When this happens it usually accelerates the settlement process because it draws the clients in from the beginning. Clients involved in disputes usually appreciate the opportunity to have someone hear them out, to get a reaction to their position from a neutral third party, and to get things off their chest. Many clients have a great deal of emotion and ego invested in their position. Encouraging them to speak out and to participate actively provides the opportunity for needed emotional catharsis. Once emotions have been vented, the clients are able to consider their alternatives more objectively. This inevitably increases the chances for compromise and settlement.

§ 12.14 Caucuses

"After the opening statements, the mediator will meet privately with the parties and attorneys on each side of the dispute. These private meetings are commonly referred to as 'caucuses'. In these sessions the mediator attempts to develop a relationship of trust with the parties and to discern the real issues involved in the dispute. How this comes about naturally depends on the style and skills of the mediator.

"For the caucus process to work, the mediator must assure each party that anything told to the mediator confidentially will not be disclosed to the other side without permission. Establishing this high level of trust is essential if the caucus process is to work. Before leaving a private session, experienced mediators will carefully review with the party exactly what will be said to the other side so that there will be no inadvertent breach of confidences.

"In the caucus the mediator may probe for and point out weaknesses in the party's position, suggest new ways of looking at their position, or open their minds to the other side's way of looking at the issues. The mediator may also explore the negotiating goals of the parties, what their real interests and objectives are, and whether they have fully taken into account the risks, expense, and uncertainties of the litigation process. Experienced mediators will attest to how the attitude and demeanor of the participants can change dramatically in the course of caucuses. Defensive posturing falls away and eventually the discussion turns to the core issues in the dispute. The mediator may become a negotiating consultant to each side, providing subtle guidance as to what may or may not be a realistic position or negotiating strategy—again, respecting the confidences of each side. Eventually a cooperative spirit can emerge, with all parties working constructively with the mediator toward the same end: a resolution of the dispute.

"As the bargaining process evolves, the mediator may engage in what might be called shuttle diplomacy, bringing offers and counter-offers from one side to the other, perhaps explaining the reasoning or motivation behind negotiating positions. The mediator also serves as a buffer for emotional responses a party may have to positions communicated from another party. A skilled mediator will allow a reasonable amount of venting of emotions to occur, because this can clear the way to better communication. Throughout this process, the mediator will continue to act as a sounding board to moderate extreme positions, point out strengths and weaknesses, and above all try to keep the dialogue and negotiations moving forward.

"Sometimes the mediator will decide to interrupt the caucus process and to bring the parties together for an open discussion with all parties present. Often this change in dynamics can precipitate a breakthrough, a change in tone, or a new idea or approach that will advance the negotiations. Perhaps the mediator will even suggest, after obtaining the permission of counsel, that the principals meet with the mediator without attorneys present. It is surprising how when attorneys are out of the room, clients will often noticeably change their demeanor and will begin to talk to each other like businessmen, rather than combatants.

"[S]ome mediators, especially family mediators, prefer not to use caucuses at all, and conduct the entire mediation with all parties present at all times. The rationale behind such an approach is that it is important for parties to hear, understand, and acknowledge the other side's position, with its full emotional impact. There is also the concern that private sessions can foster distrust. Some mediators will conduct the entire mediation by communicating only with the principals, leaving the attorneys outside the room to serve merely as advisors on legal issues. Because of this divergence in approaches, it is wise to ascertain the particular style of the mediator proposed for your case."

* * *

C.   THE ROLE OF THE MEDIATOR

Amongst mediators, there is universal consensus about the fundamental importance of neutrality. However, beyond the neutrality principle, there is little consensus about how actively the mediator should intervene in the discussions of the parties. For example, some believe that it is appropriate and even necessary for mediators to devise a proposal for settlement, while others believe that such a role is improper. Similarly, some believe that a mediator should assess the reasonableness of the parties' proposals for settlement, and again others believe that it is a breach of neutrality to do so. And there is a difference between those who advocate evaluative as opposed to facilitative mediation. Several dimensions of the debates over the mediator's role are discussed in the following passage. In reading them, consider what role the author favors and why.

The Role of the Mediator by Yaroslav Sochynsky, Esq.[7]

"[T]here is no standard mediation approach; the approach will vary with each case and with each mediator. The role of a mediator has been

---

7. YAROSLAV SOCHYNSKY, ESQ., *Mediation—A Guide for Practitioners*, CALIFORNIA ADR PRACTICE GUIDE, Ch. 12 (AMERICAN LAW INSTITUTE 1996). Reprinted with permission.

variously described as agent of reality; referee; sounding board; honest broker; intermediary; traffic cop; devil's advocate; spark plug; and lightning rod. The mediator's function is multi-faceted and of course includes elements of each of these descriptions. Naturally it will change with the character of the dispute and the dynamics of the particular mediation.

"The mediator is responsible for maintaining a modicum of order and civility in the mediation. This is not usually a problem in mediations, but occasionally tempers will flare and a skilled mediator will know how and when to intervene. In such emotionally charged cases the mediator will need to walk a fine line allowing a certain amount of latitude for venting without having the proceedings deteriorate into a shouting match.

"The mediator is also responsible for making sure that communication between the parties is clear. So often disputes are the result of inadequate communication and misunderstanding. This can be compounded in a mediation if the mediator is not alert and does not take care to clearly communicate the respective positions of the parties.

"The mediator will also act as a sounding board, giving the parties the opportunity to try out their ideas or negotiating positions on the mediator before communicating them to the other side. In this way the mediator can moderate extreme positions, and help create a climate for more principled negotiations.

"One distinguishing characteristic among mediating styles is whether the mediation will be primarily facilitative or evaluative. In the first mode, the mediator acts mostly as an intermediary and counselor, and tries to refrain from making any value judgments about the merit or lack of merit of the parties' positions. In the latter mode, the mediator is expected to and will in fact communicate assessments of the respective merits of the parties' positions, or even provide advisory opinions as to the outcome. Sometimes mediators will use a combination of these approaches, perhaps starting out in the facilitative mode and then, as the need arises, give the parties feedback on what is likely to happen in the litigation if the case is not settled.

"There is a danger, however, in the mediator providing too concrete a prediction of the eventual outcome to the parties, or telling the parties what a fair settlement would be. The vice is that such pronouncements may unjustifiably cause one party or the other to become convinced they are right and harden their position. The mediation can then become a tug of war with the mediator having taken one side over the other. When this happens, settlement will be much more difficult because one side will no longer be motivated to change its position. The true art in mediation is enabling disputing parties to reach an agreement between themselves, without imposing any particular result on them. This does not mean that a mediator will not use powers of persuasion or subtly guide the process in the direction of settlement. But it does mean that the mediator should take great care not to dictate to the parties what they can or cannot do.

"[M]ediators will also endeavor to help the parties focus on their respective interests, rather than their legal positions. In litigation, parties can become wedded to their positions and entrenched in their thinking—particularly after they have heard the same arguments repeated by their counsel throughout the litigation. The mediator's job is to give the parties a fresh perspective and to remind them that their interests may be better served by a fair compromise, rather than taking the risk of losing the case after spending a lot of money on litigation costs. The mediator will also make the parties aware of the hardships and time drain of trial preparation and trial, and how this can adversely affect their business.

"A good mediator will also be skilled in active listening—giving the party clear signals that their position and strong feelings are being understood and acknowledged, if not necessarily accepted. By this technique, the skilled mediator will progressively defuse tensions and will guide the parties to a more objective and rational assessment of their true interests. The mediator will also try to help each party understand and acknowledge the other side's point of view. This peeling away process eventually leads to bridges of understanding and empathy that can ultimately result in a breakthrough and agreement on monetary issues.

"Much is said about the mediator's role in coming up with creative compromises, forging win-win scenarios for settlement, or creating value exchanges that the parties have overlooked. There certainly are situations where a mediator will come up with an ingenious solution or novel barter arrangement that the parties had overlooked, such as an agreement to provide future services or discounts in lieu of payment of money. But the truth is that most mediations result in good settlements without miracle solutions or mediator heroics. Most creative resolutions that occur in mediations are the result of the parties' own ingenuity. It is the mediator's role to foster a fertile environment where creative thinking and brainstorming are encouraged—by asking questions, trying out new ideas, and challenging the parties to be creative. In this way, a skilled mediator can often plant the seeds of what may ultimately become a novel resolution that no one had even considered.

"Finally, the mediator's job is to make sure the negotiating process does not stall, that the energy remains at a high level, and that the parties not give up the quest for a resolution. This involves a certain amount of cheerleading and enormous stamina. Most experienced mediators who have practiced law will confirm that conducting a mediation is much more exhausting, hour for hour, than trying a case. The mediator must stay completely focused and empathetic at all times because clarity of communication is essential to the process. It is this persistence and commitment to reaching a settlement that probably distinguishes the most successful mediators....

"Once a settlement has been agreed to, most mediators will urge the parties to memorialize the agreement in a writing signed by all participants before they leave the room. This memorandum of settlement need not be typed, can expressly contemplate the preparation of a more comprehensive settlement document and should recite the essential terms of the settlement. Terms to consider are:

1.   The amount of money to be paid by whom to whom, in what form, and when

2.   Mutual general releases of all claims between the parties, including waivers of rights under [California] Code of Civil Procedure § 1542.

3.   Dismissal of all claims and cross-complaints with prejudice

4.   Payment of attorneys' fees and costs

5.   Whether there will be a confidentiality provision

6.   Any other special terms of settlement

7.   A recitation that the settlement memorandum is intended as a binding settlement agreement enforceable in court notwithstanding that it will be reduced to a more comprehensive settlement agreement

Usually, mediators will not become involved in the drafting or preparation of settlement memoranda.''

* * *

Query, why do you think that mediators do not usually become involved in the drafting of a settlement?

D.   TWO VIEWS OF DISPUTES AND HOW THEY ARE RESOLVED

In the extensive literature on mediation, there are two different views of disputes, each of which has implications for the meaning of mediator neutrality. One view is that disputes are the result of a breakdown in communications. This is the "broken telephone" view of dispute resolution.[8] Under this view, a dispute arises when a telephone breaks so the parties are not able to see that they both have a shared interest in a particular outcome. Usually the telephone breaks because personal feelings like anger, spite, or vengeance, or character traits like obstinance or pride, get in the way of rational communication. In Fuller's view, alternative dispute mechanisms such as mediation can provide a telephone repair-person—an outsider who can communicate with both sides and thus restore communications. The repair-person will help them resolve the dispute in a way that both sides really, in their rational states of mind, want.

The broken telephone view of disputes assumes that there is a win-win solution to the dispute, and that mediation provides a mechanism to help the parties find it. The same view can be found in the well-known book, GETTING TO YES by Roger Fisher and William Ury. Fisher and Ury advocate that parties engage in bargaining that focuses on interests rather than on positions. They show that parties usually have multiple interests, and that there are often multiple positions that can satisfy a parties' interests.

8.   See, e.g., Harry T. Edwards, *Alternative Dispute Resolution: Panacea or Anathema?* 99 HARV. L. REV. 668 (1986).

Parties often have shared interests as well as interests that conflict. If parties engage in interest bargaining rather than positional bargaining, they claim, it is often possible to find a position that is compatible with the interests of both sides. They term this "mutual gains" bargaining.

The GETTING TO YES view of disputes, like the broken telephone view, assumes there has been a breakdown of communications that prevents parties from perceiving the possibilities of a win-win resolution. The framework of mutual gains bargaining functions like the telephone repair-person to highlight the parties' shared interests and locate possibilities for shared gains. Many mediators use the mutual gains perspective to define their role. They speak of win-win solutions to disputes. Often such win-win solutions are possible, and the mediation literature contains many examples where mediators were able to show parties the path to those optimal results.

However, while some disputes are the result of failed communication, there are also disputes that are not amenable to a win-win solution. These are zero-sum, winner-take-all disputes, disputes in which one side's gain will necessarily be the other side's loss. An important question is, in such a "true conflict" dispute, is there any role for a mediator? For example, can mediation work to resolve a child custody dispute in a bitter divorce where both parents want custody of the children and where joint custody is not a feasible alternative either because there is too much bitterness and distrust to make it work, or because the parents are geographically separated? Similarly, it is unclear whether mediation can work in situations where the parties do not have an on-going relationship to preserve. One sees this frequently in tort cases. For example, if a bicyclist claims that a motorist negligently opened her automobile door as the cyclist was approaching, causing the cyclist injury, and the motorist denies all liability, how can a mediator find a win-win solution? Most disputes involving breach of contract where parties do not contemplate future relationships and where neither has reputational interests at stake are similarly zero-sum in structure. In these winner-take-all situations, how can a mediator help the parties to resolve the dispute?

This question stems from an alternative view of disputes. It sees disputes as the result of a fundamental conflict of interest between two parties, parties who usually possess unequal resources, knowledge, or power. In this view, the mediator's role is to attempt to get one or both parties to compromise their interests so that the dispute can be settled. That is, mediation is an effort to achieve a strategic retreat in which one side (or both) gives up something it wants.

If a dispute embodies a true conflict in which there is no mutual gains, win-win outcome, then there is a serious question about how a mediator can help parties achieve a resolution. How can the mediator get parties to compromise when they have been unable to do so out of self-interest or the settlement efforts of their attorneys? It is possible that an evaluative mediator can achieve a resolution of a true conflict dispute by convincing one side that their claim is weak, either morally or legally. But query whether such a mediator departs from the cardinal virtue of neutrality in so doing? Alternatively, a facilitative mediator might attempt to convince each side that it has more to lose than to win by litigating the issue but then maintain a posture of passivity. Such a process creates a danger that the stronger party will cajole and/or coerce the weaker one into submission, all with the tacit blessing of the mediator. This too could be described as a departure from neutrality. Thus one of the central practical and theoretical issues in mediation is what neutrality requires of a mediator in disputes which are not amenable to a mutual gains resolution. If one believes that there are no such disputes, then obviously this question does not arise. But if there are even a subset of disputes that represent true zero-sum conflicts, then the issue of the role of the mediator and the responsibility of neutrality becomes a central concern.

E.   THE DISTINCTIVE ADVANTAGES OF MEDIATION

Mediation—Its Forms and Functions by Lon L. Fuller[9]

"[C]asual treatments of the subject in the literature of sociology tend to assume that the object of mediation is to make the parties aware of the 'social norms' applicable to their relationship and to persuade them to accommodate themselves to the 'structure' imposed by these norms. From this point of view the difference between a judge and a mediator is simply that the judge orders the parties to conform themselves to the rules, while the mediator persuades them to do so. But mediation is commonly directed, not toward achieving conformity to norms, but toward the creation of the relevant norms themselves. This is true, for example, in the very common case where the mediator assists the parties in working out the terms of a contract defining their rights and duties toward one another. In such a case there is no pre-existing structure that can guide mediation; it is the mediational process that produces the structure.

"It may be suggested that mediation is always, in any event, directed toward bringing about a more harmonious relationship between the parties, whether this be achieved through explicit agreement, through a reciprocal acceptance of the 'social norms' relevant to their relationship, or simply because the parties have been helped to a new and more perceptive understanding of one another's problems. The fact that in ordinary usage the terms 'mediation' and 'conciliation' are largely interchangeable tends to reinforce this view of the matter.

"But at this point we encounter the inconvenient fact that mediation can be directed, not toward cementing a relationship, but toward terminating it. In a form of mediation that is coming to be called 'marriage therapy' mediative efforts between husband and wife may be undertaken by a psychoanalyst, a psychiatrist, a social worker, a marriage counselor, or even a friendly neighbor. In this situation it will not infrequently turn out that the most effective use of mediation will be in assisting the parties to accept

---

9. Lon L. Fuller, *Mediation—Its Forms and Functions*, 44 S. CAL. L. REV. 305 (1971) (excerpts) (citations omitted). Reprinted with permission.

the inevitability of divorce. In a radically different context one of the most dramatically successful uses of mediation I ever witnessed involved a case in which an astute mediator helped the parties rescind a business contract. Two corporations were entrapped by a long-term supply contract that had become burdensome and disadvantageous to both. Canceling it, however, was a complicated matter, requiring a period of 'phasing out' and various financial adjustments back and forth. For some time the parties had been chiefly engaged in reciprocal threats of a law suit. On the advice of an attorney for one of the parties, a mediator (whose previous experience had been almost entirely in the field of labor relations) was brought in. Within no time at all a severance of relations was accomplished and the two firms parted company happily.

"Thus we find that mediation may be directed toward, and result in discrepant and even diametrically opposed results. This circumstance argues against our being able to derive any general structure of the mediational process from some identifiable goal shared by all mediational efforts. We may, of course, indulge in observations to the effect that the mere presence of a third person tends to put the parties on their good behavior, that the mediator can direct their verbal exchanges away from recrimination and toward the issues that need to be faced, that by receiving separate and confidential communications from the parties he can gradually bring into the open issues so deep cutting that the parties themselves had shared a tacit taboo against any discussion of them and that, finally, he can by his management of the interchange demonstrate to the parties that it is possible to discuss divisive issues without either rancor or evasion. . . .

"[T]he central quality of mediation, namely, its capacity to reorient the parties toward each other, not by imposing rules on them, but by helping them to achieve a new and shared perception of their relationship, a perception that will redirect their attitudes and dispositions toward one another.

"This quality of mediation becomes most visible when the proper function of the mediator turns out to be, not that of inducing the parties to accept formal rules for the governance of their future relations, but that of helping them to free themselves from the encumbrance of rules and of accepting, instead, a relationship of mutual respect, trust and understanding that will enable them to meet shared contingencies without the aid of formal prescriptions laid down in advance. Such a mediational effort might well come into play in any of the various forms of mediation between husband and wife associated with 'family counseling' and 'marriage therapy.' In the task of re-establishing the marriage as a going concern the mediator might find it essential to break up formalized conceptions of 'duty' and to substitute a more fluid sense of mutual trust and shared responsibility. In effect, instead of working toward achieving a rule-oriented relationship he might devote his efforts, to some degree at least, in exactly the opposite direction. . . .

"[I]t is time now to bring mediation into some closer relation with the order-producing and order-restoring processes of society as a whole and in particular with those of state-made law. Some paragraphs back I spoke of the 'central quality of mediation, namely, its capacity to reorient the parties toward each other, not by imposing rules on them, but by helping them to achieve a new and shared perception of their relationship, a perception that will redirect their attitudes and dispositions toward one another.' This suggests a certain antithesis between mediational processes, on the one hand, and the standard procedures of law, on the other, for surely central to the very notion of law is the concept of *rules*.

"Insofar as our concern is with the problem of bringing laws into existence, this 'antithesis' presents no difficulty at all. It is a commonplace of democratic government that statutes quite generally express some measure of compromise between opposing points of view. Individual legislators often find themselves, at times with some reluctance, cast in the essential mediative role that will effect this compromise. The crucial problem arises when we ask, not what role mediation should play in creating law, but how far and in what respects should it enter into the administration of laws. A general answer to this question is easy: once a law has been duly enacted its interpretation and enforcement is for the courts; courts have been instituted, not to mediate disputes, but to decide them.

"It is not difficult to see why, under a system of state-made law, the standard instrument of dispute settlement should be adjudication and not mediation. If the question is whether *A* drove through a red light, or has paid his grocery bill, or has properly reported his earnings to Internal Revenue, even the most ardent advocate of conciliative procedures would hardly recommend mediation as the standard way of dealing with such problems. A pervasive use of mediation could here obliterate the essential guideposts and boundary markers men need in orienting their actions toward one another and could end by producing a situation in which no one could know precisely where he stood or how he might get where he wanted to be. As between black and white, gray may sometimes seem an acceptable compromise, but there are circumstances in which it is essential to work hard toward keeping things black and white. Maintaining a legal system in functioning order is one of those occasions.

"It is, then, not in the making of legal rules, but in their enforcement and administration that a certain incompatibility may be perceived between mediative procedures and 'the rule of law.' We may express something of the nature of this incompatibility by saying that, whereas mediation is directed toward *persons*, judgments of law are directed toward *acts*; it is acts, not people, that are declared proper or improper under the relevant provisions of law. This distinction is not quite so simple as it seems on the surface, for there are routine occasions within the operations of a legal system when judgment must be passed on persons. This necessity arises, for example, when a court must decide whether a convicted criminal should be admitted to probation or when a judge must determine which of two contesting parents should be given custody of a child. But in its core operations, in deciding, for example, whether a man has committed a crime or broken a contract, the standards of legal judgment are derived from rules defining the consequences of specific acts or failures to act; these rules do not attempt or invite any general appraisal of the qualities or dispositions of the person, exception being made, of course, for cases where the problem of legal accountability is raised, as when the defense of insanity is pleaded.

"The distinction just taken has been blurred in modern sociology by the indiscriminate use of the term 'social norm.' This expression seems to be so used as to embrace indifferently, on the one hand, rules attributing legal or social consequences to overt and specifically defined acts, and, on the other, precepts eliciting dispositions of the person, including a willingness to respond to somewhat shifting and indefinite 'role expectations.' The word 'norm' seems, indeed, to owe its popularity precisely to the circumstance that it lifts from the user the responsibility for making any such distinction. Complex and difficult as making this distinction may in some contexts become, it is vitally important to keep it in mind in any inquiry directed toward discerning the limits of the effectiveness of 'law,' or toward defining the proper place and function of the various forms of social ordering, including mediation. . . .

"[I]n seeking now to delineate, within the processes of society as a whole, the proper domain of mediation, I suggest that we may usefully apply two tests; the first of these tells us when mediation *should not* be used, the second tells us when it *cannot* be used. The two tests are as follows: *First*, is the underlying relationship such that it is best organized by impersonal act-oriented rules? If so, then mediation will generally be out of place except as it is employed to create or modify rules. *Second*, is the problem presented amenable to solution through mediational processes? Mediation is itself subject to intrinsic limitations; I have discerned two of these: (1) it cannot generally be employed when more than two parties are involved; (2) it presupposes an intermeshing of interests of an intensity sufficient to make the parties willing to collaborate in the mediational effort."

F.   QUESTIONS

In reading the mediation cases and materials that follow, consider the following questions:

1.   How does mediation differs from litigation?

2.   What is the role of the mediator? Is it appropriate for a mediator to propose a settlement? Is it improper for a mediator to do so?

3.   How does a mediator help parties reach agreement? What is it about the process of mediation (when it succeeds) that induces parties to compromise and settle?

4.   If parties have unequal power, whether in the form of unequal resources or unequal knowledge and sophistication about their legal rights, does mediation operate to equalize power by shoring up the power of the weaker party? Or, does mediation operate to disempower the weaker party

and reinforce existing power disparities? Would the answer to this question differ depending upon whether the mediator was a facilitative mediator or an evaluative one?

5.   Is it the responsibility of the mediator to attempt to equalize power relations? Or, is it the responsibility of the mediator to remain neutral, and permit power imbalances to affect the settlement?

6.   Does the mediator have responsibility for the fairness of any settlement that results from the mediation?

7.   How does one's theory of disputes—be it a broken telephone view of disputes, or a power imbalance view—affect one's view of the proper role of the mediator?

2.   LEGAL EFFECT OF AN AGREEMENT TO MEDIATE

DeValk Lincoln Mercury, Inc. v. Ford Motor Company
811 F.2d 326 (7th Cir.1987).

■ HARLINGTON WOOD, JR., CIRCUIT JUDGE.

Plaintiffs Harold DeValk, John Fitzgerald, and DeValk Lincoln Mercury, Inc. ("DLM"), appeal a grant of summary judgment in favor of defendants Ford Motor Company and Ford Leasing Development Company (collectively "Ford"). Plaintiffs DeValk and Fitzgerald were owners and managers of an automobile dealership, DeValk Lincoln Mercury, in Chicago, Illinois. In August 1979, after several months of poor performance, DLM submitted its resignation as a Lincoln–Mercury dealership to Ford. DLM and Ford then entered into negotiations to wind up the dealership's affairs and to transfer DLM's inventory back to Ford pursuant to contractual agreements. Disputes arose during these negotiations. The disputes went unresolved and plaintiffs eventually brought this lawsuit against Ford alleging violations of the Automobile Dealers Day in Court Act, 15 U.S.C. §§ 1221 et seq. (1982), breach of contract, breach of fiduciary duty, and fraud. After some of plaintiffs' claims were dismissed, defendants moved for summary judgment on the remaining claims. The district court granted defendants' motion for summary judgment on all the remaining claims. We affirm.

I.   FACTUAL BACKGROUND

In 1976 three Lincoln–Mercury dealerships served the near northwest side of Chicago, Illinois. In the spring of that year, Ford conducted a marketing study of the area and concluded that, in light of a declining market trend, consideration should be given to eliminating one of the three dealerships at the time ownership changed hands at any one of them. At the time this study was completed, and unaware of its existence, plaintiff DeValk was negotiating with Czarnowski Lincoln–Mercury, one of the three dealerships, to purchase its assets and also was approaching Ford to seek approval to operate a dealership at Czarnowski's geographic location. DeValk also worked at this time as general manager of Czarnowski. In March 1977 Ford approved DLM as a Lincoln-Mercury dealership and executed with DLM standard Lincoln and Mercury Sales and Service Agreements ("Sales Agreements") by which DLM could purchase automobiles, parts, signs, tools, and other items from Ford.

At the time control of the dealership changed hands, Czarnowski Lincoln-Mercury was struggling. It did not have floor plan financing to purchase new automobiles. It could only get parts from Ford on a C.O.D. basis. Czarnowski did not have adequate resources to perform warranty work and its reputation in the community suffered as a result. Moreover, employee morale was low.

In spite of DeValk's efforts as the new owner, the dealership continued to suffer. Throughout 1977 and into 1978, DLM experienced losses. In July 1978, based in part on the amended market study completed in the spring of 1976, Ford informed DeValk it had placed DLM on "delete status." That delete status meant that Ford would not continue a Lincoln–Mercury dealership at DLM's location once DeValk ceased to be the majority owner of the dealership. In late September or early October, DLM hired plaintiff Fitzgerald as general sales manager. Five months later, in February 1979, Fitzgerald purchased a 45% interest in DLM. In February, March, and April, DLM managed to turn a profit. By August, however, DeValk and Fitzgerald decided to terminate the dealership. DLM submitted its resignation to Ford on August 23rd to become effective in October. DLM's resignation letter made no claims against Ford and reserved no rights to pursue any action against Ford. DLM's resignation letter also requested Ford to repurchase DLM's current inventory of automobiles. Ford accepted the resignation on October 1st, and DLM ceased operations on October 11th. In late October Ford took back DLM's inventory of parts and current model automobiles and credited DLM's account for those repurchases. Negotiations ensued over the inventory repurchases and other items, which engendered the disputes eventually giving rise to this lawsuit.

II. LEGAL STANDARD

In reviewing a grant of summary judgment we decide whether the legal papers on file "show that there is no genuine issue as to any material fact and that the moving party is entitled to a judgment as a matter of law." Fed.R.Civ.P. 56(c). Our review thus takes two steps. We first determine whether there are any genuine issues of material fact. In making this determination, we draw all inferences in the light most favorable to the non-movant. Bartman v. Allis–Chalmers Corp., 799 F.2d 311, 312 (7th Cir.1986); Rodeo v. Gillman, 787 F.2d 1175 (7th Cir.1986). But in so doing, we draw only reasonable inferences, not every conceivable inference. Bartman v. Allis–Chalmers Corp., 799 F.2d 311, 312–13 (7th Cir.1986); Matthews v. Allis–Chalmers, 769 F.2d 1215, 1218 (7th Cir.1985). If we find that any genuine issues of material fact do exist, then summary judgment was improperly granted and we must reverse. If, however, we find there are no genuine issues of material fact, we then determine as a second step whether summary judgment is correct as a matter of law.

III. DISCUSSION

Plaintiffs' contentions for purposes of this appeal can be divided into two categories. One set of claims relates to paragraph 23 of the Sales Agreements between Ford and DLM and the other set relates to paragraphs 21(b) & 21(c). Before examining the two sets of claims themselves, however, we turn to choice of law considerations.

A. Choice of Law

Both sets of claims relevant to this appeal center on the Sales Agreements between Ford and DLM. The Sales Agreements contain a choice of law clause that specifies Michigan's law as the controlling law for construing the provisions of the Sales Agreements. This case, however, was brought in federal court in Illinois, not Michigan. The claims at issue here are based on diversity jurisdiction. Well settled law holds that federal courts resolving diversity claims must apply state law. Erie Railroad Co. v. Tompkins, 304 U.S. 64, 58 S.Ct. 817, 82 L.Ed. 1188 (1938). Moreover, the state law applied by federal courts must be the forum state's law on resolving conflicts of law. Klaxon Co. v. Stentor Electric Manufacturing Co., 313 U.S. 487, 61 S.Ct. 1020, 85 L.Ed. 1477 (1941) . . .

In this instance we look to the forum state, Illinois, to determine how its conflict of law principles treat choice of law clauses in contracts. We recently had occasion to make this inquiry with respect to Illinois's law and we noted that "Illinois courts, which have long allowed parties to 'substitute the laws of another place or country,' will enforce the substituted law 'where it is not dangerous, inconvenient, immoral, nor contrary to the public policy of the local [i.e., Illinois] government.' " Sarnoff v. American Home Products Corp., 798 F.2d 1075, 1081 (7th Cir.1986) (quoting McAllister v. Smith, 17 Ill. 328, 333 (1856)) . . .

A federal court sitting in Illinois, therefore, should honor a contractual choice of law clause specifying Michigan law as controlling, unless the applicable Michigan law is dangerous, inconvenient, immoral, or contrary to public policy. As will become apparent in our discussion of the construction of the Sales Agreements, the applicable Michigan law does not fall outside the bounds set by Illinois's conflict of laws principles, and will, therefore, be honored as the parties' choice of law.

B. Paragraph 23 Claims

Among other things, the Sales Agreements between Ford and DLM provide that when Ford or the dealer terminates or fails to renew the dealership, the dealer is entitled to receive certain benefits. These benefits include Ford's willingness to buy back the current inventory of automobiles and parts from the dealer. But in consideration of agreeing to buy back the inventory, the Sales Agreements provide in relevant part of paragraph 23 that the dealer will release Ford from liability except with respect to claims arising under paragraphs 19(f), 21, and 22 of the Sales Agreements:

> *[U]pon the Dealer's demand of any such benefits upon any termination or nonrenewal by the Dealer, the Company shall be released from any and all other liability to the Dealer* with respect to all relationships and actions between the Dealer and the Company, however claimed to arise, except any liability that the Company may have under subparagraph 19(f) and said paragraphs 21 and 22, and except for such amounts as the Company may have agreed in writing to pay to the Dealer. *Simultaneously with the receipt of any benefits so elected or demanded, the Dealer shall execute and deliver to the Company a general release* with exceptions, as above described, satisfactory to the Company. (emphasis added)

[The court considered and rejected the plaintiff's arguments that the release was invalid on the grounds of ambiguity, unconscionability, or waiver.]

C.   Paragraph 21(b) & 21(c) Claims

Aside from the claims arising under paragraph 23, a second set of claims arises under paragraphs 21(b) & 21(c). This second set of claims is not subject to paragraph 23's release of liability. Rather, these claims are specifically exempted from the release. Paragraph 23 releases all liability, "except any liability that the Company may have under subparagraph 19(f) and said paragraphs 21 and 22."

Although the paragraph 21(b) & 21(c) claims are not subject to paragraph 23's release, they are subject to a mediation clause. The mediation clause, found in paragraph 18(b) of the Sales Agreements, provides:

> *Any protest, controversy or claim by the Dealer* (whether for damages, stay of action or otherwise) with respect to any termination or nonrenewal of this agreement by the Company or the settlement of the accounts of the Dealer with the Company after any termination or nonrenewal of this agreement by the Company or the Dealer has become effective, *shall be appealed by the Dealer to the Policy Board* within fifteen (15) days after the Dealer's receipt of notice of termination or nonrenewal, or, as to settlement of accounts after termination or nonrenewal, within one year after the termination or nonrenewal has become effective. *Appeal to the Policy Board shall be a condition precedent to the Dealer's right to pursue any other remedy available under this agreement or otherwise available under law.* The Company, but not the Dealer, shall be bound by the decision of the Policy Board. (emphasis added).

The mediation clause is straightforward. It requires DLM to appeal any "protest, controversy or claim" it has with Ford to the Dealer Policy Board. The mediation clause further specifies that the "[a]ppeal to the Policy Board shall be a condition precedent to the Dealer's right to pursue any other remedy . . . available under law."

1. Substantial Performance

Plaintiffs concede they did not appeal their dispute with Ford to the Dealer Policy Board. But plaintiffs contend their failure to take the appeal is not fatal to their claims under paragraphs 21(b) & 21(c) because they "substantially complied" with the mediation clause's requirements.[3] Plaintiffs base this contention on their view of the underlying purpose of the mediation clause: "It must be inferred that the purpose of requiring an appeal to the Dealer Policy Board is to give Ford Motor notice of any potential claim the dealer may have with respect to matters covered under paragraph 18(b) and to allow Ford Motor an opportunity to attempt to settle the claim prior to litigation." Plaintiffs argue that their post-resignation actions fulfill this two-pronged purpose of the mediation clause, and thus represent substantial compliance with its requirements, even though an appeal was not taken to the Dealer Policy Board.

Plaintiffs believe they fulfilled the first alleged purpose of the mediation clause by writing four letters to Ford detailing DLM's grievances. Plaintiffs argue these letters gave Ford all the notice it needed of the claims with which plaintiffs were concerned. As for the second alleged purpose of the mediation clause, plaintiffs contend they presented Ford with ample opportunity to settle their claims prior to litigation. The negotiations between plaintiffs and Ford's representatives spanned over eight months. Both Ford and plaintiffs effectively articulated their respective positions during these negotiations. Plaintiffs argue this negotiation process fulfilled the purpose of allowing Ford to attempt to settle its claims with DLM.

Although it is true that "Michigan follows the substantial performance rule," P & M Construction Co. v. Hammond Ventures, Inc., 3 Mich.App. 306, 142 N.W.2d 468, 473 (1966) (citation omitted), and that in Michigan "the extent of nonperformance [is] viewed in relation to the full performance promised," Gordon v. Great Lakes Bowling Corp., 18 Mich.App. 358, 171 N.W.2d 225, 228–29 (1969), we cannot agree with plaintiffs' contention.

As an initial matter, we hesitate to apply the substantial performance rule outside the realm of cases in which that rule is applied in Michigan. The substantial performance rule in Michigan allows contractors, engineers, builders, and other construction professionals to recover a proportionate share of a contractual sum when they have substantially performed their construction obligations. See, e.g., Antonoff v. Basso, 347 Mich. 18, 78 N.W.2d 604 (1956); McCall v. Freedman, 35 Mich.App. 243, 192 N.W.2d 275 (1971). Outside of those construction-type cases, however, we are unable to find any evidence that Michigan's courts are willing to more broadly apply the substantial performance rule. Cf. Gordon v. Great Lakes Bowling Corp., 18 Mich.App. 358, 171 N.W.2d 225, 228–29 (1969) (applying substantial performance rule to lease dispute, but in addition to rent, parties argued over construction costs and construction delay).

3. Based on this language of the mediation clause, Ford contends it is released from any liability that may have arisen under paragraphs 21(b) & 21(c).

Even if we were confident that Michigan's courts would apply the substantial performance rule to a wider variety of contractual disputes, we would not apply the rule here. Although the substantial performance rule in Michigan seems to derive in part from the maxim, "The law abhors a forfeiture," we are convinced it applies only in the absence of conditions precedent. E.g., Knox v. Knox, 337 Mich. 109, 59 N.W.2d 108, 112 (1953) ("While parties to a contract may by specific provision, or by necessary implication, make performance by one party a condition precedent to liability on the part of the other, courts are not disposed, in the absence of specific provisions or reasonable implications, to give such construction to an agreement, especially if so doing brings about an unfair result."); Kachanowski v. Cohen, 305 Mich. 438, 9 N.W.2d 667, 668 (1943) ("The law is well settled that one who executes a contract may protect himself from liability by a distinct agreement that it shall not become operative until there has been compliance with certain conditions thereof.").

The mediation clause here states that it is a condition precedent to any litigation. As a result, the clause takes itself outside the sphere of influence of the substantial performance rule. Because the mediation clause demands strict compliance with its requirement of appeal to the Dealer Policy Board before the parties can litigate, plaintiffs' substantial performance arguments must fail.

2. Waiver of Mediation Clause

Undaunted, plaintiffs argue that even if the mediation clause operates as a condition precedent to litigation, Ford waived the requirements of that clause by its conduct following the final date on which an appeal could be taken to the Dealer Policy Board. The mediation clause requires the dissatisfied dealer to appeal its claims to the Dealer Policy Board "within one year after the termination or nonrenewal has become effective." Ford accepted DLM's resignation and DLM ceased operations in October 1979. Therefore, any continuing negotiations between DLM and Ford after October 1980, plaintiffs argue, constitute a waiver by Ford of the requirements of the mediation clause. As evidence of such continuing negotiations, plaintiffs point to a letter from Ford dated December 1980, an unpaid credit reflected in June 1981, and a claimed reduction in unpaid credit in October 1985; all three items addressing credits to DLM's parts account with respect to the repurchasing of parts by Ford.

Initially, we note that "a waiver of a breach of contract must be a 'voluntary, intentional relinquishment of a known right.'" Bissell v. L.W. Edison Co., 9 Mich.App. 276, 156 N.W.2d 623, 627 (1967) (quoting Don–Ray Tool & Die, Inc. v. John Hancock Mutual Life Insurance Co., 5 Mich.App. 263, 146 N.W.2d 139, 142 (1966)). We then ask, under Michigan law, what evidence is necessary to show the relinquishment of the right? The Supreme Court of Michigan has explained that "[a] waiver may be shown by proof of express language of agreement or inferably established by such declarations, acts, and conduct of the party against whom it is claimed as are inconsistent with a purpose to exact strict performance."

Strom–Johnson Construction Co. v. Riverview Furniture Co., 227 Mich. 55, 198 N.W. 714, 718 (1924). So the waiver can be express, or it may be inferred from the conduct of the nonbreaching party. Specifically, the conduct giving rise to an inference of waiver may take the form of continued performance by the breaching party without any attempt by the non-breaching party to call a halt to the performance. The Supreme Court of Michigan noted in another case that " '[i]t was the appellant's duty, when it discovered the apparent breach of the contract, if it intended to insist upon a forfeiture, to do so at once. By permitting appellees to proceed with the performance of the contract it waived a breach.' " Schnepf v. Thomas L. McNamara, Inc., 354 Mich. 393, 93 N.W.2d 230, 232 (1958) (quoting Grayson–McLeod Lumber Co. v. Slack–Kress Tie & Stave Co., 102 Ark. 79, 143 S.W. 581, 583 (1912)); accord Barton v. Chemical Bank, 577 F.2d 1329, 1337 (5th Cir.1978) ("[A] party standing silent while the other party to the contract fails to perform a condition will be estopped from later asserting the condition.").

In this regard, plaintiffs point us to the law of arbitration clauses as a closely analogous area of contractual agreement by which we should be guided. The Supreme Court of Michigan has held that an insurer "may waive the compulsory arbitration provision of its insurance policy by its conduct." Bielski v. Wolverine Insurance Co., 379 Mich. 280, 150 N.W.2d 788, 790 (1967). That court also explained:

> "A clause in an insurance policy providing for arbitration or appraisal of the loss or damage as a condition precedent to a suit by the policyholder to recover insurance is inserted wholly for the protection of the insurer and may be waived by it. Such waivers need not be expressed in terms, but may be implied by the acts, omissions, or conduct of the insurer or its agents authorized in such respect."

Id. (quoting 29A American Jurisprudence Insurance § 1617 (1960)); Capital Mortgage Corp. v. Coopers & Lybrand, 142 Mich.App. 531, 369 N.W.2d 922, 924 (1985).

Superficially, it appears that Ford's conduct after the time expired for an appeal to the Dealer Policy Board possibly constitutes a waiver. And we might find persuasive plaintiffs' arguments in this regard were it not for Ford's response, with which we agree, that Michigan's courts uphold anti-waiver clauses. Because DLM agreed in paragraph 27 of the Sales Agreements that implied waivers of Sales Agreements' provisions would not be permitted, plaintiffs' waiver argument cannot stand.

[The court then considered the plaintiff's argument that Ford's alleged material breaches of the Sales Agreements relieved DLM of any duty to appeal its grievances to the Dealer Policy Board. It concluded that because the plaintiffs had not raised this repudiation argument in the district court, they had waived it on appeal.]

IV. CONCLUSION

Even after drawing all the reasonable inferences in favor of plaintiffs' positions on this appeal from an adverse grant of summary judgment, we cannot find any genuine issues of material fact. Because there are no such issues, the judgment granted to defendants by the district judge as a matter of law is

AFFIRMED.

* * *

Questions

1. In part, the court's reasoning in *DeValk* was based on the fact that the contract had an anti-waiver provision and that Michigan upholds such anti-waiver provisions. The court applied Michigan law even though the lawsuit was brought in Illinois because it gave effect to the choice of law clause in the Sales Agreement. Under what circumstances could the court refuse to apply Michigan law despite the choice of law clause? Were those circumstances present here? If, under Illinois law, courts would not honor anti-waiver clauses, would the result be the same? How could the plaintiff argue that Illinois law rather than Michigan law should apply?

2. Note that the plaintiff's case was brought under the Automobile Dealers Day in Court Act, a federal statute designed to protect automobile dealers from unfair treatment by automobile manufacturers with whom they deal. It is a statute specifically aimed at redressing the disparity of power between the contracting parties. Can the plaintiff argue that the mediation clause in the contract reflects the very disparity in bargaining power that the statute addresses? Should that affect the court's analysis of the issues in the case? What can the plaintiff point to in the contract to make that argument convincingly? How might the defendant respond?

* * *

Kirschenman v. Superior Court of Contra Costa County

36 Cal.Rptr.2d 166 (Court of Appeal, 1st District, 1994).

■ ANDERSON, PRESIDING JUSTICE.

Petitioners (defendants below) seek a writ to vacate an order sanctioning them for failing to personally attend a mediation session and requiring them to participate in further mediation. Plaintiffs, real parties in interest, respond by urging us to rule that once an attorney orally agrees to mediate a dispute neither that attorney nor the client may withdraw consent absent court approval upon a showing of good cause; we hold otherwise. We grant relief because (1) the court had no authority to mandate mediation; (2) there was no enforceable agreement to mediate; and (3) in any event, there was no failure to comply with the court's mediation order.

Petitioners are Wayne Kirschenman and Kirschenman Enterprises, Inc. (hereafter Kirschenman) and Attorney Robert D. Patterson who represents Kirschenman (one of 14 named defendants) in the underlying multi-party commercial litigation and related cross-actions. A status conference was held in the underlying case on April 15, 1994. Patterson appeared by telephone. The court asked the attorneys present if they were "interested in any kind of mediation on the case" and Patterson replied that he "would be willing to do that on behalf of Kirschenman." Thereafter the attorneys chose private mediation and the court announced that there would be another status conference in 60 days. There was no discussion of personal appearance at the mediation by the litigants or their counsel, no minute order was entered nor was any written order signed by the court.

By letter dated May 13, 1994, Attorney Patterson informed the court that plaintiffs' counsel and the defense attorneys located in northern California were in the process of arranging to employ a mediator and that mediation was tentatively scheduled to occur in the early part of June. Patterson also stated that he had been informed by his client, Mr. Kirschenman, that Kirschenman would make no settlement of any kind. Patterson then asked to be excused from the mediation. The court denied the request. Thereupon, petitioners filed a mediation brief and paid their share of the mediation expenses. Neither Kirschenman nor Patterson appeared in person at the mediation session, which was held on June 6, 1994, but both did make themselves available by telephone.

Plaintiffs' counsel filed a motion for sanctions for failure of petitioners to participate in mediation. Petitioners opposed the motion pointing out that they had filed a brief, paid their portion of the mediation expenses, and had made themselves available by telephone for the mediation session. They also pointed out that neither the mediator nor any attorney had attempted to make telephone contact during the session. Nevertheless, respondent court granted the motion for sanctions in its entirety.

On June 17, 1994, a second status conference was held at which time the court announced that all parties were ordered to engage in further mediation before August 29, 1994. The court was asked by plaintiffs' counsel to clarify what it meant by "attendance" at mediation, and the court replied that it meant personal appearance by lawyers and either clients or their carriers, except for those out of state who were allowed to appear by telephone.

Upon application of petitioners for extraordinary relief, we stayed the order directing petitioners to participate in further mediation and the order imposing sanctions.

DISCUSSION

Our consideration of the order sanctioning petitioners for not attending the first mediation session in person and the order requiring petitioners to attend a further session commences with the proposition that the court had no statutory authority to require the parties to participate in mediation. Nor did respondent court initially purport to mandate mediation or any other form of alternative dispute resolution, but rather merely inquired of the attorneys attending the status conference if they were interested in mediation.

Thus, respondent court's authority to sanction petitioners and to make orders regarding mediation in this case rests on the court's authority to enforce the oral agreement of petitioners to participate in mediation. Plaintiff cites to federal cases which have enforced written agreements for nonbinding alternative dispute resolution. (See DeValk Lincoln Mercury, Inc. v. Ford Motor Co. (7th Cir.1987) 811 F.2d 326, 335; AMF, Inc. v. Brunswick Corp. (E.D.N.Y.1985) 621 F.Supp. 456, 463.) Plaintiff also refers to policy statements, such as that in Business and Professions Code section 465, subdivision (b), which encourage and support resolution of disputes by the use of alternatives to the courts. However, we note that even in the legislation to which plaintiff refers, the parties are specifically not prohibited from revoking consent to participate in voluntary dispute resolution. (See Bus. & Prof.Code, § 467.7.)

Petitioners timely sought to withdraw from participation in mediation prior to the appointment of the mediator. They should have been permitted to do so.

Let a peremptory writ of mandate issue directing respondent court to vacate its order imposing sanctions and its order requiring petitioners to participate in further mediation. Petitioners are to recover costs of this writ proceeding.

* * *

Questions

1. Why did the Appeals Court not require the plaintiffs to attend the mediation after they had given their consent to do so through their lawyers?

2. The court in *Kirschenman* stated that a party may revoke its consent to mediation, and if it does so in a timely fashion, the court will not force the parties to proceed with the mediation. Is there some tension between this holding and *DeValk Lincoln Mercury?* Can the two cases be distinguished?

* * *

3. CONFIDENTIALITY IN MEDIATION[1]

The success of mediation depends upon parties airing their positions fully to the mediator. Full disclosure enables the mediator to explore the issues and identify hidden sources of conflict and convergence. Candor by the parties is necessary if the mediator is to discover the true motives, beliefs, interests, and concerns of the parties. Indeed, without full disclo-

---

1. See generally, James M. Assey, Jr., *Mum's the Word on Mediation: Confidentiality and Synder–Falkingham v. Stockburger,* 9 Geo. J. of Legal Ethics 991 (1996); Alan Kirtley, *The Mediation Privilege's Transition* *from Theory to Implementation,* 1 J. of Dispute Resol. 1 (1995). For a dissenting voice, see Eric D. Green, *A Heretical View of the Mediation Privilege,* 2 J. of Dispute Resol. 1 (1996).

sure, the mediator cannot hope to be successful in helping the parties find a satisfactory settlement. Yet parties often have legitimate fears that any disclosures or concessions they might make would be used against them if mediation should fail and they face their opponent in a court of law. To the extent parties have such fears, they will withhold crucial information during mediation and make it impossible for the mediator to help them reach a settlement. Therefore protection of confidentiality is considered one of the bedrock principles of mediation.

Confidentiality plays another role in mediation in addition to encouraging candor. One of the reasons parties choose to mediate a dispute rather than pursue litigation is that they want to keep their dispute and/or settlement confidential. For example, a large corporation that produces popular name brand food items might not want the public to know that it is being sued for adulterated products. Even if the corporation were to prevail in such suit, it might fear that the reputation of its brand name products could be tarnished. Similarly, in matrimonial disputes, divorcing parents may want to shield their children from the allegations and animosity of their dispute. Or, in an employment dispute, an employee who sues her employer for discrimination might not want to get a reputation as a "trouble-maker." In these and many other situations, parties may choose mediation in part because of its ability to provide confidentiality.

The degree to which party communications in mediation is in fact confidential varies from jurisdiction to jurisdiction and is subject to evolving legal rules. There are three principal methods to ensure confidentiality in mediation: by contract, by evidentiary exclusion, and by privilege. The legal issues involved in each of these methods is addressed in the cases and materials below.

A. CONFIDENTIALITY BY CONTRACT

Mediators often ask parties to sign a Confidentiality Agreement at the commencement of a mediation. Typical of such agreements is the following:

Confidentiality Agreement

The undersigned parties are attempting to resolve a dispute. _____ has agreed to work as mediator with them. In order to promote communications among the parties and facilitate the settlement of the dispute, all parties agree as follows:

All statements made during the course of the mediation are privileged settlement discussions, are made without prejudice to any party's legal position, and are non-discoverable and inadmissible for any purpose in any legal proceeding.

Any information disclosed by any party, or by a representative of a party, or by a witness on behalf of a party, to the mediator is confidential; no privilege shall be affected by any such disclosure. The mediator shall not be an advocate for any party.

Disclosure of any records, reports or other documents received by the mediator cannot be compelled. The mediator shall not be compelled to disclose or to testify in any proceeding as to information disclosed or representations made in the course of the mediation or communicated to the mediator in confidence.

The mediator shall have no liability for any act or omission in connection with the mediation.

No aspect of the mediation shall be relied upon or introduced in evidence in any arbitral, judicial or other proceeding, including but not limited to:

a. Views expressed or suggestions made by a party with respect to a possible settlement of the dispute;

b. Admissions made in the course of the mediation proceedings; and/or

c. Proposals made or views expressed by the mediator or the response of any party thereto.

The parties agree that the breach of this agreement would cause irreparable harm and that monetary damages would be an inadequate remedy, since the parties are relying upon this agreement of confidentiality in disclosing sensitive business and/or personal information. The parties therefore agree and stipulate that any party to this agreement may obtain an injunction to prevent disclosure of any such confidential information in violation of this agreement. The parties agree that if any party breaches this agreement, that party shall be liable for and shall indemnify the mediator for all costs, expenses, liabilities and fees, including attorneys' fees, that may be incurred as a result of such breach.

DATED: _____, and signed before the commencement of the mediation by each of the persons involved in the mediation.

* * *

The foregoing form agreement contains a stipulation by the parties that in case either side breaches, the other can obtain an injunction from a court to prevent disclosure of confidential information, but such a stipulation is of dubious value. It is a general axiom that the public is entitled to every person's evidence in a court of law. Public policy forbids contracts to exclude evidence. John Henry Wigmore, EVIDENCE IN TRIALS AT COMMON LAW § 2192 (1961). So, how likely is it that a court would issue such an injunction? If a court will not issue an injunction to prevent a breach, does a confidentiality agreement provide parties with any protection against disclosure? Consider the following case:

In *Simrin v. Simrin*, 43 Cal.Rptr. 376 (Cal.Ct.App.1965), a wife filed a motion to modify the custody provisions of the parties' divorce decree. At the same time, the husband sought to modify the child custody provisions by reducing her right to have the children visit with her. The California

Superior Court found for the husband and the wife appealed. The District Court of Appeal affirmed.

In response to the wife's effort to introduce testimony concerning counseling sessions with their rabbi, the court ruled that where a rabbi had undertaken marriage counseling with husband and wife only after an express agreement that their communications to him would be confidential, the rabbi could not be compelled to relate the confidential communications. It stated:

> "A . . . question arises from the court's ruling that a rabbi who acted as a marriage counselor for the parties need not reveal conversations with them. The wife called as a witness a rabbi, who declined to testify, not on the ground of privilege, but that he undertook marriage counseling with the husband and wife only after an express agreement that their communications to him would be confidential and that neither would call him as a witness in the event of a divorce action. He imposed the condition so they would feel free to communicate with him."

The court rejected the husband's argument that the communications were privileged under a state law designed to protect the confidentiality of confessions in a church. It then addressed the validity of the confidentiality agreement:

> "As to the agreement, appellant argues that to hold her to her bargain with the rabbi and with her husband is to sanction a contract to suppress evidence contrary to public policy. However, public policy also strongly favors procedures designed to preserve marriages, and counseling has become a promising means to that end. The two policies are here in conflict and we resolve the conflict by holding the parties to their agreement. If a husband or wife must speak guardedly for fear of making an admission that might be used in court, the purpose of counseling is frustrated. One should not be permitted, under cover of suppression of evidence, to repudiate an agreement so deeply affecting the marriage relationship. For the unwary spouse who speaks freely, repudiation would prove a trap; for the wily, a vehicle for making self-serving declarations."

* * *

Questions

1. Is the reasoning of *Simrin* limited to the matrimonial context, or can it provide a basis for enforcing mediation confidentiality agreements in other settings?

2. Does the court's willingness to enforce the confidentiality agreement in *Simrin* turn in part on its desire to urge parties to use non-litigation means to resolve matrimonial issues? To what extent are courts effective in monitoring the break-up of families?

3. The foregoing Confidentiality Agreement does not permit disclosure of information produced during a mediation in a subsequent "arbitral, judicial or other proceeding." Would it prevent disclosure during the course of discovery? Would it be perjury if a party, in an answer to an interrogatory or in a deposition, denied knowledge of a fact that she had learned during a mediation session? Would a signed Confidentiality Agreement provide her with a defense?

4. The Confidentiality Agreement does not, by its terms, restrict third parties from disclosing information adduced at mediation. Thus if there are more than two parties involved in a dispute, and only two have signed the Confidentiality Agreement, as in a multi-party accident case, any nonsignatory could introduce statements made at mediation in a subsequent lawsuit. If such a nonsignatory introduced a statement from the mediation in a lawsuit against a signatory, could the signatory party rebut with information acquired during the mediation despite the prohibition of this Agreement?

* * *

B. CONFIDENTIALITY UNDER THE RULES OF EVIDENCE

Another method of ensuring protection for the confidentiality of statements made in the course of mediation is through an evidentiary exclusion. Under the common law, evidence concerning offers of settlement and compromise can be excluded on the grounds of irrelevancy. However, the common law rules do not exclude discussions held and information disclosed in the course of settlement talks. Thus, most of the discussions that transpire during mediation would not fall within the common law exclusion.

Rule 408 of the Federal Rules of Evidence creates an exclusion for compromise and offers to compromise litigation. It applies in the federal courts and those state courts that have adopted it. Rule 408 provides:

Rule 408. Compromise and Offers of Compromise

Evidence of (1) furnishing or offering or promising to furnish, or (2) accepting or accepting or promising to accept, a valuable consideration in compromising or attempting to compromise a claim which was disputed as to either validity or amount, is not admissible to prove liability or for invalidity of the claim or its amount. Evidence of conduct or statements made in compromise negotiations is likewise not admissible. This rule does not require the exclusion of any evidence otherwise discoverable merely because it is presented in the course of compromise negotiations. This rule also does not require exclusion when the evidence is offered for another purpose, such as proving bias or prejudice of a witness, negativing a contention of undue delay, or proving an effort to obstruct a criminal investigation or prosecution.

Mediation sessions are appropriately considered efforts to compromise, so under Rule 408, disclosures made in that context would be excludable as "evidence of conduct or statements made in compromise negotiations."

However, Rule 408 is of only limited usefulness in shielding mediation proceedings from disclosure.

According to its terms, Rule 408 only excludes evidence of compromise discussions that is offered to prove or disprove liability or establish its amount. The rule does not exclude evidence of compromise discussions when offered for "another purpose." As a practical matter, this exception can often swallow the rule. A skillful attorney can almost always find some other basis to admit evidence, such as to show bias of a witness or to impeach previous testimony. Further, Rule 408 only prevents evidence adduced during compromise discussions from being admitted in court. It does not prevent disclosure of such evidence during depositions or other types of discovery so long as disclosure is likely to lead to admissible evidence. Furthermore, such evidence is not excluded in an administrative hearing or a criminal proceeding, where the Federal Rules of Evidence do not apply.

C. A MEDIATION PRIVILEGE

In light of the loopholes in the confidentiality protection afforded mediation by contractual means or evidentiary rules, every state except Delaware has adopted a mediation privilege. Most have done so through legislation, but some courts have also created mediation privileges in spite of the fact that courts generally disfavor judicially-created privileges. The privileges vary greatly from state to state.[2] Some of the respects in which statutes differ are:

1. What qualifies as a mediation for purposes of claiming privilege?

If a privilege is to attach to communications made during a mediation, it is necessary for the statute to define what qualifies as a "mediation." For example, a loosely worded statute that confers a privilege on all communications "in which a third party aids in resolving a dispute" would erect a privilege every time a neighbor or friend helped two acquaintances resolve a dispute. Yet a narrow statute that only conferred a privilege when a trained and certified mediator was involved might exclude many bona fide mediations from its ambit. Some states only confer a privilege on communications made in a court-ordered mediation, thereby leaving the vast multitude of mediations outside its scope. One approach that arguably avoids both under and over-inclusiveness is found in the Washington statute, which create a mediation privilege when there is a court order to mediate or the parties execute a written agreement to mediate. WASH. REV. CODE § 5.60.060(1) (Supp. 1994).

Another approach that some states have taken is to limit the mediation privilege to processes involving mediators who have certain designated professional qualifications or specified certification. For example, Massa-

---

2. For a good discussion of the varying state privilege statutes, see Alan Kirtley, *The Mediation Privilege's Transition from Theory to Implementation*, 1 J. of Dispute Resol. 1, 22–24 (1995); James M. Assey, *Mum's the Word on Mediation*, 9 Geo. J. of Legal Ethics 991, 997 (1996).

chusetts confers a privilege when there is a mediation involving "[A] person ... has completed at least thirty hours of training in mediation and who has either four years of professional experience as a mediator or is accountable to a dispute resolution organization which has been in existence for at least three years." Mass. Gen. L. ch. 233 § 23C (1986).

2. What aspects of the mediation process are subject to the privilege?

A mediation privilege is only useful if it applies to all the discussions that transpire during the mediation sessions. Only then can it aid in promoting free and candid discussions. However, sometimes statements are made by parties in anticipation of mediation. For example, a party might make statements about its position when contacting a potential mediator or when attempting to induce the other side to agree to mediation. If the mediation goes forward, a question can arise as to whether these statements made prior to the formal mediation sessions are within the privilege. Alternatively, if one party is unsuccessful in its attempts to induce the other to agree to mediation, there is also a question whether initial exploratory efforts to mediate should be privileged. Some states include in their mediation privileges pre-mediation discussions and some do not. The Washington statute gives broad protection for pre-mediation statements by including within the privilege "any communication made or materials submitted in, or in connection with, the mediation proceeding." WASH. REV. CODE § 5.60.070 (1) (Supp. 1994).

3. Who is covered by the privilege?

Privileges also differ in regard to whose statements are covered. While it seems obvious that statements made by parties, their attorneys, and the mediator should be covered by a privilege, statutes vary as to whether statements by non-lawyer advocates or witnesses are also included.

4. To what does the privilege apply?

As discussed above, evidentiary exclusions typically only preclude evidence from being introduced at court in a civil case. A privilege can go further, and prevent disclosure during discovery and other pretrial stages, and apply to administrative proceedings and criminal matters as well as to civil trials. State mediation statutes differ on the breadth of their privileges. Some extend the privilege to civil cases only, some to "any proceeding," some to civil and criminal proceedings, and some to "all judicial or administrative proceedings." Some are silent on this issue, leaving the breadth of the privilege to be determined by the state courts. Some privileges operate at all stages of an action, and some are limited to a courtroom. Some extend the privilege to arbitration and other ADR procedures and some do not.

5. Who holds the privilege? Who can exercise it and/or waive it?

Under most statutes, the parties to a mediation are holders of the privilege. This means that either one can invoke it if the other attempts to disclose privileged communications in a subsequent proceeding. The issue arises when an attempted mediation effort fails, litigation ensues, and one side wants to introduce admissions made or matters discussed in the failed mediation. However, a more difficult issue arises when one side or both sides want to introduce testimony of the mediator. In attorney-client privilege and doctor-patient privileges, it is established that the privilege belongs to the client and/or patient, not to the attorney and/or doctor. However, in mediation there is a legitimate reason to assign the privilege to the mediator as well as to the parties. A mediator's credibility depends upon maintaining the utmost appearance of neutrality, so that to give testimony that might favor one side against the other could compromise the mediator's professional stature. Therefore mediators have an independent interest in preventing disclosures made by or to them during a mediation session.

Some statutes treat the mediation privilege as belonging to the parties, and stipulate that it can only be waived by the parties acting jointly. Thus the parties can together decide to call the mediator to testify, but neither one can do so on its own. Others bifurcate the issue, and permit the parties to waive the privilege of confidentiality of party testimony if both agree, but require that the mediator also agree to waive the privilege for mediator disclosures.

6.   What information is privileged?

State confidentiality laws differ as to what information falls within the privilege. Some state mediation privileges apply only to discussions during mediation, while some apply to notes and other physical memorabilia as well. Some apply only to discussions of the issue being mediated, while some apply to all things discussed. And some create exceptions for certain types of information. For example, the Virginia and California laws specify that the mediation privilege does not apply to financial data disclosed as part of a mediation concerning child support. VA. CODE ANN. § 8.01–576.10 (Michie 1995); CAL. EVID. CODE § SCE 1152.5 (B), (C) (Deering 1995). The Washington statute contains seven exemptions, including "(b) when the written materials or tangible evidence . . . were not prepared specifically for use in and actually used in the mediation proceeding;" and "(g) in a subsequent action between the mediator and a party to the mediation arising out of the mediation." WASH. REV. CODE § 5.60.070 (1994).

Some of the major issues concerning the scope and definition of a mediation privilege are posed in the following cases.

* * *

Harry H. Hudson v. Gloria P. Hudson

600 So.2d 7 (Dist. Ct. of Appl., 4th Dist., Florida 1992).

■ PER CURIAM.

The appellant husband has perfected this appeal from a final judgment of dissolution and from an order denying his motion to vacate said judgment.

It appears that, during the progress of the dissolution proceeding below, the trial court set the case for trial commencing April 1, 1991. In the interim, an order scheduling mediation was entered and a mediation hearing was set for March 27, 1991. At said hearing the parties arrived at what appeared to be an oral agreement settling the issues involved, but no written mediation settlement agreement was signed. Shortly thereafter, the husband apparently had second thoughts about the proposed settlement, and the parties never reduced the alleged oral agreement to writing. The trial date of April 1, 1991, came and the wife and her counsel showed up for trial but neither the husband nor his counsel appeared. The trial judge commenced the final hearing and heard the testimony of the wife and a residence witness.

The transcript of that hearing reflects that the wife apprised the court of the mediation proceeding, the negotiations toward settlement, and the proposed oral agreement. She even produced her written, unsigned version of what the parties had agreed to. Apparently to corroborate that, she had the mediator sign the back of her written version as a sort of certification that this was what the parties had agreed to at said hearing. In addition to these revelations of the "mediation agreements," the court took testimony from the wife relative to the marital property and other pertinent evidence generally submitted to arrive at a distribution of the marital estate and support needs of the parties. A final judgment was entered and in due course the husband obtained a copy. A motion to vacate the judgment was filed and a hearing held thereon, at which the trial court indicated that she did not hear a motion to enforce the oral mediation agreement, but that she tried the case on the merits and entered judgment thereon. The motion to vacate was denied.

Section 44.102(3), Florida Statutes (Supp.1990), the statutory court-ordered mediation provision, provides in pertinent part:

(3) Each party involved in a court-ordered mediation proceeding has a privilege to refuse to disclose, and to prevent any person present at the proceeding from disclosing, communications made during such proceeding. Notwithstanding the provisions of § 119.14, all oral or written communications in a mediation proceeding, other than an executed settlement agreement, shall be exempt from the requirements of chapter 119 and shall be confidential and inadmissible as evidence in any subsequent legal proceeding, unless all parties agree otherwise.

The transcript of the dissolution trial leaves little doubt that the trial court was fully apprised of the mediation proceeding and exactly what the wife perceived to have been agreed upon between the parties, albeit there was no written executed agreement. It appears to us that the injection of the so-called agreement prepared by the wife and "certified" by the mediator, and the various testimonial representations of what transpired at said hearing vis-a-vis agreements between the parties, into the trial before the court violates the spirit and letter of the mediation statute. The confidentiality of the negotiations should remain inviolate until a written agreement is executed by the parties.

Therefore, we hold that the well was poisoned by the admission of the foregoing evidence of the "agreement" and so infected the judgment reached that it should be vacated and the matter tried anew.

Accordingly, except for the provision dissolving the marriage of the parties, the final judgment is reversed and the cause is remanded for a new trial on the remaining issues.

* * *

John R. McKinlay v. Louise R. McKinlay

648 So.2d 806 (Dist. Ct. of Appl., 1st District, Florida 1995).

■ MICKLE, JUDGE.

John R. McKinlay, the former husband (Husband), appeals from an August 1991 final order disposing of real and personal property. He alleges three errors: 1) the trial court's failure to enforce the parties' mediation agreement and to impose sanctions; 2) the refusal to permit the mediator to testify in response to allegations made by Louise R. McKinlay, the former wife (Wife), who had questioned the fairness and propriety of the mediation proceedings but claimed a privilege as to mediation communications; and 3) the trial court's division of property. Finding error as to the second issue, we are constrained to reverse and remand for a full evidentiary hearing. § 90.507, Fla.Stat. (1989) (waiver of privilege by voluntary disclosure).

The original proceedings in this prolonged litigation were initiated in May 1985, when Wife filed a petition to dissolve the parties' 17–year marriage. After a hearing in 1986, the lower tribunal issued a final judgment of dissolution of marriage, which was reversed and remanded in Husband's first appeal. McKinlay v. McKinlay, 523 So.2d 182 (Fla. 1st DCA 1988).

Upon remand, the trial court issued orders in October 1989 setting the cause for final hearing but also referring the parties to mediation during the interim period. § 44.302(1), Fla.Stat. (1989) (permitting trial court to refer contested civil action to mediation). Husband, Wife, and their attorneys attended the December 8, 1989, mediation conference and, with the mediator, all signed a "Stipulation of the Parties" indicating their settlement as to terms involving the distribution of real property, an investment plan, boats, cemetery lots, personal property, life insurance policies, and attorney's fees and costs. On the "Disposition of Mediation Conference" form, the mediator checked "Agreement signed (total resolution)." The stipulation and the mediator's report were filed immediately in the trial court.

In a letter dated December 8, 1989, Wife informed her then-trial counsel, "I do not believe the stipulation agreement that we signed earlier today was fair to me." She alleged that she had been "under severe emotional distress" and had been pressured into signing the agreement. In a letter dated December 14, 1989, Wife's former trial counsel notified Husband's lawyer as follows: "Please be advised that I have been informed by Ms. McKinlay that she, as a result of numerous factors occurring at the time of the mediation, feels that she no longer wishes to abide by the terms of the mediation agreement as signed."

On February 1, 1990, Husband filed a motion to enforce the mediation agreement and to impose sanctions, noting 1) the lapse of 10 days since the filing of the stipulation and report and 2) the absence of a written objection to the stipulation by the trial court. Husband argued that the agreement had become binding on the parties pursuant to Fla.R.Civ.P. 1.730 and that Wife had failed to comply with procedural requirements for objecting to the result.

In a February 14, 1990, letter to the trial judge, Wife complained of being "trapped in a dilemma," and she alleged first that Husband's counsel had "badgered" and "intimidated" her at every deposition and hearing and had given "inaccurate information" to the mediator. Second, Wife contended that her own former counsel had instructed her to sign the mediation agreement on the ground that "his attorney fees to pursue this would be more than the outcome would be worth." Third, she stated that the mediator had pressured her into signing the agreement. Wife asserted that she had been under severe emotional distress at the time of the mediation conference because of a family health emergency, and she sought to have the agreement cancelled.

At an unreported hearing on February 15, 1990, the trial court received Wife's letter, sealed the correspondence between Wife's and Husband's counsel, and heard Wife's testimony alleging prior intimidation and indicating her wish not to abide by the "forced" terms of the mediation agreement. In a February 23, 1990, order on Husband's motion, the trial court stated:

While the Florida Rules of Civil Procedure contemplate a filed objection to the Stipulation and Agreement the court finds that the Husband was not prejudiced inasmuch as counsel for the Husband was aware that the Wife was not willing to agree by the Stipulation and Agreement. Additionally, this cause was set for final hearing prior to the time that the mediation conference [was set,] and the final hearing was not taken off the calendar or postponed as a result of the attempted mediation.

After denial of his motion for enforcement and sanctions, Husband moved for rehearing alleging 1) that the parties had entered into a valid and binding contract on December 8, 1989, prior to the submission of the mediation agreement and report to the trial court, and 2) that Husband had been severely prejudiced by having to incur the expense of trial as a result of the non-enforcement of the agreement. Subsequently, Wife hired new counsel.

Issue I

The first issue requires us to determine whether the trial court properly found that Wife's written objection and subsequent allegations warranted an evidentiary hearing. Subsection (b) of Rule 1.730, effective January 1, 1988, Rules of Civ.Proc., In re Proposed Rules for Implementation of Fla.Stat. Sections 44.301–.306, 518 So.2d 908 (Fla.1987), provided as follows:

> In cases where agreement or partial agreement is reached as to any matter or issue, including legal or factual issues to be determined by the court, such agreement shall be reduced to writing, signed by the parties and their counsel, if any, and be immediately thereafter submitted to the court. If counsel neither signs nor objects, in writing, to the agreement within 10 days of service on counsel, then the agreement is conclusively presumed to be approved by counsel and shall then be immediately submitted to the court. Once the agreement becomes binding upon the parties by their execution and that of their counsel, it may only be set aside by the court pursuant to these rules. The agreement shall set forth all relevant statements of fact and statements of future courses of conduct as agreed upon by the parties.

The record demonstrates that the mediation proceedings concluded on December 8, 1989, with a settlement stipulation signed by Husband and Wife, their attorneys, and the mediator, and with the mediator's signed disposition indicating a total resolution of issues. Both documents were filed immediately in the lower tribunal.

Written notification of objection was provided to Husband's counsel in the form of Wife's attorney's letter dated December 14, 1989. This letter indicated that "numerous factors occurring at the time of the mediation" made Wife unwilling to abide by the terms of the agreement. Although not a model of clarity, Rule 1.730 contemplates counsel's making a written objection to a mediated settlement agreement and is consistent with decisional law permitting analogous agreements to be modified or set aside upon the former spouse's establishing that it was procured by fraud, intimidation, or duress. Casto v. Casto, 508 So.2d 330, 333 (Fla.1987). The letter offered by Wife's counsel to Husband's attorney, which was dated December 14 and was received on December 16, 1989, was sufficient to apprise opposing counsel that Wife was objecting and wished not to abide by the terms of the mediation agreement. At that point, the final agreement remained subject to a modification or set-aside "by the court pursuant to these rules." Therefore, we conclude that the matter was properly before the trial court for consideration of evidence addressing the agreement's validity, enforceability, and potential modification. Work v. Provine, 632 So.2d 1119, 1121 (Fla. 1st DCA 1994) (modification of property settlement incorporated into final judgment of dissolution may be had if party seeking modification can satisfy exceptionally heavy burden of showing, e.g., fraud or duress).

Issue II

The second issue arose during the evidentiary hearing held on April 4, 1990, in part to address the issue of enforcement of the mediation agreement. In response to Wife's earlier allegations of intimidation or duress in the mediation proceedings, Husband sought to have the mediator testify. Wife's counsel objected on the ground that mediated matters are privileged and inadmissible over objection pursuant to section 44.101(3) and section 44.302(2), Florida Statutes. Husband's attorney countered that Wife had waived her privilege by challenging the conduct and integrity of the mediation proceedings, and by fully presenting her allegations in writing and in testimony at the unreported hearing. Finding that Wife had exercised her procedural right to object to the mediation results and had not waived her right to exclude testimony concerning mediation communications, the trial court refused to allow the mediator either to testify or to proffer testimony. That ruling constitutes reversible error.

The trial court based its decision first on section 44.101(3), Florida Statutes (1989), which provided in pertinent part:

> (3) Notwithstanding the provisions of § 119.14 [public meeting and record requirements], all oral or written communications in mediation proceedings are exempt from the requirements of chapter 119 and shall be confidential and inadmissible as evidence in any subsequent legal proceeding, unless both parties agree otherwise.

Second, the court relied on section 44.302(2), Florida Statutes (1989) [subsequently renumbered § 44.102(2)], which stated:

> (2) Each party involved in the mediation proceeding has a privilege to refuse to disclose, and to prevent any person present at the proceeding from disclosing, communications made during such proceeding whether or not the dispute was successfully resolved. This subsection shall not be construed to prevent or inhibit the discovery or admissibility of any information which is otherwise subject to discovery or admission under applicable law or rules of court. There is no privilege as to communications made in furtherance of the commission of a crime or fraud or as part of a plan to commit a crime or a fraud. Nothing in this subsection shall be construed so as to permit an individual to obtain immunity from prosecution for criminal conduct.

The trial court found that Wife had not waived her statutory privilege.

The parties have called our attention to Hudson v. Hudson, 600 So.2d 7 (Fla. 4th DCA 1992) (as modif. on reh'g), in which the reviewing court reversed upon a finding that admission of evidence pertaining to an oral mediation agreement had tainted the judgment. Id. at 9. Although Hudson supports Wife's position that mediation communications generally are confidential and inadmissible in a subsequent legal proceeding unless all parties agree otherwise, we find several key factual distinctions between the cases. First, the instant mediation proceedings resulted in a signed, written agreement. Cf. Gordon v. Royal Caribbean Cruises, Ltd., 641 So.2d 515 (Fla. 3d DCA 1994) (under Rule 1.730(b), "confidentiality afforded to parties involved in mediation proceedings must remain inviolate" where parties failed to effectuate a written, signed settlement agreement). Second, we note that, unlike the case sub judice, Hudson and its progeny were subject to an amendment to chapter 44, Florida Statutes, effective October 1, 1991, which provided that "[n]otwithstanding the provisions of § 119.14, all oral or written communications in a mediation proceeding, *other than an executed settlement agreement*, ... shall be confidential and inadmissible as evidence in any subsequent legal proceeding, unless all parties agree otherwise." 1990 Fla.Laws ch. 90–188, § 2, amending and renumbering § 44.302, Fla.Stat. (Emphasis added.)

Third, and most significant, is the fact that as the party who objected to the settlement based on allegations of duress and intimidation, Wife availed herself of the opportunities to file a written letter to the trial judge and to testify at the unreported February 15, 1990, hearing. However, with only her side of the story presented, she invoked a statutory privilege to preclude testimony or a proffer from other witnesses such as the mediator. These particular facts lead us to conclude that Wife waived her statutory privilege of confidentiality and that, as a result of the waiver, it was error and a breach of fair play to deny Husband the opportunity to present rebuttal testimony and evidence.

Our conclusion is bolstered by the general body of law holding that certain analogous statutory privileges, e.g., the psychotherapist-patient privilege set forth in section 90.503, Florida Statutes, and the lawyer-client privilege set forth in section 90.502, Florida Statutes, can be waived. See, e.g., Procacci v. Seitlin, 497 So.2d 969 (Fla. 3d DCA 1986) (attorney-client privilege waived by client's suit for malpractice). Section § 90.507, Florida Statutes, provides:

> A person who has a privilege against the disclosure of a confidential matter or communication waives the privilege if he, or his predecessor while holder of the privilege, voluntarily discloses or makes the communication when he does not have a reasonable expectation of privacy, or consents to disclosure of, any significant part of the matter or communication. This section is not applicable when the disclosure is itself a privileged communication.

Given that Wife invoked the privilege at the April 1990 hearing while challenging the prior conduct or statements of the attorneys and the mediator, we are drawn inescapably to conclude that she thereby voluntarily disclosed or consented to the disclosure of a significant part of the matter or communications for which the privilege was claimed. The same basic considerations involved here underlie those cases in which a party seeking the protection of the so-called Dead Man's Statute, section 90.602, Florida Statutes, has availed itself of certain testimony or other evidence, thereby "opening the door" to matters otherwise sought to be excluded and waiving the very privilege asserted. [citations omitted]. Likewise, the accountant-client privilege can be waived in certain circumstances. Savino v. Luciano, 92 So.2d 817, 819 (Fla.1957) (defendant invoking accountant-client privilege as to an audit waived the right when he relied on the audit to prove a defense and counterclaim).

Having found reversible error as to the second issue, we need not reach the final issue relating to the property distribution scheme. The order is REVERSED and the cause is REMANDED for further proceedings consistent herewith.

■ WOLF, J., concurs. WEBSTER, J., concurs in result only.

* * *

Questions

1.   Under the Florida mediation statute, is it necessary that both parties agree before there can be a waiver of the privilege of confidentiality? What does the *McKinlay* court say are the circumstances under which the mediation privilege can be waived? How heavy is the "heavy burden" that the court imposes?

2.   In *McKinlay,* could the wife have established grounds for repudiating the mediation settlement agreement without introducing evidence from the mediation sessions? If not, what remains of the privilege in cases where one side wants to impugn a mediated settlement agreement?

3.   Once one party has waived the privilege of confidentiality for purposes of showing intimidation, does it necessarily follow that the other side must also be permitted to introduce information from the mediation? Can the court hear evidence from the mediation only for the purpose of deciding the issue of intimidation? If it finds there was no intimidation, can the evidence from the mediation be used to decide other issues in dispute?

4.   Under the Florida mediation privilege statute, who is the holder of the privilege?

* * *

Note on *Folb v. Motion Picture Industry Pension & Health Plans*

In FOLB V. MOTION PICTURE INDUSTRY PENSION & HEALTH PLANS, 16 F. Supp.2d 1164 (C.D.Cal.1998), an employee of defendant, Vasquez, accused another employee, Folb, of sexually harassing her. Vasquez and the defendant entered into formal mediation of the harassment claim, and both parties signed a confidentiality agreement. They did not resolve the Vasquez dispute during mediation, but soon thereafter, the dispute was settled. Subsequently, Folb was fired by the defendant. Defendant claimed Folb was fired for sexual harassment of Vasquez, but Folb claimed he was wrongfully discharged for blowing the whistle on improper business practices of the defendant. Folb, in his suit challenging his dismissal, sought to compel disclosure of the Vasquez's mediation brief as well as correspondence about the mediation and notes prepared for the settlement negotiations. Folb claimed that in those negotiations, defendant took the position that Vasquez had not been sexually harassed, a position that was inconsistent with its position in the wrongful dismissal litigation.

The court considered at length whether or not to adopt a federal mediation privilege, if so, and how broad such a privilege should be. It stated:

"[R]ules protecting the confidentiality of mediation proceedings and rules protecting the actual or perceived impartiality of mediators serve the same ultimate purpose: encouraging parties to attend mediation and communicate openly and honestly in order to facilitate successful alternative dispute resolution.

"[C]onciliators must maintain a reputation for impartiality, and the parties to conciliation conferences must feel free to talk without any fear that the conciliator may subsequently make disclosures as a witness in some other proceeding, to the possible disadvantage of a party to the conference. If conciliators were permitted or required to testify about their activities, or if the production of notes or reports of their activities could be required, not even the strictest adherence to purely factual matters would prevent the evidence from favoring or seeming to favor one side. [citing NLRB v. Joseph Macaluso, Inc., 618 F.2d 51, 55 (9th Cir.1980)].

"Whether information divulged in mediation proceedings is disclosed through the compelled testimony of a mediator or the compelled disclosure of documents conveyed to or prepared by the mediator, the side most forthcoming in the mediation process is penalized when third parties can discover confidential communications with the mediator. Refusing to establish a privilege to protect confidential communications in mediation proceedings creates an incentive for participants to withhold sensitive information in mediation or refuse to participate at all....

"Taking the foregoing authorities en masse, the majority of courts to consider the issue appear to have concluded that the need for confidentiality and trust between participants in a mediation proceeding is sufficiently imperative to necessitate the creation of some form of privilege. This conclusion takes on added significance when considered in conjunction with the fact that many federal district courts rely on the success of ADR proceedings to minimize the size of their dockets....

"... Academic authors differ on the necessity of creating a mediation privilege, but most federal courts considering the issue have protected confidential settlement negotiations and mediation proceedings, either by relying on state law or by applying the confidentiality provisions of federal court ADR programs. Having carefully reviewed the foregoing authority, the Court concludes that the proposed blanket mediation privilege is rooted in the imperative need for confidence and trust among participants....

"Accordingly, this Court finds it is appropriate, in light of reason and experience, to adopt a federal mediation privilege applicable to all communications made in conjunction with a formal mediation ...

"The mediation underlying the instant dispute was a formal mediation with a neutral mediator, not a private settlement discussion between the parties. Accordingly, the mediation privilege adopted today applies only to information disclosed in conjunction with mediation proceedings with a neutral. Any interpretation of Rule 501 must be consistent with Rule 408. To protect settlement communications not related to mediation would invade Rule 408's domain; only Congress is authorized to amend the scope of protection afforded by Rule 408. Consequently, any post-mediation communications are protected only by Rule 408's limitations on admissibility.

"On the facts presented here, the Court concludes that communications to the mediator and communications between parties during the mediation are protected. In addition, communications in preparation for and during the course of a mediation with a neutral must be protected. Subsequent negotiations between the parties, however, are not protected even if they include information initially disclosed in the mediation. To protect additional communications, the parties are required to return to mediation. A contrary rule would permit a party to claim the privilege with respect to any settlement negotiations so long as the communications took place following an attempt to mediate the dispute."

* * *

Question

Is the rationale for a mediation privilege when one party to the mediation seeks to compel disclosure of material presented at mediation in a lawsuit against the other party the same when it is a third party seeking information about a mediation to which they did not participate? Which situation presents the stronger case for a privilege?

* * *

Snyder–Falkinham v. Stockburger

457 S.E.2d 36 (Sup. Ct. of Va. 1995).

■ COMPTON, JUSTICE.

In this dispute spawned from pending civil litigation, the questions on appeal are whether the trial court erred in ruling that the plaintiff agreed to a settlement of the underlying action and whether the trial court erred in holding that the plaintiff's trial attorneys had the authority to have the action dismissed with prejudice.

In November 1991, appellant Georgia Anne Snyder–Falkinham filed the underlying suit, a legal malpractice action, against appellees Bruce C. Stockburger, an attorney at law; Gentry, Locke, Rakes and Moore, a Roanoke law firm in which Stockburger was a partner; and certain other named partners in the law firm, seeking compensatory and punitive damages. The plaintiff asserted that, beginning in early 1980, an attorney-client relationship existed between her and defendant Stockburger. She claimed that this relationship evolved over the years "to the point where defendant Stockburger was providing legal and financial advice in all of the plaintiff's personal and business dealings."

She asserted that, with Stockburger's advice, she began a construction business that became involved in, among other things, residential housing projects in Blacksburg and Radford. She contended that she sustained actual losses of $6.7 million as the result of the defendants' alleged breach of fiduciary duties, professional negligence, and fraud and misrepresentation in handling her business affairs. In responsive pleadings, the defendants denied all the plaintiff's allegations of wrongful conduct.

As a January 31, 1994 trial date approached, defendant Stockburger, by counsel, moved that the case be referred to a dispute resolution evaluation session pursuant to Virginia's Dispute Resolution Program. Code §§ 8.01–576.4 to–576.12. The trial court granted the motion, referred the matter to such a session, and directed the parties to return to court on January 31 irrespective of the outcome of the referral.

The plaintiff and her trial attorneys, Thomas L. Rasnic and Roger E. Jenne; defendant Stockburger and his attorney; and the attorney for the other defendants appeared in Richmond on January 25 for a three-hour evaluation session. At the conclusion of the session, certain terms of agreement relating to the litigation and attributed to the plaintiff were recorded on a Mediation Memorandum of Agreement by one of the mediators.

Over the next several days, the parties continued to negotiate for a full and final settlement. On Sunday, January 30, the day before trial, the plaintiff, her trial attorneys, and the attorneys for the defendants engaged in extensive discussions in a Roanoke hotel. Late that evening, according to defendants, the plaintiff agreed to all terms of a proposed settlement, a fact that the plaintiff now denies.

The next morning, January 31, plaintiff's trial attorney Rasnic and one of defendants' attorneys went to the courthouse where the trial court entered two orders, each dismissing the underlying action with prejudice. The orders carried the endorsements of plaintiff's trial attorneys and the attorneys for the defendants. One order dismissed the law firm's individual partners, except Stockburger, and dismissed the claim for punitive damages. The other order was a general dismissal and contained a provision permitting a contempt citation for violation of the confidentiality portion of a "Mutual Release and Settlement Agreement."

Shortly after noon on January 31, plaintiff was called by one of her trial attorneys and was asked to come to Roanoke from her home in Blacksburg to execute the settlement papers memorializing the agreement. She told the attorney "that she was still thinking about" the settlement. Apparently, the plaintiff had consulted earlier that morning with another attorney, one of her present appellate counsel.

On February 3, 1994, both appellate counsel filed a praecipe noting their appearance as counsel for the plaintiff for the purpose of filing a motion to vacate the January 31 dismissal orders. Plaintiff's trial counsel then filed a notice and motion to withdraw as counsel for the plaintiff.

Plaintiff's appellate counsel then filed a motion to vacate the January 31 orders, and defendants' counsel filed a motion to confirm the settlement. On February 15, 1994, the trial court conducted a hearing on the respective motions, after entering an order relieving plaintiff's trial counsel as counsel of record.

Upon considering the testimony of 16 witnesses and reviewing numerous exhibits, the trial court, stating the decision involved a question of "credibility," found "as a fact that the plaintiff did agree to the terms of the settlement, and that the attorneys did have actual as well as implied authority to settle the case." We awarded the plaintiff an appeal from the February 15, 1994 order denying the plaintiff's motion to vacate and sustaining the defendants' motion to confirm.

On appeal, plaintiff assigns four errors. Two assigned errors invoke the provisions of Code § 8.01–576.10, which deals with the confidentiality of dispute resolution proceedings. As pertinent, the statute provides: "Any communication made in or in connection with the dispute resolution proceeding which relates to the controversy, whether made to the neutral or dispute resolution program or to a party, or to any other person if made at a dispute resolution proceeding, is confidential."

Relying on the statute, the plaintiff first contends that, during the February 15th hearing, the trial court erred when it admitted evidence of discussions and events which occurred in the court-ordered mediation proceeding bearing upon the question of whether the plaintiff's trial attorneys had authority to have her case dismissed with prejudice. Still relying on the statute, plaintiff next contends that the trial court erred by admitting in evidence the Mediation Memorandum of Agreement to establish the ultimate existence of a settlement agreement.

We do not reach for decision either of those issues because they are procedurally barred by Rule 5:25. As applicable here, this rule of appellate procedure provides that error will not be sustained to any ruling of the trial court admitting evidence unless the objection to such admission "was stated with reasonable certainty at the time of the ruling." Although admission of the evidence challenged in these two assignments of error was the subject of several objections by plaintiff's counsel during the hearing, not once did counsel cite to the trial judge or rely on Code § 8.01–576.10, or any other statute dealing with dispute resolution proceedings. Indeed, three days after entry of the February 15th order, plaintiff, by counsel, filed a ten-page Motion for Reconsideration, and did not mention any of the foregoing statutes. Thus, the trial court was never afforded the opportunity to address and rule on the issues that the plaintiff now raises, and we will not consider them for the first time on appeal.

The remaining assignments of error challenge the sufficiency of the evidence on proof of a settlement and on proof of the authority of plaintiff's trial counsel to move for entry of the orders dismissing the underlying action. Prior to a discussion of the evidence on those issues, a review of applicable, settled principles of law is appropriate.

"The law favors compromise and settlement of disputed claims." Bangor–Punta Operations, Inc. v. Atlantic Leasing, Ltd., 215 Va. 180, 183, 207 S.E.2d 858, 860 (1974). But the essential elements of a valid contract must exist to support a binding compromise settlement; there must be a complete agreement including acceptance of an offer as well as valuable consideration. Montagna v. Holiday Inns, Inc., 221 Va. 336, 346, 269 S.E.2d 838, 844 (1980). Ultimate resolution of the question whether there has been a binding settlement involves a determination of the parties' intention, as objectively manifested. Id.; Boisseau v. Fuller, 96 Va. 45, 46, 30 S.E. 457, 457 (1898).

An attorney at law, merely by virtue of being retained by the client, has no authority to compromise the client's claim without the latter's consent. Dawson v. Hotchkiss, 160 Va. 577, 581–82, 169 S.E. 564, 565 (1933). Nevertheless, the attorney has full authority to act on behalf of the client in the conduct of litigation before the court, including making admissions and factual stipulations. Harris v. Diamond Constr. Co., 184 Va. 711, 722, 36 S.E.2d 573, 578 (1946).

An attorney's general authority permits the attorney to discontinue a pending action by a dismissal without prejudice; but this general authority gives the attorney no right to discharge or terminate a cause of action by a dismissal on the merits, such as by a dismissal with prejudice, without special authority or acquiescence on the part of the client. Virginia Concrete Co. v. Board of Supervisors of Fairfax County, 197 Va. 821, 827, 91 S.E.2d 415, 420 (1956).

When a civil case is tried by a court without the intervention of a jury and, as here, a party objects to the decision on the ground that it is contrary to the evidence, the trial court's judgment will not be set aside on appeal "unless it appears from the evidence that such judgment is plainly wrong or without evidence to support it." Code § 8.01–680. The conclusions of the trial court under these circumstances are entitled to "great weight." Dawson, 160 Va. at 581, 169 S.E. at 565.

In summarizing the evidence, we shall apply established appellate principles and recite the facts in the light most favorable to the defendants, who prevailed below. Viewing the record in this manner, we hold there is competent, credible evidence to support the trial court's factual findings (1) that the parties, including the plaintiff, voluntarily entered into a complete and final settlement agreement, and (2) that the plaintiff's trial attorneys were authorized to dismiss her action with prejudice. We will assume, without deciding, that the defendants had the burden of proof on both of these issues.

The plaintiff's trial attorneys, Rasnic (a member of the Virginia Bar) and Jenne (a Tennessee lawyer), were working pursuant to a written contract of employment that provided for an attorney's fee of 40 percent of the amount recovered. The contract specified that the attorneys were "authorized to effect a settlement or compromise, subject to the client(s) approval."

The trial court's order referring the case to the dispute resolution evaluation session was entered on December 21, 1993. The order provided that if, within 14 days after entry of the order, the plaintiff objected to the referral, she would be excused from attendance at the session. As we have stated, the plaintiff appeared at the session accompanied by Rasnic and Jenne.

During the session, one of the persons conducting the proceedings asked the participants to identify themselves and said it was the practice for the individual parties to speak at the session rather than have their attorneys speak for them. At that time, the plaintiff "very clearly" made her position known. She said, "I will have my attorneys speak for me; I am not going to make any statements on my own behalf." According to the plaintiff, she spoke only "about two sentences" during the three-hour session.

During the session, the plaintiff agreed on several issues in the presence of the other participants. Each of the items was written on the Mediation Memorandum of Agreement, and the wording was read back to the participants and discussed in detail. Although her attorneys negotiated and spoke for her, the plaintiff conveyed to all present her agreement with the items discussed. The items of agreement during the session included the plaintiff's promise to waive her claim for punitive damages, her promise to waive any claim in excess of the defendant law firm's professional liability insurance policy limits, her promise to nonsuit all individual defendants other than Stockburger, and the promise of the law firm's liability insurer to withdraw its reservation of the right to deny coverage to certain defendants.

During the marathon negotiating session on January 30th at the hotel, numerous telephone and face-to-face conferences took place among counsel for the parties, with discussions between the plaintiff and her trial attorneys interspersed. Many varied topics were considered including the participation of plaintiff's two children in a release of claims, the tax consequences if the settlement involved a transfer of capital stock in an entity controlled by plaintiff and Stockburger, the disposition of a promissory note for $25,000 made by Stockburger payable to plaintiff, and, of course, the amount of money that would be paid the plaintiff in settlement of her claims.

Finally, late in the evening on January 30th, one of counsel for the defendants spoke by telephone with Jenne and advised that payment of an increased settlement amount was virtually certain to be approved. Jenne then conferred again with the plaintiff, and she agreed "to all the terms of the settlement at that time" without "any reservation."

The essence of the settlement, according to Jenne's testimony, was that "x number of dollars" was to be paid the plaintiff, "she was going to accept that amount of money" and execute a release, "she was going to cancel the $25,000 note,'' and the entire settlement was to be confidential. Jenne said the results obtained in the dispute resolution session became "more or less moot" when the final settlement was reached on January 30th and the final agreement superseded the mediation agreement.

When the compromise was reached, everyone ceased trial preparations. The plaintiff called her brother, her sister, her bookkeeper, and her son. During one of the telephone conversations, the plaintiff was overheard to say, "The case has been settled." Each of the persons called testified that plaintiff advised them late Sunday evening that the trial scheduled for Monday had been cancelled. Jenne's paralegal learned of the late developments when the plaintiff told her the case "was settled." The husband of Rasnic's paralegal, Ronnie L. Robbins, spoke with the plaintiff during Sunday evening. She told him, "You know, Ronnie, the legal system really sucks. Those people knew the case was going to settle three or four months ago, and they are dragging it out as long as they can because they are on a ticker."

On Monday morning, January 31st, Stockburger's attorney called Jenne at 7:30 a.m. to tell him that the settlement amount had received final approval late the previous night. Jenne immediately called the plaintiff, who apparently was at her Blacksburg home, and informed her of the final approval and that the settlement was "a done deal." Jenne advised that he would call her again when "we got the paperwork together" to memorialize the agreement. He also advised her that Rasnic would be "going to the courthouse" with an attorney for the defendants. Counsel met the trial judge that morning and presented drafts of the dismissal orders, which he entered.

Near 12:50 p.m. on January 31st, when the plaintiff was asked to come to Roanoke to sign the settlement papers memorializing the agreement and when she told Jenne that "she was still thinking about it," Jenne said to her, "What do you mean, you're still thinking about it . . . this deal's been settled, it's over with; we need you to get up here and get the paperwork completed." Both Jenne and the plaintiff became "angry and upset," and she told him that she had talked with one of her expert witnesses, who discussed the extent of her monetary damages and said her trial attorneys "were not prepared to fight the case for her." She stated to Jenne that "she was not going forward with it at this point" and that "we would be hearing from her new lawyer from Washington, D.C." in about an hour. Contrary to the plaintiff's testimony, there is overwhelming credible evidence to support the conclusion that this was the first time plaintiff indicated she was not pleased with the settlement terms or that she thought no settlement had been reached.

As we have indicated, the record is replete with competent evidence to support the trial court's factual finding that the plaintiff orally agreed to a binding settlement. Paraphrasing Montagna and Boisseau, we conclude that her intention to compromise was objectively manifested, as shown by the evidence we have just recited.

Once a competent party makes a settlement and acts affirmatively to enter into such settlement, her second thoughts at a later time upon the wisdom of the settlement do not constitute good cause for setting it aside. Moreland v. Suttmiller, 183 W.Va. 621, 625, 397 S.E.2d 910, 914 (1990). That is what occurred here. The record establishes conclusively that from the time of the Richmond mediation session, when several items of the compromise were negotiated, until late in the evening on January 30th, the plaintiff fully agreed to the essential terms of the settlement. Not until she had conversations with her "expert witness" and another attorney during the morning of January 31 did she voice any objection to the agreement, and embark on a campaign to repudiate it. That was too late. By that time, the settlement was a "done deal."

Contrary to the plaintiff's contention on appeal, the settlement was binding even though these parties contemplated that a formal, written "Mutual Release and Settlement Agreement" memorializing the compromise would be executed. If, as here, the parties are fully agreed upon the terms of the settlement and intend to be bound thereby, "the mere fact that a later formal writing is contemplated will not vitiate the agreement." North America Managers, Inc. v. Reinach, 177 Va. 116, 121, 12 S.E.2d 806, 808 (1941); Boisseau, 96 Va. at 46, 30 S.E. at 457.

Finally, there is no merit to the plaintiff's contention the trial court erred in ruling that her trial attorneys lacked authority to have her case dismissed with prejudice. Again, the evidence to the contrary is overwhelming.

The analysis of this issue must begin with the provisions of the contingent-fee contract of employment. It authorized plaintiff's trial attorneys "to effect a settlement or compromise" of the underlying action. Next, during the Richmond mediation session, the plaintiff "very clearly," acting consistently with the authority given in the written contract, orally empowered Rasnic and Jenne to "speak for" her during the negotiations. The record establishes that this authority was never revoked, either expressly or impliedly, until after noon on January 31st and after the settlement was consummated.

But, as we have said, the general authority of an attorney does not give counsel the right to dismiss the client's cause of action with prejudice, without "special authority or acquiescence" on the part of the client. Virginia Concrete Co., 197 Va. at 827, 91 S.E.2d at 420. Both special authority and acquiescence existed here. For example, Jenne testified that when he and Rasnic endorsed the drafts of the dismissal orders during the morning of January 31st, their "authority and direction" from the plaintiff was that the case "was settled, and that all of her claims were dismissed with prejudice." Jenne was asked, "And what was the basis upon which you held that position and that understanding with your client?" He responded, "Her direction to us."

For these reasons, we conclude that the trial court did not err, and the orders entered on January 31, 1994 and the order entered February 15, 1994 will be

Affirmed.

* * *

Questions

1.   The *Snyder–Falkinham* opinion has been criticized on the grounds that the court used a technicality to avoid an important issue of mediation confidentiality. See James M. Assey, Jr., *Mum's the Word on Mediation: Confidentiality and Snyder–Falkinham v. Stockburger*, 9 Geo. J. Of Leg. Ethics 991 (1996). Based on the information the court provides, could it be argued that the plaintiff's attorney did raise an objection to disclosure of confidential information in a timely fashion? If so, is the court justified in disposing of the confidentiality issue as it does?

2.   If the confidentiality argument had been properly raised, how should the court rule? Did the parties in fact agree to an oral settlement? When was the settlement reached?

3.   How can the existence of a verbal settlement in mediation be proved without introducing testimony concerning discussions that occurred during mediation? If the mediator in this case had insisted that the parties reduce their purported settlement agreement to writing, even though a more formal writing were contemplated, could this dispute have been avoided? How detailed would the writing have to be to avoid a subsequent change of position by one side?

4.   In *Vernon v. Acton*, 693 N.E.2d 1345 (Ind.Ct.App.1998), an automobile negligence action, the trial court admitted, over plaintiff's objection, testimony by the mediator and a third party participant that established that a verbal settlement agreement had been reached during mediation of the plaintiff's claim. The court also admitted testimony as to what the terms of the settlement were, but it refused to admit any other testimony about the mediation session. The plaintiff appealed. The appellate court held that the evidence was admissible. It stated that while there was a state law regarding confidentiality in mediation, it only applied to "civil and domestic relations actions filed in all ... courts of the state." It held that because the complaint was not filed until December 5, 1995, after the mediation had taken place, the state law did not apply. The court further held that Rule 408 did not bar the testimony because the testimony was not admitted to show liability or invalidity of claim, but was offered for "another purpose." It also held that the fact that the parties contracted to keep statements made during mediation confidential and inadmissible did not bind the court. The court therefore found on the basis of the testimony from the mediation, that the dispute had been settled at mediation and that the settlement was clear and unambiguous as to its terms.

Should the court in *Vernon v. Acton* have admitted the testimony of the mediator and third party? If parties know that such testimony might be admissible, how might it change their conduct during mediation? Could it make parties less willing to consider compromising their claims? If so, does the possibility that such testimony might be admissible threaten the mediation process?

* * *

4. COMPELLING MEDIATORS TO TESTIFY

State of Florida v. Castellano

460 So.2d 480 (Dist. Ct. of Appl., 2d Dist., Fla. 1984).

◼ GRIMES, ACTING CHIEF JUDGE.

The state seeks to appeal an order denying its motion to quash respondent's deposition subpoena of Roger Mallory. Since this is a nonappealable order, we treat the matter as a petition for writ of certiorari.

The respondent was charged with attempted first degree murder. In responding to a demand for discovery, the state listed Mallory as a person having information about the case. The respondent subpoenaed Mallory for the taking of his deposition. Mallory is a mediator in the Citizens Dispute Settlement Program (CDSP) in the Tenth Judicial Circuit.[1] The respondent asserts that Mallory will be able to testify that during the course of mediation the person who became the victim of the alleged attempted murder made life-threatening statements to the respondent. He maintains such testimony will support his contention of self-defense. The state filed a motion to quash the deposition subpoena urging that statements made to CDSP mediators were privileged. The court denied the motion to quash.

At the outset, we note that section 90.501, Florida Statutes (1983), provides:

> 90.501 Privileges recognized only as provided.—Except as otherwise provided by this chapter, any other statute, or the Constitution of the United States or of the State of Florida, no person in a legal proceeding has a privilege to:
>
> (1) Refuse to be a witness.
>
> (2) Refuse to disclose any matter.
>
> (3) Refuse to produce any object or writing.
>
> (4) Prevent another from being a witness, from disclosing any matter, or from producing any object or writing.

Thus, privileges in Florida are no longer creatures of judicial decision. Marshall v. Anderson, 459 So.2d 384 (Fla. 3d DCA 1984).

---

1. In essence, this program offers an alternative to a formal prosecution for enu-   merated misdemeanors.

In this case, the state argues for privilege on two grounds. First, the state contends that communications made by parties in the CDSP are privileged as being in the nature of offers of compromise. However, the rule protecting offers of compromise appears to be one more of admissibility than privilege. C. McCormick, McCormick on Evidence § 274 (2d ed. 1972); 4 J. Wigmore, Wigmore on Evidence § 1061 (rev. ed. 1972). The admissibility of offers to compromise is addressed in section 90.408, Florida Statutes (1983):

> 90.408 Compromise and offers to compromise.—Evidence of an offer to compromise a claim which was disputed as to validity or amount, as well as any relevant conduct or statements made in negotiations concerning a compromise, is inadmissible to prove liability or absence of liability for the claim or its value.

The plain language of the provision only excludes evidence of an offer of compromise presented to prove liability or the absence of liability for a claim or its value. Therefore, even if the admissibility of such evidence could be equated with the privilege not to disclose the evidence, there is nothing in the statute remotely applicable to the testimony sought herein. This section is simply not relevant to the situation where a mediator testifies in a criminal proceeding regarding an alleged threat made by one party to another in a prior CDSP setting.

Alternatively, the state asserts that since the CDSP is an investigatory arm of the state attorney, the privilege accorded to statements made to a prosecuting attorney should be extended to those made to a CDSP mediator. See Widener v. Croft, 184 So.2d 444 (Fla. 4th DCA), cert. denied, 192 So.2d 486 (Fla.1966). We know of no rationale to make such an extension. The parties to a CDSP program are simply attempting to resolve a dispute so that a criminal prosecution will be unnecessary. All statements are made voluntarily by persons under no legal compulsion to attend. The record reflects no authority for the mediator's statement that the parties' communications were confidential. The fact that he may have so advised the parties that their communications would be held confidential does not now excuse him from being compelled by respondent to testify concerning what was said.

There is no legal basis for a privilege which would prevent the respondent from obtaining Mallory's testimony. If confidentiality is essential to the success of the CDSP program, the legislature is the proper branch of government from which to obtain the necessary protection.

Certiorari denied.

* * *

The People of the State of New York v. George Snyder

129 Misc.2d 137, 492 N.Y.S.2d 890.
(S.Ct. Erie County, 1985).

■ JOHN J. CONNELL, ACTING JUSTICE.

The above named defendant was indicted by the Erie County Grand Jury on charges of Murder in the Second Degree and Criminal Possession of a Weapon in the Second Degree involving an alleged incident on August

16, 1983 in which William Fugate was shot to death by the defendant.

In the case at bar, the defense, both in the voir dire and opening statement to the jury, had raised the defense of justification claiming that the defendant shot and killed William Fugate in self defense. Mention was also made by defense counsel in his opening statement of the victim and defendant's participation with the Community Dispute Resolution Center prior to the fatal shooting. Because of these statements, the District Attorney subpoenaed any and all records pertaining to such mediation between the defendant and the victim and involving a third person, Deborah Nelson.

Attorneys for the Better Business Bureau Foundation which administers the Community Dispute Resolution Center program in Erie County served an Order to Show Cause on the District Attorney's Office signed June 7, 1985 and made returnable on June 10, 1985 seeking that the said subpoena be quashed pursuant to CPLR 2304. On the return date arguments were heard from the attorney for the Better Business Bureau Foundation, the District Attorney's Office and defense counsel for George Snyder. Subsequent to the oral argument, and after review of the papers submitted in support of and in opposition to the motion, and upon review of the applicable statutory law, the motion to quash the subpoena was granted. There appears to be no reported case construing Section 849–b(6) of the Judiciary Law.

The Community Dispute Resolution Center's Program was established in 1981 by the New York State Legislature to enable the creation of community dispute centers to resolve neighborhood and interpersonal disputes. The goal of the Legislature in creating these centers was to provide a "quick, inexpensive and voluntary resolution of disagreements, while at the same time serving the overall public interests by permitting the criminal justice community to concentrate its resources on more serious criminal matters." (1981 McKinney's Session Laws, p. 2630.) It was the feeling of the Legislature that in order for such programs to be successful, the parties availing themselves of the services of these forums must feel that they can air their disputes "in an informal atmosphere without restraint and intimidation." (1981 McKinney's Session Laws, pp. 1728–1729.)

In order to assure confidentiality to the parties involved, and thereby encourage their full, frank, and open participation, Section 849–b(6) of the Judiciary Law was enacted as follows:

> "Except as otherwise expressly provided in this Article, all memoranda, work products, or case files of the mediator are confidential and not subject to disclosure in any judicial or administrative proceeding. Any communication relating to the subject matter of the resolution made during the resolution process by any participant, mediator, or any

other person present at the dispute resolution shall be a confidential communication.''

In spite of the first sentence in this statute, there appears no where else in the article an exception to the restrictive language of the statute.

I find that even if the defendant can be found to have waived the confidentiality of the records pertaining to the mediation sessions in which he was involved, the statute, as drafted, permits no such waiver. The items sought by the District Attorney are by definition, ''confidential communications.''

Confidential communications are, by their very nature, guided by rules of exclusion. Most commonly rules of exclusion are drafted to prevent evidence being presented to a jury that is of no probative value or of a kind that may unfairly prejudice one of the parties or misdirect the jury's attention from the primary issue at hand. The confidentiality of certain communications, however, is meant to nurture very specific interpersonal or professional relationships that the Courts, society and the legislature deem desirable. (Fisch on NY Evidence, 2nd Edition, p. 335).

The Court of Appeals recently strictly construed Public Health Law Section 2306 which relates to information concerning sexually transmittable diseases. That section reads as follows: ''All reports or information secured by a board of health or health officer under the provisions of this article shall be confidential except in so far as is necessary to carry out the purposes of this article.'' In the Matter of Grattan v. People, 65 N.Y.2d 243, 491 N.Y.S.2d 125, 480 N.E.2d 714, the Court held that the goal of the statute cannot be defeated simply by the consent of the source to release the information. ''The requirement of confidentiality (Public Health Law Section 2306) is integral to a statutory scheme designed to encourage afflicted persons to seek and secure treatment, which in the case of communicable disease, served individual interests as well as those of society.'' (Matter of Grattan, supra, at p. 245, 491 N.Y.S.2d 125, 480 N.E.2d 714).

Section 849–b(6) is even more restrictive in its language by specifically referring to excluding disclosure from ''any judicial or administrative proceeding.'' Section 849–b(4)(a) places funding for the dispute centers in jeopardy unless '' . . . it complies with the provisions of this article and the applicable rules and regulations of the chief administrator . . .'' The intent of the Legislature to provide forums for the resolutions of disputes as alternatives to structured judicial settings is, therefore, clearly defined in the statutory language itself as well as the funding provisions for the dispute centers.

To grant the District Attorney's request to review the records of the Community Dispute Resolution Center would subvert the legislature's clear intention to guarantee the confidentiality of all such records and communications.

Accordingly, the subpoena is hereby quashed.

* * *

Andrew L. Smith v. Clayton J. Smith, et al.

154 F.R.D. 661 (N.D. Texas, 1994).

■ FITZWATER, DISTRICT JUDGE:

This is an appeal from an order of the magistrate judge quashing a trial subpoena duces tecum served on a mediator appointed by a state court. The parties who issued the subpoena contend the mediator's testimony is necessary to refute plaintiff's claims in the present suit that relate to the settlement of state court lawsuits that the witness mediated. Without approving the magistrate judge's recognition of a mediator privilege, the court discerns no basis to disturb the order and therefore affirms.

I

Plaintiff Andrew L. Smith ("Andrew") brings this action against defendants Clayton J. Smith ("Clayton"), Mark L. Smith ("Mark"), Smith Protective Services, Inc. ("SPS"), Smith Fire Equipment, Inc. ("SFE"), and Marcla, Inc. ("Marcla"). In the words of the Fifth Circuit, it "is but another chapter in a protracted internecine feud among [the Smiths]." Smith v. Ayres, 977 F.2d 946, 947 (5th Cir.1992), cert. denied, __ U.S. __, 113 S.Ct. 2342, 124 L.Ed.2d 252 (1993). Andrew alleges that his two brothers, Clayton and Mark, with the assistance of SPS' lawyer, R. Jack Ayres, Jr., Esq. ("Ayres"), colluded to seize control of SPS by rescinding a sale of SPS stock from Clayton to SPS. Andrew sued his brothers in state court, challenging their control rights in SPS, and contending he and his mother, Coralie C. Smith, were the controlling shareholders. Andrew filed a separate state court suit, seeking lost salary and other damages caused by the allegedly wrongful issuance of SPS stock to Clayton. Plaintiff also filed a derivative securities fraud action in federal district court against Ayres, the SPS attorney, alleging that Ayres was liable for his role in procuring the issuance of SPS stock to Mark and Clayton and for the two brothers' subsequent mismanagement of SPS.

With the assistance of a mediator appointed by the state district court, Andrew, his mother, and brothers settled the state court suits and executed a settlement agreement that purported to settle all claims and controversies between them. The parties also executed a release. Pursuant to the settlement agreement, plaintiff was to receive $50,000 at the time of closing the settlement agreement, $2.6 million to be paid over a period of 25 years, assignment of SPS' claims against Ayres in the derivative suit, a 1990 Cadillac sedan, and complete affidavits by Mark and Clayton setting forth their personal knowledge of the involvement of Ayres in the alleged stock fraud scheme. SPS was to purchase all but one of Andrew's shares and all of his mother's shares in SPS and SFE at their par value of one cent per share. The agreement provided that in the event of default of any covenant in the agreement, SPS would have 120 days to cure, and if it did not cure within that time, Andrew and his mother could exercise an option to purchase 65% of the authorized shares of SPS for $65,000.

Andrew brings the instant action, contending defendants misrepresented that they would make a full and complete disclosure of the involvement of Ayres in the alleged SPS stock fraud scheme, as provided in the settlement agreement, and that defendants failed to disclose the pending sale of SFE's assets to a competitor of SFE, in order to induce Andrew and his mother to sell their SFE stock to defendants for a grossly inadequate price. Andrew alleges claims for securities fraud, in violation of § 10(b) of the Securities Exchange Act of 1934, 15 U.S.C. § 78j(b), and Rule 10b–5 promulgated thereunder; breach of and conspiracy to breach fiduciary duties; violation of the Racketeer Influenced and Corrupt Organizations Act, 18 U.S.C. § 1962(b), (c), and (d) ("civil RICO"); and common law fraud. Andrew also seeks specific performance of the settlement agreement, allowing him to exercise his option to purchase 65% of SPS, and attorney's fees.

In connection with the trial setting for this case, defendants issued a subpoena duces tecum to Tom James, Esq. (the "Mediator"), the individual who mediated settlement of the state court lawsuits. The subpoena commanded that he appear as a witness at trial and produce and permit inspection and copying of all documents in his possession "relating to mediation of Cause No. 86–5798–K, Coralie Smith, et al. v. Clayton J. Smith, et al., in the 192nd Judicial District Court, Dallas County, Texas and Cause No. 84–3652–K in the 192nd Judicial District Court, Dallas County, Texas, Smith Protective Services, Inc. v. Andrew L. Smith." Defendants seek to introduce the testimony of the Mediator because Andrew contends that Mark and Clayton defrauded him into signing the settlement agreement that resulted from the mediation process. Defendants maintain that the Mediator "is the only impartial witness to the concerns and attitudes expressed by [Andrew] during the private caucus sessions concerning both the affidavits and any disclosure of the future asset sale," and that the Mediator "is the only impartial witness to defendants' conduct and their statements concerning the affidavits during their private caucus sessions." Defendants urge that "[b]ecause [Andrew] alleges fraud, his conduct, state of mind, words and actions during the mediation immediately before the time he alleges he was defrauded are highly probative of any reliance he placed upon the alleged representations." They contend their own statements and conduct during their private sessions with the Mediator are likewise "extremely important for the jury to be able to consider."

The Mediator moved to quash the subpoena or, in the alternative, for a protective order. He argued that the requested testimony was prohibited by Tex.Civ.Prac. & Rem.Code Ann. § 154.073 (West Supp.1994), and Rule 12 of the Rules for Mediation promulgated by the state District Courts of Dallas County, Texas (the "Dallas District Court Mediation Rules"), and that any evidence would be inadmissible pursuant to Fed.R.Evid. 408.

Amicus curiae The Association of Attorney–Mediators, Inc. ("AAM") supported the Mediator's motion.

The court referred the motion to the magistrate judge, who decided in favor of the Mediator and quashed the subpoena. The magistrate judge began his written order by assuming that the Mediator's testimony would not be rendered inadmissible by Rule 408. He found it unnecessary to decide whether Texas law and the Dallas District Court Mediation Rules were binding on this court because comity and the expectations of the Mediator and the parties at the time the mediation was conducted required this court to give due deference to the Texas law and rules. The magistrate judge then held that a mediator privilege applied, he assumed the privilege was a qualified one, and on the basis of the facts presented, he decided for public policy reasons that the privilege outweighed defendants' interest in obtaining the Mediator's records and testimony.

Defendants seek to overturn the magistrate judge's order on four grounds. Under the rubric "clearly erroneous" they urge that the order should be reversed because, first, there is no comity that this court must recognize since relevant Texas law empowers this court independently to determine the disclosure question; second, the expectations of the parties and the Mediator are not in issue; and third, Texas law does not prohibit disclosure of oral communications or written materials if they are otherwise admissible or discoverable independent of the alternative dispute resolution procedure. Contending fourth that the order is contrary to law, defendants urge that the magistrate judge abridged an obligation of Texas law by failing to conduct an in camera inspection, or to allow a district judge to make such an inspection, before quashing the subpoena.

The Mediator, joined by amicus curiae AAM and plaintiff Andrew, urge the court to affirm the magistrate judge's order quashing the subpoena duces tecum. . . .

III

Because the parties to this appeal have assumed the applicability of Texas law and the Dallas District Court Mediation Rules, the court briefly describes the Texas alternative dispute resolution statute and its confidentiality requirements and the local Dallas confidentiality rules.

A

The mediation that brought about the settlement of the two state court lawsuits was convened on the state court's motion pursuant to the Alternative Dispute Resolution Procedures Act ("ADR Act"), . . . Tex.Civ.Prac. & Rem.Code Ann. §§ 154.001–.073 (West Supp.1994). In 1987 the Texas Legislature enacted the ADR Act, a law that articulates the state's policy of encouraging peaceable resolution of disputes and the early settlement of pending litigation. . . . "The Texas Alternative Dispute Resolution Procedures Act . . . sets forth a comprehensive procedural framework for the use of alternative dispute resolution procedures." . . . "The Act establishes a definite state policy to encourage the early settlement of pending litigation through voluntary settlement procedures and places the responsibility for carrying out this procedure on both trial and appellate courts." Id. ... Texas state courts are admonished by § 154.003 to carry out this policy. Decker, 824 S.W.2d at 250.

The ADR Act authorizes courts to refer a pending dispute to an alternative dispute resolution procedure at any point in the trial and appellate process. ... "A court cannot force the disputants to peaceably resolve their differences, but it can compel them to sit down with each other." Decker, 824 S.W.2d at 250. "Chapter 154 contemplates mandatory referral only, not mandatory negotiation." Id. at 251. A court cannot compel the parties to negotiate in good faith. Id.

Under the Texas ADR scheme, "[t]he job of a mediator is simply to facilitate communication between the parties and thereby encourage reconciliation, settlement and understanding among them." In re Ames, 860 S.W.2d 590, 592 (Tex.App.1993, no writ) (citing § 154.023(a)). It is hoped that "mediation will assist the parties in reaching a voluntary agreement that will serve to resolve their dispute and avoid the need for traditional litigation." Id. "A mediator may not impose his own judgment on the issues for that of the parties." § 154.023(b).

B

The Texas ADR Act has been described as the most complete in conferring the cloak of confidentiality on communications made during alternative dispute resolution procedures. See Michael D. Young & David S. Ross, Confidentiality of Mediation Procedures, C879 ALI–ABA 571, 578 (1993). "Texas is in the vanguard of affording protection to communications made during ADR procedures." Id. In the ADR Act, there are two sections that impose requirements of confidentiality. Section 154.053 prescribes the standards and duties of "impartial third parties," a term that includes mediators. This section contains two provisos that relate to confidentiality, § 154.053(b) and (c):

> (b) Unless expressly authorized by the disclosing party, the impartial third party may not disclose to either party information given in confidence by the other and shall at all times maintain confidentiality with respect to communications relating to the subject matter of the dispute.

> (c) Unless the parties agree otherwise, all matters, including the conduct and demeanor of the parties and their counsel during the settlement process, are confidential and may never be disclosed to anyone, including the appointing court.

In addition to § 154.053, the Act also contains § 154.073, entitled "Confidentiality of Communications in Dispute Resolution Procedures." This section addresses the confidentiality requirements applicable to alternative dispute resolution participants and impartial third parties, including mediators. Section 154.073 states:

(a) Except as provided by Subsections (c) and (d), a communication relating to the subject matter of any civil or criminal dispute made by a participant in an alternative dispute resolution procedure, whether before or after the institution of formal judicial proceedings, is confidential, is not subject to disclosure, and may not be used as evidence against the participant in any judicial or administrative proceeding.

(b) Any record made at an alternative dispute resolution procedure is confidential, and the participants or the third party facilitating the procedure may not be required to testify in any proceedings relating to or arising out of the matter in dispute or be subject to process requiring disclosure of confidential information or data relating to or arising out of the matter in dispute.

(c) An oral communication or written material used in or made a part of an alternative dispute resolution procedure is admissible or discoverable if it is admissible or discoverable independent of the procedure.

(d) If this section conflicts with other legal requirements for disclosure of communications or materials, the issue of confidentiality may be presented to the court having jurisdiction of the proceedings to determine, in camera, whether the facts, circumstances, and context of the communications or materials sought to be disclosed warrant a protective order of the court or whether the communications or materials are subject to disclosure.

IV

Against this backdrop, the court now turns to the four grounds on which defendants seek to reverse the magistrate judge's order.

A

In their first and second arguments, defendants maintain that the magistrate judge erred when he relied upon the principle of comity and considered the expectations of the Mediator and the parties at the time the mediation was conducted.

With respect to their first ground, defendants contend there is no comity that this court must recognize. Defendants do not contest the magistrate judge's determination that Texas law applies in this case. They at least implicitly agree with the magistrate judge's decision to give the Texas ADR Act controlling effect. Instead, defendants argue that this court is fully empowered under the ADR Act to decide the confidentiality question for itself because s 154.073(d) permits the court having jurisdiction of the proceedings "to penetrate the confidentiality of alternative dispute resolution procedures."

Defendants urge second that the magistrate judge erred because neither the expectations of the parties nor of the Mediator are in issue. They posit that Andrew has no expectations of confidentiality because he has already waived the attorney-client privilege and any right of attorney work product. They urge that the Mediator has no legitimate expectations to be accounted for because the parties rather than the Mediator have the right to assert confidentiality, and because the evidence defendants seek will not be used against the Mediator.

These arguments misperceive the magistrate judge's holdings and thus present no basis to overturn his order. The magistrate judge relied upon the principle of comity and upon the expectations of the parties and the Mediator in order to give effect to the Texas ADR Act and Rule 12 of the Dallas District Court Mediation Rules. The magistrate judge wrote:

"It is not necessary to decide whether the Texas rules are binding on this court. But in considering the issues presented this court is required to give due deference to those promulgations both on the basis of comity and in considering the expectations of the mediator and the parties at the time the mediation was conducted, including the confidentiality requirements under which the mediation was held and concluded."

Because the magistrate judge relied upon comity and the parties and Mediator's expectations as bases for invoking Texas law, and since defendants do not challenge the application of Texas law—arguing instead that the ADR Act does not entitle the Mediator to relief—the court discerns no basis to reverse the order on either of the initial two grounds presented.[7]

B

In their third argument, defendants urge that the magistrate judge erred when he expressed concern that "Allowing a party to call a mediator as a witness in a subsequent proceeding would do violence to the finality of a prior dispute settled via alternative dispute resolution, even where all parties consent to a waiver of confidentiality."

Defendants contend this holding improperly overlooks that plaintiff Andrew has initiated suit based upon the mediated settlement agreement and has thus placed in issue the oral and written communications made during mediation.[8] They reason that it is error to permit Andrew to prosecute a fraud claim based on the mediated settlement agreement itself, while simultaneously depriving them of the opportunity to introduce probative evidence from the mediation process that could refute the claim. Defendants urge on the basis of § 154.073(c) that the Mediator should be compelled to testify because the oral communications and written materials in question are admissible or discoverable independent of the mediation procedure.

---

7. The magistrate judge correctly recognized that principles of comity enable a federal court to accord deference to a state-created privilege. See, e.g., United States v. One Parcel of Prop., 930 F.2d 139, 141 (2d Cir.1991) (per curiam). Such state privileges are construed narrowly, however, and must yield to federal interests that outweigh them. Id.

8. Andrew contends his claims are not based on what was said during mediation. His concession apparently is intended to comply with § 154.073(a), which prohibits the use of such communications as evidence against a participant. He also acknowledges, on the facts presented in the instant case, that he cannot call the Mediator as a witness.

Defendants' reliance on § 154.073(c) is unavailing. This proviso states that

> An oral communication or written material used in or made a part of an alternative dispute resolution procedure is admissible or discoverable if it is admissible or discoverable independent of the procedure.

The court holds that § 154.073(c) should be interpreted to have the same effect as Tex.R.Civ.Evid. 408, which states, in pertinent part:

> This rule does not require the exclusion of any evidence otherwise discoverable merely because it is presented in the course of compromise negotiations.

In other words, § 154.073(c) provides that oral communications and written materials that are otherwise admissible or discoverable are not made inadmissible or non-discoverable solely because they have been uttered or disseminated in an alternative dispute resolution proceeding. To interpret § 154.073(c) as do defendants would unjustifiably create an exception to the confidentiality proviso of § 154.073(b) that is not expressly set out in the ADR Act and that should not be impliedly recognized in the face of the Act's pellucid confidentiality requirements.

Defendants have not demonstrated that the Mediator possesses discoverable or admissible evidence derived apart from the mediation conference. This ground presents no basis to reverse the magistrate judge's order.

C

[The Court also rejected defendants' argument that the law required the magistrate to conduct an in camera inspection before quashing the subpoena.]

D

A district judge will reverse a ruling of the magistrate judge in a nondispositive matter only for clearly erroneous fact findings, a ruling that is contrary to law, or a decision that constitutes an abuse of discretion. The four grounds that defendants advance in the present appeal do not provide any basis to disturb the magistrate judge's order, and it is affirmed.

V

In the present case, defendants have assumed the applicability of the Texas ADR Act and Dallas District Court Mediation Rules in challenging the magistrate judge's order. The court need not therefore decide whether there is a mediator privilege,[11] and it declines to adopt the magistrate

---

11. By "mediator privilege" the court refers to a privilege invocable by the mediator, with or without the consent of a client or other mediation participant. In the present case the magistrate judge recognized such a privilege in granting relief to a mediator who on his own sought to quash a subpoena. In this sense a mediator privilege is unlike one, such as the attorney-client privilege, that is controlled by the client and is therefore waivable. "Legislation is not always consistent in mediation, but typically mediator-client privileges cannot be waived by the client alone." Kevin Gibson, *Confidentiality in Mediation:*

judge's recognition of such a privilege in today's case. As the court will explain, federal law governs whether there is a mediator privilege in a case like the present one, the extent to which federal courts currently recognize such a privilege is narrow, and the Supreme Court and Fifth Circuit will not confer a new privilege without carefully balancing the relevant competing interests. While confidentiality appears to be widely accepted in state law as a desirable component of the mediation process, there are legitimate countervailing interests to be accounted for in formulating a privilege that is invocable by a mediator, not the least of which is the venerable "right to every man's evidence." The privilege question should be decided only in a case that requires that the issue be resolved, and then only after carefully examining and weighing the relevant factors. . . .

B

Federal court decisions that have adopted a mediator privilege have done so principally in the context of labor mediation. The courts have relied upon explicit national policy reasons to preclude mediators from testifying. Amicus curiae AAM has cited, and the court has found, only one published federal court opinion that has recognized the privilege on the basis of state law. The court has neither located, nor been pointed to, other published opinions that support a wider application of a federal mediator privilege.

The Ninth Circuit examined whether the purpose of preserving mediator effectiveness could prevail over "the fundamental principle of Anglo–American law that the public is entitled to every person's evidence." See id. at 53–54. The panel held, given the mediator's critical role as the tiebreaker witness, that revocation of the subpoena could be permitted only if denial of the mediator's testimony "has a public good transcending the normally predominant principle of utilizing all rational means for ascertaining truth." Id. at 54 (quoting Elkins v. United States, 364 U.S. 206, 234, 80 S.Ct. 1437, 1454, 4 L.Ed.2d 1669 (1960) (Frankfurter, J., dissenting)). "The public interest protected by revocation must be substantial." Id. The court held that the public interest in maintaining the perceived and actual impartiality of federal mediators outweighed the benefits derivable from the mediator's testimony. Id. In so doing, it relied upon the policy of the United States, as articulated by the Congress when it created the FMCS. Id. The court noted the critical role that the FMCS played in resolving labor disputes, and held that any activity that would significantly decrease the effectiveness of the service could threaten the industrial stability of the nation. Id. at 55. The court declined to permit the mediator to testify to "objective facts" only, because such a limitation would not dispel the perception of partiality created by mediator testimony. Id. at 56. The court concluded that complete exclusion of mediator testimony was necessary to the preservation of an effective system of labor mediation. Id.

A Moral Reassessment, 1992 J. Disp. Resol.
25, 3 (1992) (footnote omitted).

C

[T]he Supreme Court will not "create and apply an evidentiary privilege unless it 'promotes sufficiently important interests to outweigh the need for probative evidence.' " University of Pennsylvania v. E.E.O.C., 493 U.S. 182, 189, 110 S.Ct. 577, 582, 107 L.Ed.2d 571 (1990) (quoting Trammel, 445 U.S. at 51, 100 S.Ct. at 912). Moreover, because the "testimonial exclusionary rules and privileges contravene the fundamental principle that the public has a right to every man's evidence, any such privilege must be strictly construed." Id. (quoting United States v. Bryan, 339 U.S. 323, 331, 70 S.Ct. 724, 730, 70 S.Ct. 724 (1950)) . . .

The Fifth Circuit views the role of courts in expanding privileges as a limited one. "Privileges are based upon the idea that certain societal values are more important than the search for truth. There is no question that the doctrine of privilege or immunity from testifying has been narrowly proscribed." In re Dinnan, 661 F.2d 426, 429 (5th Cir. Unit B Nov.1981), cert. denied, 457 U.S. 1106, 102 S.Ct. 2904, 73 L.Ed.2d 1314 (1982). "[J]udge-made privileges have fallen into disfavor." Id. (footnote omitted). "[T]here has been a notable hostility on the part of the judiciary to recognizing new privileges." Id. at 430 (footnote omitted). Privileges are strongly disfavored in federal practice. American Civil Liberties Union v. Finch, 638 F.2d 1336, 1344 (5th Cir. Unit A Mar.1981). "While a number of new privileges have been established recently, they generally have been statutorily created." Dinnan, 661 F.2d at 429 (footnote omitted).

To say that the Supreme Court and the Fifth Circuit will not blithely recognize a new privilege is not, of course, to reject adoption of a qualified mediator privilege in the proper case. The determination whether to recognize a *mediator* privilege should not be resolved, however, at the level of generality represented by examination of *mediation* confidentiality. To accept as a given that the process of private party mediation should take place in confidence is not of itself sufficient to excuse a mediator from an obligation of disclosure upon the request of a disputant. When the question to be resolved is whether the mediator should have protected status, the balancing of competing interests will only properly take place in the context of the mediator, not of mediation in its broadest sense.

In this narrower and more relevant setting, the court notes that "[m]ost states have passed laws protecting communications made . . . by the mediator if those communications relate to the mediation." Young & Ross, supra § III(B), at 577. "Many states grant a privilege to communications by the mediator." Id. at 575. Several states have explicitly insulated mediators from compulsory process and testimony regarding confidential oral and written communications made during the mediation process. See, e.g., Arkansas, 1993 Ark. Acts 641, § 6(b); Colorado, Colo.Rev.Stat.Ann. § 13–22–307 (West 1989 & Supp.1991); Illinois, 710 ILCS 20/6 (1992); Iowa, Iowa Code s 679.12 (1991); Massachusetts, Mass.Ann.Laws ch. 233, § 23C (Law Co-op.1985) . . .

Protections of this type are justified on various grounds. One basis is the perceived need to preserve the appearance of the mediator's impartiality and neutrality. See Macaluso, 618 F.2d at 54 (public interest in maintaining perceived and actual impartiality outweighed benefits derivable from mediator's testimony); ... Young & Ross, supra § III(B), at 577 (citing the "[n]eed to protect the mediator's reputation for neutrality"). Another is an apprehension that qualified individuals will not serve as mediators out of concern for being required to testify. See Maine Cent. R.R., 117 F.R.D. at 486–87 ("Moreover, the Court thinks it likely that it will be increasingly difficult to find able people to serve as mediators if they know that they might later have to testify concerning the manner in which their arbitrations are conducted.") ...

Yet at a time when state-law support for confidentiality in mediation is apparently increasing, the protections accorded are still characterized as uneven and lacking uniformity. See Young & Ross, supra § III(B), at 575. This is attributed to an absence of consensus concerning the scope of the right of confidentiality. "The unsettled state of the law reflects disagreement among judges and legislators on the weight of competing interests[.]" Id. Proponents of a mediator privilege must reckon with the important right of litigants to obtain all available evidence, a right that arguably is paramount to some of the interests relied upon to justify immunizing mediators from compulsory disclosure. And certain of the reasons on which advocates of a mediator privilege stand are subject to question. There are those who challenge the validity of concerns regarding an appearance of mediator impartiality. See Kevin Gibson, Confidentiality in Mediation: A Moral Reassessment, 1992 J.Disp.Resol. 25, 46, 48 (1992), available in Westlaw, JLR Database, 1992 JDR 25, at 12–13 (contending "[t]here are two dubious lines of reasoning behind the assumption that mediator testimony will inevitably compromise the perception of impartiality," and arguing that the "key premise" that confidentiality is necessary to protect the reputation of impartiality "is not as strong as it initially appears, and it alone cannot adequately justify confidentiality in all cases"). Furthermore, one can arguably question the validity of predictions of a shortage of mediators—including able ones—if a mediator privilege is not adopted. See Louis J. Weber, Jr., Court–Referred ADR and the Lawyer–Mediator: In Service of Whom?, 46 SMU L.Rev. 2113, 2114–15 (1993) (noting that following passage of Texas ADR Act in 1987, coupled with a recession and general economic downturn in Texas that soured lawyer income, ADR "suddenly" became popular; pointing out that in Dallas County, Texas, where the vast majority of court-referred mediations are made to attorneys who are on appointment lists kept by the courts or ADR coordinator, inclusion on the lists "is aggressively pursued by almost all lawyers interested in receiving court appointments;" and stating, "One has only to observe the abundant lawyer-mediator marketing as evidence of the strong revenue interest court-referred ADR has to lawyers competing in a slumping or declining lawyer economy.").

E

When a litigant seeks to assert a privilege not recognized in the common law, the court must test it by balancing the policies behind the privilege against those favoring disclosure. American Civil Liberties Union, 638 F.2d at 1343. Yet it is precisely because this process must be performed carefully, taking into account all relevant interests, that the privilege should neither be adopted nor rejected in a case such as the present one that does not squarely present the issue. The court therefore leaves the decision to the proper case. . . .

The magistrate judge's order quashing the subpoena duces tecum is AFFIRMED.

* * *

Questions

1. Are the same factors that are relevant to deciding whether to create a mediation privilege when a party seeks to avoid disclosure of the content of mediation relevant when it is a mediator seeking to avoid testifying? Which situation presents the stronger case for recognizing a privilege? Compare *Smith v. Smith* to *Folb v. Motion Picture Industry*, supra.

2. While the court in *Smith* purports to reject a general mediator privilege, it says it is not "reject[ing] adoption of a qualified privilege in the proper case." How would it know which is a "proper case?" Must a court hear a proffer of the mediator's testimony in order to determine whether it is entitled to a qualified privilege?

3. Is the argument for a mediator privilege stronger when the testimony is sought in a criminal case or in a civil case? Should trials of minor criminal infractions have the same privilege rule as trials of felonies?

4. Should criminal cases, especially felony cases, be resolved in mediation? Is the State's interests in vindication or punishment an interest amenable to compromise in a mediation context? Or, is plea bargaining a criminal law equivalent to civil law mediation?

* * *

5. MEDIATOR LIABILITY FOR NEGLIGENCE

Elizabeth P. Lange v. Richard M. Marshall

622 S.W.2d 237 (Mo. Ct. of Appls. 1981).

■ SMITH, JUDGE

Defendant appeals from a judgment based upon a jury verdict against him in the amount of $74,000. Plaintiff's action was based upon the alleged negligence of defendant as a lawyer in his representation of her in the dissolution of her marriage.

Defendant was a close personal friend of plaintiff and her former husband, Ralph Lange. When the couple reached a decision to terminate their twenty-five year old marriage, each separately approached defendant. He advised each that he would not represent one against the other, but that if they could agree on the terms of their dissolution, he would represent them jointly and prepare the necessary papers to effectuate the dissolution. Plaintiff, ill with lupus eryethemathosis, had herself admitted to the psychiatric ward of a hospital because of depression arising from her marital problems. During this admission she and her husband discussed the terms of the dissolution. A conference was held at the hospital with plaintiff, her husband, and defendant present. At that time the terms of a settlement stipulation were agreed to and subsequently put into final form by defendant. The stipulation and joint petition for dissolution were signed the day plaintiff left the hospital, three days after the hospital conference. The documents were filed the next day and the petition for dissolution was heard by a circuit judge four days later. The judge took the matter under submission and stated that he would not enter a judgment for thirty days. Within that period plaintiff had second thoughts about the settlement provisions of the stipulation and sought legal counsel.[1] The husband also sought legal counsel and defendant withdrew from the case and from any further discussions with the parties concerning it. Upon motion the matter was taken off submission, and 10 months later, following considerable discovery, was disposed of by a settlement more favorable to plaintiff. The degree to which the settlement was more favorable is strongly disputed by the parties, plaintiff contending it was substantially more favorable, defendant that it was slightly better. The record does not support a conclusion either way.

Plaintiff's charges of negligence were that defendant failed to (1) inquire as to the financial state of Ralph Lange and advise plaintiff; (2) negotiate for a better settlement for plaintiff; (3) advise plaintiff she would get a better settlement if she litigated the matter; and (4) fully and fairly disclose to plaintiff her rights as to marital property, custody and maintenance. Defendant admitted that he did none of these things and contended that he had no duty to do them. He asserted that because he undertook to represent the parties as a mediator, a status disclosed fully to both parties, that he felt it would be improper for him to do any of the four things claimed to be negligence as it would place him in the position of an advocate for one party or the other.[2] We need not resolve the exact nature of defendant's status nor the duties which that status imposed upon him. For purposes of this opinion we will assume that defendant's status

---

1. Plaintiff testified that from the time of her hospitalization until after the hearing, she was so emotionally distraught and so medicated that she didn't understand what was happening. There was substantial testimony to the contrary.

2. The parties disagree as to the nature of the obligation defendant undertook. It is

clear that he advised both parties that he would not represent either as an advocate. Although the terms "arbitrator" and "negotiator" were also used in the parties' conversations, "mediator" would appear to be the proper term to apply to defendant's role.

imposed upon him one or more of the claimed duties and that he breached that or those duties.

Accepting therefore the proposition of defendant's negligence we are unable to find that plaintiff sustained any damage as a proximate result of that negligence. Negligence alone does not warrant a recovery for plaintiff. There must also be damage proximately resulting therefrom. Mitchell v. Transamerica Ins. Co., 551 S.W.2d 586 (Ky.App.1977) (2). While the question of proximate cause is usually for the jury, in rare cases and under clear and compelling circumstances, the question becomes one of law for the court. Carter v. Boys' Club of Greater Kansas City, 552 S.W.2d 327 (Mo.App.1977) (4–6). Where the evidence connecting the injury to the negligence amounts to mere conjecture and speculation the court must not allow the case to be submitted to the jury and a contention that the evidence did not make a submissible case should be sustained. Pizzurro v. First North County Bank and Trust Co., 545 S.W.2d 348 (Mo.App.1976) (3–5). It is plaintiff's burden to establish that the negligence of defendant proximately resulted in damages to her. (citations omitted).

Plaintiff's claimed damages were for 10 months lost maintenance payments (which Ralph Lange discontinued after plaintiff obtained counsel and repudiated the original settlement), fees for accountants and private investigators (necessary to prepare for litigating a better settlement after she repudiated the original agreement), apartment rent, federal and state taxes, medical charges (which Ralph Lange agreed to pay in the original agreement and refused to pay after it was repudiated), and legal fees of $45,000 based upon a contingent fee contract with her attorneys handling the dissolution proceeding.[3]

There is no evidence in the record that had defendant done the things plaintiff contends he did not do that these items of expense would not have been incurred in order for plaintiff to achieve the settlement she considered proper. There is no evidence in the record that Ralph Lange would have voluntarily agreed to a settlement acceptable to plaintiff had defendant done the things he admittedly did not do. If anything the evidence is to the contrary. Ralph Lange testified that he intended to be fair with plaintiff but that her idea of fairness, and her attorney's idea of fairness, did not comport with his. The evidence established that plaintiff had substantial income producing assets in her own name which had come to her through large gifts from Ralph Lange's father. The evidence also established that most of the assets in Ralph Lange's name were also gifts from his father and at least arguably did not constitute marital property. There was no evidence of Ralph Lange's income or the extent to which it represented income from gifts.

It is the rankest conjecture and speculation to conclude that Ralph Lange's willingness to settle the marital affairs without litigation on the basis of the original settlement established his willingness to settle without

---

3. This contingent fee contract in a dissolution case was void as against public policy. Shanks v. Kilgore, 589 S.W.2d 318 (Mo. App.1979).

litigation at a higher figure acceptable to plaintiff. Plaintiff states in her brief that it is "obvious" that upon proper representation by defendant she would have received a far more beneficial settlement in a non-contested dissolution. She points to no evidence to support this conclusion and its "obviousness" eludes us. The parties agreed that defendant was not representing plaintiff as an advocate but in a mediation position. The ten months of heated litigation (following plaintiff's repudiation of the settlement) after both parties had obtained counsel and were fully aware of their respective rights belies the "obviousness" of plaintiff's conclusion.

Plaintiff failed to establish any damages proximately caused by defendant's claimed negligence.

Judgment reversed.

* * *

Questions

1. Was the defendant negligent in the *Lange* case? Would your position be different if the defendant had been a professional mediator rather than a family friend? What if the defendant were a professional mediator who was also a family friend?

2. Is the fact that the defendant was a lawyer relevant to the question of whether he was negligent? Do lawyers have special obligations when helping parties settle a dispute that has legal ramifications?

3. Does a mediator have an obligation to shore up the power of the weaker party in a dispute? Does the mediator have an obligation to advise parties of their legal rights? Does a mediator have an obligation to compel disclosure of relevant information? Would it be different if the mediator were a lawyer? Look at the A.B.A.'s Standards of Practice for Lawyer Mediators in Family Disputes at Appendix E, infra. What would be the result of the *Lange* case under the A.B.A. Code?

4. Look at the Society for Professionals in Dispute Resolution (SPIDR) Model Standards of Conduct for Mediators, at Appendix D, infra. Would the result be the same under this code as under the A.B.A. Code?

5. Which Code of Conduct—the ABA Code or the SPIDR Code—better embodies the ideal of mediator neutrality?

6. Over a hundred years ago, Edmund Burke wrote:

    The world is governed by go-betweens. These go-betweens influence the persons with whom they carry on the intercourse, by stating their own sense to each of them as the sense of the other; and thus they reciprocally master both sides.[1]

This suggests that neutrality by a go-between, such as a mediator, is unattainable. Do you agree? How can a mediator exercise her authority and influence without abandoning a position of neutrality?

---

1. THE WORKS OF EDMUND BURKE, 189–190 (1904).

7. What is a professional mediator? Is it someone who holds him/herself out as a full-time mediator? Should there be a licensing requirement?

* * *

Vickie Howard v. Robin Drapkin

222 Cal.App.3d 843, 271 Cal.Rptr. 893 (Ct. of Appl., 2d Dist. 1990).

■ CROSKEY, ASSOCIATE JUSTICE.

Plaintiff Vickie Howard ("plaintiff") appeals from a dismissal entered after a demurrer to her second amended complaint was sustained without leave to amend. The instant case evolved from a family law matter in which child custody and visitation were in dispute (the "underlying action"). Defendant Robin Drapkin ("defendant"), a psychologist, performed an evaluation of plaintiff and her family and plaintiff now claims that defendant acted improperly in carrying out that task.

In this appeal we are asked to determine whether the alleged wrongful actions of which plaintiff complains were performed in such a context that defendant can claim (1) common law immunity as a quasi-judicial officer participating in the judicial process or (2) statutory privilege under Civil Code section 47, subdivision (2) ("section 47(2)")[1] for a publication in a judicial proceeding. We conclude that defendant, acting in the capacity of a neutral third person engaged in efforts to effect a resolution of a family law dispute, is entitled to the protection of quasi-judicial immunity for the conduct of such dispute resolution services. We also find that the litigation privilege provided for in section 47(2) applies to the facts of this case. We therefore affirm the dismissal of plaintiff's complaint.

FACTUAL AND PROCEDURAL BACKGROUND

This case arises in the context of a family law dispute over custody and visitation rights with respect to the minor son of the plaintiff and her former husband, Robert. The dispute was one of a series and involved charges of physical and sexual abuse. Plaintiff initiated family law proceedings in which she sought to have Robert's custody and visitation rights terminated. Prior to any court hearing, plaintiff and Robert entered into a stipulation which provided that the defendant, as an independent psychologist, would evaluate the facts and circumstances and render non-binding findings and recommendations. This stipulation was ultimately signed by the court and converted into an order.

Plaintiff's claims against defendant apparently arise from (1) a single six-hour session between plaintiff and defendant, conducted pursuant to the aforesaid stipulation, in which plaintiff alleges that defendant was abusive, (2) defendant's report which plaintiff claims was negligently pre-

---

1. Civil Code section 47, subdivision 2 provides in relevant part that with certain exceptions for dissolution of marriage pro-ceedings, "A privileged publication or broadcast is one made— ... [¶] 2. In any ... (2) judicial proceeding...."

pared, included false statements and omitted crucial information and (3) defendant's alleged failure to disclose certain conflicts of interest and lack of expertise in child abuse matters. The pleading before us is plaintiff's second amended complaint in which she had pled causes of action for professional negligence, intentional infliction of emotional distress, negligent infliction of emotional distress and fraud. . . .

ISSUE PRESENTED

This appeal raises the issue of the availability of (1) quasi-judicial immunity by reason of defendant's involvement as a neutral dispute-resolving participant in the judicial process and (2) the absolute privilege under the provisions of section 47(2), as a complete bar to plaintiff's actions.

DISCUSSION

Defendant asserts both of these grounds and we have concluded that both arguments are meritorious.[2] For the historical and policy reasons discussed below, we believe that absolute quasi-judicial immunity is properly extended to neutral third persons who are engaged in mediation, conciliation, evaluation or similar dispute resolution efforts. As to defendant's second argument, the issue of section 47(2) privilege has, since the filing of the briefs herein, been resolved in defendant's favor by the Supreme Court's decision in Silberg v. Anderson (1990) 50 Cal.3d 205, 266 Cal.Rptr. 638, 786 P.2d 365.

1. *Common Law Immunity*

a. *Overview of Judicial Immunity*

The concept of judicial immunity is longstanding and absolute, with its roots in English common law. It bars civil actions against judges for acts performed in the exercise of their judicial functions[3] and it applies to all judicial determinations, including those rendered in excess of the judge's

---

2. We review this case in the context of both quasi-judicial immunity and statutory privilege out of a recognition that they are not coextensive. While on the facts here presented we will find that they both apply, the statutory privilege extends to bar liability for "communicative acts" but not conduct or "noncommunicative acts." (Kimmel v. Goland (1990) 51 Cal.3d 202, 211, 271 Cal.Rptr. 191, 793 P.2d 524); (Pacific Gas & Electric Co. v. Bear Stearns & Company (1990) 50 Cal.3d 1118, 1132, fn. 12, 270 Cal.Rptr. 1, 791 P.2d 587.) No such limitation exists for common law quasi-judicial immunity. Here, however, any conduct in which defendant engaged was secondary to and intertwined with the alleged offensive and dishonest communicative acts. Nonetheless, due to the importance of this issue and the likelihood that future cases involving neutral third persons

engaged in mediation, conciliation, evaluation or other similar dispute resolution efforts may not be so clear, we believe it necessary to base our decision on both grounds.

3. "Immunity exists for 'judicial' actions; those relating to a function normally performed by a judge and where the parties understood they were dealing with the judge in his official capacity. [Citations.]" (Olney v. Sacramento County Bar Assn. (1989) 212 Cal. App.3d 807, 811, 260 Cal.Rptr. 842.) Thus, the line is drawn "between truly judicial acts, for which immunity is appropriate, and acts that simply happen to have been done by judges. Here, as in other contexts, immunity is justified and defined by the functions it protects and serves, not by the person to whom it attaches." (Forrester v. White (1988) 484 U.S. 219, 227). Acts and decisions which

jurisdiction, no matter how erroneous or even malicious or corrupt they may be. (Turpen v. Booth (1880) 56 Cal. 65, 68; Greene v. Zank (1984) 158 Cal.App.3d 497, 507, 204 Cal.Rptr. 770.) The judge is immune unless "he has acted in the clear absence of all jurisdiction. [Citations.]" (Greene, supra, at p. 507, 204 Cal.Rptr. 770.) Beyond doubt, the doctrine of "civil immunity of the judiciary in the performance of judicial functions is deeply rooted in California law." [citations omitted].

The rationale behind the doctrine is twofold. First, it "protect[s] the finality of judgments [and] discourag[es] inappropriate collateral attacks." (Forrester v. White, supra, 484 U.S. 219, 225, 108 S.Ct. 538, 543.) Second, it "protect[s] judicial independence by insulating judges from vexatious actions prosecuted by disgruntled litigants. [Citation.]" (Ibid.) With respect to the latter reason, the immunity is necessary in order to have an independent and impartial judiciary. The public is best served when its judicial officers are free from fear of personal consequences for acts performed in their judicial capacity. (Greene v. Zank, supra, 158 Cal.App.3d at p. 508, 204 Cal.Rptr. 770.) "If judges were personally liable for erroneous decisions, the resulting avalanche of suits, most of them frivolous but vexatious, would provide powerful incentives for judges to avoid rendering decisions likely to provoke such suits. [Citation.] The resulting timidity would be hard to detect or control, and it would manifestly detract from independent and impartial adjudication." (Forrester v. White, supra, 484 U.S. 219, 226–227, 108 S.Ct. 538, 544.) "It is a judge's duty to decide all cases within his jurisdiction that are brought before him, including controversial cases that arouse the most intense feelings in the litigants. His errors may be corrected on appeal, but he should not have to fear that unsatisfied litigants may hound him with litigation charging malice or corruption. Imposing such a burden on judges would contribute not to principled and fearless decision-making but to intimidation." (Pierson v. Ray (1967) 386 U.S. 547, 554, 87 S.Ct. 1213, 1218, 18 L.Ed.2d 288, 294–295.) " 'The justification for [judicial immunity] is that it is impossible to know whether [a person's claim against an official] is well founded until the case has been tried, and that to submit all officials, the innocent as well as the guilty, to the burden of a trial and to the inevitable danger of its outcome, would dampen the ardor of all but the most resolute, or the most irresponsible, in the unflinching discharge of their duties.' " (Hardy v. Vial, supra, 48 Cal.2d at pp. 582–583, 311 P.2d 494, quoting from Gregoire v. Biddle (2d Cir.1949) 177 F.2d 579, 581.) Thus, the protection must be absolute, even to the malicious or corrupt judge. The effect of judicial

are not judicial or adjudicative, i.e., acts and decisions performed and made by a judge which are administrative or legislative, "even though they may be essential to the very functioning of the courts, have not ... been regarded as judicial acts." (Id. at p. 228, 108 S.Ct. at p. 544.) This does not mean that judges who make legislative or administrative types of decisions are not able to claim legislative immunity (Supreme Court of Va. v. Consumers Union (1980) 446 U.S. 719, 731 et seq.; Forrester v. White, supra, 484 U.S. 219, 228) or an immunity like that enjoyed by executive branch officials "when performing within the scope of their power acts which require the exercise of discretion or judgment. [Citations.]" (Hardy v. Vial (1957) 48 Cal.2d 577, 582, 311 P.2d 494; accord Forrester v. White, supra, 484 U.S. 219, 230).

immunity is that the action against the judicial officer must be dismissed. (Hardy, supra, 48 Cal.2d at p. 584, 311 P.2d 494.)

b.   *Quasi-Judicial Immunity*

Under the concept of "quasi-judicial immunity," California courts have extended absolute judicial immunity to persons other than judges if those persons act in a judicial or quasi-judicial capacity. Thus, court commissioners "acting either as a temporary judge or performing subordinate judicial duties ordered by the appointing court" have been granted quasi-judicial immunity. (Tagliavia v. County of Los Angeles, supra, 112 Cal.App.3d at p. 763, 169 Cal.Rptr. 467.) So also, quasi-judicial immunity from civil suits for acts performed in the exercise of their duties has been given to grand jurors (Turpen v. Booth, supra, 56 Cal. at p. 69); administrative law hearing officers (Taylor v. Mitzel (1978) 82 Cal.App.3d 665, 670–671, 147 Cal.Rptr. 323); arbitrators (Baar v. Tigerman (1983) 140 Cal.App.3d 979, 985, 211 Cal.Rptr. 426; Coopers & Lybrand v. Superior Court (1989) 212 Cal.App.3d 524, 534, 260 Cal.Rptr. 713);[4] organizations sponsoring an arbitrator (Olney v. Sacramento County Bar Assn., supra, 212 Cal.App.3d at pp. 814–815, 260 Cal.Rptr. 842); and prosecutors (Pearson v. Reed (1935) 6 Cal.App.2d 277, 286–288, 44 P.2d 592). Additionally, the State Bar and the Committee of Bar Examiners, as arms of the Supreme Court, and their officials, as officers of the Supreme Court, have been afforded quasi-judicial immunity from civil suits for acts performed in the exercise of their duties. (Greene v. Zank, supra, 158 Cal.App.3d at p. 513, 204 Cal.Rptr. 770.) As with the reason for granting judicial immunity, quasi-judicial immunity is given to promote uninhibited and independent decisionmaking. (Baar v. Tigerman, supra, 140 Cal.App.3d at p. 982, 211 Cal.Rptr. 426.)

As noted above, courts look at the nature of the challenged act which a judge has performed to determine if it is truly judicial and therefore deserving of judicial immunity. So also, in determining whether a person is acting in a quasi-judicial fashion, the courts look at "the nature of the duty performed [to determine] whether it is a judicial act—not the name or classification of the officer who performs it, and many who are properly classified as executive officers are invested with limited judicial powers." (Pearson v. Reed, supra, 6 Cal.App.2d at pp. 286–287, 44 P.2d 592.) In Pearson, the court found that a prosecutor, in examining evidence submitted to him and in determining whether to prosecute a case against a defendant, is performing an act that is judicial in nature, thus making him both a quasi-judicial officer and an executive branch officer. (Ibid.)

c.   *The Right to Quasi–Judicial Immunity Depends Upon a Connection to the Judicial Process*

Plaintiff seeks to establish that California's version of common law judicial and quasi-judicial immunity is applied only to *public officials* (judges, grand jurors, prosecutors, commissioners, etc.). If that were so,

---

4. The Legislature made judicial immunity for arbitrators a statutory requirement by adding section 1280.1 to the Code of Civil Procedure. (Stats.1985, ch. 709, § 1, p. 2341.) However, by its own terms, section 1280.1 remains in effect only until January 1, 1991 unless a subsequent statute is enacted to delete or extend that date. (Code Civ. Proc., § 1280.1.)

then arbitrators would not be protected by common law quasi-judicial immunity.[5] We believe that in California, it is not so much one's status as a public official which has generally been the litmus test for judicial immunity but rather the above-referenced analysis of "functions normally performed by judges." (See fn. 3, ante.) It just so happens, that with the exception of arbitrators, and sometimes referees (Park Plaza Ltd. v. Pietz (1987) 193 Cal.App.3d 1414, 1418–1419, 239 Cal.Rptr. 51), such functions have usually been performed by public officials.

The case upon which plaintiff relies for her "public official" analysis is White v. Towers (1951) 37 Cal.2d 727, 235 P.2d 209, an action for malicious prosecution against an investigator for the State Fish and Game Commission who had the duty of enforcing laws regarding the protection of fish and game. That case does speak of "the immunity from civil liability with which the law surrounds *officials directly connected with the judicial processes.*" (Id. at p. 730, 235 P.2d 209, emphasis added.) However, a reading of the court's opinion shows that the court was more interested in the "connected with the judicial process" portion of the above-quoted excerpt than with the fact that the defendant could be classified as an "official."

[I]t is the line of cases which directly concerns the application of the doctrine *to those connected with the judicial processes* which is determinative herein. Thus, it has been held almost universally that public prosecutors are entitled to immunity. [Citations.] Similarly, grand jurors were early held to be protected against civil actions for alleged malicious prosecution. [Citation.] A review of the cases which have concerned the application of the doctrine to law enforcement officers shows that the great majority of the courts have ruled in favor of the officers. (Emphasis added.) The court then went on to cite California and federal cases involving law enforcement officers such as a building inspector charged with investigating an alleged violation of a building ordinance, a deputy fire marshal charged with investigating fires, and an assistant city engineer.

Thus, the White court focused on the *importance to the judicial system* of persons charged with the duty to investigate crimes and institute criminal proceedings. The court was impressed by their connection to the judicial processes rather than the fact that they could be classified as public officials. In our judgment, that is the proper way to view the matter. We therefore reject plaintiff's efforts to place the emphasis on the status of defendant rather than upon the connection between the defendant's activity and the judicial process.

d. *Policy Considerations Support the Approach of the Federal Cases to Quasi-Judicial Immunity*

For their part, defendant and amicus ask this court to go beyond California's apparently heretofore limited application of the "persons con-

---

5. "Arbitration is the submission for determination of a disputed matter to private *unofficial* persons selected in the manner provided by law or by agreement of the parties." (Stockwell v. Equitable F. & M. Ins. Co. (1933) 134 Cal.App. 534, 540, 25 P.2d 873, emphasis added.)

nected with the judicial processes" analysis and apply common law quasi-judicial immunity like the federal courts have applied it—to people connected with the judicial process who are not "public officials," arbitrators or referees, such as (1) mediators, guardians ad litem, therapists, receivers, bankruptcy trustees and other persons appointed by the courts for their expertise and (2) persons whose work product comes into the judicial process to be used by the court even though they were not court-appointed, such as social workers and probation department employees. Defendant and amicus also argue that immunity should be extended even further to a third category of people—those persons involved in alternative methods of dispute resolution, such as mediators and "neutral fact-finders," who function apart from the courts, as did the defendant in the instant case.[6]

Such an extension of quasi-judicial immunity would find persuasive support in a number of federal cases. The federal courts have held that immunity applies to such court-appointed persons as a trust officer employed by the Oregon Department of Veterans Affairs which was acting (by court appointment) as the conservator of plaintiff's estranged husband (Mosher v. Saalfeld (9th Cir.1978) 589 F.2d 438, 442, cert. den. 442 U.S. 941, 99 S.Ct. 2883, 61 L.Ed.2d 311); a receiver appointed by a court to manage property of a marital estate during a dissolution of the marriage (New Alaska Development Corp. v. Guetschow (9th Cir.1989) 869 F.2d 1298, 1302–1303); a child protective services worker acting pursuant to a court order to take a child into custody (Coverdell v. Dept. of Social & Health Services (9th Cir.1987) 834 F.2d 758, 764–765); and guardians ad litem, psychologists and attorneys for children in child abuse actions (Myers v. Morris (8th Cir.1987) 810 F.2d 1437, 1465–1468, cert. den. 484 U.S. 828, 108 S.Ct. 97, 98 L.Ed.2d 58).

With respect to nonappointed persons whose work product comes into the judicial process, the courts have held that immunity was properly given to probation officers who prepare presentencing reports for the use by the courts (Demoran v. Witt (9th Cir.1985) 781 F.2d 155) and workers at the Michigan Department of Social Services and psychiatrists who were involved in terminating plaintiffs' parental rights (Kurzawa v. Mueller (6th Cir.1984) 732 F.2d 1456). The Kurzawa court stated that in order to protect the well-being of children, the defendants must be able to perform their jobs "without the worry of intimidation and harassment from dissatisfied parents." (Id. at p. 1458; see also, In re Alicia T. (1990) 221 Cal.App.3d __, 271 Cal.Rptr. 513, and Jenkins v. County of Orange (1989) 212 Cal.App.3d 278, 260 Cal.Rptr. 645 [following federal cases which recognize an absolute immunity for § 1983 claims against social workers who were acting within the scope of their employment in investigating allegations of child abuse and initiating dependency proceedings].)

---

6. We recognize that ultimately defendant's status in the underlying action was governed by a court order. However, in our view, that is not the crucial fact. For several months prior to when the court signed the "order" portion of the "Stipulation and Or-der for Child Custody Evaluation," the defendant worked pursuant to the private agreement of plaintiff and Robert, albeit in the shadow of pending litigation, in order to effect a resolution of their dispute.

These courts emphasized that the defendants served functions integral to the judicial process . . . For example, in Myers v. Morris, supra, 810 F.2d at p. 1467, the court said: "[T]he . . . therapists, guardians and attorney were appointed to fulfill quasi-judicial responsibilities under court direction. The family court was required to determine whether the children in its custody were neglected and to secure appropriate placements. To perform these functions, the court exercised its statutory authority to seek the assistance of experts. [Citation.] The absolute immunity which is accorded persons acting *as an integral part of the judicial process* protects them from having to litigate the manner in which they performed their delegated functions." (Emphasis added.) . . .

We are persuaded that the approach of the federal courts is consistent with the relevant policy considerations of attracting to an overburdened judicial system the independent and impartial services and expertise upon which that system necessarily depends. Thus, we believe it appropriate that these "nonjudicial persons who fulfill quasi-judicial functions intimately related to the judicial process" (Myers v. Morris, supra, 810 F.2d at p. 1466–1467) should be given absolute quasi-judicial immunity for damage claims arising from their performance of duties in connection with the judicial process. Without such immunity, such persons will be reluctant to accept court appointments or provide work product for the courts' use. Additionally, the threat of civil liability may affect the manner in which they perform their jobs. (Moses v. Parwatikar (8th Cir.1987) 813 F.2d 891, 892, cert. den. 484 U.S. 832, 108 S.Ct. 108, 98 L.Ed.2d 67.)

e. *Extension of Immunity to Persons Engaged in Neutral Dispute Resolution Is Appropriate*

In arguing for extensions of immunity to the category of persons who function apart from the courts in an attempt to resolve disputes, defendant and amicus emphasize that in this day of excessively crowded courts and long delays in bringing civil cases to trial, more reliance is being placed by both parties and the courts on alternative methods of dispute resolution. Along traditional lines, the provisions of article VI, section 22 of the Constitution, which allow the Legislature to provide for the appointment by trial courts of officers such as commissioners, referees and masters (Taglia-via v. County of Los Angeles, supra, 112 Cal.App.3d at p. 763, 169 Cal.Rptr. 467), are becoming ever more important. We have court commissioners (Code Civ. Proc., § 259) and voluntary and mandatory referees (Code Civ. Proc., § 638 et seq.). In addition, contracts for binding arbitration (Code Civ. Proc., § 1280 et seq.) and provisions for non-binding arbitration (Code Civ. Proc., § 1141.10 et seq.) help relieve court congestion. So also does Civil Code section 4607's provision for mandatory mediation of child custody and visitation disputes.

More recently, other aspects of alternative dispute resolution efforts are being used with greater frequency. There are voluntary settlement conferences which are conducted by volunteers working with the court through, for example, local bar associations. In addition, if it is necessary, the parties can choose a mediator or neutral fact-finder with the expertise to facilitate a resolution of their particular dispute. As amicus notes, mediation is traditionally a non-binding dispute resolution alternative. While most mediation is voluntary, some is compulsory, like that provided for in Civil Code section 4607.[8]

Besides relieving court congestion and speeding up the conclusion of cases, these less-traditional alternative dispute resolution procedures are often less expensive and less stressful than seeing a case through its normal trial path. Like the more formal dispute resolution procedures, they are critical to the proper functioning of our increasingly congested trial courts.

We agree with defendant and amicus that the justification for giving judicial and quasi-judicial immunity to judges, commissioners, referees, court-appointed persons (such as psychologists, guardians ad litem and receivers), and nonappointed persons (such as those who prepare probation reports and handle child abuse cases) applies with equal force to these neutral persons who attempt to resolve disputes. Although they are not "law connected," as are judges, commissioners and court-appointed experts, neither are non-judicial arbitrators. (Stockwell v. Equitable F. & M. Ins. Co., supra, 134 Cal.App. at p. 540). Similarly, referees, although appointed by the courts, may or may not be employees or officers of the court and they may be paid by the parties. (Park Plaza, Ltd. v. Pietz, supra, 193 Cal.App.3d at p. 1419).[9]

Plaintiff notes that attorneys can be held liable to their clients for professional negligence because they have a specific duty to their clients. Using a "duty to the public" vs. "duty to a client" approach, plaintiff seeks to distinguish the federal "court appointment" cases from the instant case. She argues that "It is, among other things, the absence of a public responsibility, and the presence of a duty to private clients, which distinguishes the instant case from the various authorities defendant cited ... for the proposition that court-appointed mental health professionals are immune from civil liability.... In each of the cases relied upon by the defendant, the psychologist or psychiatrist was either acting as an agent of the court pursuant to a court appointment in order to provide an opinion to the court itself [citations] or was a government official who owed a direct

8. In the instant case, plaintiff states in her opening brief that defendant was hired by herself and the child's father to provide psychological services in an attempt to resolve the family's problems outside of court, (as well as to prepare a report and potentially act as an expert witness if called by either parent). Thus, in addition to the mandatory mediation which plaintiff and her husband would receive under Civil Code section 4607, they were receiving private mediation-type services from defendant.

9. In Coopers & Lybrand v. Superior Court, supra, 212 Cal.App.3d 524, 260 Cal.

Rptr. 713 this court discussed the 1985 legislation which had expanded immunity for arbitrators. We recognized that "The law ... has come a long way from disfavoring arbitration so as not to encroach on the jurisdiction of the courts to the present policy of actively encouraging alternative dispute resolution in order to relieve the burden on the judicial system." (Id. at p. 535, 260 Cal.Rptr. 713.) In the instant opinion, we recognize the necessity for immunity for other but similar alternative dispute resolution activities.

duty to the public at large [citations] or was appointed by the court and had the responsibility of reporting to a governmental agency [citation]."

However, in reviewing the issue of immunity, we think that the focus is more correctly placed on a non-advocate vs. advocate analysis. Thus, while the criminal defense attorney who is paid with public funds has a duty to the public not to waste those funds, it is his or her job as an *advocate* for the defendant which makes him or her responsible and liable to the defendant and susceptible to a later civil action.

In contrast, the psychologist who is mediating a child custody dispute, whether by court appointment or not, is not an advocate for either parent, even if paid by them. (Cf. Park Plaza, Ltd. v. Pietz, supra, 193 Cal.App.3d at p. 1419, 239 Cal.Rptr. 51, where the court said that referees who are paid for by the parties in a law suit are not employees or independent contractors of those parties or of their attorneys.) The job of third parties such as mediators, conciliators and evaluators involves impartiality and neutrality, as does that of a judge, commissioner or referee; hence, there should be entitlement to the same immunity given others who function as neutrals in an attempt to resolve disputes. In a sense, those persons are similar to a judge who is handling a voluntary or mandatory settlement conference, no matter whether they are (1) making binding decisions (such as referees acting pursuant to Code Civ. Proc., § 638, subd. (1), and arbitrators), (2) making recommendations to the court (such as referees acting under Code Civ. Proc., § 639 or mediators acting under Civ.Code, § 4607), or (3) privately attempting to settle disputes, such as the defendant here.

We therefore hold that absolute quasi-judicial immunity is properly extended to these neutral third-parties for their conduct in performing dispute resolution services which are connected to the judicial process and involve either (1) the making of binding decisions, (2) the making of findings or recommendations to the court or (3) the arbitration, mediation, conciliation, evaluation or other similar resolution of pending disputes. As the defendant was clearly engaged in this latter activity, she is entitled to the protection of such quasi-judicial immunity. . . .

◼ DANIELSON, ASSOCIATE JUSTICE, concurring and dissenting.

I concur in the result reached in the foregoing decision, but emphatically dissent and disassociate myself from the reasoning and the holding of the majority opinion which would create, by judicial legislation, a "quasi-judicial immunity" in persons whom it vaguely designates as "neutral third party participants in the judicial process."

In the first place, the majority simply designates those upon whom it would confer this newly-created quasi-judicial immunity as "neutral," and assumes that they are, in fact, neutral. Whether or not they are truly neutral presents a very substantial question of fact, one which would not have to be decided if this appeal were decided under existing law. The litigation privilege of Civil Code section 47, subdivision (2) (hereafter section 47(2)) provides a broad privilege which will protect participants in litigation from the consequences of their communications. Thus, the immunity which the majority would create serves no recognizable useful purpose.

The Majority's Holding is Judicial Legislation

The majority frankly and honestly acknowledges that defendant has asked this court to "go beyond" California's heretofore limited application of immunity and apply it to others (1) appointed by courts for their expertise, and (2) persons whose work product comes into the judicial process to be used by the court, even though they were not court appointed, such as social workers. The majority has granted that request. The majority holds "that absolute quasi-judicial immunity is properly extended to neutral third party participants in the judicial process." But who is doing the extending? The answer is: This court. However, the majority does not identify, nor can they, their constitutional authority for "going beyond" the constitution and the laws of the State of California, and "extending" immunity to such third parties. By that act of "extending" they have created a new immunity, a new exemption from accountability, which has not existed in the laws of this state. To borrow the words of our Supreme Court in Mutual Life Ins. Co. v. City of Los Angeles (1990) 50 Cal.3d 402, 416, 267 Cal.Rptr. 589, 787 P.2d 996, this is "nothing more than judicial legislation." * * *

Judicial Immunity Is Very limited In Scope

The majority opinion presents an extensive overview of judicial immunity. In studying that overview it must be noted and then remembered that judicial immunity, even for judges, is limited to those judicial acts which are adjudicatory in nature, i.e. decision making, dispositive, and the immunity does not otherwise extend to acts which simply happen to be done by judges. It is the *function* of adjudication of an issue, the decision making function, which requires and is the basis for judicial immunity. The decision of the United States Supreme Court in Forrester v. White (1988) 484 U.S. 219, 108 S.Ct. 538, 98 L.Ed.2d 555, is controlling on that point; and it provides no basis for extending such immunity to the non-adjudicatory actions of judges, nor of their adjuncts. A fortiori, judicial immunity should not extend to persons who are neither judges nor their adjuncts, but only third-party participants in litigation, i.e., witnesses.

It is important that this limitation be kept in mind, since the effect of the majority opinion is to extend judicial immunity, termed "quasi-judicial immunity," to persons who do not adjudicate but who are, at most, "neutral third-party participants in the judicial process."

The majority's scholarly review of judicial immunity contains no valid argument to justify extending such immunity to non-judicial persons who do not perform an adjudicatory function.

The Majority's Reasoning Does Not Support Its Holding

The majority discourse at length on their perceived need for creating their new quasi-judicial immunity. The examples they cite as demonstrating a need for such immunity do not support their conclusion. Where immunity is granted to the categories of persons which they mention, that immunity is based upon the function such person is performing at the particular time, not on his or her calling or profession. As pointed out, above, judicial immunity extends to the person exercising a judicial function which is adjudicatory, decision-making, in nature. Even the act of a judge, in the performance of his duties as a judge, which is not adjudicatory in nature, is not clothed with judicial immunity. (Forrester v. White, supra, 484 U.S. 219, 108 S.Ct. 538, 98 L.Ed.2d 555.) The many categories of professionals referred to by the majority are granted immunity for their acts as adjuncts to a judge in aid of the judge's performing an adjudicatory act; they are the extension, so to speak, of the judge in those circumstances.

The Creation Of Immunity Is A Legislative Function

[I]n 1985 the Legislature granted judicial immunity to arbitrators by enacting Code of Civil Procedure section 1280.1, which provides, in part: "An arbitrator has the immunity of a judicial officer from civil liability when acting in the capacity of arbitrator under any statute or contract." If there had been any need to extend judicial immunity to those encompassed in the new immunity created by the majority opinion the Legislature could have met that need by similar legislation at that time, or if such need now exists the Legislature is the correct branch of government, and has the power and the right to do so now.

[T]he majority's discussion in support of its holding that judicial immunity should be extended to some broad, undefined, class is actually a series of arguments which might be used to support proposed legislation to create such an immunity. The reasoning might make a good law review article, but it has no place in a judicial decision. Laws should be created by legislation, not by litigation. . . .

* * *

Questions

1. The court in *Howard v. Drapkin* makes an analogy between private mediators and others who perform "judicial functions" such as grand jurors, administrative hearing officers, and prosecutors. To what extent is the analogy convincing? In what way are mediators performing judicial functions? Are mediators more judicial in their function than arbitrators? Grand jurors? Administrative hearing officers?

2. What sanctions are available for a prosecutor or an administrative hearing officer who is negligent in performing his official duties? What sanctions are available for a mediator who is negligent? What remedies are available to persons whose interests are harmed by such negligence?

3. After *Howard*, is a lawyer who attempts to settle cases immune from liability for negligence?

4. What is negligence by a mediator? Is it negligent for a mediator to permit parties to sign an agreement whereby one party unknowingly waived significant rights? Would it be negligent for a mediator to propose a settlement that failed to take into account relevant case law that is decidedly favorable to one side? It it negligent for a mediator to propose a settlement that is far less than the amount that the complainant party is asking for and is also far less than the respondent is willing to pay?

5. Suppose a mediator assists an employer and a former employee in settling a claim of wrongful dismissal claim. In the settlement, the terminated employee gets a lump sum payment equal to three months wages, and in exchange releases the employer from all claims relating to her employment. If it subsequently turned out that the employee was terminated on the basis of her race and the mediator had failed to alert the employee to her potential employment discrimination claim, has the mediator been negligent?

* * *

6. Professional Responsibility Issues in Mediation

A. Unauthorized Practice of Law

Michael Werle d/b/a Werle Consultants Family Mediation Center v. Rhode Island Bar Association

755 F.2d 195 (1st Cir.1985).

■ Coffin, Circuit Judge

The questions involved in this case are whether appellees are state actors and whether they enjoy immunity from liability under 42 U.S.C. s 1983. Appellant, Dr. Michael Werle, claims that appellees, the Rhode Island Bar Association and the members of its former Committee on the Unauthorized Practice of Law, violated his First and Fourteenth Amendment rights by sending him a letter requesting that he discontinue his divorce mediation business on the grounds that it involved him in the unauthorized practice of law. After conducting a two-day, non-jury trial, the district court determined that appellees were not state actors acting under the color of state law and dismissed Dr. Werle's case for failure to state a claim. We affirm the dismissal on somewhat different grounds.

The facts of the case are as follows. At the end of January 1981, appellee Michael Margolis, Chairman of the Bar Association's Committee on the Unauthorized Practice of Law (the "Committee"), received a copy of a brochure from Dr. Werle's business, Werle Consultants Family Mediation Center (the "Center"). The brochure, which was sent to a number of lawyers throughout Rhode Island, described the Center as a place where cooperative resolution of marital problems could be undertaken. The Center would provide, among other things, "impartial mediation and arbitration service for divorcing couples", assisting them in reaching agreement "upon division of property, support and child custody". Dr. Werle, described in the brochure as a psychologist and associate professor of psychology experienced in family mediation, was the only mediation "consultant" named in the brochure, though it also referred generally to an "advisory attorney", who was to be "called upon to provide legal and tax advice" and to draft formal settlement agreements. A couple utilizing the Center would make a deposit which was sufficient to pay for ten hours of mediation time and three hours of the advisory attorney's time.[1]

Upon receiving the brochure, Mr. Margolis compared it to the prohibitions contained in Rhode Island's unauthorized practice of law statute, Chapter 11–27 of Rhode Island's General Laws. Concluding that the brochure described practices which were in violation of Chapter 11–27, Margolis contacted all but two of the eleven or so other members of the Committee, discussed the brochure's contents, and received their unanimous concurrence that the brochure and the practice described therein probably violated Rhode Island's laws and that Dr. Werle should be informed of that fact. Margolis contacted Dr. Werle by phone and also met with him to discuss the problem. During the meeting, Margolis gave Dr. Werle a copy of the statutes allegedly being violated and indicated what he thought some of the violations were. Margolis later testified that the violations he had in mind, most, if not all of which, he identified for Dr. Werle, included the tendering of legal advice, the legal representation of an individual in a civil dispute, the drafting of legal documents, the collection of what were in effect legal fees, the advertising of legal services, and the advertising of assistance in divorce proceedings.[2] Although the two men also discussed the possibility of Dr. Werle meeting with the whole Committee at its next meeting, Dr. Werle decided not to exercise that option when he learned that the meeting would not be held until after a cease and desist letter was to be sent to him.

Also, according to the trial testimony of Dr. Werle but contrary to that of Margolis, the latter either stated, or allowed Dr. Werle to believe, the

---

1. At trial, Dr. Werle confirmed that at the time of the brochure's distribution, he was the only "consultant" or mediator at the Center and that he was still in the process of lining up individuals who would be willing and qualified to serve as advisory attorneys.

2. While a number of provisions under chapter 11–27 are involved here, it is enough for our purposes to quote from only three. First, section 11–27–2 specifies as one type of unauthorized practice of law "[t]he giving or tendering to another person for a consideration, direct or indirect, of any advice or counsel pertaining to a law question...." R.I.Gen.Laws s 11–27–2(2). Second, section 11–27–10 states that no one other than a member of the bar "shall ... advertise in any

manner that he ... will furnish or agree to furnish legal services or advice or the services of an attorney at law...." R.I.Gen.Laws s 11–27–10. Finally, section 11–27–20 states that anyone who "distributes ... any circular, pamphlet, card, handbill, advertisement, ... or notice of any kind offering to procure or to aid in procuring any divorce ... shall be fined not exceeding one hundred dollars ($100)." R.I.Gen.Laws s 11–27–20. Whether Margolis discussed with Dr. Werle all of these provisions specifically is not important. It was enough that the laws were on the books for Dr. Werle or his counsel to read and that Margolis, according to his uncontradicted testimony, gave Dr. Werle copies of most, if not all, of the relevant provisions.

following: that the Committee would recommend prosecution of Dr. Werle if he did not cease and desist, that the Committee's recommendations on such matters were always adopted by the Bar Association's Executive Committee, that the Executive Committee always forwarded the recommendations to the Attorney General of Rhode Island, and that the Attorney General always responded by commencing prosecution against the unauthorized practitioner. Whatever may have been said to Dr. Werle at the time, testimony at the trial supported the first three claims but not the fourth; the Attorney General had not commenced a prosecution for the unauthorized practice of law in approximately ten years. Apparently unaware of this fact, Dr. Werle left the meeting believing his only choice was either to discontinue his business until he determined whether it was legal or to face criminal prosecution by the Attorney General. On February 4, 1981, Margolis sent a letter on behalf of the Committee, requesting Dr. Werle to cease and desist from the unauthorized practice of law.

On February 9, 1981, Dr. Werle responded to Margolis by letter. Dr. Werle wrote, "I have concluded that there is a possibility that I would be in technical violation of the law if I were to continue offering divorce mediation through my psychological practice under the terms of the brochure that outlines the procedure." He added that he did not think that he was involved in the practice of law but that he would comply with the Committee's request until he could ascertain whether he was. Because Werle indicated he would comply with the request, the Committee took no further action on the matter.[3]

Seven months passed before Dr. Werle, in September of 1981, tried to obtain an opinion from the Attorney General as to whether the Center's mediation practice constituted a violation of the law. The Attorney General, however, refused to issue an opinion. Dr. Werle commenced this section 1983 action four months later, in January of 1982, naming as defendants not only appellees but also the Attorney General and the State of Rhode Island.

To prove his claim against each defendant, Dr. Werle had to establish that the defendant was a state actor acting under the color of state law and that the defendant had deprived Dr. Werle of a right secured by the Constitution and laws of the United States. Adickes v. S.H. Kress & Co., 398 U.S. 144, 150–52, 90 S.Ct. 1598, 1604–06, 26 L.Ed.2d 142 (1970). The district court concluded after trial, however, that the case against the Bar Association defendants should be dismissed because they were not state actors. The case against the Attorney General and Rhode Island was also dismissed, but for reasons that need not concern us here since no appeal has been taken with respect to those two parties.

3. The decision to drop the matter, as well as all the previous steps taken by Margolis and the Committee from the time the brochure was received, comported with the Committee's standard operating procedures. Even the step of conferring with the members by phone, rather than waiting for the next regularly scheduled meeting, was a procedure that had been employed in the past.

On appeal, Dr. Werle concedes that the injunctive and declarative aspects of his claim have been mooted by amendments made in 1982 to R.I.Gen. Laws s 11–27–19 that resulted in the permanent dissolution of the Committee.[4] He pursues his remaining damages claim, arguing that, contrary to the district court's findings, appellees were state actors serving a public function and exercising authority delegated to them by Rhode Island's legislature and judiciary.

Because of the nature of Dr. Werle's allegations and the evidence adduced at trial, however, we need not address this claim. On the one hand, if the district court was correct in concluding that appellees were not state actors, then it was also correct in dismissing Dr. Werle's suit for failure to state a claim. On the other hand, if the district court was wrong, i.e., even if we assume that appellees were state actors for the very reasons set forth by Dr. Werle, the evidence compels us to conclude that they enjoyed either absolute or qualified immunity from damages liability under section 1983. As the Supreme Court noted in Harlow v. Fitzgerald, 457 U.S. 800, 810–19, 102 S.Ct. 2727, 2734–39, 73 L.Ed.2d 396 (1982), prosecutors, as well as judges and legislators, acting within the scope of their official duties enjoy absolute immunity, and other government officials are accorded the lesser protection of qualified immunity. In accord with this distinction between the types of officials and the immunity they enjoy, we consider first the possibility that appellees served as "public" prosecutors and second the possibility that they were acting as "public" investigators.

Throughout this litigation, Dr. Werle has suggested that a chilling effect upon the exercise of his constitutional rights was caused by the threat of a complaint brought either by the Bar Association through its members or by the Attorney General upon the Bar Association's recommendation. Dr. Werle speaks of the Committee as if it were a surrogate for the Attorney General, bringing unauthorized practice of law claims and enforcing the relevant provisions of the Rhode Island statutes. The problem with this argument is that it cuts both ways: as much as it points to the conclusion that appellees are state actors, it also points to the conclusion that they enjoy the same absolute immunity that prosecutors enjoy.

The Supreme Court has held that state prosecutors enjoy the same absolute immunity from section 1983 liability that they enjoy under the common law.[5] Imbler v. Pachtman, 424 U.S. 409, 427, 96 S.Ct. 984, 993, 47 L.Ed.2d

---

4. Those amendments created a new unauthorized practice of law committee appointed by, and directly accountable to, the Supreme Court of Rhode Island, not the Bar Association.

5. As the Supreme Court has implied, "absolute" is really too strong a word. Prosecutors can be held criminally liable for wilfully violating someone's constitutional rights and are amenable to professional discipline by their peers. Imbler v. Pachtman, 424 U.S. 409, 428–29, 96 S.Ct. 984, 994, 47 L.Ed.2d

128 (1976). In addition, as the limiting language of Imbler makes clear, a prosecutor enjoys immunity from civil suit only with respect to actions taken within the scope of his official duties. Id. at 420, 96 S.Ct. at 990.

If, in the alternative, we assume that the role appellees played was more like that of an investigator than that of a prosecutor, then it is a lesser, qualified immunity that they enjoyed. Even in the case of a prosecutor, it has been held that the quasi-judicial, or absolute,

128 (1976). In addition, precedent and policy argue that the same privilege should be extended to those authorized in particular types of cases to serve in effect as "public" prosecutors. See, e.g., Slavin v. Curry, 574 F.2d 1256, 1266 (5th Cir.) (members of bar association's grievance committee held to enjoy absolute immunity from damages liability under section 1983 because they were performing as agents of the state's judicial department), modified on other grounds, 583 F.2d 779 (5th Cir.1978); Schneider v. Colegio de Abogados de Puerto Rico, 546 F.Supp. 1251, 1264 (D.P.R.1982) (damages claim fails because of prosecutorial immunity enjoyed by bar association); Hoke v. Board of Medical Examiners of North Carolina, 445 F.Supp. 1313, 1315–16 (W.D.N.C.1978) (members of board absolutely immune from liability for damages where their decision to prefer charges against certain physicians was found analogous to state prosecutor's initiation of criminal proceedings). Thus, if we assume, as Dr. Werle argues, that appellees had clear authority to bring a civil claim or to take steps that led directly to a criminal prosecution by the Attorney General and that it was the threat of prosecution that chilled his constitutional rights, then we are compelled to conclude that appellees were absolutely immune from damages liability under section 1983 because the conduct that was feared would have involved appellees in doing nothing more than properly fulfilling their roles as "public" prosecutors.[6]

The evidence demonstrates rather clearly that no reasonable person would have known that appellees' conduct constituted such a violation. As the district court noted in its opinion, "[t]here is no evidence of a bad faith threat of prosecution in the instant case. One could in good faith, upon reading [Dr. Werle's] brochure in conjunction with Title 11, Chapter 27 of Rhode Island General Laws, suspect that [Dr. Werle's] proposed activities would constitute the unauthorized practice of law." This is the same conclusion that Dr. Werle came to in his letter to Margolis, admitting the possibility that the procedure outlined in the brochure was in "technical violation of the law".

immunity that is enjoyed as an advocate for the state in a judicial forum should not be extended to cover whatever tangential, investigative or administrative functions the prosecutor may also perform. See, e.g., McSurely v. McClellan, 697 F.2d 309, 318–19 (D.C.Cir. 1982). When performing these secondary functions, the prosecutor is entitled only to that lesser immunity which is accorded administrative and investigative officials. Id.

Even under this qualified immunity standard, though, we find that appellees are protected from liability. In Harlow v. Fitzgerald, 457 U.S. at 818, 102 S.Ct. at 2739, the Supreme Court held that "government officials performing discretionary functions generally are shielded from liability for civil damages insofar as their conduct does not violate clearly established statutory or constitutional rights of which a reasonable person would have known." Applying the Harlow standard to this case, we conclude that as long as a reasonable person would not have known that appellees' conduct violated Dr. Werle's rights, appellees would be entitled to qualified immunity.

6. We note that there is no evidence to suggest that appellees actually knew or thought their conduct violated Dr. Werle's constitutional or statutory rights. See Harlow v. Fitzgerald, 457 U.S. at 821, 102 S.Ct. at 2740 (Brennan, J., concurring) (noting that one "who actually knows that he [is] violating the law" would not be protected under the qualified immunity standard).

Indeed, a reasonable person would almost certainly have concluded that the brochure on its face showed Dr. Werle and the Center to be in violation of at least those provisions of Rhode Island law which prohibit a non-attorney from advertising the services of an attorney and which prohibit anyone from advertising assistance in the procurement of a divorce. See supra note 2, at 196. In addition, the testimony of Dr. Werle at trial would do little to dissuade a reasonable person from believing that there was a significant probability that Dr. Werle's services, as advertised in the brochure, would involve him in advising couples on legal questions concerning custody, maintenance, and property distribution. Although Dr. Werle told Margolis at their meeting that only the "advisory attorney" would give legal advice, the fact that the role of this attorney was so vaguely defined in Dr. Werle's own mind (apparently the attorney's client was to be either the couple or the mediation process itself, not either of the spouses individually) raises significant doubts that a proper separation of the legal and psychological aspects of the counselling services had yet been worked out.

Furthermore, Dr. Werle has pointed to no authority that even suggests, let alone establishes, that the Committee might be violating his constitutional rights by enforcing the express provisions of Rhode Island's statutes.[7] Indeed, to the extent that the Supreme Court of Rhode Island has considered the validity of certain of the unauthorized practice of law provisions, or, more accurately, their predecessor provisions, the court has held them to be constitutional enactments designed to aid the court in the exercise of its authority to regulate and supervise the practice of law. Rhode Island Bar Association v. Lesser, 68 R.I. 14, 16–17, 26 A.2d 6, 7 (1942) (citing Rhode Island Bar Association v. Automobile Service Association, 55 R.I. 122, 179 A. 139 (1935); Creditors' Service Corp. v. Cummings, 57 R.I. 291, 190 A. 2 (1937)).

For all of these reasons, we hold that Margolis' conduct and that of the other appellees fell within the scope of the immunity, whether absolute or qualified, that they must have enjoyed if they were the state actors that Dr. Werle claims they were.

Accordingly, the decision of the district court is affirmed.

* * *

New Jersey Ethics Opinion, Number 676 Alternative Dispute Resolution

New Jersey Supreme Court Advisory Committee on Professional Ethics 136 N.J.L.J. 1298, NJ Atty.Advert.Op. 18 (1994).

This opinion arises from the Committee on Attorney Advertising's consideration of a grievance concerning the advertisements of five attor-

---

7. As for the argument that Margolis misrepresented that the Attorney General always prosecutes a matter referred from the Committee, we merely observe that, given a reasonable basis for suspecting punishable violations of law, Margolis would not lose his immunity by virtue of any misrepresentations about the certainty of punishment.

neys who are engaging in alternative dispute resolution (hereinafter "ADR") as arbitrators or mediators. The grievance alleges that the these attorneys are in violation of Opinion 657, 1 N.J.L. 129 (February 17, 1992), 130 N.J.L.J. 656 (February 24, 1992), in that they are practicing law and engaging in ADR-related activities in the same location, jointly advertising or marketing the two, and making no attempt to avoid any other demonstration of a relationship between them.

After careful consideration of the grievance, the advertisements which appeared in an "Alternative Dispute Resolution Directory" in the New Jersey Law Journal on May 17, 1993, and Opinion 657, the Committee raised the issue of whether alternative dispute resolution is ancillary to or part and parcel of the practice of law. Needless to say, the answer to this question would affect not only the Committee's disposition of the grievance, but also the conduct of an ever-growing segment of the Bar in this State. Consequently, the Committee enlisted the assistance of not only the respondents, but also other attorneys and entities with an interest in this matter. Given the number and nature of the responses to its request for assistance, the Committee concluded that it would be better to treat the grievance as an inquiry and issue an advisory opinion. . . .

Alternative Dispute Resolution and Complementary Dispute Resolution have apparently swept the country. Given the congestion and resultant backlogs of the courts, and the expense of the more traditional adversarial process, state and federal courts have embraced ADR and CDR as providing faster and less expensive resolution of disputes. In New Jersey, our Supreme Court has amended the Rules Governing the Courts of the State of New Jersey to include R. 1:40—"Complementary Dispute Resolution Programs."[1] In adopting this rule, which became effective September 1, 1992, the Court implemented the Report of the Supreme Court Committee on Complimentary Dispute Resolution, 130 N.J.L.J. 578, 1 N.J.L. 170 (1992), expressing the following purpose and goals:

Complementary Dispute Resolution Programs are an integral part of the Superior Court and Municipal Courts. They are intended to enhance the quality and performance of the judicial process. Lawyers should become familiar with available CDR programs and inform their clients of them. R. 1:40–1.

Among other things, the rule requires screening of all custody and visitation matters for referral to mediation, R. 1:40–5; allows for mediation of small claims and, in the discretion of the Assignment Judge, landlord-tenant disputes, R. 1:40–6; and calls for mandatory mediation of certain municipal court matters, R. 1:40–7. Of particular relevance to this opinion is R. 1:40–9 which, subject to the approval of the Assignment Judge, permits referral of matters to non-court administered dispute resolution programs (ADR).

---

1. The statutory base for ADR in New Jersey may be found in the New Jersey Alternative Procedure for Dispute Resolution Act, N.J.S.A. 2A:23A–1 et seq., and the New Jersey Arbitration Act, N.J.S.A. 2A:24–1 et seq.

The emergence of ADR has presented attorneys with new and varied ways in which to serve their clients. No longer are attorneys limited to the traditional role of advocate in civil litigation. They may now represent their clients in ADR proceedings, assist their clients in establishing dispute resolution programs and negotiate contracts requiring ADR. Not surprisingly, they are in ever increasing numbers serving as arbitrators or mediators in ADR programs.

Many lawyers are natural arbitrators. Arbitration, which in many cases closely resembles litigation, usually takes place in an adversarial setting, with the parties represented by counsel and the arbitrator(s) rendering a final and binding adjudication. Attorneys, accustomed as they are to appearing before judges, presenting evidence and engaging in oral and written advocacy in an adjudicative forum, come to the arbitrator's task enthusiastically or, as one commentator described it, "like the proverbial duck taking to water." Unquestionably, their educational training and experience make them well-suited if not uniquely qualified to serve as arbitrators.

Similarly, with training and experience beyond that necessary for and obtained through traditional lawyering, many attorneys are able to provide excellent mediation services. Unlike arbitration, which in many cases is contractually agreed upon before a dispute arises, mediation usually arises after the fact and is a voluntary process. In mediation, the parties in dispute, with or without their attorneys, and without prejudice to their rights to proceed with arbitration or litigation if the matter does not settle, meet with a neutral third party in a good-faith effort to achieve a far more economical, prompt and mutually advantageous resolution of all or part of their dispute. Given their experience weighing the merits of a case and exploring the prospects for settlement, attorneys possess qualifications that lend themselves to service as mediators.

Attorneys are also conversant with and sensitive to the ethical standards attendant upon service as a mediator or arbitrator. For example, they may not serve as mediator or arbitrator in any case in which they have a conflict of interest. Nor may they participate in ADR as mediator or arbitrator and subsequently represent either of the parties should the mediation not result in a settlement. R. 1:40–4(b). See also Opinion 521, 112 N.J.L.J. 394 (1983) (attorney may not participate in private matrimonial mediation service and subsequently represent either spouse in divorce action).

Third party neutrals are also under an obligation not to disclose any confidential information obtained during mediation unless they reasonably believe it is necessary to prevent a participant from committing a criminal or illegal act likely to result in death or serious bodily harm. R. 1:40–4(b). See Canon 5D(7), Code of Judicial Conduct (information acquired by a judge in a judicial capacity should not be used or disclosed by the judge in financial dealings or for any other purpose not related to judicial duties). Cf. RPC 1.6(b)(1) (a lawyer shall reveal to the proper authorities confidential information relating to representation of a client as soon as and to the extent the lawyer reasonably believes necessary to prevent the client from committing a criminal, illegal or fraudulent act the lawyer reasonably believes is likely to result in death or substantial bodily harm or substantial injury to the financial interest or property of another).

Unlike the situation described in Opinion 657, supra, 1 N.J.L. 129, 130 N.J.L.J. 656, respondents and most of the other commentators do not differentiate between their ADR activities and their legal practices. In their advertising, they hold themselves out as lawyers who, in addition to traditional civil and/or criminal trial work, also provide ADR services, including arbitration and mediation, both as counsel and third party neutrals. None can recall a client ever having expressed confusion or surprise over their provision of ADR services as part and parcel of their law practices. To the contrary, many of their clients retained them precisely because of their familiarity with and willingness to engage in alternative dispute resolution when practicable.

Attorneys engaged in ADR activities consider themselves professionals in dispute resolution. They report that their activities: (a) negotiating; (b) advocating in mediation, arbitration, or litigation settings; or (c) when no conflicts of interest arise, serving as third party neutrals, have been of great benefit to their client community. Their experience in ADR has also provided them with a theoretical as well as practical perspective they might not otherwise have gained and has influenced their "traditional" adversarial practice, just as their litigation practice has informed and strengthened their ADR practice.

It is therefore apparent that ADR has become part and parcel of the practice of law and constitutes a tool of equal rank with litigation to achieve, in the proper case, prompt and cost effective dispute resolution. When a lawyer (a) discusses the potential of ADR with a client; (b) participates as an advocate in mediation or arbitration; or (c) serves as a third party neutral, he or she is acting as a lawyer and is not engaging in a separate business. In fact, without exception, the commentators' professional liability insurance policies include their activities as arbitrators, mediators and third party neutrals among the coverages afforded under the policy.

This is not to say that only lawyers appropriately may provide third party neutral services. There are many trained and experienced lay arbitrators acting under the aegis of the American Arbitration Association and other recognized organizations. In fact, with certain expressed exceptions, no special occupational status or degree is required to be a mediator or receive mediation training in the CDR programs administered by the Court. R. 1:40–10, Guideline 1.1. Clearly, non-lawyers may provide ADR/CDR services as long as they do not hold themselves out as lawyers and do not engage in any activities, such as the rendering of legal advice, that might constitute the unauthorized practice of law.

However, the fact that non-lawyers may and do serve as third party neutrals does not mean that attorneys engaged in ADR are rendering non-legal services to their clients. Therefore, unlike ancillary business activities such as the medical-legal consulting service described in Opinion 657, supra, 1 N.J.L. 129, 130 N.J.L.J. 656, ADR services may be rendered in the same location as and jointly marketed or advertised with an attorney's legal practice.

* * *

Questions

1. In *Werle*, the Court found that the Rhode Island Bar Association had qualified immunity because it was acting in good faith when it threatened to refer the Family Mediation Center to the state Attorney General for prosecution. Could you argue that bad faith, or at least the possibility of bad faith, was present?

2. Was the Family Mediation Center in *Werle* engaged in the unauthorized practice of law? What is practicing law? Is it practicing law to help clients draft agreements? To advise parties of their legal rights? To define the state of the law? Were these potential activities of the Center?

3. What does the New Jersey Bar Association say about mediation services and the practice of law? Under its view, would the Family Mediation Center in *Werle* be engaged in unauthorized practice?

4. Do you believe that only lawyers should be mediators? Should mediation be a licensed degree, similar to a law degree, with state or federal licensing required?

* * *

B. CONFLICT OF INTEREST

McKenzie Construction v. St. Croix Storage Corporation

961 F.Supp. 857 (D.V.I., St. Croix Div. 1997).

■ RESNICK, UNITED STATES MAGISTRATE JUDGE.

THIS MATTER is before the Court on defendants St. Croix Storage Corp. and Sun Storage Partners, L.P.'s motion to disqualify the law firm of Rohn & Cusick as counsel for plaintiffs in this action. Plaintiffs filed an Opposition, defendant filed a Reply asserting new allegations. Plaintiffs responded further as directed by the Court and have requested "oral argument so that Attorney Moorehead can take the stand and inform the Court of the true nature of what occurred here." Plaintiffs' Reply Brief, p. 1.

Plaintiff McKenzie Construction is a local lumber retail company who brought this damages action against defendants St. Croix Storage Corp. for conversion of lumber. The Court ordered the matter submitted to mediation and later appointed Attorney Lisa Moorehead as mediator. (See Order

Appointing Mediator dated May 26, 1994). Mediation was unsuccessful and the parties have resumed preparation for trial.

In seeking to disqualify the firm of Rohn & Cusick, defendants claim that the firm's hiring of Attorney Moorehead, who was the mediator appointed by the Court to settle this case, presents an irreparable conflict of interest in contravention of the rules governing the conduct of mediators and attorneys alike. Defendants reason that Moorehead's position as mediator allowed her access to "a wide range of confidential information derived from her private consultations" with the parties. Plaintiffs responded that although Moorehead may be subject to disqualification, she is simply "of counsel" to the law firm of Rohn & Cusick and that, under Virgin Islands law, the disqualification of the law firm is not automatic. Moreover, plaintiffs assert that although no confidences were exchanged in the mediation, the firm had created a "cone of silence" around Moorehead, insulating her from the case. However, defendants countered that since being hired by Rohn & Cusick in September of 1996, Moorehead had inserted herself into the case by meeting with an investigator for defendants concerning the investigator's contact with plaintiff about the case. The Court requested that plaintiffs file a direct response to defendants' allegation. In their response, plaintiffs submit an affidavit of Attorney Moorehead in which she avers that a "cone of silence" has been erected at Rohn & Cusick and admits that she met with the investigator in order to advise him that he could be civilly liable for attempting to settle a case with a represented party. She claims that she did not discuss the merits of the instant case. Defendants also seek the imposition of sanctions against plaintiffs' law firm for filing false affidavits.

After review of the record and the submissions of the parties, this Court concludes that there exists a sufficient basis for resolution of this issue on the pleadings alone. Accordingly, the request for a hearing is denied.

DISCUSSION

A motion to disqualify counsel requires the court to balance the right of a party to retain counsel of his choice and the substantial hardship which might result from disqualification as against the public perception of and the public trust in the judicial system. Powell v. Alabama, 287 U.S. 45, 53, 53 S.Ct. 55, 58, 77 L.Ed. 158 (1932). The underlying principle in considering motions to disqualify counsel is safeguarding the integrity of the court proceedings and the purpose of granting such motions is to eliminate the threat that the litigation will be tainted. United States Football League v. National Football League, 605 F.Supp. 1448, 1464 (S.D.N.Y.1985). The district court's power to disqualify an attorney derives from its inherent authority to supervise the professional conduct of attorneys appearing before it. (citations omitted).

This case presents the question whether a law firm must be disqualified from representing a party when it employs an attorney who was formerly the mediator in the identical litigation. Plaintiffs essentially concede that Attorney Moorehead should be screened from involvement in the case. Indeed, they "do not dispute that Ms. Moorehead, herself, may be subject to disqualification." Plaintiffs' Opposition, page 1. They argue, however, that the "cone of silence" erected around Attorney Moorehead is sufficient under the rules and case law, and that the facts do not warrant disqualification of the entire firm. Defendants maintain that Moorehead's contact with the investigator, subsequent to the date that the "cone of silence" was reportedly constructed, constitutes a violation of the relevant ethical standards and presents a more compelling case for disqualification.

The leading case on attorney disqualification in this district is Bluebeard's Castle, Inc. v. Delmar Marketing, Inc., 886 F.Supp. 1204, 1207 (D.Vi.1995). In that case, this Court ruled that where an attorney accepts representation of a party adverse to a former client in a substantially related matter, the Court "presumes that confidences were disclosed during the previous relationship and that such confidences would be used against the former client ... [and] does not require that the moving party be able to show that confidences actually were passed on or to detail their contents." (citations omitted.) The Court went on to find that an attorney faced with such a prospect should, at the least, fully disclose the fact to that party or, at most, refuse such representation. Failure to honor such conflict would result in the disqualification of the attorney and his entire firm. Id. at 1208–1210. The Court relied on the Model Rules of Professional Conduct in disqualifying the attorney and his law firm....

The Bluebeard's court relied on McNamara v. Boehm, Civ. No. 92/141 (Terr.Ct.V.I.1992) where the Territorial Court ruled that an attorney who had represented a client in a divorce could not later represent an employee of that client in an action adverse to the former client. Guided by the standards set forth in Rules 1.9[2] and 1.10(a) of the Model Rules of Professional Conduct, the court announced that disqualification is required "where it appears that the subject matter of a pending suit in which the

---

2. Rule 1.9 of the ABA Model Rules of Professional Conduct reads as follows:

CONFLICT OF INTEREST: FORMER CLIENT

(a) A lawyer who has formerly represented a client in a matter shall not thereafter represent another person in the same or a substantially related matter in which that person's interests are materially adverse to the interests of the former client unless the former client consents after consultation.

(b) A lawyer shall not knowingly represent a person in the same or substantially related matter in which a firm with which the lawyer formerly was associated had previously represented a client

(1) whose interests are materially adverse to that person; and

(2) about whom the lawyer had acquired information protected by rules 1.6 and 1.9(c) that is material to the matter;

(c) A lawyer who has formerly represented a client in a matter or whose present or former firm has formerly represented a client in a matter shall not thereafter

(1) use information relating to the representation to the disadvantage of the former client except as Rule 1.6 or Rule 3.3 would permit or require with respect to a client, or when the information has become generally known; or

(2) reveal information relating to the representation except as rule 1.6 or Rule 3.3 would permit or require with respect to a client.

attorney represents an interest adverse to a prior [client] is such that during the course of the former representation the attorney 'might have acquired substantially related material.' "Id. at 4, citing Brice, at 6. The court characterized the rules as "prophylactic measures [enacted] to prevent any possibility, however slight, that confidences and secrets obtained from a client during a previous relationship may subsequently be used against him." Id. at 5.

The instant motion to disqualify differs somewhat from the cases cited above, in that it focuses on Attorney Moorehead's role as a mediator who was subsequently hired by the law firm in question. However, the analysis is the same. First, although it is arguable that mediation is not, technically, an adversarial process as is the traditional practice of law, where there is no specific rule that speaks to the issue, courts refer to the Model Rules as a guide to regulate the conduct of the attorney who serves as a mediator in Alternate Dispute Resolution [ADR] proceedings and is later involved in the matter in which he or she mediated. Daigneault, Michael G., Lawyers as Mediators: Traps ... Pitfalls ... Hazards, 43 JAN Fed. Law. 10 (and cases cited therein)[3] In both situations, the duty of loyalty is at stake. Defendants assert that as mediator Moorehead was privy to confidential information which would be relevant to the present litigation. They argue that under the existing local and ABA rules, her disqualification should be imputed to the entire firm. Mediation is defined as the private, informal dispute resolution process in which a neutral third person, the mediator, helps disputing parties to reach an agreement. Black's Law Dictionary, 6 ed. at 981.

The recent case of Poly Software International, Inc. v. Su, 880 F.Supp. 1487 (D.Utah 1995), discusses the identical issue presented in the case sub judice. In that case, two parties agreed to mediate a copyright action which they were defending. However, soon after the mediated settlement the parties sued each other. One of the parties retained the mediator as his counsel. The other party moved to disqualify the mediator-turned-attorney in light of his prior status as mediator in the previous action. The District Court disqualified the attorney and his law firm from participating in the litigation and held that an attorney who serves as a mediator cannot subsequently represent anyone in a substantially related matter without the consent of the original parties. The court reasoned that mediators routinely receive and preserve confidences in much the same manner as an attorney. The court referred to the Model Rules of Professional Conduct and concluded that where the mediator was privy to confidential information, the applicable ethical rules imposed the same responsibilities as the

---

3. Additionally, in response to the emerging problems presented by mediators turned attorneys, the American Bar Association, in conjunction with the American Arbitration Association and the Society of Professionals in Dispute Resolution, has drafted a code of professional responsibility tailored specifically for ADR mediators. The Draft Rules recommend that mediators be prohibited from representing one party to the dispute against another in future legal proceedings related to the subject of the litigation. See Smiley, Alison, Professional Codes and Neutral Lawyering: An Emerging Standard Governing Nonrepresentational Attorney Mediation, 7 Geo. J. Legal Ethics 213 (1993).

rules relating to an attorney's subsequent representation of a former client. The court also considered the rule prohibiting judges and other adjudicative officers from representing anyone in connection with a matter in which he or she participated "personally and substantially." Model Rule 1.2.

Likewise, in Cho v. Superior Court, 39 Cal.App.4th 113, 45 Cal.Rptr.2d 863 (1995), a former judge and his law firm were disqualified from representing a party in an action in which the former judge had participated in settlement conferences. That court relied on ABA Model Rule 1.12 which prohibits a lawyer who has participated personally and substantially in a matter as a judge or adjudicative officer, from representing anyone in connection with the same matter. Id. 45 Cal.Rptr.2d at 867. The Court compared the judge's role in the proceedings to that of a mediator, and found that the position necessarily involved the exchange of confidences going to the merits of the case. The court cautioned that "no amount of assurances or screening procedures, no 'cone of silence' could ever convince the opposing party that the confidences would not be used to its disadvantage." Id. 45 Cal.Rptr.2d at 869. The Court concluded that based on the nature of the attorney's prior participation, there is a presumption that confidences were revealed, and the attorney should not have "to engage in subtle evaluation of the extent to which he acquired relevant information in the first representation and of the actual use of that representation." Id. Thus, the rule of the cases is that a mediator should never represent a party to the mediation in a subsequent related or similar matter.

It is against this backdrop that this Court must determine whether Attorney Moorehead, who was the mediator in this identical action, may have received confidences which may be used to the disadvantage of defendant in this case, warranting her disqualification and that of her law firm. Guided by the case law and experience, this Court notes that the very nature of mediation requires that confidences be exchanged. Hence, Local Rule of Civil Procedure 3.2(c)(2) provides that a mediator appointed in this jurisdiction must be impartial and is required to disqualify himself or herself "in any action in which he/she would be required under Title 28, USC sec. 455 to disqualify him/herself if he/she were a judge or Magistrate Judge." Title 28, USC sec. 455 requires such a judicial officer to disqualify himself or herself (1) where the attorney served as a lawyer, the associate lawyer, a witness or a judge in the case; or (2) where the attorney has served in governmental employment and participated in the case as a counsel, adviser or material witness.

John Landers, Vice President of defendant St. Croix Storage Corp., states by affidavit that he was present during the mediation conference and met with Attorney Moorehead separately and together with the other parties. He states that he openly discussed "the facts of the matter, the financial status and capability of Sun Storage to either pay a settlement figure or to pay a verdict, the status and degree of involvement of certain of the partners ... in the management and operation ... and the trial strategy that was to be employed in the absence of settlement of this matter." Plaintiffs claim that all discussions in the case were done in a group setting and not "confidential". They further argue that any information received would have been discovered during the normal course of litigation.

Plaintiffs' entire argument against disqualification lacks credibility, is unsupported by legal analysis, and completely ignores the existing standards governing attorney conduct. This Court finds, and many commentators agree, that during mediation parties are encouraged to disclose the strengths and weaknesses of their positions, in an effort to arrive at a settlement. Protection of confidences in such a setting strengthens the incentive of parties to negotiate without fear that the mediator will subsequently use the information against them. Additionally, the rules regulating attorney conduct place the onus on the attorney to "remain conscious of the obligation to preserve confidences and maintain loyalty." 886 F.Supp. at 1207. It is clear from the record that the parties met to negotiate a settlement. It is undisputed that the mediation lasted at least one hour. It is not unreasonable to assume that in light of the nature and purpose of the proceeding, that confidential information was disclosed by the parties. Notwithstanding Attorney Moorehead's statements to the contrary, the present situation presents such a serious affront to the policy that forms the basis of the rules, that this Court has no choice but to conclude that Attorney Moorehead must be disqualified.

DISQUALIFICATION OF THE FIRM

This Court further finds that disqualification of Attorney Moorehead should be imputed to the other members of the firm. The cases and Model Rule 1.10(a)[4] require such disqualification. Plaintiffs' fixation on Brice to support their argument that such disqualification is not automatic, signifies a fundamental misunderstanding of that case. The Brice case simply held that where there is no "substantial relationship" between the former representation and the present one, disqualification was not warranted. Here, the former representation and the present are one and the same, thus obviating the need to determine the existence of a "substantial relationship", and creating a stronger case for disqualification.

In addition, the Court is disturbed by Attorney Moorehead's contact with Mr. Pierre Tepie, an investigator associated with this case. Partly in response to a Motion for Sanctions filed by plaintiffs, Mr. Tepie, who is a self-employed investigator and process server, stated, via affidavit that he was hired by Shirryl Hughes, on behalf of a defendant in this case, to attempt to negotiate an out of court settlement. He further stated that after such attempted negotiation, he was contacted by Attorney Moorehead, who attempted to persuade him to discontinue his efforts. Attorney Moorehead responded, also via affidavit, that she contacted Tepie with regard to his attempted negotiation because she "thought it was wise to inform him that he could be civilly liable for contacting a represented party." She

---

4. The rule states: "While lawyers are associated in a firm, none of them shall knowingly represent a client when any one of them practicing alone would be prohibited from doing so by Rule 1.7, 1.8(c), 1.9 or 2.2."

claims she did not know whom he worked for. Moorehead, who was reportedly excluded from the case, does not explain in her affidavit, the manner in which she learned about Tepie's involvement. In any event, this court finds that Moorehead's contact with an agent of the defendants in this very case, implicates the effectiveness of the measures allegedly adopted by her employer to avoid her involvement in this matter. Accordingly, disqualification of the law firm of Rohn & Cusick is necessary to safeguard the integrity of the ongoing litigation and to eliminate the threat that the proceedings will be tainted.

THE MOTION FOR SANCTIONS

Counsel for defendants also seek an order imposing sanctions on plaintiffs' counsel for filing false affidavits with the court. In particular, counsel refers to plaintiffs' attorneys' affidavits attesting to the exclusion of Attorney Moorehead from the case. Defendants' counsel submits that the evidence of Moorehead's subsequent involvement in the case renders the earlier affidavits false, exposing plaintiffs' counsel to sanctions ranging from suspension to disbarment.

Federal courts have inherent authority to impose sanctions upon parties and counsel for filing false or seriously misleading affidavits. Chambers v. NASCO, Inc., 501 U.S. 32, 111 S.Ct. 2123, 115 L.Ed.2d 27 (1991). However, because of their effect, inherent powers must be exercised with restraint and discretion. Id. at 44, 111 S.Ct. at 2132–33. A court's power to sanction attorneys should be reserved for those cases in which the conduct is egregious, and no other basis for sanction exists. Martin v. Brown, 63 F.3d 1252, 1265 (3d Cir.1995). Additionally, the sanctions should be tailored to address the harm identified. Republic of Philippines v. Westinghouse Elec. Corp., 43 F.3d 65 (3d Cir.1994).

The conduct under scrutiny, here, is the integrity of plaintiffs' attorneys' affidavits regarding Attorney Moorehead's involvement in this case after being hired by Rohn & Cusick. Specifically, the affidavits involved statements regarding Moorehead's contact with Mr. Tepie. It is clear from the record that the conduct of plaintiffs' attorneys is less than exemplary; however, in light of plaintiffs' final response, this Court finds that the sworn statements, taken together, are not patently false. Moreover, even absent such contact, there is ample material in the pleadings which would lead a court to conclude that Moorehead's association with the law firm of Rohn & Cusick creates a conflict of interest warranting disqualification. Accordingly, the Court's decision to disqualify the firm from litigating this action, including the loss of revenue that it portends, provides the intended result and embodies a sanction in and of itself.

CONCLUSION

Based on the foregoing, this Court finds that, as the mediator in this case, Attorney Moorehead is presumed to have received confidential information going to the merits of the case and must be disqualified. This Court also finds that in addition to the mandate of the Model Rules, the screening procedure reportedly employed at the law firm of Rohn & Cusick failed to prevent Moorehead's subsequent involvement in this matter, further bolstering the court's conclusion that the law firm of Rohn & Cusick must also be disqualified. Finally, the Court finds that plaintiffs' affidavits herein do not warrant the imposition of sanctions. Accordingly, none will be imposed.

* * *

Questions

1. Typical conflict of interest problems arise when an attorney is asked to represent a client against a former client, or an attorney is asked to engage in joint representation of two or more clients who have potentially differing interests. Under the Model Code of Professional Conduct, many of these conflicts can be resolved through disclosure and consent by all involved. For example, an attorney can normally represent a client against a former client if there is no danger that confidences will be disclosed and if both the current and the former client consent to the representation. Similarly, an attorney who represents multiple clients with potential conflicts between them can often cure a conflict of interest problem through disclosure and consent of all involved. However, disclosure and consent is only effective in curing a conflict of interest when the only harm involved is a harm to the clients themselves. If there is a potential harm to the legal system, then disclosure and consent is not sufficient, and the representation is prohibited. Should consent and disclosure be sufficient to cure a potential conflict of interest when a mediator represents one party against the other in an unsuccessful mediation? Would it matter if the mediation were successful, and the mediator were employed by one of the parties in a subsequent, unrelated dispute against the other?

2. The court in the *McKenzie Construction* case imposed a prohibition on representation by a former mediator to any matter that is substantially related to a matter in the mediation. Is the "substantially related to" standard one that will disqualify too many attorneys who have served as mediators? Will it discourage attorneys from agreeing to serve as mediators? Could the court have chosen a less restrictive standard?

3. Could the mediator have offered testimony to show that the matter involved in the current representation was not "related or similar" to the matter involved in the mediation? What type of testimony might be admissible? What objections might be raised? If such testimony is not admissible, what other evidence might be available for the lawyer/mediator to show that the current representation is not a related or similar matter, and hence not disqualifying?

4. The court rejects the possibility of the firm erecting a "cone of silence" around the former mediator in this case. But it suggests in dicta that if there is not a "substantial relationship between the former representation and the present one," then disqualification of the firm might not be required. Is this test less demanding than the test the court articulates for

disqualifying the lawyer herself? How would the court know whether there were such a substantial relationship?

* * *

7.   CRITICAL PERSPECTIVES ON MEDIATION IN FAMILY LAW

A.   MEDIATION IN DIVORCE NEGOTIATIONS

Killing Us Softly: Divorce Mediation and the Politics of Power by Penelope E. Bryan[1]

"Divorce mediation's seductive marketing rhetoric masks a political agenda: entrenchment. Recently reformed divorce law confers greater economic rights upon divorcing women. Custody law also favors women. Negotiating lawyers rely upon these legal entitlements and craft divorce agreements reflecting them, thereby loosening the control men traditionally wield over economic resources and the socialization of children. While mediation proponents employ the obscuring rhetoric of relatedness, mediation unobtrusively reduces this threat to patriarchy by returning men to their former dominant position. This article explains how mediation accomplishes this feat.

"Proponents proclaim mediation's superiority to lawyer negotiation of divorce disputes because mediation purportedly enhances autonomy and individual dignity by empowering the couple to order their post divorce lives. The first Part of this article, however, explores power disparities between husbands and wives and the impact these disparities have on the spouses' relative negotiating abilities. This exposition clarifies that, absent mediator, lawyer, or judicial intervention, mediation empowers only the already more powerful husband. . . ."

[The author discusses the many ways in which husbands tend to be more powerful than their wives in our culture, including the fact that they earn more and therefore have more resources to purchase expert advice, have higher educational levels and therefore have greater knowledge about their legal rights as well as greater negotiating skills, and tend to work in occupations like finance and law where they have greater access to legal and financial information. She also discusses the ways in which men's higher social status makes them less "influenceable," less likely to capitulate in negotiation settings. All of these factors contribute to a general pattern in which men are more powerful than their wives in divorce negotiations.]

"2.   *Conflicting Role and Ethical Prescriptions.* [O]n financial issues the mediator role requires neutrality. While some mediators cleverly ration-

---

1. Penelope E. Bryan, *Killing Us Softly: Divorce Mediation and the Politics of Power*, 40 BUFFALO L. REV. 443 (1992) (excerpts) (footnotes omitted). Reprinted with permission.

alize their way around this prescription, many others take it quite serious-ly. Neutrality, in its pure form, requires the mediator to refrain from attempting to influence the substance of mediated agreements. Mediators must not give advice on what alternatives they think superior, for doing so represents a biased infliction of the mediator's value preference upon the divorcing couple. Mediator neutrality places the responsibility for generating alternatives and outcomes solely on the parties.

"The ethic of party empowerment firmly buttresses mediator neutrality. Empowerment in mediation allegedly respects and fosters individual autonomy and dignity while simultaneously limiting state intrusion. In marketing mediation to clients mediators contrast mediation to the specter of the intrusive judge imposing formal, external, and insensitive criteria on private family matters. In place of this threatening alternative, mediators offer couples the chance to make their own decisions on how to order their post-divorce lives. Under this ethic, as with neutrality, the responsibility for generating alternatives and outcomes lies exclusively with the parties.

"Some mediators intuitively sense the tension between neutrality and empowerment and mediation's ability to protect the weaker party from unfair outcomes. Faced with this tension they do not abandon their role and ethical prescriptions. Nor do they use the drastic and time-consuming measures necessary to meaningfully power balance. Instead mediators assume they can resolve the tension and generate fair outcomes if they simply control the process of mediation while ignoring the substance of emerging agreements. Mediators believe process tactics like allowing both spouses ample opportunity to speak, or requiring both spouses to submit detailed budgets, allow them neutrally to balance power and generate fair outcomes. Yet neither these, nor other allegedly neutral process tactics, however, assure balanced power or fair outcomes. A wife actually may speak more than her husband, yet his few words may command her deference. The wife may submit a thorough budget, yet the budget may reflect her low expectations or her depression may blunt her ability to effectively negotiate for her financial needs reflected in the budget. Once the multifaceted nature of power is understood, tactics designed to control only process do little to protect the disadvantaged spouse.

"Moreover, mediators concerned with fairness cannot use substantive legal norms to balance power and assure outcomes that, at least, somewhat reflect society's perception of justice. Imposition of legal norms would violate neutrality and empowerment. Furthermore, if mental health mediators impose law or give legal advice, they expose themselves to accusations of unauthorized practice of law. Law then remains just as irrelevant to financial issues in mediation as to child custody issues. Mediators instead encourage couples to fashion idiosyncratic financial agreements unconstrained by the rigid dictates of formal law. The wife freely can relinquish her legal right to a portion of her husband's pension fund or her right to spousal maintenance. Mediation cloaks her right to forgo these legal entitlements in the seductive and obscuring rhetoric of autonomy and empowerment.

"Mediators do, however, urge the divorcing couple to treat each other with fairness. Cut loose from its moorings in formal distributional law and set upon the stormy seas of divorce negotiations, this fragile skiff of equity will not promote fair financial results for women. Because of their social power men, not women, determine and occupy the roles society perceives valuable and deserving of reward. The husband's role of primary economic provider, for instance, commands more value than the wife's provision of a clean home, properly dressed children and well prepared meals. When divorce occurs and only a vague equity norm determines a fair distribution of marital income and assets, a result giving the husband a greater share than the wife might seem equitable to the couple and the mediator because of his more deserving marital duties. Moreover, when one considers the value men attach to their income and wealth, reliance upon an unspecified norm of fairness to induce the husband to part with income or assets seems, at best, naive. The equity norm used by mediators to balance power and produce fair outcomes provides a thin reed, indeed, of protection for the disadvantaged wife.

"Since mediators cannot balance power effectively by altering the causes of power disparity, by blindly relying upon process control, by employing formal distributional law, or by appealing to an informal equity norm, mediator efforts at power balancing prove insufficient to protect the weaker wife. Mediators, however, could achieve power balancing's goal of equitable financial agreements by closely monitoring the substance of the emerging agreement, and, when necessary, intervening to promote fairness. Herein, however, lies the problem. Mediator neutrality and party empowerment norms require the mediator steadfastly to avoid interference with the parties' right to self-determination. Active substantive intervention lacks neutrality and violates party empowerment. Consequently, even a mediator concerned with fair results will feel obligated to refrain from using this tactic, and will cling, instead, to ineffective process tactics and a biased equity norm.

"Abandonment of neutrality and party empowerment as guiding principles in mediation and adoption of mediator responsibility for fair outcomes provide obvious ways for mediation to afford some protection for the weaker spouse. Mediator self-interest, however, prohibits this solution. First, mental health professionals' lack of financial expertise, their discomfort with their lack of financial sophistication, and the low value they place on financial, as opposed to emotional and relational concerns, should make them unwilling to accept responsibility for determining and imposing fair financial agreements.

"Moreover, administrators in efficiency-driven court-affiliated programs measure a mediator's success by how many agreements he can produce and how long he takes to produce them. Pressing for financial fairness might threaten a mediator's success by provoking the husband to terminate mediation before reaching an agreement. While divorcing mothers likely will succumb to the expert mediator's coercion on child issues, the husband likely will walk out in response to mediator coercion on financial issues because the mental health mediator lacks legitimate authority over financial issues. Moreover, husband resistance to mediator coercion on finances seems more likely than a mother's resistance to coercion on child issues because the mediator's insistence on financial fairness overtly conflicts with the husband's interest in retaining marital income and assets. In contrast, the mediator manipulates the traditional mother into joint custody by explaining how this custody arrangement coincides with the mother's interest in maintaining relationships. The threat then of the husband's walkout should inhibit a mediator concerned with success from pressing the husband on financial issues and should encourage mediators to retain neutrality and party empowerment as guiding principles.

"Mediators also resist abandoning these guiding principles and taking responsibility for fair financial outcomes because these norms provide several layers of insulation from malpractice liability. First, they place responsibility for substance exclusively on the parties. Additionally, the empowerment ethic creates the expectation that mediated agreements will reflect the idiosyncratic needs of the couple. No objective standard then exists against which to measure the fairness of mediated agreements. Since mediators cannot be accountable for what they do not control and the fairness of mediated agreements defies evaluation, the norms of neutrality and party empowerment artfully insulate the mediator from accountability for fair outcomes. Trading these norms for responsibility, in contrast, would expose the mediator to liability for unfair results. The spectre of malpractice provides additional disincentive for abandoning these principles.

"The judicial system, with its overwhelming concern for efficiency, also has much to lose if mediators publicly declare their intent to shape the substance of mediated financial agreements. This declaration would force the divorcing public to choose between a judge sworn to impose known substantive laws and a mediator sworn to impose his own unknown sense of fairness on the couple's financial dispute. Facing this choice the public might prefer the relative predictability of a judge sworn to impose known substantive law to a mediator whose preferences remain a mystery. If this were to happen, mediation programs would fail, forcing the legal system to reassimilate the numerous family law cases it now shuffles into mediation. Active mediator participation in financial agreements thus ultimately threatens to exacerbate the legal system's efficiency problems and judicial administrators will not encourage mediators to abandon neutrality and party empowerment norms.

"Judges, too, have a self-interest in promoting public acceptance of mediation through the promise of mediator neutrality and party empowerment. Judges do not like hearing family law cases. If mediators abandon neutrality and party empowerment and as a result the divorcing public avoids mediation, judges would be forced to entertain distasteful dissolution cases in greater numbers. Because of their interest in avoiding these cases, judges will not encourage mediators to abandon the norms and impose their sense of fairness on the divorcing couple.

"Moreover, mediator relinquishment of neutrality and party empowerment threatens the dignity and legitimacy of the formal justice system. If mediators impose their ideas of financial fairness upon divorcing couples, the distinction between mediation and judicial decisionmaking blurs. Even though the origins and content of the distributive norms employed by judges and mediators would differ, both mediators and judges would impose external norms on the divorcing couple rather than effectuate what the couple might prefer. Also, in both dispute resolution processes a third party rather than the divorcing couple would do the decisionmaking. In essence, if mediators abandon neutrality and party empowerment they would act as judges act. The realization then would emerge that the shift to divorce mediation does little more than change which third party does the decisionmaking and the public would see mediation as little more than an abdication of judicial responsibility. This perception would threaten the justice system's legitimacy. Thus, once again, little pressure from the formal justice system should exist for mediators to abandon neutrality and party empowerment norms in favor of mediator activism.

"In summary, the ethic of neutrality and party empowerment compromises any attempt by the mediator to produce fair financial agreements through power balancing because it denies mediators the opportunity to use the only effective power balancing technique: interference with the substance of financial agreements. Nor will mediators abandon these norms willingly and accept responsibility for producing fair outcomes because these norms protect several mediator self-interests as well as those of judges and efficiency minded judicial administrators. Even if mediators could, if they chose, power balance, these numerous constraints make that choice highly unlikely. Power balancing thus proves a rhetorical, rather than real, protection for the weaker spouse."

* * *

B. MEDIATION IN CHILD CUSTODY DISPUTES

Dominant Discourse, Professional Language, and Legal Change in Child Custody Decisionmaking by Martha Fineman[1]

I. INTRODUCTION

"This Article explores how the rhetoric used by social workers and mediators has been successful in appropriating the business of child custody decisionmaking. An integral part of this process has been an attack on the nature of existing rules and decisionmaking institutions, a phenomenon that can be viewed metaphorically as the claiming by the helping professions of the custody decisionmaking terrain through the rhetoric of reform. The extent to which the concepts and values put forth by the helping

---

1. Martha Fineman, *Dominant Discourse, Professional Language, and Legal Change in Child Custody Decisionmaking,* 101 HARV. L. REV. 727 (1988) (excerpts) (citations omitted). Reprinted with permission.

professions have been incorporated into and dominate the public and political language of the escalating custody debate illustrates the success of their efforts.

"The recent trend in the legal area is to mandate mediation of custody and related post-divorce disputes. Thus, contemporary shifts in custody policy are best understood in the context of the rhetoric and ideology of social workers and mediators, proponents of this trend who, as a professional group, have transformed divorce. In this Article, I argue that the establishment of mandatory mediation as the preferred process, and joint custody or shared parenting as the substantive norm, represents a significant divergence from previously accepted legal doctrine. Yet, because these changes are presented in procedural terms, the rhetoric concerning mediation has masked, at the same time that it has facilitated, the extensive shifts in substantive results. Labeling changes as procedural makes them easier to accept but also obscures the substantive changes that are taking place. . . .

"In this Article, I criticize social workers and other members of the helping professions in part because they present themselves as neutral, nonadversarial decisionmakers in contrast to attorneys, whom they characterize as both adversarial and combative. Yet social workers are not neutral; they have a professional bias in favor of a specific substantive result. That result benefits their profession by creating the need for mediation and counseling. It is this bias and self-interest that makes the process one for political consideration. The bias inherent in mediation is different from, but no less suspect than, the bias that can result from overt favoritism of one party over another. It is understood from this perspective that if no mutual, objective professional decisionmaker exists, we must confront moral, political and legal questions from which the "experts" cannot save us.

II.   CHANGES AND DISCOURSE—AN OVERVIEW

A.   The Transformation of the Custody Debate

"Divorce and child custody decisionmaking has traditionally been the preserve of legal institutions: legislatures established laws to govern 'domestic relations,' and judges decided cases presented by attorneys representing adverse parties. Early divorce reforms, which sought changes in legal rules, particularly the movement from a fault-based to a no-fault system, sought adjustments that would mediate the harshness of the legal system.

"The current debate about the content and form of child custody law, however, reflects a struggle between two professional ideologies—those of law and social work. Fundamental questions have been raised about the appropriateness of legal institutions, legal solutions, and legal processes in divorce and custody cases. Such objections have culminated in a substantial redistribution of decisionmaking authority from judges and lawyers to the helping professions. . . .

"Helping professionals and other proponents of joint custody asserted that the win/lose philosophy of naming a sole custodian was inappropriate, because parents had equal rights and responsibilities in relation to their children during marriage. In addition, they found the notion of "visiting" one's child ideologically and emotionally offensive. By contrast, the symbolic ideal of parental equality was compelling. Desirable custody policy, therefore, was post-divorce shared parenting. It was this notion of a legally mandated and constructed continuing relationship between divorced parents, so central to joint custody, that was so foreign to traditional family law policy. In essence, the social workers' ideal of shared parenting was a rejection of the desirability of a legally acknowledged sole custodian.

"As this view has become accepted, it has altered the way we articulate and conceive of custody issues. The dominant rhetoric no longer describes divorce as a process that terminates the relationship between spouses, establishing one as the custodial parent with clear responsibilities. Rather, divorce is now described as a process that, through mediation, restructures and reformulates the spouses' relationship, conferring equal or shared parental rights on both parents although one, in practice, usually assumes the primary responsibility for care of the children. This is an important substantive shift.

"The helping professions' ability to suggest and obtain such radical change in substantive policy derives in part from their ability to present the debate over divorce and custody as one involving the treatment of an emotional crisis rather than a solution to a legal problem. Custody was merely a "label"; what was really at issue was the states of mind or attitudes of the family members. In this sense, the helping professions ignored the fact of, and the justifications for, the differing legal consequences that flowed from the labels of "custodial parent" and "noncustodial parent." These designations were also considered to be offensive to noncustodial fathers, which added weight to arguments that the terms and rules had to be changed. Terms such as "shared parenting" and "periods of physical placement" replaced "physical custody" and "visitation" as the proper way to discuss custody arrangements....

"The helping professions' concern with symbols overshadowed the fact that in practice joint custody dispositions continue to resemble sole maternal custody and paternal visitation. In fact, the social role and function of a sole custodial parent continues. Whether or not custodial mothers exist as a legal category, they exist as an institution—as a practical reality experienced by many children of divorce and their mothers. The recent rhetorical disapproval of and attempts to abolish formally the institution of the sole custodial parent have not destroyed it, but only placed it in the shadows....

IV.   SOCIAL WORKERS AND DIVORCE

"Under traditional legal rules, the helping professions were confined to a supplemental role in the family court system: agency social workers functioned as counselors or custody investigators. With the changes in traditional custody decisionmaking ideology, however, social workers are moving from a supplemental role to the role of substitute decisionmaker, displacing guardians ad litem and, ultimately, replacing judges as the final arbiters of child custody. . . .

"The first expansion of the social worker's role in divorce was through conciliation courts created by many jurisdictions when they adopted no-fault legislation. These courts were designed to provide "short-contact marital counseling service for couples on the verge of separation and divorce." The proponents of such courts justified them on the ground that divorce was a social problem requiring state services to ease the crisis. These services could be provided by social workers, giving them a new role in the legal system at a time when their role was being limited elsewhere. Conciliation courts thus embodied the notion of a partnership between law and the behavioral sciences.

"These courts initially provided reconciliation counseling, but as divorce became more accepted and reconciliation a less important goal, the counseling method was replaced first by a divorce therapy model and ultimately by the contemporary mediation ideal. As the formal role of social workers evolved, so did their ideology and rhetoric. Consistent throughout the evolution of social workers' involvement with divorce, however, has been their perception that their appropriate function is to make divorce as conflict-free as possible, or at least to manage the conflict appropriately. . . .

"Currently, the language of the helping professions portrays divorce as an "emotional crisis" that has to be treated, but that can also be an occasion that provides some "unique opportunities for growth." In the rhetoric of the social workers, divorce is a crisis within the "family system"-type of "situational" crisis to be "managed." Although the profession no longer sees divorce as pathological, a negative impact on the family system is viewed as inevitable. The focus of the helping professional, under this view of divorce, is on both alleviating the initial "trauma" of divorce and managing the "external variables" that may affect the family's future "response and adjustment to divorce."

"The goal of the helping professional is to bring the parties to the recognition that the "structural dimensions" of their former marital system have not disappeared but must be reshaped into a new, though limited, "post-dissolution organization." This new organization is based on the relationship between the parents—now ex-spouses—with parent-child relationships as "sub-systems" within this paradigm. Divorce requires parents to "decouple from their former marital and nuclear roles and begin to recouple at a level of shared parenting responsibilities."

"In this framework, the role of the system is to be therapeutic—to facilitate and assist the family in adapting to a new post-divorce family structure. Attorneys, in this context, are viewed as ill-equipped to handle the crisis because of their adversarial orientation and the ways in which they impede or defeat the therapeutic ideal. By contrast, social workers and others in the helping professions are in possession or control of the therapeutic process.

C. Opportunity Seized: The Rhetorical War

"As their involvement with divorce cases through conciliation counseling and court-ordered custody evaluations increased, social workers rejected the lawyer/social worker partnership that they had initially espoused. Within the context of divorce generally—and disputed custody cases particularly—helping professionals challenged central aspects of legal ideology. With the elimination of fault-based divorce and the advent of their crisis theory of divorce, helping professionals began to assert that adversarial concepts and procedures were inappropriate for resolving divorce and custody cases. Social workers objected to the very nature of the adversarial process, asserting that it was unnecessary, inappropriate, and indicative of the outmoded notions of "winning" or "losing" custody. Divorce was a crisis to be worked through; conflict was to be recognized and managed. Spouses (with the aid of a social worker) were to be self-determining and exercise their responsibility to each other and their children to settle their differences so they could function as post-divorce parents. There simply was no room for such growth in the traditional adversarial system. Lawyers' use of adversarial procedures were especially criticized for its effect on children. In essence, social workers' attacks questioned both the appropriateness of the representation ideal and adversariness as a process by which fact-finding and decisionmaking occur.

"The helping professions tend to distinguish two aspects of divorce—the emotional divorce, which involves "feelings," and the legal divorce, which involves a division of property, a determination of support, and a decision about custody. Social workers view the legal divorce as secondary to the emotional divorce. Thus, once an emotional divorce has occurred, the legal divorce is pro forma; conversely, without an emotional divorce, no true separation can or will occur and the parties will continue to battle throughout and after the legal divorce. Some form of counseling, therapy, or mediation is seen as essential to a resolution of these emotional issues, with postdivorce shared parenting as the optimal goal.

"In this regard, social workers argued that an adversarial role was unnecessary—lawyers were not needed to prove grounds for divorce as they had been under the fault-based system. Similarly, social workers viewed lawyers as unconcerned with, and incompetent to perform, the needed therapeutic function. Lawyers could not be discarded altogether, however, as some issues still needed legal resolution. The social work literature explicitly expressed the competition between the professions, with legal personnel cast as inappropriate decisionmakers in custody cases due to their lack of training in child development and psychology.

"Although it was initially thought that no-fault divorce would eliminate conflict, social workers' involvement with the system convinced them that this legal change had no such transformative effect. In the custody area, in particular, conflict was still apparent . . .

"Social workers' criticisms of the existing no-fault system formed the basis of calls for an alternative system, reflecting even more procedural and substantive changes, such as mediation and the establishment of a shared parenting norm. These reforms were urged in rhetoric that embodied their view of litigation, conflict, and what is desirable in the post-divorce family.

"The calls for change were accompanied by assertions about what was "really" happening in the divorce context. That reality was psychological, not legal, in its focus. According to mental health professionals, the desire to litigate divorce issues, particularly custody, is the product of unresolved feelings about the termination of the marriage. Intervention by a helping professional is necessary to assist a couple in resolving these feelings so that they do not engage in protracted litigation as the extension of their emotional battles. The helping professionals' view is that litigation is harmful to all, particularly children, and that it is usually undertaken without any true legal or factual justification.

"Moreover, results achieved under a sole custody legal doctrine were objectionable from the viewpoint of social workers' "family-systems" theory. Rather than focusing on the best parent, the social worker concentrated on how to "restructure" the family. Restructuring meant allowing both parents to continue their parental relationship with the children. When forced to choose between parents, helping professionals preferred the parent who would most freely allow the child access to the other parent. The notion of "the most generous parent" became synonymous with the determination of who was the better parent.

"Given social workers' assumptions, their criticisms of the legal system, and their characterization of the divorce, it is no surprise that mediation by those trained in the helping professions emerged as the logical procedural solution. If disputed custody was really an emotional event, and the legal system and lawyers had no ability to address the problems, then a new process and new personnel were necessary. Social workers' criticisms of legal decisionmakers, processes, and results were essential to the formulation of the mediation ideal. . . .

V.   THE MANNER OF APPROPRIATION: THE USE OF NARRATIVE STRATEGIES AND THE INTERSECTION OF OTHER INTERESTS

"I believe that the rhetoric and strategy of the helping professions have been successful for two related reasons. First, the helping professions have presented their arguments in the form of "stories" that contain powerful images that are readily understood by those not familiar with the custody decisionmaking process. Second, the images that they project intersect and are compatible with the interests of significant societal groups that have facilitated the changes suggested by the stories.

A.   Narrative Strategies

One of the significant methods by which the helping professions' ideals became dominant in the custody area was through the construction and manipulation of rhetorical visions or narratives. I call these rhetorical devices narratives because they are stories with a beginning, a middle, and an end. These is competition and drama—tension and resolution—in these narratives. Their "morals" are ways of legitimating one type of substantive and procedural result to the exclusion of others. In describing or illustrating a "problem," they also suggest the "solution." This form of presentation makes the professional standards of the helping professions and the legal system concrete, understandable, and susceptible to positive action. This rhetorical strategy operates by presenting simplistic dichotomous images: negative images or "horror stories" regarding the existing (lawyer-controlled) divorce practice, and corresponding positive images or "fairy tales" of an idealized (social worker-controlled) process for purer and better decisionmaking.

"These narratives had an additional characteristic that operated to the helping professions' advantage in securing changes. They were cast in terms of mere substitution of decisionmakers rather than of alteration of results. They focused on divorce as a discrete event that had to be made less volatile through the use of trained mediators. These narratives either assumed or ignored and obscured the desirability of the substantive goal of shared parenting. The narratives confined the discussion to the desirability of a change in procedure without revealing that this would also produce a change in substance compatible with the new decisionmakers' professional ideology and norms.

"The use of rhetorical devices serves the institutional interests of those in the mediation business who wish to stake out an area for their own control. Their language, which is cast as neutral and professional, is political. This fact has been obscured, however, because their rhetoric has confined the debate to a procedural level.

1. The Horror Story.—The image of the legal system constructed by the helping professions is adversarial, combative, and productive of divisions, misunderstandings, and hostility. These negative characterizations are understood to be the inevitable product of a system controlled by attorneys and the judiciary. Social workers assert that lawyers focus on rights, claims, due process, and other things "peripheral" to the real issues.

"Those who flock to mediation as the ideal decisionmaking mechanism accuse lawyers and the adversary system of increasing trauma, escalating conflict, obstructing communication, failing to perceive the need for negotiation and counseling, and generally interfering with the development of a process that could help the parties. In their vision, the adversarial system, with its emphasis on conflict and rationality, is inherently unresponsive to the "emotions" and "feelings" associated with the divorce process, which social workers believe are more important and worthy of concern.

"Lawyers in general and judges in particular are viewed as poorly trained to deal with the psychological aspects of divorce. Because they employ what is described as "militant tunnel-vision advocacy" as a result of their "temperament and training," lawyers cannot possibly make a "success of . . . divorce." Lawyers and judges are seen as acting on their own biases and values in determining what is in the best interest of the child. A related criticism is that lawyers replace the parties in the negotiation process and thereby fail to enhance the conflict management skills of the parties and to produce agreements to which the parties are committed. Lawyers are criticized for dwelling on the past, laying blame, finding fault, and failing to focus on future conduct as do mediators. In this way, social workers' rhetoric lays the basis for their claim to control of the process. . . .

"The generic horror story therefore involves a husband, wife and child(ren) who enter the divorce process, employing two lawyers (his and hers). There is escalating bitterness, pain, and suffering. More and more money is expended. The child(ren) is(are) particularly hurt by the process, particularly since he/she(they) lose(s) a parent in the process (the "noncustodial" parent). It is a process in which there are "winners" and "losers." In other words, it seems inevitable that there will be an unhappy ending to this narrative.

2. The Fairy Tale.—In contrast to the negative images embodied in the horror stories describing the legal process, the helping professions present themselves as a distinct and preferable alternative. The ideal is established rhetorically.

"Social workers view divorce as occasioning the birth of an ongoing, albeit different, relationship, with mediators and social workers as its midwives and monitors. "Let's talk about it" seems to be the ideal, and the talk is envisioned as continuing for decades. The continued involvement is not only with each other but with the legal system as well. This ideal is obviously very different from the traditional legal system, which seeks an end or termination of a significant interaction at divorce: a division, distribution, or allocation of the things acquired during marriage—an emancipatory model—and with its "ending," the permission for a "new life" for the participants and the withdrawal of active legal interference in their relationship. . . .

"In this way, social workers and mediators set apart the concerns of the adversarial system and subordinate them to the more important concerns of their own professions. Caring, sharing, mental health, and concern for future functioning, they assert, are their exclusive preserve and cannot be attained through the adversarial process.

"In this contrasting generic fairy tale narrative, husband, wife, and child(ren) consult not two lawyers but one mediator; only one is necessary because the process is nonadversarial. The process is characterized by cooperation, caring and acceptance. It costs less money and produces a fairer result. This is obviously a narrative with a happy ending. . . .

VI. PRACTICAL CONSEQUENCES

A. Assessing the Narratives

"The discourse of the helping professions has created rather than reflected reality. In part, helping professionals have been successful in appropriating the divorce business for themselves because, in the abstract, they offer hope to those who have been hurt by divorce and custody battles. The "reality" that they construct through their rhetoric is one that many want to believe exists.

"The realistic assessment of the "fairy tale" narrative, however, is that there will be no happy ending; in fact, there will be no ending at all. The narrative assumes an ongoing relationship between the spouses—not an ending—a fact that is not apparent in the presentation of the typical adversary system versus mediation.

"The costs associated with such non-endings are also hidden. Traditional divorce was an emancipatory process that terminated the relationship and freed lives for rebuilding. The social workers' ideal of an ongoing co-parental relationship may leave little room for the formation of new relationships by parents or by children. Children may in fact suffer more from these non-endings. They may never be able to overcome the quite typical fantasy that mommy and daddy will get back together. It is not clear that non-endings will in fact be "happy" in any significant number of family situations.

"Non-endings do benefit mediators, however, who assert that only they can achieve reorganization of families (the process that produces happy non-endings). In the view of the social worker, mediation is in the first instance designated as a superior process based on informality that can therefore give full protection to the privacy and autonomy of the parties by allowing them to make important decisions for themselves. The ideal process takes place within a context of open communication and protects against the parties having issues decided for them through lawyers' adversarial tricks.

"Yet the supposed benefits of mediation are not all process related. It is also argued that the purpose of mediation—to reorient the parties toward one another—is substantially different from, and superior to, the legal ideal. Mediation discourages the focus on legal rights and seeks to help the divorcing parties achieve a new and shared post-divorce relationship, in which they redirect their attitude and disposition toward one another for post-divorce shared parenting. The ideal product of the process, in the rhetoric of the helping professions, is a restructuring of the relationship of the adults, rather than its termination. . . .

"The implications of this approach are enormous. Not only does this represent a serious decision about who it is that ultimately makes custody decisions—judge, attorney, or mediator-social worker—but, because of the inherent nature of the mediator/shared parenting ideal, adoption of this approach represents a significant opportunity for continuous and substantial intervention by social workers or other court-associated personnel. The goals of the helping professions are at odds with the traditional legal goal of divorce. Nothing is "terminated," except the formal marital bond between the adults. Because the family unit theoretically continues, it may often be in need of the services and communication skills provided by the mediator alternative to the adversarial system. Potentially, therefore, the legal system's involvement will not end either, at least until all the children reach adulthood. Coercive and continuous supervision of the restructured unit is compatible with this view. There are no legal or doctrinal impediments to reactivating the mediation system. If things are not operating to the satisfaction of one ex-spouse, the mediation mechanism can be reengaged to work things out.

"This narrative non-ending has been uncritically incorporated into reform rhetoric concerning the legal system. Recent changes in custody rules, particularly those setting forth presumptions of joint custody, are consistent with the rhetoric and the non-ending it advocates. The acceptance of this nontermination ideal is also associated to some extent with the imposition of other ideals onto family law, including the goals of equality, gender neutrality, and social restructuring. Concern with these abstract goals may overtake the desire to reach workable and practical decisions upon divorce. The entire area is permeated with symbolism that relates only tangentially to the realities of divorce.

"Ultimately, the helping professions' discourse has encompassed and absorbed traditional legal dialogue concerning custody. "Sharing" became identified as the public and political language of the escalating debate over the appropriate concept and process for resolving custody disputes. The political victory of the helping professions is manifested by the conferring of legally significant rights and obligations, through the explicit delegation of decisionmaking authority to the social workers and mediators. Legislatures and the judiciary have delegated this power both on an institutional level, as with the creation of mandatory mediation or counseling services staffed with social workers and connected to the court system, and in individual cases, in which judges seek and accept the advice of "experts" in the helping profession. This formal recognition of the helping professions' role places the state's imprimatur on their appropriation of custody decisionmaking.

B. The Politics of Rhetoric

"Lost in the rhetoric of the social worker are real concerns. There is little or no appreciation of the many real problems that joint custody and the ideal of sharing and caring can cause. The prospect of a continued relationship with an ex-spouse may be horrifying to contemplate, but the sharing ideal assumes that a relationship between the noncustodial parent and the child cannot proceed without it. Also unsettling is the extent to which allegations of mistreatment, abuse, or neglect on the part of husbands toward either their wives or children are trivialized, masked, or lost amid the psychological rhetoric that reduces mothers' desires to have custody and control of their children to pathology....

"Because social workers and others sympathetic to mediation have created and controlled the presentation of both narratives, the real nature of the competition between the legal and therapeutic models has been hidden. Notably, there are no parallel scenarios involving vindictive or greedy husbands in the mediation literature. No alternative narrative, sympathetic to single parent or sole custody and control, has gained any credibility in the literature. Nor do many stories assign different characters to the stock "victim" and "villain" roles.

"Further, by branding opposition to mediation and joint custody as the manifestation of a psychological problem to which mediation is itself the solution, mediation rhetoric forecloses any effective expression of women's legitimate concerns. As things now stand, the cries of protest over the imposition of a joint custody or shared parenting solution from mothers who will be assuming primary care for their children (but sharing control) are attributed to the fact that these mothers have not accomplished an "emotional divorce." As soon as they are able to get over "their issues" they will be able to begin "rational problem solving" and will cooperate agreeably.

"The social workers' discourse accepts without criticism the superiority of "rational decisionmaking" within the new, reconstructed family structure. Through this method, the "vindictive" woman is thwarted, the "victimized" man allowed to continue to operate as paternal familius (in an altered form, of course) by being given "equal rights" without the formal imposition of responsibility. The helping professionals believe this approach remedies the pro-mother imbalance that has existed in custody decision-making."

CHAPTER THREE

THIRD PARTY EVALUATION, FACT-FINDING, AND OMBUDSMEN

1. INTRODUCTION

There are forms of dispute resolution that utilize third parties other than mediators to help parties reach an agreement. For example, sometimes a third party is enlisted as an evaluator or appraiser. In that event, the third party is brought in to make an evaluation based on his or her professional expertise. Third parties have been used as appraisers and evaluators in many contexts, sometimes at the behest of the court and sometimes by agreement of the parties. For example, a court might ask a psychologist to evaluate a child in a contested child custody case to help the court determine the best interests of the child. Or, in an action for partition, parties might agree to obtain a valuation of the jointly-owned property by a professional real estate appraiser. In such circumstances, the third party can help the parties resolve their dispute not because the third party induces the parties to agree but because the third party applies her own expertise to an issue that divides them. The effectiveness of the third party is a function of the respect and trust that the parties place in the third party's expertise.

Another type of dispute resolution device that utilizes third party neutrals is a fact-finder. Individual fact-finders or fact-finding panels are often utilized to resolve disputes in which the government is a party, or disputes which could have an adverse impact on the public interest. Frequently, legislation requires the use of a fact-finder to resolve disputes of these types. For example, labor legislation governing the railroads, the airlines, and most public sector employees call for fact-finding panels to investigate labor disputes once they reach a certain level of severity. The same legislation usually calls upon the panels to make their findings public. The goal of this legislation is to mobilize public opinion to put pressure on the parties to settle the dispute in accord with the fact-finders' report.

Some aspects of fact-finding are described in the passage that follows:

Factfinding by Leo Kanowitz [1]

"A factfinder's role differs from that of a mediator's in a number of respects. For one thing, although the factfinder's recommendations are

1. Leo Kanowitz, *Factfinding*, in ALTERNATIVE DISPUTE RESOLUTION (1985). Reprinted with permission.

publicized, the mediator's are not. (For an exception in the area of mediation, see Cal. Civ. Code § 4607(a), examined in McLaughlin, supra, which exception suggests that the California legislature may have misla-belled what was essentially a hybrid process—mediation and factfinding combined—as strictly mediation.) For another, it is contemplated that factfinding proceedings will result in the issuance of specific recommenda-tions for a just, fair or reasonable resolution of the parties' dispute. By contrast, although mediators sometimes make specific recommendations to the parties, generally these are couched in terms of suggestions or ques-tions. Thus, a factfinder might, in a given case, properly recommend that a public employer raise the wages of its employees by $100 per month and publicize that recommendation. A mediator, in the same case, would ask the parties if an increase of $100 per month strikes them as a satisfactory way of resolving their dispute, and neither that question nor their response would become a matter of public knowledge.

"In many respects, nonbinding factfinding also resembles advisory arbitration. The essential difference, however, is that the results of adviso-ry arbitration are not publicized. By contrast, in nonbinding factfinding, publication is an essential element of the process, especially in public sector collective bargaining.

"At times, factfinding is conducted by a single factfinder. At other times, a larger group, such as a tripartite factfinding board, conducts the hearing and makes its recommendations on the basis of the facts found. It is not unusual for factfinders, whether a single person or a larger group, to issue multiple recommendations, some of which favor or adopt the position of one party, while others favor or adopt the position of the opposing party. Thus, in negotiations over a new contract between a teachers' union and a local school district, impasse might have been reached on whether, and how much of, a wage increase should be granted by the employer, whether teachers are entitled to preparation time during working hours, and over questions concerning holiday pay, vacations, fringe benefits and the like. After factfinding has been completed, the factfinder's might recommend that the position of the teachers be adopted on the issue of wages, but that of the school district on the issue of preparation time."

* * *

Another type of third party intervention in disputes that is utilized with increasing frequently in both the public and private sectors is an ombudsperson. Ombudspeople are primarily found in large organizations or government. Often they are employed to deal with employment disputes, or with disputes between a governmental agency and the public. Some corpo-rations have utilized ombudspeople to deal with consumer complaints as well.

The role of the ombudsperson is described in the passage that follows:

The Ombudsman by Linda Singer [2]

"In-house neutrals most often are called 'ombudsmen' or 'ombudspeople.' Although in the classic Scandinavian model, the ombudsman never works for the institution he or she is supposed to oversee, in this country the ombudsperson concept has appeared most frequently since the late 1960s as part of the management of a public or private organization. Here, the ombudsperson is considered a neutral member of the corporate structure, located outside the normal managerial chain of command and reporting directly to the president of the organization. The person's job is to help resolve work-related disputes through informal counseling, mediation, or, more rarely, investigation and recommendations to management.

"Perhaps because of the difficulty in combining these responsibilities with other duties to the same employer, ombudspeople have been used primarily in large corporations and universities. (However, there is no reason smaller companies could not contract with an outside neutral for more flexible, part-time service.) Approximately 200 large corporations, including McDonald's, Control Data, Federal Express, IBM, American Optical Company, AT & T Information Systems, and the Bank of America, have in-house neutrals. There are an additional 100 ombudsperson offices in colleges and universities. Recently the Internal Revenue Service established an ombudsperson to help resolve taxpayers' problems with the IRS.

"According to Mary Rowe, who has served as ombudsperson at the Massachusetts Institute of Technology for the past fourteen years, her functions cover a broad range: simply listening to employees' concerns on a confidential basis (often at night on the telephone or at restaurants or other places outside of work) and giving advice on how difficult situations might be dealt with by the people themselves; acting as a go-between between employees and their supervisors; conducting face-to-face mediation; and performing formal investigation and reporting to the university's president. More than nine out of ten corporate neutrals were chosen from within their organizations, generally because they already were seen as natural mediators. In explaining how they can be neutral when they work for the employer who is part of a dispute, these people say that their job is to assure employees of fair process and that their loyalty to the employer is satisfied when they settle disputes among employees evenhandedly.

"Ombudspeople attempt to assure employees not only that they are neutral but that they will keep all communications confidential and help to protect complaining employees from reprisals. In this regard, virtually all in-house neutrals accept anonymous complaints from employees. When dealing with sensitive areas, such as sexual harassment, experienced neutrals have found many employees embarrassed to have their identities revealed. On the other hand, it may not be practical to try to resolve some types of problems (such as complaints of nonpromotion) without determining the identity of the complainant."

* * *

2. Linda Singer, *The Ombudsman,* in
SETTLING DISPUTES, Reprinted with permission.

Some of the legal issues that arise in the use of third party neutrals as evaluators, fact-finders and ombudspersons parallel the issues we saw in Chapter 2 in the context of mediation. However, as the following cases illustrate, there are also issues that are unique to each of the particular roles that third-party play in resolving disputes.

2. LEGAL EFFECT OF AGREEMENT TO UTILIZE THIRD-PARTY EVALUATOR

AMF Incorporated v. Brunswick Corporation

621 F.Supp. 456 (S.D.N.Y. 1985).

■ WEINSTEIN, CHIEF JUDGE.

In this case of first impression, AMF Incorporated seeks to compel Brunswick Corporation to comply with their agreement to obtain a non-binding advisory opinion in a dispute over the propriety of advertising claims. For reasons indicated below, the agreement to utilize an alternative dispute resolution mechanism must be enforced.

I. FACTS

AMF and Brunswick compete nationally in the manufacture of electronic and automatic machinery used for bowling centers. In earlier litigation before this court, AMF alleged that Brunswick had advertised certain automatic scoring devices in a false and deceptive manner. Brunswick responded with counterclaims regarding advertisements for AMF's pinspotter, bowling pins and automatic scorer. In 1983 the parties ended the litigation with a settlement agreement filed with the court. Any future dispute involving an advertised claim of "data based comparative superiority" of any bowling product would be submitted to an advisory third party, the National Advertising Division ("NAD") of the Council of Better Business Bureaus, to determine whether there was experimental support for the claim.

Paragraph 9 of the agreement reads as follows:

> If either party shall hereafter publish or disseminate any claim by advertisement or promotional materials of any kind or nature, which expressly or impliedly refer to a comparative superiority of a bowling product manufactured, sold or distributed by either of them, as compared to a similar product manufactured, sold or distributed by the other, which claim shall expressly or impliedly be based on data, studies or tests (hereafter "data based comparative superiority") such claims shall be subject to the provisions of this paragraph. . . .

> Should either party make a claim to data based comparative superiority, the other may request that substantiation for the same be delivered to the agreed upon advisory third party, subject to the provisions of

this agreement, whereupon the party who has made the claim shall promptly comply.

Both parties agree to submit any controversy which they may have with respect to data based comparative superiority of any of their products over that of the other to such advisory third party for the rendition of an advisory opinion. Such opinion shall not be binding upon the parties, but shall be advisory only. . . .

NAD was created in 1971 by the American Advertising Federation, American Association of Advertising Agencies, Association of National Advertisers, and the Council of Better Business Bureaus "to help sustain high standards of truth and accuracy in national advertising." It monitors television, radio, and print advertising, and responds to complaints from individual consumers, consumer groups, local Better Business Bureaus, competitors, professional and trade associations, and state and federal agencies. If NAD finds that the advertising claims are unsupported, and the advertiser refuses to modify or discontinue the advertising, the organization will complain to the appropriate governmental authority. See Statement of Organization and Procedures of the National Advertising Review Board, at ¶ 2.1A. Voluntary compliance with NAD's decisions has been universal. Reportedly no advertiser who has participated in the complete process of a NAD investigation and NARB appeal has declined to abide by the decision.

In March and April 1985, Brunswick advertised its product, Armor Plate 3000, in a trade periodical called Bowler's Journal. Armor Plate is a synthetic laminated material used to make bowling lanes. It competes with the wood lanes produced by AMF. "The wood lane. A relic of the past," claims the advertisement, under a sketch of a horse and buggy. It goes on to detail the advantages of Armor Plate; and, as indicated in the footnote to the advertisement, strongly suggests that research supports the claim of durability as compared to wood lanes.

By replacing your worn out wood lanes with Armor Plate 3000, Brunswick's high tech laminated surface, what you're doing is saving money. Up to $500.00 per lane per year in lost revenue and upkeep.

That's because today's high technology has helped make Armor Plate 3000 so tough and good looking that it seems to last forever.*

AMF, disputing the content of the advertisement, sought from Brunswick the underlying research data referred to in the footnote. Brunswick replied that having undertaken the expense of research it would not make the results available to AMF. Thereupon AMF informed Brunswick that it was invoking Paragraph 9 of the settlement agreement and requested that Brunswick provide substantiation to an independent third party. Brunswick responded that its advertisement did not fall within the terms of the

---

* Continuing independent research projects that Armor Plate 3000 will now last over twenty years before the possible need arises to replace a small lane area much like replacing a broken board in a wood lane.

agreement. AMF now brings this action to compel Brunswick to submit its data to the NAD for nonbinding arbitration.

II.   THE AGREEMENT COVERS THE DISPUTE

The agreement on its face covers the dispute. It provides, in relevant part, that:

> If either party shall [1] *hereafter* publish or disseminate any claim by advertisement or promotional materials of any kind or nature, which [2] expressly or *impliedly refers to a comparative superiority* of a bowling product manufactured, sold or distributed by either of them, as compared to a similar product manufactured, sold or distributed by the other, [3] which claim shall expressly or *impliedly* be *based on data, studies or tests* (hereafter "data based comparative superiority") [4] such *claims shall be subject to the provisions of this* paragraph....

The advertisement (1), was published after the agreement of June 30, 1983. It (2), impliedly refers to comparative superiority of a Brunswick bowling product over one of AMF. It is (3), impliedly based on data and tests. Thus (4), the dispute is subject to the agreement.

The agreement also provides for a method of substantiation of the claim without resort to litigation. It reads:

> Should either party make a claim to data based comparative superiority, the other may request that substantiation for the same be delivered to the agreed upon advisory third party, subject to the provisions of this agreement, whereupon the party who has made the claim shall promptly comply.

> Both parties agree to submit any controversy which they may have with respect to data based comparative superiority of any of their products over that of the other to such advisory third party for the rendition of an advisory opinion. Such opinion shall not be binding upon the parties, but shall be advisory only....

The agreement specifies NAD as the appropriate third party. It states:

> The parties agree that the National Advertising Division of the Council of Better Business is agreeable to each as the advisory third party. Should NAD not agree to undertake any such advisory opinion, the parties undertake to mutually agree upon other procedures for the review of advertising claims.

NAD has agreed to undertake to examine the data and render an opinion.

III.   LAW

[First the Court considered whether the Federal Arbitration Act applied to the settlement agreement. The court concluded that even though the agreement differed from most notions of arbitration because it did not provide an effective alternative to litigation, it satisfied the policy underlying the FAA. Then, in the alternative, the Court considered whether the parties' *contract to utilize an alternative dispute resolution mechanism was enforceable under New York law.]*

B.   Contract to Employ an Alternative Dispute–Resolution Mechanism

1.   Consent Agreements as Enforceable Contracts

Whether or not the agreement be deemed one to arbitrate, it is an enforceable contract to utilize a confidential advisory process in a matter of serious concern to the parties. The agreement may be enforced in equity. Through the equitable relief of specific performance Brunswick may be compelled to surrender its "comparative data based" information to the NAD for inquiry as to deceptiveness.

The law of New York would apply since the settlement agreement was executed and filed in New York. . . . (citations omitted).

New York would be likely to enforce such an agreement whose practical commercial benefits to both parties is so clear. In the memorable language of Judge Cardozo granting equitable relief in a contract action:

> The law has outgrown its primitive stage of formalism when the precise word was the sovereign talisman, and every slip was fatal. It takes a broader view today. . . . [T]he whole writing may be "instinct with an obligation," imperfectly expressed. . . .

Wood v. Lucy, Lady Duff–Gordon, 222 N.Y. 88, 118 N.E. 214 (1917).

If the agreement's force is found in the fact that it was part of a settlement of a *federal* litigation so that, arguably, federal law applies, the result is no different. The Second Circuit has recently made clear the strong public policy requiring agreements between parties in settlement of litigation to be construed as enforceable contracts. See Berger v. Heckler, 771 F.2d 1556, 1568, (2d Cir.1985). . . .

The fact that the agreement terminating the litigation was not formally signed by the court does not affect enforceability. It is the agreement terminating the litigation, rather than the court's imprimatur, that gives rise to the obligation.

The settlement agreement evinces a clear intent by both parties to require confidential submission to the NAD of disputes concerning advertised data-based claims of superiority. This settlement facilitated the termination of AMF's lawsuit and Brunswick's counterclaim. Both parties bargained for and benefited from the stipulation.

2.   Equity Jurisdiction

Untenable is the defendant's argument that there is an adequate remedy at law so that equity is without jurisdiction. Specific performance is available as a remedy where the remedy at law is not appropriate if such equitable relief will not force a "vain order." See, e.g., Union Pacific Railroad Co. v. Chicago, R.I. & P. Co., 163 U.S. 564, 16 S.Ct. 1173, 41 L.Ed. 265 (1896); Pennington v. Ziman, 13 A.D.2d 769, 216 N.Y.S.2d 1 (1st Dep't 1961); Restatement (Second) of Contracts, §§ 357–366 (1981).

The agreement itself recognized that the legal process would not adequately address the parties' needs. Through their contract the parties have identified an "injury" sufficient to require the dispute resolution mechanism they thought most appropriate.

The alternative dispute resolution (ADR) procedure agreed upon in the settlement is designed to reduce the acrimony associated with protracted litigation and to improve the chances of resolving future advertising disputes. This form of ADR is designed to keep disputes of this kind out of court.

The value of this settlement agreement lies largely in the particular experience and skill of the NAD as a resolver of disputes. In the fourteen years since its formation, the NAD has developed its own process of reviewing complaints of deceptiveness, coupling relative informality and confidentiality with safeguards to ensure procedural fairness. See NAD Guide for Advertisers and Advertising Agencies, attached to Petitioner AMF's Supplemental Brief in Support of Its Petition for Arbitration as Exhibit 2. As the NAD puts it: "Speed, informality and modest cost are three chief benefits of [this] self-regulatory system." Id. at 3. To these advantages of the special ADR system designed by the parties is added the unique ability of the NAD to decide what is fair in advertising. A judge might make this inquiry, but ultimately it would have to defer to the very expertise that NAD offers without resort to the courts.

General public policy favors support of alternatives to litigation when these alternatives serve the interests of the parties and of judicial administration. Here AMF and Brunswick agreed in June 1983 that a special ADR mechanism would serve them better than litigation. Such decisions are encouraged by no less an observer than the Chief Justice of the United States. In his words, ADR devices are often superior to litigation "in terms of cost, time, and human wear and tear." Remarks of Warren E. Burger, Chief Justice of the United States, at the Twin Cities Advisory Council of the American Arbitration Association, St. Paul, Minn., August 21, 1985....

As suggested by the "Plan for Court–Annexed Arbitration, United States District Court, Eastern District of New York," effective January 1, 1986, the specific policy of this court is to enforce ADR agreements. In most instances they reduce the need for court trials and save clients time and money.

A remedy at law would be inadequate since it could only approximate the skilled, speedy and inexpensive efforts available by way of specific performance. A law suit would deny AMF the practical specialized experience that the parties agreed to have available for an examination of data-based comparative advertising. A court decision and an NAD decision would have different effects on the parties' reputations within the bowling products industry. In short, a remedy at law falls short of providing many of the advantages of specific performance.

To deem specific performance "a vain order" would be to say that AMF and Brunswick settled their earlier litigation with a nullity. This characterization of a valid settlement agreement filed in court is unwarranted....

IV.   CONCLUSION

The new advertisement is not so explicit in denigrating the competitor's product as the former advertisements that were subject to the prior litigation. But for the readers—purchasers of bowling alleys—the effect is much the same. The current dispute is at least as important to the parties as the former one that resulted in litigation, a settlement, and an agreement on a process for resolving further disputes about advertising.

AMF's petition to compel the submission of data pursuant to Paragraph 9 of the settlement agreement of June 30, 1983 is enforceable under the Federal Arbitration Act and pursuant to this court's equity jurisdiction.

So Ordered.

* * *

Questions

1.   Why is there no adequate remedy at law in the *AMF* case? What would the remedy at law be? Is it adequate?

2.   How does the court address the defendant's concern that it is being ordered to engage in a "vain" act? Is it vain for the court to compel a defendant to participate in a proceeding that will yield, at most, a non-binding advisory opinion by a third-party?

3.   What is the court's views of alternative dispute resolution? To what extent does the court's decision depend upon its views?

* * *

3.   LEGAL STATUS OF FACT-FINDING REPORT

Jeffery v. Weintraub

648 P.2d 914 (Wash. Ct. of Appls. 1982).

■ RINGOLD, JUDGE.

The defendants (homeowners), owners of 13 floating homes moored at a facility[1] owned and operated by plaintiffs Gordon Jeffery and Margaret Jeffery (Jeffery), appeal a summary judgment for unpaid increases in moorage fees (rent). Jeffery cross-appeals the award of a single statutory

---

1.   The moorage facility, located at Lake Union in Seattle, extends some 310 feet from shore. Jeffery owns the submerged land within 160 feet from shore, and leases the remaining 150 feet from the State of Washington.

attorneys fee in the consolidated superior court proceeding. We affirm the judgment of the superior court, but modify the effective date of the rent increase and remand for redetermination of statutory attorneys fees.

On May 29, 1979, Jeffery gave notice to the homeowners that moorage rates would increase approximately 20 percent, or $30 per month, effective July 1, 1979. The homeowners then petitioned the City of Seattle for fact-finding pursuant to Ordinance 107012.[2] A fact-finder was appointed on July

---

2. Ordinance 107012, known as the "Equity Ordinance," was codified at Seattle Municipal Code ch. 7.20 and provided in pertinent part as follows: "Section 4. If a floating home owner believes that a demanded moorage fee increase is unreasonable, such floating home owner, or any group of similarly affected floating home owners, may file a Petition for Fact-Finding with the Mayor. Such petition shall be filed within fifteen days of receipt by such floating home owner or owners of written notification of such moorage fee increase.... "Section 5. After the filing of a Petition for Fact–Finding, the Mayor shall within seven days notify the floating home moorage owner of such filing and shall within fifteen days of the filing of such petition appoint a qualified person from a panel approved by the American Arbitration Association to conduct fact-finding proceedings to consider the justification and reasonableness of the demanded moorage fee increase.... "Section 6. The fact-finder shall conduct a public hearing for the purpose of making a factual determination as to whether the demanded moorage or increase is reasonable in amount. The moorage owner or operator, whichever would benefit from the demanded moorage fee increase, shall be required to be present at the hearing. The reasonableness of the moorage fee increase shall be evaluated upon the basis of whether such moorage fee constitutes a fair and reasonable return upon the current value of the property of the owner of the floating home moorage which is devoted to such use, and in making such evaluation the fact-finder, in addition to any other factors he or she deems relevant, shall consider the following factors: '(1) increases or decreases in the Consumer Price Index for residential rents in Seattle, Washington as determined by the United States Department of Labor, Bureau of Labor Statistics; '(2) increases or decreases in property taxes placed upon the floating home moorage; '(3) increases or decreases in the expenses of operation and maintenance of the floating home moorage, provided that such expenses are for services, repairs, property maintenance, utilities, or any other such expenses which are necessary or reasonable for the continued operation of a floating home moorage. '(4) the reasonable costs of capital improvements to the floating home moorage property which benefit the floating home owners occupying moorage sites at such floating home moorage. '(5) increases or decreases in necessary or desirable services furnished by the floating home moorage owner or operator where such increased or decreased services affect the person or persons initiating the fact-finding proceedings. '(6) substantial deterioration in the facilities provided for the occupants of moorage sites at such floating home moorage due to failure of the floating home moorage owner or operator to perform ordinary repairs, replacement and maintenance of the floating home moorage property and improvements. '(7) the current fair market value of the floating home moorages. '(8) comparability with moorage fees charged for other floating home moorage sites in the City.' 'Section 7. ... After the completion of such public hearing the fact-finder shall issue a preliminary decision as to the reasonableness of the demanded moorage fee increase.' If the preliminary decision does not support the demanded moorage fee increase in whole or in part, the fact-finder shall call the parties together and suggest a resolution of the moorage fee dispute that is supported by the fact-finder's preliminary decision. If no agreement is reached by the parties, the fact-finder shall issue his final decision as to the reasonableness of the demanded moorage fee increase. The fact-finding proceedings shall be concluded either by agreement or by issuing a final decision within 60 days of the appointment of the fact-finder. No contested moorage fee increase shall take effect until the conclusion of fact-finding proceedings; provided that the moorage owner or operator may recover retroactively such increases as are found reasonable by the fact-finder. At any time during the fact-finding proceeding

9, 1979, and a hearing was held September 5, 1979. The fact-finder in his decision of September 27, 1979, concluded that not only was the proposed increase unreasonable, but "(a)ny increase in the fees currently charged would be unreasonable." Following the fact-finding, Jeffery notified the homeowners that regardless of the fact-finder's decision, the increased rental would take effect on September 8, 1979, with all arrearages due November 1, 1979. The homeowners continued to pay moorage fees but refused to pay the increase.

Jeffery brought 14 separate actions in district court against the delinquent homeowners, which were consolidated by agreement of the parties. Following judgment in Jeffery's favor, 13 of the homeowners appealed to the superior court for a trial de novo. The superior court granted Jeffery's motion for summary judgment and the homeowners appeal.

EFFECT OF FACT–FINDER'S DECISION

The homeowners contend that under the Equity Ordinance, the fact-finder's decision that the increase was unreasonable is binding on the parties and prevents Jeffery from charging an increased fee. They argue that if the city council had not intended the fact-finder's decision to be binding, the ordinance would have explicitly so provided, as in the educational employment relations act, RCW 41.59.120(2), which provides that "the fact-finder shall make findings of fact and recommend terms of settlement . . . which recommendations shall be advisory only."

Our task in construing a statute is to give effect to the intent of the legislature. Janovich v. Herron, 91 Wash.2d 767, 592 P.2d 1096 (1979). We hold that the trial court did not err in concluding that the legislature intended the fact-finder's decision to have no binding effect.[3]

The stated purpose of a statute is an important indicium of legislative intent. Whatcom County v. Langlie, 40 Wash.2d 855, 246 P.2d 836 (1952). The purpose of the ordinance, as expressed in its title, was to establish "a fact-finding process to aid the settlement of disputes over moorage fees between floating home owners and owners of floating home moorages."

---

the parties thereto by mutual voluntary written agreement may request that the fact-finder serve as an arbitrator to finally determine the dispute concerning moorage fees pursuant to R.C.W. 7.04.010 through 7.04.220, and any such arbitration shall be conducted in accordance with the Rules of the American Arbitration Association and judgment on the award may be entered in any court having jurisdiction thereof." Ordinance 107012 became effective December 21, 1977, and was repealed by the passage of Ordinance 109280, effective September 21, 1980. See Seattle Municipal Code, ch. 7.20.

3. In Kennedy v. Seattle, 94 Wash.2d 376, 617 P.2d 713 (1980), not cited by either party here, the Supreme Court upheld the constitutionality of the fact-finding provisions of the Equity Ordinance. Although the Court stated, in describing the ordinance, that "it allows a houseboat owner to have the approval of a fact-finder before any increase in rent can be made by the moorage owner," Id at 380–81, 617 P.2d 713, the issue of the binding effect, if any, of the fact-finder's decision was not before the Court; any implication that the fact-finder's decision is binding is therefore dicta.

The fact-finding is characterized as *aiding* dispute settlement, not as finally settling the dispute.

Statements by the chairperson of the committee in charge of legislation have been used by courts in determining legislative intent. Snow's Mobile Homes, Inc. v. Morgan, 80 Wash.2d 283, 494 P.2d 216 (1972). The chairman's comments indicate that the fact-finder's decision was not intended to be binding on the parties.[4]

UNCONSCIONABILITY

The homeowners next contend that by granting summary judgment to Jeffery the trial court denied them an opportunity to prove that the moorage fee increases were unconscionable, hence unenforceable at law. They cite Schroeder v. Fageol Motors, Inc., 86 Wash.2d 256, 544 P.2d 20 (1975), for the proposition that the issue of unconscionability may not be determined at summary judgment, and argue that they are entitled to a full hearing in order to present evidence of unconscionability.

While the Court in Schroeder, after exploring the concept of unconscionability under the Uniform Commercial Code (UCC),[5] stated at 262, 544 P.2d 20, "In accordance with the requisites set forth above, a court is not

---

4. At the council meeting before the ordinance was passed the chairman stated: "This is where this proposal differs from the original suggestion which had rent arbitration in it. This has a fact-finding process. And, if there is a complaint-it works on a complaint basis-from a floating home owner, they can request this fact-finding process and the owner, or he who benefits from the increase, is obliged to attend this process and justify or explain the proposed rental increase in terms of inflation, tax assessments, improvements to the property, comparable rent structures, etc. And the fact-finder will issue a report at the end stating whether he feels that this is a justifiable increase or not, and if not, why not, and what it should be and in general, try and-if it's too much, convince the owner that it is too much and maybe get an adjustment. In the end the fact-finder does not have the ability to set the rents, but it is felt that (1) a frankly unreasonable increase is less likely if there is this kind of, the prospect of this kind of a process and (2) if you're going to be a bum, you're going to be a bum in public. It's a moral suasion, it (sic) a jawboning kind of process and it is, we are hoping that that will meet the problem."

5. RCW 62A.2–302 provides: *"Unconscionable contract or clause.* (1) If the court as a matter of law finds the contract or any clause of the contract to have been unconscio-

nable at the time it was made the court may refuse to enforce the contract, or it may enforce the remainder of the contract without the unconscionable clause, or it may so limit the application of any unconscionable clause as to avoid any unconscionable result." (2) When it is claimed or appears to the court that the contract or any clause thereof may be unconscionable the parties shall be afforded a reasonable opportunity to present evidence as to its commercial setting, purpose and effect to aid the court in making the determination. "Although the contract in Schroeder v. Fageol Motors, Inc., 86 Wash.2d 256, 544 P.2d 20 (1975), arose under the UCC, the doctrine of unconscionability is available outside the UCC context. See, e.g., Christiansen Bros., Inc. v. State, 90 Wash.2d 872, 586 P.2d 840 (1978); Montgomery Ward & Co., Inc. v. Annuity Board, 16 Wash.App. 439, 556 P.2d 552 (1976). We assume without deciding that a 'reasonable opportunity to present evidence' is required in a non-UCC case as well as one claiming unconscionability under the UCC. Other courts have held, as we do now, that a hearing on a motion for summary judgment gives the parties the 'reasonable opportunity to present evidence'" contemplated under RCW 62A.2–302(2). See Earl M. Jorgensen Co. v. Mark Constr., Inc., 56 Hawaii 466, 540 P.2d 978 (1975), and cases cited therein.

authorized to dispose of this issue under the rules governing summary judgment'', this statement is dicta and not binding on this court. Schroeder was an appeal from a judgment after trial and did not concern a summary judgment. The Court made its statement as part of a general exposition on unconscionability and not as part of its holding. See, e.g., State ex rel. Johnson v. Funkhouser, 52 Wash.2d 370, 325 P.2d 297 (1958).

We see no reason why principles of summary judgment should not apply to test the legal sufficiency of the facts underlying a claim of unconscionability. Although unconscionability is a matter of law to be decided by the trial court, Schroeder 86 Wash.2d at 262, 544 P.2d 20, the decision is one based on the factual circumstances surrounding the transaction in question. Christiansen Bros., Inc. v. State, 90 Wash.2d 872, 586 P.2d 840 (1978). The purpose of summary judgment is to avoid a useless trial where there are no material facts at issue. LaPlante v. State, 85 Wash.2d 154, 531 P.2d 299 (1975). If the material facts are undisputed, and when looked at in the light most favorable to the party alleging unconscionability are insufficient to establish unconscionability, there is no need for the trial court to inquire further. Absent a threshold showing of unconscionability sufficient to survive summary judgment, the issue disappears from the case.

To prevail on summary judgment, the moving party must present facts showing that it is entitled to judgment as a matter of law. Once the initial showing is made, the nonmoving party "must set forth specific facts showing that there is a genuine issue for trial." CR 56(e); LaPlante v. State, supra. Jeffery's uncontroverted affidavit established the amount of the moorage fee increase and the homeowners' refusal to pay it, thereby meeting the initial burden. The homeowners responded with the affidavit of one of the individual homeowners, which contains the following relevant to the claimed unconscionability:

3. Because of a variety of circumstances including, most notably, a number of statutes and regulations restricting and regulating use of the waterfronts in and around Seattle, including Lake Union, there is no legal place to which she can move her floating home. There are not any additional places for existing floating homes in the Seattle area.

4. She has never had any choice as to the moorage fee to be paid to the Moorage Owners for moorage space for her floating home, or as to other terms and conditions of her tenancy. Except for the fact-finding process which enables her to obtain a determination of the reasonableness of the moorage fee demanded by the Moorage Owners, she has never had any ability to bargain about or otherwise have an effect upon the amount of the fee demanded. Her only choice other than through litigation is either to pay the amount demanded or move her floating home, and if she were to remove her floating home, she would have to dismantle it and sell it for scrap as there is no legal place in the area to put it other than where it is presently located.

6. The moorage fee demanded by the Moorage Owners is, under the circumstances, an unreasonable and unconscionable moorage fee, and should not be enforceable.

Jeffery responded with the affidavit of his attorney to the effect that at the time of the increase and continuing to the present there was an established market for the sale of floating homes at prices varying from $40,000 to $80,000, and that as of May 13, 1980, two new houseboat moorages were available for rent in the Portage Bay area. This affidavit also related that the contested increase in moorage fees was less than the corresponding rise in the Consumer Price Index for the same period. The homeowners made no further response.

While the affidavits arguably raise issues of fact, such as the scarcity of moorages and the evanescence of the homeowners' lifestyle, none is material to the issue of unconscionability. What is material, and seems to us dispositive, is the homeowners' failure to set forth unconscionable circumstances at the time of the initial contract, when they first decided to moor their homes at Jeffery's facility. The relevant inquiry when unconscionability is claimed is into the circumstances "at the time the contract is made." Restatement (Second) of Contracts § 208 (1981).[6] The record is barren as to the relative bargaining power of the parties at the time of the initial contract. The homeowners nowhere allege that the specter of moorage fee increases was not foreseeable. Nor do they contend that they were forced to live in floating homes, or that they are prevented from changing their lifestyle if they so choose. We must conclude, on this record, that they had the power, at the time of their initial bargain with Jeffery, to either contract for an acceptable moorage fee schedule or to live elsewhere. See Christiansen Bros. v. State, supra.

Synonyms for unconscionable include "shocking to the conscience" and "monstrously harsh." Montgomery Ward & Co., Inc. v. Annuity Board, 16 Wash.App. 439, 444, 556 P.2d 552 (1976). The moorage fee increase here before us is neither. In the absence of a showing of unconscionability sufficient to merit further inquiry, summary judgment was proper.

STATE ACTION IN VIOLATION OF DUE PROCESS

We understand the homeowners to argue that if state action is present an unreasonable rent increase constitutes a deprivation of property without due process of law. They claim that there was a genuine issue of material fact as to the presence of state action, because the State owns and leases to Jeffery a portion of the land on which the moorage facility is situated. They also point to the statutes and regulations governing shoreline use and argue that the State has given Jeffery monopoly power over the owners of floating homes moored at the facility.

Even if we assume that the State's ownership of part of the submerged land used for the moorage facility brings the fee increase into the realm of state action sufficient to implicate the protections of the Fourteenth

---

6. Although the contract between Jeffery and the homeowners appears at first blush to arise anew each month, we refer to conditions at the time of the initial decision to moor for our determination of conscionability. As the Court stated in Kennedy v. Seattle, supra, "If a houseboat owner is on a moorage and does not violate other portions of the houseboat ordinance, it is impossible for the houseboat owner to be evicted and impossible for the owner of the moorage to use the moorage for the owner's residence." 94 Wash.2d at 386, 617 P.2d 713. The contract is much more akin to a lease from the original date of moorage than a month to month tenancy.

Amendment,[7] the homeowners have not raised a genuine issue of material fact as to the claimed due process violation. But for the bare assertion that imposition of an "unreasonable" moorage fee increase violates the due process clause, the homeowners cite no authority to justify this request for judicial rent control. We will not consider an argument, absent citation of relevant authority, unless it is well taken on its face. State v. Kroll, 87 Wash.2d 829, 558 P.2d 173 (1976).

[The court's discussions of the issues of the effective date of the fee increase and statutory attorney's fees are omitted.]

The judgment as modified is affirmed, with costs to Jeffery, and remanded for redetermination of statutory attorneys fees.

■ DURHAM, J. and WARD WILLIAMS, J., concur in the result.

* * *

Questions

1. The court in *Jeffrey v. Weintraub* held that the fact-finding report in this case had no binding effect. What then might be the purpose of the local ordinance that required moorage facilities to engage in fact-finding proceedings over moorage fees? Is it intended as a redistributive provision, i.e., to protect floating homeowners against unreasonable increases in their fees? If so, how might the fact-finding procedure further this goal? If the legislature wanted to protect floating homeowners against unreasonable fee increases, what other options were available?

2. In footnote 7, the court raised the possibility that the state's ownership interest in the underlying waterways made the moorage fee increase state action. The court dismissed the argument summarily. However, if there were state action, might the plaintiffs have a stronger argument than the court acknowledges based on the alleged unreasonableness of the fee increase? If so, would the fact-finding report be relevant to establish unreasonableness? Would it be admissible in a court? Would the moorage facility operators have a right to cross-examine the fact-finder?

* * *

7. See, e.g., Burton v. Wilmington Parking Authority, 365 U.S. 715, 81 S.Ct. 856, 6 L.Ed.2d 45 (1961); MacLean v. First Northwest Industries of America, Inc., 24 Wash.App. 161, 600 P.2d 1027 (1979), rev'd, 96 Wash.2d 338, 635 P.2d 683 (1981). Under the present state of the law in Washington it is unclear whether the fact that the State leases property to a private person is a sufficient nexus to characterize as state action the otherwise private conduct of the lessee with regard to the leased property. The Court of Appeals in MacLean found that allegedly discriminatory "ladies' night" admission pricing for basketball games constituted state action because the games were played at a stadium leased from the City of Seattle. 24 Wash.App. at 165, 600 P.2d 1027. Although the majority opinion of the Supreme Court reversing MacLean expressed doubt as to this court's finding of state action, 96 Wash.2d at 348 n.4, 635 P.2d 683, it reversed the decision on other grounds. A strong dissent argued in part that the Court of Appeals finding of state action was correct. Id. 96 Wash.2d at 353–59, 635 P.2d 683 (Dolliver, J. dissenting).

4.   RIGHT TO CROSS-EXAMINE A THIRD PARTY EVALUATOR

McLaughlin v. Superior Court of the County of San Mateo

140 Cal.App.3d 473, 189 Cal.Rptr. 479 (Cal. Ct. of Appl., 1983).

■ RATTIGAN, ASSOCIATE JUSTICE.

Civil Code section 4607 requires prehearing mediation of child custody and visitation disputes in marital dissolution proceedings conducted pursuant to the Family Law Act. (Civ.Code, pt. 5, commencing with § 4000.) The statute also provides that, if the parties fail to agree in the mediation proceedings, the mediator "may, consistent with local court rules, render a recommendation to the court as to the custody or visitation of the child or children" involved. Pursuant to this provision, respondent superior court has adopted a "local court rule," or policy, which (1) requires the mediator to make a recommendation to the court if the parties fail to agree in the mediation proceedings, but (2) prohibits cross-examination of the mediator by the parties. We hold in this original proceeding that the policy is constitutionally invalid in significant respects.

The record in the proceeding supports the following recitals:

Petitioner Thomas J. McLaughlin and real party in interest Linda Lee McLaughlin were married in 1969. They have three children, whose ages range between 6 and 13 years. The following events occurred in 1982: On May 17, petitioner filed a petition in respondent court for dissolution of the marriage. He requested in it, among other things, that he be awarded custody of the children. Real party in interest filed a response in which she requested the court to award "joint legal" custody of the children and their "physical custody" to her.

On June 10, petitioner applied to respondent court for an order granting temporary custody of the children to him and reasonable visitation rights to real party in interest. On the same date, the court issued an order to show cause in which the questions of temporary custody and visitation were set for hearing on June 30. Real party in interest filed a responsive declaration in which she requested an order granting temporary custody to her and "[r]easonable visitation to petitioner."

The hearing on the order to show cause was commenced on June 30 as scheduled. When it was called, petitioner's counsel recited his understanding that the pending issues of temporary custody and visitation were to be "referred for mediation." Counsel also stated his view that "the mediation procedure [,] insofar as it allows the mediator to make a recommendation to the Court, and bars the introduction of any testimony from the mediator about what the parties tell him or her[,] is unconstitutional as a denial of the right to cross-examine." On that ground, counsel in effect moved for a "protective order" which would permit mediation proceedings, but which would provide that if they did not result in agreement by the parties, on the issues of temporary custody and visitation, the mediator would be prohibited from making a recommendation to the court unless petitioner were guaranteed the right to cross-examine the mediator.

Speaking to the motion, the court pointed out that Civil Code section 4607 "required" that "a contested custody or visitation matter ... be preceded ... by a session of mandatory mediation ... under the new 1980 law."[1] The court also pointed out that the required mediation proceedings were to be conducted "before the court of conciliation." In an exchange with counsel which followed, the court denied the motion on the ground that the "protective order" requested would violate a policy the court had adopted pursuant to Civil Code section 4607, subdivision (e). (See fn. 1, ante.)

The exchange produced clarification of petitioner's motion. It also included the only available description of respondent court's policy, which has apparently not been memorialized in a written rule. For these reasons, we quote pertinent passages of the exchange in the margin.[3]

1. It is undisputed that the court's reference to "the new 1980 law" was to Civil Code section 4607, which was added to title 4 of the Family Law Act in that year. (Stats. 1980, ch. 48, § 5 pp. 133–134.) The statute reads in pertinent part as follows (italics added): "4607. (a) Where it appears on the face of the petition or other application for an order or modification of an order for the custody or visitation of a child or children that either or both such issues are contested, as provided in Section 4600, 4600.1 or 4601, the matter *shall* be set for mediation of the contested issues prior to or concurrent with the setting of the matter for hearing. The purpose of such mediation proceeding shall be to reduce acrimony which may exist between the parties and to develop an agreement assuring the child or children's close and continuing contact with both parents after the marriage is dissolved. The mediator shall use his or her best efforts to effect a settlement of the custody or visitation dispute .... "(c) Mediation proceedings shall be held in private and shall be confidential, and all communications, verbal or written, from the parties to the mediator made in a proceeding pursuant to this section shall be deemed to be official information within the meaning of Section 1040 of the Evidence Code. "(d) The mediator shall have the authority to exclude counsel from participation in the mediation proceedings where, in the discretion of the mediator, exclusion of counsel is deemed by the mediator to be appropri-

ate or necessary.... "(e) The mediator *may, consistent with local court rules,* render a recommendation to the court as to the custody or visitation of the child or children. The mediator *may,* in cases where the parties have not reached agreement as a result of the mediation proceeding, recommend to the court that an investigation be conducted pursuant to Section 4602, or that other action be taken to assist the parties to effect a resolution of the controversy prior to any hearing on the issues. The mediator *may,* in appropriate cases, recommend that mutual restraining orders be issued, pending determination of the controversy, to protect the well-being of the children involved.... Any agreement reached by the parties as a result of mediation shall be reported to the court and to counsel for the parties by the mediator on the day set for mediation or any time thereafter designated by the court...."

3. "THE COURT [addressing Mr. Brunwasser, petitioner's counsel]: Some counties, as you probably know, do not permit or require a recommendation from the mediator in the event the parties are unable to agree. Some do. This county [i.e., respondent court] does, and therefore, I'm not prepared to give you the protective order you wish. The court feels that in the event the mediator were free to testify as to any of the matters mediated, that is[,] the substance of the matter as gleaned from the mediation

After the court had denied the motion, counsel for both parties agreed to a continuance of the hearing on temporary custody and visitation. They also agreed that custody would remain in "status quo" pending further proceedings. On July 6, respondent court filed a formal order in which it directed mediation of the pending issues pursuant to Civil Code section 4607, subdivision (a); denied petitioner's motion for a protective order; and continued the hearing on the pending issues to August 11.

On July 30, petitioner commenced the present proceeding by petitioning this court for a writ of prohibition restraining respondent court from "taking any further actions to enforce its order filed July 6, 1982 requiring petitioner and real party to submit their temporary custody dispute to mediation" in the absence of a "protective order" to the effect that the mediator could not make a recommendation to the court unless petitioner were permitted to cross-examine the mediator.... Petitioner also asked this court to stay the mediation proceedings pending disposition of his petition.

On August 10, this court summarily denied the petition and the request for a stay. In a petition for hearing filed in the Supreme Court on August 16, petitioner again requested a temporary stay of the mediation proceedings in respondent court. In a later communication to the Supreme Court, he stated that respondent court had meanwhile set the hearing on temporary custody and visitation for August 24. Petitioner in effect requested that the Supreme Court make an order temporarily staying the hearing in the absence of a protective order barring a recommendation to respondent court by the mediator.

On August 18, the Supreme Court made an order temporarily staying the August 24 hearing without qualification. On August 25, it made an order in which it granted the petition for hearing; returned the cause to this court with directions to issue an alternative writ; and ordered that the stay granted on August 18 was to remain in effect "pending final determination of this matter." ...

Review

[C]ivil Code section 4607, subdivision (a), clearly requires prehearing mediation of child custody and visitation disputes in marital dissolution

session, ... certainly you would have the right to cross-examine the mediator. "However, our instructions as a matter of court policy to the mediators are that they are not to state the basis for their ... recommendation....' In short, the recommendation of the mediator is simply ... a recommendation to the court without any statement of underlying basis.... That's the way we do business here.... "MR. BRUNWASSER: ... I have no objection to mediation. What I have an objection to is a procedure which allows the mediator ... to communicate with the court and not be subject to defend [sic] his or her opinion by cross-examination. "THE COURT: I understand that. I hope you equally understand that it is our policy to require a recommendation if the mediation is unsuccessful. It's a starting point which enables the court ... [,] in the absence of other evidence, to make an interim order based upon the opinion of the trained counselor, and it's a procedure we opted for when this law was enacted. We're satisfied that the law permits that, and so your motion for a protective order is denied.' "

proceedings. (See fn. 1, ante.) Subdivision (e) of the statute is also clear to the effect that the mediator "may, consistent with local court rules," make a recommendation to the court on either issue, or both, if the parties fail to reach agreement in the mediation proceedings. Subdivision (e) does not require or authorize disclosure to the parties of a recommendation made by the mediator to the court, nor of the mediator's reasons; it neither requires nor authorizes cross-examination of the mediator by the parties, which would necessarily require or bring about disclosure of the recommendation and the reasons for it; and the statute's express deference to "local court rules" has the effect of making disclosure and cross-examination matters of local option.

As we have seen, respondent court has exercised this option by adopting a policy which requires that the mediator make a recommendation to the court if the parties have failed to agree on child custody or visitation in the mediation proceedings; requires that the mediator not state his or her reasons for the recommendation; and denies the parties the right to cross-examine the mediator on the ground that the reasons have not been disclosed to the court. (See fn. 3, ante.) Amicus curiae has shown us that one large metropolitan superior court follows an entirely different procedure, and that another has adopted a policy which is essentially similar to respondent court's.[7]

---

7. Amicus curiae describes the practice of the Los Angeles County Superior Court without documentation, but without dispute by any party to this proceeding, as follows: Where prehearing mediation proceedings have been conducted in that court pursuant to Civil Code section 4607, and where the parties have not agreed on child custody or visitation (or both), the court (1) neither receives nor permits a recommendation by the mediator and (2) proceeds to hear and determine the contested issue or issues without referring to the unsuccessful mediation process in any way. Amicus curiae has filed declarations showing the related practice followed in the Superior Court for the City and County of San Francisco. Only one of the declarations shows what happens when the parties fail to agree on custody or visitation in a mediation proceeding conducted in that court. The declaration was executed by a judge of the court, who states in pertinent part: "On the morning of an initial hearing in which there is an issue of custody or visitation," the parties and a mediator are brought together. A "mediation session" is conducted at that time, after the mediator has talked to the parties' attorneys. "If there has been no agreement" at the session, the mediator "tells the attorneys in the presence of the parties what her [sic] recommendation is for the duration of the mediation," which is to continue at subsequent sessions. " . . . [N]o report is made to the attorneys nor to the court by the mediator, that is, there is no discussion of the factual detail which was presented." When the initial hearing is called on the same day, the parties' attorneys communicate the mediator's recommendation to the court. "At that time, the court inquires of the attorney who disagrees with the recommendation as to why there is a disagreement and why they [sic] feel that the recommendation should be something other than what the mediator had suggested. This commentary is then considered and the court makes an order to be in effect during the mediation period. At this hearing, if either attorney wants an adversary hearing on temporary custody or visitation, a hearing date is given to them for that adversary hearing, usually to take place within two to three weeks. . . ." This (appellate) court interprets the statement last quoted in the second paragraph (supra, commencing with "[N]o report is made . . .") to mean that the mediator's reasons for his or her recommendation are not disclosed to the parties, the attorneys, or the court when the recommendation is made in the first instance. This declaration fairly shows that the court makes the initial order on temporary custody or visitation without

The feature of respondent court's policy which prohibits cross-examination of the mediator is consistent with the provision in subdivision (c) of the statute that the mediation proceedings "shall be confidential." The requirement that the mediator not state to the court his or her reasons for the recommendation is consistent with the provision in subdivision (c) which protects the confidentiality of the parties' "communications" to the mediator by making them "official information within the meaning of Section 1040 of the Evidence Code." (See ibid.) The facts remain that the policy permits the court to receive a significant recommendation on contested issues but denies the parties the right to cross-examine its source. This combination cannot constitutionally be enforced.

In Fewel v. Fewel (1943) 23 Cal.2d 431, 144 P.2d 592, the plaintiff had appealed from successive child custody orders made by a trial court in a divorce action. (Id., at p. 433, 144 P.2d 592.) The order which was "controlling" had been "based exclusively on the *recommendation* of a court investigator...." (Ibid. [original italics].) The Supreme Court further described the recommendation, and held, as follows:

> "The recommendation ... is a recommendation for an order *and nothing more*. It contains no statement of facts or of the reasons for the conclusions suggested. The investigator was *not present for cross-examination*.... Such procedure cannot be sustained. By it the plaintiff was *denied the fair trial in open court* to which she was entitled; ... she was *precluded from cross-examination of adverse witnesses*.... Such errors require a reversal of the order."

(Fewel v. Fewel, supra, 23 Cal.2d 431 at p. 433 [italics added].) The "errors" had included actions and omissions by the trial court in addition to the denial of the right to cross-examine the investigator. (See ibid.) The Fewel court nevertheless made it clear that the denial of that right alone was reversible error, holding further:

> "The reports of ... investigators should be presented ... under oath, and an investigator, upon timely demand by any party, *must appear like any other witness and testify subject to the rules of evidence and the right of cross-examination*. It definitely is not the province of investigators to make *a private ... recommendation* to the judge, or any recommendation independent of the evidence on which it is based." (23 Cal.2d 431 at p. 436 [italics added].)

The applicability of these holdings to the comparable situation presented in respondent court is obvious....

Subdivision (a) of Civil Code section 4607 provides that contested issues of child custody and visitation "shall" be referred to prehearing mediation proceedings. (See fn. 1, ante.) Subdivision (e) of the statute provides that the mediator "may, consistent with local court rules," make a recommendation to the court if the parties fail to agree in the proceedings. (See ibid.) The use of the opposing verb forms in the same statute fairly

permitting cross-examination of the mediator. The declaration does not show whether cross-examination of the mediator is permitted at any later hearing.

reflects a legislative intent that the first provision is to be construed as mandatory and the second as permissive.... Construction of the second provision as permissive is also supported by its express deference to "local court rules."

"If 'the terms of a statute are by fair and reasonable interpretation capable of a meaning consistent with the requirements of the Constitution, the statute will be given that meaning, rather than another in conflict with the Constitution.' [Citations.]" (Metromedia, Inc. v. City of San Diego (1982) 32 Cal.3d 180, 186, 185 Cal.Rptr. 260, 649 P.2d 902.) We are therefore to construe the permissive language of Civil Code section 4607, subdivision (e), in such manner as will comport with the requirements of due process discussed above. It follows that the mediator designated by respondent court may not make a recommendation to the court subject to a "local court rule," or policy, which prohibits either party from calling the mediator and cross-examining him or her at a hearing on the contested issue or issues covered by the recommendation. (Fewel v. Fewel, supra, 23 Cal.2d 431 at pp. 433, 436, 144 P.2d 592.) For purposes of the present proceeding, it further follows that the mediator "may" not make a recommendation to respondent court in the absence of the protective order sought by petitioner, which will guarantee him the right to cross-examine the mediator.

These conclusions permit the mediation proceedings which Civil Code section 4607 requires where child custody or visitation are contested. They also permit the mediator to make a recommendation to the court if the proceedings do not produce agreement, but only if the parties are guaranteed—or waive—the right to cross-examine the mediator and other rights essential to due process. (See Fewel v. Fewel, supra, 23 Cal.2d 431 at pp. 433, 436, 144 P.2d 592.) Our conclusions are consistent with our duty to harmonize the provisions of subdivisions (a) and (e) of the statute without doing violence to its salutary purposes.... In addition, it has been shown in the present proceeding that disparities among "local court rules" adopted pursuant to subdivision (e) have had the effect of guaranteeing due process in some superior courts but not in others. (See fn. 7, ante.) Our conclusions will terminate this effect, which the Legislature obviously did not intend...

The writ of mandate ordered below permits the mediation proceedings to be conducted as previously ordered by respondent court. It also directs that the court *not* receive a recommendation from the mediator, as to any contested issue on which agreement is not reached, unless (1) the court has first made a protective order which guarantees the parties the rights to have the mediator testify and to cross-examine him or her concerning the recommendation or (2) the rights have been waived.

A peremptory writ of mandate consistent with this opinion will issue.

* * *

Questions

1.   While the legislation at issue in this case refers to the third party in child custody disputes as a ''mediator,'' it also specifies that when the parties do not reach a voluntary resolution of issue, the third party is placed in the role of an evaluator who makes a recommendation to the court. Is this type of evaluator similar to the fact-finder in the previous case? What are the similarities and differences?

2.   In *Jeffery v. Weintraub*, would there have been any constitutional problem for a court hearing the fact-finding report without giving the defendants a right to cross-examine the fact-finders? Is it a more serious constitutional issue than that posed in *McLaughlin?*

3.   What weight do you think a court should give the evaluator's report in a child custody case? How might the report be challenged?

4.   Is there a difference between a third party's conclusion when asked to find facts and a third party's conclusion when asked to make an evaluation? How might an opposing side refute a fact-finding report? How might one challenge an evaluation? In which type of case would cross-examination be more valuable?

* * *

5.   OMBUDSMEN AND PRIVILEGE

Garstang v. Superior Court of Los Angeles County and California Institute of Technology

39 Cal.App.4th 526, 46 Cal.Rptr.2d 84 (Cal. Ct. of Appl. 1995).

■ NOTT, ASSOCIATE JUSTICE.

Meg Garstang has petitioned this court for an extraordinary writ of mandate directing the superior court to set aside its order denying her motion to compel further answers to deposition questions.

We are asked to decide whether communications disclosed during mediation sessions before an ombudsperson employed by a private educational institution are privileged. We conclude they are protected by the qualified privilege set forth in this state's Constitution.

I.   FACTUAL AND PROCEDURAL BACKGROUND

Garstang worked for the California Institute of Technology (Caltech). On April 1, 1994, she sued Caltech and three co-workers, Cathy Fontenette, Kerry Etheridge and Christina Smith for slander and intentional infliction of emotional distress.

According to the complaint, Garstang was hired in 1989 as a secretary and shortly thereafter was promoted to the position of assistant to Russell Giambelluca, a division administrator. In March 1992, she was again promoted. Following these promotions the individual defendants told third persons that Garstang had "traded sexual favors for job advancement." Caltech "approved, consented to and ratified" these false statements.

In 1992 and 1993, Helen Hasenfeld, Caltech's ombudsperson, conducted a number of meetings in connection with the rumors being circulated. Ann Bussone, Caltech's director of human resources, Giambelluca, Fontenette and other Caltech employees, including David Stevenson, participated in the Hasenfeld meetings. Garstang believes that during one of the sessions an admission was made that she had been "treated unfairly." Unfortunately, the ombudsman was unable to resolve the situation and Garstang filed suit seeking general, special, and punitive damages.

In preparation for her lawsuit, Garstang deposed Etheridge, Fontenette and Stevenson and questioned them about the Hasenfeld meetings. The deponents were instructed by counsel not to answer on the basis that the statements were privileged because they were made before an ombudsperson.

Garstang moved to compel further responses to those questions regarding Hasenfeld and the deponents' conversations with her, pointing out that California does not recognize an ombudsman privilege.

Caltech and the individual defendants opposed the motion to compel arguing that because the communications were made during mediation proceedings they were privileged pursuant to Evidence Code section 1152.5. It was also contended that the California constitutional right to privacy protected the communications.

In denying Garstang's motion, the superior court opined, "[w]ell, the policy of the law, of course, is to settle cases without having to take them through the entire court process. And I think if I were to disregard this privilege, this would hamper [the] process." This petition for writ of mandate followed.

II. DISCUSSION

A. Contentions

Garstang contends the deponents were required to answer questions concerning statements made in Hasenfeld's presence because "there exists no ombudsman's privilege in California."

Real parties concur. They assert, however, that the communications are privileged because they occurred during a "mediation," and are, therefore, protected from discovery pursuant to section 1152.5. Alternatively, real parties contend that the communications are protected by the qualified privilege set forth in Article I, section 1 of this state's Constitution.

B. Mediation Privilege

Section 1152.5, as it read at the time of the Hasenfeld meetings, provided as follows:

"(a) Subject to the conditions and exceptions provided in this section, when persons agree to conduct and participate in a mediation for the purpose of compromising, settling, or resolving a dispute:

"(1) Evidence of anything said or of any admission made in the course of the mediation is not admissible in evidence, and disclosure of any such evidence shall not be compelled, in any civil action in which, pursuant to law, testimony can be compelled to be given.

"(2) Unless the document otherwise provides, no document prepared for the purpose of, or in the course of, or pursuant to, the mediation, or copy thereof, is admissible in evidence, and disclosure of any such document shall not be compelled, in any civil action in which, pursuant to law, testimony can be compelled to be given.

"(b) Subdivision (a) does not limit the admissibility of evidence if all persons who conducted or otherwise participated in the mediation consent to its disclosure.

"(c) This section does not apply unless, before the mediation begins, the persons who agree to conduct and participate in the mediation execute an agreement in writing that sets out the text of subdivisions (a) and (b) and states that the persons agree that this section shall apply to the mediation."

None of the parties participating in the Hasenfeld meetings executed the writing required by section 1152.5, subdivision (c). Thus, even if we assume Hasenfeld was conducting a "mediation" as that term is used in section 1152.5 at the time she endeavored to resolve Garstang's workplace dispute, the mediation privilege is inapplicable.

Our conclusion does not, however, render the communications discoverable. In our opinion, private institutions have a qualified privilege not to disclose communications made before an ombudsman in an attempt to mediate an employee dispute. That qualified privilege is based on California's constitutional right of privacy.

C. Qualified Privilege

In California there is no privilege to refuse to disclose any matter, or to refuse to produce any writing, object, or thing, unless the privilege is created by statute. (§ 911, subd. (b).) "[T]he privileges contained in the Evidence Code are *exclusive* and the courts are not free to create new privileges as a matter of judicial policy. [Citations.]" (Valley Bank of Nevada v. Superior Court (1975) 15 Cal.3d 652, 656, 125 Cal.Rptr. 553, 542 P.2d 977.) California, of course, does not specifically recognize an ombudsman privilege. (§ 900, et seq.)

There is, however, a right of privacy set forth in Article I, section 1 of this state's Constitution which states: "All people are by nature free and independent and have inalienable rights. Among these are enjoying and defending life and liberty, acquiring, possessing, and protecting property, and pursuing and obtaining safety, happiness, *and privacy*." (Emphasis added.) This "inalienable right" is a "fundamental interest" of our society, essential to those rights guaranteed under the federal constitution. (City of Santa Barbara v. Adamson (1980) 27 Cal.3d 123, 130, 164 Cal.Rptr. 539, 610 P.2d 436.) "The right to privacy is not absolute, but it may be abridged only when there is a compelling and opposing state interest. [Citations.]" (Kahn v. Superior Court (1987) 188 Cal.App.3d 752, 765, 233 Cal.Rptr. 662.)

One such compelling public need lies in facilitating the "ascertainment of truth" in connection with legal claims.... (Citations omitted).

In Board of Trustees v. Superior Court (1981) 119 Cal.App.3d 516, 174 Cal.Rptr. 160, the court faced a similar conflict between the "compelling" state interest in discovery and the parties' "fundamental right" of privacy. In that case, a faculty member of Stanford's school of medicine sued the university and a co-worker for, among other things, libel and "conspiracy to defame." (Id. at p. 523, 174 Cal.Rptr. 160.) Prior to trial the plaintiff demanded to inspect and copy the personnel, tenure, and promotion files of the defendant co-worker; all documents regarding his research; all documents compiled by university committees in their investigation of the plaintiff; and the personnel, tenure, and promotion files of the plaintiff himself. (Id. at p. 524, 174 Cal.Rptr. 160.) The trial court allowed partial discovery. The board of trustees sought a writ of mandate which the Court of Appeal issued. The appellate court denied disclosure of the co-worker's files on the ground that there was no "compelling state interest" in such disclosure. (Id. at pp. 526–527, 174 Cal.Rptr. 160.) It also denied disclosure of the university committee files concerning the investigation of the plaintiff, on the ground that since those committees had found no misconduct on his part, those files bore no relevance to his lawsuit. (Id. at pp. 527–528, 174 Cal.Rptr. 160.) The court did, however, allow the plaintiff to obtain his own personnel file, with the identities of contributors redacted. (Id. at p. 533, 174 Cal.Rptr. 160.)

In reconciling the competing public values advanced by the parties, the Board of Trustees court set forth two important principles. The first is that "inquiry into one's private affairs will *not* be constitutionally justified simply because inadmissible, and irrelevant, matter sought to be discovered *might* lead to other, and relevant evidence." [Citation.] " 'When compelled disclosure intrudes on constitutionally protected areas, it cannot be justified solely on the ground that it may lead to relevant information.' "[Citations.] "And even when discovery of private information is found directly relevant to the issues of ongoing litigation, it will not be automatically allowed; there must be then a 'careful balancing' of the 'compelling public need' for discovery against the fundamental right of privacy. [Citations.]" (Board of Trustees v. Superior Court, supra, 119 Cal.App.3d at p. 525, 174 Cal.Rptr. 160.) The second principle is that where the communications were tendered under a guaranty of confidentiality, they are thus manifestly within the Constitution's protected area of privacy. (Id. at p. 527, 174 Cal.Rptr. 160.)

In light of these principles we consider Garstang's request for disclosure of the communications made before Caltech's ombudsman. The participants in the ombudsman sessions were all Caltech employees. Two are named as defendants in this action. All of the participants discussed Garstang and the rumors she alleges were being circulated about her. If Garstang is denied an opportunity to depose these individuals as to what was said in the meetings with the ombudsman, her ability to ascertain the truth in connection with her lawsuit may be impaired. We are of the opinion, however, that a proper balancing of the competing values would here necessarily weigh in favor of the right of privacy of those individuals participating in the ombudsman sessions since the communications related to the private affairs of various Caltech employees, and were maintained in confidence by the institution.

In passing on a problem similar to ours, the court in Kientzy v. McDonnell Douglas Corp. (1991) 133 F.R.D. 570, 572 (Kientzy) reached the same conclusion. There, an individual sought to depose the ombudsman before whom communications were made by fellow employees. The Kientzy court held that communications received during an informal mediation before an ombudsman were privileged because the communication was one made in the belief that it would not be disclosed, confidentiality was essential to the maintenance of the relationship between the parties, the relationship was one that society considers worthy of being fostered, and the injury to the relationship incurred by disclosure would be greater than the benefit gained in the correct disposal of litigation. (Id. at p. 571.)

Evidence provided by Caltech shows that employees participating in informal mediations before its ombudsperson do so in the belief that the communications will not be disclosed. Caltech gives to all employees a strict pledge of confidentiality and assurance that they may rely on the confidentiality, independence and impartiality of the ombuds office.[5] While Caltech has formal mechanisms for resolving harassment complaints, those members of the Caltech community who elect not to avail themselves of the institute's formal complaint and resolution procedures, may utilize the services of the ombuds office which was established in 1986 to "provide the Caltech community with confidential, informal assistance in resolving intra-campus conflicts, disputes and grievances; in promoting fair and equitable treatment within the Institute, and in fostering the general well-being of the Caltech community."

---

5. Caltech pledges within information distributed to its employees that "[t]he confidences and identities of the people who consult with us will not be passed on to anyone else without express permission to do so, except to the extent required by law."

Caltech also assures its employees that "[t]he Ombudsperson does not take sides, but considers the rights and interests of all parties involved in a dispute, with the aim of achieving a fair outcome. The Ombudsperson does not arbitrate, adjudicate, or participate in the formal grievance process."

Employees are also told that "[t]he Ombudsperson will take into consideration interests and concerns of all members of the Caltech community involved in a dispute. The Ombudsperson works toward resolutions of problems based on principles of fairness, without favoritism toward any group or individual. To ensure objectivity, the office is independent of all Institute structures, while reporting to the Provost's Office on administrative and budgetary matters only."

There is no question that confidentiality is essential to the maintenance of the relationship between Caltech's employees and management. As the Kientzy court noted, "[t]he function of [an] ombudsman's office is to receive communications and to remedy workplace problems, in a strictly confidential atmosphere. Without this confidentiality, the office would be just one more non-confidential opportunity for employees to air disputes. The ombudsman's office provides an opportunity for complete disclosure, without the specter of retaliation, that does not exist in the other available, non-confidential grievance and complaint procedures." (Kientzy, supra, 133 F.R.D. at p. 572.)

It is readily apparent that the relationship between the ombuds office and Caltech's employees and management is worthy of societal support. Caltech is a large university, with a diverse student body and work force. It is important that its students and employees have "an opportunity to make confidential statements and to receive confidential guidance, information, and aid to remedy workplace problems" to benefit themselves and their community. (Kientzy, supra, 133 F.R.D. at p. 572.) "This is true in spite of the possibility that such actions may be perceived by an employee to be against company or fellow employees' interests." (Ibid.)

It is also apparent that the harm caused by the disruption of the confidential relationship between the ombuds office and others in Garstang's case would be greater than the benefit to Garstang by disclosure. "A successful ombudsman program resolves many problems informally and more quickly than other more formal procedures, including court actions." (Kientzy, supra, 133 F.R.D. at p. 572.) A court order that those participating in the sessions held by Hasenfeld disclose the information communicated in confidence would destroy the reputation and principle of confidentiality that the Caltech ombudsman program and office now enjoys and needs to perform its function. This is so because the utility of such a program and office "in resolving disputes in [the] workplace and thus diminishing the need for more formal resolution procedures, is founded on the confidentiality of its communications to and from company officials and employees." (Ibid.)

Given the valuable service an ombudsman provides, we are convinced of the propriety of affording constitutional protection to the privacy interests of individuals participating in an ombudsman program such as that established by Caltech. Garstang contends, however, that under the facts of this case the qualified privilege should not apply because (1) she was "never made aware nor did she ever have an understanding that her meetings with Hasenfeld would be kept confidential;" (2) Hasenfeld did not keep her pledge of confidentiality since she told at least one third person those things talked about in the ombudsman sessions she conducted; (3) Hasenfeld failed to bring "all of the parties together to reach any type of settlement or compromise;" and (4) Hasenfeld was not a neutral person because she is "employed by [Caltech] under their Human Resource umbrella and as such must look out for the best interests of [Caltech]."

The record reveals that every Caltech employee, including Garstang, was made aware of Hasenfeld's status as an ombudsperson, of Caltech's pledge of confidentiality, and that Caltech guaranteed the independence of the ombudsman office. Under these circumstances, and in the absence of evidence indicating that Caltech breached its confidentiality pledge and/or its guaranty that the ombudsman office would be independent, we must uphold the trial court's implied findings that Hasenfeld was acting in her capacity as an ombudsperson at the time she attempted to resolve Garstang's workplace dispute, that the individuals participating in the Hasenfeld meetings (including Garstang) did so believing their communications would not be disclosed, and that the ombudsman's office is independent of all Caltech structures.

Although not well articulated, it appears that Garstang also argues that an ombudsman is restricted in the manner in which he or she is entitled to proceed once approached with a workplace dispute. Garstang suggests that an ombudsman is required to conduct a group discussion, being careful to include those who are directly involved in the dispute, and any co-workers who may have information impacting upon the controversy, and at the conclusion of the meeting, the ombudsman is required to attempt to mediate a settlement.

Although the approach may differ from ombudsman to ombudsman, it seems obvious that before a dispute can be resolved an investigation of the facts is essential. It is only then that the nature of the controversy is revealed and the positions of the parties determined. Given the nature of workplace disputes, an ombudsman must be given the discretion to conduct a number of sessions—some of which may involve a single individual, and some of which may involve a number of individuals. At the conclusion of his or her investigation, the ombudsman must decide the likelihood of settlement. If he or she determines that resolution is unlikely the ombudsman sessions will be terminated. The decision to do so is strictly within the ombudsman's discretion, and will not be considered as evidence (in any lawsuit which may be filed) of whether a "true" mediation was being attempted.

The record here discloses that Hasenfeld acted in conformity with the authority conferred upon an ombudsperson, to wit, she discussed the problem with various individuals in order to ascertain the facts, and to determine the positions of those involved in the dispute. All this she did in an attempt to resolve a workplace dispute. We conclude, therefore, that the qualified privilege applies.

III. DISPOSITION

The petition for writ of mandate is denied. The temporary stay issued February 2, 1995, is vacated.

* * *

Carman v. McDonnell Douglas Corporation

114 F.3d 790 (8th Cir. 1997).

■ RICHARD S. ARNOLD, CHIEF JUDGE.

In October 1992, McDonnell Douglas Aircraft Corporation laid off Frank Carman as part of a reduction in force of its management staff. Carman then sued McDonnell Douglas, claiming that his termination violated the Age Discrimination in Employment Act, the Missouri Human Rights Act, and the Employee Retirement Income Security Act of 1974. In the course of discovery, the District Court denied Carman's request for the production of certain documents, holding that they were protected by the "Ombudsman Privilege." The District Court later granted summary judgment to McDonnell Douglas, a decision which Carman now appeals. Because we hold that the District Court lacked sufficient justification for creating an ombudsman privilege and denying Carman's discovery request, we reverse and remand.

I.

In June 1994, Carman requested 54 sets of documents from McDonnell Douglas. Item No. 53 was a request for "[a]ll notes and documents reflecting data known to ... Clemente [a company ombudsman] ... concerning" the plaintiff, a number of other individuals, and various topics including "[m]eeting notes regarding lay-offs in Plaintiff's Division" and "[m]eeting notes regarding Plaintiff Frank Carman." Appellant's App. 346–47. McDonnell Douglas objected to this and many other requests as vague, overbroad, and irrelevant, and further objected "with regard to documents known to Therese Clemente because her activities as an 'ombudsman' were considered confidential and any information and documents relating to her activities are immune from discovery." Id. at 358. In response, plaintiff filed a motion to compel production of certain documents. The Court granted the motion in part and ordered the defendants to produce a number of documents, including those requested in Item No. 53. Id. at 360. Two months later, however, in clarifying its order with respect to Item No. 53, the Court ruled that "defendant is not required to produce documents protected by the Ombudsman Privilege." Id. at 362. The Court also held that McDonnell Douglas did not have to produce adverse impact analyses prepared in anticipation of litigation and limited Carman's request for information about McDonnell Douglas's past reductions in force to the McDonnell Douglas Aircraft Company, the component company of McDonnell Douglas Corporation where Carman worked. In February 1996, the Court granted McDonnell Douglas's motion for summary judgment. The Court assumed that Carman had established a prima facie case of age discrimination but held that he had failed to present sufficient evidence that McDonnell Douglas's stated reasons for laying him off were pretextual. This appeal followed.

II.

[The court rejected the plaintiffs requests for documents concerning personnel files of other employees.]

III.

We now turn to the issue of the "ombudsman privilege." In the context of this case, the term "ombudsman" refers to an employee outside of the corporate chain of command whose job is to investigate and mediate workplace disputes. The corporate ombudsman is paid by the corporation and lacks the structural independence that characterizes government ombudsmen in some countries and states, where the office of ombudsman is a separate branch of government that handles disputes between citizens and government agencies. Nonetheless, the corporate ombudsman purports to be an independent and neutral party who promises strict confidentiality to all employees and is bound by the Code of Ethics of the Corporate Ombudsman Association, which requires the ombudsman to keep communications confidential. McDonnell Douglas argues for recognition of an evidentiary privilege that would protect corporate ombudsmen from having to disclose relevant employee communications to civil litigants.

The Federal Rule of Evidence 501 states that federal courts should recognize evidentiary privileges according to "the principles of the common law" interpreted "in the light of reason and experience." The beginning of any analysis under Rule 501 is the principle that "the public has a right to every man's evidence." Hardwicke, L.C.J., quoted in 12 Cobbett's Parliamentary History 675, 693 (1742) (quoted with approval in United States v. Bryan, 339 U.S. 323, 331 (1950)). Accordingly, evidentiary privileges "are not lightly created." United States v. Nixon, 418 U.S. 683, 710 (1974). A party that seeks the creation of a new evidentiary privilege must overcome the significant burden of establishing that "permitting a refusal to testify or excluding relevant evidence has a public good transcending the normally predominant principle of utilizing all rational means for ascertaining truth." Trammel v. United States, 445 U.S. 40, 50, (1980) (quoting Elkins v. United States, 364 U.S. 206, 234 (1960) (Frankfurter, J., dissenting)).

The first important factor for assessing a proposed new evidentiary privilege is the importance of the relationship that the privilege will foster. The defendant argues that ombudsmen help resolve workplace disputes prior to the commencement of expensive and time-consuming litigation. We agree that fair and efficient alternative dispute resolution techniques benefit society and are worthy of encouragement. To the extent that corporate ombudsmen successfully resolve disputes in a fair and efficient manner, they are a welcome and helpful addition to a society that is weary of lawsuits.

Nonetheless, far more is required to justify the creation of a new evidentiary privilege. First, McDonnell Douglas has failed to present any evidence, and indeed has not even argued, that the ombudsman method is more successful at resolving workplace disputes than other forms of alternative dispute resolution, nor has it even pointed to any evidence establishing that its own ombudsman is especially successful at resolving workplace disputes prior to the commencement of litigation. . . .

Second, McDonnell Douglas has failed to make a compelling argument that most of the advantages afforded by the ombudsman method would be lost without the privilege. Even without a privilege, corporate ombudsmen still have much to offer employees in the way of confidentiality, for they are still able to promise to keep employee communications confidential from management. Indeed, when an aggrieved employee or an employee-witness is deciding whether or not to confide in a company ombudsman, his greatest concern is not likely to be that the statement will someday be revealed in civil discovery. More likely, the employee will fear that the ombudsman is biased in favor of the company, and that the ombudsman will tell management everything that the employee says. The denial of an ombudsman privilege will not affect the ombudsman's ability to convince an employee that the ombudsman is neutral, and creation of an ombudsman privilege will not help alleviate the fear that she is not.

We are especially unconvinced that "no present or future [McDonnell Douglas] employee could feel comfortable in airing his or her disputes with the Ombudsman because of the specter of discovery." See Appellee's Br. 45. An employee either will or will not have a meritorious complaint. If he does not and is aware that he does not, he is no more likely to share the frivolousness of his complaint with a company ombudsman than he is with a court. If he has a meritorious complaint that he would prefer not to litigate, then he will generally feel that he has nothing to hide and will be undeterred by the prospect of civil discovery from sharing the nature of his complaint with the ombudsman. The dim prospect that the employee's complaint might someday surface in an unrelated case strikes us as an unlikely deterrent. Again, it is the perception that the ombudsman is the company's investigator, a fear that does not depend upon the prospect of civil discovery, that is most likely to keep such an employee from speaking openly.

McDonnell Douglas also argues that failure to recognize an ombudsman privilege will disrupt the relationship between management and the ombudsman's office. In cases where management has nothing to hide, this is unlikely. It is probably true that management will be less likely to share damaging information with an ombudsman if there is no privilege. Nonetheless, McDonnell Douglas has provided no reason to believe that management is especially eager to confess wrongdoing to ombudsmen when a privilege exists, or that ombudsmen are helpful at resolving disputes that involve violations of the law by management or supervisors. If the chilling of management-ombudsman communications occurs only in cases that would not have been resolved at the ombudsman stage anyway, then there is no reason to recognize an ombudsman privilege.

McDonnell Douglas relies on the analysis of the court in Kientzy, supra, apparently one of only two federal courts to have recognized a corporate-ombudsman privilege. We do not find the reasoning of that opinion convincing. For example, the Kientzy opinion argues that confidentiality is essential to ombudsman-employee relationships because the function of that relationship is to "receive communications and to remedy workplace problems, in a strictly confidential atmosphere. Without this confidentiality, the office would just be one more non-confidential opportunity for employees to air disputes. The ombudsman's office provides an opportunity for complete disclosure, without the specter of retaliation, that does not exist in the other available, non-confidential grievance and complaint procedures." 133 F.R.D. at 572. As we have said, the corporate ombudsman will still be able to promise confidentiality in most circumstances even with no privilege. To justify the creation of a privilege, McDonnell Douglas must first establish that society benefits in some significant way from the particular brand of confidentiality that the privilege affords. Only then can a court decide whether the advantages of the proposed privilege overcome the strong presumption in favor of disclosure of all relevant information. The creation of a wholly new evidentiary privilege is a big step. This record does not convince us that we should take it.

IV

We disagree with the District Court's holding that employee communications to Therese Clemente were protected from discovery by an ombudsman privilege. The judgment is reversed, and the cause remanded for further proceedings consistent with this opinion. On remand, the District Court should order the production of the evidence it had believed the privilege protected, unless there are other reasons why discovery of this evidence would not be appropriate. It should then reconsider its ruling on defendant's motion for summary judgment in light of this new evidence and the parties' arguments with respect to its significance.

It is so ordered.

* * *

Questions

1. What is an ombudsperson? How does an ombudsperson differ from a mediator? An evaluator? A fact-finder?

2. In *Garstang v. Superior Court*, the court emphasized that Caltech had given its employees reason to believe that communications to the ombudsperson would be confidential, and employees in fact believed that such communications were confidential. Are private assurances of confidentiality generally sufficient to create a judicially-recognized privilege? What other reasons might explain the court's result?

3. Can an ombudsperson be neutral in the way that a mediator can be? Is it necessary for an ombudsperson to be neutral to be effective? What does the court mean when it discusses whether the ombudsperson is "independent?"

4. Should courts create an ombudsperson privilege? Does one's position on this depend upon one's views about the values of an ombudsperson to resolve disputes?

* * *

CHAPTER FOUR
SETTLEMENT

---

1. INTRODUCTION

Most lawsuits end in a settlement between the parties. In fact, most lawsuits settle before they even get to trial. The legal system encourages parties to settle cases short of trial because to do so saves on court time and thus on public resources. At the same time, most trial lawyers prefer to settle cases rather than try them in order to save their clients the expense and uncertainty of a trial. Further, many commentators believe that a settlement is superior to a judgment from the parties' vantage point because a settlement is a consensual rather than an imposed resolution of a dispute. A settlement can be tailored to the parties' specific concerns and interests rather than embody conventional legal remedies. Thus, it is often maintained that a settlement is more likely to reflect both sides' priorities than a judgment at trial.

Many alternative dispute resolution techniques are ultimately efforts to promote settlement. Mediation, when it is successful, induces the parties to settle and helps them formulate settlement terms that both sides find acceptable. Other settlement-enhancing forms of ADR include the use of conciliation, third party evaluators, mini-trials, non-binding summary jury trials, early neutral case evaluation, and mandatory judicial settlement conferences. While settlement seems obviously preferable to litigation, settlement also has its critics. Some scholars have warned that an excessive reliance on settlement diminishes public discourse and deprives the public of the opportunity to elaborate norms for our mutual governance. Others have warned that the settlement process, if unexamined, could enable strong parties to take advantage of weaker ones and yield unfair results. Also, there are special problems posed in class action settlements where named plaintiffs and their lawyers settle disputes for parties who are not before the court. These issues are explored in the cases and materials that follow.

---

2. PERSPECTIVES ON SETTLEMENT

A. FISS ON *AGAINST SETTLEMENT*

In a series of articles in the *Yale Law Journal*, Professors Owen M. Fiss, Andrew W. Mcthenia, and Thomas L. Shaffer debated the desirability of private settlement as an alternative to judgment. Owen M. Fiss in a path-breaking article, *Against Settlement*, 93 Yale L. J. 1073 (1984), contends that alternative dispute resolution processes are highly problematic and should not be institutionalized on a wholesale and indiscriminate basis. Fiss takes issue with ADR proponents' view of the role and nature of adjudication. He claims that ADR advocates too often see adjudication as a process to resolve quarrels between neighbors who have reached an impasse and turned to a stranger for help. Fiss contends that litigation differs from this model, and instead signifies that social relations have already broken down irremediably. He criticizes attempts to negotiate what he sees as a "truce" between parties where none is possible.

For Fiss, "settlement is a capitulation to the conditions of mass society and should be neither encouraged nor praised." Settlement is simply a streamlining procedure for overcrowded dockets. In order to clear dockets, parties are shuffled into a process that Fiss sees as the civil analog to the criminal plea bargain. These settlements suffer from several defects: Consent is often coerced; the bargain may be struck by a party without authority; subsequent judicial involvement becomes problematic in the absence of judgment; and justice may not be achieved. He writes:

THE IMBALANCE OF POWER

"By viewing the lawsuit as a quarrel between two neighbors, the dispute-resolution story that underlies ADR implicitly asks us to assume a rough equality between the contending parties. It treats settlement as the anticipation of the outcome of trial and assumes that the terms of settlement are simply a product of the parties' predictions of that outcome. In truth, however, settlement is also a function of the resources available to each party to finance the litigation, and those resources are frequently distributed unequally. Many lawsuits do not involve a property dispute between two neighbors, or between AT & T and the government (to update the story), but rather concern a struggle between a member of a racial minority and a municipal police department over alleged brutality, or a claim by a worker against a large corporation over work-related injuries. In these cases, the distribution of financial resources, or the ability of one party to pass along its costs, will invariably infect the bargaining process, and the settlement will be at odds with a conception of justice that seeks to make the wealth of the parties irrelevant.

"The disparities in resources between the parties can influence the settlement in three ways. First, the poorer party may be less able to amass and analyze the information needed to predict the outcome of the litigation, and thus be disadvantaged in the bargaining process. Second, he may need the damages he seeks immediately and thus be induced to settle as a way of accelerating payment, even though he realizes he would get less now than he might if he awaited judgment. All plaintiffs want their damages immediately, but an indigent plaintiff may be exploited by a rich defendant because his need is so great that the defendant can force him to accept a sum that is less than the ordinary present value of the judgment. Third, the poorer party might be forced to settle because he does not have the resources to finance the litigation, to cover either his own projected expenses, such as his lawyer's time, or the expenses his opponent can impose through the manipulation of procedural mechanisms such as discovery. It might seem that settlement benefits the plaintiff by allowing him to avoid the costs of litigation, but this is not so. The defendant can anticipate the plaintiff's costs if the case were to be tried fully and decrease his offer by that amount. The indigent plaintiff is a victim of the costs of litigation even if he settles.

"[O]f course, imbalances of power can distort judgment as well: Resources influence the quality of presentation, which in turn has an important bearing on who wins and the terms of victory. We count, however, on the guiding presence of the judge, who can employ a number of measures to lessen the impact of distributional inequalities. He can, for example, supplement the parties' presentations by asking questions, calling his own witnesses, and inviting other persons and institutions to participate as amici. These measures are likely to make only a small contribution toward moderating the influence of distributional inequalities, but should not be ignored for that reason. Not even these small steps are possible with settlement. There is, moreover, a critical difference between a process like settlement, which is based on bargaining and accepts inequalities of wealth as an integral and legitimate component of the process, and a process like judgment, which knowingly struggles against those inequalities. Judgment aspires to an autonomy from distributional inequalities, and it gathers much of its appeal from this aspiration.

THE ABSENCE OF AUTHORITATIVE CONSENT

"The argument for settlement presupposes that the contestants are individuals. These individuals speak for themselves and should be bound by the rules they generate. In many situations, however, individuals are ensnared in contractual relationships that impair their autonomy: Lawyers or insurance companies might, for example, agree to settlements that are in their interests but are not in the best interests of their clients, and to which their clients would not agree if the choice were still theirs. But a deeper and more intractable problem arises from the fact that many parties are not individuals but rather organizations or groups. We do not know who is entitled to speak for these entities and to give the consent upon which so much of the appeal of settlement depends.

"Some organizations, such as corporations or unions, have formal procedures for identifying the persons who are authorized to speak for them. But these procedures are imperfect: They are designed to facilitate transactions between the organization and outsiders, rather than to insure that the members of the organization in fact agree with a particular decision. Nor do they eliminate conflicts of interests. The chief executive officer of a corporation may settle a suit to prevent embarrassing disclosures about his managerial policies, but such disclosures might well be in the interest of the shareholders. The president of a union may agree to a settlement as a way of preserving his power within the organization; for that very reason, he may not risk the dangers entailed in consulting the rank and file or in subjecting the settlement to ratification by the membership. Moreover, the representational procedures found in corporations, unions, or other private formal organizations are not universal. Much contemporary litigation, especially in the federal courts, involves governmental agencies, and the procedures in those organizations for generating authoritative consent are far cruder than those in the corporate context. We are left to wonder, for example, whether the attorney general should be able to bind all state officials, some of whom are elected and thus have an independent mandate from the people, or even whether the incumbent attorney general should be able to bind his successors.

"These problems become even more pronounced when we turn from organizations and consider the fact that much contemporary litigation involves even more nebulous social entities, namely, groups. Some of these groups, such as ethnic or racial minorities, inmates of prisons, or residents of institutions for mentally retarded people, may have an identity or existence that transcends the lawsuit, but they do not have any formal organizational structure and therefore lack any procedures for generating authoritative consent. The absence of such a procedure is even more pronounced in cases involving a group, such as the purchasers of Cuisinarts between 1972 and 1982, which is constructed solely in order to create funds large enough to make it financially attractive for lawyers to handle the case."

Fiss acknowledges that going to judgment does not altogether avoid the risk of unauthorized or unrepresentative actions. The Federal Rules of Civil Procedure, he notes, allow a representative to be created by self-appointment in the case of a defendant class. Fiss contends, however, that the process of litigation provides a court with the opportunity to evaluate the actions and statements of the representatives, who are contesting each other's claims. In contrast, court approval of a settlement turns merely on whether the proposed agreement, which both sides are now supporting, is close to what the court imagines a judgment after trial to be. In this situation, the contending parties have every interest in defending the settlement and convincing the court of its propriety.

Fiss also argues that in the settlement approval process, the lack of a meaningful role for the court is diminished in other ways. He writes:

"The dispute-resolution story trivializes the remedial dimensions of lawsuits and mistakenly assumes judgment to be the end of the process. It supposes that the judge's duty is to declare which neighbor is right and which wrong, and that this declaration will end the judge's involvement (save in that most exceptional situation where it is also necessary for him to issue a writ directing the sheriff to execute the declaration). Under these assumptions, settlement appears as an almost perfect substitute for judgment, for it too can declare the parties' rights. Often, however, judgment is not the end of a lawsuit but only the beginning. The involvement of the court may continue almost indefinitely. In these cases, settlement cannot provide an adequate basis for that necessary continuing involvement, and thus is no substitute for judgment.

"The parties may sometimes be locked in combat with one another and view the lawsuit as only one phase in a long continuing struggle. The entry of judgment will then not end the struggle, but rather change its terms and the balance of power. One of the parties will invariably return to the court and again ask for its assistance, not so much because conditions have changed, but because the conditions that preceded the lawsuit have unfortunately not changed. This often occurs in domestic-relations cases, where the divorce decree represents only the opening salvo in an endless series of skirmishes over custody and support.

JUSTICE RATHER THAN PEACE

"The dispute-resolution story makes settlement appear as a perfect substitute for judgment, as we just saw, by trivializing the remedial dimensions of a lawsuit, and also by reducing the social function of the lawsuit to one of resolving private disputes: In that story, settlement appears to achieve exactly the same purpose as judgment-peace between the parties-but at considerably less expense to society. The two quarreling neighbors turn to a court in order to resolve their dispute, and society makes courts available because it wants to aid in the achievement of their private ends or to secure the peace.

"In my view, however, the purpose of adjudication should be understood in broader terms. Adjudication uses public resources, and employs not strangers chosen by the parties but public officials chosen by a process in which the public participates. These officials, like members of the legislative and executive branches, possess a power that has been defined and conferred by public law, not by private agreement. Their job is not to maximize the ends of private parties, nor simply to secure the peace, but to explicate and give force to the values embodied in authoritative texts such as the Constitution and statutes: to interpret those values and to bring reality into accord with them. This duty is not discharged when the parties settle.

"In our political system, courts are reactive institutions. They do not search out interpretive occasions, but instead wait for others to bring matters to their attention. They also rely for the most part on others to investigate and present the law and facts. A settlement will thereby deprive a court of the occasion, and perhaps even the ability, to render an interpretation. A court cannot proceed (or not proceed very far) in the face of a settlement. To be against settlement is not to urge that parties be 'forced' to litigate, since that would interfere with their autonomy and distort the adjudicative process; the parties will be inclined to make the court believe that their bargain is justice. To be against settlement is only to suggest that when the parties settle, society gets less than what appears, and for a price it does not know it is paying. Parties might settle while leaving justice undone. The settlement of a school suit might secure the peace, but not racial equality. Although the parties are prepared to live under the terms they bargained for, and although such peaceful coexistence may be a necessary precondition of justice, and itself a state of affairs to be valued, it is not justice itself. To settle for something means to accept less than some ideal. . . .

THE REAL DIVIDE

"To all this, one can readily imagine a simple response by way of confession and avoidance: We are not talking about those lawsuits. Advocates of ADR might insist that my account of adjudication, in contrast to the one implied by the dispute-resolution story, focuses on a rather narrow category of lawsuits. They could argue that while settlement may have only the most limited appeal with respect to those cases, I have not spoken to the 'typical' case. My response is twofold.

"First, even as a purely quantitative matter, I doubt that the number of cases I am referring to is trivial. My universe includes those cases in which there are significant distributional inequalities; those in which it is difficult to generate authoritative consent because organizations or social groups are parties or because the power to settle is vested in autonomous agents; those in which the court must continue to supervise the parties after judgment; and those in which justice needs to be done, or to put it more modestly, where there is a genuine social need for an authoritative interpretation of law. I imagine that the number of cases that satisfy one of these four criteria is considerable; in contrast to the kind of case portrayed in the dispute-resolution story, they probably dominate the docket of a modern court system.

"Second, it demands a certain kind of myopia to be concerned only with the number of cases, as though all cases are equal simply because the clerk of the court assigns each a single docket number. All cases are not equal. The Los Angeles desegregation case, to take one example, is not equal to the allegedly more typical suit involving a property dispute or an automobile accident. The desegregation suit consumes more resources, affects more people, and provokes far greater challenges to the judicial power. The settlement movement must introduce a qualitative perspective; it must speak to these more 'significant' cases, and demonstrate the propriety of settling them. Otherwise it will soon be seen as an irrelevance, dealing with trivia rather than responding to the very conditions that give the movement its greatest sway and saliency.

"Nor would sorting cases into 'two tracks,' one for settlement, and another for judgment, avoid my objections. Settling automobile cases and leaving discrimination or antitrust cases for judgment might remove a large number of cases from the dockets, but the dockets will nevertheless remain burdened with the cases that consume the most judicial resources and represent the most controversial exercises of the judicial power. A 'two track' strategy would drain the argument for settlement of much of its appeal. I also doubt whether the 'two track' strategy can be sensibly implemented. It is impossible to formulate adequate criteria for prospectively sorting cases. The problems of settlement are not tied to the subject matter of the suit, but instead stem from factors that are harder to identify, such as the wealth of the parties, the likely post-judgment history of the suit, or the need for an authoritative interpretation of law. The authors of the amendment to Rule 68 make a gesture toward a 'two track' strategy by exempting class actions and shareholder derivative suits, and by allowing the judge to refrain from awarding attorney's fees when it is 'unjustified under all of the circumstances.' But these gestures are cramped and ill-conceived, and are likely to increase the workload of the courts by giving rise to yet another set of issues to litigate. It is, moreover, hard to see how these problems can be avoided. Many of the factors that lead a society to bring social relationships that otherwise seem wholly private (e.g., marriage) within the jurisdiction of a court, such as imbalances of power or the interests of third parties, are also likely to make settlement problematic. Settlement is a poor substitute for judgement; it is an even poorer substitute for the withdrawal of jurisdiction.

"[I]n fact, most ADR advocates make no effort to distinguish between different types of cases or to suggest that 'the gentler arts of reconciliation and accommodation' might be particularly appropriate for one type of case but not for another. They lump all cases together. This suggests that what divides me from the partisans of ADR is not that we are concerned with different universes of cases, that Derek Bok, for example, focuses on boundary quarrels while I see only desegregation suits. I suspect instead that what divides us is much deeper and stems from our understanding of the purpose of the civil law suit and its place in society. It is a difference in outlook.

"Someone like Bok sees adjudication in essentially private terms: The purpose of lawsuits and the civil courts is to resolve disputes, and the amount of litigation we encounter is evidence of the needlessly combative and quarrelsome character of Americans. Or as Bok put it, using a more diplomatic idiom: 'At bottom, ours is a society built on individualism, competition, and success.' I, on the other hand, see adjudication in more public terms: Civil litigation is an institutional arrangement for using state power to bring a recalcitrant reality closer to our chosen ideals. We turn to the courts because we need to, not because of some quirk in our personalities. We train our students in the tougher arts so that they may help secure all that the law promises, not because we want them to become gladiators or because we take a special pleasure in combat.

"To conceive of the civil lawsuit in public terms as America does might be unique. I am willing to assume that no other country-including Japan, Bok's new paragon—has a case like Brown v. Board of Education in which the judicial power is used to eradicate the caste structure. I am willing to assume that no other country conceives of law and uses law in quite the way we do. But this should be a source of pride rather than shame. What is unique is not the problem, that we live short of our ideals, but that we alone among the nations of the world seem willing to do something about it. Adjudication American-style is not a reflection of our combativeness but rather a tribute to our inventiveness and perhaps even more to our commitment."

B. McThenia and Shaffer on *For Reconciliation*

In their response to Fiss, Professors Andrew W. McThenia and Thomas L. Shaffer take issue with Fiss' conception of ADR and traditional litigation. They write in *For Reconciliation*, 94 Yale L. J. 1660 (1985):

"Fiss attacks a straw man. In our view, the models he has created for argument in other circumstances have become mechanisms of self-deception not only for him but for most of those who write about alternatives to litigation. His understanding that the plea of ADR advocates is based on efficiency reduces the entire question to one of procedures. Fiss's argument rests on the faith that justice—and he uses the word—is usually something people get from the government. He comes close to arguing that the branch of government that resolves disputes, the courts, is the principal source of justice in fragmented modern American society . . . .

"Fiss's description of traditional dispute resolution is a story of two neighbors 'in a state of nature' who each claim a single piece of property and who, when they cannot agree, turn to 'a stranger' to resolve their dispute. He asserts that traditional dispute resolution depicts a sociologically impoverished universe, operates in a state of nature where there are no public values or goals except a supposed 'natural harmony' of the status quo, and calls on the exercise of power by a stranger. That was never Fuller's position. Nor do we find much support in the literature or in reality for such a view of traditional adjudication. If there ever was such a world we expect it was 'nasty, brutish and short.' However, we don't really believe that traditional adjudication ever bore much resemblance to that story. Yet this is the view of the world that Fiss attributes to the advocates of ADR; his attack on ADR is premised on that notion.

" . . . After setting up his 'state of nature' model of dispute resolution, Fiss attributes that view of the world to the advocates of ADR. He understands pleas to consider alternatives to current means of resolving disputes as turning on the inefficiency of traditional adjudication (his negative model), and popular dissatisfaction with it. He equates the ADR movement with those who urge settlement more than judgment and who seek a 'truce more than a true reconciliation.' He argues that settlement is 'a capitulation to the conditions of mass society,' a capitulation that 'should be neither encouraged nor praised.' He assumes that the ADR movement is one that wants peace at any price and treats settlement as 'the anticipation of the outcome of trial,' that is, trial in his stranger-judge, negative model of adjudication.

"Fiss is against settlement because he views the matters that come before courts in America, and that are inappropriate for ADR, as including cases in which: (1) there are distributional inequities; (2) securing authoritative consent or settlement is difficult; (3) continued supervision following judgment is necessary; and (4) there is a genuine need for an authoritative interpretation of law. Fiss characterizes disputes in this limited way—as arguments between two neighbors, one of whom has vastly superior bargaining power over the other. It is then easy for him to prefer litigation to settlement, because litigation is a way to equalize bargaining power.

"The soundest and deepest part of the ADR movement does not rest on Fiss's two-neighbors model. It rests on values—of religion, community, and work place—that are more vigorous than Fiss thinks. In many, in fact most, of the cultural traditions that argue for ADR, settlement is neither an avoidance mechanism nor a truce. Settlement is a process of reconciliation in which the anger of broken relationships is to be confronted rather than avoided, and in which healing demands not a truce but confrontation. Instead of 'trivializing the remedial process,' settlement exalts that process. Instead of 'reducing the social function ... to one of resolving private disputes,' settlement calls on substantive community values. Settlement is sometimes a beginning, and is sometimes a postscript, but it is not the essence of the enterprise of dispute resolution. The essence of the enterprise is more like the structural injunction, about which Fiss has written so eloquently, than like an alternative to the resolution-by-stranger described by his negative model.

"The 'real divide' between us and Fiss may not be our differing views of the sorts of cases that now wind their way into American courts, but, more fundamentally, it may be our different views of justice. Fiss comes close to equating justice with law. He includes among the cases unsuited for settlement 'those in which justice needs to be done, or to put it more modestly, where there is a genuine social need for an authoritative interpretation of law.' We do not believe that law and justice are synonymous. We see the deepest and soundest of ADR arguments as in agreement with us: Justice is not usually something people get from the government. And courts (which are not, in any case, strangers) are not the only or even the most important places that dispense justice.

"Many advocates of ADR can well be taken to have asked about the law's response to disputes, and alternatives to that response, not in order to reform the law but in order to locate alternative views of what a dispute is. Such alternatives would likely advance or assume understandings of justice (or, if you like, peace) that are also radically different from justice as something lawyers administer, or peace as the absence of violence. They assume not that justice is something people get from the government but that it is something people give to one another. These advocates seek an understanding of justice in the way Socrates and Thrasymachus did in the Republic: Justice is not the will of the stronger; it is not efficiency in government; it is not the reduction of violence: Justice is what we discover—you and I, Socrates said—when we walk together, listen together, and even love one another, in our curiosity about what justice is and where justice comes from. . . .

"Thus, the procedure gives priority to restoring the relationship. Hebraic theology puts primary emphasis on relationships, a priority that is political and even ontological, as well as ethical, and therefore legal. And so, most radically, the religious tradition seeks not resolution (which connotes the sort of doctrinal integrity in the law that seems to us to be Fiss's highest priority) but reconciliation of brother to brother, sister to sister, sister to brother, child to parent, neighbor to neighbor, buyer to seller, defendant to plaintiff, and judge to both. (The Judge is also an I and a Thou.) This view of what a dispute is, and of what third parties seek when they intervene in disputes between others, provides an existing, traditional, common alternative to the law's response. The fact seems to be that this alternative has both a vigorous modern history and a studiable contemporary vitality (Jerrold Auerbach to the contrary notwithstanding)."

McThenia and Shaffer contend that American religious culture contains the theoretical basis for ADR and a way to apply theory to disputes. For them, the Torah and the Gospel are the prime sources for radical alternatives to litigation. Both Judaism and Christianity envision a religious community with the authority to resolve disputes and when gentle persuasion fails, compel obedience. The process involves conversation, mediation, and if necessary, "airing the dispute before representatives of the community." Only if the dispute goes to judgment is community pressure applied.

C. FISS RESPONDS

In a rejoinder entitled *Out of Eden,* 94 Yale L. J. 1669 (1985), Professor Fiss observed that religion can distort as well as inspire. According to Fiss, McThenia and Shaffer have mistaken "the periphery for the center" in their defense of settlement. He writes:

"Religion can inspire. It can also distort, and this is precisely what it does for Professors McThenia and Shaffer. It leads them to mistake the periphery for the center. . . .

"In my earlier article I tried to come to terms with a movement that seeks alternatives to litigation. . . .

"Professors McThenia and Shaffer now lend their voices to this movement, but in an unusual way. They add a religious dimension. They emphasize reconciliation rather than settlement, and appear to be moved by a conception of social organization that takes the insular religious community as its model: 'Justice is what we discover—you and I, Socrates said—when we walk together, listen together, and even love one another, in our curiosity about what justice is and where justice comes from.' McThenia and Shaffer speak out on behalf of social mechanisms that might restore or preserve loving relationships and, not surprisingly, they find the judicial judgment a rather inept instrument for that purpose.

"I have no special interest in countering their plea: I am as much for love as the next person. What McThenia and Shaffer say is not wrong, just beside the point: Their reasons for seeking alternatives to litigation are not those of the movement. Chief Justice Burger is not moved by love, or by a desire to find new ways to restore or preserve loving relationships, but rather by concerns of efficiency and politics. He seeks alternatives to litigation in order to reduce the caseload of the judiciary or, even more plausibly, to insulate the status quo from reform by the judiciary. Of course, McThenia and Shaffer are entitled to their own reasons for support-ing a social and political movement, but they should not delude themselves that they have given a general account of ADR or explained its saliency and sway within the bar today.

"McThenia and Shaffer should also understand that their plea for reconciliation does not respond to the primary social situation to which ADR is addressed. In their search for alternatives to litigation, the advo-cates of ADR focus on social situations in which interpersonal relationships have been so thoroughly disrupted that there is no chance of reconciliation: People turn to courts when they are at the end of the road. That is why I focused my attention on settlement rather than reconciliation. As I said in the original article, ADR proposals like those embodied in Rule 16 and in the amendments to Rule 68 picture settlement not as a reconciliation, but as a truce. To be against settlement is not to be against reconciliation but to address another social situation altogether.

"Of course, it would be nice if the blacks of Chicago, to take one example, did not have to go to court in order to obtain all that the Constitution promises, and instead were able to work things out with the school board by walking, and talking, and loving. But once they have turned to the courts, it strikes me as absurd for the legal system to create incentives or pressures that force them to settle. It is costly to litigate, as they well know, but it also is costly to settle. To ignore these costs and to disfavor litigation because you hope that social relations between the parties can be restored is like ignoring the dangers of plea bargaining and favoring it over trial because you wish the crime that gave rise to the prosecution had not occurred.

"In defending their variant of ADR, Professors McThenia and Shaffer might contest my factual premise about the divided character of our communities. They might argue that the blacks of Chicago who turn to the courts are mistaken in their belief that they cannot get justice on their own. Or McThenia and Shaffer might insist that no matter how improba-ble, reconciliation is always a possibility, at least as a logical or formal matter, and that one should not be allowed into court unless one first has attempted reconciliation—a miracle is always possible. On this account, ADR emerges as an exhaustion requirement, and at one point McThenia and Shaffer draw on the experience of the ancient Hebrews and Christians to proffer such an idea: 'The [preferred] procedure involves, first, conversa-tion; if that fails, it involves mediation; if mediation fails, it involves airing the dispute before representatives of the community.' Only if the claimant refuses to heed the advice of the community elders will he or she be allowed to turn to the courts, and then only at the greatest risk: Whatever you lose on earth should be considered lost in heaven. . . .

"[O]nce we change our perspective and consider the modern American community, whether it be a Chicago, or an Evanston, or a Gary, we can understand why an exhaustion requirement of the type Professors McThe-nia and Shaffer propose is likely only to compound the costs of justice. Society will come to have two (or more) processes where it now has one, because the claimant is not likely to be satisfied with conversation, mediation, or a lecture by the representatives of the community, and thus will eventually turn to the courts. The McThenia–Shaffer proposal is likely to obstruct access to the courts without increasing the chance that the fabric of the community will be restored. . . .

"I realize that all might not go well and that adjudication might fail. Justice is not reducible to the law or to the particular decisions of any court: It is an aspiration. The truth of the matter, however, is that all institutions—not just those of the state—stand in jeopardy of failing in this aspiration. And there is no reason whatsoever for believing that adjudication suffers this risk more than any other institution. In fact, given the inequalities and divisions that so pervade our society, and given the need for a power as great as that of the state to close the gap between our ideals and the actual conditions of our social life, adjudication is more likely to succeed in this aspiration. Adjudication is more likely to do justice than conversation, mediation, arbitration, settlement, rent-a-judge, mini-trials, community moots or any other contrivance of ADR, precisely because it vests the power of the state in officials who act as trustees for the public, who are highly visible, and who are committed to reason. What we need at the moment is not another assault on this form of public power, whether from the periphery or the center, or whether inspired by religion or politics, but a renewed appreciation of all that it promises."

D.   THE DEBATE REVISITED

Recently, several new voices have joined the debate. Professor David Luban, in an article entitled *Settlements and the Erosion of the Public Realm*, 83 Geo. L. J. 2619 (1995) is one such voice. Luban agrees with Fiss that adjudication is a central part of political life, and is necessary to articulate public values and to structure social order. Further, he acknowledges that certain settlements can realize values of legal justice and the creation of public goods. However, Luban is critical of some settlements not because that they are destructive per se, but because certain settlements have a strong negative impact on the common good. Luban considers that private settlements in such cases as class-action asbestos and antitrust claims create "self-serving public law" in which the parties "achieve mutual satisfaction at the expense of those not at the bargaining table." Luban contends that the essential question is not whether to be "for or against settlement," but rather to sort out the infrequent "bad" settlements from the routine, "good" settlements.

Professor Carrie Menkel–Meadow, in a rejoinder to Luban entitled *Whose Dispute is it Anyway?: A Philosophical and Democratic Defense of Settlement (in Some Cases)*, 83 Geo. L. J. 2663 (1995), agrees that the issue is not whether to be for or against settlement. Settlement, she states, is here to stay. Arguing that many who criticize settlement suffer from "litigation romanticism," Menkel–Meadow is more enthusiastic than Luban in her support of settlement. She sees settlement as an aspect of party autonomy and as a philosophically and instrumentally justifiable response to docket crowding in the courts. For Menkel–Meadow, private interests in settlement often outweigh the public interest in airing a dispute, and it is "antidemocratic" to insist on a public tribunal when the parties do not want one. While Menkel–Meadow concedes that some settlements improperly impinge upon the public good, she questions the courts' ability to distinguish the "bad" settlements from the "good," concluding that Luban has raised more questions than he has answered.

E.   SETTLEMENT IN THE SHADOW OF THE LAW

In an influential article, Professors Robert H. Mnookin and Lewis Kornhauser demonstrate that the settlement process is not as removed from the substantive legal rules as many theorists presume. Rather, in *Bargaining in the Shadow of the Law: The Case of Divorce*, 88 Yale L. J. 950 (1979), they demonstrate that legal rules play a powerful role in shaping the terms of bargaining and the outcomes of settlement negotiations.

"Divorcing parents do not bargain over the division of family wealth and custodial prerogatives in a vacuum; they bargain in the shadow of the law. The legal rules governing alimony, child support, marital property, and custody give each parent certain claims based on what each would get if the case went to trail. In other words, the outcome that the law will impose if no agreement is reached gives each parent certain bargaining chips—an endowment of sorts.

"A simplified example may be illustrative. Assume that in disputed custody cases the law flatly provided that all mothers had the right to custody of minor children and that all fathers only had the right to visitation two weekends a month. Absent some contrary agreement acceptable to both parents, a court would order this arrangement. Assume further that the legal rules relating to marital property, alimony, and child support gave the mother some determinate share of the family's economic resources. In negotiations under this regime, neither spouse would ever consent to a division that left him or her worse off than if he or she insisted on going to court. The range of negotiated outcomes would be limited to those that leave both parents as well off as they would be in the absence of a bargain."

Mnookin and Kornhouser show how legal rules can be analyzed and evaluated for their impact on settlement negotiations. They focus particularly on the impact of legal uncertainty on the bargaining process and on the relative power of the bargaining parties. They contend that a rule that creates discretion in the judge and thus uncertainty as to the outcome disadvantages parties who are risk-averse. For example, the best interests of child standard for awarding custody in divorce law operates, they claim, to the disadvantage of the party who is most anxious to lose custody. They write:

"Legal rules are generally not as simple or straightforward as is suggested by the last example. Often, the outcome in court is far from certain, with any number of outcomes possible. Indeed, existing legal standards governing custody, alimony, child support, and marital property are all striking for their lack of precision and thus provide a bargaining backdrop clouded by uncertainty. . . . .

"Analyzing the effects of uncertainty on bargaining is an extremely complicated task. It is apparent, however, that the effects in any particular case will depend in part on the attitudes of the two spouses toward risk—what economists call 'risk preferences.' . . . .

"There has been considerable debate about the advantages and disadvantages of legal standards that confer broad discretionary power on decision makers. But analysis has generally focused, both in the family law context and elsewhere, on the effects of discretion on the decisionmaking behavior of officials. We would like to suggest a different perspective, focusing on the implications of discretionary standards when they serve as the backdrop for out-of-court negotiations by the parties themselves.

"The effect on the process of divorce bargaining of having more or less precise standards can be fruitfully explored by comparing and contrasting the effects of three different custody standards, each of which has proponents in current policy discussion:

"1.   A *maternal-preference rule* creates a strong presumption in favor of giving custody to a mother, with the father having limited visitation rights. Until recently, this was the dominant standard.

"2.   The *best interests of the child standard* calls for a highly individualized determination, confers broad discretion on the judge, and gives no automatic preference to either parent simply on the basis of the parent's or the child's sex. This standard seems to be the dominant one today. We will assume that ordinarily the parent who is awarded custody will have care and control of the child for all but two weekends a month, during which time the other spouse will have visitation rights.

"3.   A *joint-custody rule* provides that in disputed cases each parent will have care and control of a child for half the time. Although it has been seriously proposed, no jurisdiction has adopted this rule.

"Each of these three custody standards creates its own set of bargaining endowments. Because different rules give various amounts of bargaining chips to the parties, changing the standard would affect each party's relative bargaining power and would therefore influence the range and frequency of possible negotiated outcomes.

"For example, if the legal standard were changed from a maternal-preference rule to a standard that gave no preference based on parental sex, then a father's chances of winning custody in a contested case would be improved. This in turn would affect the outcomes reached through negotiation, since it would generally increase the bargaining power of fathers as a class and decrease the bargaining power of mothers. Because of differences in parental preferences, however, not all fathers would end up with more child-time: some might simply pay less in alimony or child support. Thus, our analysis suggests that recent changes in custody law giving fathers more equal claims to custody, and in alimony law limiting the extent and availability of permanent alimony, have strengthened the relative bargaining power of husbands.

"Both the best interests standard and the joint-custody rule are 'neutral' as between the sexes; nevertheless, they have very different implications for bargaining. Under the best interests principle the outcome in court will often be uncertain: each spouse may be able to make a plausible claim for custody, and it may be impossible to predict how a court would decide a disputed case. Under the joint-custody standard, on the other hand, the parties both know what will happen in court: each will be responsible for the child half the time. Thus, comparison of these two standards allows us to explore further the effects of uncertainty on the bargaining process.

"Uncertainty has several important effects on the relative bargaining power of the parties. As suggested earlier, if there is substantial variance among the possible court-imposed outcomes, the relatively more risk-averse party is comparatively disadvantaged. The important policy implications of this fact are illustrated by the following example.

"Assume that both the parents would like to have custody. The father is risk-neutral; he would be indifferent if given a choice between (1) having custody of his child half the time; or (2) being exposed to adjudication under the best interests standard and having a fifty percent chance of winning full custodial rights and a fifty percent chance of only having visitation rights. The mother, on the other hand, we will assume is risk-averse; she would much prefer the certainty of half the child's time to the risk of adjudication with a fifty percent chance that she might end up only with visitation.

"We would predict that under the best interests standard the mother, because she is risk-averse, will accept less in order to avoid the gamble inherent in adjudication. Both custody standards are 'sex neutral,' yet the best interests standard disadvantages a risk-averse parent and the joint-custody rule does not. The fact that uncertainty about the outcome in court concerning custody disadvantages the relatively more risk-averse parent is a peculiarly ironic and tragic result. Most of us would assume that a good parent would be unwilling to take a gamble in which one outcome would substantially diminish his or her relationship with the child. And yet the consequence of a vague, discretionary rule is to disadvantage such a parent if he or she is negotiating with a spouse who is more of a gambler.

"Vague legal standards have other effects on the parties' relative bargaining power and on negotiations. Uncertainty about the outcome in court probably increases transaction costs. Imprecise legal standards require an expert to estimate the probable outcome if the parties go to court. A lawyer may be necessary simply for a person to learn what his bargaining chips are. Moreover, because there may be no objective source of information about the actual probabilities of outcome in a particular case, the parties and their representatives may spend considerable time attempting to persuade the other side that it has overestimated its prospects for success.

"It would also seem that vague legal standards give a relative advantage to the more able negotiator. As the dispersion among possible outcomes in court becomes wider, there will be a greater premium on bargaining skills, since there will be greater opportunities for strategic behavior and a wider range of possible negotiated outcomes that might leave a party better off than possible court-imposed outcomes...."

In addition, Mnookin and Kornhouser claim that some rules prevent parties from bargaining altogether, thus preventing settlement and fomenting litigation. As an example, they analyze a proposal that custodial parent have all rights, and noncustodial parent have none. Such a rule, they claim, would deprive parties of the possibility of reaching a mutually satisfactory compromise. Such a rule will promote litigation both because parties cannot compromise and because they cannot bind themselves for the future.

* * *

Questions

1. Do you agree with Menkel–Meadow that private interests in settlement outweigh the public interest in an open airing of disputes, the reasoned elaboration of legal norms, and the collective structuring of the social order? Should settlements in certain types of cases be subject to judicial scrutiny? For example, might there be a greater public interest in monitoring the terms of settlements in class action employment discrimination litigation or tobacco-related claims, than in ordinary commercial disputes that raises claims about contractual performance and breach?

2. How serious should we take Fiss' concern that in settlement, parties disregard publicly enacted legal principles to the detriment of society as a whole? Do Mnookin and Kornhouser provide a satisfactory response? If legal rules do in fact shape settlements, what is left of Fiss' position? One problem that Mnookin and Kornhouser do not discuss is that if most lawsuits are settled and not litigated, where will the legal rules come from to cast the shadow in which parties can negotiate? Must not there be at least some cases that are fully litigated to provide the kind of guidance that Mnookin and Kornhouser presume?

* * *

3. INTERPRETING SETTLEMENT AGREEMENTS

Press Machinery Corporation v. Smith R.P.M. Corporation

727 F.2d 781(8th Cir.1984).

■ LAY, CHIEF JUDGE.

Smith R.P.M. Corporation (Smith), a Missouri corporation, appeals from the district court's judgment that construed a settlement agreement between Smith and Press Machinery Corp. (PMC), an Illinois corporation. The court interpreted the settlement agreement as granting PMC a limited license under a patent subsequently issued to Smith. For reversal, Smith argues that the district court erred in considering extrinsic evidence when interpreting the settlement agreement and in applying equitable estoppel to find a limited license for PMC. We affirm.

Smith manufactures, markets and installs printing press equipment. In particular, Smith markets a system for converting newspaper letterpress presses to the offset method of printing. In 1978, Smith filed a patent application for its method of installing its press conversion system. In 1979, Smith contracted to install its system for the Los Angeles Times. Smith then subcontracted with DEV Industries, Inc. (DEV) to supply certain equipment for Smith's Los Angeles Times contract. The subcontract contained DEV's agreement not to compete with Smith for two years in the manufacture or sale of press conversion systems. Three months into the contract, however, DEV set up and incorporated PMC, hired Smith's chief engineer and its national sales manager, and thereafter entered the press conversion market in competition with Smith. PMC subsequently contracted with the Kansas City Star to install a press conversion system.

In July of 1980, Smith filed suit against its two former employees, PMC, and DEV, in a Missouri state court. Smith alleged violation of the two year restrictive covenant and sought damages and an injunction barring PMC from disclosing or using trade secrets or confidential information regarding Smith's press conversion system. Four days before trial, on July 16, 1981, the parties entered into a settlement agreement. The agreement purported to release the parties from "all claims, rights of action, causes of action and demands of every kind and character which the parties hereto now have or under any circumstances could or might have, against the other arising out of, resulting from or in any way pertaining to the agreements and matters referred to in [the pleadings]." The agreement also required PMC, inter alia, to make a cash payment of $20,000 to Smith upon execution of the agreement and monthly payments of $10,000 for two years. To protect its interests, Smith was given a security interest in PMC's rights to payment under PMC's contract with the Kansas City Star. The financial arrangement was not made public; however, PMC insisted on the following public announcement:

> The lawsuit captioned Smith R.P.M. Corporation vs. DEV Industries, Inc., Press Machinery Corporation, et al., (No. CV–80–16649, Circuit Court of Jackson County, Missouri) has been terminated to the mutual satisfaction of the parties, leaving each party on its own to compete and sell letter press to offset conversion systems.

During the state court litigation, PMC allegedly was apprised of Smith's pending patent application for its method of installing its press conversion system. Smith received oral notification that its patent would be approved in April of 1981. However, during the settlement negotiations in July, the pending patent was not discussed, nor did the agreement make any specific reference to it. The settlement agreement was effectuated on July 16, 1981; Smith's method patent was issued on September 1, 1981. Smith then contacted persons at the Kansas City Star and informed them of Smith's patent. Smith also initiated a letter campaign warning persons who had contracted with PMC of the possibility that PMC was infringing Smith's patent. For reasons in dispute, the Star suspended performance of its contract with PMC. PMC then stopped making the payments to Smith that were mandated by the settlement agreement. This action followed.

PMC charges Smith with breach of the settlement agreement and seeks a declaratory judgment of noninfringement of Smith's patent. On PMC's motion for summary judgment, the district court found that PMC had a limited license under Smith's subsequently issued method patent and that Smith was equitably estopped from asserting its patent against PMC, at least regarding the completion of the Star contract.

On appeal, Smith contends that the release is a clear and unambiguous statement. Smith asserts that the reach of any general language in the agreement must be determined solely by reference to the matters specifically raised in the state court litigation. Stutz v. Campbell, 602 S.W.2d 874 (Mo.Ct.App.1980). Smith urges that because of the theoretical and remedial differences between the two actions, a patent infringement claim is distinct from an action premised on allegations of trade secret violations. Therefore, Smith argues, the court erred in finding that Smith released its right to assert its subsequently issued patent against PMC at the same time that Smith released it's trade secrets claims against PMC. Smith also contends that there was no finding that the document was ambiguous. Absent such a finding, Smith submits that the court erred in considering surrounding circumstances and the actions of defendants when interpreting the document. Smith also contends that if considered, the extrinsic evidence supports a finding that the parties had no intention of releasing Smith's potential patent rights.

Under Missouri law, normal rules of contract construction apply to interpretation of settlement agreements. Roberts v. Browning, 610 F.2d 528, 533 (8th Cir.1979). Crucial to the construction of the settlement agreement is the intent of the parties. J.E. Hathman, Inc. v. Sigma Alpha Epsilon Club, 491 S.W.2d 261, 264 (Mo.1973) (en banc). Whether a contract is ambiguous, is a question of law. If the court determines that there is no ambiguity, then the intention of the parties and interpretation of the contract is for the court to determine, as garnered from the four corners of the document. Id. Where a contract is ambiguous, use of extrinsic evidence for interpretation is proper; the resolution of the ambiguity is a question of fact to be determined by a jury. Fitch v. Doke, 532 F.2d 115, 117 (8th Cir.1976). In determining whether a contract is ambiguous, the court must consider the whole instrument and the natural and ordinary meaning of the language. Moreover, a mere difference of opinion as to the proper interpretation does not render the contract ambiguous as a matter of law. According to Missouri law, the court's role is to determine the intention as manifested not by what the parties now say they intended but by the document. In that inquiry, however, the court is justified in considering more than the mere words of the contract. The surrounding circumstances at the time of contracting and the positions and actions of the parties are relevant to the judicial interpretation of the contract. Cure v. City of Jefferson, 380 S.W.2d 305, 310–11 (Mo.1964) (adopting Restatement (Second) of Contracts); Restatement (Second) of Contracts, ss 202, 230, 235 (1981) . . . The evidence considered by the court, however, may not be used to vary, contradict, enlarge, modify, or curtail the written terms of the agreement.

In the instant case, the trial court apparently found that the intent and knowledge of the parties in negotiating the settlement agreement were fully apparent either on the face of the agreement or from the facts as then developed. Without making an explicit finding of ambiguity, the court determined that the surrounding circumstances were an appropriate consideration in the court's interpretation of the agreement. The court went on to declare that "[t]he circumstances surrounding the Kansas City Star contract, the actions of [Smith] in regard to the Kansas City Star, and the intent of the parties as to that contract in their negotiations and execution of the settlement agreement are developed sufficiently . . . to warrant [finding a limited license]."

From our own review of the settlement agreement, we find that the document is plain and unambiguous. The trial court's consideration of the circumstances surrounding the Kansas City Star contract and the negotiations of the settlement agreement was used appropriately to determine the intent of the parties and was not used to vary the written terms of the agreement. We find that the terms of the settlement agreement clearly reach the present dispute.

The essence of Count II in the state court litigation was Smith's contention that in PMC's competition with Smith, PMC was using "trade secrets, confidential information and plans and designs owned solely and exclusively by [Smith]." Accordingly, Smith sought to enjoin PMC from using the trade secrets and confidential information relating to the Smith conversion system. Contrary to Smith's assertion, however, the settlement agreement is not limited to a release of the trade secrets claim. The only limitation on coverage is that the claim, right of action, cause of action or demand must "*somehow arise out of, result from or in some way pertain to the agreements and matters referred to [in the pleadings of the state court litigation].*" At the time suit was filed, and when it was settled, PMC was installing a press conversion system at the Kansas City Star. Presumably, PMC's installation of the press conversion system at the Star was among the actions of PMC that Smith alleged were an improper use of trade secrets and confidential information acquired from PMC's contacts with Smith. The patent asserted in the present litigation covers one method of installing Smith's conversion system. Clearly, this at least pertains to the trade secrets that were allegedly being disclosed. In this regard, we note that the license recognized by the district court extends only to PMC's method of installing the press conversion system at the Star.

Moreover, the manner and method of PMC's payments to Smith, as provided in the settlement agreement, reflect the parties' intention that PMC would continue to work on the Kansas City Star project. Smith's allegations of potential patent infringement within two months of the settlement clearly inhibited PMC's ability to complete the work.[3] Denying PMC the right to use the trade secrets and confidential information for which it had paid, would strip the agreement of much of its meaning. The agreement is broad and employs expansive terminology. The release in the settlement agreement is not limited to the cause of action then at issue; nor is it limited to resolving past disputes. The agreement was an attempt to resolve finally those disputes then at issue and those that might arise in the future. We find that, as a whole and in light of established rules of contract interpretation, the settlement agreement was intended to allow PMC to continue manufacturing, marketing and installing its conversion system at the Kansas City Star.

Because we have determined that the settlement agreement clearly grants PMC a limited license under Smith's subsequently issued patent, it is unnecessary to address Smith's contention that the district court erred in applying the doctrine of equitable estoppel.

Accordingly, the district court order is affirmed. Costs are awarded to appellee.

* * *

Questions

1. What factors led the appellate court to find that the settlement agreement was not ambiguous? If you were drafting a release as part of a settlement in this case, how could you avoid this result?

2. When parties settle disputes, it is often necessary later to determine just what they settled. Questions of parol evidence abound. For example, when a subsequent dispute arises, one side is likely to claim that the matter was already settled, and the other is likely to claim that it was not included in the prior settlement. In such case, courts are called upon to interpret the scope of a settlement. Can a court decide such questions without hearing extrinsic evidence concerning the nature of the dispute that was settled and the intent of the parties in the settlement? Did the appellate court in this case use extrinsic evidence in reaching its conclusion? Why did Smith seek to keep out the extrinsic evidence? How did it affect the court's interpretation of the settlement agreement?

3. What other defenses might a party raise to enforcement of a settlement agreement?

---

3. The district court reserved ruling on whether Smith's actions constitute a breach of the settlement agreement.

4.   Should a court enforce a settlement agreement if it was the result of an altogether baseless claim? What if one side fabricated a claim against the other in order to extort a settlement? Should a court examine the underlying claim that was settled in order to determine whether to enforce the settlement agreement? Consider the following hypothetical:

Jones and Smith own neighboring property, which is separated by a fence. For as long as either can remember, Jones has had a shed directly abutting the fence. Now Jones wants to sell her house and puts it on the market. She is planning a job relocation, and needs to sell her house quickly so that she can get resettled elsewhere. Smith, knowing the property is for sale and knowing there is some urgency, tells Jones that the property line is actually five feet to the side of the boundary fence, and that in fact, Jones' shed is wholly on Smith's property. Smith shows Jones a survey of the property that supports Smith's assertion. Smith says that he wants damages for this continuing trespass, and that if Jones refuses, he will file a lis pendens, tying up any efforts of Jones to sell her property for several years. Jones, distressed about the prospect of a lawsuit stopping a potential sale, executes a settlement agreement with Smith. As part of the settlement, Smith agrees to forgive past trespasses of Jones, Jones promises to move the shed, and Jones gives Smith a note for $5,000. Jones moves the shed, sells the house, and moves. In doing so, Jones has a new survey that shows that she was right concerning the property line, and that Smith's claim regarding the location of the property line was completely baseless. Consequently, Jones refuses to pay on the note, and Smith sues on the basis of the settlement agreement.

Who wins? What would a court need to know to decide this? Should the outcome depend upon Smith's good faith belief, or lack of good faith belief, in the validity of his claim? For example, what if Smith, in bad faith, altered a survey in order to get Jones to agree to a settlement? Alternatively, should the result depend upon the objective validity of the underlying claim? That is, what if Smith's claim was asserted in good faith, but was patently false? For example, what if he misread the survey? Should the outcome turn on the objective validity of the underlying claim that was settled? What are the problems with each approach?

The American Law Institute's Restatement of Contracts has attempted to address the problem of settlements of disputed claims by treating it as a question of consideration. According to the Restatement of Contracts 1st § 76(b), an agreement to settle a disputed claim is supported by consideration if the parties have an "honest and reasonable belief" in the "possible validity" of the claim. In contrast, the Restatement of Contracts 2nd § 74 says an agreement settling a disputed claim is not supported by consideration unless the claim that is settled is actually doubtful *or* the surrendering party has good faith belief in the validity of the claim. A third approach is found in some state courts that say that the claim on which the settlement is based must be made in good faith and must have *some* foundation, i.e. be based on a *colorable right*. If a good faith claim makes a mountain out of a molehill, it is "doubtful." But if there is no molehill, then the claim has no substance, so its settlement is not consideration. See, e.g., *Duncan v. Black,* 324 S.W.2d 483 (Mo.App.1959).

What are the problems with each approach? Which is preferable?

* * *

---

4.   THE PUBLIC STAKE IN SETTLEMENT AGREEMENTS

United States v. Bechtel Corporation

648 F.2d 660 (9th Cir.1981).

■ SKOPIL, CIRCUIT JUDGE:

INTRODUCTION

Bechtel Corporation, Bechtel Incorporated, and certain of their subsidiaries ("Bechtel") appeal the entry of a consent judgment. The decree was entered in an antitrust action based on Bechtel's alleged participation in the Arab boycott of Israel. We conclude that the acts of the government, taken after a stipulation consenting to the judgment was filed, do not require that Bechtel be relieved from its consent. We further find that the trial court did not err in determining that the decree is in the public interest. We affirm.

BACKGROUND AND PROCEEDINGS BELOW

In January 1976 the United States filed a civil action against Bechtel asserting violations of section 1 of the Sherman Act, 15 U.S.C. § 1. The complaint described the Arab boycott, whereby Arab League countries refuse to engage in commercial relations with those who engage in commerce with Israel. It alleged that Bechtel combined, conspired, and agreed with others to participate in the boycott. The government asserted that this activity restrained trade in violation of the antitrust laws, and requested declaratory and injunctive relief.

Bechtel denied the complaint's material allegations and raised eleven defenses, including estoppel, inapplicability of the antitrust laws, government sanction, sovereign compulsion, act of state, non-justiciable controversy, national interest, and failure to state a cause of action.

In January 1977 the parties proposed a consent decree and filed it with the district court, along with the competitive impact statement required by the Antitrust Procedures and Penalties Act ("APPA"), 15 U.S.C. § 16. The parties also filed a stipulation. The stipulation provided that the proposed judgment could be entered "upon the motion of either party or upon the Court's own motion, at any time after compliance with the requirements of the Antitrust Procedures and Penalties Act (15 U.S.C. §§ 16(b) et seq.) and without further notice to any party or other proceedings, provided that plaintiff (the government) has not withdrawn its consent which it may do at any time before the entry of the proposed Final Judgment by serving notice thereof on defendants and by filing that notice with the Court.''

On January 19, 1977 the proposed decree and the government's competitive impact statement were published in the Federal Register and certain newspapers. In the following sixty days the government received comments on the proposed decree from the public. The sixty-day period for public comment, provided by 15 U.S.C. § 16(d), ended on April 3, 1977.

In June 1977 Congress passed the Export Administration Amendments ("EAA") regarding foreign boycotts. 50 U.S.C.App. §§ 2401–13. Department of Commerce regulations interpreting the new law were drafted, published and finally issued in January 1978.

On March 24, 1978 the government published its response to the comments received from the public on the proposed consent decree. On May 10, 1978 it moved for entry of the proposed final judgment.

On June 30, 1978 Bechtel filed its opposition to the entry of the decree. Bechtel argued that: (1) there was no basis for entering the judgment because the government had violated the stipulation by failing to comply with the APPA; (2) Bechtel's consent was vitiated by the new interpretations the government was applying to the decree; and (3) entry of the decree was no longer in the public interest because of the conflicting interpretations and the intervening passage of the Export Administration Amendments.

The district court concluded that the United States had not violated the APPA, or at least that Bechtel had not shown sufficient prejudice from any such violation to nullify its consent. It also determined that the interpretations of the proposed judgment the government had advanced in its response to public comments did not repudiate the agreement or amount to a withdrawal of consent. Further, the court found the EAA no bar to entry of the decree. Finally, the district court found the proposed judgment in the public interest, and ordered it entered. Bechtel appealed.

We must decide: (1) whether the district court had jurisdiction to enter the decree; (2) whether the government violated the provisions of the APPA; (3) if so, whether the violation vitiated the stipulation of consent; (4) whether the interpretations of the decree presented in the government's response to public comments amounted to a repudiation by the government or relieved Bechtel of its consent; (5) what factors must be considered in determining whether the entry of a consent judgment in an antitrust case is in the public interest; and (6) whether entry of this decree is in the public interest.

DISCUSSION

Decrees entered by consent may be reviewed on appeal where there is a claim of lack of actual consent or a lack of subject matter jurisdiction. Swift & Co. v. United States, 276 U.S. 311, 48 S.Ct. 311, 72 L.Ed. 587 (1928). But a decree that " 'appears by the record to have been rendered by consent, is always affirmed, without considering the merits of the cause.' " Id. at 324,

48 S.Ct. at 314 (quoting Nashville, C. & St. L. R. Co. v. United States, 113 U.S. 261, 5 S.Ct. 460, 28 L.Ed. 971 (1885)).

We must consider only the propriety of the entry of the decree. The merits of the judgment are not before us, except for two limited purposes. The decree may have been beyond the district court's jurisdiction to enter or the substance of the decree may be contrary to the public interest.

I. Jurisdiction

Bechtel argues that its alleged boycott activities were beyond the scope of the antitrust laws. Bechtel contends this means it was beyond the power of the district court to enter the decree or contrary to the public interest for it to do so.

The jurisdictional part of this argument "fails to distinguish an error in decision from the want of power to decide." Swift & Co., supra, 276 U.S. at 330, 48 S.Ct. at 316. If Bechtel is correct in its assertion that the boycott is beyond the reach of the antitrust laws, it proves at most that the complaint failed to state a cause of action. Such a failure is not a jurisdictional defect. Bell v. Hood, 327 U.S. 678, 66 S.Ct. 773, 90 L.Ed. 939 (1946).

A judgment dismissing an action for failure to state a claim is a judgment on the merits. In dismissing an action a court must assume jurisdiction. Id. Any error by the court in refusing to enter such a judgment might be corrected on appeal if Bechtel had not waived the defect by its consent. Swift & Co., supra, 276 U.S. at 331, 48 S.Ct. at 316–317.

Bechtel was not required to give its consent to the judgment it now protests. It had a right to litigate the applicability of the antitrust laws to its alleged participation in the Arab boycott. It voluntarily surrendered that right. We cannot decide whether the complaint stated a cause of action without violating the rule against reviewing the merits of consent decrees.

II. Consent

Bechtel contends that the judgment must be vacated because the only basis for its entry, consent, was lacking. In the face of the stipulation Bechtel concededly entered, we must interpret this as an argument that the government withdrew its consent or repudiated the agreement, or that events occurring after the stipulation equitably require that Bechtel be relieved of its consent.

A. Antitrust Procedures and Penalties Act.

The stipulation filed by the parties called for the consent decree to be entered "at any time after compliance with the requirements of the Antitrust Procedures and Penalties Act" Bechtel argues that compliance with the APPA was a condition of its consent that was never met. Alternatively, Bechtel contends that the government's violation of the stipulation entitled it to relief from its consent.

Bechtel asserts that the government violated the APPA by failing to file its responses to public comment on the proposed decree until nearly one year after the close of the comment period. The APPA requires a proposed consent decree to be filed in the district court and published in the Federal Register "at least 60 days prior to the effective date of such judgment." 15 U.S.C. § 16(b). It also provides that "(a)ny written comments relating to such proposal and *any responses by the United States thereto,* shall also be filed with such district court and published by the United States in the Federal Register *within such sixty-day period.*" Id. (Emphasis added.)

Section 16(d) describes the public comment and government response procedure in more detail. It provides in part: "(d) During the 60–day period as specified in subsection (b) of this section, and such additional time as the United States may request and the court may grant, the United States shall receive and consider any written comments relating to the proposal for the consent judgment submitted under subsection (b) of this section. . . . *At the close of the period* during which such comments may be received, *the United States shall file with the district court and cause to be published in the Federal Register a response to such comments.*" (Emphasis added.)

Bechtel contends that the government had to file and publish its response to public comments within 60 days of the filing and publication of the proposed decree, unless it received an extension of time from the court. The government argues, and the district court agreed, that the sixty-day period is a minimum time for public comment between publication and entry of a proposed consent decree.

The government's interpretation of section 16(b) ignores the plain language of the statute. Not only public comments, but also the United States' responses are to be filed within the sixty-day period. While the phrase "[a]t the close of the period" in section 16(d) may indicate that the government is allowed some additional time after the end of sixty days to prepare and file responses, it does not mean at any time after the close of the period.

The government's failure to file its responses within the time contemplated by the APPA does not mean, however, that the decree could not be entered. Completion of APPA procedures was required before the judgment could be entered. This requirement was established by the terms of the stipulation, as well as by operation of the statute itself. But we decline to read the stipulation or the statute as making strict technical compliance with the APPA a condition to final entry of the decree.

The structure of the statute and its legislative history indicate that Congress was primarily concerned with allowing sufficient time for comment and response. The time provisions were not established to prevent open-ended scrutiny of a proposed consent decree. It would not advance the purposes of the statute to adopt a rule that any failure strictly to meet a time limitation precludes entry of a consent decree.

Bechtel has not persuaded us that the phrase in the stipulation "after compliance with the requirements of the Antitrust Procedures and Penalties Act" should be read any more strictly than the statute itself. The noncompliance did not go to the essence of the stipulation. Bechtel admitted at argument that it would not have objected to entry of the decree based on the lapse of time alone. Bechtel has not shown any prejudice to it arising from the government's failure to file its responses to public comments until nearly one year after the close of the comment period.

Bechtel argues that as a result of the government's delay, it has become enmeshed in a conflict between the Department of Justice and the Department of Commerce over the proper response to foreign boycotts and the interpretation of the Export Administration Amendments. Bechtel has not shown how the timely filing of the government's response to public comments would have avoided this conflict, if any. Nor has Bechtel shown that it has less protection because of the delayed filing. The district court specifically declined to decide whether the EAA would require modification of the decree after its entry.

We conclude that the government's failure strictly to comply with the APPA time requirements does not entitle Bechtel to relief from its consent.

III. Repudiation

Bechtel asserts that the government breached the stipulation and "destroyed consent" by repudiating the decree's meaning. The repudiation is said to have occurred when the government filed and published its response to public comments on the proposed decree. Bechtel alleges that the government has interpreted the judgment in a manner inconsistent with the understanding reached by the parties in their negotiations and expressed in the government's competitive impact statement. Bechtel concedes that no words have been altered, but argues that the government's interpretation changed the decree.

The government says that it has not changed its interpretation of the judgment, although it concedes that it made an incorrect statement in the competitive impact statement it filed with the proposed decree. The government characterizes the interpretation offered in its response to public comments as an effort to correct and clarify its obvious earlier mistake, not a change in position. The district court found that the government had not repudiated the proposed judgment.

Bechtel's contention imputes too much power to the government and too little power to the court. The government cannot unilaterally change the meaning of a judgment. When a consent judgment is being interpreted for enforcement purposes a court may rely on certain aids to construction, including the circumstances surrounding the formation of the order. United States v. ITT Continental Baking Co., 420 U.S. 223, 238, 95 S.Ct. 926, 935, 43 L.Ed.2d 148 (1975). In a later enforcement proceeding Bechtel may persuade a court that its interpretation of the decree is the correct one. . . .

IV. Public Interest

Bechtel asserts that the district court applied the wrong test in determining whether the consent decree was in the public interest. Furthermore, Bechtel argues, the decree is not in the public interest and the district court erred in so finding.

A.   Scope of Inquiry.

The district court stated as its "guidelines for consideration" whether the relief provided for in the proposed judgment was adequate to remedy the antitrust violations alleged in the complaint. The court concluded that the relief was adequate. Bechtel contends this view was erroneously narrow.

The APPA requires a district court to determine that consent judgment is in the public interest before it may be entered. 15 U.S.C. § 16(e). The statute suggests considerations that may be relevant: "For the purpose of such determination, the court *may* consider (1) the competitive impact of such judgment, including termination of alleged violations, provisions for enforcement and modification, duration or relief sought, anticipated effects of alternative remedies actually considered, and any other considerations bearing upon the adequacy of such judgment; (2) the impact of entry of such judgment upon the public generally and individuals alleging specific injury from the violations set forth in the complaint including consideration of the public benefit, if any, to be derived from a determination of the issues at trial." Id. (Emphasis added.)

The statute suggests that a court may, and perhaps should, look beyond the strict relationship between complaint and remedy in evaluating the public interest. We cannot agree that a district court should engage in an unrestricted evaluation of what relief would best serve the public.

The balancing of competing social and political interests affected by a proposed antitrust consent decree must be left, in the first instance, to the discretion of the Attorney General. See United States v. National Broadcasting Co., 449 F.Supp. 1127 (C.D.Cal.1978). The court's role in protecting the public interest is one of insuring that the government has not breached its duty to the public in consenting to the decree. The court is required to determine not whether a particular decree is the one that will best serve society, but whether the settlement is "within the reaches of the public interest." Id. at 1143 (quoting United States v. Gillette Co., 406 F.Supp. 713, 716 (D.Mass.1975)). More elaborate requirements might undermine the effectiveness of antitrust enforcement by consent decree.

We conclude that the inquiry undertaken by the district court was appropriate in scope. The record shows that the district court considered potential conflicts between the EAA and the decree and the government's allegedly inconsistent interpretations in its evaluation of the public interest. The only matters the court expressly refused to consider were contentions going to the merits of the underlying claims and defenses. This refusal was proper.

B.   Merits.

Finally, Bechtel argues that the district court erred in determining that the decree is in the public interest. Bechtel contends that entry of the judgment is inimical to the public interest because it increases uncertainty as to what conduct Bechtel may engage in, it will encourage litigation by others because of its ambiguity, it conflicts with the balance of national and international interests struck by Congress and the executive branch and embodied in the EAA, it is unnecessary because of the EAA, it enjoins conduct beyond the reach of the antitrust laws, it implicitly condones the government's failure to comply with the APPA, and the public would benefit from trial of the issues.

In the court below, and here, Bechtel offered only conclusory statements that increased litigation is likely as a result of this decree. Such statements are not sufficient to show that entry of the decree is not in the public interest. Likewise, Bechtel has not shown how the public would benefit from a trial of the issues any more than it would in any case that is ended by settlement.

Any uncertainty Bechtel is experiencing about what it may or may not do under the decree is not necessarily a matter of the public interest. Furthermore, the uncertainty is no greater than that which would exist without a decree at all. Bechtel is always entitled to the protection of a judicial interpretation of the judgment. Similarly, any conflict between the EAA and the decree is not relevant to a determination of the public interest. The decree contains modification provisions. If Bechtel is entitled to substantive changes in the decree it may seek them.

It is not contrary to the public interest, as contemplated by the APPA, to enter a decree that is not necessary, or that grants relief to which the government might not be strictly entitled. The public does not suffer because Bechtel consented to limitations on its activities that could not otherwise be imposed. Bechtel cannot transform self-interest to public interest by pointing to the importance of its economic activity to society. Such an argument would apply to most antitrust consent decrees.

Entry of the decree in the face of the government's failure strictly to observe the APPA time requirements does not condone or sanction such a violation. It would not serve the public interest to assure government compliance with the time limitations by refusing to enter the decree. The remedy is far too drastic and indirect. Bechtel has shown no prejudice from the delay, and the public benefit from entry of the decree far outweighs any detriment from the appearance of sanctioning a wrong.

CONCLUSION

Bechtel agreed to the entry of the judgment from which it appeals. Events occurring since it stipulated its consent do not entitle it to relief. It may seek protection through judicial interpretation or modification of the judgment. The entry of the judgment itself was proper and is AFFIRMED.

* * *

Questions

1. Should courts consider the public interest in deciding whether to approve settlement agreements? Or are such agreements merely private

contracts in which the courts' role is simply to discern and enforce the will of the parties? Should the result depend upon whether the dispute that is settled was a contractual dispute between two contracting parties, or whether it involved an allegation that one party had violated the other's statutory rights?

2. In *Coventry v. United States Steel Corp.*, 856 F.2d 514 (3d Cir. 1988), the Third Circuit imposed a stricter test for voluntariness in judging the validity of a settlement and release in a dispute involved allegations of unlawful discrimination than it would use in a settlement of a mere contractual dispute. Is this another way a court can police settlements to protect the public interest?

3. When a court considers how a settlement affects the public interest, how should it define the public interest? If a settlement results from an alleged violation of a statute, must the settlement fully replicate the result that a court would have imposed if it had adjudicated the case? What is the problem with this standard for assessing the public interest in the settlement approval process? What other standard could a court use? Can a court police settlements for consistency with the public interest without having to decide the very legal issue that the parties purported to settle?

* * *

5. SETTLING CLASS ACTIONS

A class action, formerly known as a representative action in equity, is a lawsuit in which one or more named parties serve as representatives for a defined class. The litigation is conducted by counsel for the named parties, who act as attorneys for the entire class. A judgment reached in a class action is in most cases binding on the entire class except those who are permitted to opt out. Similarly, if the named parties to a class action reach a settlement, that settlement is likewise binding upon all members of the class other than those who legitimately opted out. Thus the settlement of class actions poses unique issues of fairness and due process toward the unnamed class members. These issues are explored in this section. First, however, it is useful to review the basic structure of Rule 23.

Rule 23 of the Federal Rules of Civil Procedure sets forth the rules governing class actions in the federal courts. Rule 23(a) provides that:

(a) Prerequisites to a Class Action. One or more members of a class may sue or be sued as representative parties on behalf of all only if (1) the class is so numerous that joinder of all members is impracticable, (2) there are questions of law or fact common to the class, (3) the claims or defenses of the representative parties are typical of the claims or defenses of the class, and (4) the representative parties will fairly and adequately protect the interests of the class.

That is, to maintain a class action, the moving party must demonstrate that the Rule 23(a) prerequisites of numerosity, commonality, typicality and representativeness are satisfied. In addition, the moving party must also show that the case falls within one of the three categories in Rule 23(b). Rule 23(b) sets out three types of class actions that can be maintained.

(b) Class Actions Maintainable. An action may be maintained as a class action if the prerequisites of subdivision (a) are satisfied, and in addition:

(1) the prosecution of separate actions by or against individual members of the class would create a risk of

> (A) inconsistent or varying adjudications with respect to individual members of the class which would establish incompatible standards of conduct for the party opposing the class, or

> (B) adjudications with respect to individual members of the class which would as a practical matter be dispositive of the interests of the other members not parties to the adjudications or substantially impair or impede their ability to protect their interests; or

(2) the party opposing the class has acted or refused to act on grounds generally applicable to the class, thereby making appropriate final injunctive relief or corresponding declaratory relief with respect to the class as a whole; or

(3) the court finds that the common questions of law or fact common to the members of the class predominate over any questions affecting only individual members, and that a class action is superior to other available methods for the fair and efficient adjudication of the controversy.

Rule 23(c) sets forth the procedural aspects of class actions. It provides that once a class action is commenced, the court shall determine ''as soon as practicable'' whether it is to be so maintained. It also states that in class actions brought under Rule 23(b)(3), the class representatives must give notice to all potential class members of the pendency of the action. Such notice must advise each potential class member that he has a right to be excluded from the class should he choose to do so, and that those who request exclusion will not be bound by the judgment. In contrast, in Rule 23(b)(1) or (2) class actions, class members not have the right to opt-out. For that reason, they are known as mandatory class actions. Any judgment in Rule 23(b)(1) or (2) class actions must specify those whom the court finds to be members of the class. Rule 23(c) also provides that when appropriate, a class may be divided into subclasses, and each subclass treated as a class.

Rule 23(d) specifies the types of orders a court may issue in conducting a class action. The court's powers include devising measures to avoid repetition in the presentation of evidence and imposing conditions on representative parties and intervenors.

Rule 23(e) states that a class action ''shall not be dismissed or compromised without the approval of the court.'' It also requires that notice of a proposed dismissal or compromise be given to class members.

Thus under Rule 23(e), when parties settle a class action lawsuit, a court must determine whether the settlement is fair and reasonable. Typically a court will conduct a hearing on the fairness of the settlement and give any and all class members who object to the proposed settlement an opportunity to be heard.

* * *

A.   FAIRNESS AND ADEQUACY OF REVIEW

Parker v. Anderson

667 F.2d 1204 (5th Cir.1982).

■ POLITZ, CIRCUIT JUDGE:

We review the district court's approval of a settlement of a class action suit against Bell Helicopter Company and its award of attorneys' fees. The court's approval was granted over the objection of all but one of the eleven named plaintiffs as well as over the objections of a number of class plaintiffs. Improprieties are claimed to have occurred in the settlement negotiations and the agreement is challenged as inadequate in its terms. In addition, one of the attorneys for the class appeals the amount of attorney's fees awarded to his firm. Finding neither error nor abuse of discretion in the court's approval of the settlement and setting of attorneys' fees and costs, we affirm.

Facts

In March 1975, Sarah Parker and Curtis Ford filed a class action suit against Bell Helicopter Company, a division of Textron, Inc., and certain unions, alleging discrimination in employment against blacks and females, in violation of Title VII of the Civil Rights Act of 1964, 42 U.S.C. §§ 2000e–2000e-17. Between 1975 and 1979 six other lawsuits brought by nine plaintiffs alleged identical discrimination by Bell; two of these suits included unions as defendants. The seven suits were consolidated into the instant proceeding.

Following consolidation, because the attorneys were unable to agree to an apportionment of responsibilities, the district court designated Howard Specter as lead counsel and Huey Mitchell and James Barber as associate class counsel, and assigned them concomitant duties. On April 21, 1978, the district court conditionally certified the litigation as a class action under Rule 23(b)(2) of the Federal Rules of Civil Procedure. Extensive, reciprocal discovery on the merits began in October 1978 and continued until February 1980.

Trial was scheduled for March 3, 1980. At the pretrial conference on February 6, 1980, it appeared that a settlement might be possible; the court urged counsel to make a good faith effort to reach an agreement. On February 29, 1980, counsel reached a tentative agreement and moved jointly for a continuance. The motion was granted and the court instructed counsel to inform the court on or before April 1, 1980, whether a complete settlement could be achieved.

During March 1980, class counsel met with the various named plaintiffs and discussed the tentative settlement proposal. Each of the eleven named plaintiffs authorized their counsel to note their approval of the class settlement, subject to Bell's acceptance of their individual demands which included a demand of $100,000 for one plaintiff, $84,000 for another, and guarantees of promotion to specific jobs for others. Bell countered with an offer of $1,500 each for ten of the named plaintiffs and $2,500 plus a future promotion for the eleventh.

On March 26, 1980, associate class counsel Barber met with all named plaintiffs to discuss the suit and proposed settlement. A discussion of the evidence, particularly the statistics plaintiffs were relying on, was planned. No serious discussion of the lawsuit was possible; plaintiffs were interested primarily in discussing their personal monetary demands. Apparently convinced that Bell's offer to them was too little, nine of the eleven plaintiffs expressed opposition to the settlement.[3]

On March 29, 1980, the attorneys for the parties approved a proposed Stipulation of Compromise and Agreement which embodied 18 of the 19 points contained in the tentative agreement concluded on February 29, 1980. The proposal required Bell to deposit $1,250,000 in an interest bearing account to be distributed to the class members when and as directed by the court. Certain affirmative relief measures projected to cost Bell approximately $1,000,000 to implement and maintain, were included. The proposal was made applicable only to the members of the class; Bell agreed to sever the individual claims of the named plaintiffs. Those claims are still pending.

On April 8, 1980, lead counsel Specter met with the named plaintiffs, intending to discuss the proposed settlement and his analysis of the strengths and weaknesses of the evidentiary base of their suit. The effort was futile; the plaintiffs focused on and voiced disagreement with Bell's counter to their individual claims. Specter offered to meet separately with each plaintiff. No one accepted his invitation.

On April 10, 1980, several plaintiffs moved to enroll Charles Padorr as their attorney for purposes of objecting to the settlement. By June 21, 1980, all plaintiffs had dismissed their original attorneys except the nonobjecting Judith Anderson, who continued to be represented by Mitchell. On April 18, 1980, the proposed settlement was filed along with a motion for preliminary approval.

On May 29, 1980, the district court defined a subclass of "objectors" and appointed Padorr as their counsel with authority to conduct discovery

---

3. The trial court capsulated the evidence about the meeting as follows: Angry and offended at what seemed to them small counteroffers, and fortified with a case of beer, the plaintiffs were ill disposed to listen to any explanation of the deficiencies of the statistical case against Bell. Posturing and wild talk took the place of reasoned analysis. At the close of the meeting, the plaintiffs voted to "reject" the settlement.

into the propriety of the settlement negotiations and the fairness of the settlement. On July 25, 1980, the court preliminarily approved the settlement for purposes of notification of the class. After considering filings from all parties, including the objectors, the court approved forms of notice for dissemination to the class, direct and by publication. This notice advised that a hearing would be conducted to examine the fairness and adequacy of the settlement.

After being continued once, the hearing on the proposed settlement commenced on October 16, 1980. For two days the court received evidence from the proponents and opponents of the proposed settlement. The hearing extended into a third day, when the court received evidence on the issue of fees for the class attorneys.

On March 11, 1981, the court filed a comprehensive Memorandum Opinion and Order which found the settlement to be fair and reasonable. The court also assessed fees for the various class attorneys and allowed their recovery of costs incurred in preparing the matter for trial. On April 10, 1981, the court amended the earlier order to correct clerical errors, to effect one substantive change, and to provide for post-settlement attorney's fees and apportionment of interest accruing on the deposit. This appeal followed.

Objectors maintain that the settlement should be rejected because (1) the terms are not fair and reasonable, (2) the class attorneys did not properly represent the class in negotiations, and (3) the payment of attorneys' fees out of the class settlement fund creates an impermissible conflict of interest. Mitchell appeals his award of attorney's fees.

I.   Fairness and Adequacy of the Settlement

Rule 23(e) requires court approval of compromise settlements of class actions, but it is silent as to the standard to be applied. Nonetheless, the rubric is now well established that the court will not approve a settlement unless it is found to be fair, adequate, and reasonable. In re Corrugated Container Antitrust Litigation, 643 F.2d 195 (5th Cir.1981); Cotton v. Hinton, 559 F.2d 1326 (5th Cir.1977). In determining the adequacy and reasonableness of the proposed settlement, the court does not adjudicate the dispute, for as we noted in Young v. Katz, 447 F.2d 431, 433 (5th Cir.1971): "[I]n examining a proposed compromise ... the court does not try the case. The very purpose of the compromise is to avoid the delay and expense of such a trial." In evaluating settlement proposals, six factors should be considered: (1) whether the settlement was a product of fraud or collusion; (2) the complexity, expense, and likely duration of the litigation; (3) the stage of the proceedings and the amount of discovery completed; (4) the factual and legal obstacles prevailing on the merits; (5) the possible range of recovery and the certainty of damages; and (6) the respective opinions of the participants, including class counsel, class representative, and the absent class members. See Pettway v. American Cast Iron Pipe Co., 576 F.2d 1157 (5th Cir.1978), cert. denied, 439 U.S. 1115, 99 S.Ct. 1020, 59 L.Ed.2d 74 (1979).

Our appellate review of the district court's approval of a settlement is limited; an approved settlement will not be upset unless the court clearly abused its discretion. Young v. Katz, 447 F.2d 431, 432 (5th Cir.1971). Similar to the function of the trial court, our limited review rule is a product of the strong judicial policy favoring the resolution of disputes through settlement. United States v. City of Miami, 614 F.2d 1322 (5th Cir.1980).

In deciding whether a clear abuse of discretion has occurred, we share the view of our colleagues of the Second, Fourth and Eighth Circuits that, absent fraud or collusion, the most important factor is the probability of the plaintiffs' success on the merits. . . .

In the case at bar, the court approved a settlement which provided, because of the accrued interest, a cash recovery exceeding $1,440,000 and 15 specifications of employment enhancement which the court concluded would cost Bell approximately $1,000,000 to implement and maintain. The district court's detailed findings and conclusions, which include a thorough history and analysis of the litigation, reflect a careful evaluation of the settlement in light of the six factors set forth above.

After reviewing the entire settlement and pretrial record, the court concluded that the plaintiffs had "only a marginal chance of recovery in the five million dollar range," and that even if they were successful in recovering a judgment in the more realistic range of three to five million dollars an appeal raising serious issues was likely. Review and analysis of the plaintiffs' affidavits, testimony, and the opinion of their expert statistician, impressed the district court that substantial weaknesses existed in their case. The trial judge noted "a significant risk of failure to show liability on the major backpay issues," and that the issues concerning the validity of Bell's education and experience requirements for hundreds of different jobs would be disputed hotly at trial, with sharply conflicting testimony about the statistical evidence, presenting an "all-or-nothing confrontation of unpredictable outcome." The judge also saw difficulties with the issue of certifying a class that included unhired applicants and Bell's facility at Amarillo. Problems were presented by the question of showing discriminatory intent for Title VII claims not based on adverse impact, and the validity of the causes of action based on affirmative action plans. Weighed against this background, the court concluded that the monetary award and the provisions for affirmative relief constituted a fair, reasonable, and adequate settlement.[6]

---

6. Even if the trial judge had found a comfortable probability that plaintiffs would have recovered $5,000,000, that factor would not mandate that the order approving the settlement be vacated. We agree with the comments by the Second Circuit when it confirmed the approval of a settlement which constituted only 12% of potential recovery in City of Detroit v. Grinnell Corp.: "The fact that a proposed settlement may only amount to a fraction of the potential recovery does not, in and of itself, mean that the proposed settlement is grossly inadequate and should be disapproved." 495 F.2d at 455. The court continued in a footnote: "In fact there is no reason, at least in theory, why a satisfactory settlement could not amount to a hundredth

We are not persuaded that the trial court erred either in its assessment of the probabilities of success or the range of recovery. Objectors offered no evidence at the settlement hearing concerning these issues. They were represented then by able and experienced counsel who had been empowered to conduct all necessary discovery and allowed adequate time to do so. We find no basis in this record for the contention that the trial court abused its discretion in finding this settlement fair and reasonable.[8]

II. Fairness and Adequacy of Representation

Objectors contend that the attorneys did not represent the class fairly and adequately during negotiations. They contend that counsel failed to consult with them, withheld certain information, and misrepresented material matters. The record does not support any of these assertions.

This inquiry must be placed in proper perspective. Objectors' personal claims were not before the district court and are not before us; they were severed and are still pending. Rather, the objectors stand before us as representatives of the absentee class members. The question presented by this appeal is whether class counsel provided fair and adequate legal representation to the class as a whole. Necessarily, much of what counsel does for the class is by and through the class representatives, but that is neither the ultimate nor the key determinant. The compelling obligation of class counsel in class action litigation is to the group which makes up the class. Counsel must be aware of and motivated by that which is in the maximum best interests of the class considered as a unit.

The duty owed to the client sharply distinguishes litigation on behalf of one or more individuals and litigation on behalf of a class. Objectors emphasize the duty of counsel in non-class litigation. The prevailing principles in that situation cannot be imported wholesale into a class action setting. The fairness and adequacy of counsel's performance cannot be gauged in terms of the representation of the named plaintiffs. In addressing this point in our recent decision of Kincade v. General Tire & Rubber Co., 635 F.2d 501, 508 (5th Cir.1981), we stated: Appellants' argument that the

---

or even a thousandth part of a single percent of the potential recovery." Id. at n.2.

8. Objectors challenge the 15 affirmative relief provisions, nine because they do not go far enough and six because they duplicate existing programs. We reject the challenge as to the nine for the reasons discussed in text. The trial judge concluded that in the arms length negotiations, the strength of plaintiffs' case would not support the insistence of a more favorable result. We are not prepared to disturb this judgment call as an abuse of discretion. As to the contention that six provisions are duplicative of existing programs, we simply do not agree. As an example, objectors insist that

the provision requiring Bell to publicize the existence and purposes of its "Employee Skills Profile and Questionnaire," is duplicative and therefore meaningless. This document, when used, lists the skills, education, and work experience of Bell employees. The provision requires Bell to provide personnel to encourage and assist both old and new employees to complete and update these profiles. The record reflects that the profile program was available previously but it was not publicized and it was not implemented. The proposed program would be structured to insure utilization, to the advantage of employees. In this context, we do not find this procedure duplicative. Nor do we find the others defective for similar reasons.

settlement cannot be applied to them because they did not authorize their attorney . . . to settle the case or otherwise consent to the settlement is also easily disposed of. Because the "client" in a class action consists of numerous unnamed class members as well as the representatives, and because "[t]he class itself often speaks in several voices . . ., it may be impossible for the class attorney to do more than act in what he believes to be the best interests of the class as a whole. . . ." Pettway v. American Cast Iron Pipe Co., 576 F.2d 1157, 1216 (5th Cir.1978).

The courts have recognized that the duty owed by class counsel is to the entire class and is not dependent on the special desires of the named plaintiffs. It has been held that agreement of the named plaintiffs is not essential to approval of a settlement which the trial court finds to be fair and reasonable. "Because of the unique nature of the attorney-client relationship in a class action, the cases cited by appellants holding that an attorney cannot settle his individual client's case without the authorization of the client are simply inapplicable." Kincade, 635 F.2d at 508; Flinn v. FMC Corp., 528 F.2d 1169, 1174 n. 19 (4th Cir.1975), cert. denied, 424 U.S. 967, 96 S.Ct. 1462, 47 L.Ed.2d 734 (1976) ("Appellants do not argue, nor may they under the authorities, that the assent of the class plaintiffs is essential to the settlement, provided the trial court finds it fair and reasonable.") . . . The rationale implicit in these decisions is sound: the named plaintiffs should not be permitted to hold the absentee class hostage by refusing to assent to an otherwise fair and adequate settlement in order to secure their individual demands. The trial court was not impressed favorably by the motivation of the objectors, finding as a fact that: "Plaintiff-objectors opposed the settlement in bad faith, primarily to gain leverage in settling their individual claims against Bell at exorbitant figures."

We measure class counsel's performance of the duty to represent the class fairly and adequately as we gauge the fairness and adequacy of the settlement. It will follow generally that an attorney who secures and submits a fair and adequate settlement has represented the client class fairly and adequately. In this instance, we affirm the trial judge's findings as to the settlement and necessarily reject the contention that the attorneys' performance in confecting the settlement was inadequate.

Objectors contend that counsel did not consult with them in a meaningful way and that they failed to disclose some matters and misrepresented others. These allegations are contrary to factual findings by the trial judge and are not supported by the record.

Consultation

Objectors complain of the inadequacy of contacts between counsel and the class members, especially as regards discussions of relative strengths and weaknesses of their case. Objectors point to the paucity of contact between counsel and the class representatives, pointing particularly to the five month period immediately preceding the February 29, 1980, tentative accord. The record does not support this assertion.

We note over 30 contacts between a member of Specter's staff and the class representatives during that period. In addition, the record reflects substantial contacts between class counsel and the representatives during March and April of 1980. During that period, the class attorneys advised the representatives of the terms of the proposed settlement, evaluated the evidentiary bases for the case, held meetings to discuss the settlement, and attempted to negotiate a monetary increase for some of the individual representatives.[9] Objectors suggest that these contacts are immaterial, contending that the February 29 letter was, in effect, the final settlement agreement. This objection is not well taken. As appellees point out, the tentative agreement was conditional, incomplete, and subject to approval, including the ultimate approval of the court.

The trial court reached the following conclusions: "Counsel consulted regularly and frequently with the class representatives throughout the case"; during March "all named plaintiffs consulted their attorneys about the class action settlement and authorized them to convey binding offers to Bell and to approve class settlement on their behalf if accepted," . . .; and "lead counsel behaved appropriately in negotiating the tentative settlement as spokesman for the class, immediately advising the named plaintiffs and associate counsel of its terms by letter, and ascertaining the named plaintiffs' reaction to the settlement before presenting it to the court." We perceive no error in these findings. . . .

Misrepresentation

The letter of February 29, outlining the terms of the tentative agreement, contained no reference to a time limit for the injunctive relief against Bell. The final agreement of March 28 contained a provision limiting injunctive relief to four years. Objectors claim that the failure of class counsel to inform them of this modification was misrepresentation. To support their contention, they point to the March 25 letter from Specter to Mackey explaining the terms of the settlement; that letter did not advise of the limitation.

Specter testified at the settlement hearing that any provision in the final agreement that was not in the February 29 letter was agreed to on March 28. The four year term for injunctive relief is one of those provisions. This testimony is not controverted. Since counsel was not aware of

---

9. For example, in a letter to plaintiff Mackey, dated March 25, 1980, lead counsel devoted approximately four pages to a detailed evaluation of the strengths and weaknesses of the case. In summarizing his purpose for writing he stated: "I want you to have a clear understanding of the risks which you are running before you decide what course to take and whether to seek to settle or take your chances in court." A similar letter was sent to plaintiff Odom. In addition, on at least two occasions, it was the named plaintiffs that refused to accept counseling and evaluations offered by class counsel. After the February 29 letter but before the final settlement agreement, associate counsel Barber met with plaintiffs to discuss the case. Instead of rational discussion, he was confronted with hostility and anger. After the March 28 agreement, but before the settlement hearing, lead counsel offered to discuss settlement with plaintiffs individually. The invitation went begging.

this provision during the conferences and communications with the plaintiffs in March 1980, his failure to inform them of this element cannot constitute misrepresentation. We find no merit in this contention.

III.   Attorneys' Fees

Objectors contend the settlement should be set aside because the manner in which the attorneys' fees were awarded created an impermissible conflict of interest. We agree with objectors that awards of attorneys' fees in the class action context present a potential for abuse, but we find no impropriety in the instant case.

The fees of class action attorneys have been paid historically out of the fruits of their labors. Alyeska Pipeline Service Co. v. Wilderness Society, 421 U.S. 240, 95 S.Ct. 1612, 44 L.Ed.2d 141 (1975). The amount of the attorneys' fees must be approved by the district court at the settlement hearing required under Rule 53(e). A full hearing is required. The trial judge has a responsibility to assess the reasonableness of the attorneys' fees in light of the standards enunciated in Johnson v. Georgia Highway Express, Inc., 488 F.2d 714 (5th Cir.1974),[11] and to enter findings of fact and conclusions of law setting out the basis for the fee award. Piambino v. Bailey, 610 F.2d 1306 (5th Cir.1980). See Norwood v. Harrison, 581 F.2d 518 (5th Cir.1978). When these procedures are complied with, our review of a trial court's award is confined to determining whether the trial court abused its discretion.

In the present case, the settlement agreement provided that "all Plaintiffs' attorneys' fees, expenses, and costs awarded by the Court shall be paid from the Settlement Fund" and that Bell "would have no further liability as to fees and costs than from the Settlement Fund except with respect to fees earned or costs incurred subsequent to the date of execution of this Stipulation." The agreement did not purport to set the amount of attorneys' fees. Instead, the third day of the settlement hearing was devoted to the question of attorneys' fees. That the trial court set the fees in light of the Johnson standards is evident from its opinion which explains in detail the methodology and basis for the various awards. We find no abuse of discretion in the setting of attorney's fees.

The appellants urge us to find that regardless of the care taken by the trial judge, a settlement providing for attorneys' fees payable out of the settlement fund creates an impermissible conflict of interest, citing Piambino v. Bailey and Prandini v. National Tea Co., 557 F.2d 1015 (3d Cir.1977). Their reliance on these cases is misplaced.

---

11. The Johnson factors are: (1) the time and labor involved; (2) the novelty and difficulty of the questions; (3) the skill requisite to perform the legal service properly; (4) the preclusion of other employment by the attorney due to the acceptance of the case; (5) the customary fee; (6) whether the fee is fixed or contingent; (7) time limitations imposed by the client or the circumstances; (8) the amount involved and the results obtained; (9) the experience, reputation, and ability of the attorneys; (10) the political "undesirability" of the case; (11) the nature and length of the professional relationship with the client; and (12) awards in similar cases. 488 F.2d at 717–19. In Piambino v. Bailey, we added two additional factors: the difficulty of the case and the uncertainty of the recovery.

In Prandini, the settlement agreement provided for payment of a certain sum to the class and another set sum to counsel. The two separate funds were negotiated simultaneously and the court recognized the inherent conflict. Similarly, in Piambino, the settlement agreement provided for the payment of a specific amount of attorneys' fees out of the settlement fund. The district court did not make an independent evaluation of the reasonableness of the fees, stating that it was:

> not being asked to set a reasonable attorneys' fee in conjunction with the instant settlement; rather the court is being presented with a proposed settlement, agreed to by all parties and unopposed by the class, which incorporates an award of attorneys' fees in the amount of $750,000.00 as a vital part of the settlement.

610 F.2d at 1328. We held that the district court improperly abdicated its responsibility to assess the reasonableness of the attorneys' fees and reversed its approval of the settlement.

Neither situation is presented in the instant case. The amount of the attorneys' fees was left entirely to the discretion of the court. The evil feared in some settlements—unscrupulous attorneys negotiating large attorney's fees at the expense of an inadequate settlement for the client--can best be met by a careful district judge, sensitive to the problem, properly evaluating the adequacy of the settlement for the class and determining and setting a reasonable attorney's fee in light of the Johnson standards. We find no abuse of discretion in the present case and affirm the award of attorneys' fees and costs recoveries to the attorneys. . . .

The judgment of the district court is AFFIRMED in all respects.

* * *

Questions

1. Why does the court in *Parker* approve the class action settlement when all but one of the named plaintiff's objected? How does the court determine that the settlement was fair?

2. What kinds of evidence does the court examine to determine the plaintiff's likelihood of success on the merits? Can a court base its assessment on a review of the paper records—affidavits, depositions, and so forth? Can a court judge the fairness of a settlement if a case settles early before there has been any significant amount of discovery?

3. Is the court's scrutiny of the merits of a case when presented with a motion to approve a class action settlement the same level of scrutiny a court would give to a motion for summary judgment? What are the differences between the two types of motions? Which type of motion should have a higher level of judicial scrutiny?

4. How can a court assess the adequacy of representation by class counsel? Is the inquiry concerning adequacy of representation merely an assessment of the fairness of the settlement? If so, is the standard not redundant? Is there an independent measure of adequate representation that the court brings to bear in *Parker*? What factors should a court use to

determine adequacy of representation of class counsel in a class action that settles early before much discovery has transpired?

5. Who is the client in the class action in *Parker*? If it is the named parties, could the court have approved settlement in this case? If the client is the unnamed parties—those who comprise the abstraction known as "the class"—how can such a client exert control over its lawyer and over the conduct of the lawsuit? Is class counsel presumed to be acting in the interests of the class? Is this an irrebuttable presumption? Given the potential conflict of interest and the serious dangers of ethical lapses when a lawyer is not accountable to her client, should a judge act as the guardian of the clients' interests in a class action? Is that an apt description of the role a judge plays in deciding the propriety of the class action settlements?

* * *

J.A. Shults, et al. v. Champion Int'l Corp.

821 F.Supp. 520 (E.D.Tenn.1993).

■ HULL, DISTRICT JUDGE.

This is a class action for interference with property rights brought by riparian landowners on the Pigeon River and Douglas Lake in Cocke, Jefferson and Sevier Counties of Tennessee. The attorneys for the parties have negotiated a settlement agreement which has been submitted to the Court for approval. On January 19, 1993, after notice of the proposed settlement had issued to class members, the Court conducted a fairness hearing. Based upon the written objections signed by sixty-one (61) class members, the testimony at the fairness hearing, and the Court's personal assessment of the proposed agreement, the Court has decided not to approve the settlement.

The plaintiff class, composed of approximately two thousand, six hundred (2,600) riparian landowners and lessees, claimed that Champion's pulp and paper mill in Canton, North Carolina, discharges waste water into the Pigeon River which contains many toxic chemicals; that its paper-making process also discolors the river's water and makes it foul-smelling; that Champion's use of the river constitutes a private nuisance that unreasonably interferes with their rights as riparian property owners; and that this use is also a trespass contaminating their land and usable water. The plaintiffs sought damages to compensate for the diminution in the market value, rental value and/or use value of their realty, including compensation for the personal discomfort, stress, annoyance, and anxiety associated with this contamination of the river and lake water and their riparian properties. They also sought punitive damages and injunctive relief which would prohibit Champion from using lead, cadmium, cyanide, arsenic, elemental chlorine and chlorinated compounds in its mill processes.[1]

---

1. There were other tort theories raised in the original complaint, such as fear of cancer, but these were dismissed early in the proceedings. The pretrial order, which sup-

The case came to trial on September 14, 1992. On October 16, 1992, the Court declared a mistrial after the jury had announced that it was unable to reach a unanimous verdict. On December 21, 1992, attorneys for the parties entered into the settlement agreement now before the Court.

The proposed settlement provides for Champion to pay Six and One–Half ($6.5) Million Dollars into an interest bearing account which, after payment of the plaintiffs' litigation fees and expenses, will be used to establish a charitable fund to benefit the landowners and their communities, through environmental, educational, or other charitable activities. No compensatory or punitive damages are to be paid directly to any of the class members and no injunctive relief is to be imposed upon Champion.

The agreement not only settles the class action claims against Champion but would release Champion from liability for,

> all future claims, demands, rights of action and causes of action of every kind and character, whether arising in law or equity, both against the Settling Defendant and all other persons and entities, which each Class member, his, her or its heirs, executors, administrators, successors, and assigns, ever had, now have or hereafter may acquire, by reason of, arising out of, or in any way relating to Champion's Discharge [of waste water from its pulp and paper mill in Canton, North Carolina, into the Pigeon River and Douglas Lake].

The agreement entails the creation of The Pigeon River Endowment Fund which would be managed, invested, and administered by the already-existing East Tennessee Corporation, a tax exempt, nonprofit corporation organized under Tenn.Code Ann. § 48–52–103. The general purpose of the fund is to benefit, through environmental, educational, or other charitable activities including community or industrial development, not only those landowners who chose to be class members in this lawsuit but all landowners along the river and lake and their communities in Cocke, Sevier and Jefferson Counties. The Foundation is to establish a Board of Advisors of the Pigeon River Endowment Fund from the Pigeon River and Douglas Lake communities (not necessarily composed of class members), but is to retain control over the distribution of the funds. The document establishing the endowment specifically states its intention that the fund be continued in perpetuity. Presumably, disbursements to class members would be made only from the net income of the fund.

The objections raised by class members fall into several broad categories. Many members voiced disapproval of the fact that the settlement would allow for payment of the plaintiffs' attorneys but would not put any money directly into the pockets of the landowners.

Other objections focused on the fact that Champion accepts no blame for its long-term pollution of the river and is not being enjoined from polluting it in the future. Not surprisingly, many thought the settlement

planted the pleadings, limited the action to one sounding in trespass and nuisance. At no time was any claim raised for a physical injury such as cancer based on exposure to toxic chemicals in the waters of the river or the lake.

would give Champion a license to pollute in the future, free from any objection by those living downstream.

Even more serious objections focussed on the fact that the lawsuit was tried as one for trespass and nuisance, but the settlement would settle any claim for personal injuries which class members may now have or may learn about in the future. Several people pointed out that they only recently learned of the possible dioxin contamination of their properties and speculated that there might be other toxic agents in the river or the lake about which they still know nothing. In addition, despite assurances to the contrary by the attorneys for both parties, the agreement precludes lawsuits based on possible future misconduct on Champion's part, rather than just barring claims based on conduct prior to the effective date of the agreement.

In evaluating the fairness, reasonableness, and adequacy of the proposed settlement, the Court has considered 1) the complexity, expense, and likely duration of the litigation; 2) the factual and legal obstacles to a verdict in favor of the class; 3) the possible range of recovery and certainty of damages; 4) the number of objectors to the settlement and the nature of their objections; and 5) the impact the settlement might have on the community.

Because the proof in this lawsuit had to be presented through numerous expert witnesses, the litigation was both lengthy and expensive. In addition, the many complicated legal issues and evidentiary questions raised in this action guarantee that any verdict would have to be appealed. Nevertheless, retrial is not impossible. All of the expert testimony in this case was videotaped and could be used in a second trial to minimize expert witness fees. Further, all evidentiary questions have already been resolved and attorneys for both sides of the case know exactly what evidence will be admitted into trial. A retrial would likely be shorter and less costly than the first trial. Finally, other law firms have expressed interest in the lawsuit and may be able to contribute money and expertise to a retrial. The Court does not find the length, complexity, or expense of this case prohibitive.

The Court is aware of no legal obstacles to a plaintiffs' verdict. In the first trial of this case, none of the representative plaintiffs demonstrated evidence of substantial property damage. However, they did have credible proof of stress, annoyance, and anxiety caused by the contamination of their water. It was obvious to the Court that any hope the class might have had of obtaining a sizeable verdict depended on the availability of punitive damages. Unfortunately for the plaintiffs' case, most of the evidence of reprehensible conduct on Champion's part fell outside the statute of limitations. In the three-year period which preceded the filing of this lawsuit, the evidence showed that Champion not only stopped discharging dioxin into the Pigeon River, but embarked upon a major effort to redesign its manufacturing procedures to greatly reduce the odor and color pollution of the river. There was evidence that the water which borders the plaintiffs' properties was much more polluted when they acquired their land than it is today. Moreover, the evidence showed that Champion's discharges used to be regulated by the State of North Carolina (apparently with little concern for the people downstream in Tennessee), but are now monitored more evenhandedly by the federal Environmental Protection Agency. All these factors decrease the likelihood of a large punitive damages award. Nonetheless, the plaintiffs' case had moral strength. The undisputed evidence was that, for a great many years, Champion used the Pigeon River as its private sewer. The color contamination, which limited the depth to which light could penetrate the waters and greatly impaired normal aquatic life, and the smell associated with Champion's discharge, were obvious to even the most casual observer. Less obvious and more sinister was the fact that, historically, many toxic chemicals were released into the river with no warning to persons living downstream and no concern for possible damage to the ecosystem. The plaintiffs' outrage at this insult is justifiable and, in the Court's opinion, could support an award of punitive damages even though Champion's conduct today appears to be reasonable, and even though there is reason to believe that future contamination of the river will be held to a legal minimum.

As indicated earlier, the number of objectors is not great, but it is by no means insignificant. The objections they raise are serious ones.

Naturally, some class members objected to the fact that the only people getting any direct financial advantage from the settlement were the attorneys for the plaintiffs. However, this is not necessarily inappropriate. Only the attorneys for the plaintiffs advanced personal funds to finance the lawsuit. It is not unreasonable that some of the settlement funds be used to pay for the costs of this litigation.

In addition, while the class members may not know this, it is typical of settlement agreements that no liability be admitted by any party. This language does not disturb the Court. The Court agrees with the class members that the language of the settlement appears to give Champion a license to pollute the Pigeon River. However, the only real license given to Champion is the NPDES permit which controls and limits its waste water discharges. The Court believes that the Environmental Protection Agency will monitor Champion's activities and protect the interests of the class.

The objection which is of the gravest concern to the Court has to do with the language of the release. In the original notice of the class action sent out to all riparian property owners, the potential class members were advised,

> The class action seeks damages both for loss of value of the land and for other incidental damages attributable to the land use.... If you do not ask to be excluded, you will continue to be a part of the class, and will be bound by the Court's final decision whether Plaintiff wins or loses.

The Court is satisfied that, as of the date the class closed, those who had not opted out could be precluded from bringing a separate cause of action, such as a personal injury claim, about any condition known to them at that time. However, the Court is confidant that those who passively remained in the class had no idea that any outcome of the lawsuit could possibly preclude them (and their children and grandchildren), from ever bringing a lawsuit against Champion that "in any way related" to Champion's discharges. This release language used in the proposed settlement is peculiarly suited to lawsuits arising out of discrete events such as accidental spills of toxic material. It does not strike the Court as appropriate in a lawsuit concerning continuing conduct that might well vary in its intensity or degree. Moreover, the toxic chemicals to which the class members where exposed were not made known to them in a timely fashion. Fears that, at some future date, we may discover additional harm from agents in the water, do not seem unfounded. No settlement that precludes future, unknown causes of action can be considered fair, reasonable, or in the best interests of the class as a whole.

The final factor which the Court considered is the impact this settlement would have upon the community. There is no question that a trust fund, which could be drawn upon by all members of the community, could be highly beneficial. If it did nothing more than make a college education available to all the youth of this area, the long term salutary impact on the community would be impressive. However, this benefit has to be weighed against the disheartening and even demoralizing effect upon the community of the knowledge that its only lawsuit to redress over eighty years of harm (and possible future harm) to an important environmental asset ended with the impaired parties receiving no direct compensation for the loss they have sustained.

When all of these factors are carefully weighed, the Court must reject the settlement as now proposed.

This does not mean that the parties are forced to retry this action. The Court would, in fact, welcome a settlement agreement if one could be fashioned that met the concerns expressed in this Order. The parties are advised that, based on the meager evidence of actual damages presented at the first trial, the fact that Champion's conduct in recent years has been much more responsible to its downstream neighbors, and the fact that Champion's discharges are now subject to federal regulation, a settlement in the amount of Six and One–Half ($6.5) Million Dollars would be approved.

The Court would also approve release language that barred all trespass and nuisance claims based on known conduct prior to the effective date of the settlement and barred any class member's personal injury claim arising prior to the date the class was closed.

The Court would allow twenty percent (20%) of the settlement monies to be used for attorneys' fees and, in addition, would reimburse the plaintiffs' out-of-pocket litigation expenses from the fund.

The balance of the settlement fund would be distributed directly to the class members. The Court does not think placing the money in an endowment fund would be fair to the class for several reasons. For one thing, it is difficult to envision ways to spend the monies that would proportionately benefit all the members of the class. For another, the class members entered into this litigation with the idea that they would recover money damages for the "loss of value of the land and for incidental damages attributable to land use." They should not have their modest recovery involuntarily placed in a charity even if the charity would be beneficial to the community.

In the event that a settlement is reached, the Court would appoint a Master, pursuant to Rule 53, Federal Rules of Civil Procedure, to devise an equitable formula for distribution of the monies and to handle the actual disbursements to the class members.

If no acceptable settlement proposal is offered to the Court by August 1, 1993, the case will be reset for trial on September 7, 1993.

* * *

Questions

1. What factors were present in the settlement in *Shults* that led the court to refuse to approve it?

2. Is the release in this case similar to the release in the *Press Machinery v. Smith R.P.M.* case, supra. In the *Press Machinery* case, the court did not find the language of the release overbroad or otherwise problematic. How can we explain the court's disapproval of the release in this case?

* * *

B.   CLAIM PRECLUSION

Martin v. Wilks

490 U.S. 755, 109 S.Ct. 2180 (1989).

■ CHIEF JUSTICE REHNQUIST announced the opinion of the Court.

A group of white firefighters sued the city of Birmingham, Alabama (City), and the Jefferson County Personnel Board (Board) alleging that they were being denied promotions in favor of less qualified black firefighters. They claimed that the City and the Board were making promotion decisions on the basis of race in reliance on certain consent decrees, and that these decisions constituted impermissible racial discrimination in violation of the Constitution and federal statutes. The District Court held that the white firefighters were precluded from challenging employment decisions taken pursuant to the decrees, even though these firefighters had not been parties to the proceedings in which the decrees were entered. We think this holding contravenes the general rule that a person cannot be deprived of his legal rights in a proceeding to which he is not a party.

The litigation in which the consent decrees were entered began in 1974, when the Ensley Branch of the National Association for the Advancement of Colored People and seven black individuals filed separate class-action complaints against the City and the Board. They alleged that both had engaged in racially discriminatory hiring and promotion practices in various public service jobs in violation of Title VII of the Civil Rights Act of 1964, 42 U.S.C. § 2000e et seq., and other federal law. After a bench trial on some issues, but before judgment, the parties entered into two consent decrees, one between the black individuals and the City and the other between them and the Board. These proposed decrees set forth an extensive remedial scheme, including long-term and interim annual goals for the hiring of blacks as firefighters. The decrees also provided for goals for promotion of blacks within the fire department.

The District Court entered an order provisionally approving the decrees and directing publication of notice of the upcoming fairness hearings. App. 694–696. Notice of the hearings, with a reference to the general nature of the decrees, was published in two local newspapers. At that hearing, the Birmingham Firefighters Association (BFA) appeared and filed objections as amicus curiae. After the hearing, but before final approval of the decrees, the BFA and two of its members also moved to intervene on the ground that the decrees would adversely affect their rights. The District Court denied the motions as untimely and approved the decrees. United States v. Jefferson County, 28 FEP Cases 1834 (N.D.Ala.1981). Seven white firefighters, all members of the BFA, then filed a complaint against the City and the Board seeking injunctive relief against enforcement of the decrees. The seven argued that the decrees would operate to illegally discriminate against them; the District Court denied relief. App. to Pet. for Cert. 37a.

Both the denial of intervention and the denial of injunctive relief were affirmed on appeal. United States v. Jefferson County, 720 F.2d 1511 (C.A.11 1983). The District Court had not abused its discretion in refusing to let the BFA intervene, thought the Eleventh Circuit, in part because the firefighters could "institut[e] an independent Title VII suit, asserting specific violations of their rights." Id., at 1518. And, for the same reason, petitioners had not adequately shown the potential for irreparable harm from the operation of the decrees necessary to obtain injunctive relief. Id., at 1520.

A new group of white firefighters, the Wilks respondents, then brought suit against the City and the Board in District Court. They too alleged that, because of their race, they were being denied promotions in favor of less qualified blacks in violation of federal law. The Board and the City admitted to making race-conscious employment decisions, but argued that the decisions were unassailable because they were made pursuant to the consent decrees. A group of black individuals, the Martin petitioners, were allowed to intervene in their individual capacities to defend the decrees.

The defendants moved to dismiss the reverse discrimination cases as impermissible collateral attacks on the consent decrees. The District Court denied the motions, ruling that the decrees would provide a defense to claims of discrimination for employment decisions "mandated" by the decrees, leaving the principal issue for trial whether the challenged promotions were indeed required by the decrees. App. 237–239, 250. After trial the District Court granted the motion to dismiss. App. to Pet. for Cert. 67a. The court concluded that "if in fact the City was required to [make promotions of blacks] by the consent decree, then they would not be guilty of [illegal] racial discrimination" and that the defendants had "establish[ed] that the promotions of the black individuals ... were in fact required by the terms of the consent decree." Id., at 28a.

On appeal, the Eleventh Circuit reversed. It held that, "[b]ecause ... [the Wilks respondents] were neither parties nor privies to the consent decrees, ... their independent claims of unlawful discrimination are not precluded." In re Birmingham Reverse Discrimination Employment Litigation, 833 F.2d 1492, 1498 (1987). ... Although it recognized a "strong public policy in favor of voluntary affirmative action plans," the panel acknowledged that this interest "must yield to the policy against requiring third parties to submit to bargains in which their interests were either ignored or sacrificed." Ibid. The court remanded the case for trial of the discrimination claims....

We granted certiorari, 487 U.S. 1204, 108 S.Ct. 2843, 101 L.Ed.2d 881 (1988), and now affirm the Eleventh Circuit's judgment. All agree that "[i]t is a principle of general application in Anglo–American jurisprudence that one is not bound by a judgment in personam in a litigation in which he is not designated as a party or to which he has not been made a party by service of process." Hansberry v. Lee, 311 U.S. 32, 40, 61 S.Ct. 115, 117, 85 L.Ed. 22 (1940). This rule is part of our "deep-rooted historic tradition that everyone should have his own day in court." 18 C. Wright, A. Miller, & E. Cooper, Federal Practice and Procedure § 4449, p. 417 (1981) (hereafter 18 Wright). A judgment or decree among parties to a lawsuit resolves issues as among them, but it does not conclude the rights of strangers to those proceedings.[2]

Petitioners argue that, because respondents failed to timely intervene in the initial proceedings, their current challenge to actions taken under the consent decree constitutes an impermissible "collateral attack." They argue that respondents were aware that the underlying suit might affect them, and if they chose to pass up an opportunity to intervene, they should not be permitted to later litigate the issues in a new action. The position has sufficient appeal to have commanded the approval of the great majority of the Federal Courts of Appeals, but we agree with the contrary view expressed by the Court of Appeals for the Eleventh Circuit in these cases....

Joinder as a party, rather than knowledge of a lawsuit and an opportunity to intervene, is the method by which potential parties are subjected to the jurisdiction of the court and bound by a judgment or decree.[6] The

---

2. We have recognized an exception to the general rule when, in certain limited circumstances, a person, although not a party, has his interests adequately represented by someone with the same interests who is a party. See Hansberry v. Lee, 311 U.S. 32, 41–42.

6. The dissent argues, on the one hand, that respondents have not been "bound" by the decree but, rather, that they are only

parties to a lawsuit presumably know better than anyone else the nature and scope of relief sought in the action, and at whose expense such relief might be granted. It makes sense, therefore, to place on them a burden of bringing in additional parties where such a step is indicated, rather than placing on potential additional parties a duty to intervene when they acquire knowledge of the lawsuit. The linchpin of the "impermissible collateral attack" doctrine—the attribution of preclusive effect to a failure to intervene—is therefore quite inconsistent with Rule 19 and Rule 24.

[P]etitioners contend that a different result should be reached because the need to join affected parties will be burdensome and ultimately discouraging to civil rights litigation. Potential adverse claimants may be numerous and difficult to identify; if they are not joined, the possibility for inconsistent judgments exists. Judicial resources will be needlessly consumed in relitigation of the same question. . . .

The difficulties petitioners foresee in identifying those who could be adversely affected by a decree granting broad remedial relief are undoubtedly present, but they arise from the nature of the relief sought and not because of any choice between mandatory intervention and joinder. Rule 19's provisions for joining interested parties are designed to accommodate the sort of complexities that may arise from a decree affecting numerous people in various ways. We doubt that a mandatory intervention rule would be any less awkward. As mentioned, plaintiffs who seek the aid of the courts to alter existing employment policies, or the employer who might be subject to conflicting decrees, are best able to bear the burden of designating those who would be adversely affected if plaintiffs prevail; these parties will generally have a better understanding of the scope of likely relief than employees who are not named but might be affected. Petitioners' alternative does not eliminate the need for, or difficulty of, identifying persons who, because of their interests, should be included in a lawsuit. It merely shifts that responsibility to less able shoulders.

[P]etitioners also urge that the congressional policy favoring voluntary settlement of employment discrimination claims, referred to in cases such as Carson v. American Brands, Inc., 450 U.S. 79, 101 S.Ct. 993, 67 L.Ed.2d 59 (1981), also supports the "impermissible collateral attack" doctrine. But once again it is essential to note just what is meant by "voluntary settlement." A voluntary settlement in the form of a consent decree between one group of employees and their employer cannot possibly "settle," voluntarily or otherwise, the conflicting claims of another group of

suffering practical adverse effects from the consent decree. Post, at 2188–2190. On the other hand, the dissent characterizes respondents' suit not as an assertion of their own independent rights, but as a collateral attack on the consent decrees which, it is said, can only proceed on very limited grounds. Post, at 2195–2198. Respondents in their suit have alleged that they are being racially discriminated against by their employer in violation of Title VII: either the fact that the disputed employment decisions are being made pursuant to a consent decree is a defense to respondents' Title VII claims or it is not. If it is a defense to challenges to employment practices which would otherwise violate Title VII, it is very difficult to see why respondents are not being "bound" by the decree.

employees who do not join in the agreement. This is true even if the second group of employees is a party to the litigation:

"[P]arties who choose to resolve litigation through settlement may not dispose of the claims of a third party ... without that party's agreement. A court's approval of a consent decree between some of the parties therefore cannot dispose of the valid claims of nonconsenting intervenors." Firefighters v. Cleveland, 478 U.S. 501, 529, 106 S.Ct. 3063, 3079, 92 L.Ed.2d 405 (1986).

Insofar as the argument is bottomed on the idea that it may be easier to settle claims among a disparate group of affected persons if they are all before the court, joinder bids fair to accomplish that result as well as a regime of mandatory intervention.

For the foregoing reasons we affirm the decision of the Court of Appeals for the Eleventh Circuit. That court remanded the case for trial of the reverse discrimination claims. Birmingham Reverse Discrimination, 833 F.2d, at 1500–1502. Petitioners point to language in the District Court's findings of fact and conclusions of law which suggests that respondents will not prevail on the merits. We agree with the view of the Court of Appeals, however, that the proceedings in the District Court may have been affected by the mistaken view that respondents' claims on the merits were barred to the extent they were inconsistent with the consent decree.

Affirmed.

■ JUSTICE STEVENS, with whom JUSTICES MARSHALL, BRENNAN, and BLACKMUN join, dissenting

As a matter of law there is a vast difference between persons who are actual parties to litigation and persons who merely have the kind of interest that may as a practical matter be impaired by the outcome of a case. Persons in the first category have a right to participate in a trial and to appeal from an adverse judgment; depending on whether they win or lose, their legal rights may be enhanced or impaired. Persons in the latter category have a right to intervene in the action in a timely fashion, [Fed. R. Civ. Pro. 24(a)(2)] or they may be joined as parties against their will. [Fed. R. Civ. Pro. 19(a)] But if they remain on the sidelines, they may be harmed as a practical matter even though their legal rights are unaffected. [See Provident Tradesmens Bank & Trust Co. v. Patterson, 390 U.S. 102 (1968)] One of the disadvantages of sideline-sitting is that the bystander has no right to appeal from a judgment no matter how harmful it may be.

In these cases the Court quite rightly concludes that the white firefighters who brought the second series of Title VII cases could not be deprived of their legal rights in the first series of cases because they had neither intervened nor been joined as parties.... There is no reason, however, why the consent decrees might not produce changes in conditions at the white firefighters' place of employment that, as a practical matter, may have a serious effect on their opportunities for employment or promotion even though they are not bound by the decrees in any legal sense. The fact that one of the effects of a decree is to curtail the job opportunities of nonparties does not mean that the nonparties have been deprived of legal rights or that they have standing to appeal from that decree without becoming parties.

[T]hus, a person who can foresee that a lawsuit is likely to have a practical impact on his interests may pay a heavy price if he elects to sit on the sidelines instead of intervening and taking the risk that his legal rights will be impaired. . . .

II

Regardless of whether the white firefighters were parties to the decrees granting relief to their black co-workers, it would be quite wrong to assume that they could never collaterally attack such a decree. If a litigant has standing, he or she can always collaterally attack a judgment for certain narrowly defined defects. See, e.g., Klapprott v. United States, 335 U.S. 601, 69 S.Ct. 384, 93 L.Ed. 266 (1949); and cases cited in n. 5, supra. See also Korematsu v. United States, 584 F.Supp. 1406 (N.D.Cal.1984) (granting writ of coram nobis vacating conviction based on Government concealment of critical contradictory evidence in Korematsu v. United States, 323 U.S. 214, 65 S.Ct. 193, 89 L.Ed. 194 (1944)). On the other hand, a district court is not required to retry a case—or to sit in review of another court's judgment—every time an interested nonparty asserts that *some* error that might have been raised on direct appeal was committed. Such a broad allowance of collateral review would destroy the integrity of litigated judgments, would lead to an abundance of vexatious litigation, and would subvert the interest in comity between courts. Here, respondents have offered no circumstance that might justify reopening the District Court's settled judgment.

The implementation of a consent decree affecting the interests of a multitude of nonparties, and the reliance on that decree as a defense to a charge of discrimination in hiring and promotion decisions, raise a legitimate concern of collusion. No such allegation, however, has been raised. . . .

Nor can it be maintained that the consent judgment is subject to reopening and further litigation because the relief it afforded was so out of line with settled legal doctrine that it "was transparently invalid or had only a frivolous pretense to validity." Walker v. Birmingham, 388 U.S. 307, 315, 87 S.Ct. 1824, 1829, 18 L.Ed.2d 1210 (1967) (suggesting that a contemner might be allowed to challenge contempt citation on ground that underlying court order was "transparently invalid"). To the contrary, the type of race-conscious relief ordered in the consent decrees is entirely consistent with this Court's approach to affirmative action. Given a sufficient predicate of racial discrimination, neither the Equal Protection Clause of the Fourteenth Amendment nor Title VII of the Civil Rights Act of 1964 erects a bar to affirmative-action plans that benefit non-victims and have some adverse effect on nonwrongdoers. . . .

Hence, there is no basis for collaterally attacking the judgment as collusive, fraudulent, or transparently invalid. Moreover, respondents do not claim—nor has there been any showing of—mistake, duress, or lack of jurisdiction. Instead, respondents are left to argue that somewhat different relief would have been more appropriate than the relief that was actually granted. Although this sort of issue may provide the basis for a direct appeal, it cannot, and should not, serve to open the door to relitigation of a settled judgment.

III

The facts that respondents are not bound by the decrees and that they have no basis for a collateral attack, moreover, do not compel the conclusion that the District Court should have treated the decrees as nonexistent for purposes of respondents' discrimination suit. That the decrees may not directly interfere with any of respondents' legal rights does not mean that they may not affect the factual setting in a way that negates respondents' claim. The fact that a criminal suspect is not a party to the issuance of a search warrant does not imply that the presence of a facially valid warrant may not be taken as evidence that the police acted in good faith. ... Similarly, the fact that an employer is acting under court compulsion may be evidence that the employer is acting in good faith and without discriminatory intent. ... [27]

After reviewing the evidence, the District Court found that the City had in fact acted under compulsion of the consent decrees. App. to Pet. for Cert. 107a; In re Birmingham Reverse Discrimination Employment Litigation, 36 EPD 35022 p. 36,586 (N.D.Ala.1985). Based on this finding, the court concluded that the City carried its burden of coming forward with a legitimate business reason for its promotion policy, and, accordingly, held that the promotion decisions were "not taken with the requisite discriminatory intent" necessary to make out a claim of disparate treatment under Title VII or the Equal Protection Clause. App. to Pet. for Cert. 107a, citing United States v. Jefferson County, 720 F.2d, at 1518...

[I]n a case such as these, however, in which there has been no showing that the decree was collusive, fraudulent, transparently invalid, or entered without jurisdiction, it would be "unconscionable" to conclude that obedi-

---

27. Because consent decrees "have attributes both of contracts and judicial decrees," they are treated differently for different purposes. United States v. ITT Continental Baking Co., 420 U.S. 223, 236, n. 10, 95 S.Ct. 926, 934, n. 10, 43 L.Ed.2d 148 (1975). See also Firefighters v. Cleveland, 478 U.S., at 519, 106 S.Ct., at 3074. For example, because the content of a consent decree is generally a product of negotiations between the parties, decrees are construed for enforcement purposes as contracts. See ITT Continental Baking Co., supra, 420 U.S., at 238, 95 S.Ct., at 935; Stotts v. Memphis Fire Dept., 679 F.2d 541, 557 (C.A.6 1982), rev'd on other grounds, 467 U.S. 561, 104 S.Ct. 2576, 81 L.Ed.2d 483 (1984). For purposes of deter-mining whether an employer can be held liable for intentional discrimination merely for complying with the terms of a consent decree, however, it is appropriate to treat the consent decree as a judicial order. Unlike the typical contract, a consent decree, such as the ones at issue here, is developed in the context of adversary litigation. Moreover, the court reviews the consent decree to determine whether it is lawful, reasonable, and equitable. In placing the judicial imprimatur on the decree, the court provides the parties with some assurance that the decree is legal and that they may rely on it. Most significantly, violation of a consent decree is punishable as criminal contempt. See 18 U.S.C. §§ 401, 402; Fed.Rule Crim.Proc. 42.

ence to an order remedying a Title VII violation could subject a defendant to additional liability.... Assuming that the District Court's findings of fact were not clearly erroneous—which of course is a matter that is not before us—it seems perfectly clear that its judgment should have been affirmed. Any other conclusion would subject large employers who seek to comply with the law by remedying past discrimination to a never-ending stream of litigation and potential liability. It is unfathomable that either Title VII or the Equal Protection Clause demands such a counterproductive result.

IV

The predecessor to this litigation was brought to change a pattern of hiring and promotion practices that had discriminated against black citizens in Birmingham for decades. The white respondents in these cases are not responsible for that history of discrimination, but they are nevertheless beneficiaries of the discriminatory practices that the litigation was designed to correct. Any remedy that seeks to create employment conditions that would have obtained if there had been no violations of law will necessarily have an adverse impact on whites, who must now share their job and promotion opportunities with blacks. Just as white employees in the past were innocent beneficiaries of illegal discriminatory practices, so is it inevitable that some of the same white employees will be innocent victims who must share some of the burdens resulting from the redress of the past wrongs.

* * *

Questions

1. When parties to a lawsuit agree to a settlement, they often further agree to entry of judgment in the pending litigation in favor of one side. If they agree to enter judgment for the plaintiff, they couple it with a further entry to the effect that the judgment is satisfied. Or they may agree to enter judgment for the defendant. In either case, such consent judgment terminates the litigation and preclude another suit between the parties on the same claim. What does the majority in *Martin v. Wilks* say is the impact of a consent decree on nonparties? What is the position of the dissent? Which argument is more persuasive?

2. If nonparties cannot be bound to the terms of a Title VII consent decree, why is it that unnamed class members can be bound in a class action settlement? Can the two be distinguished according to differences in the level of scrutiny a court will give to the terms of the settlement?

3. The dissent in *Martin v. Wilks* suggests that a consent decree might be rejected if it were "so out of line with settled legal doctrine that it was 'transparently invalid or had only a frivolous pretense to validity.' " (citation omitted). It found in this case that the "type of race-conscious relief ordered in the consent decree was consistent with this Court's approach to affirmative action" and that there had been a showing of a "sufficient

predicate of racial discrimination" to permit the remedy of affirmative action. Is the dissent suggesting that a court has an obligation to engage in some review of the merits of a consent decree in a discrimination case? If so, on what basis could a court conduct such a review? How can it decide whether there is a "sufficient" showing of racial discrimination without a record akin to the type that would be produced at trial? Must there be at least some discovery or other factual record developed before a court can approve a consent decree? Similarly, how can a court know whether a decree is "consistent with" settled approaches to affirmative action without making some at least provisional ruling on the merits of the case?

* * *

C.   SPECIAL PROBLEMS OF SETTLEMENT CLASSES

In re Baldwin–United Corporation

105 F.R.D. 475 (S.D.N.Y.1984).

■ BRIEANT, DISTRICT JUDGE.

These consolidated cases, transferred to the Southern District of New York by the Judicial Panel on Multi district Litigation on February 27, 1984, arise out of the sale by insurance company subsidiaries of Baldwin–United Corporation of certain contracts known to the Court as single premium deferred annuities ("SPDAs"). These SPDAs were issued principally between 1979 and May 1983 by National Investors Life Insurance Company, an Arkansas insurance corporation, and University Life Insurance Company of America, an Indiana insurance corporation. The annuities were sold to the public on a nation-wide basis through various broker-dealers and other entities.

In July 1983, the two issuing insurance companies, as well as four companies which reinsured the SPDAs in part, were placed in rehabilitation. The ultimate corporate parent of these six companies, Baldwin–United Corporation, entered bankruptcy proceedings pursuant to voluntary and involuntary petitions for reorganization filed on September 26, 1983. During 1983 and 1984 SPDA purchasers filed more than 90 federal civil actions alleging fraud and/or violations of the federal and state securities laws and other pendent state law claims. Finding that the initial forty actions before it involved common questions of fact, the MDL Panel ordered that they be transferred to this district court for coordinated or consolidated pre-trial proceedings pursuant to 28 U.S.C. § 1407. In re Baldwin–United Corporation Litigation, No. 581, 581 F.Supp. 739 (J.P.J.L.1984).

This Court held a pre-trial conference on April 3, 1984 and thereafter entered pre-trial orders approving the creation of a plaintiff's steering committee and providing, among other things, for the filing of separate consolidated class complaints with respect to each of the unrelated broker-dealer defendants. Since that time, liaison counsel for plaintiffs and for defendants have been engaged actively in pursuing the litigation goals of the parties and have appeared frequently before the Court for coordination of pre-trial proceedings. Familiarity of the reader with all such prior proceedings is assumed.

A recent significant event with which the within motion is concerned is the filing beginning on September 21, 1984 of fourteen stipulations of settlement between plaintiffs and the defendants in fourteen of the actions (the "settling actions"). The parties to the proposed settlements now request the Court (1) to certify tentative or conditional classes solely for the purpose of considering the proposed settlement; (2) to conduct a fairness hearing on whether the proposed settlements should be approved; and (3) to order that notice of the hearing be sent to members of the proposed class and to resolve issues affecting the content of such notice.

Class Certification

Whether this Court should certify a conditional settlement class solely for purposes of approving or disapproving a settlement already formulated by the parties is a controversial issue. On one hand, the current edition of the Manual for Complex Litigation, § 1.46 (5th ed. 1982) ("Manual"), concludes that tentative classes for the purpose of settlement ordinarily should not be formed. Id. at 60. Similarly there is an apparent inconsistency between the language of Rule 23, F.R.Civ.P., and a mechanism whereby formal class certification would be bypassed until a date when first notice of the pendency of a class action and notice of a proposed settlement are sent simultaneously to prospective class members. In re Franklin National Bank Securities Litigation, 574 F.2d 662, 671–72, n. 6, modified, 599 F.2d 1109 (2d Cir.1978). Since Rule 23(c) requires that class certification take place "as soon as practicable after the commencement of an action," the practice of bypassing pre-settlement formal class certification is a subject of concern.[1] On the other hand, many courts have employed this practice in the name of judicial efficiency in order to facilitate apparently beneficial settlement proposals.

For the reasons set forth below, this Court finds that under the circumstances of the cases at bar, tentative class certification for settlement purposes only is appropriate at this time and is in the interests of Justice.

The current edition of the Manual lists nine policy reasons in support of its conclusion that settlement classes ought not be certified:

"(1) Rule 23 does not expressly authorize formation of tentative classes for the purpose of settlement. (2) There usually can be no assurance that the class members will be adequately represented in the settlement negotiations until the court makes the findings, which are a condition precedent to the formation of a class, after an opportunity for an evidentiary hearing. Formation of a tentative class for the purpose of settlement, with a requirement that the class members accept the settlement or opt out and litigate independently, might deny the members of the class the opportunity to show the inadequacy of the

---

1. See Manual for Complex Litigation, § 1.46 at 60 (5th ed. 1982) ("There is some doubt that this practice is authorized by Rule 23 as amended, even if one concedes that the courts are expected to develop new methods of employing the amended Rule 23").

representation of the class by the representative party or parties agreeing to the settlement and their counsel. (3) The appropriate membership of the class and the identity of the members ordinarily should not be determined in the absence of an opportunity for hearing and judicial findings of fact and conclusions of law. Nor can there usually be any assurance that the tentative class will be composed of members without conflicting interests. Absent such findings and conclusions, it may be difficult to determine how many members there are in a class, who they are, the aggregate of claims of all members of the class, the amount of the individual claim of each member in relation to the total claims of all members of the class and, therefore, the amount of money that will be payable to each member of the class. This information would seem to be essential for a member to make any rational choice between whether to remain in the class and accept the benefits of the settlement or to opt out. (4) If the information relevant to liability, damages, and the expenses of preparation for trial and of trial is not developed, there usually cannot be a fair recognition in settlement negotiations of the potential liability of the party or parties opposing the class and the potential damages that might be recovered for the class. (5) Formation of a tentative class for the purpose of settlement preempts determination of the question whether the claim for relief should be litigated for the members of the class or should be the subject of further pretrial preparation, with a view toward securing a better settlement or a trial on the merits. It also preempts the question of which parties and counsel should represent the tentative class, since there must be an unofficially negotiated earlier settlement for the purpose of the formation of the tentative class. (6) The formation of a tentative class for the purpose of settlement denies the class member the choice, contemplated by amended Rule 23, to become a member of the proposed class for the purpose of litigation, with adequate representation as a member of litigating class. (7) Formation of such a class denies a member of the class the right to appear in the action as a party and to maintain the position of a litigating party. (8) Formation of such a class might lead to a long delay in preparing the case for trial, for those parties who desire to litigate their claims for relief. (9) In the absence of reasonable discovery conducted on an adversary basis by counsel representing the class, it is difficult to determine whether the proposed settlement has any relation to the economic facts of life relevant to the case.''

Manual for Complex Litigation § 1.46 at 60–61 (5th ed. 1982).

In essence, most of the perceived problems relied upon by the Board of Editors of the Manual concern the risk of a premature, inadequate settlement, and the possibility that class members may be induced to accept such an improvident settlement in the absence of sufficient information to make a reasoned choice. In re Beef Industry Antitrust Litigation, 607 F.2d 167, 176 (5th Cir.1979), cert. denied, 452 U.S. 905, 101 S.Ct. 3029, 69 L.Ed.2d 405 (1981). As Judge Wisdom stated: ''The recommendations of the Manual in § 1.46 are intended to prevent collusion, individual settlement, 'buy-offs' where the class action is used to benefit some individual at the expense of absent members, and other abuses.'' 607 F.2d at 174. However, the law in this Circuit does recognize that deviation from this recommendation of the Manual may be reasonable in the appropriate case. Weinberger v. Kendrick, 698 F.2d 61, 73 (2d Cir.1982), cert. denied, ___ U.S. ___, 104 S.Ct. 77, 78 L.Ed.2d 89 (1984).

Among the policy reasons advanced by the Manual is the concern that class members will not have been represented adequately during settlement negotiations due to the fact that the negotiations precede judicial findings as to the prerequisites to class formation under Rule 23(a). See Eisen v. Carlisle & Jacquelin, 391 F.2d 555, 562–63 (2d Cir.1968), vacated and remanded on other grounds, 417 U.S. 156, 94 S.Ct. 2140, 40 L.Ed.2d 732 (1974) (court must examine whether plaintiffs' interests are antagonistic to interests of other class members); Schlesinger v. Reservists Committee to Stop the War, 418 U.S. 208, 216, 94 S.Ct. 2925, 2929, 41 L.Ed.2d 706 (1974) (court must examine whether class representatives possess the same interest and claim the same injury as other class members). The Court agrees that arguments in opposition to settlement classes have merit when they are addressed to the problem of inadequate representation or possible collusion among the named plaintiffs and some or all defendants. Rule 23(a)(4), F.R.Civ.P. However, in the case at bar, there is no danger of inadequate representation because all of the named plaintiffs have virtually identical claims for recovery which have been pursued by a steering committee and liaison counsel exclusively authorized to negotiate on behalf of the class by Pretrial Order No. 1 entered by this Court on April 11, 1984. The settlement class representatives have the same class interests as would a typical conditional class representative selected after a Rule 23 evidentiary hearing, and have no incentive to engage in collusion or recommend an improvident settlement in order to serve some unrelated purpose of their own.

This is not a case where several different counsel were competing for designation as class representatives; nor is this a case where defendants had the opportunity during negotiations to play one plaintiff's attorney off against another. See City of Detroit v. Grinnell, 495 F.2d 448, 465 (2d Cir.1974). These dangers were prevented by the early designation of a plaintiffs' steering committee in Pretrial Order No. 1, and the enumeration therein of the committee's powers and duties. No plaintiffs' counsel in this Multi district action other than members of the steering committee have had the authority to negotiate for settlements on behalf of the proposed classes in the settling actions. Thus plaintiffs have spoken with one consistent voice during settlement discussions and one of the Manual's major concerns is absent.

In the instant case, as in so many of this type, the settling defendants do not consent to class certification, solely because in the event that the settlement fails, they prefer to remain free to assert various defenses aimed at the pleadings and at the same time oppose full certification of a plaintiffs' class. Defendants may object to the contention that "the questions of law or fact common to the members of the class predominate over any questions affecting only individual members, and that a class action is superior to other available methods for the fair and efficient adjudication of the controversy." Rule 23(b)(3), F.R.Civ.P. While it ultimately might prove true that a class action is not the most efficient device for resolution of these cases, the possibility of such an ultimate finding by this Court, if made in the future after discovery and after an evidentiary hearing, should not be permitted, at this stage, to prevent SPDA holders from receiving notice of these proposed settlements, and a full hearing as to whether the Court ought to approve the proposed settlement.

Another of the policy reasons supporting the Manual's rationale against the tentative settlement class mechanism is that there can be no assurance that the membership of the class will be delineated appropriately or that the tentative class will not be composed of plaintiffs with conflicting interests. Again, this important concern is not implicated in the case at bar, because the facts show that all SPDA purchasers from the settling defendants are readily identifiable through the books and records of the issuing insurance companies, and all are treated alike by the settlements. The tentative class members thus have no conflicts among themselves; they all stand to gain the exact same relief through the proportionate formula of recovery contained in the stipulations of settlement. Here, there is no danger comparable to that perceived in Plummer v. Chemical Bank, 668 F.2d 654 (2d Cir.1982), where the court expressed its concern over preferential treatment afforded the named plaintiffs by the proposed settlement.

Yet another policy reason expressed in the Manual is that formation of a settlement class preempts determination of whether plaintiffs should continue to litigate their claims for relief with an eye towards a better settlement agreement or even a trial on the merits. In the stipulations of settlement filed herein, the class members have been provided with a full opportunity to object to the terms of the settlement while remaining a member of the class. Stipulations of Settlement, ¶ 16. As an alternative, plaintiffs can opt out of a settlement class and pursue their litigation goals either individually or as another putative class. This procedure complies with City of Detroit v. Grinnell, supra, and safeguards the individual freedom of choice of each SPDA purchaser from a settling defendant. Also it appears more sensible under the circumstances of this case to provide SPDA purchasers with the financial information contained in the settlement agreements now, so that they will have a more concrete basis for deciding whether to opt out of a plaintiffs' class, than to expect opt-out decisions to precede advisement of the possibility of settlement, as they typically must do under the policy of the Manual. See In re Mid–Atlantic Toyota Antitrust Litigation, 564 F.Supp. 1379, 1389 (D.Md.1983).

The Court of Appeals for the Second Circuit has ruled that it "refuse[s] to adopt a per se rule prohibiting approval when a class action settlement has been reached by means of settlement classes certified after the settlement, with notice simultaneous with that of the settlement...." Weinberger v. Kendrick, 698 F.2d at 73. In so holding, the Court stressed that the trial courts "are bound to scrutinize the fairness of the settlement agreement with even more than the usual care ... in order to meet the concerns noted in the Manual." Id. at 73. If the settlement agreement is found to be fair, reasonable and adequate—both in its substantive provisions and in the process of its creation—then the policy reasons behind the Manual's admonition become inapplicable.

Apart from the general difficulties which must be addressed, and indeed "scrutinized," under Weinberger v. Kendrick, supra, when a court considers whether to certify a tentative class for purposes of settlement only, a special objection has been raised by two SPDA purchasers, Bernard and Anna Shipman, who are named as plaintiffs in the consolidated amended class complaint filed in Moore v. E.F. Hutton Group, Inc., et al., 84 Civ. 7197–CLB. The Shipmans oppose certification of a national settlement class on the ground that they possess "unique" legal rights under Washington state law and that these rights will not be adequately protected by the proposed class representatives in the settling actions. (Memorandum in Opposition to Proposed Settlement and to Proposed Settlement Class, filed October 24, 1984). Even if the Washington SPDA holders who purchased from one of the fourteen settling defendants do have special or unique state law claims, the Court cannot find that these potential class members should be denied access to settlement information or denied the opportunity to decide for themselves whether or not to opt out of the proposed class.

At oral argument on November 2, 1984, counsel for the Shipmans contended that, as a practical matter, SPDA purchasers will not exercise their opt-out rights. This contention is speculative. The Court has not been provided with any data to convince it that the standard methods of class notice and opportunity to request exclusion from a class are so ineffective that the Court should not even attempt to order that the Washington SPDA purchasers be notified and furnished with access to the same information and opportunity available to others.

The better solution for this perceived problem would be to make certain that the form of notice approved by the Court is sufficiently clear and informative in its content and directions, a subject discussed more fully below. The Court has also examined the class complaint in Moore v. E.F. Hutton Group, Inc., et al. and finds that the federal complaint adequately embraces the pendent state law claims arising out of the sale of the SPDAs. The Shipmans' state law claims are not so special or unusual as to justify imposition by this Court of an involuntary exclusion from the settlement, compelling litigation and delay for Washington state SPDA purchasers from one of the broker-dealer defendants. The request by the Shipmans that any class definition exclude all persons who purchased National Investors Life Insurance Company SPDAs from E.F. Hutton Group, Inc. in the State of Washington during the relevant time period appears lacking in merit.

Similarly, objections voiced by Intervenor–Plaintiffs and plaintiff Judith A. Shay (who has proposed a statewide class in California) do not persuade the Court that a tentative class for settlement purposes should not be certified. The only objectors who have argued to the Court in opposition to the within motion are plaintiffs Shay, Bernard and Anna

Shipman, and the Intervening guaranty associations. This small amount of opposition, in view of the relatively widespread publicity and the circulation of the settlement stipulations among plaintiffs' counsel, is another factor which supports approval of tentative class certification and the scheduling of a fairness hearing. City of Detroit v. Grinnell, 495 F.2d at 462.

Upon consideration of the proposed settlement presented to this Court for preliminary approval, the Court finds that it is at least sufficiently fair, reasonable and adequate to justify notice to those affected and an opportunity to be heard. The substantive terms of the proposed agreement call for a cash payment of approximately $138,000,000 to the members of the classes in the fourteen settling actions. According to the affidavit of plaintiffs' liaison counsel, sworn to October 10, 1984, this fund "represents a payment of approximately 30% of the damages sustained by members of the class when measured by the difference between the tangible assets in the hands of the rehabilitators and the liabilities of the rehabilitators to the members of the classes." In comparing the advantages of an immediate cash payment with the risks involved in long and uncertain litigation, it appears that the settlement is sufficiently substantial at this stage to present it to the SPDA purchasers and conduct a fairness hearing on notice.[3]

The terms of the settlement also appear fair because they do not differentiate among the broker-dealer defendants in any way that would suggest collusion or abuse. Each of the defendants is to pay in the same ratio and each class member is to obtain the same proportionate settlement regardless of which broker-dealer sold the SPDA. In addition, the fact that there are several broker-defendants who were presented with the opportunity to join these settlement stipulations and declined to do so implies that the settlement terms are favorable to the plaintiffs and that the negotiations preceding settlement operated in the required adversarial posture free of any possible collusion.

In order to supplement judicial examination of the substance of a compromise agreement, and because a court cannot conduct a trial in order to avoid a trial, attention must be paid to the process by which a settlement has been reached. Weinberger, 698 F.2d at 74. The negotiations in these settling actions were conducted on behalf of plaintiffs by experienced attorneys who are familiar with this type of litigation. As a consequence, their judgment is entitled to some weight. Trainor v. Berner, 334 F.Supp. 1143, 1149 (S.D.N.Y.1971). In the opinion of these experienced attorneys the settlement is reasonable when compared with an evaluation of the probability of ultimate success on the merits. As all parties to the actions are aware, one of the hotly contested issues which has not yet been decided is whether these SPDAs fit within the definition of a "security" for purposes of 15 U.S.C. §§ 77b and 78c. The Court finds that the negotiating parties considered this and other legal issues during the course of negotia-

---

3. Plaintiff's steering committee has informed the Court that its investigation had demonstrated many SPDA holders are at or near retirement age. Accordingly, a proposed settlement that offers an early resolution to this contest may be of greater benefit.

tions and, at least based on information presently available to the Court, they have been able to assess fairly the value of the claims asserted in the class complaints against the settling broker-dealer defendants.

Both the Intervenor–Plaintiffs (six state guaranty associations) and a California plaintiff (Shay v. Merrill Lynch Pierce Fenner & Smith, Inc., et al) object that the settlements are not within the range of reasonableness because formal discovery has not occurred. While it is true that full-fledged discovery has not been had, this is not always a bar to class certification or even to approving a settlement. See Jones v. Amalgamated Warbasse Houses, Inc., 97 F.R.D. 355, 360 (S.D.N.Y.), aff'd, 721 F.2d 881 (2d Cir.1983), cert. denied, ___ U.S. ___, 104 S.Ct. 1929, 80 L.Ed.2d 474 (1984); Plummer v. Chemical Bank, 668 F.2d at 658; In re Corrugated Container Antitrust Litigation, 643 F.2d 195, 211 (5th Cir.1981), cert. denied, 456 U.S. 998, 102 S.Ct. 2283, 73 L.Ed.2d 1294 (1982); Galdi Securities v. Propp, 87 F.R.D. 6, (S.D.N.Y.1979).

In addition to discussions with defense counsel over a three-month period, plaintiffs' steering committee has had access to the expert testimony and other evidence received by the Arkansas and Indiana state courts supervising the development of rehabilitation plans. Plaintiffs' steering committee has had available for its review various documents produced by some of the settling defendants in response to plaintiffs' initial discovery requests. The Stipulations of Settlement, at ¶ 25, provide that this production will continue during the notice period. Finally, a vast amount of relevant discoverable information was available through public documents concerning the financial condition of Baldwin–United Corporation and its subsidiaries. We believe that counsel availed themselves of all of these sources of information and conducted full adversarial negotiations, as they were authorized to do by Pretrial Order No. 1.

In light of the foregoing, the Court finds that a conditional class should be certified for the purpose of considering the proposed settlements. The requirements of numerosity, typicality, common questions of law or fact, and adequacy of representation have been met and the Court finds that, under Rule 23(b)(3), the tentative class procedure presents the most efficient method for adjudication of the immediate issues presented by the parties to the settling actions. The tentative class in each of the 14 settling actions shall be composed of those persons and entities, including the settling plaintiffs, (a) who purchased single premium deferred annuities ("SPDAs"), (i) which were issued by National Investors Life Insurance Company and University Life Insurance Company of America and/or reinsured by National Investors Pension Insurance Company, Mt. Hood Pension Insurance Company, National Equity Life Insurance Company, Inc. and S & H Life Insurance Company, all of which are affiliated with Baldwin–United Corporation, and (ii) which were purchased through the respective settling broker-dealer defendants in each such action during the period January 1, 1979 through July 13, 1983, each in his, her or its individual capacity and any and all collective representative capacities, and their representatives, assigns, heirs, executors, administrators, custodians, predecessors or successors in interest and any other person having any legal or beneficial interest in any of such SPDAs, and (b) who continued to hold such SPDAs on July 13, 1983.

The respective representatives of the Class as to each of the above captioned actions shall be and are hereby certified to be as follows: 1. Donnelly v. A.G. Edward & Sons, Inc., 84 Civ. 0098–CLB, Robert C. Donnelly, Joseph Lowry and Eva Lowry; 2. Miller v. Boenning & Scattergood, Inc., 84 Civ. 2234–CLB, Sandra S. Miller; 3. Wert v. Blunt Ellis & Loewi, Inc., 84 Civ. 6575–CLB, Donald H. Wert, Elaine Meinecke, Howard M. Schudson, Jean Strike, Joseph Strike and Shirley Lerand; 4. Moffatt v. Drexel Burnham Lambert Incorporated, 84 Civ. 1673–CLB, Joseph T. Moffatt and Marvel S. Platoff; 5. Moore v. E.F. Hutton Group, Inc., 83 Civ. 7197–CLB, Ronald A. Schooling, Steven Domeny, Rose Domeny, Dennis P. Attalla, Arnold D. Jones, Stephen H. Grossman, Randy F. Grossman, Philip Rhodes, Jr., Tadako Rhodes, Charles B. Scarborough, Barbara Scarborough, Sam Gesualdo and Sharon Gesualdo; 6. Sokoloff v. Janney Montgomery Scott, Inc., 83 Civ. 8084–CLB, Sonia Sokoloff; 7. Phillips v. Kidder, Peabody & Co., Inc., 83 Civ. 8475–CLB, Thomas G. Phillips, III; 8. Factor v. Merrill Lynch & Co., Inc., 83 Civ. 7009–CLB, Harry Factor, Willa June Morgan, Douglas M. Mann, Lillie Lavin, Kenneth Tomnitz, David D. Ilgenfritz, Mary S. Ilgenfritz and Pemberton H. Shober, Jr.; 9. Dippolito v. Moseley Hallgarten Estabrook & Weeden, Inc., 84 Civ. 3084–CLB, Mary Grace Dippolito; 10. Ostin v. Oppenheimer & Co., Inc., 83 Civ. 7568–CLB, Nils Ostin and Helen E. Ostin; 11. Kissel v. Parker/Hunter, Inc., 84 Civ. 2233–CLB, Edward Kissel, Jr.; 12. Blumberg v. Prudential Bache Securities, Inc., 83 Civ. 7358–CLB, Lewis Levin, Rose Levin, Richard J. Boyle, Patricia A. Boyle, Daniel R. Cavalier and Naomi L. Cavalier; 13. Shepperd v. Smith Barney Harris Upham, Inc., 83 Civ. 8474–CLB, Francis M. Bennett (successor in interest to Plaintiff Hambleton Shepperd); and 14. Abrams v. Thomson McKinnon Securities, Inc., 83 Civ. 7359–CLB, Bernice V. Abrams, David Morris and Shirley Morris.

At this preliminary stage, the Court finds that all SPDA holders, in all fifty states, deserve to receive notice of the proposed settlements and have the opportunity to either object and remain in the class or request exclusion from the class. An order scheduling a hearing on the fairness of the stipulation of settlement is being filed simultaneously herewith. As the Intervenor-Plaintiffs did not become parties to these actions until October 5, 1984, after the dates upon which the stipulations of settlement were entered into by plaintiffs and the settling defendants, any reference in the stipulations of settlement to "parties" shall refer to the parties to the settling actions as of the dates of the stipulations of settlement, unless otherwise ordered by the Court.

Class Notice

The Court has fully considered the various forms of notice submitted to it by the settling parties as well as by the two objecting plaintiffs and the Intervenor–Plaintiffs. At the conference held on November 2, 1984, the Court requested that counsel who objected to the form of notice attached to the Order to Show Cause filed October 11, 1984, confer and present to the Court any requests for alteration. Counsel have done so and the Court has approved a form of notice which is being filed simultaneously herewith.

The approved class notice fairly apprises "prospective class members of the class action's pendency, the relevant terms of the proposed settlement[s], and their options in connection with [this] case." Weinberger, 698 F.2d at 70. The notice adequately describes, among other things, the status of the rehabilitation proceedings, the litigation posture of the plaintiffs and the settling defendants, the settlement fund, and the application for attorneys' fees and expenses. In addition the notice advises the class members as to what effect the settlements will have on the future legal rights of class members.

As to the "opt-out" provisions contained in the notice, the Court finds that these instructions and explanations are clear and easy to follow. They inform class members that if requests for exclusion are not received in the manner specified, then the class member shall be bound by any judgments rendered by the Court pursuant to the settlement of the settling actions. The notice also provides that a settling class member who has not opted out may file objections and appear at the fairness hearing. It is proper for the notice to require opt-outs to be filed prior to the fairness hearing since this procedure "places potential objectors in no worse position than occurs when formal class certification precedes settlement. . . ." Weinberger, 698 F.2d at 72.

Finally, the notice will be mailed to each class member "who can be identified through reasonable effort," Eisen v. Carlisle & Jacquelin, 417 U.S. 156, 176, 94 S.Ct. 2140, 2151, 40 L.Ed.2d 732 (1974), and will be published in the National Edition of the Wall Street Journal once a week for three consecutive weeks following the mailing of the primary notice. The individual mailings will be sent to class members at their last known addresses as set forth on the records of the Rehabilitators of the insurance companies. The use of bank and brokerage house records to compile lists for class action mailings is a procedure that has been approved by the Court of Appeals. In re Franklin National Bank Securities Litigation, 574 F.2d 662, 669–70, modified on other grounds, 599 F.2d 1109 (2d Cir.1978).

The Court finds that further detail in the content of the notice is not required in order to comply with Rule 5 of the Civil Rules of the United States District Courts for the Southern and Eastern Districts of New York. The parties to the settling actions have an interest in receiving notice of the total sum of the requested attorneys' fees, but it is not material under the circumstances of these cases to describe further how the fee will be allocated among the participating lawyers.

All of the foregoing is without prejudice to the findings the Court will make after conducting the fairness hearing, at which time all objections or arguments in opposition to the proposed settlements will be heard and considered and proponents must discharge their burden to prove that the proposed settlement agreements are fair and reasonable.

So Ordered.

* * *

Questions

1.   As discussed above, Federal Rule 23(c) provides that a motion to certify a class shall be made "as soon as practicable after the commencement of an action. . . ." In a settlement class action, a court is presented with a motion to certify a class and to approve a settlement at the same time. If the motion is made early in the litigation, before any significant discovery has transpired, how can a court determine whether the settlement is "fair, reasonable, and adequate?" If parties instead await development of a factual record before moving to certify a class, then have they violated the command of Rule 23(c) to bring such a motion "as soon as practicable?" Can parties seeking a settlement class action avoid this dilemma and satisfy Rule 23 as the rule is currently written?

2.   Did the court in *Baldwin* rule on the fairness of the proposed settlement, or merely decide to certify a class action for purposes of settlement? Can the two issues be disentangled when a court is presented with a petition to certify a class after a settlement has been reached?

3.   As you read the next two cases, compare them to the *Baldwin* case. In particular, consider what features in the *Baldwin* case makes it a relatively easy case for a court to rule on the fairness of a proposed settlement in contrast to the latter cases.

* * *

In re Silicone Gel Breast Implant Products Liability Litigation

Heidi Lindsey, et al. v. Dow Corning Corp., et al.
1994 WL 578353 (N.D.Ala.1994).

(Approval of Settlement)

■ POINTER, CHIEF JUDGE.

In April 1994, the court provisionally certified the Lindsey action (CV 94–P–11558–S) under Rule 23(b)(3) as a class action for settlement purposes and gave preliminary and conditional approval to a proposed $4,225,-070,000 class settlement, reputed to be the largest such settlement ever. Detailed information concerning the settlement, including all of the items required under Rule 23(c)(2), as well as a form for requesting exclusion from the class, was sent by first-class mail to each person, domestic and foreign, identified as possibly a breast-implant recipient. Written objections and comments from class members and others have been received and reviewed. At hearings held on August 18, 19, and 22, 1994, the court heard oral comments from all persons—regardless of whether they had legal standing to be heard or had timely requested permission—who wished to speak in favor of or in opposition to the proposed settlement. The matter was taken under submission at the conclusion of these hearings on August 22, 1994. After considering all issues and concerns presented, the court concludes that the proposed settlement, with certain clarifications and minor modifications described in this Opinion, including a redefinition of the class, should be approved.

Even its proponents do not claim this settlement is perfect or without problems. In approving the settlement, the court is heeding the admonition of Voltaire, which has been often repeated and rephrased during the hearing process: "The best is the enemy of the good."

TIMING AND NATURE OF SETTLEMENT

This is not a settlement hastily proposed at the outset of litigation before significant discovery and without the insights afforded from presentation of evidence at a trial. Breast implant litigation began more than fifteen years ago, and about a dozen cases have been tried to verdict in different federal and state courts. The deluge of new filings of cases that began in early 1992 has resulted in massive discovery efforts, involving the production and review of millions of pages of documents and the taking of hundreds of depositions. Extensive, arms-length, non-collusive, good-faith settlement negotiations were conducted over many months, even as counsel continued just as vigorously and thoroughly to prepare for potential trial of the thousands of cases already filed or expected in the future.

On the other hand, neither can this settlement be evaluated on the basis of a closed set of data from which all claims can be measured with precision or confidence. Scientific inquiries into possible linkage between breast-implantations and a variety of serious diseases and medical conditions are ongoing and will likely continue for many years. Thousands of class members have serious physical conditions they attribute to their implants. Thousands of others do not have, and may never or only many years later experience, any problems associated with their implants. Some want their implants removed immediately; some want to keep their implants in place, at least for the time being. Verdicts in the cases thus far tried have been mixed, some favorable to the defendants and some favorable to the plaintiffs. While these cases are useful in understanding the dynamics, cost, and length of trial and in considering possible settlement values, they do not provide a reliable basis for any statistical extrapolation or prediction as to outcomes of trials in the many different factual and legal settings these claims involve.

In proposing a settlement in the face of these uncertainties, the parties are recognizing that (1) the defendants' resources are not unlimited, and would be reduced, to the potential detriment of claimants, by the huge costs incurred in litigation over the coming years;[2] (2) thousands of claim-

---

2. Indeed, some have questioned whether the defendants' resources are suffi- cient to make the $4,225,070,000 payments that may be required under the settlement.

ants cannot afford to wait their turn in the judicial queues; and (3) the federal and state court systems will not be able to resolve promptly all breast implant cases without a substantial reduction in the number of cases now pending or expected. Almost 10,000 such cases, many with multiple plaintiffs, are now pending in this court, with almost as many in state courts around the country. Some implant cases have also been filed in other countries.

The terms of this complex settlement, as described in detail in the Settlement Notice with its attachments and as refined in Orders No. 15–20, will not be repeated or summarized in this Opinion except as needed when discussing particular issues. What perhaps should be noted is that—in the effort to provide a fair and workable procedure for resolving thousands of claims on an optional basis—the settlement contains many innovative provisions not found in traditional class action settlements. These features include a program for receiving claims over a 30–year period and for payments that do not depend on the amount of contributions or financial resources of the defendant that supplied the particular claimant's implants; a simplified claims procedure that does not involve adversarial proceedings or require examinations by court-appointed physicians; the initial identification of certain diseases and medical conditions for which substantial amounts—as much as $1,400,000 net after attorneys' fees—would be paid to class members who have or in the 30–year period develop such conditions, without requiring proof of causation; additional compensation should a recipient's condition or disability worsen during that period; a method for adding to this list other diseases or medical conditions (including ones affecting children of implant recipients) if justified by scientific research; procedures for later additional opt-out rights should defendants' settlement contributions prove to be inadequate to pay the full amount of the projected settlement benefits for these diseases and conditions; the protection of claimants against excessive attorney's fees or administrative expenses through a special fund and mechanism for determining and paying those fees and expenses; and the establishment of a series of special funds to provide compensation or reimbursement for medical evaluations, removal of implants, implant ruptures, and other injuries not covered under the disease compensation program, to provide for emergency situations, and to correct for inequities among class members under other parts of the settlement. . . .

After substantial investigation, Plaintiffs' Settlement Class Counsel have stipulated that adequate financial assurances have been given by the various Settling Defendants under Section XIV of the Settlement Agreement with respect to their ability to make these payments. Based on these stipulations, and after conducting an appropriate in camera review, the court has found these assurances to be satisfactory. However, it should be noted that at least some defendants might be unable to make the required payments under the settlement if the cost of defending and responding to adverse judgments outside the settlement becomes too great; this will depend not only on how many cases by opt-outs they must defend but also on how quickly those cases are brought to trial.

SUPPORT BY CLASS MEMBERS

While approval of a proposed class settlement is not a matter to be decided by a plebescite, the views of putative class members are certainly relevant and entitled to great weight. One may gauge the extent of support or opposition in this case by looking to such matters as the written submissions, the statements made during the hearing, and the number of opt-outs and early registrations.

Two general conclusions can be drawn: First, virtually all domestic class members—at least after they understand that the court has no power to order the defendants to contribute larger amounts to the settlement or to make major revisions in the terms of the settlement—want the settlement to be approved, and without delay. Second, while virtually all foreign claimants believe the proposed settlement inequitably treats foreign claimants in relation to domestic claimants, thousands of them do, at least if certain changes are made, want the settlement to be approved so they can participate, subject to their rights to opt out at a later date. Opposition to the settlement is most significant among putative class members in Australia and Canada, though even in those countries there are many wanting an opportunity to participate subject to their future opt-out rights.

The settlement notice package informed putative class members about their right to submit objections and comments respecting the proposed settlement. It also advised them that there was no need to submit comments if they supported the settlement and, indeed, that the court would assume that persons favored approval of the settlement if they did not opt out or submit any comment. (See Q42 in the "Questions-and-Answers.) Not surprisingly in light of this advice, most of the comments submitted did contain various criticisms of the proposed settlement. What was not expected and is perhaps more significant is the relative paucity of negative comments—less than 1/3 of 1% of those to whom notices were sent and only slightly more than 1% of those who have already registered under the settlement. Although considered by the court as similar to 'amicus' " submissions, many of these were from persons who opted out of the settlement or were mailed after the June 17th deadline. Most of these criticisms, moreover, reflect a misunderstanding about the court's powers—erroneously believing that the court could order major changes in the proposed settlement, such as requiring the defendants to pay greater amounts into the settlement fund.

Given the purpose of the hearing, it is likewise not surprising that a majority of the oral presentations to the court were critical of various aspects of the proposed settlement. What is most significant is that, once understanding the limitations and constraints on the court's powers in considering the proposed settlement, only a very few—indeed, only two of the domestic class members—asked the court to reject the settlement. Even among those speaking for foreign class members, most were calling for the court to use whatever powers it had to reduce perceived inequities between foreign and domestic members, rather than to reject the settlement.

Some indication of the broad support for the settlement is given by the number of early registrations. By the start of the hearing, more than 90,000 persons had already registered with the Claims Office even though the settlement had not yet been approved by the court and more than three months remained before the December 1, 1994, registration date. Tens of thousands of additional registrations could be expected by December 1, with many to be submitted, along with claim forms and supporting medical documentation, by September 16 for consideration under the Current Disease Compensation Program. There have been few registrations by foreign claimants, no doubt due in large measure to the criticisms and requests for changes being advanced by their counsel.

Two points may be made about the number of persons electing to opt out of the settlement class: (1) In absolute terms, the number of opt-outs—approximately 7,800 persons in the United States and approximately 6,500 persons outside the United States—is substantial, and indeed raises the specter that one or more defendants may elect to withdraw from the settlement in view of the risks and costs of potential litigation with these claimants. (2) In relative terms, the number of opt-outs is a small fraction—less than 5%—of the total number of persons identified as putative class members, and may be viewed as surprisingly low considering the extensive public discussions of the settlement and the fact that so many thousands already have employed attorneys and indeed have actions pending.

It would be a mistake, however, to assume that persons opting out want the settlement to be disapproved. Yes, most elected to opt out because they believed they could recover more through individual litigation than under the settlement. But most also, when informed, would understand that the settlement will serve their best interests by reducing the court congestion that could long delay judicial resolution of their individual lawsuits and by enabling the defendants to remain sufficiently viable economically as to be able to respond in damages if found liable in those lawsuits. Indeed, after the figures were released regarding the number of opt-outs, many—realizing that with so many opt-outs an early judicial resolution of their claim was unlikely, and reevaluating the benefits provided under the settlement, including the potential for later opting out—have withdrawn their exclusion and rejoined the settlement class. This trend is likely to continue for several weeks, not only by domestic claimants, but also by foreign claimants as they learn of the changes being made for their benefit.

OBJECTIONS BY CLASS MEMBERS

While, as indicated, objections and criticisms were submitted by only a minute portion of the putative class, these comments nevertheless have been given serious attention by the court. Some raise questions that merit discussion in this Opinion.

At the outset, it should be emphasized that the court is not called upon to decide the merits of the claims made on behalf of the class members or to decide whether, or to what extent, the defendants are liable to all or any of the class members. Rather, the court has been presented with an agreement between the parties for possible settlement of claims. It cannot rewrite the essential provisions of that agreement, but rather must decide whether to approve or disapprove that agreement. It cannot, for example, order the defendants to pay more money into the settlement or change the basic provisions for distribution of those proceeds as agreed to by the parties and submitted to the class members. There are, however, some details of the settlement that are within the court's power to modify at this time, as well as some that would be subject to being addressed by the court during the 30–year period for implementing the settlement. Moreover, there may be some changes to which the parties would, after having heard the comments of class members, agree and which would not require another class notification and hearing process.

Adequacy

Perhaps the most serious question relates to the "adequacy" of the Disease Compensation Program. While only a few challenge the adequacy of the amounts shown in the Schedule of Benefits, many are concerned that the defendants' contributions to the Disease Compensation Program—up to $2,715,070,000—will not be sufficient to pay benefits at the levels shown in the Schedule. More particularly, they believe the defendants' contributions to the "Current Disease" portion of this program—$1,200,000,000—will only be enough to make payments to these initial claimants at a fraction of the amounts shown in the Schedule. This potential can be demonstrated through simple mathematical calculations under various hypotheses. For example, even if all eligible Current Disease claimants were in the lowest level on the Schedule ($105,000), this level would be reduced by 50% if there were as many as 23,000 such persons.

Currently no one has reliable data to determine how many class members satisfy the symptom and disability criteria to qualify at this time under the Current Disease Compensation Program, much less to predict how many will meet those criteria during the 30–year life of the Ongoing Disease Compensation Program. The defendants may be correct in their belief—or hope—that the number of persons having the requisite symptoms and disabilities to qualify under the Disease Compensation Program will not be so large as to cause any reduction in the scheduled benefit levels or at most only a small reduction that, indeed, might be remedied through additional negotiations. If, however, as many believe, there are tens of thousands of persons who will qualify at varying benefit levels under the Current Disease Compensation Program, the reductions in scheduled benefits are likely to be so significant that a large number of class members would elect at that point to opt out and in turn the defendants would withdraw from the settlement.

The court's guess is that the $1.2 billion to be paid into the Current Disease Compensation Program will not be enough to pay all approved claims at 100% of the amounts shown on the Schedule. But the court cannot even hazard a guess as to whether such a reduction in benefits—often referred to as "ratcheting"—would be so large that it could not be remedied through further negotiations of the parties or would result in massive opt-outs from the settlement.

In approving the settlement in the face of these serious risks and uncertainties, the court is doing so primarily because of the so-called second opt-out right. Under terms of the settlement, all registered class members not opting out in the initial period will be given another right to opt out if funds paid into the Current Disease Compensation Program are insufficient to pay eligible domestic claimants the full amount of benefits shown on the Schedule. After being notified of the amount of the potential reduction in payment levels, all such persons—not just those who had submitted Current Disease claims—would be able to remove themselves from the settlement class without any penalty. They would then have full rights to institute and pursue litigation against all Settling Defendants and Released Parties, including any rights to seek punitive or multiple damages, and any applicable statutes of limitation or repose would have been suspended during the time they were members of the class.

Through this unusual procedure, it will be possible to obtain the missing information many say is critical in assessing the fairness and adequacy of the settlement; namely, information about the number of breast-implant recipients suffering from various diseases and medical conditions allegedly caused by those implants. Class members then will have an option to exclude themselves from the settlement class. In short, before class members face the loss of any rights relating to individual litigation, they will be advised of both the maximum and the minimum amounts payable under the Disease Compensation Program to current claimants. The provisions for Current Disease claims and for a second opt-out, in combination, provide a sufficient response to the concerns of those who have suggested that the court delay approval of the settlement until reliable data can be obtained about the medical conditions of implant-recipients.

It should be recognized that, if there is a reduction and second opt-out period, some delay—perhaps six months or so—in pursuing individual litigation will have been suffered by those who elect to opt out at that time, or indeed by all class members should the defendants withdraw because of the number of opt-outs. The court concludes, however, that, notwithstanding the risk of such delays, it is in the interest of the class as a whole to give the settlement the chance to succeed. Those who are convinced the settlement is doomed to fail have had, of course, the right to opt out during the initial period in order to pursue their individual claims.

Disease Compensation Program

In addition to concerns about funding of the Disease Compensation Program, discussed above, some have criticized various features of the Program itself, the Schedule of Benefits (or grid), and the Disease Schedule attached as Exhibit D to the Settlement Notice.

The most frequently expressed criticisms of the program relate to the omission of cancer—particularly breast cancer—from the list of covered diseases and the omission of children's illnesses that some attribute to the mother's implant. Many have requested that the court modify the Program to add these and other diseases and illnesses to those covered under the Current Disease Compensation Program.

As earlier indicated, the court is limited in its power to alter the agreement reached by the parties. The court is clearly precluded at this time from adding other diseases and conditions to the Schedule of Benefits or the Disease Schedule because the parties have agreed to a procedure for considering such additions. Under the agreement, a new disease or condition can be added by the court to the Ongoing Disease Compensation Program during its 30–year period, but only after a determination by a 5–person court-appointed Medical Panel that the then-existing medical and scientific evidence demonstrates that the disease or condition is caused by breast implants. The agreement expressly provides that this procedure would govern the potential addition of children's illnesses.

There can be no guarantee, of course, that any illnesses will be added to the Disease Schedule under this procedure, for even if on-going scientific research should indicate that breast implants can be a cause of some disease, the court would still have to consider whether to authorize inclusion of the disease under the Disease Compensation Program, which provides benefits without requiring proof of causation.[9] Recognizing that inclusion of new diseases is problematic at best, the settlement has, through the initial opt-out period, provided a means for implant recipients to pursue through the tort system a claim that they suffer from a serious disease which they believe was caused by a breast-implant but which is not included in the Disease Schedule. With respect to claims of injury to children from their mother's breast implant, the agreement provides an opt-out right, protected against statutes of limitation, until the later of two years after attaining their majority or after manifesting symptoms of the illness claimed to be the result of the mother's implant. The dissatisfaction and objections of those with illnesses not covered under the Disease Compensation Program, while certainly understandable, do not constitute a basis for the court's rejecting the settlement. It should be noted that, in developing criteria for distributions under the Designated Fund III–V, it may be appropriate to give some consideration to particular conditions, such as disfigurement, not included as a covered disease under the Disease Compensation Program.

A few have criticized the Schedule of Benefits for its treatment of implant recipients with multiple diseases or conditions covered under the Disease Schedule, e.g., both lupus and atypical connective tissue disease. A

---

9. The court is frankly skeptical that any disease with a high incidence rate in the general population, such as breast cancer, could be added to the Disease Schedule, unless the scientific evidence not only demonstrated that breast-implants could be a cause of the disease but also indicated particular symptoms or etiological criteria for determining that a particular person's disease was likely caused by an implant.

claimant with multiple diseases or conditions covered under the Disease Schedule is to be paid based upon the disease, severity level, and onset age that would provide the greatest payment. The critics of these provisions argue that in litigation a claimant with multiple covered diseases would be compensated for all the diseases, or at least in a greater amount than if she suffered from only the most serious disease, and that the Disease Schedule should similarly provide increased compensation for multiple diseases. While it certainly would have been rational and fair for the Disease Compensation Program to have been structured in that manner, the approach agreed to by the parties—which the court is without power to change—is also rational and fair, particularly since the few class members in that situation were given the right to opt out if they believed it was in their best interest to pursue their multiple-disease claims in separate litigation. . . .

Opt-out Rights

As mentioned earlier, the court has been accepting exclusions post-marked after the deadlines for all foreign claimants and, on a minimal showing of cause, for domestic claimants, and has also been allowing persons to withdraw their exclusions in order to rejoin the settlement class. Because of the effect on the defendants' decisions whether to withdraw from the settlement due to the number of opt-outs—decisions that are to be made by September 9, 1994—the court will scrutinize very carefully any new requests to be excluded and allow such exclusions only on a showing of compelling circumstances. Also, because of the potential effect on allocation and distribution of benefits under both the Disease Compensation Program and the Designated Funds, the court would expect final membership in the settlement class (subject to any later opt-out rights allowed under the settlement) to be fixed on the basis of materials submitted by December 1, 1994.

The agreement and settlement notice provide that, if a breast-implant recipient withdraws from the settlement class, this automatically excludes her family members and personal representatives from the settlement class. This is an appropriate provision as it relates to any derivative claims or similar claims that are based on the implant recipient's injury or death. The parties, however, are agreed that claims by children of an implant recipient for their own personal injury or death resulting from their mother's implant should be treated differently; namely, by allowing the child to remain in the settlement class with respect to such personal claims (subject to the extended special opt-out rights) even if the mother excludes herself from the settlement class. This change is approved by the court and will be effected by changing paragraph (b)(6) of the class definition.

The agreement and settlement notice also provide that family members cannot exclude themselves from the settlement class as to these derivative claims (e.g., loss of consortium, loss of services, etc.) if the implant recipient remains in the class. The reason for this restriction is obvious—the defendants would be unwilling to make a settlement with an implant recipient that could be as much as $1,400,000 if they would still be subject to potentially large expenditures of time and money in litigation with the recipient's spouse involving most of the issues that litigation with the implant recipient would entail. The objection has been raised by a few spouses that this is unfair, particularly since they are not assured of any additional payments under the settlement for their claims.

The court rejects the argument that it should disapprove the settlement unless, as has been done in a few class action settlements, some of the settlement funds are set aside to pay these derivative claims. Given the large number of potential derivative claims—probably over half of the existing lawsuits have been brought by a wife and husband—any such diversion, to be meaningful, would involve a substantial reduction in the amounts payable to the implant recipients themselves and would result in expensive and time-consuming administrative reviews. The approach of this settlement—treating the amounts offered as payments to settle both the direct and the derivative claims—is a fair and reasonable approach. If the amount offered is not considered by the wife and husband as adequate to compensate for both types of claims, they could have elected—and may again have the option—to exclude themselves from the settlement class. Should the wife and husband disagree as to whether to exclude themselves from the settlement, it is appropriate in the context of this litigation for that decision to be made by the wife. The special problems presented in a proposed class action such as this should be viewed as justifying the court's exercise of equitable powers in these circumstances, notwithstanding an arguable interference with the rights of a husband. . . .

BAR ORDER

The settlement, of course, precludes further claims by class members against the Settling Defendants and Released Parties. It does not, however, preclude class members from instituting or pursuing breast-implant litigation against others—hospitals, doctors, and non-settling manufacturers and suppliers—who have not joined in the settlement. The Settling Defendants are understandably concerned that, in addition to the $4.225 billion being paid by them in the settlement, they could be exposed to liability for still further amounts under theories of indemnification or contribution asserted by defendants in those cases. As in other similar class settlements, the Settling Defendants have, as a condition to agreeing to the settlement, insisted on protection against such claims. This protection is contained in Sections IX and XII.5 of the Settlement Agreement, which purport to bar claims against the Settling Defendants and Released Parties by such non-settling defendants seeking through indemnification or contribution to recover in whole or in part amounts that such persons may be called upon to pay to class members.

The basic problem with the bar order is obvious: it would affect potential rights of persons and entities who have not agreed to it and who are not even parties in the Lindsey action. Adhering to the teaching contained in other cases in which this problem has arisen, the court has invited these non-parties to comment on or object to the proposed bar order. Several have done so, some through motions to intervene. After considering their arguments, the court concludes that, with some modifications and clarifications, the provisions of the settlement with respect to the bar order are fair and reasonable, and can and should be approved.

First and perhaps most significantly, this approval shall not be viewed as precluding such non-settling defendants from taking advantage of any rights of setoff or credit, or similar rights to limit or reduce claims by class members, otherwise available to them have under applicable state laws based on payments made to or for the benefit of class members under this settlement. The settlement agreement is hereby deemed modified to the extent it may otherwise be read as denying such rights.

Second, these provisions bar only actions—whether based on contribution, indemnity, or other similar theories of law—in which such non-settling defendants might seek to recover from the Settling Defendants or Released Parties for liability of such non-settling defendants to class members for breast-implant related injuries or for expenses incurred in defending against such actions or claims. Approval of the settlement does not bar claims by such a non-settling defendant based on a contract between the non-settling defendant and a Settling Defendant that explicitly provides for contribution or indemnification; nor does it bar any independent claims relating to other disputes between such non-settling defendants and the Settling Defendants and Released Parties.

Third, by seeking and obtaining this bar, the Settling Defendants and Released Parties shall likewise be precluded from making similar claims against such non-settling defendants for reimbursement, indemnification, subrogation, contribution, or the like for money paid by them under the settlement. In short, the bar is a mutual bar. It may be noted that the agreement similarly precludes such claims as between or among the Settling Defendants.

Fourth, the bar order does not affect any claims between or among the Settling Defendants, Released Parties, and non-settling defendants for contribution or indemnification relating to claims made by persons who are not members of the settlement class or who opt out of the settlement class.

Fifth, the provisions of the settlement extending the statute of limitations and statute of repose for class members do not apply to claims of class members against the non-settling defendants.

Sixth, a Settling Defendant that withdraws from the Settlement pursuant to Section V of the Agreement or is determined to be in Final Default under Section XIII of the Agreement shall be treated, for purposes of the bar order, in the same manner as a manufacturer, supplier, or health-care provider that was not a party to this settlement ...

With the above modifications, the court finds and concludes that the bar order is essential to the settlement, is fair and equitable, is supported by adequate consideration, and is within the court's powers even though these other manufacturers, suppliers, and health-care providers have not agreed to the order or been named in parties in the Lindsey action. See In re U.S. Oil and Gas Litigation, 967 F.2d 489, 496 (11th Cir.1992), and In re Jiffy Lube Securities Litigation, 927 F.2d 155, 158–60 (4th Cir.1991)....

SUMMARY

The court has made a few modifications to the settlement agreement that either appear to be within the court's power or are believed to be acceptable to the parties, the major ones being a grace period for filing supporting medical documentation for current claims and certain revisions affecting foreign claimants, including clarification and improvement of potential benefits under the Disease Compensation Program, providing potential benefits under Designated Funds I–V, and redefining the class to exclude—but with provisions for purely voluntary participation—residents of Australia and the Canadian Provinces of Ontario and Quebec.

The court finds that, with these changes—

(1) the proposed settlement is a good-faith, arms-length, and non-collusive compromise and settlement of disputed claims;

(2) the proposed settlement is, from the standpoint of the class members, fair, reasonable, adequate, and in their best interests; and

(3) the proposed settlement is, from the standpoint of the defendants, a fair and reasonable compromise of each Settling Defendant's potential liabilities and legal obligations regarding claims for bodily injury or death from breast implants, which have been agreed to by defendants only after extensive negotiations conducted with the assistance of three independent persons appointed by the court, and which imposes a legal obligation upon such defendants to make the payments at the times, in the amounts, and in the manner specified in Exhibit D to the Settlement Agreement and Exhibit C to the Settlement Notice. The allocation of payments as between Designated Funds I–VI and the Disease Compensation Program does not alter the fact that the total amount to be paid by each defendant reflects that defendant's reasonable settlement of compensatory bodily injury claims.

Concurrently with this Opinion, the court is signing and entering a Final Order and Judgment that incorporates as appropriate the terms of the settlement as approved. This judgment is expressly made a final judgment under Rule 54(b), with the time for appeal commencing this date. If any Settling Defendant seeks to exercise its option to withdraw from the settlement, it should do so by means of a motion under Rule 59 filed by September 9, 1994. Any contention by Settlement Class Counsel or a Settling Defendant that the court's modifications are unacceptable and beyond the court's power should likewise be presented by a motion under Rule 59.

FINAL ORDER AND JUDGMENT (Corrected)

In accordance with the findings and conclusions contained in the Opinion filed herewith, the Settlement Agreement—with the modifications made in prior orders, in the Opinion, and in this Order—is determined to have been entered into in good faith, to be non-collusive, to be reasonable, fair, and adequate, to be in the best interests of the class, and therefore is approved. Based on, subject to, and incorporating such provisions, it is hereby ORDERED and ADJUDGED as follows:

1.   Heidi Lindsey and the other designated Representative Plaintiffs under Order No. 15 shall have and recover for themselves and other members of the plaintiffs' class:

(a) from Dow Corning Corporation the sum of $2,018,740,000.00;

(b) from Baxter Healthcare Corp. and Baxter International, Inc., the sum of $555,790,000.00;

(c) from Medical Engineering Corporation and Bristol–Myers Squibb Co. the sum of $1,154,290,000.00;

(d) from Minnesota Mining & Manufacturing Co. the sum of $325,000,-000.00;

(e) from Applied Silicone Corporation the sum of $250,000.00;

(f) from Wilshire Technologies, Inc., the sum of $8,000,000.00;

(g) from Union Carbide Corporation the sum of $138,000,000.00; and

(h) from McGhan Medical Corp. the sum of $25,000,000.00.

2.   The provisional certification of the class for settlement purposes, with certain modifications, is confirmed.

(a) Except as provided in (b), the class on whose behalf this judgment is entered consists of—

(1) all persons, wherever located, who have been implanted before June 1, 1993, with one or more breast implants (whether or not already or later removed), with respect to any claim against a Settling Defendant or Released Party for their own personal injury or death that may be asserted as due in whole or part to any breast implant;

(2) every child, wherever located, born before April 1, 1994, whose natural mother is a person described in subparagraph (1) above and who was born after the date his or her mother had a breast implant, with respect to any claim against a Settling Defendant or Released Party for his or her own personal injury or death that may be asserted as due in whole or part to his or her mother's having had a breast implant; and

(3) all persons or entities (including estates, representatives, spouses, children, relatives, and "significant others"), wherever located, with respect to any claim against a Settling Defendant or Released Party that they may assert independently or derivatively because of their personal relationship to a person described in subparagraph (1) or (2) above.

(b) Excluded from the class are the following:

(1) breast-implant recipients all of whose breast implants can be identified as manufactured or distributed by Porex Medical Technologies Corp.,

Koken Co., Ltd., or other foreign manufacturers not listed in Exhibit A or B to the Settlement Notice;

(2) breast-implant recipients who, as of April 1, 1994, were not citizens or permanent resident aliens of the United States if all of their breast implantations were performed outside the United States and—

(A) they have received any compensation for breast implant injuries or expenses from a Settling Defendant under the laws or procedures of another country; or

(B) they as of April 1, 1994, resided or were domiciled in Australia, or resided or had received a breast-implant in either the Province of Ontario or the Province of Quebec, Canada, except that such persons may, on an individual and purely "opt-in" basis, become voluntary "Foreign Claimant" members of the settlement class. To opt in, such persons must file a Registration Form with the Claims Administrator, P.O. Box 56666, Houston, Texas, USA, 77256, postmarked no later than December 1, 1994. By voluntarily opting in through this registration, such persons—

(i) will be deemed to waive any objections and to accept the general terms of the settlement applicable to Foreign Claimants, and

(ii) will have all rights and benefits accorded to Foreign Claimants, including the right to opt out after the court determines the projected amounts payable to Foreign Claimants under the Disease Compensation Schedule. If an opting-in Foreign Claimant should later elect such opt-out right, the Settling Defendants will be precluded from asserting in a defense based on a statute of limitations, statute of repose, or similar proscription the period of time from January 24, 1992, to the date that is 30 days after such person elects to opt-out of the class.

(3) breast-implant recipients who, before June 17, 1994, shall have separately settled with a Settling Defendant, providing a general release of claims related to breast implants, unless (A) they were not represented by counsel in such settlement and the settlement involved a payment of less than $15,000 or (B) they demonstrate by clear and convincing evidence that their settlement was induced by a Settling Defendant's fraud;

(4) breast-implant recipients who, before June 17, 1994, shall have obtained and collected a judgment against a Settling Defendant on a breast-implant claim or, after a trial on the merits, shall have had a final judgment entered against them on a breast-implant claim in favor of a Settling Defendant;

(5) breast-implant recipients who (during the "First Opt Out" period) elect to exclude themselves from the Settlement Class by return of a completed Exclusion Form, received or postmarked no later than June 17, 1994, or whose Exclusion Form, though received or postmarked after that date, is accepted by the Court as timely; and

(6) any person or entity described in paragraph 2(a)(3) whose status as a class member depends on class membership of a recipient excluded under paragraphs 2(b)(1) through 2(b)(5).

(c) As used in this Order and Judgment, the terms "Settling Defendants" and "Released Parties" mean those persons and entities listed or described in Schedules A and B to the Settlement Notice.

(d) A list of persons excluding themselves from the class will, in order to protect privacy interests to the extent possible, be maintained under seal by the court, with the identity of such persons subject to disclosure only to the extent necessary to protect the rights of the various parties (such as to determine whether a person is precluded from instituting or maintaining some other action).

3.   Except as otherwise provided in the terms of settlement as approved by the court:

(a) the Settling Defendants and Released Parties are forever released from any and all claims which any member of the class had, has, or may have in the future against any of such persons and entities with respect to any existing or future claim, known or unknown, accrued or unaccrued, for personal injury or death that may be asserted as due in whole or part to any breast implant;

(b) each member of the class is barred and permanently enjoined from instituting, asserting, or prosecuting against any of the Settling Defendants or Released Parties in any pending or future action in any federal or state court in this country, or in any court or tribunal in any other country, any and all claims which such individual had, has, or may have in the future against any of such persons and entities with respect to any existing or future claim, known or unknown, accrued or unaccrued, for personal injury or death that may be asserted as due in whole or part to any breast implant;

(c) other persons and entities, not parties to the settlement agreement, against whom members of the class may assert claims for breast-implant related injuries or death are barred from making claims for contribution or indemnification against the Settling Defendants and Released Parties to the extent described in the accompanying Opinion, but are not precluded from asserting any rights to set-off, credit, or reduction that may be allowed under applicable state law; and

(d) other persons and entities, not parties to the settlement agreement, who may have claims for subrogation or reimbursement arising from payment of medical expenses or providing medical services o class members, are barred from making such claims against the Settling Defendants and Released Parties, but are not by this judgment precluded from subsequently attempting to institute or pursue such claims against the settlement fund or class members.

4.   Costs are taxed against the settlement funds paid by the defendants.

5. Under Fed.R.Civ.P. 54(b), the court expressly determines that there is no just reason for delay and expressly directs that this judgment, upon filing in CV 94–P–11558–S, be deemed as a final judgment with respect to all claims by members of the class against the defendants herein with respect to breast-implant related injuries or death.

6. Without deferring or delaying the finality of this order and judgment, this court retains exclusive, general, and continuing jurisdiction as needed or appropriate in order to administer, supervise, implement, interpret, or enforce the settlement, including the investment, conservation, protection, allocation, and distribution of the settlement funds.

* * *

Questions

1. What are the pros and cons of the settlement in the Silicon Gel case? Are the objectors correct in their fears that the settlement is inadequate in amount and arbitrary as to which diseases are covered? Or, are the proponents correct that this represents the best possible, albeit imperfect, solution to a very difficult problem?

2. How could you frame objections to settlement under the terms of Rule 23? Are the prerequisites to class certification met? Is this settlement fair to future claimants, who may not know of their injury and thus do not know they are members of the class?

3. Note the impact of the settlement on third parties. It bars indemnification claims against defendants by nonparties, such as hospitals and doctors who are not part of the settlement. Is this permissible under *Martin v. Wilks?*

4. Can the objectors satisfy their concerns by choosing to opt-out? Is there any practical difference between opting-out and defeating the settlement altogether? Here the opt-outs are to be decided before the court determines whether the settlement is approved. Does that timetable create strategic dilemmas for objecting potential class members? How could such dilemmas be avoided?

5. The settlement is structured so as to set up a mini ADR mechanism to determine individual claims. Claimants only have to show that they have an enumerated medical condition and had a silicone gel implant. They do not have to prove that the injury was caused by the silicone gel product. In contrast to the tort system, in the settlement compensation is paid without proof of causation, not to mention fault. Other tort defenses, such as assumption of risk and contributory negligence are also lacking. Is this a better way to compensate victims of mass torts than the litigation system?

6. Why should those who had implants that led to a particular disease receive compensation, while others who have the same disease but no implant receive no compensation? To compensate one without proof of causality and fault, but not the other, appears arbitrary. Would it make

sense to jettison the tort system for mass toxic torts, and compensate all victims—whatever the cause of their ailment—from a social insurance fund? Note this would be a public law approach to the same problem that is currently addressed by settlement class actions. In considering the merits of a settlement class versus a public compensation system approach, does it matter whether the mass torts are the result of repeated corporate conduct rather than a single incident like an airplane crash?

7.   After the 1994 silicone gel class action settlement was approved by Judge Pointer, several problems arose. First, many women announced an intention to opt out of the class settlement and pursue their claims in state court. Furthermore, the settlement was based on an estimate that some 60,000 women would file claims. Instead, 480,000 women filed claims. As a result of these factors, Dow Corning backed out and declared bankruptcy in 1995. The other companies participating in the 1994 settlement, including Bristol–Meyers and 3M, reached a new settlement that applied to for women who received implants from companies other than Dow Corning. That settlement, involving fewer women and a fund of some $3 billion, has been approved by Judge Pointer. In the meantime, Dow Corning has reached another settlement agreement with the class that represents most of the American women with claims against the company. This new settlement requires Dow Corning to contribute $3.2 billion to a fund that will pay out up to $250,000 per claim. The U.S. Bankruptcy Court has not yet approved the settlement, but approval is anticipated.

8.   In June, 1999, the National Institute of Health issued a 450–page report on the link between silicone gel breast implants and serious or life-threatening diseases. The report, based on a review of 3,000 cases, conclud-ed that there was insufficient evidence to establish such a link. However, the Report did not give the implants a clean bill of health. Rather, it found that one in four women who has an implant requires repeat surgeries to repair leakage or remove them when they become hard and painful. It also pointed out that implants can block mammogram images, and thus impede diagnosis of other serious conditions. And it left open the possibility that other medical problems traceable to the implants may appear in the future.

Should the recent study that casts doubt on any link between silicone gel implants and serious or life-threatening diseases be a factor in a court's consideration of the fairness of the class action settlement? How much weight should such a subsequently developed scientific information be given?

9.   After protracted litigation concerning the use of Agent Orange during the Vietnam War, Judge Weinstein approved a class action settlement of $180 million for Vietnam veterans and their families who alleged serious medical conditions had resulted from exposure. *In Re "Agent Orange" Products Liability Litigation*, 597 F. Supp. 740 (E.D.N.Y. 1984). After the settlement was approved, a number of veterans opted out in order to pursue their own lawsuits. Some of these opt out cases were consolidated for trial in federal court before Judge Weinstein. Then less than one year after approving the class settlement, Judge Weinstein granted summary

judgment to defendants and dismissed the cases of 287 veterans and class members who had opted out. Judge Weinstein did so because he found no credible scientific evidence linking the medical conditions to their exposure to Agent Orange. He stated that the medical evidence on which the plaintiff's cases relied was so lacking in reliability as to be inadmissible. Judge Weinstein acknowledged that it was possible that causation could be proved at some time in the future, but there was no proof of causality at that time. *In Re Agent "Orange Product" Liability Litigation*, 611 F. Supp. 1223 (E.D.N.Y. 1985), aff'd 818 F.2d 187 (2d Cir. 1987).

Is it appropriate for a judge who believes that there is no scientific basis for a class toxic tort claim to nonetheless approve a settlement requiring the manufacturer to pay compensation to class members?

10.   Some years after the Agent Orange litigation, Weinstein wrote a law review article in which he explained why he approved the settlement despite the dearth of medical evidence to support the plaintiff's claims. He wrote:

> "In the Agent Orange case, for example, I held hearings all over the country. I listened to some 600 people, and I received hundreds of telephone and written communications. I was struck by the deep emotional underpinnings of the litigation. The fact that the law and science, in my view, did not support a viable cause of action did not warrant ignoring these heartfelt cries for justice. Obviously I was affected by the emotional appeal of veterans who thought themselves abused. Should I have allowed that factor to affect my handling of the litigation? Could I have avoided such an effect?"

Jack B. Weinstein, *Ethical Dimensions in Mass Tort Litigation*, 88 NW U. L. REV. 469, 491 (1994). Should humanitarian concerns or sympathetic community sentiment be relevant to a judge when ruling on the fairness of a class action settlement? What role should community sentiment play in a mass tort class action brought by a class of unsympathetic plaintiffs? How should such community or humanitarian concerns be weighed against scientific evidence to the contrary? See generally, See PETER H. SCHUCK, AGENT ORANGE ON TRIAL: MASS TOXIC DISASTERS IN THE COURTS (1987).

* * *

Amchem Products, Inc., et al. v. Windsor, et al.

521 U.S. 591, 117 S.Ct. 2231 (1997).

◼ JUSTICE GINSBURG delivered the opinion of the Court.

This case concerns the legitimacy under Rule 23 of the Federal Rules of Civil Procedure of a class-action certification sought to achieve global settlement of current and future asbestos-related claims. The class proposed for certification potentially encompasses hundreds of thousands, perhaps millions, of individuals tied together by this commonality: each was, or some day may be, adversely affected by past exposure to asbestos products manufactured by one or more of 20 companies. Those companies, defendants in the lower courts, are petitioners here.

The United States District Court for the Eastern District of Pennsylvania certified the class for settlement only, finding that the proposed settlement was fair and that representation and notice had been adequate. That court enjoined class members from separately pursuing asbestos-related personal-injury suits in any court, federal or state, pending the issuance of a final order. The Court of Appeals for the Third Circuit vacated the District Court's orders, holding that the class certification failed to satisfy Rule 23's requirements in several critical respects. We affirm the Court of Appeals' judgment.

I

A

The settlement-class certification we confront evolved in response to an asbestos-litigation crisis. See Georgine v. Amchem Products, Inc., 83 F.3d 610, 618, and n. 2 (C.A.3 1996) (citing commentary). A United States Judicial Conference Ad Hoc Committee on Asbestos Litigation, appointed by THE CHIEF JUSTICE in September 1990, described facets of the problem in a 1991 report:

> "[This] is a tale of danger known in the 1930s, exposure inflicted upon millions of Americans in the 1940s and 1950s, injuries that began to take their toll in the 1960s, and a flood of lawsuits beginning in the 1970s. On the basis of past and current filing data, and because of a latency period that may last as long as 40 years for some asbestos related diseases, a continuing stream of claims can be expected. The final toll of asbestos related injuries is unknown. Predictions have been made of 200,000 asbestos disease deaths before the year 2000 and as many as 265,000 by the year 2015.

> "The most objectionable aspects of asbestos litigation can be briefly summarized: dockets in both federal and state courts continue to grow; long delays are routine; trials are too long; the same issues are litigated over and over; transaction costs exceed the victims' recovery by nearly two to one; exhaustion of assets threatens and distorts the process; and future claimants may lose altogether." Report of The Judicial Conference Ad Hoc Committee on Asbestos Litigation 2–3 (Mar.1991).

Real reform, the report concluded, required federal legislation creating a national asbestos dispute-resolution scheme. See id., at 3, 27–35; see also id., at 42 (dissenting statement of Hogan, J.) (agreeing that "a national solution is the only answer" and suggesting "passage by Congress of an administrative claims procedure similar to the Black Lung legislation"). As recommended by the Ad Hoc Committee, the Judicial Conference of the United States urged Congress to act. See Report of the Proceedings of the Judicial Conference of the United States 33 (Mar. 12, 1991). To this date, no congressional response has emerged.

In the face of legislative inaction, the federal courts—lacking authority to replace state tort systems with a national toxic tort compensation regime—endeavored to work with the procedural tools available to improve management of federal asbestos litigation. Eight federal judges, experienced in the superintendence of asbestos cases, urged the Judicial Panel on Multidistrict Litigation (MDL Panel), to consolidate in a single district all asbestos complaints then pending in federal courts. Accepting the recommendation, the MDL Panel transferred all asbestos cases then filed, but not yet on trial in federal courts to a single district, the United States District Court for the Eastern District of Pennsylvania; pursuant to the transfer order, the collected cases were consolidated for pretrial proceedings before Judge Weiner. See In re Asbestos Products Liability Litigation (No. VI), 771 F.Supp. 415, 422–424 (Jud.Pan.Mult.Lit. 1991). The order aggregated pending cases only; no authority resides in the MDL Panel to license for consolidated proceedings claims not yet filed.

B

After the consolidation, attorneys for plaintiffs and defendants formed separate steering committees and began settlement negotiations. Ronald L. Motley and Gene Locks—later appointed, along with Motley's law partner Joseph F. Rice, to represent the plaintiff class in this action—co-chaired the Plaintiffs' Steering Committee. Counsel for the Center for Claims Resolution (CCR), the consortium of 20 former asbestos manufacturers now before us as petitioners, participated in the Defendants' Steering Committee. Although the MDL order collected, transferred, and consolidated only cases already commenced in federal courts, settlement negotiations included efforts to find a "means of resolving . . . future cases." Record, Doc. 3, p. 2 (Memorandum in Support of Joint Motion for Conditional Class Certification); see also Georgine v. Amchem Products, Inc., 157 F.R.D. 246, 266 (E.D.Pa.1994) ("primary purpose of the settlement talks in the consolidated MDL litigation was to craft a national settlement that would provide an alternative resolution mechanism for asbestos claims," including claims that might be filed in the future).

In November 1991, the Defendants' Steering Committee made an offer designed to settle all pending and future asbestos cases by providing a fund for distribution by plaintiffs' counsel among asbestos-exposed individuals. The Plaintiffs' Steering Committee rejected this offer, and negotiations fell apart. CCR, however, continued to pursue "a workable administrative system for the handling of future claims." Id., at 270.

To that end, CCR counsel approached the lawyers who had headed the Plaintiffs' Steering Committee in the unsuccessful negotiations, and a new round of negotiations began; that round yielded the mass settlement agreement now in controversy. At the time, the former heads of the Plaintiffs' Steering Committee represented thousands of plaintiffs with then-pending asbestos-related claims—claimants the parties to this suit call "inventory" plaintiffs. CCR indicated in these discussions that it would resist settlement of inventory cases absent "some kind of protection for the future." Id., at 294; see also id., at 295 (CCR communicated to the inventory plaintiffs' attorneys that once the CCR defendants saw a rational way to deal with claims expected to be filed in the future, those defendants would be prepared to address the settlement of pending cases).

Settlement talks thus concentrated on devising an administrative scheme for disposition of asbestos claims not yet in litigation. In these negotiations, counsel for masses of inventory plaintiffs endeavored to represent the interests of the anticipated future claimants, although those lawyers then had no attorney-client relationship with such claimants.

Once negotiations seemed likely to produce an agreement purporting to bind potential plaintiffs, CCR agreed to settle, through separate agreements, the claims of plaintiffs who had already filed asbestos-related lawsuits. In one such agreement, CCR defendants promised to pay more than $200 million to gain release of the claims of numerous inventory plaintiffs. After settling the inventory claims, CCR, together with the plaintiffs' lawyers CCR had approached, launched this case, exclusively involving persons outside the MDL Panel's province—plaintiffs without already pending lawsuits.[3]

C

The class action thus instituted was not intended to be litigated. Rather, within the space of a single day, January 15, 1993, the settling parties—CCR defendants and the representatives of the plaintiff class described below—presented to the District Court a complaint, an answer, a proposed settlement agreement, and a joint motion for conditional class certification.

The complaint identified nine lead plaintiffs, designating them and members of their families as representatives of a class comprising all persons who had not filed an asbestos-related lawsuit against a CCR defendant as of the date the class action commenced, but who (1) had been exposed—occupationally or through the occupational exposure of a spouse or household member—to asbestos or products containing asbestos attributable to a CCR defendant, or (2) whose spouse or family member had been so exposed. Untold numbers of individuals may fall within this description. All named plaintiffs alleged that they or a member of their family had been exposed to asbestos-containing products of CCR defendants. More than half of the named plaintiffs alleged that they or their family members had already suffered various physical injuries as a result of the exposure. The others alleged that they had not yet manifested any asbestos-related condition. The complaint delineated no subclasses; all named plaintiffs were designated as representatives of the class as a whole.

The complaint invoked the District Court's diversity jurisdiction and asserted various state-law claims for relief, including (1) negligent failure to warn, (2) strict liability, (3) breach of express and implied warranty, (4)

3. It is basic to comprehension of this proceeding to notice that no transferred case is included in the settlement at issue, and no case covered by the settlement existed as a civil action at the time of the MDL Panel transfer

negligent infliction of emotional distress, (5) enhanced risk of disease, (6) medical monitoring, and (7) civil conspiracy. Each plaintiff requested unspecified damages in excess of $100,000. CCR defendants' answer denied the principal allegations of the complaint and asserted 11 affirmative defenses.

A stipulation of settlement accompanied the pleadings; it proposed to settle, and to preclude nearly all class members from litigating against CCR companies, all claims not filed before January 15, 1993, involving compensation for present and future asbestos-related personal injury or death. An exhaustive document exceeding 100 pages, the stipulation presents in detail an administrative mechanism and a schedule of payments to compensate class members who meet defined asbestos-exposure and medical requirements. The stipulation describes four categories of compensable disease: mesothelioma; lung cancer; certain "other cancers" (colon-rectal, laryngeal, esophageal, and stomach cancer); and "non-malignant conditions" (asbestosis and bilateral pleural thickening). Persons with "exceptional" medical claims—claims that do not fall within the four described diagnostic categories—may in some instances qualify for compensation, but the settlement caps the number of "exceptional" claims CCR must cover.

For each qualifying disease category, the stipulation specifies the range of damages CCR will pay to qualifying claimants. Payments under the settlement are not adjustable for inflation. Mesothelioma claimants—the most highly compensated category—are scheduled to receive between $20,000 and $200,000. The stipulation provides that CCR is to propose the level of compensation within the prescribed ranges; it also establishes procedures to resolve disputes over medical diagnoses and levels of compensation.

Compensation above the fixed ranges may be obtained for "extraordinary" claims. But the settlement places both numerical caps and dollar limits on such claims.[6] The settlement also imposes "case flow maximums," which cap the number of claims payable for each disease in a given year.

Class members are to receive no compensation for certain kinds of claims, even if otherwise applicable state law recognizes such claims. Claims that garner no compensation under the settlement include claims by family members of asbestos-exposed individuals for loss of consortium, and claims by so-called "exposure-only" plaintiffs for increased risk of cancer, fear of future asbestos-related injury, and medical monitoring. "Pleural" claims, which might be asserted by persons with asbestos-related plaques on their lungs but no accompanying physical impairment, are also excluded. Although not entitled to present compensation, exposure-only claimants and pleural claimants may qualify for benefits when and if they develop a compensable disease and meet the relevant exposure and medical

---

6. Only three percent of the qualified mesothelioma, lung cancer, and "other cancer" claims, and only one percent of the total number of qualified "non-malignant condition" claims can be designated "extraordinary." Average expenditures are specified for claims found "extraordinary"; mesothelioma victims with compensable extraordinary claims, for example, receive, on average, $300,000.

criteria. Defendants forgo defenses to liability, including statute of limitations pleas.

Class members, in the main, are bound by the settlement in perpetuity, while CCR defendants may choose to withdraw from the settlement after ten years. A small number of class members—only a few per year—may reject the settlement and pursue their claims in court. Those permitted to exercise this option, however, may not assert any punitive damages claim or any claim for increased risk of cancer. Aspects of the administration of the settlement are to be monitored by the AFL–CIO and class counsel. Class counsel are to receive attorneys' fees in an amount to be approved by the District Court.

D

On January 29, 1993, as requested by the settling parties, the District Court conditionally certified, under Federal Rule of Civil Procedure 23(b)(3), an encompassing opt-out class. The certified class included persons occupationally exposed to defendants' asbestos products, and members of their families, who had not filed suit as of January 15. Judge Weiner appointed Locks, Motley, and Rice as class counsel, noting that "[t]he Court may in the future appoint additional counsel if it is deemed necessary and advisable." Record, Doc. 11, p. 3 (Class Certification Order). At no stage of the proceedings, however, were additional counsel in fact appointed. Nor was the class ever divided into subclasses. In a separate order, Judge Weiner assigned to Judge Reed, also of the Eastern District of Pennsylvania, "the task of conducting fairness proceedings and of determining whether the proposed settlement is fair to the class." See 157 F.R.D., at 258. Various class members raised objections to the settlement stipulation, and Judge Weiner granted the objectors full rights to participate in the subsequent proceedings. Ibid.

In preliminary rulings, Judge Reed held that the District Court had subject-matter jurisdiction, see Carlough v. Amchem Products, Inc., 834 F.Supp. 1437, 1467–1468 (E.D.Pa.1993), and he approved the settling parties' elaborate plan for giving notice to the class, see Carlough v. Amchem Products, Inc., 158 F.R.D. 314, 336 (E.D.Pa.1993). The court-approved notice informed recipients that they could exclude themselves from the class, if they so chose, within a three-month opt-out period.

Objectors raised numerous challenges to the settlement. They urged that the settlement unfairly disadvantaged those without currently compensable conditions in that it failed to adjust for inflation or to account for changes, over time, in medical understanding. They maintained that compensation levels were intolerably low in comparison to awards available in tort litigation or payments received by the inventory plaintiffs. And they objected to the absence of any compensation for certain claims, for example, medical monitoring, compensable under the tort law of several States. Rejecting these and all other objections, Judge Reed concluded that the settlement terms were fair and had been negotiated without collusion. See 157 F.R.D., at 325, 331–332. He also found that adequate notice had been given to class members, see id., at 332–334, and that final class certification under Rule 23(b)(3) was appropriate, see id., at 315.

As to the specific prerequisites to certification, the District Court observed that the class satisfied Rule 23(a)(1)'s numerosity requirement,[8] see ibid., a matter no one debates. The Rule 23(a)(2) and (b)(3) requirements of commonality[9] and preponderance[10] were also satisfied, the District Court held, in that

> "[t]he members of the class have all been exposed to asbestos products supplied by the defendants and all share an interest in receiving prompt and fair compensation for their claims, while minimizing the risks and transaction costs inherent in the asbestos litigation process as it occurs presently in the tort system. Whether the proposed settlement satisfies this interest and is otherwise a fair, reasonable and adequate compromise of the claims of the class is a predominant issue for purposes of Rule 23(b)(3)." Id., at 316.

The District Court held next that the claims of the class representatives were "typical" of the class as a whole, a requirement of Rule 23(a)(3),[11] and that, as Rule 23(b)(3) demands,[12] the class settlement was "superior" to other methods of adjudication. See ibid.

Strenuous objections had been asserted regarding the adequacy of representation, a Rule 23(a)(4) requirement.[13] Objectors maintained that class counsel and class representatives had disqualifying conflicts of interests. In particular, objectors urged, claimants whose injuries had become manifest and claimants without manifest injuries should not have common counsel and should not be aggregated in a single class. Furthermore, objectors argued, lawyers representing inventory plaintiffs should not represent the newly-formed class.

Satisfied that class counsel had ably negotiated the settlement in the best interests of all concerned, and that the named parties served as adequate representatives, the District Court rejected these objections. See id., at 317–319, 326–332. Subclasses were unnecessary, the District Court held, bearing in mind the added cost and confusion they would entail and the ability of class members to exclude themselves from the class during the three-month opt-out period. See id., at 318–319. Reasoning that the representative plaintiffs "have a strong interest that recovery for *all* of the medical categories be maximized because they may have claims in *any*, or several categories," the District Court found "no antagonism of interest between class members with various medical conditions, or between persons with and without currently manifest asbestos impairment." Id., at

---

8. Rule 23(a)(1) requires that the class be "so numerous that joinder of all members is impracticable."

9. Rule 23(a)(2) requires that there be "questions of law or fact common to the class."

10. Rule 23(b)(3) requires that "the [common] questions of law or fact ... predominate over any questions affecting only individual members."

11. Rule 23(a)(3) states that "the claims ... of the representative parties [must be] typical of the claims ... of the class."

12. Rule 23(b)(3) requires that "a class action [be] superior to other available methods for the fair and efficient adjudication of the controversy."

13. Rule 23(a)(4) requires that "the representative parties will fairly and adequately protect the interests of the class."

318. Declaring class certification appropriate and the settlement fair, the District Court preliminarily enjoined all class members from commencing any asbestos-related suit against the CCR defendants in any state or federal court. See Georgine v. Amchem Products, Inc., 878 F.Supp. 716, 726–727 (E.D.Pa.1994).

The objectors appealed. The United States Court of Appeals for the Third Circuit vacated the certification, holding that the requirements of Rule 23 had not been satisfied. See Georgine v. Amchem Products, Inc., 83 F.3d 610 (1996).

E

The Court of Appeals, in a long, heavily detailed opinion by Judge Becker, first noted several challenges by objectors to justiciability, subject-matter jurisdiction, and adequacy of notice. These challenges, the court said, raised "serious concerns." Id., at 623. However, the court observed, "the jurisdictional issues in this case would not exist but for the [class action] certification." Ibid. Turning to the class-certification issues and finding them dispositive, the Third Circuit declined to decide other questions.

On class-action prerequisites, the Court of Appeals referred to an earlier Third Circuit decision, In re General Motors Corp. Pick–Up Truck Fuel Tank Products Liability Litigation, 55 F.3d 768 (C.A.3), cert. denied, 516 U.S. ___, 116 S.Ct. 88, 133 L.Ed.2d 45 (1995) (hereinafter GM Trucks), which held that although a class action may be certified for settlement purposes only, Rule 23(a)'s requirements must be satisfied as if the case were going to be litigated. 55 F.3d, at 799–800. The same rule should apply, the Third Circuit said, to class certification under Rule 23(b)(3). See 83 F.3d, at 625. But cf. In re Asbestos Litigation, 90 F.3d 963, 975–976, and n. 8 (C.A.5 1996), cert. pending, Nos. 96–1379, 96–1394. While stating that the requirements of Rule 23(a) and (b)(3) must be met "without taking into account the settlement," 83 F.3d, at 626, the Court of Appeals in fact closely considered the terms of the settlement as it examined aspects of the case under Rule 23 criteria. See id., at 630–634.

The Third Circuit recognized that Rule 23(a)(2)'s "commonality" requirement is subsumed under, or superseded by, the more stringent Rule 23(b)(3) requirement that questions common to the class "predominate over" other questions. The court therefore trained its attention on the "predominance" inquiry. See id., at 627. The harmfulness of asbestos exposure was indeed a prime factor common to the class, the Third Circuit observed. See id., at 626, 630. But uncommon questions abounded.

In contrast to mass torts involving a single accident, class members in this case were exposed to different asbestos-containing products, in different ways, over different periods, and for different amounts of time; some suffered no physical injury, others suffered disabling or deadly diseases. See id., at 626, 628. "These factual differences," the Third Circuit explained, "translate [d] into significant legal differences." Id., at 627. State law governed and varied widely on such critical issues as "viability of [exposure-only] claims [and] availability of causes of action for medical monitoring, increased risk of cancer, and fear of future injury." Ibid.[14] "[T]he number of uncommon issues in this humongous class action," the Third Circuit concluded, ibid., barred a determination, under existing tort law, that common questions predominated, see id., at 630.

The Court of Appeals next found that "serious intra-class conflicts preclude[d] th[e] class from meeting the adequacy of representation requirement" of Rule 23(a)(4). Ibid. Adverting to, but not resolving charges of attorney conflict of interests, the Third Circuit addressed the question whether the named plaintiffs could adequately advance the interests of all class members. The Court of Appeals acknowledged that the District Court was certainly correct to this extent: " '[T]he members of the class are united in seeking the maximum possible recovery for their asbestos-related claims.' " Ibid. (quoting 157 F.R.D., at 317). "But the settlement does more than simply provide a general recovery fund," the Court of Appeals immediately added; "[r]ather, it makes important judgments on how recovery is to be *allocated* among different kinds of plaintiffs, decisions that necessarily favor some claimants over others." 83 F.3d, at 630.

In the Third Circuit's view, the "most salient" divergence of interests separated plaintiffs already afflicted with an asbestos-related disease from plaintiffs without manifest injury (exposure-only plaintiffs). The latter would rationally want protection against inflation for distant recoveries. See ibid. They would also seek sturdy back-end opt-out rights and "causation provisions that can keep pace with changing science and medicine, rather than freezing in place the science of 1993." Id., at 630–631. Already injured parties, in contrast, would care little about such provisions and would rationally trade them for higher current payouts. See id., at 631. These and other adverse interests, the Court of Appeals carefully explained, strongly suggested that an undivided set of representatives could not adequately protect the discrete interests of both currently afflicted and exposure-only claimants.

The Third Circuit next rejected the District Court's determination that the named plaintiffs were "typical" of the class, noting that this Rule 23(a)(3) inquiry overlaps the adequacy of representation question: "both look to the potential for conflicts in the class." Id., at 632. Evident conflict problems, the court said, led it to hold that "no set of representatives can be 'typical' of this class." Ibid.

The Court of Appeals similarly rejected the District Court's assessment of the superiority of the class action. The Third Circuit initially noted that a class action so large and complex "could not be tried." Ibid. The court elaborated most particularly, however, on the unfairness of binding exposure-only plaintiffs who might be unaware of the class action or lack

---

14. Recoveries under the laws of different States spanned a wide range. Objectors assert, for example, that 15% of current mesothelioma claims arise in California, where the statewide average recovery is $419,674—or more than 209% above the $200,000 maximum specified in the settlement for mesothelioma claims not typed "extraordinary." See Brief for Respondents George Windsor et al. 5–6, n. 5 (citing 2 App. 461).

sufficient information about their exposure to make a reasoned decision whether to stay in or opt out. See id., at 633. "A series of statewide or more narrowly defined adjudications, either through consolidation under Rule 42(a) or as class actions under Rule 23, would seem preferable," the Court of Appeals said. Id., at 634.

The Third Circuit, after intensive review, ultimately ordered decertification of the class and vacation of the District Court's anti-suit injunction. Id., at 635. Judge Wellford concurred, "fully subscrib[ing] to the decision of Judge Becker that the plaintiffs in this case ha[d] not met the requirements of Rule 23." Ibid. He added that in his view, named exposure-only plaintiffs had no standing to pursue the suit in federal court, for their depositions showed that "[t]hey claimed no damages and no present injury." Id., at 638.

We granted certiorari, 519 U.S. ___, 117 S.Ct. 379, 136 L.Ed.2d 297 (1996), and now affirm.

II

Objectors assert in this Court, as they did in the District Court and Court of Appeals, an array of jurisdictional barriers. Most fundamentally, they maintain that the settlement proceeding instituted by class counsel and CCR is not a justiciable case or controversy within the confines of Article III of the Federal Constitution. In the main, they say, the proceeding is a nonadversarial endeavor to impose on countless individuals without currently ripe claims an administrative compensation regime binding on those individuals if and when they manifest injuries.

Furthermore, objectors urge that exposure-only claimants lack standing to sue: Either they have not yet sustained any cognizable injury or, to the extent the complaint states claims and demands relief for emotional distress, enhanced risk of disease, and medical monitoring, the settlement provides no redress. Objectors also argue that exposure-only claimants did not meet the then-current amount-in-controversy requirement (in excess of $50,000) specified for federal-court jurisdiction based upon diversity of citizenship. See 28 U.S.C. § 1332(a).

As earlier recounted, see supra, at 2242, the Third Circuit declined to reach these issues because they "would not exist but for the [class action] certification." 83 F.3d, at 623. We agree that "[t]he class certification issues are dispositive," ibid.; because their resolution here is logically antecedent to the existence of any Article III issues, it is appropriate to reach them first, cf. Arizonans for Official English v. Arizona, 520 U.S. ___, ___, 117 S.Ct. 1055, 1068, 137 L.Ed.2d 170 (1997) (declining to resolve definitively question whether petitioners had standing because mootness issue was dispositive of the case). We therefore follow the path taken by the Court of Appeals, mindful that Rule 23's requirements must be interpreted in keeping with Article III constraints, and with the Rules Enabling Act, which instructs that rules of procedure "shall not abridge, enlarge or modify any substantive right," 28 U.S.C. § 2072(b). See also Fed. Rule Civ.

Proc. 82 ("rules shall not be construed to extend . . . the [subject matter] jurisdiction of the United States district courts").

III

To place this controversy in context, we briefly describe the characteristics of class actions for which the Federal Rules provide. Rule 23, governing federal-court class actions, stems from equity practice and gained its current shape in an innovative 1966 revision. See generally Kaplan, Continuing Work of the Civil Committee: 1966 Amendments of the Federal Rules of Civil Procedure (I), 81 Harv. L.Rev. 356, 375–400 (1967) (hereinafter Kaplan, Continuing Work). Rule 23(a) states four threshold requirements applicable to all class actions: (1) numerosity (a "class [so large] that joinder of all members is impracticable"); (2) commonality ("questions of law or fact common to the class"); (3) typicality (named parties' claims or defenses "are typical . . . of the class"); and (4) adequacy of representation (representatives "will fairly and adequately protect the interests of the class").

In addition to satisfying Rule 23(a)'s prerequisites, parties seeking class certification must show that the action is maintainable under Rule 23(b)(1), (2), or (3). Rule 23(b)(1) covers cases in which separate actions by or against individual class members would risk establishing "incompatible standards of conduct for the party opposing the class," Fed. Rule Civ. Proc. 23(b)(1)(A), or would "as a practical matter be dispositive of the interests" of nonparty class members "or substantially impair or impede their ability to protect their interests," Fed. Rule Civ. Proc. 23(b)(1)(B). Rule 23(b)(1)(A) "takes in cases where the party is obliged by law to treat the members of the class alike (a utility acting toward customers; a government imposing a tax), or where the party must treat all alike as a matter of practical necessity (a riparian owner using water as against downriver owners)." Kaplan, Continuing Work 388 (footnotes omitted). Rule 23(b)(1)(B) includes, for example, "limited fund" cases, instances in which numerous persons make claims against a fund insufficient to satisfy all claims. See Advisory Committee's Notes on Fed. Rule Civ. Proc. 23, 28 U.S.C.App., pp. 696–697 (hereinafter Adv. Comm. Notes).

Rule 23(b)(2) permits class actions for declaratory or injunctive relief where "the party opposing the class has acted or refused to act on grounds generally applicable to the class." Civil rights cases against parties charged with unlawful, class-based discrimination are prime examples. Adv. Comm. Notes, 28 U.S.C.App., p. 697; see Kaplan, Continuing Work 389 (subdivision (b)(2) "build[s] on experience mainly, but not exclusively, in the civil rights field").

In the 1966 class-action amendments, Rule 23(b)(3), the category at issue here, was "the most adventuresome" innovation. See Kaplan, A Prefatory Note, 10 B.C. Ind. & Com. L.Rev. 497, 497 (1969) (hereinafter Kaplan, Prefatory Note). Rule 23(b)(3) added to the complex-litigation arsenal class actions for damages designed to secure judgments binding all class members save those who affirmatively elected to be excluded. . . .

Framed for situations in which "class-action treatment is not as clearly called for" as it is in Rule 23(b)(1) and (b)(2) situations, Rule 23(b)(3) permits certification where class suit "may nevertheless be convenient and desirable." Adv. Comm. Notes, 28 U.S.C.App., p. 697. To qualify for certification under Rule 23(b)(3), a class must meet two requirements beyond the Rule 23(a) prerequisites: Common questions must "predominate over any questions affecting only individual members"; and class resolution must be "superior to other available methods for the fair and efficient adjudication of the controversy." In adding "predominance" and "superiority" to the qualification-for-certification list, the Advisory Committee sought to cover cases "in which a class action would achieve economies of time, effort, and expense, and promote . . . uniformity of decision as to persons similarly situated, without sacrificing procedural fairness or bringing about other undesirable results." Ibid. Sensitive to the competing tugs of individual autonomy for those who might prefer to go it alone or in a smaller unit, on the one hand, and systemic efficiency on the other, the Reporter for the 1966 amendments cautioned: "The new provision invites a close look at the case before it is accepted as a class action. . . ." Kaplan, Continuing Work 390.

Rule 23(b)(3) includes a nonexhaustive list of factors pertinent to a court's "close look" at the predominance and superiority criteria:

"(A) the interest of members of the class in individually controlling the prosecution or defense of separate actions; (B) the extent and nature of any litigation concerning the controversy already commenced by or against members of the class; (C) the desirability or undesirability of concentrating the litigation of the claims in the particular forum; (D) the difficulties likely to be encountered in the management of a class action."

. . . While the text of Rule 23(b)(3) does not exclude from certification cases in which individual damages run high, the Advisory Committee had dominantly in mind vindication of "the rights of groups of people who individually would be without effective strength to bring their opponents into court at all." Kaplan, Prefatory Note 497. As concisely recalled in a recent Seventh Circuit opinion:

"The policy at the very core of the class action mechanism is to overcome the problem that small recoveries do not provide the incentive for any individual to bring a solo action prosecuting his or her rights. A class action solves this problem by aggregating the relatively paltry potential recoveries into something worth someone's (usually an attorney's) labor." Mace v. Van Ru Credit Corp., 109 F.3d 338, 344 (1997).

To alert class members to their right to "opt out" of a (b)(3) class, Rule 23 instructs the court to "direct to the members of the class the best notice practicable under the circumstances, including individual notice to all members who can be identified through reasonable effort." Fed. Rule Civ. Proc. 23(c)(2). . . .

No class action may be "dismissed or compromised without [court] approval," preceded by notice to class members. Fed. Rule Civ. Proc. 23(e). The Advisory Committee's sole comment on this terse final provision of Rule 23 restates the rule's instruction without elaboration: "Subdivision (e) requires approval of the court, after notice, for the dismissal or compromise of any class action." Adv. Comm. Notes, 28 U.S.C.App., p. 699.

In the decades since the 1966 revision of Rule 23, class action practice has become ever more "adventuresome" as a means of coping with claims too numerous to secure their "just, speedy, and inexpensive determination" one by one. See Fed. Rule Civ. Proc. 1. The development reflects concerns about the efficient use of court resources and the conservation of funds to compensate claimants who do not line up early in a litigation queue. See generally J. Weinstein, Individual Justice in Mass Tort Litigation: The Effect of Class Actions, Consolidations, and Other Multiparty Devices (1995); Schwarzer, Settlement of Mass Tort Class Actions: Order out of Chaos, 80 Cornell L.Rev. 837 (1995).

Among current applications of Rule 23(b)(3), the "settlement only" class has become a stock device. See, e.g., T. Willging, L. Hooper, & R. Niemic, Empirical Study of Class Actions in Four Federal District Courts: Final Report to the Advisory Committee on Civil Rules 61–62 (1996) (noting large number of such cases in districts studied). Although all Federal Circuits recognize the utility of Rule 23(b)(3) settlement classes, courts have divided on the extent to which a proffered settlement affects court surveillance under Rule 23's certification criteria.

... A proposed amendment to Rule 23 would expressly authorize settlement class certification, in conjunction with a motion by the settling parties for Rule 23(b)(3) certification, "even though the requirements of subdivision (b)(3) might not be met for purposes of trial." Proposed Amendment to Fed. Rule Civ. Proc. 23(b), 117 S.Ct. No. 1 CXIX, CLIV to CLV (Aug.1996) (Request for Comment). In response to the publication of this proposal, voluminous public comments—many of them opposed to, or skeptical of, the amendment—were received by the Judicial Conference Standing Committee on Rules of Practice and Procedure. See, e.g., Letter from Steering Committee to Oppose Proposed Rule 23, signed by 129 law professors (May 28, 1996); Letter from Paul D. Carrington (May 21, 1996). The Committee has not yet acted on the matter. We consider the certification at issue under the rule as it is currently framed.

IV

We granted review to decide the role settlement may play, under existing Rule 23, in determining the propriety of class certification. The Third Circuit's opinion stated that each of the requirements of Rule 23(a) and (b)(3) "must be satisfied without taking into account the settlement." 83 F.3d, at 626 (quoting GM Trucks, 55 F.3d, at 799). That statement, petitioners urge, is incorrect.

We agree with petitioners to this limited extent: settlement is relevant to a class certification. The Third Circuit's opinion bears modification in that respect. But, as we earlier observed, see supra, at ___, the Court of Appeals in fact did not ignore the settlement; instead, that court homed in on settlement terms in explaining why it found the absentees' interests inadequately represented. See 83 F.3d, at 630–631. The Third Circuit's close inspection of the settlement in that regard was altogether proper.

Confronted with a request for settlement-only class certification, a district court need not inquire whether the case, if tried, would present intractable management problems, see Fed. Rule Civ. Proc. 23(b)(3)(D), for the proposal is that there be no trial. But other specifications of the rule—those designed to protect absentees by blocking unwarranted or overbroad class definitions—demand undiluted, even heightened, attention in the settlement context. Such attention is of vital importance, for a court asked to certify a settlement class will lack the opportunity, present when a case is litigated, to adjust the class, informed by the proceedings as they unfold. See Fed. Rule Civ. Proc. 23(c), (d).

And, of overriding importance, courts must be mindful that the rule as now composed sets the requirements they are bound to enforce. Federal Rules take effect after an extensive deliberative process involving many reviewers: a Rules Advisory Committee, public commenters, the Judicial Conference, this Court, the Congress. See 28 U.S.C. §§ 2073, 2074. The text of a rule thus proposed and reviewed limits judicial inventiveness. Courts are not free to amend a rule outside the process Congress ordered, a process properly tuned to the instruction that rules of procedure "shall not abridge . . . any substantive right." § 2072(b).

Rule 23(e), on settlement of class actions, reads in its entirety: "A class action shall not be dismissed or compromised without the approval of the court, and notice of the proposed dismissal or compromise shall be given to all members of the class in such manner as the court directs." This prescription was designed to function as an additional requirement, not a superseding direction, for the "class action" to which Rule 23(e) refers is one qualified for certification under Rule 23(a) and (b). Cf. Eisen, 417 U.S., at 176–177, 94 S.Ct., at 2151–2152 (adequate representation does not eliminate additional requirement to provide notice). Subdivisions (a) and (b) focus court attention on whether a proposed class has sufficient unity so that absent members can fairly be bound by decisions of class representatives. That dominant concern persists when settlement, rather than trial, is proposed.

The safeguards provided by the Rule 23(a) and (b) class-qualifying criteria, we emphasize, are not impractical impediments—checks shorn of utility—in the settlement class context. First, the standards set for the protection of absent class members serve to inhibit appraisals of the chancellor's foot kind—class certifications dependent upon the court's gestalt judgment or overarching impression of the settlement's fairness.

Second, if a fairness inquiry under Rule 23(e) controlled certification, eclipsing Rule 23(a) and (b), and permitting class designation despite the impossibility of litigation, both class counsel and court would be disarmed. Class counsel confined to settlement negotiations could not use the threat of litigation to press for a better offer, see Coffee, Class Wars: The Dilemma of the Mass Tort Class Action, 95 Colum. L.Rev. 1343, 1379–1380 (1995), and the court would face a bargain proffered for its approval without benefit of adversarial investigation, see, e.g., Kamilewicz v. Bank of Boston Corp., 100 F.3d 1348, 1352 (C.A.7 1996) (Easterbrook, J., dissenting from denial of rehearing en banc) (parties "may even put one over on the court, in a staged performance"), cert. denied, 520 U.S. ___, 117 S.Ct. 1569, 137 L.Ed.2d 714 (1997).

Federal courts, in any case, lack authority to substitute for Rule 23's certification criteria a standard never adopted—that if a settlement is "fair," then certification is proper. Applying to this case criteria the rulemakers set, we conclude that the Third Circuit's appraisal is essentially correct. Although that court should have acknowledged that settlement is a factor in the calculus, a remand is not warranted on that account. The Court of Appeals' opinion amply demonstrates why—with or without a settlement on the table—the sprawling class the District Court certified does not satisfy Rule 23's requirements.

A

We address first the requirement of Rule 23(b)(3) that "[common] questions of law or fact ... predominate over any questions affecting only individual members." The District Court concluded that predominance was satisfied based on two factors: class members' shared experience of asbestos exposure and their common "interest in receiving prompt and fair compensation for their claims, while minimizing the risks and transaction costs inherent in the asbestos litigation process as it occurs presently in the tort system." 157 F.R.D., at 316. The settling parties also contend that the settlement's fairness is a common question, predominating over disparate legal issues that might be pivotal in litigation but become irrelevant under the settlement.

The predominance requirement stated in Rule 23(b)(3), we hold, is not met by the factors on which the District Court relied. The benefits asbestos-exposed persons might gain from the establishment of a grand-scale compensation scheme is a matter fit for legislative consideration, see supra, at 2237–2238, but it is not pertinent to the predominance inquiry. That inquiry trains on the legal or factual questions that qualify each class member's case as a genuine controversy, questions that preexist any settlement.

The Rule 23(b)(3) predominance inquiry tests whether proposed classes are sufficiently cohesive to warrant adjudication by representation. See 7A Wright, Miller, & Kane 518–519. The inquiry appropriate under Rule 23(e), on the other hand, protects unnamed class members "from unjust or unfair settlements affecting their rights when the representatives become faint-hearted before the action is adjudicated or are able to secure satisfaction of their individual claims by a compromise." See 7B Wright, Miller, & Kane § 1797, at 340–341. But it is not the mission of Rule 23(e) to assure the class cohesion that legitimizes representative action in the first place. If a common interest in a fair compromise could satisfy the predominance requirement of Rule 23(b)(3), that vital prescription would be stripped of any meaning in the settlement context.

The District Court also relied upon this commonality: "The members of the class have all been exposed to asbestos products supplied by the defendants...." 157 F.R.D., at 316. Even if Rule 23(a)'s commonality requirement may be satisfied by that shared experience, the predominance criterion is far more demanding. See 83 F.3d, at 626–627. Given the greater number of questions peculiar to the several categories of class members, and to individuals within each category, and the significance of those uncommon questions, any overarching dispute about the health consequences of asbestos exposure cannot satisfy the Rule 23(b)(3) predominance standard.

The Third Circuit highlighted the disparate questions undermining class cohesion in this case:

"Class members were exposed to different asbestos-containing products, for different amounts of time, in different ways, and over different periods. Some class members suffer no physical injury or have only asymptomatic pleural changes, while others suffer from lung cancer, disabling asbestosis, or from mesothelioma.... Each has a different history of cigarette smoking, a factor that complicates the causation inquiry.

"The [exposure-only] plaintiffs especially share little in common, either with each other or with the presently injured class members. It is unclear whether they will contract asbestos-related disease and, if so, what disease each will suffer. They will also incur different medical expenses because their monitoring and treatment will depend on singular circumstances and individual medical histories." Id., at 626.

Differences in state law, the Court of Appeals observed, compound these disparities. See id., at 627 (citing Phillips Petroleum Co. v. Shutts, 472 U.S. 797, 823, 105 S.Ct. 2965, 2980, 86 L.Ed.2d 628 (1985)).

No settlement class called to our attention is as sprawling as this one. Cf. In re Asbestos Litigation, 90 F.3d, at 976, n. 8 ("We would likely agree with the Third Circuit that a class action requesting individual damages for members of a global class of asbestos claimants would not satisfy [Rule 23] requirements due to the huge number of individuals and their varying medical expenses, smoking histories, and family situations."). Predominance is a test readily met in certain cases alleging consumer or securities fraud or violations of the antitrust laws. See Adv. Comm. Notes, 28 U.S.C.App., p. 697; see also supra, at 2246. Even mass tort cases arising from a common cause or disaster may, depending upon the circumstances, satisfy the predominance requirement. The Advisory Committee for the 1966 revision of Rule 23, it is true, noted that "mass accident" cases are likely to present "significant questions, not only of damages but of liability and defenses of liability, ... affecting the individuals in different ways." Ibid. And the Committee advised that such cases are "ordinarily not appropriate" for class treatment. Ibid. But the text of the rule does not categorically exclude mass tort cases from class certification, and district courts, since the late 1970s, have been certifying such cases in increasing number. See Resnik, From "Cases" to "Litigation," 54 Law & Contemp.Prob. 5, 17–19 (Summer 1991) (describing trend). The Committee's warning, however, continues to call for caution when individual stakes are high and disparities among class members great. As the Third Circuit's opinion makes plain, the certification in this case does not follow the counsel of caution. That certification cannot be upheld, for it rests on a conception of Rule 23(b)(3)'s predominance requirement irreconcilable with the rule's design.

B

Nor can the class approved by the District Court satisfy Rule 23(a)(4)'s requirement that the named parties "will fairly and adequately protect the interests of the class." The adequacy inquiry under Rule 23(a)(4) serves to uncover conflicts of interest between named parties and the class they seek to represent. See General Telephone Co. of Southwest v. Falcon, 457 U.S. 147, 157–158, n. 13, 102 S.Ct. 2364, 2370–2371, n. 13, 72 L.Ed.2d 740 (1982). "[A] class representative must be part of the class and 'possess the same interest and suffer the same injury' as the class members." East Tex. Motor Freight System, Inc. v. Rodriguez, 431 U.S. 395, 403, 97 S.Ct. 1891, 1896, 52 L.Ed.2d 453 (1977) (quoting Schlesinger v. Reservists Comm. to Stop the War, 418 U.S. 208, 216, 94 S.Ct. 2925, 2930, 41 L.Ed.2d 706 (1974)).[20]

As the Third Circuit pointed out, named parties with diverse medical conditions sought to act on behalf of a single giant class rather than on behalf of discrete subclasses. In significant respects, the interests of those within the single class are not aligned. Most saliently, for the currently injured, the critical goal is generous immediate payments. That goal tugs against the interest of exposure-only plaintiffs in ensuring an ample, inflation-protected fund for the future. . . .

The disparity between the currently injured and exposure-only categories of plaintiffs, and the diversity within each category are not made insignificant by the District Court's finding that petitioners' assets suffice to pay claims under the settlement. See 157 F.R.D., at 291. Although this is not a "limited fund" case certified under Rule 23(b)(1)(B), the terms of the

---

20. The adequacy-of-representation requirement "tend[s] to merge" with the commonality and typicality criteria of Rule 23(a), which "serve as guideposts for determining whether ... maintenance of a class action is economical and whether the named plaintiff's claim and the class claims are so interrelated that the interests of the class members will be fairly and adequately protected in their absence." General Telephone Co. of Southwest v. Falcon, 457 U.S. 147, 157, n. 13, 102 S.Ct. 2364, 2370, n. 13, 72 L.Ed.2d 740 (1982). The adequacy heading also factors in competency and conflicts of class counsel. See id., at 157–158, n. 13, 102 S.Ct., at 2370–2371, n. 13. Like the Third Circuit, we decline to address adequacy-of-counsel issues discretely in light of our conclusions that common questions of law or fact do not predominate and that the named plaintiffs cannot adequately represent the interests of this enormous class.

settlement reflect essential allocation decisions designed to confine compensation and to limit defendants' liability. For example, as earlier described, see supra, at 2240–2241, the settlement includes no adjustment for inflation; only a few claimants per year can opt out at the back end; and loss-of-consortium claims are extinguished with no compensation.

The settling parties, in sum, achieved a global compromise with no structural assurance of fair and adequate representation for the diverse groups and individuals affected. Although the named parties alleged a range of complaints, each served generally as representative for the whole, not for a separate constituency. In another asbestos class action, the Second Circuit spoke precisely to this point:

"[W]here differences among members of a class are such that subclasses must be established, we know of no authority that permits a court to approve a settlement without creating subclasses on the basis of consents by members of a unitary class, some of whom happen to be members of the distinct subgroups. The class representatives may well have thought that the Settlement serves the aggregate interests of the entire class. But the adversity among subgroups requires that the members of each subgroup cannot be bound to a settlement except by consents given by those who understand that their role is to represent solely the members of their respective subgroups." In re Joint Eastern and Southern Dist. Asbestos Litigation, 982 F.2d 721, 742–743 (C.A.2 1992), modified on reh'g sub nom. In re Findley, 993 F.2d 7 (C.A.2 1993).

The Third Circuit found no assurance here—either in the terms of the settlement or in the structure of the negotiations—that the named plaintiffs operated under a proper understanding of their representational responsibilities. See 83 F.3d, at 630–631. That assessment, we conclude, is on the mark.

C

Impediments to the provision of adequate notice, the Third Circuit emphasized, rendered highly problematic any endeavor to tie to a settlement class persons with no perceptible asbestos-related disease at the time of the settlement. Id., at 633; cf. In re Asbestos Litigation, 90 F.3d, at 999–1000 (Smith, J., dissenting). Many persons in the exposure-only category, the Court of Appeals stressed, may not even know of their exposure, or realize the extent of the harm they may incur. Even if they fully appreciate the significance of class notice, those without current afflictions may not have the information or foresight needed to decide, intelligently, whether to stay in or opt out.

Family members of asbestos-exposed individuals may themselves fall prey to disease or may ultimately have ripe claims for loss of consortium. Yet large numbers of people in this category—future spouses and children of asbestos victims—could not be alerted to their class membership. And current spouses and children of the occupationally exposed may know nothing of that exposure.

Because we have concluded that the class in this case cannot satisfy the requirements of common issue predominance and adequacy of representation, we need not rule, definitively, on the notice given here. In accord with the Third Circuit, however, see 83 F.3d, at 633–634, we recognize the gravity of the question whether class action notice sufficient under the Constitution and Rule 23 could ever be given to legions so unselfconscious and amorphous.

V

The argument is sensibly made that a nationwide administrative claims processing regime would provide the most secure, fair, and efficient means of compensating victims of asbestos exposure. Congress, however, has not adopted such a solution. And Rule 23, which must be interpreted with fidelity to the Rules Enabling Act and applied with the interests of absent class members in close view, cannot carry the large load CCR, class counsel, and the District Court heaped upon it. As this case exemplifies, the rulemakers' prescriptions for class actions may be endangered by "those who embrace [Rule 23] too enthusiastically just as [they are by] those who approach [the rule] with distaste." C. Wright, Law of Federal Courts 508 (5th ed.1994); cf. 83 F.3d, at 634 (suggesting resort to less bold aggregation techniques, including more narrowly defined class certifications).

For the reasons stated, the judgment of the Court of Appeals for the Third Circuit is

Affirmed.

■ JUSTICE O'CONNOR took no part in the consideration or decision of this case.

■ JUSTICE BREYER, with whom JUSTICE STEVENS joins, concurring in part and dissenting in part.

Although I agree with the Court's basic holding that "settlement is relevant to a class certification," ante, at 2248, I find several problems in its approach that lead me to a different conclusion. First, I believe that the need for settlement in this mass tort case, with hundreds of thousands of lawsuits, is greater than the Court's opinion suggests. Second, I would give more weight than would the majority to settlement-related issues for purposes of determining whether common issues predominate. Third, I am uncertain about the Court's determination of adequacy of representation, and do not believe it appropriate for this Court to second-guess the District Court on the matter without first having the Court of Appeals consider it. Fourth, I am uncertain about the tenor of an opinion that seems to suggest the settlement is unfair. And fifth, in the absence of further review by the Court of Appeals, I cannot accept the majority's suggestions that "notice" is inadequate.

These difficulties flow from the majority's review of what are highly fact-based, complex, and difficult matters, matters that are inappropriate for initial review before this Court. The law gives broad leeway to district courts in making class certification decisions, and their judgments are to be reviewed by the Court of Appeals only for abuse of discretion. See Califano v. Yamasaki, 442 U.S. 682, 703, 99 S.Ct. 2545, 2558–2559, 61 L.Ed.2d 176 (1979). Indeed, the District Court's certification decision rests upon more than 300 findings of fact reached after five weeks of comprehensive hearings. Accordingly, I do not believe that we should in effect set aside the findings of the District Court. That court is far more familiar with the issues and litigants than is a court of appeals or are we, and therefore has "broad power and discretion ... with respect to matters involving the certification" of class actions. Reiter v. Sonotone Corp., 442 U.S. 330, 345, 99 S.Ct. 2326, 2334, 60 L.Ed.2d 931 (1979) ...

I do not believe that we can rely upon the Court of Appeals' review of the District Court record, for that review, and its ultimate conclusions, are infected by a legal error. E.g., Georgine v. Amchem Products, Inc., 83 F.3d 610, 626 (C.A.3 1996) (holding that *"considered as a litigation class,"* the class cannot meet Rule 23's requirements) (emphasis added). There is no evidence that the Court of Appeals at any point considered the settlement as something that would help the class meet Rule 23. I find, moreover, the fact-related issues presented here sufficiently close to warrant further detailed appellate court review under the correct legal standard. ... And I shall briefly explain why this is so.

I

First, I believe the majority understates the importance of settlement in this case. Between 13 and 21 million workers have been exposed to asbestos in the workplace—over the past 40 or 50 years—but the most severe instances of such exposure probably occurred three or four decades ago. See Report of The Judicial Conference Ad Hoc Committee on Asbestos Litigation, pp. 6–7 (Mar.1991) (Judicial Conference Report); App. 781–782, 801; B. Castleman, Asbestos: Medical and Legal Aspects 787–788 (4th ed.1996). This exposure has led to several hundred thousand lawsuits, about 15% of which involved claims for cancer and about 30% for asbestosis. See In re Joint Eastern and Southern Dist. Asbestos Litigation, 129 B.R. 710, 936–937 (E. and S.D.N.Y.1991) (Joint Litigation). About half of the suits have involved claims for pleural thickening and plaques—the harmfulness of which is apparently controversial. (One expert below testified that they "don't transform into cancer" and are not "predictor[s] of future disease," App. 781.) Some of those who suffer from the most serious injuries, however, have received little or no compensation. In re School Asbestos Litigation, 789 F.2d 996, 1000 (C.A.3 1986); see also Edley & Weiler, Asbestos: A Multi-Billion–Dollar Crisis, 30 Harv. J. Legis. 383, 384, 393 (1993) ("[U]p to one-half of asbestos claims are now being filed by people who have little or no physical impairment. Many of these claims produce substantial payments (and substantial costs) even though the individual litigants will never become impaired"). These lawsuits have taken up more than 6% of all federal civil filings in one recent year, and are subject to a delay that is twice that of other civil suits. Judicial Conference Report 7, 10–11.

Delays, high costs, and a random pattern of noncompensation led the Judicial Conference Ad Hoc Committee on Asbestos Litigation to transfer all federal asbestos personal-injury cases to the Eastern District of Pennsylvania in an effort to bring about a fair and comprehensive settlement. It is worth considering a few of the Committee's comments. See Judicial Conference Report 2 (" 'Decisions concerning thousands of deaths, millions of injuries, and billions of dollars are entangled in a litigation system whose strengths have increasingly been overshadowed by its weaknesses.' The ensuing five years have seen the picture worsen: increased filings, larger backlogs, higher costs, more bankruptcies and poorer prospects that judgments—if ever obtained—can be collected") (quoting Rand Corporation Institute for Civil Justice); id., at 13 ("The transaction costs associated with asbestos litigation are an unconscionable burden on the victims of asbestos disease," and citing Rand finding that "of each asbestos litigation dollar, 61 cents is consumed in transaction costs.... Only 39 cents were paid to the asbestos victims"); id., at 12 ("Delays also can increase transaction costs, especially the attorneys' fees paid by defendants at hourly rates. These costs reduce either the insurance fund or the company's assets, thereby reducing the funds available to pay pending and future claimants. By the end of the trial phase in [one case], at least seven defendants had declared bankruptcy (as a result of asbestos claims generally)"); see also J. Weinstein, Individual Justice in Mass Tort Litigation 155 (1995); Edley & Weiler, supra, at 389–395.

Although the transfer of the federal asbestos cases did not produce a general settlement, it was intertwined with and led to a lengthy year-long negotiation between the co-chairs of the Plaintiff's Multi–District Litigation Steering Committee (elected by the Plaintiff's Committee Members and approved by the District Court) and the 20 asbestos defendants who are before us here. Georgine v. Amchem Products, Inc., 157 F.R.D. 246, 266–267, (E.D.Pa.1994); App. 660–662. These "protracted and vigorous" negotiations led to the present partial settlement, which will pay an estimated $1.3 billion and compensate perhaps 100,000 class members in the first 10 years. 157 F.R.D., at 268, 287. . . .

The District Court, when approving the settlement, concluded that it improved the plaintiffs' chances of compensation and reduced total legal fees and other transaction costs by a significant amount. Under the previous system, according to the court, "[t]he sickest of victims often go uncompensated for years while valuable funds go to others who remain unimpaired by their mild asbestos disease." Ibid. The court believed the settlement would create a compensation system that would make more money available for plaintiffs who later develop serious illnesses.

I mention this matter because it suggests that the settlement before us is unusual in terms of its importance, both to many potential plaintiffs and to defendants, and with respect to the time, effort, and expenditure that it reflects. All of which leads me to be reluctant to set aside the District

Court's findings without more assurance than I have that they are wrong. I cannot obtain that assurance through comprehensive review of the record because that is properly the job of the Court of Appeals and that court, understandably, but as we now hold, mistakenly, believed that settlement was not a relevant (and, as I would say, important) consideration.

Second, the majority, in reviewing the District Court's determination that common "issues of fact and law predominate," says that the predominance "inquiry trains on the legal or factual questions that qualify each class member's case as a genuine controversy, questions that preexist any settlement." Ante, at 2249 (footnote omitted). I find it difficult to interpret this sentence in a way that could lead me to the majority's conclusion. If the majority means that these pre-settlement questions are what matters, then how does it reconcile its statement with its basic conclusion that "settlement is relevant" to class certification, or with the numerous lower court authority that says that settlement is not only relevant, but important? See, e. g., In re A.H. Robins Co., 880 F.2d 709, 740(C.A.4), cert. denied sub nom. Anderson v. Aetna Casualty & Surety Co., 493 U.S. 959, 110 S.Ct. 377, 107 L.Ed.2d 362 (1989) . . .

Nor do I understand how one could decide whether common questions "predominate" in the abstract—without looking at what is likely to be at issue in the proceedings that will ensue, namely, the settlement. Every group of human beings, after all, has some features in common, and some that differ. How can a court make a contextual judgment of the sort that Rule 23 requires without looking to what proceedings will follow? Such guideposts help it decide whether, in light of common concerns and differences, certification will achieve Rule 23's basic objective—"economies of time, effort, and expense." Advisory Committee's Notes on Fed. Rule Civ. Proc. 23(b)(3), 28 U.S.C.App., p. 697. As this Court has previously observed, "sometimes it may be necessary for the court to probe behind the pleadings before coming to rest on the certification question." General Telephone Co. of Southwest v. Falcon, 457 U.S. 147, 160, 102 S.Ct. 2364, 2372, 72 L.Ed.2d 740 (1982); see also C. Wright, A. Miller, & M. Kane, 7B Federal Practice and Procedure § 1785, p. 107, and n. 34 (1986). I am not saying that the "settlement counts only one way." Ante, at 2248 n. 16. Rather, the settlement may simply "add a great deal of information to the court's inquiry and will often expose diverging interests or common issues that were not evident or clear from the complaint" and courts "can and should" look to it to enhance the "ability . . . to make informed certification decisions." In re Asbestos, 90 F.3d 963, 975 (C.A.5 1996).

The majority may mean that the District Court gave too much weight to the settlement. But I am not certain how it can reach that conclusion. It cannot rely upon the Court of Appeals, for that court gave no positive weight at all to the settlement. Nor can it say that the District Court relied solely on "a common interest in a fair compromise," ante, at 2249, for the District Court did not do so. Rather, it found the settlement relevant because it explained the importance of the class plaintiffs' common features and common interests. The court found predominance in part because:

"The members of the class have all been exposed to asbestos products supplied by the defendants and all share an interest in receiving prompt and fair compensation for their claims, while minimizing the risks and transaction costs inherent in the asbestos litigation process as it occurs presently in the tort system." 157 F.R.D., at 316.

The settlement is relevant because it means that these common features and interests are likely to be important in the proceeding that would ensue—a proceeding that would focus primarily upon whether or not the proposed settlement fairly and properly satisfied the interests class members had in common. That is to say, the settlement underscored the importance of (a) the common fact of exposure, (b) the common interest in receiving *some* compensation for certain rather than running a strong risk of *no* compensation, and (c) the common interest in avoiding large legal fees, other transaction costs, and delays. Ibid.

Of course, as the majority points out, there are also important differences among class members. Different plaintiffs were exposed to different products for different times; each has a distinct medical history and a different history of smoking; and many cases arise under the laws of different States. The relevant question, however, is *how much* these differences matter in respect to the legal proceedings that lie ahead. Many, if not all, toxic tort class actions involve plaintiffs with such differences. And the differences in state law are of diminished importance in respect to a proposed settlement in which the defendants have waived all defenses and agreed to compensate all those who were injured. Id., at 292.

These differences might warrant subclasses, though subclasses can have problems of their own. "There can be a cost in creating more distinct subgroups, each with its own representation.... [T]he more subclasses created, the more severe conflicts bubble to the surface and inhibit settlement.... The resources of defendants and, ultimately, the community must not be exhausted by protracted litigation." Weinstein, Individual Justice in Mass Tort Litigation, at 66. Or these differences may be too serious to permit an effort at group settlement. This kind of determination, as I have said, is one that the law commits to the discretion of the district court—reviewable for abuse of discretion by a court of appeals. I believe that we are far too distant from the litigation itself to reweigh the fact-specific Rule 23 determinations and to find them erroneous without the benefit of the Court of Appeals first having restudied the matter with today's legal standard in mind.

Third, the majority concludes that the "representative parties" will not "fairly and adequately protect the interests of the class." Rule 23(a)(4). It finds a serious conflict between plaintiffs who are now injured and those who may be injured in the future because "for the currently injured, the critical goal is generous immediate payments," a goal that "tugs against the interest of exposure-only plaintiffs in ensuring an ample, inflation-protected fund for the future." Ante, at 2251.

I agree that there is a serious problem, but it is a problem that often exists in toxic tort cases. See Weinstein, supra, at 64 (noting that conflict "between present and future claimants" "is almost always present in some form in mass tort cases because long latency periods are needed to discover injuries"); see also Judicial Conference Report 34–35 ("Because many of the defendants in these cases have limited assets that may be called upon to satisfy the judgments obtained under current common tort rules and remedies, there is a 'real and present danger that the available assets will be exhausted before those later victims can seek compensation to which they are entitled' ") (citation omitted). And it is a problem that potentially exists whenever a single defendant injures several plaintiffs, for a settling plaintiff leaves fewer assets available for the others. With class actions, at least, plaintiffs have the consolation that a district court, thoroughly familiar with the facts, is charged with the responsibility of ensuring that the interests of no class members are sacrificed.

But this Court cannot easily safeguard such interests through review of a cold record. "What constitutes adequate representation is a question of fact that depends on the circumstances of each case." Wright, Miller, & Kane, 7A Federal Practice and Procedure, § 1765, at 271. That is particularly so when, as here, there is an unusual baseline, namely, the " 'real and present danger' " described by the Judicial Conference Report above. The majority's use of the lack of an inflation adjustment as evidence of inadequacy of representation for future plaintiffs, ante, at 2251, is one example of this difficulty. An inflation adjustment might not be as valuable as the majority assumes if most plaintiffs are old and not worried about receiving compensation decades from now. There are, of course, strong arguments as to its value. But that disagreement is one that this Court is poorly situated to resolve.

Further, certain details of the settlement that are not discussed in the majority opinion suggest that the settlement may be of greater benefit to future plaintiffs than the majority suggests. The District Court concluded that future plaintiffs receive a "significant value" from the settlement due to variety of its items that benefit future plaintiffs, such as: (1) tolling the statute of limitations so that class members "will no longer be forced to file premature lawsuits or risk their claims being time-barred"; (2) waiver of defenses to liability; (3) payment of claims, if and when members become sick, pursuant to the settlement's compensation standards, which avoids "the uncertainties, long delays and high transaction costs [including attorney's fees] of the tort system"; (4) "some assurance that there will be funds available if and when they get sick," based on the finding that each defendant "has shown an ability to fund the payment of all qualifying claims" under the settlement; and (5) the right to additional compensation if cancer develops (many settlements for plaintiffs with noncancerous conditions bar such additional claims). 157 F.R.D., at 292. For these reasons, and others, the District Court found that the distinction between present and future plaintiffs was "illusory." 157 F.R.D., at 317–318.

I do not know whether or not the benefits are more or less valuable than an inflation adjustment. But I can certainly recognize an argument that they are. (To choose one more brief illustration, the majority chastises the settlement for extinguishing loss-of-consortium claims, ante, at 2251, 2252, but does not note that, as the District Court found, the "defendants' historical [settlement] averages, upon which the compensation values are based, include payments for loss of consortium claims, and, accordingly, the Compensation Schedule is not unfair for this ascribed reason," 157 F.R.D., at 278.) The difficulties inherent in both knowing and understanding the vast number of relevant individual fact-based determinations here counsel heavily in favor of deference to district court decisionmaking in Rule 23 decisions. Or, at the least, making certain that appellate court review has taken place with the correct standard in mind.

Fourth, I am more agnostic than is the majority about the basic fairness of the settlement. Ante, at 2250–2252. The District Court's conclusions rested upon complicated factual findings that are not easily cast aside. It is helpful to consider some of them, such as its determination that the settlement provided "fair compensation . . . while reducing the delays and transaction costs endemic to the asbestos litigation process" and that "the proposed class action settlement is superior to other available methods for the fair and efficient resolution of the asbestos-related personal injury claims of class members." 157 F.R.D., at 316 (citation omitted); see also id., at 335 ("The inadequate tort system has demonstrated that the lawyers are well paid for their services but the victims are not receiving speedy and reasonably inexpensive resolution of their claims. Rather, the victims' recoveries are delayed, excessively reduced by transaction costs and relegated to the impersonal group trials and mass consolidations. The sickest of victims often go uncompensated for years while valuable funds go to others who remain unimpaired by their mild asbestos disease. Indeed, [these] unimpaired victims have, in many states, been forced to assert their claims prematurely or risk giving up all rights to future compensation for any future lung cancer or mesothelioma. The plan which this Court approves today will correct that unfair result for the class members and the . . . defendants"); id., at 279, 280 (settlement "will result in less delay for asbestos claimants than that experienced in the present tort system" and will "result in the CCR defendants paying more claims, at a faster rate, than they have ever paid before"); id., at 292; Edley & Weiler, 30 Harv. J. Legis., at 405, 407 (finding that "[t]here are several reasons to believe that this settlement secures important gains for both sides" and that they "firmly endorse the fairness and adequacy of this settlement"). Indeed, the settlement has been endorsed as fair and reasonable by the AFL–CIO (and its Building and Construction Trades Department), which represents a " 'substantial percentage' " of class members, 157 F.R.D., at 325, and which has a role in monitoring implementation of the settlement, id., at 285. I do not intend to pass judgment upon the settlement's fairness, but I do believe that these matters would have to be explored in far greater depth before I could reach a conclusion about fairness. And that task, as I have said, is one for the Court of Appeals.

Finally, I believe it is up to the District Court, rather than this Court, to review the legal sufficiency of notice to members of the class. The District Court found that the plan to provide notice was implemented at a cost of millions of dollars and included hundreds of thousands of individual notices, a wide-ranging television and print campaign, and significant additional efforts by 35 international and national unions to notify their members. 157 F.R.D., at 312–313, 336. Every notice emphasized that an individual did not currently have to be sick to be a class member. And in the end, the District Court was "confident" that Rule 23 and due process requirements were satisfied because, as a result of this "extensive and expensive notice procedure," "over six million" individuals "received actual notice materials," and "millions more" were reached by the media campaign. Id., at 312, 333, 336. Although the majority, in principle, is reviewing a Court of Appeals' conclusion, it seems to me that its opinion might call into question the fact-related determinations of the District Court. Ante, at 2252. To the extent that it does so, I disagree, for such findings cannot be so quickly disregarded. And I do not think that our precedents permit this Court to do so. See Reiter, 442 U.S., at 345, 99 S.Ct., at 2334; Yamasaki, 442 U.S., at 703, 99 S.Ct., at 2558–2559.

II

The issues in this case are complicated and difficult. The District Court might have been correct. Or not. Subclasses might be appropriate. Or not. I cannot tell. And I do not believe that this Court should be in the business of trying to make these fact-based determinations. That is a job suited to the district courts in the first instance, and the courts of appeal on review. But there is no reason in this case to believe that the Court of Appeals conducted its prior review with an understanding that the settlement could have constituted a reasonably strong factor in favor of class certification. For this reason, I would provide the courts below with an opportunity to analyze the factual questions involved in certification by vacating the judgment, and remanding the case for further proceedings.

* * *

Manual for Complex Litigation, Third

Federal Judicial Center (1995).

30.4 Class Action Settlements

30.45 SETTLEMENT CLASSES

Occasionally, before a class is certified, parties enter into settlement agreements, which provide for certification of a class as defined therein, for settlement purposes only. Such settlement classes facilitate global settlements. They also permit defendants to settle while preserving the right to contest the propriety and scope of the class allegations if the settlement is not approved and, in Rule 23(b)(3) actions, to withdraw from the settlement if too many class members opt out. The costs of litigating class certification are saved and litigation expense is generally reduced by an early settlement.[772]

For these reasons, courts permit the use of settlement classes and the negotiation of settlement before class certification.[773] Approval under Rule 23(e) of settlements involving settlement classes, however, requires closer judicial scrutiny than approval of settlements where class certification has been litigated. As noted in supra section 30.42, an early settlement will find the court and class counsel less informed than if substantial discovery had occurred. As a result, the court will find it more difficult to assess the strengths and weaknesses of the parties' claims and defenses, determine the appropriate membership of the class, and consider how class members will benefit from settlement. The court should provide an adequate opportunity for proponents and opponents to make a full showing of all relevant matters.

Settlement classes can raise numerous issues, including conflicts of interest. Some of these issues are the following:

1.   Conflicts between class counsel and counsel for individual plaintiffs. Approval of the class will in effect largely convert individual claimants falling within its definition from clients of their attorneys into clients of class counsel. It will also effectively terminate their pending individual and class actions. Because of these effects, divergent interests must be taken into account and fairly accommodated. The court should consider whether the group of counsel who have negotiated the settlement has fairly represented the interests of all.

2.   Protection of future claimants. The court should consider the impact of the settlement on persons who may not currently be aware that they have a claim or whose claim may not yet have come into existence. Since they cannot be given meaningful notice, they may be particularly prejudiced by the settlement, and their opt-out rights (in a Rule 23(b)(3) action) may be illusory.

3.   Administration of claims procedure. The court should consider whether the persons chosen to administer the procedure are disinterested or have conflicts arising from their representation of individual claimants.

4.   Partial settlements. Settlement classes present special problems when used with partial settlements. Members of the settlement class may have difficulty understanding their position in the litigation. Moreover, since they will not know whether they will be members of a class with respect to claims against nonsettling defendants, they may be unable to

---

772.   But see supra § 24.12 (attorneys' fees in common fund cases), noting the desirability of fee arrangements that reward counsel for efficiency.

773.   See, e.g., Weinberger v. Kendrick, 698 F.2d 61 (2d Cir.1982); In re Beef Indus. Antitrust Litig., 607 F.2d 167 (5th Cir.1979); cf. Plummer v. Chemical Bank, 668 F.2d 654 (2d Cir.1982); In re Franklin Nat'l Bank Sec. Litig., 574 F.2d 662 (1978), modified, 599 F.2d 1109 (2d Cir.1978). For an analysis of the factors affecting formation of a settlement class, see In re Baldwin–United Corp., 105 F.R.D. 475 (S.D.N.Y.1984). See also infra § 33.29 (mass tort settlements).

make an informed decision regarding the adequacy of the settlement. (See infra section 30.46.)

5.   Conditional settlements. The parties may propose a precertification settlement that permits the settling parties to withdraw from the settlement if a specified number of persons opt out of the class or of the settlement. Although this may promote settlement by giving a defendant greater assurance of ending the controversy and avoiding the expense of litigating numerous individual claims, it may also prolong uncertainty by delaying a final settlement. An alternate approach is to provide that the benefits paid to the class will be reduced in proportion to the number of opt outs or the total amount of their claims.

6.   Additional barred claims. Some settlements, particularly in securities litigation, are conditioned on settlors waiving claims for additional time periods not covered by the pleadings or waiving additional potential claims against the settling defendants. Because such waivers raise a potential for abuse, they should be reviewed to ascertain their justification and the compensating benefit to the class for surrendering such claims.

A settlement will occasionally cover a class different from that certified. Typically, the parties propose to enlarge the class—or the claims of the class—to give the settling defendants greater protection against future litigation, although sometimes they may seek to reduce the class. The problem presented by these requests is not the lack of sufficient information and scrutiny, but rather the possibility that fiduciary responsibilities of class counsel or class representatives may have been compromised. The parties should be required to explain in detail what new facts, changed circumstances, or earlier errors support the alteration of the original definition. If a (b)(3) class is enlarged, notice must be given to the new members of their right to opt out; if a class is reduced, notice should be given under Rule 23(d) to those being excluded, since the statute of limitations will begin to run again on their claims.

* * *

33.   Application in Particular Types of Litigation
33.2   Mass Torts

33.29   SETTLEMENT

Settlement activity in mass tort litigation tends to parallel pretrial and trial organization. Consolidated cases tend to generate settlement-related information at the same time and follow a settlement timetable driven by pretrial and trial deadlines. In general, organization of cases along individual plaintiff lines can be expected to lead to individual settlements, and organization along aggregated lines can be expected to produce aggregated settlements.[1108]

1108.   See, e.g., special master Francis McGovern's description of the settlement in Jenkins v. Raymark in Mature Mass Torts, supra note 1012, at 663–75 (1989); Mullenix, supra note 8, at 550–69 (discussing settlement activity and trial plans in Cimino v.

Although most defendants prefer to avoid bankruptcy, the bankruptcy process appears to be used with increasing frequency to achieve and implement settlement in mass tort litigation.[1109] Bankruptcy alone permits a federal court to marshal all claims against a defendant and to control both state and federal litigation. It is of limited utility, however, in disposing of litigation against numerous defendants who are unlikely to choose the same course. As an alternative to bankruptcy, it may be possible to set a ceiling on damages by certifying a mandatory "limited fund" settlement class that includes future claimants, obtaining court approval of the proposed settlement fund as fair to all members of the class, and, so long as a procedure is provided to protect future claimants, enjoining the filing of additional actions. This approach has been used in some mass tort actions, but because of the difficulty in protecting the interests of future claimants, its legality is questionable.[1110] The Fourth Circuit approved such a procedure in In re A.H. Robins, Co., Inc.,[1111] in which the district court had certified a nationwide class under Fed. R. Civ. P. 23(b)(1)(B). That case may have paved the way for similar actions, but, as noted above, at least one court of appeals has expressed the opinion that bankruptcy provides the exclusive remedy for an insolvent defendant.[1112]

Certification of settlement classes involving unidentified class members with latent injuries from exposure to toxic products raises questions of fairness and requires careful consideration by the court (see supra section 30.45).[1113] The interests of future claimants may well conflict with the interests of present claimants who seek the maximum recovery on their claims and of defendants who seek to obtain the widest possible preclusive effect of the settlement so that they can continue doing business without the threat of future litigation. Courts have taken steps to protect the interests of future claimants by obtaining estimates of the number, quality,

---

Raymark and the School Asbestos Litig.); Trends, supra note 1020, at 87. A notable exception is the "global settlement" reached in the breast implant litigation that arose out of a pretrial structure designed to support individual trials within an MDL consolidation.

1109. See generally In re A.H. Robins Co., Inc., 880 F.2d 709 (4th Cir.1989) (Dalkon Shield); Kane v. Johns–Manville Corp., 843 F.2d 636, 638–41 (2d Cir.1988) (asbestos); In re UNR Indus., Inc., 725 F.2d 1111 (7th Cir.1984) (asbestos), all of which review the history of the litigation.

1110. In re Joint E. & S. Dist. Asbestos Litig. (Keene Corp.), 14 F.3d 726 (2d Cir. 1993) (vacating preliminary injunction enjoining pending and future asbestos-related litigation against an asbestos manufacturer-plaintiff in a nationwide mandatory 23(b)(1)(B) class action filed to protect settlement discussions; the action did not present a

case or controversy under Article III and was a "a self-evident evasion of [the Bankruptcy Code, which is] the exclusive legal system established by Congress for debtors to seek relief.") . . . .

1111. 880 F.2d 709 (1989). The court found that due process was satisfied by the settlement's provision of a right to jury trial for class members who did not accept an arbitration award.

1112. In re Joint E. & S. Dist. Asbestos Litig. (Keene Corp.), 14 F.3d at 732–33.

1113. For an opinion addressing fairness issues in the context of a controversial mass tort settlement proposal, see Georgine v. Amchem Prods., Inc., 157 F.R.D. 246 (E.D.Pa.1994) (on appeal) (memorandum opinion approving class settlement); In re Silicone Breast Implant Prods. Liab. Litig., 1994 WL 578353 (N.D.Ala.) (same). . . .

and value of outstanding and anticipated claims; estimation of such claims may require expert study and testimony covering such areas as statistics and epidemiology. Conflicts may also exist between plaintiffs and their counsel, among defendants, and between defendants and their insurers, adding complexity and risk to settlement efforts.

In mass tort litigation, collecting information about past, pending, and future claims is integral to reviewing settlement. The court can often organize pretrial data-gathering so that it supports settlement as well as trial. In litigation with thousands of personal injury claims, courts have appointed special masters to assemble databases that document the main features of claims. In consolidated cases, computer-based data have been used to match individual pending cases with closed cases having similar characteristics to provide guidance for settlement.

The parties should attempt to achieve, to the extent feasible, a "global" settlement, resolving not only the defendants' potential liability to the plaintiffs, but also their liability to one another for indemnification or contribution. If the entire litigation cannot be resolved through a single settlement, partial settlements—by some defendants with all plaintiffs, by all defendants with some plaintiffs, or by some defendants with some plaintiffs—should be explored. If all efforts fail, the parties may be able to resolve a significant portion of the litigation through a series of case-by-case, party-by-party settlements. In the absence of bellwether trials or their equivalent, taking a representative sample of claims through mediation, arbitration, or another form of alternative dispute resolution can generate evaluations supporting further settlements.

Various provisions can be made in a settlement for future claims. A portion of the settlement funds may be set aside to purchase an annuity or to fund a trust to pay future benefits or provide diagnostic services to plaintiffs, depending on such factors as medical developments and expenses and economic losses after the date of the settlement. Similarly, if the defendants are concerned about the possibility of actions being instituted after the settlement—for example, by minors with respect to whom the statute of limitations may be tolled—some of the settlement funds may be reserved for a period of time contingent on such claims.

As in other types of litigation, the assigned judge should be wary of extensive involvement in settlement. Although some judges participate actively in settlement negotiations,[1123] others take care to insulate themselves from the negotiations, leaving this activity to a special master or settlement judge;[1124] where judges have been involved, they have turned

---

1123. See e.g., In re "Agent Orange" Prod. Liab. Litig., 597 F.Supp. 740, aff'd, 818 F.2d 145 (2d Cir.1987). For an assessment of the risks of such judicial involvement in settlement, see Peter Schuck, The Role of Judges in Settling Complex Cases: The Agent Orange Example, 53 U. Chi. L. Rev. 337, 359–65 (1986).

1124. See e.g., In re Silicone Gel Breast Implant Prods. Liab. Litig., MDL No. 926 (in which the transferee judge appointed three judges to act as mediators to assist in discussing a global settlement)....

over to another judge the responsibility for review and approval of the settlement.

* * *

The Corruption of the Class Action: The New Technology of Collusion by John C. Coffee [1]

"Professor Coffee argues that recent developments in the mass tort class action reveal an impending and historic shift in the function of the class action: Once a sword for plaintiffs, it is becoming a shield for defendants. Until recently, the class action primarily served as a vehicle by which plaintiffs could aggregate claims of low to moderate value, which could not be asserted in an economically feasible manner on an individual basis, into a larger collective action, thereby gaining leverage over defendants. Today, however, it is increasingly the corporate defendant that wishes to be sued in a class action and—with the help of a friendly plaintiffs' attorney—that often actively arranges for such a suit to be brought by a nominal plaintiff. The procedures by which such a collusive action can be implemented are relatively new and represent for defendants a major development in legal technology that may allow them in the future to escape or minimize their liability for most mass torts.

"The new pattern is most evident in the mass tort area for several basic reasons: (1) many mass tort victims are able to bring economically viable individual actions (and many are sufficiently high stakes plaintiffs that they would opt out of any class action—provided that the law permitted them to do so); (2) increasingly during the 1980s, mass tort claims threatened public corporations with bankruptcy (and actually bankrupted A.H. Robins, Johns Manville, National Gypsum, and others, who but for their tort liabilities would have escaped bankruptcy); and (3) particularly in the case of asbestos, mass tort claims began to cast a longer and longer shadow on the federal docket. Fearing that mass tort claims could bankrupt their corporations and swamp their dockets, both defendants and federal judges began to look for a mechanism by which to reduce the impact of such litigation.

"Rather than resist class action certification, defendants changed their tactics and began to seek provisional certification (for "settlement purposes only") because they discovered this technique could assure low cost settlements. Historically, collusive settlements in class actions were effected by plaintiffs' attorneys exchanging a low recovery for a high attorneys' fee from the defendants. However, this technique was at least potentially susceptible to judicial control—because even when the court approved the settlement, it could still reduce the fee award. The new technique that has developed in mass tort cases, however, largely outflanks the (limited)

---

1.   John C. Coffee Jr., *The Corruption of Class Action,* 80 CORNELL L. REV. 851 (1995) (delivered at conference on *Mass Torts: Serv-* *ing Up Just Desserts,* Cornell Law School, 1994 and summarized by Symposium editor).

effectiveness of judicial oversight through control over the fee award. Defendants can offer plaintiffs' attorneys a global settlement by which they agree to settle the plaintiffs' attorneys' entire inventory of existing cases at the prevailing market rate for such claims if the same attorneys will agree to bring and settle a class action on behalf of other (largely future) claimants on a less favorable basis. Uniquely, such an inventory settlement is possible in the mass tort field where the plaintiffs' attorney is likely to be a specialized practitioner handling a large volume of a specific category of personal injury claims (asbestos cases, for example), usually on a referral basis.

"Professor Coffee examines several recent examples where such an inventory settlement of existing cases has accompanied (and sometimes been clearly linked to) a class action settlement on behalf of future claimants. He predicts that the defense bar is now broadly adopting and generalizing this approach, which will be widely followed in the future to the detriment of injured tort victims unless reforms are introduced.

"In his critique of current practices, Professor Coffee focuses on three specific targets:

1.   *The "Settlement Class Action"*

"Until recently, courts did not permit a settlement of a class action until after the court "certified" the class and selected lead counsel. Often, there was a considerable struggle within the plaintiffs' camp surrounding the selection of lead counsel. At least potentially, this contest both maximized the court's discretionary control over the case and reduced (marginally) the possibility of a quiet collusive settlement. Yet in a "settlement class action," plaintiffs' lawyers and defendants typically negotiate a settlement prior to filing the class action, and the class action is certified for purposes of settlement only. Not only do the plaintiffs' attorneys abandon the right to litigation at the outset (which assures defendants that there is little downside risk from the use of this approach), but there is little opportunity for judicial oversight or intervention by other plaintiffs' attorneys.

"This was the pattern in Georgine v. Amchem Products, Inc., where, after many months of private negotiation and prior to the filing of the class action, a consortium of twenty major asbestos producers reached a global settlement covering all future asbestos personal injury claims with just two plaintiffs' law firms. The complaint, the answer, and the settlement were all filed on the same day. Although the two plaintiffs' law firms had earlier served on a nationwide steering committee of plaintiffs' attorneys, the majority of this committee had rejected a settlement with the same defendants.

"Professor Coffee argues that the critical problem with settlement class actions is that they permit the defendants to choose the plaintiffs' attorneys. Even when no discernible side payment is offered to the plaintiffs' attorneys, defendants can effectively conduct a reverse auction among plaintiffs' attorneys, seeking the lowest bidder from the large population of plaintiffs' attorneys. Because each attorney knows that there are other attorneys to whom the defendant can make the same offer, and because ultimately the most cooperative plaintiffs' attorney (that is, the lowest bidder) will win, plaintiffs' attorneys are pressured to accept settlements on terms favorable to the defendants. In effect, defendants confer a valuable property right on the "friendliest" plaintiffs' attorney: the right to represent a very large class of plaintiffs (mostly future claimants) that the attorney does not currently represent. This valuable right plus the linked ability to settle on a superior basis all the cases in the attorney's existing inventory (which cases might not otherwise be resolved for years) represents the inducement for reaching a weak settlement.

"Although courts historically viewed "settlement class actions" skeptically (and indeed mass tort class actions were themselves rarely certified at all until recently), judicial attitudes changed sharply in the late 1980s, as the federal judiciary searched for some means by which to protect itself from an inundation of individual mass tort cases. Although class actions provisionally certified "for purposes of settlement only" have now become common (in the asbestos field, breast implants, and defective product cases), the critical fact about these cases is that the dominant interpretation of Federal Rule of Civil Procedure 23 would probably prevent the same class action from being certified for purposes of trial. The doctrinal problem is the "commonality" requirement of Federal Rule of Civil Procedure 23(a), which some circuits believe cannot be satisfied in mass tort class actions for personal injuries. The consequence, however, is a profound imbalance that denies even well-meaning plaintiffs' attorneys any leverage in settlement negotiations. Put simply, plaintiffs' attorneys in such a setting have only a limited franchise: they can settle, but not fight. Given these constraints, they are effectively negotiating with at least one arm tied behind their backs. Indeed, when the class action cannot be brought to trial, the most logical reason for defendants to settle is that they believe that "a settlement class action" is cheaper than a continuing stream of individual actions. Under these circumstances, the class action becomes the defendants' weapon.

2.   *"Future Claims"*

"A unique characteristic of recent mass tort class actions has been their deliberately narrow definition of the class so as to include only those persons who had not yet filed a lawsuit on the date the class action was filed. This practice of sharply separating present from future claims both reflects the desire of counsel (on both sides) to purge from the class any present claimants (who have both the incentive and ability in "high stakes" cases to monitor their attorneys) and the defendants' primary desire, given the long latency period (possibly extending for decades) in mass tort cases, to obtain litigation closure so that plaintiffs' recoveries will not continue to spiral upward.

"If the defendant corporation waits until these injuries actually develop, the asbestos experience has taught them that an aggressive plaintiffs' bar will continue to obtain very costly individual verdicts, possibly including punitive damages. However, because only a small percentage of those exposed to the dangerous product or toxin will develop injury, defendants can anticipate that these prospective victims will take little action to protect their claims from an unfairly cheap compromise before they develop the first signs or symptoms of injury. As a result, when a mass torts class action is defined primarily to encompass future claimants, defendants can expect "rational apathy" on the part of most class members, who have little incentive to protect themselves (and no reason to opt out with regard to injuries they have not yet experienced). This, in turn, sets the stage for a collusive settlement.

"Current experience suggests that the beneficiaries of the "future claims" class action are: (1) defendants, who cap and limit their liability; (2) courts, which escape the prospect of a high volume of individual claims crowding their dockets; and (3) the plaintiffs' attorneys selected by defendants as class counsel, who are generously paid for their willingness to settle the claims of persons who have never sought to be represented by them.

3. *"Opt–Outs"*

"In some recent class actions, individual plaintiffs have been denied the right to "opt out." When such a right exists, individual plaintiffs often exercise it in large numbers (as happened in the silicone breast implants settlement). Some courts are now denying plaintiffs any right to opt out, making a class action lawsuit mandatory in order to avoid depletion of a "limited fund." Procedurally, this "limited fund" rationale for denying opt-outs has been implemented by treating the corporation's insurance policy as the limited fund. The problem with this rationale is that it permits opportunistic behavior by the corporate debtor, which can scale down its tort liabilities and avert bankruptcy. In contrast, in bankruptcy, the absolute priority rule would require that shareholders not retain any interest in the company unless creditors were first paid in full. Thus, the "limited fund" class action may serve chiefly to effect wealth transfers from a corporation's tort creditors to its shareholders.

4. *Possible Reforms*

"Professor Coffee examines a variety of possible reforms, including (1) interpreting Rule 23(a)(4) to prevent a plaintiffs' attorney from resolving future claims on a less favorable basis than the attorney has recently settled any significant number of present claims, thereby precluding the defendants' use of inventory settlements to induce the attorney to represent the future claims class; (2) modifying the right to opt-out for the special case of the future claimant so that it commences as of the claimant's discovery of his injury; and (3) representative plaintiff steering committees or an auction procedure for the choice of lead counsel to improve the accountability of the counsel selection process. Certain of these reforms may be constitutionally required by the Due Process Clause. More broadly, Professor Coffee questions whether the filing of a future claims class action based only on the fact of exposure to a toxic or dangerous product should satisfy the "case and controversy" requirement of Article III of the U.S. Constitution. Standing, he suggests, should be limited to those circumstances in which (1) class members are likely to be aware of their injuries at the time of certification (such as in the defective heart valve or breast implant cases) and (2) the class includes present and future claimants so that at least some class members are in a position to monitor the adequacy of their attorneys' representation. Finally, Professor Coffee argues that "settlement class" actions should only be tolerated where the same class action could be certified for purposes of trial. This would require the court to make the same finding of "commonality" under Federal Rule of Civil Procedure 23(a) and, in an action certified under Federal Rule of Civil Procedure 23(b)(3), the same finding that such common issues "predominate over any questions affecting only individual members"—without relying on the fairness or adequacy of the settlement as the alleged common issue. This requirement would arm plaintiffs' attorneys in settlement negotiations with the ability to go to trial.

"Ultimately, the most distinctive fact about mass tort class actions, Professor Coffee argues, is not the opportunistic behavior of the settling parties, but the palpable self-interest of distinct judges seeking to avoid a flood of individual actions. Accordingly, the likelihood of real reform, he suggests, depends upon convincing federal courts that their ends do not justify the current means, and that the necessary case load reduction can be achieved through techniques that are less invasive of plaintiffs' rights and less costly to the appearance of justice. The most important reform, he argues, may therefore be to chill "opportunistic" opt-outs and to reallocate all opt-outs equitably among judicial districts and among the state and federal systems."

* * *

Questions

1. The lower court decisions in the *Amchem Products* case (known as *Georgine v. Amchem Products*) were the subject of tremendous controversy in the legal academy. Scholars criticized the lawyers for the plaintiff class on ethical grounds, and criticized the courts for approving a settlement which, the critics claimed, was a product of dubious ethical conduct and replete with conflicts of interest. Professor Susan P. Koniak, for example, argued that in the settlement approved by the District Court in the case, the class counsel colluded with the defendants to gain high settlements for their initial clients (and high fees for themselves in these cases) while short-changing the other members of the class. *Feasting While the Widow Weeps: Georgine v. Amchem Products, Inc.*, 80 CORNELL L. REV. 1045 (1995). She writes, she says, in order "to expose the serious defects in the *Georgine* model, a model that invites defendants to who harm large groups of people to pay a premium on the first victims who file claims in exchange for lower and more limited liability to all future claimants." Id. at 1048. See also, John Leubsdorf, *Co–Opting the Class Action*, 80 CORNELL L. REV. 1222 (1995). Professor Carrie Menkel–Meadow, in *Ethics and the Settlements of Mass Torts: When the Rules Meet the Road*, 80 CORNELL L. REV. 1159 (1995), disagrees with Koniak. Menkel–Meadow believes that current ethical rules

regarding lawyer conflict of interest and ethics in negotiation and litigation derive from individual attorney-client relationships and cannot be transposed to the setting of mass tort class actions. Rather, she argues, settlements in cases such as *Georgine* must be judged not on the basis of the process by which they were reached, but on the basis of their fairness in light of a realistic assessment of the alternatives available to the claimants had there been no settlement reached at all.

The Supreme Court did not address these ethical issues in the *Amchem* opinion. If it had, on the basis of their differing views concerning settlement class actions, how do you think the majority and dissenting justices would have ruled?

2. While the *Amchem* case was pending in the lower courts, the Third Circuit rejected a class action settlement in another case involving defects in General Motors trucks. In *In Re General Motors Corp. Pick–Up Truck Fuel Tank Products Liability Litigation*, 55 F.3d 768, 777 (3d Cir. 1995), class counsel explored settlement while a motion for class certification was pending. They reached a settlement agreement pursuant to which General Motors would give each class member a coupon worth $1,000 toward the purchase of a new General Motors truck. The District Court held a brief fairness hearing, and then issued an order certifying the class and approving the settlement. Four days later, the district court approved class counsel's request for $9.5. million in attorney fees. See Koniak, *Feasting While the Widow Weeps*, 80 Cornell L. Rev. 1045, 1152 (1995) (discussing *In Re General Motors*). The Third Circuit vacated the lower court's order and and criticized the district court for failing to adequately assess the fairness of the settlement or protect the interests of absentee class members. Judge Becker, writing for the Court, gave a detailed exposition of the ethical dangers posed by settlement class actions. He stated that where the class membership is uncertain or involves future claimants, the ethical dangers are particularly pronounced. "With less information about the class, the judge cannot as effectively monitor for collusion, individual settlements, buy-outs (where some individuals use the class action device to benefit themselves at the expense of absentees), and other abuses. For example, if the court fails to define the class before settlement negotiations commence, then during the settlement approval phase the judge will have greater difficulty detecting if the parties improperly manipulated the scope of the class in order to buy the defendant's acquiescence." Id. At 787.

Is it possible that the class counsel in *Amchem* manipulated the composition of the class in order to benefit themselves and defendants? If a judge concluded that nonetheless the settlement was fair to the claimants, would such conduct by class counsel violate any ethical canons? Would it provide the basis for a court to reject an otherwise fair settlement? How can a court know if such a settlement is fair?

3. In mass tort cases stemming from a product that has produced unusual or unanticipated harms—i.e., products such as asbestos, silicone gel, or the Dalkon Shield—there are often no fully litigated cases to provide a standard against which to measure the fairness of a proposed settlement. These

types of cases involve potentially the most serious and pervasive harms, yet they are also the cases in which a court has the most difficulty judging the settlement. In such cases, what standard can a court use to judge the adequacy of a negotiated settlement? Is it possible that the settlement class action is not an appropriate vehicle for determining such claims? If it is not, what would be a preferable method?

* * *

Note on *Ortiz v. Fibreboard Corp.* and Limited Fund Class Actions

Some of the issues left unresolved in *Amchem Products v. Windsor* were addressed by the Supreme Court in ORTIZ V. FIBREBOARD CORP., ___ U.S. ___, 119 S. Ct. 2295 (1999). *Ortiz* is similar to *Amchem* in several respects. *Ortiz*, like *Amchem*, involved a major class action settlement of asbestos claims. Also, in *Ortiz*, as in *Amchem*, the class was composed both of members who were exposed but had no symptoms as well as members who had developed asbestos-related diseases. Also in both cases, the lawyers involved in the class settlement had a substantial number of pre-settlement "inventory" claims which were treated differently, and more favorably, for settlement purposes than the class claims. However, *Ortiz* differed from *Amchem* in one significant respect. The settling parties in *Ortiz* sought class certification under Rule 23(b)(1)(B), a provision that pertains to actions brought against a limited fund. Unlike Rule 23 the (b)(3) class action that was involved in *Amchem*, Rule 23(b)(1) class actions establish a mandatory class, i.e., one in which class members are not permitted to opt-out.

The parties in *Ortiz* sought certification under Rule 23(b)(1)(B) due to the unique features of the case. By the early 1990s, Fibreboard faced over a hundred thousand of claims for personal injury resulting from exposure to asbestos. At the same time, Fibreboard had two insurance policies, which it claimed, provided unlimited coverage for any asbestos liability it might have. The two insurance companies disputed the fact of such unlimited coverage, and thus Fibreboard and the insurers were locked in litigation in California state court. Fibreboard knew that if it were to lose the coverage dispute, it would be bankrupt by the pending and future asbestos claims.

On the eve of the date upon which the California appeals court announced that it would decide the coverage dispute, Fibreboard approached the two insurance companies and the asbestos plaintiffs' counsel, and proposed that they negotiate a global settlement. Fibreboard wanted a settlement before the court ruled on the coverage dispute because it feared that the appeals court might rule that the insurance policies were worthless. The asbestos plaintiffs' counsel, knowing that if Fibreboard lost the coverage dispute, it could only pay a portion of the potential asbestos-related claims, were also willing to discuss settlement. Under the ticking time-bomb of an imminent ruling in the coverage dispute, the insurance companies, Fibreboard and the plaintiffs' counsel negotiated a Trilateral Settlement Agreement.

The settlement established a fund comprised of a contribution from the insurance companies amounting to $1.535 billion, and a contribution from Fibreboard amounting to $10 million, of which all but $500,000 would come from other insurance proceeds. The fund would be used to pay class members' asbestos injury and death claims. Claimants were required to seek to settle with the trustees of the fund, and should such efforts fail, to proceed to mediation, arbitration and a mandatory settlement conference to attempt to resolve their claim. If they exhausted the process and no settlement were achieved, they could go to court against the fund, but were subject to a limit of $500,000 per claim, with punitive damages and interest barred.

The insurance companies were only willing to participate in such a settlement on the condition that it gave them global peace. Thus they insisted upon a mandatory class because they did not want to face additional liability from future opt-outs. Without a mandatory class, they maintained they would not settle, and would instead take their chances that the California court would rule that the insurance policies were worthless and thus absolve them of all liability on the plaintiffs' asbestos claims.

The district court in Ortiz initially certified the class and approved the global settlement that had been negotiated by Fibreboard, plaintiffs' lawyers, and the insurance companies. The Fifth Circuit affirmed the following year, but that decision was vacated and remanded by the Supreme Court for reconsideration in light of *Amchem*. On remand, the Fifth Circuit adhered to its view that the certification was proper and that the settlement was fair and adequate. Objectors to the settlement successfully petitioned for certiorari and the Supreme Court reversed.

In a 7–2 decision authored by Justice Souter, the Supreme Court rejected the class certification, thus rejecting the settlement. The Court discussed the classic types of limited fund class actions in equity, such as actions against trust accounts, bank accounts, company assets during liquidation, proceeds of a ship sale in maritime accident cases, and others. The Court concluded that the early limited fund class actions shared several characteristics that the drafters of Rule 23(b)(a)(B) intended to retain as necessary elements to such a class action. First, there must be a fund with a definitely ascertained limit, such that the fund is inadequate to pay the liquidated claims asserted against it. "The concept driving this type of suit was insufficiency, which alone justified the limit on an early feast to avoid a later famine." Second, the whole of the inadequate fund must be devoted to satisfying the claims. And finally, the claimants identified by a common theory of recovery must be treated equitably among themselves. It found the proposed global settlement in *Ortiz* lacking on all criteria.

In regard to the first criteria, the Court ruled that there was insufficient showing that a limited fund actually existed. The settlement fund was merely a product of the agreement between the insurance companies, Fibreboard, and the plaintiff's counsel. The Court faulted the lower court for failing to undertake an independent evaluation of potential insurance funds, instead relying upon the parties' agreement to set a maximum amount that the insurance companies would be required to pay. The Court stated that a limited fund is not one that is limited simply by the amount the parties agree to put into the settlement.

In addition, the Court stated that the limited fund class action was designed to apply to liquidated claims, not to aggregate unliquidated tort claims such as are posed in mass tort cases. While not deciding whether Rule 23(b)(1)(B) could ever be used in a mass tort case, the Court stated that there was in that area, a need for caution.

In regard to the second criteria, the Court found that the fund was not exclusively utilized to pay the class members' claims. In particular, it focused on the fact that the global settlement only required Fibreboard to contribute $500,000 to the settlement fund. From this the Court concluded that the settlement permitted Fibreboard to retain almost all its net worth. The Court opined that some of Fibreboard's considerable net worth should have gone into the limited fund, a fund that was, by definition, too small to fully compensate the victims.

In regard to the third criteria, the Court held that the settlement did not treat the different categories of class members equitably. It found that the lawyers who negotiated for the plaintiff class had serious conflicts of interest. The Court faulted the District Court for permitting the settlement to exclude plaintiffs who were part of the class counsels' existing inventory of pres-existing claims, some 45,000 inventory plaintiffs. The Court stated that "can be no question that such a mandatory settlement class will not qualify when in the very negotiations aimed at a class settlement, class counsel agree to exclude what could turn out to be as much as a third of the claimants . . . a substantial number of whom class counsel represent." The Court noted that those inventory plaintiffs, who were not part of the mandatory class, obtained more favorable settlements than the Global Settlement provided for class members.

The Court also faulted the lower court for failing to make sub-classes with separate representation as called for by its decision in *Amchem*. The *Ortiz* Court stated that it was necessary to distinguish, for purposes of sub-classes, between present and future claimants, between currently injured and exposure-only plaintiffs, and between plaintiffs who were exposed while Fibreboard had insurance coverage (and thus had more valuable claims) and those who were exposed after the coverage expired. The Court stated that these groups had conflicting interests so that separate representation was required. By treating these differently situated plaintiffs identically, the lower court had not necessarily treated them equitably. Rather, "The very decision to treat them all the same is itself an allocation decision with results almost certainly different from the results that those with immediate injuries or claims of indemnified liability would have chosen."

In overturning the class certification, the *Ortiz* Court was motivated by the same concerns of fairness to absent class members, fairness to present class members with disparate interests, the problem of future claimants, and the danger of class counsel operating with a conflict of interest that we saw in *Amchem*. These issues are posed more starkly in the 23(b)(1) context of *Ortiz* than in the Rule 23(b)(3) context of *Amchem* because in the former, class members do not have a right to opt out.

In dissent, Justices Breyer and Stevens warned that the volume of asbestos cases was threatening to create a disaster of major proportions for the civil justice system. They said that in light of the "elephantine mass of asbestos cases," it was appropriate for judges to search aggressively for ways, within the framework of existing law, to resolve the cases in a way that avoids delay and expense and does not bring about massive denial of justice. In this case, they pointed out, the district court judge who approved the settlement had considerable experience with large asbestos cases and knew first-hand the unusually high costs in delay, attorney fees and other expenses that such suits entailed. One earlier class action case handled by the same judge involved a 133 day trial, more than 500 witnesses, and a half a million pages of documents, and yet it only resolved 160 cases. Thus, the dissenting justices stated,

> "I cannot easily find a legal answer to the problems this case raises by referring, as does the majority, to our 'deep-rooted historic tradition that everyone should have his own day in court ... Instead, in these circumstances, I believe our Court should allow a district court full authority to exercise every bit of discretionary power that the law provides."

Questions

1. To what extent is the *Ortiz* majority influenced by the fact that action was a Rule 23(b)(1) class action? If the parties had proceeded under Rule 23(b)(3), how would it have come out in light of *Amchem*?

2. In a limited fund class action, does a court have to ascertain with certainty the liquidated value of the plaintiffs' claims in order to determine whether or not the fund is sufficient to pay them? If so, how should a court do so? Must it hold a hearing on the validity and amount of each members' claim in order to determine whether the class action can be maintained? Obviously such a requirement would render such the class action vehicle superfluous. On the other hand, what degree of certainty must a court have to ascertain that a limited fund is inadequate to pay the members' aggregated claims? How is a court to determine, or approximate to a lesser degree of certainty, the value of the claims?

3. Why does the *Ortiz* majority suggest that a limited fund class action might not be appropriate for a mass tort case? What if a single company is responsible for a mass tort and the company's total assets, plus available insurance, are vastly insufficient to pay any reasonable estimate of the total liability. In such a case, can a court make a determination of inadequacy in the absence of a final and precise specification of the number of class members and the value of their claims? Is there justification for permitting such a class action to be maintained?

4.   To what extent do you think that the majority in *Ortiz* is animated by concerns of potentially unethical conduct by the class counsel?

5.   How much discretion does a District Court possess in considering whether to certify a class under Rule 23? Do the decisions in *Amchem* and *Ortiz* diminish the amount of discretion that the lower courts have? Can you argue that the district court exercised its discretion appropriately in upholding the certification in *Ortiz*?

* * *

Stacey A. Williams, et al. v. General Electric Capital Auto Lease, Inc.

159 F.3d 266 (7th Cir.1998).

■ DIANE P. WOOD, CIRCUIT JUDGE.

Because class actions are brought in the names of only a few representative plaintiffs on behalf of a larger defined group, it happens from time to time that duplicate or overlapping class actions are filed. When this occurs, it normally is necessary to decide which lawsuit (if any) definitively resolves a matter between particular parties. That is the principal issue before us in this case, a class action challenging certain provisions in automobile leases issued by General Electric Capital Auto Lease, Inc. (GECAL) under the Consumer Leasing Act (CLA), 15 U.S.C. § 1667 et seq. and various Illinois statutes prohibiting unfair and deceptive trade practices. After this case was filed in the Northern District of Illinois in December 1994 at the behest of named representatives Stacey A. Williams and others, the named parties to the lawsuit consented to proceeding before a magistrate judge under 28 U.S.C. § 636(c). The court eventually certified a nationwide class, and the case was resolved when the district court approved a settlement ("the Williams suit"). Later, Gwynne Dooner and others filed essentially the same suit as a new class action against GECAL in the Middle District of Florida ("the Dooner suit"). GECAL responded (among other ways) by filing a motion in the Northern District of Illinois to enjoin further prosecution of the Dooner suit. Still acting for the district court, the magistrate judge (who has since been appointed to the United States Bankruptcy Court) granted the injunction. The Dooner plaintiffs have appealed from that order. . . .

II

To understand the Dooner plaintiffs' arguments on appeal, it is necessary to review the substantive claims of the Williams action. The Williams plaintiffs alleged that GECAL had violated the CLA and state law in several ways. First, they claimed that GECAL had failed adequately to disclose the substantial early termination and default charges in its standard form automobile leases, in violation of 15 U.S.C. § 1667a. See also Regulation M, 12 C.F.R. §§ 213.3, 213.4 (1998). Second, they alleged that the early termination charges under the leases were unreasonable, in violation of 15 U.S.C. § 1667b(b), and that the lessee's right under 15 U.S.C. § 1667b(c) to demand an appraisal of the residual value of the automobile upon early termination was, as a practical matter, unavailable in certain cases. (Specifically, the Williams plaintiffs complained that although the lessee had 10 days to obtain an appraisal before early termination, the right of appraisal as a practical matter was illusory for cases in which early termination was triggered by lessee default, since GECAL could unilaterally order early termination upon default and then repossess the car.) No class was certified until a settlement had been prepared and submitted to the court, which occurred in July 1995.

At that time, the court provisionally certified a settlement class described as:

> all persons in the United States other than residents of Connecticut who, between January 1, 1987, and July 21, 1995, entered into an automobile lease assigned to General Electric Capital Auto Lease, Inc. ("GECAL") and written on a lease form prepared by GECAL which bears one of the identification numbers [listed in the Settlement Agreement]. . . .

The court certified the class under Fed. R. Civ. P. 23(b)(3), which meant of course that absentee class members had the right to opt out of the settlement. All class members received notice by mail of the proposed settlement, and were given until November 1, 1995, to opt out or to provide notice of their intent to object to the settlement. Approximately 1,300 class members elected to opt out.

The court conducted a fairness hearing on the settlement on November 29, 1995. On January 4, 1996, it entered an order certifying the class as it had provisionally been defined and it approved the settlement. Williams v. General Electric Capital Auto Lease, Inc., No. 94–C–7410, 1995 WL 765266 (N.D.Ill. Dec. 26, 1995) (memorandum decision). Under the agreement, settling class members were entitled to receive either a $50 certificate applicable against any early termination fee, or a $100 certificate applicable against payments on a new auto lease. (One of the objectors at the fairness hearing had labeled this arrangement a "joke," pointing out that his early termination fee was more than $1,000.) The settlement agreement also contained the following language releasing the claims of the class members against GECAL:

> The settlement embodied in this Agreement shall apply to all persons in the Class as defined in paragraph 3(a) hereof and shall be in complete and final settlement of all claims asserted in the Actions, and all claims which might have been asserted in the Actions, on behalf of the plaintiffs and the Class against GECAL, its successors and assigns, . . . arising out of disclosures made on or in connection with vehicle leases assigned to GECAL, out of the reasonableness or validity of the charges and other terms contained in such leases, and out of the collection or attempted collection of charges imposed under such lease forms, except those claims excluded in paragraph 2(h) hereof.

(The excluded claims referred to those based on representations other than the written terms of the lease, vehicle defect claims, property damage or personal injury claims, and repossession or collection claims not based on the lease. They are not at issue here.) The court's final judgment roughly tracked this language and ordered that all claims asserted in the action and all claims that might have been asserted in it were dismissed with prejudice (with a similar set of exceptions). The January 4, 1996, final judgment also enjoined all "[c]lass members who did not opt out of the class ... from commencing, prosecuting, or asserting by way of counterclaim or defense against GECAL any of the claims dismissed, settled or barred pursuant to this order."

Given that language, one might wonder under what theory the Dooner plaintiffs began their class action in Florida on July 9, 1996, since they had each signed their GECAL lease between January 1, 1987, and July 21, 1995, and thus fell within the description of the class that the Williams court had used. Also, even though they apparently received the required notices about the class, none of them had opted out of the Williams litigation. What distinguished the Dooner plaintiffs was that as of July 21, 1995, the date the court provisionally approved the class certification and settlement, none of the members of the Dooner class had yet terminated their leases early or been assessed penalties. (This statement is an accurate description for the named representatives Suzanne and James Harper, Lisa and John Ward, and Dudley Williams—no relation to Stacey Williams of the Williams class—who each paid anywhere from $1,237 to $9,728 in early termination charges only after the Williams settlement. Gwynne Dooner herself, however, appears to be an improper plaintiff [because, according to] the amended Florida complaint ... "[o]n July 5, 1995, Dooner terminated the lease agreement and was assessed early termination charges." Based on this factual admission, Dooner is identically situated to the Williams settlement class ...)

In September 1996, GECAL moved in the Northern District of Illinois for an order enforcing the final judgment in Williams and enjoining the Florida action. The named Dooner plaintiffs appeared through their attorney to contest GECAL's motion. They argued that because their leases had not been terminated by July 21, 1995 (the date specified in the order certifying the class), their claims against GECAL had not been justiciable at the time the Williams settlement was approved. Accordingly, they reasoned, any effort to include them in the Williams class or to bind them to the Williams settlement was a nullity. Alternatively, conceding that they received the opt-out notice, the plaintiffs also argued that: (1) the opt-out provided was illusory as to them, and thus inconsistent with due process, since as holders of unterminated leases "they had no knowledge of an early termination claim against GECAL ... much less the value of the claim, or whether they wished to release such a claim"; and (2) they were inadequately represented by the named Williams plaintiffs because of a vague intra-class conflict. The district court rejected their justiciability arguments and entered GECAL's requested injunction without expressly entertaining the Dooner plaintiffs' collateral attack on the Williams settlement. The Dooner plaintiffs have now brought their appeal to us.

III

In order to resolve the appellants' justiciability argument, we must answer several questions: first, were the Dooner plaintiffs included within the class certified in Williams; second, did they have any claim before the court that was justiciable at that time; and third, was the Williams court empowered to enter an order affecting any future claims of the members of the Dooner class that would not have been ripe for adjudication at the time the Williams order was entered. These are all legal questions, for which our review is de novo. (Citations omitted) Only if the answer to all three of those questions is yes may we consider the district court's anti-suit injunction, which we would review under the abuse of discretion standard.

As far as the record shows, each of the appellants before us falls squarely within the class certified in Williams, which included individuals (other than Connecticut residents) who between January 1, 1987, and July 21, 1995, entered into a standard automobile lease prepared by, and assigned to, GECAL. It is also uncontested that none of the Dooner plaintiffs exercised his or her right to opt out of the Williams litigation. They do not argue that the notice they received was formally insufficient under Fed. R. Civ. P. 23(c)(2), and such an argument would be quite hard to sustain in any event given that some 1,300 people did opt out. We consider below, however, the Dooner plaintiffs' argument that the notice was "constitutionally" insufficient because a person who had not yet terminated the lease and been assessed a penalty would not know whether she had an early termination claim against GECAL and if she should pursue such a claim personally or through the class. For present purposes, it is enough to observe that the Dooner plaintiffs fell within the class description used in Williams.

A somewhat more difficult question is whether the Dooner plaintiffs had any claims that were presently justiciable at the time of the Williams litigation, settlement, and judgment. Returning to the Williams complaint, recall that there were two theories raised under federal law: (1) the claim that GECAL had failed to disclose, in an understandable manner, the substantial early termination and default charges in its standard form automobile leases; and (2) the substantive claims that the early termination charges under the leases were unreasonable and that the appraisal right under the lease was illusory. We agree with the Dooner plaintiffs that there are legitimate questions about the ripeness of the second type of claim in their cases. None of the Dooner plaintiffs had tried to terminate a lease, and so it might have been unclear how the appraisal procedures would have worked for them, or whether the amount of the early termination charge would have been reasonable. These claims arguably never actually arose and thus, as of the time of the Williams settlement, were only hypothetically available. Cf. Highsmith v. Chrysler Credit Corp., 18 F.3d 434 (7th

Cir.1994) (some doubt as to whether claim by plaintiff who had not terminated early or even expressed a desire to do so would be justiciable).

If that were all we had, then the twin problems of standing and justiciability of future claims with which other courts have grappled might be squarely presented. See, e.g., Georgine v. Amchem Products, Inc., 83 F.3d 610, 635–38 (3d Cir.1996) (Wellford, J., concurring) (arguing that claims brought by exposure-only asbestos plaintiffs are non-justiciable for lack of case or controversy), aff'd. sub nom., Amchem Prod., Inc. v. Windsor, 521 U.S. 591, ___, 117 S.Ct. 2231, 2244, 138 L.Ed.2d 689 (1997) (recognizing, but declining to reach, the justiciability question); In re Asbestos Litig., 90 F.3d 963, 1015–26 (5th Cir.1996) (Smith, J., dissenting), majority opinion vacated for consideration in light of Amchem, Flanagan v. Ahearn, ___ U.S. ___, 117 S.Ct. 2503, 138 L.Ed.2d 1008 (1997), aff'd. on remand, 134 F.3d 668 (5th Cir.1998) (per curiam), cert. granted sub nom., Ortiz v. Fibreboard Corp., ___ U.S. ___, 118 S.Ct. 2339, 141 L.Ed.2d 711 (1998). See generally John C. Coffee, Jr., Class Wars: The Dilemma of the Mass Tort Class Action, 95 Colum. L.Rev. 1343, 1422–33 (1995); Note, And Justiciability for All?: Future Injury Plaintiffs and the Separation of Powers, 109 Harv. L.Rev. 1066 (1996). Our case differs from the problems those courts discussed, however, because it is clear that the Dooner plaintiffs had at least one presently justiciable claim at the time of the Williams settlement: their claim that the disclosure provisions in the leases violated the CLA. See Highsmith, 18 F.3d at 438–40 (reaching the merits of a CLA disclosure claim even though the plaintiff had not actually terminated his lease early). That claim, as even counsel for the Dooner plaintiffs admits, was properly before the Northern District of Illinois in Williams and was subject to resolution in the settlement. We can therefore narrow the issue before us to whether any injunction against the Dooner plaintiffs' Florida litigation could reach only their disclosure claims, or whether the Illinois court could properly enjoin the entire Florida suit.

In our view, the court not only could address the entire suit, but this was the appropriate step for it to take. This conclusion follows from the law relating to releases of claims. As the Ninth Circuit wrote in an opinion addressing the massive class action settlement of the claims arising from the bond defaults of the Washington Public Power Supply System:

> [t]he weight of authority holds that a federal court may release not only those claims alleged in the complaint, but also a claim "based on the identical factual predicate as that underlying the claims in the settled class action even though the claim was not presented *and might not have been presentable in the class action*."

Class Plaintiffs v. City of Seattle, 955 F.2d 1268, 1287 (9th Cir.1992) (emphasis in original), quoting TBK Partners, Ltd. v. Western Union Corp., 675 F.2d 456, 460 (2d Cir.1982). Admittedly, both the WPPSS case and TBK Partners involved class settlements in federal court releasing state law claims that might not have been cognizable in federal court—as opposed to the release of claims that were non-justiciable in the "case or controversy" sense. However, because the logic of both cases has been subsequently applied to situations where *state* court class settlements released claims of exclusive *federal* subject matter jurisdiction, see, e.g., Matsushita Elec. Indus. Co. v. Epstein, 516 U.S. 367, 116 S.Ct. 873, 879, 881–82, 134 L.Ed.2d 6 (1996); Grimes v. Vitalink Communications Corp., 17 F.3d 1553, 1563–64 (3d Cir.1994); Nottingham Partners v. Trans–Lux Corp., 925 F.2d 29, 34 (1st Cir.1991) (all three cases citing TBK Partners with approval), it seems reasonable to read the WPPSS and TBK Partners cases as pertaining broadly to the law of "releases" rather than narrowly to the issue of federal court jurisdiction. We also note, in this connection, that nothing in the Supreme Court's Amchem decision suggested that the federal courts lacked the Article III *power* to settle future claims of class members. Instead, the Court simply did not reach the Article III justiciability issues because it found that the question whether the settlement class should have been certified was "logically antecedent" to the existence of the Article III issues. See Amchem, 117 S.Ct. at 2244.

Here, the substantive claims of the Dooner plaintiffs are based on the identical factual predicate (the leases and the potential for an early termination penalty) as the disclosure claims that we have noted were properly before the Williams court. It is possible that the appraisal procedure and the computation of the early termination payments might be ministerial at any given point in time. If that were true, then the Dooner plaintiffs perhaps could have assessed their potential liability for early termination even at the time of the Williams settlement; at a minimum, the range of statutory damages available to individual plaintiffs should have been clear. See 15 U.S.C. § 1640(a)(2)(A). We need express no opinion on these questions, however, because even if the claims were not ripe, they were closely enough related to the disclosure claims that everything could be resolved in the settlement. It is not at all uncommon for settlements to include a global release of all claims past, present, and future, that the parties might have brought against each other. See, e.g., Fair v. International Flavors & Fragrances, Inc., 905 F.2d 1114, 1115–16 (7th Cir.1990) (even though one claim was technically "nonexistent" at the time of settlement, the parties' general release was enforceable because circumstances showed that employee releasing her claims had known of, and intentionally resolved, the potential dispute that might have existed), as clarified by, Lynn v. CSX Transp., Inc., 84 F.3d 970, 975–77 (7th Cir.1996). That is all that was done here.

Finally, we turn to the plaintiffs' due process attack on the adequacy of representation and opt-out notice in the Williams certification. The plaintiffs' claim regarding adequacy of representation, which appeared in their brief in a solitary footnote, is insufficiently developed on appeal and is therefore waived. See Otto v. Variable Annuity Life Ins. Co., 134 F.3d 841, 854–55 (7th Cir.1998). The plaintiffs' second argument—that their opt-out rights were illusory since as holders of unterminated leases they lacked knowledge of what claims they held against GECAL and the value of those claims—merits scarcely more discussion. Although the court below did not expressly rule on the plaintiffs' due process collateral attack on certification, a close reading of the opinion indicates that it did so implicitly when it found that:

> The [Dooner] ... plaintiffs had the necessary incentive to read the notice of proposed settlement [in Williams] carefully. The [Dooner] plaintiffs were notified of the terms of the settlement and of the fairness hearing. Further, they were adequately equipped to make a reasoned decision, based on the likelihood of early termination and the costs/benefits of a separate legal challenge, regarding the relative merits of participating in the class or opting out.

[T]hus, in the end, the plaintiffs' due process attack on certification is little more than a gussied up version of their justiciability argument, and it fails for the same reason: all of the Dooner plaintiffs had a cognizable disclosure claim at the time of the Williams settlement that placed them on inquiry notice about the entire settlement.

With no justiciability or due process bars standing in its way, the district court did not abuse its discretion in entering an injunction against the Florida litigation. Indeed, it is hard to see how anything less than a comprehensive injunction could have protected the Illinois settlement. No one can say for sure what the settlement would have looked like if GECAL had thought that it was really resolving only the disclosure claims and leaving open a large number of substantive claims, but it is safe to say it probably would have been different. The Dooner plaintiffs did not sign their leases after the closing date for the Williams class, and thus they cannot avoid class membership that way. Had they wished to take a wait-and-see approach to their individual claims, they could have objected or opted out of the class along with the 1,300 others who took that approach. They did not, and the lower court was therefore well within its authority to prohibit them from re-litigating their claims in another forum. We therefore AFFIRM the district court's injunction.

* * *

Questions

1. How does the *Williams* court avoid the problems of standing and justiciability posed in cases where class actions attempt to settle not-yet-ripened claims? Such an issue was posed but not decided in *Amchem Products v. Windsor*.

2. If there had been no *Williams* settlement, could the Dooner plaintiffs have brought suit on the grounds of GECAL's failure to disclose the terms of its early termination charges before they had incurred such charges? Lacking any specific injury, what type of remedy could they seek? How likely is it that the Dooner plaintiffs would want to bring such an action? Is it reasonable for the court to conclude that because they had a justiciable claim at the time of the *Williams* settlement, they should be barred from litigating the disclosure claim later when it became a matter of financial importance to them?

3.   Recall that in *Shults v. Champion Int'l., supra*, the court found that the settlement was not adequate in part because it bound future claimants, whose claims were not yet ripe. Is the position of the Dooner plaintiffs similar to that of the the future claimants in *Shults*—the unborn children and grandchildren of present riparian owners?

4.   Why does the court bar not only the Dooner plaintiffs' nondisclosure claim but also their substantive objections to the unreasonableness of the lease termination charges? Is the court's reasoning convincing? Is the extension of the release to nonjusticiable claims the same as the release of state law claims in the face of identical federal law claims? Which is a stronger argument for barring the claims?

5.   Does the *Williams* court suggest that so long as individuals have at least one justiciable claim involved in a settlement class action settlement, then any future claims they might have against the settling defendant is barred? Might this give settling defendants an incentive to urge the plaintiffs attorneys to include as many possible claims in the complaint? Does the fact that this is a settlement class action in which the class certification motion is presented to the court at the same time as the proposed settlement, make such collusion more likely? Or, is the problem the same when it is a regular class action which includes future claimants with not-yet-ripe claims?

CHAPTER FIVE

ARBITRATION I: THE AGREEMENT TO ARBITRATE

1. INTRODUCTION

Arbitration is a form of dispute resolution in which a dispute is presented to one or more neutral persons who conduct a hearing and render a decision on the merits. Unlike negotiation and mediation, in arbitration a dispute is decided by the neutral arbitrator and a resolution is imposed on the parties. In mediation and negotiation, in contrast, disputes are resolved on terms that embody the assent of both parties.

Arbitration proceedings can take an almost infinite variety of forms, ranging from procedures that are highly informal and ad hoc to procedures that are as structured and formal as a court of law. Under some procedures, arbitration consists of the parties sitting around a table and taking turns telling their side of the story of the dispute to a neutral who listens and asks questions. Alternatively, some arbitrations follow formal rules of evidence and procedure, and include motion practice, stenographic records of hearings, and post-hearing briefs. Most arbitrations fall between these two extremes. But it is axiomatic that arbitrations take whatever forms the parties desire—arbitration is a creature of the parties and the parties are free to shape the scope of arbitration and the procedures to be used in whatever way they please. It is not uncommon for arbitration agreements to specify particular procedures and evidentiary rules to apply to the arbitration hearing.

Just as the procedures for arbitration vary, there are many methods of designating an arbitrator. Sometimes disputants designate an arbitrator on an ad hoc basis, after a dispute has arisen. Sometimes parties in an ongoing relationship designate a standing arbitrator, or umpire, to resolve any and all disputes that may arise between them.

Arbitration is utilized frequently in commercial disputes, where trade associations or industry-specific groups have devised industry-specific procedures for the resolution of disputes between members of the trade. These procedures often call upon respected senior members of the trade, like village elders, to hear disputes and bring their knowledge of fairness and local custom to bear in their deliberations.[1]

Arbitration is also used frequently in collective bargaining settings. It is customary for collective bargaining agreements to establish formal grievance procedures, which enable an orderly method for a union and manage-

---

1. See, Soia Mentschikoff, *Commercial Arbitration,* 61 COLUM. L. REV. 846 (1961).

ment to consult and negotiate over issues of contractual interpretation or allegations that one side has breached its contractual obligations. If agreement is not reached by the early stages of the grievance procedure, collective bargaining agreements typically specify that arbitration before an outside neutral arbitrator will be the final stage.[2]

There are a number of professional associations that parties can use to obtain qualified arbitrators. The best known is the American Arbitration Association ("AAA"), an organization founded in the 1920s at the time of the enactment of the Federal Arbitration Act. The AAA has become a large national organization with headquarters in New York and several regional offices. It maintains lists of arbitrators by speciality in specific subject areas, as well as general lists in the areas of commercial disputes, international disputes, mass torts disputes, energy disputes, labor-management disputes, individual employment disputes, and construction disputes. The AAA also has devised a set of standard arbitral rules and procedures for each of these subject areas. When parties contact the AAA in search of an arbitrator, the AAA provides the parties with a list of several arbitrators in the relevant subject area from which the parties can make their selection. The parties pay the AAA an administrative fee for its services and pay the arbitrator at an agreed-upon hourly rate.

Once an arbitrator is selected, the parties usually agree upon a written submission to the arbitrator. The submission states in concise and general terms the questions to be decided. The arbitrator's task is defined and circumscribed by the submission. For example, a typical submission in the a labor-management dispute might say:

> Did the Company violate the collective bargaining agreement when it reassigned Jones from the production department to the shipping department on February 12, 1998, and if so, what shall the remedy be?

After a hearing is held, the arbitrator issues an award. Courts treat the award as a final and binding disposition of the issues submitted to the arbitrator. The award may or may not be accompanied by a written opinion. The question of whether or under what circumstances arbitrators should write opinions is hotly debated for reasons that are addressed below. Whether or not an arbitral award is accompanied by an opinion, judicial review of arbitral awards is extremely limited. While some judicial review of arbitral awards is possible, and indeed necessary to ensure that the arbitrator has not violated the parties' agreement to arbitrate, courts avoid reviewing the merits of the dispute. Thus, from the perspective of disputants, arbitration is an alternative means of resolving a dispute that is more like a judicial resolution than the alternative dispute resolution mechanisms discussed in previous chapters.

---

2. See Harry Shulman, *Reason, Contract, and Law in Labor Relations,* 68 HARV. L. REV. 999 (1955).

A.   HISTORICAL BACKGROUND

Prior to 1920, common law courts in the United States did not grant specific performance of arbitration agreements. This meant, in practice, that if one party to an arbitration agreement refused to arbitrate, the other party was powerless to compel arbitration. The party seeking arbitration could not obtain an order compelling arbitration nor could they obtain a stay of litigation if suit were brought by the contract-breaker. In most states, the party seeking arbitration could go to a court for damages for breach of the promise to arbitrate, but courts would award a nominal amount—at most the cost of preparing for the arbitration than never occurred.[3] Federal courts followed the common law rule.

The doctrine that denied specific performance to a promise to arbitrate was called the revocability doctrine, based on an agency analogy. The arbitrator was considered the agent of both sides, so that agreements to arbitrate were revocable by either party until the arbitral award was rendered. Once an award was rendered, the legal status of the arbitration changed. At common law, arbitral awards were binding, and in many jurisdictions, they could be converted into a judgment of the court.

There were two different justifications offered for the revocability doctrine. The first was the notion that the parties were not competent, by private contract, to "oust the court of jurisdiction." This formulation originated in England, but it quickly took hold in both federal and state courts in the United States.[4] For example, the Supreme Court said in 1874 in *Insurance Co. v. Morse*, "Agreements in advance to oust the courts of the jurisdiction conferred by law are illegal and void."[5] It was sometimes said that parties could neither create nor diminish the jurisdiction of the courts by contract.[6]

The other rationale for the 19th century revocability doctrine was set out by Justice Story in 1845, in *Tobey v. County of Bristol*, 23 Fed. Cas. 1313 (1845). In the excerpt which follows, Justice Story explained that while a court of equity has no objections to arbitration tribunals, it will not compel parties to participate in an arbitration because they cannot ensure that the process will be fair and equitable. The limited-powers-of-equity rationale for the revocability doctrine has received less attention than the ouster rationale.

* * *

3. Harry Baum & Leon Pressman, *The Enforcement of Commercial Arbitration Agreements in the Federal Courts,* 8 N.Y.U.L. REV. 238, 241–42 (1930).

4. See Julius Cohen, COMMERCIAL ARBITRATION, 84–102 (tracing the history of the "oust the jurisdiction" doctrine in England and America) (1918).

5. Insurance Co. v. Morse, 87 U.S. (20 Wall) 445, 22 L.Ed. 365 (1874).

6. The "ouster" rationale is discussed and criticized by Judge Frank in the Kulukundis Shipping v. Amtorg Trading case, which appears below.

Tobey v. County of Bristol

Circuit Court, D. Massachusetts.
23 Fed.Cas. 1313 (1845).

■ STORY, CIRCUIT JUSTICE.

... Courts of equity do not refuse to interfere to compel a party specifically to perform an agreement to refer to arbitration, because they wish to discourage arbitrations, as against public policy. On the contrary, they have and can have no just objection to these domestic forums, and will enforce, and promptly interfere to enforce their awards when fairly and lawfully made, without hesitation or question. But when they are asked to proceed farther and to compel the parties to appoint arbitrators whose award shall be final, they necessarily pause to consider, whether such tribunals possess adequate means of giving redress, and whether they have a right to compel a reluctant party to submit to such a tribunal, and to close against him the doors of the common courts of justice, provided by the government to protect rights and to redress wrongs. One of the established principles of courts of equity is, not to entertain a bill for the specific performance of any agreement, where it is doubtful whether it may not thereby become the instrument of injustice, or to deprive parties of rights which they are otherwise fairly entitled to have protected. The specific performance of an agreement is, by no means, a matter of right which a party has authority to demand from a court of equity. So far from this, it is a matter of sound discretion in the court, to be granted or withheld, according to its own view of the merits and circumstances of the particular case, and never amounts to a peremptory duty. Now we all know, that arbitrators, at the common law, possess no authority whatsoever, even to administer an oath, or to compel the attendance of witnesses. They cannot compel the production of documents, and papers and books of account, or insist upon a discovery of facts from the parties under oath. They are not ordinarily well enough acquainted with the principles of law or equity, to administer either effectually, in complicated cases; and hence it has often been said, that the judgment of arbitrators is but rusticum judicium. Ought then a court of equity to compel a resort to such a tribunal, by which, however honest and intelligent, it can in no case be clear that the real legal or equitable rights of the parties can be fully ascertained or perfectly protected?

... And this leads me to remark in the second place, that it is an established principle of courts of equity never to enforce the specific performance of any agreement, where it would be a vain and imperfect act, or where a specific performance is from the very nature and character of the agreement, impracticable or inequitable, to be enforced. 2 Story, Eq. Jur. § 959a. Thus, for example, courts of equity will not decree the specific performance of an agreement for a partnership in business, where it is to be merely doing the pleasure of both parties, because it may be forthwith dissolved by either party. See Story, Partn. §§ 189, 190, and Colly. Partn. (2n Ed.) bk. 2, pp. 132, 133, c. 2, § 2; 1 Story, Eq. Jur.§ 666, and the cases there cited; Crawshay v. Maule, 1 Swanst. 515, the reporter's note. So, upon the like ground, courts of equity will not decree the specific performance of a contract by an author to write dramatic performances for a particular theatre, although it will restrain him from writing for another theatre, if he has contracted not to do so (2 Story, Eq. Jur. § 959a; Morris v. Colman, 18 Ves. 437; Clarke v. Price, 3 Wils. Ch. 157; Baldwin v. Society for Diffusion of Useful Knowledge, 9 Sim. 393); nor will they compel the specific performance of a contract by an actor to act a specified number of nights at a particular theatre (Kemble v. Kean, 6 Sim. 333); nor will they compel the specific performance of a contract to furnish maps to be engraved and published by the other party (Baldwin v. Society for Diffusion of Useful Knowledge, 9 Sim. 393). In all these cases the reason is the same, the utter inadequacy of the means of the court to enforce the due performance of such a contract. The same principle would apply to the case of a specific contract by a master to paint an historical picture, or a contract by a sculptor to carve a statute or a group, historical or otherwise. From their very nature, all such contracts must depend for their due execution, upon the skill, and will, and honor of the contracting party. Now this very reasoning applies with equal force to the case at bar. How can a court of equity compel the respective parties to name arbitrators; and a fortiori, how can it compel the parties mutually to select arbitrators, since each much, in such a case, agree to all the arbitrators? If one party refuses to name and arbitrator, how is the court to compel him to name one? If an arbitrator is named by one party, how is the court to ascertain, if the other party objects to him, whether he is right or wrong in his objection? If one party names an arbitrator, who will not act, how can the court compel him to select another? If one party names an arbitrator not agreed to by the other, how is the court to find out what are his reasons for refusing? If one party names an arbitrator whom the other deems incompetent, how is the court to decide upon the question of his competency? Take the present case, where the arbitrators are to be mutually selected, when and within that time are they to be appointed? How many shall they be,—two, three, four, five, seventeen, or even twenty? The resolve is silent as to the number. Can the court fix the number, if the parties do not agree upon it? That would be doing what has never yet been done. If either party should refuse to name any arbitrator, or to agree upon any named by the other side, has the court authority, of itself, to appoint arbitrators, or to substitute a master for them? That would be, as Sir John Leach said in Agar v. Macklen, 2 Sim. & S. 418, 423, to bind the parties contrary to their agreement; and in Milnes v. Gery, 14 Ves. 400, 408, Sir William Grant held such an appointment to be clearly beyond the authority of the court. In Wilks v. Davis, 3 Mer. 507, 509, Lord Eldon referring to the cases of Cooth v. Jackson, 6 Ves. 34; Milnes v. Gery, 14 Ves. 400, 408; and Blundell v. Brettargh, 17 Ves. 232,— said: "It has been determined in the cases referred to, that if one party agrees to sell and another to purchase, at a price to be settled by arbitrators named by the parties, if no award has been made, the court cannot decree respecting it." In Cooth v. Jackson, 6 Ves. 34, Lord Eldon said: "I am not aware of a case even at law, nor that a court of equity has ever entertained this jurisdiction, that where a reference has been made to arbitration and the judgment of the arbitrators is not given in the time and manner according to the agreement, the court have substituted themselves for the arbitrators and made the award. I am not aware that it has been done even in a case where the substantial thing to be done is agreed between the parties, but the time and manner in which it is to be done, is that which they have put upon others to execute." The same learned judge, in Blundell v. Brettargh, 17 Ves. 232, 242, affirmed the same statement, substituting only the word "prescribe" for "execute." So that we abundantly see, that the very impracticability of compelling the parties to name arbitrators, or upon their default, for the court to appoint them, constitutes, and must forever constitute, a complete bar to any attempt on the part of a court of equity to compel the specific performance of any agreement to refer to arbitration. It is essentially, in its very nature and character, an agreement which must rest in the good faith and honor of the parties, and like an agreement to paint a picture, or to carve a statute, or to write a book, or to invent patterns for prints, must be left to the conscience of the parties, or to such remedy in damages for the breach thereof, as the law has provided. . . .

* * *

Questions

1. The normal remedy for breach of contract is damages. When one side alleges a breach of a promise to arbitrate, why might that party seek specific performance instead? Could damages ever serve as an adequate remedy for breach of a promise to arbitrate?

2. How does Story's approach differ from the "ouster rationale" for refusing to grant specific performance to a promise to arbitrate discussed in the note on Historical Background, above?

3. While common law courts would not issue a specific decree to compel parties to arbitrate, if parties nonetheless choose to arbitrate a dispute and an award was rendered, the courts would enforce the arbitral award at the behest of one of the parties. Is this treatment of arbitration consistent with Story's approach in *Tobey?* Is it consistent with the "ouster rationale" for refusing to compel parties to arbitrate in the first place?

* * *

B. THE NEW YORK ARBITRATION ACT OF 1920

Modern arbitration law has its origins in the New York Arbitration Act of 1920. In the early years of the twentieth century, the commercial bar of New York mounted a concerted challenge to the revocability doctrine. Commercial trade groups used arbitration extensively, and wanted the legal system to reflect and support their arbitration practices. The role of the business community in the development and legal authorization of arbitration is described by Jerold S. Auerbach in the following passage from his book, JUSTICE WITHOUT LAW:

JUSTICE WITHOUT LAW by Jerold S. Auerbach*

"[C]ommercial arbitration ... was nourished by the convergence of business organization and government regulation during the early years of the twentieth century. After a turbulent era of competitive disorder following the Civil War, business consolidation made self-regulation possible. By the 1920s there was a high level of industrial self-government. Indeed, business interests were equated with the national interest; the ideal society was seen as a benevolent business commonwealth (although, to be sure, uncommon wealth was reserved for businessmen). As business power expanded, however, government regulatory power (with considerable lag) also expanded in an effort to contain it. But the stronger the regulatory state, the stronger the desire for spheres of voluntary activity beyond its control. The growth of the regulatory state unsettled advocates of commercial autonomy, who turned to arbitration as a shield against government intrusion. Arbitration fit neatly into their vision of industrial planning; it permitted businessmen to solve their own problems 'in their own way— without resort to the clumsy and heavy hand of Government.' Commercial arbitration revived as the indigenous demand of powerful economic groups who formed their own consensual communities of profit.

"Before World War I, commercial arbitration was confined to trade associations whose members engaged in the continuous sale or trade of a special product, commodity, or security. (Arbitration in the New York Stock Exchange, the Chicago Board of Trade, and the fur and silk industries dated back to the nineteenth century.) In such tightly organized associations the value of an enduring commercial relationship far exceeded the value of a particular commodity. Without the internal resolution of disputes through arbitration, litigation would inevitably promote 'hard feeling and ultimate disruption' of the bonds that sustained commercial relationships. As long as disputes were settled within the association, members were assured that their shared customs, however idiosyncratic, would be respected. Trade custom, which facilitated amicable relations between buyer and seller, offered far more security than the mysterious, and threatening, procedures of the law.

"Commercial arbitration was revived at the instigation of Charles L. Bernheimer, president of a cotton-goods concern, who was frustrated by the costs, delays, and uncertainties of commercial litigation. Bernheimer touted the virtues of arbitration, which resolved disputes 'in a rough and ready "Squire Justice" fashion wherein ordinary common sense, knowledge of human nature, a clean cut sense of commercial equity, patience and forbearance produce the results desired' by businessmen. More powerful than 'the force of law,' reported his Chamber of Commerce arbitration

---

* Jerold S. Auerbach, JUSTICE WITHOUT LAW (Oxford Press 1983). Reprinted with permission.

committee, was 'the collective conscience of a group.' Other businessmen were also discovering the advantages of commercial arbitration. In Illinois, where arbitration by the Chicago Board of Trade helped to rationalize the commodities market, various commodities exchanges used its arbitration processes to maintain common standards and tight discipline among members. 'Why waste time, energy and money in court trials?' read a letter of inquiry to 'Mr. Business Man' in Illinois. Arbitration 'does not result in enmity between the parties, as does the ordinary law suit.' Instead, it offered expertise, business efficiency, and just results.

"Preliminary support for the principle of arbitration came from an unexpected source: the legal profession. As the administration of justice deteriorated in urban America, lawyers were thrown on the defensive. They conceded (at least in the privacy of their own company), that there was 'a widespread feeling throughout the country that our bench and bar are not meeting the demands of the present age, that there has been manifest a growing distrust of our courts and a growing disrespect for our laws.' At the annual meeting of the Missouri Bar Association in 1914 Percy Werner, a St. Louis attorney, proposed a 'simple, dignified, honest, conciliatory, and democratic' procedure for the resolution of private disputes. Ordinary citizens were entitled to a procedure 'free from technicality and mystery, "which cut" to the marrow of a controversy in a simple, speedy, direct manner.' As government regulation increased, Werner observed, courts were inundated with an unprecedented volume of public-law issues, ranging from labor-management conflict to public utilities regulation to social legislation for working women and children. To reduce judicial congestion the ordinary private disputes of individuals should be diverted to voluntary tribunals for arbitration by a lawyer, chosen by the disputants' attorneys. Not only would these tribunals serve the public; they would benefit bench and bar. Public respect for the judiciary would increase as over-crowded dockets diminished. Since only attorneys with 'character and learning' would serve as arbitrators, 'suspicion and reproach' of the bar would recede.

"The New York Chamber of Commerce expressed interest in Werner's proposal, noting the opportunity for 'cooperative usefulness between commercial organizations and the legal profession.' The New York State Bar Association established a new committee to consider a range of alternatives that its members proposed for preventing unnecessary litigation: conciliation courts; Mormon-style mediation; arbitration; and specialized merchants' tribunals. Arbitration captured the committee's interest, but lawyers and businessmen wanted different results from it. Lawyers, defensive about criticism, were eager to improve their public image, without losing clients, while retaining control over dispute resolution. Businessmen, apprehensive about outside intrusion, wanted expeditious, inexpensive justice which comported with commercial practice, free of external legal constraints."

* * *

In 1915, Judge Charles Hough of the Southern District of New York wrote in *U.S. Asphalt Refining Co. v. Trinidad Lake Petroleum Co.*,[7] that there was no basis for the revocability doctrine other than *stare decisis*. Using this decision as its cue, the New York Chamber of Commerce decided to launch a full-scale attack on the doctrine. It participated as *amicus curiae* in another pending case regarding enforcement of arbitration agreements, and it commissioned Mr. Julius Henry Cohen, a respected member of the New York commercial bar and the Chair of the New York Bar Association's Committee on Arbitration, to represent the Chamber. Cohen's brief was then expanded into a book-length treatise on the errors of the revocability doctrine and the pressing need for reform in the law of arbitration.[8]

Cohen's book was followed by an avalanche of writings from the commercial law community urging courts and legislatures to change the law of arbitration. In 1919, the New York Chamber of Commerce joined with the New York Bar Association to draft a statute for the New York legislature changing the common law rule. The statute, drafted by Julius Cohen, was patterned on the English arbitration law of 1898, which had dealt the final blow to the revocability doctrine there. There was, however, one significant difference between the New York and British statutes. The proposed New York law did not contain a provision for de novo court review of questions of law while the British law did. There was also some dispute within the American legal community over whether arbitration agreements should be irrevocable for existing disputes or for future disputes.[9] Those who wanted to ensure that *all* agreements to arbitrate— those pertaining to future disputes as well as to existing disputes—were legally enforceable and irrevocable prevailed. In 1920, Cohen's bill passed the New York legislature and became the New York Arbitration Act.

The New York Arbitration Act of 1920 made written agreements to arbitrate existing or future disputes "valid enforceable and irrevocable, save upon such grounds as exist at law or in equity for the revocation of any contract." Ch. 275, General Laws of New York of 1920, Section 2. It further provided in Section 3 that a party aggrieved by the failure of another to submit a dispute such a dispute to arbitration could petition the state supreme court (i.e., the New York trial court) "for an order directing that such arbitration proceed in the manner provided for in such contract or submission." Section 4 contained a procedure by which the court could appoint an arbitrator in the event that a party resisting arbitration failed to cooperate in the selecting of one or if no method was specifically provided in the parties' contract. And the New York statute provided in Section 5 that once any suit or proceeding brought on a matter referable to

---

7. U.S. Asphalt Refining Co. v. Trinidad Lake Petroleum Co., 222 Fed. 1006 (S.D.N.Y.1915).

8. Charles Bernheimer, *Introduction,* in Julius Henry Cohen, COMMERCIAL ARBITRATION AND THE LAW.

9. See Alfred Heuston, *Settlement of Disputes by Arbitration,* 1 WASH. L. REV. 243, 244, n. 8 (1925).

arbitration under the statute, the court "shall stay the trial of the action until such arbitration has been had in accordance with the terms of the agreement."

The New York Arbitration Act also amended the New York Civil Practice Act in several respects to provide for arbitration. One important provision was the addition of Section 1457 of the Civil Practice Act, which specified four grounds upon which courts could vacate an arbitration award. These are:

1. Where the award was procured by corruption, fraud or other undue means.

2. Where there was evident partiality or corruption in the arbitrators or either of them.

3. Where the arbitrators were guilty of misconduct in refusing to postpone the hearing upon sufficient cause shown, or in refusing to hear evidence pertinent and material to the controversy; or of any other misbehavior by which the rights of any party have been prejudiced.

4. Where the arbitrators exceeded their powers, or so imperfectly executed them, that a mutual, final and definite award upon the subject-matter submitted was not made.

This language of the New York Arbitration Act was adopted, almost verbatim, in the Federal Arbitration Act five years later.

* * *

Questions

1. Compare the provisions of the New York Arbitration Act of 1920 with the provisions of the Federal Arbitration Act, as it appears in Appendix A. Are there any significant differences?

2. How might arbitration of a dispute between two members of a trade association differ from arbitration between two strangers, or between a member and a nonmember of a trade association? Are the reasons why courts should enforce agreements to arbitrate stronger or weaker when a dispute is between strangers who do not share such common membership?

* * *

C. THE FEDERAL ARBITRATION ACT OF 1925

In the early 1920's several states followed the lead of New York and enacted arbitration statutes to remove the common law doctrine of revocability and provide for legal enforcement of executory promises to arbitrate. At the same time, the American Bar Association began to work on a federal arbitration law, patterned on the New York statute. The A.B.A. prepared drafts for an United States Arbitration Act (USAA) in 1921, 1922, and 1923. Congress held hearings on the proposed USAA bill in January 1924, after which the bill moved with unusual dispatch through the House and Senate Committees. In 1925, the Congress unanimously passed a statute patterned on the New York Arbitration law.[10] The United States Arbitration Law, later renamed the Federal Arbitration Act (FAA), was signed by President Coolidge on February 12, 1925.

The Federal Arbitration Act says that arbitration agreements contained in contracts involving maritime transactions or interstate commerce are "valid, irrevocable, and enforceable, save upon such grounds as exist at law or in equity for the revocation of any contract." 9 U.S.C. § 2. It also empowers federal courts to grant a stay of litigation for any issue referable to arbitration under a valid arbitration agreement, 9 U.S.C. § 3, and to grant a motion to compel arbitration when one party refuses to abide by its arbitration agreement. 9 U.S.C. § 4. The text of the FAA appears in Appendix A, below.

One month after the new federal arbitration law went into effect, Julius Cohen, who played a significant role in drafting the federal arbitration law, together with Kenneth Dayton, set forth their views of the goals and effects of the new enactment in an article entitled *The New Federal Arbitration Law,* 12 VA. L. REV. 265 (1926):

"Before we analyze the machinery furnished by this statute to accomplish its purposes, we must understand the end for which systems of arbitration are devised. The evils which arbitration is intended to correct are three in number: (1) The long delay usually incident to a proceeding at law, in equity or in admiralty, especially in recent years in centers of commercial activity, where there has arisen great congestion of the court calendars. This delay arises not only from congestion of the calendars, which necessitates each case awaiting its turn for consideration, but also frequently from preliminary motions and other steps taken by litigants, appeals there from, which delay consideration of the merits, and appeals from decisions upon the merits which commonly follow the decision of any case of real importance. (2) The expense of litigation. (3) The failure, through litigation, to reach a decision regarded as just when measured by the standards of the business world. This failure may result either because the courts necessarily apply general rules which do not always fit a specific case, or because, in the ordinary jury trial, the parties do not have the benefit of the judgment of persons familiar with the peculiarities of the given controversy.

"Making an agreement to arbitrate is not always sufficient, however. If both parties are strictly honorable and if there is no misunderstanding between them as to the scope and effect of the agreement which they have made, they will carry out the contract to arbitrate and perform the award entered upon it, and there is no necessity for a statute. Unfortunately, this situation does not commonly exist. The

---

10. For a detailed history of the enactment of the USAA, see Ian R. Macneil, AMERI-CAN ARBITRATION LAW, pp. 83–101 (Oxford University Press, 1992).

party refusing to proceed may believe in good faith that for one reason or another his agreement to arbitrate does not bind him (*i.e.*, he may assert that he made no such agreement or that it was not intended to cover the particular controversy). Even without this, after a dispute has arisen, one party or the other ordinarily has a certain technical advantage which may be impaired if he submits the controversy to arbitration rather than to the courts. It may be in the application of a settled rule of law. It may be in some procedural peculiarity, or it may be merely in the delay of which he is assured by the congestion of the courts before he has to meet his obligation. The result is that this party is usually loath to surrender his supposed advantage. His unwillingness is not necessarily due to dishonesty or bad faith. Unfortunately, business has become so used to the doctrine of revocability of arbitration agreements that these clauses are not regarded in the same light as other contractual obligations, and the party who refuses to perform his agreement frequently does not realize that he is violating his word. He has no conscious intention of defaulting upon his agreement, but the rule of law has blinded him to the fact that this is an agreement. While our American courts have usually declared a friendly attitude toward arbitration, they have felt themselves bound by the long standing decisions holding that arbitration agreements were revocable at will and would not be enforced by the courts. The result has been that any party who wished to avoid an agreement which he had made to arbitrate had only to declare his refusal to proceed and the courts would not order specific performance of the contract while the alternative of a damage suit was inadequate.

"Furthermore, after the completion of an arbitration proceeding and the rendition of an award, the remedy open to the successful party if his opponent refused to perform the award was not in all respects satisfactory. To be sure, the award was usually considered a determination of the merits of the controversy, and the successful party had only to plead and prove the award to recover judgment upon it. Even this remedy, however, left room for an extended law suit because of the collateral issues of fraud and misconduct and other impropriety in the proceeding which might be introduced and which meant that the delay in finally recovering judgment was substantially as great as though action had been brought upon the original dispute. The one advantage lay in the fact that proof became simpler.

"To meet the situation where, through dishonesty or mistake or otherwise, one party to an arbitration agreement refuses to perform it, statutes such as those adopted by Congress and in New York and New Jersey are advocated and have met favor.

"The adoption of the statute does not mean that parties who have agreed to arbitrate and, after the controversy arises, are still willing to arbitrate and abide by the results must come into court or submit to any legal interference whatever. The arbitration proceeds as though the statute were non-existent. There is no interference by the courts.

"Where one party refuses to carry out the agreement, however, the other party now has a remedy formerly denied him. This remedy is not, as has been suggested, equally cumbersome with the existing actions at law, nor is there any prospect that it will ever become so.

"It has been suggested that the proposed law depends entirely for its validity upon the exercise of the interstate-commerce and admiralty powers of Congress. This is not the fact. It rests upon the constitutional provision by which Congress is authorized to establish and control inferior Federal courts. So far as congressional acts relate to the procedure in such courts, they are clearly within the congressional power. This principle is so evident and so firmly established that it cannot be seriously disputed. The statute as drawn establishes a procedure in the Federal courts for the enforcement of certain arbitration agreements. It is no infringement upon the right of each State to decide for itself what contracts shall or shall not exist under its laws. To be sure, whether or not a contract exists is a question of the substantive law of the jurisdiction wherein the contract was made. But whether or not an arbitration agreement is to be enforced is a question of the law of procedure and is determined by the law of the jurisdiction wherein the remedy is sought. That the enforcement of arbitration contracts is within the law of procedure as distinguished from substantive law is well settled by the decisions of our courts. The rule must be changed for the jurisdiction in which the agreement is sought to be enforced, and a change in the jurisdiction in which it was made is of no effect. Every one of the States in the Union might declare such agreement to be valid and enforceable, and still in the Federal courts it would remain void and unenforceable without this statute. . . .

"Arbitration under the Federal and similar statutes is simply a new procedural remedy, particularly adapted to the settlement of commercial disputes. It clearly is not outside the law because it is provided for by statute. No more is it outside the established legal system, because under these statutes the proceeding from beginning to end may be brought under the supervision of the courts if either party deems it necessary. No one is required to make an agreement to arbitrate. Such action by a party is entirely voluntary. When the agreement to arbitrate is made, it is not left outside the law. Proceedings under the new arbitration law are as much a part of our legal system as any other special proceeding or form of remedy. It is merely a new method for enforcing a contract freely made by the parties thereto."

* * *

Questions

1.   Cohen and Dayton mention three evils that the Federal Arbitration Act was intended to correct when it was enacted in the 1920s. Do these criticisms of the judicial system also pertain to the present time?

2.   Cohen and Dayton state that the enforcement of arbitration clauses under the Federal Arbitration Act is an aspect of procedural law. Can an argument be made that this is an aspect of substantive law?

3.   Note that Cohen and Dayton emphasize that the FAA does not rest on Congress' Commerce Power or its Admiralty Powers, but rather on Congress' power under Article III to establish and regulate the procedures in the federal courts. Why do you think they take this position? What would be the consequences if the FAA rested on the Commerce Power instead?

* * *

The *Kulukundis Shipping* case, which appears below, is an early attempt by a federal court to interpret and apply the then-new federal arbitration statute. In reading the opinion, consider whether Justice Frank's views are in tension with Justice Story's in the *Tobey* case.

Kulukundis Shipping Co., S/A v. Amtorg Trading Corporation

126 F.2d 978 (2d Cir. 1942).

■ FRANK, CIRCUIT JUDGE.

The libel alleged that appellant (respondent) had, through its authorized representatives, agreed to a charter party with appellee (libellant). Appellant's answer in effect denied that anyone authorized to act for it had so agreed. After a trial, the district court made the following

"Findings of Fact

"1.   Libellant, Kulukundis Shipping Co. S/A, employed Blidberg Rothchild Co. Inc. as a broker and the respondent, Amtorg Trading Corporation employed Potter & Gordon, Inc. as its broker in the negotiations for the chartering of the ship 'Mount Helmos' for a trip to Japan. On March 15, 1940, Rothchild, of the firm of Blidberg Rothchild Co. Inc., and Gordon, acting on behalf of Potter & Gordon, Inc., agreed upon a charter and closed by Gordon executing and delivering to Rothchild a fixture slip which is the usual trade practice, indicating the conclusion of charter negotiations in the trade of ship brokerage. All the material items of the bargain are set forth in the fixture slip excepting demurrage, dispatch, and the date of the commencement of the charter term which all had been agreed on but were omitted by an oversight. A number of the terms, including the War Risks Clause of 1937, were fixed by the incorporation of a reference to an earlier charter of the steamer 'Norbryn.' Gordon acted with authority.

"2. Thereafter, respondent refused to sign the charter but instead repudiated it.

"Conclusions of Law

"1. Respondent has breached a valid contract and is liable in damages to the libellant.''

Pursuant to the foregoing, the court entered an order that appellee recover from appellant the damages sustained, and referred to a named commissioner the ascertainment of the damages, to be reported to the court. . . .

The appellant, in its answer originally filed, pleaded that no contract had been made. No steps of any importance having meanwhile occurred in the suit, some nine months later and two months before the trial, it sought to amend its answer by including, as a separate defense, the fact that the alleged charter party upon which appellee was suing contained an arbitration clause, that appellee had not at any time asked appellant to proceed to arbitration, and that therefore the suit had been prematurely brought. This motion to amend was denied. If the amendment should have been allowed, the additional defense can now be urged.

The arbitration clause reads as follows: "24. Demurrage or despatch is to be settled at loading and discharging ports separately, except as per Clause 9. Owners and Charterers agree, in case of any dispute or claim, to settle same by arbitration in New York. Also, in case of a dispute of any nature whatsoever, same is to be settled by arbitration in New York. In both cases arbitrators are to be commercial men."

[The court then quoted Sections 2, 3 & 4 of the Federal Arbitration Act.]

Appellant admits—as it must—that the district court had jurisdiction to determine whether the parties had made an agreement to arbitrate.[3] Appellant contends, however, that, once the court determined in this suit that there was such an arbitration agreement, the court lost all power over the suit beyond that of staying further proceedings until there had been an arbitration as agreed to;[4] in that arbitration, argues appellant, the arbitrators will have jurisdiction to determine all issues except the existence of the arbitration clause. This jurisdiction, it is urged, is broad enough to permit an independent determination, by the arbitrator, that the contract itself is not valid or binding. Appellee asserts that the defendant had repudiated the charter-party, and that, therefore, the arbitration clause must be wholly disregarded.

In considering these contentions in the light of the precedents, it is necessary to take into account the history of the judicial attitude towards arbitration: The English courts, while giving full effect to agreements to submit controversies to arbitration after they had ripened into arbitrators' awards, would—over a long period beginning at the end of the 17th century—do little or nothing to prevent or make irksome the breach of

---

3. Under Section 3 of the Act, the court cannot grant a stay until it is "satisfied that the issue involved in such suit * * * is referable to arbitration under" an "agreement in writing for * * * arbitration." Clearly the court cannot be thus "satisfied" without a determination that the parties made such an agreement to arbitrate.

4. Of, if plaintiff had so requested, then under Section 4, directing the parties to proceed with the arbitration.

such agreements when they were still executory.[5] Prior to 1687, such a breach could be made costly: a penal bond given to abide the result of an arbitration had a real bite, since a breach of the bond's condition led to a judgment for the amount of the penalty. It was so held in 1609 in Vynoir's Case, 8 Coke Rep. 81b. To be sure, Coke there, in a dictum, citing precedents, dilated on the inherent revocability of the authority given to an arbitrator; such a revocation was not too important, however, if it resulted in a stiff judgment on a penal bond. But the Statute of Fines and Penalties (8 & 9 Wm.III c. 11, s. 8), enacted in 1687, provided that, in an action on any bond given for performance of agreements, while judgment would be entered for the penalty, execution should issue only for the damages actually sustained. Coke's dictum as to revocability, uttered seventy-eight years earlier, now took on a new significance, as it was now held that for breach of an undertaking to arbitrate the damages were only nominal. Recognizing the effect of the impact of this statute on executory arbitration agreements, Parliament, eleven years later, enacted a statute, 9 Wm.III c. 15 (1698), designed to remedy the situation by providing that, if an agreement to arbitrate so provided, it could be made a "rule of court" (i.e., a court order), in which event it became irrevocable, and one who revoked it would be subject to punishment for contempt of court; but the submission was revocable until such a rule of court had been obtained. This statute, limited in scope, was narrowly construed and was of little help.[8] The ordinary executory arbitration agreement thus lost all real efficacy since it was not specifically enforceable in equity, and was held not to constitute the basis of a plea in bar in, or a stay of, a suit on the original cause of action. In admiralty, the rulings were much the same.

It has been well said that "the legal mind must assign some reason in order to decide anything with spiritual quiet."[9] And so, by way of rationalization, it became fashionable in the middle of the 18th century to say that

---

5. The early English history of enforcement of executory arbitration agreements is not too clear. Arbitration was used by the medieval guilds and in early maritime transactions. Some persons trace an influence back to Roman law, doubtless itself affected by Greek law; others discern the influence of ecclesiastical law. See Sayre, *Development of Commercial Arbitration Law*, 37 YALE L.J. (1927) 595, 597. [additional citations omitted.]

8. See Sayre, loc. cit. at 606; Annotation, 47 L.R.A.,N.S. 436; Chaffee & Simpson, 1 Cases on Equity. (1934) 552–553.

In 1833, a statute (3 & 4 Wm.IV, c. 42) was passed which was intended to reinforce the 1680 statute, but it still left a submission revocable until an action was brought in connection with an arbitration proceeding. An Act of 1854 (17 & 19 Vict.c. 125) provided

that any arbitration agreement could be made the basis of a stay and irrevocable except by leave of court, granted in the exercise of the court's discretion.

The Arbitration Act of 1889 (52 & 53 Vict. c. 49) provided that any such agreement, unless a contrary intention is expressed therein, shall be irrevocable, except by leave of court, and shall have the same effect as if it had been made an order of court; it provided adequate court review of questions of law raised in the arbitration hearing. See Sayre, loc. cit., 606–607; 47 L.R.A.,N.S., 436ff; Chaffee & Simpson, loc. cit.

9. Hough, J., in United States Asphalt R. Co. v. Trinidad Lake P. Co., D.C. 1915, 222 F. 1006, 1008. He discusses and shows the "worthlessness" of the several "causes advanced for refusing to compel men to abide by their arbitration contracts."

such agreements were against public policy because they "oust the jurisdiction" of the courts. But that was a quaint explanation, inasmuch as an award, under an arbitration agreement, enforced both at law and in equity, was no less an ouster; and the same was true of releases and covenants not to sue, which were given full effect. Moreover, the agreement to arbitrate was not illegal, since suit could be maintained for its breach. Here was a clear instance of what Holmes called a "right" to break a contract and to substitute payment of damages for non-performance;[10] as, in this type of case, the damages were only nominal, that "right" was indeed meaningful.

An effort has been made to justify this judicial hostility to the executory arbitration agreement on the ground that arbitrations, if unsupervised by the courts, are undesirable, and that legislation was needed to make possible such supervision. But if that was the reason for unfriendliness to such executory agreements, then the courts should also have refused to aid arbitrations when they ripened into awards. And what the English courts, especially the equity courts, did in other contexts, shows that, if they had the will, they could have devised means of protecting parties to arbitrations. Instead, they restrictively interpreted successive statutes intended to give effect to executory arbitrations.... Perhaps the true explanation is the hypnotic power of the phrase, "oust the jurisdiction."[17] Give a bad dogma a good name and its bite may become as bad as its bark.

In 1855, in Scott v. Avery, 5 H.C.L. 811, the tide seemed to have turned. There it was held that if a policy made an award of damages by arbitrators a condition precedent to a suit on the policy, a failure to submit to arbitration would preclude such a suit, even if the policy left to the arbitrators the consideration of all the elements of liability. But, despite later legislation, the hostility of the English courts to executory arbitrations resumed somewhat after Scott v. Avery, and seems never to have been entirely dissipated.

That English attitude was largely taken over in the 19th century by most courts in this country. Indeed, in general, they would not go as far as Scott v. Avery, supra, and continued to use the "ouster of jurisdiction" concept: An executory agreement to arbitrate would not be given specific performance or furnish the basis of a stay of proceedings on the original cause of action.... In the case of broader executory agreements, no more than nominal dangers would be given for a breach.

Generally speaking, then, the courts of this country were unfriendly to executory arbitration agreements. The lower federal courts, feeling bound to comply with the precedents, nevertheless became critical of this judicial hostility. There were intimations in the Supreme Court that perhaps the old view might be abandoned, but in the cases hinting at that newer

---

10. Holmes, The Path of The Law, 10 Harv.L.Rev. (1897) 457....

17. Words sometimes have such potency. For an excellent 18th century American essay on "semantics" along these lines, see Mr. Justice Wilson's opinion in Chisholm v. Georgia, 1793, 2 Dall. 419, 454ff, 1 L.Ed. 440; Cf. United States v. Forness, 2 Cir., January 20, 1942, 125 F.2d 928, 934, and note 9.

attitude the issue was not raised. Effective state arbitration statutes were enacted beginning with the New York Statute of 1920.

The United States Arbitration Act of 1925 was sustained as constitutional, in its application to cases arising in admiralty. Marine Transit Corp. v. Dreyfus, 1932, 284 U.S. 263, 52 S.Ct. 166, 76 L.Ed. 282. The purpose of that Act was deliberately to alter the judicial atmosphere previously existing. The report of the House Committee stated, in part: "Arbitration agreements are purely matters of contract, and the effect of the bill is simply to make the contracting party live up to his agreement. He can no longer refuse to perform his contract when it becomes disadvantageous to him. An arbitration agreement is placed upon the same footing as other contracts, where it belongs. * * * The need for the law arises from an anachronism of our American law. Some centuries ago, because of the jealousy of the English courts for their own jurisdiction, they refused to enforce specific agreements to arbitrate upon the ground that the courts were thereby ousted from their jurisdiction. This jealousy survived for so long a period that the principle became firmly embedded in the English common law and was adopted with it by the American courts. The courts have felt that the precedent was too strongly fixed to be overturned without legislative enactment, although they have frequently criticized the rule and recognized its illogical nature and the injustice which results from it. The bill declares simply that such agreements for arbitration shall be enforced, and provides a procedure in the Federal courts for their enforcement. * * * It is particularly appropriate that the action should be taken at this time when there is so much agitation against the costliness and delays of litigation. These matters can be largely eliminated by agreements for arbitration, if arbitration agreements are made valid and enforceable."

In the light of the clear intention of Congress, it is our obligation to shake off the old judicial hostility to arbitration. Accordingly, in a case like this, involving the federal Act, we should not follow English or other decisions which have narrowly construed the terms of arbitration agreements or arbitration statutes. With this new orientation, we approach the problems here presented. They are twofold: (a) Does the arbitration provision here have the sweeping effect ascribed to it by appellant? (b) Is it, as appellee contends, wholly without efficacy because appellant asserted that there never was an agreement for a charter party? We shall consider these questions in turn:

To the appellant's sweeping contention there are several answers:

(a) Appellant, as we saw, concedes that, in such a case as this, before sending any issue to arbitrators, the court must determine whether an arbitration provision exists. As the arbitration clause here is an integral part of the charter party, the court, in determining that the parties agreed to that clause, must necessarily first have found that the charter party exists. If the court here, having so found, were now to direct the arbitrators to consider that same issue, they would be traversing ground already covered in the court trial. There would thus result precisely that needless expenditure of time and money (the "costliness and delays of litigation") which Congress sought to avoid in enacting the Arbitration Act. In the light of that fact, a reasonable interpretation of the Act compels a repudiation of appellant's sweeping contention.

(b) If the issue of the existence of the charter party were left to the arbitrators and they found that it was never made, they would, unavoidably (unless they were insane), be obliged to conclude that the arbitration agreement had never been made. Such a conclusion would (1) negate the court's prior contrary decision on a subject which, admittedly, the Act commits to the court, and (2) would destroy the arbitrators' authority to decide anything and thus make their decision a nullity. Cf. Phillips, The Paradox in Arbitration Law, 46 Harv.L.Rev. (1933) 1258, 1270–1272; Phillips, A Lawyer's Approach to Commercial Arbitration, 41 Yale L.J. (1934) 31; 6 Williston, Contracts (Rev.ed. 1938), Section 1920 (pp. 5369–5379).

(c) The Arbitration Act does not cover an arbitration agreement sufficiently broad to include a controversy as to the existence of the very contract which embodies the arbitration agreement. Section 2 of the Act describes only three types of agreement covered by the Act: One type is "an agreement * * * to submit to arbitration an existing controversy arising out of * * * a contract, transaction," etc.; thus the parties here, after a dispute had arisen as to the existence of the charter party, might have made an agreement to submit to arbitration that "existing" controversy. But that is not this case. Section 2 also includes a "provision in * * * a contract evidencing a transaction * * * to settle by arbitration a controversy thereafter arising out of such contract or transaction * * *." Plainly such a provision does not include a provision in a contract to arbitrate the issue whether the minds of the parties ever met so as to bring about the very contract of which that arbitration clause is a part; a controversy "arising out of a transaction evidenced by a contract," for if no contract existed then there was no such transaction evidenced by a contract and, therefore, no controversy arising out of that transaction. The third type of arbitration agreement described in Section 2 of the Act is a provision in a contract to settle by arbitration "a controversy thereafter arising out of * * * the refusal to perform the whole or any part thereof." This is familiar language; it refers to a controversy, which parties to a contract may easily contemplate, arising when a party to the contract, without denying that he made it, refuses performance; it does not mean a controversy arising out of the denial by one of the parties that he ever made any contract whatsoever.

It is clear then that, even assuming, arguendo, that a contract would be drawn containing an arbitration clause sufficiently broad to include a controversy as to whether the minds of the parties had ever met concerning the making of the very contract which embodies the arbitration clause, such a clause would not be within the Arbitration Act. Accordingly, it perhaps would not be immunized from the prestatutory rules inimical to arbitration, i.e., would not serve as the basis of a stay of the suit on the contract, leaving the parties to the arbitration called for by their agreement. Were the arbitration clause here sufficiently broad to call for arbitration of the dispute as to the existence of the charter party, it would, therefore, perhaps be arguable that it was entirely outside of the Act and, accordingly, irrelevant in the case before us; we need not consider that question, as we hold that the breadth of the arbitration clause is not so great and it is within the terms of Section 2 of the Act.

We conclude that it would be improper to submit to the arbitrators the issue of the making of the charter party.

But it does not follow that appellant was not entitled to a stay of the suit, under Section 3, until arbitration has been had as to the amount of the damages. Here it is important to differentiate between Sections 3 and 4 of the Act. Under Section 4, the proceeding—as the Supreme Court observed in Marine Transit Corp. v. Dreyfus, 284 U.S. 263, 278, 52 S.Ct. 166, 76 L.Ed. 516—is one for specific performance: One of the parties seeks "an order directing that * * * arbitration proceed in the manner provided for" in the arbitration clause or agreement. It may well be that in a proceeding under Section 4, there are open many of the usual defenses available in a suit for specific performance.[30] It would seem that a court, when exercising equity powers, should do so on the basis of a fully informed judgment as to all the circumstances. We recognize that some authorities have held to the contrary under similarly worded state arbitration statutes, interpreting them to require the courts automatically to decree specific performance without regard to the usual equitable considerations. It is difficult for us to believe that Congress intended us so to construe Section 4, although we do not here decide that question.[32] However that may be, the same equitable considerations should surely not be applicable when a defendant asks a stay pursuant to Section 3. For he is not then seeking specific performance (i.e., an order requiring that the parties proceed to arbitration) but merely a stay order of a kind long familiar in common law, equity and admiralty actions. His position is that when the court (to quote Section 3) is "satisfied that the issue involved in such suit * * * is referable to arbitration," the court must "stay the trial of the action until such arbitration has been had in accordance with the terms of the agreement." There is a well recognized distinction between such a stay and

---

30. Note the statement in the Congressional Committee's report: "An arbitration agreement is placed upon the same footing as other contracts, where it belongs." But no other contracts will be ordered to be specifically enforced where the customary equitable factors are absent. Other portions of that report, previously quoted, state that the purpose of the Act was to get rid of the effects of the earlier judicial hostility to arbitration contracts. To interpret the Act as precluding equitable considerations when a court is asked to order specific performance is to do far more than that.

32. Those sponsors of arbitration who insist that the valuable traditional powers of the equity courts are choked off under provisions like Section 4 are doing arbitration no real service. For where their position has been accepted, litigation—which the arbitration statutes are designed to reduce—is augmented. The more enthusiastic of those sponsors have thought of arbitration as a universal panacea. We doubt whether it will cure corns or bring general beatitude. Few panaceas work as well as advertised. Almost always those who propose one think solely of the disadvantages of an older method which they criticize, forget its advantages, and disregard evils which may attend the reform.

specific performance: The first merely arrests further action by the court itself in the suit until something outside the suit has occurred; but the court does not order that it shall be done. The second, through the exercise of discretionary equity powers, affirmatively orders that someone do (or refrain from doing) some act outside the suit.

... In the case at bar, so far as the arbitration was concerned, it was the first duty of the court, under Section 3, to determine whether there was an agreement to arbitrate and whether any of the issues raised in the suit were within the reach of that agreement. The appellant contested the existence of the charter party which contained that agreement, but also alternatively pleaded that, if it existed, then there should be a stay pending arbitration of the appropriate issues. We see no reason why a respondent should be precluded from thus pleading in the alternative.

... As Williston remarks: "A person who repudiates a contract wrongfully cannot sue upon it himself, but if he is sued upon it, he can be held liable only according to the terms of the contract. If, therefore, an arbitration clause amounts to a condition precedent to the defendant's promise to pay any insurance money, and such conditions are lawful, the defendant can be held liable only if that condition is performed, prevented or waived."

Arbitration under the charter party here was a condition precedent. At common law, or in admiralty, failure of a plaintiff to perform an ordinary condition precedent (unless excused) is the basis of a plea in bar....

The arbitration clause here was clearly broad enough to cover the issue of damages; "a clause of general arbitration does not cease to be within the statute when the dispute narrows down to damages alone."[36] It has been suggested that the arbitration clause calls for arbitrators who are "commercial men," that they are not appropriate persons to compute damages in this case where appellant has not merely breached but denied the existence of the charter party, and that, therefore, it must follow that the parties did not contemplate arbitration of such damages. But that argument is untenable, since it rests upon an unsound assumption, i.e., that damages are to be differently computed in those two kinds of situations. In truth, it is precisely this sort of case where arbitration of damages by "commercial men" may be peculiarly useful, as they are likely to be more familiar than the average lawyer who serves as special master with the relevant background of international shipping in the state of world affairs as of the period covered by the charter party.

There remains to be considered the language of Section 3 of the Act that, "on application," such a stay shall be granted "providing the applicant for the stay is not in default in proceeding with such arbitration." We take that proviso to refer to a party who, when requested, has refused to go to arbitration or who has refused to proceed with the hearing before the arbitrators once it has commenced. The appellant was never asked by

36. Shanferoke Coal & Supply Corp. v.   297, 299.
Westchester S. Corp., 2 Cir., 1934, 70 F.2d

appellee to proceed with the arbitration; indeed, it is the appellee who has objected to it. . . .

Accordingly, we conclude that the defendant here was not in default within the meaning of the proviso in Section 3. It follows that the district court should have stayed the suit, pending arbitration to determine the damages. . . .

The order of the district court is reversed and the cause is remanded with directions to proceed in accordance with the foregoing opinion.

* * *

Questions

1.   Compare the court's discussion of an arbitrator's ability to decide the validity of its enabling contractual clause in *Kulukundis* to a court's ability to determine its own jurisdiction. How do they differ? How are they similar? Should they be identical?

2.   When parties to a dispute disagree about whether a valid contract was formed, can a court decide the issue of contract formation without deciding the merits of the case? Consider the following hypothetical:

> Osborne discusses renting her recreational vehicle to Katsiff for one month, at a particular rate. Many details are discussed, including price, liability, and the fact that Katsiff wants the car on Monday, August 1 at 10:00 to begin a family vacation. Katsiff takes notes, but nothing is signed. After their discussions, Katsiff believes they have a deal. He shows up at Osborne's house on Monday to get the vehicle, but Osborne refuses to deliver it. Katsiff rents a comparable vehicle at a higher price and then sues Osborne for breach of promise to rent the vehicle. Osborne defends on the grounds that no valid contract was formed.

If the court finds there was a contract formed, has it also decided that Osborne is in breach? If it finds that no contract was formed, can it nonetheless find Osborne liable? Is this hypothetical distinguishable from the *Kulukundis Shipping* case?

3.   In the above hypothetical, suppose that the discussions between the parties included the issue of arbitration. Assume that they agreed that, should they have disagreements about the performance of the rental arrangement, they will submit the dispute to arbitration according to the AAA commercial arbitration rules. In such case, if a court decides that there was a valid contract, is the arbitration clause also valid? If so, can the arbitrator decide that no valid contract was made?

4.   Judge Frank's rendering of the history of judicial responses to arbitration concentrates on the interjurisdictional rivalry between courts and private tribunals. He offers a thorough critique of the "ouster of jurisdiction" rationale for the courts' restrictive approach. He only mentions Justice Story's opinion in the *Tobey* case in a footnote, even though Justice

Story was one of nineteenth century America's preeminent jurists. How well does he respond to the due process and equity arguments that Justice Story raised in the *Tobey* opinion?

* * *

2.   STATE VERSUS FEDERAL LAW

The Federal Arbitration Act declared arbitration agreements to be "valid, enforceable and irrevocable." It also called upon federal courts to enforce arbitration agreements by staying litigation in any suit referable to arbitration (Section 3), and by granting motions to compel recalcitrant parties to arbitrate disputes that they agreed to submit to arbitration. (Section 4). The Act, while expressly applicable to federal courts, left open many questions about the role of state law. For example, in a diversity case, is the issue of arbitration substantive or procedural for purposes of deciding whether or not to apply state substantive law under *Erie Railroad Co. v. Tompkins*? Do the provisions of the Act apply only to federal law issues in federal courts, or do they also apply to state law issues brought in federal courts pursuant to the courts' ancillary jurisdiction? Does the Act preempt conflicting state law for cases involving commerce and maritime transactions? If so, does it apply in state courts? Assuming there is preemption, does Section 3, which provides that suits brought in a *federal court* upon any issue referable to arbitration shall be stayed pending such arbitration, have any applicability in state courts? Does the exception in Section 2, which denies enforceability for arbitration agreements "upon such grounds as exist at law or in equity for the enforcement of any contract," call upon federal courts to apply state common law defenses to arbitration agreements?

The Supreme Court has addressed these issues and related issues over a forty-year period. The way in which these issues have been resolved has had significant ramifications for the role of arbitration in our civil litigation system. However, as the following cases demonstrate, the relationship between state and federal arbitration law is far from settled. There remain significant open questions and there are still vigorous dissenting views represented on the Court.

Bernhardt v. Polygraphic Company of America, Inc.

350 U.S. 198 (1956).

■ MR. JUSTICE DOUGLAS delivered the opinion of the Court.

This suit, removed from a Vermont court to the District Court on grounds of diversity of citizenship, was brought for damages for the discharge of petitioner under an employment contract. At the time the contract was made petitioner was a resident of New York. Respondent is a New York corporation. The contract was made in New York. Petitioner later became a resident of Vermont, where he was to perform his duties under the contract, and asserts his rights there.

The contract contains a provision that in case of any dispute the parties will submit the matter to arbitration under New York law by the American Arbitration Association, whose determination "shall be final and absolute." After the case had been removed to the District Court, respondent moved for a stay of the proceedings so that the controversy could go to arbitration in New York. The motion alleged that the law of New York governs the question whether the arbitration provision of the contract is binding.

The District Court ruled that under Erie R. Co. v. Tompkins, 304 U.S. 64, 58 S.Ct. 817, 82 L.Ed. 1188, the arbitration provision of the contract was governed by Vermont law and that the law of Vermont makes revocable an agreement to arbitrate at any time before an award is actually made. The District Court therefore denied the stay, 122 F.Supp. 733. The Court of Appeals reversed, 218 F.2d 948. The case is here on a petition for certiorari which we granted, 349 U.S. 943, 75 S.Ct. 873, because of the doubtful application by the Court of Appeals of Erie R. Co. v. Tompkins, supra.

A question under the United States Arbitration Act ... lies at the threshold of the case. Section 2 of that Act makes "valid, irrevocable, and enforceable" provisions for arbitration in certain classes of contracts;[1] and § 3 provides for a stay of actions in the federal courts of issues referable to arbitration under those contracts.[2] Section 2 makes "valid, irrevocable, and enforceable" only two types of contracts: those relating to a maritime transaction and those involving commerce. No maritime transaction is involved here. Nor does this contract evidence "a transaction involving commerce" within the meaning of § 2 of the Act. There is no showing that petitioner while performing his duties under the employment contract was working "in" commerce, was producing goods for commerce, or was engaging in activity that affected commerce, within the meaning of our decisions.[3]

---

1.   Section 2 provides: "A written provision in any maritime transaction or a contract evidencing a transaction involving commerce to settle by arbitration a controversy thereafter arising out of such contract or transaction, or the refusal to perform the whole or any part thereof, or an agreement in writing to submit to arbitration an existing controversy arising out of such a contract, transaction, or refusal, shall be valid, irrevocable, and enforceable, save upon such grounds as exist at law or in equity for the revocation of any contract."

2.   Section 3 provides: "If any suit or proceeding be brought in any of the courts of the United States upon any issue referable to arbitration under an agreement in writing for such arbitration, the court in which such suit is pending, upon being satisfied that the issue involved in such suit or proceeding is referable to arbitration under such an agreement, shall on application of one of the parties stay the trial of the action until such arbitration has been had in accordance with the terms of the agreement, providing the applicant for the stay is not in default in proceeding with such arbitration."

3.   Section 1 defines "commerce" as: " . . . commerce among the several States or with foreign nations, or in any Territory of the United States or in the District of Columbia, or between any such Territory and another, or between any such Territory and any State or foreign nation, or between the Dis-

The Court of Appeals went on to hold that in any event § 3 of the Act stands on its own footing. It concluded that while § 2 makes enforceable arbitration agreements in maritime transactions and in transactions involving commerce, § 3 covers all arbitration agreements even though they do not involve maritime transactions or transactions in commerce. We disagree with that reading of the Act. Sections 1, 2, and 3 are integral parts of a whole. To be sure, § 3 does not repeat the words "maritime transaction" or "transaction involving commerce", used in §§ 1 and 2. But §§ 1 and 2 define the field in which Congress was legislating. Since § 3 is a part of the regulatory scheme, we can only assume that the "agreement in writing" for arbitration referred to in § 3 is the kind of agreement which §§ 1 and 2 have brought under federal regulation. There is no intimation or suggestion in the Committee Reports that §§ 1 and 2 cover a narrower field than § 3. On the contrary, S.Rep. No. 536, 68th Cong., 1st Sess., p. 2, states that § 1 defines the contracts to which "the bill will be applicable." And H.R. Rep. No. 96, 68th Cong., 1st Sess., p. 1, states that one foundation of the new regulating measure is "the Federal control over interstate commerce and over admiralty." If respondent's contention is correct, a constitutional question might be presented. Erie R. Co. v. Tompkins indicated that Congress does not have the constitutional authority to make the law that is applicable to controversies in diversity of citizenship cases. Shanferoke Coal & Supply Corp. of Delaware v. Westchester Service Corp., 293 U.S. 449, 55 S.Ct. 313, 79 L.Ed. 583, applied the Federal Act in a diversity case. But that decision antedated Erie R. Co. v. Tompkins; and the Court did not consider the larger question presented here—that is, whether arbitration touched on substantive rights, which Erie R. Co. v. Tompkins held were governed by local law, or was a mere form of procedure within the power of the federal courts or Congress to prescribe. Our view, as will be developed, is that § 3, so read, would invade the local law field. We therefore read § 3 narrowly to avoid that issue. Federal Trade Commission v. American Tobacco Co., 264 U.S. 298, 307, 44 S.Ct. 336, 337, 68 L.Ed. 696. We conclude that the stay provided in § 3 reaches only those contracts covered by §§ 1 and 2.

The question remains whether, apart from the Federal Act, a provision of a contract providing for arbitration is enforceable in a diversity case.

The Court of Appeals, in disagreeing with the District Court as to the effect of an arbitration agreement under Erie R. Co. v. Tompkins, followed its earlier decision of Murray Oil Products Co. v. Mitsui & Co., 146 F.2d 381, 383, which held that, "Arbitration is merely a form of trial, to be adopted in the action itself, in place of the trial at common law: it is like a reference to a master, or an 'advisory trial' under Federal Rules of Civil Procedure . . .."

---

trict of Columbia and any State or Territory or foreign nation, but nothing herein contained shall apply to contracts of employment of seamen, railroad employees, or any other class of workers engaged in foreign or interstate commerce." Since no transaction involving commerce appears to be involved here, we do not reach the further question whether in any event petitioner would be included in "any other class of workers" within the exceptions of § 1 of the Act.

We disagree with that conclusion. We deal were with a right to recover that owes its existence to one of the States, not to the United States. The federal court enforces the state-created right by rules of procedure which it has acquired from the Federal Government and which therefore are not identical with those of the state courts. Yet, in spite of that difference in procedure, the federal court enforcing a state-created right in a diversity case is, as we said in Guaranty Trust Co. of New York v. York, 326 U.S. 99, 108, 65 S.Ct. 1464, 1469, 89 L.Ed. 2079, in substance "only another court of the State." The federal court therefore may not "substantially affect the enforcement of the right as given by the State." Id., 326 U.S. 109, 65 S.Ct. 1470. If the federal court allows arbitration where the state court would disallow it, the outcome of litigation might depend on the court-house where suit is brought. For the remedy by arbitration, whatever its merits or shortcomings, substantially affects the cause of action created by the State. The nature of the tribunal where suits are tried is an important part of the parcel of rights behind a cause of action. The change from a court of law to an arbitration panel may make a radical difference in ultimate result. Arbitration carries no right to trial by jury that is guaranteed both by the Seventh Amendment and by Ch. 1, Art. 12th, of the Vermont Constitution. Arbitrators do not have the benefit of judicial instruction on the law; they need not give their reasons for their results; the record of their proceedings is not as complete as it is in a court trial; and judicial review of an award is more limited than judicial review of a trial—all as discussed in Wilko v. Swan, 346 U.S. 427, 435–438, 74 S.Ct. 182, 186, 188, 98 L.Ed. 168.[4] We said in the York case that "The nub of the policy that underlies Erie R. Co. v. Tompkins is that for the same transaction the accident of a suit by a non-resident litigant in a federal court instead of in a State court a block away, should not lead to a substantially different result." 326 U.S. at 109, 65 S.Ct. 1470. There would in our judgment be a resultant discrimination if the parties suing on a Vermont cause of action in the federal court were remitted to arbitration, while those suing in the Vermont court could not be.

The District Court found that if the parties were in a Vermont court, the agreement to submit to arbitration would not be binding and could be revoked at any time before an award was made. He gave as his authority Mead's Adm'x v. Owen, 83 Vt. 132, 135, 74 A. 1058, 1059, and Sartwell v. Sowles, 72 Vt. 270, 277, 48 A. 11, 14, decided by the Supreme Court of Vermont. In the Owen case the court, in speaking of an agreement to arbitrate, held that ". . . either party may revoke the submission at any

---

4. Whether the arbitrators misconstrued a contract is not open to judicial review. The Hartbridge, 2 Cir., 62 F.2d 72. Questions of fault or neglect are solely for the arbitrators' consideration. James Richardson & Sons v. W. E. Hedger Transportation Corp., 2 Cir., 98 F.2d 55. Arbitrators are not bound by the rules of evidence.... They may draw on their personal knowledge in making an award. American Almond Products Co. v. Consolidated Pecan Sales Co., 2 Cir., 144 F.2d 448. ... Absent agreement of the parties, a written transcript of the proceedings is unnecessary. A. O. Andersen Trading Co. v. Brimberg. Swearing of witnesses may not be required. Application of Shapiro, supra. And the arbitrators need not disclose the facts or reasons behind their award. Shirley Silk Co. v. American Silk Mills, Inc., 257 App.Div. 375, 377, 13 N.Y.S.2d 309, 311.

time before the publication of an award.'' 83 Vt. at 135, 74 A. at 1059. That case was decided in 1910. But it was agreed on oral argument that there is no later authority from the Vermont courts, that no fracture in the rules announced in those cases has appeared in subsequent rulings or dicta, and that no legislative movement is under way in Vermont to change the result of those cases. Since the federal judge making those findings is from the Vermont bar, we give special weight to his statement of what the Vermont law is. . . . We agree with him that if arbitration could not be compelled in the Vermont courts, it should not be compelled in the Federal District Court. Were the question in doubt or deserving further canvass, we would of course remand the case to the Court of Appeals to pass on this question of Vermont law. But, as we have indicated, there appears to be no confusion in the Vermont decisions, no developing line of authorities that casts a shadow over the established ones, no dicta, doubts or ambiguities in the opinions of Vermont judges on the question, no legislative development that promises to undermine the judicial rule. We see no reason, therefore, to remand the case to the Court of Appeals to pass on this question of local law.

Respondent argues that since the contract was made in New York and the parties contracted for arbitration under New York law, New York arbitration law should be applied to the enforcement of the contract. A question of conflict of laws is tendered, a question that is also governed by Vermont law. See Klaxon Co. v. Stentor Electric Mfg. Co., 313 U.S. 487, 61 S.Ct. 1020, 85 L.Ed. 1477. It is not clear to some of us that the District Court ruled on that question. We mention it explicitly so that it will be open for consideration on remand of the cause to the District Court.

The judgment of the Court of Appeals is reversed and the cause is remanded to the District Court for proceedings in conformity with this opinion.

Reversed and remanded.

■ MR. JUSTICE FRANKFURTER, concurring.

It is my view that the judgment of the Court of Appeals should be reversed and the case remanded to that court and not to the District Court.

This action was brought in the Bennington County Court of the State of Vermont by petitioner, a citizen of Vermont, against respondent, a corporation of the State of New York. Respondent removed the case to the United States District Court for the District of Vermont. The subject matter of the litigation is a contract made between the parties in New York, and the sole basis of the jurisdiction of the District Court is diversity of citizenship. Not only was the contract made in New York, but the parties agreed to the following provision in it:

"Fourteenth: The parties hereto do hereby stipulate and agree that it is their intention and covenant that this agreement and performance hereunder and all suits and special proceedings hereunder be construed in accordance with and under and pursuant to the laws of the State of New York and that in any action special proceeding or other proceeding that may be brought arising out of, in connection with or by reason of this agreement, the laws of the State of New York shall be applicable and shall govern to the exclusion of the law of any other forum, without regard to the jurisdiction in which any action or special proceeding may be instituted.''

Respondent invoked another provision of the contract whereby disputes under the agreement were to be submitted to arbitration subject to the regulations of the American Arbitration Association and the pertinent provisions of the New York Arbitration Act, Civil Practice Act, § 1468 et seq. It did so by a motion to stay the proceeding in the District Court pending arbitration.

The District Court denied the stay because, on its reading of the Vermont cases, Vermont law, while recognizing the binding force of such an agreement by way of a suit for damages, does not allow specific performance or a stay pending arbitration. It rested on a decision rendered by the Supreme Court of Vermont in a bill for an accounting evidently between two Vermonters and relating wholly to a Vermont transaction, i.e., a controversy about personal property on a Vermont farm. Mead's Adm'x v. Owen, 83 Vt. 132, 74 A. 1058. This case was decided in 1910 and, in turn, relied on Aspinwall v. Tousey, 2 Tyler 328, decided in 1803, authorizing revocation of a submission to arbitration at any time before the publication of an award.

The Court of Appeals found it unnecessary to consider what the Vermont law was today, for it held that the arbitration provision did not concern a matter of ''substantive'' law, for which, in this diversity case, Vermont law would be controlling on the United States District Court sitting in Vermont. It held that the arbitration provision fell within the law of ''procedure'' governing an action in the federal court, whatever the source of the jurisdiction. So holding, the Court of Appeals found § 3 of the United States Arbitration Act, 9 U.S.C. § 3, applicable and, accordingly, directed the District Court to heed that Act and allow the matter to go to arbitration. 218 F.2d 948.

This Court explained in Guaranty Trust Co. of New York v. York, 326 U.S. 99, 65 S.Ct. 1464, 89 L.Ed. 2079, why the categories of ''substance'' and ''procedure'' are, in relation to the application of the doctrine of Erie R. Co. v. Tompkins, 304 U.S. 64, 58 S.Ct. 817, 82 L.Ed. 1188, less than self-defining. They are delusive. The intrinsic content of what is thought to be conveyed by those terms in the particular context of a particular litigation becomes the essential inquiry. This mode of approaching the problem has had several applications since the York decision. I agree with the Court's opinion that the differences between arbitral and judicial determination of a controversy under a contract sufficiently go to the merits of the outcome, and not merely because of the contingencies of different individuals passing on the same question, to make the matter one of ''substance'' in the sense relevant for Erie R. Co. v. Tompkins. In view of the ground that was taken in that case for its decision, it would raise a serious question of constitutional law whether Congress could subject to arbitration litigation in the federal courts which is there solely because it is ''between Citizens of different States'', U.S.Const. Art. III, § 2, in disregard of the law of the

State in which a federal court is sitting. Since the United States Arbitration Act of 1925 does not obviously apply to diversity cases, in the light of its terms and the relevant interpretive materials, avoidance of the constitutional question is for me sufficiently compelling to lead to a construction of the Act as not applicable to diversity cases....

Vermont law regarding such an arbitration agreement as the one before us, therefore, becomes decisive of the litigation. But what is Vermont law? One of the difficulties, of course, resulting from Erie R. Co. v. Tompkins, is that it is not always easy and sometimes difficult to ascertain what the governing state law is. The essence of the doctrine of that case is that the difficulties of ascertaining state law are fraught with less mischief than disregard of the basic nature of diversity jurisdiction, namely, the enforcement of state-created rights and state policies going to the heart of those rights. If Judge Gibson's statement of what is the contemporary Vermont law relevant to the arbitration provision now before him were determinative, that would be that. But the defendant is entitled to have the view of the Court of Appeals on Vermont law and cannot, under the Act of Congress, be foreclosed by the District Court's interpretation.

As long as there is diversity jurisdiction, "estimates" are necessarily often all that federal courts can make in ascertaining what the state court would rule to be its law.... This Court ought not to by-pass the Court of Appeals on an issue which, if the Court of Appeals had made a different estimate from the District Court's, of contemporaneous Vermont law regarding such a contract as the one before us, this Court, one can confidently say, would not have set its view of Vermont law against that of the Court of Appeals. For the mere fact that Vermont in 1910 restated its old law against denying equitable relief for breach of a promise to arbitrate a contract made under such Vermont law, is hardly a conclusive ground for attributing to the Vermont Supreme Court application of this equitable doctrine in 1956 to a contract made in New York with explicit agreement by the parties that the law of New York which allows such a stay as was here sought, New York Civil Practice Act, § 1451, should govern.... Law does change with times and circumstances, and not merely through legislative reforms. It is also to be noted that law is not restricted to what is found in Law Reports, or otherwise written. See Nashville, C. & St. L.R. Co. v. Browning, 310 U.S. 362, 369, 60 S.Ct. 968, 84 L.Ed. 1254. The Supreme Court of Vermont last spoke on this matter in 1910. The doctrine that it referred to was not a peculiar indigenous Vermont rule. The attitude reflected by that decision nearly half a century ago was the current traditional judicial hostility against ousting courts, as the phrase ran, of their jurisdiction.... To be sure, a vigorous legislative movement got under way in the 1920's expressive of a broadened outlook of view on this subject. But courts do not always wait for legislation to find a judicial doctrine outmoded....

Surely in the light of all that has happened since 1910 in the general field of the law of arbitration, it is not for us to assume that the Court of Appeals, if it had that question for consideration, could not have found that the law of Vermont today does not require disregard of a provision of a contract made in New York, with a purposeful desire to have the law of New York govern, to accomplish a result that today may be deemed to be a general doctrine of the law. Of course, if the Court of Appeals, versed in the general jurisprudence of Vermont and having among its members a Vermont lawyer, should find that the Vermont court would, despite the New York incidents of the contract, apply Vermont law and that it is the habit of the Vermont court to adhere to its precedents and to leave changes to the legislature, it would not be for the federal court to gainsay that policy. I am not suggesting what the Court of Appeals' answer to these questions would be, still less what it should be. I do maintain that the defendant does have the right to have the judgment of the Court of Appeals on that question and that it is not for us to deny him that right.

I would remand the case to the Court of Appeals for its determination of Vermont law on matters which the basis of its decision heretofore rendered it needless to consider.

■ [MR. JUSTICE HARLAN's separate concurrence and MR. JUSTICE BURTON's dissenting opinion have been omitted.]

* * *

Questions

1.   According to Justice Douglas, what is the constitutional basis of the FAA? Can his view be squared with that of Julius Cohen, who drafted the statute, as set forth in the Cohen and Dayton article, above. What is the constitutional problem with the Respondent's position in *Bernhardt*, to which Justice Douglas alludes?

2.   If Douglas had decided that the FAA is procedural rather than substantive, what would have been the outcome of this case?

3.   Once the Court decided that the FAA is substantive for purposes of *Erie*, do the provisions of the Act apply in diversity cases?

* * *

Southland Corporation v. Keating

465 U.S. 1, 104 S.Ct. 852 (1984).

■ CHIEF JUSTICE BURGER delivered the opinion of the Court.

This case presents the questions (a) whether the California Franchise Investment Law, which invalidates certain arbitration agreements covered by the Federal Arbitration Act, violates the Supremacy Clause and (b) whether arbitration under the Federal Act is impaired when a class action structure is imposed on the process by the state courts.

I

Appellant Southland Corporation is the owner and franchisor of 7–Eleven convenience stores. Southland's standard franchise agreement provides each franchisee with a license to use certain registered trademarks, a lease or sublease of a convenience store owned or leased by Southland, inventory financing, and assistance in advertising and merchandising. The franchisees operate the stores, supply bookkeeping data, and pay Southland a fixed percentage of gross profits. The franchise agreement also contains the following provision requiring arbitration:

> "Any controversy or claim arising out of or relating to this Agreement or the breach thereof shall be settled by arbitration in accordance with the Rules of the American Arbitration Association ... and judgment upon any award rendered by the arbitrator may be entered in any court having jurisdiction thereof."

Appellees are 7–Eleven franchisees. Between September 1975 and January 1977, several appellees filed individual actions against Southland in California Superior Court alleging, among other things, fraud, oral misrepresentation, breach of contract, breach of fiduciary duty, and violation of the disclosure requirements of the California Franchise Investment Law, Cal.Corp.Code § 31000 et seq. (West 1977). Southland's answer, in all but one of the individual actions, included the affirmative defense of failure to arbitrate.

In May 1977, appellee Keating filed a class action against Southland on behalf of a class that assertedly includes approximately 800 California franchisees. Keating's principal claims were substantially the same as those asserted by the other franchisees. After the various actions were consolidated, Southland petitioned to compel arbitration of the claims in all cases, and appellees moved for class certification.

The Superior Court granted Southland's motion to compel arbitration of all claims except those claims based on the Franchise Investment Law. The court did not pass on appellees' request for class certification. Southland appealed from the order insofar as it excluded from arbitration the claims based on the California statute. Appellees filed a petition for a writ of mandamus or prohibition in the California Court of Appeal arguing that the arbitration should proceed as a class action.

The California Court of Appeal reversed the trial court's refusal to compel arbitration of appellees' claims under the Franchise Investment Law. 109 Cal.App.3d 784, 167 Cal.Rptr. 481 (1980). That court interpreted the arbitration clause to require arbitration of all claims asserted under the Franchise Investment Law, and construed the Franchise Investment Law not to invalidate such agreements to arbitrate. Alternatively, the court concluded that if the Franchise Investment Law rendered arbitration agreements involving commerce unenforceable, it would conflict with § 2 of the Federal Arbitration Act, 9 U.S.C. § 2, and therefore be invalid under the Supremacy Clause. 167 Cal.Rptr. at 493–494. The Court of Appeal also determined that there was no "insurmountable obstacle" to conducting an arbitration on a classwide basis, and issued a writ of mandate directing the trial court to conduct class certification proceedings. Id., at 492.

The California Supreme Court, by a vote of 4–2, reversed the ruling that claims asserted under the Franchise Investment Law are arbitrable. Keating v. Supreme Court of Alameda County, 31 Cal.3d 584, 183 Cal.Rptr. 360, 645 P.2d 1192 (1982). The California Supreme Court interpreted the Franchise Investment Law to require judicial consideration of claims brought under that statute and concluded that the California statute did not contravene the federal Act. Id., at 604, 183 Cal.Rptr., at 371–372, 645 P.2d, at 1203–1204. The court also remanded the case to the trial court for consideration of appellees' request for classwide arbitration.

We postponed consideration of the question of jurisdiction pending argument on the merits. 459 U.S. 1101 (1983). We reverse in part and dismiss in part . . . .

III

As previously noted, the California Franchise Investment Law provides:

> "Any condition, stipulation or provision purporting to bind any person acquiring any franchise to waive compliance with any provision of this law or any rule or order hereunder is void." Cal.Corp.Code § 31512 (West 1977).

The California Supreme Court interpreted this statute to require judicial consideration of claims brought under the State statute and accordingly refused to enforce the parties' contract to arbitrate such claims. So interpreted the California Franchise Investment Law directly conflicts with § 2 of the Federal Arbitration Act and violates the Supremacy Clause.

In enacting § 2 of the federal Act, Congress declared a national policy favoring arbitration and withdrew the power of the states to require a judicial forum for the resolution of claims which the contracting parties agreed to resolve by arbitration. The Federal Arbitration Act provides:

> "A written provision in any maritime transaction or a contract evidencing a transaction involving commerce to settle by arbitration a controversy thereafter arising out of such contract or transaction, or the refusal to perform the whole or any part thereof, or an agreement in writing to submit to arbitration an existing controversy arising out of such a contract, transaction, or refusal, shall be valid, irrevocable, and enforceable, save upon such grounds as exist at law or in equity for the revocation of any contract." 9 U.S.C. § 2.

Congress has thus mandated the enforcement of arbitration agreements.

We discern only two limitations on the enforceability of arbitration provisions governed by the Federal Arbitration Act: they must be part of a written maritime contract or a contract "evidencing a transaction involving commerce" and such clauses may be revoked upon "grounds as exist at law or in equity for the revocation of any contract." We see nothing in the Act indicating that the broad principle of enforceability is subject to any additional limitations under State law.

The Federal Arbitration Act rests on the authority of Congress to enact substantive rules under the Commerce Clause. In Prima Paint Corp. v. Flood & Conklin Manufacturing Corp., 388 U.S. 395, 87 S.Ct. 1801, 18 L.Ed.2d 1270 (1967), the Court examined the legislative history of the Act and concluded that the statute "is based upon ... the incontestable federal foundations of 'control over interstate commerce and over admiralty.' " Id., at 405, 87 S.Ct., at 1806 (quoting H.R.Rep. No. 96, 68th Cong., 1st Sess. 1 (1924)). The contract in Prima Paint, as here, contained an arbitration clause. One party in that case alleged that the other had committed fraud in the inducement of the contract, although not of arbitration clause in particular, and sought to have the claim of fraud adjudicated in federal court. The Court held that, notwithstanding a contrary state rule, consideration of a claim of fraud in the inducement of a contract "is for the arbitrators and not for the courts," 388 U.S., at 400, 87 S.Ct., at 1804. The Court relied for this holding on Congress' broad power to fashion substantive rules under the Commerce Clause.

At least since 1824 Congress' authority under the Commerce Clause has been held plenary. Gibbons v. Ogden, 22 U.S. 1, 196, 9 Wheat. 1, 196, 6 L.Ed. 23 (1824). In the words of Chief Justice Marshall, the authority of Congress is "the power to regulate; that is, to prescribe the rule by which commerce is to be governed." Ibid. The statements of the Court in Prima Paint that the Arbitration Act was an exercise of the Commerce Clause power clearly implied that the substantive rules of the Act were to apply in state as well as federal courts. As Justice Black observed in his dissent, when Congress exercises its authority to enact substantive federal law under the Commerce Clause, it normally creates rules that are enforceable in state as well as federal courts. Prima Paint, 388 U.S., at 420, 87 S.Ct., at 1814 (Black, J., dissenting) ....

Although the legislative history is not without ambiguities, there are strong indications that Congress had in mind something more than making arbitration agreements enforceable only in the federal courts. The House Report plainly suggests the more comprehensive objectives:

> "The purpose of this bill is to make valid and enforceable agreements for arbitration contained *in contracts involving interstate commerce* or within the jurisdiction or [sic] admiralty, *or* which may be the subject of litigation in the Federal courts." H.R.Rep. No. 96, 68th Cong., 1st Sess. 1 (1924) (Emphasis added.)

This broader purpose can also be inferred from the reality that Congress would be less likely to address a problem whose impact was confined to federal courts than a problem of large significance in the field of commerce. The Arbitration Act sought to "overcome the rule of equity, that equity will not specifically enforce any arbitration agreement." Hearing on S. 4214 Before a Subcomm. of the Senate Comm. on the Judiciary, 67th Cong., 4th Sess. 6 (1923) (Senate Hearing) (remarks of Sen. Walsh). The House Report accompanying the bill stated:

"The need for the law arises from ... the jealousy of the English courts for their own jurisdiction.... This jealousy survived for so lon[g] a period that the principle became firmly embedded in the English common law and was adopted with it by the American courts. The courts have felt that the precedent was too strongly fixed to be overturned without legislative enactment...." H.R.Rep. No. 96, supra, 1–2.

Surely this makes clear that the House Report contemplated a broad reach of the Act, unencumbered by state law constraints. As was stated in Metro Industrial Painting Corp. v. Terminal Construction Corp., 287 F.2d 382, 387 (CA2 1961) (Lumbard, concurring), "the purpose of the act was to assure those who desired arbitration and whose contracts related to interstate commerce that their expectations would not be undermined by federal judges, or ... by state courts or legislatures." Congress also showed its awareness of the widespread unwillingness of state courts to enforce arbitration agreements, e.g., Senate Hearing, supra, at 8, and that such courts were bound by state laws inadequately providing for

"technical arbitration by which, if you agree to arbitrate under the method provided by the statute, you have an arbitration by statute[;] but [the statutes] ha[d] nothing to do with validating the contract to arbitrate." Ibid.

The problems Congress faced were therefore twofold: the old common law hostility toward arbitration, and the failure of state arbitration statutes to mandate enforcement of arbitration agreements. To confine the scope of the Act to arbitrations sought to be enforced in federal courts would frustrate what we believe Congress intended to be a broad enactment appropriate in scope to meet the large problems Congress was addressing.

JUSTICE O'CONNOR argues that Congress viewed the Arbitration Act "as a procedural statute, applicable only in federal courts." Post, at 25. If it is correct that Congress sought only to create a procedural remedy in the federal courts, there can be no explanation for the express limitation in the Arbitration Act to contracts "involving commerce." 9 U.S.C. § 2. For example, when Congress has authorized this Court to prescribe the rules of procedure in the federal Courts of Appeals, District Courts, and bankruptcy courts, it has not limited the power of the Court to prescribe rules applicable only to causes of action involving commerce. See, e.g., 28 U.S.C. §§ 2072, 2075, 2076 (1976). We would expect that if Congress, in enacting the Arbitration Act, was creating what it thought to be a procedural rule applicable only in federal courts, it would not so limit the Act to transactions involving commerce. On the other hand, Congress would need to call on the Commerce Clause if it intended the Act to apply in state courts. Yet at the same time, its reach would be limited to transactions involving interstate commerce. We therefore view the "involving commerce" requirement in § 2, not as an inexplicable limitation on the power of the federal courts, but as a necessary qualification on a statute intended to apply in state and federal courts.

Under the interpretation of the Arbitration Act urged by JUSTICE O'CONNOR, claims brought under the California Franchise Investment Law are not arbitrable when they are raised in state court. Yet it is clear beyond question that if this suit had been brought as a diversity action in a federal district court, the arbitration clause would have been enforceable.[7] Prima Paint, supra. The interpretation given to the Arbitration Act by the California Supreme Court would therefore encourage and reward forum shopping. We are unwilling to attribute to Congress the intent, in drawing on the comprehensive powers of the Commerce Clause, to create a right to enforce an arbitration contract and yet make the right dependent for its enforcement on the particular forum in which it is asserted. And since the overwhelming proportion of all civil litigation in this country is in the state courts, we cannot believe Congress intended to limit the Arbitration Act to disputes subject only to *federal* court jurisdiction.[9] Such an interpretation would frustrate Congressional intent to place "[a]n arbitration agreement ... upon the same footing as other contracts, where it belongs." H.R.Rep. No. 96, supra, 1.

In creating a substantive rule applicable in state as well as federal courts,[10] Congress intended to foreclose state legislative attempts to undercut the enforceability of arbitration agreements. We hold that § 31512 of the California Franchise Investment Law violates the Supremacy Clause....

It is so ordered.

■ JUSTICE STEVENS, concurring in part and dissenting in part.

The Court holds that an arbitration clause that is enforceable in an action in a federal court is equally enforceable if the action is brought in a

---

7. Appellees contend that the arbitration clause, which provides for the arbitration of "any controversy or claim arising out of or relating to this Agreement or the breach hereof," does not cover their claims under the California Franchise Investment Law. We find the language quoted above broad enough to cover such claims. Cf. Prima Paint, supra, 388 U.S., at 403–404, 406, 87 S.Ct., at 1805–1806, 1807 (finding nearly identical language to cover a claim that a contract was induced by fraud).

9. While the Federal Arbitration Act creates federal substantive law requiring the parties to honor arbitration agreements, it does not create any independent federal-question jurisdiction under 28 U.S.C. § 1331 (1976) or otherwise. Moses H. Cone, 103 S.Ct., at 942 n. 32. This seems implicit in the provisions in § 3 for a stay by a "court in which such suit is pending" and in § 4 that enforcement may be ordered by "any United States district court which, save for such agreement, would have jurisdiction under Title 28, in a civil action or in admiralty of the subject matter of a suit arising out of the controversy between the parties." Ibid.; Prima Paint, supra, 388 U.S., at 420 and n. 24, 87 S.Ct., at 1814 (Black, J., dissenting); Krauss Bros. Lumber Co. v. Louis Bossert & Sons, Inc., 62 F.2d 1004, 1006 (CA2 1933) (L. Hand, J.)

10. The contention is made that the Court's interpretation of § 2 of the Act renders §§ 3 and 4 "largely superfluous." Post, at 869, n. 20. This misreads our holding and the Act. In holding that the Arbitration Act preempts a state law that withdraws the power to enforce arbitration agreements, we do not hold that §§ 3 and 4 of the Arbitration Act apply to proceedings in state courts. Section 4, for example, provides that the Federal Rules of Civil Procedure apply in proceedings to compel arbitration. The Federal Rules do not apply in such state court proceedings.

state court. I agree with that conclusion. Although Justice O'CONNOR's review of the legislative history of the Federal Arbitration Act demonstrates that the 1925 Congress that enacted the statute viewed the statute as essentially procedural in nature, I am persuaded that the intervening developments in the law compel the conclusion that the Court has reached. I am nevertheless troubled by one aspect of the case that seems to trouble none of my colleagues.

For me it is not "clear beyond question that if this suit had been brought as a diversity action in a Federal District Court, the arbitration clause would have been enforceable." Ante, at 15. The general rule prescribed by § 2 of the Federal Arbitration Act is that arbitration clauses in contracts involving interstate transactions are enforceable as a matter of federal law. That general rule, however, is subject to an exception based on "such grounds as exist at law or in equity for the revocation of any contract." I believe that exception leaves room for the implementation of certain substantive state policies that would be undermined by enforcing certain categories of arbitration clauses.

The exercise of State authority in a field traditionally occupied by State law will not be deemed preempted by a federal statute unless that was the clear and manifest purpose of Congress. Ray v. Atlantic Richfield Co., 435 U.S. 151, 157, 98 S.Ct. 988, 994, 55 L.Ed.2d 179 (1978); see generally, Hamilton, The Federalist No. 32, 200 (Van Doren Ed.1945). Moreover, even where a federal statute does displace State authority, it "rarely occupies a legal field completely, totally excluding all participation by the legal systems of the states.... Federal legislation, on the whole, has been conceived and drafted on an ad hoc basis to accomplish limited objectives. It builds upon legal relationships established by the states, altering or supplanting them only so far as necessary for the special purpose." P. Bator, P. Mishkin, D. Shapiro, & H. Wechsler, Hart and Wechsler's The Federal Courts and the Federal System 470–471 (2d ed. 1973).

The limited objective of the Federal Arbitration Act was to abrogate the general common law rule against specific enforcement of arbitration agreements, S.Rep. No. 536, 68th Cong., 1st Sess., 2–3 (1924), and a state statute which merely codified the general common law rule—either directly by employing the prior doctrine of revocability or indirectly by declaring all such agreements void—would be preempted by the Act. However, beyond this conclusion, which seems compelled by the language of § 2 and case law concerning the Act, it is by no means clear that Congress intended entirely to displace State authority in this field. Indeed, while it is an understatement to say that "the legislative history of the ... Act ... reveals little awareness on the part of Congress that state law might be affected," it must surely be true that given the lack of a "clear mandate from Congress as to the extent to which state statutes and decisions are to be superseded, we must be cautious in construing the act lest we excessively encroach on the powers which Congressional policy, if not the Constitution, would reserve to the states." Metro Industrial Painting Corp. v. Terminal Construction Co., 287 F.2d 382, 386 (CA2 1961) (Lumbard, C.J., concurring).

The textual basis in the Act for avoiding such encroachment is the clause of § 2 which provides that arbitration agreements are subject to revocation on such grounds as exist at law or in equity for the revocation of any contract. The Act, however, does not define what grounds for revocation may be permissible, and hence it would appear that the judiciary must fashion the limitations as a matter of federal common law. Cf. Textile Workers v. Lincoln Mills, 353 U.S. 448, 77 S.Ct. 912, 1 L.Ed.2d 972 (1957). In doing so, we must first recognize that as the " 'saving clause' in § 2 indicates, the purpose of Congress in 1925 was to make arbitration agreements as enforceable as other contracts, but not more so." Prima Paint Corp. v. Flood & Conklin Mfg. Co., 388 U.S. 395, 404 n. 12, 87 S.Ct. 1801, 1806 n. 12, 18 L.Ed.2d 1270 (1967); see also, H.R.Rep. No. 96, 68th Cong., 1st Sess. 1 (1924). The existence of a federal statute enunciating a substantive federal policy does not necessarily require the inexorable application of a uniform federal rule of decision notwithstanding the differing conditions which may exist in the several States and regardless of the decisions of the States to exert police powers as they deem best for the welfare of their citizens.... Indeed, the lower courts generally look to State law regarding questions of formation of the arbitration agreement under § 2, see, e.g., Comprehensive Merchandising Catalogs, Inc. v. Madison Sales Corp., 521 F.2d 1210 (CA7 1975), which is entirely appropriate so long as the state rule does not conflict with the policy of § 2.

A contract which is deemed void is surely revocable at law or in equity, and the California legislature has declared all conditions purporting to waive compliance with the protections of the Franchise Investment Law, including but not limited to arbitration provisions, void as a matter of public policy. Given the importance to the State of franchise relationships, the relative disparity in the bargaining positions between the franchisor and the franchisee, and the remedial purposes of the California Act, I believe this declaration of State policy is entitled to respect.

Congress itself struck a similar balance in § 14 of the Securities Act of 1933, 15 U.S.C. § 77n, and did not find it necessary to amend the Federal Arbitration Act. Rather, this Court held that the Securities Act provision invalidating arbitration agreements in certain contexts could be reconciled with the general policy favoring enforcement of arbitration agreements. Wilko v. Swan, 346 U.S. 427, 74 S.Ct. 182, 98 L.Ed. 168 (1953). Repeals by implication are of course not favored, and we did not suggest that Congress had intended to repeal or modify the substantive scope of the Arbitration Act in passing the Securities Act. Instead, we exercised judgment, scrutinizing the policies of the Arbitration Act and their applicability in the special context of the remedial legislation at issue, and found the Arbitration Act inapplicable. We have exercised such judgment in other cases concerning the scope of the Arbitration Act, and have focused not on sterile generalization, but rather on the substance of the transaction at issue, the nature of the relationship between the parties to the agreement, and the purpose of the regulatory scheme. See, e.g., Scherk v. Alberto–Culver Co., 417 U.S. 506, 94 S.Ct. 2449, 41 L.Ed.2d 270 (1974), rev'g, 484 F.2d 611 (CA7 1973); see also, id., 484 F.2d, at 615–620 (Stevens, Circuit Judge, dissenting).

Surely the general language of the Arbitration Act that arbitration agreements are valid does not mean that all such agreements are valid irrespective of their purpose or effect. See generally, Paramount Famous Lasky Corp. v. United States, 282 U.S. 30, 51 S.Ct. 42, 75 L.Ed. 145 (1930) (holding arbitration agreement void as a restraint of trade).

We should not refuse to exercise independent judgment concerning the conditions under which an arbitration agreement, generally enforceable under the Act, can be held invalid as contrary to public policy simply because the source of the substantive law to which the arbitration agreement attaches is a State rather than the Federal Government. I find no evidence that Congress intended such a double standard to apply, and I would not lightly impute such an intent to the 1925 Congress which enacted the Arbitration Act.

A state policy excluding wage claims from arbitration, cf. Merrill Lynch, Pierce, Fenner & Smith v. Ware, 414 U.S. 117, 94 S.Ct. 383, 38 L.Ed.2d 348 (1973), or a state policy of providing special protection for franchisees, such as that expressed in California's Franchise Investment Law, can be recognized without impairing the basic purposes of the federal statute. Like the majority of the California Supreme Court, I am not persuaded that Congress intended the pre-emptive effect of this statute to be "so unyielding as to require enforcement of an agreement to arbitrate a dispute over the application of a regulatory statute which a state legislature, in conformity with analogous federal policy, has decided should be left to judicial enforcement." App. to Juris. Statement 18a.

Thus, although I agree with most of the Court's reasoning and specifically with its jurisdictional holdings, I respectfully dissent from its conclusion concerning the enforceability of the arbitration agreement. On that issue, I would affirm the judgment of the California Supreme Court.

■ JUSTICE O'CONNOR with whom JUSTICE REHNQUIST joins, dissenting.

Section 2 of the Federal Arbitration Act (FAA), 9 U.S.C. § 2, provides that a written arbitration agreement "shall be valid, irrevocable, and enforceable, save upon such grounds as exist at law or in equity for the revocation of any contract." § 2 does not, on its face, identify which judicial forums are bound by its requirements or what procedures govern its enforcement. The FAA deals with these matters in §§ 3 and 4. § 3 provides:

> "If any suit or proceeding be brought *in any of the courts of the United States* upon any issue referable to arbitration ... the court ... shall on application of one of the parties stay the trial of the action until such arbitration has been had in accordance with the terms of the agreement...."[2]

§ 4 specifies that a party aggrieved by another's refusal to arbitrate

> "may petition *any United States district court* which, save for such agreement, would have jurisdiction under Title 28, in a civil action or

---

2. 9 U.S.C. § 3 (emphasis added).

in admiralty of the subject matter ... for an order directing that such arbitration proceed in the manner provided for in such agreement...."[3]

Today, the Court takes the facial silence of § 2 as a license to declare that state as well as federal courts must apply § 2. In addition, though this is not spelled out in the opinion, the Court holds that in enforcing this newly-discovered federal right state courts must follow procedures specified in § 3. The Court's decision is impelled by an understandable desire to encourage the use of arbitration, but it utterly fails to recognize the clear congressional intent underlying the FAA. Congress intended to require federal, not state, courts to respect arbitration agreements.

I

The FAA (originally the "United States Arbitration Act") was enacted in 1925. As demonstrated below, infra, at 24–29, Congress thought it was exercising its power to dictate either procedure or "general federal law" in federal courts. The issue presented here is the result of three subsequent decisions of this Court.

In 1938 this Court decided Erie Railroad Co. v. Tompkins, 304 U.S. 64, 58 S.Ct. 817, 82 L.Ed. 1188. Erie denied the federal government the power to create substantive law solely by virtue of the Article III power to control federal court jurisdiction. Eighteen years later the Court decided Bernhardt v. Polygraphic Co., 350 U.S. 198, 76 S.Ct. 273, 100 L.Ed. 199 (1956). Bernhardt held that the duty to arbitrate a contract dispute is outcome-determinative—i.e. "substantive"—and therefore a matter normally governed by state law in federal diversity cases.

Bernhardt gave rise to concern that the FAA could thereafter constitutionally be applied only in federal court cases arising under federal law, not in diversity cases.[4] In Prima Paint v. Flood & Conklin, 388 U.S. 395, 404–405, 87 S.Ct. 1801, 1806–1807, 18 L.Ed.2d 1270 (1967), we addressed that concern, and held that the FAA may constitutionally be applied to proceedings in a federal diversity court. The FAA covers only contracts involving interstate commerce or maritime affairs, and Congress "plainly has the power to legislate" in that area. 388 U.S., at 405, 87 S.Ct., at 1807.

Nevertheless, the Prima Paint decision "carefully avoided any explicit endorsement of the view that the Arbitration Act embodied substantive policies that were to be applied to all contracts within its scope, whether sued on in state or federal courts." P. Bator, P. Mishkin, D. Shapiro, & H. Wechsler, Hart and Wechsler's The Federal Courts and the Federal System 731–732 (2d ed. 1973). Today's case is the first in which this Court has had

3. 9 U.S.C. § 4 (emphasis added). § 9, which addresses the enforcement of arbitration awards, is also relevant. "If no court is specified in the agreement of the parties, then such application may be made to the *United States court in and for the district* *within which such award was made....*" 9 U.S.C. § 9 (emphasis added).

4. Justice Frankfurter made precisely this suggestion in Bernhardt. 350 U.S., at 208, 76 S.Ct., at 279 (Frankfurter, J., concurring).

occasion to determine whether the FAA applies to state court proceedings. One statement on the subject did appear in Moses H. Cone Memorial Hospital v. Mercury Construction Corp., 460 U.S. 1 (1983), but that case involved a federal, not a state, court proceeding; its dictum concerning the law applicable in state courts was wholly unnecessary to its holding.

II

The majority opinion decides three issues. First, it holds that § 2 creates federal substantive rights that must be enforced by the state courts. Second, though the issue is not raised in this case, the Court states, ante, at 15–16, n. 9, that § 2 substantive rights may not be the basis for invoking federal court jurisdiction under 28 U.S.C. § 1331. Third, the Court reads § 2 to require state courts to enforce § 2 rights using procedures that mimic those specified for federal courts by FAA §§ 3 and 4. The first of these conclusions is unquestionably wrong as a matter of statutory construction; the second appears to be an attempt to limit the damage done by the first; the third is unnecessary and unwise.

A

One rarely finds a legislative history as unambiguous as the FAA's. That history establishes conclusively that the 1925 Congress viewed the FAA as a procedural statute, applicable only in federal courts, derived, Congress believed, largely from the federal power to control the jurisdiction of the federal courts.

In 1925 Congress emphatically believed arbitration to be a matter of "procedure." At hearings on the Act congressional subcommittees were told: "The theory on which you do this is that you have the right to tell the Federal courts how to proceed." The House Report on the FAA stated: "Whether an agreement for arbitration shall be enforced or not is a question of procedure...."[8] On the floor of the House Congressman Graham assured his fellow members that the FAA

> "does not involve any new principle of law except to provide a simple method ... in order to give enforcement.... It creates no new legislation, grants no new rights, except a remedy to enforce an agreement in commercial contracts and in admiralty contracts."[9]

A month after the Act was signed into law the American Bar Association Committee that had drafted and pressed for passage of the federal legislation wrote:

---

8. H.R.Rep. No. 96, 68th Cong., 1st Sess. 1 (1924). To similar effect, the Senate Report noted that the New York statute, after which the FAA was patterned, had been upheld against constitutional attack the previous year in Red Cross Line v. Atlantic Fruit Co., 264 U.S. 109, 44 S.Ct. 274, 68 L.Ed. 582 (1924). S.Rep. No. 536, 68th Cong., 1st Sess. 3 (1924). In Red Cross Justice Brandeis based the Court's approval of the New York statute on the fact that the statute effected no change in the substantive law.

9. 65 Cong.Rec. 1931 (1924).

"The statute establishes a procedure in the Federal courts for the enforcement of arbitration agreements.... A Federal statute providing for the enforcement of arbitration agreements does relate solely to procedure in the Federal courts.... [W]hether or not an arbitration agreement is to be enforced is a question of the law of procedure and is determined by the law of the jurisdiction wherein the remedy is sought. That the enforcement of arbitration contracts is within the law of procedure as distinguished from substantive law is well settled by the decisions of our courts."[10]

Since Bernhardt, a right to arbitration has been characterized as "substantive," and that holding is not challenged here. But Congress in 1925 did not characterize the FAA as this Court did in 1956. Congress *believed* that the FAA established nothing more than a rule of procedure, a rule therefore applicable only in the federal courts.

If characterizing the FAA as procedural was not enough, the draftsmen of the Act, the House Report, and the early commentators all flatly stated that the Act was intended to affect only federal court proceedings. Mr. Cohen, the American Bar Association member who drafted the bill, assured two congressional subcommittees in joint hearings:

"Nor can it be said that the Congress of the United States, *directing its own courts* ..., would infringe upon the provinces or prerogatives of the States.... [T]he question of the enforcement relates to the law of remedies and not to substantive law. The rule must be changed for the jurisdiction in which the agreement is sought to be enforced.... There is no disposition therefore by means of the Federal bludgeon to force an individual State into an unwilling submission to arbitration enforcement."[12]

The House Report on the FAA unambiguously stated: "Before [arbitration] contracts could be enforced in the Federal courts ... this law is essential. The bill declares that such agreements shall be recognized and enforced by the courts of the United States."

Yet another indication that Congress did not intend the FAA to govern state court proceedings is found in the powers Congress relied on in passing the Act. The FAA might have been grounded on Congress's powers to regulate interstate and maritime affairs, since the Act extends only to contracts in those areas. There are, indeed, references in the legislative history to the corresponding federal powers. More numerous, however, are the references to Congress's pre-Erie power to prescribe "general law"

---

10. Committee on Commerce, Trade and Commercial Law, The United States Arbitration Law and its Application, 11 A.B.A.J. 153, 154–155 (1925). See also Cohen & Dayton, The New Federal Arbitration Law, 12 Va.L.Rev. 265, 275–276 (1926).

12. Joint Hearing 39–40 (emphasis added). "The primary purpose of the statute is to make enforcible in the Federal courts such agreements for arbitration...." Id., at 38 (statement of Mr. Cohen). See also Senate Hearing 2 ("The bill follows the lines of the New York arbitration law applying it to fields wherein there is Federal jurisdiction").

applicable in all federal courts.[14] At the congressional hearings, for example: "Congress rests solely upon its power to prescribe the jurisdiction and duties of the Federal courts."[15] And in the House Report:

> "The matter is properly the subject of Federal action. Whether an agreement for arbitration shall be enforced or not is a question of procedure to be determined by the law court in which the proceeding is brought and not one of substantive law to be determined by the law of the forum in which the contract is made...."

Plainly, a power derived from Congress's Article III control over federal court jurisdiction would not by any flight of fancy permit Congress to control proceedings in state courts.

The foregoing cannot be dismissed as "ambiguities" in the legislative history. It is accurate to say that the entire history contains only one ambiguity, and that appears in the single sentence of the House Report cited by the Court ante, at 12–13. That ambiguity, however, is definitively resolved elsewhere in the same House Report, see supra, at 27, and throughout the rest of the legislative history.

B

The structure of the FAA itself runs directly contrary to the reading the Court today gives to § 2. §§ 3 and 4 are the implementing provisions of the Act, and they expressly apply only to federal courts. § 4 refers to the "United States district court[s]," and provides that it can be invoked only in a court that has jurisdiction under Title 28 of the United States Code. As originally enacted, § 3 referred, in the same terms as § 4, to "courts [or court] of the United States." There has since been a minor amendment in § 4's phrasing, but no substantive change in either section's limitation to federal courts.

None of this Court's prior decisions has authoritatively construed the Act otherwise. It bears repeating that both Prima Paint and Moses H. Cone involved *federal court* litigation. The applicability of the FAA to state court proceedings was simply not before the Court in either case. Justice Black would surely be surprised to find either the majority opinion or his dissent in Prima Paint cited by the Court today, as both are, ante, at 11, 12. His dissent took pains to point out:

> "The Court here does not hold ... that the body of federal substantive law created by federal judges under the Arbitration Act is required to be applied by state courts. A holding to that effect—which the Court seems to leave up in the air—would flout the intention of the framers of the Act." 388 U.S., at 424, 87 S.Ct., at 1816 (Black, J., dissenting) (footnotes omitted).

---

14. For my present purpose it is enough to recognize that Congress relied *at least in part* on its Article III power over the jurisdiction of the federal courts. See Prima Paint, 388 U.S., at 405, and n. 13, 87 S.Ct., at 1807, n. 13 (majority opinion); id., at 416–420, 87 S.Ct., at 1812–1814 (Black, J., dissenting).

15. Joint Hearing 38. See also id., at 17, 37–38.

Nothing in the Prima Paint majority opinion contradicts this statement.

The Prima Paint majority gave full but precise effect to the original congressional intent—it recognized that notwithstanding the intervention of Erie the FAA's restrictive focus on maritime and interstate contracts permits its application in federal diversity courts. Today's decision, in contrast, glosses over both the careful crafting of Prima Paint and the historical reasons that made Prima Paint necessary, and gives the FAA a reach far broader than Congress intended.[19]

III

Section 2, like the rest of the FAA, should have no application whatsoever in state courts. Assuming, to the contrary, that § 2 *does* create a federal right that the state courts must enforce, state courts should nonetheless be allowed, at least in the first instance, to fashion their own procedures for enforcing the right. Unfortunately, the Court seems to direct that the arbitration clause at issue here must be *specifically* enforced; apparently no other means of enforcement is permissible.[20]

It is settled that a state court must honor federally created rights and that it may not unreasonably undermine them by invoking contrary local procedure. "[T]he assertion of Federal rights, when plainly and reasonably made, is not to be defeated under the name of local practice." Brown v. Western R., 338 U.S. 294, 299, 70 S.Ct. 105, 108, 94 L.Ed. 100 (1949). But absent specific direction from Congress the state courts have always been permitted to apply their own reasonable procedures when enforcing federal rights. Before we undertake to read a set of complex and mandatory procedures into § 2's brief and general language, we should at a minimum allow state courts and legislatures a chance to develop their own methods for enforcing the new federal rights. Some might choose to award compensatory or punitive damages for the violation of an arbitration agreement; some might award litigation costs to the party who remained willing to arbitrate; some might affirm the "validity and enforceability" of arbitration agreements in other ways. Any of these approaches could vindicate § 2 rights in a manner fully consonant with the language and background of that provision.

---

19. The Court suggests, ante, at 12, that it is unlikely that Congress would have created a federal substantive right that the state courts were not required to enforce. But it is equally rare to find a federal substantive right that cannot be enforced in federal court under the jurisdictional grant of 28 U.S.C. § 1331. Yet the Court states, ante, at 15–16, n. 9, that the FAA must be so construed. The simple answer to this puzzle is that in 1925 Congress did not believe it was creating a substantive right at all.

20. If my understanding of the Court's opinion is correct, the Court has made § 3 of the FAA binding on the state courts. But as we have noted, supra, at 29, § 3 by its own terms governs only *federal court* proceedings. Moreover, if § 2, standing alone, creates a federal right to specific enforcement of arbitration agreements §§ 3 and 4 are, of course, largely superfluous. And if § 2 implicitly incorporates §§ 3 and 4 procedures for making arbitration agreements enforceable before arbitration begins, why not also § 9 procedures concerning venue, personal jurisdiction, and notice for enforcing an arbitrator's award after arbitration ends? One set of procedures is of little use without the other.

The unelaborated terms of § 2 certainly invite flexible enforcement. At common law many jurisdictions were hostile to arbitration agreements. Kulukundis Shipping Co. v. Amtorg Trading Corp., 126 F.2d 978, 982–984 (CA2 1942). That hostility was reflected in two different doctrines: "revocability," which allowed parties to repudiate arbitration agreements at any time before the arbitrator's award was made, and "invalidity" or "unenforceability," equivalent rules that flatly denied any remedy for the failure to honor an arbitration agreement. In contrast, common law jurisdictions that enforced arbitration agreements did so in at least three different ways—through actions for damages, actions for specific enforcement, or by enforcing sanctions imposed by trade and commercial associations on members who violated arbitration agreements. In 1925 a forum allowing *any one* of these remedies would have been thought to recognize the "validity" and "enforceability" of arbitration clauses.

This Court has previously rejected the view that state courts can adequately protect federal rights only if "such courts in enforcing the Federal right are to be treated as Federal courts and subjected pro hac vice to [federal] limitations...." Minneapolis & St. Louis R. v. Bombolis, 241 U.S. 211, 221, 36 S.Ct. 595, 598, 60 L.Ed. 961 (1916). As explained by Professor Hart,

> "The general rule, bottomed deeply in belief in the importance of state control of state judicial procedure, is that federal law takes the state courts as it finds them.... Some differences in remedy and procedure are inescapable if the different governments are to retain a measure of independence in deciding how justice should be administered. If the differences become so conspicuous as to affect advance calculations of outcome, and so to induce an undesirable shopping between forums, the remedy does not lie in the sacrifice of the independence of either government. It lies rather in provision by the federal government, confident of the justice of its own procedure, of a federal forum equally accessible to both litigants."[24]

In summary, even were I to accept the majority's reading of § 2, I would disagree with the Court's disposition of this case. After articulating the nature and scope of the federal right it discerns in § 2, the Court should remand to the state court, which has acted, heretofore, under a misapprehension of federal law. The state court should determine, at least in the first instance, what procedures it will follow to vindicate the newly articulated federal rights. Compare Missouri ex rel. Southern R. Co. v. Mayfield, 340 U.S. 1, 5, 71 S.Ct. 1, 3, 95 L.Ed. 3 (1950).

IV

The Court, ante, at 15–16, rejects the idea of requiring the FAA to be applied only in federal courts partly out of concern with the problem of forum shopping. The concern is unfounded. Because the FAA makes the

---

24. Hart, The Relations Between State and Federal Law, 54 Colum.L.Rev. 489, 508 (1954). See generally P. Bator, P. Mishkin, D. Shapiro, & H. Wechsler, supra, at 567–573.

federal courts equally accessible to both parties to a dispute, no forum shopping would be possible even if we gave the FAA a construction faithful to the congressional intent. In controversies involving incomplete diversity of citizenship there is simply no access to federal court and therefore no possibility of forum shopping. In controversies *with* complete diversity of citizenship the FAA grants federal court access equally to both parties; no party can gain any advantage by forum shopping. Even when the party resisting arbitration initiates an action in state court, the opposing party can invoke FAA § 4 and promptly secure a federal court order to compel arbitration. See, e.g., Moses H. Cone Memorial Hospital v. Mercury Construction Corp., supra.

Ironically, the FAA was passed specifically to rectify forum shopping problems created by this Court's decision in Swift v. Tyson, 41 U.S. 1, 16 Pet. 1, 10 L.Ed. 865 (1842). By 1925 several major commercial states had passed state arbitration laws, but the federal courts refused to enforce those laws in diversity cases. The drafters of the FAA might have anticipated Bernhardt by legislation and required federal diversity courts to adopt the arbitration law of the state in which they sat. But they deliberately chose a different approach. As was pointed out at congressional hearings, an additional goal of the Act was to make arbitration agreements enforceable even in federal courts located in states that had no arbitration law. The drafters' plan for maintaining reasonable harmony between state and federal practices was not to bludgeon states into compliance, but rather to adopt a uniform federal law, patterned after New York's path-breaking state statute, and simultaneously to press for passage of coordinated state legislation. The key language of the Uniform Act for Commercial Arbitration was, accordingly, identical to that in § 2 of the FAA.

In summary, forum shopping concerns in connection with the FAA are a distraction that do not withstand scrutiny. The Court ignores the drafters' carefully devised plan for dealing with those problems.

V

Today's decision adds yet another chapter to the FAA's already colorful history. In 1842 this Court's ruling in Swift v. Tyson, 41 U.S. 1, 16 Pet. 1, 10 L.Ed. 865 (1842), set up a major obstacle to the enforcement of state arbitration laws in federal diversity courts. In 1925 Congress sought to rectify the problem by enacting the FAA; the intent was to create uniform law binding only in the federal courts. In Erie R. Co. v. Tompkins, 304 U.S. 64 (1938), and then in Bernhardt v. Polygraphic Co. (1956), this Court significantly curtailed federal power. In 1967 our decision in Prima Paint upheld the application of the FAA in a federal court proceeding as a valid exercise of Congress's Commerce Clause and Admiralty powers. Today the Court discovers a federal right in FAA § 2 that the state courts must enforce. Apparently confident that state courts are not competent to devise their own procedures for protecting the newly discovered federal right, the Court summarily prescribes a specific procedure, found nowhere in § 2 or its common law origins, that the state courts are to follow.

Today's decision is unfaithful to congressional intent, unnecessary, and, in light of the FAA's antecedents and the intervening contraction of federal power, inexplicable. Although arbitration is a worthy alternative to litigation, today's exercise in judicial revisionism goes too far. I respectfully dissent.

* * *

Questions

1.   Can the Supreme Court's opinion in *Southland* be reconciled with that in *Bernhardt?*

2.   In 1924, when Congress was considering the bill that became the Federal Arbitration Act, the Committee Report on the bill stated:

> "The purpose of this bill is to make valid and enforcible [sic] agreements for arbitration contained in contracts involving interstate commerce or within the jurisdiction of [sic] admiralty, or which may be the subject of litigation in the Federal courts. . . .
>
> Whether an agreement for arbitration shall be enforced or not is a question of procedure to be determined by the law court in which the proceeding is brought and not one of substantive law to be determined by the law of the forum in which the contract is made."

Report from the Committee on the Judiciary, H. Rep. No. 96, 68th Congress, 1st Sess. (January 24, 1924).

Was the majority opinion in *Southland* faithful to this legislative history?

3.   Recall that in *Bernhardt v. Polygraphic Co.*, the Supreme Court held that for *Erie* purposes, the enforceability of an agreement to arbitrate was a matter of substantive law, and thus to be governed by state law in diversity cases. Later, in *Prima Paint v. Flood & Conklin*, 388 U.S. 395 (1967), the Court ruled that the FAA was based upon Congress' power to regulate interstate commerce, thus making it applicable in state courts as well as in federal courts by virtue of the Supremacy Clause. As a result, however, the Court created a jurisdictional anomaly: arbitration is substantive for *Erie* purposes (*Bernhardt*), but the Commerce Clause basis for the Act makes it substantive *federal* law and thus applicable in state courts and in federal courts in diversity cases. How can this anomaly be justified?

4.   In *Southland*, and in *Moses H. Cone Memorial Hospital v. Mercury Construction Corp.*, 460 U.S. 1 (1983) discussed therein, the Supreme Court stated that the FAA does not create federal question jurisdiction. Can the FAA be substantive and yet not give rise to a federal question? Why does the Court not hold that parties seeking to invoke the FAA thereby create a federal question? Is this another jurisdictional anomaly?

* * *

Note on *Perry v. Thomas*

In PERRY V. THOMAS, 482 U.S. 483, 107 S.Ct. 2520 (1987), the Supreme Court addressed the question of whether or not the FAA preempts restrictions on arbitration enacted by state legislatures. Thomas, an employee of the securities firm Kidder, Peabody, & Co., had a dispute over commissions he alleged he had earned on the sale of securities. When Thomas initially applied for employment with the firm, he had executed a Uniform Application for Securities Industry Registration, which provided for arbitration of all disputes between himself and the firm. Thomas sued for his commissions in state court, and the defendants sought to stay proceedings and compel arbitration. The California Labor Code provided that actions for the collection of wages could be maintained "without regard to the existence of any private agreement to arbitrate." CAL. LAB. CODE § 229 (West 1971).

The California Superior Court and Court of Appeal held that the claim was not subject to arbitration. It based its decision on the Supreme Court's decision in *Merrill Lynch, Pierce, Fenner & Smith v. Ware,* 414 U.S. 117 (1973), where the Court rejected a Supremacy Clause challenge to Section 229 of the California Labor Code in a case that arose under the 1934 Securities Exchange Act. Having concluded that *Merrill Lynch v. Ware,* was dispositive, the California Superior Court also did not address Thomas' alternative argument that the arbitration agreement in his case constituted an unconscionable, unenforceable contract of adhesion because "(a) the selection of arbitrators is made by the New York Stock Exchange and is presumptively biased in favor of management; and (b) the denial of meaningful ... discovery is unduly oppressive and frustrates an employee's claim for relief."

Justice Marshall, writing for the majority of the Supreme Court, reversed. He found that the California Labor Code provision was preempted by the FAA and ordered the litigation stayed and the case sent to arbitration in accordance with the FAA. The Court distinguished *Ware* on the grounds that the specific federal substantive law that was claimed to preempt state law in that case emanated from the 1934 Exchange Act, an Act which the Court interpreted to contain no policy favoring arbitration and no necessity for uniformity in "an exchange's housekeeping affairs."

"By contrast," wrote Justice Marshall, "the present appeal addresses the pre-emptive effect of the Federal Arbitration Act, a statute that embodies Congress' intent to provide for the enforcement of arbitration agreements within the full reach of the Commerce Clause. Its general applicability reflects that '[t]he preeminent concern of Congress in passing the Act was to enforce private agreements into which parties had entered.... Byrd, 470 U.S., at 221, 105 S.Ct., at 1242. We have accordingly held that these agreements must be 'rigorously enforce [d].' " Ibid.... This clear federal policy places § 2 of the Act in unmistakable conflict with California's § 229 requirement that litigants be provided a judicial forum for resolving wage disputes. Therefore, under the Supremacy Clause, the state statute must give way.

The majority also declined to address Thomas' claim that the arbitration agreement in this case constituted an unconscionable, unenforceable contract of adhesion. However, in footnote 9, Marshall added:

"We note, however, the choice-of-law issue that arises when defenses such as Thomas' so-called 'standing' and unconscionability arguments are asserted. In instances such as these, the text of § 2 provides the touchstone for choosing between state-law principles and the principles of federal common law envisioned by the passage of that statute: An agreement to arbitrate is valid, irrevocable, and enforceable, as a matter of federal law, see Moses H. Cone Memorial Hospital v. Mercury Construction Corp., 460 U.S. 1, 24, 103 S.Ct. 927, 941, 74 L.Ed.2d 765 (1983), 'save upon such grounds as exist at law or in equity for the revocation of any contract.' 9 U.S.C. § 2 (emphasis added). Thus state law, whether of legislative or judicial origin, is applicable if that law arose to govern issues concerning the validity, revocability, and enforceability of contracts generally. A state-law principle that takes its meaning precisely from the fact that a contract to arbitrate is at issue does not comport with this requirement of § 2. See Prima Paint, supra, 388 U.S., at 404, 87 S.Ct., at 1806; Southland Corp. v. Keating, 465 U.S., at 16–17, n. 11, 104 S.Ct., at 861, n. 11. A court may not, then, in assessing the rights of litigants to enforce an arbitration agreement, construe that agreement in a manner different from that in which it otherwise construes nonarbitration agreements under state law. Nor may a court rely on the uniqueness of an agreement to arbitrate as a basis for a state-law holding that enforcement would be unconscionable, for this would enable the court to effect what we hold today the state legislature cannot."

Justice O'Connor, in her dissent, argued,

"Even if I were not to adhere to my position that the Act is inapplicable to state court proceedings, however, I would still dissent. We have held that Congress can limit or preclude a waiver of a judicial forum, and that Congress' intent to do so will be deduced from a statute's text or legislative history, or 'from an inherent conflict between arbitration and the statute's underlying purposes.' Shearson/American Express Inc. v. McMahon, 482 U.S. 220, 227, 107 S.Ct. 2332, ___, 96 L.Ed.2d 185 (1987). As JUSTICE STEVENS has observed, the Court has not explained why state legislatures should not also be able to limit or preclude waiver of a judicial forum. "

"[T]he California Legislature intended to preclude waiver of a judicial forum; it is clear, moreover, that this intent reflects an important state policy. Section 229 of the California Labor Code specifically provides that actions for the collection of wages may be maintained in the state courts 'without regard to the existence of any private agreement to arbitrate.' Cal.Lab.Code Ann. § 229 (West 1971). The California Legislature thereby intended 'to protect the worker from the exploitative employer who would demand that a prospective employee sign away in advance his right to resort to the judicial system for redress of an employment grievance,' and

§ 229 has 'manifested itself as an important state policy through interpretation by the California courts.' " Merrill Lynch, Pierce, Fenner & Smith v. Ware, 414 U.S. 117, 131, 132–133, 94 S.Ct. 383, 391, 392, 38 L.Ed.2d 348 (1973).

"In my view, therefore, even if the Act applies to state court proceedings, California's policy choice to preclude waivers of a judicial forum for wage claims is entitled to respect.

Justice Stevens, also dissenting, stated that he shared Justice O'Connor's opinion that "the States' power to except certain categories of disputes from arbitration should be preserved unless Congress decides otherwise."

* * *

Questions

1. How does *Perry* differ from *Southland?* What issues are presented in *Perry* that were not already decided in *Southland*? Is *Perry* a harder or easier case than *Southland* for finding the state law claims preempted?

2. What does footnote 9 in *Perry* say about the role of state law doctrines under the FAA? According to the Court, which state law doctrines survive the very broad preemptive reach of the FAA?

* * *

Volt Information Sciences, Inc. v. Board of Trustees of Stanford University

489 U.S. 468, 109 S.Ct. 1248 (1989).

■ CHIEF JUSTICE REHNQUIST delivered the opinion of the Court.

Unlike its federal counterpart, the California Arbitration Act, Cal.Civ. Proc.Code Ann.§ 1280 et seq. (West 1982), contains a provision allowing a court to stay arbitration pending resolution of related litigation. We hold that application of the California statute is not pre-empted by the Federal Arbitration Act (FAA or Act), 9 U.S.C. § 1 et seq., in a case where the parties have agreed that their arbitration agreement will be governed by the law of California.

Appellant Volt Information Sciences, Inc. (Volt), and appellee Board of Trustees of Leland Stanford Junior University (Stanford) entered into a construction contract under which Volt was to install a system of electrical conduits on the Stanford campus. The contract contained an agreement to arbitrate all disputes between the parties "arising out of or relating to this contract or the breach thereof."[1] The contract also contained a choice-of-

---

1. The arbitration clause read in full as follows:

"All claims, disputes and other matters in question between the parties to this contract, arising out of or relating to this

law clause providing that "[t]he Contract shall be governed by the law of the place where the Project is located." App. 37. During the course of the project, a dispute developed regarding compensation for extra work, and Volt made a formal demand for arbitration. Stanford responded by filing an action against Volt in California Superior Court, alleging fraud and breach of contract; in the same action, Stanford also sought indemnity from two other companies involved in the construction project, with whom it did not have arbitration agreements. Volt petitioned the Superior Court to compel arbitration of the dispute.[2] Stanford in turn moved to stay arbitration pursuant to Cal.Civ.Proc.Code Ann. § 1281.2(c) (West 1982), which permits a court to stay arbitration pending resolution of related litigation between a party to the arbitration agreement and third parties not bound by it, where "there is a possibility of conflicting rulings on a common issue of law or fact."[3] The Superior Court denied Volt's motion to compel arbitration and stayed the arbitration proceedings pending the outcome of the litigation on the authority of § 1281.2(c). App. 59–60.

The California Court of Appeal affirmed. The court acknowledged that the parties' contract involved interstate commerce, that the FAA governs contracts in interstate commerce, and that the FAA contains no provision permitting a court to stay arbitration pending resolution of related litigation involving third parties not bound by the arbitration agreement. App. 64–65. However, the court held that by specifying that their contract would be governed by " 'the law of the place where the project is located,' " the parties had incorporated the California rules of arbitration, including § 1281.2(c), into their arbitration agreement. Id., at 65. Finally, the court rejected Volt's contention that, even if the parties had agreed to arbitrate under the California rules, application of § 1281.2(c) here was nonetheless pre-empted by the FAA because the contract involved interstate commerce. Id., at 68–80.

The court reasoned that the purpose of the FAA was " 'not [to] mandate the arbitration of all claims, but merely the enforcement . . . of

contract or the breach thereof, shall be decided by arbitration in accordance with the Construction Industry Arbitration Rules of the American Arbitration Association then prevailing unless the parties mutually agreed [sic] otherwise. . . . This agreement to arbitrate . . . shall be specifically enforceable under the prevailing arbitration law." App. 40.

2. . . . Volt also asked the court to stay the Superior Court litigation until the arbitration was completed, presumably pursuant to § 3 of the FAA, 9 U.S.C. § 3, and the parallel provision of the California Arbitration Act, Cal. Civ. Proc. Code Ann. § 1281.2(c)(3) (West 1982). App. 45–46.

3. Section 1281.2(c) provides, in pertinent part, that when a court determines that

"[a] party to the arbitration agreement is also a party to a pending court action or special proceeding with a third party, arising out of the same transaction or series of related transactions and there is a possibility of conflicting rulings on a common issue of law or fact [,] . . . the court (1) may refuse to enforce the arbitration agreement and may order intervention or joinder of all parties in a single action or special proceeding; (2) may order intervention or joinder as to all or only certain issues; (3) may order arbitration among the parties who have agreed to arbitration and stay the pending court action or special proceeding pending the outcome of the arbitration proceeding; or (4) may stay arbitration pending the outcome of the court action or special proceeding."

privately negotiated arbitration agreements.' " Id., at 70 (quoting Dean Witter Reynolds Inc. v. Byrd, 470 U.S. 213, 219, 105 S.Ct. 1238, 1242, 84 L.Ed.2d 158 (1985)). While the FAA therefore pre-empts application of state laws which render arbitration agreements unenforceable, "[i]t does not follow, however, that the federal law has preclusive effect in a case where the parties have chosen in their [arbitration] agreement to abide by state rules." App. 71. To the contrary, because "[t]he thrust of the federal law is that arbitration is strictly a matter of contract," ibid., the parties to an arbitration agreement should be "at liberty to choose the terms under which they will arbitrate." Id., at 72. Where, as here, the parties have chosen in their agreement to abide by the state rules of arbitration, application of the FAA to prevent enforcement of those rules would actually be "inimical to the policies underlying state and federal arbitration law," id., at 73, because it would "force the parties to arbitrate in a manner contrary to their agreement." Id., at 65. The California Supreme Court denied Volt's petition for discretionary review. Id., at 87. We postponed consideration of our jurisdiction to the hearing on the merits.... We now hold that we have appellate jurisdiction and affirm.

Appellant devotes the bulk of its argument to convincing us that the Court of Appeal erred in interpreting the choice-of-law clause to mean that the parties had incorporated the California rules of arbitration into their arbitration agreement.... Appellant acknowledges, as it must, that the interpretation of private contracts is ordinarily a question of state law, which this Court does not sit to review.... But appellant nonetheless maintains that we should set aside the Court of Appeal's interpretation of this particular contractual provision for two principal reasons.

Appellant first suggests that the Court of Appeal's construction of the choice-of-law clause was in effect a finding that appellant had "waived" its "federally guaranteed right to compel arbitration of the parties' dispute," a waiver whose validity must be judged by reference to federal rather than state law.... This argument fundamentally misconceives the nature of the rights created by the FAA. The Act was designed "to overrule the judiciary's longstanding refusal to enforce agreements to arbitrate," Byrd, supra, 470 U.S., at 219–220, 105 S.Ct., at 1241–1242, and place such agreements "upon the same footing as other contracts," Scherk v. Alberto–Culver Co., 417 U.S. 506, 511.... Section 2 of the Act therefore declares that a written agreement to arbitrate in any contract involving interstate commerce or a maritime transaction "shall be valid, irrevocable, and enforceable, save upon such grounds as exist at law or in equity for the revocation of any contract," 9 U.S.C. § 2, and § 4 allows a party to such an arbitration agreement to "petition any United States district court ... for an order directing that such arbitration proceed in the manner provided for in such agreement."

But § 4 of the FAA does not confer a right to compel arbitration of any dispute at any time; it confers only the right to obtain an order directing that "arbitration proceed *in the manner provided for in [the parties']* agreement." 9 U.S.C. § 4 (emphasis added). Here the Court of Appeal found that, by incorporating the California rules of arbitration into their agreement, the parties had agreed that arbitration would not proceed in situations which fell within the scope of Calif. Code Civ. Proc. Ann. § 1281.2(c) (West 1982). This was not a finding that appellant had "waived" an FAA-guaranteed right to compel arbitration of this dispute, but a finding that it had no such right in the first place, because the parties' agreement did not require arbitration to proceed in this situation. Accordingly, appellant's contention that the contract interpretation issue presented here involves the "waiver" of a federal right is without merit.

Second, appellant argues that we should set aside the Court of Appeal's construction of the choice-of-law clause because it violates the settled federal rule that questions of arbitrability in contracts subject to the FAA must be resolved with a healthy regard for the federal policy favoring arbitration. Brief for Appellant 49–52; id., at 92–96, citing Moses H. Cone Memorial Hospital v. Mercury Construction Corp., 460 U.S. 1, 24–25, 103 S.Ct. 927, 941–942, 74 L.Ed.2d 765 (1983) (§ 2 of the FAA "create[s] a body of federal substantive law of arbitrability, applicable to any arbitration agreement within the coverage of the Act," which requires that "questions of arbitrability . . . be addressed with a healthy regard for the federal policy favoring arbitration," and that "any doubts concerning the scope of arbitrable issues . . . be resolved in favor of arbitration"); Mitsubishi Motors Corp. v. Soler Chrysler–Plymouth, Inc., 473 U.S. 614, 626, 105 S.Ct. 3346, 3353, 87 L.Ed.2d 444 (1985) (in construing an arbitration agreement within the coverage of the FAA, "as with any other contract, the parties' intentions control, but those intentions are generously construed as to issues of arbitrability"). These cases of course establish that, in applying general state-law principles of contract interpretation to the interpretation of an arbitration agreement within the scope of the Act, . . . due regard must be given to the federal policy favoring arbitration, and ambiguities as to the scope of the arbitration clause itself resolved in favor of arbitration.

But we do not think the Court of Appeal offended the Moses H. Cone principle by interpreting the choice-of-law provision to mean that the parties intended the California rules of arbitration, including the § 1281.2(c) stay provision, to apply to their arbitration agreement. There is no federal policy favoring arbitration under a certain set of procedural rules; the federal policy is simply to ensure the enforceability, according to their terms, of private agreements to arbitrate. Interpreting a choice-of-law clause to make applicable state rules governing the conduct of arbitration—rules which are manifestly designed to encourage resort to the arbitral process—simply does not offend the rule of liberal construction set forth in Moses H. Cone, nor does it offend any other policy embodied in the FAA.[5]

---

5. Unlike the dissent, see post at 486–487, we think the California arbitration rules which the parties have incorporated into their contract generally foster the federal policy favoring arbitration. As indicated, the FAA itself contains no provision designed to deal with the special practical problems that arise in multiparty contractual disputes when some or all of the contracts at issue include agreements to arbitrate. California has taken the lead in fashioning a legislative response to this problem, by giving courts authority to

The question remains whether, assuming the choice-of-law clause meant what the Court of Appeal found it to mean, application of Cal. Civ. Proc. Code Ann. § 1281.2(c) is nonetheless pre-empted by the FAA to the extent it is used to stay arbitration under this contract involving interstate commerce. It is undisputed that this contract falls within the coverage of the FAA, since it involves interstate commerce, and that the FAA contains no provision authorizing a stay of arbitration in this situation. Appellee contends, however, that §§ 3 and 4 of the FAA, which are the specific sections claimed to conflict with the California statute at issue here, are not applicable in this state-court proceeding and thus cannot pre-empt application of the California statute. See Brief for Appellee 43–50. While the argument is not without some merit,[6] we need not resolve it to decide this case, for we conclude that even if §§ 3 and 4 of the FAA are fully applicable in state-court proceedings, they do not prevent application of Cal.Civ.Proc. Code Ann. § 1281.2(c) to stay arbitration where, as here, the parties have agreed to arbitrate in accordance with California law.

The FAA contains no express pre-emptive provision, nor does it reflect a congressional intent to occupy the entire field of arbitration. See Bernhardt v. Polygraphic Co., 350 U.S. 198, 76 S.Ct. 273, 100 L.Ed. 199 (1956) (upholding application of state arbitration law to arbitration provision in contract not covered by the FAA). But even when Congress has not completely displaced state regulation in an area, state law may nonetheless be pre-empted to the extent that it actually conflicts with federal law—that is, to the extent that it "stands as an obstacle to the accomplishment and execution of the full purposes and objectives of Congress." Hines v. Davidowitz, 312 U.S. 52, 67, 61 S.Ct. 399, 404, 85 L.Ed. 581 (1941). The question before us, therefore, is whether application of Cal.Civ.Proc.Code Ann. § 1281.2(c) to stay arbitration under this contract in interstate commerce, in accordance with the terms of the arbitration agreement itself, would undermine the goals and policies of the FAA. We conclude that it would not.

... In recognition of Congress' principal purpose of ensuring that private arbitration agreements are enforced according to their terms, we have held that the FAA pre-empts state laws which "require a judicial forum for the resolution of claims which the contracting parties agreed to resolve by arbitration." Southland Corp. v. Keating, 465 U.S. 1, 10 ... But

consolidate or stay arbitration proceedings in these situations in order to minimize the potential for contradictory judgments. See Calif. Civ. Proc. Code Ann. § 1281.2(c).

   6. While we have held that the FAA's "substantive" provisions—§§ 1 and 2—are applicable in state as well as federal court, see Southland Corp. v. Keating, 465 U.S. 1, 12, 104 S.Ct. 852, 859, 79 L.Ed.2d 1 (1984), we have never held that §§ 3 and 4, which by their terms appear to apply only to proceed-

ings in federal court, see 9 U.S.C. § 3 (referring to proceedings "brought in any of the courts of the United States"); § 4 (referring to "any United States district court"), are nonetheless applicable in state court. See Southland Corp. v. Keating, supra, at 16, n. 10, 104 S.Ct., at 861 n. 10 (expressly reserving the question whether "§§ 3 and 4 of the Arbitration Act apply to proceedings in state courts"); see also id., at 29, 104 S.Ct., at 867 (O'CONNOR, J., dissenting) (§§ 3 and 4 of the FAA apply only in federal court).

it does not follow that the FAA prevents the enforcement of agreements to arbitrate under different rules than those set forth in the Act itself. Indeed, such a result would be quite inimical to the FAA's primary purpose of ensuring that private agreements to arbitrate are enforced according to their terms. Arbitration under the Act is a matter of consent, not coercion, and parties are generally free to structure their arbitration agreements as they see fit. Just as they may limit by contract the issues which they will arbitrate, see Mitsubishi, supra, 473 U.S., at 628, 105 S.Ct., at 3353, so too may they specify by contract the rules under which that arbitration will be conducted. Where, as here, the parties have agreed to abide by state rules of arbitration, enforcing those rules according to the terms of the agreement is fully consistent with the goals of the FAA, even if the result is that arbitration is stayed where the Act would otherwise permit it to go forward. By permitting the courts to "rigorously enforce" such agreements according to their terms ... we give effect to the contractual rights and expectations of the parties, without doing violence to the policies behind by the FAA.

The judgment of the Court of Appeals is

Affirmed.

■ JUSTICE O'CONNOR took no part in the consideration or decision of this case.

■ JUSTICE BRENNAN, with whom JUSTICE MARSHALL joins, dissenting.

The litigants in this case were parties to a construction contract which contained a clause obligating them to arbitrate disputes and making that obligation specifically enforceable. The contract also incorporated provisions of a standard form contract prepared by the American Institute of Architects and endorsed by the Associated General Contractors of America; among these general provisions was § 7.1.1: "The Contract shall be governed by the law of the place where the Project is located." When a dispute arose between the parties, Volt invoked the arbitration clause, while Stanford attempted to avoid it (apparently because the dispute also involved two other contractors with whom Stanford had no arbitration agreements).

The Federal Arbitration Act (FAA), 9 U.S.C. § 1 et seq., requires courts to enforce arbitration agreements in contracts involving interstate commerce. See ante, at 474. The California courts nonetheless rejected Volt's petition to compel arbitration in reliance on a provision of state law that, in the circumstances presented, permitted a court to stay arbitration pending the conclusion of related litigation. Volt, not surprisingly, suggested that the Supremacy Clause compelled a different result. The California Court of Appeal found, however, that the parties had agreed that their contract would be governed solely by the law of the State of California, to the exclusion of federal law. In reaching this conclusion the court relied on no extrinsic evidence of the parties' intent, but solely on the language of the form contract that the " 'law of the place where the project is located' " would govern. App. 66–67.

This Court now declines to review that holding, which denies effect to an important federal statute, apparently because it finds no question of federal law involved. I can accept neither the state court's unusual interpretation of the parties' contract, nor this Court's unwillingness to review it. I would reverse the judgment of the California Court of Appeal.[4]

I

Contrary to the Court's view, the state court's construction of the choice-of-law clause is reviewable for two independent reasons.

A

The Court's decision not to review the state court's interpretation of the choice-of-law clause appears to be based on the principle that "the interpretation of private contracts is ordinarily a question of state law, which this Court does not sit to review." ... I have no quarrel with the general proposition that the interpretation of contracts is a matter of state law. By ending its analysis at that level of generality, however, the Court overlooks well-established precedent to the effect that, in order to guard against arbitrary denials of federal claims, a state court's construction of a contract in such a way as to preclude enforcement of a federal right is not immune from review in this Court as to its "adequacy."

Many of our cases that so hold involve, understandably enough, claims under the Contract Clause. In Appleby v. City of New York, 271 U.S. 364, 46 S.Ct. 569, 70 L.Ed. 992 (1926), for example, petitioners alleged that the city had unconstitutionally impaired their rights contained in a contract deeding them certain submerged lands in the city harbor. Chief Justice Taft stated the issue for the Court as follows:

> "The questions we have here to determine are, first, was there a contract, second, what was its proper construction and effect, and, third, was its obligation impaired by subsequent legislation as enforced by the state court? These questions we must answer independently of the conclusion of [the state] court. Of course we should give all proper weight to its judgment, but we can not perform our duty to enforce the guaranty of the Federal Constitution as to the inviolability of contracts by state legislative action unless we give the questions independent consideration." Id., at 379–380, 46 S.Ct., at 573.

. . .

Indeed, our ability to review state-law decisions in such circumstances is not limited to the interpretation of contracts. In Rogers v. Alabama, 192 U.S. 226, 24 S.Ct. 257, 48 L.Ed. 417 (1904), we noted the

---

4. I do not disagree with the Court's holding, ante, at 477–479, that the FAA does not pre-empt state arbitration rules, even as applied to contracts involving interstate commerce, when the parties have agreed to arbitrate by those rules to the exclusion of federal arbitration law. I would not reach that question, however, because I conclude that the parties have made no such agreement.

"necessary and well settled rule that the exercise of jurisdiction by this court to protect constitutional rights cannot be declined when it is plain that the fair result of a decision is to deny the rights. It is well known that this court will decide for itself whether a contract was made as well as whether the obligation of the contract has been impaired. But that is merely an illustration of a more general rule." Id., at 230, 24 S.Ct., at 258 (citation omitted).

. . .

While in this case the federal right at issue is a statutory, not a constitutional, one, the principle under which we review the antecedent question of state law is the same. Where "the existence or the application of a federal right turns on a logically antecedent finding on a matter of state law, it is essential to the Court's performance of its function that it exercise an ancillary jurisdiction to consider the state question. Federal rights could otherwise be nullified by the manipulation of state law." Wechsler, The Appellate Jurisdiction of the Supreme Court: Reflections on the Law and the Logistics of Direct Review, 34 Wash. & Lee L.Rev. 1043, 1052 (1977)....

No less than in the cited cases, the right of the instant parties to have their arbitration agreement enforced pursuant to the FAA could readily be circumvented by a state-court construction of their contract as having intended to exclude the applicability of federal law. It is therefore essential that, while according due deference to the decision of the state court, we independently determine whether we "clearly would have judged the issue differently if [we] were the state's highest court." Wechsler, supra, at 1052.

B

Arbitration is, of course, "a matter of contract and a party cannot be required to submit to arbitration any dispute which he has not agreed so to submit." Steelworkers v. Warrior & Gulf Co., 363 U.S. 574, 582, 80 S.Ct. 1347, 1353, 4 L.Ed.2d 1409 (1960). I agree with the Court that "the FAA does not require parties to arbitrate when they have not agreed to do so." Ante, at 478. Since the FAA merely requires enforcement of what the parties have agreed to, moreover, they are free if they wish to write an agreement to arbitrate outside the coverage of the FAA. Such an agreement would permit a state rule, otherwise pre-empted by the FAA, to govern their arbitration. The substantive question in this case is whether or not they have done so. And that question, we have made clear in the past, is a matter of federal law.

Not only does the FAA require the enforcement of arbitration agreements, but we have held that it also establishes substantive federal law that must be consulted in determining whether (or to what extent) a given contract provides for arbitration. We have stated this most clearly in Moses H. Cone Memorial Hospital v. Mercury Construction Corp., 460 U.S. 1, 24–25, 103 S.Ct. 927, 941–942, 74 L.Ed.2d 765 (1983):

"Section 2 [of the FAA] is a congressional declaration of a liberal federal policy favoring arbitration agreements, notwithstanding any state substantive or procedural policies to the contrary. The effect of the section is to create a body of federal substantive law of arbitrability, applicable to any arbitration agreement within the coverage of the Act...."

The Court recognizes the relevance of the Moses H. Cone principle but finds it unoffended by the Court of Appeal's decision, which, the Court suggests, merely determines what set of procedural rules will apply. Ante, at 476. I agree fully with the Court that "the federal policy is simply to ensure the enforceability, according to their terms, of private agreements to arbitrate," ibid., but I disagree emphatically with its conclusion that policy is not frustrated here. Applying the California procedural rule, which stays arbitration while litigation of the same issue goes forward, means simply that the parties' dispute will be litigated rather than arbitrated. Thus, interpreting the parties' agreement to say that the California procedural rules apply rather than the FAA, where the parties arguably had no such intent, implicates the Moses H. Cone principle no less than would an interpretation of the parties' contract that erroneously denied the existence of an agreement to arbitrate.[8]

While appearing to recognize that the state court's interpretation of the contract does raise a question of federal law, the Court nonetheless refuses to determine whether the state court misconstrued that agreement. There is no warrant for failing to do so. The FAA requires that a court determining a question of arbitrability not stop with the application of state-law rules for construing the parties' intentions, but that it also take account of the command of federal law that "those intentions [be] generously construed as to issues of arbitrability." Mitsubishi Motors, supra, 473 U.S., at 626, 105 S.Ct., at 3354. Thus, the decision below is based on both state and federal law, which are thoroughly intertwined. In such circumstances the state-court judgment cannot be said to rest on an "adequate and independent state ground" so as to bar review by this Court. See Enterprise Irrigation Dist. v. Farmers Mutual Canal Co., 243 U.S. 157, 164, 37 S.Ct. 318, 320, 61 L.Ed. 644 (1917) ("But where the non-federal ground is so interwoven with the other as not to be an independent matter ... our jurisdiction is plain")....

II

Construed with deference to the opinion of the California Court of Appeal, yet "with a healthy regard for the federal policy favoring arbitra-

---

8. Whether or not "the California arbitration rules ... generally foster the federal policy favoring arbitration," ante, at 476, n. 5, is not the relevant question. Section 2 of the FAA requires courts to enforce agreements to arbitrate, and in Moses H. Cone we held that doubts as to whether the parties had so agreed were to be resolved in favor of arbitration. Whether California's arbitration rules are more likely than federal law to foster arbitration, i.e., to induce parties to agree to arbitrate disputes, is another matter entirely. On that question it is up to Congress, not this Court, to "fashion a legislative response," ante, at 476, n. 5, and in the meantime we are not free to substitute our notions of good policy for federal law as currently written.

tion,'' Moses H. Cone, 460 U.S., at 24, 103 S.Ct., at 941, it is clear that the choice-of-law clause cannot bear the interpretation the California court assigned to it.

Construction of a contractual provision is, of course, a matter of discerning the parties' intent. It is important to recall, in the first place, that in this case there is no extrinsic evidence of their intent. We must therefore rely on the contract itself. But the provision of the contract at issue here was not one that these parties drafted themselves. Rather, they incorporated portions of a standard form contract commonly used in the construction industry. That makes it most unlikely that their intent was in any way at variance with the purposes for which choice-of-law clauses are commonly written and the manner in which they are generally interpreted.

It seems to me beyond dispute that the normal purpose of such choice-of-law clauses is to determine that the law of one State rather than that of another State will be applicable; they simply do not speak to any interaction between state and federal law. A cursory glance at standard conflicts texts confirms this observation: they contain no reference at all to the relation between federal and state law in their discussions of contractual choice-of-law clauses. See, e.g., R. Weintraub, Commentary on the Conflict of Laws § 7.3C (2d ed. 1980); E. Scoles & P. Hay, Conflict of Laws 632–652 (1982); R. Leflar, L. McDougal, & R. Felix, American Conflicts Law § 147 (4th ed. 1986). The same is true of standard codifications. See Uniform Commercial Code § 1–105(1) (1978); Restatement (Second) of Conflict of Laws § 187 (1971). Indeed the Restatement of Conflicts notes expressly that it does not deal with ''the ever-present problem of determining the respective spheres of authority of the law and courts of the nation and of the member States.'' Id., § 2, Comment c. Decisions of this Court fully bear out the impression that choice-of-law clauses do not speak to any state-federal issue. On at least two occasions we have been called upon to determine the applicability vel non of the FAA to contracts containing choice-of-law clauses similar to that at issue here. Despite adverting to the choice-of-law clauses in other contexts in our opinions, we ascribed no significance whatever to them in connection with the applicability of the FAA. Scherk v. Alberto–Culver Co., 417 U.S. 506, 94 S.Ct. 2449, 41 L.Ed.2d 270 (1974); Bernhardt v. Polygraphic Co., 350 U.S. 198, 76 S.Ct. 273, 100 L.Ed. 199 (1956). . . . Choice-of-law clauses simply have never been used for the purpose of dealing with the relationship between state and federal law. There is no basis whatever for believing that the parties in this case intended their choice-of-law clause to do so.

Moreover, the literal language of the contract—''the law of the place''—gives no indication of any intention to apply only state law and exclude other law that would normally be applicable to something taking place at that location. By settled principles of federal supremacy, the law of any place in the United States includes federal law. See Claflin v. Houseman, 93 U.S. 130, 136, 23 L.Ed. 833 (1876); Hauenstein v. Lynham, 100 U.S. 483, 490, 25 L.Ed. 628 (1879) (''[T]he Constitution, laws, and treaties of the United States are as much a part of the law of every State as its own local laws and Constitution"). As the dissenting judge below noted, "under California law, federal law governs matters cognizable in California courts upon which the United States has definitively spoken." App. 82 (opinion of Capaccioli, J.). Thus, "the mere choice of California law is not a selection of California law over federal law...." Id., at 84. In the absence of any evidence to the contrary it must be assumed that this is what the parties meant by "the law of the place where the Project is located." ...

III

Most commercial contracts written in this country contain choice-of-law clauses, similar to the one in the Stanford–Volt contract, specifying which State's law is to govern the interpretation of the contract. See Scoles & Hay, Conflict of Laws, at 632–633 ("Party autonomy means that the parties are free to select the law governing their contract, subject to certain limitations. They will usually do so by means of an express choice-of-law clause in their written contract"). Were every state court to construe such clauses as an expression of the parties' intent to exclude the application of federal law, as has the California Court of Appeal in this case, the result would be to render the Federal Arbitration Act a virtual nullity as to presently existing contracts. I cannot believe that the parties to contracts intend such consequences to flow from their insertion of a standard choice-of-law clause. Even less can I agree that we are powerless to review decisions of state courts that effectively nullify a vital piece of federal legislation. I respectfully dissent.

* * *

Questions

1.   After *Volt*, will a choice of law clause in a contract always supplant the application of the FAA? Under what circumstances will it so operate?

2.   Would the results in *Southland* or *Perry* have been different if those cases had involved a choice of law clause similar to that involved in *Volt*?

3.   How can *Perry* be distinguished from *Volt*?

4.   Is the holding of *Volt* limited to state law procedural rules regulating arbitration, or does it also apply to state law substantive rules that bear on arbitration? That is, in *Southland*, could the parties have retained the benefits of the California Franchise Investment Act by enumerating its provisions in their contract? Could they have done so by incorporating the CFIA by reference?

5.   Is *Volt* in tension with the federal policy of the FAA to favor arbitration as a means of resolving disputes?

* * *

Allied–Bruce Terminix Companies, Inc., et. al. v. G. Michael Dobson, et. al.

513 U.S. 265, 115 S.Ct. 834 (1995).

■ JUSTICE BREYER delivered the opinion of the Court.

This case concerns the reach of § 2 of the Federal Arbitration Act. That section makes enforceable a written arbitration provision in "a contract *evidencing* a transaction *involving* commerce." 9 U.S.C. § 2 (emphasis added). Should we read this phrase broadly, extending the Act's reach to the limits of Congress' Commerce Clause power? Or, do the two underscored words—"involving" and "evidencing"—significantly restrict the Act's application? We conclude that the broader reading of the Act is the correct one; and we reverse a State Supreme Court judgment to the contrary.

I

In August 1987 Steven Gwin, a respondent, who owned a house in Birmingham, Alabama, bought a lifetime "Termite Protection Plan" (Plan) from the local office of Allied–Bruce Terminix Companies, a franchise of Terminix International Company. In the Plan, Allied–Bruce promised "to protect" Gwin's house "against the attack of subterranean termites," to reinspect periodically, to provide any "further treatment found necessary," and to repair, up to $100,000, damage caused by new termite infestations. App. 69. Terminix International "guarantee[d] the fulfillment of the terms" of the Plan. Ibid. The Plan's contract document provided in writing that

> "*any controversy or claim* . . . arising out of or relating to the interpretation, performance or breach of any provision of this agreement *shall be settled exclusively by arbitration.*" Id., at 70 (emphasis added).

In the Spring of 1991 Mr. and Mrs. Gwin, wishing to sell their house to Mr. and Mrs. Dobson, had Allied–Bruce reinspect the house. They obtained a clean bill of health. But, no sooner had they sold the house and transferred the Termite Protection Plan to Mr. and Mrs. Dobson than the Dobsons found the house swarming with termites. Allied–Bruce attempted to treat and repair the house, but the Dobsons found Allied–Bruce's efforts inadequate. They therefore sued the Gwins, and (along with the Gwins, who cross-claimed) also sued Allied-Bruce and Terminix in Alabama state court. Allied–Bruce and Terminix, pointing to the Plan's arbitration clause and § 2 of the Federal Arbitration Act, immediately asked the court for a stay, to allow arbitration to proceed. The court denied the stay. Allied–Bruce and Terminix appealed.

The Supreme Court of Alabama upheld the denial of the stay on the basis of a state statute, Ala.Code § 8–1–41(3) (1993), making written, predispute arbitration agreements invalid and "unenforceable." 628 So.2d 354, 355 (Ala.1993). To reach this conclusion, the court had to find that the Federal Arbitration Act, which pre-empts conflicting state law, did not apply to the termite contract. It made just that finding. The court considered the federal Act inapplicable because the connection between the termite contract and interstate commerce was too slight. In the court's view, the Act applies to a contract only if " 'at the time [the parties entered into the contract] and accepted the arbitration clause, they *contemplated* substantial interstate activity.' " Ibid. (emphasis in original) (quoting Metro Industrial Painting Corp. v. Terminal Constr. Co., 287 F.2d 382, 387 (CA2) (Lumbard, C.J., concurring), cert. denied, 368 U.S. 817, 82 S.Ct. 31, 7 L.Ed.2d 24 (1961)). Despite some interstate activities (e.g., Allied–Bruce, like Terminix, is a multistate firm and shipped treatment and repair material from out of state), the court found that the parties "contemplated" a transaction that was primarily local and not "substantially" interstate.

Several state courts and federal district courts, like the Supreme Court of Alabama, have interpreted the Act's language as requiring the parties to a contract to have "contemplated" an interstate commerce connection. See, e.g., Burke County Public Schools Bd. of Ed. v. Shaver Partnership, 303 N.C. 408, 417–420, 279 S.E.2d 816, 822–823 (1981); R.J. Palmer Constr. Co. v. Wichita Band Instrument Co., 7 Kan.App.2d 363, 367, 642 P.2d 127, 130 (1982); Lacheney v. Profitkey Int'l, Inc., 818 F.Supp. 922, 924 (E.D.Va. 1993). Several federal appellate courts, however, have interpreted the same language differently, as reaching to the limits of Congress' Commerce Clause power. See, e.g., Foster v. Turley, 808 F.2d 38, 40 (C.A.10 1986); Robert Lawrence Co. v. Devonshire Fabrics, Inc., 271 F.2d 402, 406–407 (C.A.2 1959), cert. dism'd, 364 U.S. 801, 81 S.Ct. 27, 5 L.Ed.2d 37 (1960); cf. Snyder v. Smith, 736 F.2d 409, 417–418 (CA7), cert. denied, 469 U.S. 1037, 105 S.Ct. 513, 83 L.Ed.2d 403 (1984). We granted certiorari to resolve this conflict, 510 U.S. 1190, 114 S.Ct. 1292, 127 L.Ed.2d 646 (1994); and, as we said, we conclude that the broader reading of the statute is the right one. . . .

[R]espondents, supported by 20 state attorneys general, now ask us to overrule Southland and thereby to permit Alabama to apply its antiarbitration statute in this case irrespective of the proper interpretation of § 2. The Southland Court, however, recognized that the pre-emption issue was a difficult one, and it considered the basic arguments that respondents and amici now raise (even though those issues were not thoroughly briefed at the time). Nothing significant has changed in the 10 years subsequent to Southland; no later cases have eroded Southland's authority; and, no unforeseen practical problems have arisen. Moreover, in the interim, private parties have likely written contracts relying upon Southland as authority. Further, Congress, both before and after Southland, has enacted legislation extending, not retracting, the scope of arbitration. See, e.g., 9 U.S.C. § 15 (eliminating the Act of State doctrine as a bar to arbitration); 9 U.S.C. §§ 201–208 (international arbitration). For these reasons, we find it inappropriate to reconsider what is by now well-established law.

We therefore proceed to the basic interpretive questions aware that we are interpreting an Act that seeks broadly to overcome judicial hostility to arbitration agreements and that applies in both federal and state courts. We must decide in this case whether that Act used language about interstate commerce that nonetheless limits the Act's application, thereby carving out an important statutory niche in which a State remains free to apply its antiarbitration law or policy. We conclude that it does not.

III

The Federal Arbitration Act, § 2, provides that a "written provision in any maritime transaction or a *contract evidencing a transaction involving commerce* to settle by arbitration a controversy thereafter arising out of such contract or transaction . . . shall be valid, irrevocable, and enforceable, save upon such grounds as exist at law or in equity for the revocation of any contract." 9 U.S.C. § 2 (emphasis added).

The initial interpretive question focuses upon the words "involving commerce." These words are broader than the often-found words of art "in commerce." They therefore cover more than " 'only persons or activities *within the flow* of interstate commerce.' " United States v. American Building Maintenance Industries, 422 U.S. 271, 276, 95 S.Ct. 2150, 2154, 45 L.Ed.2d 177 (1975), quoting Gulf Oil Corp. v. Copp Paving Co., 419 U.S. 186, 195, 95 S.Ct. 392, 398, 42 L.Ed.2d 378 (1974) (defining "in commerce" as related to the "flow" and defining the "flow" to include "the generation of goods and services for interstate markets and their transport and distribution to the consumer"); see also FTC v. Bunte Brothers, Inc., 312 U.S. 349, 351, 61 S.Ct. 580, 582, 85 L.Ed. 881 (1941). But, how far beyond the flow of commerce does the word "involving" reach? Is "involving" the functional equivalent of the word "affecting?" That phrase—"affecting commerce"—normally signals a congressional intent to exercise its Commerce Clause powers to the full. See Russell v. United States, 471 U.S. 858, 859, 105 S.Ct. 2455, 2456, 85 L.Ed.2d 829 (1985). We cannot look to other statutes for guidance for the parties tell us that this is the only federal statute that uses the word "involving" to describe an interstate commerce relation.

After examining the statute's language, background, and structure, we conclude that the word "involving" is broad and is indeed the functional equivalent of "affecting." For one thing, such an interpretation, linguistically speaking, is permissible. The dictionary finds instances in which "involve" and "affect" sometimes can mean about the same thing. V Oxford English Dictionary 466 (1st ed. 1933) (providing examples dating back to the mid-nineteenth century, where "involve" means to "include or affect in . . . operation"). For another, the Act's legislative history, to the extent that it is informative, indicates an expansive congressional intent. See, e.g., H.R.Rep. No. 96, 68th Cong., 1st Sess., 1 (1924) (the Act's "control over interstate commerce reaches not only the actual physical interstate shipment of goods but also contracts relating to interstate commerce"); 65 Cong.Rec. 1931 (1924) (the Act "affects contracts relating to interstate subjects and contracts in admiralty") (remarks of Rep. Graham); Joint Hearings on S. 1005 and H.R. 646 before the Subcommittees of the Committees on the Judiciary, 68th Cong., 1st Sess., 7 (1924) (hereinafter Joint Hearings) (testimony of Charles L. Bernheimer, chairman of the

Committee on Arbitration of the Chamber of Commerce of the State of New York, agreeing that the proposed bill "relates to contracts arising in interstate commerce"); id., at 16 (testimony of Julius H. Cohen, drafter for the American Bar Association of much of the proposed bill's language, that the Act reflects part of a strategy to rid the law of an "anachronism" by "get[ting] a Federal law to cover interstate and foreign commerce and admiralty"); see also 9 U.S.C. § 1 (defining the word "commerce" in the language of the Commerce Clause itself).

Further, this Court has previously described the Act's reach expansively as coinciding with that of the Commerce Clause. See, e.g., Perry v. Thomas, 482 U.S. 483, 490, 107 S.Ct. 2520, 2525–26, 96 L.Ed.2d 426 (1987) (the Act "embodies Congress' intent to provide for the enforcement of arbitration agreements within the full reach of the Commerce Clause"); Southland Corp. v. Keating, 465 U.S., at 14–15, 104 S.Ct., at 860 (the " 'involving commerce' " requirement is a constitutionally "necessary qualification" on the Act's reach, marking its permissible outer limit); see also Prima Paint Corp. v. Flood & Conklin Mfg. Co., 388 U.S., at 407, 87 S.Ct., at 1807–08 (Harlan, J., concurring) (endorsing Robert Lawrence Co. v. Devonshire Fabrics, Inc., 271 F.2d 402, 407 (CA2 1959) (Congress, in enacting the FAA, "took pains to utilize as much of its power as it could . . .")).

Finally, a broad interpretation of this language is consistent with the Act's basic purpose, to put arbitration provisions on "the same footing" as a contract's other terms. Scherk v. Alberto–Culver Co., 417 U.S., at 511, 94 S.Ct., at 2453. Conversely, a narrower interpretation is not consistent with the Act's purpose, for (unless unreasonably narrowed to the flow of commerce) such an interpretation would create a new, unfamiliar, test lying somewhere in a no-man's land between "in commerce" and "affecting commerce," thereby unnecessarily complicating the law and breeding litigation from a statute that seeks to avoid it.

We recognize arguments to the contrary: The pre-New Deal Congress that passed the Act in 1925 might well have thought the Commerce Clause did not stretch as far as has turned out to be so. But, it is not unusual for this Court in similar circumstances to ask whether the scope of a statute should expand along with the expansion of the Commerce Clause power itself, and to answer the question affirmatively—as, for the reasons set forth above, we do here. See, e.g., McLain v. Real Estate Bd. of New Orleans, Inc., 444 U.S. 232, 241, 100 S.Ct. 502, 508–509, 62 L.Ed.2d 441 (1980); Hospital Building Co. v. Trustees of Rex Hospital, 425 U.S. 738, 743, n. 2, 96 S.Ct. 1848, 1852, n. 2, 48 L.Ed.2d 338 (1976). . . .

The Gwins and Dobsons, with far better reason, point to a different case, Bernhardt v. Polygraphic Co. of America, 350 U.S. 198, 76 S.Ct. 273, 100 L.Ed. 199 (1956). In that case, Bernhardt, a New York resident, had entered into an employment contract (containing an arbitration clause) in New York with Polygraphic, a New York corporation. But, Bernhardt "was to perform" that contract after he "later became a resident of Vermont." Id., at 199, 76 S.Ct., at 274. This Court was faced with the question whether, in light of Erie, a federal court should apply the Federal Arbitration Act in a diversity case when faced with state law hostile to arbitration. 350 U.S., at 200, 76 S.Ct., at 274–75. The Court did not reach that question, however, for it decided that the contract itself did not "involv[e]" interstate commerce and therefore fell outside the Act. Id., at 200–202, 76 S.Ct., at 274–276. Since Congress, constitutionally speaking, *could* have applied the Act to Bernhardt's contract, say the parties, how then can we say that the Act's word "involving" reaches as far as the Commerce Clause itself?

The best response to this argument is to point to the way in which the Court reasoned in Bernhardt, and to what the Court said. It said that the *reason* the Act did not apply to Bernhardt's contract was that there was

> "*no showing that petitioner* while performing his duties under the employment contract was working 'in' commerce, was producing goods for commerce, or *was engaging in activity that affected commerce*, within the meaning of our decisions." Bernhardt, supra, at 200–201, 76 S.Ct., at 274–275 (emphasis added) (footnote omitted).

Thus, the Court interpreted the words "involving commerce" as broadly as the words "affecting commerce"; and, as we have said, these latter words normally mean a full exercise of constitutional power. At the same time, the Court's opinion does not discuss the implications of the "interstate" facts to which the respondents now point. For these reasons, Bernhardt does not require us to narrow the scope of the word "involving." And, we conclude that the word "involving," like "affecting," signals an intent to exercise Congress's commerce power to the full.

IV

Section 2 applies where there is "a contract *evidencing a transaction* involving commerce." 9 U.S.C. § 2 (emphasis added). The second interpretive question focuses on the underscored words. Does "evidencing a transaction" mean only that the transaction (that the contract "evidences") must turn out, *in fact*, to have involved interstate commerce? Or, does it mean more?

Many years ago, Second Circuit Chief Judge Lumbard said that the phrase meant considerably more. He wrote: "The significant question … is not whether, in carrying out the terms of the contract, the parties did cross state lines, but whether, *at the time they entered into it* and accepted the arbitration clause, they *contemplated* substantial interstate activity. Cogent evidence regarding their state of mind at the time would be the terms of the contract, and if it, on its face, evidences interstate traffic …, the contract should come within § 2. In addition, evidence as to how the parties expected the contract to be performed and how it was performed is relevant to whether substantial interstate activity was contemplated." Metro Industrial Painting Corp. v. Terminal Constr. Co., 287 F.2d 382, 387 (C.A.2 1961) (Lumbard, C.J., concurring) (second emphasis added).

The Supreme Court of Alabama, and several other courts, have followed this view, known as the "contemplation of the parties" test. See supra, at 269–270.

We find the interpretive choice difficult, but for several reasons we conclude that the first interpretation ("commerce in fact") is more faithful to the statute than the second ("contemplation of the parties"). First, the "contemplation of the parties" interpretation, when viewed in terms of the statute's basic purpose, seems anomalous. That interpretation invites litigation about what was, or was not, "contemplated." Why would Congress intend a test that risks the very kind of costs and delay through litigation (about the circumstances of contract formation) that Congress wrote the Act to help the parties avoid? See Moses H. Cone Memorial Hospital v. Mercury Constr. Corp., 460 U.S. 1, 29, 103 S.Ct. 927, 944, 74 L.Ed.2d 765 (1983) (the Act "calls for a summary and speedy disposition of motions or petitions to enforce arbitration clauses").

Moreover, that interpretation too often would turn the validity of an arbitration clause on what, from the perspective of the statute's basic purpose, seems happenstance, namely whether the parties happened to think to insert a reference to interstate commerce in the document or happened to mention it in an initial conversation. After all, parties to a sales contract with an arbitration clause might naturally think about the goods sold, or about arbitration, but why should they naturally think about an interstate commerce connection?

Further, that interpretation fits awkwardly with the rest of § 2. That section, for example, permits parties to agree to submit to arbitration "an existing controversy arising out of" a contract made earlier. Why would Congress want to risk non-enforceability of this *later* arbitration agreement (even if fully connected with interstate commerce) simply because the parties did not properly "contemplate" (or write about) the interstate aspects of the earlier contract? The first interpretation, requiring only that the "transaction" *in fact* involve interstate commerce, avoids this anomaly, as it avoids the other anomalous effects growing out of the "contemplation of the parties" test.

Second, the statute's language permits the "commerce in fact" interpretation. That interpretation, we concede, leaves little work for the word "evidencing" (in the phrase "a contract evidencing a transaction") to perform, for every contract evidences some transaction. But, perhaps Congress did not want that word to perform much work. The Act's history, to the extent informative, indicates that the Act's supporters saw the Act as part of an effort to make arbitration agreements universally enforceable. They wanted to "get a Federal law" that would "cover" areas where the Constitution authorized Congress to legislate, namely "interstate and foreign commerce and admiralty." Joint Hearings, at 16 (testimony of Julius H. Cohen). They urged Congress to model the Act after a New York statute that made enforceable a written arbitration provision "in a written contract," Act of Apr. 19, 1920, ch. 275, § 2, 1920 N.Y.Laws 803, 804. Hearing on S. 4213 and S. 4214 before the Subcommittee of the Senate Committee on the Judiciary, 67th Cong., 4th Sess., 2 (1923) (testimony of Charles L. Bernheimer). Early drafts made enforceable a written arbitration provision "in *any contract* or maritime transaction or transaction involving commerce." S. 4214, 67th Cong., 4th Sess. § 2 (1922) (emphasis added); S. 1005, 68th Cong., 1st Sess. (1923); H.R. 646, 68th Cong., 1st Sess. (1924). Members of Congress, looking at that phrase, might have thought the words "any contract" standing alone went beyond Congress's constitutional authority. And, if so, they might have simply connected those words with the later words "transaction involving commerce," thereby creating the phrase that became law. Nothing in the Act's history suggests any other, more limiting, task for the language.

Third, the basic practical argument underlying the "contemplation of the parties" test was, in Judge Lumbard's words, the need to "be cautious in construing the act lest we excessively encroach on the powers which Congressional policy, if not the Constitution, would reserve to the states." Metro Industrial Painting Corp., supra, at 386 (Lumbard, C.J., concurring). The practical force of this argument has diminished in light of this Court's later holdings that the Act does displace state law to the contrary. See Southland Corp. v. Keating, 465 U.S., at 10–16, 104 S.Ct., at 858–861; Perry v. Thomas, 482 U.S., at 489–492, 107 S.Ct., at 2525–2527.

Finally, we note that an amicus curiae argues for an "objective" ("reasonable person" oriented) version of the "contemplation of the parties" test on the ground that such an interpretation would better protect consumers asked to sign form contracts by businesses. We agree that Congress, when enacting this law, had the needs of consumers, as well as others, in mind. See S.Rep. No. 536, 68th Cong., 1st Sess., 3 (1924) (the Act, by avoiding "the delay and expense of litigation," will appeal "to big business and little business alike, ... corporate interests [and] ... individuals"). Indeed, arbitration's advantages often would seem helpful to individuals, say, complaining about a product, who need a less expensive alternative to litigation. See, e.g., H.R.Rep. No. 97–542, p. 13 (1982) ("The advantages of arbitration are many: it is usually cheaper and faster than litigation; it can have simpler procedural and evidentiary rules; it normally minimizes hostility and is less disruptive of ongoing and future business dealings among the parties; it is often more flexible in regard to scheduling of times and places of hearings and discovery devices ..."). And, according to the American Arbitration Association (also an amicus here), more than one-third of its claims involve amounts below $10,000, while another third involve claims of $10,000 to $50,000 (with an average processing time of less than six months). App. to Brief for American Arbitration Association as Amicus Curiae 26–27.

We are uncertain, however, just how the "objective" version of the "contemplation" test would help consumers. Sometimes, of course, it would permit, say, a consumer with potentially large damage claims, to disavow a contract's arbitration provision and proceed in court. But, if so, it would equally permit, say, local business entities to disavow a contract's arbitration provisions, thereby leaving the typical consumer who has only a small damage claim (who seeks, say, the value of only a defective refrigerator or television set) without any remedy but a court remedy, the costs and delays of which could eat up the value of an eventual small recovery.

In any event, § 2 gives States a method for protecting consumers against unfair pressure to agree to a contract with an unwanted arbitration provision. States may regulate contracts, including arbitration clauses, under general contract law principles and they may invalidate an arbitration clause "upon such grounds as exist at law or in equity for the revocation of *any* contract." 9 U.S.C. § 2 (emphasis added). What States may not do is decide that a contract is fair enough to enforce all its basic terms (price, service, credit), but not fair enough to enforce its arbitration clause. The Act makes any such state policy unlawful, for that kind of policy would place arbitration clauses on an unequal "footing," directly contrary to the Act's language and Congress's intent. See Volt Information Sciences, Inc., 489 U.S., at 474, 109 S.Ct., at 1253.

For these reasons, we accept the "commerce in fact" interpretation, reading the Act's language as insisting that the "transaction" in fact "involve" interstate commerce, even if the parties did not contemplate an interstate commerce connection.

V

The parties do not contest that the transaction in this case, in fact, involved interstate commerce. In addition to the multistate nature of Terminix and Allied–Bruce, the termite-treating and house-repairing material used by Allied–Bruce in its (allegedly inadequate) efforts to carry out the terms of the Plan, came from outside Alabama.

Consequently, the judgment of the Supreme Court of Alabama is reversed and the case is remanded for further proceedings consistent with this opinion.

It is so ordered.

■ JUSTICE O'CONNOR, concurring.

I agree with the Court's construction of § 2 of the Federal Arbitration Act. As applied in federal courts, the Court's interpretation comports fully with my understanding of congressional intent. A more restrictive definition of "evidencing" and "involving" would doubtless foster prearbitration litigation that would frustrate the very purpose of the statute. As applied in state courts, however, the effect of a broad formulation of § 2 is more troublesome. The reading of § 2 adopted today will displace many state statutes carefully calibrated to protect consumers, see, e.g., Mont.Code Ann. § 27–5–114(2)(b) (1993) (refusing to enforce arbitration clauses in consumer contracts where the consideration is $5,000 or less), and state procedural requirements aimed at ensuring knowing and voluntary consent, see, e.g., S.C.Code Ann. § 15–48–10(a) (Supp.1993) (requiring that notice of arbitration provision be prominently placed on first page of contract). I have long adhered to the view, discussed below, that Congress designed the Federal Arbitration Act to apply only in federal courts. But if we are to apply the Act in state courts, it makes little sense to read § 2 differently in that context. In the end, my agreement with the Court's construction of § 2 rests largely on the wisdom of maintaining a uniform standard.

I continue to believe that Congress never intended the Federal Arbitration Act to apply in state courts, and that this Court has strayed far afield in giving the Act so broad a compass. See Southland Corp. v. Keating, 465 U.S. 1, 21–36, 104 S.Ct. 852, 863–871, 79 L.Ed.2d 1 (1984) (O'CONNOR, J., dissenting); see also Perry v. Thomas, 482 U.S. 483, 494–495, 107 S.Ct. 2520, 2528, 96 L.Ed.2d 426 (1987) (O'CONNOR, J., dissenting); . . . We have often said that the pre-emptive effect of a federal statute is fundamentally a question of congressional intent. See, e.g., Cipollone v. Liggett Group, Inc., 505 U.S. 504, 516, 112 S.Ct. 2608, 120 L.Ed.2d 407 (1992); . . . Indeed, we have held that " '[w]here . . . the field which Congress is said to have pre-empted' includes areas that have 'been traditionally occupied by the States,' congressional intent to supersede state laws must be 'clear and manifest.' " English, supra, 496 U.S., at 79, 110 S.Ct., at 2275, quoting Jones v. Rath Packing Co., 430 U.S. 519, 525, 97 S.Ct. 1305, 1309, 51 L.Ed.2d 604 (1977). Yet, over the past decade, the Court has abandoned all pretense of ascertaining congressional intent with respect to the Federal Arbitration Act, building instead, case by case, an edifice of its own creation. See Perry v. Thomas, supra, 482 U.S., at 493, 107 S.Ct., at 2527–2528 (STEVENS, J., dissenting) ("It is only in the last few years that the Court has effectively rewritten the statute to give it a pre-emptive scope that Congress certainly did not intend"). I have no doubt that Congress could enact, in the first instance, a federal arbitration statute that displaces most state arbitration laws. But I also have no doubt that, in 1925, Congress enacted no such statute.

Were we writing on a clean slate, I would adhere to that view and affirm the Alabama court's decision. But, as the Court points out, more than 10 years have passed since Southland, several subsequent cases have built upon its reasoning, and parties have undoubtedly made contracts in reliance on the Court's interpretation of the Act in the interim. After reflection, I am persuaded by considerations of *stare decisis*, which we have said "have special force in the area of statutory interpretation," Patterson v. McLean Credit Union, 491 U.S. 164, 172–173, 109 S.Ct. 2363, 2370–2371, 105 L.Ed.2d 132 (1989), to acquiesce in today's judgment. Though wrong, Southland has not proved unworkable, and, as always, "Congress remains free to alter what we have done." Ibid.

Today's decision caps this Court's effort to expand the Federal Arbitration Act. Although each decision has built logically upon the decisions preceding it, the initial building block in Southland laid a faulty foundation. I acquiesce in today's judgment because there is no "special justification" to overrule Southland. Arizona v. Rumsey, 467 U.S. 203, 212, 104 S.Ct. 2305, 2310–11, 81 L.Ed.2d 164 (1984). It remains now for Congress to correct this interpretation if it wishes to preserve state autonomy in state courts.

■ JUSTICE THOMAS, with whom JUSTICE SCALIA joins, dissenting.

I disagree with the majority at the threshold of this case, and so I do not reach the question that it decides. In my view, the Federal Arbitration Act (FAA) does not apply in state courts. I respectfully dissent.

I

In Southland Corp. v. Keating, 465 U.S. 1, 104 S.Ct. 852, 79 L.Ed.2d 1 (1984), this Court concluded that § 2 of the FAA "appl[ies] in state as well as federal courts," id., at 12, 104 S.Ct., at 859, and "withdr[aws] the power of the states to require a judicial forum for the resolution of claims which the contracting parties agreed to resolve by arbitration," id., at 10, 104 S.Ct., at 858. In my view, both aspects of Southland are wrong.

A

Section 2 of the FAA declares that an arbitration clause contained in "a contract evidencing a transaction involving commerce" shall be "valid, irrevocable, and enforceable, save upon such grounds as exist at law or in equity for the revocation of any contract." 9 U.S.C. § 2.... On its face, and considered out of context, § 2 draws no apparent distinction between federal courts and state courts. But not until 1959—nearly 35 years after Congress enacted the FAA—did any court suggest that § 2 applied in state courts. See Robert Lawrence Co. v. Devonshire Fabrics, Inc., 271 F.2d 402, 407 (C.A.2 1959), cert. dism'd, 364 U.S. 801, 81 S.Ct. 27, 5 L.Ed.2d 37 (1960). No state court agreed until the 1960's. See, e.g., REA Express v. Missouri Pacific R. Co., 447 S.W.2d 721, 726 (Tex.Civ.App.1969) (stating that the FAA applies but noting that it had been waived in the case at hand); cf. Rubewa Products Co. v. Watson's Quality Turkey Products, Inc., 242 A.2d 609, 613 (D.C.1968) (same). This Court waited until 1984 to conclude, over a strong dissent by Justice O'CONNOR, that § 2 extends to the States. See Southland, supra, 465 U.S., at 10–16, 104 S.Ct., at 858–861.

The explanation for this delay is simple: the statute that Congress enacted actually applies only in federal courts. At the time of the FAA's passage in 1925, laws governing the enforceability of arbitration agreements were generally thought to deal purely with matters of procedure rather than substance, because they were directed solely to the mechanisms for resolving the underlying disputes. As then-Judge Cardozo explained: "Arbitration is a form of procedure whereby differences may be settled. It is not a definition of the rights and wrongs out of which differences grow." Berkovitz v. Arbib & Houlberg, Inc., 230 N.Y. 261, 270, 130 N.E. 288, 290 (1921) (holding the New York arbitration statute of 1920, from which the FAA was copied, to be purely procedural). It would have been extraordinary for Congress to attempt to prescribe procedural rules for *state* courts. See, e.g., Ex parte Gounis, 304 Mo. 428, 437, 263 S.W. 988, 990 (1924) (describing the rule that Congress cannot "regulate or control [state courts'] modes of procedure" as one of the "general principles which have come to be accepted as settled constitutional law"). And because the FAA was enacted against this general background, no one read it as such an attempt. See, e.g., Baum & Pressman, The Enforcement of Commercial Arbitration Agreements in the Federal Courts, 8 N.Y.U.L.Q.Rev. 428, 459 (1931) (noting that the FAA "does not purport to extend its teeth to state proceedings," though arguing that it constitutionally could have done so); 6 S. Williston & G. Thompson, Law of Contracts 5368 (rev. ed. 1938) ("Inasmuch as arbitration acts are deemed procedural, the [FAA] applies only to the federal courts ..." (footnote omitted)); cf. Southland, 465 U.S., at 25–29, 104 S.Ct., at 865–868 (O'CONNOR, J., dissenting) (describing "unambiguous" legislative history to this effect).

Indeed, to judge from the reported cases, it appears that no state court was even *asked* to enforce the statute for many years after the passage of the FAA. Federal courts, for their part, refused to apply state arbitration statutes in cases to which the FAA was inapplicable. See, e.g., California Prune & Apricot Growers' Assn. v. Catz American Co., 60 F.2d 788 (C.A.9 1932). Their refusal was not the outgrowth of this Court's decision in Swift v. Tyson, 41 U.S. (16 Pet.) 1, 10 L.Ed. 865 (1842), which held that certain categories of state judicial decisions were not "laws" for purposes of the Rules of Decision Act and hence were not binding in federal courts; even under Swift, state statutes unambiguously constituted "laws." Rather, federal courts did not apply the state arbitration statutes because the statutes were not considered *substantive* laws. See California Prune, supra, at 790 ("It is undoubtedly true that a federal court in proper cases may enforce state laws; but this principle is applicable only when the state legislation invoke[d] creates or establishes a substantive or general right"). In short, state arbitration statutes prescribed rules for the state courts, and the FAA prescribed rules for the federal courts.

It is easy to understand why lawyers in 1925 classified arbitration statutes as procedural. An arbitration agreement is a species of forum-selection clause: without laying down any rules of decision, it identifies the adjudicator of disputes. A strong argument can be made that such forum-selection clauses concern procedure rather than substance. Cf. Fed.Rules Civ.Proc. 73 (district court, with consent of the parties, may refer case to magistrate for resolution), 53 (district court may refer issues to special master). And if a contractual provision deals purely with matters of judicial procedure, one might well conclude that questions about whether and how it will be enforced also relate to procedure. . . .

Despite the FAA's general focus on the federal courts, of course, § 2 itself contains no such explicit limitation. But the text of the statute nonetheless makes clear that § 2 was not meant as a statement of substantive law binding on the States. After all, if § 2 really was understood to "creat[e] federal substantive law requiring the parties to honor arbitration agreements," Southland, 465 U.S., at 15, n. 9, 104 S.Ct., at 860, n. 9, then the breach of an arbitration agreement covered by § 2 would give rise to a federal question within the subject-matter jurisdiction of the federal district courts. See 28 U.S.C. § 1331. Yet the ensuing provisions of the Act, without expressly taking away this jurisdiction, clearly rest on the assumption that federal courts have jurisdiction to enforce arbitration agreements only when they would have had jurisdiction over the underlying dispute. See 9 U.S.C. §§ 3, 4, 8. In other words, the FAA treats arbitration simply as one means of resolving disputes that lie within the jurisdiction of the federal courts; it makes clear that the breach of a covered arbitration agreement does not itself provide any independent basis for such jurisdiction. Even the Southland majority was forced to acknowledge this point, conceding that § 2 "does not create any independent federal-question jurisdiction under 28 U.S.C. § 1331 or otherwise." 465 U.S., at 15, n. 9, 104 S.Ct., at 860, n. 9. But the *reason* that § 2 does not give rise to federal-question jurisdiction is that it was enacted as a purely procedural provision. For the same reason, it applies only in the federal courts.

The distinction between "substance" and "procedure" acquired new meaning after Erie Railroad Co. v. Tompkins, 304 U.S. 64, 58 S.Ct. 817, 82 L.Ed. 1188 (1938). Thus, in 1956 we held that for Erie purposes, the question whether a court should stay litigation brought in breach of an arbitration agreement is one of "substantive" law. Bernhardt v. Polygraphic Co. of America, Inc., 350 U.S. 198, 203–204, 76 S.Ct. 273, 276–277, 100 L.Ed. 199. But this later development could not change the original meaning of the statute that Congress enacted in 1925. Although Bernhardt classified portions of the FAA as "substantive" rather than "procedural," it does not mean that they were so understood in 1925 or that Congress extended the FAA's reach beyond the federal courts.

When Justice O'CONNOR pointed out the FAA's original meaning in her Southland dissent, see 465 U.S., at 25–30, 104 S.Ct., at 865–868, the majority offered only one real response. If § 2 had been considered a purely procedural provision, the majority reasoned, Congress would have extended it to all contracts rather than simply to maritime transactions and "contract[s] evidencing a transaction involving [interstate or foreign] commerce." See id., at 14, 104 S.Ct., at 860. Yet Congress might well have thought that even if it *could* have called upon federal courts to enforce arbitration agreements in every single case that came before them, there was no federal interest in doing so unless interstate commerce or maritime transactions were involved. This conclusion is far more plausible than Southland's idea that Congress both viewed § 2 as a statement of substantive law and believed that it created no federal-question jurisdiction.

Even if the interstate commerce requirement raises uncertainty about the original meaning of the statute, we should resolve the uncertainty in light of core principles of federalism. While "Congress may legislate in areas traditionally regulated by the States" as long as it "is acting within the powers granted it under the Constitution," we assume that "Congress does not exercise [this power] lightly." Gregory v. Ashcroft, 501 U.S. 452, 460, 111 S.Ct. 2395, 2400–2401, 115 L.Ed.2d 410 (1991). To the extent that federal statutes are ambiguous, we do not read them to displace state law. Rather, we must be "absolutely certain" that Congress intended such displacement before we give preemptive effect to a federal statute. Id., at 464, 111 S.Ct., at 2402–2403. In 1925, the enactment of a "substantive" arbitration statute along the lines envisioned by Southland would have displaced an enormous body of state law: outside of a few States, predispute arbitration agreements either were wholly unenforceable or at least were not subject to specific performance. See generally Note to Williams v. Branning Mfg. Co., 47 LRA (n.s.) 337 (1914) (detailed listing of state cases). Far from being "absolutely certain" that Congress swept aside these state rules, I am quite sure that it did not.

B

Suppose, however, that the first aspect of Southland was correct: § 2 requires States to enforce the covered arbitration agreements and pre-empts all contrary state law. There still would be no textual basis for Southland's suggestion that § 2 requires the States to enforce those agreements through the remedy of specific performance—that is, by forcing the parties to submit to arbitration. A contract surely can be "valid, irrevocable and enforceable" even though it can be enforced only through actions for damages. Thus, on the eve of the FAA's enactment, this Court described executory arbitration agreements as being "valid" and as creating "a perfect obligation" under federal law even though federal courts refused to order their specific performance. See Red Cross Line v. Atlantic Fruit Co., 264 U.S. 109, 120–123, 44 S.Ct. 274, 275–277, 68 L.Ed. 582 (1924).

To be sure, §§ 3 and 4 of the FAA require that *federal* courts specifically enforce arbitration agreements. These provisions deal, respectively, with the potential plaintiffs and the potential defendants in the underlying dispute: § 3 holds the plaintiffs to their promise not to take their claims straight to court, while § 4 holds the defendants to their promise to submit to arbitration rather than making the other party sue them. Had this case arisen in one of the "courts of the United States," it is § 3 that would have been relevant. Upon proper motion, the court would have been obliged to grant a stay pending arbitration, unless the contract between the parties did not "evidenc[e] a transaction involving [interstate] commerce." See Bernhardt, 350 U.S., at 202, 76 S.Ct., at 275–276 (holding that § 3 is limited to the arbitration agreements that § 2 declares valid). Because this case arose in the courts of Alabama, however, petitioners are forced to contend that § 2 imposes precisely the same obligation on *all* courts (both federal and state) that § 3 imposes solely on *federal* courts. Though Southland supports this argument, it simply cannot be correct, or § 3 would be superfluous.

Alabama law brings these issues into sharp focus. Citing "public policy" grounds that reach back to Bozeman v. Gilbert, 1 Ala. 90 (1840), Alabama courts have declared that predispute arbitration agreements are "void." See, e.g., Wells v. Mobile County Bd. of Realtors, 387 So.2d 140, 144 (Ala.1980). But a separate state statute also includes "[a]n agreement to submit a controversy to arbitration" among the obligations that "cannot be specifically enforced" in Alabama. Ala.Code § 8–1–41 (1975). Especially in light of the Gregory v. Ashcroft presumption, § 2—even if applicable to the States—is most naturally read to pre-empt only Alabama's common-law rule and not the state statute; the statute does not itself make executory arbitration agreements invalid, revocable, or unenforceable, any more than the inclusion of "[a]n obligation to render personal service" in the same statutory provision means that employment contracts are invalid in Alabama. In the case at hand, the specific-enforcement statute appears to provide an adequate ground for the denial of petitioners' motion for a stay.

II

Rather than attempting to defend Southland on its merits, petitioners rely chiefly on the doctrine of *stare decisis* in urging us to adhere to our mistaken interpretation of the FAA. See Reply Brief for Petitioners 3–6. In my view, that doctrine is insufficient to save Southland.

The majority (ante, at 272–273) and Justice O'CONNOR (ante, at 283–284) properly focus on whether overruling Southland would frustrate the legitimate expectations of people who have drafted and executed contracts in the belief that even state courts will strictly enforce arbitration clauses. I do not doubt that innumerable contracts containing arbitration clauses have been written since 1984, or that arbitrable disputes might yet arise out of a large proportion of these contracts. Some of these contracts might well have been written differently in the absence of Southland. Still, I see no reason to think that the costs of overruling Southland are unacceptably high. Certainly no reliance interests are involved in cases like the present one, where the applicability of the FAA was not within the contemplation of the parties at the time of contracting. In many other cases, moreover, the parties will simply comply with their arbitration agreement, either on the theory that they should live up to their promises or on the theory that arbitration is the cheapest and best way of resolving their dispute. In a fair number of the remaining cases, the party seeking to enforce an arbitration agreement will be able to get into federal court, where the FAA will apply. And even if access to federal court is impossible (because § 2 creates no independent basis for federal-question jurisdiction), many cases will arise in States whose own law largely parallels the FAA. Only Alabama, Mississippi, and Nebraska still hold all executory arbitration agreements to be unenforceable, though some other States refuse to enforce particular classes of such agreements. See Strickland, The Federal Arbitration Act's Interstate Commerce Requirement: What's Left for State Arbitration Law?, 21 Hofstra L.Rev. 385, 401–403, and n. 93 (1992).

Quoting Arizona v. Rumsey, 467 U.S. 203, 212, 104 S.Ct. 2305, 2310–2311, 81 L.Ed.2d 164 (1984), Justice O'CONNOR nonetheless acquiesces in the majority's judgment "because there is no 'special justification' to overrule Southland." Ante, at 844. Even under this approach, the necessity of "preserv[ing] state autonomy in state courts," ibid., seems sufficient to me.

But suppose that *stare decisis* really did require us to abide by Southland's holding that § 2 applies to the States. The doctrine still would not require us to follow Southland's suggestion that § 2 requires the specific enforcement of the arbitration agreements that it covers. We accord no precedential weight to mere dicta, and this latter suggestion was wholly unnecessary to the decision in Southland. The arbitration agreement at issue there, if valid at all with respect to the particular claims in dispute, clearly was subject to specific performance under state law; indeed, the state trial court had already compelled arbitration for all the other claims raised in the complaint. See Southland, 465 U.S., at 4, 104 S.Ct., at 855; Cal.Code Civ.Proc.Ann. §§ 1281.2, 1281.4 (West 1982). Accordingly, the only question properly before the Southland Court was whether § 2 pre-empted a separate state law declaring the arbitration agreement "void" as applied to the remaining claims. See 465 U.S., at 10, 104 S.Ct., at 858 (discussing Cal.Corp.Code Ann. § 1512 (West 1977)). The same can be said for Perry v. Thomas, 482 U.S. 483, 107 S.Ct. 2520, 96 L.Ed.2d 426 (1987), in which we again held that § 2 pre-empted a California statute that (as we had observed in a prior case, see Merrill Lynch, Pierce, Fenner & Smith, Inc. v. Ware, 414 U.S. 117, 133, 94 S.Ct. 383, 392–393, 38 L.Ed.2d 348 (1973)) made certain arbitration clauses "unenforceable." We have subsequently reserved judgment about the extent to which state courts must enforce arbitration agreements through the mechanisms that §§ 3 and 4 of the FAA prescribe for the *federal* courts. See Volt Information Sciences, Inc. v. Board of Trustees of Leland Stanford Junior Univ., 489 U.S. 468, 477, 109 S.Ct. 1248, 1254–1255, 103 L.Ed.2d 488 (1989). Cf. McDermott Int'l, Inc. v. Lloyds Underwriters of London, 944 F.2d 1199, 1210 (C.A.5 1991) ("We conclude from the Supreme Court's opinions that state courts do not necessarily have to grant stays of conflicting litigation or compel arbitration in compliance with the FAA's sections 3 and 4"). In short, we have never actually held, as opposed to stating or implying in dicta, that the FAA requires a state court to stay lawsuits brought in violation of an arbitration agreement covered by § 2.

Because I believe that the FAA imposes no such obligation on state courts, and indeed that the statute is wholly inapplicable in those courts, I would affirm the Alabama Supreme Court's judgment.

[Justice SCALIA wrote a separate dissenting opinion in which he argued that "Adhering to Southland entails a permanent, unauthorized eviction of state-court power to adjudicate a potentially large class of disputes." He also stated that he "stand[s] ready to join four other Justices in overruling [Southland], since Southland will not become more correct over time, ... the course of future lawmaking seems unlikely to be affected by its existence, and the accumulated private reliance will not likely increase beyond the level it has already achieved (few contracts not terminable at will have more than a 5–year term)".]

* * *

Note on *United States v. Lopez*

Ruling on the breadth of the FAA, the Court in *Perry* determined that Congress intended that the statute be enforceable to "the full reach of the Commerce Clause." The Court reiterated and amplified this holding in *Allied-Bruce Terminex,* but in that same term the Court also decided a case that may have far-reaching implications for the scope of the Commerce Power.

In UNITED STATES V. LOPEZ, 514 U.S. 549, 115 S.Ct. 1624 (1995), the Supreme Court, for the first time in almost sixty years and the ninth time in its history, struck down a federal statute for exceeding the scope of Congress' authority under the Commerce Clause. The Respondent, Alfonso Lopez, was convicted under the Gun–Free School Zones Act of 1990, which made the carrying of a gun within 1,000 feet of a school a federal offense. Lopez was convicted in district court, and the conviction was reversed by the Fifth Circuit. A five-justice majority invalidated the statute.

The majority in *Lopez* reaffirmed Congress's power to regulate commerce in "three broad areas": (1) "the use of the channels of interstate commerce;" (2) "the instrumentalities of interstate commerce, or persons or things in interstate commerce, even though the threat [against which legislation is directed] may come only from intrastate activities;" and (3) those activities having a substantial relation to interstate commerce." The *Lopez* case involved the third (and historically broadest) basis of the Commerce power. The Court reasoned that Congress can only regulate activities that "substantially affect interstate commerce" under the *NLRB v. Jones & Laughlin Steel Co.* line of cases if the activities so regulated are "commercial" in nature. Finding that "the possession of a gun in a local school zone is in no sense an economic activity," the Court, speaking through Chief Justice Rehnquist, concluded that the federal sovereign had no authority to criminalize the activity. In doing so, the Court rejected the government's proffered syllogism: the presence of weapons in or around schools interferes with the educational mission of schools; education is central to the national economy; therefore, the presence of guns in the vicinity of the nation's schools has predictably dire consequences for national productivity and thereby affects commerce.

The majority conceded that its distinction between commercial and noncommercial activity "may in some cases result in legal uncertainty." In an apparent effort to provide some guidance for future cases, the Court staked out certain areas of activity in which the states "have historically been sovereign," and which are thus by implication off limits to federal regulation: "family law ... (including marriage, divorce, and child custody) ... criminal law enforcement or education."

Justices Kennedy and Thomas concurred separately. Justice Kennedy emphasized the need for the regulated activity to have a "commercial character" and for the legislation itself to "have an evident commercial nexus" to withstand Commerce Clause scrutiny. Justice Breyer wrote the principal dissent, in which Justices Ginsburg, Souter and Stevens joined.

* * *

Questions

1. The language of the FAA does not merely require a transaction "involving commerce"—a term which Justice Breyer equates with "affecting commerce" in *Allied-Bruce Terminex*—it also requires that there be a contract "evidencing" a transaction involving commerce. Was the Dobsons'

contract to exterminate pests in their home clearly a "contract evidencing a transaction involving interstate commerce?"

2. Can a court determine whether a contract involves interstate commerce without examining the facts of the case? If a court examines the facts, is it displacing the role of the arbitrator?

3. The FAA was enacted in 1925, before the expansion of Congress' Commerce Power in the 1930s. Leaving aside the issue of whether the statutory grant should expand with the expanding interpretations of the Commerce Power, does the fact that the statute was passed before it was evident that the Commerce Power would be interpreted expansively suggest that the basis for the statute might have been Article III rather than the Commerce Power, as the dissenters in *Allied-Bruce* suggest?

4. What, if anything, does the holding in *Lopez* do to the reach of the FAA? Does it portend anything for the FAA or for other statutes based on the Commerce Power?

* * *

---

3. ENFORCEABILITY OF AGREEMENTS TO ARBITRATE

It is frequently stated that arbitration is a creature of contract. This axiom means that arbitration cannot be imposed on parties without their consent and that the form of arbitration to be utilized is determined by the parties' agreement. Similarly, the issues subject to arbitration are determined by the agreement between the parties. Traditionally, parties in contractual relations have used arbitration to resolve disputes that arise during the course of their contractual relationship about issues of contract interpretation, performance, and breach. The contractual core of arbitration means that arbitrators are expected to base their awards on the terms of the parties' agreement.[1]

Contracting parties often include broadly worded arbitration clauses in their agreements. Typical is a clause whereby the parties promise to arbitrate "all disputes that arise out of or in relation" to a specified transaction. In such cases, courts are called upon to decide how broadly to interpret the arbitration clause. For example, should a broad boilerplate arbitration clause be deemed to refer only to disputes over contractual interpretation and performance, or should it be deemed to refer as well to disputes that arise outside of the parties' contractual obligations? For example, should a boilerplate clause obligate parties to arbitrate tort-law

---

1. In the past, arbitrators in some settings such as trade associations and craft guilds have utilized customs and norms of the trade as well as express contractual terms to inform their decisions. In these settings, the parties arguably understood that the arbitrator's role was not merely to interpret the parties' agreement, but it was also to impose on the parties the norms of the community within which the parties were mutually engaged. See, e.g. Katherine Van Wezel Stone, *Rustic Justice: Community and Coercion Under the Federal Arbitration Act*, 77 UNIV. N.CAR. L. REV. 931 (1999).

claims that arise incidentally to their contractual dealings? Should such a clause compel arbitration of disputes over public law claims—claims that one side or the other has violated a statute? Or, to put it differently, should parties be able to use private contracting to take public law claims out of the courts and place them in an arbitral forum instead? To what extent should courts permit parties to select the forum for resolving their disputes when the disputes implicate issues of statutory or common law rights?

The Supreme Court has grappled with these questions in relation to the Federal Arbitration Act for fifty years. Initially the Court interpreted the Federal Arbitration Act to compel arbitration of parties' contractual disputes, but not to compel arbitration of ancillary statutory or tort law claims. But in a series of cases in the 1980s, the Court reversed its previous position and found a large number of public law claims to be amenable to arbitration. These cases define the scope of arbitration today.

Wilko v. Swan

346 U.S. 427, 74 S.Ct. 182 (1953).

■ MR. JUSTICE REED delivered the opinion of the Court.

This action by petitioner, a customer, against respondents, partners in a securities brokerage firm, was brought in the United States District Court for the Southern District of New York, to recover damages under § 12(2) of the Securities Act of 1933.[1] The complaint alleged that on or about January 17, 1951, through the instrumentalities of interstate commerce, petitioner was induced by Hayden, Stone and Company to purchase 1,600 shares of the common stock of Air Associates, Incorporated, by false representations that pursuant to a merger contract with the Borg Warner Corporation, Air Associates' stock would be valued at $6.00 per share over the then current market price, and that financial interests were buying up the stock for the speculative profit. It was alleged that he was not told that Haven B. Page (also named as a defendant but not involved in this review), a director of, and counsel for, Air Associates was then selling his own Air Associates' stock, including some or all that petitioner purchased. Two

---

1. 15 U.S.C. § 77l(2), provides: "Any person who—* * *

"(2) sells a security (whether or not exempted by the provisions of section 77c of this title, other than paragraph (2) of subsection (a) of section 77c of this title), by the use of any means or instruments of transportation or communication in interstate commerce or of the mails, by means of a prospectus or oral communication, which includes an untrue statement of a material fact or omits to state a material fact necessary in order to make the statements, in the light of the circumstances under which they were made, not misleading (the purchaser not knowing of such untruth or omission), and who shall not sustain the burden of proof that he did not know, and in the exercise of reasonable care could not have known, of such untruth or omission, shall be liable to the person purchasing such security from him, who may sue either at law or in equity in any court of competent jurisdiction, to recover the consideration paid for such security with interest thereon, less the amount of any income received thereon, upon the tender of such security, or for damages if he no longer owns the security."

weeks after the purchase, petitioner disposed of the stock at a loss. Claiming that the loss was due to the firm's misrepresentations and omission of information concerning Mr. Page, he sought damages.

Without answering the complaint, the respondent moved to stay the trial of the action pursuant to § 3 of the United States Arbitration Act until an arbitration in accordance with the terms of identical margin agreements was had. An affidavit accompanied the motion stating that the parties' relationship was controlled by the terms of the agreements and that while the firm was willing to arbitrate petitioner had failed to seek or proceed with any arbitration of the controversy.

Finding that the margin agreements provide that arbitration should be the method of settling all future controversies, the District Court held that the agreement to arbitrate deprived petitioner of the advantageous court remedy afforded by the Securities Act, and denied the stay. A divided Court of Appeals concluded that the Act did not prohibit the agreement to refer future controversies to arbitration, and reversed.

The question is whether an agreement to arbitrate a future controversy is a "condition, stipulation, or provision binding any person acquiring any security to waive compliance with any provision" of the Securities Act which § 14[6] declares "void." We granted certiorari, 345 U.S. 969, 73 S.Ct. 1112, to review this important and novel federal question affecting both the Securities Act and the United States Arbitration Act ...

As the margin agreement in the light of the complaint evidenced a transaction in interstate commerce, no issue arises as to the applicability of the provisions of the United States Arbitration Act to this suit, based upon the Securities Act. 9 U.S.C. (Supp. V, 1952) § 2, 9 U.S.C.A. § 2. . . .

In response to a Presidential message urging that there be added to the ancient rule of *caveat emptor* the further doctrine of "let the seller also beware," Congress passed the Securities Act of 1933. Designed to protect investors, the Act requires issuers, underwriters, and dealers to make full and fair disclosure of the character of securities sold in interstate and foreign commerce and to prevent fraud in their sale. To effectuate this policy, § 12(2) created a special right to recover for misrepresentation which differs substantially from the common-law action in that the seller is made to assume the burden of proving lack of scienter. The Act's special right is enforceable in any court of competent jurisdiction—federal or state—and removal from a state court is prohibited. If suit be brought in a federal court, the purchaser has a wide choice of venue, the privilege of nation-wide service of process and the jurisdictional $3,000 requirement of diversity cases is inapplicable.

The United States Arbitration Act establishes by statute the desirability of arbitration as an alternative to the complications of litigation. The

---

6. 48 Stat. 84, 15 U.S.C. § 77n, 15 U.S.C. § 77n. § 14 provides:

'Any condition, stipulation, or provision binding any person acquiring any securi-ty to waive compliance with any provision of this subchapter or of the rules and regulations of the Commission shall be void."

reports of both Houses on that Act stress the need for avoiding the delay and expense of litigation, and practice under its terms raises hope for its usefulness both in controversies based on statutes or on standards otherwise created. This hospitable attitude of legislatures and courts toward arbitration, however, does not solve our question as to the validity of petitioner's stipulation by the margin agreements, set out below, to submit to arbitration controversies that might arise from the transactions.[15]

Petitioner argues that § 14, note 6, supra, shows that the purpose of Congress was to assure that sellers could not maneuver buyers into a position that might weaken their ability to recover under the Securities Act. He contends that arbitration lacks the certainty of a suit at law under the Act to enforce his rights. He reasons that the arbitration paragraph of the margin agreement is a stipulation that waives "compliance with" the provision of the Securities Act, set out in the margin, conferring jurisdiction of suits and special powers.

Respondent asserts that arbitration is merely a form of trial to be used in lieu of a trial at law, and therefore no conflict exists between the Securities Act and the United States Arbitration Act either in their language or in the congressional purposes in their enactment. Each may function within its own scope, the former to protect investors and the latter to simplify recovery for actionable violations of law by issuers or dealers in securities.

Respondent is in agreement with the Court of Appeals that the margin agreement arbitration paragraph, note 15, supra, does not relieve the seller from either liability or burden of proof, note 1, supra, imposed by the Securities Act. We agree that in so far as the award in arbitration may be affected by legal requirements, statutes or common law, rather than by considerations of fairness, the provisions of the Securities Act control. This is true even though this proposed agreement has no requirement that the arbitrators follow the law. This agreement of the parties as to the effect of the Securities Act includes also acceptance of the invalidity of the paragraph of the margin agreement that relieves the respondent sellers of liability for all "representation or advice by you or your employees or agents regarding the purchase or sale by me of any property...."

The words of § 14, note 6, supra, void any "stipulation" waiving compliance with any "provision" of the Securities Act. This arrangement to arbitrate is a "stipulation," and we think the right to select the judicial forum is the kind of "provision" that cannot be waived under § 14 of the Securities Act. That conclusion is reached for the reasons set out above in the statement of petitioner's contention on this review. While a buyer and

---

15. "Any controversy arising between us under this contract shall be determined by arbitration pursuant to the Arbitration Law of the State of New York, and under the rules of either the Arbitration Committee of the Chamber of Commerce of the State of New York, or of the American Arbitration Association, or of the Arbitration Committee of the New York Stock Exchange or such other Exchange as may have jurisdiction over the matter in dispute, as I may elect. Any arbitration hereunder shall be before at least three arbitrators."

seller of securities, under some circumstances, may deal at arm's length on equal terms, it is clear that the Securities Act was drafted with an eye to the disadvantages under which buyers labor. Issuers of and dealers in securities have better opportunities to investigate and appraise the prospective earnings and business plans affecting securities than buyers. It is therefore reasonable for Congress to put buyers of securities covered by that Act on a different basis from other purchasers.

When the security buyer, prior to any violation of the Securities Act, waives his right to sue in courts, he gives up more than would a participant in other business transactions. The security buyer has a wider choice of courts and venue. He thus surrenders one of the advantages the Act gives him and surrenders it at a time when he is less able to judge the weight of the handicap the Securities Act places upon his adversary.

Even though the provisions of the Securities Act, advantageous to the buyer, apply, their effectiveness in application is lessened in arbitration as compared to judicial proceedings. Determination of the quality of a commodity or the amount of money due under a contract is not the type of issue here involved. This case requires subjective findings on the purpose and knowledge of an alleged violator of the Act. They must be not only determined but applied by the arbitrators without judicial instruction on the law. As their award may be made without explanation of their reasons and without a complete record of their proceedings, the arbitrators' conception of the legal meaning of such statutory requirements as "burden of proof," "reasonable care" or "material fact," see, note 1, supra, cannot be examined. Power to vacate an award is limited. While it may be true, as the Court of Appeals thought, that a failure of the arbitrators to decide in accordance with the provisions of the Securities Act would "constitute grounds for vacating the award pursuant to section 10 of the Federal Arbitration Act," that failure would need to be made clearly to appear. In unrestricted submission, such as the present margin agreements envisage, the interpretations of the law by the arbitrators in contrast to manifest disregard are not subject, in the federal courts, to judicial review for error in interpretation. The United States Arbitration Act contains no provision for judicial determination of legal issues such as is found in the English law. As the protective provisions of the Securities Act require the exercise of judicial direction to fairly assure their effectiveness, it seems to us that Congress must have intended § 4, note 6, supra, to apply to waiver of judicial trial and review.

This accords with Boyd v. Grand Trunk Western R. Co., 338 U.S. 263, 70 S.Ct. 26, 94 L.Ed. 55. We there held invalid a stipulation restricting an employee's choice of venue in an action under the Federal Employers' Liability Act, 45 U.S.C.A. § 51 et seq. Section 6 of that Act permitted suit in any one of several localities and s 5 forbade a common carrier's exempting itself from any liability under the Act.[28] Section 5 had been

---

28. Sec. 5 of the Federal Employers' Liability Act, 35 Stat. 66, 45 U.S.C. § 55, 45 U.S.C.A. § 55, provides: "Any contract, rule, regulation, or device whatsoever, the purpose

adopted to avoid contracts waiving employers' liability. It is to be noted that in words it forbade exemption only from "liability." We said the right to select the "forum" even after the creation of a liability is a "substantial right" and that the agreement, restricting that choice, would thwart the express purpose of the statute. We need not and do not go so far in this present case. By the terms of the agreement to arbitrate, petitioner is restricted in his choice of forum prior to the existence of a controversy. While the Securities Act does not require petitioner to sue, a waiver in advance of a controversy stands upon a different footing.

Two policies, not easily reconcilable, are involved in this case. Congress has afforded participants in transactions subject to its legislative power an opportunity generally to secure prompt, economical and adequate solution of controversies through arbitration if the parties are willing to accept less certainty of legally correct adjustment. On the other hand, it has enacted the Securities Act to protect the rights of investors and has forbidden a waiver of any of those rights. Recognizing the advantages that prior agreements for arbitration may provide for the solution of commercial controversies, we decide that the intention of Congress concerning the sale of securities is better carried out by holding invalid such an agreement for arbitration of issues arising under the Act.

Reversed.

■ MR. JUSTICE JACKSON, concurring.

I agree with the Court's opinion insofar as it construes the Securities Act to prohibit waiver of a judicial remedy in favor of arbitration by agreement made before any controversy arose. I think thereafter the parties could agree upon arbitration. However, I find it unnecessary in this case, where there has not been and could not be any arbitration, to decide that the Arbitration Act precludes any judicial remedy for the arbitrators' error of interpretation of a relevant statute.

■ MR. JUSTICE FRANKFURTER, whom MR. JUSTICE MINTON joins, dissenting.

If arbitration inherently precluded full protection of the rights § 12(2) of the Securities Act affords to a purchaser of securities, or if there were no effective means of ensuring judicial review of the legal basis of the arbitration, then, of course, an agreement to settle the controversy by arbitration would be barred by § 14, the anti-waiver provision, of that Act.

There is nothing in the record before us, nor in the facts of which we can take judicial notice, to indicate that the arbitral system as practiced in the City of New York, and as enforceable under the supervisory authority of the District Court for the Southern District of New York, would not afford the plaintiff the rights to which he is entitled.[1]

---

or intent of which shall be to enable any common carrier to exempt itself from any liability created by this chapter, shall to that extent be void * * *."

1. Under the rules of the American Arbitration Association, available to the plaintiff under his contract, the procedure for selection of arbitrators is as follows: The Association submits a list of potential arbi-

The impelling considerations that led to the enactment of the Federal Arbitration Act are the advantages of providing a speedier, more economical and more effective enforcement of rights by way of arbitration than can be had by the tortuous course of litigation, especially in the City of New York. These advantages should not be assumed to be denied in controversies like that before us arising under the Securities Act, in the absence of any showing that settlement by arbitration would jeopardize the rights of the plaintiff.

Arbitrators may not disregard the law. Specifically they are, as Chief Judge Swan pointed out, "bound to decide in accordance with the provisions of section 12(2)." On this we are all agreed. It is suggested, however, that there is no effective way of assuring obedience by the arbitrators to the governing law. But since their failure to observe this law "would ... constitute grounds for vacating the award pursuant to section 10 of the Federal Arbitration Act," 201 F.2d 439, 445, appropriate means for judicial scrutiny must be implied, in the form of some record or opinion, however informal, whereby such compliance will appear, or want of it will upset the award.

We have not before us a case in which the record shows that the plaintiff in opening an account had no choice but to accept the arbitration stipulation, thereby making the stipulation an unconscionable and unenforceable provision in a business transaction. The Securities and Exchange Commission, as amicus curiae, does not contend that the stipulation which the Court of Appeals respected, under the appropriate safeguards defined by it, was a coercive practice by financial houses against customers incapable of self-protection. It is one thing to make out a case of overreaching as between parties bargaining not at arm's length. It is quite a different thing to find in the anti-waiver provision of the Securities Act a general limitation on the Federal Arbitration Act.

On the state of the record before us, I would affirm the decision of the Court of Appeals.

* * *

Questions

1. According to Justice Reed, what particular features of the Securities Act of 1933 suggest a Congressional intent to override the FAA? Could these features be interpreted in any other way?

trators qualified by experience to adjudicate the particular controversy. In the City of New York, the list would be drawn from a panel of 4,400 persons, 1,275 of whom are lawyers. Each party may strike off the names of any unacceptable persons and number the remaining in order of preference. The Association then designates the arbitrators on the basis of the preferences expressed by both parties. See "Questions and Answers," Pamphlet of American Arbitration Association. In short, those who are charged to enforce the rights are selected by the parties themselves from among those qualified to decide.

2.   Justice Frankfurter suggests that courts have the authority to overturn arbitration decisions that do not follow the law. Does the majority agree? Is Frankfurter basing this claim on the FAA? If not, then on what authority does he rely?

3.   Justice Frankfurter's dissent suggests that arbitrators have an obligation to explain their awards with written opinions. Yet the American Arbitration Association takes the opposite position in its Commercial Arbitration Rules. Rather, the AAA advises arbitrators in commercial cases not to write opinions unless both parties request them to do so. What are the pros and cons of Frankfurter's position? Why might the AAA take the position it does?

* * *

Dean Witter Reynolds, Inc. v. Byrd

470 U.S. 213, 105 S.Ct. 1238 (1985).

■ JUSTICE MARSHALL delivered the opinion of the Court.

The question presented is whether, when a complaint raises both federal securities claims and pendent state claims, a Federal District Court may deny a motion to compel arbitration of the state-law claims despite the parties' agreement to arbitrate their disputes. We granted certiorari to resolve a conflict among the Federal Courts of Appeals on this question. 467 U.S. 1240, 104 S.Ct. 3509, 82 L.Ed.2d 818 (1984).

I

In 1981, A. Lamar Byrd sold his dental practice and invested $160,000 in securities through Dean Witter Reynolds Inc., a securities broker-dealer. The value of the account declined by more than $100,000 between September 1981 and March 1982. Byrd filed a complaint against Dean Witter in the United States District Court for the Southern District of California, alleging a violation of §§ 10(b), 15(c), and 20 of the Securities Exchange Act of 1934, 15 U.S.C. §§ 78j(b), 78o(c), and 78t, and of various state-law provisions. Federal jurisdiction over the state-law claims was based on diversity of citizenship and the principle of pendent jurisdiction. In the complaint, Byrd alleged that an agent of Dean Witter had traded in his account without his prior consent, that the number of transactions executed on behalf of the account was excessive, that misrepresentations were made by an agent of Dean Witter as to the status of the account, and that the agent acted with Dean Witter's knowledge, participation, and ratification.

When Byrd invested his funds with Dean Witter in 1981, he signed a Customer's Agreement providing that "[a]ny controversy between you and the undersigned arising out of or relating to this contract or the breach thereof, shall be settled by arbitration." App. to Pet. for Cert. 11. Dean Witter accordingly filed a motion for an order severing the pendent state claims, compelling their arbitration, and staying arbitration of those claims pending resolution of the federal-court action. App. 12. It argued that the Federal Arbitration Act (Arbitration Act or Act), 9 U.S.C. §§ 1–14, which provides that arbitration agreements "shall be valid, irrevocable, and enforceable, save upon such grounds as exist at law or in equity for the revocation of any contract," § 2, required that the District Court compel arbitration of the state-law claims. The Act authorizes parties to an arbitration agreement to petition a federal district court for an order compelling arbitration of any issue referable to arbitration under the agreement. §§ 3, 4. Because Dean Witter assumed that the federal securities claim was not subject to the arbitration provision of the contract and could be resolved only in the federal forum, it did not seek to compel arbitration of that claim.[1] The District Court denied in its entirety the motion to sever and compel arbitration of the pendent state claims, and on an interlocutory appeal the Court of Appeals for the Ninth Circuit affirmed. 726 F.2d 552 (1984).

II

Confronted with the issue we address[2]—whether to compel arbitration of pendent state-law claims when the federal court will in any event assert jurisdiction over a federal-law claim—the Federal Courts of Appeals have adopted two different approaches. Along with the Ninth Circuit in this case, the Fifth and Eleventh Circuits have relied on the "doctrine of intertwining." When arbitrable and nonarbitrable claims arise out of the same transaction, and are sufficiently intertwined factually and legally, the district court, under this view, may in its discretion deny arbitration as to the arbitrable claims and try all the claims together in federal court. These

---

1. In Wilko v. Swan, 346 U.S. 427, 74 S.Ct. 182, 98 L.Ed. 168 (1953), this Court held that a predispute agreement to arbitrate claims that arise under § 12(2) of the Securities Act of 1933, 15 U.S.C. § 77l (2), was not enforceable. The Court pointed to language in § 14 of the Securities Act of 1933, 15 U.S.C. § 77n, which declares "void" any "stipulation" waiving compliance with any "provision" of the Securities Act, and held that an agreement to arbitrate amounted to a stipulation waiving the right to seek a judicial remedy, and was therefore void. 346 U.S., at 434–435, 74 S.Ct., at 186. Years later, in Scherk v. Alberto–Culver Co., 417 U.S. 506, 94 S.Ct. 2449, 41 L.Ed.2d 270 (1974), this Court questioned the applicability of Wilko to a claim arising under § 10(b) of the Securities Exchange Act of 1934, or under Rule 10b–5, because the provisions of the 1933 and 1934 Acts differ, and because, unlike § 12(2) of the 1933 Act, § 10(b) of the 1934 Act does not expressly give rise to a private cause of action.... The Court did not, however, hold that Wilko would not apply in the context of

a § 10(b) or Rule 10b–5 claim, and Wilko has retained considerable vitality in the lower federal courts. Indeed, numerous District Courts and Courts of Appeals have held that the Wilko analysis applies to claims arising under § 10(b) of the Securities Exchange Act of 1934, 15 U.S.C. § 78j(b), and that agreements to arbitrate such claims are therefore unenforceable.... Dean Witter and amici representing the securities industry urge us to resolve the applicability of Wilko to claims under § 10(b) and Rule 10b–5. We decline to do so. In the District Court, Dean Witter did not seek to compel arbitration of the federal securities claims. Thus, the question whether Wilko applies to § 10(b) and Rule 10b–5 claims is not properly before us.

2. Respondent Byrd also argues that as a contract of adhesion this arbitration agreement is subject to close judicial scrutiny, and that it should not routinely be enforced. Byrd did not present this argument to the courts below, and we decline to address it in the first instance. We therefore express no view on the merits of the argument.

courts acknowledge the strong federal policy in favor of enforcing arbitration agreements but offer two reasons why the district courts nevertheless should decline to compel arbitration in this situation. First, they assert that such a result is necessary to preserve what they consider to be the court's exclusive jurisdiction over the federal securities claim; otherwise, they suggest, arbitration of an "intertwined" state claim might precede the federal proceeding and the fact finding done by the arbitrator might thereby bind the federal court through collateral estoppel. The second reason they cite is efficiency; by declining to compel arbitration, the court avoids bifurcated proceedings and perhaps redundant efforts to litigate the same factual questions twice.

In contrast, the Sixth, Seventh, and Eighth Circuits have held that the Arbitration Act divests the district courts of any discretion regarding arbitration in cases containing both arbitrable and nonarbitrable claims, and instead requires that the courts compel arbitration of arbitrable claims, when asked to do so. These courts conclude that the Act, both through its plain meaning and the strong federal policy it reflects, requires courts to enforce the bargain of the parties to arbitrate, and "not substitute [its] own views of economy and efficiency" for those of Congress. Dickinson v. Heinold Securities, Inc., 661 F.2d 638, 646 (C.A.7 1981).

We agree with these latter courts that the Arbitration Act requires district courts to compel arbitration of pendent arbitrable claims when one of the parties files a motion to compel, even where the result would be the possibly inefficient maintenance of separate proceedings in different forums. Accordingly, we reverse the decision not to compel arbitration.

III

The Arbitration Act provides that written agreements to arbitrate controversies arising out of an existing contract "shall be valid, irrevocable, and enforceable, save upon such grounds as exist at law or in equity for the revocation of any contract." 9 U.S.C. § 2. By its terms, the Act leaves no place for the exercise of discretion by a district court, but instead mandates that district courts *shall* direct the parties to proceed to arbitration on issues as to which an arbitration agreement has been signed. §§ 3, 4. Thus, insofar as the language of the Act guides our disposition of this case, we would conclude that agreements to arbitrate must be enforced, absent a ground for revocation of the contractual agreement.

It is suggested, however, that the Act does not expressly address whether the same mandate—to enforce arbitration agreements—holds true where, as here, such a course would result in bifurcated proceedings if the arbitration agreement is enforced. Because the Act's drafters did not explicitly consider the prospect of bifurcated proceedings, we are told, the clear language of the Act might be misleading. Thus, courts that have adopted the view of the Ninth Circuit in this case have argued that the Act's goal of speedy and efficient decision making is thwarted by bifurcated proceedings, and that, given the absence of clear direction on this point, the intent of Congress in passing the Act controls and compels a refusal to compel arbitration. They point out, in addition, that in the past the Court on occasion has identified a contrary federal interest sufficiently compelling to outweigh the mandate of the Arbitration Act, see n. 1, supra, and they conclude that the interest in speedy resolution of claims should do so in this case. See, e.g., Miley v. Oppenheimer & Co., 637 F.2d 318, 336 (C.A.5 1981); Cunningham v. Dean Witter Reynolds, Inc., 550 F.Supp. 578, 585 (E.D.Cal.1982).

We turn, then, to consider whether the legislative history of the Act provides guidance on this issue. The congressional history does not expressly direct resolution of the scenario we address. We conclude, however, on consideration of Congress' intent in passing the statute, that a court must compel arbitration of otherwise arbitrable claims, when a motion to compel arbitration is made.

The legislative history of the Act establishes that the purpose behind its passage was to ensure judicial enforcement of privately made agreements to arbitrate. We therefore reject the suggestion that the overriding goal of the Arbitration Act was to promote the expeditious resolution of claims. The Act, after all, does not mandate the arbitration of all claims, but merely the enforcement—upon the motion of one of the parties—of privately negotiated arbitration agreements. The House Report accompanying the Act makes clear that its purpose was to place an arbitration agreement "upon the same footing as other contracts, where it belongs," H.R.Rep. No. 96, 68th Cong., 1st Sess., 1 (1924), and to overrule the judiciary's longstanding refusal to enforce agreements to arbitrate.[6] This is not to say that Congress was blind to the potential benefit of the legislation for expedited resolution of disputes. Far from it, the House Report expressly observed:

> "It is practically appropriate that the action should be taken at this time when there is so much agitation against the costliness and delays of litigation. These matters can be largely eliminated by agreements for arbitration, if arbitration agreements are made valid and enforceable." Id., at 2.

Nonetheless, passage of the Act was motivated, first and foremost, by a congressional desire to enforce agreements into which parties had entered, and we must not overlook this principal objective when construing the

---

6. According to the Report: "The need for the law arises from an anachronism of our American law. Some centuries ago, because of the jealousy of the English courts for their own jurisdiction, they refused to enforce specific agreements to arbitrate upon the ground that the courts were thereby ousted from their jurisdiction. This jealousy survived for so long a period that the principle became firmly embedded in the English common law and was adopted with it by the American courts. The courts have felt that the prece- dent was too strongly fixed to be overturned without legislative enactment, although they have frequently criticized the rule and recognized its illogical nature and the injustice which results from it. This bill declares simply that such agreements for arbitration shall be enforced, and provides a procedure in the Federal courts for their enforcement." H.R.Rep. No. 96, 68th Cong., 1st Sess., 1–2 (1924). See also Cohn & Dayton, The New Federal Arbitration Act, 12 Va.L.Rev. 265, 283–284 (1926).

statute, or allow the fortuitous impact of the Act on efficient dispute resolution to overshadow the underlying motivation. . . .

We therefore are not persuaded by the argument that the conflict between two goals of the Arbitration Act—enforcement of private agreements and encouragement of efficient and speedy dispute resolution—must be resolved in favor of the latter in order to realize the intent of the drafters. The preeminent concern of Congress in passing the Act was to enforce private agreements into which parties had entered, and that concern requires that we rigorously enforce agreements to arbitrate, even if the result is "piecemeal" litigation, at least absent a countervailing policy manifested in another federal statute. See n. 1, supra. By compelling arbitration of state-law claims, a district court successfully protects the contractual rights of the parties and their rights under the Arbitration Act.

IV

It is also suggested, however, and some Courts of Appeals have held, that district courts should decide arbitrable pendent claims when a nonarbitrable federal claim is before them, because otherwise the findings in the arbitration proceeding might have collateral-estoppel effect in a subsequent federal proceeding. This preclusive effect is believed to pose a threat to the federal interest in resolution of securities claims, and to warrant a refusal to compel arbitration. Other courts have held that the claims should be separately resolved, but that this preclusive effect warrants a stay of arbitration proceedings pending resolution of the federal securities claim. In this case, Dean Witter also asked the District Court to stay the arbitration proceedings pending resolution of the federal claim, and we suspect it did so in response to such holdings.

We believe that the preclusive effect of arbitration proceedings is significantly less well settled than the lower court opinions might suggest, and that the consequences of this misconception has been the formulation of unnecessarily contorted procedures. We conclude that neither a stay of proceedings, nor joined proceedings, is necessary to protect the federal interest in the federal-court proceeding, and that the formulation of collateral-estoppel rules affords adequate protection to that interest.

Initially, it is far from certain that arbitration proceedings will have any preclusive effect on the litigation of nonarbitrable federal claims. Just last Term, we held that neither the full-faith-and-credit provision of 28 U.S.C. § 1738, nor a judicially fashioned rule of preclusion, permits a federal court to accord res judicata or collateral-estoppel effect to an unappealed arbitration award in a case brought under 42 U.S.C. § 1983. McDonald v. West Branch, 466 U.S. 284, 104 S.Ct. 1799, 80 L.Ed.2d 302 (1984). The full-faith-and-credit statute requires that federal courts give the same preclusive effect to a State's *judicial proceedings* as would the courts of the State rendering the judgment, and since arbitration is not a judicial proceeding, we held that the statute does not apply to arbitration awards. Id., at 287–288, 104 S.Ct., at 1801–1802. The same analysis inevitably would apply to any unappealed state arbitration proceedings. We also declined, in McDonald, to fashion a federal common-law rule of preclusion, in part on the ground that arbitration cannot provide an adequate substitute for a judicial proceeding in protecting the federal statutory and constitutional rights that § 1983 is designed to safeguard. We therefore recognized that arbitration proceedings will not necessarily have a preclusive effect on subsequent federal-court proceedings.

Significantly, McDonald also establishes that courts may directly and effectively protect federal interests by determining the preclusive effect to be given to an arbitration proceeding. Since preclusion doctrine comfortably plays this role, it follows that neither a stay of the arbitration proceedings, nor a refusal to compel arbitration of state claims, is *required* in order to assure that a precedent arbitration does not impede a subsequent federal-court action. The Courts of Appeals that have assumed collateral-estoppel effect must be given to arbitration proceedings have therefore sought to accomplish indirectly that which they erroneously assumed they could not do directly.

The question of what preclusive effect, if any, the arbitration proceedings might have is not yet before us, however, and we do not decide it. The collateral-estoppel effect of an arbitration proceeding is at issue only after arbitration is completed, of course, and we therefore have no need to consider now whether the analysis in McDonald encompasses this case. Suffice it to say that in framing preclusion rules in this context, courts shall take into account the federal interests warranting protection. As a result, there is no reason to require that district courts decline to compel arbitration, or manipulate the ordering of the resulting bifurcated proceedings, simply to avoid an infringement of federal interests.

Finding unpersuasive the arguments advanced in support of the ruling below, we hold that the District Court erred in refusing to grant the motion of Dean Witter to compel arbitration of the pendent state claims. Accordingly, we reverse the decision of the Court of Appeals insofar as it upheld the District Court's denial of the motion to compel arbitration, and we remand for further proceedings consistent with this opinion.

It is so ordered.

■ JUSTICE WHITE, concurring.

I join the Court's opinion. I write separately only to add a few words regarding two issues that it leaves undeveloped.

The premise of the controversy before us is that respondent's claims under the Securities Exchange Act of 1934 are not arbitrable, notwithstanding the contrary agreement of the parties. The Court's opinion rightly concludes that the question whether that is so is not before us. Ante, at 216, n. 1. Nonetheless, I note that this is a matter of substantial doubt. In Wilko v. Swan, 346 U.S. 427, 74 S.Ct. 182, 98 L.Ed. 168 (1953), the Court held arbitration agreements unenforceable with regard to claims under § 12(2) the 1933 Act. . . .

Wilko's reasoning cannot be mechanically transplanted to the 1934 Act. While § 29 of that Act, 15 U.S.C. § 78cc(a), is equivalent to § 14 of the

1933 Act, counterparts of the other two provisions are imperfect or absent altogether. Jurisdiction under the 1934 Act is narrower, being restricted to the federal courts. 15 U.S.C. § 78aa. More important, the cause of action under § 10(b) and Rule 10b–5, involved here, is implied rather than express.... The phrase "waive compliance with any *provision of this chapter*," 15 U.S.C. § 78cc(a) (emphasis added), is thus literally inapplicable. Moreover, Wilko's solicitude for the federal cause of action—the "special right" established by Congress, 346 U.S., at 431, 74 S.Ct., at 184—is not necessarily appropriate where the cause of action is judicially implied and not so different from the common-law action.

... The Court's opinion makes clear that a district court should not stay arbitration, or refuse to compel it at all, for fear of its preclusive effect. And I can perceive few, if any, other possible reasons for staying the arbitration pending the outcome of the lawsuit. Belated enforcement of the arbitration clause, though a less substantial interference than a refusal to enforce it at all, nonetheless significantly disappoints the expectations of the parties and frustrates the clear purpose of their agreement. In addition, once it is decided that the two proceedings are to go forward independently, the concern for speedy resolution suggests that neither should be delayed. While the impossibility of the lawyers being in two places at once may require some accommodation in scheduling, it seems to me that the heavy presumption should be that the arbitration and the lawsuit will each proceed in its normal course. And while the matter remains to be determined by the District Court, I see nothing in the record before us to indicate that arbitration in the present case should be stayed.

* * *

Questions

1. To what extent do the majority and concurring opinions in *Dean Witter Reynolds v. Byrd* modify the holding of *Wilko*?

2. What does the Court in *Dean Witter Reynolds* say about the effect of an arbitral ruling on a federal court's subsequent determination of a federal claim? Is it possible that an arbitral award, while not technically preclusive, could have a *de facto* preclusive effect? Is the Court's analogy to its treatment of full-faith-and-credit preclusion persuasive? What are the relevant differences?

3. Does the Court suggest that federal courts should decide what collateral-estoppel effect to give an arbitral award on a case-by-case basis? If so, what factors should a court use to make that determination? Can a court make that determination without considering the merits of the arbitrated claim? Does this amount to de facto judicial review of the merits of an arbitration award?

4. The Court in *Dean Witter Reynolds* states that there is a tension between two goals of the FAA—to provide expeditious resolution of disputes and to enforce private agreements to arbitrate? It concludes that

when these goals are in tension, the latter should take precedence. On what basis is it making this choice? What are the consequences of this interpretation for the FAA?

* * *

Scherk v. Alberto–Culver Co.

417 U.S. 506, 94 S.Ct. 2449 (1974).

■ MR. JUSTICE STEWART delivered the opinion of the Court.

Alberto–Culver Co., the respondent, is an American company incorporated in Delaware with its principal office in Illinois. It manufactures and distributes toiletries and hair products in this country and abroad. During the 1960's Alberto–Culver decided to expand its overseas operations, and as part of this program it approached the petitioner Fritz Scherk, a German citizen residing at the time of trial in Switzerland. Scherk was the owner of three interrelated business entities, organized under the laws of Germany and Liechtenstein, that were engaged in the manufacture of toiletries and the licensing of trademarks for such toiletries. An initial contact with Scherk was made by a representative of Alberto–Culver in Germany in June 1967, and negotiations followed at further meetings in both Europe and the United States during 1967 and 1968. In February 1969 a contract was signed in Vienna, Austria, which provided for the transfer of the ownership of Scherk's enterprises to Alberto–Culver, along with all rights held by these enterprises to trademarks in cosmetic goods. The contract contained a number of express warranties whereby Scherk guaranteed the sole and unencumbered ownership of these trademarks. In addition, the contract contained an arbitration clause providing that "any controversy or claim [that] shall arise out of this agreement or the breach thereof" would be referred to arbitration before the International Chamber of Commerce in Paris, France, and that "[t]he laws of the State of Illinois, U.S.A. shall apply to and govern this agreement, its interpretation and performance."[1]

The closing of the transaction took place in Geneva, Switzerland, in June 1969. Nearly one year later Alberto–Culver allegedly discovered that the trademark rights purchased under the contract were subject to substantial encumbrances that threatened to give others superior rights to the trademarks and to restrict or preclude Alberto–Culver's use of them.

---

1. The arbitration clause relating to the transfer of one of Scherk's business entities, similar to the clauses covering the other two, reads in its entirety as follows:

"The parties agree that if any controversy or claim shall arise out of this agreement or the breach thereof and either party shall request that the matter shall be settled by arbitration, the matter shall be settled exclusively by arbitration in accordance with the rules then obtaining of the International Chamber of Commerce, Paris, France.... All arbitration proceedings shall be held in Paris, France, and each party agrees to comply in all respects with any award made in any such proceeding and to the entry of a judgment in any jurisdiction upon any award rendered in such proceeding. The laws of the State of Illinois, U.S.A. shall apply to and govern this agreement, its interpretation and performance."

Alberto–Culver thereupon tendered back to Scherk the property that had been transferred to it and offered to rescind the contract. Upon Scherk's refusal, Alberto–Culver commenced this action for damages and other relief in a Federal District Court in Illinois, contending that Scherk's fraudulent representations concerning the status of the trademark rights constituted violations of § 10(b) of the Securities Exchange Act of 1934, . . . and Rule 10b–5 promulgated thereunder . . . .

In response, Scherk filed a motion to dismiss the action for want of personal and subject-matter jurisdiction as well as on the basis of *forum non conveniens*, or, alternatively, to stay the action pending arbitration in Paris pursuant to the agreement of the parties. Alberto–Culver, in turn, opposed this motion and sought a preliminary injunction restraining the prosecution of arbitration proceedings. On December 2, 1971, the District Court denied Scherk's motion to dismiss, and, on January 14, 1972, it granted a preliminary order enjoining Scherk from proceeding with arbitration. In taking these actions the court relied entirely on this Court's decision in Wilko v. Swan, 346 U.S. 427, 74 S.Ct. 182, 98 L.Ed. 168, which held that an agreement to arbitrate could not preclude a buyer of a security from seeking a judicial remedy under the Securities Act of 1933, in view of the language of § 14 of that Act, barring "(a)ny condition, stipulation, or provision binding any person acquiring any security to waive compliance with any provision of this subchapter . . . ." . . . The Court of Appeals for the Seventh Circuit, with one judge dissenting, affirmed, upon what it considered the controlling authority of the Wilko decision. 484 F.2d 611. Because of the importance of the question presented we granted Scherk's petition for a writ of certiorari. 414 U.S. 1156, 94 S.Ct. 913, 39 L.Ed.2d 108.

I

The United States Arbitration Act, now 9 U.S.C. § 1 et seq., reversing centuries of judicial hostility to arbitration agreements, was designed to allow parties to avoid "the costliness and delays of litigation," and to place arbitration agreements "upon the same footing as other contracts . . . ." . . . Accordingly the Act provides that an arbitration agreement such as is here involved "shall be valid, irrevocable, and enforceable, save upon such grounds as exist at law or in equity for the revocation of any contract." 9 U.S.C. § 2. The Act also provides in § 3 for a stay of proceedings in a case where a court is satisfied that the issue before it is arbitrable under the agreement, and § 4 of the Act directs a federal court to order parties to proceed to arbitration if there has been a "failure, neglect, or refusal" of any party to honor an agreement to arbitrate.

In Wilko v. Swan, supra, this Court acknowledged that the Act reflects a legislative recognition of the "desirability of arbitration as an alternative to the complications of litigation," 346 U.S., at 431, 74 S.Ct., at 185, but nonetheless declined to apply the Act's provisions . . . [6]

6. The arbitration agreement involved in Wilko was contained in a standard form margin contract. But see the dissenting opinion of Mr. Justice Frankfurter, 346 U.S. 427,

Thus, Wilko's advance agreement to arbitrate any disputes subsequently arising out of his contract to purchase the securities was unenforceable under the terms of § 14 of the Securities Act of 1933.

Alberto–Culver, relying on this precedent, contends that the District Court and Court of Appeals were correct in holding that its agreement to arbitrate disputes arising under the contract with Scherk is similarly unenforceable in view of its contentions that Scherk's conduct constituted violations of the Securities Exchange Act of 1934 and rules promulgated thereunder. For the reasons that follow, we reject this contention and hold that the provisions of the Arbitration Act cannot be ignored in this case.

At the outset, a colorable argument could be made that even the semantic reasoning of the Wilko opinion does not control the case before us. Wilko concerned a suit brought under § 12(2) of the Securities Act of 1933, which provides a defrauded purchaser with the "special right" of a private remedy for civil liability, 346 U.S., at 431, 74 S.Ct., at 184. There is no statutory counterpart of § 12(2) in the Securities Exchange Act of 1934, and neither § 10(b) of that Act nor Rule 10b–5 speaks of a private remedy to redress violations of the kind alleged here. While federal case law has established that § 10(b) and Rule 10b–5 create an implied private cause of action, see 6 L. Loss, Securities Regulation 3869–3873 (1969) and cases cited therein; . . . the Act itself does not establish the "special right" that the Court in Wilko found significant. Furthermore, while both the Securities Act of 1933 and the Securities Exchange Act of 1934 contain sections barring waiver of compliance with any "provision" of the respective Acts, certain of the "provisions" of the 1933 Act that the Court held could not be waived by Wilko's agreement to arbitrate find no counterpart in the 1934 Act. In particular, the Court in Wilko noted that the jurisdictional provision of the 1933 Act, 15 U.S.C. § 77v, allowed a plaintiff to bring suit "in any court of competent jurisdiction—federal or state—and removal from a state court is prohibited." 346 U.S., at 431, 74 S.Ct., at 184. The analogous provision of the 1934 Act, by contrast, provides for suit only in the federal district courts that have "exclusive jurisdiction," 15 U.S.C. § 78aa, thus significantly restricting the plaintiff's choice of forum.

Accepting the premise, however, that the operative portions of the language of the 1933 Act relied upon in Wilko are contained in the Securities Exchange Act of 1934, the respondent's reliance on Wilko in this case ignores the significant and, we find, crucial differences between the agreement involved in Wilko and the one signed by the parties here. Alberto–Culver's contract to purchase the business entities belonging to

439, 440, 74 S.Ct. 182, 189, concluding that the record did not show that "the plaintiff [Wilko] in opening an account had no choice but to accept the arbitration stipulation. . . ." The petitioner here would limit the decision in Wilko to situations where the parties exhibit a disparity of bargaining power, and contends that, since the negotiations leading to the present contract took place over a number of years and involved the participation on both sides of knowledgeable and sophisticated business and legal experts, the Wilko decision should not apply. See also the dissenting opinion of Judge Stevens of the Court of Appeals in this case, 484 F.2d 611, 615. Because of our disposition of this case on other grounds, we need not consider this contention.

Scherk was a truly international agreement. Alberto–Culver is an American corporation with its principal place of business and the vast bulk of its activity in this country, while Scherk is a citizen of Germany whose companies were organized under the laws of Germany and Liechtenstein. The negotiations leading to the signing of the contract in Austria and to the closing in Switzerland took place in the United States, England, and Germany, and involved consultations with legal and trademark experts from each of those countries and from Liechtenstein. Finally, and most significantly, the subject matter of the contract concerned the sale of business enterprises organized under the laws of and primarily situated in European countries, whose activities were largely, if not entirely, directed to European markets.

Such a contract involves considerations and policies significantly different from those found controlling in Wilko. In Wilko, quite apart from the arbitration provision, there was no question but that the laws of the United States generally, and the federal securities laws in particular, would govern disputes arising out of the stock-purchase agreement. The parties, the negotiations, and the subject matter of the contract were all situated in this country, and no credible claim could have been entertained that any international conflict-of-laws problems would arise. In this case, by contrast, in the absence of the arbitration provision considerable uncertainty existed at the time of the agreement, and still exists, concerning the law applicable to the resolution of disputes arising out of the contract.

Such uncertainty will almost inevitably exist with respect to any contract touching two or more countries, each with its own substantive laws and conflict-of-laws rules. A contractual provision specifying in advance the forum in which disputes shall be litigated and the law to be applied is, therefore, an almost indispensable precondition to achievement of the orderliness and predictability essential to any international business transaction. Furthermore, such a provision obviates the danger that a dispute under the agreement might be submitted to a forum hostile to the interests of one of the parties or unfamiliar with the problem area involved.[10]

A parochial refusal by the courts of one country to enforce an international arbitration agreement would not only frustrate these purposes, but would invite unseemly and mutually destructive jockeying by the parties to secure tactical litigation advantages. In the present case, for example, it is not inconceivable that if Scherk had anticipated that Alberto–Culver would be able in this country to enjoin resort to arbitration he might have sought an order in France or some other country enjoining Alberto–Culver from proceeding with its litigation in the United States. Whatever recognition

---

10.   See Quigley, Accession by the United States to the United Nations Convention on the Recognition and Enforcement of Foreign Arbitral Awards, 70 Yale L.J. 1049, 1051 (1961). For example, while the arbitration agreement involved here provided that the controversies arising out of the agreement be resolved under "(t)he laws of the State of Illinois," supra, n. 1, a determination of the existence and extent of fraud concerning the trademarks would necessarily involve an understanding of foreign law on that subject.

the courts of this country might ultimately have granted to the order of the foreign court, the dicey atmosphere of such a legal no-man's-land would surely damage the fabric of international commerce and trade, and imperil the willingness and ability of businessmen to enter into international commercial agreements.[11]

The exception to the clear provisions of the Arbitration Act carved out by Wilko is simply inapposite to a case such as the one before us. In Wilko the Court reasoned that "(w)hen the security buyer, prior to any violation of the Securities Act, waives his right to sue in courts, he gives up more than would a participant in other business transactions. The security buyer has a wider choice of courts and venue. He thus surrenders one of the advantages the Act gives him...." 346 U.S., at 435, 74 S.Ct., at 187. In the context of an international contract, however, these advantages become chimerical since, as indicated above, an opposing party may by speedy resort to a foreign court block or hinder access to the American court of the purchaser's choice.

Two Terms ago in The Bremen v. Zapata Off–Shore Co., 407 U.S. 1, 92 S.Ct. 1907, 32 L.Ed.2d 513, we rejected the doctrine that a forum-selection clause of a contract, although voluntarily adopted by the parties, will not be respected in a suit brought in the United States "unless the selected state would provide a more convenient forum than the state in which suit is brought." Id., at 7, 92 S.Ct., at 1912. Rather, we concluded that a "forum clause should control absent a strong showing that it should be set aside." Id., at 15, 92 S.Ct., at 1916. We noted that "much uncertainty and possibly great inconvenience to both parties could arise if a suit could be maintained in any jurisdiction in which an accident might occur or if jurisdiction were left to any place [where personal or in rem jurisdiction might be established]. The elimination of all such uncertainties by agreeing in advance on a forum acceptable to both parties is an indispensable element in international trade, commerce, and contracting." Id., at 13....

An agreement to arbitrate before a specified tribunal is, in effect, a specialized kind of forum-selection clause that posits not only the situs of suit but also the procedure to be used in resolving the dispute. The

---

11. The dissenting opinion argues that our conclusion that Wilko is inapplicable to the situation presented in this case will vitiate the force of that decision because parties to transactions with many more direct contacts with this country than in the present case will nonetheless be able to invoke the "talisman" of having an "international contract." Post, at 529. Concededly, situations may arise where the contacts with foreign countries are so insignificant or attenuated that the holding in Wilko would meaningfully apply. Judicial response to such situations can and should await future litigation in concrete cases. This case, however, provides no basis for a judgment that only United States laws and United States courts should determine this controversy in the face of a solemn agreement between the parties that such controversies be resolved elsewhere. The only contact between the United States and the transaction involved here is the fact that Alberto–Culver is an American corporation and the occurrence of some—but by no means the greater part—of the pre-contract negotiations in this country. To determine that "American standards of fairness," post, at 528, must nonetheless govern the controversy demeans the standards of justice elsewhere in the world, and unnecessarily exalts the primacy of United States law over the laws of other countries.

invalidation of such an agreement in the case before us would not only allow the respondent to repudiate its solemn promise but would, as well, reflect a "parochial concept that all disputes must be resolved under our laws and in our courts.... We cannot have trade and commerce in world markets and international waters exclusively on our terms, governed by our laws, and resolved in our courts." Id., at 9, 92 S.Ct., at 1912.

For all these reasons we hold that the agreement of the parties in this case to arbitrate any dispute arising out of their international commercial transaction is to be respected and enforced by the federal courts in accord with the explicit provisions of the Arbitration Act.

Accordingly, the judgment of the Court of Appeals is reversed and the case is remanded to that court with directions to remand to the District Court for further proceedings consistent with this opinion.

■ MR. JUSTICE DOUGLAS, with whom MR. JUSTICE BRENNAN, MR. JUSTICE WHITE, and MR. JUSTICE MARSHALL concur, dissenting.

... The basic dispute between the parties concerned allegations that the trademarks which were basic assets in the transaction were encumbered and that their purchase was induced through serious instances of fraudulent representations and omissions by Scherk and his agents within the jurisdiction of the United States. If a question of trademarks were the only one involved, the principle of The Bremen v. Zapata Off–Shore Co., 407 U.S. 1, 92 S.Ct. 1907, 32 L.Ed.2d 513, would be controlling.

We have here, however, questions under the Securities Exchange Act of 1934, which in § 3(a)(10) defines "security" as including any "note, stock, treasury stock, bond, debenture, certificate of interest or participation in any profit-sharing agreement...." 15 U.S.C. § 78c(a)(10). We held in Tcherepnin v. Knight, 389 U.S. 332, 88 S.Ct. 548, 19 L.Ed.2d 564, as respects § 3(a)(10):

"(R)emedial legislation should be construed broadly to effectuate its purposes. The Securities Exchange Act quite clearly falls into the category of remedial legislation. One of its central purposes is to protect investors through the requirement of full disclosure by issuers of securities, and the definition of security in § 3(a)(10) necessarily determines the classes of investments and investors which will receive the Act's protections. Finally, we are reminded that, in searching for the meaning and scope of the word 'security' in the Act, form should be disregarded for substance and the emphasis should be on economic reality." Id., at 336, 88 S.Ct., at 553. (Footnote omitted.)

Section 10(b) of the 1934 Act makes it unlawful for any person by use of agencies of interstate commerce or the mails "[t]o use or employ, in connection with the purchase or sale of any security," whether or not registered on a national securities exchange, "any manipulative or deceptive device or contrivance in contravention of such rules and regulations as the Commission may prescribe." 15 U.S.C. § 78j (b).

Alberto–Culver, as noted, is not a private person but a corporation with publicly held stock listed on the New York Stock Exchange. If it is to be believed, if in other words the allegations made are proved, the American company has been defrauded by the issuance of "securities" (promissory notes) for assets which are worthless or of a much lower value than represented. Rule 10b–5 of the Securities and Exchange Commission states:

"It shall be unlawful for any person, directly or indirectly, by the use of any means or instrumentality of interstate commerce, or of the mails or of any facility of any national securities exchange,

"(a) To employ any device, scheme, or artifice to defraud,

"(b) To make any untrue statement of a material fact or to omit to state a material fact necessary in order to make the statements made, in the light of the circumstances under which they were made, not misleading, or

"(c) To engage in any act, practice, or course of business which operates or would operate as a fraud or deceit upon any person,

"in connection with the purchase or sale of any security." 17 CFR § 240.10b–5.

Section 29(a) of the Act provides:

"Any condition, stipulation, or provision binding any person to waive compliance with any provision of this chapter or of any rule or regulation thereunder, or of any rule of an exchange required thereby shall be void." 15 U.S.C. § 78cc(a).

And § 29(b) adds that "[e]very contract" made in violation of the Act "shall be void." No exception is made for contracts which have an international character.

The Securities Act of 1933, 48 Stat. 84, 15 U.S.C. § 77n, has a like provision in its § 14:

"Any condition, stipulation, or provision binding any person acquiring any security to waive compliance with any provision of this subchapter or of the rules and regulations of the Commission shall be void."

... It could perhaps be argued that Wilko does not govern because it involved a little customer pitted against a big brokerage house, while we deal here with sophisticated buyers and sellers: Scherk, a powerful German operator, and Alberto–Culver, an American business surrounded and protected by lawyers and experts. But that would miss the point of the problem. The Act does not speak in terms of "sophisticated" as opposed to "unsophisticated" people dealing in securities. The rules when the giants play are the same as when the pygmies enter the market.

If there are victims here, they are not Alberto–Culver the corporation, but the thousands of investors who are the security holders in Alberto–Culver. If there is fraud and the promissory notes are excessive, the impact is on the equity in Alberto–Culver.

Moreover, the securities market these days is not made up of a host of small people scrambling to get in and out of stocks or other securities. The markets are overshadowed by huge institutional traders. The so-called "off-shore funds," of which Scherk is a member, present perplexing problems under both the 1933 and 1934 Acts. The tendency of American investors to invest indirectly as through mutual funds may change the character of the regulation but not its need.

There has been much support for arbitration of disputes; and it may be the superior way of settling some disagreements. If A and B were quarreling over a trade-mark and there was an arbitration clause in the contract, the policy of Congress in implementing the United Nations Convention on the Recognition and Enforcement of Foreign Arbitral Awards, as it did in 9 U.S.C. § 201 et seq., would prevail. But the Act does not substitute an arbiter for the settlement of disputes under the 1933 and 1934 Acts. Art. II(3) of the Convention says:

> "The court of a Contracting State, when seized of an action in a matter in respect of which the parties have made an agreement within the meaning of this article, shall, at the request of one of the parties, refer the parties to arbitration, unless it finds that the said agreement is null and void, inoperative or incapable of being performed."[5] ...

But § 29(a) of the 1934 Act makes agreements to arbitrate liabilities under § 10 of the Act "void" and "inoperative." Congress has specified a precise way whereby big and small investors will be protected and the rules under which the Alberto–Culvers of this Nation shall operate. They or their lawyers cannot waive those statutory conditions, for our corporate giants are not principalities of power but guardians of a host of wards unable to care for themselves. It is these wards that the 1934 Act tries to protect.... It is peculiarly appropriate that we adhere to Wilko—more so even than when Wilko was decided. Huge foreign investments are being made in our companies. It is important that American standards of fairness in security dealings govern the destinies of American investors until Congress changes these standards.

... The Court appears to attach some significance to the fact that the specific provisions of the 1933 Act involved in Wilko are not duplicated in the 1934 Act, which is involved in this case. While Alberto–Culver would not have the right to sue in either a state or federal forum as did the plaintiff in Wilko, 346 U.S., at 431, 74 S.Ct., at 184, the Court deprives it of its right to have its Rule 10b–5 claim heard in a federal court. We spoke at length in Wilko of this problem, elucidating the undesirable effects of remitting a securities plaintiff to an arbitral, rather than a judicial, forum. Here, as in Wilko, the allegations of fraudulent misrepresentation will involve "subjective findings on the purpose and knowledge" of the defen-

---

5. The Convention also permits that arbitral awards not be recognized and enforced when a court in the country where enforcement is sought finds that "[t]he recognition or enforcement of the award would be contrary to the public policy of that country." Art. V(2)(b); [1970] 3 U.S.T. 2517, 2520, T.I.A.S. No. 6997. It also provides that recognition of an award may be refused when the arbitration agreement "is not valid under the law to which the parties have subjected it," in this case the laws of Illinois. Art. V(1)(a). See n. 10, infra.

dant, questions ill-determined by arbitrators without judicial instruction on the law. See id., at 435, 74 S.Ct., at 187. An arbitral award can be made without explication of reasons and without development of a record, so that the arbitrator's conception of our statutory requirement may be absolutely incorrect yet functionally unreviewable, even when the arbitrator seeks to apply our law. We recognized in Wilko that there is no judicial review corresponding to review of court decisions. Id., at 436–437, 74 S.Ct., at 187–188. The extensive pretrial discovery provided by the Federal Rules of Civil Procedure for actions in district court would not be available. And the wide choice of venue provided by the 1934 Act, 15 U.S.C. § 78aa, would be forfeited. See Wilko v. Swan, supra, at 431, 435, 74 S.Ct. at 186. The loss of the proper judicial forum carries with it the loss of substantial rights.

When a defendant, as alleged here, has, through proscribed acts within our territory, brought itself within the ken of federal securities regulation, a fact not disputed here, those laws—including the controlling principles of Wilko—apply whether the defendant is foreign or American, and whether or not there are transnational elements in the dealings. Those laws are rendered a chimera when foreign corporations or funds—unlike domestic defendants—can nullify them by virtue of arbitration clauses which send defrauded American investors to the uncertainty of arbitration on foreign soil, or, if those investors cannot afford to arbitrate their claims in a far-off forum, to no remedy at all.

Moreover, the international aura which the Court gives this case is ominous. We now have many multinational corporations in vast operations around the world—Europe, Latin America, the Middle East, and Asia. The investments of many American investors turn on dealings by these companies. Up to this day, it has been assumed by reason of Wilko that they were all protected by our various federal securities Acts. If these guarantees are to be removed, it should take a legislative enactment. I would enforce our laws as they stand, unless Congress makes an exception.

* * *

Questions

1.   How does the *Scherck* Court interpret the Court's previous holding in *Wilko*? How does the dissent's interpretation differ? Which is the better reading of the text?

2.   What are the special concerns the majority gives for upholding arbitration awards in international agreements? Does it suggest that the holding of *Scherck* is limited to the international context? Or, is the reasoning in *Scherck* applicable in a purely domestic context? Does the dissent agree that international arbitration poses unique concerns that are not present in domestic arbitrations?

3.   According to the majority, what will protect investors against an international commercial arbitrator misconstruing or misapplying U.S.

securities laws? How does the majority address the concerns about the procedural inadequacy of arbitration that are raised by the dissent?

* * *

Mitsubishi Motors Corp. v. Soler Chrysler–Plymouth, Inc.

473 U.S. 614, 105 S.Ct. 3346 (1985).

■ JUSTICE BLACKMUN delivered the opinion of the Court.

The principal question presented by these cases is the arbitrability, pursuant to the Federal Arbitration Act, 9 U.S.C. § 1 et seq., and the Convention on the Recognition and Enforcement of Foreign Arbitral Awards (Convention), [1970] 21 U.S.T. 2517, T.I.A.S. No. 6997, of claims arising under the Sherman Act, 15 U.S.C. § 1 et seq., and encompassed within a valid arbitration clause in an agreement embodying an international commercial transaction.

I

Petitioner-cross-respondent Mitsubishi Motors Corporation (Mitsubishi) is a Japanese corporation which manufactures automobiles and has its principal place of business in Tokyo, Japan. Mitsubishi is the product of a joint venture between, on the one hand, Chrysler International, S.A. (CISA), a Swiss corporation registered in Geneva and wholly owned by Chrysler Corporation, and, on the other, Mitsubishi Heavy Industries, Inc., a Japanese corporation. The aim of the joint venture was the distribution through Chrysler dealers outside the continental United States of vehicles manufactured by Mitsubishi and bearing Chrysler and Mitsubishi trademarks. Respondent-cross-petitioner Soler Chrysler–Plymouth, Inc. (Soler), is a Puerto Rico corporation with its principal place of business in Pueblo Viejo, Guaynabo, Puerto Rico.

On October 31, 1979, Soler entered into a Distributor Agreement with CISA which provided for the sale by Soler of Mitsubishi-manufactured vehicles within a designated area, including metropolitan San Juan. . . . On the same date, CISA, Soler, and Mitsubishi entered into a Sales Procedure Agreement (Sales Agreement) which, referring to the Distributor Agreement, provided for the direct sale of Mitsubishi products to Soler and governed the terms and conditions of such sales. . . . Paragraph VI of the Sales Agreement, labeled "Arbitration of Certain Matters," provides:

> "All disputes, controversies or differences which may arise between [Mitsubishi] and [Soler] out of or in relation to Articles I–B through V of this Agreement or for the breach thereof, shall be finally settled by arbitration in Japan in accordance with the rules and regulations of the Japan Commercial Arbitration Association." . . .

Initially, Soler did a brisk business in Mitsubishi-manufactured vehicles. As a result of its strong performance, its minimum sales volume, specified by Mitsubishi and CISA, and agreed to by Soler, for the 1981 model year was substantially increased.... In early 1981, however, the new-car market slackened. Soler ran into serious difficulties in meeting the expected sales volume, and by the spring of 1981 it felt itself compelled to request that Mitsubishi delay or cancel shipment of several orders.... About the same time, Soler attempted to arrange for the transshipment of a quantity of its vehicles for sale in the continental United States and Latin America. Mitsubishi and CISA, however, refused permission for any such diversion, citing a variety of reasons,[1] and no vehicles were transshipped. Attempts to work out these difficulties failed. Mitsubishi eventually withheld shipment of 966 vehicles, apparently representing orders placed for May, June, and July 1981 production, responsibility for which Soler disclaimed in February 1982....

The following month, Mitsubishi brought an action against Soler in the United States District Court for the District of Puerto Rico under the Federal Arbitration Act and the Convention.[2] Mitsubishi sought an order, pursuant to 9 U.S.C. §§ 4 and 201, to compel arbitration in accord with ¶ VI of the Sales Agreement.... Shortly after filing the complaint, Mitsubishi filed a request for arbitration before the Japan Commercial Arbitration Association....

Soler denied the allegations and counterclaimed against both Mitsubishi and CISA. It alleged numerous breaches by Mitsubishi of the Sales Agreement,[5] raised a pair of defamation claims, and asserted causes of action under the Sherman Act, 15 U.S.C. § 1 et seq.; the federal Automobile Dealers' Day in Court Act, 70 Stat. 1125, 15 U.S.C. § 1221 et seq.; the Puerto Rico competition statute, P.R.Laws Ann., Tit. 10, § 257 et seq. (1976); and the Puerto Rico Dealers' Contracts Act, P.R.Laws Ann., Tit. 10, § 278 et seq. (1978 and Supp.1983). In the counterclaim premised on the Sherman Act, Soler alleged that Mitsubishi and CISA had conspired to divide markets in restraint of trade. To effectuate the plan, according to

1. The reasons advanced included concerns that such diversion would interfere with the Japanese trade policy of voluntarily limiting imports to the United States, App. 143, 177–178; that the Soler-ordered vehicles would be unsuitable for use in certain proposed destinations because of their manufacture, with use in Puerto Rico in mind, without heaters and defoggers, id., at 182; that the vehicles would be unsuitable for use in Latin America because of the unavailability there of the unleaded, high-octane fuel they required, id., at 177, 181–182; that adequate warranty service could not be ensured, id., at 176, 182; and that diversion to the mainland would violate contractual obligations between CISA and Mitsubishi, id., at 144, 183.

2. The complaint alleged that Soler had failed to pay for 966 ordered vehicles; that it

had failed to pay contractual "distress unit penalties," intended to reimburse Mitsubishi for storage costs and interest charges incurred because of Soler's failure to take shipment of ordered vehicles; that Soler's failure to fulfill warranty obligations threatened Mitsubishi's reputation and goodwill; that Soler had failed to obtain required financing; and that the Distributor and Sales Agreements had expired by their terms or, alternatively, that Soler had surrendered its rights under the Sales Agreement. Id., at 11–14.

5. The alleged breaches included wrongful refusal to ship ordered vehicles and necessary parts, failure to make payment for warranty work and authorized rebates, and bad faith in establishing minimum-sales volumes. Id., at 97–101.

Soler, Mitsubishi had refused to permit Soler to resell to buyers in North, Central, or South America vehicles it had obligated itself to purchase from Mitsubishi; had refused to ship ordered vehicles or the parts, such as heaters and defoggers, that would be necessary to permit Soler to make its vehicles suitable for resale outside Puerto Rico; and had coercively attempted to replace Soler and its other Puerto Rico distributors with a wholly owned subsidiary which would serve as the exclusive Mitsubishi distributor in Puerto Rico. . . .

After a hearing, the District Court ordered Mitsubishi and Soler to arbitrate each of the issues raised in the complaint and in all the counterclaims save two and a portion of a third. With regard to the federal antitrust issues, it recognized that the Courts of Appeals, following American Safety Equipment Corp. v. J.P. Maguire & Co., 391 F.2d 821 (C.A.2 1968), uniformly had held that the rights conferred by the antitrust laws were " 'of a character inappropriate for enforcement by arbitration.' " . . . The District Court held, however, that the international character of the Mitsubishi–Soler undertaking required enforcement of the agreement to arbitrate even as to the antitrust claims. It relied on Scherk v. Alberto–Culver Co., 417 U.S. 506, 515–520, 94 S.Ct. 2449, 2455–2458, 41 L.Ed.2d 270 (1974), in which this Court ordered arbitration, pursuant to a provision embodied in an international agreement, of a claim arising under the Securities Exchange Act of 1934 notwithstanding its assumption, arguendo, that Wilko, supra, which held nonarbitrable claims arising under the Securities Act of 1933, also would bar arbitration of a 1934 Act claim arising in a domestic context.

The United States Court of Appeals for the First Circuit affirmed in part and reversed in part. 723 F.2d 155 (1983). It first rejected Soler's argument that Puerto Rico law precluded enforcement of an agreement obligating a local dealer to arbitrate controversies outside Puerto Rico. It also rejected Soler's suggestion that it could not have intended to arbitrate statutory claims not mentioned in the arbitration agreement. Assessing arbitrability "on an allegation-by-allegation basis," id., at 159, the court then read the arbitration clause to encompass virtually all the claims arising under the various statutes, including all those arising under the Sherman Act.

Finally, after endorsing the doctrine of American Safety, precluding arbitration of antitrust claims, the Court of Appeals concluded that neither this Court's decision in Scherk nor the Convention required abandonment of that doctrine in the face of an international transaction. 723 F.2d, at 164–168. Accordingly, it reversed the judgment of the District Court insofar as it had ordered submission of "Soler's antitrust claims" to arbitration. Affirming the remainder of the judgment, the court directed the District Court to consider in the first instance how the parallel judicial and arbitral proceedings should go forward.

We granted certiorari primarily to consider whether an American court should enforce an agreement to resolve antitrust claims by arbitration when that agreement arises from an international transaction. . . .

II

At the outset, we address the contention raised in Soler's cross-petition that the arbitration clause at issue may not be read to encompass the statutory counterclaims stated in its answer to the complaint. In making this argument, Soler does not question the Court of Appeals' application of ¶ VI of the Sales Agreement to the disputes involved here as a matter of standard contract interpretation. Instead, it argues that as a matter of law a court may not construe an arbitration agreement to encompass claims arising out of statutes designed to protect a class to which the party resisting arbitration belongs "unless [that party] has expressly agreed" to arbitrate those claims, see Pet. for Cert. in No. 83–1733, pp. 8, I, by which Soler presumably means that the arbitration clause must specifically mention the statute giving rise to the claims that a party to the clause seeks to arbitrate. See 723 F.2d, at 159. Soler reasons that, because it falls within the class for whose benefit the federal and local antitrust laws and dealers' Acts were passed, but the arbitration clause at issue does not mention these statutes or statutes in general, the clause cannot be read to contemplate arbitration of these statutory claims.

We do not agree, for we find no warrant in the Arbitration Act for implying in every contract within its ken a presumption against arbitration of statutory claims. The Act's centerpiece provision makes a written agreement to arbitrate "in any maritime transaction or a contract evidencing a transaction involving commerce ... valid, irrevocable, and enforceable, save upon such grounds as exist at law or in equity for the revocation of any contract." 9 U.S.C. § 2. The "liberal federal policy favoring arbitration agreements," Moses H. Cone Memorial Hospital v. Mercury Construction Corp., 460 U.S. 1, 24, 103 S.Ct. 927, 941, 74 L.Ed.2d 765 (1983), manifested by this provision and the Act as a whole, is at bottom a policy guaranteeing the enforcement of private contractual arrangements: the Act simply "creates a body of federal substantive law establishing and regulating the duty to honor an agreement to arbitrate." Id., at 25, n. 32, 103 S.Ct., at 942, n. 32. As this Court recently observed, "[t]he preeminent concern of Congress in passing the Act was to enforce private agreements into which parties had entered," a concern which "requires that we rigorously enforce agreements to arbitrate." Dean Witter Reynolds Inc. v. Byrd, 470 U.S. 213, 221 . . . .

Accordingly, the first task of a court asked to compel arbitration of a dispute is to determine whether the parties agreed to arbitrate that dispute. The court is to make this determination by applying the "federal substantive law of arbitrability, applicable to any arbitration agreement within the coverage of the Act." Moses H. Cone Memorial Hospital, 460 U.S., at 24, 103 S.Ct., at 941 . . . . And that body of law counsels

> "that questions of arbitrability must be addressed with a healthy regard for the federal policy favoring arbitration. . . . The Arbitration Act establishes that, as a matter of federal law, any doubts concerning the scope of arbitrable issues should be resolved in favor of arbitration, whether the problem at hand is the construction of the contract

language itself or an allegation of waiver, delay, or a like defense to
arbitrability." Moses H. Cone Memorial Hospital, 460 U.S., at 24–25,
103 S.Ct., at 941–942.

See, e.g., Steelworkers v. Warrior & Gulf Navigation Co., 363 U.S. 574,
582–583, 80 S.Ct. 1347, 1352–1353, 4 L.Ed.2d 1409 (1960). Thus, as with
any other contract, the parties' intentions control, but those intentions are
generously construed as to issues of arbitrability.

There is no reason to depart from these guidelines where a party
bound by an arbitration agreement raises claims founded on statutory
rights. Some time ago this Court expressed "hope for [the Act's] usefulness
both in controversies based on statutes or on standards otherwise created,"
Wilko v. Swan, 346 U.S. 427, 432 (1953) (footnote omitted); . . . and we are
well past the time when judicial suspicion of the desirability of arbitration
and of the competence of arbitral tribunals inhibited the development of
arbitration as an alternative means of dispute resolution. Just last Term in
Southland Corp., supra, where we held that § 2 of the Act declared a
national policy applicable equally in state as well as federal courts, we
construed an arbitration clause to encompass the disputes at issue without
pausing at the source in a state statute of the rights asserted by the parties
resisting arbitration. 465 U.S., at 15, and n. 7, 104 S.Ct., at 860, and n. 7.
Of course, courts should remain attuned to well-supported claims that the
agreement to arbitrate resulted from the sort of fraud or overwhelming
economic power that would provide grounds "for the revocation of any
contract." 9 U.S.C. § 2; . . . But, absent such compelling considerations, the
Act itself provides no basis for disfavoring agreements to arbitrate statutory claims by skewing the otherwise hospitable inquiry into arbitrability.

That is not to say that all controversies implicating statutory rights are
suitable for arbitration. There is no reason to distort the process of contract
interpretation, however, in order to ferret out the inappropriate. Just as it
is the congressional policy manifested in the Federal Arbitration Act that
requires courts liberally to construe the scope of arbitration agreements
covered by that Act, it is the congressional intention expressed in some
other statute on which the courts must rely to identify any category of
claims as to which agreements to arbitrate will be held unenforceable. See
Wilko v. Swan, 346 U.S., at 434–435, 74 S.Ct., at 186–187; Southland Corp.,
465 U.S., at 16, n. 11, 104 S.Ct., at 861, n.11; Dean Witter Reynolds Inc.,
470 U.S., at 224–225, 105 S.Ct., at 1244–1245 (concurring opinion). For
that reason, Soler's concern for statutorily protected classes provides no
reason to color the lens through which the arbitration clause is read. By
agreeing to arbitrate a statutory claim, a party does not forgo the substantive rights afforded by the statute; it only submits to their resolution in an
arbitral, rather than a judicial, forum. It trades the procedures and opportunity for review of the courtroom for the simplicity, informality, and
expedition of arbitration. We must assume that if Congress intended the
substantive protection afforded by a given statute to include protection
against waiver of the right to a judicial forum, that intention will be

deducible from text or legislative history. See Wilko v. Swan, supra. Having made the bargain to arbitrate, the party should be held to it unless Congress itself has evinced an intention to preclude a waiver of judicial remedies for the statutory rights at issue. Nothing, in the meantime, prevents a party from excluding statutory claims from the scope of an agreement to arbitrate. See Prima Paint Corp., 388 U.S., at 406, 87 S.Ct., at 1807.

In sum, the Court of Appeals correctly conducted a two-step inquiry, first determining whether the parties' agreement to arbitrate reached the statutory issues, and then, upon finding it did, considering whether legal constraints external to the parties' agreement foreclosed the arbitration of those claims. We endorse its rejection of Soler's proposed rule of arbitration-clause construction.

III

We now turn to consider whether Soler's antitrust claims are nonarbitrable even though it has agreed to arbitrate them. In holding that they are not, the Court of Appeals followed the decision of the Second Circuit in American Safety Equipment Corp. v. J.P. Maguire & Co., 391 F.2d 821 (1968). Notwithstanding the absence of any explicit support for such an exception in either the Sherman Act or the Federal Arbitration Act, the Second Circuit there reasoned that "the pervasive public interest in enforcement of the antitrust laws, and the nature of the claims that arise in such cases, combine to make ... antitrust claims ... inappropriate for arbitration." Id., at 827–828. We find it unnecessary to assess the legitimacy of the American Safety doctrine as applied to agreements to arbitrate arising from domestic transactions. As in Scherk v. Alberto-Culver Co., 417 U.S. 506, 94 S.Ct. 2449, 41 L.Ed.2d 270 (1974), we conclude that concerns of international comity, respect for the capacities of foreign and transnational tribunals, and sensitivity to the need of the international commercial system for predictability in the resolution of disputes require that we enforce the parties' agreement, even assuming that a contrary result would be forthcoming in a domestic context.

Even before Scherk, this Court had recognized the utility of forum-selection clauses in international transactions ... Recognizing that "agreeing in advance on a forum acceptable to both parties is an indispensable element in international trade, commerce, and contracting," id., at 13–14, 92 S.Ct., at 1914–1916 the decision in The Bremen clearly eschewed a provincial solicitude for the jurisdiction of domestic forums. . . .

The Bremen and Scherk establish a strong presumption in favor of enforcement of freely negotiated contractual choice-of-forum provisions. Here, as in Scherk, that presumption is reinforced by the emphatic federal policy in favor of arbitral dispute resolution. And at least since this Nation's accession in 1970 to the Convention, see [1970] 21 U.S.T. 2517, T.I.A.S. 6997, and the implementation of the Convention in the same year by amendment of the Federal Arbitration Act, that federal policy applies with special force in the field of international commerce. Thus, we must weigh the concerns of American Safety against a strong belief in the efficacy of arbitral procedures for the resolution of international commercial disputes and an equal commitment to the enforcement of freely negotiated choice-of-forum clauses.

At the outset, we confess to some skepticism of certain aspects of the American Safety doctrine. As distilled by the First Circuit, 723 F.2d, at 162, the doctrine comprises four ingredients. First, private parties play a pivotal role in aiding governmental enforcement of the antitrust laws by means of the private action for treble damages. Second, "the strong possibility that contracts which generate antitrust disputes may be contracts of adhesion militates against automatic forum determination by contract." Third, antitrust issues, prone to complication, require sophisticated legal and economic analysis, and thus are "ill-adapted to strengths of the arbitral process, i.e., expedition, minimal requirements of written rationale, simplicity, resort to basic concepts of common sense and simple equity." Finally, just as "issues of war and peace are too important to be vested in the generals, . . . decisions as to antitrust regulation of business are too important to be lodged in arbitrators chosen from the business community—particularly those from a foreign community that has had no experience with or exposure to our law and values." See American Safety, 391 F.2d, at 826–827.

Initially, we find the second concern unjustified. The mere appearance of an antitrust dispute does not alone warrant invalidation of the selected forum on the undemonstrated assumption that the arbitration clause is tainted. A party resisting arbitration of course may attack directly the validity of the agreement to arbitrate. See Prima Paint Corp. v. Flood & Conklin Mfg. Co., 388 U.S. 395, 87 S.Ct. 1801, 18 L.Ed.2d 1270 (1967). Moreover, the party may attempt to make a showing that would warrant setting aside the forum-selection clause—that the agreement was "[a]ffected by fraud, undue influence, or overweening bargaining power"; that "enforcement would be unreasonable and unjust"; or that proceedings "in the contractual forum will be so gravely difficult and inconvenient that [the resisting party] will for all practical purposes be deprived of his day in court." The Bremen, 407 U.S., at 12, 15, 18, 92 S.Ct., at 1914, 1916, 1917. But absent such a showing—and none was attempted here—there is no basis for assuming the forum inadequate or its selection unfair.

Next, potential complexity should not suffice to ward off arbitration. We might well have some doubt that even the courts following American Safety subscribe fully to the view that antitrust matters are inherently insusceptible to resolution by arbitration, as these same courts have agreed that an undertaking to arbitrate antitrust claims entered into after the dispute arises is acceptable.... And the vertical restraints which most frequently give birth to antitrust claims covered by an arbitration agreement will not often occasion the monstrous proceedings that have given antitrust litigation an image of intractability. In any event, adaptability and access to expertise are hallmarks of arbitration. The anticipated subject matter of the dispute may be taken into account when the arbitrators are appointed, and arbitral rules typically provide for the participation of experts either employed by the parties or appointed by the tribunal. Moreover, it is often a judgment that streamlined proceedings and expeditious results will best serve their needs that causes parties to agree to arbitrate their disputes; it is typically a desire to keep the effort and expense required to resolve a dispute within manageable bounds that prompts them mutually to forgo access to judicial remedies. In sum, the factor of potential complexity alone does not persuade us that an arbitral tribunal could not properly handle an antitrust matter.

For similar reasons, we also reject the proposition that an arbitration panel will pose too great a danger of innate hostility to the constraints on business conduct that antitrust law imposes. International arbitrators frequently are drawn from the legal as well as the business community; where the dispute has an important legal component, the parties and the arbitral body with whose assistance they have agreed to settle their dispute can be expected to select arbitrators accordingly. We decline to indulge the presumption that the parties and arbitral body conducting a proceeding will be unable or unwilling to retain competent, conscientious, and impartial arbitrators.

We are left, then, with the core of the American Safety doctrine—the fundamental importance to American democratic capitalism of the regime of the antitrust laws. . . . Without doubt, the private cause of action plays a central role in enforcing this regime. . . . As the Court of Appeals pointed out:

> " 'A claim under the antitrust laws is not merely a private matter. The Sherman Act is designed to promote the national interest in a competitive economy; thus, the plaintiff asserting his rights under the Act has been likened to a private attorney-general who protects the public's interest.' " 723 F.2d, at 168, quoting American Safety, 391 F.2d, at 826.

The treble-damages provision wielded by the private litigant is a chief tool in the antitrust enforcement scheme, posing a crucial deterrent to potential violators. . . .

The importance of the private damages remedy, however, does not compel the conclusion that it may not be sought outside an American court. Notwithstanding its important incidental policing function, the treble-damages cause of action conferred on private parties by § 4 of the Clayton Act, 15 U.S.C. § 15, and pursued by Soler here by way of its third counterclaim, seeks primarily to enable an injured competitor to gain compensation for that injury. . . .

After examining the respective legislative histories, the Court in Brunswick [Corp. v. Peublo–Bowl–O–Mat, Inc.] recognized that when first enacted in 1890 as § 7 of the Sherman Act, 26 Stat. 210, the treble-damages provision "was conceived of primarily as a remedy for '[t]he people of the United States as individuals,' " 429 U.S., at 486, n. 10, 97 S.Ct., at 696, n. 10, quoting 21 Cong.Rec. 1767–1768 (1890) (remarks of Sen. George); when reenacted in 1914 as § 4 of the Clayton Act, 38 Stat. 731, it was still "conceived primarily as 'open[ing] the door of justice to every man, whenever he may be injured by those who violate the antitrust laws, and giv[ing] the injured party ample damages for the wrong suffered.' " 429 U.S., at 486, n. 10, 97 S.Ct., at 696, n. 10, quoting 51 Cong.Rec. 9073 (1914) (remarks of Rep. Webb). And, of course, the antitrust cause of action remains at all times under the control of the individual litigant: no citizen is under an obligation to bring an antitrust suit, see Illinois Brick Co. v. Illinois, 431 U.S. 720, 746, 97 S.Ct. 2061, 2074, 52 L.Ed.2d 707 (1977), and the private antitrust plaintiff needs no executive or judicial approval before settling one. It follows that, at least where the international cast of a transaction would otherwise add an element of uncertainty to dispute resolution, the prospective litigant may provide in advance for a mutually agreeable procedure whereby he would seek his antitrust recovery as well as settle other controversies.

There is no reason to assume at the outset of the dispute that international arbitration will not provide an adequate mechanism. To be sure, the international arbitral tribunal owes no prior allegiance to the legal norms of particular states; hence, it has no direct obligation to vindicate their statutory dictates. The tribunal, however, is bound to effectuate the intentions of the parties. Where the parties have agreed that the arbitral body is to decide a defined set of claims which includes, as in these cases, those arising from the application of American antitrust law, the tribunal therefore should be bound to decide that dispute in accord with the national law giving rise to the claim.... And so long as the prospective litigant effectively may vindicate its statutory cause of action in the arbitral forum, the statute will continue to serve both its remedial and deterrent function.

Having permitted the arbitration to go forward, the national courts of the United States will have the opportunity at the award-enforcement stage to ensure that the legitimate interest in the enforcement of the antitrust laws has been addressed. The Convention reserves to each signatory country the right to refuse enforcement of an award where the "recognition or enforcement of the award would be contrary to the public policy of that country." ... While the efficacy of the arbitral process requires that substantive review at the award-enforcement stage remain minimal, it would not require intrusive inquiry to ascertain that the tribunal took cognizance of the antitrust claims and actually decided them.

As international trade has expanded in recent decades, so too has the use of international arbitration to resolve disputes arising in the course of that trade. The controversies that international arbitral institutions are called upon to resolve have increased in diversity as well as in complexity. Yet the potential of these tribunals for efficient disposition of legal disagreements arising from commercial relations has not yet been tested. If they are to take a central place in the international legal order, national courts will need to "shake off the old judicial hostility to arbitration," Kulukundis Shipping Co. v. Amtorg Trading Corp., 126 F.2d 978, 985 (C.A.2 1942), and also their customary and understandable unwillingness to cede jurisdiction of a claim arising under domestic law to a foreign or transnational tribunal. To this extent, at least, it will be necessary for national courts to subordinate domestic notions of arbitrability to the international policy favoring commercial arbitration. See Scherk, supra.[21]

Accordingly, we "require this representative of the American business community to honor its bargain," Alberto–Culver Co. v. Scherk, 484 F.2d 611, 620 (C.A.7 1973) (Stevens, J., dissenting), by holding this agreement to arbitrate "enforce[able] . . . in accord with the explicit provisions of the Arbitration Act." Scherk, 417 U.S., at 520, 94 S.Ct., at 2457

The judgment of the Court of Appeals is affirmed in part and reversed in part, and the cases are remanded for further proceedings consistent with this opinion.

It is so ordered.

■ JUSTICE POWELL took no part in the decision of these cases.

■ JUSTICE STEVENS, with whom JUSTICE BRENNAN joins, and with whom JUSTICE MARSHALL joins except as to Part II, dissenting.

. . . This Court agrees with the Court of Appeals' interpretation of the scope of the arbitration clause, but disagrees with its conclusion that the clause is unenforceable insofar as it purports to cover an antitrust claim against a Japanese company. This Court's holding rests almost exclusively on the federal policy favoring arbitration of commercial disputes and vague notions of international comity arising from the fact that the automobiles involved here were manufactured in Japan. Because I am convinced that the Court of Appeals' construction of the arbitration clause is erroneous, and because I strongly disagree with this Court's interpretation of the relevant federal statutes, I respectfully dissent. In my opinion, (1) a fair construction of the language in the arbitration clause in the parties' contract does not encompass a claim that auto manufacturers entered into a conspiracy in violation of the antitrust laws; (2) an arbitration clause should not normally be construed to cover a statutory remedy that it does not expressly identify; (3) Congress did not intend § 2 of the Federal Arbitration Act to apply to antitrust claims; and (4) Congress did not intend the Convention on the Recognition and Enforcement of Foreign Arbitral Awards to apply to disputes that are not covered by the Federal Arbitration Act.

---

21. We do not quarrel with the Court of Appeals' conclusion that Art. II(1) of the Convention, which requires the recognition of agreements to arbitrate that involve "subject matter capable of settlement by arbitration," contemplates exceptions to arbitrability grounded in domestic law. . . .

Doubtless, Congress may specify categories of claims it wishes to reserve for decision by our own courts without contravening this Nation's obligations under the Convention. But we decline to subvert the spirit of the United States' accession to the Convention by recognizing subject-matter exceptions where Congress has not expressly directed the courts to do so.

I

On October 31, 1979, respondent, Soler Chrysler–Plymouth, Inc. (Soler), entered into a "distributor agreement" to govern the sale of Plymouth passenger cars to be manufactured by petitioner, Mitsubishi Motors Corporation of Tokyo, Japan (Mitsubishi). Mitsubishi, however, was not a party to that agreement. Rather the "purchase rights" were granted to Soler by a wholly owned subsidiary of Chrysler Corporation that is referred to as "Chrysler" in the agreement. The distributor agreement does not contain an arbitration clause. Nor does the record contain any other agreement providing for the arbitration of disputes between Soler and Chrysler.

Paragraph 26 of the distributor agreement authorizes Chrysler to have Soler's orders filled by any company affiliated with Chrysler, that company thereby becoming the "supplier" of the products covered by the agreement with Chrysler. Relying on paragraph 26 of their distributor agreement, Soler, Chrysler, and Mitsubishi entered into a separate Sales Procedure Agreement designating Mitsubishi as the supplier of the products covered by the distributor agreement. The arbitration clause the Court construes today is found in that agreement. As a matter of ordinary contract interpretation, there are at least two reasons why that clause does not apply to Soler's antitrust claim against Chrysler and Mitsubishi.

First, the clause only applies to two-party disputes between Soler and Mitsubishi. The antitrust violation alleged in Soler's counterclaim is a three-party dispute. Soler has joined both Chrysler and its associated company, Mitsubishi, as counter defendants. The pleading expressly alleges that both of those companies are "engaged in an unlawful combination and conspiracy to restrain and divide markets in interstate and foreign commerce, in violation of the Sherman Antitrust Act and the Clayton Act." . . . It is further alleged that Chrysler authorized and participated in several overt acts directed at Soler. At this stage of the case we must, of course, assume the truth of those allegations. Only by stretching the language of the arbitration clause far beyond its ordinary meaning could one possibly conclude that it encompasses this three-party dispute.

Second, the clause only applies to disputes "which may arise between MMC and BUYER out of or in relation to Articles I–B through V of this Agreement or for the breach thereof. . . ." Id., at 52. Thus, disputes relating to only 5 out of a total of 15 Articles in the Sales Procedure Agreement are arbitrable. Those five Articles cover: (1) the terms and conditions of direct sales (matters such as the scheduling of orders, deliveries, and payment); (2) technical and engineering changes; (3) compliance by Mitsubishi with customs laws and regulations, and Soler's obligation to inform Mitsubishi of relevant local laws; (4) trademarks and patent rights; and (5) Mitsubishi's right to cease production of any products. It is immediately obviously that Soler's antitrust claim did not arise out of Articles I–B through V and it is not a claim "for the breach thereof." The question is whether it is a dispute "in relation to" those Articles.

Because Mitsubishi relies on those Articles of the contract to explain some of the activities that Soler challenges in its antitrust claim, the Court of Appeals concluded that the relationship between the dispute and those Articles brought the arbitration clause into play. I find that construction of the clause wholly unpersuasive. The words "in relation to" appear between the references to claims that arise under the contract and claims for breach of the contract; I believe all three of the species of arbitrable claims must be predicated on contractual rights defined in Articles I–B through V.

The federal policy favoring arbitration cannot sustain the weight that the Court assigns to it. A clause requiring arbitration of all claims "relating to" a contract surely could not encompass a claim that the arbitration clause was itself part of a contract in restraint of trade.... Nor in my judgment should it be read to encompass a claim that relies, not on a failure to perform the contract, but on an independent violation of federal law. The matters asserted by way of defense do not control the character, or the source, of the claim that Soler has asserted. Accordingly, simply as a matter of ordinary contract interpretation, I would hold that Soler's antitrust claim is not arbitrable.

II

Section 2 of the Federal Arbitration Act describes three kinds of arbitrable agreements. Two—those including maritime transactions and those covering the submission of an existing dispute to arbitration—are not involved in this case. The language of § 2 relating to the Soler–Mitsubishi arbitration clause reads as follows:

> "A written provision in ... a contract evidencing a transaction involving commerce to settle by arbitration a controversy thereafter arising out of such contract ... or the refusal to perform the whole or any part thereof, ... shall be valid, irrevocable, and enforceable, save upon such grounds as exist at law or in equity for the revocation of any contract."

The plain language of this statute encompasses Soler's claims that arise out of its contract with Mitsubishi, but does not encompass a claim arising under federal law, or indeed one that arises under its distributor agreement with Chrysler. Nothing in the text of the 1925 Act, nor its legislative history, suggests that Congress intended to authorize the arbitration of any statutory claims.[11]

---

11. In his dissent in Prima Paint Corp. v. Flood & Conklin Mfg. Co., 388 U.S., at 415, 87 S.Ct., at 1811 Justice Black quoted the following commentary written shortly after the statute was passed:

"Not all questions arising out of contracts ought to be arbitrated. It is a remedy peculiarly suited to the disposition of the ordinary disputes between merchants as to questions of fact—quantity, quality, time of delivery, compliance with terms of payment, excuses for non-performance, and the like. It has a place also in the determination of the simpler questions of law—the questions of law which arise out of these daily relations between merchants as to the passage of title, the existence of warranties, or the questions of law which are complementary to the questions of fact which we have just mentioned." Cohen & Dayton, The New Federal Arbitration Law, 12 Va.L.Rev. 265, 281 (1926).

In the Prima Paint case the Court held that the Act applied to a claim of fraud in the inducement of the contract, but did not intimate that it might also cover federal statutory claims....

Until today all of our cases enforcing agreements to arbitrate under the Arbitration Act have involved contract claims. In one, the party claiming a breach of contractual warranties also claimed that the breach amounted to fraud actionable under § 10(b) of the Securities Exchange Act of 1934. Scherk v. Alberto–Culver Co., 417 U.S. 506, 94 S.Ct. 2449, 41 L.Ed.2d 270 (1974). But this is the first time the Court has considered the question whether a standard arbitration clause referring to claims arising out of or relating to a contract should be construed to cover statutory claims that have only an indirect relationship to the contract. In my opinion, neither the Congress that enacted the Arbitration Act in 1925, nor the many parties who have agreed to such standard clauses, could have anticipated the Court's answer to that question.

On several occasions we have drawn a distinction between statutory rights and contractual rights and refused to hold that an arbitration barred the assertion of a statutory right. Thus, in Alexander v. Gardner–Denver Co., 415 U.S. 36, 94 S.Ct. 1011, 39 L.Ed.2d 147 (1974), we held that the arbitration of a claim of employment discrimination would not bar an employee's statutory right to damages under Title VII of the Civil Rights Act of 1964, 42 U.S.C. §§ 2000e—2000e–17, notwithstanding the strong federal policy favoring the arbitration of labor disputes. In that case the Court explained at some length why it would be unreasonable to assume that Congress intended to give arbitrators the final authority to implement the federal statutory policy:

"[W]e have long recognized that 'the choice of forums inevitably affects the scope of the substantive right to be vindicated.' U.S. Bulk Carriers v. Arguelles, 400 U.S. 351, 359–360 [91 S.Ct. 409, 413–414, 27 L.Ed.2d 456] (1971) (Harlan, J., concurring). Respondent's deferral rule is necessarily premised on the assumption that arbitral processes are commensurate with judicial processes and that Congress impliedly intended federal courts to defer to arbitral decisions on Title VII issues. We deem this supposition unlikely.

"Arbitral procedures, while well suited to the resolution of contractual disputes, make arbitration a comparatively inappropriate forum for the final resolution of rights created by Title VII. This conclusion rests first on the special role of the arbitrator, whose task is to effectuate the intent of the parties rather than the requirements of enacted legislation.... But other facts may still render arbitral processes comparatively inferior to judicial processes in the protection of Title VII rights. Among these is the fact that the specialized competence of arbitrators pertains primarily to the law of the shop, not the law of the land. United Steelworkers of America v. Warrior & Gulf Navigation Co., 363 U.S. 574, 581–583, [80 S.Ct. 1347, 1352–1353, 4 L.Ed.2d 1409] (1960). Parties usually choose an arbitrator because they trust his knowledge and judgment concerning the demands and norms of industrial relations. On the other hand, the resolution of statutory or constitutional issues is a primary responsibility of courts, and judicial construction has proved especially necessary with respect to Title VII, whose broad language frequently can be given meaning only by reference to public law concepts."

415 U.S., at 56–57, 94 S.Ct., at 1023–1024 (footnote omitted).

In addition, the Court noted that the informal procedures which make arbitration so desirable in the context of contractual disputes are inadequate to develop a record for appellate review of statutory questions. Such review is essential on matters of statutory interpretation in order to assure consistent application of important public rights.

In Barrentine v. Arkansas–Best Freight System, Inc., 450 U.S. 728, 101 S.Ct. 1437, 67 L.Ed.2d 641 (1981), we reached a similar conclusion with respect to the arbitrability of an employee's claim based on the Fair Labor Standards Act, 29 U.S.C. §§ 201–219. We again noted that an arbitrator, unlike a federal judge, has no institutional obligation to enforce federal legislative policy:

> "Because the arbitrator is required to effectuate the intent of the parties, rather than to enforce the statute, he may issue a ruling that is inimical to the public policies underlying the FLSA, thus depriving an employee of protected statutory rights.

> "Finally, not only are arbitral procedures less protective of individual statutory rights than are judicial procedures, see Gardner–Denver, supra [415 U.S.], at 57–58 [94 S.Ct., at 1024–1025], but arbitrators very often are powerless to grant the aggrieved employees as broad a range of relief. Under the FLSA, courts can award actual and liquidated damages, reasonable attorney's fees, and costs. 29 U.S.C. § 216(b). An arbitrator, by contrast, can award only that compensation authorized by the wage provision of the collective-bargaining agreement.... It is most unlikely that he will be authorized to award liquidated damages, costs, or attorney's fees." 450 U.S., at 744–745, 101 S.Ct., at 1446–1447 (footnote omitted) ...

The Court's opinions in Alexander, Barrentine, McDonald, and Wilko all explain why it makes good sense to draw a distinction between statutory claims and contract claims. In view of the Court's repeated recognition of the distinction between federal statutory rights and contractual rights, together with the undisputed historical fact that arbitration has functioned almost entirely in either the area of labor disputes or in "ordinary disputes between merchants as to questions of fact," see n. 11, supra, it is reasonable to assume that most lawyers and executives would not expect the language in the standard arbitration clause to cover federal statutory claims. Thus, in my opinion, both a fair respect for the importance of the interests that Congress has identified as worthy of federal statutory protection, and a fair appraisal of the most likely understanding of the parties who sign agreements containing standard arbitration clauses, support a presumption that such clauses do not apply to federal statutory claims.

III

The Court has repeatedly held that a decision by Congress to create a special statutory remedy renders a private agreement to arbitrate a federal

statutory claim unenforceable.... The reasons that motivated those decisions apply with special force to the federal policy that is protected by the
antitrust laws....

The Sherman and Clayton Acts reflect Congress' appraisal of the value
of economic freedom; they guarantee the vitality of the entrepreneurial
spirit. Questions arising under these Acts are among the most important in
public law.

The unique public interest in the enforcement of the antitrust laws is
repeatedly reflected in the special remedial scheme enacted by Congress.
Since its enactment in 1890, the Sherman Act has provided for public
enforcement through criminal as well as civil sanctions. The pre-eminent
federal interest in effective enforcement once justified a provision for
special three-judge district courts to hear antitrust claims on an expedited
basis, as well as for direct appeal to this Court bypassing the courts of
appeals. See, e.g., United States v. National Assn. of Securities Dealers,
Inc., 422 U.S. 694, 95 S.Ct. 2427, 45 L.Ed.2d 486 (1975).

The special interest in encouraging private enforcement of the Sherman Act has been reflected in the statutory scheme ever since 1890.
Section 7 of the original Act, used the broadest possible language to
describe the class of litigants who may invoke its protection. "The Act is
comprehensive in its terms and coverage, protecting all who are made
victims of the forbidden practices by whomever they may be perpetrated."
Mandeville Island Farms, Inc. v. American Crystal Sugar Co., 334 U.S. 219,
236, 68 S.Ct. 996, 1006, 92 L.Ed. 1328, (1948); see also Associated General
Contractors of California, Inc. v. Carpenters, 459 U.S. 519, 529, 103 S.Ct.
897, 904, 74 L.Ed.2d 723 (1983).

The provision for mandatory treble damages—unique in federal law
when the statute was enacted—provides a special incentive to the private
enforcement of the statute, as well as an especially powerful deterrent to
violators. What we have described as "the public interest in vigilant
enforcement of the antitrust laws through the instrumentality of the
private treble-damage action," Lawlor v. National Screen Service Corp.,
349 U.S. 322, 329, 75 S.Ct. 865, 869, 99 L.Ed. 1122 (1955), is buttressed by
the statutory mandate that the injured party also recover costs, "including
a reasonable attorney's fee." 15 U.S.C. § 15(a). The interest in wide and
effective enforcement has thus, for almost a century, been vindicated by
enlisting the assistance of "private Attorneys General"; we have always
attached special importance to their role because "[e]very violation of the
antitrust laws is a blow to the free-enterprise system envisaged by Congress." Hawaii v. Standard Oil Co., 405 U.S. 251, 262, 92 S.Ct. 885, 891, 31
L.Ed.2d 184 (1972).

There are, in addition, several unusual features of the antitrust en-
forcement scheme that unequivocally require rejection of any thought that
Congress would tolerate private arbitration of antitrust claims in lieu of the
statutory remedies that it fashioned. As we explained in Blumenstock
Brothers Advertising Agency v. Curtis Publishing Co., 252 U.S. 436, 440, 40
S.Ct. 385, 386, 64 L.Ed. 649 (1920), an antitrust treble-damages case "can

only be brought in a District Court of the United States." The determination that these cases are "too important to be decided otherwise than by competent tribunals" surely cannot allow private arbitrators to assume a jurisdiction that is denied to courts of the sovereign States....

In view of the history of antitrust enforcement in the United States, it is not surprising that all of the federal courts that have considered the question have uniformly and unhesitatingly concluded that agreements to arbitrate federal antitrust issues are not enforceable. In a landmark opinion for the Court of Appeals for the Second Circuit, Judge Feinberg wrote:

> "A claim under the antitrust laws is not merely a private matter. The Sherman Act is designed to promote the national interest in a competitive economy; thus, the plaintiff asserting his rights under the Act has been likened to a private attorney-general who protects the public's interest.... Antitrust violations can affect hundreds of thousands—perhaps millions—of people and inflict staggering economic damage.... We do not believe that Congress intended such claims to be resolved elsewhere than in the courts. We do not suggest that all antitrust litigations attain these swollen proportions; the courts, no less than the public, are thankful that they do not. But in fashioning a rule to govern the arbitrability of antitrust claims, we must consider the rule's potential effect. For the same reason, it is also proper to ask whether contracts of adhesion between alleged monopolists and their customers should determine the forum for trying antitrust violations." American Safety Equipment Corp. v. J.P. Maguire & Co., 391 F.2d 821, 826–827 (1968) (footnote omitted).

This view has been followed in later cases from that Circuit and by the First, Fifth, Seventh, Eighth, and Ninth Circuits....

This Court would be well advised to endorse the collective wisdom of the distinguished judges of the Courts of Appeals who have unanimously concluded that the statutory remedies fashioned by Congress for the enforcement of the antitrust laws render an agreement to arbitrate antitrust disputes unenforceable. Arbitration awards are only reviewable for manifest disregard of the law, 9 U.S.C. §§ 10, 207, and the rudimentary procedures which make arbitration so desirable in the context of a private dispute often mean that the record is so inadequate that the arbitrator's decision is virtually unreviewable.[31] Despotic decision making of this kind is fine for parties who are willing to agree in advance to settle for a best approximation of the correct result in order to resolve quickly and inexpensively any contractual dispute that may arise in an ongoing commercial relationship. Such informality, however, is simply unacceptable when every error may have devastating consequences for important businesses in our

---

31. The arbitration procedure in this case does not provide any right to evidentiary discovery or a written decision, and requires that all proceedings be closed to the public. App. 220–221. Moreover, Japanese arbitrators do not have the power of compulsory process to secure witnesses and documents, nor do witnesses who are available testify under oath. Id., at 218–219. Cf. 9 U.S.C. § 7 (arbitrators may summon witnesses to attend proceedings and seek enforcement in a district court).

national economy and may undermine their ability to compete in world markets. Instead of "muffling a grievance in the cloakroom of arbitration," the public interest in free competitive markets would be better served by having the issues resolved "in the light of impartial public court adjudication." See Merrill Lynch, Pierce, Fenner & Smith, Inc. v. Ware, 414 U.S. 117, 136 (1973).

IV

The Court assumes for the purposes of its decision that the antitrust issues would not be arbitrable if this were a purely domestic dispute, ante, at 3355, but holds that the international character of the controversy makes it arbitrable. The holding rests on vague concerns for the international implications of its decision and a misguided application of Scherk v. Alberto–Culver, Co., 417 U.S. 506, 94 S.Ct. 2449, 41 L.Ed.2d 270 (1974).

International Obligations of the United States

Before relying on its own notions of what international comity requires, it is surprising that the Court does not determine the specific commitments that the United States has made to enforce private agreements to arbitrate disputes arising under public law. As the Court acknowledges, the only treaty relevant here is the Convention on the Recognition and Enforcement of Foreign Arbitral Awards. [1970] 21 U.S.T. 2517, T.I.A.S. No. 6997. The Convention was adopted in 1958 at a multilateral conference sponsored by the United Nations. This Nation did not sign the proposed convention at that time; displaying its characteristic caution before entering into international compacts, the United States did not accede to it until 12 years later.

As the Court acknowledged in Scherk v. Alberto–Culver Co., 417 U.S., at 520, n. 15, 94 S.Ct., at 2457, n. 15, the principal purpose of the Convention "was to encourage the recognition and enforcement of commercial arbitration agreements in international contracts and to unify the standards by which agreements to arbitrate are observed and arbitral awards are enforced in the signatory countries." However, the United States, as amicus curiae, advises the Court that the Convention "clearly contemplates" that signatory nations will enforce domestic laws prohibiting the arbitration of certain subject matters. Brief for United States as Amicus Curiae 28. This interpretation of the Convention was adopted by the Court of Appeals, 723 F.2d, at 162–166, and the Court declines to reject it, ante, at 639–640, n. 21. The construction is beyond doubt. . . .

This construction is confirmed by the provisions of the Convention which provide for the enforcement of international arbitration awards. Article III provides that each "Contracting State shall recognize arbitral awards as binding and enforce them." However, if an arbitration award is "contrary to the public policy of [a] country" called upon to enforce it, or if it concerns a subject matter which is "not capable of settlement by arbitration under the law of that country," the Convention does not require that it be enforced. Arts. V(2)(a) and (b). Thus, reading Articles II and V together, the Convention provides that agreements to arbitrate disputes which are nonarbitrable under domestic law need not be honored, nor awards rendered under them enforced. . . .

International Comity

It is clear then that the international obligations of the United States permit us to honor Congress' commitment to the exclusive resolution of antitrust disputes in the federal courts. The Court today refuses to do so, offering only vague concerns for comity among nations. The courts of other nations, on the other hand, have applied the exception provided in the Convention, and refused to enforce agreements to arbitrate specific subject matters of concern to them.

It may be that the subject-matter exception to the Convention ought to be reserved—as a matter of domestic law—for matters of the greatest public interest which involve concerns that are shared by other nations. The Sherman Act's commitment to free competitive markets is among our most important civil policies. Supra, at 650–657. This commitment, shared by other nations which are signatory to the Convention, is hardly the sort of parochial concern that we should decline to enforce in the interest of international comity. . . .

Lacking any support for the proposition that the enforcement of our domestic laws in this context will result in international recriminations, the Court seeks refuge in an obtuse application of its own precedent, Scherk v. Alberto–Culver Co., 417 U.S. 506, 94 S.Ct. 2449, 41 L.Ed.2d 270 (1974), in order to defend the contrary result. . . .

Thus, in its opinion in Scherk, the Court distinguished Wilko because in that case "no credible claim could have been entertained that any international conflict-of-laws problems would arise." 417 U.S., at 516, 94 S.Ct., at 2455. That distinction fits this case precisely, since I consider it perfectly clear that the rules of American antitrust law must govern the claim of an American automobile dealer that he has been injured by an international conspiracy to restrain trade in the American automobile market.

The critical importance of the foreign-law issues in Scherk was apparent to me even before the case reached this Court. See n. 12, supra. For that reason, it is especially distressing to find that the Court is unable to perceive why the reasoning in Scherk is wholly inapplicable to Soler's antitrust claims against Chrysler and Mitsubishi. The merits of those claims are controlled entirely by American law. It is true that the automobiles are manufactured in Japan and that Mitsubishi is a Japanese corporation, but the same antitrust questions would be presented if Mitsubishi were owned by two American companies instead of by one American and one Japanese partner. When Mitsubishi enters the American market and plans to engage in business in that market over a period of years, it must recognize its obligation to comply with American law and to be subject to the remedial provisions of American statutes. . . .

V

The Court's repeated incantation of the high ideals of "international arbitration" creates the impression that this case involves the fate of an institution designed to implement a formula for world peace. But just as it is improper to subordinate the public interest in enforcement of antitrust policy to the private interest in resolving commercial disputes, so is it equally unwise to allow a vision of world unity to distort the importance of the selection of the proper forum for resolving this dispute. Like any other mechanism for resolving controversies, international arbitration will only succeed if it is realistically limited to tasks it is capable of performing well—the prompt and inexpensive resolution of essentially contractual disputes between commercial partners. As for matters involving the political passions and the fundamental interests of nations, even the multilateral convention adopted under the auspices of the United Nations recognizes that private international arbitration is incapable of achieving satisfactory results.

In my opinion, the elected representatives of the American people would not have us dispatch an American citizen to a foreign land in search of an uncertain remedy for the violation of a public right that is protected by the Sherman Act. This is especially so when there has been no genuine bargaining over the terms of the submission, and the arbitration remedy provided has not even the most elementary guarantees of fair process. Consideration of a fully developed record by a jury, instructed in the law by a federal judge, and subject to appellate review, is a surer guide to the competitive character of a commercial practice than the practically unreviewable judgment of a private arbitrator.

Unlike the Congress that enacted the Sherman Act in 1890, the Court today does not seem to appreciate the value of economic freedom. I respectfully dissent.

* * *

Questions

1. Do you agree with the *Mitsubishi* Court that an arbitration clause should be treated the same as a choice of forum clause in the international context? Are there differences between the types of clauses that the Court is ignoring that might argue for a different outcome in this case?

2. What features of the Sherman Antitrust Act led some lower courts to hold that Sherman Act claims are inappropriate for arbitration? How does the Supreme Court majority in *Mitsubishi* respond to these objections? What other federal statutes might be amenable to arbitration? What types of statutes would not be amenable?

3. How important to the majority's reasoning is the availability of judicial review for arbitration awards that construe the Sherman Act?

4. Does the Court's opinion leave the *American Safety* doctrine intact for wholly domestic disputes involving arbitration of antitrust claims?

* * *

Shearson/American Express, Inc. v. McMahon

482 U.S. 220, 107 S.Ct. 2332 (1987).

■ JUSTICE O'CONNOR delivered the opinion of the Court.

This case presents two questions regarding the enforceability of predispute arbitration agreements between brokerage firms and their customers. The first is whether a claim brought under § 10(b) of the Securities Exchange Act of 1934 (Exchange Act), 48 Stat. 891, 15 U.S.C. § 78j(b), must be sent to arbitration in accordance with the terms of an arbitration agreement. The second is whether a claim brought under the Racketeer Influenced and Corrupt Organizations Act (RICO), 18 U.S.C. § 1961 et seq., must be arbitrated in accordance with the terms of such an agreement.

I

Between 1980 and 1982, respondents Eugene and Julia McMahon, individually and as trustees for various pension and profit-sharing plans, were customers of petitioner Shearson/American Express Inc. (Shearson), a brokerage firm registered with the Securities and Exchange Commission (SEC or Commission). Two customer agreements signed by Julia McMahon provided for arbitration of any controversy relating to the accounts the McMahons maintained with Shearson. The arbitration provision provided in relevant part as follows:

> "Unless unenforceable due to federal or state law, any controversy arising out of or relating to my accounts, to transactions with you for me or to this agreement or the breach thereof, shall be settled by arbitration in accordance with the rules, then in effect, of the National Association of Securities Dealers, Inc. or the Boards of Directors of the New York Stock Exchange, Inc. and/or the American Stock Exchange, Inc. as I may elect." 618 F.Supp. 384, 385 (1985).

In October 1984, the McMahons filed an amended complaint against Shearson and petitioner Mary Ann McNulty, the registered representative who handled their accounts, in the United States District Court for the Southern District of New York. The complaint alleged that McNulty, with Shearson's knowledge, had violated § 10(b) of the Exchange Act and Rule 10b–5, 17 CFR § 240.10b–5 (1986), by engaging in fraudulent, excessive trading on respondents' accounts and by making false statements and omitting material facts from the advice given to respondents. The complaint also alleged a RICO claim, 18 U.S.C. § 1962(c), and state law claims for fraud and breach of fiduciary duties.

Relying on the customer agreements, petitioners moved to compel arbitration of the McMahons' claims pursuant to § 3 of the Federal Arbitration Act, 9 U.S.C. § 3. The District Court granted the motion in part. 618 F.Supp. 384 (1985). The court first rejected the McMahons' contention that the arbitration agreements were unenforceable as contracts of adhesion. It then found that the McMahons' § 10(b) claims were arbitrable under the terms of the agreement, concluding that such a result followed from this Court's decision in Dean Witter Reynolds Inc. v. Byrd, 470 U.S. 213, 105 S.Ct. 1238, 84 L.Ed.2d 158 (1985), and the "strong national policy favoring the enforcement of arbitration agreements." 618 F.Supp., at 388. The District Court also held that the McMahons' state law claims were arbitrable under Dean Witter Reynolds Inc. v. Byrd, supra. It concluded, however, that the McMahons' RICO claim was not arbitrable "because of the important federal policies inherent in the enforcement of RICO by the federal courts." 618 F.Supp., at 387.

The Court of Appeals affirmed the District Court on the state law and RICO claims, but it reversed on the Exchange Act claims. 788 F.2d 94 (1986). With respect to the RICO claim, the Court of Appeals concluded that "public policy" considerations made it "inappropriat[e]" to apply the provisions of the Arbitration Act to RICO suits. Id., at 98. The court reasoned that RICO claims are "not merely a private matter." Ibid. Because a RICO plaintiff may be likened to a "private attorney general" protecting the public interest, ibid., the Court of Appeals concluded that such claims should be adjudicated only in a judicial forum. It distinguished this Court's reasoning in Mitsubishi Motors Corp. v. Soler Chrysler–Plymouth, Inc., 473 U.S. 614, 105 S.Ct. 3346, 87 L.Ed.2d 444 (1985), concerning the arbitrability of antitrust claims, on the ground that it involved international business transactions and did not affect the law "as applied to agreements to arbitrate arising from domestic transactions." 788 F.2d, at 98.

With respect to respondents' Exchange Act claims, the Court of Appeals noted that under Wilko v. Swan, 346 U.S. 427, 74 S.Ct. 182, 98 L.Ed. 168 (1953), claims arising under § 12(2) of the Securities Act of 1933 (Securities Act), 48 Stat. 84, 15 U.S.C. § 77l(2), are not subject to compulsory arbitration. The Court of Appeals observed that it previously had extended the Wilko rule to claims arising under § 10(b) of the Exchange Act and Rule 10b–5.... The court acknowledged that Scherk v. Alberto–Culver Co., 417 U.S. 506, 94 S.Ct. 2449, 41 L.Ed.2d 270 (1974), and Dean Witter Reynolds Inc. v. Byrd, supra, had "cast some doubt on the applicability of Wilko to claims under § 10(b)." 788 F.2d, at 97. The Court of Appeals nevertheless concluded that it was bound by the "clear judicial precedent in this Circuit," and held that Wilko must be applied to Exchange Act claims. 788 F.2d, at 98.

We granted certiorari, 479 U.S. 812, 107 S.Ct. 60, 93 L.Ed.2d 20 (1986), to resolve the conflict among the Courts of Appeals regarding the arbitrability of § 10(b) and RICO claims.

II

The Federal Arbitration Act, 9 U.S.C. § 1 et seq., provides the starting point for answering the questions raised in this case. The Act was intended to "revers[e] centuries of judicial hostility to arbitration agreements," Scherk v. Alberto–Culver Co., supra, 417 U.S., at 510, 94 S.Ct., at 2453, by "plac[ing] arbitration agreements 'upon the same footing as other contracts.'" 417 U.S., at 511, 94 S.Ct., at 2453, quoting H.R.Rep. No. 96, 68th Cong., 1st Sess., 1, 2 (1924). The Arbitration Act accomplishes this purpose by providing that arbitration agreements "shall be valid, irrevocable, and enforceable, save upon such grounds as exist at law or in equity for the revocation of any contract." 9 U.S.C. § 2. The Act also provides that a court must stay its proceedings if it is satisfied that an issue before it is arbitrable under the agreement, § 3; and it authorizes a federal district court to issue an order compelling arbitration if there has been a "failure, neglect, or refusal" to comply with the arbitration agreement, § 4.

The Arbitration Act thus establishes a "federal policy favoring arbitration," Moses H. Cone Memorial Hospital v. Mercury Construction Corp., 460 U.S. 1, 24, 103 S.Ct. 927, 941, 74 L.Ed.2d 765 (1983), requiring that "we rigorously enforce agreements to arbitrate." Dean Witter Reynolds Inc. v. Byrd, supra, 470 U.S., at 221, 105 S.Ct., at 1242. This duty to enforce arbitration agreements is not diminished when a party bound by an agreement raises a claim founded on statutory rights. As we observed in Mitsubishi Motors Corp. v. Soler Chrysler–Plymouth, Inc., "we are well past the time when judicial suspicion of the desirability of arbitration and of the competence of arbitral tribunals" should inhibit enforcement of the Act "'in controversies based on statutes.'" 473 U.S., at 626–627, 105 S.Ct., at 3354, quoting Wilko v. Swan, supra, 346 U.S., at 432, 74 S.Ct., at 185. Absent a well-founded claim that an arbitration agreement resulted from the sort of fraud or excessive economic power that "would provide grounds 'for the revocation of any contract,'" 473 U.S., at 627, 105 S.Ct., at 3354, the Arbitration Act "provides no basis for disfavoring agreements to arbitrate statutory claims by skewing the otherwise hospitable inquiry into arbitrability." Ibid.

The Arbitration Act, standing alone, therefore mandates enforcement of agreements to arbitrate statutory claims. Like any statutory directive, the Arbitration Act's mandate may be overridden by a contrary congressional command. The burden is on the party opposing arbitration, however, to show that Congress intended to preclude a waiver of judicial remedies for the statutory rights at issue. See id., at 628, 105 S.Ct., at 3354. If Congress did intend to limit or prohibit waiver of a judicial forum for a particular claim, such an intent "will be deducible from [the statute's] text or legislative history," ibid., or from an inherent conflict between arbitration and the statute's underlying purposes. . . .

To defeat application of the Arbitration Act in this case, therefore, the McMahons must demonstrate that Congress intended to make an exception to the Arbitration Act for claims arising under RICO and the Exchange Act, an intention discernible from the text, history, or purposes of the statute.

We examine the McMahons' arguments regarding the Exchange Act and RICO in turn.

III

When Congress enacted the Exchange Act in 1934, it did not specifically address the question of the arbitrability of § 10(b) claims. The McMahons contend, however, that congressional intent to require a judicial forum for the resolution of § 10(b) claims can be deduced from § 29(a) of the Exchange Act, 15 U.S.C. § 78cc(a), which declares void "[a]ny condition, stipulation, or provision binding any person to waive compliance with any provision of [the Act]."

First, we reject the McMahons' argument that § 29(a) forbids waiver of § 27 of the Exchange Act, 15 U.S.C. § 78aa. Section 27 provides in relevant part:

> "The district courts of the United States ... shall have exclusive jurisdiction of violations of this title or the rules and regulations thereunder, and of all suits in equity and actions at law brought to enforce any liability or duty created by this title or the rules and regulations thereunder."

The McMahons contend that an agreement to waive this jurisdictional provision is unenforceable because § 29(a) voids the waiver of "any provision" of the Exchange Act. The language of § 29(a), however, does not reach so far. What the antiwaiver provision of § 29(a) forbids is enforcement of agreements to waive "compliance" with the provisions of the statute. But § 27 itself does not impose any duty with which persons trading in securities must "comply." By its terms, § 29(a) only prohibits waiver of the substantive obligations imposed by the Exchange Act. Because § 27 does not impose any statutory duties, its waiver does not constitute a waiver of "compliance with any provision" of the Exchange Act under § 29(a).

We do not read Wilko v. Swan, 346 U.S. 427, 74 S.Ct., 182, 98 L.Ed. 168 (1953), as compelling a different result. In Wilko, the Court held that a predispute agreement could not be enforced to compel arbitration of a claim arising under § 12(2) of the Securities Act, 15 U.S.C. § 77l(2). The basis for the ruling was § 14 of the Securities Act, which, like § 29(a) of the Exchange Act, declares void any stipulation "to waive compliance with any provision" of the statute. At the beginning of its analysis, the Wilko Court stated that the Securities Act's jurisdictional provision was "the kind of 'provision' that cannot be waived under § 14 of the Securities Act." 346 U.S., at 435, 74 S.Ct., at 186. This statement, however, can only be understood in the context of the Court's ensuing discussion explaining why arbitration was inadequate as a means of enforcing "the provisions of the Securities Act, advantageous to the buyer." Ibid. The conclusion in Wilko was expressly based on the Court's belief that a judicial forum was needed to protect the substantive rights created by the Securities Act: "As the protective provisions of the Securities Act require the exercise of judicial direction to fairly assure their effectiveness, it seems to us that Congress must have intended § 14 ... to apply to waiver of judicial trial and review." Id., at 437, 74 S.Ct., at 188. Wilko must be understood, therefore, as holding that the plaintiff's waiver of the "right to select the judicial forum," id., at 435, 74 S.Ct., at 186, was unenforceable only because arbitration was judged inadequate to enforce the statutory rights created by § 12(2).

Indeed, any different reading of Wilko would be inconsistent with this Court's decision in Scherk v. Alberto–Culver Co., 417 U.S. 506, 94 S.Ct. 2449, 41 L.Ed.2d 270 (1974). In Scherk, the Court upheld enforcement of a predispute agreement to arbitrate Exchange Act claims by parties to an international contract.... The decision in Scherk thus turned on the Court's judgment that under the circumstances of that case, arbitration was an adequate substitute for adjudication as a means of enforcing the parties' statutory rights. Scherk supports our understanding that Wilko must be read as barring waiver of a judicial forum only where arbitration is inadequate to protect the substantive rights at issue. At the same time, it confirms that where arbitration does provide an adequate means of enforcing the provisions of the Exchange Act, § 29(a) does not void a predispute waiver of § 27—Scherk upheld enforcement of just such a waiver.

The second argument offered by the McMahons is that the arbitration agreement effects an impermissible waiver of the substantive protections of the Exchange Act. Ordinarily, "[b]y agreeing to arbitrate a statutory claim, a party does not forgo the substantive rights afforded by the statute; it only submits to their resolution in an arbitral, rather than a judicial, forum." Mitsubishi Motors Corp. v. Soler Chrysler–Plymouth, Inc., 473 U.S., at 628, 105 S.Ct., at 3354. The McMahons argue, however, that § 29(a) compels a different conclusion. Initially, they contend that predispute agreements are void under § 29(a) because they tend to result from broker overreaching. They reason, as do some commentators, that Wilko is premised on the belief "that arbitration clauses in securities sales agreements generally are not freely negotiated." See, e.g., Sterk, Enforceability of Agreements to Arbitrate: An Examination of the Public Policy Defense, 2 Cardozo L.Rev. 481, 519 (1981). According to this view, Wilko barred enforcement of predispute agreements because of this frequent inequality of bargaining power, reasoning that Congress intended for § 14 generally to ensure that sellers did not "maneuver buyers into a position that might weaken their ability to recover under the Securities Act." 346 U.S., at 432, 74 S.Ct., at 185. The McMahons urge that we should interpret § 29(a) in the same fashion.

We decline to give Wilko a reading so far at odds with the plain language of § 14, or to adopt such an unlikely interpretation of § 29(a). The concern that § 29(a) is directed against is evident from the statute's plain language: it is a concern with whether an agreement "waive[s] compliance with [a] provision" of the Exchange Act. The voluntariness of the agreement is irrelevant to this inquiry: if a stipulation waives compliance with a statutory duty, it is void under § 29(a), whether voluntary or not. Thus, a customer cannot negotiate a reduction in commissions in exchange for a waiver of compliance with the requirements of the Exchange Act, even if the customer knowingly and voluntarily agreed to the bargain. Section 29(a) is concerned, not with whether brokers "maneuver[ed customers] into" an agreement, but with whether the agreement "weaken[s] their ability to recover under the [Exchange] Act." 346 U.S., at 432, 74 S.Ct., at 185. The former is grounds for revoking the contract under ordinary principles of contract law; the latter is grounds for voiding the agreement under § 29(a).

The other reason advanced by the McMahons for finding a waiver of their § 10(b) rights is that arbitration does "weaken their ability to recover under the [Exchange] Act." Ibid. That is the heart of the Court's decision in Wilko, and respondents urge that we should follow its reasoning. Wilko listed several grounds why, in the Court's view, the "effectiveness [of the Act's provisions] in application is lessened in arbitration." 346 U.S., at 435, 74 S.Ct., at 185. First, the Wilko Court believed that arbitration proceedings were not suited to cases requiring "subjective findings on the purpose and knowledge of an alleged violator." Id., at 435–436, 74 S.Ct., at 186–187. Wilko also was concerned that arbitrators must make legal determinations "without judicial instruction on the law," and that an arbitration award "may be made without explanation of [the arbitrator's] reasons and without a complete record of their proceedings." Id., at 436, 74 S.Ct., at 187. Finally, Wilko noted that the "[p]ower to vacate an award is limited," and that "interpretations of the law by the arbitrators in contrast to manifest disregard are not subject, in the federal courts, to judicial review for error in interpretation." Id., at 436–437, 74 S.Ct., at 187–188. Wilko concluded that in view of these drawbacks to arbitration, § 12(2) claims "require[d] the exercise of judicial direction to fairly assure their effectiveness." Id., at 437, 74 S.Ct., at 187.

As Justice Frankfurter noted in his dissent in Wilko, the Court's opinion did not rest on any evidence, either "in the record . . . [or] in the facts of which [it could] take judicial notice," that "the arbitral system . . . would not afford the plaintiff the rights to which he is entitled." Id., at 439, 74 S.Ct., at 189. Instead, the reasons given in Wilko reflect a general suspicion of the desirability of arbitration and the competence of arbitral tribunals—most apply with no greater force to the arbitration of securities disputes than to the arbitration of legal disputes generally. It is difficult to reconcile Wilko's mistrust of the arbitral process with this Court's subsequent decisions involving the Arbitration Act. . . .

The suitability of arbitration as a means of enforcing Exchange Act rights is evident from our decision in Scherk. Although the holding in that case was limited to international agreements, the competence of arbitral tribunals to resolve § 10(b) claims is the same in both settings. Courts likewise have routinely enforced agreements to arbitrate § 10(b) claims where both parties are members of a securities exchange or the National Association of Securities Dealers (NASD), suggesting that arbitral tribunals are fully capable of handling such matters. . . . And courts uniformly have concluded that Wilko does not apply to the submission to arbitration of existing disputes, see, e.g., Gardner v. Shearson, Hammill & Co., 433 F.2d 367 (C.A.5 1970); Moran v. Paine, Webber, Jackson & Curtis, 389 F.2d 242 (C.A.3 1968), even though the inherent suitability of arbitration as a means of resolving § 10(b) claims remains unchanged. Cf. Mitsubishi, 473 U.S., at 633, 105 S.Ct., at 3357.

Thus, the mistrust of arbitration that formed the basis for the Wilko opinion in 1953 is difficult to square with the assessment of arbitration that has prevailed since that time. This is especially so in light of the intervening changes in the regulatory structure of the securities laws. Even if Wilko's assumptions regarding arbitration were valid at the time Wilko was decided, most certainly they do not hold true today for arbitration procedures subject to the SEC's oversight authority.

In 1953, when Wilko was decided, the Commission had only limited authority over the rules governing self-regulatory organizations (SROs)— the national securities exchanges and registered securities associations— and this authority appears not to have included any authority at all over their arbitration rules. See Brief for Securities and Exchange Commission as *Amicus Curiae* 14–15. Since the 1975 amendments to § 19 of the Exchange Act, however, the Commission has had expansive power to ensure the adequacy of the arbitration procedures employed by the SROs. No proposed rule change may take effect unless the SEC finds that the proposed rule is consistent with the requirements of the Exchange Act, 15 U.S.C. § 78s(b)(2); and the Commission has the power, on its own initiative, to "abrogate, add to, and delete from" any SRO rule if it finds such changes necessary or appropriate to further the objectives of the Act, 15 U.S.C. § 78s(c). In short, the Commission has broad authority to oversee and to regulate the rules adopted by the SROs relating to customer disputes, including the power to mandate the adoption of any rules it deems necessary to ensure that arbitration procedures adequately protect statutory rights.

In the exercise of its regulatory authority, the SEC has specifically approved the arbitration procedures of the New York Stock Exchange, the American Stock Exchange, and the NASD, the organizations mentioned in the arbitration agreement at issue in this case. We conclude that where, as in this case, the prescribed procedures are subject to the Commission's § 19 authority, an arbitration agreement does not effect a waiver of the protections of the Act. While stare decisis concerns may counsel against upsetting Wilko's contrary conclusion under the Securities Act, we refuse to extend Wilko's reasoning to the Exchange Act in light of these intervening regulatory developments. The McMahons' agreement to submit to arbitration therefore is not tantamount to an impermissible waiver of the McMahons' rights under § 10(b), and the agreement is not void on that basis under § 29(a).

The final argument offered by the McMahons is that even if § 29(a) as enacted does not void predispute arbitration agreements, Congress subsequently has indicated that it desires § 29(a) to be so interpreted. According to the McMahons, Congress expressed this intent when it failed to make more extensive changes to § 28(b), 15 U.S.C. § 78bb(b), in the 1975 amendments to the Exchange Act. Before its amendment, § 28(b) provided in relevant part:

> "Nothing in this chapter shall be construed to modify existing law (1) with regard to the binding effect on any member of any exchange of any action taken by the authorities of such exchange to settle disputes between its members, or (2) with regard to the binding effect of such action on any person who has agreed to be bound thereby, or (3) with regard to the binding effect on any such member of any disciplinary action taken by the authorities of the exchange." 48 Stat. 903.

The chief aim of this provision was to preserve the self-regulatory role of the securities exchanges, by giving the exchanges a means of enforcing their rules against their members.... In 1975, Congress made extensive revisions to the Exchange Act intended to "clarify the scope of the self-regulatory responsibilities of national securities exchanges and registered securities associations ... and the manner in which they are to exercise those responsibilities." S.Rep. No. 94–75, p. 22 (1975). In making these changes, the Senate Report observed: "The self-regulatory organizations must exercise governmental-type powers if they are to carry out their responsibilities under the Exchange Act. When a member violates the Act or a self-regulatory organization's rules, the organization must be in a position to impose appropriate penalties or to revoke relevant privileges." Id., at 24....

Thus, the amended version of § 28(b), like the original, mentions neither customers nor arbitration. It is directed at an entirely different problem: enhancing the self-regulatory function of the SROs under the Exchange Act.

The McMahons nonetheless argue that we should find it significant that Congress did *not* take this opportunity to address the general question of the arbitrability of Exchange Act claims. Their argument is based entirely on a sentence from the Conference Report, which they contend amounts to a ratification of Wilko's extension to Exchange Act claims. The Conference Report states:

> "The Senate bill amended section 28 of the Securities Exchange Act of 1934 with respect to arbitration proceedings between self-regulatory organizations and their participants, members, or persons dealing with members or participants. The House amendment contained no comparable provision. The House receded to the Senate. It was the clear understanding of the conferees that this amendment did not change existing law, as articulated in Wilko v. Swan, 346 U.S. 427 [74 S.Ct. 182, 98 L.Ed. 168] (1953), concerning the effect of arbitration proceedings provisions in agreements entered into by persons dealing with members and participants of self-regulatory organizations." ...

The McMahons contend that the conferees would not have acknowledged Wilko in a revision of the Exchange Act unless they were aware of lower court decisions extending Wilko to § 10(b) claims and intended to approve them. We find this argument fraught with difficulties. We cannot see how Congress could extend Wilko to the Exchange Act without enacting into law any provision remotely addressing that subject. See Train v. City of New York, 420 U.S. 35, 45, 95 S.Ct. 839, 845, 43 L.Ed.2d 1 (1975). And even if it could, there is little reason to interpret the Report as the McMahons suggest. At the outset, the committee may well have mentioned Wilko for a reason entirely different from the one postulated by the McMahons—lower courts had applied § 28(b) to the Securities Act, see, e.g., Axelrod & Co. v. Kordich, Victor & Neufeld, supra, at 843, and the committee may simply have wished to make clear that the amendment to § 28(b) was not otherwise intended to affect Wilko' s construction of the Securities Act. Moreover, even if the committee were referring to the arbitrability of § 10(b) claims, the quoted sentence does not disclose what committee members thought "existing law" provided. The conference members might have had in mind the two Court of Appeals decisions extending Wilko to the Exchange Act, as the McMahons contend. See Greater Continental Corp. v. Schechter, 422 F.2d 1100 (C.A.2 1970); Moran v. Paine, Webber, Jackson & Curtis, 389 F.2d 242 (C.A.3 1968). It is equally likely, however, that the committee had in mind this Court's decision the year before expressing doubts as to whether Wilko should be extended to § 10(b) claims. See Scherk v. Alberto–Culver Co., 417 U.S., at 513, 94 S.Ct., at 2454 ("[A] colorable argument could be made that even the semantic reasoning of the Wilko opinion does not control [a case based on § 10(b)]"). Finally, even assuming the conferees had an understanding of existing law that all agreed upon, they specifically disclaimed any intent to change it. Hence, the Wilko issue was left to the courts: it was unaffected by the amendment to § 28(b). This statement of congressional inaction simply does not support the proposition that the 1975 Congress intended to engraft onto unamended § 29(a) a meaning different from that of the enacting Congress.

We conclude, therefore, that Congress did not intend for § 29(a) to bar enforcement of all predispute arbitration agreements. In this case, where the SEC has sufficient statutory authority to ensure that arbitration is adequate to vindicate Exchange Act rights, enforcement does not effect a waiver of "compliance with any provision" of the Exchange Act under § 29(a). Accordingly, we hold the McMahons' agreements to arbitrate Exchange Act claims "enforce[able] ... in accord with the explicit provisions of the Arbitration Act." Scherk v. Alberto–Culver Co., supra, at 520, 94 S.Ct., at 2457.

IV

Unlike the Exchange Act, there is nothing in the text of the RICO statute that even arguably evinces congressional intent to exclude civil RICO claims from the dictates of the Arbitration Act. This silence in the text is matched by silence in the statute's legislative history. The private treble-damages provision codified as 18 U.S.C. § 1964(c) was added to the House version of the bill after the bill had been passed by the Senate, and it received only abbreviated discussion in either House. See Sedima, S.P.R.L.

v. Imrex Co., 473 U.S. 479, 486–488, 105 S.Ct. 3275, 3280–3281, 87 L.Ed.2d 346 (1985). There is no hint in these legislative debates that Congress intended for RICO treble-damages claims to be excluded from the ambit of the Arbitration Act. See Genesco, Inc. v. T. Kakiuchi & Co., Ltd., 815 F.2d 840, 850–851 (C.A.2 1987); Mayaja, Inc. v. Bodkin, 803 F.2d 157, 164 (C.A.5 1986).

Because RICO's text and legislative history fail to reveal any intent to override the provisions of the Arbitration Act, the McMahons must argue that there is an irreconcilable conflict between arbitration and RICO's underlying purposes. Our decision in Mitsubishi Motors Corp. v. Soler Chrysler-Plymouth, Inc., 473 U.S. 614, 105 S.Ct. 3346, 87 L.Ed.2d 444 (1985), however, already has addressed many of the grounds given by the McMahons to support this claim. . . .

Not only does Mitsubishi support the arbitrability of RICO claims, but there is even more reason to suppose that arbitration will adequately serve the purposes of RICO than that it will adequately protect private enforcement of the antitrust laws. Antitrust violations generally have a widespread impact on national markets as a whole, and the antitrust treble-damages provision gives private parties an incentive to bring civil suits that serve to advance the national interest in a competitive economy. See Lindsay, "Public" Rights and Private Forums: Predispute Arbitration Agreements and Securities Litigation, 20 Loyola (LA) L.Rev. 643, 691–692 (1987). RICO's drafters likewise sought to provide vigorous incentives for plaintiffs to pursue RICO claims that would advance society's fight against organized crime. See Sedima, S.P.R.L. v. Imrex Co., supra, at 498, 105 S.Ct., at 3286. But in fact RICO actions are seldom asserted "against the archetypal, intimidating mobster." Id., at 499, 105 S.Ct., at 3286; see also id., at 506, 105 S.Ct., at 3295 (MARSHALL, J., dissenting) ("[O]nly 9% of all civil RICO cases have involved allegations of criminal activity normally associated with professional criminals"). The special incentives necessary to encourage civil enforcement actions against organized crime do not support nonarbitrability of run-of-the-mill civil RICO claims brought against legitimate enterprises. The private attorney general role for the typical RICO plaintiff is simply less plausible than it is for the typical antitrust plaintiff, and does not support a finding that there is an irreconcilable conflict between arbitration and enforcement of the RICO statute.

In sum, we find no basis for concluding that Congress intended to prevent enforcement of agreements to arbitrate RICO claims. The McMahons may effectively vindicate their RICO claim in an arbitral forum, and therefore there is no inherent conflict between arbitration and the purposes underlying § 1964(c). Moreover, nothing in RICO's text or legislative history otherwise demonstrates congressional intent to make an exception to the Arbitration Act for RICO claims. Accordingly, the McMahons, "having made the bargain to arbitrate," will be held to their bargain. Their RICO claim is arbitrable under the terms of the Arbitration Act.

V

Accordingly, the judgment of the Court of Appeals for the Second Circuit is reversed, and the case is remanded for further proceedings consistent with this opinion.

It is so ordered.

■ JUSTICE BLACKMUN, with whom JUSTICE BRENNAN and JUSTICE MARSHALL join, concurring in part and dissenting in part.

I concur in the Court's decision to enforce the arbitration agreement with respect to respondents' RICO claims and thus join Parts I, II, and IV of the Court's opinion. I disagree, however, with the Court's conclusion that respondents' § 10(b) claims also are subject to arbitration.

Both the Securities Act of 1933 and the Securities Exchange Act of 1934 were enacted to protect investors from predatory behavior of securities industry personnel. In Wilko v. Swan, 346 U.S. 427, 74 S.Ct. 182, 98 L.Ed. 168 (1953), the Court recognized this basic purpose when it declined to enforce a predispute agreement to compel arbitration of claims under the Securities Act. Following that decision, lower courts extended Wilko's reasoning to claims brought under § 10(b) of the Exchange Act, and Congress approved of this extension. In today's decision, however, the Court effectively overrules Wilko by accepting the Securities and Exchange Commission's newly adopted position that arbitration procedures in the securities industry and the Commission's oversight of the self-regulatory organizations (SROs) have improved greatly since Wilko was decided. The Court thus approves the abandonment of the judiciary's role in the resolution of claims under the Exchange Act and leaves such claims to the arbitral forum of the securities industry at a time when the industry's abuses towards investors are more apparent than ever.

I

At the outset, it is useful to review the manner by which the issue decided today has been kept alive inappropriately by this Court. As the majority explains, Wilko was limited to the holding "that a predispute agreement could not be enforced to compel arbitration of a claim arising under § 12(2) of the Securities Act." Ante, at 228. Relying, however, on the reasoning of Wilko and the similarity between the pertinent provisions of the Securities Act and those of the Exchange Act, lower courts extended the Wilko holding to claims under the Exchange Act and refused to enforce predispute agreements to arbitrate them as well. . . .

If, however, there could have been any doubts about the extension of Wilko's holding to § 10(b) claims, they were undermined by Congress in its 1975 amendments to the Exchange Act. The Court questions the significance of these amendments, which, as it notes, concerned, among other things, provisions dealing with dispute resolution and disciplinary action by an SRO towards its own members. See ante, at 235–236. These amendments, however, are regarded as "the 'most substantial and significant revision of this country's Federal securities laws since the passage of the

Securities Exchange Act in 1934.' " . . . More importantly, in enacting these amendments, Congress specifically was considering exceptions to § 29(a), 15 U.S.C. § 78cc, the nonwaiver provision of the Exchange Act, a provision primarily designed with the protection of investors in mind. The statement from the legislative history, cited by the Court, ante, at 236–237, on its face indicates that Congress did not want the amendments to overrule Wilko. Moreover, the fact that this statement was made in an amendment to the Exchange Act suggests that Congress was aware of the extension of Wilko to § 10(b) claims. Although the remark does not necessarily signify Congress' endorsement of this extension, in the absence of any prior congressional indication to the contrary, it implies that Congress was not concerned with arresting this trend. Such inaction during a wholesale revision of the securities laws, a revision designed to further investor protection, would argue in favor of Congress' approval of Wilko and its extension to § 10(b) claims. . . .

One would have thought that, after these amendments, the matter of Wilko's extension to Exchange Act claims at last would be uncontroversial. In the years following the Scherk decision, *all* the Courts of Appeals treating the issue so interpreted Wilko. In Dean Witter Reynolds Inc. v. Byrd, 470 U.S. 213, 105 S.Ct. 1238, 84 L.Ed.2d 158 (1985), this Court declined to address the extension issue, which was not before it, but recognized the development in the case law. Id., at 215, n. 1, 105 S.Ct., at 1240, n. 1. Yet, like a ghost reluctant to accept its eternal rest, the "colorable argument" surfaced again, this time in a concurring opinion. See id., at 224, 105 S.Ct., at 1244 (WHITE, J.). . . .

II

There are essentially two problems with the Court's conclusion that predispute agreements to arbitrate § 10(b) claims may be enforced. First, the Court gives Wilko an overly narrow reading so that it can fit into the syllogism offered by the Commission and accepted by the Court, namely, (1) Wilko was really a case concerning whether arbitration was adequate for the enforcement of the substantive provisions of the securities laws; (2) all of the Wilko Court's doubts as to arbitration's adequacy are outdated; (3) thus Wilko is no longer good law. . . . Second, the Court accepts uncritically petitioners' and the Commission's argument that the problems with arbitration, highlighted by the Wilko Court, either no longer exist or are not now viewed as problems by the Court. This acceptance primarily is based upon the Court's belief in the Commission's representations that its oversight of the SROs ensures the adequacy of arbitration.

A

I agree with the Court's observation that, in order to establish an exception to the Arbitration Act, 9 U.S.C. § 1 et seq., for a class of statutory claims, there must be "an intention discernible from the text, history, or purposes of the statute." Ante, at 227. Where the Court first goes wrong, however, is in its failure to acknowledge that the Exchange Act, like the Securities Act, constitutes such an exception. This failure is made possible only by the unduly narrow reading of Wilko that ignores the Court's determination there that the Securities Act *was* an exception to the Arbitration Act. The Court's reading is particularly startling because it is in direct contradiction to the interpretation of Wilko given by the Court in Mitsubishi Motors Corp. v. Soler Chrysler–Plymouth, Inc., 473 U.S. 614, 105 S.Ct. 3346, 87 L.Ed.2d 444 (1985), a decision on which the Court relies for its strong statement of a federal policy in favor of arbitration. But we observed in Mitsubishi:

> "Just as it is the congressional policy manifested in the Federal Arbitration Act that requires courts liberally to construe the scope of arbitration agreements covered by that Act, it is the congressional intention expressed in some other statute on which the courts must rely to identify any category of claims as to which agreements to arbitrate will be held unenforceable. See Wilko v. Swan, 346 U.S., at 434–435 [74 S.Ct., at 186–187].... We must assume that if Congress intended the substantive protection afforded by a given statute to include protection against waiver of the right to a judicial forum, that intention will be deducible from text or legislative history. See Wilko v. Swan, supra." Id., at 627–628, 105 S.Ct., at 3354.

Such language clearly suggests that, in Mitsubishi, we viewed Wilko as holding that the text and legislative history of the Securities Act—not general problems with arbitration—established that the Securities Act constituted an exception to the Arbitration Act. In a surprising display of logic, the Court uses Mitsubishi as support for the virtues of arbitration and thus as a means for undermining Wilko's holding, but fails to take into account the most pertinent language in Mitsubishi.

It is not necessary to rely just on the statement in Mitsubishi to realize that in Wilko the Court had before it the issue of congressional intent to exempt statutory claims from the reach of the Arbitration Act. One has only to reread the Wilko opinion without the constricted vision of the Court. The Court's misreading is possible because, while extolling the policies of the Arbitration Act, it is insensitive to, and disregards the policies of, the Securities Act. This Act was passed in 1933, eight years *after* the Arbitration Act of 1925, see 43 Stat. 883, and in response to the market crash of 1929. The Act was designed to remedy abuses in the securities industry, particularly fraud and misrepresentation by securities-industry personnel, that had contributed to that disastrous event. See Malcolm & Segall 730–731. It had as its main goal investor protection, which took the form of an effort to place investors on an equal footing with those in the securities industry by promoting full disclosure of information on investments. See L. Loss, Fundamentals of Securities Regulation 36 (1983).

The Court in Wilko recognized the policy of investor protection in the Securities Act. It was this recognition that animated its discussion of whether § 14, 48 Stat. 84, 15 U.S.C. § 77n, the nonwaiver provision of the Securities Act, applied to § 22(a), 48 Stat. 86, as amended, 15 U.S.C. § 77v(a), the provision that gave an investor a judicial forum for the resolution of securities disputes. In the Court's words, the Securities Act, "[d]esigned to protect investors, ... requires issuers, underwriters, and dealers to make full and fair disclosure of the character of securities sold in interstate and foreign commerce and to prevent fraud in their sale." 346 U.S., at 431, 74 S.Ct., at 184. The Court then noted that, to promote this policy in the Act, Congress had designed an elaborate statutory structure: it gave investors a "special right" of suit under § 12(2); they could bring the suit in federal or state court pursuant to § 22(a); and, if brought in federal court, there were numerous procedural advantages, such as nationwide service of process. Ibid. In reasoning that a predispute agreement to arbitrate § 12(2) claims would constitute a "waiver" of a provision of the Act, i.e., the right to the judicial forum embodied in § 22(a), the Court specifically referred to the policy of investor protection underlying the Act:

> "While a buyer and seller of securities, under some circumstances, may deal at arm's length on equal terms, it is clear that the Securities Act was drafted with an eye to the disadvantages under which buyers labor. Issuers of and dealers in securities have better opportunities to investigate and appraise the prospective earnings and business plans affecting securities than buyers. It is therefore reasonable for Congress to put buyers of securities covered by that Act on a different basis from other purchasers.

> "When the security buyer, prior to any violation of the Securities Act, waives his right to sue in courts, he gives up more than would a participant in other business transactions. The security buyer has a wider choice of courts and venue. He thus surrenders one of the advantages the Act gives him and surrenders it at a time when he is less able to judge the weight of the handicap the Securities Act places upon his adversary." Id., at 435, 74 S.Ct., at 186–187.

In the Court's view, the express language, legislative history, and purposes of the Securities Act all made predispute agreements to arbitrate § 12(2) claims unenforceable despite the presence of the Arbitration Act.[9]

Accordingly, the Court seriously errs when it states that the result in Wilko turned only on the perceived inadequacy of arbitration for the enforcement of § 12(2) claims. It is true that the Wilko Court discussed the

---

9. In discussing the similar nonwaiver provision under the Exchange Act, § 29(a), 48 Stat. 903, as amended, 15 U.S.C. § 78cc(a), the Court now suggests that it can be read only to mean that an investor cannot waive security-investment personnel's "compliance" with a duty under the statute. See ante, at 228. The Court implies that the literal language of § 29(a) does not apply to an investor's waiver of his own action.... It appears, however, that in Wilko the Court understood the nonwaiver provision *also* to mean that, at least in the predispute context, an investor could not waive *his* compliance with the provision for dispute resolution in the courts. This reading of the antiwaiver provision makes sense in terms of the policy of investor protection. To counteract the inherent superior position of the securities-industry professional, up to and including the time when a dispute might occur between a broker and the investor, Congress intended to place the investor on "a different basis from other purchasers." 346 U.S., at 435, 74 S.Ct., at 187. Construing § 14 not to allow the investor to waive his right to a judicial forum in the predispute setting serves this congressional purpose of maintaining the investor in a special position....

inadequacies of this process, 346 U.S., at 435–437, 74 S.Ct., at 186–188, and that this discussion constituted one ground for the Court's decision. The discussion, however, occurred *after* the Court had concluded that the language, legislative history, and purposes of the Securities Act mandated an exception to the Arbitration Act for these securities claims.

The Court's decision in Scherk is consistent with this reading of Wilko, despite the Court's suggestion to the contrary. See ante, at 229. Indeed, in reading Scherk as a case turning on the adequacy of arbitration, the Court completely ignores the central thrust of that decision. As the Court itself notes, ante, at 229, in Scherk the Court assumed that Wilko's prohibition on enforcing predispute arbitration agreements ordinarily would extend to § 10(b) claims, such as those at issue in Scherk. The Scherk Court relied on a crucial difference between the international business situation presented to it and that before the Court in Wilko, where the laws of the United States, particularly the securities laws, clearly governed the dispute....

In light of a proper reading of Wilko, the pertinent question then becomes whether the language, legislative history, and purposes of the Exchange Act call for an exception to the Arbitration Act for § 10(b) claims. The Exchange Act waiver provision is virtually identical to that of the Securities Act. More importantly, the same concern with investor protection that motivated the Securities Act is evident in the Exchange Act, although the latter, in contrast to the former, is aimed at trading in the secondary securities market.... We have recognized that both Acts were designed with this common purpose in mind.... Indeed, the application of both Acts to the same conduct, ... suggests that they have the same basic goal. And we have approved a cumulative construction of remedies under the securities Acts to promote the maximum possible protection of investors....

In sum, the same reasons that led the Court to find an exception to the Arbitration Act for § 12(2) claims exist for § 10(b) claims as well. It is clear that Wilko, when properly read, governs the instant case and mandates that a predispute arbitration agreement should not be enforced as to § 10(b) claims.

B

Even if I were to accept the Court's narrow reading of Wilko, as a case dealing only with the inadequacies of arbitration in 1953,[14] I do not think that this case should be resolved differently today so long as the policy of investor protection is given proper consideration in the analysis. Despite improvements in the process of arbitration and changes in the judicial attitude towards it, several aspects of arbitration that were seen by the

---

14. This argument, in essence, is a functional one. It suggests that, although Congress *intended* to protect investors through the provision of a judicial forum for the enforcement of their rights under the securities Acts, this intention will not be con-travened by sending these claims to arbitration because arbitration is now the "functional equivalent" of the courts. See Brief for Securities and Exchange Commission as Amicus Curiae 12; see also Maryland Comment 373.

Wilko court to be inimical to the policy of investor protection still remain. Moreover, I have serious reservations about the Commission's contention that its oversight of the SROs' arbitration procedures will ensure that the process is adequate to protect an investor's rights under the securities Acts.

As the Court observes, ante, at 231, in Wilko the Court was disturbed by several characteristics of arbitration that made such a process inadequate to safeguard the special position in which the Securities Act had placed the investor. The Court concluded that judicial review of the arbitrators' application of the securities laws would be difficult because arbitrators were required neither to give the reasons for their decisions nor to make a complete record of their proceedings. See 346 U.S., at 436, 74 S.Ct., at 187. The Court also observed that the grounds for vacating an arbitration award were limited. The Court noted that, under the Arbitration Act, there were only four grounds for vacation of an award: fraud in procuring the award, partiality on the part of arbitrators, gross misconduct by arbitrators, and the failure of arbitrators to render a final decision. Id., at 436, n. 22, 74 S.Ct., at 187, n. 22, quoting 9 U.S.C. § 10 (1952 Ed., Supp. V). The arbitrators' interpretation of the law would be subject to judicial review only under the "manifest disregard" standard. 346 U.S., at 436, 74 S.Ct., at 187.

The Court today appears to argue that the Wilko Court's assessment of arbitration's inadequacy is outdated, first, because arbitration has improved since 1953, and, second, because the Court no longer considers the criticisms of arbitration made in Wilko to be valid reasons why statutory claims, such as those under § 10(b), should not be sent to arbitration. It is true that arbitration procedures in the securities industry have improved since Wilko's day. Of particular importance has been the development of a code of arbitration by the Commission with the assistance of representatives of the securities industry and the public. . . .

Even those who favor the arbitration of securities claims do not contend, however, that arbitration has changed so significantly as to eliminate the essential characteristics noted by the Wilko Court. Indeed, proponents of arbitration would not see these characteristics as "problems," because, in their view, the characteristics permit the unique "streamlined" nature of the arbitral process. As at the time of Wilko, preparation of a record of arbitration proceedings is not invariably required today. Moreover, arbitrators are not bound by precedent and are actually discouraged by their associations from giving reasons for a decision. See R. Coulson, Business Arbitration—What You Need to Know 29 (3d ed. 1986) ("Written opinions can be dangerous because they identify targets for the losing party to attack"); see also Duke Note 553; Fletcher 456–457. Judicial review is still substantially limited to the four grounds listed in § 10 of the Arbitration Act and to the concept of "manifest disregard" of the law. . . .

The Court's "mistrust" of arbitration may have given way recently to an acceptance of this process, not only because of the improvements in arbitration, but also because of the Court's present assumption that the distinctive features of arbitration, its more quick and economical resolution of claims, do not render it inherently inadequate for the resolution of statutory claims. See Mitsubishi Motors Corp. v. Soler Chrysler–Plymouth, Inc., 473 U.S., at 633, 105 S.Ct., at 3357. Such reasoning, however, should prevail only in the absence of the congressional policy that places the statutory claimant in a special position with respect to possible violators of his statutory rights. As even the most ardent supporter of arbitration would recognize, the arbitral process *at best* places the investor on an equal footing with the securities-industry personnel against whom the claims are brought.

Furthermore, there remains the danger that, *at worst*, compelling an investor to arbitrate securities claims puts him in a forum controlled by the securities industry. This result directly contradicts the goal of both securities Acts to free the investor from the control of the market professional. The Uniform Code provides some safeguards[19] but despite them, and indeed because of the background of the arbitrators, the investor has the impression, frequently justified, that his claims are being judged by a forum composed of individuals sympathetic to the securities industry and not drawn from the public. It is generally recognized that the codes do not define who falls into the category "not from the securities industry." ... Accordingly, it is often possible for the "public" arbitrators to be attorneys or consultants whose clients have been exchange members or SROs. See Panel of Arbitrators 1987–1988, CCH American Stock Exchange Guide 158–160 (1987) (71 out of 116 "public" arbitrators are lawyers). The uniform opposition of investors to compelled arbitration and the overwhelming support of the securities industry for the process suggest that there must be *some* truth to the investors' belief that the securities industry has an advantage in a forum under its own control....

More surprising than the Court's acceptance of the present adequacy of arbitration for the resolution of securities claims is its confidence in the Commission's oversight of the arbitration procedures of the SROs to ensure this adequacy. Such confidence amounts to a wholesale acceptance of the Commission's *present* position that this oversight undermines the force of Wilko and that arbitration therefore should be compelled because the Commission has supervisory authority over the SROs' arbitration procedures. The Court, however, fails to acknowledge that, until it filed an amicus brief in this case, the Commission consistently took the position that § 10(b) claims, like those under § 12(2), should not be sent to arbitration, that predispute arbitration agreements, where the investor was not advised of his right to a judicial forum, were misleading, and that the

---

19. The Uniform Code mandates that a majority of an arbitration panel, usually composed of between three to five arbitrators, be drawn from outside the industry. Fifth SICA Report § 8(a), p. 31. Each arbitrator, moreover, is directed to disclose "any circumstances which might preclude such arbitrator from rendering an objective and impartial determination." § 11, p. 32. In addition, the parties are informed of the business associations of the arbitrators, § 9, and each party has the right to one peremptory challenge and to unlimited challenges for cause, § 10, p. 32. The arbitrators are usually individuals familiar with the federal securities laws. See Brener v. Becker Paribas Inc., 628 F.Supp. 442, 448 (S.D.N.Y.1985).

very regulatory oversight upon which the Commission now relies could not alone make securities-industry arbitration adequate. It is most questionable, then, whether the Commission's recently adopted position is entitled to the deference that the Court accords it.

... Moreover, the Commission's own description of its enforcement capabilities contradicts its position that its general overview of SRO rules and procedures can make arbitration adequate for resolving securities claims. The Commission does not pretend that its oversight consists of anything other than a general review of SRO rules and the ability to require that an SRO adopt or delete a particular rule. It does not contend that its "sweeping authority," Brief 16, includes a review of specific arbitration proceedings. It thus neither polices nor monitors the results of these arbitrations for possible misapplications of securities laws or for indications of how investors fare in these proceedings. Given, in fact, the present constraints on the Commission's resources in this time of market expansion, ... it is doubtful whether the Commission could undertake to conduct any such review....

In the meantime, the Court leaves lower courts with some authority, albeit limited, to protect investors before Congress acts. Courts should take seriously their duty to review the results of arbitration to the extent possible under the Arbitration Act. As we explained in Mitsubishi Motors Corp. v. Soler Chrysler–Plymouth, Inc., "courts should remain attuned to well-supported claims that the agreement to arbitrate resulted from the sort of fraud or overwhelming economic power that would provide grounds 'for the revocation of any contract.'" 473 U.S., at 627, 105 S.Ct., at 3354, quoting 9 U.S.C. § 2. Indeed, in light of today's decision compelling the enforcement of predispute arbitration agreements, it is likely that investors will be inclined, more than ever, to bring complaints to federal courts that arbitrators were partial or acted in "manifest disregard" of the securities laws. See Brown, Shell, & Tyson at 36. It is thus ironic that the Court's decision, no doubt animated by its desire to rid the federal courts of these suits, actually may *increase* litigation about arbitration.

I therefore respectfully dissent in part.

■ JUSTICE STEVENS, concurring in part and dissenting in part.

Gaps in the law must, of course, be filled by judicial construction. But after a statute has been construed, either by this Court or by a consistent course of decision by other federal judges and agencies, it acquires a meaning that should be as clear as if the judicial gloss had been drafted by the Congress itself. This position reflects both respect for Congress' role, see Boys Markets, Inc. v. Retail Clerks, 398 U.S. 235, 257–258, 90 S.Ct. 1583, 1595–1596, 26 L.Ed.2d 199 (1970) (Black, J., dissenting), and the compelling need to preserve the courts' limited resources, see B. Cardozo, The Nature of the Judicial Process 149 (1921).

During the 32 years immediately following this Court's decision in Wilko v. Swan, 346 U.S. 427, 74 S.Ct. 182, 98 L.Ed. 168 (1953), each of the eight Circuits that addressed the issue concluded that the holding of Wilko was fully applicable to claims arising under the Securities Exchange Act of 1934. See ante, at 248, n. 6 (opinion of BLACKMUN, J.). This longstanding interpretation creates a strong presumption, in my view, that any mistake that the courts may have made in interpreting the statute is best remedied by the Legislative, not the Judicial, Branch. The history set forth in Part I of Justice BLACKMUN's opinion adds special force to that presumption in this case.

For this reason, I respectfully dissent from the portion of the Court's judgment that holds Wilko inapplicable to the 1934 Act. Like Justice BLACKMUN, however, I join Parts I, II, and IV of the Court's opinion.

* * *

Questions

1. Do the provisions of the Securities and Exchange Act of 1934 differ sufficiently from those of the Securities Act of 1933 to warrant the conclusion that the latter but not the former statute was intended to override the FAA?

2. How convincing is Justice O'Connor's interpretation of the 1975 amendments to the Securities Acts? Is there another view of those amendments that might argue for a different result in this case?

3. Compare the interpretation of *Wilko* by the majority and the dissent in *Shearson/American Express v. McMahon*. How do the two opinions differ as to what was held in that previous case?

4. Is there tension between Justice O'Connor's opinion in this case and her dissent in *Southland*? Can these two opinions be reconciled?

5. What are the differing views of the majority and dissent about the virtues and shortcomings of the arbitration process?

* * *

Rodriguez De Quijas v. Shearson/American Express, Inc.

490 U.S. 477, 109 S.Ct. 1917 (1989).

■ JUSTICE KENNEDY delivered the opinion of the Court.

The question here is whether a predispute agreement to arbitrate claims under the Securities Act of 1933 is unenforceable, requiring resolution of the claims only in a judicial forum.

I

Petitioners are individuals who invested about $400,000 in securities. They signed a standard customer agreement with the broker, which included a clause stating that the parties agreed to settle any controversies "relating to [the] accounts" through binding arbitration that complies with specified procedures. The agreement to arbitrate these controversies is unqualified, unless it is found to be unenforceable under federal or state law. Customer's Agreement ¶ 13. The investments turned sour, and petitioners eventually sued respondent and its broker-agent in charge of the accounts, alleging that their money was lost in unauthorized and fraudulent transactions. In their complaint they pleaded various violations of federal and state law, including claims under § 12(2) of the Securities Act of 1933, 15 U.S.C. § 77l(2), and claims under three sections of the Securities Exchange Act of 1934.

The District Court ordered all the claims to be submitted to arbitration except for those raised under § 12(2) of the Securities Act. It held that the latter claims must proceed in the court action under our clear holding on the point in Wilko v. Swan, 346 U.S. 427, 74 S.Ct. 182, 98 L.Ed. 168 (1953). The District Court reaffirmed its ruling upon reconsideration and also entered a default judgment against the broker, who is no longer in the case. The Court of Appeals reversed, concluding that the arbitration agreement is enforceable because this Court's subsequent decisions have reduced Wilko to "obsolescence." Rodriguez de Quijas v. Shearson/Lehman Bros., Inc., 845 F.2d 1296, 1299 (C.A.5 1988). We granted certiorari, 488 U.S. 954, 109 S.Ct. 389, 102 L.Ed.2d 379 (1988).

II

The Wilko case, decided in 1953, required the Court to determine whether an agreement to arbitrate future controversies constitutes a binding stipulation "to waive compliance with any provision" of the Securities Act, which is nullified by § 14 of the Act. 15 U.S.C. § 77n. The Court considered the language, purposes, and legislative history of the Securities Act and concluded that the agreement to arbitrate was void under § 14. But the decision was a difficult one in view of the competing legislative policy embodied in the Arbitration Act, which the Court described as "not easily reconcilable," and which strongly favors the enforcement of agreements to arbitrate as a means of securing "prompt, economical and adequate solution of controversies." 346 U.S., at 438, 74 S.Ct., at 188.

It has been recognized that Wilko was not obviously correct, for "the language prohibiting waiver of 'compliance with any provision of this title' could easily have been read to relate to substantive provisions of the Act without including the remedy provisions." Alberto–Culver Co. v. Scherk, 484 F.2d 611, 618, n. 7 (C.A.7 1973) (Stevens, J., dissenting), rev'd, 417 U.S. 506, 94 S.Ct. 2449, 41 L.Ed.2d 270 (1974)....

The Court's characterization of the arbitration process in Wilko is pervaded by what Judge Jerome Frank called "the old judicial hostility to arbitration." Kulukundis Shipping Co. v. Amtorg Trading Corp., 126 F.2d 978, 985 (C.A.2 1942). That view has been steadily eroded over the years, beginning in the lower courts. See Scherk, supra, at 616 (Stevens, J., dissenting) (citing cases).... To the extent that Wilko rested on suspicion of arbitration as a method of weakening the protections afforded in the substantive law to would-be complainants, it has fallen far out of step with our current strong endorsement of the federal statutes favoring this method of resolving disputes.

Once the outmoded presumption of disfavoring arbitration proceedings is set to one side, it becomes clear that the right to select the judicial forum and the wider choice of courts are not such essential features of the Securities Act that § 14 is properly construed to bar any waiver of these provisions. Nor are they so critical that they cannot be waived under the rationale that the Securities Act was intended to place buyers of securities on an equal footing with sellers. Wilko identified two different kinds of provisions in the Securities Act that would advance this objective. Some are substantive, such as the provision placing on the seller the burden of proving lack of scienter when a buyer alleges fraud. See 346 U.S., at 431, 74 S.Ct., at 184, citing 15 U.S.C. § 77l(2). Others are procedural. The specific procedural improvements highlighted in Wilko are the statute's broad venue provisions in the federal courts; the existence of nationwide service of process in the federal courts; the extinction of the amount-in-controversy requirement that had applied to fraud suits when they were brought in federal courts under diversity jurisdiction rather than as a federal cause of action; and the grant of concurrent jurisdiction in the state and federal courts without possibility of removal. See 346 U.S., at 431, 74 S.Ct., at 184, citing 15 U.S.C. § 77v(a).

There is no sound basis for construing the prohibition in § 14 on waiving "compliance with any provision" of the Securities Act to apply to these procedural provisions. Although the first three measures do facilitate suits by buyers of securities, the grant of concurrent jurisdiction constitutes explicit authorization for complainants to waive those protections by filing suit in state court without possibility of removal to federal court. These measures, moreover, are present in other federal statutes which have not been interpreted to prohibit enforcement of predispute agreements to arbitrate. See Shearson/American Express Inc. v. McMahon, supra (construing the Securities Exchange Act of 1934; see 15 U.S.C. § 78aa); ibid. (construing the RICO statutes; see 18 U.S.C. § 1965); Mitsubishi Motors Corp. v. Soler Chrysler–Plymouth, Inc., supra (construing the antitrust laws; see 15 U.S.C. § 15).

Indeed, in McMahon the Court declined to read § 29(a) of the Securities Exchange Act of 1934, the language of which is in every respect the same as that in § 14 of the 1933 Act, compare 15 U.S.C. § 77v(a) with § 78aa, to prohibit enforcement of predispute agreements to arbitrate. The only conceivable distinction in this regard between the Securities Act and the Securities Exchange Act is that the former statute allows concurrent federal-state jurisdiction over causes of action and the latter statute provides for exclusive federal jurisdiction. But even if this distinction were thought to make any difference at all, it would suggest that arbitration agreements, which are "in effect, a specialized kind of forum-selection clause," Scherk v. Alberto–Culver Co., 417 U.S. 506, 519, 94 S.Ct. 2449, 2457, 41 L.Ed.2d 270 (1974), should not be prohibited under the Securities Act, since they, like the provision for concurrent jurisdiction, serve to advance the objective of allowing buyers of securities a broader right to select the forum for resolving disputes, whether it be judicial or otherwise . . . .

Finally, in McMahon we stressed the strong language of the Arbitration Act, which declares as a matter of federal law that arbitration agreements "shall be valid, irrevocable, and enforceable, save upon such grounds as exist at law or in equity for the revocation of any contract." 9 U.S.C. § 2. Under that statute, the party opposing arbitration carries the burden of showing that Congress intended in a separate statute to preclude a waiver of judicial remedies, or that such a waiver of judicial remedies inherently conflicts with the underlying purposes of that other statute. 482 U.S., at 226–227, 107 S.Ct., at 2337–2338. But as Justice Frankfurter said in dissent in Wilko, so it is true in this case: "There is nothing in the record before us, nor in the facts of which we can take judicial notice, to indicate that the arbitral system . . . would not afford the plaintiff the rights to which he is entitled." 346 U.S., at 439, 74 S.Ct., at 189. Petitioners have not carried their burden of showing that arbitration agreements are not enforceable under the Securities Act.

The language quoted above from § 2 of the Arbitration Act also allows the courts to give relief where the party opposing arbitration presents "well-supported claims that the agreement to arbitrate resulted from the sort of fraud or overwhelming economic power that would provide grounds 'for the revocation of any contract.'" Mitsubishi, 473 U.S., at 627, 105 S.Ct., at 3354. This avenue of relief is in harmony with the Securities Act's concern to protect buyers of securities by removing "the disadvantages under which buyers labor" in their dealings with sellers. Wilko, supra, 346 U.S., at 435, 74 S.Ct., at 187. Although petitioners suggest that the agreement to arbitrate here was adhesive in nature, the record contains no factual showing sufficient to support that suggestion.

III

We do not suggest that the Court of Appeals on its own authority should have taken the step of renouncing Wilko. If a precedent of this Court has direct application in a case, yet appears to rest on reasons rejected in some other line of decisions, the Court of Appeals should follow the case which directly controls, leaving to this Court the prerogative of overruling its own decisions. We now conclude that Wilko was incorrectly decided and is inconsistent with the prevailing uniform construction of other federal statutes governing arbitration agreements in the setting of business transactions. Although we are normally and properly reluctant to overturn our decisions construing statutes, we have done so to achieve a uniform interpretation of similar statutory language, Commissioner v. Estate of Church, 335 U.S. 632, 649–650, 69 S.Ct. 322, 330–331, 93 L.Ed. 288 (1949), and to correct a seriously erroneous interpretation of statutory language that would undermine congressional policy as expressed in other legislation, see, e.g., Boys Markets, Inc. v. Retail Clerks, 398 U.S. 235, 240–241, 90 S.Ct. 1583, 1586–1587, 26 L.Ed.2d 199 (1970) (overruling Sinclair

Refining Co. v. Atkinson, 370 U.S. 195, 82 S.Ct. 1328, 8 L.Ed.2d 440 (1962)). Both purposes would be served here by overruling the Wilko decision.

It also would be undesirable for the decisions in Wilko and McMahon to continue to exist side by side. Their inconsistency is at odds with the principle that the 1933 and 1934 Acts should be construed harmoniously because they "constitute interrelated components of the federal regulatory scheme governing transactions in securities." Ernst & Ernst v. Hochfelder, 425 U.S. 185, 206, 96 S.Ct. 1375, 1387, 47 L.Ed.2d 668 (1976). In this case, for example, petitioners' claims under the 1934 Act were subjected to arbitration, while their claim under the 1933 Act was not permitted to go to arbitration, but was required to proceed in court. That result makes little sense for similar claims, based on similar facts, which are supposed to arise within a single federal regulatory scheme. In addition, the inconsistency between Wilko and McMahon undermines the essential rationale for a harmonious construction of the two statutes, which is to discourage litigants from manipulating their allegations merely to cast their claims under one of the securities laws rather than another. For all of these reasons, therefore, we overrule the decision in Wilko.

... The judgment of the Court of Appeals is

Affirmed.

■ JUSTICE STEVENS, with whom JUSTICE BRENNAN, JUSTICE MARSHALL, and JUSTICE BLACKMUN join, dissenting.

The Court of Appeals refused to follow Wilko v. Swan, 346 U.S. 427, 74 S.Ct. 182, 98 L.Ed. 168 (1953), a controlling precedent of this Court. As the majority correctly acknowledges, ante, at 484, the Court of Appeals therefore engaged in an indefensible brand of judicial activism. We, of course, are not subject to the same restraint when asked to upset one of our own precedents. But when our earlier opinion gives a statutory provision concrete meaning, which Congress elects not to amend during the ensuing 3 1/2 decades, our duty to respect Congress' work product is strikingly similar to the duty of other federal courts to respect our work product.

In the final analysis, a Justice's vote in a case like this depends more on his or her views about the respective lawmaking responsibilities of Congress and this Court than on conflicting policy interests. Judges who have confidence in their own ability to fashion public policy are less hesitant to change the law than those of us who are inclined to give wide latitude to the views of the voters' representatives on nonconstitutional matters.... As I pointed out years ago, Alberto–Culver Co. v. Scherk, 484 F.2d 611, 615–620 (C.A.7 1973) (dissenting opinion), rev'd, 417 U.S. 506, 94 S.Ct. 2449, 41 L.Ed.2d 270 (1974), there are valid policy and textual arguments on both sides regarding the interrelation of federal securities and arbitration Acts. See ante, at 479–484. None of these arguments, however, carries sufficient weight to tip the balance between judicial and legislative authority and overturn an interpretation of an Act of Congress that has been settled for many years.

I respectfully dissent.

* * *

Questions

1. Was the result in *Rodriguez* inevitable in light of the reasoning in *Scherck, Mitsubishi,* and *McMahon?*

2. Is the Court's statement that *Wilko*'s reasoning "has fallen far out of step with our current strong endorsement" of arbitration based on anything other than its own opinions in post-*Wilko* cases? If that is the only basis for the statement, is the Court's reasoning anything more than bootstrapping?

3. Does the Court accept a distinction between a waiver of the substantive provisions of a statute and a waiver of a remedy, as was mentioned in dicta in *Scherck* and quoted herein? Is this distinction a useful means to determine whether claims arising under the Securities Act are amenable to arbitration? Does this distinction help determine whether other statutory claims are amenable to arbitration? Is there some other basis for deciding which statutory claims are amenable to arbitration and which are not?

* * *

Gilmer v. Interstate/Johnson Lane Corp.

500 U.S. 20, 111 S.Ct. 1647 (1991).

■ JUSTICE WHITE delivered the opinion of the Court.

The question presented in this case is whether a claim under the Age Discrimination in Employment Act of 1967 (ADEA), 81 Stat. 602, as amended, 29 U.S.C. § 621 et seq., can be subjected to compulsory arbitration pursuant to an arbitration agreement in a securities registration application. The Court of Appeals held that it could, 895 F.2d 195 (C.A.4 1990), and we affirm.

I

Respondent Interstate/Johnson Lane Corporation (Interstate) hired petitioner Robert Gilmer as a Manager of Financial Services in May 1981. As required by his employment, Gilmer registered as a securities representative with several stock exchanges, including the New York Stock Exchange (NYSE). See App. 15–18. His registration application, entitled "Uniform Application for Securities Industry Registration or Transfer," provided, among other things, that Gilmer "agree[d] to arbitrate any dispute, claim or controversy" arising between him and Interstate "that is required to be arbitrated under the rules, constitutions or by-laws of the organizations with which I register." Id., at 18. Of relevance to this case, NYSE Rule 347 provides for arbitration of "[a]ny controversy between a registered representative and any member or member organization arising out of the employment or termination of employment of such registered representative." App. to Brief for Respondent 1.

Interstate terminated Gilmer's employment in 1987, at which time Gilmer was 62 years of age. After first filing an age discrimination charge with the Equal Employment Opportunity Commission (EEOC), Gilmer subsequently brought suit in the United States District Court for the Western District of North Carolina, alleging that Interstate had discharged him because of his age, in violation of the ADEA. In response to Gilmer's complaint, Interstate filed in the District Court a motion to compel arbitration of the ADEA claim. In its motion, Interstate relied upon the arbitration agreement in Gilmer's registration application, as well as the Federal Arbitration Act (FAA), 9 U.S.C. § 1 et seq. The District Court denied Interstate's motion, based on this Court's decision in Alexander v. Gardner–Denver Co., 415 U.S. 36, 94 S.Ct. 1011, 39 L.Ed.2d 147 (1974), and because it concluded that "Congress intended to protect ADEA claimants from the waiver of a judicial forum." App. 87. The United States Court of Appeals for the Fourth Circuit reversed, finding "nothing in the text, legislative history, or underlying purposes of the ADEA indicating a congressional intent to preclude enforcement of arbitration agreements." 895 F.2d, at 197. We granted certiorari, 498 U.S. 809, 111 S.Ct. 41, 112 L.Ed.2d 18 (1990), to resolve a conflict among the Courts of Appeals regarding the arbitrability of ADEA claims.

II

The FAA was originally enacted in 1925, 43 Stat. 883, and then reenacted and codified in 1947 as Title 9 of the United States Code. Its purpose was to reverse the longstanding judicial hostility to arbitration agreements that had existed at English common law and had been adopted by American courts, and to place arbitration agreements upon the same footing as other contracts. Dean Witter Reynolds Inc. v. Byrd, 470 U.S. 213, 219–220, and n. 6 (1985); Scherk v. Alberto–Culver Co., 417 U.S. 506, 510, n. 4 (1974). Its primary substantive provision states that "[a] written provision in any maritime transaction or a contract evidencing a transaction involving commerce to settle by arbitration a controversy thereafter arising out of such contract or transaction ... shall be valid, irrevocable, and enforceable, save upon such grounds as exist at law or in equity for the revocation of any contract." 9 U.S.C. § 2. The FAA also provides for stays of proceedings in federal district courts when an issue in the proceeding is referable to arbitration, § 3, and for orders compelling arbitration when one party has failed, neglected, or refused to comply with an arbitration agreement, § 4. These provisions manifest a "liberal federal policy favoring arbitration agreements." Moses H. Cone Memorial Hospital v. Mercury Construction Corp., 460 U.S. 1, 24, 103 S.Ct. 927, 941, 74 L.Ed.2d 765 (1983).[2]

---

2. Section 1 of the FAA provides that "nothing herein contained shall apply to contracts of employment of seamen, railroad employees, or any other class of workers engaged in foreign or interstate commerce." 9 U.S.C. § 1. Several amici curiae in support of

It is by now clear that statutory claims may be the subject of an arbitration agreement, enforceable pursuant to the FAA. Indeed, in recent years we have held enforceable arbitration agreements relating to claims arising under the Sherman Act, 15 U.S.C. §§ 1–7; § 10(b) of the Securities Exchange Act of 1934, 15 U.S.C. § 78j(b); the civil provisions of the Racketeer Influenced and Corrupt Organizations Act (RICO), 18 U.S.C. § 1961 et seq.; and § 12(2) of the Securities Act of 1933, 15 U.S.C. § 77l(2). See Mitsubishi Motors Corp. v. Soler Chrysler–Plymouth, Inc., 473 U.S. 614, 105 S.Ct. 3346, 87 L.Ed.2d 444 (1985); Shearson/American Express Inc. v. McMahon, 482 U.S. 220, 107 S.Ct. 2332, 96 L.Ed.2d 185 (1987); Rodriguez de Quijas v. Shearson/American Express, Inc., 490 U.S. 477, 109 S.Ct. 1917, 104 L.Ed.2d 526 (1989). In these cases we recognized that "[b]y agreeing to arbitrate a statutory claim, a party does not forgo the substantive rights afforded by the statute; it only submits to their resolution in an arbitral, rather than a judicial, forum." Mitsubishi, 473 U.S., at 628, 105 S.Ct., at 3354.

Although all statutory claims may not be appropriate for arbitration, "[h]aving made the bargain to arbitrate, the party should be held to it unless Congress itself has evinced an intention to preclude a waiver of judicial remedies for the statutory rights at issue." Ibid. In this regard, we note that the burden is on Gilmer to show that Congress intended to preclude a waiver of a judicial forum for ADEA claims. See McMahon, 482 U.S., at 227, 107 S.Ct., at 2337. If such an intention exists, it will be discoverable in the text of the ADEA, its legislative history, or an "inherent conflict" between arbitration and the ADEA's underlying purposes. See ibid. Throughout such an inquiry, it should be kept in mind that "questions of arbitrability must be addressed with a healthy regard for the federal policy favoring arbitration." Moses H. Cone, supra, 460 U.S., at 24, 103 S.Ct., at 941.

Gilmer argue that section excludes from the coverage of the FAA all "contracts of employment." Gilmer, however, did not raise the issue in the courts below, it was not addressed there, and it was not among the questions presented in the petition for certiorari. In any event, it would be inappropriate to address the scope of the § 1 exclusion because the arbitration clause being enforced here is not contained in a contract of employment. The FAA requires that the arbitration clause being enforced be in writing. See 9 U.S.C. §§ 2, 3. The record before us does not show, and the parties do not contend, that Gilmer's employment agreement with Interstate contained a written arbitration clause. Rather, the arbitration clause at issue is in Gilmer's securities registration application, which is a contract with the securities exchanges, not with Interstate. The lower courts addressing the issue uniformly have concluded that the exclusionary clause of § 1 of the FAA is inapplicable to arbitration clauses contained in such registration applications. ... We implicitly assumed as much in Perry v. Thomas, 482 U.S. 483, 107 S.Ct. 2520, 96 L.Ed.2d 426 (1987), where we held that the FAA required a former employee of a securities firm to arbitrate his statutory wage claim against his former employer, pursuant to an arbitration clause in his registration application. Unlike the dissent, see post, at 1659–1660, we choose to follow the plain language of the FAA and the weight of authority, and we therefore hold that § 1's exclusionary clause does not apply to Gilmer's arbitration agreement. Consequently, we leave for another day the issue raised by amici curiae.

III

Gilmer concedes that nothing in the text of the ADEA or its legislative history explicitly precludes arbitration. He argues, however, that compulsory arbitration of ADEA claims pursuant to arbitration agreements would be inconsistent with the statutory framework and purposes of the ADEA. Like the Court of Appeals, we disagree.

A

Congress enacted the ADEA in 1967 "to promote employment of older persons based on their ability rather than age; to prohibit arbitrary age discrimination in employment; [and] to help employers and workers find ways of meeting problems arising from the impact of age on employment." 29 U.S.C. § 621(b). To achieve those goals, the ADEA, among other things, makes it unlawful for an employer "to fail or refuse to hire or to discharge any individual or otherwise discriminate against any individual with respect to his compensation, terms, conditions, or privileges of employment, because of such individual's age." § 623(a)(1). This proscription is enforced both by private suits and by the EEOC. In order for an aggrieved individual to bring suit under the ADEA, he or she must first file a charge with the EEOC and then wait at least 60 days. § 626(d). An individual's right to sue is extinguished, however, if the EEOC institutes an action against the employer. § 626(c)(1). Before the EEOC can bring such an action, though, it must "attempt to eliminate the discriminatory practice or practices alleged, and to effect voluntary compliance with the requirements of this chapter through informal methods of conciliation, conference, and persuasion." § 626(b); see also 29 CFR § 1626.15 (1990).

As Gilmer contends, the ADEA is designed not only to address individual grievances, but also to further important social policies. See, e.g., EEOC v. Wyoming, 460 U.S. 226, 231, 103 S.Ct. 1054, 1057–1058, 75 L.Ed.2d 18 (1983). We do not perceive any inherent inconsistency between those policies, however, and enforcing agreements to arbitrate age discrimination claims. It is true that arbitration focuses on specific disputes between the parties involved. The same can be said, however, of judicial resolution of claims. Both of these dispute resolution mechanisms nevertheless also can further broader social purposes. The Sherman Act, the Securities Exchange Act of 1934, RICO, and the Securities Act of 1933 all are designed to advance important public policies, but, as noted above, claims under those statutes are appropriate for arbitration. "[S]o long as the prospective litigant effectively may vindicate [his or her] statutory cause of action in the arbitral forum, the statute will continue to serve both its remedial and deterrent function." Mitsubishi, supra, 473 U.S., at 637, 105 S.Ct., at 3359.

We also are unpersuaded by the argument that arbitration will undermine the role of the EEOC in enforcing the ADEA. An individual ADEA claimant subject to an arbitration agreement will still be free to file a charge with the EEOC, even though the claimant is not able to institute a private judicial action. Indeed, Gilmer filed a charge with the EEOC in this case. In any event, the EEOC's role in combating age discrimination is not dependent on the filing of a charge; the agency may receive information concerning alleged violations of the ADEA "from any source," and it has independent authority to investigate age discrimination. See 29 CFR §§ 1626.4, 1626.13 (1990). Moreover, nothing in the ADEA indicates that Congress intended that the EEOC be involved in all employment disputes. Such disputes can be settled, for example, without any EEOC involvement. . . .[3] Finally, the mere involvement of an administrative agency in the enforcement of a statute is not sufficient to preclude arbitration. For example, the Securities Exchange Commission is heavily involved in the enforcement of the Securities Exchange Act of 1934 and the Securities Act of 1933, but we have held that claims under both of those statutes may be subject to compulsory arbitration. See Shearson/American Express Inc. v. McMahon, 482 U.S. 220, 107 S.Ct. 2332, 96 L.Ed.2d 185 (1987); Rodriguez de Quijas v. Shearson/American Express, Inc., 490 U.S. 477, 109 S.Ct. 1917, 104 L.Ed.2d 526 (1989).

Gilmer also argues that compulsory arbitration is improper because it deprives claimants of the judicial forum provided for by the ADEA. Congress, however, did not explicitly preclude arbitration or other nonjudicial resolution of claims, even in its recent amendments to the ADEA. "[I]f Congress intended the substantive protection afforded [by the ADEA] to include protection against waiver of the right to a judicial forum, that intention will be deducible from text or legislative history." Mitsubishi, 473 U.S., at 628, 105 S.Ct., at 3354. Moreover, Gilmer's argument ignores the ADEA's flexible approach to resolution of claims. The EEOC, for example, is directed to pursue "informal methods of conciliation, conference, and persuasion," 29 U.S.C. § 626(b), which suggests that out-of-court dispute resolution, such as arbitration, is consistent with the statutory scheme established by Congress. In addition, arbitration is consistent with Congress' grant of concurrent jurisdiction over ADEA claims to state and federal courts, see 29 U.S.C. § 626(c)(1) (allowing suits to be brought "in any court of competent jurisdiction"), because arbitration agreements, "like the provision for concurrent jurisdiction, serve to advance the objective of allowing [claimants] a broader right to select the forum for resolving disputes, whether it be judicial or otherwise." Rodriguez de Quijas, supra, at 483, 109 S.Ct., at 1921.

B

In arguing that arbitration is inconsistent with the ADEA, Gilmer also raises a host of challenges to the adequacy of arbitration procedures. Initially, we note that in our recent arbitration cases we have already rejected most of these arguments as insufficient to preclude arbitration of statutory claims. Such generalized attacks on arbitration "res[t] on suspicion of arbitration as a method of weakening the protections afforded in the

---

3. In the recently enacted Older Workers Benefits Protection Act, Pub.L. 101–433, 104 Stat. 978, Congress amended the ADEA to provide that "[a]n individual may not waive any right or claim under this Act unless the waiver is knowing and voluntary." See § 201. Congress also specified certain conditions that must be met in order for a waiver to be knowing and voluntary. Ibid.

substantive law to would-be complainants," and as such, they are "far out of step with our current strong endorsement of the federal statutes favoring this method of resolving disputes." Rodriguez de Quijas, supra, at 481, 109 S.Ct., at 1920. Consequently, we address these arguments only briefly.

Gilmer first speculates that arbitration panels will be biased. However, "[w]e decline to indulge the presumption that the parties and arbitral body conducting a proceeding will be unable or unwilling to retain competent, conscientious and impartial arbitrators." Mitsubishi, supra, 473 U.S., at 634, 105 S.Ct., at 3357–3358. In any event, we note that the NYSE arbitration rules, which are applicable to the dispute in this case, provide protections against biased panels. The rules require, for example, that the parties be informed of the employment histories of the arbitrators, and that they be allowed to make further inquiries into the arbitrators' backgrounds. See 2 CCH New York Stock Exchange Guide ¶ 2608, p. 4314 (Rule 608) (1991) (hereinafter 2 N.Y.S.E. Guide). In addition, each party is allowed one peremptory challenge and unlimited challenges for cause. Id., ¶ 2609, at 4315 (Rule 609). Moreover, the arbitrators are required to disclose "any circumstances which might preclude [them] from rendering an objective and impartial determination." Id., ¶ 2610, at 4315 (Rule 610). The FAA also protects against bias, by providing that courts may overturn arbitration decisions "[w]here there was evident partiality or corruption in the arbitrators." 9 U.S.C. § 10(b). There has been no showing in this case that those provisions are inadequate to guard against potential bias.

Gilmer also complains that the discovery allowed in arbitration is more limited than in the federal courts, which he contends will make it difficult to prove discrimination. It is unlikely, however, that age discrimination claims require more extensive discovery than other claims that we have found to be arbitrable, such as RICO and antitrust claims. Moreover, there has been no showing in this case that the NYSE discovery provisions, which allow for document production, information requests, depositions, and subpoenas, see 2 N.Y.S.E. Guide ¶ 2619, pp. 4318–4320 (Rule 619); Securities and Exchange Commission Order Approving Proposed Rule Changes by New York Stock Exchange, Inc., Nat. Assn. of Securities Dealers, Inc., and the American Stock Exchange, Inc., Relating to the Arbitration Process and the Use of Predispute Arbitration Clauses, 54 Fed.Reg. 21144, 21149–21151 (1989), will prove insufficient to allow ADEA claimants such as Gilmer a fair opportunity to present their claims. Although those procedures might not be as extensive as in the federal courts, by agreeing to arbitrate, a party "trades the procedures and opportunity for review of the courtroom for the simplicity, informality, and expedition of arbitration." Mitsubishi, supra, at 628, 105 S.Ct., at 3354. Indeed, an important counterweight to the reduced discovery in NYSE arbitration is that arbitrators are not bound by the rules of evidence. See 2 N.Y.S.E. Guide ¶ 2620, p. 4320 (Rule 620).

A further alleged deficiency of arbitration is that arbitrators often will not issue written opinions, resulting, Gilmer contends, in a lack of public knowledge of employers' discriminatory policies, an inability to obtain effective appellate review, and a stifling of the development of the law. The NYSE rules, however, do require that all arbitration awards be in writing, and that the awards contain the names of the parties, a summary of the issues in controversy, and a description of the award issued. See id., ¶¶ 2627(a), (e), at 4321 (Rules 627(a), (e)). In addition, the award decisions are made available to the public. See id., ¶ 2627(f), at 4322 (Rule 627(f)). Furthermore, judicial decisions addressing ADEA claims will continue to be issued because it is unlikely that all or even most ADEA claimants will be subject to arbitration agreements. Finally, Gilmer's concerns apply equally to settlements of ADEA claims, which, as noted above, are clearly allowed.[4]

It is also argued that arbitration procedures cannot adequately further the purposes of the ADEA because they do not provide for broad equitable relief and class actions. As the court below noted, however, arbitrators do have the power to fashion equitable relief. 895 F.2d, at 199–200. Indeed, the NYSE rules applicable here do not restrict the types of relief an arbitrator may award, but merely refer to "damages and/or other relief." 2 N.Y.S.E. Guide ¶ 2627(e), p. 4321 (Rule 627(e)). The NYSE rules also provide for collective proceedings. Id., ¶ 2612(d), at 4317 (Rule 612(d)). But "even if the arbitration could not go forward as a class action or class relief could not be granted by the arbitrator, the fact that the [ADEA] provides for the possibility of bringing a collective action does not mean that individual attempts at conciliation were intended to be barred." Nicholson v. CPC Int'l Inc., 877 F.2d 221, 241 (C.A.3 1989) (Becker, J., dissenting). Finally, it should be remembered that arbitration agreements will not preclude the EEOC from bringing actions seeking class-wide and equitable relief.

C

An additional reason advanced by Gilmer for refusing to enforce arbitration agreements relating to ADEA claims is his contention that there often will be unequal bargaining power between employers and employees. Mere inequality in bargaining power, however, is not a sufficient reason to hold that arbitration agreements are never enforceable in the employment context. Relationships between securities dealers and investors, for example, may involve unequal bargaining power, but we nevertheless held in Rodriguez de Quijas and McMahon that agreements to arbitrate in that context are enforceable. See 490 U.S., at 484, 109 S.Ct., at 1921–1922; 482 U.S., at 230, 107 S.Ct., at 2339–2340. As discussed above, the FAA's purpose was to place arbitration agreements on the same footing as other contracts. Thus, arbitration agreements are enforceable "save upon such grounds as exist at law or in equity for the revocation of any contract." 9 U.S.C. § 2. "Of course, courts should remain attuned to well-supported claims that the agreement to arbitrate resulted from the sort of

---

4. Gilmer also contends that judicial review of arbitration decisions is too limited. We have stated, however, that "although judicial scrutiny of arbitration awards necessarily is limited, such review is sufficient to ensure that arbitrators comply with the requirements of the statute" at issue. Shearson/American Express Inc. v. McMahon, 482 U.S. 220, 232, 107 S.Ct. 2332, 2340, 96 L.Ed.2d 185 (1987).

fraud or overwhelming economic power that would provide grounds 'for the revocation of any contract.' " Mitsubishi, 473 U.S., at 627, 105 S.Ct., at 3354. There is no indication in this case, however, that Gilmer, an experienced businessman, was coerced or defrauded into agreeing to the arbitration clause in his registration application. As with the claimed procedural inadequacies discussed above, this claim of unequal bargaining power is best left for resolution in specific cases.

IV

In addition to the arguments discussed above, Gilmer vigorously asserts that our decision in Alexander v. Gardner–Denver Co., 415 U.S. 36, 94 S.Ct. 1011, 39 L.Ed.2d 147 (1974), and its progeny—Barrentine v. Arkansas–Best Freight System, Inc., 450 U.S. 728, 101 S.Ct. 1437, 67 L.Ed.2d 641 (1981), and McDonald v. West Branch, 466 U.S. 284, 104 S.Ct. 1799, 80 L.Ed.2d 302 (1984)—preclude arbitration of employment discrimination claims. Gilmer's reliance on these cases, however, is misplaced.

In Gardner–Denver, the issue was whether a discharged employee whose grievance had been arbitrated pursuant to an arbitration clause in a collective-bargaining agreement was precluded from subsequently bringing a Title VII action based upon the conduct that was the subject of the grievance. In holding that the employee was not foreclosed from bringing the Title VII claim, we stressed that an employee's contractual rights under a collective-bargaining agreement are distinct from the employee's statutory Title VII rights: "In submitting his grievance to arbitration, an employee seeks to vindicate his contractual right under a collective-bargaining agreement. By contrast, in filing a lawsuit under Title VII, an employee asserts independent statutory rights accorded by Congress. The distinctly separate nature of these contractual and statutory rights is not vitiated merely because both were violated as a result of the same factual occurrence." 415 U.S., at 49–50, 94 S.Ct., at 1020.

We also noted that a labor arbitrator has authority only to resolve questions of contractual rights. Id., at 53–54, 94 S.Ct., at 1022–1023. The arbitrator's "task is to effectuate the intent of the parties" and he or she does not have the "general authority to invoke public laws that conflict with the bargain between the parties." Id., at 53, 94 S.Ct., at 1022. By contrast, "in instituting an action under Title VII, the employee is not seeking review of the arbitrator's decision. Rather, he is asserting a statutory right independent of the arbitration process." Id., at 54, 94 S.Ct., at 1022. We further expressed concern that in collective-bargaining arbitration "the interests of the individual employee may be subordinated to the collective interests of all employees in the bargaining unit." Id., at 58, n. 19, 94 S.Ct., at 1024, n. 19.

Barrentine and McDonald similarly involved the issue whether arbitration under a collective-bargaining agreement precluded a subsequent statutory claim. In holding that the statutory claims there were not precluded, we noted, as in Gardner–Denver, the difference between contractual rights under a collective-bargaining agreement and individual statutory rights, the potential disparity in interests between a union and an employee, and the limited authority and power of labor arbitrators.

There are several important distinctions between the Gardner–Denver line of cases and the case before us. First, those cases did not involve the issue of the enforceability of an agreement to arbitrate statutory claims. Rather, they involved the quite different issue whether arbitration of contract-based claims precluded subsequent judicial resolution of statutory claims. Since the employees there had not agreed to arbitrate their statutory claims, and the labor arbitrators were not authorized to resolve such claims, the arbitration in those cases understandably was held not to preclude subsequent statutory actions. Second, because the arbitration in those cases occurred in the context of a collective-bargaining agreement, the claimants there were represented by their unions in the arbitration proceedings. An important concern therefore was the tension between collective representation and individual statutory rights, a concern not applicable to the present case. Finally, those cases were not decided under the FAA, which, as discussed above, reflects a "liberal federal policy favoring arbitration agreements." Mitsubishi, 473 U.S., at 625, 105 S.Ct., at 3353. Therefore, those cases provide no basis for refusing to enforce Gilmer's agreement to arbitrate his ADEA claim.

V

We conclude that Gilmer has not met his burden of showing that Congress, in enacting the ADEA, intended to preclude arbitration of claims under that Act. Accordingly, the judgment of the Court of Appeals is

Affirmed.

■ JUSTICE STEVENS, with whom JUSTICE MARSHALL joins, dissenting.

Section 1 of the Federal Arbitration Act (FAA) states:

"[N]othing herein contained shall apply to contracts of employment of seamen, railroad employees, or any other class of workers engaged in foreign or interstate commerce." 9 U.S.C. § 1.

The Court today, in holding that the FAA compels enforcement of arbitration clauses even when claims of age discrimination are at issue, skirts the antecedent question whether the coverage of the Act even extends to arbitration clauses contained in employment contracts, regardless of the subject matter of the claim at issue. In my opinion, arbitration clauses contained in employment agreements are specifically exempt from coverage of the FAA, and for that reason respondent Interstate/Johnson Lane Corporation cannot, pursuant to the FAA, compel petitioner to submit his claims arising under the Age Discrimination in Employment Act of 1967 (ADEA), 29 U.S.C. § 621 et seq., to binding arbitration.

I

Petitioner did not, as the majority correctly notes, ante, at 1651–1652, n. 2, raise the issue of the applicability of the FAA to employment contracts at any stage of the proceedings below. Nor did petitioner raise the coverage issue in his petition for writ of certiorari before this Court. It was amici who first raised the argument in their briefs in support of petitioner prior to oral argument of the case. See Brief for American Federation of Labor and Congress of Industrial Organizations as Amicus Curiae; Brief for American Association of Retired Persons as Amicus Curiae; Brief for Lawyers' Committee for Civil Rights Under Law as Amicus Curiae 17–18.

Notwithstanding the apparent waiver of the issue below, I believe that the Court should reach the issue of the coverage of the FAA to employment disputes because resolution of the question is so clearly antecedent to disposition of this case. On a number of occasions, this Court has considered issues waived by the parties below and in the petition for certiorari because the issues were so integral to decision of the case that they could be considered "fairly subsumed" by the actual questions presented....

In my opinion the considerations in favor of reaching an issue not presented below or in the petition for certiorari are more compelling in this case than in the cited cases. Here the issue of the applicability of the FAA to employment contracts was adequately briefed and raised by the amici in support of petitioner. More important, however, is that respondent and its amici had full opportunity to brief and argue the same issue in opposition. See Brief for Respondent 42–50; Brief for Securities Industry Association, Inc., as Amicus Curiae 18–20; Brief for Equal Employment Advisory Council et al. as Amici Curiae 14–16. Moreover, the Court amply raised the issue with the parties at oral argument, at which both sides were on notice and fully prepared to argue the merits of the question. Finally, as in Arcadia, the issue whether the FAA even covers employment disputes is clearly "antecedent ... and ultimately dispositive" of the question whether courts and respondent may rely on the FAA to compel petitioner to submit his ADEA claims to arbitration.

II

The Court, declining to reach the issue for the reason that petitioner never raised it below, nevertheless concludes that "it would be inappropriate to address the scope of the § 1 exclusion because the arbitration clause being enforced here is not contained in a contract of employment.... Rather, the arbitration clause at issue is in Gilmer's securities registration application, which is a contract with the securities exchanges, not with Interstate." Ante, at 1651–1652, n. 2. In my opinion the Court too narrowly construes the scope of the exclusion contained in § 1 of the FAA.

There is little dispute that the primary concern animating the FAA was the perceived need by the business community to overturn the common-law rule that denied specific enforcement of agreements to arbitrate in contracts between business entities. The Act was drafted by a committee of the American Bar Association (ABA), acting upon instructions from the ABA to consider and report upon "the further extension of the principle of commercial arbitration." Report of the Forty-third Annual Meeting of the ABA, 45 A.B.A.Rep. 75 (1920). At the Senate Judiciary Subcommittee hearings on the proposed bill, the chairman of the ABA committee responsible for drafting the bill assured the Senators that the bill "is not intended [to] be an act referring to labor disputes, at all. It is purely an act to give the merchants the right or the privilege of sitting down and agreeing with each other as to what their damages are, if they want to do it. Now that is all there is in this." Hearing on S. 4213 and S. 4214 before a Subcommittee of the Senate Committee on the Judiciary, 67th Cong., 4th Sess., 9 (1923). At the same hearing, Senator Walsh stated:

> "The trouble about the matter is that a great many of these contracts that are entered into are really not [voluntary] things at all. Take an insurance policy; there is a blank in it. You can take that or you can leave it. The agent has no power at all to decide it. Either you can make that contract or you can not make any contract. It is the same with a good many contracts of employment. A man says, 'These are our terms. All right, take it or leave it.' Well, there is nothing for the man to do except to sign it; and then he surrenders his right to have his case tried by the court, and has to have it tried before a tribunal in which he has no confidence at all." Ibid.

Given that the FAA specifically was intended to exclude arbitration agreements between employees and employers, I see no reason to limit this exclusion from coverage to arbitration clauses contained in agreements entitled "Contract of Employment." In this case, the parties conceded at oral argument that Gilmer had no "contract of employment" as such with respondent. Gilmer was, however, required as a condition of his employment to become a registered representative of several stock exchanges, including the New York Stock Exchange (NYSE). Just because his agreement to arbitrate any "dispute, claim or controversy" with his employer that arose out of the employment relationship was contained in his application for registration before the NYSE rather than in a specific contract of employment with his employer, I do not think that Gilmer can be compelled pursuant to the FAA to arbitrate his employment-related dispute. Rather, in my opinion the exclusion in § 1 should be interpreted to cover any agreements by the employee to arbitrate disputes with the employer arising out of the employment relationship, particularly where such agreements to arbitrate are conditions of employment.

My reading of the scope of the exclusion contained in § 1 is supported by early judicial interpretations of the FAA. As of 1956, three Courts of Appeals had held that the FAA's exclusion of "contracts of employment" referred not only to individual contracts of employment, but also to collective-bargaining agreements. See Lincoln Mills of Ala. v. Textile Workers Union of America, 230 F.2d 81 (C.A.5 1956), rev'd, 353 U.S. 448, 77 S.Ct. 912, 1 L.Ed.2d 972 (1957); United Electrical, Radio & Machine Workers of America v. Miller Metal Products, Inc., 215 F.2d 221 (C.A.4 1954); Amalgamated Assn. of Street, Electric R. and Motor Coach Employees of America v. Pennsylvania Greyhound Lines, Inc., 192 F.2d 310 (C.A.3 1951). Indeed, the application of the FAA's exclusionary clause to arbitration provisions in collective-bargaining agreements was one of the issues raised in the petition for certiorari and briefed at great length in Lincoln

Mills and its companion cases, Goodall–Sanford, Inc. v. Textile Workers, 353 U.S. 550, 77 S.Ct. 920, 1 L.Ed.2d 1031 (1957), and General Electric Co. v. Electrical Workers, 353 U.S. 547, 77 S.Ct. 921, 1 L.Ed.2d 1028 (1957). Although the Court decided the enforceability of the arbitration provisions in the collective-bargaining agreements by reference to § 301 of the Labor Management Relations Act, 1947, 29 U.S.C. § 185, it did not reject the Courts of Appeals' holdings that the arbitration provisions would not otherwise be enforceable pursuant to the FAA since they were specifically excluded under § 1. In dissent, Justice Frankfurter perceived a "rejection, though not explicit, of the availability of the Federal Arbitration Act to enforce arbitration clauses in collective-bargaining agreements in the silent treatment given that Act by the Court's opinion. If an Act that authorizes the federal courts to enforce arbitration provisions in contracts generally, but specifically denies authority to decree that remedy for 'contracts of employment,' were available, the Court would hardly spin such power out of the empty darkness of § 301. I would make this rejection explicit, recognizing that when Congress passed legislation to enable arbitration agreements to be enforced by the federal courts, it saw fit to exclude this remedy with respect to labor contracts." Textile Workers v. Lincoln Mills, 353 U.S., at 466, 77 S.Ct., at 926.

III

Not only would I find that the FAA does not apply to employment-related disputes between employers and employees in general, but also I would hold that compulsory arbitration conflicts with the congressional purpose animating the ADEA, in particular. As this Court previously has noted, authorizing the courts to issue broad injunctive relief is the corner-stone to eliminating discrimination in society. Albemarle Paper Co. v. Moody, 422 U.S. 405, 415, 95 S.Ct. 2362, 2370, 45 L.Ed.2d 280 (1975). The ADEA, like Title VII of the Civil Rights Act of 1964, authorizes courts to award broad, class-based injunctive relief to achieve the purposes of the Act. 29 U.S.C. § 626(b). Because commercial arbitration is typically limited to a specific dispute between the particular parties and because the available remedies in arbitral forums generally do not provide for class-wide injunctive relief, see Shell, ERISA and Other Federal Employment Statutes: When is Commercial Arbitration an "Adequate Substitute" for the Courts?, 68 Texas L.Rev. 509, 568 (1990), I would conclude that an essential purpose of the ADEA is frustrated by compulsory arbitration of employment discrimination claims. Moreover, as Chief Justice Burger explained:

> "Plainly, it would not comport with the congressional objectives behind a statute seeking to enforce civil rights protected by Title VII to allow the very forces that had practiced discrimination to contract away the right to enforce civil rights in the courts. For federal courts to defer to arbitral decisions reached by the same combination of forces that had long perpetuated invidious discrimination would have made the foxes guardians of the chickens." Barrentine v. Arkansas–Best Freight System, Inc., 450 U.S. 728 (1981) (dissenting opinion).

In my opinion the same concerns expressed by Chief Justice Burger with regard to compulsory arbitration of Title VII claims may be said of claims arising under the ADEA. The Court's holding today clearly eviscerates the important role played by an independent judiciary in eradicating employment discrimination.

IV

When the FAA was passed in 1925, I doubt that any legislator who voted for it expected it to apply to statutory claims, to form contracts between parties of unequal bargaining power, or to the arbitration of disputes arising out of the employment relationship. In recent years, however, the Court "has effectively rewritten the statute", and abandoned its earlier view that statutory claims were not appropriate subjects for arbitration. See Mitsubishi Motors v. Soler Chrysler–Plymouth, Inc., 473 U.S. 614, 646–651, 105 S.Ct. 3346, 3363–3367, 87 L.Ed.2d 444 (1985) (STEVENS, J., dissenting). Although I remain persuaded that it erred in doing so, the Court has also put to one side any concern about the inequality of bargaining power between an entire industry, on the one hand, and an individual customer or employee, on the other. See ante, at 1655–1656. Until today, however, the Court has not read § 2 of the FAA as broadly encompassing disputes arising out of the employment relationship. I believe this additional extension of the FAA is erroneous. Accordingly, I respectfully dissent.

* * *

Questions

1.   What does the *Gilmer* opinion have to say about how a court should determine which statutory claims are amenable to arbitration? How does the Court address the plaintiff's argument that the Age Discrimination Act embodies important policies that should be determined by a public tribunal?

2.   Why might an employee prefer to litigate rather than arbitrate an age discrimination claim?

3.   Does the Court's opinion in *Gilmer* mean that employees of brokerage firms who have Title VII claims must submit those claims to arbitration? A study by the General Accounting Office found that in 1992, 89 per cent of the arbitrators serving on stock exchange arbitration panels were white males over the age of 60. How might that fact affect a female employee's confidence in the fairness of arbitration if she had a sexual harassment complaint to bring? Would the GAO study be relevant to the court's analysis of whether the claim was amenable to arbitration? Should it?

4.   Are there special concerns about the use of arbitration in the employment area that should lead the Court to impose stricter scrutiny on the bargaining process that led the parties to conclude an arbitration agree-

ment? Should a court also impose a stricter scrutiny on the arbitration procedures when employment claims are asserted?

5. Does the *Gilmer* court impose a set of minimal due process norms on arbitration? If so, what are they? Should an award that results from an arbitration proceeding that does not contain the Gilmer procedures be vacated by a court?

* * *

4. ARBITRATION UNDER THE LABOR MANAGEMENT RELATIONS ACT—AN ALTERNATIVE STATUTORY FRAMEWORK

Arbitration has been a prominent feature of American collective bargaining agreements since World War II. At present, approximately 95 per cent of collective bargaining agreements contain grievance procedures that utilize in arbitration as the last step. Thus arbitration has become the primary method for interpreting and enforcing collective bargaining agreements in the United States.

Labor arbitration pursuant to a collective bargaining agreement is governed by a federal labor statute—Section 301(a) of the Labor Management Relations Act.[1] Ironically, Section 301, which was enacted in 1947, does not mention arbitration at all. Rather, it creates jurisdiction in federal courts to enforce collective bargaining agreements. It was enacted to enable employers to enforce promises not to strike that were contained in collective bargaining agreements. Section 301 (a) says:

> "Suits for violation of contacts between an employer and a labor organization representing employees in an industry affecting commerce as defined in this Act, or between any such labor organizations, may be brought in any district court of the United States having jurisdiction of the parties, without respect to the amount in controversy or without regard to the citizenship of the parties." 29 U.S.C. § 185(a).

Despite its brevity, Section 301 has generated considerable judicial and scholarly attention. The bare words of the statute have served as a foundation upon which has been built an entire legal structure for regulating collective bargaining. Through a process of inventive judicial construction which began with the Supreme Court decision in *Textile Workers v. Lincoln Mills, infra,* 353 U.S. 448 (1957), Section 301 has generated a common law of labor relations centered on judicial support for labor arbitration.

Section 301 and the federal common law of labor arbitration defined the role of arbitration within the American collective bargaining system. In a series of cases interpreting Section 301, the Supreme Court has delineat-

---

1. The application of the FAA to collective bargaining agreements has recently become a subject of controversy. See, Pryner v. Tractor Supply Co., 109 F.3d 354, 154 LRRM (BNA) 2806 (7th Cir. 1997) (holding that collective bargaining agreements are governed by both the Federal Arbitration Act and Section 301). See also Textile Workers v. Lincoln Mills, 353 U.S. 448 (1957) (Frankfurter dissent).

ed a delicate relationship between the judicial system and private labor arbitration. These doctrines have been a major influence on the law of arbitration in other areas as well. Indeed, many of the expansive interpretations of the Federal Arbitration Act in the 1980s are based upon labor precedents from Section 301 cases in the 1950s and 1960s. Thus it is instructive to study the evolution of the legal doctrines under Section 301 both to understand the role of law in labor arbitration, and to understand the evolving law of arbitration in the nonlabor areas that are governed by the Federal Arbitration Act.

Textile Workers Union of America v. Lincoln Mills of Alabama

353 U.S. 448, 77 S.Ct. 912 (1957).

■ MR. JUSTICE DOUGLAS delivered the opinion of the Court.

Petitioner-union entered into a collective bargaining agreement in 1953 with respondent-employer, the agreement to run one year and from year to year thereafter, unless terminated on specified notices. The agreement provided that there would be no strikes or work stoppages and that grievances would be handled pursuant to a specified procedure. The last step in the grievance procedure—a step that could be taken by either party—was arbitration.

This controversy involves several grievances that concern work loads and work assignments. The grievances were processed through the various steps in the grievance procedure and were finally denied by the employer. The union requested arbitration, and the employer refused. Thereupon the union brought this suit in the District Court to compel arbitration.

The District Court concluded that it had jurisdiction and ordered the employer to comply with the grievance arbitration provisions of the collective bargaining agreement. The Court of Appeals reversed by a divided vote. 230 F.2d 81. It held that, although the District Court had jurisdiction to entertain the suit, the court had no authority founded either in federal or state law to grant the relief. The case is here on a petition for a writ of certiorari which we granted because of the importance of the problem and the contrariety of views in the courts. 352 U.S. 821, 77 S.Ct. 54, 1 L.Ed.2d 46.

The starting point of our inquiry is § 301 of the Labor Management Relations Act of 1947, 61 Stat. 156, 29 U.S.C. § 185, 29 U.S.C.A. § 185, which provides:

(a) "Suits for violation of contracts between an employer and a labor organization representing employees in an industry affecting commerce as defined in this chapter, or between any such labor organizations, may be brought in any district court of the United States having jurisdiction of the parties, without respect to the amount in controversy or without regard to the citizenship of the parties."

(b) "Any labor organization which represents employees in an industry affecting commerce as defined in this chapter and any employer whose activities affect commerce as defined in this chapter shall be bound by the acts of its agents. Any such labor organization may sue or be sued as an entity and in behalf of the employees whom it represents in the courts of the United States. Any money judgment against a labor organization in a district court of the United States shall be enforceable only against the organization as an entity and against its assets, and shall not be enforceable against any individual member or his assets."

There has been considerable litigation involving § 301 and courts have construed it differently. There is one view that § 301(a) merely gives federal district courts jurisdiction in controversies that involve labor organizations in industries affecting commerce, without regard to diversity of citizenship or the amount in controversy. Under that view § 301(a) would not be the source of substantive law; it would neither supply federal law to resolve these controversies nor turn the federal judges to state law for answers to the questions. Other courts—the overwhelming number of them—hold that § 301(a) is more than jurisdictional—that it authorizes federal courts to fashion a body of federal law for the enforcement of these collective bargaining agreements and includes within that federal law specific performance of promises to arbitrate grievances under collective bargaining agreements. Perhaps the leading decision representing that point of view is the one rendered by Judge Wyzanski in Textile Workers Union v. American Thread Co., 113 F.Supp. 137. That is our construction of § 301(a), which means that the agreement to arbitrate grievance disputes, contained in this collective bargaining agreement, should be specifically enforced.

From the face of the Act it is apparent that § 301(a) and § 301(b) supplement one another. Section 301(b) makes it possible for a labor organization, representing employees in an industry affecting commerce, to sue and be sued as an entity in the federal courts. Section 301(b) in other words provides the procedural remedy lacking at common law. Section 301(a) certainly does something more than that. Plainly, it supplies the basis upon which the federal district courts may take jurisdiction and apply the procedural rule of § 301(b). The question is whether § 301(a) is more than jurisdictional.

The legislative history of § 301 is somewhat cloudy and confusing. But there are a few shafts of light that illuminate our problem.

The bills, as they passed the House and the Senate, contained provisions which would have made the failure to abide by an agreement to arbitrate an unfair labor practice. S.Rep. No. 105, 80th Cong., 1st Sess., pp. 20–21, 23; H.R.Rep. No. 245, 80th Cong., 1st Sess., p. 21. This feature of the law was dropped in Conference. As the Conference Report stated, "Once parties have made a collective bargaining contract, the enforcement of that contract should be left to the usual processes of the law and not to the National Labor Relations Board." H.R.Conf.Rep. No. 510, 80th Cong., 1st Sess., p. 42.

Both the Senate and the House took pains to provide for "the usual processes of the law" by provisions which were the substantial equivalent of § 301(a) in its present form. Both the Senate Report and the House Report indicate a primary concern that unions as well as employees should be bound to collective bargaining contracts. But there was also a broader concern—a concern with a procedure for making such agreements enforceable in the courts by either party. At one point the Senate Report, supra, p. 15, states, "We feel that the aggrieved party should also have a right of action in the Federal courts. Such a policy is completely in accord with the purpose of the Wagner Act which the Supreme Court declared was 'to compel employers to bargain collectively with their employees to the end that an employment contract, binding on both parties, should be made....' "

Congress was also interested in promoting collective bargaining that ended with agreements not to strike. The Senate Report, supra, p. 16 states:

> "If unions can break agreements with relative impunity, then such agreements do not tend to stabilize industrial relations. The execution of an agreement does not by itself promote industrial peace. The chief advantage which an employer can reasonably expect from a collective labor agreement is assurance of uninterrupted operation during the term of the agreement. Without some effective method of assuring freedom from economic warfare for the term of the agreement, there is little reason why an employer would desire to sign such a contract.

> "Consequently, to encourage the making of agreements and to promote industrial peace through faithful performance by the parties, collective agreements affecting interstate commerce should be enforceable in the Federal courts. Our amendment would provide for suits by unions as legal entities and against unions as legal entities in the Federal courts in disputes affecting commerce."

Thus collective bargaining contracts were made "equally binding and enforceable on both parties." Id., p. 15. As stated in the House Report, supra, p. 6, the new provision "makes labor organizations equally responsible with employers for contract violations and provides for suit by either against the other in the United States district courts." ...

Plainly the agreement to arbitrate grievance disputes is the *quid pro quo* for an agreement not to strike. Viewed in this light, the legislation does more than confer jurisdiction in the federal courts over labor organizations. It expresses a federal policy that federal courts should enforce these agreements on behalf of or against labor organizations and that industrial peace can be best obtained only in that way.

To be sure, there is a great medley of ideas reflected in the hearings, reports, and debates on this Act. Yet, to repeat, the entire tenor of the history indicates that the agreement to arbitrate grievance disputes was considered as quid pro quo of a no-strike agreement. And when in the House the debate narrowed to the question whether § 301 was more than jurisdictional, it became abundantly clear that the purpose of the section was to provide the necessary legal remedies. Section 302 of the House bill, the substantial equivalent of the present § 301, was being described by Mr. Hartley, the sponsor of the bill in the House:

> Mr. Barden. Mr. Chairman, I take this time for the purpose of asking the Chairman a question, and in asking the question I want it understood that it is intended to make a part of the record that may hereafter be referred to as history of the legislation.
>
> It is my understanding that section 302, the section dealing with equal responsibility under collective bargaining contracts in strike actions and proceedings in district courts contemplates not only the ordinary lawsuits for damages but also such other remedial proceedings, both legal and equitable, as might be appropriate in the circumstances; in other words, proceedings could, for example, be brought by the employers, the labor organizations, or interested individual employees under the Declaratory Judgments Act in order to secure declarations from the Court of legal rights under the contract.
>
> Mr. Hartley. The interpretation the gentleman has just given of that section is absolutely correct. 93 Cong.Rec. 3656–3657.

It seems, therefore, clear to us that Congress adopted a policy which placed sanctions behind agreements to arbitrate grievance disputes,[6] by implication rejecting the common-law rule, discussed in Red Cross Line v. Atlantic Fruit Co., 264 U.S. 109, 44 S.Ct. 274, 68 L.Ed. 582, against enforcement of executory agreements to arbitrate. We would undercut the Act and defeat its policy if we read § 301 narrowly as only conferring jurisdiction over labor organizations.

The question then is, what is the substantive law to be applied in suits under § 301(a)? We conclude that the substantive law to apply in suits under § 301(a) is federal law, which the courts must fashion from the policy of our national labor laws. See Mendelsohn, Enforceability of Arbitration Agreements Under Taft–Hartley Section 301, 66 Yale L.J. 167. The Labor Management Relations Act expressly furnishes some substantive law. It points out what the parties may or may not do in certain situations. Other problems will lie in the penumbra of express statutory mandates. dates. Some will lack express statutory sanction but will be solved by looking at the policy of the legislation and fashioning a remedy that will effectuate that policy. The range of judicial inventiveness will be determined by the nature of the problem.... Federal interpretation of the federal law will govern, not state law.... But state law, if compatible with

---

6. Association of Westinghouse Salaried Employees v. Westinghouse Corp., 348 U.S. 437, 75 S.Ct. 489, 99 L.Ed. 510, is quite a different case. There the union sued to recover unpaid wages on behalf of some 4,000 employees. The basic question concerned the standing of the union to sue and recover on those individual employment contracts. The question here concerns the right of the union to enforce the agreement to arbitrate which it has made with the employer.

the purpose of § 301, may be resorted to in order to find the rule that will best effectuate the federal policy.... Any state law applied, however, will be absorbed as federal law and will not be an independent source of private rights.

It is not uncommon for federal courts to fashion federal law where federal rights are concerned. See Clearfield Trust Co. v. United States, 318 U.S. 363, 366—367 ... Congress has indicated by § 301(a) the purpose to follow that course here. There is no constitutional difficulty. Article III, § 2, extends the judicial power to cases "arising under . . . the Laws of the United States..." The power of Congress to regulate these labor-management controversies under the Commerce Clause is plain. Houston East & West Texas R. Co. v. United States, 234 U.S. 342, 34 S.Ct. 833, 58 L.Ed. 1341; National Labor Relations Board v. Jones & Laughlin Corp., 301 U.S. 1, 57 S.Ct. 615, 81 L.Ed. 893. A case or controversy arising under s 301(a) is, therefore, one within the purview of judicial power as defined in Article III. . . .

The judgment of the Court of Appeals is reversed and the cause is remanded to that court for proceedings in conformity with this opinion.

Reversed.

■ MR. JUSTICE BLACK took no part in the consideration or decision of this case.

■ MR. JUSTICE FRANKFURTER (dissenting).

The Court has avoided the difficult problems raised by § 301 of the Taft-Hartley Act, ... by attributing to the section an occult content. This plainly procedural section is transmuted into a mandate to the federal courts to fashion a whole body of substantive federal law appropriate for the complicated and touchy problems raised by collective bargaining. I have set forth in my opinion in Association of Westinghouse Salaried Employees v. Westinghouse Electric Corp. the detailed reasons why I believe that § 301 cannot be so construed, even if constitutional questions cannot be avoided. 348 U.S. 437. But the Court has a "clear" and contrary conclusion emerge from the "somewhat," to say the least, "cloudy and confusing legislative history." This is more than can be fairly asked even from the alchemy of construction. Since the Court relies on a few isolated statements in the legislative history which do not support its conclusion, however favorably read, I have deemed in necessary to set forth in an appendix the entire relevant legislative history of the Taft–Hartley Act and its predecessor, the Case Bill. This legislative history reinforces the natural meaning of the statute as an exclusively procedural provision, affording, that is, an accessible federal forum for suits on agreements between labor organizations and employers, but not enacting federal law for such suits. . . .

It should also be noted that whatever may be a union's ad hoc benefit in a particular case, the meaning of collective bargaining for labor does not remotely derive from reliance on the sanction of litigation in the courts. Restrictions made by legislation like the Clayton Act of 1914, ... and the Norris–LaGuardia Act of 1932, ... upon the use of familiar remedies theretofore available in the federal courts, reflected deep fears of the labor movement of the use of such remedies against labor. But a union, like any other combatant engaged in a particular fight, is ready to make an ally of an old enemy, and so we also find unions resorting to the otherwise much excoriated labor injunction. Such intermittent yielding to expediency does not change the fact that judicial intervention is ill-suited to the special characteristics of the arbitration process in labor disputes; nor are the conditions for its effective functioning thereby altered.

"The arbitration is an integral part of the system of self-government. And the system is designed to aid management in its quest for efficiency, to assist union leadership in its participation in the enterprise, and to secure justice for the employees. it is a means of making collective bargaining work and thus preserving private enterprise in a free government. When it works fairly well, it does not need the sanction of the law of contracts or the law of arbitration. It is only when the system breaks down completely that the courts' aid in these respects is invoked. But the courts cannot, by occasional sporadic decision, restore the parties' continuing relationship; and their intervention in such cases may seriously affect the going systems of self-government. When their autonomous system breaks down, might not the parties better be left to the usual methods for adjustment of labor disputes rather than to court actions on the contract or on the arbitration award?" Shulman, Reason, Contract, and Law in Labor Relations, 68 Harv.L.Rev. 999, 1024.

These reflections summarized the vast and extraordinarily successful experience of Dean Harry Shulman as labor arbitrator, especially as umpire under the collective-bargaining contract between the Ford Motor Co. and the UAW—CIO.... Arbitration agreements are for specific terms, generally much shorter than the time required for adjudication of a contested lawsuit through the available stages of trial and appeal. Renegotiation of agreements cannot await the outcome of such litigation; nor can the parties' continuing relation await it. Cases under § 301 will probably present unusual rather than representative situations. A "rule" derived from them is more likely to discombobulate than to compose. A "uniform corpus" cannot be expected to evolve, certainly not within a time to serve its assumed function....

Even on the Court's attribution to § 301 of a direction to the federal courts to fashion, out of bits and pieces elsewhere to be gathered, a federal common law of labor contracts, it still does not follow that Congress has enacted that an agreement to arbitrate industrial differences be specifically enforceable in the federal courts. On the contrary, the body of relevant federal law precludes such enforcement of arbitration clauses in collective-bargaining agreements.

Prior to 1925, the doctrine that executory agreements to arbitrate any kind of dispute would not be specifically enforced still held sway in the federal courts.... Legislation was deemed necessary to assure such power to the federal courts. In 1925, Congress passed the United States Arbitration Act, ... making executory agreements to arbitrate specifically enforce-able in the federal courts, but explicitly excluding "contracts of employ-ment" of workers engaged in interstate commerce from its scope. Naturally enough, I find rejection, though not explicit, of the availability of the Federal Arbitration Act to enforce arbitration clauses in collective-bargain-ing agreements in the silent treatment given that Act by the Court's opinion. If an Act that authorizes the federal courts to enforce arbitration provisions in contracts generally, but specifically denies authority to decree that remedy for "contracts of employment," were available, the Court would hardly spin such power out of the empty darkness of § 301. I would make this rejection explicit, recognizing that when Congress passed legisla-tion to enable arbitration agreements to be enforced by the federal courts, it saw fit to exclude this remedy with respect to labor contracts....

Even though the Court glaringly ignores the Arbitration Act, it does at least recognize the common-law rule against enforcement of executory agreements to arbitrate. It nevertheless enforces the arbitration clause in the collective-bargaining agreements in these cases. It does so because it finds that Congress "by implication" rejected the common-law rule. I would add that the Court, in thus deriving power from the unrevealing words of the Taft–Hartley Act, has also found that Congress "by implication" repealed its own statutory exemption of collective-bargaining agreements in the Arbitration Act, an exemption made as we have seen for well-defined reasons of policy.

... [T]he rule that is departed from "by implication" had not only been "judicially formulated" but had purposefully been congressionally formulated in the Arbitration Act of 1925. And it is being departed from on the tenuous basis of the legislative history of § 301, for which the utmost that can be claimed is that insofar as there was any expectation at all, it was only that conventional remedies, including equitable remedies, would be available. But of course, as we have seen, "equitable remedies" in the federal courts had traditionally excluded specific performance of arbitration clauses, except as explicitly provided by the 1925 Act. Thus, even assuming that § 301 contains directions for some federal substantive law of labor contracts, I see no justification for translating the vague expectation concerning the remedies to be applied into an overruling of previous federal common law and, more particularly, into the repeal of the previous congres-sional exemption of collective-bargaining agreements from the class of agreements in which arbitration clauses were to be enforced.

The second ground of my dissent from the Court's action is more fundamental. Since I do not agree with the Court's conclusion that federal substantive law is to govern in actions under § 301, I am forced to consider the serious constitutional question that was adumbrated in the Westing-house case, 348 U.S. at 449–452, the constitutionality of a grant of jurisdiction to federal courts over contracts that came into being entirely by virtue of state substantive law, a jurisdiction not based on diversity of citizenship, yet one in which a federal court would, as in diversity cases, act in effect merely as another court of the State in which it sits. The scope of allowable federal judicial power that this grant must satisfy is constitutionally described as "Cases, in Law and Equity, arising under this Constitution, the Laws of the United States, and Treaties made, or which shall be made, under their Authority." Art. III, § 2....

Almost without exception, decisions under the general statutory grants have tested jurisdiction in terms of the presence, as an integral part of plaintiff's cause of action, of an issue calling for interpretation or application of federal law.... Although it has sometimes been suggested that the "cause of action" must derive from federal law, ... it has been found sufficient that some aspect of federal law is essential to plaintiff's success.... The litigation-provoking problem has been the degree to which federal law must be in the forefront of the case and not collateral, peripheral or remote...

To be sure, the full scope of a substantive regulation is frequently in dispute and must await authoritative determination by courts. Congress declares its purpose imperfectly or partially, and compatible judicial construction completes it. But in this case we start with a provision that is wholly jurisdictional and as such bristles with constitutional problems under Article III. To avoid them, interpolation of substantive regulation has been proposed. From what materials are we to draw a determination that § 301 is something other than what it declares itself? Is the Court justified in creating all the difficult problems of choice within a sphere of delicate policy without any direction from Congress and merely for the sake of giving effect to a provision that seems to deal with a different subject? . . .

Assuming, however, that we would be justified in pouring substantive content into a merely procedural vehicle, what elements of federal law could reasonably be put into the provisions of § 301? The suggestion that the section permits the federal courts to work out, without more, a federal code governing collective-bargaining contracts must, for reasons that have already been stated, be rejected. Likewise the suggestion that § 301 may be viewed as a congressional authorization to the federal courts to work out a concept of the nature of the collective-bargaining contract, leaving detailed questions of interpretation to state law....

Nor will Congress' objective be furthered by an attempt to limit the grant of a federal forum to certain types of actions between unions and employers. It would be difficult to find any basis for, or principles of, selection, either in the terms of § 301 or in considerations relevant to promotion of stability in labor relations. It is true that a fair reading of § 301 in the context of its enactment shows that the suit that Congress primarily contemplated was the suit against a union for strike in violation of contract. From this it might be possible to imply a federal right to bring an action for damages based on such an event. In the interest of mutuality, so close to the heart of Congress, we might in turn find a federal right in the union to sue for a lockout in violation of contract. But neither federal right would be involved in the present cases. Moreover, it bears repetition that Congress chose not to make this the basis of federal law, i.e., it chose not to make such conduct an unfair labor practice. . . .

In the wise distribution of governmental powers, this Court cannot do what a President sometimes does in returning a bill to Congress. We cannot return this provision to Congress and respectfully request that body to face the responsibility placed upon it by the Constitution to define the jurisdiction of the lower courts with some particularity and not to leave these courts at large. Confronted as I am, I regretfully have no choice. For all the reasons elaborated in this dissent, even reading into § 301 the limited federal rights consistent with the purposes of that section, I am impelled to the view that it is unconstitutional in cases such as the present ones where it provides the sole basis for exercise of jurisdiction by the federal courts.

[The concurring opinion of Mr. Justice Burton, with which Mr. Justice Harlan joins, has been omitted.]

* * *

Questions

1. Why was this case brought under Section 301 of the Labor Management Relations Act rather than under the FAA?

2. Why does Justice Douglas emphasize that Section 301 is not merely procedural? What constitutional problem would be posed if it were merely procedural?

3. Justice Douglas ultimately concludes that Section 301 is substantive. What is the substance that he finds in the provision? From what source does he derive it? How does he use the substance he attributes to the statute to decide the narrow question in the case? What is the specific issue in the case?

4. What does Justice Douglas mean by his statement that no-strike clauses and arbitration promises stand in a *quid pro quo* relationship to each other? Is this an empirical claim that the clauses are in fact negotiated and found together in collective bargaining agreements? If so, does he give any evidence for that? What kind of evidence might be relevant to support such a claim? Alternatively, is Douglas' assertion of a *quid pro quo* relationship between arbitration and a no-strike promise a logical claim, i.e., a claim that if there is one clause in a collective bargaining agreement, the other must also be present? Does the opinion provide any reasoning to support such a logical linkage? Or does Douglas mean there is some relationship between the two clauses other than an empirical or logical link? If so, what does he mean by his statement that there is a *quid pro quo* relationship between arbitration and a no-strike promise?

5. What is Justice Frankfurter's view about the constitutionality of Section 301?

6.   When he was Professor Frankfurter, a law professor at Harvard Law School, Justice Frankfurter drafted the Norris–LaGuardia Act. That statute withdraws the power of a federal court to issue an injunction in a labor dispute except under narrowly defined circumstances not present in the *Lincoln Mills* case. Is Frankfurter's dissent herein based solely on his view that the Norris–LaGuardia Act prohibits an injunctive decree in a labor dispute, or does he have another ground for his objection? What is Justice Frankfurter's view on the power of courts to grant specific performance to promises to arbitrate?

7.   What evidence is there that Congress intended, when it enacted Section 301, to create a federal common law of collective bargaining agreements? Does not the simple language of Section 301(a) suggest otherwise? The decision in *Lincoln Mills* has been criticized as an extreme and illegitimate instance of judicial law-making? Is judicial law-making justified in this case? Is it ever justified?

* * *

Note on *Local 174, Teamsters v. Lucas Flour Company*

In LOCAL 174, TEAMSTERS, CHAUFFEURS, WAREHOUSEMEN & HELPERS OF AMERICA v. LUCAS FLOUR COMPANY, 369 U.S. 95 (1962), the company and union had a collective bargaining agreement that called for arbitration of "any difference as to the true interpretation of this agreement." It further provided that "during such arbitration, there shall be no suspension of work." The contract also stated that "[t]he Employer reserves the right to discharge any man in his employ if his work is not satisfactory."

In May, 1958, the company fired an employee for unsatisfactory work after the employee damaged a fork-lift truck. The union called a strike to protest the discharge, and the strike lasted eight days. After the strike ended, the union submitted the issue of the employee's dismissal to arbitration. Five months later, the arbitration board ruled in favor of the employer. In the meantime, the employer brought an action against the union in state court seeking damages caused by the strike. The state court applied state law and awarded damages to the employer. While the union had not violated any express term of the no-strike clause, the state court stated, "the strike was a violation of the collective bargaining contract, because it was an attempt to coerce the employer to forego his contractual right to discharge an employee for unsatisfactory work." The Supreme Court granted certiorari on two issues: Should the state court apply state or federal law, and was the union in violation of its collective bargaining agreement?

The Court first held that the state court erred in applying state law to a Section 301 case. It said, "The dimensions of § 301 require the conclusion that substantive principles of federal labor law must be paramount in the area covered by the statute. Comprehensiveness is inherent in the process by which the law is to be formulated under the mandate of Lincoln Mills, requiring issues raised in suits of a kind covered by § 301 to be decided according to the precepts of federal labor policy.

"More important, the subject matter of § 301(a) 'is peculiarly one that calls for uniform law.' ... The possibility that individual contract terms might have different meanings under state and federal law would inevitably exert a disruptive influence upon both the negotiation and administration of collective agreements. Because neither party could be certain of the rights which it had obtained or conceded, the process of negotiating an agreement would be made immeasurably more difficult by the necessity of trying to formulate contract provisions in such a way as to contain the same meaning under two or more systems of law which might someday be invoked in enforcing the contract. Once the collective bargain was made, the possibility of conflicting substantive interpretation under competing legal systems would tend to stimulate and prolong disputes as to its interpretation. Indeed, the existence of possibly conflicting legal concepts might substantially impede the parties' willingness to agree to contract terms providing for final arbitral or judicial resolution of disputes.

"The importance of the area which would be affected by separate systems of substantive law makes the need for a single body of federal law particularly compelling. The ordering and adjusting of competing interests through a process of free and voluntary collective bargaining is the keystone of the federal scheme to promote industrial peace. State law which frustrates the effort of Congress to stimulate the smooth functioning of that process thus strikes at the very core of federal labor policy. With due regard to the many factors which bear upon competing state and federal interests in this area ... we cannot but conclude that in enacting § 301 Congress intended doctrines of federal labor law uniformly to prevail over inconsistent local rules."

Having determined that federal law applied, the Court applied the evolving federal law of Section 301 to decide the ultimate issue in the case—whether the union violated the agreement. The union argued that there was no violation of the collective bargaining agreement because there was not a no-strike clause in the contract that explicitly pertained to the strike. The Court disagreed:

"The collective bargaining contract expressly imposed upon both parties the duty of submitting the dispute in question to final and binding arbitration. In a consistent course of decisions the Courts of Appeals of at least five Federal Circuits have held that a strike to settle a dispute which a collective bargaining agreement provides shall be settled exclusively and finally by compulsory arbitration constitutes a violation of the agreement.... We approve that doctrine. To hold otherwise would obviously do violence to accepted principles of traditional contract law. Even more in point, a contrary view would be completely at odds with the basic policy of national labor legislation to promote the arbitral process as a substitute for economic warfare....

"What has been said is not to suggest that a no-strike agreement is to be implied beyond the area which it has been agreed will be exclusively covered by compulsory terminal arbitration. Nor is it to suggest that there may not arise problems in specific cases as to whether compulsory and binding arbitration has been agreed upon, and, if so, as to what disputes have been made arbitrable. But no such problems are present in this case. The grievance over which the union struck was, as it concedes, one which it had expressly agreed to settle by submission to final and binding arbitration proceedings. The strike which it called was a violation of that contractual obligation."

JUSTICE BLACK, in a strongly worded dissent, accused the majority of rewriting the contract between the parties. He said:

"The Court now finds—out of clear air, so far as I can see—that the union, without saying so in the agreement, not only agreed to arbitrate such differences, but also promised that there would be no strike while arbitration of a dispute was pending under this provision. And on the basis of its 'discovery' of this additional unwritten promise by the union, the Court upholds a judgment awarding the company substantial damages for a strike in breach of contract...."

Justice Black also questioned what principles of "traditional contract law" the Court referred to when it so disregarded the parties express contractual language. "I had supposed, however—though evidently the Court thinks otherwise—that the job of courts enforcing contracts was to give legal effect to what the contracting parties actually agree to do, not to what courts think they ought to do. In any case, I have been unable to find any accepted principle of contract law—traditional or otherwise—that permits courts to change completely the nature of a contract by adding new promises that the parties themselves refused to make in order that the new court-made contract might better fit into whatever social, economic, or legal policies the courts believe to be so important that they should have been taken out of the realm of voluntary contract by the legislative body and furthered by compulsory legislation."

* * *

Questions

1. How does the relationship between state and federal law in the *Lucas Flour* case compare to the relationship set out in *Volt v. Board of Trustees?*

2. Justice Black accuses the majority of departing from ordinary notions of contractual consent by implying a no-strike clause where none exists. What doctrines of "traditional contract law" was the majority referring to? Is Justice Black correct—has the court rewritten the agreement between the parties, or has it merely interpreted the agreement?

3. Can parties counteract the impact of *Lucas Flour* by expressly stating, in their collective agreement, that even though there is an arbitration provision, there is no obligation of the union to refrain from striking in

certain specified situations, such as in disputes concerning imminent threat to safety? After *Lucas Flour*, will courts enforce those private agreements? If so, does *Lucas Flour* really signify a court disregarding the parties' intent, or is it a rule of construction that applies when the parties are silent as to their intent?

4.   After *Lucas Flour*, courts can imply a no-strike clause into a collective agreement that has an applicable arbitration clause. However, courts do not imply an arbitration clause where there is an applicable no-strike clause. What do you think accounts for this difference in treatment? Is this a departure from the notion that the two clauses are mirror images of each other as the *quid pro quo* language of *Lincoln Mills* would suggest?

* * *

United Steelworkers of America v. American Manufacturing Co.

363 U.S. 564, 80 S.Ct. 1343 (1960).

■ Opinion of the Court by MR. JUSTICE DOUGLAS, announced by MR. JUSTICE BRENNAN.

This suit was brought by petitioner union in the District Court to compel arbitration of a "grievance" that petitioner, acting for one Sparks, a union member, had filed with the respondent, Sparks' employer. The employer defended on the ground (1) that Sparks is estopped from making his claim because he had a few days previously settled a workmen's compensation claim against the company on the basis that he was permanently partially disabled, (2) that Sparks is not physically able to do the work, and (3) that this type of dispute is not arbitrable under the collective bargaining agreement in question.

The agreement provided that during its term there would be "no strike," unless the employer refused to abide by a decision of the arbitrator. The agreement sets out a detailed grievance procedure with a provision for arbitration (regarded as the standard form) of all disputes between the parties "as to the meaning, interpretation and application of the provisions of this agreement."[1]

---

1.   The relevant arbitration provisions read as follows: "Any disputes, misunderstandings, differences or grievances arising between the parties as to the meaning, interpretation and application of the provisions of this agreement, which are not adjusted as herein provided, may be submitted to the Board of Arbitration for decision....

"The arbitrator may interpret this agreement and apply it to the particular case under consideration but shall, however, have no authority to add to, subtract from, or modify the terms of the agreement. Disputes relating to discharges or such matters as might involve a loss of pay for employees may carry an award of back pay in whole or in part as may be determined by the Board of Arbitration.

"The decision of the Board of Arbitration shall be final and conclusively binding upon both parties, and the parties agree to observe and abide by same...."

The agreement reserves to the management power to suspend or discharge any employee "for cause." It also contains a provision that the employer will employ and promote employees on the principle of seniority "where ability and efficiency are equal." Sparks left his work due to an injury and while off work brought an action for compensation benefits. The case was settled, Sparks' physician expressing the opinion that the injury had made him 25% "permanently partially disabled." That was on September 9. Two weeks later the union filed a grievance which charged that Sparks was entitled to return to his job by virtue of the seniority provision of the collective bargaining agreement. Respondent refused to arbitrate and this action was brought. The District Court held that Sparks, having accepted the settlement on the basis of permanent partial disability, was estopped to claim any seniority or employment rights and granted the motion for summary judgment. The Court of Appeals affirmed, 264 F.2d 624, for different reasons. After reviewing the evidence it held that the grievance is "a frivolous, patently baseless one, not subject to arbitration under the collective bargaining agreement." Id., at page 628. The case is here on a writ of certiorari, 361 U.S. 881.

Section 203(d) of the Labor Management Relations Act, 1947, 61 Stat. 154, 29 U.S.C. § 173(d), 29 U.S.C.A. § 173(d), states, "Final adjustment by a method agreed upon by the parties is hereby declared to be the desirable method for settlement of grievance disputes arising over the application or interpretation of an existing collective-bargaining agreement...." That policy can be effectuated only if the means chosen by the parties for settlement of their differences under a collective bargaining agreement is given full play.

A state decision that held to the contrary announced a principle that could only have a crippling effect on grievance arbitration. The case was International Ass'n of Machinists v. Cutler–Hammer, Inc., 271 App.Div. 917, 67 N.Y.S.2d 317, affirmed 297 N.Y., 519, 74 N.E.2d 464. It held that "If the meaning of the provision of the contract sought to be arbitrated is beyond dispute, there cannot be anything to arbitrate and the contract cannot be said to provide for arbitration." 271 App.Div. at page 918, 67 N.Y.S.2d, at 318. The lower courts in the instant case had a like preoccupation with ordinary contract law. The collective agreement requires arbitration of claims that courts might be unwilling to entertain. In the context of the plant or industry the grievance may assume proportions of which judges are ignorant. Yet, the agreement is to submit all grievances to arbitration, not merely those that a court may deem to be meritorious. There is no exception in the "no strike" clause and none therefore should be read into the grievance clause, since one is the *quid pro quo* for the other. The question is not whether in the mind of the court there is equity in the claim. Arbitration is a stabilizing influence only as it serves as a vehicle for handling any and all disputes that arise under the agreement.

The collective agreement calls for the submission of grievances in the categories which it describes, irrespective of whether a court may deem them to be meritorious. In our role of developing a meaningful body of law to govern the interpretation and enforcement of collective bargaining agreements, we think special heed should be given to the context in which collective bargaining agreements are negotiated and the purpose which they are intended to serve. See Lewis v. Benedict Coal Corp., 361 U.S. 459, 468, 80 S.Ct. 489, 495, 4 L.Ed.2d 442. The function of the court is very limited when the parties have agreed to submit all questions of contract interpretation to the arbitrator. It is confined to ascertaining whether the party seeking arbitration is making a claim which on its face is governed by the contract. Whether the moving party is right or wrong is a question of contract interpretation for the arbitrator. In these circumstances the moving party should not be deprived of the arbitrator's judgment, when it was his judgment and all that it connotes that was bargained for.

The courts, therefore, have no business weighing the merits of the grievance, considering whether there is equity in a particular claim, or determining whether there is particular language in the written instrument which will support the claim. The agreement is to submit all grievances to arbitration, not merely those which the court will deem meritorious. The processing of even frivolous claims may have therapeutic values of which those who are not a part of the plant environment may be quite unaware.

The union claimed in this case that the company had violated a specific provision of the contract. The company took the position that it had not violated that clause. There was, therefore, a dispute between the parties as to "the meaning, interpretation and application" of the collective bargaining agreement. Arbitration should have been ordered. When the judiciary undertakes to determine the merits of a grievance under the guise of interpreting the grievance procedure of collective bargaining agreements, it usurps a function which under that regime is entrusted to the arbitration tribunal.

Reversed.

■ MR. JUSTICE FRANKFURTER concurs in the result

■ MR. JUSTICE WHITTAKER, believing that the District Court lacked jurisdiction to determine the merits of the claim which the parties had validly agreed to submit to the exclusive jurisdiction of a Board of Arbitrators (Textile Workers v. Lincoln Mills, 353 U.S. 448) concurs in the result of this opinion.

* * *

Questions

1. Does the Court in *American Manufacturing* decide that an employer must arbitrate any grievance a union wants to arbitrate, no matter how frivolous? Suppose an employee filed a grievance claiming that she is entitled to overtime pay for a certain day, and it turns out, on investigation, that the employee did not work at all on that day because she was away on vacation. Should the employer be forced to arbitrate her claim?

Are there costs in requiring an employer to arbitrate all frivolous cases? What is the countervailing benefit, if any?

2.   What are the reasons Justice Douglas advances for holding that all cases, even frivolous ones, must be arbitrated? Could he have interpreted the parties agreement in this case to mean that they agree to arbitrate all *reasonable* grievances? Would the latter approach change the role of arbitration in the collective bargaining system?

3.   According to Justice Douglas, what is the role of a court when presented with a petition to compel arbitration? Is it to simply rubber stamp the petition as "granted?" Or must the court engage in some sort of review?

4.   Why does the Court impliedly limit arbitration to claims that on their face are covered by an arbitration clause? Why not hold that all disputes must be arbitrated?

5.   Can courts rule on the issue of arbitrability without considering the merits of a dispute? Even with the light once-over look that Douglas calls for, are courts required to make some initial foray into the merits of the dispute? Could the court have formulated a test for arbitrability that avoids this result?

* * *

United Steelworkers of America v. Warrior and Gulf Navigation Co.

363 U.S. 574, 80 S.Ct. 1347 (1960).

■ Opinion of the Court by MR. JUSTICE DOUGLAS, announced by MR. JUSTICE BRENNAN.

Respondent transports steel and steel products by barge and maintains a terminal at Chickasaw, Alabama, where it performs maintenance and repair work on its barges. The employees at that terminal constitute a bargaining unit covered by a collective bargaining agreement negotiated by petitioner union. Respondent between 1956 and 1958 laid off some employees, reducing the bargaining unit from 42 to 23 men. This reduction was due in part to respondent contracting maintenance work, previously done by its employees, to other companies. The latter used respondent's supervisors to lay out the work and hired some of the laid-off employees of respondent (at reduced wages). Some were in fact assigned to work on respondent's barges. A number of employees signed a grievance which petitioner presented to respondent, the grievance reading:

"We are hereby protesting the Company's actions, of arbitrarily and unreasonably contracting out work to other concerns, that could and previously has been performed by Company employees.

"This practice becomes unreasonable, unjust and discriminatory in lieu (sic) of the fact that at present there are a number of employees that have been laid off for about 1 and 1/2 years or more for allegedly lack of work.

"Confronted with these facts we charge that the Company is in violation of the contract by inducing a partial lock-out, of a number of the employees who would otherwise be working were it not for this unfair practice."

The collective agreement had both a "no strike" and a "no lockout" provision. It also had a grievance procedure which provided in relevant part as follows:

"Issues which conflict with any Federal statute in its application as established by Court procedure or matters which are strictly a function of management shall not be subject to arbitration under this section.

"Should differences arise between the Company and the Union or its members employed by the Company as to the meaning and application of the provisions of this Agreement, or should any local trouble of any kind arise, there shall be no suspension of work on account of such differences but an earnest effort shall be made to settle such differences immediately in the following manner:

"A. For Maintenance Employees:

"First, between the aggrieved employees, and the Foreman involved;

"Second, between a member or members of the Grievance Committee designated by the Union, and the Foreman and Master Mechanic. . . .

"Fifth, if agreement has not been reached the matter shall be referred to an impartial umpire for decision. The parties shall meet to decide on an umpire acceptable to both. If no agreement on selection of an umpire is reached, the parties shall jointly petition the United States Conciliation Service for suggestion of a list of umpires from which selection shall be made. The decision of the umpire will be final."

Settlement of this grievance was not had and respondent refused arbitration. This suit was then commenced by the union to compel it.

The District Court granted respondent's motion to dismiss the complaint. 168 F.Supp. 702. It held after hearing evidence, much of which went to the merits of the grievance, that the agreement did not "confide in an arbitrator the right to review the defendant's business judgment in contracting out work." Id., at 705. It further held that "the contracting out of repair and maintenance work, as well as construction work, is strictly a function of management not limited in any respect by the labor agreement involved here." Ibid. The Court of Appeals affirmed by a divided vote, 269 F.2d 633, the majority holding that the collective agreement had withdrawn from the grievance procedure "matters which are strictly a function of management" and that contracting out fell in that exception. The case is here on a writ of certiorari. 361 U.S. 912.

We held in Textile Workers v. Lincoln Mills, 353 U.S. 448, that a grievance arbitration provision in a collective agreement could be enforced by reason of § 301(a) of the Labor Management Relations Act and that the policy to be applied in enforcing this type of arbitration was that reflected in our national labor laws.... The present federal policy is to promote industrial stabilization through the collective bargaining agreement.... A major factor in achieving industrial peace is the inclusion of a provision for arbitration of grievances in the collective bargaining agreement.[4]

Thus the run of arbitration cases, illustrated by Wilko v. Swan, 346 U.S. 427, becomes irrelevant to our problem. There the choice is between the adjudication of cases or controversies in courts with established procedures or even special statutory safeguards on the one hand and the settlement of them in the more informal arbitration tribunal on the other. In the commercial case, arbitration is the substitute for litigation. Here arbitration is the substitute for industrial strife. Since arbitration of labor disputes has quite different functions from arbitration under an ordinary commercial agreement, the hostility evinced by courts toward arbitration of commercial agreements has no place here. For arbitration of labor disputes under collective bargaining agreements is part and parcel of the collective bargaining process itself.

The collective bargaining agreement states the rights and duties of the parties. It is more than a contract; it is a generalized code to govern a myriad of cases which the draftsmen cannot wholly anticipate.... The collective agreement covers the whole employment relationship. It calls into being a new common law—the common law of a particular industry or of a particular plant. As one observer has put it:[6]

" . . . (I)t is not unqualifiedly true that a collective-bargaining agreement is simply a document by which the union and employees have imposed upon management limited, express restrictions of its otherwise absolute right to manage the enterprise, so that an employee's claim must fail unless he can point to a specific contract provision upon which the claim is founded,. There are too many people, too many problems, too many unforeseeable contingencies to make the words of the contract the exclusive source of rights and duties. One cannot reduce all the rules governing a community like an industrial plant to fifteen or even fifty pages. Within the sphere of collective bargaining, the institutional characteristics and the governmental nature of the collective-bargaining process demand a common law of the shop which implements and furnishes the context of the agreement. We must assume that intelligent negotiators acknowledged so plain a need unless they stated a contrary rule in plain words."

A collective bargaining agreement is an effort to erect a system of industrial self-government. When most parties enter into contractual relationship they do so voluntarily, in the sense that there is no real compul-

---

4. Complete effectuation of the federal policy is achieved when the agreement contains both an arbitration provision for all unresolved grievances and an absolute prohibition of strikes, the arbitration agreement being the "quid pro quo" for the agreement not to strike. Textile Workers v. Lincoln Mills, 353 U.S. 448, 455, 77 S.Ct. 912, 917.

6. Cox, Reflections Upon Labor Arbitration, 72 Harv.L.Rev. 1482, 1498–1499 (1959).

sion to deal with one another, as opposed to dealing with other parties. This is not true of the labor agreement. The choice is generally not between entering or refusing to enter into a relationship, for that in all probability pre-exists the negotiations. Rather it is between having that relationship governed by an agreed-upon rule of law or leaving each and every matter subject to a temporary resolution dependent solely upon the relative strength, at any given moment, of the contending forces. The mature labor agreement may attempt to regulate all aspects of the complicated relationship, from the most crucial to the most minute over an extended period of time. Because of the compulsion to reach agreement and the breadth of the matters covered, as well as the need for a fairly concise and readable instrument, the product of negotiations (the written document) is, in the words of the late Dean Shulman, "a compilation of diverse provisions: some provide objective criteria almost automatically applicable; some provide more or less specific standards which require reason and judgment in their application; and some do little more than leave problems to future consideration with an expression of hope and good faith." Shulman, supra, at 1005. Gaps may be left to be filled in by reference to the practices of the particular industry and of the various shops covered by the agreement. Many of the specific practices which underlie the agreement may be unknown, except in hazy form, even to the negotiators. Courts and arbitration in the context of most commercial contracts are resorted to because there has been a breakdown in the working relationship of the parties; such resort is the unwanted exception. But the grievance machinery under a collective bargaining agreement is at the very heart of the system of industrial self-government. Arbitration is the means of solving the unforeseeable by molding a system of private law for all the problems which may arise and to provide for their solution in a way which will generally accord with the variant needs and desires of the parties. The processing of disputes through the grievance machinery is actually a vehicle by which meaning and content are given to the collective bargaining agreement.

Apart from matters that the parties specifically exclude, all of the questions on which the parties disagree must therefore come within the scope of the grievance and arbitration provisions of the collective agreement. The grievance procedure is, in other words, a part of the continuous collective bargaining process. It, rather than a strike, is the terminal point of a disagreement.

The labor arbitrator performs functions which are not normal to the courts; the considerations which help him fashion judgments may indeed by foreign to the competence of courts.

"A proper conception of the arbitrator's function is basic. He is not a public tribunal imposed upon the parties by superior authority which the parties are obliged to accept. He has no general charter to administer justice for a community which transcends the parties. He is rather part of a system of self-government created by and confined to the parties. . . . " Shulman, supra, at 1016.

The labor arbitrator's source of law is not confined to the express provisions of the contract, as the industrial common law—the practices of the industry and the shop—is equally a part of the collective bargaining agreement although not expressed in it. The labor arbitrator is usually chosen because of the parties' confidence in his knowledge of the common law of the shop and their trust in his personal judgment to bring to bear considerations which are not expressed in the contract as criteria for judgment. The parties expect that his judgment of a particular grievance will reflect not only what the contract says but, insofar as the collective bargaining agreement permits, such factors as the effect upon productivity of a particular result, its consequence to the morale of the shop, his judgment whether tensions will be heightened or diminished. For the parties' objective in using the arbitration process is primarily to further their common goal of uninterrupted production under the agreement, to make the agreement serve their specialized needs. The ablest judge cannot be expected to bring the same experience and competence to bear upon the determination of a grievance, because he cannot be similarly informed.

The Congress, however, has by § 301 of the Labor Management Relations Act, assigned the courts the duty of determining whether the reluctant party has breached his promise to arbitrate. For arbitration is a matter of contract and a party cannot be required to submit to arbitration any dispute which he has not agreed so to submit. Yet, to be consistent with congressional policy in favor of settlement of disputes by the parties through the machinery of arbitration, the judicial inquiry under § 301 must be strictly confined to the question whether the reluctant party did agree to arbitrate the grievance or did agree to give the arbitrator power to make the award he made. An order to arbitrate the particular grievance should not be denied unless it may be said with positive assurance that the arbitration clause is not susceptible of an interpretation that covers the asserted dispute. Doubts should be resolved in favor of coverage.

We do not agree with the lower courts that contracting-out grievances were necessarily excepted from the grievance procedure of this agreement. To be sure, the agreement provides that "matters which are strictly a function of management shall not be subject to arbitration." But it goes on to say that if "differences" arise or if "any local trouble of any kind" arises, the grievance procedure shall be applicable.

Collective bargaining agreements regulate or restrict the exercise of management functions; they do not oust management from the performance of them. Management hires and fires, pays and promotes, supervises and plans. All these are part of its function, and absent a collective bargaining agreement, it may be exercised freely except as limited by public law and by the willingness of employees to work under the particular, unilaterally imposed conditions. A collective bargaining agreement may treat only with certain specific practices, leaving the rest to management but subject to the possibility of work stoppages. When, however, an absolute no-strike clause is included in the agreement, then in a very real sense everything that management does is subject to the agreement, for either management is prohibited or limited in the action it takes, or if not, it is protected from interference by strikes. This comprehensive reach of the collective bargaining agreement does not mean, however, that the language, "strictly a function of management," has no meaning.

"Strictly a function of management" might be thought to refer to any practice of management in which, under particular circumstances prescribed by the agreement, it is permitted to indulge. But if courts, in order to determine arbitrability, were allowed to determine what is permitted and what is not, the arbitration clause would be swallowed up by the exception. Every grievance in a sense involves a claim that management has violated some provision of the agreement.

Accordingly, "strictly a function of management" must be interpreted as referring only to that over which the contract gives management complete control and unfettered discretion. Respondent claims that the contracting out of work falls within this category. Contracting out work is the basis of many grievances; and that type of claim is grist in the mills of the arbitrators. A specific collective bargaining agreement may exclude contracting out from the grievance procedure. Or a written collateral agreement may make clear that contracting out was not a matter for arbitration. In such a case a grievance based solely on contracting out would not be arbitrable. Here, however, there is no such provision. Nor is there any showing that the parties designed the phrase "strictly a function of management" to encompass any and all forms of contracting out. In the absence of any express provision excluding a particular grievance from arbitration, we think only the most forceful evidence of a purpose to exclude the claim from arbitration can prevail, particularly where, as here, the exclusion clause is vague and the arbitration clause quite broad. Since any attempt by a court to infer such a purpose necessarily comprehends the merits, the court should view with suspicion an attempt to persuade it to become entangled in the construction of the substantive provisions of a labor agreement, even through the back door of interpreting the arbitration clause, when the alternative is to utilize the services of an arbitrator.

The grievance alleged that the contracting out was a violation of the collective bargaining agreement. There was, therefore, a dispute "as to the meaning and application of the provisions of this Agreement" which the parties had agreed would be determined by arbitration.

The judiciary sits in these cases to bring into operation an arbitral process which substitutes a regime of peaceful settlement for the older regime of industrial conflict. Whether contracting out in the present case violated the agreement is the question. It is a question for the arbiter, not for the courts.

Reversed.

■ MR. JUSTICE FRANKFURTER concurs in the result.

■ MR. JUSTICE BLACK took no part in consideration or decision of this case.

■ MR. JUSTICE WHITTAKER, dissenting.

Until today, I have understood it to be the unquestioned law, as this Court has consistently held, that arbitrators are private judges chosen by the parties to decide particular matters specifically submitted; that the contract under which matters are submitted to arbitrators is at once the source and limit of their authority and power; and that their power to decide issues with finality, thus ousting the normal functions of the courts, must rest upon a clear, definitive agreement of the parties, as such powers can never be implied. United States v. Moorman, 338 U.S. 457, 462 ... I believe that the Court today departs from the established principles announced in these decisions.

Here, the employer operates a shop for the normal maintenance of its barges, but it is not equipped to make major repairs, and accordingly the employer has, from the beginning of its operations more than 19 years ago, contracted out its major repair work. During most, if not all, of this time the union has represented the employees in that unit. The District Court found that "[t]hroughout the successive labor agreements between these parties, including the present one, . . . (the union) has unsuccessfully sought to negotiate changes in the labor contracts, and particularly during the negotiation of the present labor agreement, . . . which would have limited the right of the [employer] to continue the practice of contracting out such work." 168 F.Supp. 702, 704–705.

The labor agreement involved here provides for arbitration of disputes respecting the interpretation and application of the agreement and, arguably, also some other things. But the first paragraph of the arbitration section says: "[M]atters which are strictly a function of management shall not be subject to arbitration under this section." Although acquiescing for 19 years in the employer's interpretation that contracting out work was "strictly a function of management," and having repeatedly tried—particularly in the negotiation of the agreement involved here—but unsuccessfully, to induce the employer to agree to a covenant that would prohibit it from contracting out work, the union, after having agreed to and signed the contract involved, presented a "grievance" on the ground that the employer's contracting out work, at a time when some employees in the unit were laid off for lack of work, constituted a partial "lockout" of employees in violation of the antilockout provision of the agreement.

Being unable to persuade the employer to agree to cease contracting out work or to agree to arbitrate the "grievance," the union brought this action in the District Court, under § 301 of the Labor Management Relations Act, 29 U.S.C. § 185, 29 U.S.C.A. § 185, for a decree compelling the employer to submit the "grievance" to arbitration. The District Court, holding that the contracting out of work was, and over a long course of dealings had been interpreted and understood by the parties to be, "strictly a function of management," and was therefore specifically excluded from arbitration by the terms of the contract, denied the relief prayed, 168 F.Supp. 702. The Court of Appeals affirmed, 269 F.2d 633, and we granted certiorari. 361 U.S. 912, 80 S.Ct. 255, 4 L.Ed.2d 183.

The Court now reverses the judgment of the Court of Appeals. It holds that the arbitrator's source of law is "not confined to the express provisions of the contract," that arbitration should be ordered "unless it may be said with positive assurance that the arbitration clause is not susceptible of an interpretation that covers the asserted dispute," that "[d]oubts [of arbitrability] should be resolved in favor of coverage," and that when, as here, "an absolute no-strike clause is included in the agreement, then . . . everything that management does is subject to [arbitration]." I understand the Court thus to hold that the arbitrators are not confined to the express provisions of the contract, that arbitration is to be ordered unless it may be said with positive assurance that arbitration of a particular dispute is excluded by the contract, that doubts of arbitrability are to be resolved in favor of arbitration, and that when, as here, the contract contains a no-strike clause, everything that management does is subject to arbitration.

This is an entirely new and strange doctrine to me. I suggest, with deference, that it departs from both the contract of the parties and the controlling decisions of this Court. I find nothing in the contract that purports to confer upon arbitrators any such general breadth of private judicial power. The Court cites no legislative or judicial authority that creates for or gives to arbitrators such broad general powers. And I respectfully submit that today's decision cannot be squared with the statement of Judge, later Mr. Justice, Cardozo in Marchant that "No one is under a duty to resort to these conventional tribunals, however helpful their processes, *except to the extent that he has signified his willingness. Our own favor or disfavor of the cause of arbitration is not to count as a factor in the appraisal of the thought of others.*" (emphasis added), 252 N.Y., at 299, 169 N.E., at 391; nor with his statement in that case that "(t)he question is one of intention, to be ascertained by the same tests that are applied to contracts generally," id.; nor with this Court's statement in Moorman, "that the intention of the parties to submit their contractual disputes to final determination outside the courts *should be made manifest by plain language*" (emphasis added), 338 U.S., at 462, 70 S.Ct. at page 291; nor with this Court's statement in Hensey that: "To make such (an arbitrator's) certificate conclusive *requires plain language in the contract. It is not to be implied.*" (Emphasis added.) 205 U.S., at page 309, 27 S.Ct. at page 539. "A party is never required to submit to arbitration any question which he has not agreed so to submit, and *contracts providing for arbitration will be carefully construed in order not to force a party to submit to arbitration a question which he did not intend to be submitted.*" (Emphasis added.) Fernandez & Hnos. v. Rickert Rice Mills, supra, 1 Cir., 119 F.2d at page 815.

With respect, I submit that there is nothing in the contract here to indicate that the employer "signified [its] willingness" (Marchant, supra, 252 N.Y. at page 299, 169 N.E. at page 391) to submit to arbitrators whether it must cease contracting out work. Certainly no such intention is "made manifest by plain language" (Moorman, supra, 338 U.S. at page 462, 70 S.Ct. at page 291), as the law "requires," because such consent "is not to be implied." Hensey, supra, 205 U.S. at page 309, 27 S.Ct. at page 539.

To the contrary, the parties by their conduct over many years interpreted the contracting out of major repair work to be "strictly a function of management," and if, as the concurring opinion suggests, the words of the contract can "be understood only by reference to the background which gave rise to their inclusion," then the interpretation given by the parties over 19 years to the phrase "matters which are strictly a function of management" should logically have some significance here. By their contract, the parties agreed that "matters which are strictly a function of management shall not be subject to arbitration." The union over the course of many years repeatedly tried to induce the employer to agree to a covenant prohibiting the contracting out of work, but was never successful. The union again made such an effort in negotiating the very contract involved here, and, failing of success, signed the contract, knowing, of course, that it did not contain any such covenant, but that, to the contrary, it contained, just as had the former contracts, a covenant that "matters which are strictly a function of management shall not be subject to arbitration." Does not this show that, instead of signifying a willingness to submit to arbitration the matter of whether the employer might continue to contract out work, the parties fairly agreed to exclude at least that matter from arbitration? Surely it cannot be said that the parties agreed to such a submission by any "plain language." Moorman, supra, 338 U.S. at page 462, 70 S.Ct. at 291, and Hensey, supra, 205 U.S. at page 309, 27 S.Ct. at 539. Does not then the Court's opinion compel the employer "to submit to arbitration [a] question which (it) has not agreed so to submit"? Fernandez & Hnos., supra, 119 F.2d at 815.

Surely the question whether a particular subject or class of subjects is or is not made arbitrable by a contract is a judicial question, and if, as the concurring opinion suggests, "the court may conclude that [the contract] commits to arbitration any [subject or class of subjects]." it may likewise conclude that the contract does not commit such subject or class of subjects to arbitration, and "[w]ith that finding the court will have exhausted its function" no more nor less by denying arbitration than by ordering it. Here the District Court found, and the Court of Appeals approved its finding, that by the terms of the contract, as interpreted by the parties over 19 years, the contracting out of work was "strictly a function of management" and "not subject to arbitration." That finding, I think, should be accepted here. Acceptance of it requires affirmance of the judgment....

* * *

Questions

1. Consider the following hypothetical:

    A collective bargaining agreement contains a provision stating that disputes over safety issues are subject to arbitration but disputes over job assignments are not. The agreement also states that in the event of a safety dispute, an employee is entitled to refuse to perform unsafe work if an expedited grievance is filed. One day an employee named

Fletcher is given an assignment that she claims is dangerous. She refuses to perform and instead files a grievance seeking to arbitrate. The employer claims that it is not arbitrable because it is a job assignment dispute, and disciplines Fletcher for refusing the assignment. The union grieves the discipline action and the employer refuses to arbitrate. The union brings suit to compel arbitration.

How should the court rule?

2.   Suppose the employer, in the previous hypothetical, has evidence that shows that Fletcher fabricated her safety concerns in order to obtain arbitration of the job assignment. Would that alter the outcome under the *Warrior and Gulf* court's analysis? What would Justice Whittaker say about the relevance and admissibility of the employer's evidence? What would the majority say?

3.   It is often said that the decision in *Warrior and Gulf* creates a presumption of arbitrability for cases arising under Section 301 of the Labor Management Relations Act. In what sense is it a presumption? Is it a conclusive presumption? How can a party challenging arbitrability overcome the presumption? What reasons does the Court give for creating such a presumption?

* * *

CHAPTER SIX

ARBITRATION II: DEFENSES TO ARBITRATION

The decision to utilize arbitration rather than litigation to resolve a dispute is a practical question that can have enormous strategic and tactical consequences for the parties. The issue can arise at two points in time—at the time that a contract is drafted, or during the course of performance, after a dispute has arisen. Even if parties have inserted an arbitration clause into their initial agreement, it is not uncommon for one side to attempt to resist arbitration at the time the dispute arises.

When the prospect of arbitration arises in the context of an actual dispute, parties often bring different considerations to bear on the issue than they did at the contract-drafting stage. Whether it is in a party's interest to utilize arbitration rather than litigation depends upon many factors, such as the nature of the dispute, the nature of the arbitral tribunal, the types of procedures utilized in the procedure, the method of selecting the arbitrators, and the types of remedies sought. Many of these factors were not present at the time the contract was drafted. In addition, by the time there is a dispute requiring resolution, the parties usually perceive themselves as being in an adversarial rather than cooperative relationship with each other, i.e., a relationship in which one party's gain will be the other party's loss. The zero-sum framework applies not only to the anticipated outcome of the dispute, it also applies to the issue of whether or not to utilize arbitration. That is, when one side wants to arbitrate a dispute, the other side usually does not. The party seeking to utilize arbitration does so because it believes it will obtain a strategic or practical advantage in the arbitral forum. But in the looking glass logic of litigation, where one party sees its interest to lie, the other party sees its interest to avoid. Thus parties who might have agreed to arbitration clauses at the time of contract drafting often find themselves seeking to avoid arbitration at the time of disputing.

On some occasions, a party's resistance to arbitration is well grounded. A party may fear that the particular makeup of the arbitral panel or the method of selection will yield an arbitrator who will be unsympathetic to its position. Or, the party may want to raise certain legal claims or defenses that it believes an arbitrator will not adequately understand or weigh in the determination. Or, the party resisting arbitration may want the discovery tools or remedy powers available only in a court. Thus there are many reasons why a party might seek to avoid arbitration.

This chapter explores the question, under what circumstances can a party avoid an arbitration clause under the Federal Arbitration Act? Section 2 of the Federal Arbitration Act states that:

> A written provision in any maritime transaction or a contract evidencing a transaction involving commerce to settle by arbitration a controversy arising thereafter arising out of such contract or transaction, or the refusal to perform the whole or any part thereof, or an agreement in writing to submit to arbitration an existing controversy arising out of such a contract, transaction, or refusal, shall be valid, irrevocable and enforceable, *save upon such grounds as exist at law or in equity for the revocation of any contract.* (Emphasis supplied).

According to this provision, a party can resist arbitration if it can effectively assert a defense that would constitute grounds at law or in equity for the revocation of any contract. As we saw in Chapter 5, a court will look to state law to govern such a defense. See, e.g. *Volt v. Board of Trustees*, supra. However, we also saw that to succeed, a state law defense to arbitration must be a matter of general state law, not state law specific to arbitration. See *Perry v. Thomas*, supra.

Defenses to arbitration are raised in two contexts. First, if one party to a dispute brings an action in court on its claim, the opponent can move for a stay of the judicial proceedings under Section 3 of the FAA on the ground that the dispute is subject to arbitration. Section 3 states:

> If any suit or proceeding be brought in any of the courts of the United States upon any issue referable to arbitration under an agreement in writing for such arbitration, the court in which the suit is pending, upon being satisfied that the issue involved in such suit or proceeding is referable to arbitration under such an agreement, *shall on application of one of the parties stay the trial of the action until such arbitration has been had in accordance with the terms of the agreement* . . . (Emphasis supplied).

If there is a written arbitration clause that comes under the FAA, the plaintiff that originally brought the action in court has the burden of showing why the arbitration clause should not be enforced.

Alternately, a party seeking arbitration can bring a petition under Section 4 of the FAA for a motion to compel its opponent to arbitrate. Section 4 provides that:

> A party aggrieved by the alleged failure, neglect, or refusal of another to arbitrate under a written agreement for arbitration may petition any United States district court . . . for an order directing that such arbitration proceed in the manner provided for in such agreement. . . . The court shall hear the parties, and upon being satisfied that the making of the agreement for arbitration or the failure to comply therewith is not in issue, *the court shall make an order directing the parties to proceed to arbitration* in accordance with the terms of the agreement. (Emphasis supplied).

In such case, the party resisting arbitration must assert a valid defense.

Whether a defense to arbitration is raised by a plaintiff in response to a defendant's motion under § 3 to stay litigation, or by a defendant in response to a plaintiff's § 4 petition to compel arbitration, the principles that a court will apply are the same. The following cases demonstrate how courts treat the most common defenses to arbitration.

1.   ARBITRABILITY

Country Mutual Insurance Company v. Kosmos

116 Ill.App.3d 914, 452 N.E.2d 547 (Ill. Appl. 1 Dist. 1983).

■ ROMITI, PRESIDING JUSTICE:

The sole issue in this case is whether an insurer can be forced to arbitrate an uninsured motorist claim even where it is clear as a matter of law from the pleadings that there is no coverage. We hold there is no duty to arbitrate under such circumstances and reverse the trial court which ordered arbitration.

Plaintiff Country Mutual Insurance Company filed this action to obtain a declaration that there was no insurance coverage and no duty to arbitrate. In its complaint the insurer alleged that the insured, after suffering an accident, made a claim and demanded arbitration. When interviewed the insured stated that the accident occurred when as a result of swerving to avoid another motor vehicle his car left the roadway and collided with a light pole. The insurer thereupon denied coverage since there was no contact with another motor vehicle.

The insured has never denied that there was no contact, either in the trial court or on appeal.

As required by statute, the automobile liability policy issued by Country Mutual to defendant provided uninsured motorist coverage including accidents caused by hit and run vehicles. (Ill.Rev.Stat.1979, ch. 73, par. 755a.) It is well established in Illinois that a provision, statutory or otherwise, limiting coverage to accidents caused by hit and run vehicles affords coverage only where the hit and run vehicle makes contact with the insured or his vehicle. Finch v. Central National Insurance Group of Omaha (1974), 59 Ill.2d 123.

The insurance policy does provide for arbitration but only where the parties disagree over whether the insured is "legally entitled to recover damages from the owner or operator of an uninsured motor vehicle" or the amount of such damages. Under this provision only questions of negligence and damages can be submitted to the arbitrator. (Flood v. Country Mutual Insurance Co. (1968), 41 Ill.2d 91, 242 N.E.2d 149.) Questions of law or fact concerning coverage cannot, under this clause, be submitted to arbitration. (Flood; Liberty Mutual Fire Insurance Co. v. Loring (1968), 91 Ill.App.2d 372, 235 N.E.2d 418.) Thus the question whether there was contact is not arbitrable under this clause but is decided by the trial court in a declaratory judgment action. (Loring.) "[I]f no contact; no hit-and-run automobile. If no uninsured motorist; no right to arbitration * * *." Cruger v. Allstate Insurance Co. (Fla.App.1964), 162 So.2d 690, 693...

The insured contends that this limitation on the right to arbitration is invalid in light of the 1978 amendment to the statute providing in part:

> "No such policy shall be renewed or delivered or issued for delivery in this State after July 1, 1978 unless it is provided therein that any dispute with respect to such coverage shall be submitted for arbitration to the American Arbitration Association or for determination in the following manner: Upon the insured requesting arbitration, each party to the dispute shall select an arbitrator and the two arbitrators so named shall select a third arbitrator. If such arbitrators are not selected within 45 days from such request, either party may request that such arbitration be submitted to the American Arbitration Association." (Ill.Rev.Stat.1979, ch. 73, par. 755a.)

If, in fact, the policy provision is in conflict with the statute then of course the statute is controlling.... If not, then the parties are bound by the policy provisions.

The language "disputes with respect to such coverage" is ambiguous. It is not clear whether it refers to issues of the existence of coverage or merely disputes arising under the policy provision where coverage is established. Accordingly, it would be appropriate to look at the construction of the legislature when enacting the bill.... But the legislative debates, as cited by the insurer (80th Illinois General Assembly, Third Reading of Senate Bill 1041, May 23, 1977, pp. 46–47), indicate that the statute was enacted solely to curb delays in arbitration and not to extend the scope of arbitration.

However we need not resolve that question because in this case no bona fide dispute has been raised by the pleadings. As already noted, the insurer alleged that there was no contact and the insured has not alleged that there was contact. Yet absent an allegation of physical contact with the unidentified driver, the insured's claim is insufficient and must be dismissed. (Finch v. Central National Insurance Group of Omaha (1974), 59 Ill.2d 123, 319 N.E.2d 468.) To allow an arbitrator to rule for an insured despite the clearly established absence of coverage would be to give the arbitrator unconstitutional powers to decide questions solely of law..., and to overrule the Illinois Supreme Court, something even this court cannot do.

Accordingly, the judgment of the trial court is reversed and judgment entered for the plaintiff.

■ JOHNSON and JIGANTI, JJ., concur.

* * *

Questions

1. Why do you think the insurance company in this case seeks to avoid arbitration where the facts seem to favor its position so clearly?

2. The court finds that there is "clearly established absence of coverage." Is this so clear? Is the question "solely a matter of law" as the court suggests? Is the court using its power to determine questions of law or fact concerning the scope of coverage to pre-screen the insured's claim?

3. Should there be a general requirement for pleadings in arbitration to set out the factual basis for a legal claim? If not, how would arbitrability be determined under the standard of the Illinois Court of Appeals?

4. How is the court interpreting the 1978 amendment to the state statute? Can there be arbitration "with respect to such coverage" without an arbitrator considering the scope of coverage? What, in the court's view, is left for an arbitrator to decide concerning coverage? Why does the court believe it should not permit an arbitrator to decide the scope of coverage?

5. Note that the court says it would be unconstitutional to submit questions of law to the arbitrator. *Country Mutual Insurance* was decided in 1983, the same year as *Southland* and two years before *Mitsubishi Motors,* which were studied in the last chapter. Do you think the court would take the same position today?

* * *

John V. Bowmer v. Dorothy B. Bowmer

50 N.Y.2d 288, 406 N.E.2d 760 (1980).

■ FUCHSBERG, JUDGE.

Confronting in this case the increasingly common use of arbitration in the context of a dispute between former spouses, we hold that a separation agreement's broadly worded arbitration clause, which additionally draws attention to matters specifically made arbitrable elsewhere in the agreement, does not confer authority upon the arbitrator to pass on the husband's claim that changed circumstances warranted a downward modification of the agreement's support provisions.

After nearly 17 years of marriage, in April of 1972 John and Dorothy Bowmer entered into a lengthy and detailed separation agreement which, as later incorporated but not merged in a judgment of divorce, provided for the husband's payment of alimony and support for their three minor children pursuant to a carefully arranged formula. Its arbitration clause, numbered paragraph 17, reads in pertinent part: "Any claim, dispute or misunderstanding arising out of or in connection with this Agreement, or any breach hereof, or any default in payment by the Husband, or any matter herein made the subject matter of arbitration, shall be arbitrated".

As the clause suggests, at various points the agreement delineated certain matters that were expressly made arbitrable, including adjustments in the support formula (upon the stated contingencies that the tax laws were amended to make support payments taxable to the husband and that the Government's cost of living index was discontinued or its method of publication altered) and in the extent of the husband's obligation to underwrite college costs should the parties disagree over the husband's ability to meet them.

The present dispute had its genesis in July, 1977, when Bowmer informed his former wife that, because of changed circumstances, as of February, 1978 he would reduce his support payments by almost $1,000 per month and make no further tuition payments.[1] She refused to accede to this plan or to his alternative informal request that they submit the question to arbitration. Thereafter, when he nevertheless unilaterally undertook to make these downward adjustments, Ms. Bowmer invoked the arbitration clause to compel him to pay the arrearages. Her former husband then commenced this proceeding to stay the arbitration she had commenced and to compel arbitration on the issues of whether he was entitled to downward modification of his monetary obligations consistent with the steps he had taken. Contemporaneously, Bowmer filed his own demand for arbitration on these and a third issue.[2] She, in turn, cross-moved to stay the arbitration he had initiated, contending that, except for the question of his deferment of the children's educational expenses, the issues he raised were nonarbitrable.[3] In due course, Special Term consolidated both arbitration proceedings, denied her motion and directed that arbitration proceed on the issues Bowmer had raised.

But, on Ms. Bowmer's appeal from so much of the order that directed arbitration on the issue of reduction in the level of support payments, the Appellate Division modified, holding that issue to be nonarbitrable (67 A.D.2d 8, 10, 414 N.Y.S.2d 340). On the former husband's appeal to us, therefore, the sole question is whether the arbitrator may properly consider the claim for downward modification on the support obligations. For the reasons which follow, we conclude he may not and, therefore, we now affirm the order from which this appeal arises.

Arbitration clauses are by now familiar provisos in separation agreements. Indeed, aside from expressing the parties' preference for a means of dispute resolution more informal, more expedient and possibly less costly than litigation (Matter of Siegel [Lewis], 40 N.Y.2d 687, 689, 389 N.Y.S.2d 800, 358 N.E.2d 484), an arbitration provision may well have been intended to furnish insulation from the potential for notoriety and other stresses that so often accompanies the airing of marital disputes in court (see Matter of Lasek v. Lasek, 13 A.D.2d 242, 244, 215 N.Y.S.2d 983). Moreover,

---

1. Petitioner asserted that it was no longer economically feasible for him to meet the support obligations in the agreement because his second wife was no longer employed and because, with all three children in college, the additional payments for educational expenses had grown to $12,000 per year.

2. In his demand, Bowmer also sought to direct the sale of the marital abode, reading the agreement as permitting his former spouse to reside there only while the children, then attending college away from home, lived there on a full-time basis. Although Ms.

Bowmer unsuccessfully contested the arbitrability of this issue below, it was not appealed to the Appellate Division.

3. The separation agreement specifically provided: "If the Husband is of the opinion that he cannot afford to pay for the (college) education of a particular Child, and if the Wife does not agree with his alleged inability to do so, she shall have the right to have the matter arbitrated, pursuant to Article '17' of this Agreement".

resort to the arbitral forum may afford the spouses an opportunity to have their grievances heard by someone who they think may be especially well qualified in matrimonial matters.

But as with such provisions in the commercial context generally, the rule is clear that unless the agreement to arbitrate expressly and unequivocally encompasses the subject matter of the particular dispute, a party cannot be compelled to forego the right to seek judicial relief and instead submit to arbitration.... Examining the clause in paragraph 17 with this precept in mind, we first observe the standard, broadly framed directive to submit to arbitration "Any claim, dispute or misunderstanding arising out of or in connection with" the agreement.... However, there is more. As indicated earlier, the clause goes on to state that elsewhere in the agreement particular matters, apparently of special import to the spouses, are expressly made arbitrable. Paragraph 17 therefore seems to be something of a hybrid, containing wording ordinarily present in both broad and limited arbitration clauses; hence, we should not reflexively attribute to the parties an intention to have every possible dispute go to arbitration....

For, though the parties might well have thought that the particularized matters were subsumed under the general arbitration language—in which case they could be understood as merely intending to emphasize the arbitrability of certain disputes—the inclusion perhaps more reasonably suggests that the spouses viewed the general language somewhat qualifiedly. This accords with the rule of construction that, in such cases, the specific provisions tend to restrict the general (see 4 Williston, Contracts (3d ed.), § 624, pp. 822–825). Thus, rather than place reliance on a single boilerplate proviso, the parties were careful to direct explicitly that arbitration be the remedy for several critical and foreseeable conflicts on the extent of the husband's support obligation.

Further evidence that the arbitration clause was not intended to encompass the dispute here comes from the fact that the support provisions themselves were particularly detailed and drawn flexibly to anticipate changes in the spouses' circumstances. Exemplifying this is the agreement's design for a sliding scale of support payments equivalent to 50% of the husband's gross income, but in no event less than $14,000 or more than $30,000, less an amount equivalent to one half of the wife's gross income over $9,000. "Gross income" was itself meticulously defined and made to reflect, at least in part, the financial condition of the parties: for instance, depending on whether Bowmer's gross income was below or above $50,000 he was either to include or exclude from that figure payments from his employer's profit-sharing plan. On top of all this, of course, the cost of living index guaranteed a broader kind of responsiveness to economic variations.

The sense of these provisions, taken together, is to indicate that the parties gave their attention to the possibility of changed circumstances and tried to address the problem by injecting elasticity into the support formula itself. Given this and the fact that the husband's obligation to pay for the costs of his children's college education was expressly made modifiable under changed circumstances and specifically made the subject of arbitration, it is significant that neither the modification nor arbitrability of the more fundamental support obligation is addressed by any term of the 37–page separation agreement.

The omission becomes especially important in light of the inability of courts to effect any change in an adequate level of support fixed by a valid and unimpeached separation agreement unless it has been merged in a judgment of divorce. . . . Of course, had they so intended, the parties could have agreed that the support provisions be modifiable by judicial proceedings under appropriate circumstances. . . . But they did not. And, although the power to alter the support provisions in a separation agreement may likewise be conferred upon an arbitrator . . ., the cases so holding have involved contracts explicitly authorizing such relief (see Braverman v. Braverman, 9 Misc.2d 661, 168 N.Y.S.2d 348, supra; Storch v. Storch, 38 A.D.2d 904, 329 N.Y.S.2d 474). Against this background—the frame of reference of the drafters of this detailed and comprehensive document—appellant's claim that a downward modification of support "arises out of or in connection with" the terms of the agreement is hardly persuasive.

More fundamentally, what appellant seeks, in essence, is to have the arbitrator rewrite the terms of the agreement because he now views them as onerous. This cannot be considered merely a claim arising from the contract. Instead, it requires the making of a new contract, not by the parties, but by the arbitrator. Obviously, the parties never agreed to such a procedure for it would mean that, once the agreement made provision for arbitration, the arbitrator would be completely unfettered by the terms of the contract in resolving disputes. Nor is our refusal to place the power to change the support provisions within the scope of the arbitration clause to be considered an impermissible attempt to precensor the type of relief available to the arbitrator. While, as a general rule, once a controversy is properly before the arbitrator he has wide discretion in his choice of remedies . . ., the power to formulate flexible solutions cannot be used as a bootstrap for an unpredictable expansion of the parameters of arbitral authority (cf. Garrity v. Lyle Stuart, Inc., 40 N.Y.2d 354).

Appellant insists that our decision in Matter of SCM Corp. (Fisher Park Lane Co.), 40 N.Y.2d 788, sanctions such an arbitral rewriting. However, the rationale of that case was considerably more limited. There, though holding that a landlord's counterclaim for reformation was time-barred, we took the occasion to state that the arbitrator, acting pursuant to a broad arbitration clause, could permissibly reform the terms of a lease on the landlord's assertion that the instrument failed to conform to the parties' original intent (40 N.Y.2d, supra, at pp. 792-794). Reformation of a contract to express what the parties in fact agreed upon has been held to be a claim which arises out of the contract, in contradistinction to modification of contract terms to reflect changed circumstances, a claim of a fundamentally different nature, which finds no basis at all in the agreement. . . . Pointedly, appellant nowhere suggests that by reason of accident, mistake or fraud the agreement failed to express the real intentions of the contracting parties...; he seeks instead to create a wholly new contract.

... Accordingly, the order of the Appellate Division should be affirmed.

■ GABRIELLI, JUDGE (dissenting).

I am impelled to dissent, for I cannot concur in the misapplication of previously well-settled principles of law to this rather simple case. The dispositive issue presented by this appeal is whether a separation agreement requiring arbitration of "(a)ny claim, dispute or misunderstanding arising out of or in connection with" the agreement authorizes arbitration of the husband's claim that his support obligations under the agreement should be modified because of a change in circumstances. Also implicated, because of the analysis employed by the majority of this court, is whether an arbitrator's power to grant certain requested relief may be challenged by an application to stay arbitration.

... It is beyond dispute that the parties to a separation agreement may agree to arbitrate disputes concerning the support provisions of that agreement (see Hirsch v. Hirsch, 37 N.Y.2d 312, 372 N.Y.S.2d 71, 333 N.E.2d 371). Hence, the only issue in this case is whether in fact the Bowmers have so agreed. As is noted above, the agreement provides for arbitration of "[a]ny claim, dispute or misunderstanding arising out of or in connection with" the separation agreement, it is difficult to conceive of a broader declaration of arbitrability. Appellant's claim, whether it be viewed as an attempt to modify the agreement or, more accurately, as a claim that the agreement itself impliedly contemplated modification of the support obligation by an arbitrator, certainly must fall within the purview of that wide-sweeping language. Hence, it appears evident that the instant dispute is arbitrable.

The majority, however, now concludes that this seemingly broad language does not truly mean what it says, but is instead limited in some inarticulable manner and to some uncertain extent. Unfortunately, there exists no support for such an interpretation in the language of the agreement. As noted above, the arbitration clause explicitly provides for arbitration of "(a)ny claim, dispute or misunderstanding arising out of or in connection with this Agreement, or any breach hereof, or any default in payment by the Husband, or any matter herein made the subject matter of arbitration". The majority suggests that the provision for the arbitration of "any claim, dispute or misunderstanding arising out of or in connection with" the agreement has no real application or meaning, and that the only controversies actually made arbitrable by the agreement are those involving "any breach hereof, or any default in payment by the Husband, or any matter herein made the subject matter of arbitration". To so hold is to simply read the opening words of the arbitration provision out of existence entirely, and that is something which a court may not do under the guise of contract interpretation. Had the parties desired to provide for arbitration of only those disputes mentioned in the latter phrases of the arbitration clause, there would have been no reason to include the broad opening words. However, that language was made an integral part of the agreement and should be given effect by the courts.

This judicial evisceration of an extremely broad arbitration provision portends a return to that outmoded and heavy-handed judicial scrutiny of arbitration agreements which I had thought this court had abandoned by its decision in Matter of Weinrott (Carp), 32 N.Y.2d 190, 344 N.Y.S.2d 848, 298 N.E.2d 42. Today's decision resurrects, in new guise, the so-called "specifically enumerated" approach to arbitration clauses which we explicitly rejected in Weinrott. The effect of this decision is to render meaningless the otherwise broad provisions of any arbitration agreement in which the parties, possibly from an excess of caution, have taken the care to specify those particular types of disputes which they feared might not be covered by the general language of the arbitration agreement. I cannot concur in such an approach. It serves no valid purpose where, as here, the intent of the parties is plainly to submit to arbitration all disputes "arising out of or in connection with" the separation agreement. Rather, it will merely encourage those who wish to delay final resolution of a dispute to turn to the courts in the hope of preventing the submission to arbitration of matters clearly intended to be determined in that forum.

No more persuasive is the majority's suggestion that the instant dispute is not arbitrable because appellant is attempting to have the arbitrator "rewrite" the agreement and not merely interpret it. Initially, I note that there exists no reason why two persons may not enter into an agreement authorizing an arbitrator to modify the terms of that agreement upon the application of one of the parties. Any objections to the concept of an arbitrator "rewriting" a contract for the parties stems not from some evil inherent in the idea itself, but rather from the more general doctrine that, at least in the area of consensual arbitration, a party may be bound by the decision of an arbitrator only to the extent that he has agreed to be bound. Normally, the parties to an agreement will not wish to confer upon an arbitrator the power to modify their agreement, and it is for that reason that the arbitrator will lack the power to "rewrite" the agreement. Such objections, however, pertain not to the arbitrability of a dispute, but rather to the power of the arbitrator to provide certain relief, and as such may only be raised by application to vacate an award, not by application to stay arbitration (compare CPLR 7503, with 7511; see Board of Educ. v. Barni, 49 N.Y.2d 311, 425 N.Y.S.2d 554, 401 N.E.2d 912).

That the instant application to stay involves no more than a premature contention that the arbitrator will exceed his power is shown by the fact that regardless of the outcome of this appeal, arbitration will proceed on the question of appellant's obligations under the contract. The only effect of this proceeding can be to limit the range of remedies which the arbitrator may employ in an attempt to resolve the dispute between the Bowmers. The expenditure of so much time and effort merely to inform an arbitrator in advance of arbitration that he may not grant certain requested relief is hardly consistent with the function of arbitration as an inexpensive and swift alternative forum. Moreover, it serves to take from the arbitrator the power to determine, at least in the first instance, the range of remedies authorized by the agreement, and creates yet another preliminary inquiry to be made by the courts before ordering arbitration.

Accordingly, I vote to reverse the order of the Appellate Division and reinstate the order of Supreme Court.

■ JASEN, JONES, WACHTLER and MEYER, JJ., concur with FUCHSBERG, J.

■ GABRIELLI, J., dissents and votes to reverse in a separate opinion in which COOKE, C. J., concurs.

* * *

Questions

1.   How does the majority reach its conclusion on the issue of arbitrability? Is the disagreement between the majority and the dissent a disagreement about how to interpret the contractual provision or a difference in attitude about arbitration?

2.   What would be wrong with permitting an arbitrator to rewrite an agreement in light of changed circumstances? In some situations, of which family law is a prime example, courts have the power to revise contracts in light of changed circumstances. If that were the case under New York's matrimonial law, should an arbitrator also have that power? Is there a difference between permitting a court to revise a contract and permitting an arbitrator to do so?

3.   Consider the following hypothetical:

A landowner, who owns a large apartment complex, of 1,000 units, gets into a dispute with a tenant. The lease, which is a standard lease that he uses for all his units, states:

Landlord will maintain premises and make reasonable repairs. If damage requiring repair is the result of Tenant's intentional act or negligence, Landlord has the right to bill Tenant for the cost of repairs, and if said bill is not paid promptly, Landlord may treat the repair bill as rent for purposes of remedies.

The lease also states:

Tenant will keep apartment in reasonable repair, and refrain from any activity that will cause undue damage or undue wear and tear.

All obligations concerning condition of the apartment are subject to arbitration.

Also under the lease, the tenant has the usual obligation to pay rent every month, and the obligations of tenant to pay rent are subject to state law, which gives landlord a right to evict after 10 days notice.

A dispute arises when the tenant's upstairs neighbor leaves his bathtub running and it overflows, dripping water through tenant's kitchen ceiling. The water gets into the tenant's light fixtures, causing the lights to short out. The tenant tries to get the landlord to repair the damage, but the landlord does not do so. After two weeks in which the tenant has no lights in her kitchen, she withholds rent, and sends the landlord a letter explaining that she will pay rent when her ceiling and kitchen light is repaired. The landlord sends her a notice that continued nonpayment of rent for 10 days will give him right to evict. After 10 days, he moves to evict in state court. The tenant makes a motion to stay the proceeding and compel arbitration. The state has an arbitration law identical to FAA.

How would you argue this case for the tenant? Would the approach of the majority or the dissent in *Bowmer* be more useful to cite in favor or your position? How should a court decide the issue?

* * *

Moses H. Cone Memorial Hospital v. Mercury Construction Corp.

460 U.S. 1, 103 S.Ct. 927 (1983).

■ JUSTICE BRENNAN delivered the opinion of the Court.

This case, commenced as a petition for an order to compel arbitration under § 4 of the United States Arbitration Act of 1925 (Arbitration Act or Act), 9 U.S.C. § 4, presents the question whether, in light of the policies of the Act and of our decisions in Colorado River Water Conservation District v. United States, 424 U.S. 800 (1976), and Will v. Calvert Fire Insurance Co., 437 U.S. 655 (1978), the District Court for the Middle District of North Carolina properly stayed this diversity action pending resolution of a concurrent state-court suit. The Court of Appeals for the Fourth Circuit reversed the stay. We granted certiorari.... We affirm.

I

Petitioner Moses H. Cone Memorial Hospital (Hospital) is located in Greensboro, North Carolina. Respondent Mercury Construction Corp. (Mercury), a construction contractor, has its principal place of business in Alabama. In July 1975, Mercury and the Hospital entered into a contract for the construction of additions to the Hospital building. The contract, drafted by representatives of the Hospital, included provisions for resolving disputes arising out of the contract or its breach. All disputes involving interpretation of the contract or performance of the construction work were to be referred in the first instance to J.N. Pease Associates (Architect), an independent architectural firm hired by the Hospital to design and oversee the construction project. With certain stated exceptions, any dispute decided by the Architect (or not decided by it within a stated time) could be submitted by either party to binding arbitration under a broad arbitration clause in the contract:

> "All claims, disputes and other matters in question arising out of, or relating to, this Contract or the breach thereof, ... shall be decided

by arbitration in accordance with the Construction Industry Arbitration Rules of the American Arbitration Association then obtaining unless the parties mutually agree otherwise. This agreement to arbitrate shall be specifically enforceable under the prevailing arbitration law. The award rendered by the arbitrators shall be final, and judgment may be entered upon it in accordance with applicable law in any court having jurisdiction thereof." App. 29–30.

The contract also specified the time limits for arbitration demands.

Construction on the project began in July 1975. Performance was to be completed by October 1979. In fact, construction was substantially completed in February 1979, and final inspections were made that June.

At a meeting in October 1977 (during construction), attended by representatives of Mercury, the Hospital, and the Architect, Mercury agreed, at the Architect's request, to withhold its claims for delay and impact costs (i.e., claims for extended overhead or increase in construction costs due to delay or inaction by the Hospital) until the work was substantially completed. On this record, the Hospital does not contest the existence of this agreement, although it asserts that the Architect lacked authority to agree to a delay in presentation of claims or to entertain claims after the contract work was completed.

In January 1980, Mercury submitted to the Architect its claims for delay and impact costs. Mercury and the Architect discussed the claims over several months, substantially reducing the amount of the claims. According to the Hospital, it first learned of the existence of Mercury's claims in April 1980; its lawyers assumed active participation in the claim procedure in May. The parties differ in their characterizations of the events of the next few months—whether there were "ongoing negotiations," or merely an "investigation" by the Hospital. In any event, it appears from the record that lawyers for the Hospital requested additional information concerning Mercury's claims. As a result, on August 12, 1980, Mercury gave a detailed presentation of its claims at a meeting attended by Mercury's representatives and lawyers, the Hospital's representatives and lawyers, and representatives of the Architect. Mercury agreed to send copies of its files to an expert hired by the Hospital, and the parties agreed to meet again on October 13.

On October 6, Mercury's counsel telephoned the Hospital's counsel to confirm that the scheduled meeting would go forward. The Hospital's counsel said he would call back the next day. When he did, he informed Mercury's counsel that the Hospital would pay nothing on Mercury's claim. He also said that the Hospital intended to file a declaratory judgment action in North Carolina state court.

True to its word, the Hospital filed an action on the morning of October 8 in the Superior Court of Guilford County, North Carolina, naming Mercury and the Architect as defendants. The complaint alleged that Mercury's claim was without factual or legal basis and that it was barred by the statute of limitations. It alleged that Mercury had lost any right to arbitration under the contract due to waiver, laches, estoppel, and failure to make a timely demand for arbitration. The complaint also alleged various delinquencies on the part of the Architect. As relief, the Hospital sought a declaration that there was no right to arbitration; a stay of arbitration; a declaration that the Hospital bore no liability to Mercury; and a declaration that if the Hospital should be found liable in any respect to Mercury, it would be entitled to indemnity from the Architect. The complaint was served on Mercury on October 9. On that same day, Mercury's counsel mailed a demand for arbitration.

On October 15, without notice to Mercury, the Hospital obtained an ex parte injunction from the state court forbidding Mercury to take any steps directed toward arbitration. Mercury objected, and the stay was dissolved on October 27. As soon as the stay was lifted, Mercury filed the present action in the District Court, seeking an order compelling arbitration under § 4 of the Arbitration Act, 9 U.S.C. § 4.[4] Jurisdiction was based on diversity of citizenship. On the Hospital's motion, the District Court stayed Mercury's federal-court suit pending resolution of the state-court suit because the two suits involved the identical issue of the arbitrability of Mercury's claims. . . .

Mercury sought review of the District Court's stay by both a notice of appeal and a petition for mandamus. A panel of the Court of Appeals for the Fourth Circuit heard argument in the case, but before the panel issued any decision, the Court informed the parties that it would consider the case en banc. After reargument, the en banc Court held that it had appellate jurisdiction over the case under 28 U.S.C. § 1291. It reversed the District Court's stay order and remanded the case to the District Court with instructions for entry of an order to arbitrate.

[The District Court's stay] was plainly erroneous in view of Congress's clear intent, in the Arbitration Act, to move the parties to an arbitrable dispute out of court and into arbitration as quickly and easily as possible. The Act provides two parallel devices for enforcing an arbitration agreement: a stay of litigation in any case raising a dispute referable to arbitration, 9 U.S.C. § 3, and an affirmative order to engage in arbitration, § 4. Both of these sections call for an expeditious and summary hearing, with only restricted inquiry into factual issues. Assuming that the state court would have granted prompt relief to Mercury under the Act, there still would have been an inevitable delay as a result of the District Court's stay. The stay thus frustrated the statutory policy of rapid and unobstructed enforcement of arbitration agreements.

. . . [T]he basic issue presented in Mercury's federal suit was the arbitrability of the dispute between Mercury and the Hospital. Federal law in the terms of the Arbitration Act governs that issue in either state or federal court. Section 2 is the primary substantive provision of the Act,

---

4. Simultaneously, Mercury filed a petition for removal of the Hospital's state-court action. The District Court remanded the removed case on the ground that, because the Hospital and the Architect are both North Carolina corporations, there was no complete diversity. The propriety of the removal or remand is not before this Court.

declaring that a written agreement to arbitrate "in any maritime transaction or a contract evidencing a transaction involving commerce ... shall be valid, irrevocable, and enforceable, save upon such grounds as exist at law or in equity for the revocation of any contract." 9 U.S.C. § 2. Section 2 is a congressional declaration of a liberal federal policy favoring arbitration agreements, notwithstanding any state substantive or procedural policies to the contrary. The effect of the section is to create a body of federal substantive law of arbitrability, applicable to any arbitration agreement within the coverage of the Act. In Prima Paint Corp. v. Flood & Conklin Mfg. Corp., 388 U.S. 395, 87 S.Ct. 1801, 18 L.Ed.2d 1270 (1967), for example, the parties had signed a contract containing an arbitration clause, but one party alleged that there had been fraud in the inducement of the entire contract (although the alleged fraud did not go to the arbitration clause in particular). The issue before us was whether the issue of fraud in the inducement was itself an arbitrable controversy. We held that the language and policies of the Act required the conclusion that the fraud issue was arbitrable. Id., at 402–404, 87 S.Ct., at 1805–06. Although our holding in Prima Paint extended only to the specific issue presented, the courts of appeals have since consistently concluded that questions of arbitrability must be addressed with a healthy regard for the federal policy favoring arbitration. We agree. The Arbitration Act establishes that, as a matter of federal law, any doubts concerning the scope of arbitrable issues should be resolved in favor of arbitration, whether the problem at hand is the construction of the contract language itself or an allegation of waiver, delay, or a like defense to arbitrability.

To be sure, the source-of-law factor has less significance here than in Calvert, since the federal courts' jurisdiction to enforce the Arbitration Act is concurrent with that of the state courts.[32] But we emphasize that our task in cases such as this is not to find some substantial reason for the *exercise* of federal jurisdiction by the district court; rather, the task is to ascertain whether there exist "exceptional" circumstances, the "clearest of justifications," that can suffice under Colorado River to justify the *surrender* of that jurisdiction. Although in some rare circumstances the presence of state-law issues may weigh in favor of that surrender . . ., the presence of

---

32. See n. 34, infra. The Arbitration Act is something of an anomaly in the field of federal-court jurisdiction. It creates a body of federal substantive law establishing and regulating the duty to honor an agreement to arbitrate, yet it does not create any independent federal-question jurisdiction under 28 U.S.C. § 1331 (1976 ed., Supp. IV) or otherwise. Section 4 provides for an order compelling arbitration only when the federal district court would have jurisdiction over a suit on the underlying dispute; hence, there must be diversity of citizenship or some other independent basis for federal jurisdiction before the order can issue. E.g., Commercial Metals Co. v. Balfour, Guthrie, & Co., 577 F.2d 264, 268–269 (C.A.5 1978), and cases cited. Section 3 likewise limits the federal courts to the extent that a federal court cannot stay a suit pending before it unless there is such a suit in existence. Nevertheless, although enforcement of the Act is left in large part to the state courts, it nevertheless represents federal policy to be vindicated by the federal courts where otherwise appropriate. We need not address whether a federal court might stay a state-court suit pending arbitration under 28 U.S.C. § 2283.

federal-law issues must always be a major consideration weighing against surrender. . . .

Finally, in this case an important reason against allowing a stay is the probable inadequacy of the state-court proceeding to protect Mercury's rights. We are not to be understood to impeach the competence or procedures of the North Carolina courts. Moreover, state courts, as much as federal courts, are obliged to grant stays of litigation under § 3 of the Arbitration Act.[34] It is less clear, however, whether the same is true of an order to compel arbitration under § 4 of the Act.[35] We need not resolve that question here; it suffices to say that there was, at a minimum, substantial room for doubt that Mercury could obtain from the state court an order compelling the Hospital to arbitrate.[36] In many cases, no doubt, a § 3 stay is quite adequate to protect the right to arbitration. But in a case such as this, where the party opposing arbitration is the one from whom payment or performance is sought, a stay of litigation alone is not enough. It leaves the recalcitrant party free to sit and do nothing—neither to litigate nor to arbitrate. If the state court stayed litigation pending arbitration but declined to compel the Hospital to arbitrate, Mercury would have no sure way to proceed with its claims except to return to federal court to obtain a § 4 order—a pointless and wasteful burden on the supposedly summary and speedy procedures prescribed by the Arbitration Act.

[I]n addition to reversing the District Court's stay, the Court of Appeals decided that the underlying contractual dispute between Mercury and the Hospital is arbitrable under the Arbitration Act and the terms of the parties' arbitration agreement. It reversed the District Court's judg-

---

34. Although § 3 refers ambiguously to a suit "in any of the courts of the United States," the state courts have almost unanimously recognized that the stay provision of § 3 applies to suits in state as well as federal courts, requiring them to issue the same speedy relief when a dispute is referable to arbitration. (The North Carolina Supreme Court has so held, although not until after the District Court ordered this stay. Burke County Public Schools Board of Education v. Shaver Partnership, 303 N.C. 408, 279 S.E.2d 816 (1981).) This is necessary to carry out Congress's intent to mandate enforcement of all covered arbitration agreements; Congress can hardly have meant that an agreement to arbitrate can be enforced against a party who attempts to litigate an arbitrable dispute in federal court, but not against one who sues on the same dispute in state court. See also Prima Paint, 388 U.S., at 404, 87 S.Ct., at 1806.

35. Section 4, unlike § 3, speaks only of a petition to "any United States district court." Nonetheless, at least one state court has held that § 4 does require state courts to

issue § 4 orders to arbitrate where the section's conditions are met. Main v. Merrill Lynch, Pierce, Fenner & Smith Inc., 67 Cal. App.3d 19, 24–25, 136 Cal.Rptr. 378, 380–381 (1977).

36. As a historical matter, there was considerable doubt at the time of the District Court's stay that the North Carolina court would have granted even a § 3 stay of litigation. The then-controlling precedent in North Carolina was to the effect that a contract such as that between Mercury and the Hospital was not subject to the Arbitration Act at all, on the reasoning that a construction project is not "commerce" within the meaning of §§ 1 and 2 of the Act. Burke County Public Schools Board of Education v. Shaver Partnership, 46 N.C.App. 573, 265 S.E.2d 481 (1980); Bryant–Durham Electric Co. v. Durham County Hospital Corp., 42 N.C.App. 351, 256 S.E.2d 529 (1979). The North Carolina Supreme Court has, however, since repudiated those decisions. Burke County Public Schools Board of Education v. Shaver Partnership, 303 N.C. 408, 279 S.E.2d 816 (1981).

ment and remanded the case "with instructions to proceed in conformity herewith." 656 F.2d, at 946. In effect, the Court of Appeals directed the District Court to enter a § 4 order to arbitrate.

In this Court, the Hospital does not contest the substantive correctness of the Court of Appeals's holding on arbitrability. It does raise several objections to the procedures the Court of Appeals used in considering and deciding this case. In particular, it points out that the only issue formally appealed to the Court of Appeals was the propriety of the District Court's stay order. Ordinarily, we would not expect the Court of Appeals to pass on issues not decided in the District Court. In the present case, however, we are not disposed to disturb the Court's discretion in its handling of the case in view of the special interests at stake and the apparent lack of any prejudice to the parties. Title 28 U.S.C. § 2106 gives a court of appeals some latitude in entering an order to achieve justice in the circumstances. The Arbitration Act calls for a summary and speedy disposition of motions or petitions to enforce arbitration clauses. The Court of Appeals had in the record full briefs and evidentiary submissions from both parties on the merits of arbitrability, and held that there were no disputed issues of fact requiring a jury trial before a § 4 order could issue. Under these circumstances, the Court acted within its authority in deciding the legal issues presented in order to facilitate the prompt arbitration that Congress envisaged.

Affirmed.

■ JUSTICE REHNQUIST, with whom THE CHIEF JUSTICE and JUSTICE O'CONNOR join, dissent.

* * *

Questions

1.   What is the issue of arbitrability in this case? In what way does it differ from the issue of arbitrability that is posed in the *Bowmer* case?

2.   How does the Court decide the question of arbitrability in *Moses H. Cone*? Is the standard for arbitrability the court applied in *Moses H. Cone* different from the one it applied in *Bowmer*? How can we account for the difference?

3.   One commentator has written that while a presumption of arbitrability is justifiable in the labor relations context due to the role of arbitration in preserving labor peace, such a presumption cannot be justified in the interpretation of the Federal Arbitration Act. In the latter context, "The Supreme Court has no clear expression of congressional policy upon which to base its own program of promoting commercial arbitration." Jonathan R. Nelson, *Judge-Made Law and the Presumption of Arbitrability*, 58 Brook. L. Rev. 279, 328 (1992). Do you agree? Suppose Congress made a declaration that arbitration is a valuable device for resolving disputes because it conserves on scarce judicial resources and provides an efficient and speedy method of resolving most disputes. Would this statement then

support the presumption of arbitrability in the FAA context? Could one infer such a statement from Congress' silence in the face of the numerous Supreme Court decisions in the past decade that have expanded the role of arbitration in commercial and other settings under the FAA?

4.   In cases arising under Section 301 of the Labor Management Relations Act, the Supreme Court has determined that issues of procedural arbitrability are to be treated differently than questions of substantively arbitrability for purposes of whether a court or arbitrator is to decide them. See *John Wiley & Sons v. Livingston*, 376 U.S. 543 (1964). From what we have seen to date, does the Court make the same distinction in the FAA cases? Should it make such a distinction?

* * *

First Options of Chicago, Inc. v. Kaplan

514 U.S. 938, 115 S.Ct. 1920 (1995).

■ JUSTICE BREYER delivered the opinion of the Court.

In this case we consider two questions about how courts should review certain matters under the Federal Arbitration Act, 9 U.S.C. § 1 et seq. (1988 Ed. and Supp. V): (1) how a district court should review an arbitrator's decision that the parties agreed to arbitrate a dispute, and (2) how a court of appeals should review a district court's decision confirming, or refusing to vacate, an arbitration award.

I

The case concerns several related disputes between, on one side, First Options of Chicago, Inc., a firm that clears stock trades on the Philadelphia Stock Exchange, and, on the other side, three parties: Manuel Kaplan; his wife, Carol Kaplan; and his wholly owned investment company, MK Investments, Inc. (MKI), whose trading account First Options cleared. The disputes center around a "workout" agreement, embodied in four separate documents, which governs the "working out" of debts to First Options that MKI and the Kaplans incurred as a result of the October 1987 stock market crash. In 1989, after entering into the agreement, MKI lost an additional $1.5 million. First Options then took control of, and liquidated, certain MKI assets; demanded immediate payment of the entire MKI debt; and insisted that the Kaplans personally pay any deficiency. When its demands went unsatisfied, First Options sought arbitration by a panel of the Philadelphia Stock Exchange.

MKI, having signed the only workout document (out of four) that contained an arbitration clause, accepted arbitration. The Kaplans, however, who had not personally signed that document, denied that their disagreement with First Options was arbitrable and filed written objections to that effect with the arbitration panel. The arbitrators decided that they had the power to rule on the merits of the parties' dispute, and did so in favor of First Options. The Kaplans then asked the Federal District Court to vacate the arbitration award, see 9 U.S.C. § 10 (1988 Ed., Supp. V), and First Options requested its confirmation, see § 9. The court confirmed the award. Nonetheless, on appeal the Court of Appeals for the Third Circuit agreed with the Kaplans that their dispute was not arbitrable; and it reversed the District Court's confirmation of the award against them.

We granted certiorari to consider two questions regarding the standards that the Court of Appeals used to review the determination that the Kaplans' dispute with First Options was arbitrable. First, the Court of Appeals said that courts "should *independently* decide whether an arbitration panel has jurisdiction over the merits of any particular dispute." 19 F.3d, at 1509 (emphasis added). First Options asked us to decide whether this is so (i.e., whether courts, in "reviewing the arbitrators' decision on arbitrability," should "apply a *de novo* standard of review or the more deferential standard applied to arbitrators' decisions on the merits") when the objecting party "submitted the issue to the arbitrators for decision." Pet. for Cert. I. Second, the Court of Appeals stated that it would review a district court's denial of a motion to vacate a commercial arbitration award (and the correlative grant of a motion to confirm it) "*de novo*." 19 F.3d, at 1509. First Options argues that the Court of Appeals instead should have applied an "abuse of discretion" standard. See Robbins v. Day, 954 F.2d 679, 681–682 (C.A.11 1992).

II

The first question—the standard of review applied to an arbitrator's decision about arbitrability—is a narrow one. To understand just how narrow, consider three types of disagreement present in this case. First, the Kaplans and First Options disagree about whether the Kaplans are personally liable for MKI's debt to First Options. That disagreement makes up the *merits* of the dispute. Second, they disagree about whether they agreed to arbitrate the merits. That disagreement is about the *arbitrability* of the dispute. Third, they disagree about *who should have the primary power to decide the second matter*. Does that power belong primarily to the arbitrators (because the court reviews their arbitrability decision deferentially) or to the court (because the court makes up its mind about arbitrability independently)? We consider here only this third question.

Although the question is a narrow one, it has a certain practical importance. That is because a party who has not agreed to arbitrate will normally have a right to a court's decision about the merits of its dispute (say, as here, its obligation under a contract). But, where the party has agreed to arbitrate, he or she, in effect, has relinquished much of that right's practical value. The party still can ask a court to review the arbitrator's decision, but the court will set that decision aside only in very unusual circumstances. See, e.g., 9 U.S.C. § 10 (award procured by corruption, fraud, or undue means; arbitrator exceeded his powers); Wilko v. Swan, 346 U.S. 427, 436–437, 74 S.Ct. 182, 187–188, 98 L.Ed. 168 (1953) (parties bound by arbitrator's decision not in "manifest disregard" of the law), overruled on other grounds, Rodriguez de Quijas v. Shearson/American Express, Inc., 490 U.S. 477 (1989). Hence, who–court or arbitrator–has the primary authority to decide whether a party has agreed to arbitrate can make a critical difference to a party resisting arbitration.

We believe the answer to the "who" question (i.e., the standard-of-review question) is fairly simple. Just as the arbitrability of the merits of a dispute depends upon whether the parties agreed to arbitrate that dispute, see, e.g., Mastrobuono v. Shearson Lehman Hutton, Inc., 514 U.S. 52, 58, 115 S.Ct. 1212, 1216, 131 L.Ed.2d 76 (1995); Mitsubishi Motors Corp. v. Soler Chrysler–Plymouth, Inc., 473 U.S. 614, 626 (1985), so the question "who has the primary power to decide arbitrability" turns upon what the parties agreed about *that* matter. Did the parties agree to submit the arbitrability question itself to arbitration? If so, then the court's standard for reviewing the arbitrator's decision about *that* matter should not differ from the standard courts apply when they review any other matter that parties have agreed to arbitrate. See AT & T Technologies, Inc. v. Communications Workers, 475 U.S. 643, 649, 106 S.Ct. 1415, 1418, 89 L.Ed.2d 648 (1986) (parties may agree to arbitrate arbitrability); Steelworkers v. Warrior & Gulf Navigation Co., 363 U.S. 574, 583, n. 7, 80 S.Ct. 1347, 1353, n. 7, 4 L.Ed.2d 1409 (1960) (same). That is to say, the court should give considerable leeway to the arbitrator, setting aside his or her decision only in certain narrow circumstances. See, e.g., 9 U.S.C. § 10. If, on the other hand, the parties did *not* agree to submit the arbitrability question itself to arbitration, then the court should decide that question just as it would decide any other question that the parties did not submit to arbitration, namely independently. These two answers flow inexorably from the fact that arbitration is simply a matter of contract between the parties; it is a way to resolve those disputes—but only those disputes—that the parties have agreed to submit to arbitration. See, e.g., AT & T Technologies, supra, at 649, 106 S.Ct., at 1418; Mastrobuono, supra, at 58–60, and n. 9, 115 S.Ct., at 1216–1217, and n. 9 . . . (additional citations omitted).

We agree with First Options, therefore, that a court must defer to an arbitrator's arbitrability decision when the parties submitted that matter to arbitration. Nevertheless, that conclusion does not help First Options win this case. That is because a fair and complete answer to the standard-of-review question requires a word about how a court should decide whether the parties have agreed to submit the arbitrability issue to arbitration. And, that word makes clear that the Kaplans did not agree to arbitrate arbitrability here.

When deciding whether the parties agreed to arbitrate a certain matter (including arbitrability), courts generally (though with a qualification we discuss below) should apply ordinary state-law principles that govern the formation of contracts. See, e.g., Mastrobuono, supra, at 62–64, and n. 9, 115 S.Ct., at 1219, and n. 9. . . . The relevant state law here, for example, would require the court to see whether the parties objectively revealed an intent to submit the arbitrability issue to arbitration. See, e.g., Estate of Jesmer v. Rohlev, 241 Ill.App.3d 798, 803, 182 Ill.Dec. 282, 286, 609 N.E.2d 816, 820 (1993) (law of the State whose law governs the workout agreement); ... See generally Mitsubishi Motors, supra, at 626, 105 S.Ct., at 3353.

This Court, however, has (as we just said) added an important qualification, applicable when courts decide whether a party has agreed that arbitrators should decide arbitrability: Courts should not assume that the parties agreed to arbitrate arbitrability unless there is "clea[r] and unmistakabl[e]" evidence that they did so. AT & T Technologies, supra, at 649, 106 S.Ct., at 1418–1419; see Warrior & Gulf, supra, at 583, n. 7, 80 S.Ct., at 1353, n. 7. In this manner the law treats silence or ambiguity about the question "*who* (primarily) should decide arbitrability" differently from the way it treats silence or ambiguity about the question "*whether* a particular merits-related dispute is arbitrable because it is within the scope of a valid arbitration agreement"—for in respect to this latter question the law reverses the presumption. See Mitsubishi Motors, supra, at 626, 105 S.Ct., at 3353 (" '[A]ny doubts concerning the scope of arbitrable issues should be resolved in favor of arbitration' ") (quoting Moses H. Cone Memorial Hospital v. Mercury Constr. Corp., 460 U.S. 1, 24–25, 103 S.Ct. 927, 941, 74 L.Ed.2d 765 (1983)); Warrior & Gulf, supra, at 582–583, 80 S.Ct., at 1352–1353.

But, this difference in treatment is understandable. The latter question arises when the parties have a contract that provides for arbitration of some issues. In such circumstances, the parties likely gave at least some thought to the scope of arbitration. And, given the law's permissive policies in respect to arbitration, see, e.g., Mitsubishi Motors, supra, at 626, 105 S.Ct., at 3353, one can understand why the law would insist upon clarity before concluding that the parties did *not* want to arbitrate a related matter. See Domke § 2.02, p. 156 (issues will be deemed arbitrable unless "it is clear that the arbitration clause has not included" them). On the other hand, the former question—the "who (primarily) should decide arbitrability" question—is rather arcane. A party often might not focus upon that question or upon the significance of having arbitrators decide the scope of their own powers. Cf. Cox, Reflections Upon Labor Arbitration, 72 Harv.L.Rev. 1482, 1508–1509 (1959), cited in Warrior & Gulf, 363 U.S., at 583, n. 7, 80 S.Ct., at 1353, n. 7. And, given the principle that a party can be forced to arbitrate only those issues it specifically has agreed to submit to arbitration, one can understand why courts might hesitate to interpret silence or ambiguity on the "who should decide arbitrability" point as giving the arbitrators that power, for doing so might too often force unwilling parties to arbitrate a matter they reasonably would have thought a judge, not an arbitrator, would decide. Ibid. See generally Dean Witter Reynolds Inc. v. Byrd, 470 U.S. 213, 219–220, 105 S.Ct. 1238, 1241–1242, 84 L.Ed.2d 158 (1985) (Arbitration Act's basic purpose is to "ensure judicial enforcement of privately made agreements to arbitrate").

On the record before us, First Options cannot show that the Kaplans clearly agreed to have the arbitrators decide (i.e., to arbitrate) the question of arbitrability. First Options relies on the Kaplans' filing with the arbitrators a written memorandum objecting to the arbitrators' jurisdiction. But merely arguing the arbitrability issue to an arbitrator does not indicate a clear willingness to arbitrate that issue, i.e., a willingness to be effectively bound by the arbitrator's decision on that point. To the contrary, insofar as the Kaplans were forcefully objecting to the arbitrators deciding their dispute with First Options, one naturally would think that they did *not* want the arbitrators to have binding authority over them. This conclusion draws added support from (1) an obvious explanation for the Kaplans' presence before the arbitrators (i.e., that MKI, Mr. Kaplan's wholly owned firm, was arbitrating workout agreement matters); and (2) Third Circuit law that suggested that the Kaplans might argue arbitrability to the arbitrators without losing their right to independent court review, Teamsters v. Western Pennsylvania Motor Carriers Assn., 574 F.2d 783, 786–788 (1978); see 19 F.3d, at 1512, n. 13.

First Options makes several counter arguments: (1) that the Kaplans had other ways to get an independent court decision on the question of arbitrability without arguing the issue to the arbitrators (e.g., by trying to enjoin the arbitration, or by refusing to participate in the arbitration and then defending against a court petition First Options would have brought to compel arbitration, see 9 U.S.C. § 4); (2) that permitting parties to argue arbitrability to an arbitrator without being bound by the result would cause delay and waste in the resolution of disputes; and (3) that the Arbitration Act therefore requires a presumption that the Kaplans agreed to be bound by the arbitrators' decision, not the contrary. The first of these points, however, while true, simply does not say anything about whether the Kaplans intended to be bound by the arbitrators' decision. The second point, too, is inconclusive, for factual circumstances vary too greatly to permit a confident conclusion about whether allowing the arbitrator to make an initial (but independently reviewable) arbitrability determination would, in general, slow down the dispute resolution process. And, the third point is legally erroneous, for there is no strong arbitration-related policy favoring First Options in respect to its particular argument here. After all, the basic objective in this area is not to resolve disputes in the quickest manner possible, no matter what the parties' wishes, Dean Witter Reynolds, supra, at 219–220, 105 S.Ct., at 1241–1242, but to ensure that commercial arbitration agreements, like other contracts, " 'are enforced according to their terms,' " Mastrobuono, 514 U.S., at 54, 115 S.Ct., at 1214 (quoting Volt Information Sciences, 489 U.S., at 479, 109 S.Ct., at 1256), and according to the intentions of the parties, Mitsubishi Motors, 473 U.S., at 626, 105 S.Ct., at 3353. See Allied–Bruce, 513 U.S., at 268–69, 115 S.Ct., at 837. That policy favors the Kaplans, not First Options.

We conclude that, because the Kaplans did not clearly agree to submit the question of arbitrability to arbitration, the Court of Appeals was correct in finding that the arbitrability of the Kaplan/First Options dispute was subject to independent review by the courts.

III

We turn next to the standard a court of appeals should apply when reviewing a district court decision that refuses to vacate, see 9 U.S.C. § 10 (1988 Ed., Supp. V), or confirms, see § 9, an arbitration award. Although the Third Circuit sometimes used the words *"de novo"* to describe this standard, its opinion makes clear that it simply believes (as do all Circuits but one) that there is no *special* standard governing its review of a district court's decision in these circumstances. Rather, review of, for example, a district court decision confirming an arbitration award on the ground that the parties agreed to submit their dispute to arbitration, should proceed like review of any other district court decision finding an agreement between parties, i.e., accepting findings of fact that are not "clearly erroneous" but deciding questions of law *de novo*. See 19 F.3d, at 1509.

One Court of Appeals, the Eleventh Circuit, has said something different. Because of federal policy favoring arbitration, that court says that it applies a specially lenient "abuse of discretion" standard (even as to questions of law) when reviewing district court decisions that confirm (but not those that set aside) arbitration awards. See, e.g., Robbins v. Day, 954 F.2d, at 681–682. First Options asks us to hold that the Eleventh Circuit's view is correct.

We believe, however, that the majority of Circuits is right in saying that courts of appeals should apply ordinary, not special, standards when reviewing district court decisions upholding arbitration awards. For one thing, it is undesirable to make the law more complicated by proliferating review standards without good reasons. More importantly, the reviewing attitude that a court of appeals takes toward a district court decision should depend upon "the respective institutional advantages of trial and appellate courts," not upon what standard of review will more likely produce a particular substantive result. Salve Regina College v. Russell, 499 U.S. 225, 231–233 (1991). The law, for example, tells all courts (trial and appellate) to give administrative agencies a degree of legal leeway when they review certain interpretations of the law that those agencies have made. See, e.g., Chevron U.S.A. Inc. v. Natural Resources Defense Council, Inc., 467 U.S. 837, 843–844 (1984). But, no one, to our knowledge, has suggested that this policy of giving leeway to agencies means that a court of appeals should give *extra* leeway to a district court decision that upholds an agency. Similarly, courts grant arbitrators considerable leeway when reviewing most arbitration decisions; but that fact does not mean that appellate courts should give *extra* leeway to district courts that uphold arbitrators. First Options argues that the Arbitration Act is special because the Act, in one section, allows courts of appeals to conduct interlocutory review of certain anti-arbitration district court rulings (e.g., orders enjoining arbitrations), but not those upholding arbitration (e.g., orders refusing to enjoin arbitrations). 9 U.S.C. § 16 (1988 Ed., Supp. V). But that portion of the Act governs the timing of review; it is therefore too weak a support for the distinct claim that the court of appeals should use a different *standard* when reviewing certain district court decisions. The Act says nothing about standards of review.

We conclude that the Court of Appeals used the proper standards for reviewing the District Court's arbitrability determinations.

IV

Finally, First Options argues that, even if we rule against it on the standard-of-review questions, we nonetheless should hold that the Court of

Appeals erred in its ultimate conclusion that the merits of the Kaplan/First Options dispute were not arbitrable. This factbound issue is beyond the scope of the questions we agreed to review.

The judgment of the Court of Appeals is affirmed.

* * *

Questions

1.   If parties can consent to have an arbitrator to determine the issue of arbitrability, and if, as *Moses Cone* concludes, there is a presumption of arbitrability for issues of contract construction, then why does the Court not order the parties to arbitrate the issue of arbitrability in *First Options*? Is *First Options* consistent with *Moses Cone*? Or, does *First Options* represent a retreat from the expansive conception of arbitrability enunciated in *Moses Cone*?

2.   Why does the Court not apply the presumption of arbitrability in *First Options*? Why does it require "clear and unmistakable evidence" of such an intent on the issue of who is to decide arbitrability, but not on other issues concerning arbitrability? Does the Court make a serious encroachment on the presumption of arbitrability by doing so? Is the Court distinguishing arbitrability determinations on the basis of its own view as to which issues the parties are likely to have considered and which ones they are not likely to have considered in the contract formation process? What is the basis for the Court's conclusion that the parties were not likely to have considered the issue of who is to decide arbitrability? Are there other types of issues that parties are unlikely to consider at the time of contract formation? Should those likewise be excluded from the presumption of arbitrability?

3.   Is there a conflict between a liberal federal policy favoring arbitration and the Court's commitment to treating arbitration agreements like ordinary contracts? Can the result in *First Options* be explained on the basis of the court's desire to enforce the will of the parties or is it an instance of the court enforcing a federal policy favoring arbitration?

4.   In decisions of arbitrability, what are the respective institutional advantages of arbitrators and district courts? How should this affect the standard of review by district courts of arbitral decisions on arbitrability? Should it affect the standard of review on the merits of a dispute?

* * *

2.   FRAUD IN THE INDUCEMENT

Ericksen v. 100 Oak Street

35 Cal.3d 312, 673 P.2d 251 (1983).

■ GRODIN, JUSTICE.

The question presented here is whether a party to an agreement which includes an arbitration clause may bypass the arbitral process, and invoke the jurisdiction of the courts, by asserting that the agreement itself was the product of fraud. We conclude, in accord with the United States Supreme Court and the overwhelming majority of state courts which have considered the question, that the arbitration commitment is severable from the underlying agreement and that where, as in this case, the arbitration clause may reasonably be construed to encompass the fraud claim, the entire dispute should be resolved through arbitration.

Facts and Procedural History

The underlying dispute concerns a lease executed by plaintiff and respondent Ericksen, Arbuthnot, McCarthy, Kearney and Walsh, Inc., an Oakland law firm, hereinafter referred to as Ericksen, and 100 Oak Street, a California limited partnership which owns a three-story office building in Oakland. The lease, dated August 15, 1979, was for a five-year term and provided that Ericksen would occupy the first floor of the 100 Oak Street building, starting November 15, 1979.

Shortly after it occupied the premises, Ericksen began complaining that the air conditioning in the building was defective. Halfway through the lease term, Ericksen vacated the premises, moving to another office during Memorial Day weekend, 1982.

Notwithstanding a lease clause in which it agreed to arbitrate "[i]n the event of any dispute between the parties hereto with respect to the provisions of this Lease exclusive of those provisions relating to payment of rent," Ericksen filed suit on June 30, 1982. The complaint sought damages and declaratory relief and alleged a breach of the implied covenant of quiet enjoyment; breach of the implied warranty of habitability; frustration of purpose; simple breach of contract; constructive eviction; and fraud. Ericksen claimed it was entitled to rescind the agreement, and sought general and punitive damages.

Within a few days after it was served with the complaint, 100 Oak Street filed a petition to compel arbitration of the dispute (Code Civ.Proc., § 1281.2), and to stay the civil proceedings. Ericksen filed a response in which it admitted that it and 100 Oak Street had "entered into a written agreement requiring that the controversy alleged in the petition to be submitted to arbitration," but asserted that "[g]rounds exist for revocation of the agreement to arbitrate the alleged controversy in that [Ericksen] was falsely and fraudulently induced to enter into the lease agreement." On the basis of this general and unverified allegation,[1] the trial court denied 100 Oak Street's petition, and this appeal followed.

---

1. Ericksen's complaint, also unverified, alleged in part that before and after the signing of the lease defendants "falsely and fraudulently, and with intent to deceive and defraud the plaintiff, represented to plaintiff that the leased premises were in a tenantable condition," and that those representations were false, and known to be false, because "in truth the air conditioning was inadequate, making the leased premises untenantable." At oral argument before this court, Ericksen's attorney confirmed that this was

Discussion

Code of Civil Procedure section 1281.2 provides, in relevant part: "On the petition of a party to an arbitration agreement alleging the existence of a written agreement to arbitrate a controversy and that a party thereto refuses to arbitrate such controversy, the court shall order the petitioner and the respondent to arbitrate the controversy if it determines that an agreement to arbitrate the controversy exists, unless it determines that: . . . [¶] (b) Grounds exist for the revocation of the agreement."

The language of the statute on its face would not appear to countenance the trial court's view that the mere general assertion of fraud in an unverified response is sufficient basis for the denial of a petition to compel arbitration. Rather, the statute calls for a "determination" by the court as to the existence of the requisite agreement, and manifestly no such determination has been made.

There exists a more fundamental question, however, and that is whether the California Arbitration Act contemplates that a court, confronted with an agreement containing an arbitration clause and a petition to compel arbitration, will preliminarily entertain and decide a party's claim that the underlying agreement (as distinguished from the agreement to arbitrate) was produced by fraud. The question is one of first impression in this state. . . . We therefore turn to decisions of the federal courts and the courts of our sister states for guidance.

I.   The Federal Rule

In Robert Lawrence Company v. Devonshire Fabrics, Inc. (2d Cir.1959) 271 F.2d 402, cert. dism. (1960) 364 U.S. 801, 81 S.Ct. 27, 5 L.Ed.2d 37, plaintiff sought damages for allegedly fraudulent misrepresentations made by defendant in inducing it to pay for a quantity of woolen fabric, which, plaintiff claimed, was not of "first quality" as the agreement provided. Defendant moved to stay the suit pending arbitration pursuant to a provision of the sales agreement calling for arbitration of "[a]ny complaint, controversy or question which may arise with respect to this contract that cannot be settled by the parties thereto." The trial court denied the stay on the ground that the existence of a valid contract was a question which must first be determined by the court.

The court of appeals, in what proved to be a seminal decision on this issue, reversed. Calling the trial court's approach an "oversimplification of the problem," the court held that the federal arbitration statute "envisages a distinction between the entire contract between the parties on the one hand and the arbitration clause of the contract on the other." (271 F.2d at p. 409.) Such a construction was compelled, the court reasoned, not only by the language of the statute but also by other pertinent considerations as well. "Historically arbitration clauses were treated as separable parts of the

the fraud referred to in its response to the petition to compel arbitration. Ericksen's complaint also asserted that there had been a mutual rescission of the agreement, but this was not a stated ground for opposing arbitration in the trial court.

contract, although such treatment generally meant the agreement was being deprived of its efficacy. [Citations.] And since the passage of the [federal] Arbitration Act, the courts have similarly held that the illegality of part of the contract does not operate to nullify an agreement to arbitrate. [Citations.] Nor does the alleged breach or repudiation of the contract preclude the right to arbitrate. [Citations.] [¶] Finally, any doubts as to the construction of the Act ought to be resolved in line with its liberal policy of promoting arbitration both to accord with the original intention of the parties and to help ease the current congestion of court calendars. Such policy has been consistently reiterated by the federal courts and we think it deserves to be heartily endorsed." (271 F.2d at p. 410.)

Referring to the case before it, the court observed that "[t]he issue of fraud seems inextricably enmeshed in the other factual issues of the case. Indeed, the difference between fraud in the inducement and mere failure of performance by delivery of defective merchandise depends upon little more than legal verbiage and the formulation of legal conclusions. Once it is settled that arbitration agreements are 'valid, irrevocable, and enforceable' we know of no principle of law that stands as an obstacle to a determination by the parties to the effect that arbitration should not be denied or postponed upon the mere cry of fraud in the inducement, as this would permit the frustration of the very purposes sought to be achieved by the agreement to arbitrate, i.e. a speedy and relatively inexpensive trial before commercial specialists." (Id., at p. 410, emphasis added.) It would be different, the court suggested, if there were a claim, supported by a showing of substance, that the arbitration clause was itself induced by fraud, but "[i]t is not enough that there is substance to the charge that the contract to deliver merchandise of a certain quality was induced by fraud." (Id., at p. 411.) Since the contract language was broad enough to include a claim of fraud in the inducement of the contract itself, that was a question for the arbitrator to determine.

In Prima Paint v. Flood & Conklin (1967) 388 U.S. 395, 87 S.Ct. 1801, 18 L.Ed.2d 1270 the United States Supreme Court confronted the Devonshire issue in the context of a consulting agreement in which Flood & Conklin agreed to perform certain services for and not to compete with Prima Paint. The agreement contained an arbitration clause providing that " '[a]ny controversy or claim arising out of or relating to this Agreement . . . shall be settled by arbitration in the City of New York, . . .' " (388 U.S. at p. 398, 87 S.Ct. at p. 1803.) Flood & Conklin, contending that Prima had failed to make a payment under the contract, sent Prima a notice requesting arbitration. Prima responded with an action in federal district court to rescind the entire consulting agreement on the ground of fraud. The fraud allegedly consisted of Flood & Conklin's misrepresentation at the time the contract was made, that it was solvent and able to perform the agreement, when in fact it was completely insolvent. Flood & Conklin moved to stay Prima's lawsuit pending arbitration of the fraud issue. The lower courts, relying on the Second Circuit's decision in Devonshire, held that the action should be stayed to permit arbitration of the issue.

The Supreme Court noted it was the view of the Second Circuit in Devonshire and other cases that "except where the parties otherwise intend—arbitration clauses . . . are 'separable' from the contracts in which they are embedded, and that where no claim is made that fraud was directed to the arbitration clause itself, a broad arbitration clause will be held to encompass arbitration of the claim that the contract itself was induced by fraud. [Fn. omitted.]" (388 U.S. at p. 402, 87 S.Ct. at p. 1805, emphasis in original.) And, the high court adopted the Devonshire rule as a proper interpretation of the federal statute, binding upon federal courts in suits involving agreements subject to that statute—i.e., maritime contracts and those evidencing transactions in "commerce." (388 U.S. at pp. 403–404, 87 S.Ct. at pp. 1805–1806.) "In so concluding," the court stated, "we not only honor the plain meaning of the statute but also the unmistakably clear congressional purpose that the arbitration procedure, when selected by the parties to a contract, be speedy and not subject to delay and obstruction in the courts." (Id., at p. 404, 87 S.Ct. at 1806.)

The United States Supreme Court in Moses H. Cone Memorial Hosp. v. Mercury Const., supra, 460 U.S. 1, 103 S.Ct. 927, 74 L.Ed.2d 765 has recently reconfirmed Prima Paint, stating its holding in broad terms, and approving an even broader, derivative, proposition which had been accepted by the courts of appeals: "that questions of arbitrability must be addressed with a healthy regard for the federal policy favoring arbitration. . . . The Arbitration Act establishes that, as a matter of federal law, any doubts concerning the scope of arbitrable issues should be resolved in favor of arbitration, whether the problem at hand is the construction of the contract language itself or an allegation of waiver, delay, or a like defense to arbitrability." (103 S.Ct. at pp. 941–942.)

II.   The Rule in Other States

The high courts of our sister states with cognate arbitration acts have followed the rule in Prima Paint with near unanimity. The only exceptions appear to be Louisiana . . . and Minnesota. . . .

The treatment of this issue in New York, where courts have had the longest and most extensive exposure to arbitration law, is particularly instructive. In 1957, prior to Prima Paint, the New York Court of Appeals interpreted that state's arbitration law to mean that fraud in the inducement of a contract was an issue for the court, and not for the arbitrators. (Wrap–Vertiser Corporation v. Plotnick (1957) 3 N.Y.2d 17, 163 N.Y.S.2d 639, 143 N.E.2d 366.) After Prima Paint the court reversed itself and adopted the federal rule on the basis of legal and policy arguments which it found "compelling." (Weinrott v. Carp (1973) 32 N.Y.2d 190, 344 N.Y.S.2d 848, 856, 298 N.E.2d 42, 47.) The theoretical underpinning of its prior rule had been the concept that an arbitration agreement was not separable from the principal contract, so that if the substantive provisions of the contract were to fall, the entire contract including an arbitration clause would fall with it. (Id., 344 N.Y.S.2d at p. 854, 298 N.E.2d at p. 46.) But the court observed, "[j]udicial intervention, based upon a nonseparability contract theory in arbitration matters prolongs litigation, and defeats, as this case conclusively demonstrates, two of arbitration's primary virtues, speed and finality [citations]." (Id., 344 N.Y.S.2d at p. 855 . . .) Such conduct "has the effect of frustrating both the initial intent of the parties as well as legislative policy." (Ibid.)

An "additional and desirable result" of its decision, the New York court noted, was to bring that state's law in accord with federal law as declared in Prima Paint, thus avoiding the awkwardness of applying different rules depending upon whether the case involved a contract subject to the federal statute. "[I]t is a rather technical distinction to apply one law or another depending on whether interstate commerce is involved. If we were to adhere to our former approach, we would be making the existence of interstate commerce (or the lack of it) determinative with respect to the application of the arbitration provision. Clearly no party makes a decision on the scope of arbitration based on whether the contract in question involves interstate commerce." (344 N.Y.S.2d at p. 857, fn. 2, 298 N.E.2d at p. 48, fn. 2.)

III.   Evaluation

Contrary to plaintiff's contention, the majority rule, as reflected in cases like Prima Paint, Devonshire, and Weinrott, is compatible with California's arbitration statute. The difference between Code of Civil Procedure section 1281.2, which calls for arbitration unless grounds exist for revocation of the agreement, and the federal statute, which mandates arbitration "save upon such grounds as exist at law or in equity for the revocation of any contract" is inconsequential, and does not require or point to a different rule. Likewise, the New York statute, calling for arbitration when "there is no substantial question whether a valid agreement was made or complied with" (N.Y.Civ.Prac.Law, § 7503, subd. (a) (1980 McKinney)), is harmonious. As in the case of these statutes, the term "agreement" may properly be construed to refer to the agreement to arbitrate, as distinguished from the overall contract in which that agreement is contained. (Weinrott v. Carp, supra, 344 N.Y.S.2d at p. 855, 298 N.E.2d at p. 47.)

In addition, the majority rule is in accord with this state's strong public policy in favor of arbitration as a speedy and relatively inexpensive means of dispute resolution. . . . This is particularly true in cases such as this, where parties of presumptively equal bargaining power have entered into an agreement containing a commitment to arbitrate by a procedure of unchallenged fairness, and one of the parties seeks to avoid arbitration by asserting that the other party fraudulently induced the agreement because he never intended to perform. (See fn. 1, ante.) The difference between a breach of contract and such fraudulent inducement turns upon determination of a party's state of mind at the time the contract was entered into, and we ought not close our eyes to the practical consequences of a rule which would allow a party to avoid an arbitration commitment by relying upon that distinction.

California courts have observed in other contexts the dangers inherent in committing preliminary issues to the courts. "If participants in the arbitral process begin to assert all possible legal or procedural defenses in court proceedings before the arbitration itself can go forward, 'the arbitral wheels would very soon grind to a halt.'" ... And, we have recently warned against "procedural gamesmanship" aimed at undermining the advantages of arbitration. (Christensen v. Dewor Developments, supra, 33 Cal.3d 778, 784, 191 Cal.Rptr. 8, 661 P.2d 1088.) A statutory interpretation which would yield such results is not to be preferred.

We conclude that this court should adopt the majority rule. The scope of arbitration is, of course, a matter of agreement between the parties, and if they choose to limit that scope so as to exclude questions of fraud in the inducement of the contract that choice must be respected. In this state, as under federal law ... doubts concerning the scope of arbitrable issues are to be resolved in favor of arbitration.... Therefore, in the absence of indication of contrary intent, and where the arbitration clause is reasonably susceptible of such an interpretation, claims of fraud in the inducement of the contract (as distinguished from claims of fraud directed to the arbitration clause itself) will be deemed subject to arbitration.

We proceed to apply these principles to the instant case, where the parties agreed to arbitrate "any dispute between the parties hereto with respect to the provisions of this Lease exclusive of those provisions relating to payment of rent." Although this language is not as broad as that considered in Prima Paint other cases have found allegations of fraud covered by quite similar arbitration clauses. (See, e.g., J.P. Stevens & Co., Inc. v. Harrell International, Inc. (Fla.App.1974) 299 So.2d 69, cert. dism. (Fla.1975) 313 So.2d 707.) Moreover, as in Devonshire, the issue of fraud which is asserted here "seems inextricably enmeshed in the other factual issues of the case." (271 F.2d at p. 410; see also Comprehensive Merch. Cat., Inc. v. Madison Sales Corp. (7th Cir.1975) 521 F.2d 1210, 1214.) Indeed, the claim of substantive breach—that the air conditioning did not perform properly—is totally embraced within the claim of fraud—that the lessor knew, at the time of the lease, that the air conditioning would not perform. Thus, if the trial court were to proceed to determine the fraud claim it would almost certainly have to decide the claim of substantive breach as well, and the original expectations of the parties—that such questions would be determined through arbitration—would be totally defeated. However the fraud claim were determined, there would be virtually nothing left for the arbitrator to decide. We conclude that the arbitration clause is broad enough to include this claim of fraud in the inducement.

Accordingly, the judgment is reversed and the superior court is directed to vacate its order denying 100 Oak Street's petition to compel arbitration and to enter an order granting the petition.

■ RICHARDSON, KAUS, BROUSSARD and REYNOSO, JJ., concur.

■ MOSK, JUSTICE, dissenting.

The majority establish a rule that earns a high rank in the cart-before-the-horse category. Instead of first requiring determination of whether the entire agreement was induced by fraud and then, if it was not, proceeding to arbitrate the issue of compliance with its terms, my colleagues order arbitration first and then sometime in the vague future the underlying validity of the very agreement which provided, among other matters, for the arbitration, is to be ascertained. This is resupination: logic and procedure turned upside down.

Code of Civil Procedure section 1281.2 provides that the court shall order arbitration "unless it determines that: ... [¶](b) Grounds exist for the revocation of the agreement." It seems obvious that the "it" refers to the court, and that the Legislature intended the court, not the arbitrator, to determine if grounds exist for revocation of the agreement.

The majority rather curiously admit that the statute calls for determination by the court whether a valid agreement exists, and then they announce that "manifestly no such determination has been made." Obviously. Nor will it be made if the matter must proceed to arbitration before a court can ascertain whether the agreement was induced by fraud.

Another paragraph in Code of Civil Procedure section 1281.2 makes clear the legislative intent in a situation comparable to that before us. The statute declares: "If *the court determines* that there are other issues between the petitioner and the respondent which are not subject to arbitration and which are the subject of *a pending action* or special proceeding *between the petitioner and the respondent* and that a determination of such issues *may make the arbitration unnecessary*, the court may delay its order to arbitrate until the determination of such other issues or until such earlier time as the court specifies" (italics added).

Here again, the Legislature refers to "the court determines," not the arbitrator. It seems to cover our case: if the court finds there was fraud in the inducement of the underlying contract "a determination of such issues may make the arbitration unnecessary"; therefore the court may delay any order for arbitration until the fraud issue is heard and decided. As Justice Black said in another context, the language raises no doubts about its meaning "except to someone anxious to find doubts." (Prima Paint v. Flood & Conklin (1967) 388 U.S. 395, 412, 87 S.Ct. 1801, 1810, 18 L.Ed.2d 1270 (dis. opn.).)

Pursuant to that section, the Court of Appeal in Gustafson v. State Farm Mut. Auto. Ins. Co. (1973) 31 Cal.App.3d 361, 107 Cal.Rptr. 243, held that the trial court should have determined the issue of waiver before ordering arbitration—that it was a matter for the court, not the arbitrator.

I cannot quarrel with federal decisions relied on by the majority, since they are based on provisions of the federal arbitration act, which in turn is bottomed on admiralty and the commerce clause of the federal Constitution. I must concede, however, that I find the decisions unpersuasive, for the federal act specifically exempts from arbitration all contracts that are invalid "upon such grounds as exist at law or in equity for the revocation of any contract." (9 U.S.C. § 2.) This would certainly seem to embrace fraud in the inducement, as alleged in the instant case.

That was the view expressed in the irrefutable dissent by Justices Black, Douglas and Stewart in Prima Paint v. Flood & Conklin, supra, 388 U.S. 395, 412–413, 87 S.Ct. 1801, 1810, 18 L.Ed.2d 1270: "Let us look briefly at the language of the Arbitration Act itself as Congress passed it. Section 2, the key provision of the Act, provides that '[a] written provision in . . . a contract . . . involving commerce to settle by arbitration a controversy thereafter arising out of such contract . . . shall be valid, irrevocable, and enforceable, save upon such grounds as exist at law or in equity for the revocation of any contract.' (Emphasis added.) Section 3 provides that '[i]f any suit . . . be brought . . . upon any issue referable to arbitration under an agreement in writing for such arbitration, the court . . . upon being satisfied that the issue involved in such suit . . . is referable to arbitration under such an agreement, shall . . . stay the trial of the action until such arbitration has been had. . . .' (Emphasis added.) The language of these sections could not, I think, raise doubts about their meaning except to someone anxious to find doubts. They simply mean this: an arbitration agreement is to be enforced by a federal court unless the court, not the arbitrator, finds grounds 'at law or in equity for the revocation of any contract.' Fraud, of course, is one of the most common grounds for revoking a contract. If the contract was procured by fraud, then, unless the defrauded party elects to affirm it, there is absolutely no contract, nothing to be arbitrated. Sections 2 and 3 of the Act assume the existence of a valid contract. They merely provide for enforcement where such a valid contract exists. These provisions were plainly designed to protect a person against whom arbitration is sought to be enforced from having to submit his legal issues as to validity of the contract to the arbitrator. The legislative history of the Act makes this clear." (Fn. omitted.)

Justice Fortas' prevailing opinion in *Prima Paint* observes that the First Circuit in *Lummus Company v. Commonwealth Oil Refining Co.* (1960) 280 F.2d 915, held that if the arbitration clause is regarded by a state as an inseparable part of the contract, a claim of fraud in the inducement must be decided by the court. The high court did not disapprove Lummus; it merely went on to distinguish federal court proceedings, based as they were in Prima Paint on a maritime contract.

. . . While there are a number of other state courts that support the conclusion of the majority here, I am persuaded by the Louisiana court. In George Engine Co., Inc. v. Southern Shipbldg. Corp. (La.1977) 350 So.2d 881, 884–885, the court held that the issue of misrepresentation in the inducement of a contract is not to be submitted to arbitration even though the contract contains an arbitration clause. The court observed that under the Louisiana arbitration act an arbitration agreement was to be judicially enforced unless a court, not an arbitrator, found grounds at law or in equity for revocation of the contract. It reasoned that courts historically have had jurisdiction over legal issues presented by a petition to rescind a contract because of error in its inducement. Fraud in the inducement therefore was to be decided by the courts. The function of arbitrators, the court declared, is to resolve factual controversies arising out of valid contracts. It added that the courts are much better equipped than arbitrators to determine the legal question of misrepresentation or of fraud in the inducement of a contract.

It is one of the essential elements of a contract that the parties enter into it knowingly and consensually, not through fraud, duress, menace, undue influence or mistake. If consent to entering into a contract is obtained by any of the foregoing elements, a court may declare the entire contract to be unenforceable—the entire contract, without exception for any single provision. I can see no reason for selecting one provision of a potentially unenforceable contract, the arbitration clause, and stamping it with our imprimatur.

I would affirm the judgment.

■ BIRD, C.J., concurs.

* * *

Note on *Prima Paint v. Flood & Conklin*

Before 1967, most courts held that if a party raised a contractual defense grounded in state law that would render the entire contract unenforceable or void, a court rather than an arbitrator must rule on the defense.[1] They reasoned that if the contract is invalid, then so too is any promise to arbitrate contained in the contract.[2] But in PRIMA PAINT V. FLOOD & CONKLIN, 388 U.S. 395 (1967), discussed in *Ericksen v. 100 Oak Street*, supra., the Supreme Court rejected this approach, and instead ruled that allegations of fraud in the inducement did not defeat a duty to arbitrate under the contract.

In *Prima Paint*, the plaintiff and Flood & Conklin Mfg. (F & C) entered into two contracts pursuant to which Prima Paint purchased F & C's paint business, F & C provided Prima Paint with current customer lists, and F & C promised not to compete for existing customers or within existing sales areas. F & C also promised to provide consulting services in connection with its manufacturing operations, sales and service for six years. The contract had a broad arbitration clause, covering "any controversy or claim arising out of or relating to this Agreement." One week after the contract was signed, F & C filed for bankruptcy under Chapter XI of the Bankruptcy Act. Prima Paint, which had promised to provide F & C a percentage of receipts from the former F & C customers, ceased making payments.

F & C sought to arbitrate the payment dispute, and Prima Paint sued in District Court seeking recission of the consulting agreement on the basis

---

1. See Linda R. Hirshman, *The Second Arbitration Trilogy: The Federalization of Arbitration Law*, 71 Va. L. Rev. 1305, 1330 (1985).

2. See, e.g., American Airlines v. Louisville and Jefferson County Air Board, 269 F.2d 811, 816–17 (6th Cir. 1959); Kulukundis Shipping v. Amtorg Trading Corp., 126 F.2d 978 (2d Cir. 1942). But see, Robert Lawrence Co. v. Devonshire Fabrics, Inc., 271 F.2d 402 (2d Cir. 1959) (adopting and explaining separability doctrine).

of alleged fraudulent inducement. Jurisdiction was based on diversity of citizenship. Prima Paint also moved to enjoin the pending arbitration and F & C responded with a motion to stay litigation pending arbitration pursuant to Section 3 of the FAA. F & C contended that the issue of fraud in the inducement was an issue for the arbitrator to decide, not an issue to be decided by the court.

The District Court granted F & C's motion and stayed the litigation. It relied on an earlier Second Circuit case, *Robert Lawrence Co. v. Devonshire Fabrics, Inc.*, 271 F.2d 402 (2d Cir.1959), which held that an allegation of fraud in the inducement of a contract generally—as opposed to an allegation of fraud in the inducement of an arbitration clause itself—was a matter for an arbitrator, not a court, to decide. The Court of Appeals affirmed, and the Supreme Court accepted review.

The Supreme Court affirmed the lower courts. Justice Fortas, writing for the majority, endorsed the view of the Second Circuit that *"except where the parties otherwise intend*—arbitration clauses as a matter of federal law are 'separable' from the contracts in which they are embedded, and that where no claim is made that fraud was directed to the arbitration clause itself, a broad arbitration clause will be held to encompass arbitration of the claim that the contract itself was induced by fraud." 388 U.S. at 402 (emphasis in original). Fortas found support for the "separability doctrine" in Section 4 of the FAA, which states that courts must compel parties to arbitrate a dispute "once it is satisfied that 'the making of the agreement for arbitration or the failure to comply [with the arbitration agreement] is not in issue.' " 388 U.S. at 403. He reasoned that Section 4, and Section 3 by analogy, means that "if the claim is fraud in the inducement of the arbitration clause itself—an issue which goes to the 'making' of the agreement to arbitrate—the federal court may proceed to adjudicate it. But the statutory language does not permit the federal court to consider claims of fraud in the inducement of the contract generally." Id. at 403–04.

Justice Black, along with Justices Douglas and Stewart, dissented. He argued that:

> "The Court here holds that the United States Arbitration Act, 9 U.S.C. §§ 1–14, as a matter of federal substantive law, compels a party to a contract containing a written arbitration provision to carry out his 'arbitration agreement' even though a court might, after a fair trial, hold the entire contract—including the arbitration agreement—void because of fraud in the inducement. The Court holds, what is to me fantastic, that the legal issue of a contract's voidness because of fraud is to be decided by persons designated to arbitrate factual controversies arising out of a valid contract between the parties. And the arbitrators who the Court holds are to adjudicate the legal validity of the contract need not even be lawyers, and in all probability will be nonlawyers, wholly unqualified to decide legal issues, and even if qualified to apply the law, not bound to do so. I am by no means sure that thus forcing a person to forgo his opportunity to try his legal issues in the courts where, unlike the situation in arbitration, he may have a jury trial and right to appeal, is not a denial of due process of law. I am satisfied,

however that Congress did not impose any such procedures in the Arbitration Act.''

"... The plain purpose of the Act as written by Congress was this and no more: Congress wanted federal courts to enforce contracts to arbitrate and plainly said so in the Act. But Congress also plainly said that whether a contract containing an arbitration clause can be rescinded on the ground of fraud is to be decided by the courts and not by the arbitrators. Prima here challenged in the courts the validity of its alleged contract with F & C as a whole, not in fragments. If there has never been any valid contract, then there is not now and never has been anything to arbitrate. If Prima's allegations are true, the sum total of what the Court does here is to force Prima to arbitrate a contract which is void and unenforceable before arbitrators who are given the power to make final legal determinations of their own jurisdiction, not even subject to effective review by the highest court in the land. That is not what Congress said Prima must do. It seems to be what the Court thinks would promote the policy of arbitration. I am completely unable to agree to this new version of the Arbitration Act.''

The separability doctrine of *Prima Paint* applies not only to the defense of fraud in the inducement, but also to other contractual defenses, such as unconscionability, lack of consent , illegality and so forth. It operates as a severe restriction on the types of contractual defenses that can be raised as a bar to arbitration.

* * *

Questions

1. What reasons does the *Ericksen* court give for the separability doctrine? Is the doctrine consistent with the holding of *First Options*? Is it consistent with ordinary contract law?

2. Could the court have decided the issue of fraud in the inducement without deciding the issue of breach of the agreement?

3. What does the *Ericksen* court and the Supreme Court in *Prima Paint* mean by an allegation of fraud going to the arbitration clause itself? What might that consist of? Should a court distinguish between fraud in the inducement and fraud in the factum or execution for purposes of the separability doctrine?

* * *

3. ADHESION CONTRACTS, DURESS AND UNCONSCIONABILITY

Graham v. Scissor–Tail, Inc.

28 Cal.3d 807, 623 P.2d 165 (Cal. 1981).

■ THE COURT:

These are two consolidated appeals. Plaintiff Graham appeals from a judgment confirming the award of an arbitrator.... Defendant Scissor–

Tail, Inc., appeals from a special order after judgment taxing costs relating to attorney's fees.... We will reverse the judgment confirming the award, directing the trial court to vacate its order compelling arbitration (see fn. 1, ante) and conduct further proceedings. We will dismiss the appeal from the special order after judgment as moot, 103 Cal.App.3d 115, 162 Cal.Rptr. 798.

I

Plaintiff Bill Graham is an experienced promoter and producer of musical concerts. Defendant C. Russell Bridges, also known as Leon Russell (Russell), is a successful performer and recording artist and the leader of a musical group; he is also a member of the American Federation of Musicians (A.F. of M.). Defendant Scissor–Tail, Inc. (Scissor–Tail) is a California corporation, wholly owned by Russell, which serves as the vehicle by which the services of Russell and his group are marketed. Defendant David Forest Agency, Ltd. (Forest) was, at the time here relevant, acting in the capacity of booking agent for Scissor–Tail.

Early in 1973, Scissor–Tail and Russell decided to formulate and structure a personal appearance tour for the latter and his group. Forest was engaged to assist in this project, and at the suggestion of Dennis Cordell, Russell's personal manager and an officer of Scissor–Tail, contacted plaintiff Graham, who had previously promoted a number of Russell concerts, to request that he provide his services for four of the twelve concerts on the projected tour. A series of four contracts was prepared covering, respectively, concerts at Ontario, Oakland, Long Island, and Philadelphia. Graham signed all four contracts; Scissor–Tail (per Dennis Cordell), for reasons to appear, signed only those relating to the Ontario and Oakland concerts, which were to occur on July 29 and August 5, 1973.

The four contracts in question were all prepared on an identical form known in the industry as an A.F. of M. Form B Contract; in this case each bore the heading of the Forest agency. Aside from matters such as date and time, they differed from one another in only two areas—i. e., the contents of the blanks designated "hours of employment" and "wage agreed upon." The former dealt with matters such as hours of performance and the provision of a guest artist to appear on the program prior to the Russell group. The latter provided that payment was to be "applicable A.F. of M. scale" or a specified percentage (85 percent in the case of Ontario, Oakland, and Philadelphia; 90 percent in the case of Long Island) "of the gross receipts after bonafide, receipted, sanctioned expenses and taxes, whichever is greater." Also here indicated in each case was the capacity of the concert site, the price of tickets, and the potential gross.

The contracts designated Graham as the "purchaser of music" or "employer," the seven members of the group as "musicians." They did not speak explicitly to the question of who was to bear any eventual net losses. The contract forms also provided: "9. In accordance with the Constitution,

By-laws, Rules and Regulations of the Federation, the parties will submit every claim, dispute, controversy or difference involving the musical services arising out of or connected with this contract and the engagement covered thereby for determination by the International Executive Board of the Federation or a similar board of an appropriate local thereof and such determination shall be conclusive, final and binding upon the parties."

As indicated above, all four contracts were signed by plaintiff Graham, his signature appearing below his typed name on a blank designated "signature of employer." Only those contracts relating to the Ontario and Oakland concerts bore a corresponding signature; on those contracts, below the typed name "Scissor–Tail, Inc. by C. Russell Bridges aka Leon Russell" and on a blank designated "signature of leader," is the signature of Dennis Cordell, who as above indicated was Russell's personal manager and an officer of Scissor–Tail.

On the second page of each contract is a list of the seven musicians involved (including Russell), together with an indication of the A.F. of M. local of each.

The Ontario concert took place as scheduled and had gross receipts of $173,000 (out of a potential gross reflected in the contract of "$450,000 plus"), with expenses of $236,000, resulting in a net loss of some $63,000. The Oakland concert also took place, resulting in a net profit of some $98,000. Following this second concert a dispute arose among the parties over who was to bear the loss sustained in the Ontario concert and whether that loss could be offset against the profits of the Oakland concert— Scissor–Tail and Forest taking the position that under the contract Graham was to bear all losses from any concert without offset, Graham urging that under standard industry practice and custom relating to 85/15 and 90/10 contracts such losses should accrue without offset to Scissor–Tail, et al. This dispute remaining unresolved,[3] Scissor–Tail declined to execute the contracts for the Long Island and Philadelphia concerts; apparently these concerts took place as scheduled, but some party other than Graham performed the promotional services.

In October 1973, Graham filed an action for breach of contract, declaratory relief, and rescission against all defendants. Scissor–Tail responded with a petition to compel arbitration. After once ordering arbitration, the trial court in 1974 granted reconsideration in order to permit discovery "limited to the issues of whether an agreement to arbitrate was entered into and whether grounds exist to rescind such agreement...."[4]

3. It appears that in the course of discussions relating to this dispute the question of arbitration before the A.F. of M. was prominently raised by both parties. Graham, in a telegram to Forest dated August 7, 1973, indicated that unless defendants agreed to a compromise suggested by him "we will have to file charges with A.F. of M. based on Leon's breach of these four contracts."

4. Section 1281.2 of the Code of Civil Procedure, as here relevant, provides: "On petition of a party to an arbitration agreement alleging the existence of a written agreement to arbitrate a controversy and that a party thereto refuses to arbitrate such controversy, the court shall order the petitioner and the respondent to arbitrate the controversy if it determines that an

Following such discovery, and in light of resulting depositions lodged with it, the court in March of 1976 finally granted the petition and ordered arbitration. Along with its order, and at Graham's request, the court filed formal findings of fact and conclusions of law.[5]

By letter dated April 12, 1976, the A.F. of M. was advised of the court's order. By late June, however, no hearing date had been set and counsel for Scissor–Tail wrote to the union requesting that a date be set and suggesting certain dates convenient to him. Rather than comply with this request, however, the union, through its International Executive Board, on July 6 issued its decision awarding the full amount of Scissor–Tail's claim against Graham, or some $53,000.[6] Counsel for Graham, protesting against this procedure, was informed by the A.F. of M. that it conformed with normal practice, which contemplated the entry of award without hearing. Thereupon counsel for Graham enlisted the assistance of Scissor–Tail's counsel in the matter and, upon securing the latter's consent, was successful in reopening the matter and having it set for hearing.

In the meantime, on August 10, 1976, Graham had been placed on the union's "defaulter's list"—apparently a list of persons with whom union members may not do business.

On September 10, 1976, Scissor–Tail increased the claim by $20,000 to a total of some $73,000, urging that some of the expenses claimed by Graham with respect to the two concerts were improper. Scissor–Tail further requested interest on the award and $15,000 as attorney's fees.

On October 29, 1976, a hearing was held at the union's western (Hollywood) office before a "referee" appointed by the union president. The referee was a former executive officer and a long-time member of the union; he had acted as a hearing officer in many previous union matters. All parties (excluding Russell himself) and counsel were present. Graham sought to have the proceedings transcribed by a court reporter brought by him; the request was denied and the reporter excused. The hearing thereupon proceeded. Graham produced considerable evidence—consisting of his own testimony, the testimony of another promoter, the stipulated testimony of a third promoter, and three sworn statements by others engaged in the popular music concert field—to the effect that under common and widely held custom and practice in the industry, the promoter under a 90/10 or 85/15 contract was understood to bear no risk of loss because his

agreement to arbitrate the controversy exists, unless it determines that: (a) The right to compel arbitration has been waived by the petitioner; or (b) Grounds exist for the revocation of the agreement...."

5. The court made the following specific findings: "A. Scissor–Tail has not waived its right to compel arbitration; B. Plaintiff Graham did not enter into the arbitration agreements under mistake and no grounds exist for the rescission or revocation of the arbitration agreements, or any of them; and C. That

all of the issues which are raised by the Complaint and First Amended Complaint of Graham, are subject to arbitration."

6. This amount represented 85 percent of the net receipts from the Oakland concert less an advance by Graham to Scissor–Tail prior to the concert. (Apparently Graham had retained the net proceeds of the Oakland concert as an offset against the loss sustained in the Ontario concert.)

share of the profits under such contracts was considerably smaller than under the "normal" contract, under which the promoter takes a larger percentage of the profits but is understood to bear the risk of loss; no contrary evidence was offered by Scissor–Tail. The referee also heard evidence regarding the propriety of certain expenses claimed by Graham and questioned by Scissor–Tail.

On November 5, 1976, in his report to the union's International Executive Board, the referee recommended that Graham be ordered to pay to Scissor–Tail the amount of its original claim (some $53,000; see fn. 6, ante). The balance of the claim—consisting of the items added by Scissor–Tail's September 10 request—was denied, the referee noting that the union had issued no directions to him regarding it.

On February 22, 1977, the union's International Executive Board made its award in conformity with the recommendation of the referee.

Scissor–Tail thereupon filed a petition in the superior court to confirm the award; Graham filed a petition to vacate it. (See Code Civ.Proc., § 1285.) The court granted the former petition and denied the latter; judgment was entered accordingly. (Code Civ.Proc., § 1287.4.)

After entry of judgment Scissor–Tail filed a cost bill which included an item of some $16,000 for attorney's fees. The court granted Graham's motion to tax costs, striking this item on the basis of the arbitrator's (referee's) determination.

Graham appeals from the judgment confirming the arbitrator's award. Scissor-Tail appeals from the order taxing costs.

II

We first turn our attention to the validity of the order compelling arbitration. Plaintiff, as we have indicated, is entitled to challenge this order on the instant appeal. (See fn. 1, ante.)

Plaintiff's basic contention in this respect is that the order compelling arbitration was in error because the underlying agreement—at least insofar as it required arbitration of disputes before the A.F. of M.—was an unenforceable contract of adhesion. Two separate questions are thus presented, each of which requires separate consideration: (1) Is this a contract of adhesion? (2) If so, is it unenforceable?

A.

The term "contract of adhesion," now long a part of our legal vocabulary, has been variously defined in the cases and other legal literature. The serviceable general definition first suggested by Justice Tobriner in 1961, however, has well stood the test of time and will bear little improvement: "The term signifies a standardized contract, which, imposed and drafted by the party of superior bargaining strength, relegates to the subscribing party only the opportunity to adhere to the contract or reject it." (Neal v. State Farm Ins. Cos. (1961) 188 Cal.App.2d 690, 694, 10 Cal.Rptr. 781.)

Such contracts are, of course, a familiar part of the modern legal landscape, in which the classical model of "free" contracting by parties of equal or near-equal bargaining strength is often found to be unresponsive to the realities brought about by increasing concentrations of economic and other power. They are an inevitable fact of life for all citizens—business-man and consumer alike. While not lacking in social advantages, they bear within them the clear danger of oppression and overreaching. It is in the context of this tension—between social advantage in the light of modern conditions on the one hand, and the danger of oppression on the other—that courts and legislatures have sometimes acted to prevent perceived abuses.

We believe that the contract here in question, in light of all of the circumstances presented, may be fairly described as adhesive. Although defendant and its supporting amicus curiae are strenuous in their insistence that Graham's prominence and success in the promotion of popular music concerts afforded him considerable bargaining strength in the subject negotiations, the record before us fairly establishes that he, for all his asserted stature in the industry, was here reduced to the humble role of "adherent." It appears that all concert artists and groups of any significance or prominence are members of the A.F. of M.; that pursuant to express provision of the A.F. of M.'s constitution and bylaws members are not permitted to sign any form of contract other than that issued by the union; that the A.F. of M. Form B. Contract in use at the time here relevant included the arbitration provisions here in question (see fn. 2, ante, and accompanying text); and that Scissor–Tail insisted upon the use of 85/15 and 90/10 contractual arrangements. In these circumstances it must be concluded that Graham, whatever his asserted prominence in the industry, was required by the realities of his business as a concert promoter to sign A.F. of M. form contracts with any concert artist with whom he wished to do business—and that in the case before us he, wishing to promote the Russell concerts, was presented with the nonnegotiable option of accepting such contracts on an 85/15 or 90/10 basis or not at all.

It is argued, however, that other provisions of the contract—e. g., those relating to the length, time, and date of the concert and the selection of a special guest artist to appear on the program preceding the Russell group—were subject to negotiation and that this consideration operated to mitigate or remove all adhesive characteristics from the contract. We do not agree.... The terms here asserted to be subject to negotiation, assuming that they were in fact so, were of relatively minor significance in comparison to those imposed by Scissor-Tail, which included not only the provision concerning the manner and rate of compensation but that dictating a union forum for the resolution of any disputes. In these circumstances we cannot conclude that the presence of other assertedly negotiable terms acted to remove the taint of adhesion.

B.

To describe a contract as adhesive in character is not to indicate its legal effect. It is, rather, "the beginning and not the end of the analysis insofar as enforceability of its terms is concerned.'' (Wheeler v. St. Joseph Hospital, supra, 63 Cal.App.3d 345, 357, 133 Cal.Rptr. 775.) Thus, a contract of adhesion is fully enforceable according to its terms ... unless certain other factors are present which, under established legal rules—legislative or judicial—operate to render it otherwise.

Generally speaking, there are two judicially imposed limitations on the enforcement of adhesion contracts or provisions thereof. The first is that such a contract or provision which does not fall within the reasonable expectations of the weaker or ''adhering'' party will not be enforced against him.... The second—principle of equity applicable to all contracts generally—is that a contract or provision, even if consistent with the reasonable expectations of the parties, will be denied enforcement if, considered in its context, it is unduly oppressive or ''unconscionable.'' ... We proceed to examine whether the instant contract, and especially that provision thereof requiring the arbitration of disputes before the A.F. of M., should have been denied enforcement under either of these two principles.

We cannot conclude on the record before us that the contractual provision requiring arbitration of disputes before the A.F. of M. was in any way contrary to the reasonable expectations of plaintiff Graham. By his own declarations and testimony, he had been a party to literally thousands of A.F. of M. contracts containing a similar provision; indeed it appears that during the 3 years preceding the instant contracts he had promoted 15 or more concerts with Scissor-Tail, on each occasion signing a contract containing arbitration provisions similar to those here in question. It also appears that he had been involved in prior proceedings before the A.F. of M. regarding disputes with other musical groups arising under prior contracts. Finally, the discussions taking place following the Oakland concert, together with his telegram indicating that he himself would file charges with the A.F. of M. if the matter were not settled to his satisfaction (see fn. 3, ante), all strongly suggest an abiding awareness on his part that all disputes arising under the contracts were to be resolved by arbitration before the A.F. of M. For all of these reasons it must be concluded that the provisions requiring such arbitration (see fn. 2, ante, and accompanying text) were wholly consistent with Graham's reasonable expectations upon entering into the contract.

We are thus brought to the question whether the contract provision requiring the arbitration of disputes *before the A.F. of M.* because it designates an arbitrator who, by reason of its status and identity, is presumptively biased in favor of one party—is for that reason to be deemed unconscionable and unenforceable. Graham, although couching his arguments in other terminology, essentially maintains that it is—the thrust of his position being that to allow the A.F. of M. to sit in judgment of a dispute arising between one of its members and a contracting nonmember is so inimical to fundamental notions of fairness as to require nonenforcement. We proceed to a consideration of this contention.

We are met at the outset of our inquiry with certain provisions of the California Arbitration Act which, it would seem, contemplate complete contractual autonomy in the choice of an arbitrator. Section 1281.6 of the Code of Civil Procedure provides that "[I]f the arbitration agreement provides a method of appointing an arbitrator, such method shall be followed." Section 1282 of the same code states that *"(u)nless the arbitration agreement otherwise provides"* (italics added) arbitration shall be by a neutral arbitrator either alone or in combination with other neutral and/or nonneutral arbitrators. Subsection (d) of the same section provides: *"If there is no neutral arbitrator,* the powers and duties of a neutral arbitrator may be exercised by a majority of the arbitrators." (Italics added.)

In Federico v. Frick (1970) 3 Cal.App.3d 872, 84 Cal.Rptr. 74, a case factually similar to that here before us, it was held that these provisions "expressly permit[ ] the parties to an arbitration to agree to the conduct of arbitration proceedings by a nonneutral arbitrator.... [A]rbitration being a creature of statute, the statute controls." (3 Cal.App.3d at p. 876, fn. omitted.) This result followed, the court concluded, even though "[e]lementary fairness may seem to demand that arbitration proceedings be under the control of a neutral and impartial arbitrator, ..." (Id.) The court noted by way of footnote that "many government contracts customarily provide that all disputes arising under them shall be arbitrated by a specified official of the governmental entity which is one of the contracting parties."...

The case of Gear v. Webster (1968) 258 Cal.App.2d 57, 65 Cal.Rptr. 255 reached a similar result on the same statutory grounds. It should be noted, however, that this case, concerning a dispute between a salesman and a broker, both members of the arbitrating local board of realtors, was intra-organizational in nature. Federico and the instant case, of course, are not.

There have been a substantial number of California cases involving the compulsion of unwilling contractual parties (both employees and customers) to arbitrate disputes with members of the New York Stock Exchange before the latter body.... All but one have ordered arbitration before that body, but only the two first cited have given explicit attention to the issue we now consider—i. e., whether potential bias said to arise from the composition of the arbitral body should preclude enforcement of a contractual provision requiring arbitration before it. Even in these cases the issue was clouded by other factors. Thus, in the Arrieta case the court, citing Federico, stated that "(p)otential unfairness from the non-neutral nature of an arbitrator is not a ground for vacation of the arbitration award," but it was noted that under the applicable arbitration rules there existed procedures for the disqualification of biased arbitrators—a factor not here present. (59 Cal.App.3d at p. 330, 130 Cal.Rptr. 534.) In Richards, on the other hand, the court refused to compel arbitration on the ground, inter alia, that there was "basic apparent unfairness in requiring the nonmember to submit to arbitrators, all of whom have been appointed by the Exchange of which Merrill Lynch is a member." (64 Cal.App.3d at p. 903, 135 Cal.Rptr. 26, fn. omitted.) It was there made clear, however, that it was this factor *in combination with others* which required the result reached.

There are, of course, a host of cases from other jurisdictions which bear upon the problem. We here note only one, which we consider of particular interest. In the Matter of Cross & Brown Company (1957) 4 A.D.2d 501, 167 N.Y.S.2d 573, the court considered the validity of a contractual provision in an employment contract which provided that any dispute under the contract was to be arbitrated before the employer, whose decision was to be final. The court, in essence, found the provision unconscionable; enforcement was denied. "A well-recognized principle of 'natural justice,'" the court stated, "is that a man may not be a judge in his own cause. Irrespective of any proof of actual bias or prejudice, the law presumes that a party to a dispute cannot have that disinterestedness and impartiality necessary to act in a judicial or quasi-judicial capacity regarding that controversy. This absolute disqualification to act rests upon sound public policy. Any other rule would be repugnant to a proper sense of justice." (Id., at p. 575.) The court went on, however, to explain the limits of its holding in the following terms: "As a general rule, since arbitration is a contractual method of settling disputes, whom the parties choose to act as an arbitrator is a matter of their own judgment. An interest in the dispute or a relationship with a party, if known to the parties to the agreement when the arbitrator is chosen, will not disqualify the arbitrator from acting. In Lipschutz v. Gutwirth, 304 N.Y. 58, 61–62, 106 N.E.2d 8, 10, the Court said: 'The spirit of the arbitration law being the fuller effectuation of contractual rights, the method for selecting arbitrators and the composition of the arbitral tribunal have been left to the contract of the parties.' ... By our decision herein we do not intend to limit the power of contracting parties to designate arbitrators who, with the knowledge of the parties, may have an interest in the dispute or who sustain some relationship to a party which would otherwise disqualify the arbitrator from serving. What we do hold is that no party to a contract, or someone so identified with the party as to be in fact, even though not in name, the party, can be designated as an arbitrator to decide disputes under it. Apart from outraging public policy, such an agreement is illusory; for while in form it provides for arbitration, in substance it yields the power to an adverse party to decide disputes under the contract." (Id., at p. 576.)

We believe that what was said in the Cross & Brown case, viewed against the provisions of our arbitration act, provides an instructive framework for the consideration of cases such as that now confronting us. The arbitration act, as we read it, expressly recognizes the right of contractual parties to provide for the resolution of contractual disputes by arbitral machinery of their own design and composition.... In so doing we do not believe—and the Arbitration Act does not require—that the parties are or should be strictly precluded from designating as arbitrator a person or entity who, by reason of relationship to a party or some similar factor, can be expected to adopt something other than a "neutral" stance in determining disputes. At the same time we must note that when as here the contract designating such an arbitrator is the product of circumstances suggestive of adhesion, the possibility of overreaching by the dominant party looms large; contracts concluded in such circumstances, then, must be scrutinized with particular care to insure that the party of lesser bargaining power, in agreeing thereto, is not left in a position depriving him of any realistic and fair opportunity to prevail in a dispute under its terms.

As the United States Supreme Court has said in a related context, "Congress has put its blessing on private dispute settlement arrangements ..., but it was anticipated, we are sure, that the contractual machinery would operate within some minimum levels of integrity." (Hines v. Anchor Motor Freight (1976) 424 U.S. 554, 571, 96 S.Ct. 1048, 1059, 47 L.Ed.2d 231.) By the same token it appears that the Legislature has determined that the parties shall have considerable leeway in structuring the dispute settlement arrangements by which they are bound; while recognizing that the leeway may permit the establishment of arrangements which vary to some extent from the dead-center of "neutrality," we at the same time must insist—and most especially in circumstances smacking of adhesion— that certain "minimum levels of integrity" be achieved if the arrangement in question is to pass judicial muster.

It is for the courts of course to determine—largely on a case by case basis—what these "minimum levels of integrity" shall be. In doing so it must not be lost sight of that the "contractual machinery" of the parties is intended by them to serve as a substitute for—although of course not a duplicate of—formal judicial proceedings. What is contemplated, then, is a *tribunal* i.e., an entity or body which "hears and decides" disputes. (See Webster's New Internat. Dict. (2d ed. 1941) p. 2707.) As the Cross & Brown case indicates, an entity or body which by its nature is incapable of "deciding" on the basis of what it has "heard"—as, in that case, one of the principal parties to the contract—does not qualify. "Unless we close our eyes to realities," the court there said, "the agreement here becomes, not a contract to arbitrate, but an engagement to capitulate." (167 N.Y.S.2d at p. 576.) The same result would follow, the court there suggests, when one "so identified with the party as to be in fact, even though not in name, the party" is designated. (Id.) In such cases as this, the agreement to *arbitrate* is essentially illusory. Here, clearly, "minimum levels of integrity" are not achieved, and the "agreement to arbitrate" should be denied enforcement on grounds of unconscionability.

There is we think a second basis, related to that just discussed, for denying enforcement on such grounds. The fact that an entity or body designated by contract to act as arbitrator of contractual disputes is one capable of acting as a *tribunal* i.e., in the sense of *hearing* a dispute and *deciding* fairly and rationally on the basis of what it has heard is of little consequence if it proceeds under rules which deny a party the fair opportunity to present his side of the dispute. Thus, if a party resisting arbitration can show that the rules under which arbitration is to proceed will operate to deprive him of what we in other contexts have termed the common law right of fair procedure, the agreement to arbitrate should not be enforced. In this respect it is well to reiterate, adapting it to the present context, what we said in the seminal case on this subject. "The common law requirement of a fair procedure does not compel formal proceedings with all the embellishments of a court trial (citation), nor adherence to a single mode of process. It may be satisfied by any one of a variety of procedures which afford a fair opportunity for (a disputant) to present his position. As such, this court should not attempt to fix a rigid procedure that must invariably be observed." (Pinsker v. Pacific Coast Society of Orthodontists (1974) 12 Cal.3d 541, 555, 116 Cal.Rptr. 245.) When it can be demonstrated, however, that the clear effect of the established procedure of the arbitrator will be to deny the resisting party a fair opportunity to present his position, the court should refuse to compel arbitration.[23]

We thus return to the narrow question here before us: Is the contract we here consider, insofar as it requires the arbitration of all disputes arising thereunder before the A.F. of M., to be deemed unconscionable and unenforceable?

The answer to this question, we have concluded, must clearly be yes. Although our review of the record has disclosed nothing which would indicate that A.F. of M. procedures operate to deny any party a fair opportunity to present his position prior to decision, we are of the view that the "minimum levels of integrity" which are requisite to a contractual arrangement for the nonjudicial resolution of disputes are not achieved by an arrangement which designates the union of one of the parties as the arbitrator of disputes arising out of employment—especially when, as here, the arrangement is the product of circumstances indicative of adhesion.

As we have indicated above, drawing from the teaching of the Cross & Brown case, a contract which purports to designate one of the parties as the arbitrator of all disputes arising thereunder is to this extent illusory— the reason being that the party so designated will have an interest in the outcome which, in the view of the law, will render fair and reasoned decision, based on the evidence presented, a virtual impossibility. Because, as we have explained, arbitration (as a contractually structured substitute for formal judicial proceedings) contemplates just such a decision, a contractual party may not act in the capacity of arbitrator—and a contractual provision which designates him to serve in that capacity is to be denied enforcement on grounds of unconscionability. We have also indicated that the same result would follow, and for the same reasons, when the designated arbitrator is not the party himself but one whose interests are so allied with those of the party that, for all practical purposes, he is subject to the same disabilities which prevent the party himself from serving. Again, a contractual provision designating such an entity as arbitrator must be denied enforcement on the ground that it would be unconscionable to permit that entity to so serve.

A labor union is an association or combination of workers organized for the purpose of securing through united action the most favorable condi-

---

23. Enforcement of an agreement to arbitrate should be denied on this ground, we think, only in the clearest of cases, i.e., when the applicable procedures essentially preclude the possibility of a fair hearing. In all other cases the matter should be permitted to proceed to arbitration. If, in the course of arbitration proceedings, the resisting party is actually denied a fair opportunity to present his position, ample means for relief are available through a subsequent petition to vacate the award. . . .

tions as regards wages or rates of pay, hours, and conditions of employment for its members; the primary function of such an organization is that of bargaining with employers on behalf of its membership in order to achieve these objectives.... By its very nature, therefore, a labor union addresses disputes concerning compensation arrangements between its members and third parties with interests identical to those of the affected members; to suppose that it would do otherwise is to suppose that it would act in a manner inconsistent with its reason for being.

In the view of these considerations we think it must be concluded that a contractual provision designating the union of one of the parties to the contract as the arbitrator of all disputes arising thereunder—including those concerning the compensation due under the contract—does not achieve the "minimum levels of integrity" which we must demand of a contractually structured substitute for judicial proceedings. Such a provision, being inimical to the concept of arbitration as we understand it, would be denied enforcement in any circumstances; clearly it cannot stand in a case which, like that before us, requires the careful and searching scrutiny appropriate to a contract with manifestly adhesive characteristics. The trial court's order compelling arbitration in the instant case was therefore in error and must be reversed.

III

[The Court rejected the Defendant's argument that the agreement was arbitrable under § 301 of the LMRA.]

IV

We have held that the provision of the instant contract requiring arbitration of disputes arising thereunder before the A.F. of M. is unconscionable and unenforceable, and that the order compelling arbitration pursuant to it was in error. In light of the strong public policy of this state in favor of resolving disputes by arbitration, however, we do not believe that the parties herein should for this reason be precluded from availing themselves of nonjudicial means of settling their differences. The parties have indeed agreed to arbitrate, but in so doing they have named as sole and exclusive arbitrator an entity which we cannot permit to serve in that broad capacity. In these circumstances we do not believe that the parties should now be precluded from attempting to agree on an arbitrator who is not subject to the disabilities we have discussed. We therefore conclude that upon remand the trial court should afford the parties a reasonable opportunity to agree on a suitable arbitrator and, failing such agreement, the court should on petition of either party appoint the arbitrator. (See and cf. Code Civ.Proc., § 1281.6.) In the absence of an agreement or petition to appoint, the court should proceed to a judicial determination of the controversy.

The judgment is reversed and the cause remanded to the trial court with directions to vacate its order compelling arbitration and undertake further proceedings in conformity with the views expressed in this opinion.

Scissor–Tail's appeal from the special order after judgment taxing costs relating to attorney's fees is dismissed as moot.

* * *

Questions

1.   Under the court's reasoning, if Graham were to obtain a membership in the American Federation of Musicians, would the arbitration agreement still be unconscionable?

2.   Does the reasoning in this case suggest that a securities industry arbitration panel, as described in the next case, would also be treated as unconscionable?

3.   Can parties decide on any arbitration process they choose? Suppose, for example, two parties agree to an arbitration procedure in which the brother-in-law of one of them will to decide who wins and who loses in any dispute that might arise? Would this be enforceable? Can parties decide to toss a coin in the event of a dispute? Can they decide that one of the parties will decide all disputes? Or, does the *Graham v. Scissor–Tail* court suggest that there is some essential minimum due process built into the concept of "arbitration" itself? If so, what kinds of minimal procedures are required? What kinds of procedures would so violate that essential meaning of the term arbitration as to no longer come under the FAA?

* * *

Hope v. Superior Court of the County of Santa Clara

175 Cal.Rptr. 851 (Cal.Ct.App.1981).

■ GRODIN, ASSOCIATE JUSTICE.

In Graham v. Scissor–Tail, Inc. (1981) 28 Cal.3d 807, 171 Cal.Rptr. 604, 623 P.2d 165, the California Supreme Court established certain guidelines for determining when an arbitration agreement constitutes an unenforceable contract of adhesion. In this proceeding we are called upon to apply those guidelines to contracts of employment between a securities brokerage firm and two of its account executives, calling for settlement of a broad range of disputes through arbitration procedures prescribed in the constitution and rules of the New York Stock Exchange. We shall hold that the agreement for arbitration in this case is a contract of adhesion under applicable principles, and that the procedures for arbitration prescribed by the constitution and rules of the New York Stock Exchange are so one-sided, as applied to employer-employee disputes, as to render the agreement unenforceable.

Background.

Petitioners Robert W. Hope and K. James Pond were employed as account executives in the Palo Alto office of real party in interest Shearson

Hayden Stone, Inc. (Shearson). In February 1979, they were both given the option of resigning or being terminated. They left, went to work for a competitor of Shearson's, and later sued Shearson in respondent superior court claiming that Shearson owed them more than $100,000 for commissions. They also claimed that Shearson had tortiously interfered with their advantageous business relationships and engaged in unfair competition by misrepresenting their honesty and skill to Shearson's clients, by making false and derogatory comments about their abilities and experience to local brokerage firms, and by delaying or refusing to transfer accounts to their new brokerage firm.

Shearson moved to stay the proceedings (Code Civ.Proc., § 1281.4) and to compel arbitration (Code Civ.Proc., § 1281.2) on the basis of a provision contained in a seven-page "Application for Approval of Employment" which each petitioner had signed when he was first employed by Shearson. The application is a form (No. RE–1) supplied by the New York Stock Exchange, of which Shearson is a member. The provision reads: "I agree that any controversy between me and any member or member organization or affiliate or subsidiary thereof arising out of my employment or the termination of my employment shall be settled by arbitration at the instance of any such party in accordance with the arbitration procedure prescribed in the Constitution and rules then obtaining of the New York Stock Exchange, Inc."

The constitution of the New York Stock Exchange is a formidable document of some seventy pages. Provisions relating to arbitration are found in article VIII.[1] Under these provisions, the chairman of the board of directors of the Exchange (subject to approval by the board itself) appoints a board of arbitration composed of such number of members and allied members of the Exchange as he deems necessary, and two panels of arbitrators "composed of persons who are residents of or have their places of business in the Metropolitan area of the City of New York." The first panel is composed of persons engaged in the securities business, and the second of persons not so engaged. The chairman is empowered to appoint similar panels to serve outside the City of New York. In addition, he is called upon to designate one of the officers or other employees of the Exchange as arbitration director.

Controversies between a non-member and a member of the Exchange (as in the present case), unless they involve a public customer or less than $100,000, are heard and determined by five arbitrators selected by the arbitration director, at least three of whom must be from the second panel unless the non-member requests a greater number from the first panel. Such arbitration proceedings are to be held "where designated by the Exchange" and conducted "in such manner and pursuant to such rules as the Board of Directors shall from time to time adopt." Subject to rules of

---

1. Article VIII, and the rules of the board of directors pertaining to arbitration, have been amended in certain relevant respects since the trial court's ruling. The par- ties stipulated at oral argument that the case should be decided on the basis of the current rules.

the board, the arbitrators determine the amount chargeable to the parties as costs, to cover the expense of the hearings.

Current rules of the board pertaining to arbitration provide that a party may peremptorily challenge one member of the arbitration panel. In addition, arbitrators are required to disclose to the director of arbitration "any circumstances which might preclude such arbitrator from rendering an objective and impartial determination," and the director is empowered to remove "an arbitrator who discloses such information." The rules also contain a schedule of fees which must be deposited by a claimant with the Exchange in advance of arbitration, unless the deposit is waived by the director of arbitration. Where the amount in dispute is $100,000 and over, the amount of the required deposit is $550.

Petitioners argued to the trial court, among other things, that they never saw the relevant provisions of the Exchange's constitution and bylaws, and that in any event they should not be bound by those provisions, which were adhesive and unfair. When the trial court ordered arbitration nevertheless, petitioners sought relief through a petition for writ of mandate, filed in this court and then in the Supreme Court. The Supreme Court issued an alternative writ and, after its decision in Graham v. Scissor–Tail, Inc., supra, 28 Cal.3d 807, 171 Cal.Rptr. 604 transferred the case to this court for reconsideration and determination in light of that opinion.

At oral argument before this court, the parties agreed that under Labor Code section 229, as applied in Ware v. Merrill Lynch, Pierce, Fenner & Smith, Inc. (1972) 24 Cal.App.3d 35, 43–45, 100 Cal.Rptr. 791, affd. 414 U.S. 117, 94 S.Ct. 383, 38 L.Ed.2d 348, petitioners' claim against Shearson for commissions due is exempt from arbitration as a matter of state policy.[3] This leaves at issue petitioners' tort claims for interference with advantageous business relationships and unfair competition. Petitioners' contention that these claims are not within the scope of arbitration is without merit: the arbitration provision contained in the employment application form is broadly phrased to include "any controversy . . . arising out of my employment *or the termination of my employment*" (emphasis added), and in Lewsadder v. Mitchum, Jones & Templeton, Inc., supra, 36 Cal.App.3d at p. 259, 111 Cal.Rptr. 405, an agreement which did not contain the emphasized language was held broad enough to include tort claims arising out of termination. We therefore proceed to consider the issues posed by the Supreme Court's transfer order.

The Scissor–Tail Opinion.

In Graham v. Scissor–Tail, Inc., supra, 28 Cal.3d 807, Bill Graham, promoter and producer of musical concerts, entered into a series of con-

---

3. Section 229 provides: "Actions to enforce the provisions of this article for the collection of due and unpaid wages claimed by an individual may be maintained without regard to the existence of any private agreement to arbitrate. This section shall not apply to claims involving any dispute concerning the interpretation or application of any collective bargaining agreement containing such an arbitration agreement." . . .

tracts with a group of musicians and their representatives on forms provided by the American Federation of Musicians (A.F. of M.), a labor union which included the contracting musicians as members...

The Supreme Court first determined that the contracts involved were, in light of all the circumstances, contracts of adhesion...

The court went on to observe that, while the adhesive character of a contract will not itself preclude enforcement, "there are two judicially imposed limitations on the enforcement of adhesion contracts or provisions thereof. The first is that such a contract or provision which does not fall within the reasonable expectations of the weaker or 'adhering' party will not be enforced against him. (Citations; fn. omitted.) The second—a principle of equity application to all contracts generally—is that a contract or provision, even if consistent with the reasonable expectations of the parties, will be denied enforcement if, considered in its context, it is unduly oppressive or 'unconscionable.' (Citations)." (Id., at p. 820, 171 Cal.Rptr. 604, 623 P.2d 165.)

Finally, the court concluded that the contractual provision requiring arbitration of disputes before the A.F. of M., while not contrary to the reasonable expectations of the parties, was nevertheless unconscionable, and therefore unenforceable "because it designates an arbitrator who, by reason of its status and identity, is presumptively biased in favor of one party." (Id., at p. 821, 171 Cal.Rptr. 604, 623 P.2d 165.) Though the California Arbitration Act does not strictly preclude parties from designating a non-neutral arbitrator "when ... the contract designating such an arbitrator is the product of circumstances suggestive of adhesion, the possibility of overreaching by the dominant party looms large; contracts concluded in such circumstances, then, must be scrutinized with particular care to insure that the party of lesser bargaining power, in agreeing thereto, is not left in a position depriving him of any realistic and fair opportunity to prevail in a dispute under its terms." (Id., at pp. 824–825, 171 Cal.Rptr. 604, 623 P.2d 165.) Thus, "certain 'minimum levels of integrity' [must] be achieved if the arrangement in question is to pass judicial muster."

Application of Scissor–Tail.

Here, as in Scissor–Tail, the contract containing the arbitration provision was adhesive in nature. It consisted of a standard employment application form, prepared by the New York Stock Exchange, and imposed by Shearson upon all applicants for employment. Shearson does not claim that petitioners had any options other than "to adhere to the contract or reject it." (28 Cal.3d at p. 817, 171 Cal.Rptr. 604, 623 P.2d 165.) Petitioners' bargaining strength in relation to Shearson was patently less than was Graham's in relation to the musicians and their representatives.

We must also conclude on the basis of the standards set forth in Scissor–Tail that the arbitration provisions contained in the contract were unconscionable, and therefore unenforceable. Whether or not those provisions were contrary to the reasonable expectations of the parties is an issue we cannot determine on this record; but here, as is Scissor–Tail, the arbitral body is so associated with a party to the contract, i.e., Shearson, as to be presumptively biased in favor of that party.

The board of directors of the New York Stock Exchange consists of twenty directors elected by members of the Exchange and a chairman of the board elected by the board. Ten of the directors are required to be representatives of the public, none of whom are, or are affiliated with, brokers or dealers in securities; the remaining ten must be members or allied members of the Exchange bearing specified relationships to member corporations or firms. The constitution provides for "allied members" and this category of membership can include a principal executive officer of a member corporation, or a person who controls such a corporation, but it does not include employees in the category of petitioners, and even "allied members" do not vote for the board of directors.

The New York Stock Exchange, and thus its board of directors, performs a variety of quasi-public functions; but insofar as the board of directors functions in disputes between member firms and their employees, it is presumptively biased in favor of management in the same way that the Supreme Court deemed the International Executive Board of the A.F. of M. to be presumptively biased in favor of member musicians. This is not to say that members of the board of directors are in fact biased, or that they would necessarily exercise their authority in a consciously biased fashion; it is to say that the structure of governance of the Exchange is such that there exists a presumptive *institutional* bias in favor of member firms and members who constitute the electoral constituency of the board. Petitioners, being outside that constituency (cf. Gear v. Webster (1968) 258 Cal.App.2d 57, 65 Cal.Rptr. 255; Graham v. Scissor–Tail, Inc., supra, 28 Cal.3d 807, 822, 171 Cal.Rptr. 604, 623 P.2d 165) have legitimate cause to complain.

It does not serve adequately to distinguish Scissor–Tail that the arbitration tribunal in that case was the governing board of the union while here it is not the board itself but a panel of arbitrators appointed by the chairman with the approval of the board. The presumption of bias does not disappear simply because the decisional power is delegated. Nor is the presumption dispelled by rules requiring the arbitrators to be persons not engaged in the securities business, or giving the non-member one peremptory challenge, or granting the director of arbitration authority to disqualify an arbitrator. Evenhandedness could be assured by a procedure which permits selection of arbitrators by the parties to the dispute or, failing that, through the auspices of some truly neutral party. In the absence of such a procedure we must conclude, as in Scissor–Tail, that the arbitration procedures of the New York Stock Exchange fail to meet minimal levels of integrity.

In Scissor–Tail the court remanded with instructions that the trial court should afford the parties a reasonable opportunity to agree on a suitable arbitrator and, failing such agreement, the court itself should on petition of either party appoint the arbitrator. (28 Cal.3d at p. 831, 171

Cal.Rptr. 604, 623 P.2d 165.) Neither party requests such a procedure here. Moreover, arbitration of the tort issues would be somewhat complicated by the non-arbitrable nature of related issues based upon petitioners' claim for commissions due. We consider that justice would be better served in this case by allowing petitioners to proceed with their action in court.

Accordingly, a peremptory writ will issue requiring the respondent court to vacate its order of July 10, 1979, granting the petition of real parties in interest for an order to arbitrate the dispute therein pursuant to the rules of the New York Stock Exchange, and to enter an order denying said petition.

■ ELKINGTON, ACTING P. J., and NEWSOM, J., concur.

* * *

Questions

1.   Does the court in *Hope* apply the same standard for finding unconscionability as it applied in *Graham v. Scissor–Tail*? Is this an easier or a harder case?

2.   How would this case come out if it had been decided after *Rodriguez*, *McMahon* and *Gilmer*, all of which dealt with securities industry arbitration panels?

* * *

Broemmer v. Abortion Services of Phoenix, Ltd.

173 Ariz. 148, 840 P.2d 1013 (Ariz. 1992).

■ MOELLER, VICE CHIEF JUSTICE.

Melinda Kay Broemmer (plaintiff) asks this court to review a court of appeals opinion that held that an "Agreement to Arbitrate" which she signed prior to undergoing a clinical abortion is an enforceable, albeit an adhesive, contract. Broemmer v. Otto, 169 Ariz. 543, 821 P.2d 204 (1991). The opinion affirmed the trial court's grant of summary judgment in favor of Abortion Services of Phoenix and Dr. Otto (defendants). Because we hold the agreement to arbitrate is unenforceable as against plaintiff, we reverse the trial court and vacate in part the court of appeals opinion. We have jurisdiction pursuant to Ariz. Const. art. 6, § 5(3) and A.R.S. § 12–120.24.

FACTS AND PROCEDURAL HISTORY

In December 1986, plaintiff, an Iowa resident, was 21 years old, unmarried, and 16 or 17 weeks pregnant. She was a high school graduate earning less than $100.00 a week and had no medical benefits. The father-to-be insisted that plaintiff have an abortion, but her parents advised against it. Plaintiff's uncontested affidavit describes the time as one of considerable confusion and emotional and physical turmoil for her.

Plaintiff's mother contacted Abortion Services of Phoenix and made an appointment for her daughter for December 29, 1986. During their visit to the clinic that day, plaintiff and her mother expected, but did not receive, information and counseling on alternatives to abortion and the nature of the operation. When plaintiff and her mother arrived at the clinic, plaintiff was escorted into an adjoining room and asked to complete three forms, one of which is the agreement to arbitrate at issue in this case. The agreement to arbitrate included language that "any dispute aris[ing] between the Parties as a result of the fees and/or services" would be settled by binding arbitration and that "any arbitrators appointed by the AAA [American Arbitration Association] shall be licensed medical doctors who specialize in obstetrics/gynecology." The two other documents plaintiff completed at the same time were a 2–page consent-to-operate form and a questionnaire asking for a detailed medical history. Plaintiff completed all three forms in less than 5 minutes and returned them to the front desk. Clinic staff made no attempt to explain the agreement to plaintiff before or after she signed, and did not provide plaintiff with copies of the forms. After plaintiff returned the forms to the front desk, she was taken into an examination room where pre-operation procedures were performed. She was then instructed to return at 7:00 a.m. the next morning for the termination procedure. Plaintiff returned the following day and Doctor Otto performed the abortion. As a result of the procedure, plaintiff suffered a punctured uterus that required medical treatment.

Plaintiff filed a malpractice complaint in June 1988, approximately 1½ years after the medical procedure. By the time litigation commenced, plaintiff could recall completing and signing the medical history and consent-to-operate forms, but could not recall signing the agreement to arbitrate. Defendants moved to dismiss, contending that the trial court lacked subject matter jurisdiction because arbitration was required. In opposition, plaintiff submitted affidavits that remain uncontroverted. The trial court considered the affidavits, apparently treated the motion to dismiss as one for summary judgment, and granted summary judgment to the defendants. Plaintiff's motion to vacate, quash or set aside the order, or to stay the claim pending arbitration, was denied.

On appeal, the court of appeals held that although the contract was one of adhesion, it was nevertheless enforceable because it did not fall outside plaintiff's reasonable expectations and was not unconscionable.... We granted plaintiff's petition for review ...

We will resolve the one issue which is dispositive: Under the undisputed facts in this case, is the agreement to arbitrate enforceable against plaintiff? We hold that it is not.

DISCUSSION

I.   The Contract is One of Adhesion

When the facts are undisputed, this court is not bound by the trial court's conclusions and may make its own analysis of the facts or legal instruments on which the case turns. Tovrea Land & Cattle Co. v. Linsenmeyer, 100 Ariz. 107, 114, 412 P.2d 47, 51 (1966). A.R.S. § 12–1501 authorizes written agreements to arbitrate and provides that they are "valid, enforceable and irrevocable, save upon such grounds as exist at law or in equity for the revocation of any contract." Thus, the enforceability of the agreement to arbitrate is determined by principles of general contract law. The court of appeals concluded, and we agree, that, under those principles, the contract in this case was one of adhesion.

An adhesion contract is typically a standardized form "offered to consumers of goods and services on essentially a 'take it or leave it' basis without affording the consumer a realistic opportunity to bargain and under such conditions that the consumer cannot obtain the desired product or services except by acquiescing in the form contract." Wheeler v. St. Joseph Hosp., 63 Cal.App.3d 345, 356, 133 Cal.Rptr. 775, 783 (1976) (citations omitted); see also Burkons v. Ticor Title Ins. Co. of Cal., 165 Ariz. 299, 311, 798 P.2d 1308, 1320 (App.1989), rev'd on other grounds, 168 Ariz. 345, 813 P.2d 710 (1991) (essence of adhesion contract is that it is offered to consumers on essentially a "take it or leave it" basis). The Wheeler court further stated that "[t]he distinctive feature of a contract of adhesion is that the weaker party has no realistic choice as to its terms." 63 Cal.App.3d at 356, 133 Cal.Rptr. at 783 (citations omitted). Likewise, in *Contractual Problems in the Enforcement of Agreements to Arbitrate Medical Malpractice*, 58 Va.L.Rev. 947, 988 (1972), Professor Stanley Henderson recognized "the essence of an adhesion contract is that bargaining position and leverage enable one party 'to select and control risks assumed under the contract.'" (quoting Friedrich Kessler, *Contracts of Adhesion—Some Thoughts About Freedom of Contract*, 43 Colum.L.Rev. 629 (1943)).

The printed form agreement signed by plaintiff in this case possesses all the characteristics of a contract of adhesion. The form is a standardized contract offered to plaintiff on a "take it or leave it" basis. In addition to removing from the courts any potential dispute concerning fees or services, the drafter inserted additional terms potentially advantageous to itself requiring that any arbitrator appointed by the American Arbitration Association be a licensed medical doctor specializing in obstetrics/gynecology. The contract was not negotiated but was, instead, prepared by defendant and presented to plaintiff as a condition of treatment. Staff at the clinic neither explained its terms to plaintiff nor indicated that she was free to refuse to sign the form; they merely represented to plaintiff that she had to complete the three forms. The conditions under which the clinic offered plaintiff the services were on a "take it or leave it" basis, and the terms of service were not negotiable. Applying general contract law to the undisputed facts, the court of appeals correctly held that the contract was one of adhesion.

II. Reasonable Expectations

Our conclusion that the contract was one of adhesion is not, of itself, determinative of its enforceability. "[A] contract of adhesion is fully enforceable according to its terms [citations omitted] unless certain other factors are present which, under established legal rules—legislative or judicial—operate to render it otherwise." Graham v. Scissor–Tail, Inc., 28 Cal.3d 807, (1981) (footnotes omitted). To determine whether this contract of adhesion is enforceable, we look to two factors: the reasonable expectations of the adhering party and whether the contract is unconscionable. . . .

Plaintiff argues that the trial court should have adopted, and we should now adopt, the analysis provided in Obstetrics & Gynecologists v. Pepper, 101 Nev. 105, 693 P.2d 1259 (1985), because it is virtually indistinguishable from the present case. In Pepper, the patient was required to sign an agreement before receiving treatment which waived her right to jury trial and submitted all disputes to arbitration. The clinic did not explain the contents of the agreement to the patient. The clinic's practice was to have staff instruct patients to complete two medical history forms and the agreement to arbitrate and to inform patients that any questions would be answered. If the patient refused to sign the agreement, the clinic refused treatment.

The plaintiff in Pepper signed the agreement, but did not recall doing so, nor did she recall having the agreement explained to her. The plaintiff later brought suit for injuries suffered due to improperly prescribed oral contraceptives. The trial court made no findings of fact or conclusions of law, but the Nevada Supreme Court, upon review of the record before it, held the agreement unenforceable because plaintiff did not give a knowing consent to the agreement to arbitrate.

The facts in the instant case present an even stronger argument in favor of holding the agreement unenforceable than do the facts in Pepper. In both cases, plaintiffs stated that they did not recall signing the agreement to arbitrate or having it explained to them. Unlike the clinic in Pepper, the clinic in this case did not show that it was the procedure of clinic staff to offer to explain the agreement to patients. The clinic did not explain the purpose of the form to plaintiff and did not show whether plaintiff was required to sign the form or forfeit treatment. In Pepper, the fact that both parties were waiving their right to a jury trial was explicit, which is not so in the present case.

Clearly, the issues of knowing consent and reasonable expectations are closely related and intertwined. In Darner Motor Sales, Inc. v. Universal Underwriters Ins. Co., 140 Ariz. 383, 682 P.2d 388 (1984), this court used the Restatement (Second) of Contracts § 211 (Standardized Agreements), as a guide to analyzing, among other things, contracts that contain non-negotiated terms. The comment to subsection (3), quoted with approval in Darner, states in part:

> Although customers typically adhere to standardized agreements and are bound by them without even appearing to know the standard terms in detail, they are not bound to unknown terms which are beyond the range of reasonable expectation.

See 140 Ariz. at 391, 682 P.2d at 396.

The Restatement focuses our attention on whether it was beyond plaintiff's reasonable expectations to expect to arbitrate her medical malpractice claims, which includes waiving her right to a jury trial, as part of the filling out of the three forms under the facts and circumstances of this case. Clearly, there was no conspicuous or explicit waiver of the fundamental right to a jury trial or any evidence that such rights were knowingly, voluntarily and intelligently waived. The only evidence presented compels a finding that waiver of such fundamental rights was beyond the reasonable expectations of plaintiff. Moreover, as Professor Henderson writes, "[i]n attempting to effectuate reasonable expectations consistent with a standardized medical contract, a court will find less reason to regard the bargaining process as suspect if there are no terms unreasonably favorable to the stronger party." Henderson, supra, at 995. In this case failure to explain to plaintiff that the agreement required all potential disputes, including malpractice disputes, to be heard only by an arbitrator who was a licensed obstetrician/gynecologist requires us to view the "bargaining" process with suspicion. It would be unreasonable to enforce such a critical term against plaintiff when it is not a negotiated term and defendant failed to explain it to her or call her attention to it.

Plaintiff was under a great deal of emotional stress, had only a high school education, was not experienced in commercial matters, and is still not sure "what arbitration is." Given the circumstances under which the agreement was signed and the nature of the terms included therein, our reading of Pepper, Darner, the Restatement and the affidavits in this case compel us to conclude that the contract fell outside plaintiff's reasonable expectations and is, therefore, unenforceable. Because of this holding, it is unnecessary for us to determine whether the contract is also unconscionable.

III.   A Comment on The Dissent

In view of the concern expressed by the dissent, we restate our firm conviction that arbitration and other methods of alternative dispute resolution play important and desirable roles in our system of dispute resolution. We encourage their use. When agreements to arbitrate are freely and fairly entered, they will be welcomed and enforced. They will not, however, be exempted from the usual rules of contract law, as A.R.S. § 12–1501 itself makes clear....

The dissent is concerned that our decision today sends a "mixed message." It is, however, our intent to send a clear message. That message is: Contracts of adhesion will not be enforced unless they are conscionable and within the reasonable expectations of the parties. This is a well-established principle of contract law; today we merely apply it to the undisputed facts of the case before us.

DISPOSITION

Those portions of the opinion of the court of appeals inconsistent with this opinion are vacated. The judgment of the trial court is reversed and this case is remanded for further proceedings consistent with this opinion. Because plaintiff has successfully overcome defendant's claimed contractual defense, the trial court may entertain an application for fees incurred at the trial court and appellate level. Wagenseller v. Scottsdale Memorial Hosp., 147 Ariz. 370, 391–95, 710 P.2d 1025, 1046–50 (1985).

■ FELDMAN, C.J., and CORCORAN and ZLAKET, JJ., concur.

■ MARTONE, JUSTICE, dissenting.

The court's conclusion that the agreement to arbitrate was outside the plaintiff's reasonable expectations is without basis in law or fact. I fear today's decision reflects a preference for litigation over alternative dispute resolution that I had thought was behind us. I would affirm the court of appeals.

We begin with the undisputed facts that the court ignores. Appendix "A" to this dissent is the agreement to arbitrate. At the top it states in bold capital letters "PLEASE READ THIS CONTRACT CAREFULLY AS IT EFFECTS [sic] YOUR LEGAL RIGHTS." Directly under that in all capital letters are the words "AGREEMENT TO ARBITRATE." The recitals indicate that "the Parties deem it to be in their respective best interest to settle any such dispute as expeditiously and economically as possible." The parties agreed that disputes over services provided would be settled by arbitration in accordance with the rules of the American Arbitration Association. They further agreed that the arbitrators appointed by the American Arbitration Association would be licensed medical doctors who specialize in obstetrics/gynecology. Plaintiff, an adult, signed the document.

Under A.R.S. § 12–1501, a written contract to submit to arbitration *any* controversy that might arise between the parties is "valid, enforceable and irrevocable, save upon such grounds as exist at law or in equity for the revocation of any contract." The statute applies to any controversy. Under A.R.S. § 12–1503, if the arbitration agreement provides a method of appointment of arbitrators, "this method shall be followed." Under A.R.S. § 12–1518, the American Arbitration Association is expressly acknowledged as an entity that the state itself may use in connection with arbitration. There is judicial review of any award. A.R.S. § 12–1512. Thus, on the face of it, the contract to arbitrate is plainly reasonable and enforceable unless there are grounds to revoke it. A.R.S. § 12–1501.

The court seizes upon the doctrine of reasonable expectations to revoke this contract. But there is nothing in this record that would warrant a finding that an agreement to arbitrate a malpractice claim was not within the reasonable expectations of the parties. On this record, the exact opposite is likely to be true. For all we know, both sides in this case might wish to avoid litigation like the plague and seek the more harmonious waters of alternative dispute resolution. Nor is there anything in this record that would suggest that arbitration is bad. Where is the harm? In the end, today's decision reflects a preference in favor of litigation that is not shared by the courts of other states and the courts of the United States.

In Doyle v. Giuliucci, 62 Cal.2d 606, 43 Cal.Rptr. 697, 699, 401 P.2d 1, 3 (1965), Chief Justice Roger J. Traynor of the California Supreme Court said, in connection with a medical malpractice claim, that "[t]he arbitration provision in such contracts is a reasonable restriction, for it does no more than specify a forum for the settlement of disputes." And, in Madden v. Kaiser Foundation Hospitals, 17 Cal.3d 699, 131 Cal.Rptr. 882, 890, 552 P.2d 1178, 1186 (1976), the California Supreme Court outlined "the benefits of the arbitral forum":

> [t]he speed and economy of arbitration, in contrast to the expense and delay of jury trial, could prove helpful to all parties; the simplified procedures and relaxed rules of evidence in arbitration may aid an injured plaintiff in presenting his case. Plaintiffs with less serious injuries, who cannot afford the high litigation expenses of court or jury trial, disproportionate to the amount of their claim, will benefit especially from the simplicity and economy of arbitration; that procedure could facilitate the adjudication of minor malpractice claims which cannot economically be resolved in a judicial forum.[2]

The Federal Arbitration Act, 9 U.S.C. § 2, is just like Arizona's, A.R.S. § 12–1501. There was a time when judicial antipathy towards arbitration prevailed. Poor Justice Frankfurter had to say in dissent in Wilko v. Swan, 346 U.S. 427, 439, 74 S.Ct. 182, 189, 98 L.Ed. 168 (1953) that "[t]here is nothing in the record before us, nor in the facts of which we can take judicial notice, to indicate that the arbitral system ... would not afford the plaintiff the rights to which he is entitled."

Justice Frankfurter's views have now been vindicated. The Supreme Court of the United States has upheld arbitration agreements under the Federal Arbitration Act in a variety of contexts, from the commercial setting in Shearson/American Express Inc. v. McMahon, 482 U.S. 220 (1987) (Securities Exchange Act of 1934 and RICO claims) and Rodriguez de Quijas v. Shearson/American Express, Inc., 490 U.S. 477 (1989) (Securities Act of 1933) to employment discrimination claims. Gilmer v. Interstate/Johnson Lane Corp., 500 U.S. 20, 111 S.Ct. 1647 (1991) (Age Discrimination in Employment Act claim).

Indeed, in Gilmer, the Supreme Court expressly rejected the arguments that regrettably this court has accepted. 500 U.S. at 32–33, 111 S.Ct. at 1654–55. The Supreme Court has expressly rejected the "outmoded presumption" and "suspicion of arbitration as a method of weakening the protections afforded in the substantive law." Rodriguez de Quijas, 490 U.S. at 481, 109 S.Ct. at 1920.

Against this background, how does this court reach its conclusion that arbitration is beyond the reasonable expectations of the parties? Its reli-

---

2. Following these decisions, the California legislature adopted Cal.Civ.Proc.Code § 1295, which expressly regulates such provisions. California has acknowledged the validity of contracts in compliance with the statute even where the patient is illiterate and, as here, claims not to remember signing it. Bolanos v. Khalatian, 231 Cal.App.3d 1586, 283 Cal.Rptr. 209, 211 (1991).

Michigan has a statute similar to California's, Mich.Stat.Ann. §§ 27A.5040–27A.5065, and its court has rejected arguments that arbitration agreements in compliance with the statute are adhesive, unconscionable, or deny people their rights to jury trials. Morris v. Metriyakool, 418 Mich. 423, 344 N.W.2d 736 (1984).

ance on Obstetrics and Gynecologists v. Pepper, 101 Nev. 105, 693 P.2d 1259 (1985), Darner Motor Sales, Inc. v. Universal Underwriters Insurance Co., 140 Ariz. 383, 682 P.2d 388 (1984), and the Restatement (Second) of Contracts § 211 (1979), is misplaced.

Pepper is a brief per curiam opinion of the Nevada Supreme Court which merely affirmed the finding of a trial court. The trial court held a hearing to determine whether there was an enforceable arbitration contract. However, the trial court did not make findings of facts and conclusions of law. That court simply denied a motion to stay pending arbitration. The Nevada Supreme Court said "[t]he district court could certainly have found that the arbitration agreement was an adhesion contract." 693 P.2d at 1260. It then said "[s]ince appellant's counsel failed to pursue the entry of findings of facts and conclusions of law, we are bound to presume that the district court found that respondent did not give a knowing consent to the arbitration agreement prepared by appellant clinic." Id., 693 P.2d at 1261. If Pepper stands for anything, it stands for the proposition that "knowing consent" is a factual question, and that an appellate court will affirm a factual finding if there is any evidence to support it. The basis for the court's decision was "knowing consent" under Nevada law, not reasonable expectations under ours.

Nor are Darner and the Restatement support for this court's conclusion. Darner held that an adhesive contract term that is "contrary to the negotiated agreement made by the parties," 140 Ariz. at 387, 682 P.2d at 392, will not be enforced because it collides with expectations that "have been induced by the making of a promise." 140 Ariz. at 390, 682 P.2d at 395 (quoting 1 Corbin, Contracts § 1 at 2 (1963)). The defendant here did not promise the plaintiff that malpractice claims could be litigated. Thus, the agreement to arbitrate is not contrary to any negotiated deal.

Gordinier v. Aetna Casualty & Surety Co., 154 Ariz. 266, 742 P.2d 277 (1987), of course, extended Darner to the entire scope of the Restatement (Second) of Contracts § 211 (1979). But even that section does not support today's decision. Under Restatement (Second) of Contracts § 211(3), standardized agreements are enforceable except where a party has reason to believe that the other party would not manifest assent if he knew that the writing contained a particular term. Comment f to § 211 tells us:

> Such a belief or assumption may be shown by the prior negotiations or inferred from the circumstances. Reason to believe may be inferred from the fact that the term is bizarre or oppressive, from the fact that it eviscerates the non-standard terms explicitly agreed to, or from the fact that it eliminates the dominant purpose of the transaction. The inference is reinforced if the adhering party never had an opportunity to read the term, or if it is illegible or otherwise hidden from view.

Plainly, there are no facts in this case to support any of these factors. There were no prior negotiations that were contrary to arbitration. An agreement to arbitrate is hardly bizarre or oppressive. It is a preferred method of alternative dispute resolution that our legislature has expressly acknowledged in A.R.S. § 12–1501. Arbitration does not eviscerate any agreed terms. Nor does it eliminate the dominant purpose of the transaction. The plaintiff here had an opportunity to read the document, the document was legible and was hardly hidden from plaintiff's view. This arbitration agreement was in bold capital letters. Thus, the reasonable expectations standard of the Restatement (Second) of Contracts § 211 does not support this court's conclusion.

There is another reason why § 211(3) fails to support the court's conclusion. The Restatement (Second) of Contracts chapter 8 describes the whole range of unenforceable contracts. Its introductory note states:

> A particularly important change has been effected by statutes relating to arbitration, which have now been enacted in so many jurisdictions that it seems likely that even in the remaining states, there has been a change in the former judicial attitude of hostility toward agreements to arbitrate future disputes.... Such agreements are now widely used and serve the public interest by saving court time. *The rules stated in this Chapter do not preclude their enforcement even in the absence of legislation.*

Restatement (Second) of Contracts ch. 8, intro. note at 4 (emphasis added). It is difficult to reconcile the court's reliance on the Restatement in light of this....

Today's decision sends a mixed message. In light of all of these developments, how can it be that an agreement to arbitrate "fell outside plaintiff's reasonable expectations?" The court's answer, Part III, ante, at 152, 840 P.2d at 1017, merely confuses the concept of a contract of adhesion with the doctrine of reasonable expectations. The court says it will enforce arbitration agreements "freely and fairly entered," ante, at 153, 840 P.2d at 1018, and that "the document involved is a contract of adhesion." Id. But the court's own framework of analysis acknowledges that its "conclusion that the contract was one of adhesion is not, of itself, determinative of its enforceability." Ante, at 151, 840 P.2d at 1016. It acknowledges that once it is determined that an adhesive contract exists, one looks to (1) reasonable expectations and (2) conscionability. Id. No one doubts that this was a contract of adhesion. And the court holds that because "the contract fell outside plaintiff's reasonable expectations" it is unenforceable, and therefore it is not necessary "to determine whether the contract is also unconscionable." Ante, at 152, 840 P.2d at 1017. Thus the court does not reach conscionability.

The only basis for the court's decision is "reasonable expectations," but words such as "freely and fairly entered," or "contract of adhesion" are irrelevant to that inquiry. If it is not "free" it is a contract of adhesion. If it is "unfair" it is unconscionable. Nowhere does the court's "Comment on The Dissent" provide the basis for its legal conclusion that this adhesive agreement to arbitrate fell outside of plaintiff's reasonable expectations. In the end we are left to conclude that people reasonably expect litigation over alternative dispute resolution. For all these reasons, I dissent.

* * *

Questions

1. Was the arbitration agreement in this case unconscionable? Given that the plaintiff was a literate adult, was the court's decision really based on the lack of consent, or was it based on the court's view of the oppressiveness of the terms?

2. How would the case come out if instead of an arbitration clause, the contract had specified a very short statute of limitations? How would it have been decided if it specified a low cap on damages?

3. In evaluating an arbitration clause in a contract of adhesion, how should the reasonable expectations of the parties be determined? Is an arbitration clause truly beyond the *reasonable* expectations of the parties? Would the case come out differently in a locality where medical forms frequently contained arbitration provisions?

4. The dissent argues that arbitration "does not eviscerate any agreed terms" of the contract. Do you agree? In what respect might it be argued that an arbitration clause does just that? Would one know *ex ante*, or is it necessary to await the result of an arbitration to know whether agreed terms were eviscerated or not?

* * *

Note on Consent in Consumer Arbitration[1]

Consumers who are given form contracts by a large manufacturer that contain arbitration provisions hidden in a sea of standardized terms often resist arbitration on the ground that they did not truly assent. The problem arises most acutely when one of the parties is a member of an industry or trade association that advocates a standard arbitration procedure for its members to use. Such entities frequently give their customers contracts that state the contract incorporates the rules of a given trade association without mentioning that an arbitration procedure is one component of the rules. When a dispute subsequently arises, the consumer claims that she had no knowledge of the arbitration term, and thus did not consent to be bound.

It is a well known principle of contract law that parties are responsible for the contracts they sign, even if they have not read them. See, John D. Calamari, *Duty to Read—A Changing Concept*, 43 Fordham L. Rev. 341, 341 (1974). This "duty to read" means, *inter alia*, that courts hold parties to terms that they have incorporated by reference into their contracts, even if the party seeking to avoid the incorporated term had no knowledge of these terms at the time the contract was made. E. Allen Farnsworth, CONTRACTS 2d Edition, 195 & 295 (1982); John D. Calamari and Joseph M. Perillo, CONTRACTS, 3rd Edition, 410 (1987). However, a competing principle of contract law says that a party is not bound by a contractual term of

1. See Katherine Van Wezel Stone, *Rustic Justice*: *Community and Coercion Un-* *der the Federal Arbitration Act*, 77 N. CAR. L. REV. 931 (1999).

which he was unaware and which he had no reason to suspect was in the agreement. "A person is not bound by the terms of a written agreement if he had no knowledge of its terms because the manner in which they are embodied in the instrument would not lead a reasonable person to suspect that the terms are part of the contract." *Drans v. Providence College*, 119 R.I. 845, 853, 383 A.2d 1033, 1037–38 (R.I. 1978). This principle is embodied in § 211 of the RESTATEMENT OF CONTRACTS (2d), which states:

(1) Except as stated in Subsection (3), where a party to an agreement signs or otherwise manifests assent to a writing ... he adopts the writing as an integrated agreement with respect to the terms included in the writing.

. . .

(3) Where the other party has reason to believe that the party manifesting such assent would not do so if he knew that the writing contained a particular term, the term is not part of the agreement.

One application of the no-enforcement-of-unexpected-terms principle is that courts scrutinize contracts and invalidate terms if the terms are oppressive and not within a party's reasonable expectation, i.e., not within the range of terms the offeree could reasonably expect to find in the contract. The same principle applies to terms contained in standard form contracts but which are either buried in a sea of fine print or otherwise not conspicuous to the signing party. See, *Williams v. Walker–Thomas Furniture Co.*, 350 F.2d 445 (C.A.D.C. 1965); *Henningsen v. Bloomfield Motors, Inc.*, 32 N.J. 358 (1960).

Because courts exercise a policing role when confronted with one-sided incorporated terms in contracts generally, one might also expect courts to police arbitration agreements that are incorporated by reference for unfairness, oppression, or surprise. Until the late 1980s, this was the case. Courts were reluctant to uphold arbitration clauses when the arbitration provision was contained in a document that parties incorporated by reference into their contracts but did not mention expressly. See e.g., *Medical Development Corp. v. Industrial Molding*, 479 F.2d 345 (10th Cir.1973); *C. Itoh & Co. v. Jordan Int'l*, 552 F.2d 1228 (7th Cir.1977); *Amoco Oil v. M.T. Mary Ellen*, 529 F.Supp. 227 (S.D.N.Y.1981). See generally, Robert Whitman, *Incorporation by Reference in Commercial Contracts*, 21 Md. L. Rev. 1, 16–17 (1961). For example, the New York courts adopted a principle that "an agreement to arbitrate must be clear and direct, and must not depend upon implication, inveiglement or subtlety" to be enforceable. *Matter of Doughboy Industries*, 233 N.Y.S.2d 488, 493 (1962) (J. Breitel). The New York Court of Appeals stated in 1954, "[P]arties are not to be led into arbitration unwittingly through subtlety." *Riverdale Fabrics v. Tillinghast–Stiles Co.*, 306 N.Y. 288, 291 (1954).

Until the 1980s, courts were particularly skeptical of arbitration clauses in contracts in which the drafter was a member of the trade association and the party seeking to avoid arbitration was not. The New York Court of Appeals noted that such contracts appear to have been drafted with a deliberate intent of avoiding the mention of arbitration, leaving "unwary traders" to learn of the arbitration provision only when a dispute arose. *Riverdale Fabrics v. Tillinghast–Stiles*, 306 N.Y. at 292. It said: "The form of words favored by these trade associations appears to have been designed to avoid any resistance that might arise if arbitration were brought to the attention of the contracting parties as the exclusive remedy in case of disputes." Id. at 292.

In the late 1980s, state courts abandoned their policing approach to arbitration clauses incorporated by reference. Instead, they began to enforce arbitration clauses which were incorporated by reference even when the contract was silent on the existence of the arbitration clause. In part, the change was the result of the Supreme Court's opinion in 1987 in *Perry v. Thomas*, 482 U.S. 483 (1987), discussed in Chapter 5 above. In *Perry*, the Court held that under the FAA the existence of a valid agreement to arbitrate must be determined by reference to state law, but any state law or legal doctrine which is specific to arbitration is preempted by the FAA. Thus, only state laws governing the enforceability of contracts generally can be used as a defense to arbitration under the FAA. Id. at 492 & n. 9. *Perry's* admonition that courts may not rely on arbitration-specific doctrines to invalidate arbitration agreements led courts to hold that state law doctrines that required strict scrutiny of arbitration clauses that were incorporated by reference were no longer valid. See e.g., *Progressive Casualty Insurance Co. v. C.A. Reaseguradora Nacional De Venezuela*, 991 F.2d 42, 46 (2d Cir.1993); *Cook Chocolate Co. v. Salomon, Inc.*, 684 F.Supp. 1177, 1182 (S.D.N.Y.1988). Similarly, state contract law doctrines that required there to be an explicit and unequivocal waiver of a right to sue before finding that parties had agreed to binding arbitration were held to be preempted. *Progressive Casualty Insurance Co. v. C.A. Reaseguradora Nacional De Venezuela*, 991 F.2d at 45–46. The result was that whereas general contract law provides latitude for courts to protect consumers in their dealings with large organized interests by relieving them of oppressive and unexpected contractual terms, many courts interpreted *Perry* to deny courts that same latitude when they were dealing with arbitration clauses.

Recently in the employment context, some courts have begun to lean in the other direction, holding that a form contract drafted by an employer that incorporates an arbitration process without giving an employee fair notice that arbitration is included will not be enforceable. For example, in *Rosenberg v. Merrill Lynch, Pierce, Fenner & Smith*, 163 F.3d 53 (1st Cir.1998), the First Circuit held that a standard form an employee was required to sign to register with the New York Stock Exchange that required her to arbitrate "any dispute, claim or controversy that may arise that is required to be arbitrated under the rules, constitutions or by-laws of the [New York Stock Exchange]" did not require her to arbitrate her employment discrimination claims against her brokerage firm employer. The court reasoned that the form arbitration agreement:

> "was incomplete; it failed to define the range of claims subject to arbitration. It referred only to arbitration of such claims as were

required to be arbitrated by the NYSE rules. But those rules were not given to Rosenberg or described to her. The question then becomes which party should bear the risk of such incompleteness. Merrill Lynch should, we believe, bear that risk."

It remains to be seen whether courts will similarly shift the burden of uncertainty to manufacturers in situations where consumers find they lose their rights to sue because of arbitration provisions buried in fine print or hidden in incorporated terms.

* * *

4.   STATE CONSUMER PROTECTION LAW

Casarotto v. Lombardi and Doctor's Associates, Inc.
268 Mont. 369, 886 P.2d 931 (Mt. S.Ct. 1994).

■ TREIWEILER, Justice.

Plaintiffs Paul and Pamela Casarotto filed this suit in the District Court for the Eighth Judicial District in Cascade County to recover damages which they claim were caused by the defendants' breach of contract and tortious conduct. Defendants Nick Lombardi and Doctor's Associates, Inc. (DAI), moved the District Court for an order dismissing plaintiffs' complaint, or in the alternative, staying further judicial proceedings pending arbitration of plaintiffs' claims pursuant to a provision in DAI's franchise agreement with plaintiffs which required that disputes "arising out of or relating to" that contract be settled by arbitration. The District Court granted defendants' motion, and ordered that further judicial proceedings be stayed until arbitration proceedings were completed in accordance with the terms of the parties' agreement. Plaintiffs appeal from that order. We reverse the order of the District Court.

The issues raised on appeal are:

1.   Based on conflict of law principles, is the franchise agreement entered into between the Casarottos and DAI governed by Connecticut law or Montana law?

2.   If the contract is governed by Montana law, is the notice requirement in § 27–5–114(4), MCA, of Montana's Uniform Arbitration Act, preempted by the Federal Arbitration Act found at 9 U.S.C. §§ 1–15 (1988)?

FACTUAL BACKGROUND

On October 29, 1992, Paul and Pamela Casarotto filed an amended complaint naming Doctor's Associates, Inc., and Nick Lombardi as defendants. For purposes of our review of the District Court's order, we presume the facts alleged in the complaint to be true.

DAI is a Connecticut corporation which owns Subway Sandwich Shop franchises, and Lombardi is their development agent in Montana. The

Casarottos entered into a franchise agreement with DAI which allowed them to open a Subway Sandwich Shop in Great Falls, Montana. However, they were told by Lombardi that their first choice for a location in Great Falls was unavailable.

According to their complaint, the Casarottos agreed to open a shop at a less desirable location, based on a verbal agreement with Lombardi that when their preferred location became available, they would have the exclusive right to open a store at that location. Contrary to that agreement, the preferred location was subsequently awarded by Lombardi and DAI to another franchisee. As a result, the Casarottos' business suffered irreparably, and they lost their business, along with the collateral which secured their SBA loan.

This action is based on the Casarottos' allegation that Lombardi and DAI breached their agreement with the Casarottos, defrauded them, breached the covenant of good faith and fair dealing, and engaged in other tortious conduct, all of which directly caused the Casarottos loss of business and the resulting damage.

DAI's franchise agreement with the Casarottos was executed on April 25, 1988. There was no indication on the first page of the contract that it was subject to arbitration. However, paragraph 10(c) of the contract, found on page 9, included the following provision:

> Any controversy or claim arising out of or relating to this contract or the breach thereof shall be settled by Arbitration in accordance with the Commercial Arbitration Rules of the American Arbitration Association at a hearing to be held in Bridgeport, Connecticut and judgment upon an award rendered by the Arbitrator(s) may be entered in any court having jurisdiction thereof. The commencement of arbitration proceedings by an aggrieved party to settle disputes arising out of or relating to this contract is a condition precedent to the commencement of legal action by either party. The cost of such a proceeding will be born equally by the parties.

On January 29, 1993, DAI moved the District Court to dismiss the Casarottos' complaint, or at least stay further judicial proceedings, pending arbitration pursuant to paragraph 10(c) of the franchise agreement. DAI alleged that the franchise agreement affected interstate commerce, and therefore, was subject to the Federal Arbitration Act found at 9 U.S.C. §§ 1–15 (1988). They sought a stay of proceedings pursuant to § 3 of that Act. . . .

DAI claimed that Montana law could not be raised as a bar to enforcement of the arbitration provision for two reasons: First, the contract specifically called for the application of Connecticut law; and second, Montana law was preempted by the Federal Arbitration Act.

The Casarottos opposed DAI's motion on the grounds that Montana law applied, in spite of the choice of law provision in the contract, and that based on § 27–5–114(4), MCA, the contract's arbitration provision was unenforceable because DAI had not provided notice on the first page of the agreement that the contract was subject to arbitration.

On June 2, 1993, the District Court issued its order granting DAI's motion to stay further judicial proceedings pursuant to 9 U.S.C. § 3....

ISSUE 1

Based on conflict of law principles, is the franchise agreement entered into between the Casarottos and DAI governed by Connecticut law or Montana law?

Paragraph 12 of the franchise agreement entered into between the parties provides as follows: "This agreement shall be governed by and construed in accordance with the laws of the State of Connecticut and contains the entire understanding of the parties." DAI contends that, therefore, Connecticut law governs our interpretation of the contract and that since Connecticut law is identical to the Federal Arbitration Act see Conn.Gen.Stat. § 52–409 (1993), conspicuous notice that the contract was subject to arbitration was not required and we need not concern ourselves with the issue of whether Montana law is preempted.

The Casarottos respond that the issue of whether to apply Connecticut or Montana law involves a conflict of law issue and that the answer can be found in our prior decisions. We agree....

In this case, there is a choice of law provision in the parties' contract. The question is whether it was an "effective" choice. We recently held in Youngblood v. American States Ins. Co. (1993), 262 Mont. 391, 394, 866 P.2d 203, 205, that this State's public policy will ultimately determine whether choice of law provisions in contracts are "effective." In that case, we stated:

> [T]he choice of law provision will be enforced unless enforcement of the contract provision requiring application of Oregon law as regards subrogation of medical payments violates Montana's public policy or is against good morals.

Youngblood, 866 P.2d at 205.

Based on our conclusion in that case that subrogation of medical payment benefits was contrary to our public policy, we held that:

> [T]he choice of law provision in the insurance contract would result in medical payment subrogation under Oregon law. Because such subrogation violates Montana's public policy, that term of the insurance contract at issue here is not enforceable.

Youngblood, 866 P.2d at 208.

Restatement (Second) of Conflict of Laws § 187(2) (1971) is consistent with our decision in Youngblood, and expands upon the factors to be considered under the circumstances in this case. It provides that:

> (2) The law of the state chosen by the parties to govern their contractual rights and duties will be applied, even if the particular issue is one

which the parties could not have resolved by an explicit provision in their agreement directed to that issue, unless either

(a) the chosen state has no substantial relationship to the parties or the transaction and there is no other reasonable basis for the parties' choice, or

(b) application of the law of the chosen state would be contrary to a fundamental policy of a state which has a materially greater interest than the chosen state in the determination of the particular issue and which, under the rule of § 188, would be the state of the applicable law in the absence of an effective choice of law by the parties.

Adopting § 187, then, as our guide, we first look to § 188 to determine whether Montana law would be applicable absent an "effective" choice of law by the parties.

According to the affidavit of Paul Casarotto filed in opposition to DAI's motion to dismiss, he executed the contract in neither Connecticut nor Montana. It was executed while he was traveling in New York. However, it appears from that same affidavit, and from the allegations in the complaint, that original negotiations were conducted by him in Great Falls, the contract was to be performed in Great Falls, the subject matter of the contract (the Subway Sandwich Shop) was located in Great Falls, and that he and Pamela Casarotto resided in Great Falls at the time that the contract was executed. The only connection to Connecticut was that DAI was incorporated in that state and apparently had its home office in that state at the time of the parties' agreement. We conclude that based upon the application of the criteria set forth in § 188, and our prior decision in Emerson, Montana has a materially greater interest than Connecticut in the contract issue that is presented, and that absent an "effective" choice of law by the parties, Montana law would apply.

Our remaining inquiry, then, is whether application of Connecticut law would be contrary to a fundamental policy of this State by eliminating the requirement that notice be provided when a contract is subject to arbitration.

In Trammel v. Brotherhood of Locomotive Firemen and Enginemen (1953), 126 Mont. 400, 409, 253 P.2d 329, 334, we held that the public policy of a state is established by its express legislative enactments. Here, the legislative history for § 27–5–114(4), MCA, makes clear that the legislative committee members considering adoption of the Uniform Arbitration Act had two primary concerns. First, they did not want Montanans to waive their constitutional right of access to Montana's courts unknowingly, and second, they were concerned about Montanans being compelled to arbitrate disputes at distant locations beyond the borders of our State.

The facts in this case, and our recent decision in another case, justify those concerns.

Regardless of the amount in controversy between these parties, the arbitration clause in the Subway Sandwich Shop Franchise Agreement requires that the Casarottos travel thousands of miles to Connecticut to have their dispute arbitrated. Furthermore, it requires that they share equally in the expense of arbitration, regardless of the merits of their claim. Presumably, that expense could be substantial, since under the Commercial Arbitration Rules of the American Arbitration Association (1992), those expenses would, at a minimum, include: the arbitrator's fees and travel expenses, the cost of witnesses chosen by the arbitrator, the American Arbitration Association's administrative charges, and a filing fee of up to $4000, depending on the amount in controversy. For a proceeding involving multiple arbitrators, the administrative fee alone, for which the Casarottos would be responsible, is $150 a day. In addition, since the contract called for the application of Connecticut law, the Casarottos would be required to retain the services of a Connecticut attorney.

In spite of the expense set forth above, the procedural safeguards which have been established in Montana to assure the reliability of the outcome in dispute resolutions are absent in an arbitration proceeding. The extent of pretrial discovery is within the sole discretion of the arbitrator and the rules of evidence are not applicable. The arbitrator does not have to follow any law, and there does not have to be a factual basis for the arbitrator's decision. See May v. First National Pawn Brokers, Ltd. (Mont. 1994), ___ Mont. ___, 887 P.2d 185.

Based upon the determination by the Legislature of this State that the citizens of this State are at least entitled to notice before entering into an agreement which will limit their future resolution of disputes to a procedure as potentially inconvenient, expensive, and devoid of procedural safeguards as the one provided for by the rules of the American Arbitration Association, and the terms of this contract, we conclude that the notice requirement of § 27–5–114, MCA, does establish a fundamental public policy in Montana, and that the application of Connecticut law would be contrary to that policy. Therefore, we conclude that the law of Montana governs the franchise agreement entered into between the Casarottos and Doctor's Associates, Inc.

ISSUE 2

If the contract is governed by Montana law, is the notice requirement in § 27–5–114(4), MCA, of Montana's Uniform Arbitration Act, preempted by the Federal Arbitration Act found at 9 U.S.C. §§ 1–15 (1988)?

DAI contends that even if Montana law is applicable, § 27–5–114(4), MCA, is preempted by the Federal Arbitration Act because it would void an otherwise enforceable arbitration agreement. In support of its argument, DAI relies on U.S. Supreme Court decisions in Perry v. Thomas (1987), 482 U.S. 483, 107 S.Ct. 2520, 96 L.Ed.2d 426, Southland Corp. v. Keating (1984), 465 U.S. 1, 104 S.Ct. 852, 79 L.Ed.2d 1, and Moses H. Cone Memorial Hospital v. Mercury Construction Corp. (1983), 460 U.S. 1, 103 S.Ct. 927, 74 L.Ed.2d 765. These cases have been referred to as "[a] trilogy of United States Supreme Court cases" which "developed the federal policy favoring arbitration and the principle that the FAA is substantive law enacted pursuant to Congress's commerce powers that preempts contrary state provisions." David P. Pierce, The Federal Arbitration Act: Conflicting Interpretations of its Scope 61 Cinn.L.Rev. 623, 630 (1992). From this trilogy, Southland and Perry appear to be closest on point and warrant some discussion.

Southland Corporation was the owner and franchisor of 7–Eleven Convenience Stores. Its standard franchise agreements, like DAI's included an arbitration provision. Southland was sued in California by several of its franchisees, based on claims which included violations of the disclosure requirements of the California Franchise Investment Law, Cal.Corp.Code § 31000, et seq. (West 1977). The California Supreme Court held that the Franchise Investment Law required judicial consideration of claims brought under that statute, and therefore, held that arbitration could not be compelled. The U.S. Supreme Court disagreed, and held that:

> In creating a substantive rule applicable in state as well federal courts, Congress intended to foreclose state legislative attempts to undercut the enforceability of arbitration agreements. We hold that § 31512 of the California Franchise Investment Law violates the Supremacy Clause.

Southland, 465 U.S. at 16, 104 S.Ct. at 861 (footnotes omitted).

In Perry, the Supreme Court was called upon to reconcile 9 U.S.C. § 2 which mandates enforcement of arbitration agreements, with § 229 of the California Labor Code, "which provides that actions for the collection of wages may be maintained 'without regard to the existence of any private agreement to arbitrate.'" Perry, 482 U.S. at 484, 107 S.Ct. at 2523 (quoting Cal.Lab.Code § 229 (West 1971)). In that case, Kenneth Thomas sued his former employer for commissions he claimed were due for the sale of securities. His employer sought to stay the proceedings pursuant to §§ 2 and 4 of the Federal Arbitration Act, based on the arbitration provision found in Thomas's application for employment. Perry, 482 U.S. at 484–85, 107 S.Ct. at 2522–23. In an opinion affirmed by the California Court of Appeals and the California Supreme Court, the California Superior Court denied the motion to compel arbitration. On appeal, the U.S. Supreme Court held that § 2 of the FAA reflected a strong national policy favoring arbitration agreements, notwithstanding "state substantive or procedural policies to the contrary." Perry, 482 U.S. at 489, 107 S.Ct. at 2525. Citing its decision in Southland, the Court held that:

> "Congress intended to foreclose state legislative attempts to undercut the enforceability of arbitration agreements." Id. [465 U.S.] at 16 [104 S.Ct. at 858] (footnote omitted). Section 2, therefore, embodies a clear federal policy of requiring arbitration unless the agreement to arbitrate is not part of a contract evidencing interstate commerce or is revocable "upon such grounds as exist at law or in equity for the revocation of any contract." 9 U.S.C. § 2. "We see nothing in the Act indicating that the broad principle of enforceability is subject to any additional limitations under state law." Keating, supra, 465 U.S. at 11 [104 S.Ct. at 858].

Perry, 482 U.S. at 489–90, 107 S.Ct. at 2525.

As additional authority, DAI cites to our own previous decisions which have enforced arbitration agreements in Montana based on Southland and Perry. See Downey v. Christensen (1992), 251 Mont. 386, 825 P.2d 557; Vukasin v. D.A. Davidson & Co. (1990), 241 Mont. 126, 785 P.2d 713; William Gibson, Jr., Inc. v. James Graff Communications (1989), 239 Mont. 335, 780 P.2d 1131; Larsen v. Opie (1989), 237 Mont. 108, 771 P.2d 977; Passage v. Prudential–Bache Securities, Inc. (1986), 223 Mont. 60, 727 P.2d 1298.

The Casarottos, however, contend that Southland and Perry must be considered in light of the Supreme Court's more recent decision in Volt Information Sciences, Inc. v. Board of Trustees of Leland Stanford Junior University (1989), 489 U.S. 468, 109 S.Ct. 1248, 103 L.Ed.2d 488, and that our prior arbitration decisions did not deal with the enforceability of arbitration agreements which violated Montana's statutory law. We agree.

In Volt, the parties entered into a construction contract which contained an agreement to arbitrate all disputes between the parties relating to the contract. The contract also provided that it would be governed by the law in the state where the project was located. Volt, 489 U.S. at 470, 109 S.Ct. at 1251.

As a result of a contract dispute between the parties, Stanford filed an action in California Superior Court naming Volt and two other companies involved in the construction project. Volt petitioned the Superior Court to compel arbitration of the dispute. However, the California Arbitration Act found at Cal.Civ.Proc.Code § 1280, et seq. (West 1982), contained a provision allowing the court to stay arbitration pending resolution of related litigation. On that basis, the Superior Court denied Volt's motion to compel arbitration, and instead, stayed arbitration proceedings pending outcome of the litigation. The California Court of Appeals affirmed that decision, and the California Supreme Court denied Volt's petition for discretionary review. The U.S. Supreme Court granted review and affirmed the decision of the California courts. Volt, 489 U.S. at 471–73, 109 S.Ct. at 1251–52.

On appeal, the Supreme Court considered Volt's argument that California's arbitration laws were preempted by the Federal Arbitration Act. In its analysis of the preemption issue, the Supreme Court stated that:

> The FAA contains no express pre-emptive provision, nor does it reflect a congressional intent to occupy the entire field of arbitration. But even when Congress has not completely displaced state regulation in an area, state law may nonetheless be pre-empted to the extent that it actually conflicts with federal law—that is, to the extent that it "stands as an obstacle to the accomplishment and execution of the full purposes and objectives of Congress." Hines v. Davidowitz, 312 U.S. 52, 67 [61 S.Ct. 399, 404, 85 L.Ed. 581] (1941). *The question before us, therefore, is whether application of Cal.Civ.Proc.Code Ann. § 1281.2(c) to stay arbitration under this contract in interstate commerce, in accor-*

dance with the terms of the arbitration agreement itself, would under-
mine the goals and policies of the FAA. We conclude that it would not.

Volt, 489 U.S. at 477–78, 109 S.Ct. at 1255 (citation omitted; emphasis added).

The Supreme Court explained that the purpose of the Federal Arbitration Act was to enforce lawful agreements entered into by the parties, and not to impose arbitration on the parties involuntarily. It noted that in this case the parties' agreement was to be bound by the arbitration rules from California. Therefore, it held that:

> Where, as here, the parties have agreed to abide by state rules of arbitration, enforcing those rules according to the terms of the agreement is fully consistent with the goals of the FAA, even if the result is that arbitration is stayed where the Act would otherwise permit it to go forward. By permitting the courts to "rigorously enforce" such agreements according to their terms, see [Dean Witter Reynolds, Inc. v.] Byrd, [470 U.S. 213] at 221 [105 S.Ct. 1238, 1242, 84 L.Ed.2d 158 (1985)], we give effect to the contractual rights and expectations of the parties, without doing violence to the policies behind the FAA.

Volt, 489 U.S. at 479, 109 S.Ct. at 1256.

While the Court in Volt applied state laws that had been chosen by the parties in their contract, and this case involves state law which is applied pursuant to conflict of law principles, it has been observed that:

> The real significance of the Volt decision is not in the Court's holding, but rather in what the Court failed to hold. For example, the Court found no preemption of the California arbitration law by the FAA. Instead, the Court merely stated that Congress did not intend that the FAA occupy the entire field of arbitration law. Thus, enforcing the California law was merely a procedural issue and did not frustrate the policy behind the FAA of enforcing the agreement.

David P. Pierce, The Federal Arbitration Act: Conflicting Interpretations of its Scope 61 Cinn.L.Rev. 623, 635 (1992) (footnotes omitted). . . .

Based upon the Supreme Court's decision in Volt, we conclude that the nature of our inquiry is whether Montana's notice requirement found at § 27–5–114(4), MCA, would "undermine the goals and policies of the FAA." We conclude that it does not. . . .

Our conclusion that Montana's notice requirement does not undermine the policies of the FAA is based on the Supreme Court's conclusion that it was never Congress's intent when it enacted the FAA to preempt the entire field of arbitration, and its further conclusion that the FAA does not require parties to arbitrate when they have not agreed to do so. That Court held that the purpose of the FAA is simply to enforce arbitration agreements into which parties had entered, and acknowledged that the interpretation of contracts is ordinarily a question of state law. Volt, 489 U.S. at 474, 109 S.Ct. at 1253.

Presumably, therefore, the Supreme Court would not find it a threat to the policies of the Federal Arbitration Act for a state to require that before arbitration agreements are enforceable, they be entered knowingly. To hold otherwise would be to infer that arbitration is so onerous as a means of dispute resolution that it can only be foisted upon the uninformed. That would be inconsistent with the conclusion that the parties to the contract are free to decide how their disputes should be resolved.

Montana's notice requirement does not preclude parties from knowingly entering into arbitration agreements, nor do our courts decline to enforce arbitration agreements which are entered into knowingly.

Therefore, we conclude that Montana's notice statute found at § 27–5–114(4), MCA, would not undermine the goals and policies of the FAA, and is not preempted by 9 U.S.C. § 2 (1988).

Because the agreement of the parties in this case did not comply with Montana's statutory notice requirement, it is not subject to arbitration, according to the law of Montana. The District Court's order dated June 2, 1993, is, therefore, reversed, and this case is remanded to the District Court for further proceedings consistent with this opinion.

■ HARRISON, HUNT and NELSON, JJ., concur.

■ TRIEWEILER, JUSTICE, specially concurring.

The majority opinion sets forth principles of law agreeable to the majority of this Court in language appropriate for judicial precedent. I offer this special concurring opinion as my personal observation regarding many of the federal decisions which have been cited to us as authority.

To those federal judges who consider forced arbitration as the panacea for their "heavy case loads" and who consider the reluctance of state courts to buy into the arbitration program as a sign of intellectual inadequacy, I would like to explain a few things.

In Montana, we are reasonably civilized and have a sophisticated system of justice which has evolved over time and which we continue to develop for the primary purpose of assuring fairness to those people who are subject to its authority.

Over the previous 100 years of our history as a state, our courts have developed rules of evidence for the purpose of assuring that disputes are resolved on the most reliable bases possible.

Based on the presumption that all men and women are fallible and make mistakes, we have developed standards for appellate review which protect litigants from human error or the potential arbitrariness of any one individual.

We believe in the rule of law so that people can plan their commercial and personal affairs. If our trial courts decline to follow those laws, our citizens are assured that this Court will enforce them.

We have rules for venue, and jurisdictional requirements based on the assumption that it is unfair to force people to travel long distances from their homes at great expense and inconvenience to prosecute or defend against lawsuits.

We believe that our courts should be accessible to all, regardless of their economic status, or their social importance, and therefore, provide courts at public expense and guarantee access to everyone.

We have developed liberal rules of discovery (patterned after the federal courts) based on the assumption that the open and candid exchange of information is the surest way to resolve claims on their merits and avoid unnecessary trials.

We have contract laws and tort laws. We have laws to protect our citizens from bad faith, fraud, unfair business practices, and oppression by the many large national corporations who control many aspects of their lives but with whom they have no bargaining power.

While our system of justice and our rules are imperfect, they have as their ultimate purpose one overriding principle. They are intended, and continue to evolve, for the purpose of providing fairness to people, regardless of their wealth or political influence.

What I would like the people in the federal judiciary, especially at the appellate level, to understand is that due to their misinterpretation of congressional intent when it enacted the Federal Arbitration Act, and due to their naive assumption that arbitration provisions and choice of law provisions are knowingly bargained for, all of these procedural safeguards and substantive laws are easily avoided by any party with enough leverage to stick a choice of law and an arbitration provision in its pre-printed contract and require the party with inferior bargaining power to sign it.

The procedures we have established, and the laws we have enacted, are either inapplicable or unenforceable in the process we refer to as arbitration.

I am particularly offended by the attitude of federal judges, typified by the remarks of Judge Selya in the First Circuit, which were articulated in Securities Industry Ass'n v. Connolly (1st Cir.1989), 883 F.2d 1114, cert. denied (1990), 495 U.S. 956, 110 S.Ct. 2559, 109 L.Ed.2d 742.

Judge Selya considered "[i]ncreased resort to the courts" as the cause for "tumefaction of already-swollen court calendars." He refers to arbitration as "a contractual device that relieves some of the organic pressure by operating as a shunt, allowing parties to resolve disputes outside of the legal system." Connolly, 883 F.2d at 1116. He states that "[t]he hope has long been that the Act could serve as a therapy for the ailment of the crowded docket." Connolly, 883 F.2d at 1116. He then bemoans that fact that, "[a]s might be expected, there is a rub: the patient, and others in interest, often resist the treatment." Connolly, 883 F.2d at 1116.

Judge Selya refers to the preference in the various state jurisdictions to resolve disputes according to traditional notions of fairness, and then suggests that "[t]he FAA was enacted to overcome this 'anachronism'." Connolly, 883 F.2d at 1119 (citation omitted). He considers it the role of federal courts to be "on guard for artifices in which the ancient suspicion of arbitration might reappear." Connolly, 883 F.2d at 1119.

This type of arrogance not only reflects an intellectual detachment from reality, but a self-serving disregard for the purposes for which courts exist.

With all due respect, Judge Selya's opinion illustrates an all too frequent preoccupation on the part of federal judges with their own case load and a total lack of consideration for the rights of individuals. Nowhere in Judge Selya's lengthy opinion is there any consideration for the total lack of procedural safeguards inherent in the arbitration process. Nowhere in his opinion does he consider the financial hardship that contracts, like the one in this case, impose on people who simply cannot afford to enforce their rights by the process that has been forced upon them. Nowhere does Judge Selya acknowledge that the "patient" (presumably courts like this one) who resists the "treatment" (presumably the imposition of arbitration in lieu of justice) has a case load typically three times as great as Justice Selya's case load.

The notion by federal judges, like Judge Selya, that people like the Casarottos have knowingly and voluntarily bargained and agreed to resolve their contractual disputes or tort claims by arbitration, is naive at best, and self-serving and cynical at worst. To me, the idea of a contract or agreement suggests mutuality. There is no mutuality in a franchise agreement, a securities brokerage agreement, or in any other of the agreements which typically impose arbitration as the means for resolving disputes. National franchisors, like the defendant in this case, and brokerage firms, who have been the defendants in many other arbitration cases, present form contracts to franchisees and consumers in which choice of law provisions and arbitration provisions are not negotiable, and the consequences of which are not explained. The provision is either accepted, or the business or investment opportunity is denied. Yet these provisions, which are not only approved of, but encouraged by people like Judge Selya, do, in effect, subvert our system of justice as we have come to know it. If any foreign government tried to do the same, we would surely consider it a serious act of aggression.

Furthermore, if the Federal Arbitration Act is to be interpreted as broadly as some of the decisions from our federal courts would suggest, then it presents a serious issue regarding separation of powers. What these interpretations do, in effect, is permit a few major corporations to draft contracts regarding their relationship with others that immunizes them from accountability under the laws of the states where they do business, and by the courts in those states. With a legislative act, the Congress, according to some federal decisions, has written state and federal courts out of business as far as these corporations are concerned. They are not subject to California's labor laws or franchise laws, they are not subject to our contract laws or tort laws. They are, in effect, above the law.

These insidious erosions of state authority and the judicial process threaten to undermine the rule of law as we know it.

Nothing in our jurisprudence appears more intellectually detached from reality and arrogant than the lament of federal judges who see this system of imposed arbitration as "therapy for their crowded dockets." These decisions have perverted the purpose of the FAA from one to accomplish judicial neutrality, to one of open hostility to any legislative effort to assure that unsophisticated parties to contracts of adhesion at least understand the rights they are giving up.

It seems to me that judges who have let their concern for their own crowded docket overcome their concern for the rights they are entrusted with should step aside and let someone else assume their burdens. The last I checked, there were plenty of capable people willing to do so.

■ WEBER, JUSTICE, dissents as follows.

I respect the majority opinion in its expression of the deeply held conviction that arbitration of the type expressed in the contract in this case should not be enforced in Montana and thereby deprive the parties of access to the court system. . . .

The majority opinion analyzes the United States Supreme Court's decision in Volt and from that concludes that the nature of the inquiry is whether Montana's notice requirement under (§ 27–5–11494), MCA, would undermine the goals and policy of the FAA and further concludes it does not. I disagree with that analysis of Volt.

. . . It is essential to keep in mind that the key holding of Volt as expressed by the United State Supreme Court was that the agreement to arbitrate should be enforced according to its terms—and that allowed application of the California law which provided for the stay in proceedings where other parties besides the arbitration parties were involved in the case. That conclusion does not assist the majority opinion. The rationale of the Volt decision in the present case would require enforcement of the contract as agreed upon by the parties—which would require application of the American Arbitration Association rules as well as the laws of the State of Connecticut. I conclude that the contract here should be enforced to require application of the American Arbitration Association Rules and the laws of the State of Connecticut under Volt.

In addition to the conclusion reached under Volt, I will discuss several cases which have concluded that a statutory provision similar to Montana's statutory requirement of a statement in capital letters on page one of a contract is in conflict with the Federal Arbitration Act and therefore not enforceable. In David L. Threlkeld and Co. v. Metallgesellschaft Ltd. (2nd Cir.1991), 923 F.2d 245, Threlkeld asserted that Vermont law voided any arbitration agreement which does not have a specific acknowledgment of arbitration signed by both parties and where the agreement to arbitrate has not been displayed prominently in the contract. The circuit court acknowledged that Threlkeld was correct in asserting that the contracts did not comply with the rigorous Vermont standard. The circuit court then concluded that the Vermont statute is preempted by federal law and stated:

Because federal arbitration law governs this dispute, we must determine whether the Vermont statute is sufficiently consistent with federal law that the two may peacefully coexist.... The First Circuit has recently held that restrictive provisions similar to those found in the Vermont statute are preempted by federal law....

We agree with the First Circuit that state statutes such as the Vermont statute directly clash with the Convention and with the Arbitration Act because they effectively reincarnate the former judicial hostility towards arbitration. Accordingly *we hold that the Convention and the Arbitration Act preempt the Vermont statute, and that the ... arbitration provisions, as drafted, are not enforceable.* (Emphasis supplied.)

Threlkeld, 923 F.2d at 250. Threlkeld is clear authority for concluding that the Montana statute directly clashes with the Federal Arbitration Act and therefore is not enforceable.

In a similar manner, Bunge Corp. v. Perryville Feed and Produce (Mo.1985), 685 S.W.2d 837, addresses a similar issue. As pointed out by the Missouri court in Bunge, the Missouri statute is based on the Uniform Arbitration Act (as is the Montana statute) and contains a provision that each contract shall include a statement in 10 point capital letters which reads substantially as follows: THIS CONTRACT CONTAINS A BINDING ARBITRATION PROVISION WHICH MAY BE ENFORCED BY THE PARTIES. The Missouri Supreme Court then stated:

It is clear that § 435.460, if applied to this case, seeks to impose a requirement for contracts to arbitrate which is in addition to the requirements of the Federal Arbitration Act. All that is apparently required under that act is contractual language and format sufficient for an ordinarily written contract.... *If the Missouri statute applies, then a commercial contract sufficient under federal law would be in violation.*

There is a manifest violation of the supremacy clause if our statute is so applied. The Federal Arbitration Act was passed by Congress pursuant to its power to regulate interstate commerce.... Any requirement of state law which adds a burden not imposed by Congress is in derogation of the Congressional power, and pro tanto invalid. A very recent case so holding is Southland Corp. v. Keating....

We do not hold that the Missouri statute is unconstitutional. We simply hold that it may not be applied to defeat the arbitration provision of a contract which is within the coverage of the federal statute.... (Citations omitted.) (Emphasis supplied.)

Bunge, 685 S.W.2d at 839. The Bunge conclusion is directly applicable to our present case. If our Montana statute applies to the present case, then a commercial contract sufficient under federal law would be in violation of the Montana statute even though it meets the requirement of the Federal Arbitration Act. As a result, even if we accept the majority opinion conclusion that the Montana code section applies, I would hold that

Montana law may not be applied to defeat the arbitration principles of a contract which is clearly within the coverage of the Federal Arbitration Act. The District Court held that the Federal Arbitration Act required that the present suit should be stayed until the arbitration has been held in accordance with the terms of the agreement. I would affirm that holding.

■ TURNAGE, C.J., concurs in the foregoing dissent. The dissenting opinion of JUSTICE GRAY is omitted.

* * *

Questions

1.   In the foregoing case, suppose the Montana and Connecticut common law differ with respect to the standard for establishing liability on the basis of promissory estoppel, or the relevant statute of limitations. Which state's law would apply? Why might the choice of law analysis be different for an arbitration clause? Do all laws of a state reflect the state's public policies? If so, for a contract entered into or performed in Montana, would a choice of law other than Montana ever be effective?

2.   If the court's decision means that Montana arbitration law is somehow more reflective of public policies than other state laws, is the state applying an arbitration-specific doctrine in contravention to the rule of *Perry v. Thomas,* supra. that only state law defenses of a general type can be raised to defeat arbitration?

3.   Does the Supreme Court's decision in *Volt* require that the nature of the inquiry into the validity of the Montana notice requirement be based on whether the requirement would "undermine the goals and policies of the FAA?" Under that standard, how should this case come out?

4.   This case was remanded by the Supreme Court in light of *Allied–Bruce Terminex v. Dobson,* 513 U.S. 265 (1995). See 515 U.S. 1129 (1995). What in the *Allied–Bruce Terminex* case might be relevant for the Montana Supreme Court on remand?

On remand, the Montana court adhered to its earlier opinion. Subsequently, the case was appealed to the Supreme Court again on a petition for *certiorari*. The Court accepted the case and rendered the following opinion.

* * *

Doctor's Associates, Inc. v. Casarotto
517 U.S. 681, 116 S.Ct. 1652 (1996).

■ JUSTICE GINSBURG delivered the opinion of the Court.

This case concerns a standard form franchise agreement for the operation of a Subway sandwich shop in Montana. When a dispute arose between parties to the agreement, franchisee Paul Casarotto sued franchisor Doctor's Associates, Inc. (DAI) and DAI's Montana development agent, Nick Lombardi, in a Montana state court. DAI and Lombardi sought to stop the litigation pending arbitration pursuant to the arbitration clause set out on page nine of the franchise agreement.

The Federal Arbitration Act (FAA or Act) declares written provisions for arbitration "valid, irrevocable, and enforceable, save upon such grounds as exist at law or in equity for the revocation of any contract." 9 U.S.C. § 2. Montana law, however, declares an arbitration clause unenforceable unless "[n]otice that [the] contract is subject to arbitration" is "typed in underlined capital letters on the first page of the contract." Mont.Code Ann. § 27–5–114(4) (1995). The question here presented is whether Montana's law is compatible with the federal Act. We hold that Montana's first-page notice requirement, which governs not "any contract," but specifically and solely contracts "subject to arbitration," conflicts with the FAA and is therefore displaced by the federal measure.

I

Petitioner DAI is the national franchisor of Subway sandwich shops. In April 1988, DAI entered a franchise agreement with respondent Paul Casarotto, which permitted Casarotto to open a Subway shop in Great Falls, Montana. The franchise agreement stated, on page nine and in ordinary type: "Any controversy or claim arising out of or relating to this contract or the breach thereof shall be settled by Arbitration. . . ." App. 75.

In October 1992, Casarotto sued DAI and its agent, Nick Lombardi, in Montana state court, alleging state-law contract and tort claims relating to the franchise agreement. DAI demanded arbitration of those claims, and successfully moved in the Montana trial court to stay the lawsuit pending arbitration. Id., at 10–11.

The Montana Supreme Court reversed. Casarotto v. Lombardi, 268 Mont. 369, 886 P.2d 931 (1994). That court left undisturbed the trial court's findings that the franchise agreement fell within the scope of the FAA and covered the claims Casarotto stated against DAI and Lombardi. The Montana Supreme Court held, however, that Mont.Code Ann. § 27–5–114(4) rendered the agreement's arbitration clause unenforceable. The Montana statute provides:

> "Notice that a contract is subject to arbitration . . . shall be typed in underlined capital letters on the first page of the contract; and unless such notice is displayed thereon, the contract may not be subject to arbitration."

Notice of the arbitration clause in the franchise agreement did not appear on the first page of the contract. Nor was anything relating to the clause typed in underlined capital letters. Because the State's statutory notice requirement had not been met, the Montana Supreme Court declared the parties' dispute "not subject to arbitration." 268 Mont., at 382, 886 P.2d, at 939.

DAI and Lombardi unsuccessfully argued before the Montana Supreme Court that § 27–5–114(4) was preempted by § 2 of the FAA. DAI and Lombardi dominantly relied on our decisions in Southland Corp. v. Keating, 465 U.S. 1, 104 S.Ct. 852, 79 L.Ed.2d 1 (1984), and Perry v. Thomas, 482 U.S. 483, 107 S.Ct. 2520, 96 L.Ed.2d 426 (1987). In Southland, we held that § 2 of the FAA applies in state as well as federal courts, see 465 U.S., at 12, 104 S.Ct., at 859, and "withdr[aws] the power of the states to require a judicial forum for the resolution of claims which the contracting parties agreed to resolve by arbitration," id., at 10, 104 S.Ct., at 858. We noted in the pathmarking Southland decision that the FAA established a "broad principle of enforceability," id., at 11, 104 S.Ct., at 858, and that § 2 of the federal Act provided for revocation of arbitration agreements only upon "grounds as exist at law or in equity for the revocation of any contract." In Perry, we reiterated: "[S]tate law, whether of legislative or judicial origin, is applicable *if* that law arose to govern issues concerning the validity, revocability, and enforceability of contracts generally. A state-law principle that takes its meaning precisely from the fact that a contract to arbitrate is at issue does not comport with [the text of § 2]." 482 U.S., at 492, n. 9, 107 S.Ct., at 2527, n. 9.

The Montana Supreme Court, however, read our decision in Volt Information Sciences, Inc. v. Board of Trustees of Leland Stanford Junior Univ., 489 U.S. 468, 109 S.Ct. 1248, 103 L.Ed.2d 488 (1989), as limiting the preemptive force of § 2 and correspondingly qualifying Southland and Perry. 268 Mont., at 378–381, 886 P.2d, at 937–939. As the Montana Supreme Court comprehended Volt, the proper inquiry here should focus not on the bare words of § 2, but on this question: Would the application of Montana's notice requirement, contained in § 27–5–114(4), "undermine the goals and policies of the FAA." 268 Mont., at 381, 886 P.2d, at 938 (internal quotation marks omitted). Section 27–5–114(4), in the Montana court's judgment, did not undermine the goals and policies of the FAA, for the notice requirement did not preclude arbitration agreements altogether; it simply prescribed "that before arbitration agreements are enforceable, they be entered knowingly." Id., at 381, 886 P.2d, at 939.

DAI and Lombardi petitioned for certiorari. Last Term, we granted their petition, vacated the judgment of the Montana Supreme Court, and remanded for further consideration in light of Allied–Bruce Terminix Cos. v. Dobson, 513 U.S. 265, 115 S.Ct. 834, 130 L.Ed.2d 753 (1995). See 515 U.S. 1129, 115 S.Ct. 2552, 132 L.Ed.2d 807 (1995). In Allied–Bruce, we restated what our decisions in Southland and Perry had established:

> "States may regulate contracts, including arbitration clauses, under general contract law principles and they may invalidate an arbitration clause 'upon such grounds as exist at law or in equity for the revocation of *any* contract.' 9 U.S.C. § 2 (emphasis added). What States may not do is decide that a contract is fair enough to enforce all its basic terms (price, service, credit), but not fair enough to enforce its arbitration clause. The Act makes any such state policy unlawful, for that kind of policy would place arbitration clauses on an unequal 'footing,'

directly contrary to the Act's language and Congress's intent." 513 U.S. at 281, 115 S.Ct. at 843.

On remand, without inviting or permitting further briefing or oral argument,[2] the Montana Supreme Court adhered to its original ruling. The court stated: "After careful review, we can find nothing in the [Allied–Bruce] decision which relates to the issues presented to this Court in this case." Casarotto v. Lombardi, 274 Mont. 3, 7, 901 P.2d 596, 598 (1995). Elaborating, the Montana court said it found "no suggestion in [Allied–Bruce] that the principles from Volt on which we relied [to uphold § 27–5–114(4)] have been modified in any way." Id., at 8, 901 P.2d, at 598–599. We again granted certiorari, 516 U.S. 1036, 116 S.Ct. 690, 133 L.Ed.2d 594 (1996), and now reverse.

II

Section 2 of the FAA provides that written arbitration agreements "shall be valid, irrevocable, and enforceable, save upon such grounds as exist at law or in equity for the revocation of *any* contract." 9 U.S.C. § 2 (emphasis added). Repeating our observation in Perry, the text of § 2 declares that state law may be applied "*if* that law arose to govern issues concerning the validity, revocability, and enforceability of contracts generally." 482 U.S., at 492, n. 9, 107 S.Ct., at 2527, n. 9. Thus, generally applicable contract defenses, such as fraud, duress or unconscionability, may be applied to invalidate arbitration agreements without contravening § 2. See Allied–Bruce, 513 U.S., at 281, 115 S.Ct., at 842–843; Rodriguez de Quijas v. Shearson/American Express, Inc., 490 U.S. 477, 483–484, 109 S.Ct. 1917, 1921–1922, 104 L.Ed.2d 526 (1989); Shearson/American Express Inc. v. McMahon, 482 U.S. 220, 226, 107 S.Ct. 2332, 2337, 96 L.Ed.2d 185 (1987).

Courts may not, however, invalidate arbitration agreements under state laws applicable *only* to arbitration provisions. See Allied–Bruce, 513 U.S., at 281, 115 S.Ct., at 842–843; Perry, 482 U.S., at 492, n. 9, 107 S.Ct., at 2527, n. 9. By enacting § 2, we have several times said, Congress precluded States from singling out arbitration provisions for suspect status, requiring instead that such provisions be placed "upon the same footing as other contracts." Scherk v. Alberto–Culver Co., 417 U.S. 506, 511, 94 S.Ct. 2449, 2453, 41 L.Ed.2d 270 (1974) (internal quotation marks omitted). Montana's § 27–5–114(4) directly conflicts with § 2 of the FAA because the State's law conditions the enforceability of arbitration agreements on compliance with a special notice requirement not applicable to contracts generally. The FAA thus displaces the Montana statute with respect to arbitration agreements covered by the Act. See 2 I. Macneil, R. Speidel, T. Stipanowich, & G. Shell, Federal Arbitration Law § 19.1.1, pp. 19:4–19:5 (1995) (under Southland and Perry, "state legislation requiring greater

---

2. Dissenting Justice Gray thought it "cavalier" of her colleagues to ignore the defendants' request for an "opportunity to brief the issues raised by the ... remand and to present oral argument." Casarotto v. Lombardi, 274 Mont. 3, 9–10, 901 P.2d 596, 599–600 (1995).

information or choice in the making of agreements to arbitrate than in other contracts is preempted").[3]

The Montana Supreme Court misread our Volt decision and therefore reached a conclusion in this case at odds with our rulings. Volt involved an arbitration agreement that incorporated state procedural rules, one of which, on the facts of that case, called for arbitration to be stayed pending the resolution of a related judicial proceeding. The state rule examined in Volt determined only the efficient order of proceedings; it did not affect the enforceability of the arbitration agreement itself. We held that applying the state rule would not "undermine the goals and policies of the FAA," 489 U.S., at 478, 109 S.Ct., at 1255, because the very purpose of the Act was to "ensur[e] that private agreements to arbitrate are enforced according to their terms," id., at 479, 109 S.Ct., at 1256.

Applying § 27–5–114(4) here, in contrast, would not enforce the arbitration clause in the contract between DAI and Casarotto; instead, Montana's first-page notice requirement would invalidate the clause. The "goals and policies" of the FAA, this Court's precedent indicates, are antithetical to threshold limitations placed specifically and solely on arbitration provisions. Section 2 "mandate[s] the enforcement of arbitration agreements," Southland, 465 U.S., at 10, 104 S.Ct., at 858, "save upon such grounds as exist at law or in equity for the revocation of any contract," 9 U.S.C. § 2. Section 27–5–114(4) of Montana's law places arbitration agreements in a class apart from "any contract," and singularly limits their validity. The State's prescription is thus inconsonant with, and is therefore preempted by, the federal law.

For the reasons stated, the judgment of the Supreme Court of Montana is reversed, and the case is remanded for further proceedings not inconsistent with this opinion.

It is so ordered.

---

3. At oral argument, counsel for Casarotto urged a broader view, under which § 27–5–114(4) might be regarded as harmless surplus. See Tr. of Oral Arg. 29–32. Montana could have invalidated the arbitration clause in the franchise agreement under general, informed consent principles, counsel suggested. She asked us to regard § 27–5–114(4) as but one illustration of a cross-the-board rule: unexpected provisions in adhesion contracts must be conspicuous. See also Brief for Respondents 21–24. But the Montana Supreme Court announced no such sweeping rule. The court did not assert as a basis for its decision a generally applicable principle of "reasonable expectations" governing any standard form contract term. Cf. Transamerica Ins.

Co. v. Royle, 202 Mont. 173, 180, 656 P.2d 820, 824 (1983) (invalidating provision in auto insurance policy that did not "honor the reasonable expectations" of the insured). Montana's decision trains on and upholds a particular statute, one setting out a precise, arbitration-specific limitation. We review that disposition, and no other. It bears reiteration, however, that a court may not "rely on the uniqueness of an agreement to arbitrate as a basis for a state-law holding that enforcement would be unconscionable, for this would enable the court to effect what . . . the state legislature cannot." Perry v. Thomas, 482 U.S. 483, 492, n. 9, 107 S.Ct. 2520, 2527, n. 9, 96 L.Ed.2d 426 (1987).

■ JUSTICE THOMAS, dissenting.

For the reasons given in my dissent last term in Allied–Bruce Terminix Cos. v. Dobson, 513 U.S. 265, 115 S.Ct. 834, 130 L.Ed.2d 753 (1995), I remain of the view that § 2 of the Federal Arbitration Act, 9 U.S.C. § 2, does not apply to proceedings in state courts. Accordingly, I respectfully dissent.

* * *

Questions

1.   How does the majority reinterpret *Volt?* Is this the only reading of *Volt* that is possible?

2.   Does footnote 3 raise the possibility of challenges to arbitration clauses based on unconscionability or lack of consent? How must such challenges to framed in order to succeed?

* * *

5.   PUBLIC INTEREST

Faherty v. Faherty
97 N.J. 99, 477 A.2d 1257 (S.Ct. N.J. 1984).

■ GARIBALDI, J.

The question posed in this appeal is whether an arbitration provision in a separation agreement, entered into by the parties prior to their divorce and incorporated in their divorce judgment, is enforceable. The Chancery Division and the Appellate Division enforced the arbitration provision. We granted certification, 94 N.J. 616, 468 A.2d 245 (1983), and now modify and affirm, as modified, the Appellate Division's judgment.

I

Susan Faherty (Susan) and J. Roger Faherty (Roger) were divorced in 1977 after seventeen years of marriage. At that time, they had four dependent children. Prior to their divorce, the parties, both of whom were represented by counsel, negotiated and executed a Property Settlement Agreement (Agreement). The trial court incorporated the Agreement in the final judgment of divorce, which expressly recited that the court had made no "findings as to the reasonableness thereof."

The Agreement is detailed and governs equitable distribution, spousal support, child custody, and child support. Paragraph 25 of the Agreement provides that any financial dispute arising out of the Agreement must be arbitrated as a condition precedent to court action; the arbitration must be conducted under the rules of the American Arbitration Association (AAA); and the arbitrator's decision is binding on the parties. Paragraph 20 permits modification of payments due to changed circumstances but, in the event of a dispute over the necessity for such modification, requires arbitration as a condition precedent to judicial relief.

The Agreement also contains several paragraphs dealing with the equitable distribution of the parties' assets. Under the terms of the Agreement, Roger transferred the marital home in Summit, New Jersey to Susan, who also retained all the tangible personal property in the home and a Jeep. Paragraph 7 required Roger, over a ten-year period, to pay Susan ten promissory notes totaling $165,000 as "an adjustment of accounts as part of the division in lieu of statutory equitable distribution of marital assets." In the event of Roger's death, the notes were to be treated as a debt of his estate. As security for the payment of the notes, Roger was required to furnish stock to be held in an escrow account and to secure a $100,000 term life insurance policy.

Paragraph 29 provides for adjustment of support under certain circumstances. Roger was a successful investment banker employed by his closely-held family corporation. The parties recognized that Roger's ability to meet his spousal-support obligations under the Agreement was contingent on his company's earnings. To avoid the possibly unjust consequences of requiring Roger to pay the full support required in the Agreement in years when his company did not make a profit, the parties in paragraph 29 provided:

29. (a) The parties to this Agreement recognize that the husband's obligation provided for in paragraph 2 may, under the circumstances that his employer, Faherty & Swartwood, Inc., may not have substantial pre-tax earnings, be difficult for him to perform.

(b) Any arrearages which may develop in payment of the obligations provided for in paragraph 2 shall be *weighed* in connection with the amount of his fixed annual salary and the fiscal year-end pre-tax earnings of the said employer, since a distribution of said earnings or a loan on the basis of such earnings is expected to be the sole way in which the husband could meet the said obligations, or make up any arrearages which may accumulate thereunder.

(c) Nothing in this paragraph shall be deemed to apply to, modify or *limit any portion of this Agreement* with the exception of the said paragraph 2. [Emphasis added.]

Further, the Agreement included the following clauses: a release by each party of all equitable division of marital assets and all community property interests except for those provided in the Agreement; an integration clause stating that the Agreement represented the parties' entire understanding and that "there are no representations, promises, warranties, covenants or undertakings other than those expressly set forth herein"; a default clause, whereby Roger agreed that if he should default in performing any obligation under the Agreement, he would pay to Susan counsel fees she reasonably incurred to enforce her rights under the Agreement; and a provision that the Agreement shall be governed by the laws of New Jersey.

The present case arose when Susan moved in the Chancery Division for an order fixing past-due alimony and child support and compelling discovery of defendant's business records. Susan claimed that Roger was in arrears of $25,400 in support payments and had defaulted on one of the equitable-distribution promissory notes of $25,000. Roger cross-moved, seeking to compel arbitration of the arrearages pursuant to paragraphs 20 and 25 and seeking arbitration as to the amounts of future payments because he claimed significantly changed circumstances. The Chancery Division issued an order compelling arbitration of arrearages of alimony and child support as well as the issue of modification of future payments of alimony and child support in accordance with the Agreement.

Subsequently, the parties selected an arbitrator according to the rules of the AAA. The issues submitted to arbitration were Susan's claims for arrearages in alimony and child support, for future alimony and child support, as well as Roger's claim that both the arrearages in alimony and child support and future payments thereof should be reduced due to his changed circumstances.

The arbitration took several months. It included several lengthy days of examination, cross-examinations, exchange of post-hearing and reply briefs, and, finally, the entry of the arbitrator's award on January 18, 1981. The arbitrator made no written findings of fact and neither of the parties requested a written transcript.

The arbitrator's award fixed the alimony arrearages of $37,648 and child support arrearages of $12,284. The award also denied Roger's requests for reduction in future alimony, if any, and future child support. Thereafter, Susan moved in the Chancery Division to confirm the arbitration award. Roger cross-moved to vacate the arbitrator's award and to obtain court hearings for modification of his prior and future payments due to his changed circumstances and for modification of his payments in lieu of equitable distribution.

The Chancery Division confirmed the arbitration award and denied Roger's motion. Although Roger had originally petitioned the court to compel arbitration, in his appeal to the Appellate Division, for the first time, he challenged the validity of the arbitration clause and also sought to overturn the Chancery Division's confirmation of the arbitration award. The Appellate Division, in a brief per curiam opinion, found that all issues of law raised by Roger were clearly without merit.

Roger makes two basic claims. The first is that arbitration of domestic disputes between former spouses regarding alimony and child support should not, as a matter of public policy, be permitted to be settled outside the courts, and therefore the arbitration clause in the Agreement should not be enforced. The second is that the arbitration award in this case was erroneous and should be overturned.

II

Although it is clear that marital separation agreements are enforceable in this state insofar as "they are just and equitable," Schlemm v. Schlemm,

31 N.J. 557, 158 A.2d 508 (1960), this Court has never before addressed the question of the enforceability of an arbitration clause in a separation agreement.

In this state, as in most American jurisdictions, arbitration is a favored remedy. It permits parties to agree to resolve disputes outside of the court system. A court generally will enforce an arbitration agreement unless it violates public policy. E.g., Barcon Assocs., Inc. v. Tri–County Asphalt Corp., 86 N.J. 179, 186, 430 A.2d 214 (1981) (arbitration favored by the courts of this state). . . .

In recent years arbitration has been used more frequently as a viable means of resolving domestic disputes that arise under separation agreements. See Comment, "The Enforceability of Arbitration Clauses in North Carolina Separation Agreements," 15 Wake Forest L.Rev. 487 (1979). In other jurisdictions around the country courts have consistently enforced arbitration clauses to settle matrimonial disputes. See Sterk, "Enforceability of Agreements to Arbitrate: An Examination of the Public Policy Defense," 2 Cardozo L.Rev. 481, 493 (1981). . . .

III

Our arbitration statute, N.J.S.A. 2A:24–1 to–11, recognizes the validity of arbitration as a means of resolving contractual disputes between parties. As discussed earlier in this opinion, New Jersey has long recognized the validity and enforceability of separation agreements between divorcing spouses. See Schlemm, supra, 31 N.J. 557, 158 A.2d 508. Enforcement of arbitration clauses pertaining to alimony as within such agreements is a logical extension of the view, expressed in Schlemm, that parties should be granted as much autonomy as possible in the ordering of their personal lives. Since parties may settle spousal support rights and obligations by contract, Schlemm, supra, 31 N.J. at 581, 158 A.2d 508, there is no policy reason to prohibit their submitting disputes arising out of such contracts to binding arbitration. It is fair and reasonable that parties who have agreed to be bound by arbitration in a formal, written separation agreement should be so bound. Rather than frowning on arbitration of alimony disputes, public policy supports it. We recognize that in many cases arbitration of matrimonial disputes may offer an effective alternative method of dispute resolution. As commentators have noted, the advantages of arbitration of domestic disputes include reduced court congestion, the opportunity for resolution of sensitive matters in a private and informal forum, reduction of the trauma and anxiety of marital litigation, minimization of the intense polarization of parties that often occurs, and the ability to choose the arbitrator. See Comment, 15 Wake Forest L.Rev., supra, at 490. In this sensitive and intensely private area of domestic disputes, arbitration expressly contracted for by the spouses is highly desirable. We accordingly hold today that under the laws of New Jersey, parties may bind themselves in separation agreements to arbitrate disputes over alimony. As is the case with other arbitration awards, an award determining spousal support would be subject to the review provided in N.J.S.A. 2A:24–8.

IV

Our inclination to embrace arbitration in all phases of matrimonial disputes is tempered, however, by our knowledge that in such cases competing public policy considerations abound. Accordingly, the principle issue involved here is whether public policy prohibits arbitration from resolving child support and custody disputes.

Although it is generally accepted that spouses may enter enforceable agreements to arbitrate alimony disputes, some commentators have suggested that arbitration is unsatisfactory to resolve disputes concerning child support or custody because of the court's traditional role as parens patriae. Traditionally, courts under the doctrine of parens patriae have been entrusted to protect the best interests of children. Children's maintenance, custody-visitation, and overall best interests have always been subject to the close scrutiny and supervision of the courts despite any agreements to the contrary. Some commentators see arbitration as a dangerous encroachment on this jurisdiction. See Holman & Noland, "Agreement and Arbitration: Relief to over-litigation in domestic relations disputes in Washington," 12 Willamette L.J. 527, 537 (1976). Since parents cannot by agreement deprive the courts of their duty to promote the best interests of their children, it is argued that they cannot do so by arbitration.

Detractors notwithstanding, there has been a growing tendency to recognize arbitration in child support clauses. We do not agree with those who fear that by allowing parents to agree to arbitrate child support, we are interfering with the judicial protection of the best interests of the child. We see no valid reason why the arbitration process should not be available in the area of child support; the advantages of arbitration in domestic disputes outweigh any disadvantages.

Nevertheless, we recognize that the courts have a nondelegable, special supervisory function in the area of child support that may be exercised upon review of an arbitrator's award. We therefore hold that whenever the validity of an arbitration award affecting child support is questioned on the grounds that it does not provide adequate protection for the child, the trial court should conduct a special review of the award. This review should consist of a two step analysis. First, as with all arbitration awards, the courts should review child support awards as provided by N.J.S.A. 2A:24–8.[3] Second, the courts should conduct a de novo review unless it is clear on

---

3. 2A:24–8. Vacation of award; rehearing The court shall vacate the award in any of the following cases: a. Where the award was procured by corruption, fraud or undue means; b. Where there was either evident partiality or corruption in the arbitrators, or any thereof; c. Where the arbitrators were guilty of misconduct in refusing to postpone the hearing, upon sufficient cause being shown therefor, or in refusing to hear evidence, pertinent and material to the controversy, or of any other misbehaviors prejudicial to the rights of any party; d. Where the arbitrators exceeded or so imperfectly executed their powers that a mutual, final and definite award upon the subject matter submitted was not made. When an award is vacated and the time within which the agreement required the award to be made has not

the face of the award that the award could not adversely affect the substantial best interests of the child.

An arbitrator's award that grants all the requested child support would generally satisfy this second test because it is always in the child's best interest to have as much support as possible. Clearly such an award does not adversely affect the best interest of the child. In such cases, the spouse challenging the award would be limited to the statutory grounds for vacation or modification provided in N.J.S.A. 2A:24–8 because the state's interest in protecting the child has already been established. Thus, only an arbitrator's award that either reduced child support or refused a request for increased support could be subject to court review beyond the review provided by statute, because only such an award could adversely affect the interests of the child. However, even awards reducing support would be subject to court review only if they adversely affected the substantial best interests of the child. The substantial best interests of the child are not affected when the reduction in support or the denial of additional support is petty or frivolous, but only when it actually and materially affects the child's standard of living.

While several states have enforced agreements to arbitrate child support disputes, arbitration of custody and visitation issues has been deemed to be an unacceptable infringement of the court's parens patriae role. We do not reach the question of whether arbitration of child custody and visitation rights is enforceable since that issue is not before us. However, we note that the development of a fair and workable mediation or arbitration process to resolve these issues may be more beneficial to the children of this state than the present system of courtroom confrontation. See Schepard, Philbrick & Rabino, "Ground Rules for Custody Mediation and Modification," 48 Alb.L.Rev. 616 (1984). Accordingly, the policy reasons for our holding today with respect to child support may be equally applicable to child custody and visitation cases.

As we gain experience in the arbitration of child support and custody disputes, it may become evident that a child's best interests are as well protected by an arbitrator as by a judge. If so, there would be no necessity for our de novo review. However, because of the Court's parens patriae tradition, at this time we prefer to err in favor of the child's best interest.

V

Finally, we must decide whether the arbitrator's award should be confirmed in the present case. N.J.S.A. 2A:24–1 to–11 grants arbitrators "extremely broad powers and extends judicial support to the arbitration process subject only to limited review." Barcon Assocs., Inc. v. Tri–County Asphalt Corp., supra, 86 N.J. at 187, 430 A.2d 214.

Before turning to the facts of the present case, we note that the arbitrator made no written findings of fact. The AAA rules do not require such findings, but because alimony and child support are always subject to

expired, the court may, in its discretion, direct a rehearing by the arbitrators.

modification for changed circumstances, we suggest, but do not mandate, that the arbitrator in all future domestic dispute arbitrations make reasonably detailed findings of fact upon which she or he bases the arbitration award. Such findings will aid not only the court's review of the award but also will aid later arbitrators in determining requests for modification. Certainly, such findings of fact should be prepared if requested by either of the parties.

With these admonitions in mind, we find that in this case, the arbitrator's award is not subject to heightened scrutiny to protect the interests of the children because the award enforced their rights and protected their interests against Roger's claim of changed circumstances. In this case the state's interest in the welfare of the children has been protected and there is no public policy reason to subject the award to de novo review.

Of the statutory grounds for vacation of an arbitration award, Roger relies on N.J.S.A. 2A:24–8d, which provides that an arbitration award may be vacated:

> d. Where the arbitrators exceeded or so imperfectly executed their powers that a mutual, final and definite award upon the subject matter submitted was not made.

Roger bases his claim on the contention that the arbitrator failed to weigh the evidence presented to him. Roger first claims that if the arbitrator had weighed the evidence of his income and his closely-held corporations' earnings, as required by paragraph 29(b) of the Agreement, he could not have made the award that he made. We have no record in this case and Roger has failed to provide any support for this contention. Next, Roger claims that the promissory notes, which, under the terms of the Agreement, were equitable distribution, were actually disguised alimony and as such should be subject to modification for changed circumstances. In the absence of any evidence to the contrary and in view of the language of the clause in issue, we hold that Roger failed to show that the arbitrator violated N.J.S.A. 2A:24–8d. Accordingly, there is no reason to vacate or modify the award on these grounds.

* * *

Questions

1. The court states that an arbitral award that granted all requested child support would automatically qualify as an award that was in the child's best interest. Do you agree? Is it possible that such an award, if it were frivolous or so confiscatory as to impoverish the other parent, might not be in the child's best interest?

2. Does this case create a special rule for judicial review in cases involving children, or does it create a standard of review that could be applied to

other cases? What other types of cases might there be a sufficient public interest to warrant a heightened level of scrutiny of arbitral awards?

* * *

6. CONTRACTS OF EMPLOYMENT

The following group of cases address an aspect of *Gilmer v. Interstate/Johnson Lane Co.,* 500 U.S. 20 (1991), supra. that was not addressed earlier. Recall that in the *Gilmer* case, an employee of a brokerage house sued his employer alleging a violation of the Age Discrimination in Employment Act. In finding the dispute to be amenable to arbitration, the Court refused to address an argument that had been raised by *amicus curiae* on appeal. *Amicus* argued that the FAA did not compel arbitration of the plaintiff's claim because the arbitration clause was part of a contract of employment, and thus was excluded from the coverage of the FAA. The FAA states, in Section 1 that:

> nothing herein shall apply to contracts of employment of seamen, railroad employees, or any other class of workers engaged in foreign or interstate commerce. 9 U.S.C. 1.

The *Gilmer* majority refused to consider the argument on the ground that it had not been raised below. 500 U.S. at 21 & n. 2. Furthermore, it said that the arbitration agreement at issue was not between the plaintiff and his employer but rather was concluded with a third party, the National Association of Security Dealers, so arguably the exclusion would not apply.

Since *Gilmer*, lower courts have grappled with questions about how to interpret the contracts of employment exception contained in the FAA and to what extent the FAA applies in the employment context. The following cases are representative of some of the issues that arise.

Tenney Engineering, Inc. v. United Electrical Radio & Machine Workers of America, (U.E.) Local 437

207 F.2d 450 (3d Cir. 1953).

■ Before BIGGS, CHIEF JUDGE, and MARIS, GOODRICH, McLAUGHLIN, KALODNER, STALEY and HASTIE, CIRCUIT JUDGES.

■ MARIS, CIRCUIT JUDGE.

The plaintiff, a manufacturing corporation, brought an action in the District Court for the District of New Jersey under Section 301 of the Labor Management Relations Act, 1947, 29 U.S.C.A. § 185, commonly called the Taft–Hartley Act, against the defendant, a labor union, for damages for breach of contract. The breach alleged was a strike of the plaintiff's employees called by the defendant in violation of a collective bargaining agreement between the parties. The agreement contained an arbitration clause and the defendant moved for a stay of the suit pending arbitration, pursuant to Section 3 of title 9, United States Code, entitled "Arbitration". The parties stipulated that the plaintiff is engaged in the manufacture of goods for sale in interstate commerce and that its employees, represented by the defendant, are all engaged in such manufacture and incidental plant maintenance. The district court denied the stay and the defendant thereupon took the appeal now before us.

This appeal presents the question whether Section 3 of title 9 is applicable to a collective bargaining agreement between parties in the situation of those in this suit. For if the section is not so applicable the action of the district court in denying a stay under it was right. The answer to this question in turn depends upon the construction which is to be placed upon the final clause of Section 1 of title 9 which reads "nothing herein contained shall apply to contracts of employment of seamen, railroad employees, or any other class of workers engaged in foreign or interstate commerce." It has been held that the "contracts of employment" to which this clause refers include collective bargaining agreements and that the clause is a limitation upon the operation of all the sections of title 9. The majority of the court would not disturb this holding. The answer to the question accordingly turns upon whether the plaintiff's employees, who are engaged in the manufacture of goods for commerce and plant maintenance incidental thereto, are to be regarded as a "class of workers engaged in foreign or interstate commerce" within the meaning of the exclusionary clause.

The Arbitration Act, which was codified and enacted as title 9 of the United States Code in 1947, was originally enacted by the Act of February 12, 1925. Our problem, therefore, is to determine the meaning which Congress in 1925 intended to give to the phrase "workers engaged in foreign or interstate commerce". Was it intended to include only those employees actually engaged in the channels of interstate or foreign commerce or did it comprehend all those engaged in activities affecting such commerce, such as the production of goods destined for sale in it? The legislative history furnishes little light on the point. The bill was drafted by the Committee on Commerce, Trade and Commercial Law of the American Bar Association and sponsored by the Association. The only reference to the clause in question appears in a report of the Bar Association committee in which it was stated:

> "Objections to the bill were urged by Mr. Andrew Furuseth as representing the Seamen's Union, Mr. Furuseth taking the position that seamen's wages came within admiralty jurisdiction and should not be subject to an agreement to arbitrate. In order to eliminate this opposition, the committee consented to an amendment to Section 1 as follows: 'but nothing herein contained shall apply to contracts of employment of seamen, railroad employees or any other class of workers engaged in foreign or interstate commerce.' "

It thus appears that the draftsmen of the Act were presented with the problem of exempting seamen's contracts. Seamen constitute a class of workers as to whom Congress had long provided machinery for arbitration.

In exempting them the draftsmen excluded also railroad employees, another class of workers as to whom special procedure for the adjustment of disputes had previously been provided. Both these classes of workers were engaged directly in interstate or foreign commerce. To these the draftsmen of the Act added "any other class of workers engaged in foreign or interstate commerce." We think that the intent of the latter language was, under the rule of ejusdem generis, to include only those other classes of workers who are likewise engaged directly in commerce, that is, only those other classes of workers who are actually engaged in the movement of interstate or foreign commerce or in work so closely related thereto as to be in practical effect part of it. The draftsmen had in mind the two groups of transportation workers as to which special arbitration legislation already existed and they rounded out the exclusionary clause by excluding all other similar classes of workers.

It must be remembered that the Arbitration Act of 1925 was drawn and passed at a time when the concept of Congressional power over individuals whose activities affected interstate commerce had not developed to the extent to which it was expanded in the succeeding years. The area in which Congress then generally legislated is illustrated by the Federal Employers' Liability Act of 1908 which applied to a railroad employee injured "while he is employed by such carrier (by railroad) in such (interstate or foreign) commerce". This language had been construed by the Supreme Court to include only employees engaged in interstate transportation or in work so closely related to it as to be practically a part of it.[11] In incorporating almost exactly the same phraseology into the Arbitration Act of 1925 its draftsmen and the Congress which enacted it must have had in mind this current construction of the language which they used.

Moreover when Congress later proceeded to exercise power under the commerce clause in the expanded area, to which we have referred, it continued to use the phrase "engaged in commerce" in the narrower sense while using other and more precise language to include activities merely affecting commerce. Thus Congress made the Fair Labor Standards Act applicable not only to employees "engaged in commerce" but also to those engaged "in the production of goods for commerce". Congress, as the Supreme Court pointed out in McLeod v. Threlkeld, 1943, 319 U.S. 491, 63 S.Ct. 1248, 87 L.Ed. 1538, has thus used precise language in this field to carry out its intentions. We think it did so in the Arbitration Act of 1925.

In the case before us the plaintiff's employees are engaged in the production of goods for subsequent sale in interstate commerce. Thus while their activities will undoubtedly affect interstate commerce they are not acting directly in the channels of commerce itself. They are, therefore, not a "class of workers engaged in * * * interstate commerce" within the meaning of Section 1 of title 9. . . .

11. Shanks v. Delaware, L. & W. R. Co., 1916, 239 U.S. 556, 558, 36 S.Ct. 188, 60 L.Ed. 436.

The collective bargaining agreement here involved, not being excluded by Section 1, undoubtedly is within the purview of Section 3 of title 9. For it is settled that Section 3, being a purely procedural section, applies to all contracts for arbitration which may be involved in suits properly brought in the federal courts and not merely to those maritime transactions or contracts evidencing transactions involving interstate, foreign or territorial commerce the arbitration clauses of which are made valid and enforceable by the substantive provisions of Section 2 of title 9. We, therefore, do not have to decide whether the collective bargaining agreement between the present parties is a contract evidencing a transaction involving interstate commerce within the meaning of Section 2. It may well be, however, that the concept of a "transaction involving commerce" contained in that section was intended to be broader in its scope than that of "workers engaged in * * * commerce", the language of the exclusionary clause of Section 1 which we have considered. It would seem reasonable to assume that Congress intended the benefits of Section 2 to apply to all contracts within its power to regulate under the Commerce Clause of the Constitution.

We conclude that the defendant is entitled to a stay of proceedings under Section 3 of title 9, United States Code, if the collective bargaining agreement between the parties, properly construed and applied, provides for arbitration of the issues raised by the complaint and if the defendant is itself not in default in proceeding with such arbitration. Since these questions cannot be determined on the present record the case must be remanded for their determination and the entry of an appropriate stay order if the defendant is found to be entitled to it.

Our conclusion that Section 3 is applicable makes it unnecessary for us to consider whether the defendant would be entitled to the relief its seeks, by way of a counterclaim for specific performance of the arbitration clause of the agreement, under Section 301 of the Labor Management Relations Act. In this connection see the well considered opinion of Judge Wyzanski in Textile Workers Union of America, C.I.O. v. American Thread Co., D.C.Mass. 1953, 113 F.Supp. 137, which holds that such a remedy is afforded by that Act.

The order of the district court will be vacated and the cause will be remanded for further proceedings not inconsistent with this opinion.

■ BIGGS, CHIEF JUDGE (concurring).

This court should expressly overrule its decisions in Amalgamated Ass'n v. Pennsylvania Greyhound Lines, 3 Cir., 1951, 192 F.2d 310, 313, and Pennsylvania Greyhound Lines v. Amalgamated Ass'n, 3 Cir., 1952, 193 F.2d 327, holding that a collective bargaining agreement is a "contract of employment" within the purview of Section 1 of the Act. A collective bargaining agreement is not a contract of employment. Cf. J. I. Case Co. v. National Labor Relations Board, 1944, 321 U.S. 332, 334–336, 64 S.Ct. 576, 88 L.Ed. 762. The exclusionary provisions of Section 1 are therefore inapplicable under the circumstances at bar.

The majority view, limiting, in this case, the exclusionary provisions of Section 1 to contracts of employment of workers engaged in transporting goods in foreign or interstate commerce, is too narrow to be supportable. The exclusion embraces contracts of workers engaged in the production of goods for interstate commerce.

I cannot accept the plaintiff's contention that the legislative history of the Act compels the conclusion that the Act was intended to apply to commercial disputes only and not to labor disputes. The legislative history is of a kind that possesses little weight and should not be considered. Duplex Printing Press Co. v. Deering, 1921, 254 U.S. 443, 474, 41 S.Ct. 172, 65 L.Ed. 349, and United States v. Kung Chen Fur Co., 1951, 188 F.2d 577, 584, 38 Cust. & Pat.App. 107. The face of the statute must control the relief to be granted under it.

I agree with the majority that if the collective bargaining agreement provides for arbitration of the issues raised by the complaint and if Local 427 is not in default, it would be entitled to a stay under Section 3 of the Act. I, therefore, join in vacating the judgment of the court below and remanding the case for further proceedings . . .

■ McLAUGHLIN, CIRCUIT JUDGE (dissenting).

Although the legislative history of the Arbitration Act is admittedly not helpful in directly determining what scope Congress intended to give the phrase "workers engaged in foreign or interstate commerce" as found in Section 1, it does show that the statute was enacted to provide solely for arbitration in commercial disputes. As the majority notes, the bill from which the Act emerged was originally drafted by the Committee on Commerce, Trade and Commercial Law of the American Bar Association. Mr. Piatt, the chairman of this committee, in testifying before the Senate subcommittee which considered the bill said, *"It was not the intention of the bill to make an industrial arbitration in any sense."* (Emphasis supplied.) Discussion of the bill on the floor of Congress also indicates this purpose. . .

The view that there can be no compulsory arbitration under this Act of collective bargaining agreements of employees similarly situated to appellants finds solid support in the three other circuits which have considered the question. The Sixth Circuit Gatliff Coal case, supra, unlike our own coal cases, held that Section 1 was a limitation on the whole Act. Cox, the plaintiff, *who was employed in defendant's power house,* brought suit to recover wages due him under a collective bargaining agreement. Defendant moved to stay the proceedings pending arbitration. The denial of that motion was affirmed on appeal, the court holding that the agreement was within the exception of Section 1. Implicit in that decision and necessary to the holding is the determination that the contract was that of an employee engaged in interstate commerce.

International Union v. Colonial Hardwood Flooring Co., 4 Cir., 1948, 168 F.2d 33, a case very similar to the instant one, was a suit by an employer under the Labor Management Relations Act of 1947, 29 U.S.C.A.

§ 185 et seq., to recover damages on account of a strike. The Fourth Circuit affirmed the denial of the defendant union's motion to stay the proceedings so that there could be arbitration pursuant to the Arbitration Act, the court holding that the collective bargaining agreement was within the exclusionary clause of Section 1. The members of the defendant union *were employed in plaintiff's woodworking establishment* in the city of Hagerstown, Md.[23] There again the implicit holding is that the employees were engaged in interstate commerce within the Arbitration Act. The court said at 168 F.2d 36:

> "It is perfectly clear, we think, that it was the intention of Congress to exclude contracts of employment from the operation of all of these provisions (Sections 2, 3 and 4 of the Act). Congress was steering clear of compulsory arbitration of labor disputes * * *."[24]

In Mercury Oil Refining Co. v. Oil Workers International Union, 10 Cir., 1951, 187 F.2d 980, the labor organization brought an action to enforce an arbitration award made under the terms of its collective bargaining agreement. The district court invalidated the award and ordered further arbitration. Both parties appealed. The Tenth Circuit reversed that part of the judgment directing additional arbitration on the ground that labor contracts are specifically excluded from the Arbitration Act. There is nothing to indicate that the oil workers affected were engaged in the transportation industry...

Opposed to these views there is not a single decision delimiting the phrase "contracts of employment of * * * workers engaged in foreign or interstate commerce" as the majority has here done.

We are told by the majority that the exclusionary clause was intended by the draftsmen of the Act to embrace two groups of transportation workers, seamen and railroad employees, as to which special arbitration legislation already existed "and they [the draftsmen] rounded out the exclusionary clause by excluding all other similar classes of workers." The sole reason advanced for this attempted construction is the statement that the rule of ejusdem generis controls. Since the intention of Congress manifestly was to confine the Act to commercial disputes, ejusdem generis has no possible relevancy here. As said in Gooch v. United States, 297 U.S. 124, 128, 56 S.Ct. 395, 397, 80 L.Ed. 522, " * * * it [the rule of ejusdem generis] may not be used to defeat the obvious purpose of legislation." ... It should be noted that if only classes of workers as to which arbitration procedure existed were intended by Congress to be excluded from the Arbitration Act it would have been a simple task to have so worded the Act.

23. See the district court opinion, D.C.D. Md. 1948, 76 F.Supp. 493.

24. Similar language was used by this court in the first Greyhound case, 3 Cir., 192 F.2d 310, 313: "For Congress to have included in the Arbitration Act judicial intervention in the arbitration of disputes about collective bargaining involving these two classes would have created pointless friction in an already sensitive area as well as wasteful duplication. It is reasonable, therefore, to believe that the avoidance of an undesirable consequence in the field of collective bargaining *was a principal purpose of excepting contracts of employment from the Act.*" (Emphasis supplied).

Similarly, if transportation workers alone were to have been excluded Congress could have used more appropriate language to indicate such intention.

We would come closer to effecting Congressional intent if we gave proper emphasis to the words "contracts of employment" rather than narrowly construed the phrase "workers engaged in * * * interstate commerce" in the exclusionary clause. To suggest that the 1925 concept of interstate commerce should restrict the exclusionary language of the Act in 1953 is unrealistic for three reasons. In the first place, Congress was not restricted in 1925 to *excluding* only employment contracts of workers engaged in the "direct channels" of interstate commerce—it could have provided that no employment contracts, whether they involved interstate or intrastate labor, would be subjected to compulsory arbitration in the federal courts. Second, even if it be agreed, as it must be, that the concept of interstate commerce was much narrower then than now, we need not now be bound by the older view. An analogous situation would be the case of an old statute requiring that something be done according to due process of law. Would anyone argue that in interpreting such a statute today we would be limited to a consideration of what constituted due process at the time the legislation was enacted, despite the fact that our concept of that term had greatly changed in the interim? In my opinion the law is not so inflexible. Third, although the statute was originally enacted in 1925, it was reenacted and codified as Title 9 of the U.S. Code in 1947. It was because of the change in the catch line of Section 1 at that time that we held in the first Pennsylvania Greyhound case, supra, that the section applied to the whole Act. Therefore the broader view of interstate commerce as it was understood in 1947 rather than the relatively narrow view extant in 1925 should be our present guide in interpreting Section 1.

For the reasons stated I would affirm.

* * *

Questions

1. How could you answer the majority's argument in *Tenney* about *ejusdem generis*? Does the principle of construction require that the contracts of employment exclusion be interpreted narrowly, or is there a competing principle of construction that might argue for a broad interpretation?

2. In 1925, Congress believed that it only had the power to regulate employment relations of seamen and railroad workers, due to the Supreme Court's narrow view of the scope of the commerce power. Since then its view has changed dramatically so that today Congress and the courts view congressional power under the Commerce Clause as permitting Congress to regulate widely in private sector employment. See, *NLRB v. Jones & Laughlin Steel Corp.*, 301 U.S. 1 (1937). How might this change in the

power of Congress to regulate private employment affect the reasoning in *Tenney* concerning congressional intent?

3.   How is it possible, according to the *Tenney* majority, for a court to invoke section 3 of the FAA without reaching the question of whether there is a transaction involving commerce? Recall that the Supreme Court rejected this view in 1956, in the *Bernhardt* case, supra, when it rejected the view that the FAA contained two different definitions of interstate commerce. How does the Supreme Court's ruling that the statute contains only one definition of "commerce" affect the reasoning in *Tenney*?

* * *

After *Gilmer*, almost every federal circuit court adopted the approach of the *Tenney* court and applied the FAA to employment cases except where the worker-plaintiff directly transported goods across state lines. However, in *Craft v. Campbell Soup*, 177 F.3d 1083 (9th Cir.1999), the Ninth Circuit took a different approach. Addressing the question of the FAA's application to employment disputes as a case of first impression, the Ninth Circuit rejected the *Tenney* court's reasoning about the history and proper construction of the FAA's employment exclusion. In reading the majority and dissenting opinions in *Craft*, consider which position represents a better reading of the statute.

Craft v. Campbell Soup Company

177 F.3d 1083 (9th Cir.1999).

I.

Per Curiam.

Anthony I. Craft was an employee of Campbell Soup and a member of the Food Process Workers and Warehousemen and Helpers Local Union 228 ("Union"). The collective bargaining agreement ("CBA") between Campbell Soup and the Union includes a nondiscrimination clause which provides in part that "[d]isputes under this provision shall be subject to the grievance and arbitration procedure [provided in the CBA]."

Craft filed a grievance alleging racial discrimination, harassment, health and safety concerns, and other claims. The grievance was not resolved in the initial grievance stages and the Union referred it to arbitration. While the grievance was still pending, Craft filed this action in district court. He alleged claims for race discrimination and retaliation in violation of Title VII of the Civil Rights Act of 1964, as amended, 42 U.S.C. § 2000e et seq. ("Title VII"), and state law claims for assault and emotional distress.

[The district court granted Campbell Soup's motion to compel arbitration of Craft's state law claims. However, it held that arbitration of Craft's Title VII claims could not be compelled. Campbell Soup brought an interlocutory appeal of the denial of the order to arbitrate the Craft's Title VII claims.]

II.

A.

"When interpreting a statute, this court looks first to the words that Congress used." Sanchez v. Pacific Powder Co., 147 F.3d 1097, 1099 (9th Cir.1998). "Rather than focusing just on the word or phrase at issue, this court looks to the entire statute to determine Congressional intent." Id. Applying those principles here, we begin with § 2 of the FAA, which provides for the enforcement of certain arbitration provisions:

> A written provision in any maritime transaction or a *contract evidencing a transaction involving commerce* to settle by arbitration a controversy thereafter arising out of such contract or transaction, or the refusal to perform the whole or any part thereof, or an agreement in writing to submit to arbitration an existing controversy arising out of such a contract, transaction, or refusal, shall be valid, irrevocable, and enforceable, save upon such grounds as exist at law or in equity for the revocation of any contract.

9 U.S.C. § 2 (emphasis added).

The FAA does not define the phrase "contract evidencing a transaction involving commerce," so we turn to the "ordinary, contemporary and common meaning" of that phrase. See United States v. Iverson, 162 F.3d 1015, 1022 (9th Cir.1998). A collective bargaining agreement or an individual employment contract would not seem to fall within the ordinary concept of a contract "evidencing a transaction," even if it involves interstate commerce.

As pertinent, when Congress passed the FAA in 1925, the term "transaction" commonly meant "[a] business deal; an act involving buying and selling." Webster's Int'l Dictionary 2688 (2d ed. unabridged 1939).... An employment relationship, however, is not commonly referred to as a "business deal" or as "an act involving buying and selling." Instead, the connotation of the phrase "transaction involving commerce"—as Congress would have understood it in 1925—was of a commercial deal or merchant's sale. Therefore, the coverage section of the FAA, § 2, appears not to encompass employment contracts at all.... [citations omitted].

Section 1 of the FAA, however, contains definitions and, with respect to "commerce," concludes that "nothing herein contained shall apply to contracts of employment of seamen, railroad employees, or any other class of workers engaged in foreign or interstate commerce." 9 U.S.C. § 1. This latter provision might suggest that Congress intended for § 2 to apply to some collective bargaining agreements and employment contracts. Viewed as a whole, the statute is ambiguous.

Courts have developed two interpretations of these provisions: (1) Congress did not intend for the FAA to apply to any employment contracts; and (2) Congress intended for the FAA to apply to all employment contracts, except for the contracts of employees who actually transport people or goods in interstate commerce. Craft does not actually transport people or goods in interstate commerce. Thus, if the latter view applies, the FAA governs this action, and we have jurisdiction to decide this appeal....

B.

Courts that have adopted the latter view have relied on a contemporary understanding of the terms used in the FAA.[6] The FAA, however, is not a modern statute. As noted above, the FAA, including §§ 1 and 2, was enacted in 1925, before the Supreme Court dramatically expanded the meaning of interstate commerce in the 1930s. Thus, to understand whether Congress intended for the FAA to apply to employment contracts, we need to understand Congress' commerce power in 1925.

Before Congress enacted the FAA, the Supreme Court decided Hammer v. Dagenhart, 247 U.S. 251, 38 S.Ct. 529, 62 L.Ed. 1101 (1918), overruled by United States v. Darby, 312 U.S. 100, 61 S.Ct. 451, 85 L.Ed. 609 (1941). In Hammer, the Court invalidated a federal child labor law, holding that Congress' commerce power did not extend to intrastate employees whose work involved interstate commerce. Hammer defined the scope of the Commerce Clause as quite limited:

> Commerce consists of intercourse and traffic ... and includes the transportation of persons and property, as well as the purchase, sale and exchange of commodities. The making of goods and the mining of coal are not commerce, nor does the fact that these things are to be afterwards shipped or used in interstate commerce, make their production a part thereof.

> Over interstate transportation, or its incidents, the regulatory power of Congress is ample, but the production of articles, intended for interstate commerce, is a matter of local regulation.

Id. at 272 (citation and internal quotation marks omitted)....

This narrow understanding of Congress' Commerce Clause power continued through the period of the drafting and enacting of the FAA. ...

---

6. The majority of circuits have interpreted the FAA to apply to all employment contracts, except for the contracts of employees who actually transport people or goods in interstate commerce. See McWilliams v. Logicon, Inc., 143 F.3d 573, 576 (10th Cir.1998) (ignoring conflicting precedent in United Food Workers, Local Union No. 7R v. Safeway Stores, Inc., 889 F.2d 940, 943–44 (10th Cir.1989)); O'Neil v. Hilton Head Hosp., 115 F.3d 272, 274 (4th Cir.1997) (ignoring conflicting precedent in Domino Sugar Corp. v. Sugar Workers Local Union 392, 10 F.3d 1064, 1067–68 (4th Cir.1993)); Pryner v. Tractor Supply Co., 109 F.3d 354, 356–58 (7th Cir.), cert. denied, ___ U.S. ___, 118 S.Ct. 295, 139 L.Ed.2d 227 (1997); Cole v. Burns Int'l Sec. Serv., 105 F.3d 1465, 1470– 72 (D.C.Cir.1997); Rojas v. TK Communications, Inc., 87 F.3d 745, 747–48 (5th Cir. 1996); Asplundh Tree Expert Co. v. Bates, 71 F.3d 592, 596–601 (6th Cir.1995); Erving v. Virginia Squires Basketball Club, 468 F.2d 1064, 1069 (2d Cir.1972); Dickstein v. du-Pont, 443 F.2d 783, 785 (1st Cir.1971); Tenney Eng'g, Inc. v. United Elec. Workers, Local 437, 207 F.2d 450, 452–53 (3d Cir.1953). A few courts, however, have held that the FAA does not apply to any employment contracts. See Domino Sugar Corp., 10 F.3d at 1067–68; Pritzker v. Merrill Lynch, Pierce, Fenner & Smith, Inc., 7 F.3d 1110, 1120 (3d Cir.1993) (ignoring conflicting Third Circuit precedent in Tenney); United Food Workers, 889 F.2d at 943–44.

Thus, Congress' Commerce Clause power at the time of the FAA's enactment was limited to employees who actually transported people or goods in interstate commerce.

Under these circumstances, when Congress drafted § 2, that section could only apply to those employees. Section 1, however, exempts those very same employees from the scope of the FAA. Thus, when Congress drafted the FAA in 1925, the Act did not apply to any labor or employment contracts.

... Campbell Soup's interpretation of the FAA would require us to hold that Congress intended *to include* some employment contracts within the scope of the FAA *prospectively*, even though it *initially excluded* all employment contracts. That approach attributes to Congress the ability to foresee the New Deal's expansion of the Commerce Clause. We refuse to adopt such an interpretation without any indication that Congress actually had such a counterintuitive intent. As Professor Epstein has observed:

> The 1925 reading of the commerce clause gave to the phrase "involving commerce" a reading that reached the instrumentalities of interstate commerce, but not retail trades and manufacturing. Because the original coverage was so defined, it was easy to read the tag end of the employee exemption in harmony with the basic coverage provision. The only workers whose contracts were shielded from arbitration were those who plied the narrow paths of interstate and foreign commerce before 1937. Since the FAA itself does not reach manufacturing and retail trades, the exemption is coordinated with the basic provision.

> Come the undeniable transformation of 1937, and what should be done to the pre–1937 statute? The phrase "involving commerce" has now been recast to cover all productive activities. The only way to reach this conclusion is to assume that Congress meant for the FAA to grow in scope with the commerce power, even when Congress was quite mistaken (along with everyone else) about its prospects for growth....

> ... But once the FAA is (mistakenly) expanded, what fate befalls its exclusion? ... Under current law, the right answer is that the FAA keeps to its 1925 contours.... By venturing into the waters of partial translation, both sides to the present dispute get the arguments confused. First they wrongly expand the coverage "involving commerce" to keep the FAA in play; then they give the 1925 exemption its 1925 plain meaning.

Richard A. Epstein, Fidelity Without Translation, 1 Green Bag 2d 21, 27–29 (1997).

C.

To determine whether Congress intended for the FAA to apply prospectively to some labor and employment contracts, even though it did not apply to any at its enactment, we next turn to legislative history.... We hold that the legislative history supports the conclusion that we have tentatively reached from interpreting (a) the statutory term "transaction" and (b) the scope of Congress' commerce power as understood in 1925.

Specifically, the legislative history demonstrates that the Act's purpose was solely to bind merchants who were involved in commercial dealings. See Local 205, United Elec. Workers v. General Elec. Co., 233 F.2d 85, 99 (1st Cir.1956) (noting that "congressional attention was being directed at the time solely toward the field of commercial arbitration"), aff'd on other grounds, 353 U.S. 547, 77 S.Ct. 921, 1 L.Ed.2d 1028 (1957). Before the Senate Committee on the Judiciary held hearings on the FAA, the draft bill made valid and enforceable "a written provision in *any contract or* maritime transaction *or* transaction involving commerce to settle by arbitration a controversy thereafter arising.". . .

At the hearing, the chair of the ABA committee that drafted the bill that became the FAA, W.H.H. Piatt, testified that the bill was partly in reaction to intense judicial hostility toward arbitration of merchants' disputes. 67th Cong. 1, 8 (1923) (statement of W.H.H. Piatt). Despite that purpose, concern was expressed over whether the bill would apply to workers' contracts. Id. Piatt emphasized that the bill was not intended to apply to those contracts:

> It is not intended that this shall be an act referring to labor disputes *at all*. It is purely an act to give the merchants the right or the privilege of sitting down and agreeing with each other as to what their damages are, if they want to do it. Now that is all there is in this.

Id. at 9 (emphasis added). However, Piatt suggested that, if Congress felt that "there is any danger of that," they could add an employment exclusion. Id.

Before that same committee, the Secretary of Commerce, Herbert Hoover, similarly suggested that, if Congress wanted to ensure that "workers' contracts" were excluded from the bill, "it might well be amended by stating 'but nothing herein contained shall apply to contracts of employment of seamen, railroad employees, or any other class of workers engaged in interstate or foreign commerce.'" Id. at 14. Thereafter, Congress amended what became § 2 of the FAA so that it applied only to "contracts evidencing a transaction" (not to all contracts) and added the employment exclusion.

As can be seen from the hearing before the Senate Committee on the Judiciary, as well as from the subsequent amendments that Congress made to the proposed legislation, the FAA was part of an effort to gain uniformity in the application of agreements to arbitrate sales and commercial disputes. Congress never intended for the FAA to apply to employment contracts of any sort . . . (citations omitted).

D.

While neither this court nor the Supreme Court has definitively ruled on whether the FAA applies to labor and employment contracts, both courts have suggested that it does not. [The court then drew inferences from the Supreme Court's failure to apply the FAA in Textile Workers Union v. Lincoln Mills, 353 U.S. 448 (1957), and General Elec. Co. v. United Elec. Workers, 353 U.S. 547, 77 S.Ct. 921, 1 L.Ed.2d 1028 (1957).] . . .

We have also stated our own inclination not to apply the FAA to those disputes . . .

Binding precedent thus supports, albeit not strongly, the conclusion that we have reached from interpreting (a) the statutory term "transaction," (b) the scope of Congress' commerce power as understood in 1925, and (c) the legislative history of the FAA.

E.

The interpretation of the FAA has remained confused, however, because many courts (and the dissent here) have focused on the FAA's exclusion provision, § 1, and not its coverage provision, § 2. However, when interpreting a statute, we logically should look first to the coverage provision (regardless of its number).

As noted, the "transaction" requirement suggests that Congress did not intend for § 2 to apply to any employment contracts. At its broadest, however, Congress intended for § 2 to apply only to contracts of workers who transport people or goods in interstate commerce—the full reach of its commerce power in 1925. In § 1, Congress excluded those same workers from the reach of the FAA. Reading § 2 and § 1 together, as we must, demonstrates that Congress did not intend for the FAA to apply to any employment contracts. See Bernhardt v. Polygraphic Co. of Am., 350 U.S. 198, 201, 76 S.Ct. 273, 100 L.Ed. 199 (1956) (holding that courts must read the provision of the FAA together, because "[s]ections 1, 2, and 3 are integral parts of a whole").

Other circuits (and the dissent here) have refused to follow that approach, which is why they have reached the wrong result. In the process, they have provided anachronistic "explanations" in support of their conclusions that the FAA applies to some employment contracts.

One such explanation, cited by Campbell Soup, was provided by the Third Circuit in Tenney, which concluded that the Act excluded only those workers for whom there already was special arbitration. 207 F.2d at 452–53. As Professor Finkin has argued, however, "the court reasoned backward and so got it wrong." Finkin, 17 Berkeley J. Emp. & Lab. L. at 291. Congress could not have intended for the FAA to exclude only employees who already had existing arbitration procedures available, because transportation workers had no alternative arbitration system at the time. Id. Only seamen and railroad workers had arbitration alternatives and, if Congress wanted to limit the exclusion clause to these groups, it would have done so explicitly. Transportation workers were a large and important part of interstate commerce during the early 1920s and unquestionably a critical subject of Congress' interstate commerce power. Further, the visibility of these enterprises politically was increased by the legal contest over their regulatory status at the time. See id. The exclusion of these workers could not be justified by an alternate arbitration system. That being so, we decline to adopt that anachronistic "explanation."

Campbell Soup also relies on the rule of *ejusdem generis* to interpret narrowly the employment exclusion. The rule of *ejusdem generis* "limits general terms which follow specific ones to matters similar to those specified." Cole, 105 F.3d at 1471. Accordingly, the general phrase "any other class of workers engaged in foreign or interstate commerce" in the exclusion clause takes its meaning from the specific terms preceding it— "seamen" and "railroad employees"—and includes only those other classes of workers who, similarly, are working in commerce. Id.

This line of reasoning, however, is inapplicable to the FAA. As indicated above, this approach impermissibly focuses solely on § 1, without first taking a step back and looking at section § 2. Moreover, as the dissent in Tenney convincingly argues:

> Since the intention of Congress manifestly was to confine the Act to commercial disputes, ejusdem generis has no possible relevancy here. As said in Gooch v. United States, 297 U.S. 124, 128 [1936], it [the rule of ejusdem generis] may not be used to defeat the obvious purpose of legislation.

Tenney, 207 F.2d at 458 (McLaughlin, J., dissenting) (citations and internal quotation marks omitted). The meaning of § 2, the 1925 scope of Congress' commerce power, and the legislative history of the FAA demonstrate the obvious scope and purpose of the FAA, which *ejusdem generis* cannot be used to defeat. . . .

III.

Based on the wording of § 2, the pre-New Deal scope of Congress' commerce power, the legislative history of the FAA, and the suggestions gleaned from Lincoln Mills, Misco, Gilmer, and Terminix, we hold that the FAA does not apply to labor or employment contracts. Thus, the FAA is inapplicable to the CBA that governs Craft's employment. . . . Accordingly . . . this appeal is hereby

DISMISSED

■ BRUNETTI, CIRCUIT JUDGE, Dissenting.

Today, the majority goes against the great weight of circuit court authority by holding that exclusionary clause of § 1 of the Federal Arbitration Act ("FAA") applies to all contracts of employment within the scope of the Commerce Clause and that we therefore lack jurisdiction to hear this interlocutory appeal. Because I find that the plain language of statute dictates a contrary result, I respectfully dissent. . . .

The plain language of the exclusionary clause states that the Act does not "apply to contracts of employment of seamen, railroad employees, or any other class of worker engaged in foreign or interstate commerce." 9 U.S.C. § 1 (1994). A natural reading of this language indicates that

Congress intended to exclude three specific types of employment contracts from the scope of the FAA. If one reads, as the majority does, the final phrase—"any other class of workers engaged in foreign or interstate commerce"—to exclude all contracts of employment then the specific pronouncements that seamen and railroad workers' employment contracts do not fall within the purview of the Act are drained of all meaning. . . .

The "cardinal principle of statutory construction" instructs that a court has a "duty to give effect, if possible, to every clause and word of a statute." Bennett v. Spear, 520 U.S. 154, 173, 117 S.Ct. 1154, 137 L.Ed.2d 281 (1997) (internal citations omitted). Here, we can fulfill this duty by concluding that the phrase "workers engaged in interstate commerce" refers only to those workers who are themselves engaged in the movement of goods in interstate commerce. Congress with ease could have drafted § 1 to read "nothing herein shall apply to contracts of employment." Cole, 105 F.3d at 1471. This, however, is not the language Congress enacted into law and I would decline to say that Congress included the words "seamen" and "railroad employees" for no purpose.

As the majority notes, the rule of *ejusdem generis* also suggests that § 1 should be interpreted narrowly. Application of this principle here indicates that the general reference to "any other class of workers engaged in foreign or interstate commerce" is most reasonably construed to include only workers who, like "seamen" and "railroad employees," are themselves engaged directly in the movement of goods in interstate commerce. . . .

Congress' phraseology in § 2, the primary substantive provision of the FAA, also supports a narrow interpretation of the employment exclusion clause. See Asplundh Tree, 71 F.3d at 601; Allied–Bruce Terminix Companies, Inc. v. Dobson, 513 U.S. 265, 273, 115 S.Ct. 834, 130 L.Ed.2d 753 (1995); Cole, 105 F.3d at 1471–72. Section 2 states that arbitration agreements in contracts "evidencing a transaction *involving commerce*" are enforceable in federal courts. 9 U.S.C. § 2 (1994). Section 1, by contrast, excludes employment contracts of "workers *engaged in . . . interstate commerce*." The fact that Congress used different phrases to define the scope of the FAA generally on the one hand and the transactions that are excluded from the Act on the other indicates that Congress did not intend these sections to have the same scope. While some commentators and the majority here suggest that the distinction between the phrases "involving commerce" and "engaged in commerce" was not recognized in 1925 when the FAA was enacted, the Supreme Court has indicated that the term "in commerce" when used in statutes of this era should be interpreted narrowly. . . . This textual argument is particularly persuasive here in light of the fact that when Congress reenacted the FAA in 1947 it was settled law that the phrase "engaged in commerce" was not coextensive with the limits of the power of Congress over interstate commerce. . . .

By utilizing the traditional tools of statutory construction, the plain meaning of the exclusionary clause becomes clear: employment contracts for seamen, railroad workers, and other workers actually involved in the flow of commerce are excluded from the scope of the FAA. "The plain meaning of legislation should be conclusive, except in the rare case in which the literal application of a statute will produce a result demonstrably at odds with the intention of its drafters." United States v. Ron Pair Enters., 489 U.S. 235, 243, 109 S.Ct. 1026, 103 L.Ed.2d 290 (1989)....

For the foregoing reasons, I would find that, because Craft does not work in interstate commerce, this court has jurisdiction to hear this appeal under the FAA and would decide the case on the merits.

* * *

Question

Which court, *Tenney* or *Craft*, has the better argument on the meaning of the Section 1 exclusion?

* * *

Note on Employment Arbitration

The use of arbitration in the employment context poses interpretive and practical problems that go beyond the problem of interpreting the Section 1 exclusion in the FAA. The *Gilmer* case opened the door for employers to utilize arbitration for nonunion employees in a wide range of settings, and it has had a significant impact on employment discrimination and unjust dismissal litigation. A survey by the Government Accounting Office in 1997 found that approximately 10 percent of private sector employers are using nonunion arbitration systems, and another 8 percent intend to implement one in the near future. U.S. Government Accounting Office, *Alternative Dispute Resolution: Employer's Experience with ADR in the Workplace* (August, 1997). Often these employment arbitration systems, designed by an employer and presented to an employee as a precondition of hire, contain serious due process deficiencies. For example, some make it more difficult than in a court for employees to prevail by such means as shifting the burden of proof, shortening the limitations periods, or eliminating the possibility for discovery. In addition, some impose strict limitations on remedies or impose high costs on employees to have their cases heard. In response to such "cowboy arbitrations," employees have brought challenges on many grounds, including lack of consent, unconscionability, and inadequate due process. See, Katherine Van Wezel Stone, *Mandatory Arbitration of Individual Employment Rights: The Yellow Dog Contract of the 1990s*, 73 DENVER L. REV. 1017 (1996). The cases that follow illustrate some of the issues that have been raised in the evolving law of employment arbitration.

* * *

Prudential Insurance Co. of America v. Lai

42 F.3d 1299 (9th Cir.1994).

■ Before: HUG, SCHROEDER, and WILLIAM A. NORRIS, CIRCUIT JUDGES.

■ SCHROEDER, CIRCUIT JUDGE:

This is an appeal from a district court order compelling arbitration, under the Federal Arbitration Act, of statutory sexual harassment and discrimination claims. The appellants filed their claims in state court, alleging that while employed by appellee Prudential Insurance Company in 1989 and 1990, they were the victims of serious sexual discrimination and abuse by their supervisor. Prudential then filed this independent action in federal court to compel arbitration.

The district court entered an order compelling arbitration and staying the state court proceedings, based upon the arbitration clause incorporated into the Standard Applications for Securities Industry Registration ("the U-4 forms") appellants signed. We hold that the district court's order is appealable, and we reverse because appellants did not knowingly enter into any agreement to arbitrate employment disputes.

I. BACKGROUND

Justine Lai and Elvira Viernes were employed as sales representatives by the Prudential Insurance Company of America. When applying for their positions, appellants were required to sign U-4 forms containing agreements "to arbitrate any dispute, claim or controversy that . . . is required to be arbitrated under the rules, constitutions, or bylaws of the organizations with which I register." Plaintiffs subsequently registered with the National Association of Securities Dealers, which requires that disputes "arising in connection with the business" of its members be arbitrated.

Plaintiffs allege that when they signed the U-4 form, they were told only that they were applying to take a test which was required for their employment by Prudential, and that they were simply directed to sign in the relevant place without being given an opportunity to read the forms. Arbitration was never mentioned, and plaintiffs were never given a copy of the NASD Manual, which contains the actual terms of the arbitration agreement.

On November 30, 1990, appellants sued Prudential and their immediate supervisor in state court on a variety of state law claims, alleging that the supervisor had raped, harassed, and sexually abused them in a number of ways. Prudential then filed this action in federal district court, asking the court to compel arbitration of appellants' state law claims, and to stay the state court proceedings. The district court granted both of Prudential's motions.

* * *

III. ARBITRABILITY

The only agreement to arbitrate that appellants actually executed was contained in the U-4 form. Item number 5 on page 4 of the U-4 form states:

> I agree to arbitrate any dispute, claim or controversy that may arise between me or my firm, or a customer, or any other person, that is

required to be arbitrated under the rules, constitutions, or bylaws of the organizations with which I register. . . .

This provision does not in and of itself bind appellants to arbitrate any particular dispute. To see what appellants possibly could have agreed to arbitrate, we must turn to the arbitration requirements of the NASD, which appellants eventually joined. The NASD manual states:

Any dispute, claim or controversy eligible for submission under part I of this Code between or among members and/or associated persons . . . arising in connection with the business of such member(s) or in connection with the activities of such associated person(s), shall be arbitrated under this Code. . . .

NASD Manual, Code of Arbitration Procedure ¶ 3708.

Appellants contend that these provisions do not bind them to arbitrate their employment discrimination claims because they were unaware that they signed any document that contained an arbitration clause, they were never given copies of the NASD manual, and they were not otherwise on notice that they might be agreeing to arbitrate employment disputes. They further contend that even if they had known that they were agreeing to the NASD arbitration provision, its language does not cover employment disputes.

Appellants rely on Alexander v. Gardner–Denver, 415 U.S. 36, 94 S.Ct. 1011, 39 L.Ed.2d 147 (1974), to support their argument that they are not bound to arbitrate their statutory claims. Alexander held that an arbitration clause contained in a collective bargaining agreement could not supplant Title VII's statutory remedies, and the decision was widely interpreted as prohibiting any form of compulsory arbitration of Title VII claims. . . . The Supreme Court, however, without overruling Alexander, subsequently held that individuals may contractually agree to arbitrate employment disputes and thereby waive the statutory rights to which they would otherwise be entitled. Gilmer v. Interstate/Johnson Lane Corp., 500 U.S. 20, 111 S.Ct. 1647, 114 L.Ed.2d 26 (1991).

Gilmer, upon which Prudential heavily relies, made it clear that the ADEA does not bar agreements to arbitrate federal age discrimination in employment claims. Our circuit has extended Gilmer to employment discrimination claims brought under Title VII. Mago v. Shearson Lehman Hutton, Inc., 956 F.2d 932 (9th Cir.1992); see also Spellman v. Securities, Annuities, & Ins. Svc., 8 Cal.App.4th 452, 10 Cal.Rptr.2d 427 (1992) (applying Gilmer to state statutory employment discrimination claims). The issue before us, however, is not whether employees may ever agree to arbitrate statutory employment claims; they can. The issue here is whether these particular employees entered into such a binding arbitration agreement, thereby waiving statutory court remedies otherwise available.

The district court did not decide whether the arbitration clause was enforceable, agreeing with Prudential's threshold argument that enforceability of appellants' agreement to arbitrate is a question for the arbitrator to decide in the first instance. . . . Questions of whether Congress intended, in the enactment of other statutes, to prevent or limit the arbitrability of statutory claims have routinely been decided by the courts. See, e.g., Gilmer, 500 U.S. 20, 111 S.Ct. 1647 (court decided whether or not employment disputes were arbitrable by looking to whether Congress intended to preclude arbitration of those claims).... Thus, the issue of arbitrability in this case is for the court.

Appellants contend in effect that even after the Supreme Court's decision in Gilmer, employees cannot be bound by an agreement to arbitrate employment discrimination claims unless they knowingly agreed to arbitrate such claims. We agree with appellants that Congress intended there to be at least a knowing agreement to arbitrate employment disputes before an employee may be deemed to have waived the comprehensive statutory rights, remedies and procedural protections prescribed in Title VII and related state statutes. Such congressional intent, which has been noted in other judicial decisions, is apparent from the text and legislative history of Title VII.

Prior to 1991, of course, Title VII had been interpreted to prohibit any waiver of its statutory remedies in favor of arbitration, even a knowing waiver. See, e.g., Children's Hospital Medical Center, 719 F.2d at 1431 (relying on Alexander, 415 U.S. at 47–51, 94 S.Ct. at 2667–69). As the Supreme Court recognized:

> Legislative enactments in this area have long evinced a general intent to accord parallel or overlapping remedies against discrimination. In the Civil Rights Act of 1964, Congress indicated that they considered the policy against discrimination to be of the "highest priority." Consistent with this view, Title VII provides for consideration of employment discrimination claims in several forums. And, in general submission of a claim to one forum does not preclude a later submission to another. Moreover, the legislative history of Title VII manifests a congressional intent to allow an individual to pursue independently his rights under both Title VII and other applicable state and federal statutes.

415 U.S. at 47–48, 94 S.Ct. at 1019.

This conclusion was reinforced by the recent enactment of the Civil Rights Act of 1991. Section 118 of that Act states: "Where appropriate and to the extent authorized by law, the use of alternative means of dispute resolutions including, ... arbitration, is encouraged to resolve disputes arising under the Acts or provisions of Federal law amended by this title." § 118 of Pub.L. 102–166, set forth in the notes following 42 U.S.C. § 1981 (Supp.1994). One House report explained that the purpose of that section was to increase the possible remedies available to civil rights plaintiffs:

> Section 216 [of the 1991 Act] encourages the use of alternative means of dispute resolution ... where appropriate and to the extent authorized by law.... The committee emphasizes ... that the use of alternative dispute resolution mechanisms is intended to supplement, not supplant, the remedies provided by Title VII. Thus, for example,

the committee believes that any agreement to submit disputed issues to arbitration, whether in the context of a collective bargaining agreement or in an employment contract, does not preclude the affected person from seeking relief under the enforcement provisions of Title VII. This view is consistent with the Supreme Court's interpretation of Title VII in Alexander v. Gardner–Denver Co., 415 U.S. 36 [94 S.Ct. 1011, 39 L.Ed.2d 147] (1974). The committee does not intend for the inclusion of this section to be used to preclude rights and remedies that would otherwise be available.

HR Rep. No. 40(I) 102nd Cong. 1st Sess., reprinted in 1991 U.S.C.C.A.N. 549, 635. Speaking of proposed § 118, Senator Dole explicitly declared that the arbitration provision encourages arbitration only "where the parties knowingly and voluntarily elect to use these methods." 137 Cong.Rec.S. 15472, S. 15478 (Daily Ed. October 30, 1991, statement of Senator Dole).

This congressional concern that Title VII disputes be arbitrated only "where appropriate," and only when such a procedure was knowingly accepted, reflects our public policy of protecting victims of sexual discrimination and harassment through the provisions of Title VII and analogous state statutes. See Alexander, 415 U.S. at 47, 94 S.Ct. at 1019. This is a policy that is at least as strong as our public policy in favor of arbitration. Although the Supreme Court has pointed out that plaintiffs who arbitrate their statutory claims do not "forego the substantive rights afforded by the statute," Mitsubishi Motors, 473 U.S. at 628, 105 S.Ct. at 3354, the remedies and procedural protections available in the arbitral forum can differ significantly from those contemplated by the legislature. In the sexual harassment context, these procedural protections may be particularly significant.[4] Thus, we conclude that a Title VII plaintiff may only be forced to forego her statutory remedies and arbitrate her claims if she has knowingly agreed to submit such disputes to arbitration. See Civil Rights Act of 1991; cf. Gardner, 415 U.S. at 51–52, 94 S.Ct. at 1021–22 (discussing possible waiver of Title VII rights); Gilmer, 500 U.S. 20, 111 S.Ct. 1647 (clause providing for arbitration of disputes "arising out of the employment or termination of employment" binding on "experienced businessman"); Mago, 956 F.2d 932 (same); Spellman v. Securities Annuities and Insurance Services, 8 Cal.App.4th 452, 10 Cal.Rptr.2d 427 (1992) (same).

In this case, even assuming that appellants were aware of the nature of the U–4 form, they could not have understood that in signing it, they were agreeing to arbitrate sexual discrimination suits. The U–4 form did not purport to describe the types of disputes that were to be subject to arbitration. Moreover, even if appellants had signed a contract containing

---

4. In California, for example, the privacy rights of victims of sexual harassment are protected by statutes limiting discovery and admissibility of plaintiffs' sexual history in a judicial proceeding. E.g. Cal.Evid.Code §§ 782, 1106; Cal.Civ.Proc.Code § 2017(d). In addition, in an area as personal and emo-tionally charged as sexual harassment and discrimination, the procedural right to a hearing before a jury of one's peers, rather than a panel of the National Association of Securities Dealers, may be especially important.

the NASD arbitration clause, it would not put them on notice that they were bound to arbitrate Title VII claims. That provision did not even refer to employment disputes. Indeed, in a case involving an age discrimination claimant, the Seventh Circuit has held that as a matter of law the NASD provision relevant to this appeal did not cover employment disputes. Farrand v. Lutheran Broth., 993 F.2d 1253 (7th Cir.1993); but see Kidd v. Equitable Life Assurance Society, 32 F.3d 516 (11th Cir.1994). Our decision does not rest exclusively upon the precise language of the clause in the U–4 manual, for it is clear and undisputed on this record that the employment contract with Prudential that plaintiffs executed did not describe any disputes the parties agreed to arbitrate.

We therefore hold that appellants were not bound by any valid agreement to arbitrate these employment disputes, because they did not knowingly contract to forego their statutory remedies in favor of arbitration.

The order of the district court is VACATED AND THE MATTER REMANDED for the district court to dismiss Prudential's complaint.

The concurring opinion of CIRCUIT JUDGE WILLIAM A. NORRIS is omitted.

* * *

Questions

1. Does this court have the same view of the adequacy of the arbitral forum for the enforcement of statutory rights as the Supreme Court expressed in *Mitsubishi*? What kinds of empirical evidence might be relevant to determine which view is the better one?

2. What would be needed to satisfy the court's requirement that an arbitration agreement be entered into knowingly and voluntarily? Is the "knowing" requirement the same as the "voluntary" requirement, or could we imagine instances in which an agreement was entered into knowingly but not voluntarily, or vice versa? On the problematic nature of consent in the employment setting, see Stephen J. Ware, *Employment Arbitration and Voluntary Consent*, 25 HOFSTRA L. REV. 83 (1996); Jeffrey W. Stempel, *Reconsidering the Employment Contract Exclusion in Section 1 of the Federal Arbitration Act*, 1991 J. DISPUTE RESOLUTION 259 (1991); Jean Sternlight, *Rethinking the Constitutionality of the Supreme Court's Preference for Binding Arbitration*, 72 TULANE L. REV. 1 (1997).

* * *

Pony Express Courier Corp. v. Morris

921 S.W.2d 817 (Tex.Ct.App. 1996).

■ PER CURIAM.

This interlocutory appeal questions whether an arbitration agreement is unconscionable as a matter of law. Appellants, Pony Express Corporation and Charles Bouie, moved to stay litigation and compel arbitration on the basis of an arbitration agreement with the appellee, Diane Morris. Without an evidentiary hearing, the trial court found the agreement unconscionable and denied the appellants' motion. We conclude the trial court abused its discretion in finding the agreement unconscionable per se, and we reverse and remand.

Summary of Facts

According to Morris's petition and the appellants' brief, Pony Express employed Morris as a full-time warehouse worker and Bouie as a night dispatch operator. Morris contends Bouie sexually harassed her at work. She sued the appellants for negligence, gross negligence, sexual harassment, assault and battery, intentional infliction of emotional distress, discrimination, retaliation, and violations of the Texas Commission on Human Rights Act, the Texas Labor Code, and Texas OSHA statutes.

When Morris applied for work at Pony Express's warehouse, she signed an arbitration agreement that provided as follows:

> If employed, I agree that all claims relating to my employment, other than worker's compensation claims or claims arising under a non-compete agreement, shall be settled exclusively by expedited arbitration, without discovery. There shall be one arbitrator, chosen by the American Arbitration Association and the claim otherwise processed in accordance with AAA rules. Any award to me shall be limited to the lesser of (i) any actual lost wages, (ii) an amount not to exceed six months' wages, or (iii) in an appropriate case, reinstatement. The cost of arbitration shall be shared equally between me and the company.

> You may wish to consult an attorney prior to signing this application. If so, please take this form with you. However, you will not be offered employment until it is signed without modification and returned.[1]

Based on this agreement, the appellants moved to stay the litigation and compel arbitration. The motion attached the arbitration agreement but did not include the preceding portions of Morris's job application or any other supporting evidence. Morris did not file a written response. Although the trial court held a hearing on appellants' motion, it found the arbitration agreement unconscionable without hearing evidence.

Arguments on Appeal

In one point of error, the appellants maintain the trial court erred in denying their motion to compel because (1) there was no evidence of unconscionability; (2) there was no pleading of unconscionability; and (3) the arbitration agreement was valid....

3.   Validity of the Agreement

The appellants assert the trial court erred in denying their motion to compel because their arbitration agreement is valid. Specifically, they

---

1. For ease of reading, all capitals altered to upper and lower case.

maintain that arbitration agreements between employers and employees should be enforced under Gilmer v. Interstate/Johnson Lane Corp., 500 U.S. 20, 111 S.Ct. 1647, 114 L.Ed.2d 26 (1991).

In Gilmer, the Supreme Court held that a federal claim for age discrimination was subject to a compulsory arbitration agreement in a securities registration application. 500 U.S. at 35, 111 S.Ct. at 1657. Although the court rejected the plaintiff's claim of unequal bargaining power, it recognized that such claims were best left to individual resolution. Id. 500 U.S. at 33, 111 S.Ct. at 1655–56. In addition, while Gilmer describes the arbitrability of statutory claims, it does not address the enforceability of arbitration agreements. Here, the issue is not whether Morris' claims are arbitrable at all, but whether they are arbitrable under this particular arbitration agreement. Thus, Gilmer is instructive but not dispositive.

An agreement to arbitrate is valid absent grounds for the revocation of a contract, such as unconscionability.... In general, the term "unconscionability" describes a contract that is unfair because of its overall one-sidedness or the gross one-sidedness of one of its terms.... "Unconscionability" has no precise legal definition because it is not a concept but a determination to be made in light of a variety of factors. Southwestern Bell Tel. Co. v. DeLanney, 809 S.W.2d 493, 498 (Tex.1991) (Gonzalez, J., concurring) (citing 1 J. WHITE & R. SUMMERS, UNIFORM COMMERCIAL CODE § 4–3 at 203 (3d ed. 1988)); see also RESTATEMENT (SECOND) OF CONTRACTS § 208, comment a (1979) (including "weaknesses in the contracting process" and related public policy concerns).

Although no single formula exists, proof of unconscionability begins with two broad questions: (1) How did the parties arrive at the terms in controversy; and (2) Are there legitimate commercial reasons justifying the inclusion of the terms? DeLanney, 809 S.W.2d at 498–99 (Gonzalez, J., concurring). The first question, often described as the procedural aspect of unconscionability, is concerned with assent and focuses on the facts surrounding the bargaining process. Id. at 499; Tri–Continental Leasing Corp., 710 S.W.2d at 609. The second question, often described as the substantive aspect of unconscionability, is concerned with the fairness of the resulting agreement. DeLanney, 809 S.W.2d at 499 (Gonzalez, J., concurring); Wade v. Austin, 524 S.W.2d 79, 86 (Tex.Civ.App.—Texarkana 1975, no writ). In short, unconscionability must be determined on a case-by-case basis. Pearce v. Pearce, 824 S.W.2d 195, 199 (Tex.App.—El Paso 1991, writ denied). For that reason, there is nothing unconscionable per se about an arbitration contract. See Peel, 920 S.W.2d at 402 (basing its conclusion on contract principles and the atmosphere favoring arbitration).

The arbitration agreement in this case excludes other remedies, eliminates discovery, limits damages and the choice of arbitrators, and allocates costs equally between the parties. Morris contends that, taken together, these factors make the provision unconscionable.

Although binding arbitration seems harsh, it is a permissible alternative that favors neither party.... For that reason, equal cost sharing is not only enforceable, ... but is also a standard feature of arbitration clauses.

See, e.g., Fridl, 908 S.W.2d at 510. . . . Likewise, by allowing the American Arbitration Association to assign the arbitrator, neither party to this agreement is favored in the choice of the arbitrator.

In Gilmer, the court observed that parties who arbitrate agree to trade the procedures of the courtroom for the simplicity, informality, and expediency of arbitration. 500 U.S. at 31, 111 S.Ct. at 1655. Discovery may be limited as in Gilmer, see id., or eliminated as in some federal courts, see CIVIL JUSTICE EXPENSE & DELAY REDUCTION PLAN (1991), reprinted in TEXAS RULES OF COURT: FEDERAL (West 1995) (adopted by the U.S. District Courts for the Eastern District of Texas). As for the limitation on damages, we note that federal policy allows such limitations when statutory rights are not mandated. . . .

Individually, the provisions of Morris's arbitration agreement are not unconscionable. Without the circumstances surrounding the agreement, we cannot determine whether, taken together, the provisions are unconscionable. Morris asserts that she is a minimum wage employee, without equal bargaining power, who was economically coerced into signing the agreement by a national corporation. These facts were not before the trial court and are not before us. We therefore conclude the trial court abused its discretion in finding the arbitration agreement unconscionable. Cf. Peel, 920 S.W.2d at 402–03 (finding no evidence to support the contention that an arbitration agreement in an earnest money contract was unconscionable).

Conclusion

We sustain the appellants' point of error but do not compel arbitration. In those cases in which the appellate court reversed the trial court's order denying arbitration and also compelled arbitration, the appellate court applied the "no evidence" standard of review and rendered the judgment the trial court should have rendered. We find that action inappropriate in this case, given the appropriate standard of review and lack of factual development. We reverse the trial court's order denying arbitration and remand the cause for further proceedings consistent with this opinion.

* * *

Questions

1. The court in *Pony Express* states that whether an arbitration clause in an employment contract is unconscionable depends upon, *inter alia*, the existence of "legitimate commercial reasons" to justify it. Did the employer have to have legitimate reasons in the *Pony Express* case? If the employer could show that it inserted an arbitration term into the employment contract to protect the firm against large judgments and high legal fees in employment litigation, would that be a legitimate reason to justify such a clause? Is a "legitimate commercial reason" the appropriate test for determining unconscionability in the employment setting? Or should the uncon-

scionability decision be based on other factors? If so, what kinds of factors might be relevant?

2. Suppose an employer gives an employee an employment manual at the time of hire. The manual is a 16 page booklet that contains many terms, including a description of the company's sick leave provisions, a discussion of pension plan, rules concerning use of the parking lot, and a list of holiday and vacation benefits. Also buried on the last page of the manual is a provision stating "All disputes concerning employment at this company shall be submitted to arbitration under the rules and procedures that the employer adopts." If the employee later has an industrial accident and seeks to file a worker's compensation claim, must that claim be arbitrated? If she brings a sex discrimination claim, must that be arbitrated? If she brings a claim for unjust dismissal under state common law, must that claim be arbitrated? Is there any reason to treat these types of claims differently for purposes of the arbitration provision?

* * *

Note on Unconscionability in Employment Arbitration Agreements

Several courts have addressed challenges to nonunion arbitration agreements on the grounds of unconscionability. For example, in STIRLEN V. SUPERCUTS, 51 Cal.App.4th 1519, 60 Cal.Rptr.2d 138 (Ct. App. 1st Dist., Div. 2, 1997), an arbitration clause in a written employment contract provided that an employee was bound to arbitrate any dispute that might arise, including discrimination claims, and imposed restrictions on any potential remedies an employee could recover in arbitration to actual damages for breach of contract, while simultaneously providing that the employer retained its right to bring suit in a federal or state court. The California court found the arbitration provision unconscionable, stating:

> [T]he arbitration clause provides the employer with more rights and greater remedies than would otherwise be available and concomitantly deprives employees of significant rights and remedies they would normally enjoy. considering the terms of the arbitration clause in the light of the commercial context in which it operates and the legitimate needs of the parties at the time it was entered into, we have little difficulty concluding that its terms are " 'so extreme as to appear unconscionable according to the mores and business practices of the time and place.' " (quoting Williams v. Walker–Thomas Furniture Co., (D.C.Cir.1965) 350 F.2d 445, 449–50.)

In contrast, in COLE V. BURNS INTERNATIONAL SECURITY SERVICES, 105 F.3d 1465 (D.C.Cir.1997), the D.C. Circuit upheld an employment arbitration agreement that was similarly one-sided. The agreement that Burns required employees to sign provided that

> "In consideration for the Company employing you, you and the Company each agree that, in the event either party ... brings an action in a court of competent jurisdiction relating to your recruitment, employment with, or termination of employment from the Company, the plaintiff in such action agrees to waive his, her or its right to a trial by

jury.... [You] further agree that, in the event that you seek relief in a court of competent jurisdiction for a dispute covered by this Agreement, the Company may, ... at its option, require all or part of the dispute to be arbitrated by one arbitrator in accordance with the rules of the American Arbitration Association.... You understand and agree that, if the Company exercises its option, any dispute arbitrated will be heard solely by the arbitrator, and not by a court."

While the court upheld the agreement despite its asymmetrical obligation to arbitration, it added in dicta that if the arbitration clause meant that the employee was required to pay any portion of the arbitration fees, it would be unconscionable. "[W]here arbitration has been imposed by the employer as a condition of employment and occurs only at the option of the employer—arbitrator's fees should be borne solely by the employer." Judge Henderson, concurring and dissenting, accused the majority of "engag[ing] in pure judicial fee shifting which finds no support in the FAA, Gilmer or the parties' agreement."

Most recently, in HOOTERS OF AMERICA, INC. V. PHILLIPS, 173 F.3d 933 (4th Cir.1999), an employee quit her job and threatened to bring a Title VII claim over allegations of sexual harassment. Two years earlier, the employer had instituted an alternative dispute resolution program and had conditioned eligibility for raises and promotions on employees signing an "agreement to arbitrate employment-related disputes." The agreement provided that the "employee and the company agree to resolve any claims pursuant to the company's rules and procedures for alternative resolution of employment-related disputes, as promulgated by the company from time to time." Phillips had twice signed the agreement, but neither she nor any other employee was given a copy of Hooter's arbitration rules and procedures. Two years later, when she raised sexual harassment allegations, the employer filed suit seeking to compel arbitration of her claims pursuant to the alternative dispute resolution program under the Federal Arbitration Act. Phillips counterclaimed for violations of Title VII and for a declaration that the employer's arbitration agreement was unenforceable. The District Court denied the employer's motions to compel arbitration and the employer appealed.

The Fourth Circuit held that the employer materially breached the agreement to arbitrate by promulgating egregiously unfair arbitration rules. The court stated:

"Hooters argues that Phillips gave her assent to a bilateral agreement to arbitrate. That contract provided for the resolution by arbitration of all employment-related disputes, including claims arising under Title VII. Hooters claims the agreement to arbitrate is valid because Phillips twice signed it voluntarily. Thus, it argues the courts are bound to enforce it and compel arbitration.

"We disagree. The judicial inquiry, while highly circumscribed, is not focused solely on an examination for contractual formation defects such as lack of mutual assent and want of consideration.... Courts also can investigate the existence of 'such grounds as exist at law or in equity for the revocation of any contract.' 9 U.S.C. § 2. However, the grounds for revocation must relate specifically to the arbitration clause and not just to the contract as a whole. Prima Paint Corp. v. Flood & Conklin Mfg. Co., 388 U.S. 395, 402–04, 87 S.Ct. 1801, 18 L.Ed.2d 1270 (1967) ... In this case, the challenge goes to the validity of the arbitration agreement itself. Hooters materially breached the arbitration agreement by promulgating rules so egregiously unfair as to constitute a complete default of its contractual obligation to draft arbitration rules and to do so in good faith.

"Hooters and Phillips agreed to settle any disputes between them not in a judicial forum, but in another neutral forum—arbitration. Their agreement provided that Hooters was responsible for setting up such a forum by promulgating arbitration rules and procedures. To this end, Hooters instituted a set of rules in July 1996.

"The Hooters rules when taken as a whole, however, are so one-sided that their only possible purpose is to undermine the neutrality of the proceeding. The rules require the employee to provide the company notice of her claim at the outset, including 'the nature of the Claim' and 'the specific act(s) or omissions(s) which are the basis of the Claim.' Rule 6–2(1), (2). Hooters, on the other hand, is not required to file any responsive pleadings or to notice its defenses. Additionally, at the time of filing this notice, the employee must provide the company with a list of all fact witnesses with a brief summary of the facts known to each. Rule 6–2(5). The company, however, is not required to reciprocate.

"The Hooters rules also provide a mechanism for selecting a panel of three arbitrators that is crafted to ensure a biased decisionmaker. Rule 8. The employee and Hooters each select an arbitrator, and the two arbitrators in turn select a third. Good enough, except that the employee's arbitrator and the third arbitrator must be selected from a list of arbitrators created exclusively by Hooters. This gives Hooters control over the entire panel and places no limits whatsoever on whom Hooters can put on the list. Under the rules, Hooters is free to devise lists of partial arbitrators who have existing relationships, financial or familial, with Hooters and its management. In fact, the rules do not even prohibit Hooters from placing its managers themselves on the list. Further, nothing in the rules restricts Hooters from punishing arbitrators who rule against the company by removing them from the list. Given the unrestricted control that one party (Hooters) has over the panel, the selection of an impartial decision maker would be a surprising result.

"Nor is fairness to be found once the proceedings are begun. Although Hooters may expand the scope of arbitration to any matter, 'whether related or not to the Employee's Claim,' the employee cannot raise 'any matter not included in the Notice of Claim.' Rules 4–2, 8–9. Similarly, Hooters is permitted to move for summary dismissal of employee claims before a hearing is held whereas the employee is not permitted to seek summary judgment. Rule 14–4. Hooters, but not the employee, may record the arbitration hearing 'by audio or videotaping or by verbatim transcription.' Rule 18–1. The rules also grant Hooters the right to bring suit in court to vacate or modify an arbitral award when it can show, by a preponderance of the evidence, that the panel exceeded its authority. Rule 21–4. No such right is granted to the employee.

"In addition, the rules provide that upon 30 days notice Hooters, but not the employee, may cancel the agreement to arbitrate. Rule 23–1.

Moreover, Hooters reserves the right to modify the rules, 'in whole or in part,' whenever it wishes and 'without notice' to the employee. Rule 24–1. Nothing in the rules even prohibits Hooters from changing the rules in the middle of an arbitration proceeding. . . .

"We hold that the promulgation of so many biased rules—especially the scheme whereby one party to the proceeding so controls the arbitral panel—breaches the contract entered into by the parties. The parties agreed to submit their claims to arbitration—a system whereby disputes are fairly resolved by an impartial third party. Hooters by contract took on the obligation of establishing such a system. By creating a sham system unworthy even of the name of arbitration, Hooters completely failed in performing its contractual duty. . . .

"By promulgating this system of warped rules, Hooters so skewed the process in its favor that Phillips has been denied arbitration in any meaningful sense of the word. To uphold the promulgation of this aberrational scheme under the heading of arbitration would undermine, not advance, the federal policy favoring alternative dispute resolution. This we refuse to do."

* * *

Questions

1. Which feature(s) of the Hooter's arbitration system make it egregiously unfair? Is it unconscionable?

2. Would a nonunion arbitration agreement that imposed on an employee the obligation to bring all disputes to arbitration and to prove any allegation of discrimination beyond a reasonable doubt be unconscionable?

3. Would it be unconscionable for an employer to require an employee to agree, as a condition of hire, to waive all rights to bring a discrimination complaints?

4. Can an employer require an employee, at the time of hire, to agree to arbitrate any dispute that might arise, including complaints of discrimination, before an arbitrator designated by the employer's vice president for human relations?

* * *

7.   SUCCESSORS AND ASSIGNS

Kaufman v. William Iselin & Co.

74 N.Y.S.2d 23 (N.Y.App.Div.1947).

■ Before PECK, P. J., and GLENNON, DORE, VAN VOORHIS, and SHIENTAG, JJ.

■ SHIENTAG, JUSTICE.

J. B. Kaufman Co., petitioner (hereinafter called "Kaufman"), brought this proceeding to compel appellant factor, William Iselin & Co., Inc.

(hereinafter called "Iselin"), to arbitrate an alleged dispute arising out of the purchase by Kaufman of certain goods from Crest–Tex Mills, Inc. (hereinafter called "Crest–Tex"). Iselin was not a party to the contract of sale of the goods made between Kaufman and Crest–Tex. The claim against Iselin is based upon the proposition that when a seller's factor receives an assignment of invoices of accounts and of the merchandise covered thereby, that transfer carries with it as matter of law an assignment pro tanto of the contract to which the invoices relate and the assignee becomes bound by the terms of the seller's agreement with the buyer.

In the instant proceeding the buyer claims that after the merchandise was received and after the invoices had been paid to the factor, certain defects were discovered and it was found that the goods delivered were not in accordance with the specifications originally agreed upon. Notice of the defect was given to the seller Crest–Tex, to its selling agent, and to the seller's factor, Iselin. The invoices were paid by the buyer to Iselin, the seller's factor, in accordance with the billing requirements, and prior to the discovery that the merchandise was defective.

Under the agreement between the buyer and seller, it was provided that "Any controversy arising under or in relation to this contract shall be settled by arbitration."

The terms under which Iselin received the assignment of the invoices are as follows:

"This bill is assigned to and payable only to our factors William Iselin & Co., Inc., 357 Fourth Avenue, New York 10, N. Y., to whom notice must be given of any merchandise returns or claims for shortage, nondelivery or for other grounds."

"In consideration of $1.00 and other valuable consideration receipt of which is hereby acknowledged, we hereby sell, assign and transfer to William Iselin & Co., Inc., in confirmation of their title thereto, all our right, title and interest in and to the above stated accounts, invoices numbered ___ to ___ inclusive and in and to the merchandise therein described, and we hereby fully guarantee the validity and correctness of said accounts and due acceptance of said merchandise by the purchasers named without objection or claim."

"This assignment is made pursuant to the written agreement."

On petitioner's motion, the court at Special Term directed arbitration of the controversy between buyer and seller and factor. The only appellant is the factor, Iselin, who contends that as assignee of certain specific invoices, which were paid before the proceeding began, it is not subject to any claim for defective goods. The factor argues that it had no interest in the contract other than a security interest to cover advances made to the seller of the goods, that as an assignee with merely a security title it had no duty to perform in relation to delivery of goods of any special quality, and, finally, it claims that the mere assignment of a security title does not bind the assignee to any of the terms of the contract including the provision for arbitration.

The only question to be decided at this time is whether the petition supports a claim, at least prima facie, that Iselin is bound in any respect by the arbitration clause in the contract between the buyer and seller.

The question whether an assignee assumes the duties as well as the rights under an assigned contract was considered at length by the Court of Appeals in Langel v. Betz, 250 N.Y. 159, 163, 164 N.E. 890, 891. There, the court took up the American Law Institute's Restatement of the Law of Contracts, Section 164(2), which reads as follows:

> "(2) Acceptance by the assignee of such an assignment is interpreted, in the absence of circumstances showing a contrary intention, as both an assent to become an assignee of the assignor's rights and as a promise to the assignor to assume the performance of the assignor's duties."

In referring to this provision of the Restatement the Court of Appeals said:

> "This promise to the assignor would then be available to the other party to the contract. Lawrence v. Fox, 20 N.Y. 268; I Williston on Contracts, § 412. The proposed change is a complete reversal of our present rule of interpretation as to the probable intention of the parties. It is, perhaps, more in harmony with modern ideas of contractual relations than is 'the archaic view of a contract as creating a strictly personal obligation between the creditor and debtor' (Pollock on Contracts [9th Ed.] 232), which prohibited the assignee from suing at law in his own name and which denied a remedy to third party beneficiaries. 'The fountains out of which these resolutions issue' have been broken up if not destroyed (Seaver v. Ransom, 224 N.Y. 233, 237, 120 N.E. 639 [640], 2 A.L.R. 1187), but the law remains that no promise of the assignee to assume the assignor's duties is to be inferred from the acceptance of an assignment of a bilateral contract, in the absence of circumstances surrounding the assignment itself which indicate a contrary intention."

The court finally took the position that one must consider the dealings between the parties to discover whether the assignee entered into such agreements that it might be said to have assumed the duty of performance of the contract.

Obviously, the mere assignment of an invoice and of the merchandise covered thereby for purposes of securing a loan made by a commercial banker is not a situation in which it may be said that it was the intention of the parties that the factor should assume performance of the basic contract. Since that is all that is here present, we find that there is no showing of the assumption of contract duties by the appellant, Iselin.

We limit our decision to holding that on the present record no case is made out to justify a finding that the factor, under the conditions herein presented, has assumed the duty to arbitrate. This is not a situation where the assignee has taken any affirmative action under the contract to enforce its terms; in such event it is proper to hold that having taken steps to adopt the terms of the contract he had assumed the obligations as well as the rights thereunder. (Citations omitted) Here, no affirmative action having been taken by the assignee, the factor, the situation may be said to be analogous to that present in Langel v. Betz, 250 N.Y. 159, 164 N.E. 890, supra.

The order, in so far as it directs William Iselin & Co., Inc., to proceed to arbitration, should be reversed with $20 costs and disbursements to the appellant against the petitioners-respondents and the motion to that extent denied.

All concur.

* * *

Questions

1. Under the *Kaufman* court's reasoning, is there any circumstance in which an assignee would assume a contractual duty to arbitrate? What might those circumstances be? Are there circumstances in which a third party beneficiary can be forced to arbitrate a claim based on a contract between two contracting parties? Would the same reasoning apply? See *Marathon Oil v. Ruhrgas*, 115 F.3d 315 (5th Cir.1997).

2. Does the court apply the same reasoning to the assignability of an obligation to arbitrate as it would to the assignability of contractual obligations generally?

* * *

Note on Assignment of Obligation to Arbitrate

In GRUNTAL & CO. v. STEINBERG, 854 F.Supp. 324 (D.N.J.1994), Gruntal, a securities broker, acquired the assets of Philips, another broker pursuant to an Asset Purchase Agreement. The Purchase Agreement purported to include customer accounts. Subsequently, one of Philips' customers, Steinberg, sought to arbitrate a claim regarding the account under the arbitration procedures of the NASD. Gruntal sought a declaratory judgment that it did not have an obligation to arbitrate Philips' customers complaints for transactions that predated Gruntal's accession to the accounts. The District Court held that while there was an arbitration provision in the contract between the original broker and customers, the agreement did not bind the successor broker to arbitrate. The court explained:

"The Steinbergs do not argue that they and Gruntal are signatories to a contract to arbitrate. Ronald Steinberg, in fact, testified at trial that he never signed an agreement of any sort with Gruntal. Instead, the Steinbergs rely on two alternative bases for Gruntal's asserted obligation to arbitrate in the Arbitration Proceedings: (1) the transfer of the Steinberg Accounts, and the arbitration clauses in the accompanying Philips Contracts, to Gruntal as a result of the Asset Purchase Agreement and (2) Gruntal's membership in the NASD.

"Significant doubt exists as to whether the Steinberg Accounts and the attendant Philips Contracts were ever transferred to Gruntal pursuant to the transfer provision in the Asset Purchase Agreement.... It is not necessary, however, to conclusively decide this issue here. Even if the Steinberg Accounts and Philips Contracts were transferred to Gruntal, such a transfer cannot, by itself, create an obligation to arbitrate on Gruntal's part.

"Under New York law, made applicable by [the Asset Purchase Agreement], the assignee of rights under a bilateral contract is not bound to perform the assignor's duties unless he expressly assumes to do so." Lachmar v. Trunkline LNG Co., 753 F.2d 8, 9–10 (2d Cir.1985) ... "Included among the duties to which this rule has reference is the duty to arbitrate." Lachmar, 753 F.2d at 10; Kaufman v. William Iselin & Co., 272 A.D. 578, 581–82, 74 N.Y.S.2d 23 (App.Div. 1st Dept.1947)....

"In the instant case, the record establishes conclusively that Gruntal never expressly assumed Philips' duty to arbitrate in the Arbitration Proceedings. As indicated, the Arbitration Proceedings involve transactions and events which took place on or before 15 February 1988, over two months prior to the Closing Date [of the Purchase Agreement]. Also as indicated, Gruntal, by the Asset Purchase Agreement, expressly renounced any obligations of Philips, to arbitrate or otherwise, 'arising as a result of or in connection with the business or activities of [Philips] at the [Fort Lee] Office prior to the Closing Date.' Asset Purchase Agreement, 2. Silverman, the Gruntal officer who negotiated the Asset Purchase Agreement with Philips, testified at Trial that Gruntal had no intention of assuming any responsibilities of Philips which arose prior to the Closing Date."

* * *

Question

Has the court in *Gruntal & Co.* ignored the presumption of arbitrability? Has it disregarded the rule of *Perry v. Thomas* that state law arbitration-specific doctrines should not be utilized to defeat arbitration? Can this opinion be understood as consistent with prevailing arbitration law under the FAA?

* * *

CHAPTER SEVEN

ARBITRATION III: DUE PROCESS, REMEDIES, AND JUDICIAL REVIEW

1. INTRODUCTION

Arbitration is a term that applies to an almost infinite variety of types of procedures. There is no one standard, or even dominant, off-the-rack arbitration procedure. This is because arbitration procedure, like an initial promise to arbitrate, is a matter of private contract. Sometimes contracting parties set out detailed arbitration procedures in their initial agreement to arbitrate. At other times, parties may contractually incorporate a pre-existing arbitration procedure, such as the Commercial Procedures of the American Arbitration Association (see Appendix C), or the procedures of a trade association to which the contracting parties belong. However, if an arbitration agreement is silent on the procedures to be followed, then courts generally assume that the parties have delegated the task of determining procedures to the arbitrator.

Courts have grappled with the problem of determining how far a party's and/or arbitrator's control over procedure in arbitration should go, and the extent to which courts should police such proceedings for minimum due process concerns. Questions arise such as, which elements of due process can the parties waive? Does the arbitrator have ultimate control over the proceeding, or will an award be vacated that does not rise to some minimal level of due process? If there is some due process minima that courts will impose on arbitration proceedings, of what is it comprised? Should courts require arbitration to provide a "full and fair hearing?" What are the elements of such a hearing? We cannot expect courts to import the entire Federal Rules of Civil Procedure into arbitration, for if they did so, arbitration would lose its distinctive advantages of providing flexibility, informality, and speed in the resolution of disputes. We expect arbitration procedures to be more informal and to contain fewer procedural protections than a full-blown trial. Yet the question remains, how relaxed can arbitration procedures be and still accord with fundamental notions of due process? Due process concerns are particularly salient now that courts are asked to defer to arbitration for the resolution of not only contractual but also statutory disputes. Are there minimal due process norms that courts must impose in order to justify such delegation of authority?

Section 10 of the Federal Arbitration Act sets out four grounds on which a court may vacate an arbitral award:

(a) Where the award was procured by corruption, fraud, or undue means.

(b) Where there was evident partiality or corruption in the arbitrators, or either of them.

(c) Where the arbitrators were guilty of misconduct in refusing to postpone the hearing, upon sufficient cause shown, or in refusing to hear evidence pertinent and material to the controversy; or in any other misbehavior by which the rights of any party have been prejudiced.

(d) Where the arbitrators exceeded their powers, or so imperfectly executed them that a mutual, final, and definite award upon the subject matter was not made.

Of the statutory grounds for vacating arbitral awards, the first three, (a), (b) and (c), are directed toward the arbitral process rather than the merits of a final arbitral award. The fourth, (d) seems to address both procedural and substantive concerns. In the cases that follow, we see how courts have interpreted the four statutory grounds for vacating awards. In addition, some courts hold that the statutory grounds do not exhaust the grounds for setting aside awards. Some courts have found an additional ground for vacating an award when the process is found to be "fundamentally unfair." Some courts have added, as additional factors to their scrutiny of the merits, that they should vacate awards that do not "draw their essence" from the parties' agreement or are "fundamentally irrational."

The scope of fundamental fairness, minimal due process, and judicial review in arbitration, both within the statutory framework and as judge-made common law, are explored in the materials that follow.[1]

2. NOTICE, EX PARTE HEARINGS, AND DEFAULT

Gingiss International, Inc. v. Norman E. Bormet

58 F.3d 328 (7th Cir.1995).

■ BAUER, CIRCUIT JUDGE.

Gingiss International, Inc. ("Gingiss") and H–K Formalwear Corporation ("H–K Formalwear") entered into a franchise agreement on December 18, 1984, under which H–K Formalwear was granted the right to operate a Gingiss Formalwear Center store in Industry, California. The franchise agreement contained an arbitration clause which provided that all disputes between the parties relating to the agreement would be subject to arbitration in Chicago under the Federal Arbitration Act ("FAA"), 9 U.S.C. §§ 1–16, and the Rules of the American Arbitration Association ("AAA"), unless Gingiss elected to pursue certain claims in a judicial forum. The franchise agreement also contained a California choice-of-law provision. Norman E.

---

1. For a review of scholarship about the nature of due process in labor arbitration, see Jay E. Grenit, *When Due Process is Due: The* *Courts and Labor Arbitration*, 1995 DET. C.L. REV. 889 (1995).

Bormet and Phyllis M. Bormet were officers of H–K Formalwear,[1] and each owned one-third of the shares of the corporation. The store was managed by Mrs. Bormet's son, Howard Parks, who was also the president of H–K Formalwear and owned one-third of its shares.

Gingiss entered into a Shareholder's and Officer's Agreement with the Bormets and Parks contemporaneously with the franchise agreement. The Shareholder's and Officer's Agreement provided that the Bormets and Parks agreed to be bound by all obligations of H–K Formalwear under the franchise agreement as if each was the franchisee. The Bormets and Parks also agreed to be bound by all obligations of H–K Formalwear under a related sublease of the California store.

In December 1993, following the expiration of the franchise agreement, Gingiss initiated arbitration proceedings against H–K Formalwear, the Bormets, and Parks. Gingiss sought damages for several breaches of the franchise agreement and the sublease, including the failure to pay royalties and advertising fund contributions. Gingiss also sought damages for trademark infringement and unfair competition under the Lanham Act, 15 U.S.C. §§ 1051–1128, and its attorney's fees incurred in prosecuting an earlier unlawful detainer action against H–K Formalwear in California state court.

Gingiss' attorney sent a copy of Gingiss' arbitration demand by regular mail to the Bormets at a post office box in Old Fort, North Carolina. This was the same address to which Gingiss had previously sent correspondence to the Bormets, and the Bormets had regularly replied. The AAA sent a letter by regular mail to the same address on December 30, 1993, notifying the Bormets of the arbitration proceeding. The AAA sent three additional letters concerning the arbitration proceeding by regular mail to the Bormets at this address in January 1994. Neither Gingiss' arbitration demand nor any of the AAA's letters was ever returned as undelivered.

An arbitration hearing was held on March 30, 1994, at the AAA's offices in Chicago. The Bormets and Parks did not appear at the hearing. Gingiss, nonetheless, presented evidence in support of its claims pursuant to the AAA's Commercial Arbitration Rule 30. On April 14, 1994, the arbitrator awarded Gingiss $60,629.25 against H–K Formalwear, the Bormets, and Parks jointly and severally. This award remains unsatisfied. The arbitrator awarded Gingiss an additional $57,142.44 against H–K Formalwear and Parks.

Gingiss then filed this application in the district court to confirm the arbitration award rendered against the Bormets. 9 U.S.C. § 9. Jurisdiction was premised upon diversity of citizenship. The Bormets petitioned to vacate the award on several grounds. 9 U.S.C. § 10(a). The district court granted Gingiss' motion for summary judgment and confirmed the award.

---

1. Norman Bormet was the vice-president and treasurer of H–K Formalwear, and   Phyllis Bormet was the secretary.

The Bormets assert that the arbitrator exceeded his power because the arbitrator had no jurisdiction over them. 9 U.S.C. § 10(a)(4). The Bormets point out that they were not parties to the franchise agreement, and the Shareholder's and Officer's Agreement did not contain an arbitration clause. Only parties to an arbitration agreement can be compelled to arbitrate. Morrie Mages and Shirlee Mages Found. v. Thrifty Corp., 916 F.2d 402, 406 n. 1 (7th Cir.1990). The Shareholder's and Officer's Agreement incorporated the franchise agreement by reference and imposed on the Bormets all the obligations of H–K Formalwear under that agreement. Paragraph six of the Shareholder's and Officer's Agreement expressly incorporated the arbitration clause. Under federal law,[3] a subcontract with a guarantor or surety may incorporate a duty to arbitrate by reference to an arbitration clause in a general contract. Maxum Founds., Inc. v. Salus Corp., 779 F.2d 974, 978 (4th Cir.1985); Exchange Mut. Ins. Co. v. Haskell Co., 742 F.2d 274, 276 (6th Cir.1984). The Bormets therefore were obligated to arbitrate Gingiss' claims pursuant to the arbitration clause.

. . . The Bormets contend that the arbitration award should be vacated because they did not receive proper notice of the arbitration proceedings. We have repeatedly held that 9 U.S.C. § 10(a) provides the exclusive grounds for setting aside an arbitration award under the FAA. E.g., Baravati v. Josephthal, Lyon & Ross, Inc., 28 F.3d 704, 706 (7th Cir.1994); Eljer, 14 F.3d at 1256; Moseley, Hallgarten, Estabrook & Weeden, Inc. v. Ellis, 849 F.2d 264, 267 (7th Cir.1988) (collecting cases). Inadequate notice is not one of these grounds, and the Bormets' claim therefore fails.

To the extent that the Bormets are asserting that the arbitrator committed misconduct by failing to notify them of the arbitration, 9 U.S.C. § 10(a)(3), their argument is without merit. Under the AAA's Commercial Arbitration Rule 40, notice "may be served on a party by mail addressed to the party or its representative at the last known address." Gingiss sent a copy of its arbitration demand by regular mail to the Bormets at their last known address, a post office box in Old Fort, North Carolina, and the AAA sent four letters by regular mail to the Bormets at this address. None of these notices was ever returned as undelivered. The Bormets nevertheless claim that they did not receive any of these notices.

The Bormets had no right under the franchise agreement to receive actual notice of the arbitration. Rule 40 does not require that notice be served by certified or registered mail. Although the Bormets point out that both Illinois and California state law require notice by registered mail or

---

3. Because the franchise agreement involved interstate commerce, the FAA applies. 9 U.S.C. §§ 1, 2; Allied–Bruce Terminix Cos., Inc. v. Dobson, ___ U.S. ___, ___, 115 S.Ct. 834, 841–43, 130 L.Ed.2d 753 (1995). The FAA authorizes federal courts to create a federal substantive law of arbitrability applicable to any arbitration agreement within the coverage of the FAA, Moses H. Cone Memorial Hosp. v. Mercury Constr. Corp., 460 U.S. 1, 24–25 and n. 32, 103 S.Ct. 927, 941–42, and n. 32, 74 L.Ed.2d 765 (1983); Baravati v. Josephthal, Lyon & Ross, Inc., 28 F.3d 704, 707 (7th Cir.1994), unless the parties have agreed to submit the question of arbitrability to arbitration, which Gingiss and the Bormets have not done. First Options of Chicago, Inc. v. Kaplan, ___ U.S. ___, ___–___, 115 S.Ct. 1920, 1923–24, 131 L.Ed.2d 985 (1995).

personal service, 710 ILCS 5/5(a); Cal Code Civ.Proc. § 1282.2(a)(1), these laws are inapplicable. The parties expressly agreed in the arbitration clause that the AAA's Rules would govern in the arbitration proceeding. See Volt Info. Sciences, Inc. v. Board of Trustees of Leland Stanford Junior Univ., 489 U.S. 468, 479, 109 S.Ct. 1248, 1256, 103 L.Ed.2d 488 (1989) (the parties may specify by contract the rules under which arbitration will be conducted). The Bormets' reliance on section eighteen of the franchise agreement, which provided that "[a]ll written notices permitted or required to be delivered by the provisions of this Agreement" shall be delivered by hand or by registered or certified mail, is also misplaced. "[A] document should be read to give effect to all its provisions and to render them consistent with each other." Mastrobuono v. Shearson Lehman Hutton, Inc., ___ U.S. ___, ___, 115 S.Ct. 1212, 1219, 131 L.Ed.2d 76 (1995). Section eighteen, by its terms, applied only to notices which were required to be sent under the franchise agreement, such as default or termination notices. The arbitration clause, which is contained in section sixteen of the agreement, governed the notice procedures in the arbitration.

The Bormets next contend that the arbitration award "was procured by corruption, fraud, or undue means," 9 U.S.C. § 10(a)(1), because Gingiss caused an indispensable party, Howard Parks, to be absent from the arbitration hearing. In order to vacate the award on these grounds, the Bormets must demonstrate that the corruption, fraud, or undue means was (1) not discoverable upon the exercise of due diligence prior to the arbitration; (2) materially related to an issue in the arbitration; and (3) established by clear and convincing evidence. A.G. Edwards & Sons, Inc. v. McCollough, 967 F.2d 1401, 1404 (9th Cir.1992) (citation omitted), cert. denied, ___ U.S. ___, 113 S.Ct. 970, 122 L.Ed.2d 126 (1993). On March 30, 1994, the date of the hearing, Parks was required by a municipal court order to attend a judgment-debtor's proceeding in Glendale, California, in connection with the unlawful detainer action brought by Gingiss against H–K Formalwear. Neither Parks nor H–K Formalwear requested a continuance of the judgment-debtor's proceeding from the California municipal court or a postponement of the arbitration hearing from the arbitrator because of this scheduling conflict. The Bormets also did not request that the arbitrator postpone the hearing because of Parks' absence. The Bormets thus have failed to show that Parks' absence was procured by Gingiss or could not have been prevented by Parks or the Bormets.

The Bormets' remaining claims that (1) their liability to Gingiss under the Shareholder's and Officer's Agreement terminated on October 31, 1993; and (2) Gingiss failed to prove any damages caused by the Bormets, are nothing more than thinly veiled attempts to obtain appellate review of the arbitrator's decision, which is not permitted under the FAA.... Factual or legal errors by arbitrators—even clear or gross errors—"do not authorize courts to annul awards." Widell, 43 F.3d at 1151; accord Misco, 484 U.S. at 38, 108 S.Ct. at 371. With respect to the Bormets' proof of damages claim, moreover, we held in Eljer that insufficiency of the evidence is not a ground for setting aside an arbitration award under the FAA. Eljer, 14 F.3d at 1256. The Bormets also briefly assert that the arbitrator deprived them of due process of law by failing to render the award in a "just, independent and deliberate manner." This argument was not raised in the district court and therefore has been waived. E.g., United States v. Rode Corp., 996 F.2d 174, 179 (7th Cir.1993). We add that if the Bormets are merely casting their other challenges to the arbitration award in constitutional terms, their argument fails for the reasons we have discussed. The arbitration award is valid under 9 U.S.C. § 10(a), and the judgment of the district court confirming the award is therefore

AFFIRMED.

* * *

Amalgamated Cotton Garment & Allied Industries Fund v. J.B.C. Company of Madera, Inc.

608 F.Supp. 158 (W.D.Pa.1984).

■ MANSMANN, DISTRICT JUDGE.

Plaintiff Amalgamated Cotton Garment & Allied Industries Fund (the "Fund") brought this action to recover contributions allegedly due the Fund on behalf of the employees of Campo Slacks, Inc. ("Campo Slacks") and J & E Sportswear, Inc. ("J & E Sportswear"). The Fund seeks to recover these contributions from Defendants J.B.C. Company of Madera, Inc. ("J.B.C."), Joseph Campolong, Betty Campolong and David Campolong, all of whom are allegedly jointly and severally liable for said contributions. The case was tried before this Court nonjury. We hereby make the following findings of fact and conclusions of law pursuant to Fed.R.Civ.P. 52(a):

FINDINGS OF FACT

The Fund is an "employee benefit plan" within the meaning of § 3(3) of the Employee Retirement Security Act of 1974, as amended ("ERISA"), 29 U.S.C. § 1002(3).

J.B.C. is a Pennsylvania corporation.

Joseph Campolong, Betty Campolong and David Campolong are officers of J.B.C. and reside in this District.

Joseph Campolong is and was the president and sole shareholder of J.B.C. during all times pertinent to this action. Betty Campolong, wife of Joseph Campolong, is and was the secretary of J.B.C. during all times pertinent to this action. David Campolong, the son of Joseph Campolong, is and was the vice-president of J.B.C. during all times pertinent hereto. None of them, however, are or were the "alter egos" of J.B.C.

On or about October 1, 1973, Joseph Campolong, in his capacity as president of J.B.C., Campo Slacks, J & E Sportswear and Madera Business Systems, Inc., and Betty Campolong, in her capacity as secretary of those corporations, executed Articles of Merger ("Articles") which were filed with the Pennsylvania Department of State on or about January 21, 1974.

Under the Articles, Campo Slacks, J & E Sportswear and Madera Business Systems, Inc. merged into J.B.C., with J.B.C. being the surviving corporation. All assets and liabilities of the merging corporations were transferred or assumed by J.B.C. The employees of Campo Slacks and J & E Sportswear effectively became the employees of J.B.C.

The Articles have remained effective to this date. Thus, Campo Slacks and J & E Sportswear have not legally existed as separate corporate entities since at least January 21, 1974. Further, the former employees of Campo Slacks and J & E Sportswear are and have been employees of J.B.C. since at least 1974.

Nevertheless, Joseph Campolong continued to use the names of the defunct corporations, Campo Slacks and J & E Sportswear, for certain purposes. For example, during the period following the merger, Joseph Campolong executed collective bargaining agreements with the Amalgamated Clothing and Textile Workers Union (the "Union") to cover persons allegedly employed by Campo Slacks and J & E Sportswear. Pursuant to those agreements, Campo Slacks and J & E Sportswear, as the "employers," were obligated to make certain contributions to the Fund on behalf of "their" employees. Quarterly reports were prepared and sent to the Fund for these employees. Mr. Campolong signed the summary sheets which accompanied the reports.

The reports indicate that no contributions were made to the Fund for these employees for the period April 1979 through August 21, 1981 (Campo Slacks) and for the period February 25, 1979 through August 11, 1979 (J & E Sportswear).

The auditor for the Fund audited the "books" of J.B.C. at J.B.C.'s offices, examining records and reports supplied to him by J.B.C. His audit confirmed the delinquency already indicated by the quarterly reports. The total amount in delinquency is $70,191.12.

In the meantime, the Fund, pursuant to the collective bargaining agreements, initiated several arbitration proceedings against Joseph Campolong and J.B.C., as "alter egos" of Campo Slacks and J & E Sportswear, to recover delinquent contributions. The arbitrator found that due notice was given to the parties for each proceeding yet neither Mr. Campolong nor J.B.C. entered an appearance at any of the arbitration hearings.[3]

The arbitrator issued four arbitration awards in which he found Joseph Campolong and J.B.C. jointly and severally liable for the delinquent contributions. Specifically, the arbitrator found as a factual matter that Joseph Campolong, J.B.C., Campo Slacks and J & E Sportswear constitute a single joint enterprise.[4]

---

3. The evidence at trial showed that for each arbitration proceeding, a notice of intention to arbitrate was sent by certified mail to Joseph Campolong and J.B.C. In every instance, the certified mail was marked "unclaimed" and returned to the Fund.

4. The evidence showed that upon the issuance of each arbitration award, the Fund mailed a copy of the award to Joseph Campolong and J.B.C. by certified mail. Each arbitration award, as with the notices of intention to arbitrate, was returned unclaimed.

Joseph Campolong and J.B.C. did not move to vacate or to modify any of the arbitration awards until filing a counterclaim to this action more than a year after the fourth arbitration decision.

Joseph Campolong and J.B.C. have failed and refused to pay the amount of the delinquency.

The Fund brought the present action to confirm the arbitration awards pursuant to § 301 of the Labor Management Relations Act of 1947, as amended ("LMRA"), 29 U.S.C. § 185. Jurisdiction is also predicated upon ERISA and the Federal Arbitration Act, 9 U.S.C. § 1 et seq. Furthermore, the Fund seeks to hold the three individual Defendants liable pursuant to the Pennsylvania Wage Payment and Collection Law ("WPCL") 43 P.S. § 260.1 et seq. (Purdon 1964).[5]

Defendants have counterclaimed to vacate the arbitration awards. In addition, at trial, the three individual Defendants orally moved for dismissal of the case against them.

We find that Defendants are indeed jointly and severally liable for the amount of the delinquency, $70,191.12, as more fully explained in our conclusions of law.

CONCLUSIONS OF LAW

* * *

III. SECTION 301 CLAIM

Defendants assert that the Fund lacks standing to sue under § 301 of the LMRA and that this Court is therefore without subject matter jurisdiction under § 301.

We have already addressed this contention in our previous Opinion. We held that the Fund does have standing to pursue its claim under § 301. Defendant has proffered no cases to the contrary. Furthermore, we perceive no significant distinction between the Fund and its trustees, at least for the purpose of maintaining this suit under § 301. Any concern in this regard may be remedied by a simple amendment to the Complaint that adds the names of the trustees to the case caption. We will therefore permit Plaintiff to amend the Amended Complaint, adding the names of the trustees to the caption.

A.

Plaintiff postured this action as an action to confirm or enforce arbitration awards pursuant to § 301 of the LMRA.

This Court has the jurisdiction and power to confirm and enforce arbitration awards pursuant to § 301. See Sheet Metal Ass'n of N.Y. City v.

---

5. At trial, the Fund further amended its Amended Complaint to allege, inter alia, that J.B.C. and the three individual defen- dants are also liable as "employers" under the LMRA and under ERISA.

Local Union No. 28 of Sheet Metal Workers, 301 F.Supp. 553, 555 (S.D.N.Y. 1969).

We held in our previous Opinion that we must look to Pennsylvania law to determine the appropriate limitations period(s) for Plaintiff's action to confirm and any action to vacate the arbitration awards. Since Pennsylvania provides a 30–day statute of limitations for actions to vacate an arbitration award, Defendants' counterclaim to vacate the arbitration awards would ordinarily be time-barred.[13]

Regardless, we cannot enforce an arbitration award where the evidence does not establish that the parties did in fact receive proper notice and the opportunity to be present at the arbitration proceeding. In this regard, it is axiomatic that all parties to an arbitration hearing must be given an opportunity to be heard, which implies the right to receive notice of the hearing. See Ryan–Walsh Stevedoring Co. v. General Longshore Workers Union, Local No. 3000, 509 F.Supp. 463, 467 (E.D.La.1981); Wright–Bernet, Inc. v. Amalgamated Local Union No. 41, 501 F.Supp. 72, 74 (S.D.Ohio 1980).

We believe that failure to receive proper notice precludes our enforcement of the arbitration awards in question regardless of whether Pennsylvania law or New York law applies to our review of the awards.[14] ...

In Local 149, Boot and Shoe Workers Union v. Faith Shoe Co., supra, the court, in an action to enforce an arbitration award, examined the question of whether an ex parte arbitration award was void and unenforceable. The court essentially held that an ex parte award was enforceable if the other side received notice of the time and place of the hearing but did not request an adjournment or otherwise object. Since the court was considering the matter on a Fed.R.Civ.P. 12(b) Motion to Dismiss, the court took the allegations of the Complaint as stating the facts. The Complaint alleged that formal notice of the hearing had been given to Defendant and Defendant's counsel. The Complaint further alleged that on the day of the hearing, Defendant's counsel was notified again of the arbitration hearing. Upon being informed by Defendant's counsel that Defendant would not appear or be represented at the hearing, the other party advised that the

---

13. It could be argued that failure to receive notice of the arbitration awards should toll the time for filing actions to vacate. In this event, however, the statute of limitations would at least commence running on the date Defendants did receive notice of the arbitration awards. In this case, we find that Plaintiff's evidence did not establish that Defendants received timely notice of the arbitration proceedings or of the arbitration awards. Nonetheless, the evidence presented at trial did not show when Defendants actually did receive notice of the awards.

14. Under Pennsylvania law, Defendants' failure to timely file an action to va-

cate the awards would preclude them from challenging the merits of the arbitration awards. See Service Employees Int'l Union, Local No. 36 v. Office Center Services, Inc., 670 F.2d at 412; Western Kraft East, Inc. v. United Paperworkers Int'l Union, Local 375, 531 F.Supp. at 671. Under New York law, Defendants may make certain challenges to the arbitration awards in an action to confirm brought by the other party even if Defendants failed to file a timely action to vacate the awards. See §§ 7510 and 7511 of the New York Civil Practice Law and Rules.

hearing would proceed without representation by the Defendant. The court therefore concluded that the absent party had waived its right to be present and heard.

In the instant case, we cannot conclude that Joseph Campolong and J.B.C. waived their right to be present and heard at the arbitration hearings since the evidence at trial did not establish that Mr. Campolong and J.B.C. received notice of the arbitration proceedings. In this regard, there is no evidence that personal service was made or that the Fund telephonically contacted Defendants or their counsel regarding the arbitration proceedings. Moreover, the certified notices sent to Mr. Campolong and J.B.C. were never claimed and were therefore returned to the Fund.[16]

Since the evidence does not show that the absent parties received notice of the arbitration hearings, we cannot find that they waived their right to be present. Therefore, we cannot enforce the ex parte arbitration awards as requested by the Fund....

* * *

Questions

1.   Is there a right to notice of arbitral proceedings?

2.   If an arbitration agreement is silent on the question of notice, should a court imply a notice requirement? What should the implied notice requirement be? Should it require actual notice, or should constructive notice by mail or by publication be sufficient?

3.   If an arbitration agreement permits arbitration hearings to be scheduled with no notice given to one of the contracting parties, and if an arbitration is then held to which that party was not notified, is there any basis for a court to vacate the award?

4.   Do the standards for due process in arbitration vary depending upon whether the FAA, state arbitration statutes, or Section 301 of the LMRA govern the proceedings?

* * *

Waterspring, S.A. and Trans Marketing Houston Inc.

717 F.Supp. 181 (S.D.N.Y.1989).

■ LEISURE, DISTRICT JUDGE:

Waterspring, S.A. ("Waterspring," "Owner," or "petitioner"), brought this petition, as Owner of the M.T. OCEANIA GLORY, for an order pursuant to Section 4 of Title 9, United States Code, compelling respondent, Trans Marketing Houston, Inc. ("TMHI," "Charterer," or "Owner"),

---

16. We note in this regard that the certified notices were not marked "refused" as they could have been if Defendants had received them but refused to accept them. Rather, they were marked "unclaimed."

as Charterer to proceed to arbitration before a panel comprised of Stephen H. Busch ("Busch"), Manfred W. Arnold ("Arnold") and Hammond L. Cederholm ("Cederholm"), in accordance with the terms and conditions of a certain contract of charter party allegedly entered into between petitioner and respondent. TMHI has cross-moved to vacate the partial final arbitration award dated December 5, 1988.

FACTUAL BACKGROUND

A charter party agreement for the M/V COUNTESS, owned by Astor Marine S.A. and operated by Adriatic Tankers Shipping Company ("Adriatic"), was fixed on July 6, 1988 (the "Charter"). The fixture telex confirming the agreement incorporated the terms of a standard form charter party commonly know as the Asbatankvoy form. The fixture telex also provided for arbitration in New York. The COUNTESS became delayed and the Charter was amended to change the vessel to the OCEANIA GLORY, owned by Waterspring, and operated by Adriatic. The amendment was confirmed by telex. Affidavit of Glen T. Oxton, Esq., sworn to on February 15, 1989 ("Oxton Affidavit"), Exhibit 37.

The OCEANIA GLORY carried cargoes for TMHI from Houston to Santo Tomas, Guatemala and Guayaquil, Ecuador, pursuant to the Charter. Discharging in Guayaquil was completed on September 8, 1988. On September 20, 1988, the Owner submitted an invoice for demurrage in the amount of $58,122. Oxton Affidavit, Exhibit 3. Subsequently, Charterer paid $88,754.84 to Owner and withheld payment of the balance of $194,367 due to the alleged wrongful presentation of cargo documents by Owner. Oxton Affidavit, Exhibit 4.

As noted, the Charter is under the Asbatankvoy form, which provides for arbitration. Owner demanded arbitration, requested an immediate partial final award for freight and demurrage and appointed its arbitrator by a letter to Charterer sent by facsimile and mail on October 12, 1988. Oxton Affidavit, Exhibit 6. On October 25, 1988, Charterer requested time to discuss the merits of the dispute with its broker. Affidavit of Richard M. Ziccardi, Esq., sworn to on March 3, 1989 ("Ziccardi Affidavit"), Exhibit 5. On November 2, 1988, Owner, asserting that Charterer failed to appoint its arbitrator within 20 days as provided in Clause 24 of the Charter, appointed Manfred Arnold on Charterer's behalf. Oxton Affidavit, Exhibit 9. On November 10, 1988 Cederholm and Arnold appointed Busch as the third arbitrator and set the first hearing date for November 23, 1988. Oxton Affidavit, Exhibit 10.

On or about November 10, 1988, TMHI was advised by petitioner's counsel that an arbitration hearing had been scheduled for November 23, 1988 in New York City. Ziccardi Affidavit, Exhibit 9. TMHI retained counsel, who wrote to the arbitration panel on November 16, 1988, to request an adjournment. Ziccardi Affidavit, Exhibit 12. This counsel requested an extension of time from the panel on the grounds that the scheduled arbitration hearing was for the Wednesday before Thanksgiving making travel arrangements impossible and that retained counsel was previously scheduled to be in California on that day. This request was initially refused by the arbitration panel in New York, which then tied further consideration of such request to a demand for full security of the petitioner's claim. On November 22, 1988, Charterer attempted to appoint its arbitrator, Richard E. Repetto.

On December 5, 1988, the arbitration panel granted Waterspring a partial final arbitration award of $100,000. TMHI paid $100,000 to Waterspring. TMHI contends that this payment was based upon its own good faith determination that such amount was due and owing. Allegedly, the decision to pay this amount was made in advance of any knowledge on the part of TMHI of the contents of the partial final award dated December 5, 1988. Reply Memorandum of Law in Support of Counter–Motion to Vacate Partial Final Award at 4. Owner asserts it is still owed freight and demurrage aggregating $94,367.10 plus interest, costs and attorneys' fees.

DISCUSSION

MOTION TO COMPEL ARBITRATION

Petitioner presently seeks an order pursuant to Section 4 of Title 9, United States Code, compelling respondent, TMHI to proceed to arbitration before a panel comprised of Stephen H. Busch, Manfred W. Arnold and Hammond L. Cederholm, in accordance with the terms and conditions of the Charter allegedly entered into between petitioner and respondent. Respondent opposes the motion on various grounds.

A. Standing

Section 4 of the Federal Arbitration Act, 9 U.S.C. § 4 provides, inter alia:

> A party aggrieved by the alleged failure, neglect, or refusal of another to arbitrate under a written agreement for arbitration may petition any United States district court ... for an order directing that such arbitration proceed in the manner provided for in such agreement.... (emphasis added).

Clause 24 of the charter party at issue, provides in pertinent part as follows:

> Either party hereto may call for such arbitration by service upon any officer of the other, wherever he may be found, of a written notice specifying the name and address of the arbitrator chosen by the first moving party and a brief description of the disputes or differences which such party desires to put to arbitration. If the other party shall not, by notice served upon an officer of the first moving party within twenty days of the service of such notice, appoint its arbitrator to arbitrate the dispute or differences specified, then the first moving party shall have the right without further notice to appoint a second arbitrator, who shall be a disinterested person with precisely the same force and effect as if said second arbitrator has been appointed by the other party. In the event that the two arbitrators fail to appoint a third arbitrator within twenty days of the appointment of the second arbitra-

tor, either arbitrator may apply to a Judge of any court of maritime jurisdiction in the city above-mentioned for the appointment of a third arbitrator, and the appointment of such arbitrator by such Judge on such application shall have precisely the same force and effect as if such arbitrator had been appointed by the two arbitrators....

Oxton Affidavit, Exhibit 1.

TMHI urges that before seeking relief from this Court under the Arbitration Act, petitioner must exhaust its remedies under the arbitration agreement by proceeding with the arbitration to a conclusion, even though TMHI does not participate. Charterer contends that Waterspring is not a party aggrieved by a failure, neglect or refusal to arbitrate within the meaning of § 4 of the Act as it can proceed with an ex parte arbitration.

Petitioner, on the other hand, contends that before arbitration can continue, the Court must determine whether or not Waterspring is a party to the arbitration agreement, and whether the panel is properly constituted. It points out that, if it continues to go through with the arbitration, it may prove to be a nullity, and urges that this makes it an aggrieved party entitled to relief under the Act.

Section 4 of the Arbitration Act permits "a party aggrieved by the alleged failure, neglect, or refusal of another to arbitrate" under a written arbitration agreement to petition the court to compel arbitration. The basic question here is whether or not the petitioner is a party who is aggrieved by a failure to arbitrate. Unless it is, it cannot maintain this proceeding.

The arbitration agreement at issue has a self-executing mechanism. It provides that, in the event the opposing party fails to appoint its arbitrator within 20 days, the moving party may then appoint a disinterested person as the second arbitrator. The two arbitrators are then to select a third arbitrator. Thus, in the event of failure of the opposing party to appoint an arbitrator the agreement entered into by the parties provides its own remedies. If this arbitration clause is properly invoked, a duly constituted panel is formed regardless of respondent's actions and without the need to resort to Federal Court intervention. Indeed, the very purpose of such a self-executing mechanism in an arbitration clause is to avoid the time and expense of Federal Court motion practice. The case at bar is before this Court because petitioner voluntarily suspended the ex parte arbitration in order to seek an order from this Court which, in essence, would represent a retroactive approval of petitioner's actions thus far, as well as sanction future acts by the arbitrators. Such a declaratory judgment is not provided for in Title 9 of the United States Code. A/S Ganger Rolf v. Zeeland Transportation Ltd., 191 F.Supp. 359, 362–63 (S.D.N.Y.1961).

It is true that the issue of whether or not Waterspring was in fact a party to this charter and bound by the arbitration clause is not one for the arbitrators and must be passed upon by the court at some time. See, e.g., Kulukundis Shipping Co. S/A v. Amtorg Trading Corp., 126 F.2d 978 (2d Cir.1942); A/S Ganger Rolf, supra. But it does not necessarily follow that this issue must be determined prior to the conclusion of the arbitration proceeding. An ex parte arbitration under the terms of an arbitration clause like the one in the case at bar is valid and an award made thereunder is enforceable against a party bound by the clause. See, e.g., Corallo v. Merrick Central Carburetor, 733 F.2d 248 (2d Cir.1984); Standard Magnesium Corp. v. Fuchs, 251 F.2d 455 (10th Cir.1957); A/S Ganger Rolf, supra.

Such an ex parte arbitration involves risks both to the moving party and to the party which did not appoint its own arbitrator. If the assertion of the petitioner that the panel is properly constituted and that they are parties to the agreement is unfounded petitioner may find that the arbitration was in fact a useless gesture and it was put to unnecessary expense. But it is hardly in a position to complain if its unfounded assertion leads to that result.

On the other hand, if petitioner's assertions turn out to be well-founded and the panel is properly constituted, TMHI is in the position, by its own default, of being precluded from contesting the merits. It may not complain that it has not been heard on the merits before the arbitrators since it waived the right to do so, granted to it by the arbitration agreement by which it bound itself.

The Court notes that the object of the Arbitration Act contemplates only the enforcement of the arbitration agreement made by the parties themselves in the manner they themselves provide. "Having designed their own remedy for recalcitrance [petitioner] cannot, over respondent's objection, ignore that remedy and pursue another." A/S Ganger, supra, 191 F.Supp. at 362.

"What petitioner[ ] really want[s] here is a judgment declaring [the parties bound by the arbitration clause] in advance of arbitration as insurance against the possibility that [it] may be mistaken in [its] assertion that it is so bound. It does not seem to me that Sections 4, 5 and 6 of the Act contemplate such a declaratory judgment or authorize the Court to render it. These sections are designed only to insure that the parties proceed in the manner provided by the arbitration agreement which they themselves fashioned." Id. at 362–63.

Since the contract permitted petitioner to proceed with the arbitration without respondent's cooperation, petitioner is not a "party aggrieved" and 9 U.S.C. § 4 does not apply. A/S Ganger Rolf, supra, 191 F.Supp. 362–363; Cf. Aaacon Auto Transport, Inc. v. Barnes, 603 F.Supp. 1347, 1349 (S.D.N.Y.1985) (party cannot compel arbitration where other side had demanded arbitration in another forum); Koreska v. Perry–Sherwood Corp., 253 F.Supp. 830, 832 (S.D.N.Y.1965) (court cannot compel arbitration anywhere when parties have already submitted to arbitration in accordance with terms of contract), aff'd, 360 F.2d 212 (2d Cir.1966) (mem.).

Accordingly, petitioner's motion to compel the continuation of the arbitration before the present panel is denied. . . .

* * *

Questions

1.   In *Totem Marine Tug & Barge, Inc. v. North American Towing, Inc.*, 607 F.2d 649 (5th Cir.1979), an arbitration panel awarded the prevailing party an item of damages that had not been specifically requested. To determine the amount to award for the unrequested item, the arbitrators telephoned the counsel for the prevailing party after the hearing had been closed, and asked that a figure be supplied. The other side was not notified of the call nor given an opportunity to to contest the figure. The court found that this *ex parte* communication violated the Commercial Arbitration Rules of the American Arbitration Association, which require that "(a)ll evidence shall be taken in the presence of all the parties, except where any of the parties is absent, in default, or has waived his right to be present." The court further found that by receiving the ex parte communication, the arbitrators had engaged in prejudicial arbitral misconduct under Section 10(c) of the FAA. It vacated the award without prejudice so that it could be resubmitted to a new arbitration panel. Can this case be distinguished from *Waterspring v. TransMarketing Housing, Inc.*?

2.   Is it ever appropriate for an arbitration to proceed *ex parte* if there is no specific self-executing mechanism in the agreement? Who should make such determination? At what stage in the proceeding?

* * *

3.   RIGHT TO AN EVIDENTIARY HEARING

Federal Deposit Insurance Corporation v. Air Florida System, Inc.

822 F.2d 833 (9th Cir.1987).

■ FLETCHER, CIRCUIT JUDGE.

The FDIC appeals a judgment refusing to rescind its contract with Air Florida and enforcing an arbitration award in Air Florida's favor. We reverse in part, vacate in part, and remand.

BACKGROUND

In its capacity as receiver of the United States National Bank, the FDIC became a major creditor of the Westgate–California Corporation ("Westgate"). As such, the FDIC was entitled to a large block of Westgate stock once Westgate's reorganization in bankruptcy was completed. In 1980, the FDIC sold its Westgate interests to Air Florida for $15.4 million. As part of the agreement, Air Florida promised to make a general public offer for outstanding Westgate common shares at no less than the price it paid the FDIC. If Air Florida acquired more than 80% of Westgate's common stock, and if it paid more per share to tender-offerees than the

FDIC received, the FDIC was entitled to additional compensation to afford it the same price per share paid the tender-offerees.

Air Florida purchased the Westgate stock in order to acquire Air California, a Westgate controlled corporation. After Air Florida purchased the FDIC's interest in Westgate, however, Westgate's bankruptcy trustees arranged, and the district court approved, the sale of Air California to a third party for $61.5 million. The sale caused a substantial increase in the trading price of outstanding shares of Westgate common stock. Air Florida had paid approximately $18 per share for the stock, but after Air California's sale, Westgate shares traded between $21 and $26.50 per share.

In February 1982, Air Florida informed the FDIC that it had decided not to make a tender offer. On April 1, 1982, Westgate's directors announced that Westgate would be liquidated with shareholders receiving $28.25 per share of common stock.[1] On April 30, the FDIC brought suit against Air Florida seeking rescission and restitution because Air Florida had failed to make the tender offer. In defense, Air Florida denied that it had a contractual duty to make an offer at a price exceeding the price paid to the FDIC and argued that the rise in Westgate's market price excused its tender offer obligation. The FDIC asserted that Air Florida was required to make an offer reasonably calculated to acquire the shares, no matter what the market price.

Air Florida counterclaimed for $2 million it alleged was owing under a separate provision in the contract that required adjustment of the purchase price of the stock upon sale of a cannery owned by Westgate. After a bench trial, the district court adopted Air Florida's interpretation of the contract, holding that Air Florida had not breached its agreement with FDIC. FDIC v. Air Florida Sys., Inc., No. 85–0525–N(H) (S.D.Cal. Jan. 6, 1983) (Findings of Fact and Conclusions of Law). Having rejected the FDIC's rescission claim, the district court held that the contract, including the cannery adjustment provision, remained in effect. The amount of the adjustment was left open until "determined by the parties, the parties' designated accountants or an independent accountant pursuant to the arbitration procedures set forth in ... the [purchase] Agreement." Id. at 9.

When neither the parties nor their accountants could reach an agreement on the cannery adjustment, the contractual arbitration process was invoked. Following the arbitration, which resulted in a $1,486,000 adjustment in favor of Air Florida, the FDIC moved to vacate the award because of the arbitrator's failure to hold an oral hearing. The district court held that "the arbitrator's election to resolve the question ... based on written submissions alone, did not deny the FDIC a fundamentally fair hearing." FDIC v. Air Florida, No. 82–0525–N(I) (C.D.Cal. July 10 1984) (unpublished order). The court granted Air Florida's cross-motion to enter the

---

1. The liquidating dividend was paid on May 3, 1982. Air Florida realized a gain of more than $10 per share over the price paid to the FDIC, a $3.86 million profit on its Westgate common shares.

arbitration award as part of the judgment and allowed prejudgment interest on the award. . . .

Right to an Oral Hearing

FDIC asserts that the arbitrator's refusal to hold an oral hearing on the issue of contractual intent violated its rights and rendered the arbitration unenforceable. The arbitrator, who was an accountant, did meet with the FDIC and Air Florida accountants, but he then refused the FDIC's request to hold a further evidentiary hearing. Rather, he requested the parties to submit in written form the materials they wished to have considered. In support of its interpretation of the cannery adjustment provision, FDIC submitted the affidavit of the attorney who negotiated the Agreement for the FDIC. The FDIC concedes that it could have submitted additional written documentation had it chosen to do so.

There is no disagreement that the federal Arbitration Act, 9 U.S.C. §§ 1–14 governs this dispute. Where the Act applies, it "provides the exclusive grounds for challenging an arbitration award within its purview." Lafarge Conseils et Etudes, S.A. v. Kaiser Cement & Gypsum Corp., 791 F.2d 1334, 1338 (9th Cir.1986). Section 10 of the Act sets forth the circumstances under which a district court may vacate an arbitration award. 9 U.S.C. § 10. The FDIC relies on section 10(c) to support its claim of procedural deficiency. Section 10(c) permits vacation of an award

> [w]here the arbitrators were guilty of misconduct in refusing to postpone the hearing, upon sufficient cause shown, or in refusing to hear evidence pertinent and material to the controversy; or of any other misbehavior by which the rights of any party have been prejudiced.

9 U.S.C. § 10(c).

While section 10(c) assumes that the parties to an arbitration will be afforded a hearing, neither in this section nor anywhere else in the Act are hearing procedures, much less oral hearing procedures, explicitly provided for. Certainly the parties may agree upon appropriate procedures by contract, but, where they do not, procedural matters "become part of the bundle of issues committed to decisions by the arbitrator." Sheet Metal Workers Int'l Ass'n, Local 420 v. Kinney Air Conditioning Co., 756 F.2d 742, 744 (9th Cir.1985). An arbitration award should not be vacated on procedural grounds unless the procedure employed was a "sham, substantially inadequate or substantially unavailable." Harris v. Chemical Leaman Tank Lines, 437 F.2d 167, 171 (5th Cir.1971), quoted in Dogherra v. Safeway Stores, Inc., 679 F.2d 1293, 1296 (9th Cir.), cert. denied, 459 U.S. 990, 103 S.Ct. 346, 74 L.Ed.2d 386 (1982). So long as the hearing provided is "full and fair," a procedural attack must fail. Coast Trading Co. v. Pacific Molasses Co., 681 F.2d 1195, 1198 (9th Cir.1982). Applying section 10(c), a hearing is full and fair unless the arbitrator (1) despite a showing of cause, refuses a postponement; (2) refuses to hear pertinent and material evidence; or (3) engages in misbehavior that prejudices the rights of a party. 9 U.S.C. § 10(c). The FDIC did not request a postponement and there is no allegation that the arbitrator refused to consider evidence the FDIC submitted. Finally, the failure to hold an oral hearing cannot be deemed misbehavior that prejudiced the FDIC's rights because the FDIC has not shown that its evidence was not amenable to presentation in written form. Admittedly, a "paper hearing" often will be an inadequate means to determine the facts upon which an arbitration decision must rely. In this case, however, the nature of the decision to be made leads us to conclude that the "paper hearing" was adequate.[9] As the district court noted:

> [W]hat the parties bargained for was not a quasi-judicial proceeding conducted by lawyers, but [rather] the professional opinion of an independent accountant on an accounting issue—the value of a business. Accountants derive their calculations not from evidentiary hearings, but from working papers and discussions with other accountants. Thus, it was predictable that the instant arbitrator would base his decision on this information. Nothing in the parties' contractual sequential valuation process manifests an intent to require an oral evidentiary hearing. Had the parties intended the arbitration to resolve primarily legal issues through evidentiary hearings, they surely would have agreed to use a lawyer, not an accountant, as the arbitrator, or declared arbitration rules as governing. Instead the parties instructed an accountant to resolve the dispute . . ., leaving the procedure to the arbitrator's sound discretion.

FDIC v. Air Florida, No. 82–0525–N(I) at 8–9 (July 10, 1984) (unpublished order).

* * *

Casualty Indemnity Exchange v. Jack Yother

439 So.2d 77 (Ala.1983).

■ SHORES, JUSTICE.

This case grew out of the following facts:

In May 1982, Jack Yother, d/b/a Mickey Motors, purchased an automobile policy of insurance from Casualty Indemnity Exchange (CIE), covering Yother's 1979 International Harvester tractor-truck. During the pre-dawn hours of August 1, 1982, while this policy was in full force and effect, the tractor was stolen from the insured's place of business. The tractor was never recovered. It is undisputed that there was a loss, and that it was covered by the aforesaid policy.

---

9. The FDIC argues also that it had a due process right to an oral hearing. The arbitration involved here was private, not state, action; it was conducted pursuant to contract by a private arbitrator. Although Congress, in the exercise of its commerce power, has provided for some governmental regulation of private arbitration agreements, we do not find in private arbitration proceedings the state action requisite for a constitutional due process claim.

Yother submitted proof of loss for the stolen tractor to his insurance agent, claiming a loss of $40,000, the policy limit. In response, he received the following letter:

"Dear Mr. Yother:

"This is to inform you that Casualty Indemnity Exchange has rejected your Proof of Loss which you submitted to them on September 17, 1982.

"The reason for the rejection is that they are not in agreement with actual cash value you have placed on the 1979 International Tractor. They consider the tractor to have a value no greater than $35,000.00.

"Since a dispute has arisen you are entitled to call upon that provision of your policy which provides for arbitration.

"Please follow the procedure outlined in the provision and direct your correspondence to the writer.

"Yours truly,

"Robert C. Carroll, Adjuster"

The provision of the insurance policy referred to in Carroll's letter states:

"2. Appraisal. If the insured and the company fail to agree as to the amount of loss, each shall, on the written demand of either, made within sixty days after receipt of proof of loss by the company, select a competent and disinterested appraiser, and the appraisal shall be made at a reasonable time and place. The appraisers shall first select a competent and disinterested umpire, and failing for fifteen days to agree upon such umpire, then, on the request of the insured or the company, such umpire shall be selected by a judge of a court of record in the county and state in which such appraisal is pending. The appraisers shall then appraise the loss, stating separately the actual cash value at the time of loss and the amount of loss, and failing to agree shall submit their differences to the umpire. An award in writing of any two shall determine the amount of loss. The insured and the company shall each pay his or its chosen appraiser and shall bear equally the other expenses of the appraisal and umpire."

The insured notified CIE by letter that he had elected to invoke the arbitration clause to settle the dispute over the actual cash value of his tractor. The insured and CIE subsequently executed a "Memorandum of Appraisal," in which the insured appointed Elmer Mann as his appraiser, and CIE named Buddy O'Neal as its appraiser.

Mann, a local International Harvester truck and tractor dealer, had sold the insured the 1979 International Harvester tractor-truck. Mann was familiar with both the features and condition of the tractor at the time it was stolen. O'Neal, owner of a truck lot, had never seen the tractor and had no personal knowledge of its condition. After a telephone conversation and a personal meeting, the two men failed to agree on the value of the tractor.

Pursuant to the policy provision, Mann and O'Neal selected and appointed Leon Lucas, an employee of International Harvester Company, as umpire. Prior to submitting the matter to Lucas, however, Mann and O'Neal executed an instrument divided into the following sections: "(1) Declaration of Appraisers"; (2) "Selection of Umpire"; (3) "Qualification of Umpire"; and (4) "Award." The first three sections relate to acknowledgment by the appraisers and the umpire of their respective duties. The fourth section, entitled "Award," states that the undersigned appraisers and umpire "have appraised and determined and do hereby award as the actual value" of the stolen property, and provides a space for the amount of the award to be inserted. Although the two appraisers were still not in agreement as to the value to be awarded, both signed the form in blank and forwarded it to Lucas. Lucas, without consulting either appraiser or the insured, entered a figure of $36,500 and signed the form, dated December 16, 1982. The insured received notice of the award on January 10, 1983.

The insured appealed from the Award of Arbitration, as provided by § 6–6–15, Code 1975, and asked the circuit court to set it aside. He alleged that the award was void because it was not made in substantial compliance with applicable provisions of the Alabama Code, and because the insured was not given notice of the hearing and was not allowed to present any evidence of the value of the tractor. The award was entered as a judgment in the records of the Circuit Court of Marshall County, pursuant to § 6–6–15, Code.

Following a hearing, the trial court set aside the award, stating in part:

"(a) That the procedure contemplated in Code Sections 6–6–1 through 6–6–16 was not substantially followed in that no notice of any kind was given to the plaintiff, Jack Yother, and he had no opportunity to present any evidence to any of the arbitrators or appraisers except to the arbitrator or appraiser designated by him.

"(b) That said statutory scheme referred to in said Code Sections was not otherwise substantially followed.

". . .

"(d) That the parties hereto did not agree for the dispute between them to be resolved pursuant to said Code Sections."

CIE appeals, and we affirm.

CIE argues that the procedure employed in determining the actual cash value of Yother's tractor was an appraisal, *not* an arbitration. As such, CIE contends that the trial court, by relying on § 6–6–1, et seq., to vacate the award, erred because those Code provisions do not apply to an "appraisal award" made pursuant to an insurance contract. We agree that an appraisal is distinguishable from arbitration and is not subject to the various procedural requirements imposed upon the arbitration process. But whether the procedures required are those of an arbitration or of an appraisal must be determined from the intent of the disputants or from the character of the questions and issues to be answered, or both. 5 Am.Jur.2d *Arbitration and Award*, § 3 (1962).

CIE claims that Yother knowingly entered into an appraisal agreement to resolve the dispute over the actual cash value of his tractor, and that neither party intended for that determination to be subjected to the various procedural requirements under the arbitration article of the Code; in support of that agreement, CIE points out that neither the policy provision nor the "Memorandum of Appraisal," signed by the insured, uses the word "arbitration." However, we note that the letter from CIE's adjuster, rejecting the insured's original loss claim, advises him that he is entitled to "call upon that provision of [his] policy which provides for arbitration." And the insured responded that he desired to exercise his right "as per policy agreements of arbitration."

Arbitration and appraisal are generally distinguished in the following manner:

"A distinction is often drawn between an arbitration and a mere appraisal or valuation, or proceeding in the nature of an appraisal, the fundamental difference between the two proceedings being held to lie in the procedure to be followed and the effect of the findings. In other words, the point is made that appraisers, unlike arbitrators, act without hearing or judicial inquiry upon their own knowledge or information acquired independent of the evidence of witnesses; and that the appraisal ordinarily settles only a subsidiary or incidental matter rather than the main controversy as does an arbitration award."

6 C.J.S. *Arbitration*, § 3 (1975).

"An agreement for arbitration ordinarily encompasses the disposition of the entire controversy between the parties upon which award a judgment may be entered, whereas an agreement for appraisal extends merely to the resolution of the specific issues of actual cash value and the amount of loss, all other issues being reserved for determination in a plenary action before the court. Furthermore, appraisers are generally expected to act on their own skill and knowledge; they may reach individual conclusions and are required to meet only for the purpose of ironing out differences in the conclusions reached; and they are not obliged to give the rival claimants any formal notice or to hear evidence, but may proceed by ex parte investigation so long as the parties are given opportunity to make statements and explanations with regard to matters in issue."

5 Am.Jur.2d *Arbitration and Award*, § 3 (1962).

Conceding, as CIE argues, that the two proceedings are different, we hold that the trial court did not err in setting aside the award in this case, whether it is labeled arbitration or appraisal.

First, because the insured was given no notice of the hearing, he was denied the opportunity to offer testimony or other evidence of the condition and value of his tractor at the time of loss. He testified that he requested, on two separate occasions, that he be permitted to appear before the hearing. The insured stated that he made one request to Mann, his appraiser, and another request to his insurance agent, Gerald Martin. He further testified that Martin told him that his request would be forwarded to CIE. This evidence was not challenged. The fact that neither the policy provision nor the agreement expressly provides for notice to the parties is not determinative.

> "It has been held that even though neither the insurance policy nor the arbitration or appraisal agreement provides for it, notice to the parties of a hearing before the appraisers or arbitrators appointed to determine the amount of a loss under the policy is nevertheless necessary when ne of the parties manifests a desire to be heard."

Annot., 25 A.L.R.3d 711 (1969).

Secondly, a hearing was never conducted. It is undisputed that the two appraisers signed a blank award form without having agreed upon a value for the tractor-truck, and that Lucas, the umpire, entered the amount of the award without having consulted the appraisers or having received evidence from the insured as to the tractor's condition. Thus, the policy provision was not complied with. It requires concurrences of two of the three, i.e., the two appraisers and the umpire, and it is not controverted that Lucas alone made the award without notice to the insured, without a hearing, and without any evidence. Mann's testimony in this regard was undisputed:

"Q.   Did you sign each of these documents on the same day?

"A.   The two of us, yes.

"Q.   And Mr. O'Neal signed on the same day?

"A.   Yes.

"Q.   Now, the bottom document says in part: We hereby certify that we have truly and conscientiously performed, et cetera, and do hereby award as the actual cash value of the property on the 16th day of December, 1982, the amount of the loss thereto by ... blank ... on that day ... the following sum, to-wit: actual cash value $36,500. Was that figure, $36,500, in this document when you signed it?

"A.   No.

"Q.   Was it in this document when Mr. O'Neal signed it?

"A.   No.

"Q.   Did you agree that $36,500 was the actual cash value of Mr. Yother's truck?

"A.   No.

"Q.   Why did you sign the bottom document?

"A.   Well, the idea I had and that Mr. O'Neal had on arbitration, we thought that if he and I couldn't agree ... if we picked a third party, we were bound by his appraisal.

"Q.   And you all couldn't agree?

"A.   No.

In Dufresne v. Marine Ins. Co., 157 Minn. 390, 196 N.W. 560, 562 (1923), a case involving facts similar to those of the present case, the Supreme Court of Minnesota stated:

"[S]ince the universal idea of a proper determination of a controverted matter between man and man rests upon a fair hearing of both sides, it would seem to follow that an arbitration without such hearing should not be upheld, unless it satisfactorily is made to appear either that a hearing was not contemplated or else that it was waived. The court expressly found that plaintiff did not waive notice of the hearing, and that he expected and intended to be present and give evidence, but was prevented from attending and presenting his evidence because of lack of notice and knowledge of the meeting of the appraisers. The finding is sustained, we think. The claim cannot be successfully maintained that this is a case where no hearing was contemplated either because of the character of the subject to be appraised or because of the expert qualifications of the appraisers selected. Two of the appraisers had never seen the automobile. It could not be produced. They could therefore act only upon information obtained from others. And naturally, in such a case, the owner who has sustained the loss should have an opportunity to adduce evidence as to the value and qualities of the article."

It is fundamental that one is entitled to notice and an opportunity to be heard where property rights are affected. The insured asserted that right, and it was denied. CIE argues only that the policy provision is silent with respect to notice and, because it is, that the insured was entitled to none. We cannot agree, where the evidence is undisputed that he demanded notice and an opportunity to produce evidence. The foregoing statement by the Minnesota court is applicable under the facts of this case, whether it is considered a hearing held by "appraisers" or an arbitration hearing.

The judgment of the trial court is affirmed.

AFFIRMED.

■ TORBERT, C.J., and MADDOX, JONES and BEATTY, JJ., concur.

* * *

Questions

1. Do parties have a right to be present at their own arbitration proceedings? Does a "full and fair" hearing require an oral evidentiary hearing at all? If not, what does it require?

2. Common notions of due process would require that parties have a right to receive notice, to be present and to give evidence in support of their claims. However, not all arbitration procedures grant parties such rights. Some expressly deny some of these due process elements in the arbitration agreements. Some permit arbitrators to fashion procedures, even procedures that might fall short of an ideal due process norm. Is the right to be

present a right which parties can waive by agreement prior to a dispute arising? Is it a right a party can waive in the course of resolving an existing dispute? Or, is it a right which cannot be waived at all?

3. What is the difference between an appraisal and an arbitration? In *Casualty Indemnity*, did the court ultimately decide whether the contract called for an arbitration or an appraisal proceeding? Does it give any guidance as to how a court can determine whether parties intended to devise an appraisal procedure or an arbitration proceeding? What indicia of intent could a court use? Can it rely on the language the parties use to describe their procedure? Note that Mann's testimony in *Casualty Indemnity* uses the term "arbitration" and "appraisal" interchangeably in the same sentence. If the language of the principals is not dispositive, what other evidence could a court use to determine intent?

4. Can a court determine whether the parties' agreement called for an appraisal or an arbitration by looking at the type of procedure the parties impliedly set forth? Or, should it make a determination on the basis of the procedural consequences that follow from the particular label they select? In this case, is there a problem of circularity?

5. The court in *Casualty Indemnity* says that the distinctive feature of an appraisal proceeding that justifies the lack of an evidentiary hearing is that it relies on the expertise of the decision-making. But we have seen that one of the primary reasons that parties chose arbitration, and an important rationale for judicial delegation to arbitration, is the expertise of the decision-makers. If it is true that both arbitration and appraisal proceedings are chosen for the decision-maker's expertise, then why is a hearing required in the former case and not in the latter?

* * *

4.   RIGHT TO COUNSEL

Mikel v. Scharf

444 N.Y.S.2d 690 (N.Y.App.Div.1981).

MEMORANDUM BY THE COURT.

In a proceeding to confirm an arbitration award made by a religious tribunal, in which proceeding respondents cross-petitioned to vacate the award, petitioner appeals from a judgment of the Supreme Court, Kings County, dated October 16, 1980, 105 Misc.2d 548, 432 N.Y.S.2d 602, that denied the petition, granted the cross petition and vacated the award.

Judgment affirmed, with costs.

CPLR 7506 (subd. [c]) provides, as here relevant, that the parties at an arbitration hearing are "entitled to be heard, to present evidence and to cross-examine witnesses." Furthermore, "[a] party has the right to be represented by an attorney * * * [and t]his right may not be waived" (CPLR 7506, subd. [d]).

Proper procedure was not followed by the religious tribunal which rendered the subject award and that failure is fatal to confirmation of the award (see CPLR 7511, subd. [b], par. 1, cl. [iv]). The tribunal only permitted respondents' attorney to address it after considerable pleading on the part of respondent Asher Scharf and, even then, the attorney was not permitted to introduce evidence or to cross-examine witnesses, despite his attempts to do so. Furthermore, when respondents were notified of a second meeting of the tribunal, they were expressly told not to bring their attorney. The tribunal could not preclude that representation nor deny respondents the right to present evidence and the right to cross-examine (see CPLR 7506). This failure to observe statutory procedure was prejudicial to the respondents. Accordingly, the award was properly vacated.

We have examined petitioner's remaining contentions and find them to be without merit.

* * *

Outdoor Services, Inc. v. Pabagold, Inc.

185 Cal.App.3d 676, 230 Cal.Rptr. 73 (Cal.App.1986).

■ BARRY-DEAL, ASSOCIATE JUSTICE.

BACKGROUND

In March 1981, Pabagold entered into a written contract with Mediasmith, by which Mediasmith agreed to plan and place an advertising campaign for Pabagold's product, Hawaiian Gold Pabatan suntan lotion. The contract authorized Mediasmith to enter into contracts with third parties in order to effectuate the advertising program and to make timely payments to those third parties for goods and services for Pabagold's account. Pabagold was to be fully responsible to Mediasmith for all authorized expenditures. Pabagold agreed to pay Mediasmith's fee for services, including agreed-upon special services and out-of-pocket expenses. The contract contained a provision for the recovery of attorney's fees and costs incurred in enforcing the agreement, as well as a clause that any dispute arising under the contract would be settled by arbitration.

In April 1981, Mediasmith entered into an oral contract with Outdoor Services, by which Outdoor Services agreed to purchase outdoor advertising space for Pabagold's account in exchange for a 5 percent commission on the gross billings for the advertising placements. As required by the contract, Mediasmith provided Pabagold with a written media estimate for the outdoor advertising, which was signed and authorized by Pabagold's vice president, Frank T. Fitzsimmons, Jr. Outdoor Services was not mentioned on the estimate.

Outdoor Services purchased from billboard advertisers $187,244.60 worth of posting and maintenance of outdoor advertising displays and earned $8,545.42 in commissions. Upon Outdoor Services' demand upon Mediasmith for payment, Mediasmith requested payment from Pabagold. Pabagold failed to pay Mediasmith, which in turn did not pay Outdoor Services. Certain outdoor advertising companies began claiming independent liability on the part of Outdoor Services.

Mediasmith filed a complaint for breach of contract against Pabagold in San Francisco Superior Court in July 1981 and on three occasions unsuccessfully sought a writ of attachment against Pabagold. Thereafter, in November 1981, Gannett, one of the outdoor billboard companies with whom Outdoor Services had placed advertising pursuant to its contract with Mediasmith, filed a complaint against Outdoor Services.

On November 20, 1981, Outdoor Services filed a demand against Pabagold with the American Arbitration Association for arbitration as a third party beneficiary of the Pabagold–Mediasmith contract. Mediasmith, on December 14, 1981, filed a cross-demand with the American Arbitration Association for arbitration against Pabagold. On January 5, 1982, Outdoor Services filed an answer and a cross-complaint against Mediasmith and Pabagold in the Gannett action.

The American Arbitration Association granted jurisdiction over the arbitration between Mediasmith and Pabagold based on the arbitration clause contained in their contract, but required Outdoor Services to get either the consent of the parties to the arbitration or a court order as to the ability of Outdoor Services to participate in the arbitration. Pabagold refused its consent, but on March 22, 1982, Outdoor Services' petition to compel arbitration was granted by the San Francisco Superior Court.

On May 26, 1982, counsel for Pabagold failed to appear at a duly noticed prehearing conference at which the parties were to have set a hearing date for the arbitration. On the following day, Pabagold's counsel requested a continuance, and the arbitration was continued to September 1982. Pabagold's counsel again failed to appear at a duly noticed prearbitration conference on August 27, 1982.

On September 1, 1982, officers of Pabagold informed Outdoor Services that Pabagold would represent itself at the arbitration hearing. No mention was made that Pabagold was seeking new counsel. On September 6, Pabagold requested and obtained from all counsel a stipulation to continue the arbitration one day to September 8. However, on September 8, Pabagold appeared and requested a 60–day continuance in order to obtain counsel. The arbitrator denied the request, stating that Pabagold's conduct did not entitle it to a continuance.

On September 16, after the hearing had commenced, the arbitrator granted a continuance until October 25 because Stuart G. Sall, one of Pabagold's officers who was representing Pabagold at the arbitration, was experiencing health problems. The arbitrator rendered his decision in favor of Outdoor Services on November 11. On January 21, 1983, an order confirming arbitration award and a judgment were entered. This appeal followed.

DISCUSSION

* * *

[The court held that Outdoor Services was entitled to enforce the arbitration clause as a third-party beneficiary and that Outdoor Services did not waive the right to arbitrate.]

Denial of Continuance

Pabagold lastly contends that the judgment should be vacated because the arbitrator refused to continue the hearing so that Pabagold could seek new counsel. The contention lacks merit.

A party to an arbitration has the right to be represented by counsel at any arbitration proceeding. (Code Civ.Proc., § 1282.4.) The court shall vacate an arbitration award if the rights of a party were substantially prejudiced by the refusal of the arbitrators to postpone the hearing upon sufficient cause being shown therefor. (Code Civ.Proc., § 1286.2, subd. (e).)

Pabagold argues that because its counsel announced his refusal to proceed on the eve of the arbitration proceeding, Pabagold should have been granted a continuance to secure new counsel.

Contrary to appellant's assertion, there is no due process right to be represented by counsel at arbitration. (Horn v. Gurewitz (1968) 261 Cal. App.2d 255, 262, 67 Cal.Rptr. 791.) Additionally, Pabagold has failed to show sufficient cause for postponing the hearing. As early as January 26, 1982, Pabagold's counsel failed to appear at duly noticed depositions. Counsel also did not attend the prearbitration conference on May 26, 1982. However, on May 27, 1982, Pabagold's counsel requested a continuance of the arbitration scheduled for June 7, 1982. The arbitration was continued to September 7, 1982. Counsel again failed to appear at the August 27, 1982, prearbitration conference.

On September 1, 1982, Pabagold informed Outdoor Services that it would represent itself at the hearing. On September 6, 1982, Pabagold requested and obtained a stipulation by all parties to continue the arbitration for one day to September 8. On September 8, Pabagold appeared and requested a 60–day continuance to obtain new counsel. The arbitrator denied the request.

Any problems that Pabagold had with its counsel predate by several months the September arbitration. Pabagold had ample time to obtain other representation. Therefore, the arbitrator properly denied the request for a continuance.

Pabagold's lack of diligence distinguishes this case from Vann v. Shilleh (1975) 54 Cal.App.3d 192, 126 Cal.Rptr. 401. In that case, the appellant's counsel withdrew on the eve of trial because his client rejected a negotiated settlement. (Id., at p. 197.) This court held that the trial court abused its discretion in denying the appellant's motion for continuance to retain an attorney because counsel had improperly abandoned his client without advance warning. (Id., at pp. 196–197.)

Here, Pabagold was well aware that its counsel had not been diligent. Pabagold had ample time to substitute counsel, but failed to do so. Under the circumstances, no continuance was justified. . . .

* * *

Questions

1.   Is there a due process right to have an attorney represent one at an arbitration? Would it violate due process if parties agreed upon an arbitration procedure in which neither one could use an attorney? What if an attorney could be present but was not permitted to speak to the arbitration panel or to question witnesses?

2.   Would it violate due process if an arbitrator declared that no attorney shall be present in a hearing she is conducting?

* * *

5.   PROVISIONAL REMEDIES

In disputes that are scheduled for arbitration, as with disputes pending in a court, one party may be concerned that while the case is pending an intervening event, such as the dissipation of the respondent's assents, may render any award in their favor ineffectual. While some arbitration procedures permit interim remedies to issue, there remains a danger that assets may be dissipated before an arbitration panel can be constituted. One response to this concern has been for parties to an arbitration to apply to a court to obtain preliminary relief such as an injunction or other provisional remedy pending the arbitration. Typically parties ask the court for an injunction to maintain the *status quo* pending the ultimate outcome of the dispute at arbitration. Courts are divided over the question of whether such an injunction may issue under the Federal Arbitration Act, as the cases below illustrate.

Merrill Lynch, Pierce, Fenner & Smith, Inc. v. Hovey

726 F.2d 1286(8th Cir.1984).

■ LAY, CHIEF JUDGE.

Merrill Lynch, Pierce, Fenner & Smith, Inc. sought injunctive relief against five former employees to prevent their use of Merrill Lynch's records and their solicitation of Merrill Lynch clients. The employees counterclaimed seeking to compel arbitration under the Federal Arbitration

Act, 9 U.S.C. §§ 1–4 (1982). The district court granted injunctive relief and refused to submit the dispute to arbitration. The employees have appealed.

As former account executives with Merrill Lynch, Ivan Hovey, Mary Wichmann, Bruce Markey, and Richard Kadry each signed employment agreements. The agreement provides, inter alia, that certain records "shall remain the property of Merrill Lynch at all times during my employment with Merrill Lynch and after termination of my employment ... with Merrill Lynch" and prohibits former account executives from removing or retaining copies thereof; and it purports to prohibit these employees from "soliciting" clients of Merrill Lynch for one year after the termination of employment. The employees subsequently resigned from Merrill Lynch and joined E.F. Hutton, a competitor. The employees admit that they have retained some limited information entrusted to them by clients whom they had serviced while at Merrill Lynch. Moreover, the employees admit that they have solicited these customers while at E.F. Hutton. (Appellant's Brief at 4). On appeal, we are not addressing whether this constitutes a breach of the employment agreement nor do we address the validity of the clauses that purport to prohibit this conduct. The issue presented on appeal is whether the dispute is subject to arbitration or whether Merrill Lynch may properly proceed in the federal district court.

I.   Arbitrability

We initially address three issues: (1) whether there exists a valid agreement to arbitrate; (2) whether the subject matter of this dispute is covered by the agreement; and if so, (3) whether there has been a breach of the agreement. ...

Merrill Lynch and Hovey, Markey, and Wichmann are members of the NYSE. As members of the NYSE, they have agreed to comply with the NYSE rules, including the dispute resolution procedures detailed in Rule 347. The employees seek arbitration under the Federal Arbitration Act, 9 U.S.C. §§ 3, 4 based on NYSE Rule 347. Rule 347 provides:

> Any controversy between a registered representative and any member or member organization arising out of the employment or termination of employment of such registered representative by and with such member or member organization shall be settled by arbitration, at the instance of any such party, in accordance with the arbitration procedure described elsewhere in these rules.

It is readily apparent that this rule is binding on its signatories and is part of the employment agreement between the employees and Merrill Lynch. ... Moreover, we find that Rule 347 constitutes a valid written agreement to arbitrate which is governed by the Federal Arbitration Act. 9 U.S.C. §§ 1–4 ....

On the other hand, Kadry and Erickson are not members of the NYSE, nor do their employment contracts contain an arbitration agreement. Kadry and Erickson rely primarily on Article VIII of the NYSE Constitution to support their claim for arbitration. Article VIII allows nonmembers to compel arbitration of any controversy "arising out of the business" of a member.[7] Merrill Lynch contends that the employees' reliance on Article VIII is misplaced. Merrill Lynch urges that Article VIII's reference to "business" reflects that the provision's intention is to allow *customers*, not employees, to compel arbitration. We find, however, that the provision is not so limited. The article of the Constitution reflects the self-regulation of the securities industry, as well as the effort to provide an integrated method of resolving disputes involving the affairs of the NYSE. We find that Article VIII constitutes an agreement to arbitrate, upon which Kadry and Erickson may rely.

In accordance with the Federal Arbitration Act we also find that all of the employees have timely and properly requested arbitration. The remaining issue is whether the arbitration agreement reaches the subject matter of the dispute here. . . .

The district court found that the solicitation and record duplication took place *after* the employment relationship between the parties had been terminated. Employing essentially a temporal analysis, the court concluded that the violations, therefore, could not have "aris[en] out of the employment or termination of employment." On appeal, Merrill Lynch reasserts the contention that only those disputes which occurred during the employment relationship are arbitrable. On the other hand, the employees contend that, although the dispute occurred after their termination, it is still within the scope of the arbitration agreement. Upon analysis of the applicability of the Federal Arbitration Act and the Rules and Constitution of the NYSE, along with a plain reading of the arbitration agreement, we find that the dispute is arbitrable.

Under the Federal Arbitration Act, 9 U.S.C. §§ 1–4 (1982), where the parties have agreed to seek dispute resolution by arbitration, the courts are asked to stay their hand. Moses H. Cone Memorial Hospital v. Mercury Construction Corp., 460 U.S. 1, 103 S.Ct. 927, 74 L.Ed.2d 765 (1983). The scope of the arbitration agreement will be interpreted liberally and "any doubts concerning the scope of arbitrable issues should be resolved in favor of arbitration." Moses H. Cone, 103 S.Ct. at 941 & n. 27; Johnson Controls, 713 F.2d at 373. "[T]he court's function in an action to compel arbitration may not extend beyond ascertaining whether the party seeking arbitration has made a claim which *on its face* is governed by the contract." National R.R. Passenger Corp., 501 F.2d at 427 (emphasis original). The presumption of arbitrability, however, is tempered by the caveat that parties cannot be forced to arbitrate controversies that they have not agreed to submit to arbitration. United Steelworkers of America v. Warrior & Gulf Navigation Co., 363 U.S. 574, 582, 80 S.Ct. 1347, 1352, 4 L.Ed.2d 1409 (1960).

To support its argument that the present dispute is not arbitrable, Merrill Lynch relies primarily on Coudert v. Paine Webber Jackson &

---

7. "Any controversy between parties who are members, . . . member firms . . . and any controversy between a non-member and a member . . . arising out of the business of such member, . . . shall at the instance of any such party, be submitted for arbitration, in accordance with the provisions of the Constitution and the Rules of the Board of Directors." NYSE Const. art. VIII, § 1.

Curtis, 705 F.2d 78 (2d Cir.1983) and the district court opinion in Downey v. Merrill Lynch, Pierce, Fenner & Smith, Inc., No. 83 Civ. 4312 (S.D.N.Y. Aug. 18, 1983), in which the appeal was pending. In Coudert, a divided panel of the Second Circuit held that a dispute involving a defamation claim of a former account executive was not arbitrable where the alleged defamation took place after the account executive had resigned. In Downing, a district court extended this holding to a dispute involving a violation of the solicitation clause after the employee had resigned and joined a competing firm. On appeal, however, the Second Circuit reversed the district court's extension, finding that "a dispute over such a contract term would clearly be arbitrable notwithstanding the time at which the dispute arose." Downing v. Merrill Lynch, Pierce, Fenner & Smith, No. 83–7710 slip op. at 5 (2d Cir. 1984) (remanded to determine whether there was an agreement to arbitrate).

The sole issue in Coudert was the arbitrability under the Rules of the NYSE of a grievance arising out of an employer's allegedly tortious conduct. The majority in Coudert distinguished "grievance[s] *arising after* the termination of the agreement to arbitrate" from grievances that are based on *conditions that arise during* the term of the agreement to arbitrate. 705 F.2d at 81. The former are not arbitrable; the latter, however, are arbitrable regardless of whether the agreement to arbitrate has since ceased. In Coudert, the majority found that the basis of the grievance was the employer's conduct after the termination of the employment relationship and therefore also after the termination of the agreement to arbitrate. Id. at 82. Accordingly, the dispute was not found to be subject to the arbitration agreement. Id. Our case is distinguishable from Coudert and we decline to extend a rigid temporal approach to the determination of arbitrability in the situation before us.

To interpret the arbitration agreement in the manner asserted by Merrill Lynch would require reading the words "arising out of" as synonymous with "during." This interpretation is inconsistent with the words chosen and the intent of the parties. The language of the agreement is broad and the term "arising out of" contemplates that for some controversies the arbitration agreement will survive the employment relationship....

For the reasons discussed, we hold that the present controversy "arise[s] out of the employment or termination of employment." At least as to the construction and applicability of these conditions, we conclude that the arbitration agreement remains viable beyond the employment relationship of the parties.

II. Preliminary Injunction

In addition to determining that the controversy was nonarbitrable, the district court granted a preliminary injunction. We consistently have held that the grant of preliminary relief is within the district court's discretion. Dataphase Systems, Inc. v. C L Systems, Inc., 640 F.2d 109, 114 (8th Cir.1981); Planned Parenthood of Minnesota, Inc. v. Citizens for Community Action, 558 F.2d 861, 866 (8th Cir.1977). In light of our determination that the controversy is arbitrable, however, we find that the issuance of injunctive relief abrogates the intent of the Federal Arbitration Act and consequently was an abuse of discretion. Cf. Merrill Lynch, Pierce, Fenner & Smith, Inc. v. Scott, No. 83–1480 (10th Cir. May 12, 1983) (summary order staying the injunction pending arbitration).

Merrill Lynch urges this court to continue the preliminary injunction during the arbitration procedures. Merrill Lynch asserts that the continuance of the injunction is necessary to avoid irreparable harm and to assure the viability of an adequate remedy at law. The cases cited by Merrill Lynch support the contention that injunctions can be granted to preserve the status quo.[10] However, in view of our determination that the Federal Arbitration Act applies, we decline to pass on these contentions. The parties have not alleged that the contract provides for or contemplates injunctive relief along the lines granted. Accordingly, the Act directs the court to stay the judicial action. 9 U.S.C. § 3.

The congressional intent revealed in the Arbitration Act is to facilitate quick, expeditious arbitration.... Here, the judicial inquiry requisite to determine the propriety of injunctive relief necessarily would inject the court into the merits of issues more appropriately left to the arbitrator. See Prima Paint Corp. v. Flood & Conklin Manufacturing Co., 388 U.S. 395, 87 S.Ct. 1801, 18 L.Ed.2d 1270 (1967) (issue of fraud in inducement of contract was for arbitrator); see also Buffalo Forge Co. v. United Steelworkers of America, AFL–CIO, 428 U.S. 397, 412, 96 S.Ct. 3141, 3149, 49 L.Ed.2d 1022 (1976). In Buffalo Forge, the Court refused to enjoin a strike pending arbitration of the validity of the strike. The Court recognized that sanctioning judicial intervention at this preliminary stage would eviscerate the intent of arbitration agreements. Id. at 412, 96 S.Ct. at 3149.

We find this compelling authority to hold that, where the Arbitration Act is applicable and no qualifying contractual language has been alleged, the district court errs in granting injunctive relief. In doing so, we sustain not only "the plain meaning of the statute but also the unmistakably clear congressional purpose that the arbitration procedure, when selected by the parties to a contract, be speedy and not subject to delay and obstruction in the courts." Prima Paint Corp., 388 U.S. at 404, 87 S.Ct. at 1806.

---

10.   To support its claim for injunctive relief Merrill Lynch relies on Erving v. Virginia Squires Basketball Club, 468 F.2d 1064 (2d Cir.1972). In Erving, the Second Circuit found that the dispute was arbitrable; however, it also granted injunctive relief for the purpose of maintaining the status quo. Id. at 1067. Although Erving does provide some support for Merrill Lynch, the case is distinguishable. First, the employee's contract stipulated that his services were exceptional and unique and that the loss of them to the Squires would be unestimatable and not compensable by damages. In light of these stipulations, the contract expressly provided for injunctive relief, pending completion of the arbitration process. Id. at 1006 n. 1. Second, the issues addressed by the court to determine the propriety of injunctive relief were not the same ones that would ultimately be determinative of the merits of the dispute. In contrast, in our case we do not have such a contract provision and, moreover, the evidentiary foray necessary to satisfy the Dataphase criteria are essentially the same that we have determined are more properly left to arbitration....

For the reasons stated above, we reverse and remand to the district court for proceedings consistent with the determinations here.

* * *

Merrill Lynch, Pierce, Fenner & Smith, Inc. v. Bradley

756 F.2d 1048 (4th Cir.1985).

■ CHAPMAN, CIRCUIT JUDGE:

This expedited appeal involves a dispute between Merrill Lynch, Pierce, Fenner and Smith, Inc. (Merrill Lynch) and one of its former account executives, Kenneth D. Bradley. Merrill Lynch brought this action against Bradley seeking damages as well as injunctive relief to prevent him from using Merrill Lynch's records and soliciting Merrill Lynch's clients. On July 26, 1984, the district court held a hearing on Merrill Lynch's motion for a temporary restraining order and Bradley's motion to stay the trial and compel arbitration pursuant to the Federal Arbitration Act, 9 U.S.C. §§ 1–14 (1982). At the conclusion of the hearing, the district court granted Merrill Lynch a preliminary injunction, denied Bradley's motion to stay the injunction, and ordered expedited arbitration of the parties' dispute. Bradley appeals from the district court's order granting Merrill Lynch a preliminary injunction pending arbitration. 28 U.S.C. § 1292(a)(1). We affirm.

I

On December 16, 1981, Merrill Lynch hired Bradley to serve as an account executive at its office in Newport News, Virginia. At that time Merrill Lynch and Bradley entered into an Account Executive Agreement which provides, inter alia, the following:

1. All records of Merrill Lynch, including the names and addresses of its clients, are and shall remain the property of Merrill Lynch at all times during my employment with Merrill Lynch and after termination for any reason of my employment with Merrill Lynch, and that none of such records or any part of them is to be removed from the premises of Merrill Lynch either in original form or in duplicated or copied form, and that the names, addresses, and other facts in such records are not to be transmitted verbally except in the ordinary course of conducting business for Merrill Lynch.

2. In the event of termination of my services with Merrill Lynch for any reason, I will not solicit any of the clients of Merrill Lynch whom I served or whose names became known to me while in the employ of Merrill Lynch in any community or city served by the office of Merrill Lynch, or any subsidiary thereof, at which I was employed at any time for a period of one year from the date of termination of my employment. In the event that any of the provisions contained in this paragraph and/or paragraph (1) above are violated I understand that I will be liable to Merrill Lynch for any damage caused thereby.

The Account Executive Agreement also provides that "any controversy between myself [Bradley] and Merrill Lynch arising out of my employment, or the termination of my employment with Merrill Lynch for any reason whatsoever shall be settled by arbitration. . . ." In addition, Bradley was required to sign New York Stock Exchange Form U–4 when he registered with the Exchange and began his employment at Merrill Lynch. Like his employment agreement, this form requires that any controversy between Bradley and any member organization of the New York Stock Exchange shall be settled by arbitration. Finally, both Rule 347 of the Rules of the New York Stock Exchange and Article VIII, Section One of the Exchange Constitution provide that all controversies between members of the Exchange arising out of the business of the members shall be settled by arbitration in accordance with the Rules of the New York Stock Exchange.

At approximately 4:00 p.m. on Friday, July 20, 1984, Bradley tendered his resignation to Merrill Lynch and announced that he had accepted a position with Prudential–Bache Securities, Inc. at its office in Virginia Beach, Virginia. Merrill Lynch alleges that as early as the day following his resignation Bradley telephoned most or all of his Merrill Lynch customers and urged them to transfer their accounts from Merrill Lynch to Prudential–Bache. Merrill Lynch learned of Bradley's actions and filed suit on Monday, July 23, 1984, alleging breach of contract, breach of fiduciary duty, and violation of Va.Code § 18.2–499.

. . . The district court's preliminary injunction prohibits Bradley from soliciting any customers whom he had serviced or learned about while employed by Merrill Lynch. The injunction further prohibits Bradley from participating in the servicing of these customers by Prudential–Bache, including any referrals to other personnel of Prudential–Bache. At the request of Bradley's counsel, however, the district court's order was modified to delete the requirement that the New York Stock Exchange conduct arbitration in an expedited fashion.

II

Merrill Lynch and Bradley both agree that the dispute between them is subject to mandatory arbitration and that Bradley is not in default in proceeding with arbitration. Thus, the principal issue on appeal is whether § 3 of the Federal Arbitration Act, 9 U.S.C. § 3 (1982), absolutely precludes a district court from granting one party a preliminary injunction to preserve the status quo pending the arbitration of the parties' dispute.

Bradley argues that the district court abused its discretion in granting Merrill Lynch a preliminary injunction because § 3 precludes a court from considering the merits of a controversy when the dispute is subject to mandatory arbitration. Bradley cites two recent decisions to support his argument. Merrill Lynch, Pierce, Fenner & Smith, Inc. v. Hovey, 726 F.2d 1286 (8th Cir.1984); Merrill Lynch, Pierce, Fenner & Smith, Inc. v. Scott, No. 83–1480 (10th Cir. May 12, 1983). . . .

In Hovey the Eighth Circuit held that § 3 precludes a court from granting Merrill Lynch a preliminary injunction against its former account executives pending arbitration. The court stated that "where the Arbitration Act is applicable and no qualifying contractual language has been alleged, the district court errs in granting injunctive relief." 726 F.2d at 1292. In Scott the Tenth Circuit vacated, by order and without formal written opinion, a preliminary injunction which the district court had granted pending arbitration. Nevertheless, for the reasons that follow, we decline to follow Hovey and Scott and instead hold that, under certain circumstances, a district court has the discretion to grant one party a preliminary injunction to preserve the status quo pending the arbitration of the parties' dispute.

The starting point for our inquiry, of course, is the language of § 3:

> If any suit or proceeding be brought in any of the courts of the United States upon any issue referable to arbitration under an agreement in writing for such arbitration, *the court in which such suit is pending*, upon being satisfied that the issue involved in such suit or proceeding is referable to arbitration under such an agreement, *shall on application of one of the parties stay the trial of the action* until such arbitration has been had in accordance with the terms of the agreement, providing the applicant for the stay is not in default in proceeding with such arbitration.

9 U.S.C. § 3 (emphasis added). Section 3 does not contain a clear command abrogating the equitable power of district courts to enter preliminary injunctions to preserve the status quo pending arbitration. Instead, § 3 states only that the court shall stay the "trial of the action"; it does not mention preliminary injunctions or other pre-trial proceedings. Certainly Congress knows how to draft a statute which addresses all actions within the judicial power.[3] Furthermore, nothing in the statute's legislative history suggests that the word "trial" should be given a meaning other than its common and ordinary usage: the ultimate resolution of the dispute on the merits. See Senate Rep. No. 536, 68th Cong., 1st Sess. (1924); H.R.Rep. No. 96, 68th Cong., 1st Sess. (1924).

We do not believe that Congress would have enacted a statute intended to have the sweeping effect of stripping the federal judiciary of its equitable powers in all arbitrable commercial disputes without undertaking a comprehensive discussion and evaluation of the statute's effect. Accordingly, we conclude that the language of § 3 does not preclude a district court from granting one party a preliminary injunction to preserve the status quo pending arbitration.

---

3. For example, 28 U.S.C. § 2283 provides:

> A court of the United States may not grant an injunction to stay *proceedings* in a State court except as expressly authorized by Act of Congress, or where necessary in aid of its jurisdiction, or to protect or effectuate its judgments.

(emphasis added). See also 11 U.S.C. § 362(a)(1) (filing of bankruptcy petition operates as a stay of any "judicial, administrative, or other proceeding against the debtor").

Our interpretation of § 3 is not inconsistent with this Court's decision in In re Mercury Construction Corp., 656 F.2d 933 (4th Cir.1981) (en banc), aff'd sub nom. Moses H. Cone Memorial Hospital v. Mercury Construction Corp., 460 U.S. 1, 103 S.Ct. 927, 74 L.Ed.2d 765 (1983). Bradley relies upon an isolated phrase in In re Mercury Construction Corp. to support his argument that § 3 requires the stay of "all proceedings" pending arbitration. See 656 F.2d at 939 ("Section 3 requires a stay of all proceedings until such arbitration has been had in accordance with the terms of the agreement ..."). This reliance is misplaced, however, because that decision did not turn in any way on the meaning of the term "trial" as used in § 3. Rather, In re Mercury Construction Corp. involved the unrelated question of whether a federal court may compel arbitration under § 4 even though one of the parties has instituted a state court action. 656 F.2d at 938. Thus, the "all proceedings" language is dicta....

This Court's decisions in Lever Brothers Co. v. International Chemical Workers Union, Local 217, 554 F.2d 115 (4th Cir.1976), and Drivers, Chauffeurs, Warehousemen & Helpers Teamsters Local Union No. 71 v. Akers Motor Lines, Inc., 582 F.2d 1336 (4th Cir.1978), provide additional support for our decision here....

In Lever Brothers this court adopted the following standard for preliminary injunctions of labor disputes subject to mandatory arbitration:

> An injunction to preserve the status quo pending arbitration may be issued either against a company or against a union in an appropriate Boys Markets case where it is necessary to prevent conduct by the party enjoined from rendering the arbitral process a hollow formality in those instances where, as here, the arbitral award when rendered could not return the parties substantially to the status quo ante.

554 F.2d at 123. Similarly, in Akers Motor Lines we stated that if the enjoined conduct would render the arbitration process a "hollow formality," the clear language of the Norris–LaGuardia Act must give way to the congressional policy favoring arbitration. 582 F.2d at 1341.

We think the Lever Brothers—Akers Motor Lines standard represents a sound approach for determining whether a district court has abused its discretion in granting a preliminary injunction pending arbitration. Accordingly, we hold that where a dispute is subject to mandatory arbitration under the Federal Arbitration Act, a district court has the discretion to grant a preliminary injunction to preserve the status quo pending the arbitration of the parties' dispute if the enjoined conduct would render that process a "hollow formality." The arbitration process would be a hollow formality where "the arbitral award when rendered could not return the parties substantially to the status quo ante." Lever Brothers, 554 F.2d at 123. The instant case is just such a case.

We think that our decision will further, not frustrate, the policies underlying the Federal Arbitration Act. In this case preliminary injunctive relief pending arbitration furthers congressional policy by ensuring that the dispute resolution would be a meaningful process because, without such an injunction, Bradley's conduct might irreversibly alter the status quo. When an account executive breaches his employment contract by soliciting his former employer's customers, a nonsolicitation clause requires immediate application to have any effect. An injunction even a few days after solicitation has begun is unsatisfactory because the damage is done. The customers cannot be "unsolicited." It may be impossible for the arbitral award to return the parties substantially to the status quo ante because the prevailing party's damages may be too speculative.

We cannot accept Bradley's argument that preliminary injunctions support the congressional policy favoring arbitration of labor disputes but undermine the congressional policy favoring arbitration of commercial and maritime matters. Nor can we accept Bradley's argument that the district court's preliminary injunction will prejudice the arbitrator's subsequent decision on the merits. The arbitrators are sworn to render a decision based solely upon the evidence presented to them. We must assume that the arbitrators will perform their task conscientiously. Furthermore, we do not believe that Congress intended § 3 to tie a district court's hands while one party, pending the arbitration of the parties' dispute, deliberately and irreversibly altered the status quo and thereby deprived the other party of a meaningful arbitration process. . . .

III

The final issue is whether the district court abused its discretion in granting the injunction. Under the balance of hardship test the district court must consider, in "flexible interplay," the following four factors in determining whether to issue a preliminary injunction: (1) the likelihood of irreparable harm to the plaintiff without the injunction; (2) the likelihood of harm to the defendant with an injunction; (3) the plaintiff's likelihood of success on the merits; and (4) the public interest. Blackwelder Furniture Co. v. Seilig Manufacturing Co., 550 F.2d 189, 193–96 (4th Cir.1977). Under this test the district court must first compare the likelihood of irreparable harm to the plaintiff with the potential harm the defendant will experience from the grant of preliminary injunctive relief. If the balance of hardship tips decidedly in the plaintiff's favor, then the district court may grant a preliminary injunction if it determines that the dispute presents a serious issue for litigation and that the injunction will serve the public interest. Id. at 194–95. Accord, North Carolina State Ports Authority v. Dart Containerline Co., 592 F.2d 749, 750 (4th Cir.1979). Because these determinations involve findings of fact, a district court's order granting preliminary injunctive relief may be reversed only if an abuse of discretion is shown. West Virginia Highlands Conservancy v. Island Creek Coal Co., 441 F.2d 232, 235 (4th Cir.1971); Singleton v. Anson County Board of Education, 387 F.2d 349, 350 (4th Cir.1967).

We are unable to conclude that the district court abused its discretion in granting a preliminary injunction pending arbitration. We think that the district court was within its discretion in concluding that the balance of hardship test tips decidedly in Merrill Lynch's favor because Bradley did not establish that the preliminary injunction pending expedited arbitration would cause him harm and because Merrill Lynch faced irreparable, non-compensable harm in the loss of its customers. This court has recognized that "irreparability of harm includes the 'impossibility of ascertaining with any accuracy the extent of the loss.' " Blackwelder Furniture Co., 550 2d at 197 (quoting Foundry Services Inc. v. Beneflux Corp., 206 F.2d 214, 216 (2d Cir.1953)). Thus, the district court implicitly found that arbitration of this dispute would be a hollow formality absent preliminary relief. Accordingly, the order of the district court is AFFIRMED.

* * *

Note on Criteria for Imposing Provisional Remedies Pending Arbitration

The Fourth Circuit's position in *Merrill Lynch, et. al. v. Bradley*, has subsequently been adopted by the First, Second, Third, Seventh, Ninth and Tenth Circuits. In the circuits that have held that district courts can grant preliminary injunctions to maintain the *status quo* pending arbitration, the courts must determine what criteria justify the granting of such an injunction. The conventional factors a court considers in ruling on an application for a preliminary injunction include probability of success on the merits, irreparable harm, a balance of equities favoring the moving party, and the impact of the injunction on the public interest. Often these factors are formulated somewhat differently, or assigned different weights by different courts. For example, the Fifth Circuit has a four factor test in which the movant must show:

> (1) a substantial likelihood of prevailing on the merits; (2) a substantial threat of irreparable harm if not granted (3) that the threatened injury outweighs any damage that the injunction might cause the defendant; and (4) that the injunction will not disserve the public interest.

Sunbeam Products, Inc. v. West Bend Co., 123 F.3d 246 (5th Cir.1997). In contrast, the Ninth Circuit determines whether to issue a preliminary injunction by considering:

> (1) the likelihood of the moving party's success on the merits; (2) the possibility of irreparable injury to the moving party if relief is not granted; (3) the extent to which the balance of hardships favors the respective parties; and (4) in certain cases, whether the public interest will be advanced by granting the preliminary relief.

Maui Land & Pineapple Co. v. Occidental Chemical Corp., 24 F.Supp.2d 1083 (D.Haw. 1998). The Second Circuit departs significantly from the other circuits. It applies a two-prong test alternative test to determine whether to issue a preliminary injunction:

> It is by this time black-letter law that the party seeking a preliminary injunction must establish that: (1) absent injunctive relief, it will suffer an irreparable injury; and (2) *either* (a) a likelihood of success on the

merits *or* (b) sufficiently serious questions going to the merits to make them a fair ground for litigation and the balance of hardships tips in favor of the movant.

Alliance Bond Fund, Inc. v. Grupo Mexicano de Desarrollo, S.A., 143 F.3d 688, 696 (2d Cir.1998) (citing *Jackson Dairy v. H.P. Hood & Sons*, 596 F.2d 70, 72 (2d Cir.1979) (emphasis supplied).

Several problems emerge when courts attempt to adapt the conventional factors governing preliminary injunctions to an injunction that is sought prior to an arbitration. One is that it is often difficult for a court to determine whether or not an injunction should issue without inquiring into the merits of the case. Another is that there is a danger that a court will introduce a degree of delay and formality into the proceedings that the choice of the arbitral forum was designed to avoid. An even more troubling question is whether it is possible for a court to make such a determination without substituting a judicial decision on the merits for the arbitral decision that the parties have contracted for. The difficulties involved in deciding whether to grant a preliminary injunction are illustrated in the *Performance Unlimited v. Questar Publisher* case that follows:

* * *

Performance Unlimited, Inc. v. Questar Publishers, Inc.
52 F.3d 1373 (6th Cir. 1995).

■ MILBURN, CIRCUIT JUDGE.

This is a case of first impression in this circuit involving the question of whether a district court can issue a preliminary injunction under § 3 of the Federal Arbitration Act, 9 U.S.C. § 3 (1982), when the parties to this action have agreed that arbitration "shall be the sole and exclusive remedy for resolving any disputes between the parties arising out of or involving [the] Agreement" sued upon. Plaintiff Performance Unlimited, Inc. ("Performance") appeals the district court's order denying its motion for a preliminary injunction, filed pursuant to 28 U.S.C. §§ 1332(a)(1), 2201, and 2202, which would have required defendant Questar Publishers, Inc. ("Questar") to pay royalties to Performance while their contract dispute was resolved in arbitration. On appeal, the issues are (1) whether the district court erred in finding that it was precluded from issuing a preliminary injunction because of the mandatory arbitration provision in the parties' licensing agreement and (2) whether the district court erred in finding that Performance did not satisfy the four factors considered in its decision to grant or deny a preliminary injunction. For the reasons that follow, we reverse and remand.

I.

A.

This is an action for breach of contract, for a declaration of the parties' contractual rights, and for a preliminary injunction arising from the nonpayment of royalties pursuant to a licensing agreement between Performance and Questar. The royalties which are at the core of the parties dispute stem from the publication of The Beginner's Bible, a compilation of children's bible stories.

Don Wise, the president of Performance, developed the idea of publishing a series of children's bible stories, illustrated with drawings that would appeal to small children and aimed toward beginning readers. This concept was developed into a series of bible story books which were written by Karyn Henley and were sold under the name Dovetales. James R. Leininger invested in Performance in order to develop and promote the Dovetales books.

Eventually, however, Wise and Leininger agreed to separate their activities. As a result, Leininger received ownership of the copyrights and trademarks in the Dovetales product. Leininger licensed the rights to publish the Dovetales stories to Performance. In turn, Wise entered into a license agreement, a sublicense, with Questar to publish a book containing all of the original Dovetales stories along with some additional stories written by Karyn Henley, titled The Beginner's Bible. The license agreement between Performance and Questar is dated June 22, 1989, and is the subject of this action.

Pursuant to the license agreement, Questar published and began to sell The Beginner's Bible. Further, the license agreement obligated Questar to make semi-annual royalty payments to Performance based upon the sales of The Beginner's Bible. Questar regularly made the royalty payments to Performance until July of 1994. However, in a letter, dated July 28, 1994, Questar informed Performance that Performance had breached the license agreement. Furthermore, Questar refused to pay the accrued royalties to Performance, indicating in its letter that it wished to initiate a "mediation/arbitration process pursuant to paragraph 11 of the [license] agreement." J.A. 20. Instead, on July 29, 1994, Questar opened an account, the "Beginner's Bible Royalty Escrow Account," at the United States National Bank of Oregon in Sisters, Oregon, and deposited $184,484.94, the accrued royalties, into that account. J.A. 65.

The license agreement between Questar and Performance includes a provision for resolution of disputes. Paragraph 11 of the agreement provides in relevant part:

> The Licensor [Performance] and the Publisher [Questar] agree that God, In His Word, forbids Christians to bring lawsuits against other Christians in secular courts of law ... and that God desires Christians to be reconciled to one another when disputes of any nature arise between them....

> [I]n their resolution of any disputes that may arise under this Agreement, each party agrees that the provisions for mediation and arbitration set forth below shall be the sole and exclusive remedy for resolving any disputes between the parties arising out of or involving this Agreement.

It is further agreed that the Licensor and the Publisher hereby waive whatever right they might otherwise have to maintain a lawsuit-against the other in a secular court of law, on any disputes arising out of or involving this Agreement.

In the event of such a dispute, the Licensor and the Publisher agree to take the following steps, in the order indicated, until such a dispute is resolved:

(1) the Licensor and the Publisher shall meet together, pray together, and purpose to be reconciled. . . .

(2) The Licensor and the Publisher shall invite other witnesses, who may have knowledge of the actual facts of the dispute or whose knowledge would be helpful in resolving the dispute, to meet together with both parties, to pray together, and to purpose to be reconciled. . . .

(3) Both the Licensor and the Publisher shall each appoint one person as a Mediator; these two persons chosen shall then appoint a third Mediator. The three Mediators shall together determine the process of mediation, to which the Licensor and the Publisher agree to comply, and shall be free to act as Arbitrators, to whose authority the Licensor and the Publisher agree to submit. The three Mediators shall also determine to what degree the Licensor and the Publisher shall be liable for all costs related to the mediation process. . . .

B.

On August 10, 1994, Performance filed a complaint in district court, asserting a claim of breach of contract based upon Questar's refusal to pay accrued royalties due and owing to Performance pursuant to the licensing agreement between the parties and seeking a declaration of the parties' rights under the agreement. At the same time that it filed its complaint, Performance filed a motion for a preliminary injunction, seeking to enjoin Questar from refusing to pay the royalties due and owing to Performance under the license agreement and directing that Questar pay the royalties to Performance as provided in the agreement. Questar filed a brief in opposition to the motion for a preliminary injunction on August 24, 1994.

Pursuant to the agreement of the parties, the motion for a preliminary injunction was submitted to the district court based upon the documentary evidence in the record. Oral argument on the motion was held before the district court on August 25, 1994; however, the parties presented no testimonial evidence to the district court at that time.

On September 2, 1992, the district court denied Performance's motion for a preliminary injunction. Specifically, in denying Performance's motion, the district court found that it need not address the issue of whether Performance was likely to succeed on the merits of its claim that Questar breached the license agreement, "because the agreement has a mandatory arbitration provision." J.A. 26. The district court further concluded that it should not involve itself in the merits of a dispute when the parties, in their agreement, have clearly provided that arbitration is the sole and exclusive means to remedy disputes....

In summary, the Court does not feel that Performance is likely to succeed on the merits given the mandatory arbitration provision in the agreement.

J.A. 27–28.

Furthermore, the district court stated that while it

realize[d] that the royalties [provided for in the licensing agreement] are necessary for the operation of Performance's business, ... because Performance has come to the Court with "unclean hands," the Court concludes it should not grant Performance's request for equitable relief even though Performance's business might suffer irreparable harm.

J.A. 28–29. This timely appeal followed.

II.

A.

Performance argues that the district court erred in finding that it could not issue injunctive relief because of the mandatory mediation/arbitration provision in the agreement between the parties. Performance asserts that the district court's refusal to grant injunctive relief because of the mandatory arbitration provision is contrary to the rule adopted by the majority of the United States Circuit Courts of Appeals. Performance further asserts that injunctive relief is appropriate in this case to preserve the status quo pending the arbitration of the parties' dispute, because absent injunctive relief Performance will suffer irreparable harm; namely, the collapse of its business, which will render the process of arbitration a hollow and meaningless formality.

In its opinion, the district court acknowledged that this issue was one of first impression in the Sixth Circuit. The district court further acknowledged that a number of other Circuits have held that district courts may issue injunctive relief under appropriate circumstances pending arbitration. Nevertheless, the district court rejected that approach, concluding instead "that it should not involve itself in the merits of a dispute when the parties, in their agreement, have clearly provided that arbitration is the sole and exclusive means to remedy disputes." J.A. 27–18.

... The issue of whether a district court has subject matter jurisdiction to entertain a motion for preliminary injunctive relief in an arbitrable dispute is an issue of first impression in this circuit. Moreover, the issue of "[w]hether the Arbitration Act deprives the district court of subject matter jurisdiction to enter preliminary injunctive relief is an issue of law subject to plenary review." Ortho Pharmaceutical Corp. v. Amgen, Inc., 882 F.2d 806, 812 n. 6 (3d Cir.1989).

... After a thorough review of the relevant case law, we adopt the reasoning of the First, Second, Third, Fourth, Seventh, and arguably the

Ninth, Circuits and hold that in a dispute subject to mandatory arbitration under the Federal Arbitration Act, a district court has subject matter jurisdiction under § 3 of the Act to grant preliminary injunctive relief provided that the party seeking the relief satisfies the four criteria which are prerequisites to the grant of such relief. We further conclude that a grant of preliminary injunctive relief pending arbitration is particularly appropriate and furthers the Congressional purpose behind the Federal Arbitration Act, where the withholding of injunctive relief would render the process of arbitration meaningless or a hollow formality because an arbitral award, at the time it was rendered, " 'could not return the parties substantially to the status quo ante.' "Bradley, 756 F.2d at 1053 (quoting Lever Bros. Co. v. International Chemical Workers Union, Local 217, 554 F.2d 115, 123 (4th Cir.1976)).

Accordingly, we hold that the district court erred as a matter of law when it found that it could not enter preliminary injunctive relief in this case because the dispute between the parties was the subject of mandatory arbitration.

B.

Performance next argues that the district court erred in finding that it did not satisfy the four factors necessary for the grant of a preliminary injunction. The four factors are: (1) the likelihood of the plaintiff's success on the merits; (2) whether the injunction will save the plaintiff from irreparable injury; (3) whether the injunction would harm others; and (4) whether the public interest would be served. ... "A district court is required to make specific findings concerning each of the four factors, unless fewer are dispositive of the issue." Id. Moreover, the four factors are not prerequisites to be met, but rather must be balanced as part of a decision to grant or deny injunctive relief. In re DeLorean, 755 F.2d at 1229.

As was noted above, our review of this issue is limited to determining if the district court abused its discretion in denying preliminary relief. Gaston Drugs, 823 F.2d at 988. " 'A district court abuses its discretion when it relies on clearly erroneous findings of fact, or when it improperly applies the law or uses an erroneous legal standard.' "Id. (quoting Christian Schmidt Brewing Co, 753 F.2d at 1356). We review the district court's factual findings under a clearly erroneous standard, and its legal conclusions de novo. City of Mansfield, 866 F.2d at 166. Furthermore, in a case such a this, where "the district court's decision was made on the basis of a paper record, without a evidentiary hearing, we are in as good a position as the district judge to determine the propriety of granting a preliminary injunction." Roso–Lino, 749 F.2d at 125.

First, Performance argues that it has established that it would suffer irreparable injury in the absence of injunctive relief; namely, that it has shown that in the absence of royalty payments from Questar, its business would be destroyed or driven into insolvency. Performance further argues that this irreparable injury is the type of irreparable injury which would render the arbitration process either meaningless or a hollow formality because a decision from the arbitrator ordering Questar to pay the accrued royalties from The Beginner's Bible to Performance could not return Performance to the status quo ante if its business were destroyed.

In that regard, the record contains the affidavit of Jerry Wise, Performance's president dated August 9, 1994, in which Wise states that "[t]he license agreement between Performance Unlimited and Questar is by far the single most significant royalty-producing license agreement that Performance Unlimited has, and royalties received from the license constitute the single largest amount of royalty income received by Performance Unlimited yearly." J.A. 38. Wise further stated that "[i]f Questar does not pay its accrued royalties, Performance Unlimited will not be able to meet payroll, pay federal withholding taxes, pay vendors, pay royalties owed to licensees, or indeed continue to operate more than another two to three weeks." J.A. 40. The record also contains the affidavit of Richard Hilicki, Performance's Vice President of Finance, dated August 9, 1994, in which Hilicki stated that the accrued royalties of $184,000 that Questar had declined to pay to Performance, "constitute[d] in excess of 60% of the total projected revenues of Performance Unlimited for the second half of 1994." J.A. 42. Hilicki also stated that "[b]ecause of Questar's refusal to pay its royalties, Performance Unlimited has been unable to pay many of its vendors in a timely fashion ..." and that "Performance Unlimited will be unable to secure additional supplies and materials from its vendors." J.A. 43. Finally, Hilicki stated that Questar was holding approximately $45,000 in accrued royalties in addition to the $184,000 which it had deposited into the escrow account, and that royalties on The Beginner's Bible were accruing at a rate of about $30,000 to $35,000 per month. J.A. 44.

Although Questar asserts that Performance's claims of irreparable injury are pretextual, the statements of Wise and Hilicki are the only evidence of record concerning the financial condition of Performance. Accordingly, we conclude that the uncontradicted statements of Wise and Hilicki dated August 4, 1994 establish that in the absence of injunctive relief, i.e., without the payment of royalties by Questar, Performance will be unable to operate its business and the business will suffer economic collapse or insolvency....

Moreover, the district court acknowledged as much in its opinion when it stated:

> Performance notes that the $184,000 in royalties is its largest source of revenue and without the royalties, in cannot continue to operate its business....

> [T]he Court realizes that the royalties are necessary for the operation of Performance's business ...

J.A. 28.

The impending loss or financial ruin of Performance's business constitutes irreparable injury. "An injury is irreparable if it cannot be undone through monetary remedies." Interox Am. v. PPG, Indus., Inc., 736 F.2d

194, 202 (5th Cir.1984). "As a general rule, a movant has not established irreparable harm where damages would adequately compensate the movant for the asserted harm. Yet, irreparable injury has been characterized as loss of a movant's enterprise." Ryko Mfg. Corp. v. Delta Servs., Inc., 625 F.Supp. 1247, 1248 (S.D.Iowa 1985) (citation omitted). See also Roso–Lino, 749 F.2d at 125–26 ("The loss of [plaintiff's] distributorship, an ongoing business ... constitutes irreparable harm. What plaintiff stands to lose cannot be fully compensated by subsequent money damages.").

Furthermore, the type of irreparable harm which Performance is likely to suffer, the loss of its business, is precisely the type of harm which necessitates the granting of preliminary injunctive relief pending arbitration, because the arbitration will be a meaningless or hollow formality unless the status quo is preserved pending arbitration. "The Supreme Court has held that a preliminary injunction, designed to freeze the status quo and protect the damages remedy is an appropriate form of relief when it is shown that the defendant is likely to be insolvent at the time of judgement." Teradyne, 797 F.2d at 52 (citing Deckert v. Independence Shares Corp., 311 U.S. 282, 61 S.Ct. 229, 85 L.Ed. 189 (1940)). ...

> [Defendant] directs our attention to cases holding that a preliminary injunction is an inappropriate remedy where the potential harm to the movant is strictly financial. This is true as a general rule but an exception exists where the potential economic loss is so great as to threaten the existence of the movant's business. See Wright and Miller, Federal Practice and Procedure: Civil § 2948 ...

Second, Performance argues that the district court erred in finding that Performance was not entitled to equitable relief because Performance had "unclean hands." The district court stated that it

> realizes that the royalties are necessary for the operation of Performance's business, [but was] ... concerned that Performance has come to it for equitable relief with unclean hands.

J.A. 28. The district court then stated the reasons why it believed that Performance had unclean hands:

> First, there appears to be an ongoing dispute between Performance and Mr. Leininger, in that Leininger has made claims to Performance for unpaid royalties. Thus, there is a possibility that Performance has breached its license agreement with Leininger. Second, there is also the possibility that Performance has breached their sublicense agreement with Questar by allowing a third party publisher, David C. Cook Company, to publish *The Beginner's Bible* [Curriculum], even though Questar has exclusive publishing rights under the agreement. Finally, there are other claims on the very same royalties Performance seeks. Of the $184,000, Mr. Leininger is due approximately $4,300 and the Henleys, writers of the *Dovetales* stories, are due $79,000.

J.A. 28–29.

"Ordinarily, an abuse of discretion standard applies to ... review of a district court's application of the unclean hands doctrine." Northeast

Women's Center, Inc. v. McMonagle, 868 F.2d 1342, 1354 (3d Cir.) ... The doctrine of unclean hands requires that the alleged misconduct on the part of the plaintiff relate directly to the transaction about which the plaintiff has made a complaint. Dollar Systems, Inc. v. Avcar Leasing Sys., Inc., 890 F.2d 165, 173 (9th Cir.1989). ... Finally, "the doctrine is not to be used as a loose cannon, depriving a plaintiff of an equitable remedy to which he is otherwise entitled merely because he is guilty of unrelated misconduct." American Hosp. Supply Corp. v. Hospital Products, Ltd., 780 F.2d 589, 601 (7th Cir.1986).

In this case, there is no evidence of record that Performance is guilty of any misconduct that rises to the level of fraud, deceit, unconscionability, or bad faith. The disputes between Performance and Questar, and Performance and Leininger are bona fide commercial disputes. The dispute between Performance and Questar centers around the issue of whether Performance could license David C. Cook Publishers to publish *The Beginner's Bible New Testament* as part of its *The Beginner's Bible Curriculum*. Further, the dispute between Performance and Leininger centers around the question as to whether Performance could deduct legal fees from its royalty payments to Leininger. In this case, the district court made no findings as to the merits of the disputes between Performance and Questar and Performance and Leininger. Thus, the district court found that Performance had unclean hands based upon nothing more than the "possibility" that the arbitrator could determine that Performance had breached its license agreement with Questar, or that Performance had breached its license agreement with Leininger, or that Performance had breached both license agreements. This is not the required finding that Performance's actions rose to the level of fraud, deceit, unconscionability, or bad faith.

Furthermore, it is undisputed between the parties that out of the approximately $185,000 in royalty payments which are due to Performance, approximately $4,300 is due to be paid to Leininger and $79,000 is due to be paid to Karyn Henley. However, the district court cannot find that Performance has unclean hands because it has not been able to pay to Henley and Leininger moneys that Questar has refused to pay over to it. Accordingly, we conclude that the district court abused its discretion when it applied the doctrine of unclean hands to bar equitable relief, namely, the grant of a preliminary injunction to Performance.

Third, Performance argues that the district court erred in finding that the public interest would be served by denying Performance's motion for injunctive relief. The district court stated that it

> finds that public policy dictates that the arbitration provision in the agreement between Performance and Questar be enforced. The agreement provides for arbitration and explicitly states that the parties shall not bring their disputes to "secular courts." The parties should work out their disputes as provided in the agreement they both freely signed.

J.A. 29.

However, we believe that in this case the public interest would be served by granting injunctive relief to Performance "because there is a strong policy in favor of carrying out commercial arbitration when a contract contains an arbitration clause. Arbitration lightens courts' workloads, and it usually results in a speedier resolution of controversies." Sauer–Getriebe, 715 F.2d at 352. As was discussed above, we believe that in the absence of injunctive relief, Performance faces its destruction as an ongoing enterprise, and, consequently, without injunctive relief, the arbitration process agreed to by Performance and Questar in their licensing agreement will become a hollow formality. In light of the strong public policy encouraging parties in commercial disputes to submit their disagreements to the speedier resolution of arbitration where the parties have agreed to a contract containing an arbitration clause, we believe that preliminary injunctive relief is in the public interest in this case. Performance and Questar agreed to a contract containing an arbitration clause; however, in the absence of preliminary injunctive relief Performance may well lose its business. Thus, were we to reach the same conclusion as did the district court, private commercial parties will have little incentive to agree to contracts containing provisions for arbitration of their disputes, if by agreeing to arbitration of their disputes they are unable to obtain injunctive relief even when they face destruction. Therefore, the district court's finding that the denial of preliminary injunctive relief in this case would serve the public interest is clearly erroneous. Rather, the public interest is best served by the granting of preliminary injunctive relief in this case because it will foster agreements to arbitrate as a means of resolving disputes between private parties.

Fourth, Performance argues that the district court erred in finding that others, particularly Questar, would be harmed by the grant of preliminary injunctive relief. The district court found that

> [i]f the Court were to grant the preliminary injunction, and Performance still does not rectify the outstanding dispute with Leininger, then Leininger could terminate his license agreement with Performance. As a consequence, Questar's sublicense with Performance would be void. On the other hand, if the Court were to deny the preliminary injunction, and the parties continue to refuse to submit their disputes to arbitration, as provided in their agreement, then Performance will likely be forced to close its doors. As a consequence, Questar's sublicense with Performance would still be void.

J.A. 30.

We conclude that the district court's finding that Questar would be harmed by the grant of injunctive relief is clearly erroneous. The evidence shows that in the absence of injunctive relief Performance will likely collapse, thereby voiding the license agreement between Performance and Questar.

However, the district court concluded that if Performance does not rectify its dispute with Leininger, Leininger could terminate his licensing agreement with Performance, thereby also voiding Performance's license agreement with Questar. Performance and Leininger have disagreed as to whether Performance could properly deduct legal fees from its royalty payments to Leininger. However, "a bona fide dispute concerning royalty payments does not, as a matter of law, establish a material breach justifying recision of the contract absent an express provision in the contract." Arthur Guinness & Sons, PLC v. Sterling Pub. Co., 732 F.2d 1095, 1101 (2d Cir.1984). Thus, it is not at all clear that the dispute between Performance and Leininger will result in the recision of the licensing agreement between Performance and Leininger. Furthermore, there is no indication in the record that Leininger has sought arbitration or has filed a lawsuit against Performance over their dispute, much less any evidence that Leininger has sought to terminate his license agreement with Performance. Thus, the evidence shows that Questar is likely to suffer harm in the absence of preliminary injunctive relief, regardless of the outcome of the dispute between Performance and Leininger.

Finally, Performance argues that the district court erred in finding that it had little likelihood of success on the merits. As noted above, the district court concluded that it would not address the issue of the likelihood of Performance's success on the merits because this is an arbitrable dispute. The district court then stated that it did "not feel that Performance [was] likely to succeed on the merits given the mandatory arbitration provision in the agreement." J.A. 28.

" '[W]e do not consider the merits of [a] case further than to determine whether the District Judge abused his discretion in denying the preliminary injunction.' " Mason County Medical Ass'n v. Knebel, 563 F.2d 256, 261 (6th Cir.1977) ... Moreover, "it is improper for a court to decide a contractual dispute relegated to arbitration." Sauer–Getriebe, 715 F.2d at 352. Nevertheless, Performance "has demonstrated enough probable success on the merits to warrant relief." Id.

In balancing the four factors for injunctive relief, "[t]he moving party must show a strong likelihood of success on the merits if all other factors militate against granting a preliminary injunction. Similarly, the moving party need show less likelihood of success on the merits if the other facts indicate that the Court should issue a preliminary injunction." Merrill Lynch, Pierce, Fenner & Smith, Inc. v. Grall, 836 F.Supp. 428, 432 (W.D.Mich.1993) (citing In re DeLorean, 755 F.2d at 1229)). As was discussed above, the other three factors in this case weigh strongly in favor of granting the preliminary injunction requested by Performance. Thus, Performance need show less likelihood of success on the merits to obtain injunctive relief.

In this case it is undisputed that if the arbitrator finds that Performance has not breached the license agreement with Questar, Performance is entitled to the entire amount of money which Questar has placed in escrow. Further, the evidence shows that Questar has placed a substantial amount of money, approximately $185,000 in escrow, and that additional royalties due and owing to Performance under the license agreement are accruing at a significant rate, approximately $30,000 to $35,000 monthly.

Thus, even if the arbitrator determines that Performance has breached the contract and awards damages to Questar, given the amount of royalties in escrow, there is every likelihood that Performance will be entitled to at least some portion of the royalties being held in escrow. Consequently, because Performance will, as the result of the arbitration, most likely receive some portion, if not all, of the funds in the escrow account, Performance has a likelihood of success on the merits.

Furthermore, we believe that the district court can, and must, tailor any injunctive relief it grants in this case both to preserve Performance as an ongoing enterprise and to preserve Questar's right to damages, if any, out of the funds now held in escrow if it prevails on its claim of breach of damages. In Grall, the court noted that a "district court's authority to issue [preliminary] injunctive relief extends only until the arbitrators can determine the temporary injunctive relief necessary to maintain the status quo." Grall, 836 F.Supp. at 430 (citing Merrill Lynch, Pierce, Fenner & Smith, Inc. v. Salvano, 999 F.2d 211, 215 (7th Cir.1993). "Once assembled, an arbitration panel can enter whatever temporary injunctive relief it deems necessary to maintain the status quo ... '[C]ourts are ill-advised to extend the injunction once arbitration proceeds.'" Id. at 431 (quoting Salvano, 999 F.2d at 215)). Likewise, because the ultimate decision on the merits of this contractual dispute is for the arbitrators, the district court in its grant of preliminary injunctive relief should order Questar to pay only that amount of royalties necessary to ensure that Performance is not driven out of business prior to the time the arbitration proceeds. Furthermore, once the arbitration begins, it is for the arbitrators to decide how to maintain the status quo during the pendency of the arbitration process. This approach will both minimize the district court's involvement in the merits of this contractual dispute, and it will preserve the ability of the arbitration panel to fully address the merits of the dispute.

Accordingly, we hold that the district court erred in denying Performance's motion for a preliminary injunction. Therefore, the district court should grant preliminary injunctive relief to Performance pending arbitration within the parameters we have discussed above.

III.

For the reasons stated, the district court's judgment denying Performance's motion for a preliminary injunction is REVERSED and the case is REMANDED to the district court for the issuance of a preliminary injunction consistent with this opinion.

* * *

Questions

1. Who should decide requests for provisional relief—an arbitrator or a judge? If it is decided by a judge, what factors should a court use to determine whether a provisional remedy may issue? Can a court hold a hearing to determine whether these factors require the relief? Must a court

hold a hearing? What problems are posed for the authority of the arbitrator when a court makes such a determination?

2. If a request for provisional relief is directed to an arbitrator and the arbitration agreement is silent on the power to grant such relief, can an arbitrator grant the relief or not? If an arbitrator grants provisional relief in such a situation, could a court set the arbitral award aside on the grounds that it is in excess in the arbitrator's powers? Or should the power to grant provisional relief be implied in all arbitration clauses that do not explicitly deny an arbitrator that power?

3. On what basis should an arbitrator determine whether a provisional remedy should issue? Should she apply the same standard a court would apply? If so, must there be a preliminary hearing comparable to a hearing on a preliminary injunction, followed by a final arbitral hearing on the merits? Would such a two-part process undermine the rationale for utilizing arbitration rather than a court?

4. If an arbitrator awards a provisional remedy, can the movant go to court to enforce it? What test should a court apply to determine whether to enforce such a provisional award? Is it the same standard that the court would itself apply when determining whether to issue preliminary relief? Is it the same standard a court would apply to a final arbitral award? Is there some intermediate standard that would be more appropriate?

* * *

6. DISCOVERY

Mississippi Power Company v. Peabody Coal Company

69 F.R.D. 558 (S.D.Miss.1976).

■ COLEMAN, CIRCUIT JUDGE.

I. Background

Mississippi Power Company (MPC), plaintiff, has filed a civil action against Peabody Coal Company (Peabody) and Commercial Transport Corporation (Commercial), seeking $346,318,012.00 in damages for the alleged breach of a coal supply contract. Also sought were (1) a declaratory judgment that Peabody's force majeure excuse for nonperformance of the contract is not valid; (2) a judgment requiring Peabody to specifically perform said coal supply contract; and (3) an injunction, pendente lite, requiring Peabody to continue to supply the full tonnage of coal called for in the coal supply contract. Against Commercial MPC sought only a declaration that MPC was relieved from tendering for transport the minimum tonnage required by its barge contract with Commercial. MPC also sought discovery in the form of interrogatories and requests for production of documents.

The coal supply contract had an arbitration clause. Pursuant to the Federal Arbitration Act, Peabody moved for a stay pending arbitration. Peabody also filed a motion to postpone discovery, except as related to issues raised by its motion to stay while the court was considering the motion to stay.

After briefing and oral argument, District Judge Harold Cox filed a memorandum opinion on July 23, 1975. This was followed by an "Order for Arbitration" entered August 6, 1975. The opinion and order found: (1) that the contract between MPC and Peabody was one involving and affecting interstate commerce; (2) that it contained an agreement to arbitrate any unresolved controversy between the parties or claims of one party against the other under the rules of the American Arbitration Association. The Court therefore ordered the parties to proceed with such arbitration, but retained full jurisdiction of the case to make available to the parties all discovery processes provided by the Federal Rules of Civil Procedure. In this respect the order provided:

> This Court expressly retains full jurisdiction of this case and in the meantime, will make available to the parties all discovery processes provided by the Civil Rules of Federal Procedure to the extent that it may be necessary to the presentation and decision of any disputed facts in the case as may be helpful under Civil Rule 81(a)(c) [sic, 81(a)(3)] of the Federal Rules of Civil Procedure. In the meantime, this proceeding shall be stayed in this Court without prejudice or advantage to either party. The plaintiff may continue all discovery processes and have the processes of this Court available to enforce answers thereto within the time contemplated by such rules. The defendant (Peabody Coal Company) shall answer any interrogatories presently outstanding within 15 days. Further discovery processes shall be commenced and concluded within ninety days after this date.

Peabody appealed only that portion of the order which provided discovery under the Federal Rules of Civil Procedure. October 6, 1975, Peabody's appeal was dismissed because it was not taken from a final appealable order.

Subsequently, Judge Cox recused himself. Sitting by designation as a District Judge for the Southern District of Mississippi, the author of this opinion took over the case.

Discovery proceeded, but Peabody objected to certain of Miss. Power Company's interrogatories and requests for production of documents. Peabody refused certain MPC requests for production of particular documents on the ground that they were not relevant to the issues presented for arbitration and were overly broad and all-inclusive. MPC filed a motion to compel discovery. An extended hearing was held in chambers on November 21, 1975 in Ackerman, Mississippi. This Court, sua sponte, questioned Miss. Power Company's right to discovery and requested that the issue be briefed.

II. Issues

Accordingly, we now confront the task of deciding one issue, possibly two:

(1) Judge Cox having ordered that discovery may proceed under the auspices of the Court in an arbitrable case, does that order bind a superseding judge when he comes to consider the enforcement of the order?;

(2) When a Court stays a suit in order that arbitration may be had, does it have any further authority or jurisdiction to order that discovery may proceed, either as to the merits of the suit or in aid of arbitration?

Obviously, if the answer to Question No. 1 is negative, I do not reach Question No. 2 . . . . [The court then held that one District Judge may overrule or set aside the motion granted by another "where justified by sound discretion exercised in the interest of justice."]

The issue now before us arises from the following portion of Judge Cox's order of August 5, 1975:

[T]his Court expressly retains jurisdiction of this case and will make available to the parties all federal discovery procedures *to the extent that it may be necessary to the presentation and decision by the board of any disputed facts.* (Emphasis ours.)

The first sentence of Section 30 of the Commercial Arbitration Rules of the American Arbitration Association provides:

The parties may offer such evidence as they desire *and shall produce* (emphasis added) such additional evidence as the arbitrator may deem necessary to an understanding and determination of the dispute.

Title 9 of the United States Code, Section 7, authorizes arbitrators to summon witnesses, books, records, documents, and papers deemed material as evidence in the case. United States district courts may compel compliance with the summons.

It is thus readily apparent that under the contract which the parties made, under Rule 30, and under the applicable federal statute the arbitrator can compel the production (discovery) of every book, record, document and paper deemed material to the appropriate resolution of the controversy between Mississippi Power and Peabody.

With reference to discovery, however, Judge Cox's order left the parties standing with one foot in the district court and the other in the arbitrator's office. If arbitration is to proceed, and the law looks with disfavor on delays, two discovery proceedings could be in progress simultaneously, one under the direction of the Court and the other under the control of the arbitrator.

Considerable discovery has been accomplished in compliance with Judge Cox's order, but Peabody objects on numerous grounds to additional extensive discovery proposed by the plaintiff. Plaintiff has countered with a motion to compel discovery. This motion is the issue now before this Court.

Upon a thorough exploration of the applicable law the Court concludes that the motion to compel discovery should be denied and that the arbitration process should be set in motion without further delay.

The Law as to Discovery Pending Arbitration

So far as I have been able to discover, the Court of Appeals for the Fifth Circuit has had only one occasion to consider this question. This is to be found in the per curiam opinion in Local 66, International Ass'n of Heat and Frost Insulators and Asbestos Workers v. Leona Lee Corp., 5 Cir. 1970, 434 F.2d 192. This case appears to approve discovery *on the merits* prior to arbitration. It categorically stated, 434 F.2d at 194:

> Also, the District Court did not err when it specifically made available to the parties federal discovery procedures "to the extent necessary for the presentation of matters submitted for Trade Board and Arbitration determination." Such order is consistent with the District Court's retention of jurisdiction and effectuates the policy favoring arbitration. (footnote omitted).

This sweeping declaration appears to come down emphatically in support of the proposition that in a case ordered to arbitration discovery may proceed simultaneously in the courts and before the arbitrator. This District Court is, of course, obligated to follow the outstanding, unreversed precedents of the Fifth Circuit. The difficulty here, however, is that the Leona Lee per curiam never mentions, and does not discuss, outstanding judicial precedent; it does not explicate the reasoning upon which the declaration was grounded. It makes no effort to demonstrate how simultaneous discovery in arbitration cases "is consistent with the District Court's retention of jurisdiction and effectuates the policy of favoring arbitration". It is against the overwhelming weight of authority. I feel, therefore, that the decision in Leona Lee must have been grounded on some factor not made clear in the opinion and is not a controlling precedent.

The great weight of authority is clearly to the effect that discovery on the subject matter of a dispute to be arbitrated will be denied. See 7 Moore's Fed.Practice ¶ 81.05[7] at 81–82. . . .

One of the earliest cases to declare that discovery was inappropriate after a stay action was Commercial Solvents Corp. v. Louisiana Liquid Fertilizer Co., S.D.N.Y.1957, 20 F.R.D. 359. There one party had served notice on the other party to arbitrate a dispute in accordance with the terms of their contract. An ex parte order allowing the taking of depositions was obtained and it was from this order that an appeal was taken. The Court found no authority to compel discovery in aid of arbitration, noting:

> By voluntarily becoming a party to a contract in which arbitration was the agreed mode for settling disputes thereunder respondent chose to avail itself of procedures peculiar to the arbitral process rather than those used in judicial determinations. "A main object of a voluntary submission to arbitration is the avoidance of formal and technical preparation of a case for the usual procedure of a judicial trial." 1 Wigmore, Evidence § 4(e) (3d ed. 1940). Arbitration may well have

advantages but where the converse results a party having chosen to arbitrate cannot then vacillate and successfully urge a preference for a unique combination of litigation and arbitration.

20 F.R.D. at 361.

Numerous other district court cases have declared for various reasons that discovery as to the merits of a suit that has been stayed for arbitration is improper and should not be allowed. See Econo–Car Internat'l, Inc. v. Antilles Car Rentals, Inc., D.V.I.1973, 61 F.R.D. 8, 10, rev'd on other grounds, 3 Cir. 1974, 499 F.2d 1391 . . .

Some district courts have said that discovery may be ordered in "exceptional circumstances". See Ferro Union Corp. v. SS Ionic Coast, S.D.Tex.1967, 43 F.R.D. 11 (exceptional circumstances found where ship crew was about to leave the country and might never return to U.S. waters) . . .

One district court in dictum drew a distinction between "trial" and "proceedings" maintaining that the Arbitration Act compelled a stay of the trial but not a general stay of proceedings. See Donahue v. Susquehanna Collieries Co., M.D.Pa.1943, 49 F.Supp. 843, 844, rev'd, 3 Cir. 1943, 138 F.2d 3 (Court of Appeals did not discuss the extent of the stay). This argument has been rejected as unsound by recent authority. See Dickstein v. duPont, D.Mass.1970, 320 F.Supp. 150, 154, aff'd, 1st Cir. 1971, 443 F.2d 783 and cases cited therein.

From the above discussion it is apparent that the vast majority of courts that have considered the matter have concluded that allowing discovery on the merits of a case prior to arbitration is inconsistent with the aims of arbitration. The Harvard Law Review aptly stated this conclusion in one of its surveys on discovery, as follows:[4]

> As to arbitration, discovery is generally not available as an incident of the arbitration proceeding itself. Discovery is expensive and time-consuming, and is thus inconsistent with the desires of parties who refer their disputes to arbitrators rather than to formal judicial tribunals. Moreover, discovery by a collateral application in a court, although authorized in some states, is allowed with reluctance, as it tends to reduce the arbitrator's control of the proceeding. When an arbitration issue is before a court—as in a motion to stay an action allegedly referable to arbitration—discovery has usually been denied unless the stay is refused; again it is thought that the expense of discovery should not be forced on a party who has agreed to submit a controversy to a less costly method of adjudication.

See also 4 Moore's Fed.Practice ¶ 26.54 (2nd ed. 1975) (depositions are properly taken only for the purpose of preparing for trial in a pending action in the district court and not to aid in the disposition of a collateral proceeding such as arbitration).

---

4.   74 Harv.L.Rev. 940, 943 (1961).

The Decision

Within the parameters of this case, the merits of this controversy, including its evidentiary aspects, should be left to the arbitrator.

In reaching this conclusion I need not hold that discovery pending arbitration is never to be allowed, nor am I required to hold,/ as pontificated in Leona Lee, supra, that it is always to be permitted.

Instead, the parties should be held to their agreement and to the availability of Rule 30 of the Rules of the American Arbitration Association. Backed up by the federal statute, this rule allows the arbitrator, in his discretion, to permit any discovery necessary to the performance of his function. There should be no necessity for double-barreled discovery, proceeding simultaneously under the supervision of the Court, on one hand, and under the supervision of the arbitrator, on the other, a situation fraught with the likelihood of conflicts, duplications, hindrances and delays, all basically in conflict with the arbitration process, as demonstrated by the many cases hereinabove cited. This course avoids anything inimical to the obligation to arbitrate, yet it will not deprive the plaintiff of the benefits of discovery, which can be had, if needed, at the hands of the arbitrator and under his direction.

V. Conclusion

Under the facts, circumstances, and governing law of this case I hold that I am not bound by Judge Cox's original order which allowed discovery to proceed on the merits of this controversy pending arbitration or while arbitration is in progress. It need not be said, but I say it nevertheless, that this indicates no disrespect whatever for the prior views of Judge Cox or for his position as a Judge of the same court in which I am now sitting. . . .

Finding that by Section 23 the parties have contracted to submit all unresolved controversies or claims by one party against the other to arbitration, *including adjustment for gross inequities* (Section 18 of the contract), the Court directs that arbitration shall proceed without further delay.

* * *

Recognition Equipment, Inc. v. NCR Corporation

532 F.Supp. 271 (N.D.Tex.1981).

■ ROBERT W. PORTER, DISTRICT JUDGE.

Currently pending before the Court is the motion of Defendant NRC Corporation to stay all further proceedings in this action pursuant to section 3 of the Federal Arbitration Act, 9 U.S.C. § 3. Defendant's motion presents the Court with two distinct issues for consideration: first, whether the commercial contract entered into among the respective parties to this action provides for reference of the pertinent issues in dispute to arbitration; and second, assuming a stay is granted, whether or not the Court should allow discovery under the Federal Rules of Civil Procedure, pending arbitration. Jurisdiction over this action is predicated upon 28 U.S.C. § 1332, there being complete diversity of citizenship among the parties.

Recognition Equipment, Inc., Plaintiff herein, brings this action to recover monies it asserts are due and owing from the Defendant as a consequence of a sale of certain mechanical goods and related parts. Plaintiff alleges that it provided the Defendant with said goods and related parts but received payment from the Defendant which was erroneously based upon the wrong price list. The action was originally brought in state court, but there being complete diversity among the parties, the Defendant petitioned for removal to federal court. The agreement in question has two provisions which the parties assert are relevant to the Court's decision as to whether to submit the dispute to arbitration. The first is found in paragraph 18 of the contract, entitled "DEFAULT AND TERMINATION." There the parties provided specific remedies with respect to any failure on the part of the Plaintiff seller to deliver goods meeting the specifications set forth in the contract. Among the remedies available to NCR are the termination of the agreement and/or the granting of a license from Recognition to NCR covering the products in question. In paragraph 18.4 the parties provided that "[i]n the event of any other default hereunder [aside from that discussed above], either party may seek relief as would be appropriate at law or in equity." Towards the end of the contract at paragraph 28.11, the parties agreed to the following arbitration clause:

> "11. Arbitration. Any controversy or claim arising out of or relating to this Agreement or the breach thereof, shall be settled by arbitration in accordance with the Rules of the American Arbitration Association and judgment upon the award rendered by the Arbitrator(s) may be entered in any Court having jurisdiction thereof."

Recognition contends that paragraph 18.4 shows that, contrary to Paragraph 28.11, the parties intended to resolve this dispute in the courts. Paragraph 18.4, however, relates to a specific type of default enumerated therein by the parties-the failure of Recognition to provide products meeting the specifications set forth in the contract for any consecutive four month period. Paragraph 18 delineates the substantive remedies available to the parties in such event. Paragraph 18.4 merely limits the contractual remedies set forth in paragraph 18 to the specific type of default discussed above. It certainly evidences no intention that all other disputes were to be resolved in the courts, especially when read in conjunction with paragraph 28.11.

The pertinent authority with respect to the determination of a motion to stay brought pursuant to section 3 of the Federal Arbitration Act is found in Seaboard Coast Line Railroad Co. v. National Rail Passenger Corp., 554 F.2d 657, 660 (5th Cir.1977):

> "We must, therefore, look to ..., the arbitration provision, ... to determine whether the referral to arbitration was proper. At the outset, we note that the policy of the Federal Arbitration Act is to encourage arbitration and to relieve the congestion in the courts. An applicant for a § 3 stay is entitled to obtain it, if he makes 'a claim [to

arbitration] which on its face is one governed by the (applicable) agreement.' Galt v. Libbey–Owens–Ford Glass Co., 7 Cir. 1967, 376 F.2d 711, 714. And the court should grant the stay 'unless it may be said with positive assurance that the arbitration clause is not susceptible of an interpretation that covers the asserted dispute.' United Steelworkers of America v. American Manufacturing Co., 363 U.S. 564, 582–83, 80 S.Ct. 1343, 1353, 4 L.Ed.2d 1403.''

The agreement at bar is clearly susceptible to the interpretation that Paragraph 28.11 covers the dispute in question. The language of paragraph 18.4 in no way modifies this construction. As noted above, that paragraph merely limits the substantive remedies set forth in paragraph 18 to the specific type of default enumerated therein. Paragraph 18 does not modify the procedural remedy agreed upon by the parties. Hence, the Court is of the opinion that the dispute in question is properly referable to arbitration as set out in the agreement, and that consequently, Defendant's motion to stay pursuant to section 3 of the Federal Arbitration Act should be granted.

The second issue before the Court is more troublesome. Plaintiff maintains that, assuming the Court grants Defendant's motion to stay, the parties are entitled to go forward with discovery under the Federal Rules of Civil Procedure. In support of its contention Plaintiff notes that section 3 of the Federal Arbitration Act provides only for a stay of "the trial of the action," and also cites Int'l Assoc. of Heat and Frost Insulators and Asbestos Workers v. Leona Lee Corp., 434 F.2d 192 (5th Cir.1970) (per curiam). In Leona Lee the Fifth Circuit, in an action brought under section 301 of the Labor Management Relations Act, 29 U.S.C. § 185, affirmed an order of the lower court staying trial of the action and permitting discovery pursuant to the Federal Rules to the extent necessary for the presentation of the dispute to an arbitral forum. In so doing, the court stated that such a procedure was consistent with the lower court's retention of jurisdiction and that it effectuated the policy favoring arbitration. A later opinion by Circuit Judge Coleman, sitting by designation as a Judge of the United States District Court for the Southern District of Mississippi, however, undercuts the broad and sweeping language in Leona Lee. In Mississippi Power Company v. Peabody Coal Co., 69 F.R.D. 558 (S.D.Miss.1976), Judge Coleman, in a case similar to the one at bar, concluded that discovery under the Federal Rules of Civil Procedure during a section 3 stay was improper, at least on the facts of that specific case. Judge Coleman noted numerous problems with allowing parties the opportunity to engage in discovery under the Federal Rules during a section 3 stay. First and foremost is that the Federal Arbitration Act provides for discovery by the arbitrator in section 7 of the Act, 9 U.S.C. § 7, and thus additional discovery under the Federal Rules would create "dual discovery." Second, he noted that the majority of the courts which have faced the issue have decided against allowing discovery to proceed under the rules. Third, those courts which have allowed discovery to proceed pending arbitration have noted "exceptional circumstances" in the facts before them to justify the decision. Finally, Judge Coleman also noted that the purpose of arbitration is to avoid the attendant delay and expense of litigation....

Subsequent to the Mississippi Power case, the Fifth Circuit has recognized the issue raised by Judge Coleman concerning "dual discovery" preceding arbitration. Yeargin Construction Co. v. Parsons & Whittemore Alabama Machinery and Services Corp., 609 F.2d 829, 831 (5th Cir.1980). In addition, the United States Supreme Court has cited the Mississippi Power case with approval for the proposition that "when the purpose of a discovery request is to gather information for use in proceedings other than the pending suit, discovery is properly denied." Oppenheimer Fund, Inc. v. Sanders, 437 U.S. 340, 352 n. 17, 98 S.Ct. 2380, 2390 n. 17, 57 L.Ed.2d 253 (1978) (dictum).

The Court is persuaded that Judge Coleman's opinion in Mississippi Power accurately reflects the law with respect to discovery under the Federal Rules pending arbitration under the Federal Arbitration Act. Perhaps the greatest distinction between the Mississippi Power case, and Leona Lee, is that the latter case was brought under section 301 of the LMRA, 29 U.S.C. § 185. There is nothing in the opinion to indicate that the arbitral forum which would hear the claim in Leona Lee had any discovery powers. Thus, "dual discovery" may not have been an issue there and this aspect of the case could be the "factor not made clear" of which Judge Coleman spoke. Therefore, the Court is of the opinion that Leona Lee is not binding precedent for the instant case. In addition, for the reasons set forth so persuasively in Mississippi Power, the Court is of the opinion that, on the facts of this case, discovery under the Federal Rules should not proceed pending arbitration. Time and again courts have concluded that the purposes of arbitration under the Federal Arbitration Act are to facilitate and expedite the resolution of disputes, ease court congestion, and provide disputants with a less costly alternative to litigation....

The Court in Mississippi Power did not hold that discovery pending arbitration is never to be permitted and acknowledged other decisions in which it was held that such discovery may be granted under "exceptional circumstances." 69 F.R.D. at 566–67, citing Ferro Union Corp. v. SS Ionic Coast, 43 F.R.D. 11 (S.D.Tex.1967). In the immediate action Plaintiff has failed to demonstrate any "exceptional circumstances" which would justify pre-arbitration discovery. Some courts have stated that the granting of discovery during a stay lies within the Court's discretion. Bigge Crane and Rigging Co. v. Docutel Corp., 371 F.Supp. 240 (E.D.N.Y.1973). The Court is of the opinion that the better exercise of discretion in the instant case is to deny Plaintiff's request for pre-arbitration discovery.[4] Accordingly,

It is ORDERED that Defendant's motion for a stay or proceedings in this action pending arbitration of the dispute raised by the original complaint is GRANTED: the parties are directed to submit the matter to arbitration in a manner consistent with paragraph 28.11 of the contract in

---

4. A further reason for denying discovery pending arbitration lies in the potential for interference with the arbitral function. By retaining jurisdiction over this action and allowing pre-arbitration discovery the Court would be duty bound to administer the discovery process. In so doing, there is a likelihood that its administration of the discovery issues could preshape the issues before the arbitrator.

issue and the Court retains jurisdiction over the matter to enforce sections 4 and 7 of the Federal Arbitration Act;

It is further ORDERED that the Plaintiff's request for discovery pursuant to the Federal Rules of Civil Procedure pending arbitration is DENIED.

* * *

Questions

1. What is the problem of dual discovery that the court mentions in *Recognition Equipment*? Could the problem be overcome without denying parties access to the discovery provisions of the Federal Rules of Civil Procedure?

2. Under what circumstances might a court order discovery pending arbitration? What authority or policy rationale might justify such judicial action? How much weight should a court or arbitrator give to an argument that discovery will delay resolution of a dispute and undermine the rationale that led the parties to select arbitration in the first place? See Note, *Arbitration and Award—Discovery—Court May Permit Discovery on the Merits When It Will Not Delay Arbitration*, 44 U. CINN. L. REV. 151 (1975).

3. If a court were to hear discovery requests in matters in which arbitration was pending, presumably the court would have to determine which discovery requests were reasonable and relevant. How can a court determine issues of reasonableness and relevance without some attention to the merits of the underlying dispute? Must an arbitrator who hears discovery requests also make a pre-determination as to reasonableness and relevancy? Is such a determination subject to judicial review?

4. Some arbitration procedures provide for limited discovery. See, e.g., C. Edward Fletcher III, *Privatizing Securities Disputes through the Enforcement of Arbitration Agreements*, 71 MINN. L. REV. 393 (1987) (describing discovery provisions of securities industry arbitrations). Should a court presume that an arbitration procedure that does not expressly provide for discovery intend to preclude parties from engaging in discovery?

* * *

Meadows Indemnity Company, Limited v. Nutmeg Insurance Co.

157 F.R.D. 42 (M.D.Tenn.1994).

■ SANDIDGE, UNITED STATES MAGISTRATE JUDGE.

By Order entered May 27, 1993 (Docket Entry No. 16), the Court referred the following motion to the Magistrate Judge for consideration and disposition under 28 U.S.C. § 636(b)(1)(A): the motion of Willis Corroon

Corporation ("Willis Corroon") for a Protective Order (filed March 26, 1993; Docket Entry No. 1).

Oral argument on the motion was held before the undersigned on June 21, 1993. For the reasons set forth below, Willis Corroon's motion for a protective order is denied.

I. BACKGROUND

The referred matter comes to the Court on the Court's general docket as a small scene from a larger litigation picture which includes a currently pending arbitration action as well as lawsuits in New York and California. The underlying theme behind these proceedings involves events related to the operation of a casualty insurance/reinsurance pool. For the purposes of the matter before the Court, it is unnecessary to extensively relate the history of these proceedings and only a brief summary of events is provided.

In 1989, Meadows Indemnity Company, Ltd. ("Meadows") filed a lawsuit in the Eastern District of New York against several insurance companies and other related companies. Willis Corroon is the successor in interest to one defendant in the lawsuit, the Corroon & Black Corporation, and wholly owns another defendant, Baccala & Shoop Insurance Services ("BSIS"). Meadows complains that beginning in the late 1970's and continuing into the 1980's, BSIS established and managed an insurance/reinsurance pool ("the pool") and acted as an agent with respect to the pool for several policy issuing insurance companies. Meadows alleges, among other things, that BSIS and the companies, individually and in conspiracy, gained excessive commissions and fees from the pool and fraudulently concealed information from reinsurers participating in the pool regarding premium inadequacy, severity of expected loss, amount of commissions and fees diverted from premiums, etc.

The District Court in New York ordered arbitration of Meadows' claims against the defendant insurance companies and stayed the claims against BSIS and Willis Corroon until completion of the arbitration proceedings. Shortly thereafter, several of the defendant insurance companies filed suit against Meadows in California. The California lawsuit is also stayed pending the arbitration results.

The arbitration currently underway involves Meadows' claims against the several insurance companies, one of which is the Hartford Group. As part of the arbitration, Meadows petitioned the arbitration panel to subpoena certain documents and records of BSIS because of its role as agent for Hartford and as manager of the pool. Hartford objected to the petition and the panel heard both written and oral arguments from both sides as to Meadows' request. On February 22, 1993, the arbitration panel issued the subpoena to BSIS, in the care of Willis Corroon, requiring the production of documents according to a schedule of documents attached to the subpoena. The schedule sets out 53 categories or types of documents which are to be produced pursuant to the subpoena, and states that production of the documents is to take place at Willis Corroon's Nashville, Tennessee office or at another location as agreed to by the parties. It appears from the parties' briefs that the documents covered by the subpoena are in fact located in a California warehouse. See Docket Entry No. 13.

At oral argument the Court was informed by the parties that the District Court in New York had recently issued an order, on June 14, 1993, which vacated the stay of proceedings in the New York lawsuit to the extent that Meadows is allowed to proceed with pretrial discovery against BSIS.

II. ANALYSIS

The only issue before the Court is whether Willis Corroon, which is not a party to the arbitration proceedings, must comply with an order from the arbitration panel requiring it to produce numerous documents, not for the panel's review at a hearing, but for inspection and copying by Meadows prior to a hearing before the panel.

Section 7 of the Federal Arbitration Act, 9 U.S.C. §§ 1–307, provides in relevant part:

> The arbitrators ... may summon in writing any person to attend before them or any of them as a witness and in a proper case to bring with him or them any book, record, document, or paper which may be deemed material as evidence in the case ...

Willis Corroon's main argument for the protective order is that the arbitration panel has acted beyond their statutory authority by ordering production of documents unrelated to an order to appear before the arbitration panel, and by ordering production of the documents for review not by the arbitration panel but by a party to the arbitration. Willis Corroon's arguments are unpersuasive and I find that the arbitration panel's action of issuing the subpoena is within its authority under the Federal Arbitration Act.

Initially, I note that the arbitration panel has already determined that the documents to be provided are relevant to the arbitration proceedings. Given this Court's minimal contact with the issues involved in the litigation surrounding the pool, and the arbitration panel's expertise in this matter, there is no reason to second guess the panel's determination as to relevance.[1]

There is little dispute the arbitration panel, pursuant to its authority under Section 7, could require a witness in the name of Willis Corroon to appear before the panel and bring all of the documents at issue to a hearing. Considering the sheer number of documents addressed by the subpoena, however, this scenario seems quite fantastic and practically unreasonable. With this in mind, the arbitration panel issued the disputed subpoena as a method of dealing with complex and voluminous discovery matters in an orderly and efficient manner. See Docket Entry No. 9.

---

1. The District Court in New York appears to agree with the arbitration panel's determination of initial relevance, stating in its order, "[g]ood and sufficient reasons exist requiring the production of the documents in question at the arbitration proceeding."

Mindful that one of the ultimate goals of the arbitration panel is to make a full and fair determination of the issues involved, and the underlying policies behind arbitration include the resolution of issues in an efficient and less costly manner, the panel's decision to issue the subpoena seems entirely reasonable.

Contrary to the arguments of Willis Corroon, I find that Section 7 authorizes the action taken by the arbitration panel. Stanton v. Paine Webber Jackson & Curtis, 685 F.Supp. 1241 (S.D.Fla.1988). The power of the panel to compel production of documents from third-parties for the purposes of a hearing implicitly authorizes the lesser power to compel such documents for arbitration purposes prior to a hearing. Willis Corroon's argument requires adoption of an unnecessarily constrictive and unreasonable reading of Section 7 which would limit the ability of the arbitration panel to deal effectively with a large and complex case such as the one at hand, and generally hamper the use of arbitration as a forum for dispute resolution.

With respect to Willis Corroon's arguments about the burdensome nature of the subpoena, nothing has been presented which indicates that producing the documents will in fact be unduly burdensome. While Willis Corroon and BSIS are not parties to the arbitration, they are intricately related to the parties involved in the arbitration and are not mere third-parties who have been pulled into this matter arbitrarily. The documents appear to be at a central location to which Meadows has agreed to travel. The burden of sifting through the documents and copying those needed is on Meadows. At this stage there is simply no merit to Willis Corroon's arguments about an undue burden on them. If one should arise during the course of the document production, Willis Corroon may seek protection through the appropriate district court.

It appears that whether through the arbitration proceedings or the lawsuit in New York, the documents possessed by Willis Corroon relating to the pool are going to be produced for Meadows' review. As I find that the arbitration panel acted within its authority, I see no reason to grant the protective order sought by Willis Corroon and further delay the arbitration proceedings.

The arbitration panel's subpoena is valid under the Federal Arbitration Act. The requested documents should be produced at a time and location agreed on by the parties and should be made available for inspection by Meadows. Meadows shall be responsible, at its own costs, of arranging for the copying of any documents desired. An order denying the motion for a protective order will be entered.

* * *

Integrity Insurance Co. v. American Centennial Insurance Co.

885 F.Supp. 69 (S.D.N.Y.1995).

■ SCHEINDLIN, DISTRICT JUDGE.

Thomas Lennon and Eugene McGee petition this Court to quash subpoenas duces tecum issued by an arbitrator pursuant to a dispute between Integrity Insurance Company, in liquidation ("Integrity"), and American Centennial Insurance Company ("ACIC"). The subpoenas were issued by the arbitrator at the request of ACIC, and direct the petitioners to appear for pre-hearing depositions and to produce documents.

BACKGROUND

The dispute between Integrity and ACIC arises from a number of reinsurance agreements. See Affidavit of Brendan M. Kennedy ("Kennedy Aff."), Attorney for Integrity, at ¶ 2. The Liquidator instituted arbitration proceedings against ACIC pursuant to those agreements. Id. Separate and apart from the arbitration proceeding, the Liquidator has filed an action in New Jersey on behalf of Integrity's policyholders, creditors, reinsurers and others, against former officers and directors of Integrity, including petitioner McGee ("D & O action"). See Affidavit of Eugene Wollan, Attorney for ACIC, in Support of Petition ("Wollan Aff.") at ¶ 8. McGee is a former Vice President of Integrity and Lennon is McGee's attorney in the D & O action. Petition ("Pet.") at ¶¶ 3-4. Lennon also represents Leonard Stern, a former President of Integrity and a defendant in the D & O action. Wollan Aff. at ¶ 8. Discovery in the D & O action has been stayed pending the outcome of settlement negotiations. Pet. at ¶ 7.

Neither petitioner is a party to the arbitration proceeding. The subpoenas require them to appear for a deposition and to produce all relevant documents relating to the reinsurance agreements at issue between ACIC and Integrity. The subpoenas further require production of documents relating to the D & O action. Wollan Aff. at ¶ 8. Additionally, ACIC seeks to depose Lennon in order to learn the whereabouts of Stern, so that Stern can be served with a deposition subpoena. Lennon has refused to voluntarily disclose Stern's address, claiming that it is privileged. Wollan Aff. at ¶ 9; Brief in Support of Petition at 9.

Petitioners request that this Court quash these subpoenas, on the grounds that an arbitrator has no authority to compel a non-party to appear at a deposition prior to an arbitration hearing. Petitioners also question the materiality of the information sought.

DISCUSSION

A. Depositions of Nonparties

The issue of whether an arbitrator has the authority to compel a nonparty to appear at a pre-hearing deposition appears to be a case of first impression within this district. This Court recognizes that federal policy strongly favors arbitration as an alternative dispute resolution process, see Moses H. Cone Memorial Hosp. v. Mercury Constr. Corp., 460 U.S. 1, 24, 103 S.Ct. 927, 941, 74 L.Ed.2d 765 (1983), and that courts should interpret the Federal Arbitration Act ("FAA"), 9 U.S.C. §§ 1 et seq., so "as to further, rather than impede, arbitration." Bigge Crane and Rigging Co. v. Docutel Corp., 371 F.Supp. 240, 246 (E.D.N.Y.1973).

Arbitration is, however, a creation of contract, bargained for and voluntarily agreed to by the parties. The petitioners, who are not parties to the arbitration agreement, never bargained for or voluntarily agreed to participate in an arbitration. After weighing the policy favoring arbitration against the rights and privileges of nonparties, this Court concludes that an arbitrator does not have the authority to compel nonparty witnesses to appear for pre-arbitration depositions.

To determine the extent of an arbitrator's authority, one must begin with the source of that authority. An arbitrator's power *over the parties* derives from both the arbitration agreement and the FAA. Arbitrators can exert no more control over parties than that which the parties, through their agreements, granted to the arbitrators. The four reinsurance agreements contain different arbitration clauses. Agreements 1080 and 4013 state "[t]he arbitrators ... are relieved of all judicial formalities and may abstain from following the strict rules of law." Agreements 1021 and 978 state: "[t]he arbitrators will not be obliged to follow judicial formalities or the rules of evidence except to the extent required by the state law of the site of arbitration.... Except as provided above, arbitration will be based upon the procedures of the American Arbitration Association [('AAA')]." The rules of the AAA state that "[a]n arbitrator or other person authorized by law to subpoena witnesses or documents may do so upon the request of any party." American Arbitration Association, *Commercial Arbitration Rules*, Rule 31 (1993). Thus, there is nothing within the reinsurance agreements that explicitly limits the power of an arbitrator to order discovery. See Chiarella v. Viscount Indus. Co. Ltd., No. 92 Civ. 9310, 1993 WL 497967 (S.D.N.Y. Dec. 1, 1993).

Because the parties to a contract cannot bind nonparties, they certainly cannot grant such authority to an arbitrator. Thus, an arbitrator's power *over nonparties* derives solely from the FAA. The contested subpoenas were issued by the arbitrator pursuant to section 7 of the FAA.

> The arbitrators ... may summon in writing any person to attend before them or any of them as a witness and in a proper case to bring with him or them any book, record, document, or paper which may be deemed material as evidence in the case.... [I]f any person or persons so summoned to testify shall refuse or neglect to obey said summons, upon petition the United States district court for the district in which such arbitrators, or a majority of them, are sitting may compel the attendance of such person or persons before said arbitrator or arbitrators, or punish said person or persons for contempt in the same manner provided by law for securing the attendance of witnesses or their punishment for neglect or refusal to attend in the courts of the United States.

9 U.S.C. § 7.

Implicit within the power to compel compliance with an arbitrator's summons must be the power to quash that summons if it was improperly issued. Oceanic Transport Corp. v. Alcoa S.S. Co., 129 F.Supp. 160 (S.D.N.Y.1954) (rejecting petition to sanction nonparty for failure to comply and vacating subpoena because evidence sought was not material). The court may also consider a petition to quash; there is no requirement that a petition to compel be made first. See Commercial Metals Co. v. International Union Marine Corp., 318 F.Supp. 1334 (S.D.N.Y.1970) (denying motion to quash subpoena duces tecum issued by arbitrator because evidence sought by arbitrator—documents from a party—was relevant to inquiry).

Though the language of the statute speaks only to the arbitrators power to summon a witness to "attend before them," i.e. at the hearing, the courts have permitted arbitrators to order prehearing discovery of parties. See, e.g., In re Technostroyexport, 853 F.Supp. 695, 697 (S.D.N.Y. 1994) (pre-hearing discovery *between parties* is "a matter governed by the applicable arbitration rules (as distinct from court rules) and by what the arbitrator decides."); Chiarella v. Viscount Indus. Co. Ltd., No. 92 Civ. 9310, 1993 WL 497967 (S.D.N.Y. Dec. 1, 1993) (arbitrators did not exceed authority by ordering *the parties* "to mutually exchange all documents and witness lists (i.e. full discovery)"). Two cases from other districts address discovery from nonparties and appear to be the most closely analogous to the instant case.

In Stanton v. Paine Webber Jackson & Curtis, Inc., 685 F.Supp. 1241 (S.D.Fla.1988) the arbitrator, at the request of the defendants, had issued subpoenas to nonparties, requiring prehearing production of documents. The plaintiff objected, contending that issuance of the subpoenas was improper, and constituted impermissible pre-hearing discovery. The court held that:

> [the] plaintiffs . . . are asking the court to impose judicial control over the arbitration proceedings. Such action by the court would vitiate the purposes of the Federal Arbitration Act: 'to facilitate and expedite the resolution of disputes, ease court congestion, and provide disputants with a less costly alternative to litigation.' Recognition Equip., Inc. v. NCR Corp., 532 F.Supp. 271, 275 (N.D.Tex.1981).

> Furthermore, the court finds that under the Arbitration Act, the arbitrators may order and conduct such discovery as they find necessary. See Corcoran v. Shearson/American Express, Inc., 596 F.Supp. 1113, 1117 (N.D.Ga.1984); Mississippi Power Co. v. Peabody Coal Co., 69 F.R.D. 558 (S.D.Miss.1976). . . . Plaintiff's contention that § 7 of the Arbitration Act only permits the arbitrators to compel witnesses at the hearing, and prohibits pre-hearing appearances, is unfounded.

Stanton, 685 F.Supp. at 1242–43. Stanton differs from the instant case in two significant ways. First, the objections to the subpoenas in Stanton were made by one of the parties to the arbitration, not by the subpoenaed nonparty. Second, the subpoenas in Stanton were for the production of documents, and did not require pre-hearing depositions.

When contracting parties stipulate that disputes will be arbitrated, they agree to submit to arbitration procedures rather than court procedures.

> [F]ull scale discovery is not automatically available in arbitration, as it is in litigation. Everyone knows that is so; thus the unavailability of the full panoply of discovery devices, with their attendant burdens of time and expense, may fairly be regarded as one of the bargained-for benefits (or burdens, depending on one's subsequent point of view) of arbitration.

Commonwealth Ins. Co. v. Beneficial Corp., No. 87–Civ.–5056, 1987 WL 17951 (S.D.N.Y. Sept. 29, 1987); accord Oriental Commercial & Shipping Co., Ltd. v. Rosseel, N.V., 125 F.R.D. 398, 400 (S.D.N.Y.1989). Thus, if an arbitrator either refuses to permit, or limits, discovery, courts will seldom order additional discovery in aid of arbitration when requested by a party. This is motivated both by avoidance of wasteful "dual discovery," see Corcoran v. Shearson/American Express, 596 F.Supp. 1113, 1117 (N.D.Ga. 1984), and to give effect to the arbitration process that the parties bargained for. See Commonwealth, supra.

At issue here, however, is an objection by *nonparties*. Petitioners are not parties to the reinsurance agreements nor did they agree to arbitration; there is no "bargained for" advantage to the nonparty. Thus, references to cases concerning pre-hearing discovery disputes *between parties* are not persuasive.

The only reported case that explicitly addresses the plight of a nonparty who objects to arbitrator-ordered discovery is Meadows Indem. Co., Ltd. v. Nutmeg Ins. Co., 157 F.R.D. 42 (M.D.Tenn.1994). There, an arbitration panel ordered a nonparty to produce documents, for inspection by a party, prior to the arbitration hearing. Upon the nonparty's motion for a protective order, the court ruled that the arbitrators' subpoena was valid under the FAA.

> The power of the panel to compel production of documents from third-parties for the purposes of a hearing implicitly authorizes the lesser power to compel such documents for arbitration purposes prior to a hearing. [Movant's] argument requires adoption of an unnecessarily constrictive and unreasonable reading of Section 7 which would limit the ability of the arbitration panel to deal effectively with a large and complex case such as the one at hand, and generally hamper the use of arbitration as a forum for dispute resolution.

Id. at 45. The court further noted that because the documents requested would ultimately have to be produced at the hearing, if not prior to it, no added burden was placed on the nonparty. Id.

It is the burden placed on the nonparty that distinguishes Meadows from the instant case. Documents are only produced once, whether it is at the arbitration or prior to it. Common sense encourages the production of documents prior to the hearing so that the parties can familiarize themselves with the content of the documents. Depositions, however, are quite different. The nonparty may be required to appear twice—once for deposition and again at the hearing. That a nonparty might suffer this burden in a litigation is irrelevant; arbitration is not litigation, and the nonparty never consented to be a part of it. Furthermore, as the deposition is not held before the arbitrator, there is nothing to protect the nonparty from harassing or abusive discovery. The nonparty would, of necessity, turn to the court, obligating the court to become enmeshed in the merits of the matter being arbitrated. This would leave "the parties with one foot in court and the other in arbitration." Mississippi Power Co. v. Peabody Coal Co., 69 F.R.D. 558, 564 (S.D.Miss.1976). Though the Mississippi Power court was addressing "dual discovery"—discovery proceeding simultaneously under the direction of the court and the arbitrators—the considerations of "minimizing the time, expense, and formality of arbitration; preventing duplicative efforts by the federal courts and the arbitrators; and avoiding interference with the arbitrators," Thompson v. Zavin, 607 F.Supp. 780, 782–83 (N.D.Cal.1984), is equally applicable here.

Thus, an arbitrator may not compel attendance of a nonparty at a pre-hearing deposition. The subpoenas issued by the arbitrators are modified accordingly. . . .

* * *

Questions

1. Should the same considerations govern discovery directed to non-parties as those pertaining to parties? What would a non-party have to do to quash an arbitral discovery subpoena? Is a court more likely to quash an arbitral subpoena issued to a non-party than to a party? Which decision-maker has more authority to order discovery of non-parties—courts under the Federal Rules or arbitrators under the FAA?

2. Does the same policy rationale that supports broad discovery power by judges in a federal court support broad discovery power for arbitrators?

* * *

Golub v. Spivey

70 Md.App. 147, 520 A.2d 394 (Md.App. 1987).

■ KARWACKI, JUDGE.

This case commenced with the filing of a claim in the Health Claims Arbitration Office (HCAO) under the provisions of the Health Care Malpractice Claims Act. Md.Code (1974, 1984 Repl.Vol., 1986 Supp.), §§ 3–2A–01 to 3–2A–09 of the Courts and Judicial Proceedings article.[1] Following an arbitration award of $150,000 in favor of the appellee, Shelia D. Nagle Spivey, against the appellant, David D. Golub, M.D., Dr. Golub took steps to reject the award in compliance with procedures delineated in § 3–2A–06 and Rule BY2. Mrs. Spivey then filed a declaration in the Circuit Court for Baltimore City pursuant to Rule BY4. The case was tried before a jury

---

1. All further statutory references will be to this Article of the Code.

whose verdict agreed with the award of the arbitration panel. Dr. Golub appeals from the judgment entered pursuant to that verdict.

FACTS

On July 25, 1979, Mrs. Spivey (Ms. Nagle at that time) was sent by her personal physician to Dr. Golub, a radiologist, for an intravenous pyelogram, a procedure permitting study of a patient's kidney function. Although the pyelogram administered by Dr. Golub revealed inflammation and dysfunction of the left kidney, Dr. Golub erroneously reported a negative finding, i.e., a normal pyelogram. In reliance on Dr. Golub's inaccurate report, Mrs. Spivey's treating physicians failed to provide the immediate care required by her condition. The condition went untreated until the spring of 1980 when Mrs. Spivey visited a urologist. The urologist conducted tests which disclosed that Mrs. Spivey had suffered permanent damage to her left kidney due to an untreated infection.

Mrs. Spivey filed a claim with the Director of the HCAO in August 1980. In addition to Dr. Golub, other health care providers named as defendants in the statement of claim were Richard Berkowitz, M.D., and George N. Karkar, M.D. An arbitration panel consisting of an attorney, a health care provider, and a lay person was appointed pursuant to § 3–2A–04(c) to (e).

On September 9, 1983, three days before the scheduled start of the arbitration hearing, Mrs. Spivey filed a motion in limine seeking to preclude Dr. Golub from presenting expert testimony at the hearing. Previously, on February 17, 1983, the panel chairman had issued an order requiring all counsel in the case to provide the names of experts to each other by July 15, 1983. The other two defendant health care providers each provided the names of two experts by that date, but Dr. Golub did not identify any experts. The panel granted Mrs. Spivey's motion in limine over Dr. Golub's objection that he intended to call the experts named by the other defendant health care providers. The panel also denied Dr. Golub's request for a continuance.

A hearing was conducted before the arbitration panel on September 15 and 16, 1983. At the beginning of the hearing, Mrs. Spivey voluntarily dismissed Dr. Berkowitz and Dr. Karkar as defendants. Dr. Golub admitted liability at the hearing, and at its conclusion on September 16, the arbitration panel rendered an award against Dr. Golub in the amount of $150,000. In accordance with § 3–2A–05(g), written notice of the award was delivered to the Director of the HCAO, who mailed copies of it to counsel for all parties on October 24, 1983.

On November 18, 1983, Dr. Golub filed a Notice of Rejection with the Director of the HCAO pursuant to § 3–2A–06(a). At the same time he also filed a Notice of Action to Nullify Award in the Circuit Court for Baltimore City, in compliance with § 3–2A–06(b)(1) and Rule BY2. Copies of both notices were mailed to counsel for Mrs. Spivey on November 17, 1983, according to the attached certificates of service. The attorneys for Mrs. Spivey did not receive either notice and did not learn of their filing until

December 22, 1983, when one of them checked the docket at HCAO after Mrs. Spivey had inquired of him as to when she could expect payment of the arbitration award.

On December 23, 1983, 35 days after Dr. Golub's Notice of Action to Nullify Award was filed, Mrs. Spivey filed a declaration in the Circuit Court for Baltimore City. In response to that declaration, Dr. Golub filed a Motion Raising Preliminary Objection and a Motion Ne Recipiatur or to Strike. The basis for both motions was Mrs. Spivey's failure to file her declaration within 30 days after the filing of Dr. Golub's Notice of Action to Nullify Award, as required by Rule BY4 a.1. Dr. Golub also filed a Motion to Vacate Award in which he challenged the propriety of the panel's decisions granting Mrs. Spivey's motion in limine prior to the arbitration hearing and refusing to grant Dr. Golub's request for a continuance.

Although the certificates of service attached to each of the three motions filed by Dr. Golub indicate that they were mailed to counsel for Mrs. Spivey on January 9, 1984, those documents, like the previously filed notices, were not received. It was not until February 10, 1984, when Mrs. Spivey's attorneys received a copy of Judge Thomas Ward's order granting Dr. Golub's motions, that they became aware of the filing of those motions. Mrs. Spivey immediately filed a motion to set aside Judge Ward's order, citing a lack of notice as to the filing of the three motions. Mrs. Spivey's motion was supported by an affidavit by two of her attorneys attesting to their lack of notice of the three motions granted by Judge Ward as well as of Dr. Golub's Notice of Rejection and Notice of Action to Nullify Award.

On September 7, 1984, Judge Ward conducted a hearing concerning Mrs. Spivey's motion to set aside his earlier order granting Dr. Golub's three preliminary motions. In a memorandum opinion filed November 14, 1984, Judge Ward vacated his order. Judge Ward found that Dr. Golub was not prejudiced by Mrs. Spivey's filing of her declaration five days late, thereby rejecting the basis for Dr. Golub's Motion Raising Preliminary Objection and Motion Ne Recipiatur. In a separate order filed the same day, Judge Ward denied Dr. Golub's Motion to Vacate Award.

A jury trial was conducted in the Circuit Court for Baltimore City (John N. Maguire, J., presiding) on November 4 and 5, 1985. Dr. Golub again admitted liability at the trial, but he presented an expert who testified on the issues of causation and damages. The jury returned a verdict of $150,000 in favor of Mrs. Spivey.

Dr. Golub presents three questions for our consideration:

I. Whether the Circuit Court erred in denying Dr. Golub's preliminary defenses to the declaration when the declaration was not timely filed in accordance with the Health Care Malpractice Claims Act and the Maryland Rules of Procedure?

II. Whether the Circuit Court erred in denying Dr. Golub's Motion to Vacate Award in the face of improprieties in the arbitration proceeding?

III. Whether the Circuit Court erred in permitting prejudicial cross-examination of Dr. Golub's expert witness?

. . .

II.

The second issue raised by Dr. Golub concerns the Circuit Court's denial of his Motion to Vacate Award. Unless it is vacated by the court, an award rendered by a health claims arbitration panel is admissible as evidence in a subsequent court action to nullify the award. If admissible, the award is presumed correct, and the burden is on the party rejecting it to prove that it is not correct. § 3–2A–06(d); Rule BY5. Section 3–2A–06(d) states that an arbitration award is admissible "[u]nless vacated by the court pursuant to subsection (c)." Subsection (c) provides, in pertinent part:

> An allegation that an award is improper because of any ground stated in § 3–223(b) or § 3–224(b)(1), (2), (3), or (4) of this article shall be made by preliminary motion, and shall be determined by the court without a jury prior to trial.... If the court finds that a condition stated in § 3–224(b)(1), (2), (3), or (4) exists, it shall vacate the award, and trial of the case shall proceed as if there had been no award.

In his motion to vacate, Dr. Golub relied on § 3–224(b)(4), which states:

> The court shall vacate an award if:

> * * *

> (4) The arbitrators refused to postpone the hearing upon sufficient cause being shown for the postponement, refused to hear evidence material to the controversy, or otherwise so conducted the hearing, contrary to the provisions of § 3–213, as to prejudice substantially the rights of a party.

Dr. Golub contends that the arbitration panel, in granting Mrs. Spivey's motion in limine precluding Dr. Golub from presenting expert testimony at the arbitration hearing, "refused to hear evidence material to the controversy." Furthermore, Dr. Golub posits that the surprise caused by the granting of the motion in limine just prior to the scheduled start of the hearing constituted "sufficient cause" for granting his requested postponement. We think the court was correct in denying Dr. Golub's Motion to Vacate Award. Dr. Golub's argument overlooks the arbitration panel's basis for granting Mrs. Spivey's motion in limine. A deadline for naming experts had been established by the panel chairman in a scheduling order issued on February 17, 1983. That deadline was July 15, 1983. Dr. Golub not only failed to name any experts by that date, but he did not provide any names until the motion in limine was filed on September 9, 1983, at which point he sought to claim as his own the experts identified by the other two defendants.

The panel chairman in a health claims arbitration proceeding has the authority to decide all prehearing procedures including issues relating to discovery. § 3–2A–05(c). We believe exclusion of expert testimony on Dr. Golub's behalf was an appropriate sanction for Dr. Golub's failure to comply with the discovery deadline in the panel chairman's scheduling order.[4] Therefore, the Circuit Court did not err in denying Dr. Golub's Motion to Vacate Award. . . .

JUDGMENT AFFIRMED; COSTS TO BE PAID BY THE APPELLANT.

* * *

Questions

1. Are the arbitrators and court in *Golub* importing judicial procedures into the arbitral setting? Is this appropriate?

2. The court in *Golub* states that the arbitrators have authority over all pre-hearing procedures. Are there limits on the arbitrator's authority over the conduct of pre-hearing procedures? Should there be? Should there be limits to the arbitrator's authority over hearing procedures?

* * *

7. EVIDENCE

Totem Marine Tug & Barge, Inc. v. North American Towing, Inc.

607 F.2d 649 (5th Cir.1979).

■ REAVLEY, CIRCUIT JUDGE:

North American Towing, Inc. (North American) applied for confirmation of an arbitration award against Totem Marine Tug and Barge, Inc. (Totem), which sought to vacate or modify the award. The arbitrators' decision held that Totem had breached the charter agreement between the parties and awarded North American damages of $74,568.08. The district court confirmed the award. 429 F.Supp. 452 (E.D.La.1977). Because of irregularities in the conduct of the arbitration hearing which materially prejudiced Totem, we reverse.

FACTS

On June 19, 1975, Totem and North American entered a six month time charter agreement for the M/V KIRT CHOUEST owned by North American. The vessel was to be delivered to Totem at Galliano, Louisiana, and to be returned there or to any other mutually agreed port at the

---

4. If Dr. Golub intended to call the experts named by the other defendants, he should have made this known to the other parties and the HCAO panel prior to the discovery deadline.

expiration of the charter term. Totem was to use the vessel to tow a loaded barge from Houston through the Panama Canal and into the Pacific, to Los Angeles and then Seattle, and finally to Anchorage, Alaska. On October 19, 1975, Totem terminated the charter allegedly because of excessive repairs and delays caused by the vessel. North American requested arbitration. Totem responded by seeking a clarification of North American's claim. North American provided an itemized statement of the claim, the first and largest item being the "Specific contract amount for returning vessel $45,000.00" (R. at 29). Totem counterclaimed alleging that the vessel was unfit for the purposes of the charter and that the vessel had been redelivered at a mutually agreed port: Anchorage.

Although North American never requested damages for charter hire, the contract amount for use of the vessel between October 19 (the date of Totem's alleged breach) and December 19 (the end of the charter term), the arbitration panel awarded it nonetheless. The panel stated: "North American erroneously asked only for its return expense (plus some miscellaneous accounting items) in damages. The proper measure of North American's damages was the balance of charter hire due under the charter less the earnings of the vessel during that period." (R. at 118). Totem contends that by this action the arbitrators exceeded their powers and awarded on a matter not submitted to them, thereby impairing the award under the provisions of 9 U.S.C.A. § 10(d) and § 11(b) (1970).

The panel then computed North American's damages as the charter hire due under the contract from October 19 to December 19, less the earnings of the KIRT CHOUEST during the same time period, plus some miscellaneous expenses. It is undisputed that after the close of the arbitration proceedings, during deliberations, the arbitrators realized that each had a different figure in his notes on the earnings of the KIRT CHOUEST from October to December. The arbitrator appointed by North American then telephoned North American's counsel who supplied the figure which the arbitrators used to complete their computations. Totem was neither notified of this telephone conversation nor given any opportunity to respond to the figure provided by North American. Totem contends that this ex parte communication constituted prejudicial misconduct by the arbitrators in violation of 9 U.S.C.A. § 10(c).

UNLAWFUL EXTENSION OF SUBJECT MATTER

Totem contends that the issue of charter hire was never placed in issue in the arbitration proceeding and that an award on that basis denied it due process. North American acknowledges that it never specifically requested damages for charter hire but claims that the matter was naturally intertwined in the general scope of the breach of contract claim.

An arbitration proceeding is much less formal than a trial in court. "In handling evidence an arbitrator need not follow all the niceties observed by the federal courts. He need only grant the parties a fundamentally fair hearing." Bell Aerospace Co. Div. of Textron, Inc. v. Local 516, UAW, 500 F.2d 921, 923 (2d Cir. 1974). All parties in an arbitration proceeding are entitled to notice and an opportunity to be heard. Citizens Bldg. of West Palm Beach, Inc. v. Western Union Tel. Co., 120 F.2d 982, 984 (5th Cir.1941); Seldner Corp. v. W. R. Grace & Co., 22 F.Supp. 388, 391–93 (D.Md. 1938). Although arbitrators enjoy a broad grant of authority to fashion remedies (Commercial Arbitration Rules of the American Arbitration Association § 42),[2] arbitrators are restricted to those issues submitted. . . .

Arbitration is contractual and arbitrators derive their authority from the scope of the contractual agreement. United Steelworkers of America v. Enterprise Wheel and Car Corp., 363 U.S. 593, 597, 80 S.Ct. 1358, 4 L.Ed.2d 1424 (1960); Gulf and South America Steamship Co., Inc. v. National Maritime Union of America, 360 F.2d 63, 65 (5th Cir.1966). The award of an arbitration panel may be vacated where the arbitrators exceed their powers. 9 U.S.C.A. § 10(d) (1970). . . .

The arbitration panel exceeded its powers by awarding damages for charter hire to North American. Not only did North American fail to list charter hire in its itemized statement of damages submitted to Totem, but in its brief submitted to the arbitration panel, North American conceded that charter hire was not an issue in the arbitration. Totem prepared and argued a case in which return expenses, and not charter hire, was the main issue. North American originally claimed damages totalling $74,713.63, later amended to a total of $87,047.82, the first and largest item claimed being $45,000.00 for return of the vessel. With the exception of the $45,000 claim for returning the vessel, and a few other very minor exceptions totalling less than $1,000, the arbitration panel fully upheld North American's claim. In place of the $45,000 North American requested for return of the vessel, the arbitrators awarded charter hire totalling $117,440.00, bringing the total damages due North American to $157,887.63, before Totem's offsets and counterclaims. It is anomalous for the arbitration panel to award an unrequested item of damages three times larger than any item claimed by North American and then to hear the panel action supported with an argument that the awarded item was naturally intertwined within the scope of the arbitration.

In its letter of February 4, 1976, responding to Totem's request for a clarification of the matters to be submitted to arbitration, North American set forth the nature of the dispute and the amount involved by itemizing its damages.[3] Although return expenses were specifically listed, damages for charter hire were not. By awarding charter hire, the arbitrators ignored the

---

2. Section 42. SCOPE OF AWARD The Arbitrator may grant any remedy or relief which he deems just and equitable and within the scope of the agreement of the parties, including, but not limited to, specific performance of a contract. The Arbitrator, in his award, shall assess arbitration fees and expenses in favor of any party and, in the event any administrative fees or expenses are due the AAA, in favor of the AAA.

3. The Commercial Arbitration Rules of the American Arbitration Association provide as follows:

Section 7. Initiation under an Arbitration Provision in a Contract Arbitration under an arbitration provision in a contract may be initiated in the following manner: (a) The initiating party may give notice to the other party which notice shall contain a statement setting

arbitral dispute submitted by the parties and dispensed their "own brand of industrial justice." United Steelworkers of America v. Enterprise Wheel and Car Corp., supra, 363 U.S. at 597, 80 S.Ct. 1358.

EX PARTE COMMUNICATION

After the arbitrators decided to base North American's damages on charter hire instead of the expenses of returning the vessel, it became necessary to determine the earnings of the KIRT CHOUEST between October and December as an offset. Because charter hire had never been placed in issue and the vessel's earnings had arisen only as related to the issue of whether the vessel had been returned to North American at Anchorage, each of the arbitrators had a different figure in his notes and none were confident that he had the correct figure. Consequently, although the hearings had been closed several days earlier, and despite the fact that the office of Totem's counsel was in the same building in which the arbitrators were deliberating, a long distance call was placed to North American's counsel to ascertain the earnings of the KIRT CHOUEST. The figure supplied by North American's counsel was adopted by the panel although it matched none of their figures. Totem was never notified of the call or given any opportunity to contest the figure supplied.

In clause twenty-four of the charter agreement, Totem and North American incorporated the Commercial Arbitration Rules of the American Arbitration Association for the resolution of any dispute between them. Section thirty of the Arbitration Rules states that "(a)ll evidence shall be taken in the presence of all the parties, except where any of the parties is absent in default or has waived his right to be present."[5] Evidence was received from North American's counsel out of Totem's presence when the telephone call was made and the figure given by North American was adopted by the arbitrators as the basis for their computations. Totem neither defaulted nor waived its rights, but instead, timely filed a motion to vacate in district court. The arbitration rules provide specific procedures for the receipt of evidence[7] and the close of hearings,[8] procedures violated by the ex parte communication with North American.

After the arbitration panel improperly extended the scope of arbitration to include charter hire, the extent of Totem's liability hinged on the

---

forth the nature of the dispute, the amount involved, if any, the remedy sought....

5. Section 30 provides as follows:

Section 30. EVIDENCE

The parties may offer such evidence as they desire and shall produce such additional evidence as the Arbitrator may deem necessary to an understanding and determination of the dispute. When the Arbitrator is authorized by law to subpoena witnesses or documents, he may do so upon his own initiative or upon the request of any party. The Arbitrator shall be the judge of the relevancy and

materiality of the evidence offered and conformity to legal rules of evidence shall not be necessary. All evidence shall be taken in the presence of all of the Arbitrators and of all the parties, except where any of the parties is absent in default or has waived his right to be present.

7. Section 31 provides as follows:

Section 31. EVIDENCE BY AFFIDAVIT AND FILING OF DOCUMENTS

The Arbitrator shall receive and consider the evidence of witnesses by affidavit, but shall give it only such weight as he deems it entitled to after consideration of any objec-

determination of the earnings of the KIRT CHOUEST between October and December. The ex parte receipt of evidence bearing on this matter constituted misbehavior by the arbitrators prejudicial to Totem's rights in violation of 9 U.S.C.A. § 10(c); E. g., Chevron Transport Corp. v. Astro Vencedor Compania Naviera, S. A., 300 F.Supp. 179 (S.D.N.Y.1969) (the failure of maritime arbitrators to make the ship's logs in the hand of one party fully and timely available to the other party was considered sufficient grounds for vacating the award where the party could show that he was thereby prejudiced); Katz v. Uvegi, 18 Misc.2d 576, 187 N.Y.S.2d 511 (Sup.Ct.1959), aff'd, 11 A.D.2d 773, 205 N.Y.S.2d 972 (App.Div.1960): "Arbitrators cannot conduct ex parte hearings or receive evidence except in the presence of each other and of the parties, unless otherwise stipulated." 18 Misc.2d at 583, 187 N.Y.S.2d at 518.

We vacate the award without prejudice to the resubmission of the dispute between the parties before a new arbitration panel in accordance with the terms of the contract.

* * *

Questions

1. In *Totem Marine Tug & Barge*, suppose the rules governing the arbitration were silent about whether the parties should be present for all evidence. How would the case have been decided in that event?

2. How can a court know if the evidence heard *ex parte* was prejudicial? Can it interrogate the arbitrator to find out?

* * *

Michael and Mary Smaligo, Administrators of the Estate of Elizabeth Smaligo, Deceased v. Fireman's Fund Insurance Company

432 Pa. 133, 247 A.2d 577 (Pa. S.Ct. 1968).

■ JONES, JUSTICE.

Michael and Mary Smaligo, as personal representatives of their daughter's estate, instituted arbitration proceedings to recover for the daughter's

tions made to its admission. All documents not filed with the Arbitrator at the hearing, but arranged for at the hearing or subsequently by agreement of the parties, shall be filed with the AAA for transmission to the Arbitrator. All parties shall be afforded opportunity to examine such documents.

8. Section 34 provides as follows:

Section 34. CLOSING OF HEARINGS

The Arbitrator shall specifically inquire of all parties whether they have any further proofs to offer or witnesses to be heard. Upon receiving negative replies, the Arbitrator shall declare the hearings closed and a minute thereof shall be recorded. If briefs are to be filed, the hearings shall be declared closed as of the final date set by the Arbitrator for the receipt of briefs. If documents are to be filed as provided for in Section 31 and the date set for their receipt is later than that set for the receipt of briefs, the later date shall be the date of closing the hearing. The time limit within which the Arbitrator is required to make his award shall commence to run, in the absence of other agreements by the parties, upon the closing of the hearings.

death caused by a hit-and-run driver on March 27, 1967, at a time said daughter, aged 37, was on a home week-end visit from Mayview State Hospital where she had been a patient since 1962. Arbitration proceeded under the "Uninsured Motorist Clause" of Smaligos' policy of insurance with Fireman's Fund Insurance Company, which resulted in an award to Smaligos of only $243.00 (a figure which represented one-third of the cost of the family memorial monument).

Smaligos moved to vacate the award on the ground of certain irregularities in the arbitration proceedings, to-wit: (1) that the arbitrator proceeded to make an award even though informed by Smaligos' counsel of their acceptance of a settlement offer made prior to the arbitration proceedings, which offer Smaligos claimed was still outstanding; and (2) that the arbitrator denied a request of Smaligos' counsel for a recess to obtain the testimony of Dr. Parsons, decedent's attending physician, as to decedent's future work expectancy, the arbitrator holding such testimony not to be necessary. Smaligos argued that these irregularities resulted in an unjust, inequitable and unconscionable award for the death of a 37–year old woman who had been gainfully employed prior to her commitment to Mayview State Hospital in 1962. After a hearing on Smaligos' motion the court below issued an order vacating the award and remanding the case for hearing *de novo* before another arbitrator to be selected from the American Arbitration Association Panel.

The insurance company has appealed from said order, contending that, since the proceedings were admittedly under the common law, the court was bound by the arbitrator's action. In making this argument, the insurance company relies on our holding in Harwitz v. Selas Corporation of America, 406 Pa. 539, 178 A.2d 617 (1962), as follows: "If the appeal is from a common law award, Appellant, to succeed, must show by clear, precise and indubitable evidence that he was denied a hearing, or that there was fraud, misconduct, corruption or some other irregularity of this nature on the part of the arbitrator which caused him to render an unjust, inequitable and unconscionable award, the arbitrator being the final judge of both law and fact, his award not being subject to disturbance for a mistake of either."

A review of the record reveals the following facts: Elizabeth Smaligo, the decedent—a high school graduate who had also attended night classes at Duquesne University—had been gainfully employed as a secretary by Westinghouse Electric Corporation from 1949 until October, 1962, when she was admitted to Western Psychiatric Hospital and there diagnosed as schizophrenic. Later she was committed to Mayview State Hospital and, at the time of her death, was still so committed though permitted to visit her home on weekends and holidays. During such a home a weekend stay she was struck by a hit-and-run driver on March 27, 1967. Smaligos then made claim against their insurance company under the terms of the Uninsured Motorist Provisions of an automobile liability policy that had been issued to them by that company wherein the company had agreed to pay "all sums which the insured or his legal representative shall be legally entitled to recover as damages." The company refused to pay the $9,750.00 asked by Smaligos in settlement and on July 27, 1967 the company notified Smaligos' counsel by letter as follows: "We concede that there is a settlement value to the case but that it is not worth $9750. as demanded by you. In an effort to avoid further expenses and time to both, I will now make an offer to conclude this claim on an amicable basis and for the sum of $7500. which you may convey to your clients. If the offer of $7500. is not acceptable, I would then suggest that your arbitration papers be prepared as we have no intention of increasing this offer, feeling that it is fair and just to all parties concerned."

On August 30, 1967, Smaligos' counsel made a demand for arbitration to the American Arbitration Association and on October 11, 1967 Thomas J. Reinstadtler, Jr., Esquire, was appointed as arbitrator. A hearing was held on December 18, 1967 which, as before stated, resulted in the arbitrator awarding only $243, being one-third of the cost of a family memorial monument. The arbitrator determined that the funeral bill of $1016.30 was payable under the Medical Payment Clause of the policy and thus not recoverable under the Uninsured Motorist Clause.

It must be conceded that there was no evidence in the record that decedent would ever again be gainfully employed. However, Smaligos' counsel testified at the hearing on the motion to vacate that he had asked the arbitrator for a continuance in order to secure the expert testimony of Dr. Parsons on the question of decedent's future earning ability and capacity and that the arbitrator stated that such testimony was not necessary. Dr. Parsons was decedent's attending physician. The arbitrator, on the other hand, testified that no formal motion for continuance was made and that he could not remember "specifically what Mr. Maurizi asked or what my response was," although he did not deny that he had said Dr. Parsons' testimony was unnecessary. In fact, counsel who had represented defendant company during the arbitration proceedings testified that the arbitrator did state that the doctor's testimony was unnecessary.

Whether or not a formal motion for continuance was made is not as governing as the arbitrator seeks to make it. The important fact that stands clear is that Smaligos' counsel did proffer medical testimony which was relevant and of great import in the determination of loss of future earnings of the decedent and that the arbitrator determined such testimony was not necessary. It may be true that Smaligos' counsel should have come prepared with the medical testimony at the time of the hearing and that perhaps the necessity of such testimony came to him as an "afterthought" (as stated by the arbitrator), but such observations cannot militate from the all-important fact that counsel did at the time of the hearing make an offer to present the medical testimony and the arbitrator viewed such testimony as "unnecessary".

This was not a mere mistake of law or of fact binding upon all parties and the court. The arbitrator's failure to regard Dr. Parsons' testimony of any import resulted in Smaligos being denied a full and fair hearing. That an award is not binding where there has been a denial of a hearing has been clearly stated by this Court on several occasions. In Newspaper Guild of Greater Philadelphia v. Philadelphia Daily News, Inc., 401 Pa. 337, 346, 164 A.2d 215, 220 (1960), we stated: "The defenses available to the News in a proceeding to enforce a common law award are extremely limited. Such an award of arbitrators is conclusive and binding and cannot be attacked unless it can be shown by clear, precise and indubitable evidence that the parties were denied a hearing, or that there was fraud, misconduct, corruption or some other irregularity of this nature on the part of the arbitrators which caused them to render an unjust, inequitable and unconscionable award." We repeated this holding in Harwitz v. Selas Corporation of America, 406 Pa. 539, 542, 178 A.2d 617, 619 (1962), the very case relied upon by defendant as hereinbefore quoted and again here quoted as follows: "If the appeal is from a common law award, Appellant, to succeed, must show by clear, precise and indubitable evidence that he was denied a hearing, or that there was fraud, misconduct, corruption or some other irregularity of this nature on the part of the arbitrator which caused him to render an unjust, inequitable and unconscionable award, the arbitrator being the final judge of both law and fact, his award not being subject to disturbance for a mistake of either. Newspaper Guild of Greater Philadelphia v. Philadelphia Daily News, Inc., 401 Pa. 337, 164 A.2d 215 (1960); Freeman v. Ajax Foundry Products, Inc., 20 Pa.Dist. & Co. [R.]2d 128, affirmed 398 Pa. 457, 159 A.2d 708 (1960); Capecci v. Capecci, Inc., 11 Pa.Dist. & Co. (R.)2d 459, affirmed 392 Pa. 32, 139 A.2d 563 (1958)."

Though the arbitrator's conduct in this case may not have constituted fraud, misconduct, corruption or some other irregularity "of this nature", yet it was conduct which amounted to a denial of a full and fair hearing of Smaligos' cause of action. It is our opinion, therefore, that the court below properly vacated the award and remanded it for arbitration before another arbitrator.

We deem it unnecessary to make any determination of the issue raised as to the propriety of the arbitrator's holding the funeral bill to be payable under the "Medical Payments" clause and thus not recoverable under the "Uninsured Motorist" clause. The record is clear as to the willingness of the insurance company to pay the funeral bill under the "Medical Payments" clause and it should make no difference to Smaligos under which clause they recover the $1016.30.

Smaligos further argue that there was an offer and acceptance of a settlement in the amount of $7500. However, we are constrained to agree with the reasoning of the lower court that, when Smaligos filed for arbitration of the dispute, they rejected the offer of settlement. The letter hereinbefore quoted offering the said $7500 clearly stated that the company was "now" offering the same and that if it is not acceptable then Smaligos should proceed to arbitration. By proceeding to arbitration, Smaligos showed the offer was not acceptable and such conduct clearly showed that Smaligos did not intend to accept the offer nor take it under further advisement. As stated in section 36 of the Restatement of the Law of Contracts: "An offer is rejected when the offeror is justified in inferring from the words or conduct of the offeree that the offeree intends not to accept the offer or to take it under further advisement." We cannot agree with Smaligos' interpretation of the phrase "as we have no intention of increasing this offer" as meaning that the offer was to stand firm at $7500 even though arbitration was sought. The company, as stated in the letter, made the offer "in an effort to avoid further expenses and time to both"; certainly that offer cannot be viewed as still standing after the company was required to proceed to arbitration.

Order affirmed.

■ MUSMANNO, COHEN and ROBERTS, JJ., did not participate in this decision.

* * *

Questions

1. The court in *Smalgio* decided that the disputed evidence was relevant and therefore should have been admitted by the arbitrator. How can a court determine the relevance of the evidence in an arbitration proceeding? To what degree does this require the court to consider the merits of the case?

2. What does the *Smalgio* decision indicate about the minimal due process protections required to constitute a "full and fair" hearing?

* * *

Note on *Robins v. Day*:

In ROBINS V. DAY, 954 F.2d 679 (11th Cir.1992), the plaintiffs initiated arbitration proceedings against the defendant-stockbrokers based on a claim of excessive trading constituting churning of the plaintiffs' accounts. At arbitration, the defendant-stockbrokers asserted the Fifth Amendment's provision against self-incrimination and refused to testify because they were under indictment for securities fraud arising from the same set of facts. The stockbrokers also sought to continue the hearing until after the securities fraud trial was completed. The plaintiffs opposed the continuance, which was refused on the ground that the stockbrokers' testimony was unimportant to the proceedings. The stockbrokers prevailed in the arbitration. Subsequently, in seeking to have the award vacated, the plaintiffs argued that the arbitrators should have compelled the stockbrokers to testify. The Eleventh Circuit refused to vacate, noting that, "A federal court may vacate an arbitrator's award ... only if the arbitrator's refusal to hear pertinent and material evidence prejudices the rights of the parties and denies them a fair hearing. Further, an arbitration award must not be set aside for the arbitrator's refusal to hear evidence that is cumulative or irrelevant."

In reaching its decision to not vacate the award, the court emphasized the systemic virtues of arbitration:

"In applying the statutory grounds for the granting of a motion to vacate an award, we always bear in mind that the basic policy of conducting arbitration is to offer a means of deciding disputes expeditiously and at lower costs. Thus the Federal Arbitration Act allows arbitration to proceed with only a summary hearing and with restricted inquiry into factual issues. The arbitrator is not bound to hear all the evidence tendered by the parties; he need only give each party the opportunity to present its arguments and evidence. ... We will not undermine the expediency of arbitration to determine the materiality or pertinence of excluded evidence that the moving party agreed was unimportant."

How might a court go about determining whether excluded evidence is "cumulative or irrelevant" or "central and decisive"? Suppose an arbitration award was not accompanied by an opinion, but merely stated which party prevailed and the amount of monetary damages. How should a reviewing court evaluate the relevance of excluded evidence in that case?

* * *

Bonar v. Dean Witter Reynolds, Inc.

835 F.2d 1378 (11th Cir.1988).

■ KRAVITCH, CIRCUIT JUDGE:

Arbitrators of a dispute between the Bonars and Dean Witter Reynolds awarded punitive as well as compensatory damages to the Bonars. Dean Witter claims that the district court abused its discretion in refusing to vacate the award of punitive damages because (1) it was obtained through fraud; (2) the arbitrators lacked authority to award punitive damages; (3) the appellees contractually waived any right they may have had to punitive damages; and (4) the punitive damages award was so irrational as to be an abuse of the arbitrators' discretion. Concluding that the district court abused its discretion in not vacating the award on the ground of fraud, we reverse and remand for a new hearing on the issue of punitive damages.

I.

[In July, 1982, appellees James and Beverly Bonar opened a securities trading account at Dean Witter's Orlando, Florida office, with an initial deposit of $16,436.77. Their account executive, Ed Leavenworth, stole funds from their account so that, by November, 1983, it was depleted. Leavenworth stole funds from another account in 1984, and deposited those stolen funds into appellees account. In September, 1984, Leavenworth left the employ of Dean Witter and went to another investment firm. Appellees closed their Dean Witter account and moved it to Leavenworth's new firm. When they closed their Dean Witter Account, it had a market value of $11,489.90. In January, 1985, Dean Witter discovered Leavenworth's embezzlement and notified all his former customers, including appellees. In addition, Dean Witter turned over the results of its investigation to the State Attorney for Orange County, Florida, and assisted in the criminal prosecution and ultimate incarceration of Leavenworth.]

On August 9, 1985, the appellees filed a complaint and demand for arbitration with the American Arbitration Association alleging violations of various state and federal laws, breach of fiduciary duty, negligence, and gross negligence in the handling of their account. The complaint, seeking compensatory and punitive damages, named as defendants Dean Witter, John McNally, Jr., the branch manager of the Orlando office, and Leavenworth. Leavenworth was never served with process and thus never became a party to the arbitration proceedings.

A three member arbitration panel heard the appellees' case on May 8–9, 1986. At the hearing, Dean Witter and McNally admitted liability for compensatory damages.[2] Because of this admission, the central factual issue for the arbitrators to decide was whether the conduct of Dean Witter and McNally justified the imposition of punitive damages. At the hearing, in addition to the testimony from lay witnesses, the appellees presented the testimony of two expert witnesses to support their claim for punitive damages. The second expert, Thomas E. Nix, testified that he was president and owner of an investment advisory firm, that he graduated from the University of Alabama in 1980 with a bachelor's degree in finance and that in 1981 he attended Columbia University and received a bachelor's degree in accounting. Nix further testified that after his graduation from Columbia he worked for St. Paul in New York as the money manager of a $30 million portfolio and that in the summer of 1985 he received an honorary doctorate in finance from the Technical University of Vienna.

During voir dire, Nix admitted that he was not, and never had been, a licensed securities broker or branch manager of a securities brokerage house. Based on this, Dean Witter requested that Nix not be allowed to testify on the ground that he was "not qualified as an expert to render testimony on the trading in any account." After the panel rejected this request, Nix testified that, in his opinion, the trading in the appellees' account was excessive, and that Dean Witter and McNally had not properly supervised the appellees' account. On June 5, 1986, the arbitrators assessed compensatory damages against both Dean Witter and McNally, and punitive damages of $150,000 against Dean Witter alone. Following the award, Dean Witter applied to the arbitration panel for a reduction in, or the elimination of, the award of punitive damages. The arbitrators denied that application on July 15, 1986.

On July 30, 1986, Dean Witter moved to vacate or modify the arbitration award pursuant to the Federal Arbitration Act, 9 U.S.C. §§ 10 and 11, (the "Arbitration Act") on the grounds that the arbitrators lacked authori-

---

2. McNally and Dean Witter admitted liability for compensatory damages in the amount of $5,886.77. This figure represents the appellees' original deposit of $16,436.77, less the $11,489.90 value of the stock transferred to appellees when they closed their account, plus interest of 12%.

ty to award punitive damages, that the appellees contractually waived any right to punitive damages, and that the punitive damage award was based upon a manifest disregard of the evidence and was so irrational as to be an abuse of the arbitrators' discretion. Before the district court decided this motion, Dean Witter discovered that the credentials asserted by Nix as a basis for his testimony as an expert witness were completely false. Nix was an engineering student at the University of Alabama and never graduated from that institution. Furthermore, he never attended Columbia University or worked for St. Paul.

Accordingly, on November 20, 1986, Dean Witter filed an amended motion to vacate or modify the arbitration award adding as grounds that the award should be vacated under 9 U.S.C. § 10(a) because it was procured through fraud.... Shortly thereafter, the appellees filed motions to confirm the arbitration award, ... and to strike as untimely Dean Witter's amended motion to vacate. In the motion to strike, the appellees admitted that Nix had committed perjury at the arbitration hearing.

By orders dated December 9, 1986, the district court granted appellees' motion to confirm the arbitration award, denied Dean Witter's amended motion to vacate or modify the award, and denied all other motions of both parties. The district court took the above actions by stamping GRANTED or DENIED on the face of the parties' motions. As a result, there is no written order explaining the basis for these decisions. The district court entered a final judgment based on the arbitration award against Dean Witter and McNally on April 2, 1987 and this appeal followed.

II.

. . .

B.

... [W]e must now decide whether the district court, in denying the motion, abused its discretion under the Arbitration Act. Section 10 of the Arbitration Act specifies the grounds for vacating an arbitration award and provides as follows:

> In either of the following cases the United States court in and for the district wherein the award was made may make an order vacating the award upon the application of any party to the arbitration award—

> (a) Where the award was procured by corruption, fraud, or undue means.

In reviewing cases under § 10(a), courts have relied upon a three part test to determine whether an arbitration award should be vacated for fraud.[7] First, the movant must establish the fraud by clear and convincing evi-

---

7. There is no doubt that perjury constitutes fraud within the meaning of the Arbitration Act. Dogherra v. Safeway Stores, Inc., 679 F.2d 1293, 1297 (9th Cir.1982), cert. denied, 459 U.S. 990, 103 S.Ct. 346, 74 L.Ed.2d 386 (1982); cf. Harre v. A.H. Robins, 750 F.2d 1501, 1503 (11th Cir.1985) (perjury constitutes fraud under Fed.R.Civ.P. 60(b)(3)) (see infra note 8).

dence. Lafarge Conseils et Etudes, S.A. v. Kaiser Cement, 791 F.2d 1334, 1339 (9th Cir.1986); Dogherra v. Safeway Stores, Inc., 679 F.2d 1293, 1297 (9th Cir.), cert. denied, 459 U.S. 990, 103 S.Ct. 346, 74 L.Ed.2d 386 (1982). Second, the fraud must not have been discoverable upon the exercise of due diligence prior to or during the arbitration. Karppinen v. Karl Kiefer Machine Co., 187 F.2d 32, 35 (2d Cir.1951) (A. Hand, J.); see also Kaiser Cement, 791 F.2d at 1339; Dogherra, 679 F.2d at 1297. Third, the person seeking to vacate the award must demonstrate that the fraud materially related to an issue in the arbitration. Kaiser Cement, 791 F.2d at 1339; Dogherra, 679 F.2d at 1297; see also Newark Stereotypers' Union No. 18 v. Newark Morning Ledger Co., 397 F.2d 594, 599 (3d Cir.) (fraud must deprive party of fair hearing), cert. denied, 393 U.S. 954, 89 S.Ct. 378, 21 L.Ed.2d 365 (1968); cf. Rozier v. Ford Motor Co., 573 F.2d 1332, 1339 (5th Cir.1978) (relief from judgment under Fed.R.Civ.P. 60(b)(3) requires showing that perjury prevented losing party from "fully and fairly presenting his case or defense");[8] Harre v. A.H. Robins, 750 F.2d 1501, 1503 (11th Cir.1985) (same). This last element does not require the movant to establish that the result of the proceedings would have been different had the fraud not occurred. Cf. Wilson v. Thompson, 638 F.2d 801, 804 (5th Cir.Unit B March 1981) (60(b)(3)).

Mindful that we are reviewing the district court's refusal to vacate under the narrow "abuse of discretion" standard, we nevertheless hold that under the above test, Nix's perjury requires vacation of the punitive damages portion of the arbitration award. First, along with its amended motion to vacate the award, Dean Witter submitted to the district court clear and convincing evidence of Nix's perjury. Letters from the relevant university officials revealed that, contrary to his testimony, Nix had never graduated from the University of Alabama and had never attended Columbia University. Furthermore, an affidavit from the Human Resources Officer at St. Paul Fire and Marine Insurance Company confirmed that Nix had never worked for either St. Paul or its banking subsidiary. Second, Dean Witter has shown that it could not have discovered Nix's perjury before or during the arbitration hearing. Because the rules of the American

---

8. In pertinent part, Rule 60(b) provides as follows: **(b) Mistakes; Inadvertence; Excusable Neglect; Newly Discovered Evidence; Fraud, etc.** On motion and upon such terms as are just, the court may relieve a party or a party's legal representative from a final judgment, order, or proceeding for the following reasons: (3) fraud (whether heretofore denominated intrinsic or extrinsic), misrepresentation, or other misconduct of an adverse party. . . .

The standard for determining whether a party should be relieved of a final judgment under 60(b)(3) is nearly identical to the standard for determining whether an award should be vacated for fraud under § 10(a).

See Harre v. A.H. Robins, 750 F.2d at 1503. This is not surprising considering that both statutes serve the same function of permitting the reopening of an otherwise final judgment upon a demonstration of fraud in the proceedings, and both counteract the strong policy favoring the finality of awards and judgments. See Bankers Mortgage Co. v. United States, 423 F.2d 73, 77 (5th Cir.) (finality of judgments), cert. denied, 399 U.S. 927, 90 S.Ct. 2242, 26 L.Ed.2d 793 (1970); Newark Stereotypers' Union, 397 F.2d at 598 (finality of arbitration awards). Thus, cases arising under Rule 60(b)(3) are persuasive authority in deciding cases under § 10(a).

Arbitration Association do not provide for a pre-hearing exchange of witness lists, Dean Witter did not know who would testify as appellees' expert witnesses until the time of the hearing. Without a pre-hearing opportunity to thoroughly investigate Nix's credentials, Dean Witter could not have known the extent to which he lied about them at the hearing.

Dean Witter has also demonstrated that Nix's perjury materially related to an issue in the arbitration, thus satisfying its burden under the third prong of the test. As Dean Witter stressed in its brief, because the appellants admitted liability for compensatory damages, the only factual issue before the arbitrators was whether the appellants' conduct was negligent enough to justify the imposition of punitive damages. In support of the appellees' claim for punitive damages, Nix testified at considerable length about how, in his opinion, Dean Witter had mishandled the appellees' account. For example, Nix testified that compared to the average turnover in a portfolio with objectives similar to the appellees' objectives, the turnover rate he calculated for the appellees' account was "extremely high." In addition, when asked whether he thought the appellees' account had been excessively traded, Nix responded: "Briefly I would have to say that it was not so [sic only] excessive but gross and abusive." Appellees' counsel ended his direct examination by asking Nix for his expert opinion as to whether there had been a disregard for the best interests of the customer. Nix responded:

> Yes, I do. Mr. Leavenworth and Dean Witter were the fiduciaries for the Bonars' account, in my opinion. They had control, they ran the show. Ed Leavenworth may have been the first mate on the ship, but John McNally was the captain. John McNally may have delegated the responsibility of reviewing the checks, reviewing transactions, the daily blotter, whatever, but ultimately it comes back down to him.
>
> With regard to that you can't dismiss the responsibility involved here. The ultimate responsibility comes back down to the office manager. There was disregard for the customer. They embezzled from them. They embezzled from other people to put money into their account, they churned it. They even went so far as to run an excessive margin balance for three months.
>
> And from all appearances here and from the testimony it would seem that while Mr. McNally did show concern and couldn't understand why it went for ninety days or more, the evidence from my perspective during that time frame is that Dean Witter didn't care. You wouldn't let a margin balance run for ninety days if you did care.

If Nix had not committed perjury by falsifying his credentials, it is extremely doubtful that he would have been permitted to testify as an expert, and the arbitrators would have heard none of the above testimony.[11]

---

11. Under Federal Rule of Evidence 702, Nix would not have qualified as an expert witness. However, as arbitrators are not bound by the Federal Rules of Evidence, see Section 30, American Arbitration Association Commercial Arbitration Rules, there is a chance, albeit almost nonexistent, that the arbitrators would have allowed Nix to testify

The arbitrators' written award, although brief, reflects the influence of Nix's testimony. Nix was the only expert, and in fact the only witness, who unequivocally pinpointed Dean Witter as the party who "didn't care," and who testified that McNally was less culpable for showing some concern over the state of the appellees' account. The arbitrators' award of punitive damages against Dean Witter, but not against McNally, unquestionably reflects the influence of this testimony. Thus, by establishing the foundation that allowed the panel to hear influential expert testimony on the central issue of negligent supervision, the fraud materially related to an issue in the arbitration.[12]

. . . Accordingly, Dean Witter is entitled to a new hearing on the issue of punitive damages before a different panel of arbitrators.[14]

III.

[The court also considered and rejected Dean Witter's arguments that the arbitrators exceeded their powers by awarding punitive damages, and that appellees had waived their right to punitive damages by agreeing to the customer agreement in this case.]

* * *

as an expert despite his lack of credentials. The slight chance of this happening does not, however, change our decision, because even if Nix had been permitted to testify, his credentials as an expert would have been so weak as to render his opinions meaningless.

12.   The appellees argue that Nix's testimony was merely cumulative and therefore could not have prejudiced Dean Witter's case. To support this argument, the appellees point out that Paul Landauer, the expert who testified before Nix, also opined that the appellees' account had been excessively traded and negligently supervised. This, however, does not mean that the arbitrators ignored Nix's testimony on the same subject. In fact, given that only two experts testified on the crucial issue of negligent supervision, Nix's testimony was invaluable to the appellees in that it corroborated the testimony of their only other expert witness. Perhaps if Nix's testimony had followed a number of other experts who had all testified that the account had been negligently supervised, we would agree that his testimony was merely cumulative. On these facts, however, the appellees' characterization of Nix's testimony as merely "cumulative" unfairly minimizes its importance in these proceedings.

The appellees also argue that Nix's testimony on negligent supervision "merely reflects the obvious, and the conclusion—unsat-

isfactory supervision—is something counsel on these facts could argue even in the absence of expert testimony." They argue that testimony from Dean Witter employees, revealing that Dean Witter did not follow its own internal guidelines for safeguarding investors, was enough to support the arbitrators' award of punitive damages. However, what appellees *could* have done is irrelevant; what matters is that they *did* offer Nix's extensive "expert" testimony to buttress testimony of lay witnesses and now must live with the consequences of that decision.

14.   The appellees argue that if this court reverses the judgment and vacates the arbitration award, the matter should be remanded to the original panel of arbitrators, who should then state the weight given to Nix's testimony, and whether they would have made the same award in the absence of that testimony. Although we are authorized to remand to the original panel, see 9 U.S.C. § 10(e), we are not required to do so, see Electronics Corp. of America v. International Union of Electrical, Radio & Machine Workers, Local 272, 492 F.2d 1255, 1257 (1st Cir. 1974). In a case such as this, where the perjury of an expert witness has so tainted the proceedings, we agree with Dean Witter that it would be difficult for the arbitrators now to determine the importance or weight given to Nix's testimony.

Questions

1. To what extent does the test for vacating an award due to perjury require a court to examine the conduct of the hearing or the merits of the underlying dispute? In the *Bonar* case, the court quotes testimony from the hearing in order to establish that the Nix's perjury was "materially related to an issue in the arbitration." Could the movant have established grounds to vacate if there had been no record of such testimony? Without a transcript, how can a party meet the test for vacating an award due to perjury? Can the movant subpoena the arbitrator to testify to the materiality of the false testimony? Is there any other means by which a court could make such a determination?

2. One of the grounds for vacating the award is that Dean Witter could not have discovered the perjury before or during the hearing due to the absence of pre-hearing exchange of witness lists under the American Arbitration Association rules. To what degree should the court remedy deficiencies in the procedural rules the parties themselves have selected? Would it be preferable to require as a general rule that arbitration rules meet certain procedural standards to obviate the necessity of *post hoc* judicial intervention?

* * *

8. CONFIDENTIALITY OF ARBITRAL TRANSCRIPTS

Industrotech Constructors, Inc. v. Duke University

67 N.C.App. 741, 314 S.E.2d 272 (N.C. App. 1984).

■ PHILLIPS, JUDGE.

Plaintiff was one of numerous prime contractors who worked on the new Duke University Medical Center. It filed an action against Duke University for damages arising from various breaches of their construction contract. The sole issue presented by this appeal concerns the propriety of an order directing defendant, under certain protective restrictions, to produce transcripts of an arbitration proceeding involving defendant and another prime contractor on the same job. . . .

Defendant appellant first argues that the parties to the arbitration stipulated that the proceedings would remain confidential; but no such stipulation appears in the record. The appellant has the duty of ensuring that the record is property made up and includes all matters necessary for decision. Rule 9(a), N.C.Rules of Appellate Procedure; Mooneyham v. Mooneyham, 249 N.C. 641, 107 S.E.2d 66 (1959). The stipulation does not constitute a matter of which we may take judicial notice. See West v. G.D. Reddick, Inc., 302 N.C. 201, 274 S.E.2d 221 (1981). Therefore, this argument must fail.

Even absent evidence of a stipulation of confidentiality, argues defendant, the strong public policy in favor of arbitration requires confidentiality. Defendant contends that the order appealed from, by tending to expose normally relaxed arbitration proceedings to public scrutiny, will cause parties to such proceedings to become circumspect and overly litigious and thus chill the informal process. Defendant cites no case law for this proposition. We note that the Construction Industry Arbitration Rules, under which the subject arbitration took place, provide that attendance of non-parties at the hearings lies within the discretion of the arbitrator, not the parties. Furthermore, the arbitrator *must* release, upon application of *one* party, copies of all documents in the arbitrator's possession which "may be required in judicial proceedings relating to the arbitration." These provisions suggest a somewhat diminished expectation of confidentiality. Nothing in the North Carolina statutes governing arbitration requires strict confidentiality. See G.S. 1–567.1 et seq. In at least one New York case, transcripts of arbitration have been held discoverable, without mention of the policy of confidentiality. Milone v. General Motors Corp., 84 A.D.2d 921, 446 N.Y.S.2d 650 (1981). Thus the law and the contract do not appear to bar disclosure.

In addition, defendant admits that in at least one instance it has already disclosed the transcripts to a non-party. It is well established in this state that even absolutely privileged matter may be inquired into where the privilege has been waived by disclosure. See State v. Murvin, 304 N.C. 523, 284 S.E.2d 289 (1981) [attorney-client privilege waived as to affidavit where two others present during execution] ... In the circumstances of the case, then, we must conclude that confidentiality does not require reversal of the court's order. Defendant contends that the arbitration transcripts are materials "prepared in anticipation of litigation" under Rule 26(b)(3) of the N.C.Rules of Civil Procedure. And defendant further contends that good cause was not shown. Before examining the question of cause, however, we must determine the correctness of defendant's assertion that the transcripts were "prepared in anticipation of litigation." The protective order entered by the court, and defendant's own application for stay, recite only the "compelling" nature of the confidentiality considerations discussed. The record contains no indication and defendant advances nothing but conclusory statements as to what, if any, litigation the transcripts were prepared in anticipation of. In fact, this argument, taken at face value, confounds the traditional notion that the law favors arbitration as a means of *avoiding* litigation.

Privilege, of course, is determined by the court, not by the party asserting it. Midgett v. Crystal Dawn Corp., 58 N.C.App. 734, 294 S.E.2d 386 (1982). The matter cannot rest upon the *ipse dixit* of the defendant. Id.; Allred v. Graves, 261 N.C. 31, 134 S.E.2d 186 (1964). Thus, the burden of establishing, at least as a preliminary matter, that the materials were prepared in anticipation of litigation and are therefore privileged was on the defendant. Heathman v. United States Dist. Court for the Cent. Dist. of Cal., 503 F.2d 1032 (9th Cir.1974); 23 Am.Jur.2d Depositions and Discovery § 29 (1983); 27 C.J.S. Discovery § 35 at 118 (1959). This burden has not been met, as the record contains no basis for the privilege that defendant claims.

Finally, defendant argues that plaintiff should not be permitted to see the transcripts because they are "peppered" with the opinions, legal theories, and other work product of its attorneys. But this problem was solved by the court permitting defendant to excise such portions of the transcript, with plaintiff bearing the costs. The terms of the order indicate the court's concern for defendant's rights and appear to guarantee defendant such protection as it is entitled to. Nor are the terms unduly burdensome. In both Spivey v. Zant, 683 F.2d 881 (5th Cir.1982) and Resident Advisory Board v. Rizzo, 97 F.R.D. 749 (E.D.Pa.1983), it was held that excising work product portions of otherwise discoverable papers is a proper means of complying with Rule 26(b)(3).

The order entered not having been shown to be erroneous, it must be and is affirmed.

* * *

Questions

1. What effect would a confidentiality clause in the original arbitration agreement have had in the *Industrotech* case?

2. What remedy might a party have if portions of an arbitral transcript, instead of being subject to a discovery order, had been published in a newspaper? Might the fear of such publicity inhibit the arbitration process?

* * *

9. ARBITRAL BIAS AND MISCONDUCT

Commonwealth Coatings Corp. v. Continental Casualty Co.

393 U.S. 145, 89 S.Ct. 337 (1968).

■ MR. JUSTICE BLACK delivered the opinion of the Court.

At issue in this case is the question whether elementary requirements of impartiality taken for granted in every judicial proceeding are suspended when the parties agree to resolve a dispute through arbitration.

The petitioner, Commonwealth Coatings Corporation, a subcontractor, sued the sureties on the prime contractor's bond to recover money alleged to be due for a painting job. The contract for painting contained an agreement to arbitrate such controversies. Pursuant to this agreement petitioner appointed one arbitrator, the prime contractor appointed a second, and these two together selected the third arbitrator. This third arbitrator, the supposedly neutral member of the panel, conducted a large business in Puerto Rico, in which he served as an engineering consultant for various people in connection with building construction projects. One of his regular customers in this business was the prime contractor that petitioner sued in this case. This relationship with the prime contractor was in a sense sporadic in that the arbitrator's services were used only from time to time at irregular intervals, and there had been no dealings between them for about a year immediately preceding the arbitration. Nevertheless, the prime contractor's patronage was repeated and significant, involving fees of about $12,000 over a period of four of five years, and the relationship even went so far as to include the rendering of services on the very projects involved in this lawsuit. An arbitration was held, but the facts concerning the close business connections between the third arbitrator and the prime contractor were unknown to petitioner and were never revealed to it by this arbitrator, by the prime contractor, or by anyone else until after an award had been made. Petitioner challenged the award on this ground, among others, but the District Court refused to set aside the award. The Court of Appeals affirmed, 382 F.2d 1010 (C.A.1st Cir. 1967), and we granted certiorari, 390 U.S. 979, 88 S.Ct. 1098, 19 L.Ed.2d 1276 (1968).

In 1925 Congress enacted the United States Arbitration Act, 9 U.S.C. §§ 1–14, which sets out a comprehensive plan for arbitration of controversies coming under its terms, and both sides here assume that this Federal Act governs this case. Section 10, quoted below, sets out the conditions upon which awards can be vacated.[1] The two courts below held, however, that § 10 could not be construed in such a way as to justify vacating the award in this case. We disagree and reverse. Section 10 does authorize vacation of an award where it was "procured by corruption, fraud, or undue means" or "[w]here there was evident partiality * * * in the arbitrators." These provisions show a desire of Congress to provide not merely for *any* arbitration but for an impartial one. It is true that petitioner does not charge before us that the third arbitrator was actually guilty of fraud or bias in deciding this case, and we have no reason, apart from the undisclosed business relationship, to suspect him of any improper motives. But neither this arbitrator nor the prime contractor gave to petitioner even an intimation of the close financial relations that had existed between them for a period of years. We have no doubt that if a litigant could show that a foreman of a jury or a judge in a court of justice

---

1. "In either of the following cases the United States court in and for the district wherein the award was made may make an order vacating the award upon the application of any party to the arbitration—(a) Where the award was procured by corruption, fraud, or undue means, (b) Where there was evident partiality or corruption in the arbitrators, or either of them, (c) Where the arbitrators were guilty of misconduct in refusing to postpone the hearing, upon sufficient cause shown, or in refusing to hear evidence pertinent and material to the controversy; or of any other misbehavior by which the rights of any party have been prejudiced, (d) Where the arbitrators exceeded their powers, or so imperfectly executed them that a mutual, final, and definite award upon the subject matter submitted was not made, (e) Where an award is vacated and the time within which the agreement required there award to be made has not expired the court may, in its discretion, direct a rehearing by the arbitrators."

had, unknown to the litigant, any such relationship, the judgment would be subject to challenge. This is shown beyond doubt by Tumey v. State of Ohio, 273 U.S. 510, 47 S.Ct. 437, 71 L.Ed. 749 (1927), where this Court held that a conviction could not stand because a small part of the judge's income consisted of court fees collected from convicted defendants. Although in Tumey it appeared the amount of the judge's compensation actually depended on whether he decided for one side or the other, that is too small a distinction to allow this manifest violation of the strict morality and fairness Congress would have expected on the part of the arbitrator and the other party in this case. Nor should it be at all relevant, as the Court of Appeals apparently thought it was here, that "[t]he payments received were a very small part of (the arbitrator's) income * * *."[2] For in Tumey the Court held that a decision should be set aside where there is "the slightest pecuniary interest" on the part of the judge, and specifically rejected the State's contention that the compensation involved there was "so small that it is not to be regarded as likely to influence improperly a judicial officer in the discharge of his duty ...".[3] Since in the case of courts this is a *constitutional* principle, we can see no basis for refusing to find the same concept in the broad statutory language that governs arbitration proceedings and provides that an award can be set aside on the basis of "evident partiality" or the use of "undue means." See also Rogers v. Schering Corp., 165 F.Supp. 295, 301 (D.C.N.J.1958). It is true that arbitrators cannot sever all their ties with the business world, since they are not expected to get all their income from their work deciding cases, but we should, if anything, be even more scrupulous to safeguard the impartiality of arbitrators than judges, since the former have completely free rein to decide the law as well as the facts and are not subject to appellate review. We can perceive no way in which the effectiveness of the arbitration process will be hampered by the simple requirement that arbitrators disclose to the parties any dealings that might create an impression of possible bias.

While not controlling in this case, § 18 of the Rules of the American Arbitration Association, in effect at the time of this arbitration, is highly significant. It provided as follows:

"Section 18. Disclosure by Arbitrator of Disqualification—At the time of receiving his notice of appointment, the prospective Arbitrator is requested to disclose any circumstances likely to create a presumption of bias or which he believes might disqualify him as an impartial Arbitrator. Upon receipt of such information, the Tribunal Clerk shall immediately disclose it to the parties, who if willing to proceed under the circumstances disclosed, shall, in writing, so advise the Tribunal Clerk. If either party declines to waive the presumptive disqualification, the vacancy thus created shall be filled in accordance with the applicable provisions of this Rule."

---

2. 382 F.2d, at 1011.

3. 273 U.S., at 524, 47 S.Ct., at 441.

And based on the same principle as this Arbitration Association rule is that part of the 33d Canon of Judicial Ethics which provides:

"33. Social Relations. . . . [A judge] should, however, in pending or prospective litigation before him be particularly careful to avoid such action as may reasonably tend to awaken the suspicion that his social or business relations or friendships, constitute an element in influencing his judicial conduct".

This rule of arbitration and this canon of judicial ethics rest on the premise that any tribunal permitted by law to try cases and controversies not only must be unbiased but also must avoid even the appearance of bias. We cannot believe that it was the purpose of Congress to authorize litigants to submit their cases and controversies to arbitration boards that might reasonably be thought biased against one litigant and favorable to another.

Reversed.

■ MR. JUSTICE WHITE, with whom MR. JUSTICE MARSHALL joins, concurring.

While I am glad to join my Brother BLACK'S opinion in this case, I desire to make these additional remarks. The Court does not decide today that arbitrators are to be held to the standards of judicial decorum of Article III judges, or indeed of any judges. It is often because they are men of affairs, not apart from but of the marketplace, that they are effective in their adjudicatory function. Cf. United Steelworkers of America v. Warrior & Gulf Navigation Co., 363 U.S. 574, 80 S.Ct. 1347, 4 L.Ed.2d 1409 (1960). This does not mean the judiciary must overlook outright chicanery in giving effect to their awards; that would be an abdication of our responsibility. But it does mean that arbitrators are not automatically disqualified by a business relationship with the parties before them if both parties are informed of the relationship in advance, or if they are unaware of the facts but the relationship is trivial. I see no reason automatically to disqualify the best informed and most capable potential arbitrators.

The arbitration process functions best when an amicable and trusting atmosphere is preserved and there is voluntary compliance with the decree, without need for judicial enforcement. This end is best served by establishing an atmosphere of frankness at the outset, through disclosure by the arbitrator of any financial transactions which he has had or is negotiating with either of the parties. In many cases the arbitrator might believe the business relationship to be so insubstantial that to make a point of revealing it would suggest he is indeed easily swayed, and perhaps a partisan of that party. But if the law requires the disclosure, no such imputation can arise. And it is far better that the relationship be disclosed at the outset, when the parties are free to reject the arbitrator or accept him with knowledge of the relationship and continuing faith in his objectivity, than to have the relationship come to light after the arbitration, when a suspicious or disgruntled party can seize on it as a pretext for invalidating the award. The judiciary should minimize its role in arbitration as judge of the arbitrator's impartiality. That role is best consigned to the parties, who are the architects of their own arbitration process, and are far better informed of the prevailing ethical standards and reputations within their business.

Of course, an arbitrator's business relationships may be diverse indeed, involving more or less remote commercial connections with great numbers of people. He cannot be expected to provide the parties with his complete and unexpurgated business biography. But it is enough for present purposes to hold, as the Court does, that where the arbitrator has a substantial interest in a firm which has done more than trivial business with a party, that fact must be disclosed. If arbitrators err on the side of disclosure, as they should, it will not be difficult for courts to identify those undisclosed relationships which are too insubstantial to warrant vacating an award.

■ MR. JUSTICE FORTAS, with whom MR. JUSTICE HARLAN and MR. JUSTICE STEWART join, dissenting.

I dissent and would affirm the judgment.

The facts in this case do not lend themselves to the Court's ruling. The Court sets aside the arbitration award despite the fact that the award is unanimous and no claim is made of actual partiality, unfairness, bias, or fraud.

The arbitration was held pursuant to provisions in the contracts between the parties. It is not subject to the rules of the American Arbitration Association. It is governed by the United States Arbitration Act, 9 U.S.C. §§ 1–14.

Each party appointed an arbitrator and the third arbitrator was chosen by those two. The controversy relates to the third arbitrator.

. . . The third arbitrator is a leading and respected consulting engineer who has performed services for "most of the contractors in Puerto Rico." He was well known to petitioner's counsel and they were personal friends. Petitioner's counsel candidly admitted that if he had been told about the arbitrator's prior relationship "I don't think I would have objected because I know Mr. Capacete (the arbitrator)."

Clearly, the District Judge's conclusion, affirmed by the Court of Appeals for the First Circuit, was correct, that "the arbitrators conducted fair, impartial hearings; that they reached a proper determination of the issues before them, and that plaintiff's objections represent a 'situation where the losing party to an arbitration is now clutching at straws in an attempt to avoid the results of the arbitration to which it became a party.' "

The Court nevertheless orders that the arbitration award be set aside. It uses this singularly inappropriate case to announce a per se rule that in my judgment has no basis in the applicable statute or jurisprudential principles: that, regardless of the agreement between the parties, if an arbitrator has any prior business relationship with one of the parties of which he fails to inform the other party, however innocently, the arbitration award is always subject to being set aside. This is so even where the award is unanimous; where there is no suggestion that the nondisclosure indicates partiality or bias; and where it is conceded that there was in fact no irregularity, unfairness, bias, or partiality. Until the decision today, it has not been the law that an arbitrator's failure to disclose a prior business relationship with one of the parties will compel the setting aside of an arbitration award regardless of the circumstances.

I agree that failure of an arbitrator to volunteer information about business dealings with one party will, prima facie, support a claim of partiality or bias. But where there is no suggestion that the nondisclosure was calculated, and where the complaining party disclaims any imputation of partiality, bias, or misconduct, the presumption clearly is overcome.[2]

I do not believe that it is either necessary, appropriate, or permissible to rule, as the Court does, that, regardless of the facts, innocent failure to volunteer information constitutes the "evident partiality" necessary under § 10(b) of the Arbitration Act to set aside an award. "Evident partiality" means what it says: conduct—or at least an attitude or disposition—by the arbitrator favoring one party rather than the other. This case demonstrates that to rule otherwise may be a palpable injustice, since all agree that the arbitrator was innocent of either "evident partiality" or anything approaching it.

Arbitration is essentially consensual and practical. The United States Arbitration Act is obviously designed to protect the integrity of the process with a minimum of insistence upon set formulae and rules. The Court applies to this process rules applicable to judges and not to a system characterized by dealing on faith and reputation for reliability. Such formalism is not contemplated by the Act nor is it warranted in a case where no claim is made of partiality, of unfairness, or of misconduct in any degree.

* * *

Questions

1.   Is it a fundamental requirement of due process to have one's case decided by an impartial decision-maker? Should arbitrators be held to the same standard of impartiality as judges? Why does Justice Black contend that an even higher standard of impartiality should apply to arbitrators than to judges? Do the other justices agree? For a detailed comparison of the standards of impartiality of arbitrators and judges, see Steven J. Goering, *The Standard of Impartiality As Applied to Arbitrators by Federal Courts and Codes of Ethics*, 3 GEO. J. LEG. ETHICS 821 (1990).

2.   At the time of the contract and the arbitration herein, § 18 of the Rules of the American Arbitration Association, which the Court quotes, was phrased merely in terms of a "request" that the arbitrator "disclose any circumstances likely to create a presumption of bias or which he believes might disqualify him as an impartial Arbitrator." In 1964, the rule was changed to provide that "the prospective neutral Arbitrator *shall* disclose any circumstances likely to create a presumption of bias or which he believes might disqualify him as an impartial Arbitrator." (Emphasis supplied.)

2. What are the dangers of having a biased decision-maker? Is the presence or absence of bias an all-or-nothing proposition, or can there be degrees of bias and partiality? If so, how much bias and how far a departure from impartiality render a proceeding fundamentally unfair?

3. In *Commonwealth Coatings*, Justices White and Marshall take the position that arbitrators should not automatically be disqualified on the basis of a prior business relationship so long as the prior relationship is disclosed. Why, in their view, is disclosure a sufficient protection against the dangers of bias? Do you agree? Does disclosure and consent address all the problems of bias in a decision-maker? If a party consents on the basis of full information to an arbitration process that is loaded in favor of the other side, should the court ever set the award aside? What if the party consents because she was in desperate need of the contracted-for service? See, e.g., *Broemmer v. Abortion Services*, supra. Would it matter whether the disclosure was made at the time of contracting or after the dispute arose? What standard for demonstrating consent should be imposed?

4. What is the relationship between disclosure and bias? Should nondisclosure of a significant prior business relationship give rise to an inference of bias? Is such an inference justified? Is the opposite inference that non-disclosure gives rise to an inference of no bias–equally plausible?

5. What is the basis for Justice Fortas' conclusion that there was no actual bias involved in this case? How can a court tell whether an arbitrator was biased? Might not an arbitrator who had a prior business relationship with one party have an incentive to conceal the prior relationship in order to be retained as an arbitrator? Would such an arbitrator necessarily be biased? Would Fortas advocate that a court should hold an evidentiary hearing in order to determine whether an arbitrator was actually biased? See, e.g., *Sanko Steamship Co. v. Cook Industries*, 495 F.2d 1260 (2d Cir.1973); *Totem Marine Tug & Barge, Inc. v. North American Towing*, 607 F.2d 649 (5th Cir.1979). What kinds of evidence might bear on the issue? Would it be appropriate to call the arbitrator to testify? See *Legion Insurance Co. v. Insurance General Agency, Inc.*, 822 F.2d 541 (5th Cir.1987), supra.

6. Should an arbitrator be disqualified whenever there is a possibility of bias? A probability of bias? A showing of actual bias? What factors would be relevant to establish each?

* * *

Merit Insurance Company v. Leatherby Insurance Company

714 F.2d 673 (7th Cir.1983).

■ Before CUMMINGS, CHIEF JUDGE, POSNER, CIRCUIT JUDGE, and FAIRCHILD, SENIOR CIRCUIT JUDGE.

■ POSNER, CIRCUIT JUDGE.

This appeal from an order under Rule 60(b) of the Federal Rules of Civil Procedure setting aside an arbitration award requires us to decide whether the failure of one of the arbitrators to disclose a prior business relationship with a principal of one of the parties to the arbitration justified the district court in using its powers under Rule 60(b) and the United States Arbitration Act, 9 U.S.C. §§ 1 et seq., to set aside the award.

In 1972 Merit Insurance Company made a contract with Leatherby Insurance Company to reinsure claims under certain insurance policies that Leatherby had issued. Merit later sued Leatherby in federal district court for fraud in inducing the contract. Jurisdiction was based on diversity of citizenship. Leatherby moved the court for an order under 9 U.S.C. § 4 directing the parties to arbitrate their dispute in accordance with the arbitration clause in the contract, and in 1977 the district court entered such an order. See Merit Ins. Co. v. Leatherby Ins. Co., 581 F.2d 137, 139 (7th Cir.1978), and for collateral litigation Merit Ins. Co. v. Colao, 603 F.2d 654 (7th Cir.1979).

The arbitration was conducted under the auspices of the American Arbitration Association. Each party appointed one arbitrator and together the parties appointed from a list formulated by the AAA the third or "neutral" arbitrator, a Chicago lawyer named Jack Clifford. At the first meeting of the arbitration panel the panel agreed that the other two arbitrators would also be neutrals, rather than representatives of the parties that had appointed them.

After an arbitration that lasted three years and produced a hearing transcript of 16,000 pages, the panel on December 1, 1980, unanimously awarded Merit $10,675,000 on its claim. Merit petitioned the district court to confirm the award under 9 U.S.C. § 9. Leatherby opposed confirmation in part on the ground that the arbitrators had been biased, as indicated by certain evidentiary rulings in Merit's favor and by a comment the arbitrator appointed by Merit had made in the course of the proceedings. No charge of bias was leveled against Clifford specifically. The district judge rejected all of Leatherby's arguments and on November 19, 1981, confirmed the award. A month later he rejected Leatherby's first motion under Rule 60(b) to set it aside. Leatherby appealed to this court from both the order confirming the award and the order denying the Rule 60(b) motion. On May 12, 1982, while the appeal was pending, Leatherby filed a second Rule 60(b) motion, this one based on Leatherby's alleged discovery the previous month that Clifford had once worked under Merit's president and principal stockholder, Jerome Stern, at Cosmopolitan Insurance Company. The appeal was dismissed on Leatherby's motion, and an evidentiary hearing on its new charge of bias was held in the district court at the end of August. On November 4, 1982, in an oral opinion, the court granted Leatherby's Rule 60(b) motion and set aside the arbitration award, and Merit has appealed under 28 U.S.C. § 1291. See University Life Ins. Co. of America v. Unimarc Ltd., 699 F.2d 846, 848 (7th Cir.1983).

The hearing in the district court brought out the following facts. The chairman of the board of Cosmopolitan had hired Clifford late in 1960 to be head of the claims department. At the same time Stern had been promoted to executive vice-president of the company. As the vice-president in charge of the claims department Clifford reported to Stern. This relationship lasted till the beginning of 1963 when Stern left Cosmopolitan to enter private practice. Clifford left Cosmopolitan shortly afterward. Clifford and Stern both testified that they had had little professional contact while at Cosmopolitan and no social contacts then or since. Clifford had been promised substantial autonomy by the chairman of the board when he took over the claims department, and Stern—who had no background in claims evaluation and was preoccupied with corporate acquisitions and other matters unrelated to Clifford's responsibilities—gave Clifford a loose rein. Their principal contact came in meetings held at intervals of several months between Stern and the department heads who reported to him. They also had occasional brief discussions over specific claims; once Clifford was asked to review the claims reserves of an insurance company that Cosmopolitan was thinking of buying; and, on orders from above, Stern once required all of his subordinates, including Clifford, to take lie-detector tests. After Clifford and Stern entered private practice they spoke to each other on the phone on one or two occasions but these contacts were of no significance, and until the arbitration the two men had not met face to face since 1963. Rotheiser, a vice-president of Merit, was also employed at Cosmopolitan during Clifford's tenure, but he was the head of a separate department and according to both his testimony and Clifford's they had no dealings with one another.

The foregoing account is drawn in large part from the testimony of Clifford himself, of whom the district judge stated, "I do not find Mr. Clifford to be a credible witness." But read in context this statement principally refers not to Clifford's testimony about his time at Cosmopolitan—testimony corroborated by Stern and Rotheiser, whom the district judge did not find to be incredible and who were not contradicted by any other witness—but to Clifford's explanation of why he omitted to mention his affiliation with Cosmopolitan either when he filled out the forms that the American Arbitration Association requires from its prospective arbitrators or when he first saw Stern at the arbitration hearing. In 1975 the AAA had sent Clifford a "panel data sheet" which contained a space headed, "My prior occupational affiliations have been...." All that Clifford listed in this space (having listed private practice as his current occupation) was his job as claims manager for Firemen's Fund American Insurance Companies from 1949 to 1960. Clifford testified that he had not mentioned Cosmopolitan in part because he was not interested in doing the kind of arbitration for which his experience there would have been relevant. The judge disbelieved this because it was the same kind of work Clifford had done at Firemen's Fund. (The judge made no comment on Clifford's other, and more plausible, explanation for not mentioning his work for Cosmopolitan: it was not a useful reference. Since the company had been liquidated, getting an evaluation of Clifford's work for the company would have been difficult.) But the judge could not have believed that the purpose of the omission was to prevent Clifford from being disqualified as an arbitrator, for the Merit–Leatherby arbitration was still two years in the future when Clifford mailed back the form. The judge conjectured, rather, that Clifford had been embarrassed to broadcast his relationship with Cosmopolitan, because after he had left it the company had gone broke, which resulted, in the district judge's words, in "an explosion in the industry." But when Clifford filled out another panel data sheet at the AAA's request three years later, he again omitted any reference to his work at Cosmopolitan; and when the arbitration began and Clifford recognized Stern and realized that the president of Merit and the former executive vice-president of Cosmopolitan were one and the same, he had said nothing.

Leatherby argues that by failing at each of these junctures to disclose his former relationship with Stern, Clifford violated the ethical norms applicable to arbitrators, and that the only effective sanction for such a violation is to set aside the arbitration award. It also argues that Clifford did more than just fail to disclose his former relationship with Stern, that he tried to put Leatherby off the scent by calling Stern "Mr. Stern" rather than calling him by his first name; but there is no evidence that Clifford was doing anything other than maintaining the decorum of the arbitration proceeding.

The panel data sheet that the American Arbitration Association requires prospective arbitrators to fill out does not indicate that the information sought is for the purpose of determining whether grounds for disqualification exist, so no significance can be attached to Clifford's initial omission of his job history with Cosmopolitan. But section 18 of the AAA's Commercial Arbitration Rules requires the neutral arbitrator to "disclose to the AAA any circumstances likely to affect his impartiality, including any bias or any financial or personal interest in the result of the arbitration or any past or present relationship with the parties or their counsel." And Canon IIA of the Code of Ethics for Arbitrators in Commercial Disputes (jointly adopted by the American Arbitration Association and the American Bar Association) requires arbitrators to disclose "any existing or past financial, business, professional, family or social relationships which are likely to affect impartiality or which might reasonably create an appearance of partiality or bias." The requirement of disclosure is a continuing one, so the fact that Clifford's failure to disclose his relationship with Cosmopolitan in his first panel data sheet was innocent could not excuse his later failure to disclose the relationship when he accepted appointment as an arbitrator of the Merit–Leatherby dispute and when he recognized Stern on the first day of the arbitration hearing.

Notwithstanding the broad language of section 18, no one supposes that either the Commercial Arbitration Rules or the Code of Ethics for Arbitrators requires disclosure of every former social or financial relationship with a party or a party's principals. The Code states that its provisions relating to disclosure "are intended to be applied realistically so that the burden of detailed disclosure does not become so great that it is impractical for persons in the business world to be arbitrators, thereby depriving the parties of the services of those who might be best informed and qualified to decide particular types of cases." Quoting from Justice White's concurring opinion in Commonwealth Coatings Corp. v. Continental Casualty Co., 393 U.S. 145, 150–52, 89 S.Ct. 337, 340–41, 21 L.Ed.2d 301 (1968)—of which more anon—the Code states that although "arbitrators 'should err on the side of disclosure' ..., it must be recognized that 'an arbitrator's business relationships may be diverse indeed, involving more or less remote commercial connections with great numbers of people' [so that] an arbitrator 'cannot be expected to provide the parties with his complete and unexpurgated business biography,' ... [or] to disclose interests or relationships which are merely 'trivial.' "

The ethical obligations of arbitrators can be understood only by reference to the fundamental differences between adjudication by arbitrators and adjudication by judges and jurors. No one is forced to arbitrate a commercial dispute unless he has consented by contract to arbitrate. The voluntary nature of commercial arbitration is an important safeguard for the parties that is missing in the case of the courts. See Corey v. New York Stock Exchange, 691 F.2d 1205, 1210 (6th Cir.1982). Courts are coercive, not voluntary, agencies, and the American people's traditional fear of government oppression has resulted in a judicial system in which impartiality is prized above expertise. Thus, people who arbitrate do so because they prefer a tribunal knowledgeable about the subject matter of their dispute to a generalist court with its austere impartiality but limited knowledge of subject matter. "The professional competence of the arbitrator is attractive to the businessman because a commercial dispute arises out of an environment that usually possesses its own folkways, mores, and technology. Most businessmen interviewed contended that commercial disputes should be considered within the framework of such an environment. No matter how determinedly judge and lawyer work to acquire an understanding of a given business or industry, they cannot hope to approximate the practical wisdom distilled from 30 or 40 years of experience." American Management Ass'n, Resolving Business Disputes 51 (1965).

There is a tradeoff between impartiality and expertise. The expert adjudicator is more likely than a judge or juror not only to be precommitted to a particular substantive position but to know or have heard of the parties (or if the parties are organizations, their key people). "Expertise in an industry is accompanied by exposure, in ways large and small, to those engaged in it...." Andros Compania Maritima, S.A. v. Marc Rich & Co., 579 F.2d 691, 701 (2d Cir.1978). The different weighting of impartiality and expertise in arbitration compared to adjudication is dramatically illustrated by the practice whereby each party appoints one of the arbitrators to be his representative rather than a genuine umpire. See Note, The Use of Tripartite Boards in Labor, Commercial, and International Arbitration, 68 Harv. L.Rev. 293 (1954). No one would dream of having a judicial panel composed of one part-time judge and two representatives of the parties, but that is the standard arbitration panel, the panel Leatherby chose—presumably because it preferred a more expert to a more impartial tribunal—when it wrote an arbitration clause into its reinsurance contract with Merit.

If Leatherby had wanted its dispute with Merit resolved by an Article III judge (to whom it had access under the diversity jurisdiction), it would not have inserted an arbitration clause in the contract, or having done so move for arbitration against Merit's wishes. Leatherby wanted something different from judicial dispute resolution. It wanted dispute resolution by experts in the insurance industry, who were bound to have greater knowledge of the parties, based on previous professional experience, than an Article III judge, or a jury. The parties to an arbitration choose their method of dispute resolution, and can ask no more impartiality than inheres in the method they have chosen. Cf. American Almond Products Co. v. Consolidated Pecan Sales Co., 144 F.2d 448, 451 (2d Cir.1944) (L. Hand, J.).

It is no surprise, therefore, that the standards for disqualification in the Commercial Arbitration Rules and the Code of Ethics for Arbitrators are not so stringent as those in the federal statutes on judges, see, e.g., 28 U.S.C. § 455, or in Canons 2 and 3(C) of the Code of Judicial Conduct for United States Judges and the ABA's Code of Judicial Conduct. (In fact the arbitration rules and code do not contain any standards for disqualification as such, though such standards are implicit in the disclosure requirements of the AAA's Rules and the AAA–ABA Code.) We thus do not agree with Leatherby that the test for disqualification here is whether the former relationship between Stern and Clifford was "trivial" in relation to the subject matter of the arbitration. If it were trivial Clifford would not have had to disqualify himself even if he had been a judge. See, e.g., Chitimacha Tribe of Louisiana v. Harry L. Laws Co., 690 F.2d 1157, 1166 (5th Cir.1982)....

Maybe it was trivial. Chitimacha held that a district judge did not have to disqualify himself from a case in which the defendant was a corporation that the judge had represented when he was in private practice, since the representation had terminated at least six years before. That was a professional relationship, like Clifford's with Stern—only a more recent one. But the test in this case is not whether the relationship was trivial; it is whether, having due regard for the different expectations regarding impartiality that parties bring to arbitration than to litigation, the relationship between Clifford and Stern was so intimate—personally, socially, professionally, or financially—as to cast serious doubt on Clifford's impartiality. Although Stern had been Clifford's supervisor for two years and was a key witness in an arbitration where the stakes to the party of which he was the president and principal shareholder were big, their relationship had ended 14 years before, Clifford had no possible financial stake in the outcome of the arbitration, and his relationship with Stern during their period together at Cosmopolitan had been distant and impersonal. The fact that they had never socialized, either while working for the same company or afterward (though both were practicing law in Chicago all this time), indicates a lack of intimacy. And when a former employee sits in judgment on a former employer there is no presumption that he will be biased in favor of the former employer; he may well be prejudiced against him. The fact that Clifford passed his lie-detector test with flying colors might have made him grateful to Stern, or might have fanned the flames of outrage at having been subjected to such an indignity, or more likely made no difference at all because it happened so long ago. Time cools emotions, whether of gratitude or resentment.

Section 18 of the Commercial Arbitration Rules makes the AAA itself the final arbiter of disqualification once the arbitrator has been appointed, subject only (so far as relevant here) to the limited judicial review allowed by section 10 of the Arbitration Act, 9 U.S.C. § 10, after an arbitration award is made and judicial confirmation of it sought. On the basis of the facts reviewed above, considered in the light of the less stringent standards applicable to disqualification of arbitrators than to disqualification of judges, we doubt that the AAA would have disqualified Clifford—or that Leatherby would have wanted it to.

But even if the failure to disclose was a material violation of the ethical standards applicable to arbitration proceedings, it does not follow that the arbitration award may be nullified judicially. Although we have great respect for the Commercial Arbitration Rules and the Code of Ethics for Arbitrators, they are not the proper starting point for an inquiry into an award's validity under section 10 of the United States Arbitration Act and Rule 60(b) of the Federal Rules of Civil Procedure. The arbitration rules and code do not have the force of law. If Leatherby is to get the arbitration award set aside it must bring itself within the statute and the federal rule. The statute specifies limited grounds for setting aside an arbitration award. The only one relevant here is, "Where there was evident partiality or corruption in the arbitrators, or either of them." 9 U.S.C. § 10(b). (Leatherby does not argue that the award can be set aside on any other ground in the statute, such as "misbehavior" of an arbitrator, in section 10(c).) This is strong language. It makes the grounds for setting aside an arbitrator's award because of bias narrower than the grounds for disqualification in the arbitration rules and code, not to mention the statutes and ethical codes pertaining to judges. Read literally, section 10(b) would require proof of actual bias ("evident partiality"). And not only the arbitrator appointed by Merit, as one might expect, but also the arbitrator appointed by Leatherby—a member of a distinguished Chicago law firm—gave a detailed affidavit denying absolutely and in detail that Clifford had ever evinced any partiality during the three years of the arbitration.

Of course actual bias might be present yet impossible to prove; Clifford might have given no indication of his vote yet have been irrevocably committed to Merit out of some obscure sense of gratitude toward, or exaggerated respect for, Stern. If circumstances are such that a man of average probity might reasonably be suspected of partiality, maybe the language of section 10(b) can be stretched to require disqualification. But the circumstances must be powerfully suggestive of bias, and are not here.

The American Arbitration Association is in competition not only with other private arbitration services but with the courts in providing—in the case of the private services, selling—an attractive form of dispute settlement. It may set its standards as high or as low as it thinks its customers want. The statute has a different purpose—to make arbitration effective by putting the coercive force of the federal courts behind arbitration decrees that affect interstate commerce or are otherwise of federal concern. See 9 U.S.C. § 1; S.Rep. No. 536, 68th Cong., 1st Sess. 3 (1924). The statute does not provide a dispute settlement mechanism; it facilitates private dispute settlement. The standards for judicial intervention are therefore narrowly drawn to assure the basic integrity of the arbitration process without meddling in it. Section 10 is full of words like corruption and misbehavior and fraud. The standards it sets are minimum ones. The ethical concerns expressed by Leatherby are remote from the draftsmen's concerns. The Senate Report, for example, refers approvingly to " 'arrangements for avoiding the delay and expense of litigation and referring a dispute to friends ...,'" S.Rep. No. 536, supra, at 3. The fact that the AAA went beyond the statutory standards in drafting its own code of ethics does not lower the threshold for judicial intervention. If Clifford violated current ethical norms for commercial arbitrators, his was at worst a technical violation that does not justify setting aside an arbitration award on the statutory ground of evident partiality or corruption. Concern with professional reputation will provide some deterrent to such violations, especially where the arbitrator is a lawyer, as he was here.

We have discussed the issue of the award's validity as if it had to be decided on the basis of first principles—as it very largely does. Prior cases involve factual situations very different from the one here and do not yield general principles. The only Supreme Court decision, Commonwealth Coatings Corp. v. Continental Casualty Co., 393 U.S. 145, 89 S.Ct. 337, 21 L.Ed.2d 301 (1968), provides little guidance because of the inability of a majority of Justices to agree on anything but the result. Justice Black, joined by three other Justices, took a very hard line on the ethical standards of arbitrators. His opinion contains language suggesting that arbitrators are subject to the same ethical standards as judges, although this is dictum because the facts of the case required disqualification even under a narrow reading of section 10(b): the "neutral" arbitrator was a regular supplier of one of the parties to the arbitration, and had even rendered services on projects involved in the arbitration. Justice White, concurring, purported to join Justice Black's opinion but actually took a quite different tack, the sense of which is captured in the passages we quoted earlier from the Code of Ethics for Arbitrators—which treats Justice White's opinion as a surer guide to the view of a majority of the Supreme Court than Justice Black's. Justice White stated, "The Court does not decide today that arbitrators are to be held to the standards of judicial decorum of Article III judges," 393 U.S. at 150, 89 S.Ct. at 340, and since his vote was essential to a majority, what he said the Court did not decide the Court did not decide, whatever Justice Black may have hoped. Our court, in United States Wrestling Federation v. Wrestling Division of AAU, Inc., 605 F.2d 313, 319 (7th Cir.1979), treated Justice White's opinion as authoritative.

Although it is difficult to extract from the cases more than a mood, the mood is one of reluctance to set aside arbitration awards for failure of the arbitrator to disclose a relationship with a party. See, e.g., Andros Compania Maritima, S.A. v. Marc Rich & Co., supra, 579 F.2d at 700. In Andros, the arbitration award was confirmed although the neutral arbitrator, Nelson, had not disclosed that he had in the recent past sat on 19 arbitration panels with the president of one of the firms involved in the arbitration and in 12 of these panels the president had been one of the arbitrators who had selected Nelson to be the neutral. Disqualification of the neutral arbitrator was also rejected in International Produce, Inc. v. A/S Rosshavet, 638 F.2d 548, 551 (2d Cir.1981), even though, during the arbitration, he had been a witness in another case between the same law firms that were trying the arbitration matter before him. In Middlesex Mutual Ins. Co. v. Levine, 675 F.2d 1197 (11th Cir.1982) (per curiam), an arbitration award was set aside for "evident partiality," but there a company owned by the neutral arbitrator's family was entangled in a dispute with the parties to the litigation in which he personally had lost $85,000, and he also was under investigation for alleged unethical conduct involving those parties.

The suggestion in Tamari v. Bache Halsey Stuart Inc., 619 F.2d 1196 (7th Cir.1980), that "appearance of bias" is a proper standard for disqualification of arbitrators is not inconsistent with anything in our present opinion; it just means that it is unnecessary to demonstrate—what is almost impossible to demonstrate—that the arbitrator had an actual bias. The standard is an objective one, but less exacting than the one governing judges.

... Furthermore, as it is likely that if Leatherby had known about Clifford's former relationship with Stern it would not have cared, because it would not have been able to figure out any more than we can how that relationship would cut in terms of partiality toward or prejudice against Merit, we think Leatherby was required, and it failed, to support its Rule 60(b) motion with affidavits that its officers did not know of the relationship. It had to negate any inference that it had implicitly consented to have Clifford as an arbitrator knowing all it now knows but saying nothing. We note in this regard the perfunctory investigation that Leatherby made into Clifford's background when the AAA first listed him as a possible arbitrator. Leatherby argues that it would have been burdensome to investigate all 26 names on the list and that it was entitled to trust any potential arbitrator to comply with the AAA's disclosure requirements. It points out that the cost of arbitration will be increased if parties, not being able to trust the disclosure requirements, must conduct elaborate background investigations. It is true that the disclosure requirements are intended in part to avoid the costs of background investigations. But this is a $10 million case. If Leatherby had been worried about putting its fate into the hands of someone who might be linked in the distant past to the adversary's principal, it would have done more than it did to find out about Clifford. That it did so little suggests that its fear of a prejudiced panel is a tactical response to having lost the arbitration.

We do not want to encourage the losing party to every arbitration to conduct a background investigation of each of the arbitrators in an effort to uncover evidence of a former relationship with the adversary. This would only increase the cost and undermine the finality of arbitration, contrary to the purpose of the United States Arbitration Act of making arbitration a swift, inexpensive, and effective substitute for judicial dispute resolution. This lawsuit is already eight years old. To uphold the district court's vacation of the arbitration award in the absence of evidence of actual or probable partiality or corruption would open a new and, we fear, an interminable chapter in the efforts of people who have chosen arbitration and been disappointed in their choice to get the courts—to which they could have turned in the first instance for resolution of their disputes—to undo the results of their preferred method of dispute resolution.

The judgment of the district court setting aside his earlier judgment confirming the arbitration award in favor of Merit is reversed, and the case is remanded with directions to reinstate the previous judgment.

* * *

Questions

1.   What is Judge Posner's view on the standard for impartiality that should apply under the FAA? Does he believe that there can be degrees of impartiality and bias? In his view, how much bias is grounds to set aside an arbitral award? How can parties ensure total impartiality? Can they bargain for an arbitration procedure that guarantees the parties total impartiality?

2.   Why does Judge Posner say there is a tradeoff between impartiality and expertise? How does expertise purge prior relationships that raise a potential for bias? Is Posner relying on a view of professionalism that says experts, like professionals, can ignore self-interest and prior relationships when asked to apply professional judgment? Or is he saying that bias is not objectionable when parties have consented to it? Would he take the consent rationale so far as to uphold an arbitral award that was rendered by a relative of one of the parties when the initial agreement provided for the relative to arbitrate all disputes that arise?

3.   Does Posner's position rest primarily on consent or on the indeterminate nature of the bias that is produced by the prior employer-employee relationship? If it is the latter, cannot relations between siblings also be indeterminate in terms of creating either good will or ill-will? Or, parent-child relations, or even spousal relations? Should an award by an arbitrator who is a close relative of one of the parties also be upheld if there was initial consent? What if the other contracting party did not know that the arbitrator was a relation of one of the parties? Can such a scenario be distinguished from the facts of *Merit Insurance v. Leatherby*?

4.   Posner gives, as one reason for his refusal to set aside the award on grounds of bias, the explanation that there is no a priori way to know

whether the prior relationship of employer-employee created bias in favor of or in opposition to the party who is the former employer. While a judge may not know the answer to that question, presumably the former employer knows, or at least has a reasonably good guess. If the former employer believes that the former employee will be hostile, we can expect that party to speak up rather than remain silent on the issue of bias. Can we not assume, then, that if the party who is the former employer remains silent on the issue, it is because he believes that the prior relationship may be beneficial to him? Is not the existence of important information that is available only to one side, be it helpful or harmful, an element of impermissible bias?

* * *

Morris v. Metriyakool

418 Mich. 423, 344 N.W.2d 736 (1984).

■ KAVANAGH, JUSTICE.

These cases concern arbitration of medical malpractice claims. The most significant issue presented is whether the malpractice arbitration act of 1975, M.C.L. § 600.5040 et seq.; M.S.A. § 27A.5040 et seq., deprives plaintiffs of constitutional rights to an impartial decision maker. We hold that it does not.

Plaintiff Diane Jackson was treated in November, 1977, at defendant Detroit Memorial Hospital by defendant Dr. William J. Bloom for a dental malady. At that time, plaintiff agreed to submit to arbitration "any claims or disputes (except for disputes over charges for services rendered) which may arise in the future out of or in connection with the health care rendered to me * * * by this hospital, its employees and those of its independent staff doctors and consultants who have agreed to arbitrate". In August, 1979, plaintiff brought action for malpractice against defendants in the Wayne Circuit Court. Defendants moved for accelerated judgment, on the basis of the agreement to arbitrate. After a hearing, the court found the act constitutional and, finding no duress, mistake, or incompetency in the execution of the agreement, granted defendants' motion.

The Court of Appeals reversed, holding that M.C.L. § 600.5044(2); M.S.A. § 27A.5044(2) violates the constitutional guarantee of due process by " 'forcing the litigant to submit his or her claim to a tribunal which is composed in such a way that a high probability exists that such tribunal will be biased against the claimant without mandating the use of an arbitration form explicitly detailing the nature of the panel's makeup' ". Jackson v. Detroit Memorial Hospital, 110 Mich.App. 202, 204, 312 N.W.2d 212 (1981), quoting Morris v. Metriyakool, 107 Mich.App. 110, 134, 309 N.W.2d 910 (1981) (Bronson, J., dissenting in part and concurring in part). The court also held that the arbitration agreement is not a contract of adhesion and that, on the present facts, it is not unconscionable. Defendants applied for leave to appeal, and plaintiffs sought leave to cross-appeal, which we granted. 412 Mich. 885 (1981).

In the second case before us, plaintiff Delores M. Morris was admitted to defendant South Memorial Hospital on November 9, 1976. At the time of her admission, plaintiff executed an agreement similar to the one executed by plaintiff Jackson to arbitrate any claims against defendant hospital and defendant Dr. S. Metriyakool arising out of her treatment for a hysterectomy. Subsequently, plaintiff brought suit against defendants alleging negligence in the surgical procedure, which caused her to develop peritonitis, and negligence in failing to promptly diagnose and treat the condition. Defendants each moved to submit plaintiff's claims to arbitration in accordance with the agreement. The trial court dismissed plaintiff's complaint with prejudice, but without prejudice to her right to file a claim for arbitration.

The Court of Appeals rejected plaintiff's argument that the composition of the arbitration panel was unconstitutionally biased. It also held that the act does not unconstitutionally or unconscionably deprive a patient of a meaningful opportunity to decide whether to relinquish access to a court and a jury trial. The Court further held that the agreement was not a contract of adhesion. Judge Bronson dissented from the holding of constitutionality. Morris v. Metriyakool, supra. We granted plaintiff's application for leave to appeal. 412 Mich. 884 (1981).

The malpractice arbitration act provides that a patient "may, if offered, execute an agreement to arbitrate a dispute, controversy, or issue arising out of health care or treatment by a health care provider", M.C.L. § 600.5041(1); M.S.A. § 27A.5041(1), or by a hospital, M.C.L. § 600.5042(1); M.S.A. § 27A.5042(1). A patient executing such an agreement with a health-care provider may revoke it within 60 days after execution, M.C.L. § 600.5041(3); M.S.A. § 27A.5041(3), or, in the case of a hospital, within 60 days after discharge, M.C.L. § 600.5042(3); M.S.A. § 27A.5042(3), options which must be stated in the agreement. All such agreements must provide in 12–point boldface type immediately above the space for the parties' signatures that agreement to arbitrate is not a prerequisite to the receipt of health care. M.C.L. §§ 600.5041(5), 600.5042(4); M.S.A. §§ 27A.5041(5), 27A.5042(4).

For those who have elected arbitration, the act requires a three-member panel composed of an attorney, who shall be chairperson, a physician, preferably from the respondent's medical specialty, and a person who is not a licensee of the health care profession, involved, a lawyer, or a representative of a hospital or an insurance company. M.C.L. § 600.5044(2); M.S.A. § 27A.5044(2). Where the claim is against a hospital only, a hospital administrator may be substituted for the physician. If the claim is against a health-care provider other than a physician, a licensee of the health-care profession involved shall be substituted.

Defendants Detroit Memorial Hospital and Dr. Bloom appeal from the holding that the presence of the medical member unconstitutionally created a biased panel. First, they argue that because the state does not compel arbitration, but only regulates it, state action is not involved.

A basic requirement of due process is a "fair trial in a fair tribunal". In re Murchison, 349 U.S. 133, 136, 75 S.Ct. 623, 625, 99 L.Ed. 942 (1955.... Essential to this notion is a fair and impartial decision maker. Crampton v. Department of State, 395 Mich. 347, 351, 235 N.W.2d 352 (1975). The Due Process Clause, ... limits state action.... Private conduct abridging individual rights does not implicate the Due Process Clause unless to some significant extent the state, in any of its manifestations, has been found to have become involved in it, see Burton v. Wilmington Parking Authority, 365 U.S. 715, 81 S.Ct. 856, 6 L.Ed.2d 45 (1961), or to have compelled the conduct, Flagg Brothers, Inc. v. Brooks, 436 U.S. 149, 164, 98 S.Ct. 1729, 1737, 56 L.Ed.2d 185 (1978)....

We find it unnecessary, however, to determine here whether the state has significantly involved itself in the challenged action because, even if we were to find so, we have concluded that the composition of the arbitration panel does not offend guarantees of due process.

In holding the act unconstitutional, the Court of Appeals in Jackson agreed with Judge Bronson's partial dissent in Morris that the arbitration panel presents too high a probability of actual bias to be constitutionally tolerable. In his partial dissent in Morris, Judge Bronson found the statute creating the panel unconstitutional because the medical member of the arbitration panel had such an interest in the outcome that there is too great a risk that he will not be impartial. Judge Bronson cited two affidavits submitted in Morris from malpractice insurance underwriters. They averred that any hospital administrator or physician would have a direct and substantial interest in the outcome of arbitrated cases because the cost and availability of medical malpractice insurance would be affected. Judge Bronson also said that the act in question is supported by health care professionals, which indicates that they believe they will fare better under this type of system. He also concluded that anti-plaintiff attitudes exist among large numbers of doctors. "Their 'function and frame of reference' may be expected to make them partisans of their professional colleagues." Morris, 107 Mich.App. 110, 309 N.W.2d 910 (Bronson, J., dissenting in part and concurring in part).

No showing of actual bias on the part of a particular arbitration panel is claimed, the parties having appealed from motions for accelerated judgment and no arbitration panel having been convened. That does not prevent a party from claiming that the risk of actual bias is too high to be constitutionally tolerable. "[O]ur system of law has always endeavored to prevent even the probability of unfairness." Murchison, supra, 349 U.S. 136, 75 S.Ct. 625. "In pursuit of this end, various situations have been identified in which experience teaches that the probability of actual bias on the part of the judge or decision maker is too high to be constitutionally tolerable." Withrow, supra, 421 U.S. 47, 95 S.Ct. 1464. Included in those situations is that of a decision maker who has a direct or substantial pecuniary interest in the outcome of the controversy. E.g., Gibson v.

Berryhill, 411 U.S. 564, 93 S.Ct. 1689, 36 L.Ed.2d 488 (1973); see Crampton, supra, 395 Mich. 351–355, 235 N.W.2d 352.

Such a pecuniary interest is claimed here—the decision maker's interest in lower malpractice insurance premiums will influence his decision towards reducing the number and size of malpractice awards. In their affidavits, the underwriters averred that physicians and hospital administrators have a vested interest in the medical malpractice claims made against others; the claims made do affect the rate of insurance premiums and the availability of insurance. Premium rates for all doctors, they averred, are generally determined by the number of all claims, settlements, and judgments against physicians and hospitals in Michigan. The effect of an arbitration award on insurance rates is thus said to be direct and substantial.

This situation is aggravated, contends plaintiff Jackson, by the composition of the advisory committee, which selects the pool of candidates from which all members of the arbitration panel are chosen. The statute provides:

> "An arbitration advisory committee is created within the bureau of insurance and shall be appointed by the commission and shall consist of 18 members. One-half of the advisory committee shall be broadly composed of licensed physicians and other health care providers, licensed hospital or institutional health care providers, malpractice insurance carriers and licensed legal practitioners. One-half shall be broadly composed of nongovernmental, nonlawyer, nonhealth care provider, and noninsurance carrier persons. The committee may appoint 1 or more specialized subcommittees with the approval of the commissioner." M.C.L. § 500.3054; M.S.A. § 24.13054.

The medical part of the committee, which includes the malpractice insurance carriers and health-care providers, has a direct interest in reducing the number and size of malpractice awards. There is a substantial possibility, plaintiff Jackson insists, that they will select candidates who are similarly inclined.

All that has been shown here with any degree of certainty is that there is a relationship between the number and size of malpractice awards on the one hand, and the cost and availability of malpractice insurance on the other. This may be taken for granted. It may also be assumed that, because physicians and hospital administrators are concerned with the cost and availability of malpractice insurance, they are members of a class which is affected by the decision in a case between other parties. See Tumey v. Ohio, 273 U.S. 510, 522, 47 S.Ct. 437, 441, 71 L.Ed. 749, 50 A.L.R. 1243 (1927). More than that must be shown, however, to make out a case which offends due process.

In Tumey, the village mayor was disqualified from sitting as a judge where he was compensated from fines imposed for violation of the state prohibition act. The Court concluded that the mayor "had a direct, personal, pecuniary interest in convicting the defendant who came before him for trial, in the twelve dollars of costs imposed in his behalf, which he would not have received if the defendant had been acquitted." Tumey, p. 523, 47 S.Ct. p. 441.

In Ward v. Monroeville, 409 U.S. 57, 93 S.Ct. 80, 34 L.Ed.2d 267 (1972), although the mayor was not directly compensated from fines imposed for traffic offenses, he held wide executive powers and was responsible for village finances. The Court disqualified the mayor from sitting as a judge because the mayor's executive responsibilities for village finances might have made him partisan to maintain the high level of contribution from the mayor's court. Revenue from fines, costs, and fees collected in the mayor's court annually contributed almost half of the total village revenues.

Also, in Gibson, supra, the Court affirmed the district court's finding that the Alabama Board of Optometry was biased and could not provide a fair and impartial hearing to optometrists charged with unprofessional conduct for working for a corporation. The board was composed solely of independent doctors not employed by corporations. The Court held that the board had a substantial pecuniary interest in the proceedings because what was sought was the revocation of the licenses of nearly half of all optometrists in the state which, if successful, would possibly redound to the personal benefit of members of the board.

In the present case, by contrast, it has not been demonstrated that the medical members of these panels have a direct pecuniary interest or that their decision may have any substantial effect on the availability of insurance or insurance premiums. We have been shown no grounds sufficient for us to conclude that these decision makers will not act with honesty and integrity. We look for a pecuniary interest which creates a probability of unfairness, a risk of actual bias which is too high to be constitutionally tolerable. It has not been shown here.

Plaintiff Jackson also argues that as a class physicians and hospital administrators possess a subliminal bias against patients who claim medical malpractice.

We interpret this as a claim made out under Crampton, supra. In Crampton, we held that the probability of actual bias was too high where a prosecutor and a police officer sat on an appeal board to review the revocation of Crampton's driver's license for refusal to submit to a chemical test upon arrest for driving under the influence of intoxicating liquor. Police officers and prosecutors are full-time law enforcement officials, we said, deeply and personally involved in the fight against law violators. "[T]hey are identified and aligned with the state as the adversary of the citizen who is charged with violation of the law. Their function and frame of reference may be expected to make them 'partisan to maintain' their own authority and that of their fellow officers." Crampton, supra, 395 Mich. 357, 235 N.W.2d 352.

We do not believe that the medical members of these panels are so identified and aligned with respondents in malpractice cases that they may be expected to favor the respondents. Physicians and other health professionals are trained in the medical arts and are oath-bound to treat the ill. Hospital administrators are trained in the proper functioning of hospitals. Neither physicians nor hospital administrators have professional interests that are adverse to patients or even malpractice claimants on a consistent, daily basis. Any identity of interest with respondents is not so strong as to create a subliminal bias for one side and against the other.

. . . Plaintiffs next argue that the arbitration agreement waives constitutional rights to a jury trial and access to a court. Because these fundamental rights are waived, they say, the burden should rest with the defendants to show a valid contract, which they can only do by showing that the waiver was made voluntarily, knowingly, and intelligently. The burden of showing a voluntary waiver is not an easy one, argue plaintiffs, because the arbitration agreement was offered at the time of admission to the hospital in an atmosphere infected with implicit coercion. Additionally, plaintiffs argue that a knowing and intelligent waiver will not be easily shown because the defendants are chargeable with constructive fraud. Constructive fraud is said to arise out of the agreement's failure to highlight the fact of waiver, failure to disclose the composition of the arbitration panel (even though this information is contained in an informational booklet accompanying the agreement), and failure to disclose the attitudes of physicians in general, that they and hospital administrators may be biased and the reasonable probability that insurance rates are affected by awards.

. . . Answering the merits of plaintiffs' questions, defendants contend that arbitration is a matter of contract and that one who signs a written agreement is presumed to understand it. The act presumes a conforming agreement to be valid, M.C.L. §§ 600.5041(7), 600.5042(8); M.S.A. §§ 27A.5041(7), 27A.5042(8). Therefore, the burden of disproving this arbitration agreement rests with plaintiffs. Moreover, say defendants, the burden of establishing a constitutional violation rests with the party asserting it. The arbitration agreement and informational booklet reasonably indicated that arbitration was an exclusive alternative to trial by jury. Plaintiffs expressly waived their rights to trial by jury. Arbitration is voluntary and not required, which the agreement plainly states in capital letters above the signature. The form of the agreement and the information booklet is strictly controlled, M.C.L. §§ 500.3053, 500.3060, 600.5041, 600.5042; M.S.A. §§ 24.13053, 24.13060, 27A.5041, 27A.5042, and was approved by the Michigan Commissioner of Insurance.

Plaintiffs, contend defendants, have failed to demonstrate that they were coerced into signing the agreement. Answering the argument of constructive fraud, defendants say that the information booklet given to plaintiffs states that a doctor or hospital administrator serves on the arbitration panel. A chart in the booklet also states that a court case is heard by a judge and jury while an arbitration case is heard by the three-member panel.

We reject plaintiffs' allocation of the burden of proof to defendants. The burden of avoiding these arbitration agreements, as with other contracts, rests with those who would avoid them. The act states that an agreement to arbitrate which includes the statutory provisions shall be presumed valid. M.C.L. §§ 600.5041(7), 600.5042(8); M.S.A. §§ 27A.5041(7), 27A.5042(8).

The burden of showing some ground for rescinding or invalidating a contract is not altered merely because the contract entails eschewal of constitutional rights. Plaintiffs' allegations of coercion, like other contract defenses of mistake, duress, and fraud, must be proven by the party seeking to avoid the contract on such grounds.

Plaintiff Jackson contends that the arbitration agreement is a contract of adhesion, the terms of which exceeded her reasonable expectations. She claims that by not stating explicitly that court access with the right to jury trial was waived, this fact was in effect concealed and hence the contract is unconscionable.

Contracts of adhesion are characterized by standardized forms prepared by one party which are offered for rejection or acceptance without opportunity for bargaining and under the circumstances that the second party cannot obtain the desired product or service except by acquiescing in the form agreement. Steven v. Fidelity & Casualty Co. of New York, 58 Cal.2d 862, 879, 27 Cal.Rptr. 172, 377 P.2d 284 (1962).... Regardless of any possible perception among patients that the provision of optimal medical care is conditioned on their signing the arbitration agreement, we believe that the sixty-day rescission period, of which patients must be informed, fully protects those who sign the agreement. The patients' ability to rescind the agreement after leaving the hospital allows them to obtain the desired service without binding them to its terms. As a result, the agreement cannot be considered a contract of adhesion.

We also reject plaintiff's claim that the arbitration agreement is unconscionable. According to the record before us, the arbitration agreement signed by plaintiff Jackson is six paragraphs long. The first sentence of the first paragraph begins, "I understand that this hospital and I by signing this document agree to arbitrate any claims or disputes". The first two sentences of the second paragraph state:

> "I understand that Michigan Law gives me the choice of trial by judge or jury or of arbitration. I understand that arbitration is a procedure by which a panel that is either mutually agreed upon or appointed decides the dispute rather than a judge or jury."

This was not a long contract covering different terms, only one of which, obscured among many paragraphs, concerned arbitration. Arbitration was the essential and singular nature of the agreement. We do not believe that an ordinary person signing this agreement to arbitrate would reasonably expect a jury trial. We also reject plaintiffs' argument that the agreement is unconscionable for failure to highlight these terms. See

Williams v. Walker–Thomas Furniture Co., 121 U.S.App.D.C. 315, 319, 350 F.2d 445, 18 A.L.R.3d 1297 (1965).

Finally, both plaintiffs ask that we find constructive fraud and hold that the agreements are unconscionable because of failure of the contracts to disclose the composition of the panel, the attitudes of physicians, the fact that the medical member of the panel may be intrinsically biased against plaintiffs, and the reasonable probability that malpractice rates are affected by awards in medical malpractice cases.

We decline. We do not believe that the agreements are unconscionable for failing to include plaintiffs' recommendations. Nor do we believe that defendants have breached a legal or equitable duty which has had the effect of deceiving plaintiffs, nor have defendants received an unmerited benefit. Goodrich v. Waller, 314 Mich. 456, 462, 22 N.W.2d 862 (1946).

In Jackson, we reverse the finding of unconstitutionality and reinstate the order of the trial court submitting the matter to arbitration.

In Morris, we affirm.

■ CAVANAGH, JUSTICE (dissenting).

The central issue in these two cases is whether the Due Process Clauses of the United States Constitution, and the Michigan Constitution, which bar the state from depriving any person of life, liberty, or property without due process of law, are violated by the medical malpractice arbitration act of 1975, M.C.L. § 600.5040 et seq.; M.S.A. § 27A.5040 et seq. I am persuaded that they are because the act unconstitutionally deprives these plaintiffs of their due process rights to a fair hearing before an impartial decision maker.

Accepting in principle the analytical approach advanced by my brother Ryan, I am convinced that (1) plaintiffs have been deprived of the constitutionally cognizable right to a fair hearing before an impartial decision maker, (2) because of state action, (3) without due process of law.

I

While it is difficult to know whether to classify the right to a fair hearing before an impartial decision maker as a liberty or property right, there can be no doubt that it is a constitutionally cognizable right. Indeed, a basic tenet of due process is that decision makers must be unbiased and impartial. As the Supreme Court stated in In re Murchison, 349 U.S. 133 (1955):

"A fair trial in a fair tribunal is a basic requirement of due process. Fairness of course requires an absence of actual bias in the trial of cases. But our system of law has always endeavored to prevent even the probability of unfairness. To this end no man can be a judge in his own case and no man is permitted to try cases where he has an interest in the outcome. That interest cannot be defined with precision. Circumstances and relationships must be considered. This Court has said, however, that 'every procedure which would offer a possible temptation to the average man as a judge * * * not to hold the balance nice, clear and true between the State and the accused, denies the latter due process of law.' Tumey v. Ohio, 273 U.S. 510 (1927). Such a stringent rule may sometimes bar trial by judges who have no actual bias and who would do their very best to weigh the scales of justice equally between contending parties. But to perform its high function in the best way 'justice must satisfy the apparance of justice.' Offutt v. United States, 348 U.S. 11, 14 (1954)."

Thus, the potential for actual bias on the part of the decision maker may be too great in some circumstances for our system of justice to risk, despite the fact that such potential might never be realized.

One situation which presents too great a probability of actual bias is when the decision maker has a direct or substantial pecuniary interest in the outcome of the controversy. Crampton v. Department of State, 395 Mich. 347, 351, 235 N.W.2d 352 (1975). This is what the plaintiffs claim exists here, i.e., that a health care provider who must decide a medical malpractice case will be inclined to minimize the size of any award because the number and size of malpractice awards directly affect the availability and cost of medical malpractice insurance coverage.[6]

There is no dispute that the medical malpractice arbitration act was the legislative response to an alleged malpractice insurance crisis which supposedly resulted from the spiraling costs of insurance coverage for health-care providers and the reduction in actual availability of such coverage. Submission of malpractice controversies to arbitration was perceived as a way to reduce the costs of such disputes because arbitration is less complicated and quicker than litigation and usually results in a decision that is final. A reduction in the costs of bringing malpractice disputes to a resolution was to then result in a reduction in the costs of malpractice insurance coverage for health-care providers. However, since the relationship between malpractice controversies and malpractice insurance rates is so direct, it is clear that a reduction in the number and size of malpractice awards, in addition to a reduction in the costs of resolving such disputes, would be of substantial benefit to those paying for the cost of malpractice insurance coverage.

The cost of malpractice insurance premiums has a significant effect on a health-care provider's ability to practice in the medical profession. If the number and size of malpractice awards directly affect the cost of these premiums so that the premiums are more costly after an increase in the number and size of such awards, then health-care providers have a direct pecuniary interest in seeing that the number and size of malpractice awards remain small, and they have the opportunity to further this interest when they sit as decision makers in medical malpractice cases.

---

6. The affidavits of experienced underwriters of medical malpractice insurance, which are part of this record, specifically aver that any malpractice award in favor of a plaintiff affects the availability and cost of malpractice insurance coverage and thus any health care provider would have a direct and substantial interest in the outcome of arbitrated malpractice cases.

The fact that the direct effect of a particular malpractice award upon a single health-care provider's insurance rate may be minimal does not make the health-care provider's potential for bias on the basis of a pecuniary interest remote enough to be constitutionally permissible. Since the overall effect of malpractice claims and awards significantly affects insurance rates, the threat of a subliminal systematic bias exists in the medical profession. This results in a temptation for the medical-member decision maker to forget the requisite burden of proof and fail to hold the balance true and clear between the adverse parties.

The interests of health-care providers may vary according to the situation in which they find themselves. When a patient is sick and in need of treatment, the health-care provider's interests are clearly not adverse to the patient. At this point the patient's welfare is undoubtedly of paramount importance to the members of the medical profession. However, in a malpractice case the focus of attention is no longer on how to make the patient well; rather, it is on whether the patient is entitled to compensation for any mistreatment received from a member of the medical profession and, if so, the amount of compensation due. Members of the medical profession are no longer in a position to use their skills to improve the patient's health. At this point they are solely in a position of choosing whether to award the patient any money for alleged wrongful medical treatment. I believe that in this situation the interests of the health-care providers in relation to those of the patient change and, in light of the effect a malpractice award may have on their pecuniary interests, the health care providers may be expected to align themselves with and favor a member of their own profession.

This is not to say that health-care providers as a group are not fair-minded. However, in the context of medical malpractice litigation, their function as arbitrators and their frame of reference may make them partisans of their professional colleagues, producing partisan results. This situation thus presents too high a risk of actual bias on the part of the medical-member decision makers to be constitutionally permissible.

In light of this potential for bias on the part of health-care providers deciding malpractice cases, I conclude that the medical malpractice arbitration act's requirement of a health-care provider in the composition of the arbitration panel violates the plaintiffs' constitutional right to a fair hearing before an impartial decision maker. . . .

* * *

Questions

1.   The majority says that there was no showing of actual bias in this case. What evidence does it use to reach this conclusion? Do you agree? Is the court insisting that there be actual bias, or does it suggest that potential bias would be grounds to set aside an arbitral award in some circumstances? How does the majority distinguish *Gibson v. Berryhill*, the optome-

trist case? What does the dissent mean by "subliminal systematic bias"? Would Judge Posner find "subliminal systematic bias" to be grounds to invalidate an arbitration award? Should it be?

2.   How central is it to the court's reasoning that the parties had a sixty-day period in which to rescind their arbitration agreement? This factor suggests that issues of consent to arbitrate are bound up with questions of due process—the more confident the court is that there is genuine consent to arbitration, the less it needs to police the process for due process shortcomings. Should judicial scrutiny to ensure for consent to arbitration agreements obviate all scrutiny of due process concerns?

3.   Suppose there were a state law that said in all arbitrations of malpractice claims, the arbitration agreement must appear in bold print on the first page of a contract, must be in type size no smaller than 14 point, and must contain an explanation of the legal consequences of arbitration. Would such a law be enforceable after *Southland?* Would the result be different if the state law allocated the burden of proof for malpractice arbitrations, specified the composition of the arbitration panel, or mandated a 60–day rescission period? *See Doctor's Associates v. Cassaratto,* supra.

* * *

10.   ARBITRATOR IMMUNITY AND TESTIMONY

Corey v. New York Stock Exchange

691 F.2d 1205 (6th Cir.1982).

■ KENNEDY, CIRCUIT JUDGE.

Corey appeals from the District Court's dismissal of his lawsuit against the New York Stock Exchange (NYSE) in which he claimed that the procedures followed in an arbitration proceeding sponsored by the NYSE and to which he was a party were wrongful and caused him injury. Corey sought to hold the NYSE liable for the conduct of the arbitrators and the NYSE's arbitration director, Cavell. We agree with the District Court that Corey's claims against the NYSE for the acts of the arbitrators are barred by arbitral immunity and those based on Cavell's acts constitute no more than an impermissible collateral attack on the arbitrators' award.

In 1965, Corey began to invest in the stock market under the guidance of a long-time friend, Wright, who was an account executive with Merrill Lynch, Pierce, Fenner & Smith (Merrill Lynch). Wright suffered a paralyzing stroke in 1968, but returned to work thereafter and reestablished his business relationship with Corey. In 1972 and 1973, Corey invested heavily in the stock market, allegedly because of Wright's advice. Medical concerns prompted Wright's retirement in 1973 and Corey's account was transferred to another Merrill Lynch employee. The stock in Corey's portfolio depreciated in value and he was forced to liquidate it to meet the margin requirements of his account. Corey claims to have lost approximately $175,000 as a result of the liquidation.

Corey elected to initiate arbitration proceedings against Merrill Lynch in April 1976. Article VIII of the Constitution of the NYSE, gives non-members the option of submitting a claim against a member brokerage corporation for arbitration, instead of pursuing remedies at law. In his statement of claim Corey alleged that his loss resulted directly from Wright's impaired judgment as a result of his stroke and from the negligence of Merrill Lynch in permitting Wright to return to work before he was capable of intelligently advising customers. The rules of the NYSE, which sponsored the arbitration, governed the selection of the five arbitrators responsible for Corey's case as well as the procedural rules to be followed. Cavell, the Assistant Arbitration Director for the NYSE, administered arbitrations between members and non-members of the NYSE. He was responsible for overseeing the preliminary arrangements for arbitrations, including the obtaining of written submissions, arranging for the appointment of arbitration panels, scheduling hearing dates, acting as a moderator on behalf of the arbitration panel and furnishing the parties with written notification of arbitration decisions. Upon selection of the arbitration panel, two hearings were held in Detroit at which Corey appeared without counsel. In March 1977, the arbitrators dismissed Corey's claim against Merrill Lynch and assessed $700 in costs against him. Cavell mailed a copy of this decision to Corey in early April 1977. Corey was not informed of his right to appeal and did not avail himself of the appeal provisions of the federal Arbitration Act. 9 U.S.C. §§ 1 et seq.

In early 1978, Corey filed suit in Ingham County Circuit Court against Merrill Lynch claiming Merrill Lynch and the NYSE conspired to deprive him of a fair hearing before the arbitrators. Neither the NYSE, Cavell nor the individual arbitrators were named as defendants. Corey challenged the composition of the arbitration panel as violative of the NYSE rules and asserted procedural irregularities that prevented him from submitting evidence, caused hearings to be postponed over his objection and allowed the arbitrators to dominate the proceedings with the purpose of defeating his claims. A motion for accelerated judgment was granted in favor of Merrill Lynch on the ground that the arbitrators' award was final and binding and that the court lacked jurisdiction over the parties and the subject matter of the suit. Corey did not appeal this decision.

In August 1978, Corey filed suit against the NYSE in Ingham County Circuit Court making allegations virtually identical to those in his suit against Merrill Lynch. He did not name Cavell or the individual arbitrators as defendants, although complaining of their acts, presumedly pursuing the NYSE on some theory of vicarious liability. Specifically, Corey alleged that the acts of Cavell during the arbitration hearings sponsored by the NYSE deprived him of a fair hearing because Cavell selected members of the arbitration panel in violation of the NYSE rules and adjourned and rescheduled hearings over Corey's objection. Although the wrongdoing is alleged to be that of Cavell, other allegations address matters unique to the arbitrators, such as their alleged refusal to allow Corey to present evidence and their prejudgment as to the merit of Corey's claims. Corey sought $1,000,000 in punitive damages for mental anguish and long-standing physical problems brought about as a result of these acts.

Following the removal of this action to federal district court, the NYSE successfully moved for summary judgment. Corey v. New York Stock Exchange, 493 F.Supp. 51 (W.D.Mich.1980). Corey appeals this determination.

I. ARBITRAL IMMUNITY

To the extent that Corey's complaint may be construed to allege wrongdoing by the arbitrators for which the NYSE is liable, we agree with the District Court that the NYSE, acting through its arbitrators, is immune from civil liability for the acts of the arbitrators arising out of contractually agreed upon arbitration proceedings. Our decision to extend immunity to arbitrators and the boards which sponsor arbitration finds support in the case law, the policies behind the doctrines of judicial and quasi-judicial immunity and policies unique to contractually agreed upon arbitration proceedings.

The Supreme Court has long recognized that there are certain persons whose special functions require a full exemption from liability for acts committed within the scope of their duties.[4] The rationale behind the Supreme Court decisions is that the independence necessary for principled and fearless decision-making can best be preserved by protecting these persons from bias or intimidation caused by the fear of a lawsuit arising out of the exercise of official functions within their jurisdiction.... In Butz the Court stated that immunity is not extended to individuals because of their particular location in government but because of the special nature of their responsibilities. Butz, supra, 438 U.S. at 511, 98 S.Ct. at 2913. The Court said that the relevant consideration in evaluating whether immunity should attach to the acts of persons in certain roles and with certain responsibilities was the "functional comparability" of their judgments to those of a judge. Id. 512, 98 S.Ct. at 2913; Imbler, supra, 424 U.S. at 423 n. 20, 96 S.Ct. at 991 n. 20. In each instance, safeguards were present to protect other participants and the integrity of the decision-making process. Paramount among these safeguards is the right of judicial review. Butz,

---

4. The principle behind the doctrine of judicial immunity first adopted by the Supreme Court in Bradley v. Fisher, 80 U.S. 335, 20 L.Ed. 646 (1871), has been extended to state judges, Pierson v. Ray, 386 U.S. 547, 87 S.Ct. 1213, 18 L.Ed.2d 288 (1967) (judicial immunity), to federal prosecutors, Yaselli v. Goff, 275 U.S. 503, 48 S.Ct. 155, 72 L.Ed. 395 (1927), aff'g, 12 F.2d 396 (2d Cir.1926) (quasi-judicial immunity), and state prosecutors, Imbler v. Pachtman, 424 U.S. 409, 96 S.Ct. 984, 47 L.Ed.2d 128 (1976) (quasi-judicial immunity). The principle in Bradley has also been extended to federal agency examiners, administrative law judges and agency officials performing functions analogous to prosecutors, Butz v. Economou, 438 U.S. 478, 98 S.Ct. 2894, 57 L.Ed.2d 895 (1978) (quasi-judicial immunity). To ensure unintimidated independence of action, legislators also enjoy complete immunity, Tenney v. Brandhove, 341 U.S. 367, 71 S.Ct. 783, 95 L.Ed. 1019 (1951).

supra, 438 U.S. at 512–14, 98 S.Ct. at 2913–14; Pierson v. Ray, 386 U.S. 547, 554, 87 S.Ct. 1213, 1217, 18 L.Ed.2d 288 (1967).

We believe that determinations made by the panel of arbitrators in the case on appeal are functionally comparable to those of a judge or an agency hearing examiner even though this was not a statutory arbitration or one where the arbitrators were court appointed. In Burchell v. Marsh, 58 U.S. 344, 15 L.Ed. 96 (1854), the Supreme Court stated that "[a]rbitrators are judges chosen by the parties to decide the matters submitted to them...." Id. 58 U.S. at 349. The submission of the parties replaces a statute or court order as the source of the arbitrators' power with regard to subject matter and procedural rules. The arbitrators in this case were appointed by private agreement of the parties and empowered by the parties to resolve disputes between them. By agreement, the parties invoked the arbitrators' independent judgment and discretion.... By private agreement the parties have substituted the arbitrators for a judge as the decision-maker in their case. Jurisdiction by consent is recognized by reviewing and enforcing courts. See 9 U.S.C. §§ 2, 9, 10, 11....

Several safeguards exist to protect the participants in the decision-making process and the integrity of the arbitration proceedings. First, arbitration proceedings resemble judicial proceedings in several respects. Arbitration is adversarial. Both parties had a right to be represented by an attorney—a right Corey did not exercise. Discovery was available and hearings were held at which the arbitrators received evidence and entertained arguments. Both parties had the opportunity to present witnesses and other evidence and to cross-examine or impeach those of their adversary. After a period of deliberation, the arbitrators issued a written opinion deciding the claim. The second safeguard is the automatic right of judicial review provided by the federal Arbitration Act, 9 U.S.C. §§ 1 et seq., applicable because of the commerce clause nexus present in transactions involving the purchase and sale of securities.... Judicial review by a district court in the jurisdiction where the award by an arbitrator is made is provided for in sections 9, 10 and 11 of the Arbitration Act. Although the scope of review differs slightly, the same protection is present in judicial review of arbitrators' decisions under the Arbitration Act as is present in the review of judicial or administrative decisions. The circumstances under which an award may be vacated include procurement of an award by fraud, corruption, undue means, partiality or corruption in the arbitrators, misconduct on the part of the arbitrators in refusing to hear pertinent evidence, arbitrators acting in excess of their powers, arbitrators committing errors of law, etc. 9 U.S.C. §§ 9, 10, 11. The district court has the power to modify or correct an award or direct a rehearing by the arbitrators. Id. §§ 9, 10. The final safeguard is the voluntary use of arbitration as a means of dispute resolution. A person such as Corey could elect to submit his claim to arbitration or pursue his remedy at law. Presumedly, individuals will not avail themselves of arbitration by contractual agreement if they lack confidence in the impartiality and reliability of the arbitration process. In light of these safeguards, the risk of a wrongful act by the arbitrators is outweighed by the need for preserving the independence of their decision-making. See Butz, supra, 514, 98 S.Ct. at 2914.

A number of policy arguments support our decision. From Butz it is clear that immunity does not depend upon the source of the decision-making power but rather upon the nature of that power. Accordingly, the limits of immunity should be fixed in part by federal policy. The functional comparability of the arbitrators' decision-making process and judgments to those of judges and agency hearing examiners generates the same need for independent judgment, free from the threat of lawsuits. Immunity furthers this need. As with judicial and quasi-judicial immunity, arbitral immunity is essential to protect the decision-maker from undue influence and protect the decision-making process from reprisals by dissatisfied litigants. Federal policy, as manifested in the Arbitration Act and case law, favors final adjudication of differences by a means selected by the parties.... Because federal policy encourages arbitration and arbitrators are essential actors in furtherance of that policy, it is appropriate that immunity be extended to arbitrators for acts within the scope of their duties and within their jurisdiction. Corbin, supra, 396–97; Hill, supra, 326. The extension of immunity to arbitrators where arbitration is pursuant to a private agreement between the parties is especially compelling because arbitration is the means selected by the parties themselves for disposing of controversies between them. By immunizing arbitrators and their decisions from collateral attacks, arbitration as the contractual choice of the parties is respected yet the arbitrators are protected. Arbitrators have no interest in the outcome of the dispute and should not be compelled to become parties to that dispute. Tamari, supra, 781. "[I]ndividuals cannot be expected to volunteer to arbitrate disputes if they can be caught up in the struggle between the litigants and saddled with the burdens of defending a lawsuit." Tamari, supra, 781. Accord, Raitport, supra, 527. An aggrieved party alleging a due process violation in the conduct of the proceedings, fraud, misconduct, a violation of public policy, lack of jurisdiction, etc., by arbitrators should pursue remedies against the "real" adversary through the appeal process. To allow a collateral attack against arbitrators and their judgments would also emasculate the appeal provisions of the federal Arbitration Act. 9 U.S.C. §§ 9, 10. For these reasons we believe that arbitral immunity is essential to the maintenance of arbitration by contractual agreement as a viable alternative to the judicial process for the settlement of controversies and must be applied in this case.

Extension of arbitral immunity to encompass boards which sponsor arbitration is a natural and necessary product of the policies underlying arbitral immunity; otherwise the immunity extended to arbitrators is illusionary. It would be of little value to the whole arbitral procedure to merely shift the liability to the sponsoring association.

II. ARBITRATION ACT AS EXCLUSIVE REMEDY

Corey's complaint may also be construed as alleging wrongdoing by Cavell for which the NYSE is liable, such as improper selection of the panel of five arbitrators so that they were biased against Corey and adjournments of Corey's hearing dates which caused him prejudice. It is implicit in Corey's complaint that these acts compromised the arbitration award thereby causing him mental anguish and physical problems. We agree with the District Court that the federal Arbitration Act provides the exclusive remedy for challenging acts that taint an arbitration award and that Corey's attempt to sue the NYSE for the acts of Cavell is no more, in substance, than an impermissible collateral attack on the award itself.[6]

Sections 10, 11 and 12 of the Arbitration Act provide a mechanism whereby parties to an arbitration proceeding may obtain judicial review in the federal district court in the district in which the arbitration award is made. The scope of review is limited by these provisions. Section 10 provides that an award may be vacated if it was procured by fraud, corruption or undue means, where there has been evident partiality or corruption in the arbitrators, where there has been misconduct or misbehavior by which the rights of any party may have been prejudiced and where the arbitrators exceeded their powers. A rehearing by the arbitrators may be ordered in certain circumstances. Section 11 allows a district court to modify or correct an order for any miscalculation of figures or mistake in description, where the arbitrators have awarded upon a matter not submitted to them and where the award is imperfect in a matter of form not affecting the merits of the controversy. An order so compromised may be modified or corrected to effect the intent of the award and promote justice between the parties. Section 12 of the Arbitration Act requires that notice of a motion to vacate, modify or correct an award must be served on the adverse party or his attorney within three months after the award is filed or delivered. Failure to comply with this statutory precondition of timely service of notice forfeits the right to judicial review of the award. Piccolo v. Dain, Kalman & Quail, Inc., 641 F.2d 598, 600 (8th Cir.1981). ... Allegations of wrongdoing raised by Corey in his complaint are squarely within the scope of section 10 of the Arbitration Act. Evident partiality on the part of the arbitrators toward Merrill Lynch as a result of the manner in which they were selected is covered by section 10(b). Adjournments allegedly causing prejudice are reviewable under section 10(c). The issues raised by Corey's complaint could have been resolved by timely pursuit of a remedy under this section.

The federal Arbitration Act provides the exclusive remedy for challenging an award on the grounds raised by Corey. Section 2 of the Arbitration Act states that a contractual provision wherein the parties agree to submit a dispute to arbitration is valid, irrevocable and enforceable, except on such grounds in law or equity as exist for the revocation of the contract to arbitrate. Once an arbitrator has rendered a decision the award is binding on the parties unless they challenge the underlying contract to arbitrate pursuant to section 2 or avail themselves of the review provisions of sections 10 and 11. Corey has not alleged that there was any defect in the

---

6. This same argument may be made with respect to the allegations against arbitrators which we have found to be protected by arbitral immunity.

underlying agreement to arbitrate the dispute with Merrill Lynch, which he himself initiated, which would provide a basis for revoking that agreement. Nor has he availed himself of the review provisions of sections 10 and 11. Barring these two situations, the Arbitration Act provides no other avenue by which an arbitration award may be challenged. Two circuit courts have held that allegations within the purview of section 10 are reviewable only under the authority of the federal Arbitration Act. Piccolo, supra, 600 (alleged no fair and impartial hearing); Tamari v. Bache & Co., 565 F.2d 1194, 1202 (7th Cir.1977), cert. denied, 435 U.S. 905, 98 S.Ct. 1450, 55 L.Ed.2d 495 (1978) (arbitrators biased).

To confine challenges to an award within the scope of section 10 and 11 exclusively to the review provisions of the Arbitration Act is also consistent with section 12 of that Act. The three month notice requirement in section 12 for an appeal of the award on section 10 or 11 grounds is meaningless if a party to the arbitration proceedings may bring an independent direct action asserting such claims outside of the statutory time period provided for in section 12.

Corey's claims constitute a collateral attack against the award even though Corey is presently suing a different defendant than his original adversary in the arbitration proceeding and is requesting damages for the acts of wrongdoing rather than the vacation, modification or correction of the arbitration award. Corey was not harmed by the selection of the arbitrators and the adjournments of the hearings in and of themselves; he did not and cannot raise a constitutional due process claim. Rather, he was harmed by the impact these acts had on the award. Corey's complaint has no purpose other than to challenge the very wrongs affecting the award for which review is provided under section 10 of the Arbitration Act. The mere presence of the NYSE, Cavell or the arbitrators or the prayer for damages does not change the substance of his claim. Very simply, Corey did not avail himself of the review provisions of section 10 of the Arbitration Act and may not transform what would ordinarily constitute an impermissible collateral attack into a proper independent direct action by changing defendants and altering the relief sought.

Accordingly, the judgment of the District Court is affirmed.

* * *

Note on *Baar v. Tigerman*

In BAAR V. TIGERMAN, 140 Cal.App.3d 979, 211 Cal. Rptr. 426 (Cal.Ct. App.1983), defendant was the arbitrator in an arbitration hearing that lasted four years and involved 43 days of evidentiary hearings and 10 days of closing arguments. Once final briefs were submitted, on July 18, 1980, the AAA deemed the matter submitted and set the arbitrator's award deadline for 30 days later, as required by the AAA rules. On August 20, the AAA requested an extension until November 30 for Tigerman to issue his award, and the parties agreed. Tigerman did not make the new deadline, nor had he issued an award after seven months. As a result, Tigerman lost the authority vested in him by the AAA rules to render an award. The plaintiff sued Tigerman and the AAA for breach of contract and negligence for failing to issue a timely arbitration award.

The California trial court dismissed the complaint, ruling that the defendants were protected by arbitral immunity. The appellate court reversed. It held that arbitral immunity covers only the arbitrator's quasi-judicial actions, not the ministerial action of rendering, or failing to render, an award. The court reasoned as follows:

"Courts of this country have long recognized immunity to protect arbitrators from civil liability for actions taken in the arbitrator's quasi-judicial capacity. Arbitral immunity, like judicial immunity, promotes fearless and independent decision making.... To this end, the courts have refused to hold judges and arbitrators liable for their judicial actions. As Judge Duniway of the Ninth Circuit wrote: 'If [the arbitrator's] decisions can thereafter be questioned in suits brought against them by either party, there is a real possibility that their decisions will be governed more by the fear of such suits than by their own unfettered judgment as to the merits of the matter they must decide.' (Lundgren v. Freeman (9th Cir.1962) 307 F.2d 104, 117) ...

"Respondents' contention that this court should extend immunity to an arbitrator who never renders an award fails to appreciate the nature of the arbitrator-party relationship and misperceives the policy underlying arbitral immunity. To date, no case has extended arbitral immunity to cover such a situation. Indeed, the only court to address this question denied immunity....

"Although the courts have looked favorably upon arbitration as an alternative to litigation in the courts, arbitration remains essentially a private contractual arrangement between parties. As the New York Court of Appeals observed, '[a]rbitration is essentially a creature of contract, a contract in which the parties themselves charter a private tribunal for the resolution of their disputes.'" (Astoria Medical Group v. Health Ins. Plan (1962) 11 N.Y.2d 128, 132–133, 227 N.Y.S.2d 401, 182 N.E.2d 85.)

"The contractual agreement in this case specifically sets forth the time period within which Tigerman had to render his award. A judge has discretion in terms of when a decision is made, but an arbitrator loses jurisdiction if a timely award is not forthcoming. While we must protect an arbitrator acting in a quasi-judicial capacity, we must also uphold the contractual obligations of an arbitrator to the parties involved."

The court further held that arbitral immunity does not protect the sponsoring organization when the arbitrator is not immune from liability. It said that those few cases which have addressed the question of immunity for organizations that sponsor and administer arbitrations provide that these organizations derive their immunity from the arbitrator. It quoted from the Sixth Circuit opinion in *Corey v. New York Stock Exchange, supra,* which stated: "[E]xtension of arbitral immunity to encompass boards which sponsor arbitration is a natural and necessary product of the policies underlying arbitral immunity; otherwise the immunity extended to arbitrators is illusionary." (Corey v. New York Stock Exchange, 691 F.2d at p. 1211.) Thus, the court concluded, when immunity does not attach to the arbitrator, it cannot protect the sponsor.

* * *

Questions

1. To what extent are arbitrators similar to federal prosecutors, hearing agency examiners, administrative law judges and legislators, as the *Corey* court suggests? Do these similarities compel the conclusion that arbitrators should be granted the same level of immunity that these other officials enjoy? Are there significant differences which might point toward a different result on the issue of immunity?

2. The *Corey* court noted that there were safeguards to protect participants in arbitration even in the face of arbitrator immunity. The safeguards include assurances of certain minimal due process protections, a right of judicial review, the ability to vacate an award on the basis of fraud or partiality, and the fact that arbitration is voluntary in the first place. How effective are these safeguards under current interpretations of the FAA?

3. Can *Baar v. Tigerman* be distinguished from *Corey?* The court attempts to distinguish arbitral action that is quasi-judicial from arbitral action that is contractual in nature, but is not the arbitrator's entire responsibility defined by the contract between the parties? Is an arbitrator's failure to abide by a contractual timetable any different than an arbitrator's failure to hold a fair hearing or render a fair award for purposes of immunity?

4. How does the *Corey* court justify extending arbitral immunity to boards which sponsor arbitration? Is this a valid reason to expand immunity? Are there countervailing factors which should be considered?

* * *

Legion Insurance Company v. Insurance General Agency, Inc.

822 F.2d 541 (5th Cir.1987).

■ Before POLITZ, WILLIAMS, and JONES, CIRCUIT JUDGES.

■ EDITH H. JONES, CIRCUIT JUDGE:

Insurance General Agency, Inc. ("IGAI") appeals the district court's entry of judgment pursuant to 9 U.S.C. § 9 confirming an adverse arbitration award. Confronted with a motion to confirm the arbitration award by Legion and with a cross-motion to vacate or correct under 9 U.S.C. §§ 10,

11 by IGAI, the district court concluded that Legion had failed to meet its burden of proof in challenging the award. We AFFIRM.

Legion first asserts that the district court's entry of judgment on the basis of the parties' cross-motions and supporting documents, without a hearing, was inappropriate and prejudicial because it denied them fair notice and an opportunity to be heard. This argument is merit less. Title 9 U.S.C. § 6 provides that "[a]ny application to the court hereunder shall be made and heard in the manner provided by law for the making and hearing of motions...." Under this directive both parties specifically requested the court to enter an order pursuant to their respective motions. Neither party requested a hearing. Appellant cannot complain on appeal that the district court erred in granting relief specifically requested by the parties under the statutory scheme for confirming or vacating arbitration awards.

Appellant also claims that the district court's failure to take evidence, other than that submitted in the parties' motion papers, severely prejudiced its ability to present the merits of its claim. Specifically, appellant claims that the district court's decision, based solely on the motion papers and supporting exhibits, was in direct violation of the Federal Rules of Civil Procedure.[1] See Fed.R.Civ.P. 81(a)(3) (Federal Rules applicable to proceedings under Title 9 U.S.C.). We are equally unpersuaded.

Appellant cited the following bases under 9 U.S.C. §§ 10, 11 for vacating or modifying the arbitration tribunal's award: (1) The award was clearly erroneous because it exceeded the damages requested and was unsupported by the evidence; (2) The arbitrators exceeded their authority in awarding a sum which was greater than Legion's proven claim; (3) No evidence was offered supporting an award of $269,091.00, making the award irrational; (4) The arbitrators failed to adhere to the agreement providing for arbitration because it is unclear whether they considered the calculations submitted by the defendant, or, alternatively, they failed to consider the calculations which constituted material evidence; (5) The award was a result of material miscalculation of figures; and (6) The award was based on a matter not submitted to the tribunal.

The district court had before it and analyzed the relevant records from the arbitration hearing, comprising 10 documents including the arbitration agreement, the demand for arbitration, calculations setting forth the specific amount of requested damages, memoranda submitted by both parties, and the premium rates and commission schedules upon which Legion based its claim. The arbitration proceeding was not transcribed. The district court determined that there was no support for assertions 1, 2, and 6; the district court also rejected challenges 3, 4, and 5 based on the documentary evidence. Technically, the documentation before the district court was not "in evidence" because its admissibility was not supported by affidavits until after the court entered judgment. Neither party disputed the authen-

---

1. We are called upon in this appeal to consider only whether the district court abused its discretion by deciding the motion based solely on documents submitted by the parties rather than by receiving evidence. Appellant does not now reassert its challenges to the arbitration tribunal's award.

ticity of the documents, however, and the district court evidently relied upon them as if admitted by stipulation.

We recognize that some motions challenging arbitration awards may require evidentiary hearings outside the scope of the pleadings and arbitration record. Appellant cites, for example, Sanko Steamship Co. v. Cook Industries, 495 F.2d 1260, 1265 (2d Cir.1973), in which the court of appeals reversed an order confirming an arbitration award when the question of an arbitrator's impartiality was decided on an incomplete record. There the court determined that discrepancies between the judge's opinion and the facts in the record required remand to explore fully the relationships between the arbitrator and the parties involved. See also Totem Marine Tug & Barge, Inc. v. North American Towing, 607 F.2d 649 (5th Cir.1979) (hearing held and arbitral award vacated because of prejudicial misbehavior of arbitrators). Such matters as misconduct or bias of the arbitrators cannot be gauged on the face of the arbitral record alone.

No such case is here presented. The district court was not required by the Federal Rules to conduct a full hearing on appellant's motion. See Fed.R.Civ.P. 43(e) (providing that court may direct that motions be decided on the papers rather than after oral testimony); Fed.R.Civ.P. 78 (providing that court may decide motions on written statements of reasons in support and opposition to expedite business). See also Commerce Park at DFW Freeport v. Mardian Construction Co., 729 F.2d 334, 340–41 (5th Cir.1984) (holding that unsupported assertions on the issue of arbitrability did not require evidentiary hearing under 9 U.S.C. § 3); Imperial Ethiopian Gov't v. Baruch–Foster Corp., 535 F.2d 334, 337 n. 10 (5th Cir.1976) (holding that under Convention on the Recognition and Enforcement of Foreign Arbitral Awards, 9 U.S.C. §§ 201–208, which involves summary procedures, district court "was not required to resort to the formal taking of testimony or deposition procedures in order to determine" the issue before it). The error in Appellant's argument with respect to its case is exposed by the remedy it would adopt. Although it asserts no fact sought to be proved if we were to remand for evidentiary development, appellant suggests it would depose "anyone present" at the arbitration proceeding, including the arbitrators, to "recreate the evidence presented as completely as possible." Appellant's bases for vacating or modifying the arbitration award amounted, however, to evidentiary challenges and unsupported assertions that the arbitrators impermissibly calculated the award. Courts have repeatedly condemned efforts to depose members of an arbitration panel to impeach or clarify their awards. See, e.g., Andros Compania Maritima v. Marc Rich & Co., 579 F.2d 691, 702 (2d Cir.1978). To permit time-consuming, costly discovery simply to replicate the substance of the arbitration would thwart its goal. The statutory bases for overturning an arbitral tribunal are precisely and narrowly drawn to prohibit such complete de novo review of the substance of the award, as distinguished from gross calculation errors or inadequacies in the makeup of the tribunal itself. The district court was well within its discretion to dispose of the issues before it on the record submitted by the parties.[3]

Arbitration proceedings are summary in nature to effectuate the national policy favoring arbitration, and they require "expeditious and summary hearing, with only restricted inquiry into factual issues." Moses H. Cone Memorial Hospital v. Mercury Construction Corp., 460 U.S. 1, 22, 103 S.Ct. 927, 940, 74 L.Ed.2d 765 (1983). This case posed no factual issues that required the court, pursuant to the Arbitration Act, to delve beyond the documentary record of the arbitration and the award rendered. Discovery of the sort desired by IGAI would result in the court's reviewing the factual and legal accuracy of the award, a task this circuit has foreclosed. Local Union 59, Int'l. Brotherhood of Elec. Workers, AFL–CIO v. Green Corp., 725 F.2d 264, 268 (5th Cir.), cert. denied, 469 U.S. 833, 105 S.Ct. 124, 83 L.Ed.2d 66 (1984). The policy of expediting judicial enforcement of arbitral awards, albeit confuted here, counsels our courts to pierce the rhetoric of parties like IGAI who would embark on a costly legal path solely to challenge the factual or legal accuracy of an arbitration award.

The judgment of the district court is AFFIRMED.

* * *

Questions

1. Why do courts reject efforts to depose or compel testimony of arbitrators to impeach their awards? Is it merely to avoid delay, or are there additional reasons not to compel such testimony? Why does the court state that allegations of misconduct or bias by arbitrators may justify an evidentiary hearing but allegations concerning arbitrability or gross error do not?

2. We saw in Chapter 3 that courts are reluctant to compel testimony by mediators due to the need to ensure confidentiality in the mediation process and to preserve neutrality by the mediator, as well as to encourage candor between the parties. Are these same factors relevant to the issue of whether to compel arbitrators to testify?

* * *

3. Appellant asserts two additional points of error. First, appellant claims it was prejudiced by the district court's issuance of a standard "Status Report Order" pertaining to discovery and trial preparation. Appellant argues that it relied on the suggestion in the report that trial on the merits was expected. This argument ignores the summary aspect of this type of proceeding: the district court is directed to summarily dispose of these motions with limited factual inquiry to effect the intention of the parties to resolve their dispute through arbitration. More pointedly, IGAI never moved for reconsideration or otherwise urged upon the trial court its expecta-tion that further opportunities to develop and submit evidence would be provided. Nor did IGAI commence discovery of any kind after filing its cross-motion to vacate the award. Second, appellant claims for the first time on appeal that based upon further investigation, Legion's rate increase, which led to this imbroglio, was not approved by the Arizona Board of Insurance, ostensibly making the award improper. This evidence was not presented to the district court and does not appear in the record; therefore, we need not inquire whether such a revelation would have justified the relief sought by IGAI.

---

11.   STANDARD OF REVIEW OF ARBITRAL AWARDS

A.   JUDICIAL REVIEW UNDER SECTION 301 OF THE LABOR MANAGEMENT RELATIONS ACT

United Steelworkers of America v. Enterprise Wheel and Car Corp.

363 U.S. 593, 80 S.Ct. 1358 (1960).

■ Opinion of the Court by MR. JUSTICE DOUGLAS, announced by MR. JUSTICE BRENNAN.

Petitioner union and respondent during the period relevant here had a collective bargaining agreement which provided that any differences "as to the meaning and application" of the agreement should be submitted to arbitration and that the arbitrator's decision "shall be final and binding on the parties." Special provisions were included concerning the suspension and discharge of employees. The agreement stated:

"Should it be determined by the Company or by an arbitrator in accordance with the grievance procedure that the employee has been suspended unjustly or discharged in violation of the provisions of this Agreement, the Company shall reinstate the employee and pay full compensation at the employee's regular rate of pay for the time lost."

The agreement also provided:

"* * * It is understood and agreed that neither party will institute civil suits or legal proceedings against the other for alleged violation of any of the provisions of this labor contract; instead all disputes will be settled in the manner outlined in this Article III—Adjustment of Grievances."

A group of employees left their jobs in protest against the discharge of one employee. A union official advised them at once to return to work. An official of respondent at their request gave them permission and then rescinded it. The next day they were told they did not have a job any more "until this thing was settled one way or the other."

A grievance was filed; and when respondent finally refused to arbitrate, this suit was brought for specific enforcement of the arbitration provisions of the agreement. The District Court ordered arbitration. The arbitrator found that the discharge of the men was not justified, though their conduct, he said, was improper. In his view the facts warranted at most a suspension of the men for 10 days each. After their discharge and before the arbitration award the collective bargaining agreement had expired. The union, however, continued to represent the workers at the plant. The arbitrator rejected the contention that expiration of the agreement barred reinstatement of the employees. He held that the provision of the agreement above quoted imposed an unconditional obligation on the employer. He awarded reinstatement with back pay, minus pay for a 10–day suspension and such sums as these employees received from other employment.

Respondent refused to comply with the award. Petitioner moved the District Court for enforcement. The District Court directed respondent to comply. 168 F.Supp. 308. The Court of Appeals, while agreeing that the District Court had jurisdiction to enforce an arbitration award under a collective bargaining agreement, held that the failure of the award to specify the amounts to be deducted from the back pay rendered the award unenforceable. That defect, it agreed, could be remedied by requiring the parties to complete the arbitration. It went on to hold, however, that an award for back pay subsequent to the date of termination of the collective bargaining agreement could not be enforced. It also held that the requirement for reinstatement of the discharged employees was likewise unenforceable because the collective bargaining agreement had expired. 269 F.2d 327. We granted certiorari. 361 U.S. 929, 80 S.Ct. 371.

The refusal of courts to review the merits of an arbitration award is the proper approach to arbitration under collective bargaining agreements. The federal policy of settling labor disputes by arbitration would be undermined if courts had the final say on the merits of the awards. As we stated in United Steelworkers of America v. Warrior & Gulf Navigation Co., 363 U.S. 574, 80 S.Ct. 1347, the arbitrators under these collective agreements are indispensable agencies in a continuous collective bargaining process. They sit to settle disputes at the plant level—disputes that require for their solution knowledge of the custom and practices of a particular factory or of a particular industry as reflected in particular agreements.

When an arbitrator is commissioned to interpret and apply the collective bargaining agreement, he is to bring his informed judgment to bear in order to reach a fair solution of a problem. This is especially true when it comes to formulating remedies. There the need is for flexibility in meeting a wide variety of situations. The draftsmen may never have thought of what specific remedy should be awarded to meet a particular contingency. Nevertheless, an arbitrator is confined to interpretation and application of the collective bargaining agreement; he does not sit to dispense his own brand of industrial justice. He may of course look for guidance from many sources, yet his award is legitimate only so long as it draws its essence from the collective bargaining agreement. When the arbitrator's words manifest an infidelity to this obligation, courts have no choice but to refuse enforcement of the award.

The opinion of the arbitrator in this case, as it bears upon the award of back pay beyond the date of the agreement's expiration and reinstatement, is ambiguous. It may be read as based solely upon the arbitrator's view of the requirements of enacted legislation, which would mean that he exceeded the scope of the submission. Or it may be read as embodying a construction of the agreement itself, perhaps with the arbitrator looking to "the law" for help in determining the sense of the agreement. A mere ambiguity in the opinion accompanying an award, which permits the inference that the arbitrator may have exceeded his authority, is not a reason for refusing to enforce the award. Arbitrators have no obligation to the court to give their reasons for an award. To require opinions free of ambiguity may lead arbitrators to play it safe by writing no supporting opinions. This would be undesirable for a well-reasoned opinion tends to engender confidence in the integrity of the process and aids in clarifying the underlying agreement. Moreover, we see no reason to assume that this arbitrator has abused the trust the parties confided in him and has not stayed within the areas marked out for his consideration. It is not apparent that he went beyond the submission. The Court of Appeals' opinion refusing to enforce the reinstatement and partial back pay portions of the award was not based upon any finding that the arbitrator did not premise his award on his construction of the contract. It merely disagreed with the arbitrator's construction of it.

The collective bargaining agreement could have provided that if any of the employees were wrongfully discharged, the remedy would be reinstatement and back pay up to the date they were returned to work. Respondent's major argument seems to be that by applying correct principles of law to the interpretation of the collective bargaining agreement it can be determined that the agreement did not so provide, and that therefore the arbitrator's decision was not based upon the contract. The acceptance of this view would require courts, even under the standard arbitration clause, to review the merits of every construction of the contract. This plenary review by a court of the merits would make meaningless the provisions that the arbitrator's decision is final, for in reality it would almost never be final. This underlines the fundamental error which we have alluded to in United Steelworkers of America v. American Manufacturing Co., 363 U.S. 564, 80 S.Ct. 1343. As we there emphasized, the question of interpretation of the collective bargaining agreement is a question for the arbitrator. It is the arbitrator's construction which was bargained for; and so far as the arbitrator's decision concerns construction of the contract, the courts have no business overruling him because their interpretation of the contract is different from his.

[T]he judgment of the District Court should be modified so that the amounts due the employees may be definitely determined by arbitration. In all other respects we think the judgment of the District Court should be affirmed. Accordingly, we reverse the judgment of the Court of Appeals. . . .

* * *

Questions

1. What does the *Enterprise Wheel & Car* case say are the grounds for overturning an arbitral award in a labor arbitration under Section 301 of the Labor Management Relations Act? Justice Reed, writing in 1953 in *Wilko v. Swan*, suggested that an arbitral award under the FAA could be overturned if it exhibited a "manifest disregard of the law." Are these

standards of review the same? How do they differ? Which one sets a higher standard?

2.   Why is the court reluctant to review the merits of a labor arbitration award? Does the *Enterprise* test prevent courts from scrutinizing the merits of an arbitral award? Without some consideration of the merits and some view of the meaning of the contract, can a court determine whether the arbitrator's award drew its essence from the contract?

3.   When the court states that if there is "mere ambiguity," the award should be enforced, is it creating a presumption in favor of arbitral awards? What is the presumption, and is it rebuttable? What would it take to overcome the presumption?

* * *

United Paperworkers International Union v. Misco, Inc.
484 U.S. 29, 108 S.Ct. 364 (1987).

JUSTICE WHITE delivered the opinion of the Court.

The issue for decision involves several aspects of when a federal court may refuse to enforce an arbitration award rendered under a collective-bargaining agreement.

I

Misco, Inc. (Misco, or the Company), operates a paper converting plant in Monroe, Louisiana. The Company is a party to a collective-bargaining agreement with the United Paperworkers International Union, AFL–CIO, and its union local (the Union); the agreement covers the production and maintenance employees at the plant. Under the agreement, the Company or the Union may submit to arbitration any grievance that arises from the interpretation or application of its terms, and the arbitrator's decision is final and binding upon the parties. The arbitrator's authority is limited to interpretation and application of the terms contained in the agreement itself. The agreement reserves to management the right to establish, amend, and enforce "rules and regulations regulating the discipline or discharge of employees" and the procedures for imposing discipline. Such rules were to be posted and were to be in effect "until ruled on by grievance and arbitration procedures as to fairness and necessity." For about a decade, the Company's rules had listed as causes for discharge the bringing of intoxicants, narcotics, or controlled substances on to plant property or consuming any of them there, as well as reporting for work under the influence of such substances. At the time of the events involved in this case, the Company was very concerned about the use of drugs at the plant, especially among employees on the night shift.

Isiah Cooper, who worked on the night shift for Misco, was one of the employees covered by the collective-bargaining agreement. He operated a slitter-rewinder machine, which uses sharp blades to cut rolling coils of paper. The arbitrator found that this machine is hazardous and had caused numerous injuries in recent years. Cooper had been reprimanded twice in a few months for deficient performance. On January 21, 1983, one day after the second reprimand, the police searched Cooper's house pursuant to a warrant, and a substantial amount of marijuana was found. Contemporaneously, a police officer was detailed to keep Cooper's car under observation at the Company's parking lot. At about 6:30 p.m., Cooper was seen walking in the parking lot during work hours with two other men. The three men entered Cooper's car momentarily, then walked to another car, a white Cutlass, and entered it. After the other two men later returned to the plant, Cooper was apprehended by police in the backseat of this car with marijuana smoke in the air and a lighted marijuana cigarette in the front-seat ashtray. The police also searched Cooper's car and found a plastic scales case and marijuana gleanings. Cooper was arrested and charged with marijuana possession.[3]

On January 24, Cooper told the Company that he had been arrested for possession of marijuana at his home; the Company did not learn of the marijuana cigarette in the white Cutlass until January 27. It then investigated and on February 7 discharged Cooper, asserting that in the circumstances, his presence in the Cutlass violated the rule against having drugs on the plant premises. Cooper filed a grievance protesting his discharge the same day, and the matter proceeded to arbitration. The Company was not aware until September 21, five days before the arbitration hearing was scheduled, that marijuana had been found in Cooper's car. That fact did not become known to the Union until the hearing began. At the hearing it was stipulated that the issue was whether the Company had "just cause to discharge the Grievant under Rule II.1" and, "[i]f not, what if any should be the remedy." App. to Pet. for Cert. 26a.

The arbitrator upheld the grievance and ordered the Company to reinstate Cooper with back pay and full seniority. The arbitrator based his finding that there was not just cause for the discharge on his consideration of seven criteria.[5] In particular, the arbitrator found that the Company failed to prove that the employee had possessed or used marijuana on company property: finding Cooper in the backseat of a car and a burning cigarette in the front-seat ashtray was insufficient proof that Cooper was using or possessed marijuana on company property. Id., at 49a–50a. The arbitrator refused to accept into evidence the fact that marijuana had been found in Cooper's car on company premises because the Company did not know of this fact when Cooper was discharged and therefore did not rely on it as a basis for the discharge.

The Company filed suit in District Court, seeking to vacate the arbitration award on several grounds, one of which was that ordering

---

3. Cooper later pleaded guilty to that charge, which was not related to his being in a car with a lighted marijuana cigarette in it. The authorities chose not to prosecute for the latter incident.

5. These considerations were the reasonableness of the employer's position, the notice given to the employee, the timing of the investigation undertaken, the fairness of the investigation, the evidence against the employee, the possibility of discrimination, and the relation of the degree of discipline to the nature of the offense and the employee's past record.

reinstatement of Cooper, who had allegedly possessed marijuana on the plant premises, was contrary to public policy. The District Court agreed that the award must be set aside as contrary to public policy because it ran counter to general safety concerns that arise from the operation of dangerous machinery while under the influence of drugs, as well as to state criminal laws against drug possession. The Court of Appeals affirmed, with one judge dissenting. The court ruled that reinstatement would violate the public policy "against the operation of dangerous machinery by persons under the influence of drugs or alcohol." 768 F.2d 739, 743 (CA5 1985). The arbitrator had found that Cooper was apprehended on company premises in an atmosphere of marijuana smoke in another's car and that marijuana was found in his own car on the company lot. These facts established that Cooper had violated the Company's rules and gave the Company just cause to discharge him. The arbitrator did not reach this conclusion because of a "narrow focus on Cooper's procedural rights" that led him to ignore what he "knew was in fact true: that Cooper *did* bring marijuana onto his employer's premises." Ibid. Even if the arbitrator had not known of this fact at the time he entered his award, "it is doubtful that the award should be enforced today in light of what is now known." Ibid.

Because the Courts of Appeals are divided on the question of when courts may set aside arbitration awards as contravening public policy, we granted the Union's petition for a writ of certiorari, 479 U.S. 1029, 107 S.Ct. 871, 93 L.Ed.2d 826 (1987), and now reverse the judgment of the Court of Appeals.

II

The Union asserts that an arbitral award may not be set aside on public policy grounds unless the award orders conduct that violates the positive law, which is not the case here. But in the alternative, it submits that even if it is wrong in this regard, the Court of Appeals otherwise exceeded the limited authority that it had to review an arbitrator's award entered pursuant to a collective-bargaining agreement. Respondent, on the other hand, defends the public policy decision of the Court of Appeals but alternatively argues that the judgment below should be affirmed because of erroneous findings by the arbitrator. We deal first with the opposing alternative arguments.

A

... The reasons for insulating arbitral decisions from judicial review are grounded in the federal statutes regulating labor-management relations. These statutes reflect a decided preference for private settlement of labor disputes without the intervention of government ... The courts have jurisdiction to enforce collective-bargaining contracts; but where the contract provides grievance and arbitration procedures, those procedures must first be exhausted and courts must order resort to the private settlement mechanisms without dealing with the merits of the dispute. Because the parties have contracted to have disputes settled by an arbitrator chosen by them rather than by a judge, it is the arbitrator's view of the facts and of the meaning of the contract that they have agreed to accept. Courts thus do not sit to hear claims of factual or legal error by an arbitrator as an appellate court does in reviewing decisions of lower courts.... As the Court has said, the arbitrator's award settling a dispute with respect to the interpretation or application of a labor agreement must draw its essence from the contract and cannot simply reflect the arbitrator's own notions of industrial justice. But as long as the arbitrator is even arguably construing or applying the contract and acting within the scope of his authority, that a court is convinced he committed serious error does not suffice to overturn his decision. Of course, decisions procured by the parties through fraud or through the arbitrator's dishonesty need not be enforced. But there is nothing of that sort involved in this case.

B

The Company's position, simply put, is that the arbitrator committed grievous error in finding that the evidence was insufficient to prove that Cooper had possessed or used marijuana on company property. But the Court of Appeals, although it took a distinctly jaundiced view of the arbitrator's decision in this regard, was not free to refuse enforcement because it considered Cooper's presence in the white Cutlass, in the circumstances, to be ample proof that Rule II.1 was violated. No dishonesty is alleged; only improvident, even silly, fact finding is claimed. This is hardly a sufficient basis for disregarding what the agent appointed by the parties determined to be the historical facts.

Nor was it open to the Court of Appeals to refuse to enforce the award because the arbitrator, in deciding whether there was just cause to discharge, refused to consider evidence unknown to the Company at the time Cooper was fired. The parties bargained for arbitration to settle disputes and were free to set the procedural rules for arbitrators to follow if they chose. Article VI of the agreement, entitled "Arbitration Procedure," did set some ground rules for the arbitration process. It forbade the arbitrator to consider hearsay evidence, for example, but evidentiary matters were otherwise left to the arbitrator. App. 19. Here the arbitrator ruled that in determining whether Cooper had violated Rule II.1, he should not consider evidence not relied on by the employer in ordering the discharge, particularly in a case like this where there was no notice to the employee or the Union prior to the hearing that the Company would attempt to rely on after-discovered evidence. This, in effect, was a construction of what the contract required when deciding discharge cases: an arbitrator was to look only at the evidence before the employer at the time of discharge. As the arbitrator noted, this approach was consistent with the practice followed by other arbitrators. And it was consistent with our observation in John Wiley & Sons, Inc. v. Livingston, 376 U.S. 543, 557 (1964), that when the subject matter of a dispute is arbitrable, "procedural" questions which grow out of the dispute and bear on its final disposition are to be left to the arbitrator....

C

[The Court of Appeals] ... held that the evidence of marijuana in Cooper's car required that the award be set aside because to reinstate a person who had brought drugs onto the property was contrary to the public policy "against the operation of dangerous machinery by persons under the influence of drugs or alcohol." 768 F.2d, at 743. We cannot affirm that judgment.

A court's refusal to enforce an arbitrator's award under a collective-bargaining agreement because it is contrary to public policy is a specific application of the more general doctrine, rooted in the common law, that a court may refuse to enforce contracts that violate law or public policy.... That doctrine derives from the basic notion that no court will lend its aid to one who founds a cause of action upon an immoral or illegal act, and is further justified by the observation that the public's interests in confining the scope of private agreements to which it is not a party will go unrepresented unless the judiciary takes account of those interests when it considers whether to enforce such agreements.... In the common law of contracts, this doctrine has served as the foundation for occasional exercises of judicial power to abrogate private agreements.

In W.R. Grace, we recognized that "a court may not enforce a collective-bargaining agreement that is contrary to public policy," and stated that "the question of public policy is ultimately one for resolution by the courts." 461 U.S., at 766. We cautioned, however, that a court's refusal to enforce an arbitrator's *interpretation* of such contracts is limited to situations where the contract as interpreted would violate "some explicit public policy" that is "well defined and dominant, and is to be ascertained 'by reference to the laws and legal precedents and not from general considerations of supposed public interests.'" Ibid.... Two points follow from our decision in W.R. Grace. First, a court may refuse to enforce a collective-bargaining agreement when the specific terms contained in that agreement violate public policy. Second, it is apparent that our decision in that case does not otherwise sanction a broad judicial power to set aside arbitration awards as against public policy. Although we discussed the effect of that award on two broad areas of public policy, our decision turned on our examination of whether the award created any explicit conflict with other "laws and legal precedents" rather than an assessment of "general considerations of supposed public interests." 461 U.S., at 766 ...

As we see it, the formulation of public policy set out by the Court of Appeals did not comply with the statement that such a policy must be "ascertained 'by reference to the laws and legal precedents and not from general considerations of supposed public interests.'" Ibid. (quoting Muschany v. United States, supra, 324 U.S., at 66, 65 S.Ct., at 451). The Court of Appeals made no attempt to review existing laws and legal precedents in order to demonstrate that they establish a "well-defined and dominant" policy against the operation of dangerous machinery while under the influence of drugs. Although certainly such a judgment is firmly rooted in common sense, we explicitly held in W.R. Grace that a formulation of public policy based only on "general considerations of supposed public interests" is not the sort that permits a court to set aside an arbitration award that was entered in accordance with a valid collective-bargaining agreement.

Even if the Court of Appeals' formulation of public policy is to be accepted, no violation of that policy was clearly shown in this case . . . [T]he assumed connection between the marijuana gleanings found in Cooper's car and Cooper's actual use of drugs in the workplace is tenuous at best and provides an insufficient basis for holding that his reinstatement would actually violate the public policy identified by the Court of Appeals "against the operation of dangerous machinery by persons under the influence of drugs or alcohol." 768 F.2d, at 743. A refusal to enforce an award must rest on more than speculation or assumption.

In any event, it was inappropriate for the Court of Appeals itself to draw the necessary inference. To conclude from the fact that marijuana had been found in Cooper's car that Cooper had ever been or would be under the influence of marijuana while he was on the job and operating dangerous machinery is an exercise in fact finding about Cooper's use of drugs and his amenability to discipline, a task that exceeds the authority of a court asked to overturn an arbitration award. The parties did not bargain for the facts to be found by a court, but by an arbitrator chosen by them who had more opportunity to observe Cooper and to be familiar with the plant and its problems. . . .

The judgment of the Court of Appeals is reversed.

[The concurring opinion of JUSTICE BLACKMUN, with whom JUSTICE BRENNAN joins, has been omitted.]

* * *

Questions

1. How does the Court apply the *Enterprise Wheel* "essence test" in this case? How does the court evaluate the company's claim that the arbitrator's fact-finding was erroneous?

2. The Court suggests it has the power to overturn an award on the grounds of public policy. Where does this additional standard of review come from? How is applied in this case? Who decides issues of public policy—an arbitrator or a court? Given that there is a strong public policy against illicit drugs embodied in the criminal laws of all states and the federal government, why does the court refuse to vacate the awards on public policy grounds?

* * *

B.   JUDICIAL REVIEW UNDER THE FEDERAL ARBITRATION ACT

Sobel v. Hertz, Warner & Co.
469 F.2d 1211 (2d Cir.1972).

I

■ JUDGE FEINBERG:

The arbitration that led to this appeal was first requested in November 1967 by appellee Herbert Sobel, who was a customer of appellant Hertz,

Warner & Co., a stock brokerage firm and a member of the New York Stock Exchange. As a customer, Sobel had the right under Article VIII of the Constitution of the New York Stock Exchange to demand arbitration of any controversy he might have with a member firm growing out of its "business."[2] Briefly, Sobel claimed that between December 1965 and March 1966 he had purchased 10,200 shares of the common stock of Hercules Galion Products, Inc., upon the recommendation of his long-time broker, Edward Wetzel, and Michael Geier, both then employed by Hertz, Warner, and that Wetzel and Geier had made fraudulent misstatements and omissions of material facts on which Sobel had relied to his detriment. As their employer, Hertz, Warner was, according to Sobel, liable for the damages he had suffered. Sobel continued to hold his Hercules shares until Hertz, Warner demanded, in connection with the arbitration, that they be sold to fix damages. This was done in May 1968, and Sobel thereafter claimed a direct loss of about $34,000.

In 1970, both parties signed a formal submission to arbitration pursuant to the provisions of the Stock Exchange Constitution and the rules of the Board of Governors. Under the Constitution, Sobel's claim was heard by a panel consisting of two persons "engaged in the securities business" and three not so engaged. The panel held two hearings at which it heard the testimony of three witnesses and received documentary evidence. At the hearings, of which there is a full transcript, both sides were ably represented by counsel.

In May 1971, the panel issued the following decision:

> We, the undersigned, being the arbitrators selected to hear and determine a matter in controversy between the above-mentioned claimant and respondents set forth in a submission to arbitration signed by the parties on April 6, 1970 and April 10, 1970 respectively;
>
> And having heard and considered the proofs of the parties, have decided and determined that the claim of the claimant be and hereby is in all respects dismissed;
>
> That the costs, $240.00, be and hereby are assessed against the claimant.

After an unsuccessful request to the arbitrators for reconsideration, Sobel moved in the Southern District under 9 U.S.C. § 10 to vacate the arbitration award on the grounds that it had been "procured by undue means" and "that the Award is contrary to public policy, in that the arbitrators refused to make their Award in accordance with the applicable Federal Securities laws." Judge Pollack heard argument on the motion to vacate and concluded, in an exhaustive opinion, that he could not decide the

---

2. Article VIII provided, in relevant part: Sec. 1. Any controversy . . . between a non-member and a . . . member firm . . . arising out of the business of such . . . member firm, . . . shall, at the instance of such non-member, be submitted for arbitration, in accordance with the provisions of the constitution and the rules of the Board of Governors.

question without "an indication, now wholly lacking from the record, of the basis on which the petitioner's claim was dismissed." 338 F.Supp. at 289. Holding that "a District Court is justified in requiring some statement of the facts the arbitrators found decisive," id. at 298, the judge remanded the controversy to the arbitrators for that purpose. Thereafter, he certified as an interlocutory appeal under 28 U.S.C. § 1292(b) the question whether his action was proper, and we permitted the appeal.

II

Although Sobel's claims before the arbitrators rested on state statutory law and common law fraud concepts, as well as on federal securities acts, only the last are significant on this appeal. The district judge was clearly disturbed by Sobel's claim that the arbitrators must have ignored the prohibitions of sections 12(2) and 17(a) of the Securities Act of 1933, 15 U.S.C. §§ 77*l*(2), 77q(a), section 10(b) of the Securities Exchange Act of 1934, 15 U.S.C. § 78j(b), and Rule 10b–5 promulgated thereunder. The judge's opinion emphasized that Wetzel and Geier had been indicted in 1967—not long after the transactions complained of by Sobel—for conspiring to create market activity in the Hercules shares and to induce the purchase of the security by others, and that in 1971 Wetzel had pleaded guilty to the conspiracy charge and Geier had been found guilty of that and other counts after a jury trial. Sobel argued to the district court that unless the arbitrators explained their decision, there was no way of telling whether it was in "manifest disregard" of the provisions of the securities acts. The quotation is from Wilko v. Swan, 346 U.S. 427, 74 S.Ct. 182, 98 L.Ed. 168 (1953), which—oddly enough, in the context of Sobel's use of it here—stands primarily for the proposition that certain kinds of claims cannot be forced to arbitration despite a pre-dispute agreement to arbitrate. Wilko v. Swan held that an agreement to arbitrate future controversies was an impermissible waiver of the plaintiff customer's right to have his claim of securities act violations heard in court. In the course of its opinion, however, the Court also said:

> Power to vacate an award is limited. While it may be true, as the Court of Appeals thought, that a failure of the arbitrators to decide in accordance with the provisions of the Securities Act would "constitute grounds for vacating the award pursuant to section 10 of the Federal Arbitration Act," that failure would need to be made clearly to appear. In unrestricted submissions, such as the present margin agreements envisage, the interpretations of the law by the arbitrators *in contrast to manifest disregard* are not subject, in the federal courts, to judicial review for error in interpretation. [Emphasis added; footnotes omitted.]

Id. at 436–437, 74 S.Ct. at 187. The district judge agreed with Sobel that unless the arbitrators in this case stated the basis of their decision, the judge could not determine whether it was in "manifest disregard" of the law.

... [W]e believe that the issue before us is whether the arbitrators here are required to disclose the reasoning underlying their award.

The question so phrased, of course, is still a narrow one. We are not asked to decide whether arbitration was an inappropriate forum here in the first place.... Neither party questions the arbitrability of Sobel's claims under the securities acts. See, e. g., Axelrod & Co. v. Kordich, Victor & Neufeld, 451 F. 2d 838, 841–843 (2d Cir.1971) (nonmember firm seeks arbitration under Exchange rules with member firm).... Nor must we determine all the circumstances in which a court may vacate an arbitrator's award.

Nonetheless, the extent of an arbitrator's obligation to explain his award is necessarily related to the scope of judicial review of it. That issue, insofar as it leads to attempts to define "manifest disregard," is particularly troublesome.... It is a truism that an arbitration award will not be vacated for a mistaken interpretation of law ..... But if the arbitrators simply ignore the applicable law, the literal application of a "manifest disregard" standard should presumably compel vacation of the award. The problem is how a court is to be made aware of the erring conduct of the arbitrators. Obviously, a requirement that arbitrators explain their reasoning in every case would help to uncover egregious failures to apply the law to an arbitrated dispute. But such a rule would undermine the very purpose of arbitration, which is to provide a relatively quick, efficient and informal means of private dispute settlement. The sacrifice that arbitration entails in terms of legal precision is recognized, e. g., Bernhardt v. Polygraphic Co., 350 U.S. 198, 203, 76 S.Ct. 273, 100 L.Ed. 199 (1956), and is implicitly accepted in the initial assumption that certain disputes are arbitrable.... Given that acceptance, the primary consideration for the courts must be that the system operate expeditiously as well as fairly.

Presumably based upon the foregoing considerations, the Supreme Court has made it clear that there is no general requirement that arbitrators explain the reasons for their award. In Wilko v. Swan, supra, just before the language quoted above at page 1213 the Court pointed out that an award by arbitrators "may be made without explanation of their reasons and without a complete record of their proceedings...." 346 U.S. at 436, 74 S.Ct. at 187. This statement is especially significant because Mr. Justice Frankfurter in dissent made exactly the opposite point. A little over two years later, the Court observed that "Arbitrators ... need not give their reasons for their results...." Bernhardt v. Polygraphic Co., supra, 350 U.S. at 203, 76 S.Ct. at 276. These statements were, of course, known to the district judge; he even quoted them in his opinion. The argument, then, must be that there is something about this particular case that justifies the extraordinary requirement of the district court's order. We fail to see what that is. There was a complete transcript here of the arbitration proceeding. The arbitrators-and the district court-also had the benefit of an extremely detailed submission to arbitration, including Sobel's Statement of Claim and Hertz, Warner's Reply, excellent memoranda of law and summations of counsel, all of which indicate a number of theories upon which the arbitrators may have decided.[6] Cf. Ludwig Honold Mfg. Co. v. Fletcher, 405 F.2d 1123, 1128 (3d Cir.1969). It is true that claims under the securities acts are frequently complicated, although those made here seem less so than usual. And the same public interest that led to the enactment of the securities acts makes it desirable that such claims be decided correctly. But there is also a public interest, manifested in the United States Arbitration Act, 9 U.S.C. § 1 et seq., in the proper functioning of the arbitral process. It would be destructive of that process if we approved the district judge's requirement here that the arbitrators give reasons for their decision. Arbitration may not always be the speedy and economical remedy its admirers claim it is—this case is proof enough of that. But forcing arbitrators to explain their award even when grounds for it can be gleaned from the record will unjustifiably diminish whatever efficiency the process now achieves.[7]

Sobel cites a number of cases in support of the district court order. Courts have, on occasion, remanded awards to arbitrators for clarification, but they generally have done so to find out whether an issue has already been decided in arbitration rather than to discover whether the arbitrators had good reasons for their award. E. g., Galt v. Libbey–Owens–Ford Glass Co., 397 F.2d 439 (7th Cir.), cert. denied, 393 U.S. 925, 89 S.Ct. 258, 21 L.Ed.2d 262 (1968) (arbitrators report on remand that payment clause was not covered by arbitration provision, so district court reserves payment clause issues for itself) . . . Such decisions do not support a requirement that the arbitrators in this case explain their award. Sobel also relies on Granite Worsted Mills, Inc. v. Aaronson, Cowen, Ltd., 25 N.Y.2d 451, 306 N.Y.S.2d 934, 255 N.E. 2d 168 (1969), but in that 4–3 decision there was no record of the proceedings before the arbitrator to indicate a possible basis for his failure to apply a damage limitation clause. Apart from this distinction, we find most persuasive Judge Breitel's dissent, joined by Chief

6. E. g., the representations to Sobel may have been true when made, or Hertz, Warner may have exercised reasonable supervision over its employees and not had reason to know of their fraudulent activities. Cf. Kamen & Co. v. Paul H. Aschkar & Co., 382 F.2d 689 (9th Cir.1967), cert. denied, 393 U.S. 801, 89 S.Ct. 40, 21 L.Ed.2d 85 (1968). We do not imply any view as to the validity of the theories underlying such possible grounds for the award. But reliance by the arbitrators on such theories would not provide a basis for vacating the award.

7. The New York Stock Exchange in an amicus brief suggests that in the context now before us such a requirement may put an end to arbitration altogether. The district court noted that the Exchange was not required to arbitrate non-member disputes. 338 F.Supp. at 296 n. 25. The implied suggestion was, as the amicus brief points out, that if the Exchange is unable to act with the formality thought desirable by the district judge, it should decline to hear such disputes. The Exchange notes that its arbitrators dispose of hundreds of disputes a year and that if written decisions were required the system would be seriously delayed. Thus, it concludes that a decision not to afford arbitration procedures "may, to some extent, outline the only practical course for the Exchange," Amicus Brief at 4, despite the encouragement by the Securities and Exchange Commission of informal procedures for settling non-member disputes. See 2 S.E.C., Reports of Special Study of Securities Markets 559–61 (1963). But cf. Ellenbogen, English Arbitration Practice, 17 Law & Contemp.Prob. 656, 668, 678 (1952) (favorable appraisal of English system, which provides for judicial determination of questions of law at instance of arbitrator or parties).

Judge Fuld and Judge Jasen, reasoning that if a ground for the arbitrator's decision can be inferred from the facts of the case, the award should be confirmed. See also Lentine v. Fundaro, 29 N.Y.2d 382, 328 N.Y.S.2d 418, 278 N.E. 2d 633 (1972).

In short, we believe that the district court erred in remanding the arbitration proceeding to the arbitrators. We do not agree with its conclusion that "the present state of the record is not sufficient to justify final determination of the issues petitioner has raised." 338 F.Supp. at 289. Those issues are whether the arbitration award was procured by "undue means," 9 U.S.C. § 10(a), or is void as against public policy. Both parties have urged us to decide those questions. While we are tempted to do so in order to bring this litigation to an end, orderly administration suggests that the district court should rule upon them first.

Case remanded for further proceedings consistent with this opinion.

* * *

Questions

1.   Does Section 10 of the FAA contain all the grounds for challenging an arbitral award under the FAA, or are there additional grounds for judicial review of an arbitration award? What authority does the *Sobel* court give for the "manifest disregard of the law" standard of review? Is this a higher standard or a lower standard than the one the court adopted in *United Steelworkers v. Enterprise* for Section 301 cases?

2.   Under the "manifest disregard" standard, does the court engage in any review of the merits of an arbitral award? Is *disregarding* the law the same as *incorrectly applying* the law? Is it the same as deciding a case on the basis of an incorrect understanding of the law? What does the "manifest" requirement add to the standard?

3.   How can a court decide if an arbitrator "manifestly disregarded" the law? If a court cannot require an arbitrator to write an opinion, should a court conduct an evidentiary hearing and elicit testimony to determine the extent of the arbitrator's regard, or lack of regard, of the law? How else might a court decide? Should it review the evidence of the case to determine whether the award has any basis in law or in the factual record? What problems would such an approach entail? Is there any other way a court can police arbitral awards for "manifest disregard of the law?"

4.   *Sobel* was decided in 1972, when *Wilko v. Swan* was still good law, and before the Supreme Court held in *Mitsubishi* and its progeny that federal statutory claims were enforceable in arbitration. Should a higher standard of review apply today in cases in which arbitrators are called upon to interpret statutes? In such statutory cases, should courts be especially vigilant to ensure that arbitral awards do not manifestly disregard the law? Could one justify imposing a higher standard of review in such cases on the

grounds that the courts are protecting the public interest embodied in the relevant statute? Does *Misco* support such an approach?

* * *

Swift Industries, Inc. v. Botany Industries, Inc.

466 F.2d 1125 (3d Cir.1972).

EDWARD R. BECKER, DISTRICT JUDGE.

I

This is a commercial arbitration case. It comes before us on cross appeals from the judgment of the District Court for the Western District of Pennsylvania confirming in part and vacating in part the Award of an arbitrator in a dispute concerning the contractual obligations of Botany Industries, Inc. ("Botany")[2] to Swift Industries, Inc. ("Swift"). The dispute arose out of an Agreement for Exchange of Stock and Plan of Reorganization ("Agreement") dated as of August 10, 1961, among Swift, Botany and the stockholders of Swift pursuant to which, on October 2, 1961, Botany transferred to Swift the shares of two corporations, Allegheny Mortgage Company ("Allegheny") and Lincoln Homes Company ("Lincoln") in exchange for stock in Swift. Prior to the acquisition of Allegheny and Lincoln stock by Botany, Allegheny and Lincoln had been wholly owned subsidiaries of Premier Corporation of America ("Premier"), a subsidiary of Botany.[4] During the period that Allegheny and Lincoln were owned by Premier, they were included in Premier's consolidated federal income tax return.

Among the many provisions of the Agreement were warranties from Botany to Swift to the effect that there were no income taxes due the government from Allegheny and Lincoln such as are the precipitating factor in this litigation. Section 12.02 of the Agreement also contains provisions for payment by Botany to Swift in the event of a breach of that warranty. In pertinent part, § 12.02 provides that should Lincoln, Allegheny, or Swift suffer any loss resulting from liabilities of Lincoln or Allegheny for taxes attributable to ownership of property or operation of their business for any taxable period ended prior to the closing date under the Agreement (other than as provided for in certain schedules appended to the Agreement), Botany is obligated to:

> "pay Swift in cash an amount equal to all losses, liabilities and expenses *incurred or suffered* by Lincoln, Allegheny or Swift ..."

by reason thereof (emphasis added).

---

2. On April 25, 1972, Botany filed a petition for an arrangement under Chapter XI of the Bankruptcy Act. Receivers have been appointed and the affairs of Botany are presently being conducted under the aegis of the Bankruptcy Court. Moreover, virtually all of Botany's operating subsidiaries have filed similar Chapter XI petitions.

4. Premier then transferred the stock of Lincoln and Allegheny to Botany pursuant to an intercorporate arrangement.

On October 24, 1968, Premier notified Allegheny and Lincoln that the District Director of Internal Revenue in New York City had issued a letter and report (consisting of some 140 pages and 59 schedules) adjusting the income tax liability of Premier and its subsidiaries for the years 1959–62 and determining that there were deficiencies which, with interest to September 15, 1971, totaled some $8,402,670. Premier also advised Lincoln and Allegheny that under the applicable tax regulations, Premier and *each* of its subsidiaries were jointly and severally liable for the entire consolidated tax liability for each year that they were included in the consolidated return. The potential liability of Allegheny and Lincoln (including interest) for the years 1960 and 1961 was calculated to be $6,033,480. Swift viewed this situation with alarm, since the potential claim exceeded the combined net worth of Allegheny and Lincoln and approximated the consolidated net worth of Swift itself. Prior to the receipt of notification of the Premier tax letter and report, Swift had embarked upon a program of corporate growth through mergers and other transactions, but the balance sheet notation required by its auditors of the possible tax liability impaired its growth program and Swift's ability to borrow.

The claims asserted by the Internal Revenue Service ("IRS") were at once disputed by Premier and Botany. On November 4, 1968, Swift notified Botany that it deemed Botany responsible for taxes or liabilities together with all expenses incurred or suffered by Allegheny, Lincoln, or Swift in connection therewith. However, on December 5, 1968, Botany, through counsel, disclaimed liability. In another development, on November 26, 1968, seven former subsidiaries of Premier (which by this time was insolvent) entered into an agreement to apportion among themselves any ultimate income tax liability and the costs of the tax litigation ("Sharing Agreement"). On February 6, 1970, the District Director in New York issued to Premier a so-called 90–day letter, or statutory notice of deficiency. This notice was contested by Premier and the parties to the Sharing Agreement by appeal to the Tax Court of the United States. The tax litigation is still pending in the Tax Court and it is presently uncertain as to how or when it will terminate.

The foregoing recital is obviously the stuff of which lawsuits are made. The lawsuit which emerged was shaped by the Agreement, which had provided that disputes arising therefrom be adjudicated in the forum of commercial arbitration governed by the rules of the American Arbitration Association (AAA). In accordance with those rules, Swift filed a Demand for Arbitration with the AAA. In addition to asking for a declaration that Botany was liable to pay any taxes, penalties, and interest that might be determined to be due at the conclusion of the tax deficiency proceedings, Swift also requested that Botany undertake and pay the cost of defense of the deficiency proceedings. After much preliminary skirmishing, the arbitration finally got underway. Botany zealously argued that it was not responsible for any deficiency. During the course of the arbitration proceedings, Swift advanced the contention that only the delivery by Botany to Swift of a cash or surety bond protecting Swift against the possible tax deficiency would afford complete relief to all parties.

On June 30, 1970, the arbitrator entered his award, which consisted of five lettered paragraphs. The arbitrator's first finding (Paragraph A) was that Botany was liable to Swift for the federal tax deficiencies of Lincoln and Allegheny for the years 1960 and 1961. That finding is no longer a subject of dispute between the parties and the judgment of the District Court confirming it is not before us. Paragraph B of the award provided that Botany should deliver to Swift the sum of $6,000,000 or, in lieu thereof, a surety bond, to protect Allegheny, Lincoln, and Swift against the tax liability as finally determined. Paragraph C required Botany to reimburse Swift in the sum of approximately $100.000 for its counsel fees and expenses to that date. This sum included fees and expenses incurred in connection with both the tax deficiency proceedings and the commercial arbitration proceedings.

The provisions of paragraphs B and C of the Award, providing for payment of $6 million cash or the surety bond and for the payment of all counsel fees, are in bitter dispute and constitute the sinews of this appeal. On January 21, 1971, the District Court, acting on Swift's petition to confirm the Award and Botany's motion to vacate it, entered its judgment in which it confirmed paragraph C (as to fees) but vacated paragraph B in its entirety on the grounds that the award of a bond was improper because: (1) relief was not specifically requested in the prayer of the original arbitration demand; and (2) the Agreement did not specify that a bond could be awarded for a breach of warranty. Swift's motion to amend the Opinion, Order and Judgment was denied.

While we will perforce come to grips with the questions raised by the appeal from the award of counsel fees, the preeminent question before us relates to the propriety of the award of the bond, viewed in either of its aspects: (1) as a $6 million cash bond; or (2) as a surety bond. Swift maintains that even though award of a bond was not expressly contemplated in the Agreement, it was authorized by Rule 42 of the Commercial Arbitration Rules which the parties adopted by virtue of the arbitration clause of the Agreement. Rule 42 authorizes the arbitrator to grant "any remedy or relief which he deems just and equitable and within the scope of the agreement of the parties." Botany, on the other hand, argues that the award failed to draw its essence from the Agreement and went beyond the scope of the submission; Botany also contends that the award was completely irrational.

The conflicting contentions of the parties require us to apply to the commercial arbitration field those principles enunciated in a labor arbitration context by the Supreme Court in the case of United Steelworkers of America v. Enterprise Wheel & Car Corp., 363 U.S. 593, 80 S.Ct. 1358, 4 L.Ed.2d 1424 (1960), and by this Court in Ludwig Honold Mfg. Co. v. Fletcher, 405 F.2d 1123 (3d Cir.1969). Although we decide the case on a different basis than the District Court, we affirm.

II

We turn first to an exegesis of *Enterprise* and *Honold* and of the general principles of law governing the matter before us. *Enterprise* is the leading Supreme Court case enunciating the general principles that govern the disputes as to the authority of the arbitrator to fashion relief, which is the threshold question in this case. Although *Enterprise* is a labor arbitration case, its principles have been generally applied to the commercial arbitration field as well, keynoted by the oft quoted words of Mr. Justice Douglas, who delivered the Opinion of the Court:

"When an arbitrator is commissioned to interpret and apply the collective bargaining agreement, he is to bring his informed judgment to bear in order to reach a fair solution of a problem. This is especially true when it comes to formulating remedies. There the need is for flexibility in meeting a wide variety of situations. The draftsmen may never have thought of what specific remedy should be awarded to meet a particular contingency. Nevertheless, an arbitrator is confined to interpretation and application of the collective bargaining agreement; he does not sit to dispense his own brand of industrial justice. He may of course look for guidance from many sources, *yet his award is legitimate only so long as it draws its essence from the collective bargaining agreement*. When the arbitrator's words manifest an infidelity to this obligation, courts have no choice but to refuse enforcement of the award." (emphasis added.)

In the *Honold* case, which followed in the wake of *Enterprise*, resolution of the issues made it necessary for this Court to elucidate upon the general principles announced in *Enterprise*, and thus to define still more sharply the general principles governing the scope of federal judicial review of an arbitrator's award. Judge Aldisert did so, inter alia, in the following terms:

"[A] labor arbitrator's award does 'draw its essence from the collective bargaining agreement' if the interpretation can in any rational way be derived from the agreement, viewed in the light of its language, its context, and any other indicia of the parties' intention; only where there is a manifest disregard of the agreement, totally unsupported by principles of contract construction and the law of the shop, may a reviewing court disturb the award."[11]

Honold was, like *Enterprise*, a labor arbitration case; however, in his discussion of the scope of federal judicial review of an arbitrator's award, Judge Aldisert did not limit himself to labor arbitration cases, drawing upon precedent in the commercial arbitration field as well ... He then went on to recite principles of review concededly applicable in commercial arbitration cases:

"[I]t has been held that a 'mere error in the law or failure on the part of the arbitrators to understand or apply the law' will not justify judicial intervention, and that the courts' function in confirming or vacating a commercial award is 'severely limited....' "

---

11. These principles are consistent with the provisions of the Federal Arbitration Act, 9 U.S.C. § 10(d), which permits a court to vacate an award when the arbitrators have "exceeded their powers."

"[T]he interpretation of . . . arbitrators must not be disturbed as long as they are not in 'manifest disregard' of the law. [Wilko v. Swan, 346 U.S. 427, 436, 74 S.Ct. 182, 98 L.Ed. 168]."

A careful reading of *Honold* indicates that the principles governing labor and commercial arbitration cases are similar, and we therefore consider the principles of *Honold* with respect to the authority of the arbitrator to fashion an award and the scope of judicial review to be applicable in commercial arbitration cases as well. However, even though the principles are similar, there are differences in the rigor of judicial review, depending upon whether we are dealing with a labor or commercial arbitration case.

In United Steelworkers of America v. Warrior & Gulf Navigation Co., 363 U.S. 574, 578, 80 S.Ct. 1347, 1351, 4 L.Ed.2d 1409 (1960), the Court explained the different policy considerations applicable to commercial and labor arbitration cases:

"In the commercial case, arbitration is the substitute for litigation. Here arbitration is the substitute for industrial strike. Since arbitration of labor disputes has quite different functions from arbitration under an ordinary commercial agreement, the hostility evinced by courts toward arbitration of commercial agreements has no place here . . ."

. . . The facts of this case require that we highlight one additional principle of review that emanates from *Honold*. For, in holding that an arbitrator's award does not draw its essence from the agreement if the arbitrator's interpretation cannot be rationally derived therefrom, *Honold* has, in addition to limiting the arbitrator's authority to fashion relief, also established that an award may not stand if it does not meet the test of fundamental rationality. The New York Court of Appeals, whose opinions are the source of much instruction in this field, has held that an award of an arbitrator is not subject to judicial revision unless it is "completely irrational," Lentine v. Fundaro, 29 N.Y.2d 382, 328 N.Y.S.2d 418, 278 N.E.2d 633 (1972). We consider this formulation to be a fair rendering of *Honold*. In any event, it is an accurate statement of the law.

At this juncture, we must turn to the application of the principles of *Honold* to the facts at bar, keeping in mind that while our scope of review is limited, it is not as limited as in a labor arbitration case. We will first examine the question of the authority of the arbitrator to award a cash or surety bond as a form of relief, then the question of the inherent rationality or irrationality of the terms of the award, and finally, the appropriateness of the award of counsel fees.

III

As we have already noted, the threshold question in the case is the extent of the arbitrator's authority to fashion relief. It is, of course, fundamental that the authority of the arbitrator springs from the agreement to arbitrate. The arbitration clause in the Agreement in question (§ 14.08) is the standard AAA arbitration clause:

> "Section 14.08. Arbitration. Any controversy or dispute arising under this Agreement shall be settled by arbitration in accordance with the rules of the American Arbitration Association. . . ."

This clause in turn invokes § 42 of the AAA rules which provides:

> "SCOPE OF AWARD—The Arbitrator may grant any remedy or relief which he deems just and equitable and within the scope of the agreement of the parties, including, but not limited to, specific performance of a contract. . . ."

In our preliminary statement, we summarized the provisions of the Agreement providing for Botany's obligations to Swift in the event it owes federal taxes or has certain liabilities or commits breaches of covenant. Neither in those provisions nor elsewhere in the Agreement is there mention of a bond as a form of remedy in the event of breach. It is apparent that the parties never contemplated a bond as the means of making an aggrieved party whole. Swift, nonetheless, submits that, far from limiting the power of the arbitrator to consider the question of a bond, the adoption in the Agreement of the AAA rules, thereby invoking Rule 42, constitutes an articulation of the power of the arbitrator to award "any remedy or relief" including a bond. Swift also notes that § 14.04 of the Agreement provides:

> "It is not intended that the rights of Swift under . . . § 12.02 . . . shall be its exclusive remedy for the breach of any . . . warranties,"

and argues that the presence of this section reinforces a conclusion as to the efficacy of Rule 42 in this case. At this juncture, reversing the coin, as it were, Swift adds that, in any event, the Agreement contains no provision *excluding* the consideration of the bond from arbitration and that, since the AAA clause is a so-called "broad" arbitration clause under the umbrella of which every controversy or dispute is included unless, by express language, the particular dispute is excluded, see Boston & Maine Corp. v. Illinois Central RR, 396 F.2d 425 (2d Cir.1968), the arbitrator's award of the bond was proper.

Needless to reiterate, Botany dissents from these propositions; hence it is necessary to discuss those aspects of the Agreement which shed light on the question of the authority of the arbitrator to award a bond. Before doing so, it is important to place the nature of the arbitrator's award in perspective. In our view, the arbitrator's alternative award is tantamount to a $6 million cash bond. At oral argument, Swift placed heavy accent on that portion of the arbitrator's award that provided for the posting of a surety bond in lieu of cash, intimating that a bond premium (of approximately $17,800 per year) was the full extent of Botany's liability. However, under interrogation by the Court, Swift conceded that surety companies do not idly issue six million dollar bonds upon the mere payment of premium, but indeed require in addition a demonstration of immaculate credit standing or else the encumbering of viable assets (perhaps to the extent of

$6 million). At that juncture in the case it was apparent that the award was in fact tantamount to a $6 million cash bond. Although it does not influence our decision, Botany's recently acquired status as a Chapter XI debtor (see n. 2) underscores this conclusion.

The Agreement provides that, in the event of a breach of warranty, Botany will pay to Swift in cash an amount equal to "all losses, liabilities and expenses *incurred or suffered* by Lincoln, Allegheny or Swift by reason of any of the events specified...." (emphasis added). Botany asserts that no party, including Lincoln, Allegheny, or Swift, has yet, within the meaning of the Agreement, incurred or suffered any liability, expense, or loss as the result of the asserted tax deficiencies. We agree. The pending tax claim is clearly not an expense or loss. The question then is whether it is a liability in the legal sense. Within the 90–day period following issuance of the Statutory Notice of Deficiency, the matter was appealed to the Tax Court, where it now resides as an open matter to be determined by that court. The Statutory Notice of Deficiency does not constitute an assessment of liability; it constitutes the assertion of the government's claim. While responsible auditors may deem it necessary to *note* the issuance of the Statutory Notice on a financial statement, what they do is to note it, not list it as a legal liability, which it is not. This conclusion is unaltered by the fact that the Commissioner's determination is considered to be presumptively correct, for the burden of proof is still upon the government. See Psaty v. United States, 442 F.2d 1154 (3d Cir.1971).

Swift and Botany have always concurred that the Agreement conferred upon the arbitrator the power to *declare* whether or not Botany might be liable to Swift for any tax deficiency with which Lincoln and Allegheny might ultimately be charged. What Botany has questioned is whether there may be drawn from the Agreement the authority to award what is tantamount to a six million dollar cash bond to cover a liability which has not only not yet been "incurred or suffered," but which may or may not ever accrue (or which may accrue only in part). Botany points to the absence from the Agreement of any provisions which would secure either party against breaches of warranty by the other. Such provisions are frequent in agreements of this type, and we cannot assume that their absence was accidental. Botany contends that the absence of security provisions means that the parties were relying on each other's general credit with respect to repairing any breach, and certainly we cannot gainsay that this is so.

We have sought to distill from the Agreement the essence of the arbitrator's authority. Whatever that authority may be, it is clear to us that it does *not* include the authority to award a six million dollar cash bond to cover a liability which contrary to the requirements of the applicable breach of warranty clause, has not yet been (and may not be) "incurred or suffered," in a situation where the parties did not provide for such security in their agreement, although they might have done so. In our view, to award, as an adjunct to declaratory relief, a form of prejudgment execution which the Agreement by its lack of reference to security seems to exclude rather than to intend, is to eclipse the framework of the agreement and to venture onto unprotected ground. We subscribe to the observations of the *Enterprise* court that the draftsmen may be unable to perceive in advance what specific remedy should be awarded to meet a particular contingency and that in arbitration flexibility is important. But the principle of flexibility of relief cannot be permitted to obscure or to effect a metamorphosis of the claim itself. That untoward event would occur if we were to permit the arbitrator's award to stand in this case. . . .

Having reviewed the Agreement in the light of its language, its context, and the parties' apparent intent, and in terms of the question of the arbitrator's authority to fashion relief, we conclude that the arbitrator's award of a six million dollar cash surety bond does not draw its essence therefrom and that it is in manifest disregard thereof and must be set aside.

IV

Assuming, arguendo, that the arbitrator had authority to award a bond, Botany nonetheless attacks the award on a second basis: that its terms are completely irrational. We approach this allegation cautiously, for, although the complete irrationality of an award is a basis for setting it aside, the irrationality principle must be applied with a view to the narrow scope of review in arbitration cases. The basis of Botany's "irrationality" attack is the Sharing Agreement.

The Sharing Agreement was executed by the then solvent former subsidiaries of Premier after receipt of the 30 day letter. Its purpose was to provide for the orderly prosecution of the Premier tax controversy, to arrange in advance a fair allocation of and a fund for defraying its costs, and to determine in advance a fair allocation of the deficiencies finally determined to be due. . . .

The tax deficiency asserted by the government was $1,019,619.60 for the year 1960 and $2,783,698.17 for the year 1961. Thus, under the sharing agreement, the maximum tax liability of Lincoln and Allegheny exclusive of interest would be $98,658.04 for 1960 and $930,979.65 for 1961 for a total of $1,029,637.69. With interest, the maximum tax liability of Lincoln and Allegheny would be approximately $1.5 million, and then only if Premier were unsuccessful in *all* of its contentions before the Tax Court. Can a $6 million cash bond award be deemed rational in view of a maximum $1.5 million liability under the Sharing Agreement? We think not. . . .

We therefore hold that there is a second ground supporting Judge Weber's action in setting aside paragraph B of the Award—its complete lack of rationality.

* * *

Questions

1. Why does the court in *Swift Industries* use the *Honold* case, a Section 301 case, as authority on the scope of judicial review of arbitration awards?

What proposition does it derive from *Honold* for FAA cases? Why does the court conclude that it should impose more scrutiny on arbitral awards under the FAA than it does under Section 301?

2.   What is the basis of the court's statement that it should scrutinize arbitral awards for "fundamental rationality"? Does the court consider fundamental rationality an alternative formulation of the "manifest disregard" standard, a substitute for the "manifest disregard" standard, or an additional standard of review? Does the court consider the "manifest disregard" standard identical to the "essence test" from Section 301 cases?

3.   Could it be argued that the arbitral award of a bond in this case was within the arbitrator's authority to devise flexible remedies? Did the arbitrator manifestly disregard the law? Did he manifestly disregard the contract? If not, then what was the basis for the court's decision to vacate the award?

4.   What led the court to find that the award was lacking in fundamental rationality? To what extent did it review the merits of the case to reach this conclusion? What evidence did it use? Does the fundamental rationality standard of review invite a court to retry arbitration cases on the merits? Can the standard be applied without a de novo trial of the case?

* * *

Quick & Reilly, Inc. v. Jacobson

126 F.R.D. 24 (S.D.N.Y.1989).

■ SAND, DISTRICT JUDGE.

Quick & Reilly, Inc. ("Quick & Reilly") commenced a special proceeding in state court to vacate an arbitration award, which action was removed by defendant to this Court. Defendant by way of counterclaim seeks to confirm the award and to recover costs and sanctions pursuant to Fed. R.Civ.P. 11. Both parties have moved for summary judgment.

Richard O. Jacobson maintained a sizeable brokerage account at Quick & Reilly's San Diego brokerage office, which was liquidated after a margin call on October 20, 1987. Prior to liquidation, the branch manager of this Quick & Reilly office had a conversation with Mr. Jacobson concerning what action would satisfy the maintenance call and result in the account not being liquidated. The branch manager testified at the arbitration proceeding as to this conversation and also testified that Mr. Jacobson in fact complied with the Quick & Reilly request although there was testimony that Jacobson sought to withdraw this compliance. On the afternoon of October 20, 1987, Mr. Jacobson's portfolio was liquidated on the order of Leo C. Quick, Jr., Chairman of the Board and Chief Executive Officer of Quick & Reilly. Jacobson's subsequent demands for reinstatement of the account went unheeded and on November 24, 1987, Mr. Jacobson initiated arbitration proceedings pursuant to the rules of the New York Stock Exchange.

The arbitration was held after the parties had engaged in depositions and an exchange of documents. Two days of hearings were held during which time the panel heard expert testimony as well as fact witnesses. Following the hearing, the panel requested and received memoranda concerning damages. The record of the arbitration proceedings reflects that a knowledgeable and experienced panel, including two members of the securities industry and three attorneys, meticulously examined the evidence and the claims of the parties.

The arbitration panel awarded Jacobson $1,850,170.30 plus interest. The panel wrote no opinion and did not make detailed findings.

Quick & Reilly seeks to vitiate the arbitration award urging that it was entitled to liquidate the margin account at its discretion. Quick & Reilly also contends that the panel's damage award indicates that the panel construed the Margin Agreement to give the client a ten-day grace period not intended by or contained in that agreement and that such a determination exceeded the arbitrators' authority.

We note that N.Y.Civ.Prac.L. & R. § 7511(b)(1)(iii), pursuant to which Quick & Reilly seeks to vacate the award, and § 10(d) of the Federal Arbitration Act, 9 U.S.C. § 10(d) (1970), contain virtually identical provisions, so that no significant choice of law question is presented. The New York statute provides that an arbitration award may be vacated if "an arbitrator, or agency or person making the award exceeded his power or so imperfectly executed it that a final and definite award upon the subject matter submitted was not made." It is Quick & Reilly's claim that the panel exceeded its authority by interpreting the margin agreement in a manner that did not give it "the right at any point in time with or without notice to liquidate the account." Tr. at 6 (Apr. 19, 1989) (argument on motion for summary judgment).

Although Quick & Reilly of necessity frames its contention in terms of arbitrators having exceeded their authority, the claim is in fact nothing more than a claim that the arbitrators reached an erroneous decision. Mr. Quick testified before the arbitrators as to his belief that he had the right to liquidate the account during the tumultuous hours of the October 1987 crash. The panel, having been fully briefed on this issue by counsel and having heard the testimony concerning the agreements reached by Mr. Jacobson and the Quick & Reilly branch manager, concluded otherwise.

If Quick & Reilly is correct that arbitrators are not free to conclude that an account was liquidated improperly in light of evidence such as was adduced here of an explicit agreement not to do so if certain conditions were met, then the entire force of New York Stock Exchange and similar arbitration proceedings is undermined significantly.

... In sum, this Court concludes that Quick & Reilly had a full and fair determination of its claims before a New York Stock Exchange arbitration panel. No challenge—other than vague and unfortunate aspersions as to the lack of sophistication of Iowans and their inability to appreciate the chaotic state of the market during the October 1987 crash—is made to the composition of the panel or to the manner in which the proceedings were conducted. Quick & Reilly's claim, although couched in the statutory language of an excess of authority, is simply a challenge to the correctness of the panel's determination. The law is clear that such a challenge will not lie and indeed is antithetical to the very nature and purpose of arbitration—to obtain an expeditious, efficient and definitive resolution of controversies. Shearson/American Express v. McMahon, 482 U.S. 220, 107 S.Ct. 2332, 96 L.Ed.2d 185 (1987).

The motion of Quick & Reilly to set aside the arbitration award is denied and the motion by Jacobson to confirm the award is granted.

Rule 11 Sanctions

More troublesome than the decision on the motions to vacate or confirm the arbitration award is Jacobson's application for costs and sanctions pursuant to Rule 11. "Of all the duties of the judge, imposing sanctions on lawyers is perhaps the most unpleasant." Schwarzer, *Sanctions Under the New Federal Rule 11—A Closer Look*, 104 F.R.D. 181, 205 (1985).

There are two components to this application. [The first component concerned Jacobson's claim of lost income due to a difference on the interest rates for margin accounts and for arbitration awards. The Court rejected that claim on the grounds that Jacobson "has not shown that the delay in collection of the arbitration award in fact caused him to incur greater interest costs."]

The second aspect of Jacobson's application relates to legal fees. Jacobson's counsel asserts:

> "A cursory reading of the Petition demonstrates that this action has been filed for an improper purpose and that, after reasonable inquiry, a competent attorney could not form a reasonable belief as a matter of law that the pleading is well grounded in fact and is warranted by existing law or a good faith argument for the extension, modification, or reversal of existing law. See Eastway Construction Corp. v. City of New York, 762 F.2d 243 (2d Cir.1985), cert. denied, 484 U.S. 918, 108 S.Ct. 269 (1987). There is *no* existing law ... that could possibly warrant the relief sought by Quick and Reilly."

Memorandum of Law in Support of Respondent's Motion for Sanctions at 2. . . .

Jacobson's most vigorously pressed claim for sanctions relates to the nature of the proceeding itself and to the incongruity of a member of the security industry seeking so substantially to undermine the arbitration process that that industry has championed so vigorously. . . .

We believe, however, that Quick & Reilly's ability to challenge the arbitration award is in no way diminished because it is one member of an industry that as a whole, strongly favors arbitration. Were there merit to Quick & Reilly's claim, we would not penalize it because of the overall position of the security industry.

In response, counsel for Quick & Reilly renews its protestations that the arbitration award was indeed subject to attack because it "deviate[d] from the parties' agreement either by rewriting it, and fostering a result inconsistent with public policy, or departing from the 'essence' of their agreement." Q & R Supp. Memo. at 5–6. Moreover, Quick & Reilly's counsel asserts that, even if erroneous, the position it took was colorable and was not intended to harass, cause delay or needlessly increase the cost of litigation.

Counsel for Quick & Reilly asserts that:

> Moreover, since arbitration awards are not self-executing, Jacobson would have to go to court—as he, in fact, did in Iowa—to confirm the arbitration award and convert it to a judgment. Jacobson thus necessarily would have to deal with Quick & Reilly's objections to the award, and resolve their dispute through judicial intervention....

We reject this reasoning insofar as it assumes that judicial intervention is inevitable. When an arbitration award is not subject to valid legal challenge, it should be honored without the need for either party to resort to the courts.

We find that Jacobson is entitled to recover a portion of the reasonable attorneys' fees incurred directly as a result of this proceeding. Recognizing that Rule 11 was not intended to abrogate the general American rule that each party is to bear its own legal expenses, we believe that the claims advanced by Quick & Reilly were so totally devoid of merit as to warrant imposition of Rule 11 sanctions. Perhaps counsel acted in subjective good faith; we have no reason to believe that this is not so, but this is no longer the criterion for Rule 11 determinations.

The zeal of an attorney who lost the arbitration proceeding cannot overcome the lack of merit in the claims and the fact that objective counsel should have recognized the futility of the challenge....

Conclusion

We are mindful of the admonition of the Court of Appeals for the Second Circuit that

> Rule 11 sanctions should be applied only where "after reasonable inquiry, a competent attorney could not form a reasonable belief that the pleading is well grounded in fact and is warranted by existing law or a good faith argument for the extension, modification or reversal of existing law." Eastway Construction Corp. v. City of New York, 762 F.2d 243, 254 (2d Cir.1985).

Mercado v. U.S. Customs Service, 873 F.2d 641, 646 (2d Cir.1989).

We believe that pursuant to this standard, Rule 11 sanctions in the amount stated above are appropriate in this proceeding.

* * *

Questions

1. In *Quick & Reilly*, the arbitrator rendered an award that arguably suffered from defects similar to those in the arbitral award the court vacated in *Swift v. Botany*. In both cases, the losing party complained that the arbitrator implied terms into the agreement that had no basis in the agreement itself. Why then is this award not overturned? Can the cases be distinguished? Can we distinguish a claim that an arbitral award is in excess of the arbitrator's powers under an agreement from a claim that an award that is an erroneous interpretation of an agreement?

2. How does the court justify the imposition of Rule 11 sanctions? Was the claim in fact "totally devoid of merit" as the court says? Is the standard for imposing Rule 11 sanctions another means courts use to limit judicial review of arbitral awards?

* * *

Moncharsh v. Heily & Blase

3 Cal.4th 1, 832 P.2d 899 (1992).

■ LUCAS, CHIEF JUSTICE.

We granted review in this case to decide, inter alia, the extent to which a trial court may review an arbitrator's decision for errors of law. For the reasons discussed below, we conclude an arbitrator's decision is not generally reviewable for errors of fact or law, whether or not such error appears on the face of the award and causes substantial injustice to the parties. There are, however, limited exceptions to this general rule, which we also discuss below.

FACTS

On June 16, 1986, appellant Philip Moncharsh, an attorney, was hired by respondent Heily & Blase, a law firm. As a condition of employment as an associate attorney in the firm, Moncharsh signed an agreement containing a number of provisions governing various aspects of his employment. One provision (hereafter referred to as "paragraph X–C") stated: "X C. EMPLOYEE–ATTORNEY agrees not to do anything to cause, encourage, induce, entice, recommend, suggest, mention or otherwise cause or contribute to any of FIRM'S clients terminating the attorney-client relationship with FIRM, and/or substituting FIRM and retaining or associating EMPLOYEE–ATTORNEY or any other attorney or firm as their legal counsel. In the event that any FIRM client should terminate the attorney-client relationship with FIRM and substitute EMPLOYEE–ATTORNEY or another attorney or law firm who[m] EMPLOYEE–ATTORNEY suggested, recommended or directed as client's successor attorney, then, in addition to any costs which client owes FIRM up to the time of such substitution, as to all fees which EMPLOYEE–ATTORNEY may actually receive from that client or that client's successor attorney on any such cases, BLASE will receive eighty percent (80%) of said fee and EMPLOYEE–ATTORNEY will receive twenty percent (20%) of said fee.''

Moncharsh terminated his employment with Heily & Blase on February 29, 1988. DeWitt Blase, the senior partner at Heily & Blase, contacted 25 or 30 of Moncharsh's clients, noted that they had signed retainer agreements with his firm, and explained that he would now be handling their cases. Five clients, whose representation by Moncharsh predated his association with Heily & Blase, chose to have Moncharsh continue to represent them. A sixth client, Ringhof, retained Moncharsh less than two weeks before he left the firm. Moncharsh continued to represent all six clients after he left the firm.

When Blase learned Moncharsh had received fees at the conclusion of these six cases, he sought a quantum meruit share of the fees as well as a percentage of the fees pursuant to paragraph X–C of the employment agreement. Blase rejected Moncharsh's offer to settle the matter for only a quantum meruit share of the fees. The parties then invoked the arbitration clause of the employment agreement[1] and submitted the matter to an arbitrator.

The arbitrator heard two days of testimony and the matter was submitted on the briefs and exhibits. In his brief, Moncharsh argued (1) Heily & Blase was entitled to only a quantum meruit share of the fees, (2) Moncharsh and Blase had an oral agreement to treat differently the cases Moncharsh brought with him to Heily & Blase, (3) the employment agreement had terminated and was therefore inapplicable, (4) the agreement was one of adhesion and therefore unenforceable, and (5) paragraph X–C is unenforceable because it violates public policy, the Rules of Professional Conduct of the State Bar, and because it is inconsistent with Fracasse v. Brent (1972) 6 Cal.3d 784, 100 Cal.Rptr. 385, 494 P.2d 9, and Champion v. Superior Court (1988) 201 Cal.App.3d 777, 247 Cal.Rptr. 624.

In its brief, Heily & Blase contended paragraph X–C (1) is clear and unequivocal, (2) is not unconscionable, and (3) represented a reasonable attempt to avoid litigation and was thus akin to a liquidated damages provision. In addition, "To the extent it becomes important to the Arbitrator's decision," Heily & Blase alleged that Moncharsh solicited the six clients to remain with him, and further suggested that Moncharsh retained those six because it was probable that financial settlements would soon be forthcoming in all six matters. Heily & Blase contrasted these six matters with the other cases Moncharsh left with the firm, all of which allegedly required a significant amount of additional legal work.

The arbitrator ruled in Heily & Blase's favor, concluding that any oral side agreement between Moncharsh and Blase was never documented and

---

1. The arbitration clause provided: "Any dispute arising out of this Agreement shall be subject to arbitration under the rules of the American Arbitration Association. No arbitrator shall have any power to alter, amend, modify or change any of the terms of this agreement. The decision of the arbitrator shall be final and binding on FIRM and EMPLOYEE–ATTORNEY." None of the rules of the American Arbitration Association have any bearing on the issues raised in this case.

that Moncharsh was thus bound by the written employee agreement. Further, the arbitrator ruled that, "except for client Ringhof, [paragraph X–C] is not unconscionable, and it does not violate the rules of professional conduct. At the time MR. MONCHARSH agreed to the employment contract, he was a mature, experienced attorney, with employable skills. Had he not been willing to agree to the eighty/twenty (80/20) split on termination, he could simply have refused to sign the document, negotiated something different, or if negotiations were unsuccessful, his choice was to leave his employment.... [¶] ... The Arbitrator excludes the Ringhof client from the eighty/twenty (80/20) split because that client was obtained at the twilight of MR. MONCHARSH'S relationship with HEILY & BLASE, and an eighty/twenty (80/20) split with respect to that client would be unconscionable."

Moncharsh petitioned the superior court to vacate and modify the arbitration award. (Code Civ.Proc., § 1286.2; all subsequent statutory references are to this code unless otherwise stated.) Heily & Blase responded by petitioning the court to confirm the award. (§ 1285.) The court ruled that, "The arbitrator's findings on questions of both law and fact are conclusive. A court cannot set aside an arbitrator's error of law no matter how egregious." The court allowed an exception to this rule, however, "where the error appears on the face of the award." Finding no such error, the trial court denied Moncharsh's petition to vacate and granted Heily & Blase's petition to confirm the arbitrator's award.

On appeal, the Court of Appeal also recognized the rule, announced in previous cases, generally prohibiting review of the merits of the arbitrator's award. It noted, however, that an exception exists when "an error of law appears on the face of the ruling and then only if the error would result in substantial injustice." Although Moncharsh claimed paragraph X–C violated law, public policy, and the State Bar Rules of Professional Conduct, the appellate court disagreed and affirmed the trial court judgment.

We granted review and directed the parties to address the limited issue of whether, and under what conditions, a trial court may review an arbitrator's decision.

DISCUSSION

1. The General Rule of Arbitral Finality

The parties in this case submitted their dispute to an arbitrator pursuant to their written agreement. This case thus involves private, or nonjudicial, arbitration. (See Blanton v. Womancare, Inc. (1985) 38 Cal.3d 396, 401–402 & fn. 5, 212 Cal.Rptr. 151, 696 P.2d 645 [discussing the differences between judicial and nonjudicial arbitration].) In cases involving private arbitration, "[t]he scope of arbitration is ... a matter of agreement between the parties" (Ericksen, Arbuthnot, McCarthy, Kearney & Walsh, Inc. v. 100 Oak Street (1983) 35 Cal.3d 312, 323, 197 Cal.Rptr. 581, 673 P.2d 251 [hereafter Ericksen]), and " '[t]he powers of an arbitrator are limited and circumscribed by the agreement or stipulation of submission.' "(O'Malley v. Petroleum Maintenance Co. (1957) 48 Cal.2d 107, 110,

308 P.2d 9 [hereafter O'Malley], quoting Pacific Fire etc. Bureau v. Bookbinders' Union (1952) 115 Cal.App.2d 111, 114, 251 P.2d 694.)

Title 9 of the Code of Civil Procedure, as enacted and periodically amended by the Legislature, represents a comprehensive statutory scheme regulating private arbitration in this state. (§ 1280 et seq.) Through this detailed statutory scheme, the Legislature has expressed a "strong public policy in favor of arbitration as a speedy and relatively inexpensive means of dispute resolution." (Ericksen, supra, 35 Cal.3d at p. 322, 197 Cal.Rptr. 581, 673 P.2d 251) ... Consequently, courts will " 'indulge every intendment to give effect to such proceedings.' "(Doers v. Golden Gate Bridge etc. Dist. (1979) 23 Cal.3d 180, 189, 151 Cal.Rptr. 837, 588 P.2d 1261, quoting Pacific Inv. Co. v. Townsend (1976) 58 Cal.App.3d 1, 9, 129 Cal.Rptr. 489....)

The arbitration clause included in the employment agreement in this case specifically states that the arbitrator's decision would be both binding and final. The parties to this action thus clearly intended the arbitrator's decision would be final. Even had there been no such expression of intent, however, it is the general rule that parties to a private arbitration impliedly agree that the arbitrator's decision will be both binding and final.[3] Indeed, "The very essence of the term 'arbitration' [in this context] connotes a binding award." (Blanton v. Womancare, Inc., supra, 38 Cal.3d at p. 402, 212 Cal.Rptr. 151, 696 P.2d 645, citing Domke on Commercial Arbitration (rev. ed. 1984) p. 1 [hereafter Domke].) ...

This expectation of finality strongly informs the parties' choice of an arbitral forum over a judicial one. The arbitrator's decision should be the end, not the beginning, of the dispute. (See Feldman, *Arbitration Modernized—The New California Arbitration Act* (1961) 34 So.CAL.L.REV. 413, 414, fn. 11.) Expanding the availability of judicial review of such decisions "would tend to deprive the parties to the arbitration agreement of the very advantages the process is intended to produce." (Victoria v. Superior Court, supra, 40 Cal.3d at p. 751, 222 Cal.Rptr. 1, 710 P.2d 833 [dis. opn. of Lucas, J.]; see generally, *Judicial Deference*, supra, 23 UCLA L.REV. at p. 949.)

Ensuring arbitral finality thus requires that judicial intervention in the arbitration process be minimized.... Because the decision to arbitrate grievances evinces the parties' intent to bypass the judicial system and thus avoid potential delays at the trial and appellate levels, arbitral finality is a core component of the parties' agreement to submit to arbitration. Thus, an arbitration decision is final and conclusive *because the parties have agreed that it be so.* By ensuring that an arbitrator's decision is final and binding, courts simply assure that the parties receive the benefit of their bargain.

---

3. We assume for this discussion of general principles that an enforceable arbitration agreement exists. We do not address here the situation where one party advances a legal theory that would vitiate the parties' voluntary agreement to submit to arbitration. (See § 1281.2 [court will not order arbitration if "[g]rounds exist for the revocation of the agreement"].)

Moreover, "[a]rbitrators, unless specifically required to act in conformity with rules of law, may base their decision upon broad principles of justice and equity, and in doing so may expressly or impliedly reject a claim that a party might successfully have asserted in a judicial action." (Sapp v. Barenfeld (1949) 34 Cal.2d 515, 523, 212 P.2d 233.) As early as 1852, this court recognized that, "The arbitrators are not bound to award on principles of dry law, but may decide on principles of equity and good conscience, and make their award *ex aequo et bono* [according to what is just and good]." (Muldrow v. Norris (1852) 2 Cal. 74, 77.) "As a consequence, arbitration awards are generally immune from judicial review. 'Parties who stipulate in an agreement that controversies that may arise out of it shall be settled by arbitration, may expect not only to reap the advantages that flow from the use of that nontechnical, summary procedure, but also to find themselves bound by an award reached by paths neither marked nor traceable and not subject to judicial review.' (Case v. Alperson (1960) 181 Cal.App.2d 757, 759, 5 Cal.Rptr. 635 . . .)" (Nogueiro v. Kaiser Foundation Hospitals (1988) 203 Cal.App.3d 1192, 1195, 250 Cal.Rptr. 478.)

Thus, both because it vindicates the intentions of the parties that the award be final, and because an arbitrator is not ordinarily constrained to decide according to the rule of law, it is the general rule that, "The merits of the controversy between the parties are not subject to judicial review." (O'Malley, supra, 48 Cal.2d at p. 111, 308 P.2d 9, Pacific Vegetable Oil Corp. v. C.S.T. Ltd. (1946), 29 Cal.2d 228, 233, 174 P.2d 441 [hereinafter Pacific Vegetable].) More specifically, courts will not review the validity of the arbitrator's reasoning. (Grunwald–Marx, Inc. v. L.A. Joint Board, supra, 52 Cal.2d at p. 589, 343 P.2d 23.) Further, a court may not review the sufficiency of the evidence supporting an arbitrator's award. (Morris v. Zuckerman, supra, 69 Cal.2d at 691, 72 Cal.Rptr. 880, 446 P.2d 1000.)

Thus, it is the general rule that, with narrow exceptions, an arbitrator's decision cannot be reviewed for errors of fact or law. In reaffirming this general rule, we recognize there is a risk that the arbitrator will make a mistake. That risk, however, is acceptable for two reasons. First, by voluntarily submitting to arbitration, the parties have agreed to bear that risk in return for a quick, inexpensive, and conclusive resolution to their dispute. (See That Way Production Co. v. Directors Guild of America, Inc. (1979) 96 Cal.App.3d 960, 965, 158 Cal.Rptr. 475 [hereafter That Way].) As one commentator explains, "the parties to an arbitral agreement knowingly take the risks of error of fact or law committed by the arbitrators and that this is a worthy 'trade-off' in order to obtain speedy decisions by experts in the field whose practical experience and worldly reasoning will be accepted as correct by other experts." (Sweeney, *Judicial Review of Arbitral Proceedings* (1981–1982) 5 FORDHAM INT'L L.J. 253, 254.) "In other words, it is within the power of the arbitrator to make a mistake either legally or factually. When parties opt for the forum of arbitration they agree to be bound by the decision of that forum knowing that arbitrators, like judges, are fallible." (*That Way*, supra, at p. 965, 158 Cal.Rptr. 475.)

· · ·

A second reason why we tolerate the risk of an erroneous decision is because the Legislature has reduced the risk to the parties of such a decision by providing for judicial review in circumstances involving serious problems with the award itself, or with the fairness of the arbitration process. As stated ante, private arbitration proceedings are governed by title 9 of the Code of Civil Procedure, sections 1280–1294.2. Section 1286.2 sets forth the grounds for vacation of an arbitrator's award. It states in pertinent part: "[T]he court shall vacate the award if the court determines that: [¶] (a) The award was procured by corruption, fraud or other undue means; [¶] (b) There was corruption in any of the arbitrators; [¶] (c) The rights of such party were substantially prejudiced by misconduct of a neutral arbitrator; [¶] (d) The arbitrators exceeded their powers and the award cannot be corrected without affecting the merits of the decision upon the controversy submitted; or [¶] (e) The rights of such party were substantially prejudiced by the refusal of the arbitrators to postpone the hearing upon sufficient cause being shown therefor or by the refusal of the arbitrators to hear evidence material to the controversy or by other conduct of the arbitrators contrary to the provisions of this title."

In addition, section 1286.6 provides grounds for correction of an arbitration award. That section states in pertinent part: "[T]he court, unless it vacates the award pursuant to Section 1286.2, shall correct the award and confirm it as corrected if the court determines that: [¶] (a) There was an evident miscalculation of figures or an evident mistake in the description of any person, thing or property referred to in the award; [¶] (b) The arbitrators exceeded their powers but the award may be corrected without affecting the merits of the decision upon the controversy submitted; or [¶] (c) the award is imperfect in a matter of form, not affecting the merits of the controversy."

The Legislature has thus substantially reduced the possibility of certain forms of error infecting the arbitration process itself (§ 1286.2, subds. (a), (b), (c)), of an arbitrator exceeding the scope of his or her arbitral powers (§§ 1286.2, subd. (d), 1286.6, subd. (b)), of some obvious and easily correctable mistake in the award (§ 1286.6, subd. (a)), of one party being unfairly deprived of a fair opportunity to present his or her side of the dispute (§ 1286.2, subd. (e)), or of some other technical problem with the award (§ 1286.6, subd. (c)). In light of these statutory provisions, the residual risk to the parties of an arbitrator's erroneous decision represents an acceptable cost—obtaining the expedience and financial savings that the arbitration process provides—as compared to the judicial process.

Although it is thus the general rule that an arbitrator's decision is not ordinarily reviewable for error by either the trial or appellate courts, Moncharsh contends three exceptions to the general rule apply to his case. First, he claims a court may review an arbitrator's decision if an error of law is apparent on the face of the award and that error causes substantial injustice. Second, he claims the arbitrator exceeded his powers. (§ 1286.2, subd. (d).) Third, he argues courts will not enforce arbitration decisions that are illegal or violate public policy. We discuss each point seriatim.

2.   Error on the Face of the Arbitration Decision

A review of the pertinent authorities yields no shortage of proclamations that a court may vacate an arbitrator's decision when (i) an error of law appears on the face of the decision, and (ii) the error causes substantial injustice. (See, e.g., Abbott v. California State Auto. Assn. (1977) 68 Cal.App.3d 763, 771, 137 Cal.Rptr. 580.) Indeed, some cases hold the error need only appear on the face of the award, with no mention of resulting injustice. (See, e.g., Park Plaza, Ltd. v. Pietz (1987) 193 Cal.App.3d 1414, 1420, 239 Cal.Rptr. 51.) As previously noted, however, the Legislature has set forth grounds for vacation (§ 1286.2) and correction (§ 1286.6) of an arbitration award and "[a]n error of law is not one of the grounds." (Nogueiro v. Kaiser Foundation Hospitals, supra, 203 Cal.App.3d at p. 1195, 250 Cal.Rptr. 478, and cases cited.) Because Moncharsh contends that an additional exception to the general rule for errors of law is authorized by both common law and statute, we next determine the genesis of that notion as well as its continuing validity.

a.   The Early Common Law Rule

We begin with Muldrow v. Norris, supra, 2 Cal. 74 [hereafter Muldrow], a case arising before the enactment of any arbitration statutes in this state. In Muldrow, a dispute arose between the parties and they agreed to submit the matter to a panel of three arbitrators, whose decision "should be final and conclusive." (Ibid.) The arbitrators reached a decision and Norris, the losing party, sought to vacate the award. This court ruled in his favor, and we quote the opinion at length because it exemplifies the contradictory rule of judicial review that has been repeated in modified form since those early days:

"The first point we propose to examine, is, as to the power of the Court below to inquire into the award now before us. It is a well settled principle that courts of equity, in the absence of statutes, will set aside awards for fraud, mistake, or accident, and it makes no difference whether the mistake be one of fact or law. It is true, under a general submission, arbitrators have power to decide upon the law and facts: and a mere mistake of law cannot be taken advantage of. The arbitrators are not bound to award on principles of dry law, but may decide on principles of equity and good conscience, and make their award *ex aequo et bono*. If, however, they mean to decide according to the law, and mistake the law, the courts will set their award aside. A distinction seems to have been taken in the books between general and special awards. In the case of a general finding, it appears to be well settled that courts will not inquire into mistakes by evidence *aliunde*: but where the arbitrators have made any point a matter of judicial inquiry by spreading it upon the record, and they mistake the law in a palpable and material point, their award will be set aside. [Citation.] The mere act of setting forth their reasons must be considered for the purpose of enabling those dissatisfied to take advantage of them. [Citation.] In all cases where the arbitrators give the reasons of their finding, they are supposed to have intended to decide according to law, and to refer the point for the opinion of the Court. In such cases, if they mistake the law, the award must be set aside; for it is not the opinion they intended to give, the same having been made through mistake. [Citation.] In the case already cited, the Court says, 'these special awards are not to be commended, as arbitrators may often decide with perfect equity between parties, and not give good reasons for their decision; but when a special award is once before the Court, it must stand or fall by its own intrinsic correctness, tested by legal principles.' [Citations.]" (2 Cal. at pp. 77–78.)

The Muldrow court concluded: "In the case before us, the arbitrators have set forth the particular grounds upon which their finding was based: and it follows from the authorities already cited, that the correctness of the principles by which they must be supposed to have been governed is a proper subject for judicial inquiry." (2 Cal. at p. 78.)

Although Muldrow, supra, thus acknowledged that, at common law, an arbitrator need not follow the law in arriving at a decision, and that "a mere mistake of law cannot be taken advantage of" (2 Cal. at p. 77), the opinion qualified that statement and held that an award reached by an arbitrator may nevertheless be reversed if the error is "spread[ ] . . . upon the record" and the mistake is on a "palpable and material point." (Ibid.) Muldrow also stated that when an arbitrator gives reasons to support his decision, the award was subject to full-blown judicial oversight, and "must stand and fall by its own intrinsic correctness, tested by legal principles." (Id. at p. 78.)[5]

Later that same term, this court again addressed the issue. In Tyson v. Wells (1852) 2 Cal. 122, the parties agreed to submit their commercial dispute to a referee, whose decision was to be final. When the losing party challenged the referee's ruling, this court concluded the finality accorded a referee's report pursuant to statute was the same as for an arbitrator's ruling at common law. (Id. at p. 130.) This time avoiding any suggestion that an arbitrator's decision was subject to unqualified judicial review, we stated: "it may be regarded as the settled rule, that the Court will not disturb the award of an arbitrator . . . unless the error which is complained of, whether it be of law or fact, appears on the face of the award." (Id. at p. 131.) Although the court purported to be following Muldrow, supra, 2 Cal. 74, there was no qualification that the error must be on a "palpable and material point." (Id. at p. 77.)

---

5. By ensuring some measure of judicial control over arbitral awards, Muldrow, supra, was typical of courts from that early era in exhibiting suspicion of private arbitration as a means of dispute resolution. Thus, for example, courts had held that a common law submission to arbitration was revocable at any time prior to the award. (See California Academy of Sciences v. Fletcher (1893) 99 Cal. 207, 209, 33 P. 855; 3 Cal.Jur., Arbitration and Award § 19, p. 55.) In addition, early courts held agreements to arbitrate future disputes were unenforceable, both at common law and under the early statutes. (Blodgett Co. v. Bebe Co. (1923) 190 Cal. 665, 214 P. 38; Feldman, *Arbitration Law in California: Private Tribunals for Private Government*, supra, 30 So.Cal.L.Rev. at p. 382.) Even under the initial arbitration statutes, courts held invalid an agreement that the arbitrator's decision was final and that no appeal could be taken therefrom. (Kreiss v. Hotaling (1892) 96 Cal. 617, 621, 31 P. 740; In re Joshua Hendy Machine Works v. Gray (1908) 9 Cal.App. 610, 611, 99 P. 1110.)

Six months later, we addressed the issue again. In Headley v. Reed (1852) 2 Cal. 322, another case involving a reference, we wrote, "According to the rule settled in [Muldrow], the decision of the referee can only be set aside on account of fraud or *gross error of law or fact apparent on its face.*" (Id. at p. 325, italics added.) The Headley court thus injected a new factor into the Muldrow test—gross error—but did not repeat Muldrow's assertion that an arbitrator's decision was subject to full-blown judicial review.

These three early cases—Muldrow, Tyson, Headley—involved arbitration (or a reference, which was considered functionally equivalent to arbitration) at common law. From them, we can perceive the beginnings of the rule permitting judicial review of an arbitrator's ruling if error appeared on the face of the award. . . .

[The Court then expounded on the history of the California arbitration statute and the judicial interpretations thereof.]

The law has thus evolved from its common law origins and moved towards a more clearly delineated scheme rooted in statute. A majority of California appellate decisions have followed the modern rule, established by Pacific Vegetable, supra, 29 Cal.2d 228, 174 P.2d 441, and Crofoot, supra, 119 Cal.App.2d 156, 260 P.2d 156, and generally limit judicial review of private arbitration awards to those grounds specified in sections 1286.2 and 1286.6. (See, e.g., Severtson v. Williams Construction Co. (1985) 173 Cal.App.3d 86, 92–93, 220 Cal.Rptr. 400.)

This view is consistent with a large majority of decisions in other states. Although California has not adopted the Uniform Arbitration Act, more than half the states have done so. (See 7 West's U. Laws Ann. (1985) U. Arbitration Act, 1991 Cum.Ann. Pocket Pt., p. 1.) The statutory grounds to vacate a private arbitration award set forth in the uniform law largely mirror those codified in section 1286.2, however,[12] and most states have concluded that these grounds are exclusive. (See, e.g., Verdex Steel and Const. Co. v. Board of Supervisors (1973) 19 Ariz.App. 547 [509 P.2d 240.)

Although the matter would seem to have been put to rest, several California decisions rendered since the 1961 statutory amendments have inexplicably resurrected the view in Utah Const., supra, 174 Cal. 156, 162 P. 631, that an arbitration award may be vacated when an error appears on

---

12. Section 12 of the Uniform Arbitration Act states in pertinent part: "(a) Upon application of a party, the court shall vacate an award where: '(1) The award was procured by corruption, fraud or other undue means;' '(2) There was evident partiality by an arbitrator appointed as a neutral or corruption in any of the arbitrators or misconduct prejudicing the rights of any party;' '(3) The arbitrators exceeded their powers;' '(4) The arbitrators refused to postpone the hearing upon sufficient cause being shown therefor or refused to hear evidence material to the controversy or otherwise so conducted the hearing, contrary to the provisions of Section 5, as to prejudice substantially the rights of a party;' or '(5) There was no arbitration agreement and the issue was not adversely determined in proceedings under Section 2 and the party did not participate in the arbitration hearing without raising the objection;' but the fact that the relief was such that it could not or would not be granted by a court of law or equity is not a ground for vacating or refusing to confirm the award." (7 West's U.Laws Ann. (1985) U. Arbitration Act, § 12, subd. (a).)

the face of the award and causes substantial injustice. (See, e.g., Schneider v. Kaiser Foundation Hospitals (1989) 215 Cal.App.3d 1311, 1317, 264 Cal.Rptr. 227; Park Plaza, Ltd. v. Pietz, supra, 193 Cal.App.3d at p. 1420, 239 Cal.Rptr. 51.)

In light of the development of decisional law embracing as exclusive the statutory grounds to vacate an arbitration award, as well as the apparent intent of the Legislature to generally exclude nonstatutory grounds to vacate an award, we adhere to the Pacific Vegetable/Crofoot line of cases that limit judicial review of private arbitration awards to those cases in which there exists a statutory ground to vacate or correct the award. Those decisions permitting review of an award where an error of law appears on the face of the award causing substantial injustice have perpetuated a point of view that is inconsistent with the modern view of private arbitration and are therefore disapproved.

3.   The Arbitrator Did Not Exceed His Powers

Section 1286.2, subdivision (d), provides for vacation of an arbitration award when "The arbitrators exceeded their powers and the award cannot be corrected without affecting the merits of the decision upon the controversy submitted." Moncharsh argues this statutory exception to the rule generally precluding judicial review of arbitration awards applies to his case. It is unclear, however, on what theory Moncharsh would have us conclude the arbitrator exceeded his powers. It is well settled that "arbitrators do not exceed their powers merely because they assign an erroneous reason for their decision." (O'Malley, supra, 48 Cal.2d at p. 111, 308 P.2d 9; Hacienda Hotel v. Culinary Workers Union (1985) 175 Cal.App.3d 1127, 1133, 223 Cal.Rptr. 305.) A contrary holding would permit the exception to swallow the rule of limited judicial review; a litigant could always contend the arbitrator erred and thus exceeded his powers. To the extent Moncharsh argues his case comes within section 1286.2, subdivision (d) merely because the arbitrator reached an erroneous decision, we reject the point.

Moreover, consistent with our arbitration statutes and subject to the limited exceptions discussed in section 4 post, it is within the "powers" of the arbitrator to resolve the entire "merits" of the "controversy submitted" by the parties. (§ 1286.2, subd. (d); § 1286.6, subd. (b), (c).) Obviously, the "merits" include all the contested issues of law and fact submitted to the arbitrator for decision. The arbitrator's resolution of these issues is what the parties bargained for in the arbitration agreement. Moncharsh does not argue that the arbitrator's award strayed beyond the scope of the parties' agreement by resolving issues the parties did not agree to arbitrate. The agreement to arbitrate encompassed "[a]ny dispute arising out of" the employment contract. The parties' dispute over the allocation of attorney's fees following termination of employment clearly arose out of the employment contract; the arbitrator's award does no more than resolve that dispute. Under these circumstances, the arbitrator was within his "powers" in resolving the questions of law presented to him. The award is not subject to vacation or correction based on any of the statutory grounds asserted by Moncharsh.

4.   Illegality of the Contract Permits Judicial Review

Moncharsh next contends the arbitrator's award is subject to judicial review because paragraph X–C of the employment agreement is illegal and in violation of public policy. Focussing on the fee-splitting provision of the employment agreement, he contends that despite the limited scope of judicial review of arbitration awards, such review has historically been available when one party alleges the underlying contract, a portion thereof, or the resulting award, is illegal or in violation of public policy. . . .

Although Moncharsh acknowledges the general rule that an arbitrator's legal, as well as factual, determinations are final and not subject to judicial review, he argues that judicial review of the arbitrator's decision is warranted on the facts of this case. In support, he claims that the fee-splitting provision of the contract that was interpreted and enforced by the arbitrator was "illegal" and violative of "public policy" as reflected in several provisions of the Rules of Professional Conduct. Such illegality, he claims, has been recognized as a ground for judicial review as stated in a line of cases emanating from this court's decision in Loving & Evans v. Blick (1949) 33 Cal.2d 603, 204 P.2d 23 [hereafter Loving & Evans].

Loving & Evans, supra, 33 Cal.2d 603, 204 P.2d 23, involved a dispute about money due on a construction contract for remodeling done on appellant Blick's premises. In his pleading before the arbitrator, Blick claimed as a "separate and special defense" that respondent contractors could not legally recover because they were unlicensed in violation of the Business and Professions Code. The arbitrator found in respondents' favor, and they moved to confirm the award. Blick objected to the award on grounds that one of the respondents was unlicensed in violation of the code. The trial court granted the motion to confirm, but that judgment was reversed by this court. Although we recognized the general rule that the merits of a dispute before an arbitrator are not subject to judicial review, "the rules which give finality to the arbitrator's determination of ordinary questions of fact or of law are inapplicable *where the issue of illegality of the entire transaction* is raised in a proceeding for the enforcement of the arbitrator's award." (Id. at p. 609, 204 P.2d 23, italics added.)

The Court of Appeal reached a similar result in All Points Traders, Inc. v. Barrington Associates (1989) 211 Cal.App.3d 723, 259 Cal.Rptr. 780 [hereafter All Points Traders]. In that case, Barrington Associates (hereafter Barrington), an investment banking firm, sought payment of a commission for its assistance in negotiating the transfer of all the corporate stock of appellant All Points Traders. The arbitrator found in Barrington's favor and the trial court confirmed the award. Nevertheless, the Court of Appeal reversed, finding the commission agreement between the parties was invalid and unenforceable in its entirety because Barrington did not hold a real estate broker's license as required by Business and Professions Code section 10130 et seq. The appellate court reasoned that "The Legislature selected the specific means to protect the public and has expressed its intention in section 10136 [prohibiting an unlicensed broker from bringing an action to collect a commission]," and that "Enforcement of the contract for a commission would be in direct contravention of the statute and against public policy.'' (All Points Traders, supra, at p. 738, 259 Cal.Rptr. 780 [italics added].)

Both Loving & Evans, supra, 33 Cal.2d 603, 204 P.2d 23, and All Points Traders, supra, 211 Cal.App.3d 723, 259 Cal.Rptr. 780, permitted judicial review of an arbitrator's ruling where a party claimed the entire contract or transaction was illegal. By contrast, Moncharsh challenges but a single provision of the overall employment contract. Accordingly, neither Loving & Evans, supra, nor All Points Traders, supra, authorizes judicial review of his claim . . . .

Without an explicit legislative expression of public policy, however, courts should be reluctant to invalidate an arbitrator's award on this ground. The reason is clear: the Legislature has already expressed its strong support for private arbitration and the finality of arbitral awards in title 9 of the Code of Civil Procedure. (§ 1280 et seq.) Absent a clear expression of illegality or public policy undermining this strong presumption in favor of private arbitration, an arbitral award should ordinarily stand immune from judicial scrutiny.

Moncharsh contends, as he did before the arbitrator, that paragraph X–C is illegal and violates public policy because, inter alia, it violates former rules 2–107 [prohibiting unconscionable fees], 2–108 [prohibiting certain types of fee splitting arrangements], and 2–109 [prohibiting agreements restricting an attorney's right to practice], of the Rules of Professional Conduct of State Bar. We perceive, however, nothing in the Rules of Professional Conduct at issue in this case that suggests resolution by an arbitrator of what is essentially an ordinary fee dispute would be inappropriate or would improperly protect the public interest. Accordingly, judicial review of the arbitrator's decision is unavailable.

CONCLUSION

We conclude that an award reached by an arbitrator pursuant to a contractual agreement to arbitrate is not subject to judicial review except on the grounds set forth in sections 1286.2 (to vacate) and 1286.6 (for correction). Further, the existence of an error of law apparent on the face of the award that causes substantial injustice does not provide grounds for judicial review.

Finally, the normal rule of limited judicial review may not be avoided by a claim that a provision of the contract, construed or applied by the arbitrator, is ''illegal,'' except in rare cases when according finality to the arbitrator's decision would be incompatible with the protection of a statutory right. We conclude that Moncharsh has demonstrated no reason why the strong presumption in favor of the finality of the arbitral award should not apply here.

The judgment of the Court of Appeal is affirmed.

■ PANELLI, ARABIAN, BAXTER and GEORGE, JJ., concur.

■ KENNARD, JUSTICE, concurring and dissenting.

The majority holds that when a trial court is presented with an arbitration award that is erroneous on its face and will cause substantial injustice, the court has no choice but to confirm it. (Maj. opn., ante, at pp. 184, 203 of 10 Cal.Rptr.2d, at pp. 900, 919 of 832 P.2d.) Because an order confirming an arbitration award results in the entry of a judgment with the same force and effect as a judgment in a civil action (Code Civ. Proc., § 1287.4), the majority's holding requires our trial courts not only to tolerate substantial injustice, but to become its active agent.

I cannot join the majority opinion. I will not agree to a decision inflicting upon this state's trial courts a duty to promote injustice by confirming arbitration awards they know to be manifestly wrong and substantially unjust. Nor can I accept the proposition, necessarily implied although never directly stated in the majority opinion, that the general policy in favor of arbitration is more important than the judiciary's solemn obligation to do justice.

Nothing in this state's statutory or decisional law compels the rule the majority announces. On the contrary, the majority has misperceived legislative intent, misconstrued the relevant statute, and misunderstood the decisional law establishing the scope of review for arbitration decisions. Worst of all, the majority has forsaken the goal that has defined and legitimized the judiciary's role in society—to strive always for justice.

I

The object of government is justice. "Justice is the end of government. It is the end of civil society. It ever has been, and ever will be pursued, until it be obtained, or until liberty be lost in the pursuit." (James Madison, *The Federalist*, No. 51.) As the preamble to the United States Constitution affirms, our country was founded to "establish justice."

Justice is a special obligation of the judiciary. Every court has the power and the duty to "amend and control its process and orders so as to make them conform to law and justice." (Code Civ.Proc., § 128, subd. (a)(8).) When they construe statutes, courts are enjoined to do so in a way that will promote justice. (E.g., Civ.Code, § 4; Code Civ. Proc., § 4; Ed. Code, § 2; Pen.Code, § 4.) And, because the very purpose of our legal system is to do justice between the parties (Sand v. Concrete Service Co. (1959) 176 Cal.App.2d 169, 172, 1 Cal.Rptr. 257), the interests of justice are paramount in all legal proceedings (Travis v. Southern Pacific Co. (1962) 210 Cal.App.2d 410, 425, 26 Cal.Rptr. 700). In short, justice is the "sole justification of our law and courts." (Gitelson & Gitelson, *A Trial Judge's Credo Must Include His Affirmative Duty to be an Instrumentality of Justice* (1966) 7 SANTA CLARA LAW. 7, 8).

The majority never mentions the judiciary's paramount obligation to do justice, and the rule it announces—which requires trial courts to endorse decisions known to be substantially unjust—is its very antithesis. By filling its discussion with references to the expectations of the parties, the development of decisional law over the course of a century, and legislative intent as evidenced in our statute, the majority implies both that these considerations support its holding and that they are more important than doing justice.

The majority is wrong on both counts. For the judiciary, nothing can be more important than justice. This proposition is so self-evident that no further elaboration is necessary. Moreover, as we shall see, respect for parties' freedom to contract, the development of decisional law, the relevant statute, and ascertainable legislative intent belie rather than support the majority's holding.

II

As a method of dispute resolution, arbitration is generally faster and cheaper than judicial proceedings, but it has fewer safeguards against error. For this reason, parties who agree to binding arbitration must be deemed to have accepted the increased risk of error inherent in their chosen system. The majority takes this proposition, unobjectionable in itself, and from it jumps to the conclusion that parties who agree to arbitration thereby agree also to be bound by an award that on its face is manifestly erroneous and results in substantial injustice. But the conclusion defies both logic and experience. Reasonable contracting parties would never assume a risk that is so unnecessary and self-destructive.

The majority goes astray when it equates substantial injustice with a mere mistake. The two are not the same. Mistakes commonly occur in the course of dispute resolution proceedings without producing substantial injustice. As our state Constitution recognizes, determining whether a mistake has been made, and determining whether an injustice has occurred, are separate and distinct inquiries. (Cal. Const., art. VI, § 13 [court cannot set aside a judgment for error unless the error resulted in a miscarriage of justice].)

Parties who agree to resolve their disputes by arbitration should not and do not expect busy trial courts to comb the records of arbitration proceedings to determine whether any error has occurred and, if so, the effect of the error. But they no doubt do expect, and ought to be able to expect, that if the award on its face is erroneous and results in substantial injustice, a court asked to confirm the award will not turn a blind eye to the consequences of its action, but will instead take the only course consistent with its fundamental mandate, and will vacate the award.

Moreover, even if the parties were to do what is virtually inconceivable by expressly agreeing that the arbitrator's award would be binding even if substantially unjust, the agreement would not bind the judiciary. The exercise of judicial power cannot be controlled or compelled by private agreement or stipulation. (See California State Auto. Assn. Inter–Ins. Bureau v. Superior Court (1990) 50 Cal.3d 658, 664, 268 Cal.Rptr. 284, 788 P.2d 1156; Clarendon Ltd. v. Nu–West Industries, Inc. (3d Cir.1991) 936 F.2d 127, 129 ["action by the court can be neither purchased nor parlayed by the parties"].) As the United States Supreme Court has remarked, a court should refuse to be "the abettor of iniquity." (Precision Co. v. Automotive Co. (1945) 324 U.S. 806, 814, 65 S.Ct. 993, 997, 89 L.Ed. 1381.)

III

To support its holding radically curtailing judicial review of arbitration awards, the majority surveys the decisional law of California since 1850. Undeterred by the plain language of the decisions, which is almost uniformly contrary to the majority's holding, the majority attempts to penetrate the surface of the opinions in order to trace the ebb and flow of more than a century's dark currents of judicial thought. Thus, the majority relies on what it terms "subtle shifts" in the decisions, "transmogrification" of principles, and citations in one opinion that on "close scrutiny" are alleged to be at odds with a clear statement of law in the opinion's text. (Maj. opn., ante, at pp. 193, 194 of 10 Cal.Rptr.2d, at pp. 909, 910 of 832 P.2d.) As an exercise in divination or telepathy, the majority's discussion is fascinating. But as sober legal analysis, the majority's discussion is simply wrong. From the outset, this court has consistently—until now—acknowledged that courts should refuse to permit use of the judiciary's awesome coercive power to perpetrate a substantial injustice.

In the first decision cited by the majority, Muldrow v. Norris (1852) 2 Cal. 74, this court held that it would not enforce an erroneous arbitration award when the error was on a "palpable and material point." (Id. at p. 77.) Although this court used a verbal formulation—"palpable and material point"—different from the term "substantial injustice" that became the standard expression in later cases (e.g., Utah Const. Co. v. Western Pac. Ry. Co. (1916) 174 Cal. 156, 160–161, 162 P. 631), the concept is the same. To be on a "palpable and material point," an error must be of real importance or great consequence (Webster's Ninth New Collegiate Dict. (1988) p. 733), or, in other words, an error that causes substantial injustice.

Other early decisions used the term "gross error" to describe the very same ground for vacating an arbitration award. (E.g., Headley v. Reed (1852) 2 Cal. 322, 325; In re Connor (1900) 128 Cal. 279, 282, 60 P. 862.) An error is "gross" if it is glaringly noticeable "because of inexcusable badness or objectionableness." (Webster's Ninth New Collegiate Dict., supra, p. 538.) Thus, the term "gross error," like the "palpable and material point" formulation, represents an early articulation of what has subsequently become known as error causing substantial injustice.

Fairly read, the decisions of this court, although varying semantically, uniformly and firmly support the proposition that the judiciary will not knowingly perpetuate and enforce an arbitration award that is substantially unjust. This court has adopted the same standard for determining when a court should decline to follow the rule known as law of the case. (See People v. Shuey (1975) 13 Cal.3d 835, 846, 120 Cal.Rptr. 83, 533 P.2d 211 ["a manifest misapplication of existing principles resulting in substantial injustice"]; accord, George Arakelian Farms, Inc. v. Agricultural Labor Relations Bd. (1989) 49 Cal.3d 1279, 1291, 265 Cal.Rptr. 162, 783 P.2d 749.)

The Courts of Appeal have correctly interpreted our decisions. In case after case, they have reaffirmed the rule that a court will vacate an arbitration award when error appears on the face of the award and causes substantial injustice. (E.g., Cobler v. Stanley, Barber, Southard, Brown & Associates (1990) 217 Cal.App.3d 518, 526, 265 Cal.Rptr. 868....

Searching for some departure from this prominent line of authority, the majority relies heavily on the Court of Appeal decision in Crofoot v. Blair Holdings Corp. (1953) 119 Cal.App.2d 156, 260 P.2d 156 (disapproved on another ground in Posner v. Grunwald–Marx, Inc. (1961) 56 Cal.2d 169, 183, 14 Cal.Rptr. 297, 363 P.2d 313), but its reliance is misplaced. Crofoot cites this court's opinion in Pacific Vegetable Oil Corp. v. C.S.T., Ltd. (1946) 29 Cal.2d 228, 174 P.2d 441, for the proposition that courts had recently narrowed somewhat the judicial review of arbitration awards for legal error. (Crofoot, supra, 119 Cal.App.2d at p. 185, 260 P.2d 156.) But neither Crofoot nor Pacific Vegetable suggests that review had become so narrow that courts were obliged to confirm awards containing obvious error causing substantial injustice....

As the majority notes, the Crofoot opinion does state that the merits of an arbitration award may not be judicially reviewed except as provided in the statute. (Crofoot v. Blair Holdings Corp., supra, 119 Cal.App.2d 156, 186, 260 P.2d 156.) Because the relevant statute, Code of Civil Procedure section 1286.2, does not say in so many words that an arbitration award may be challenged for obvious error causing substantial injustice, the majority concludes that a court may not vacate an award on this ground. But this conclusion is wrong. Our statute does not, by negative implication or otherwise, mandate injustice.

IV

Code of Civil Procedure section 1286.2 lists five grounds for vacating an arbitration award. This statutory list is reproduced in the margin.[1] Although the statute states only that a court "shall vacate the award" if any of these grounds is present, the majority construes the statute as precluding a court from vacating an arbitration award on any ground not specifically defined in the statute. In thus construing the statutory list, the majority ignores the statute's legislative history.

... The Legislature enacted section 1286.2 in its present form in 1961 (Stats.1961, ch. 461, § 2, p. 1540) following a recommendation and study of the California Law Revision Commission. (Recommendation and Study Relating to Arbitration (Dec.1960) 3 Cal.Law Revision Com.Rep. (1961), p. G–1 et seq.) In its report to the Legislature, the commission separately and expressly addressed the subject of judicial review of arbitration awards. Because the commission accurately stated California law on this subject,

---

1. "(a) The award was procured by corruption, fraud or other undue means; [¶] (b) There was corruption in any of the arbitrators; [¶] (c) The rights of such party were substantially prejudiced by misconduct of a neutral arbitrator; [¶] (d) The arbitrators exceeded their powers and the award cannot be corrected without affecting the merits of the decision upon the controversy submitted; or [¶] (e) The rights of such party were substantially prejudiced by the refusal of the arbitrators to postpone the hearing upon sufficient cause being shown therefor or by the refusal of the arbitrators to hear evidence material to the controversy or by other conduct of the arbitrators contrary to the provisions of this title."

and because its statement belies the majority's reading of the statute, the commission's comment is worth quoting in some detail:

"Nothing in the California statute defines the permissible scope of review by the courts. Numerous court rulings have, however, developed the following basic principles which set the limits for any court review: ... [¶] (5) Statutory provisions for a review of arbitration proceedings are for the sole purpose of preventing misuse of the proceedings where corruption, fraud, misconduct, gross error or mistake has been carried into the award to the substantial prejudice of a party to the proceedings.... [¶] Neither the Uniform Arbitration Act nor other state statutes attempt to express the exact limits of court review of arbitration awards. And no good reason exists to codify into the California statute the case law as it presently exists." (Recommendation and Study Relating to Arbitration, supra, 3 Cal.Law Revision Com.Rep., pp. G–53–G–54, fns. omitted, italics added.)

The commission, in other words, did not intend to either alter or codify the judicially established grounds for challenging an arbitration award. Contrary to the majority's view, Code of Civil Procedure section 1286.2 was never meant to define the "permissible scope of review by the courts" or to "express the exact limits of court review of arbitration awards." Thus, the statute does not preclude a court from vacating an arbitration award on a ground well established by decisional law.

In words that closely track the language this court used in Pacific Vegetable Oil Corp. v. C.S.T., Ltd., supra, 29 Cal.2d 228, 240, 174 P.2d 441, the commission acknowledged that one purpose of judicial review is to prevent gross errors or mistakes from being carried into an award to the substantial prejudice of a party, that is, substantial injustice. (Recommendation and Study Relating to Arbitration, supra, 3 Cal.Law Revision Com. Rep. (1961), p. G-55.) Code of Civil Procedure section 1286.2 may not be read as barring a court from vacating an arbitration award when these conditions are present. ...

V

Despite my disagreement with the reasoning of the majority opinion, I agree with the result it reaches. This is not a case in which error appearing on the face of an arbitration award would cause a substantial injustice.

The agreement was negotiated between sophisticated parties; the disparity in bargaining power between the parties was not substantial; there is no indication of harm to the clients or other third parties; and there is no basis in the arbitrator's award for finding that the fees were wholly disproportionate to the services rendered. Therefore, the award was not substantially unjust.

CONCLUSION

Although I concur in the result, I cannot join the majority to support judicially sanctioned and enforced substantial injustice. The majority's holding violates the most basic obligation of the judiciary, and is inconsistent with both our well-established decisional law and our statute.

MOSK, J., concurs.

* * *

Questions

1. Does the court in *Moncharsh* apply the "manifest disregard of the law" standard? If not, what standard does it apply for judicial review of arbitral

Is this a different interpretation of the manifest disregard of the law standard than that used in the previous cases? awards?The Fifth Circuit suggests that the "manifest disregard" standard has a different meaning in statutory cases than it does

2. The majority distinguishes the *Loving & Evans* and *All Points Traders* in non-statutory ones. What does the court suggest the standard in non-statutory cases should be? What kinds of evidence cases on the grounds that they involve an assertion that the entire would a court use to determine whether under "all the circumstances of the case," significant injustice will result from transaction is illegal. But is not the same type of illegality alleged here, enforcement of the award? What does the court mean by drawing attention to the powers of arbitrators to judge "norms where one side is challenging the lawfulness of a fee-sharing agreement? appropriate to the relations of the parties"? Does this interpretation restrict or enlarge the scope of judicial review? Can these cases be distinguished on some other ground?How does it compare to *Moncarsch?*

3. In *Williams v. Cigna Financial Advisors, Inc.,* ___ F.3d ___ (5th Cir.1999), 1999 WL 1101178, the Fifth Circuit affirmed an arbitration award denying recovery in an age discrimination lawsuit. The Fifth Circuit expounded upon the standard of review for arbitral awards in Title VII cases, stating that in cases involving arbitration of federal statutory employment rights, "the 'manifest disregard of the law' standard 'must be sufficient to ensure that arbitrators comply with the requirements of the statute at issue.' " The court then defined the manifest disregard of the law standard in the statutory context to mean:

> "First, where on the basis of the information available to the court it is not manifest that the arbitrators acted contrary to the applicable law, the award should be upheld. Second, where on the basis of the information available to the court it is manifest that the arbitrators acted contrary to the applicable law, the award should be upheld unless it would result in significant injustice, taking into account all the circumstances of the case, including powers of arbitrators to judge norms appropriate to the relations between the parties."

Is this a different interpretation of the manifest disregard of the law standard than that used in the previous cases? The Fifth Circuit suggests that the "manifest disregard" standard has a different meaning in statutory cases than it does in non-statutory ones. What does the court suggest the standard in non-statutory cases should be? What kinds of evidence would a court use to determine whether the arbitrator acted "contrary to the applicable law"? What kinds of information can it use to determine whether under "all the circumstances of the case," significant injustice will result from enforcement of the award? What does the court mean by drawing attention to the powers of arbitrators to judge "norms appropriate to the relations of the parties"? Does this interpretation restrict or enlarge the scope of judicial review? How does it compare to *Moncarsch?*

4.   When should a court look to public policy to overturn an arbitral award? If public policy is embodied in legislation or common law, do courts have an obligation to ensure that such policies are not evaded by arbitral awards. If not, can parties always use arbitration as a means to enforce an otherwise illegal transaction?

5.   Is the *Moncharsh* court's view of public policy the same as the view the Supreme Court adopted in *Misco?* Which view permits more judicial scrutiny of arbitral awards?

6.   Does a court have an independent obligation to review arbitral awards to avoid substantial injustice?

* * *

Note on Modification of Arbitral Awards and the Doctrine of *Functus Officio*

Occasionally an arbitrator issues an award that is ambiguous, contains an error of calculation, or fails to address a matter that has been submitted. In such event, the party who is disadvantaged by the error or omission will often ask the arbitrator to clarify, correct, or complete the award. If the arbitrator does so and issues a revised award, the other side may raise an objection to enforcement of the revised award on the grounds of *functus officio.*

Functus officio is Latin for a task performed. Black's Law Dictionary defines the term as "having fulfilled the function, discharged the office, or accomplished the purpose, and therefore [having] no further force or authority." As applied to arbitrators, *functus officio* means that once an arbitral panel has issued an award, it becomes "*functus officio* and lacks any further power to act." *Ottley v. Schwartzberg*, 819 F.2d 373, 376 (2d Cir.1987). The doctrine is usually justified on the grounds that arbitrators are merely ad hoc judges, so that once the case is decided and an award issued, their decision-making power ceases. In practical terms, the doctrine reflects the policy of arbitral finality. Without the doctrine, it is feared, parties would try to pressure arbitrators to modify decisions to their own advantage.

Some commentators oppose the doctrine of *functus officio*, and argue that it is a vestige of the old days of judicial hostility to arbitration and should be abandoned. As a result, the doctrine has been relaxed in recent years. At present, most courts have recognized exceptions to the doctrine in the following situations:

1.   An arbitrator can correct a mistake that is apparent on the face of the award;

2.   An arbitrator may subsequently decide issues that were submitted but not decided in the earlier award;

3.   The arbitrator may clarify an ambiguity in an award.

These exceptions are often interpreted expansively so that they can seem to swallow the *functus officio* doctrine altogether. The following cases demonstrate how courts are reaching to find exceptions to the doctrine and thereby permit arbitrators to modify their awards.

In *Colonial Penn Insurance Co. v. Omaha Indemnity Co.*, 943 F.2d 327 (3d Cir. 1991), an arbitration panel heard a case concerning indemnification under a reinsurance agreement. The panel awarded Colonial Penn a sum of $10 million in cash plus $8 million in the form of directing Omaha to release its claim to $8 million of Colonial Penn's reserves. Upon receipt of the award, counsel for Colonial Penn informed the arbitrator and the opposing counsel that the award contained a mistake. The award assumed that Colonial Penn held $8 million in reserve to which Omaha had a claim, when in fact there were no such reserves. The arbitrator agreed that the matter should be clarified, but opposing counsel responded that the award was clear and unambiguous as written. Despite Omaha's objection, the panel issued a revised award that deleted mention of the reserves and ordered Omaha to pay the additional $8 million outright. It also sent both parties a letter explaining that the original award was based on a mistaken assumption that Colonial Penn was holding some of Omaha's assets in reserves.

When Colonial Penn attempted to enforce the revised award, Omaha objected on grounds of *functus officio* and cross-motioned to enforce the initial award. The district court ruled for Colonial Penn. On appeal, the Third Circuit held that it was improper for an arbitration panel to impeach its own award. Further, it held that if there had been a mistake, it was not a "mistake on the face of the award," so that the mistake exception to the *functus officio* doctrine did not apply. It said:

> "The exception for mistakes apparent on the face of the award is applied to clerical mistakes or obvious errors in arithmetic computation. Possibly, it could also be applied in a situation where the award on its face is contrary to a fact so well known as to be subject to judicial notice, but we take no position on that here.

> In this case, it was not possible to tell from the face of the award either that Colonial Penn held no reserves to which Omaha might have a claim or that Omaha had not submitted a claim for any reserves allegedly held by Colonial Penn ... In extending the limited exception for mistakes apparent on the face of the award to a situation where extraneous facts must be considered, the district court opened a Pandora's box ... Parties could, under the guise of a mistake in fact, seek recourse directly from the arbitrators in an attempt to overturn an adverse award." Id. at 333.

After rejecting the application of the mistake exception to the *functus officio* doctrine, the appeals court nonetheless remanded the issue to the arbitrators. The court made an analogy to Sec. 11 of the FAA, which permits a court to modify or correct an award under certain narrowly defined circumstances. The court explained:

> "Although there is no explicit provision in the Act for such a remand, courts have uniformly stated that a remand to the arbitration panel is

appropriate in cases where the award is ambiguous.... [While] a remand that allows a court to reconsider the merits is not permissible, ... when the remedy awarded by the arbitrators is ambiguous, a remand for clarification of the intended meaning of an arbitration award is appropriate.... Such a remand avoids the court's misinterpretation of the award and is therefore more likely to give the parties the award for which they bargained....

"Unlike the exception to the *functus officio* doctrine which confines the arbitrators to correcting mistakes apparent on the face of the award, an ambiguity in the award for which the court may remand to the arbitrators may be shown not only from the face of the award but from an extraneous but objectively ascertainable fact." Id. at 334.

In *Clarendon National Insurance Co. v. TIG Co.*, 183 F.R.D. 112 (S.D.N.Y. 1998), the court took a different approach to the mistake exception to the *functus officio* doctrine. In a dispute between two insurance companies, an arbitration panel ruled for the plaintiff. However, the panel made an arithmetic error in its calculation of the award. The arbitrators subsequently corrected the error at the urging of Clarendon National Insurance, the party that was harmed by the error. TIG objected to the modification and moved to vacate it on the grounds of *functus officio*. The court found that the exception to the doctrine of *functus officio* for correcting a mistake of fact did not apply. It said:

"the exemption to the *functus officio* doctrine must be stretched beyond the mistake category, since although there was an obvious mathematical error that they intended to take into account but failed to do so in their original award, ... the error was not obvious on the face of the award." Id. at 116.

Nor did the court find that the arbitrator's revision of the award completed an incomplete award or clarified an ambiguous award. Nonetheless, the court enforced the modified award, stating the arbitrators had simply corrected a mathematical error. "The spirit and basic effect of the award was not modified." It stated:

"In cases like this one, the *functus officio* doctrine may simply have outlived its usefulness. Arbitrators should simply be permitted to correct errors—but only errors.... This holding in no way gives arbitrators carte blanche to alter any decision previously rendered." Id. at 117.

* * *

Questions

1. Why are courts resistant to permitting one party to attempt to convince an arbitrator to modify an award after it has been issued?

2. Without strict application of *functus officio*, how can a court determine whether one side has utilized improper pressures to induce an arbitrator to

modify an award? What kinds of evidence could the party opposing the modification proffer to establish that the arbitrator was improperly pressured? Can the opposing party subpoena the arbitrator to testify? What other kinds of evidence might be relevant?

3. Why is the mistake exception, in its original form, limited to mistakes evident from the face of the award? What problems arise once courts expand the exception to mistakes that require further evidence to discern?

4. It is sometimes the practice in labor arbitration for an arbitration panel to circulate a draft award to the parties before issuing a final one. This process is intended to enable parties to determine whether there are serious errors, omissions or ambiguities in the award that need to be corrected. Is this a practice that could obviate the problem posed by the preceding cases? What additional dangers might such an approach create?

5. In *Colonial Penn*, the court states that it has the power to order an arbitrator to reconsider an award on the grounds of mistake or ambiguity, even in circumstances in which arbitrator does not have the power to do so on its own initiative. Does the possibility of a court-ordered modification of an award create the same dangers that the *functus officio* doctrine attempts to address?

6. Should a court ever permit an arbitrator to modify an award for mistake over the objection of one of the parties? Under what circumstances? Which approach—that of *Colonial Penn* or of *Clarendon*—is the preferable means of determining whether to enforce such a modification?

---

12. REMEDIES IN ARBITRATION

While the issue of preliminary relief in arbitration has been considered as an element of due process protections for the arbitral hearing, here we address the issue of what types of remedies an arbitrator can issue. While courts have the power to award many types of remedies, including compensatory damages, consequential damages, punitive damages, attorney fees, and interest in appropriate cases, the remedy power of arbitrators is not so well established. One remedy that has generated considerable controversy in the field of arbitration is punitive damages. The cases that follow exemplify the conflicting views in this area.

* * *

Garrity v. Lyle Stuart, Inc.

40 N.Y.2d 354, 353 N.E.2d 793 (1976).

■ BREITEL, CHIEF JUDGE.

Plaintiff author brought this proceeding under CPLR 7510 to confirm an arbitration award granting her $45,000 in compensatory damages and $7,500 in punitive damages against defendant publishing company. Supreme Court confirmed the award. The Appellate Division affirmed, one Justice dissenting, and defendant appeals.

The issue is whether an arbitrator has the power to award punitive damages.

The order of the Appellate Division should be modified to vacate the award of punitive damages and otherwise affirmed. An arbitrator has no power to award punitive damages, even if agreed upon by the parties (Matter of Publishers' Ass'n of N.Y. City [Newspaper Union], 280 App.Div. 500, 504–506, 114 N.Y.S.2d 401, 404–406). Punitive damages is a sanction reserved to the State, a public policy of such magnitude as to call for judicial intrusion to prevent its contravention. Since enforcement of an award of punitive damages as a purely private remedy would violate strong public policy, an arbitrator's award which imposes punitive damages should be vacated.

Plaintiff is the author of two books published by defendant. While the publishing agreements between the parties contained broad arbitration clauses, neither of the agreements provided for the imposition of punitive damages in the event of breach.

A dispute arose between the parties and in December, 1971 plaintiff author brought an action for damages alleging fraudulent inducement, "gross" underpayment of royalties, and various "malicious" acts designed to harass her. That action is still pending.

In March, 1974, plaintiff brought a new action alleging that defendant had wrongfully withheld an additional $45,000 in royalties. Defendant moved for a stay pending arbitration, which was granted, and plaintiff demanded arbitration. The demand requested the $45,000 withheld royalties and punitive damages for defendant's alleged "malicious" withholding of royalties, which plaintiff contended was done to coerce her into withdrawing the 1971 action.

Defendant appeared at the arbitration hearing and raised objections concerning plaintiff's standing and the conduct of the arbitration hearing. Upon rejection of these objections by the arbitrators, defendant walked out.

After hearing testimony, and considering an "informal memorandum" on punitive damages submitted by plaintiff at their request, the arbitrators awarded plaintiff both compensatory and punitive damages. On plaintiff's motion to confirm the award, defendant objected upon the ground that the award of punitive damages was beyond the scope of the arbitrators' authority.

Arbitrators generally are not bound by principles of substantive law or rules of evidence, and thus error of law or fact will not justify vacatur of an award (see Matter of Associated Teachers of Huntington v. Board of Educ., 33 N.Y.2d 229, 235, 351 N.Y.S.2d 670, 674, 306 N.E.2d 791, 795, and cases cited). It is also true that arbitrators generally are free to fashion the remedy appropriate to the wrong, if they find one, but an authentic remedy is compensatory and measured by the harm caused and how it may be corrected (Matter of Staklinski [Pyramid Elec. Co.], 6 N.Y.2d 159, 163, 188

N.Y.S.2d 541, 542, 160 N.E.2d 78, 79; see Matter of Paver & Wildfoerster [Catholic High School Ass'n.], 38 N.Y.2d 669, 677, 382 N.Y.S.2d 22, 26, 345 N.E.2d 565, 569, and cases cited). These broad principles are tolerable so long as arbitrators are not thereby empowered to ride roughshod over strong policies in the law which control coercive private conduct and confine to the State and its courts the infliction of punitive sanctions on wrongdoers.

The court will vacate an award enforcing an illegal agreement or one violative of public policy.... Since enforcement of an award of punitive damages as a purely private remedy would violate public policy, an arbitrator's award which imposes punitive damages, even though agreed upon by the parties, should be vacated....

Matter of Associated Gen. Contrs., N.Y. State Chapter (Savin Bros.), 36 N.Y.2d 957 is inapposite. That case did not involve an award of punitive damages. Instead, the court permitted enforcement of an arbitration award of treble liquidated damages, amounting to a penalty, assessed however in accordance with the express terms of a trade association membership agreement. The court held that the public policy against permitting the awarding of penalties was not of "such magnitude as to call for judicial intrusion" (p. 959). In the instant case, however, there was no provision in the agreements permitting arbitrators to award liquidated damages or penalties. Indeed, the subject apparently had never ever been considered.

The prohibition against an arbitrator awarding punitive damages is based on strong public policy indeed. At law, on the civil side, in the absence of statute, punitive damages are available only in a limited number of instances ... As was stated in Walker v. Sheldon (supra): "[p]unitive or exemplary damages have been allowed in cases where the wrong complained of is morally culpable, or is actuated by evil and reprehensible motives, not only to punish the defendant but to deter him, as well as others who might otherwise be so prompted, from indulging in similar conduct in the future." It is a social exemplary "remedy", not a private compensatory remedy.

It has always been held that punitive damages are not available for mere breach of contract, for in such a case only a private wrong, and not a public right, is involved....

Even if the so-called "malicious" breach here involved would permit of the imposition of punitive damages by a court or jury, it was not the province of arbitrators to do so. Punitive sanctions are reserved to the State, surely a public policy "of such magnitude as to call for judicial intrusion" (Matter of Associated Gen. Contrs., N.Y. State Chapter [Savin Bros.], 36 N.Y.2d 957, 959) The evil of permitting an arbitrator whose selection is often restricted or manipulatable by the party in a superior bargaining position, to award punitive damages is that it displaces the court and the jury, and therefore the State, as the engine for imposing a social sanction. As was so wisely observed by Judge, then Mr. Justice, Bergan in Matter of Publishers' Ass'n of N.Y. City (Newspaper Union), 280 App.Div. 500, 503, supra:

"The trouble with an arbitration admitting a power to grant unlimited damages by way of punishment is that if the court treated such an award in the way arbitration awards are usually treated, and followed the award to the letter, it would amount to an unlimited draft upon judicial power. In the usual case, the court stops only to inquire if the award is authorized by the contract; is complete and final on its face; and if the proceeding was fairly conducted.

"Actual damage is measurable against some objective standard—the number of pounds, or days, or gallons or yards; but punitive damages take their shape from the subjective criteria involved in attitudes toward correction and reform, and courts do not accept readily the delegation of that kind of power. Where punitive damages have been allowed for those torts which are still regarded somewhat as public penal wrongs as well as actionable private wrongs, they have had rather close judicial supervision. If the usual rules were followed there would be no effective judicial supervision over punitive awards in arbitration."

The dissent appears to have recognized the danger in permitting an arbitrator in his discretion to award unlimited punitive damages. Thus, it notes that the award made here was neither "irrational" nor "unjust" ... Standards such as these are subjective and afford no practical guidelines for the arbitrator and little protection against abuse, and would, on the other hand, contrary to the sound development of arbitration law, permit the courts to supervise awards for their justness (cf. Lentine v. Fundaro, 29 N.Y.2d 382, 386).

Parties to arbitration agree to the substitution of a private tribunal for purposes of deciding their disputes without the expense, delay and rigidities of traditional courts. If arbitrators were allowed to impose punitive damages, the usefulness of arbitration would be destroyed. It would become a trap for the unwary given the eminently desirable freedom from judicial overview of law and facts. It would mean that the scope of determination by arbitrators, by the license to award punitive damages, would be both unpredictable and uncontrollable. It would lead to a Shylock principle of doing business without a Portia-like escape from the vise of a logic foreign to arbitration law.

In imposing penal sanctions in private arrangements, a tradition of the rule of law in organized society is violated. One purpose of the rule of law is to require that the use of coercion be controlled by the State (Kelsen, General Theory of Law and State, p. 21). In a highly developed commercial and economic society the use of private force is not the danger, but the uncontrolled use of coercive economic sanctions in private arrangements. For centuries the power to punish has been a monopoly of the State, and not that of any private individual (Kelsen, loc. cit., supra). The day is long past since barbaric man achieved redress by private punitive measures.

The parties never agreed or, for that matter, even considered punitive damages as a possible sanction for breach of the agreement (see dissenting opn. below by Mr. Justice Capozzoli, 48 A.D.2d 814, 370 N.Y.S.2d 6). Here there is no pretense of agreement, although plaintiff author argues feebly that the issue of punitive damages was "waived" by failure to object originally to the demands for punitive damages, but only later to the award. The law does not and should not permit private persons to submit themselves to punitive sanctions of the order reserved to the State. The freedom of contract does not embrace the freedom to punish, even by contract. On this view, there was no power to waive the limitations on privately assessed punitive damages and, of course, no power to agree to them by the failure to object to the demand for arbitration (cf. Brooklyn Sav. Bank v. O'Neil, 324 U.S. 697, 704, 65 S.Ct. 895, 900, 89 L.Ed. 1296, affg., 293 N.Y. 666, 56 N.E.2d 259 ["waiver" of right "charged or colored with the public interest" is ineffective]. . . .

Under common-law principles, there is eventual supervision of jury awards of punitive damages, in the singularly rare cases where it is permitted, by the trial court's power to change awards and by the Appellate Division's power to modify such awards [see Walker v. Sheldon, 10 N.Y.2d 401, 405, n. 3, 223 N.Y.S.2d 488, 491, 179 N.E.2d 497, 499, supra]. That the award of punitive damages in this case was quite modest is immaterial. Such a happenstance is not one on which to base a rule.

Accordingly, the order of the Appellate Division should be modified, without costs, to vacate so much of the award which imposes punitive damages, and otherwise affirmed.

■ GABRIELLI, JUDGE (dissenting).

. . . The basic issue presented for our determination is whether, in an arbitration proceeding brought pursuant to a contract containing a broad arbitration clause, an award of punitive damages is violative of public policy.

[In this case], the arbitrators awarded plaintiff $45,000 on her claim for royalties and $7,500 in punitive damages plus interest and fees. When plaintiff moved to confirm the award, defendant objected, for the first time, that an award of punitive damages is violative of public policy and beyond the scope of the authority of the arbitrators. Special Term confirmed the award and the Appellate Division upheld that determination. I would affirm.

In doing so, I would reject the notion that this award of punitive damages is violative of public policy. We have only recently treated with a somewhat similar argument in Matter of Associated Gen. Contrs., N.Y. State Chapter (Savin Bros.), 36 N.Y.2d 957. There we considered the effect of a public policy argument against penalty awards with respect to an arbitration commenced by a national trade association in the construction industry against one of its employer-members pursuant to the provisions of a broad arbitration clause contained in the association agreement. Specifically at issue was whether an arbitration award of treble liquidated damages, assessed in accordance with the express terms of the agreement, was enforceable. We held that since the arbitration was in consequence of a broad arbitration clause and concerned no third-party interests which could be said to transcend the concerns of the parties to the arbitration, there was present . . . "no question involving public policy of such magnitude as to call for judicial intrusion". . . .

The case at bar falls within the rationale and rule of the Associated Gen. Contrs. case. Controlling here, as there, is the fact that the arbitration clause is broad indeed; there are no third-party interests involved; and the public policy against punitive damages is not so commanding that the Legislature has found it necessary to embody that policy into law, especially one that would apply to all cases involving such damages irrespective of the amount sought, the relative size of the award, or the punishable actions of the parties. Or, put another way, the public policy which "favors the peaceful resolutions of disputes through arbitration" (Associated Gen. Contrs., supra, at p. 959, 373 N.Y.S.2d at p. 556, 335 N.E.2d at p. 859) outweighs the public policy disfavoring the assessment of punitive damages in this instance, where the unjustifiable conduct complained of is found to be with malice. I would conclude, therefore, that any public policy limiting punitive damage awards does not rise to that level of significance in this case as to require judicial intervention.

The majority would distinguish the Associated Gen. Contrs. case (supra) upon the thin ground that the enforcement of a treble liquidated damages clause which was applicable to numerous nationwide contracts that conceivably could have amounted to astronomical sums is not the equivalent of the enforcement of an award of penalty damages. However, as Mr. Justice Greenblott specifically stated for the majority below in that case, and in an opinion expressly approved by this court, the amount of damages therein computed in the arbitration bore *"no reasonable relationship to the amount of damages which may be sustained"* (emphasis added; 45 A.D.2d 136, 140, 356 N.Y.S.2d 374, 378); and a contract clause which is grossly disproportionate to the presumable damage or readily ascertainable loss is a penalty clause, irrespective of its label [Equitable Lbr. Corp. v. IPA Land Development Corp., 38 N.Y.2d 516, 521–522, 381 N.Y.S.2d 459, 462–463, 344 N.E.2d 391, 395–396]. . . .

An affirmance here would do no violence to precedents in this court. In at least two varied circumstances we have held that although public policy would bar a civil suit for relief, that same public policy was not of such overriding import as to preclude confirmation of an arbitration award (Matter of Staklinski [Pyramid Elec. Co.], 6 N.Y.2d 159, 188 N.Y.S.2d 541, 160 N.E.2d 78; Matter of Ruppert [Egelhofer], 3 N.Y.2d 576, 170 N.Y.S.2d 785, 148 N.E.2d 129). In Ruppert was permitted the enjoining of a work stoppage in a labor dispute by arbitration despite the fact that the issuance of such relief by a court was prohibited by statute (then Civil Practice Act, § 876—a). Similarly, in Staklinski, citing Ruppert, we upheld an arbitration award of specific performance of an employment contract in the face of the public policy against compelling a corporation to continue the services of an officer whose services were unsatisfactory to the board of directors. The rule to be distilled these cases, therefore, is that only where the public interest clearly supersedes the concerns of the parties should courts intervene and assert exclusive dominion over disputes in arbitration. . . .

Nor can we hold, as defendant also urges, that the arbitrators exceeded their authority in awarding punitive damages to plaintiff. Arbitrators are entitled to "do justice". It has been said that, short of "complete irrationality", "they may fashion the law to fit the facts before them" (Lentine v. Fundaro, 29 N.Y.2d 382, 386, 328 N.Y.S.2d 418, 422, 278 N.E.2d 633, 636).... The award made here was neither irrational nor unjust. Indeed, defendant has not denied that its actions were designed to harass and intimidate plaintiff, as she claimed and the arbitrators obviously concluded. Hence, the award was within the power vested in the arbitrator.

As we have noted, plaintiff sought punitive damages as listed and set forth in the demand for arbitration, presenting of course a threshold question to which defendant failed to respond and, in fact, summarily refused to address himself. In effect, therefore, defendant's failure to act, respond or contest the claim is tantamount to a waiver of any objection thereto and, indeed, is equivalent to an agreement to arbitrate the allegation now complained of.

Accordingly, the order of the Appellate Division should be affirmed.

■ JASEN, FUCHSBERG and COOKE, JJ., concur with BREITEL. C.J. GABRIELLI, J., dissents and votes to affirm in a separate opinion in which JONES and WACHTLER, JJ., concur.

* * *

Antonio Mastrobuono and Diana G. Mastrobuono v. Shearson Lehman Hutton, Inc.

514 U.S. 52, 115 S.Ct. 1212 (1995).

■ JUSTICE STEVENS delivered the opinion of the Court.

New York law allows courts, but not arbitrators, to award punitive damages. In a dispute arising out of a standard-form contract that expressly provides that it "shall be governed by the laws of the State of New York," a panel of arbitrators awarded punitive damages. The District Court and Court of Appeals disallowed that award. The question presented is whether the arbitrators' award is consistent with the central purpose of the Federal Arbitration Act to ensure "that private agreements to arbitrate are enforced according to their terms." Volt Information Sciences, Inc. v. Board of Trustees of Leland Stanford Junior Univ., 489 U.S. 468, 479, 109 S.Ct. 1248, 1256, 103 L.Ed.2d 488 (1989).

I

In 1985 petitioners, Antonio Mastrobuono, then an assistant professor of medieval literature, and his wife Diana Mastrobuono, an artist, opened a securities trading account with respondent Shearson Lehman Hutton, Inc. (Shearson), by executing Shearson's standard-form Client's Agreement. Respondent Nick DiMinico, a vice president of Shearson, managed the Mastrobuonos' account until they closed it in 1987. In 1989, petitioners filed this action in the United States District Court for the Northern District of Illinois, alleging that respondents had mishandled their account and claiming damages on a variety of state and federal law theories.

Paragraph 13 of the parties' agreement contains an arbitration provision and a choice-of-law provision. Relying on the arbitration provision and on §§ 3 and 4 of the Federal Arbitration Act (FAA), 9 U.S.C. §§ 3, 4, respondents filed a motion to stay the court proceedings and to compel arbitration pursuant to the rules of the National Association of Securities Dealers. The District Court granted that motion, and a panel of three arbitrators was convened. After conducting hearings in Illinois, the panel ruled in favor of petitioners.

In the arbitration proceedings, respondents argued that the arbitrators had no authority to award punitive damages. Nevertheless, the panel's award included punitive damages of $400,000, in addition to compensatory damages of $159,327. Respondents paid the compensatory portion of the award but filed a motion in the District Court to vacate the award of punitive damages. The District Court granted the motion, 812 F.Supp. 845 (ND Ill.1993), and the Court of Appeals for the Seventh Circuit affirmed. 20 F.3d 713 (1994). Both courts relied on the choice-of-law provision in paragraph 13 of the parties' agreement, which specifies that the contract shall be governed by New York law. Because the New York Court of Appeals has decided that in New York the power to award punitive damages is limited to judicial tribunals and may not be exercised by arbitrators, Garrity v. Lyle Stuart, Inc., 40 N.Y.2d 354, 386 N.Y.S.2d 831, 353 N.E.2d 793 (1976), the District Court and the Seventh Circuit held that the panel of arbitrators had no power to award punitive damages in this case.

We granted certiorari, 513 U.S. ___, 115 S.Ct. 305, 130 L.Ed.2d 218 (1994), because the Courts of Appeals have expressed differing views on whether a contractual choice-of-law provision may preclude an arbitral award of punitive damages that otherwise would be proper.... We now reverse.

II

Earlier this Term, we upheld the enforceability of a predispute arbitration agreement governed by Alabama law, even though an Alabama statute provides that arbitration agreements are unenforceable. Allied–Bruce Terminix Cos. v. Dobson, 513 U.S. ___, 115 S.Ct. 834, 130 L.Ed.2d 753 (1995). Writing for the Court, Justice Breyer observed that Congress passed the FAA "to overcome courts' refusals to enforce agreements to arbitrate." Id., at ___, 115 S.Ct. at 838. See also Volt Information Sciences, Inc. v. Board of Trustees of Leland Stanford Junior Univ., 489 U.S. at 474, 109 S.Ct. at 1253; Dean Witter Reynolds Inc. v. Byrd, 470 U.S. 213, 220, 105 S.Ct. 1238, 1242, 84 L.Ed.2d 158 (1985). After determining that the FAA applied to the parties' arbitration agreement, we readily concluded that the federal statute pre-empted Alabama's statutory prohibition. Allied–Bruce, 513 U.S., at 272–73, 281–82, 115 S.Ct. at 839, 843.

Petitioners seek a similar disposition of the case before us today. Here, the Seventh Circuit interpreted the contract to incorporate New York law, including the Garrity rule that arbitrators may not award punitive damages. Petitioners ask us to hold that the FAA pre-empts New York's prohibition against arbitral awards of punitive damages because this state law is a vestige of the " ' "ancient" ' " judicial hostility to arbitration. See Allied–Bruce, 513 U.S., at ——, 115 S.Ct. at 838, quoting Bernhardt v. Polygraphic Co. of America, Inc., 350 U.S. 198, 211, n. 5, 76 S.Ct. 273, 281, n. 5, 100 L.Ed. 199 (1956) (Frankfurter, J., concurring). Petitioners rely on Southland Corp. v. Keating, 465 U.S. 1, 104 S.Ct. 852, 79 L.Ed.2d 1 (1984), and Perry v. Thomas, 482 U.S. 483, 107 S.Ct. 2520, 96 L.Ed.2d 426 (1987), in which we held that the FAA pre-empted two California statutes that purported to require judicial resolution of certain disputes. In Southland, we explained that the FAA not only "declared a national policy favoring arbitration," but actually "withdrew the power of the states to require a judicial forum for the resolution of claims which the contracting parties agreed to resolve by arbitration." 465 U.S., at 10, 104 S.Ct. at 858.

Respondents answer that the choice-of-law provision in their contract evidences the parties' express agreement that punitive damages should not be awarded in the arbitration of any dispute arising under their contract. Thus, they claim, this case is distinguishable from Southland and Perry, in which the parties presumably desired unlimited arbitration but state law stood in their way. Regardless of whether the FAA pre-empts the Garrity decision in contracts not expressly incorporating New York law, respondents argue that the parties may themselves agree to be bound by Garrity, just as they may agree to forgo arbitration altogether. In other words, if the contract says "no punitive damages," that is the end of the matter, for courts are bound to interpret contracts in accordance with the expressed intentions of the parties—even if the effect of those intentions is to limit arbitration.

We have previously held that the FAA's pro-arbitration policy does not operate without regard to the wishes of the contracting parties. In Volt Information Sciences, Inc. v. Board of Trustees of Leland Stanford Junior Univ., 489 U.S. 468, 109 S.Ct., 1248, 103 L.Ed.2d 488 (1989), the California Court of Appeal had construed a contractual provision to mean that the parties intended the California rules of arbitration, rather than the FAA's rules, to govern the resolution of their dispute. Id., at 472, 109 S.Ct., at 1252. Noting that the California rules were "manifestly designed to encourage resort to the arbitral process," id., at 476, 109 S.Ct., at 1254, and that they "generally foster[ed] the federal policy favoring arbitration," id., at 476, n. 5, 109 S.Ct., at 1254 n. 5, we concluded that such an interpretation was entirely consistent with the federal policy "to ensure the enforceability, according to their terms, of private agreements to arbitrate." Id., at 476, 109 S.Ct., at 1254. After referring to the holdings in Southland and Perry, which struck down state laws limiting agreed-upon arbitrability, we added:

"But it does not follow that the FAA prevents the enforcement of agreements to arbitrate under different rules than those set forth in the Act itself. Indeed, such a result would be quite inimical to the FAA's primary purpose of ensuring that private agreements to arbitrate are enforced according to their terms. Arbitration under the Act is a matter of consent, not coercion, and parties are generally free to structure their arbitration agreements as they see fit. Just as they may limit by contract the issues which they will arbitrate, see Mitsubishi [v. Soler Chrysler–Plymouth, 473 U.S. 614, 628, 105 S.Ct. 3346, 3354–55, 87 L.Ed.2d 444 (1985)], so too may they specify by contract the rules under which that arbitration will be conducted." Volt, 489 U.S., at 479, 109 S.Ct., at 1256.

Relying on our reasoning in Volt, respondents thus argue that the parties to a contract may lawfully agree to limit the issues to be arbitrated by waiving any claim for punitive damages. On the other hand, we think our decisions in Allied–Bruce, Southland, and Perry make clear that if contracting parties agree to include claims for punitive damages within the issues to be arbitrated, the FAA ensures that their agreement will be enforced according to its terms even if a rule of state law would otherwise exclude such claims from arbitration. Thus, the case before us comes down to what the contract has to say about the arbitrability of petitioners' claim for punitive damages.

III

Shearson's standard-form "Client Agreement," which petitioners executed, contains 18 paragraphs. The two relevant provisions of the agreement are found in paragraph 13.[2] The first sentence of that paragraph provides, in part, that the entire agreement "shall be governed by the laws of the State of New York." App. to Pet. for Cert. 44. The second sentence provides that "any controversy" arising out of the transactions between the parties "shall be settled by arbitration" in accordance with the rules of the National Association of Securities Dealers (NASD), or the Boards of Directors of the New York Stock Exchange and/or the American Stock Exchange. Ibid. The agreement contains no express reference to claims for punitive damages. To ascertain whether Paragraph 13 expresses an intent to include or exclude such claims, we first address the impact of each of the two relevant provisions, considered separately. We then move on to the more important inquiry: the meaning of the two provisions taken together. See Restatement (Second) of Contracts § 202(2) (1979) ("A writing is interpreted as a whole").

---

2. Paragraph 13 of the Client's Agreement provides: "This agreement shall inure to the benefit of your [Shearson's] successors and assigns[,] shall be binding on the undersigned, my [petitioners'] heirs, executors, administrators and assigns, and shall be governed by the laws of the State of New York. Unless unenforceable due to federal or state law, any controversy arising out of or relating to [my] accounts, to transactions with you, your officers, directors, agents and/or employees for me or to this agreement or the breach thereof, shall be settled by arbitration in accordance with the rules then in effect, of the National Association of Securities Dealers, Inc. or the Boards of Directors of the New York Stock Exchange, Inc. and/or the American Stock Exchange Inc. as I may elect.... Judgment upon any award rendered by the arbitrators may be entered in any court have jurisdiction thereof...."

The choice-of-law provision, when viewed in isolation, may reasonably be read as merely a substitute for the conflict-of-laws analysis that otherwise would determine what law to apply to disputes arising out of the contractual relationship. Thus, if a similar contract, without a choice-of-law provision, had been signed in New York and was to be performed in New York, presumably "the laws of the State of New York" would apply, even though the contract did not expressly so state. In such event, there would be nothing in the contract that could possibly constitute evidence of an intent to exclude punitive damages claims. Accordingly, punitive damages would be allowed because, in the absence of contractual intent to the contrary, the FAA would pre-empt the Garrity rule. See supra, at 4.

Even if the reference to "the laws of the State of New York" is more than a substitute for ordinary conflict-of-laws analysis and, as respondents urge, includes the caveat, "detached from otherwise-applicable federal law," the provision might not preclude the award of punitive damages because New York allows its courts, though not its arbitrators, to enter such awards. See Garrity, 40 N.Y.2d, at 358, 386 N.Y.S.2d at 834, 353 N.E.2d, at 796. In other words, the provision might include only New York's substantive rights and obligations, and not the State's allocation of power between alternative tribunals. Respondents' argument is persuasive only if "New York law" means "New York decisional law, including that State's allocation of power between courts and arbitrators, notwithstanding otherwise-applicable federal law." But, as we have demonstrated, the provision need not be read so broadly. It is not, in itself, an unequivocal exclusion of punitive damages claims.[4]

The arbitration provision (the second sentence of Paragraph 13) does not improve respondents' argument. On the contrary, when read separately this clause strongly implies that an arbitral award of punitive damages is appropriate. It explicitly authorizes arbitration in accordance with NASD rules;[5] the panel of arbitrators in fact proceeded under that set of rules. The NASD's Code of Arbitration Procedure indicates that arbitrators may award "damages and other relief." NASD Code of Arbitration Procedure P

---

4. The dissent makes much of the similarity between this choice-of-law clause and the one in Volt, which we took to incorporate a California statute allowing a court to stay arbitration pending resolution of related litigation. In Volt, however, we did not interpret the contract de novo. Instead, we deferred to the California court's construction of its own state's law. 489 U.S., at 474, 109 S.Ct., at 1253 ("[T]he interpretation of private contracts is ordinarily a question of state law, which this Court does not sit to review"). In the present case, by contrast, we review a *federal* court's interpretation of this contract, and our interpretation accords with that of the only decision-maker arguably entitled to deference—the arbitrator. See n. 1, *supra*.

5. The contract also authorizes (at petitioners' election) that the arbitration be governed by the rules of the New York Stock Exchange or the American Stock Exchange, instead of those of the NASD. App. to Pet. for Cert. 44. Neither set of alternative rules purports to limit an arbitrator's discretion to award punitive damages. Moreover, even if there were any doubt as to the ability of an arbitrator to award punitive damages under the Exchanges' rules, the contract expressly allows petitioners, the claimants in this case, to choose NASD rules; and the panel of arbitrators in this case in fact proceeded under NASD rules.

3741(e) (1993). While not a clear authorization of punitive damages, this provision appears broad enough at least to contemplate such a remedy. Moreover, as the Seventh Circuit noted, a manual provided to NASD arbitrators contains this provision:

B. Punitive Damages "The issue of punitive damages may arise with great frequency in arbitrations. Parties to arbitration are informed that arbitrators can consider punitive damages as a remedy." 20 F.3d, at 717. Thus, the text of the arbitration clause itself surely does not support— indeed, it contradicts—the conclusion that the parties agreed to foreclose claims for punitive damages.[7]

Although neither the choice-of-law clause nor the arbitration clause, separately considered, expresses an intent to preclude an award of punitive damages, respondents argue that a fair reading of the entire Paragraph 13 leads to that conclusion. On this theory, even if "New York law" is ambiguous, and even if "arbitration in accordance with NASD rules" indicates that punitive damages are permissible, the juxtaposition of the two clauses suggests that the contract incorporates "New York law relating to arbitration." We disagree. At most, the choice-of-law clause introduces an ambiguity into an arbitration agreement that would otherwise allow punitive damages awards. As we pointed out in Volt, when a court interprets such provisions in an agreement covered by the FAA, "due regard must be given to the federal policy favoring arbitration, and ambiguities as to the scope of the arbitration clause itself resolved in favor of arbitration." 489 U.S., at 476, 109 S.Ct., at 1254. . . .

Moreover, respondents cannot overcome the common-law rule of contract interpretation that a court should construe ambiguous language against the interest of the party that drafted it. . . . Respondents drafted an ambiguous document, and they cannot now claim the benefit of the doubt. The reason for this rule is to protect the party who did not choose the language from an unintended or unfair result. That rationale is well-suited to the facts of this case. As a practical matter, it seems unlikely that petitioners were actually aware of New York's bifurcated approach to punitive damages, or that they had any idea that by signing a standard-form agreement to arbitrate disputes they might be giving up an important

---

7. "Were we to confine our analysis to the plain language of the arbitration clause, we would have little trouble concluding that a contract clause which bound the parties to 'settle' 'all disputes' through arbitration conducted according to rules which allow any form of 'just and equitable' 'remedy of relief' was sufficiently broad to encompass the award of punitive damages. Inasmuch as agreements to arbitrate are 'generously construed,' Mitsubishi Motors Corp. v. Soler Chrysler–Plymouth, [473 U.S. 614, 626, 105 S.Ct. 3346, 3353–54, 87 L.Ed.2d 444 (1985)], it would seem sensible to interpret the 'all disputes' and 'any remedy or relief' phrases to indicate, at a minimum, an intention to resolve through arbitration any dispute that would otherwise be settled in a court, and to allow the chosen dispute resolvers to award the same varieties and forms of damages or relief as a court would be empowered to award. Since courts are empowered to award punitive damages with respect to certain types of claims, the Raytheon–Automated arbitrators would be equally empowered." Raytheon Co. v. Automated Business Systems, Inc., 882 F.2d 6, 10 (C.A.1 1989).

substantive right. In the face of such doubt, we are unwilling to impute this intent to petitioners.

Finally the respondents' reading of the two clauses violates another cardinal principle of contract construction: that a document should be read to give effect to all its provisions and to render them consistent with each other.... Restatement (Second) of Contracts § 203(a) and Comment b § 202(5). We think the best way to harmonize the choice-of-law provision with the arbitration provision is to read "the laws of the State of New York" to encompass substantive principles that New York courts would apply, but not to include special rules limiting the authority of arbitrators. Thus, the choice-of-law provision covers the rights and duties of the parties, while the arbitration clause covers arbitration; neither sentence intrudes upon the other. In contrast, respondents' reading sets up the two clauses in conflict with one another: one foreclosing punitive damages, the other allowing them. This interpretation is untenable.

We hold that the Court of Appeals misinterpreted the parties' agreement. The arbitral award should have been enforced as within the scope of the contract. The judgment of the Court of Appeals is, therefore, reversed.

It is so ordered.

■ JUSTICE THOMAS, dissenting.

In Volt Information Sciences, Inc. v. Board of Trustees of Leland Stanford Junior University, 489 U.S. 468, 478, 109 S.Ct. 1248, 1255, 103 L.Ed.2d 488 (1989), we held that the Federal Arbitration Act (FAA) simply requires courts to enforce private contracts to arbitrate as they would normal contracts—according to their terms. This holding led us to enforce a choice-of-law provision that incorporated a state procedural rule concerning arbitration proceedings. Because the choice-of-law provision here cannot reasonably be distinguished from the one in Volt, I dissent.

I

A

In Volt, Stanford University had entered into a construction contract under which Volt Information Sciences, Inc. was to install certain electrical systems on the Stanford campus. The contract contained an agreement to arbitrate all disputes arising out of the contract. A choice-of-law clause in the contract provided that "[t]he Contract shall be governed by the law of the place where the Project is located," 489 U.S., at 470, 109 S.Ct., at 1254, which happened to be California. When a dispute arose regarding compensation, Volt invoked arbitration. Stanford filed an action in state court, however, and moved to stay arbitration pursuant to California rules of civil procedure. Cal.Civ.Proc.Code Ann. § 1281.2(c) (West 1982). Opposing the stay, Volt argued that the relevant state statute authorizing the stay was pre-empted by the FAA, 9 U.S.C. § 1 et seq.

We concluded that even if the FAA preempted the state statute as applied to other parties, the choice-of-law clause in the contract at issue demonstrated that the parties had agreed to be governed by the statute....

We so held in Volt because we concluded that the FAA does not force arbitration on parties who enter into contracts involving interstate commerce. Instead, the FAA requires only that "arbitration proceed in the manner provided for in [the parties'] agreement." 9 U.S.C. § 4....

B

In this case, as in Volt, the parties agreed to mandatory arbitration of all disputes. As in Volt, the contract at issue here includes a choice-of-law clause. Indeed, the language of the two clauses is functionally equivalent: whereas the choice-of-law clause in Volt provided that "[t]he Contract shall be governed by the law of [the State of California]," ... the one before us today states, in Paragraph 13 of the Client's Agreement, that "[t]his agreement ... shall be governed by the laws of the State of New York." New York law forbids arbitrators from awarding punitive damages, Garrity v. Lyle Stuart, Inc., 40 N.Y.2d 354, 386 N.Y.S.2d 831, 353 N.E.2d 793 (1976), and permits only courts to award such damages. As in Volt, petitioners here argue that the New York rule is "anti-arbitration," and hence is pre-empted by the FAA. In concluding that the choice-of-law clause is ambiguous, the majority essentially accepts petitioners' argument. Volt itself found precisely the same argument irrelevant, however, and the majority identifies no reason to think that the state law governing the interpretation of the parties' choice-of-law clause supports a different result.

The majority claims that the incorporation of New York law "need not be read so broadly" as to include both substantive and procedural law, and that the choice of New York law "is not, in itself, an unequivocal exclusion of punitive damages claims." Ante, at 1217. But we rejected these same arguments in Volt, and the Garrity rule is just the sort of "state rule[ ] governing the conduct of arbitration" that Volt requires federal courts to enforce. 489 U.S., at 476, 109 S.Ct., at 1254. "Just as [the parties] may limit by contract the issues which they will arbitrate, so too may they specify by contract the rules under which that arbitration will be conducted." Id., at 479, 109 S.Ct., at 1256 (citation omitted). To be sure, the majority might be correct that Garrity is a rule concerning the State's allocation of power between "alternative tribunals," ante, at 1217, although Garrity appears to describe itself as substantive New York law.[2] Nonetheless, Volt makes no distinction between rules that serve only to distribute authority between courts and arbitrators (which the majority finds unenforceable) and other types of rules (which the majority finds enforceable). Indeed, the California rule in Volt could be considered to be one that allocates authority between arbitrators and courts, for it permits California courts to stay arbitration pending resolution of related litigation. See Volt, 489 U.S., at 471, 109 S.Ct., at 1251–52.

---

2. The New York Court of Appeals rested its holding on the principle that punitive damages are exemplary social remedies intended to punish, rather than to compensate. Because the power to punish can rest only in the hands of the State, the Court found that private arbitrators could not wield the authority to impose such damages. Garrity, 386 N.Y.S.2d at 833–835, 353 N.E.2d, at 796–797.

II

The majority relies upon two assertions to defend its departure from Volt. First, it contends that "[a]t most, the choice-of-law clause introduces an ambiguity into an arbitration agreement." Ante, at 1218. We are told that the agreement "would otherwise allow punitive damages awards," because of Paragraph 13's statement that arbitration would be conducted "in accordance with the rules then in effect, of the National Association of Securities Dealers, Inc. [NASD]" It is unclear which NASD "rules" the parties mean, although I am willing to agree with the majority that the phrase refers to the NASD Code of Arbitration Procedure. But the provision of the NASD Code offered by the majority simply does not speak to the availability of punitive damages. It only states:

"The award shall contain the names of the parties, the name of counsel, if any, a summary of the issues, including the type(s) of any security or product, in controversy, the damages and other relief requested, the damages and other relief awarded, a statement of any other issues resolved, the names of the arbitrators, the dates the claim was filed and the award rendered, the number and dates of hearing sessions, the location of the hearings, and the signatures of the arbitrators concurring in the award." NASD Code of Arbitration Procedure § 41(e) (1985).

It is clear that § 41(e) does not define or limit the powers of the arbitrators; it merely describes the form in which the arbitrators must announce their decision. The other provisions of § 41 confirm this point. See, e.g., § 41(a) ("All awards shall be in writing and signed by a majority of the arbitrators . . ."); § 41(c) ("Director of Arbitration shall endeavor to serve a copy of the award" to the parties); § 41(d) (arbitrators should render an award within 30 days); § 41(f) (awards shall be "publicly available"). The majority cannot find a provision of the NASD Code that specifically addresses punitive damages, or that speaks more generally to the types of damages arbitrators may or may not allow. Such a rule simply does not exist. The Code certainly does not *require* that arbitrators be empowered to award punitive damages; it leaves to the parties to define the arbitrators' remedial powers.

The majority also purports to find a clear expression of the parties' agreement on the availability of punitive damages in "a manual provided to NASD arbitrators." Ante, at 1218. But Paragraph 13 of the Client Agreement nowhere mentions this manual; it mentions only "the rules then in effect of the [NASD]." The manual does not fit either part of this description: it is neither "of the [NASD]," nor a set of "rules."

First, the manual apparently is not an official NASD document. The manual was not promulgated or adopted by the NASD. Instead, it apparently was compiled by members of the Securities Industry Conference on Arbitration (SICA) as a supplement to the Uniform Code of Arbitration, which the parties clearly did not adopt in paragraph 13. Petitioners present no evidence that the NASD has a policy of giving this specific manual to its arbitrators. Nor do petitioners assert that this manual was even used in the arbitration that gave rise to this case. More importantly, there is no indication in the text of the Client's Agreement that the parties intended this manual to be used by the arbitrators.

Second, the manual does not provide any "rules" in the sense contemplated by Paragraph 13; instead, it provides general information and advice to the arbitrator, such as "Hints for the Chair." SICA, Arbitrator's Manual 21 (1992). The manual is nothing more than a sort of "how to" guide for the arbitrator. One bit of advice, for example, states: "Care should be exercised, particularly when questioning a witness, so that the arbitrator does not indicate disbelief. Grimaces, frowns, or hand signals should all be avoided. A 'poker' face is the goal." Id., at 19.

Even if the parties had intended to adopt the manual, it cannot be read to resolve the issue of punitive damages. When read in context, the portion of the SICA manual upon which the majority relies seems only to explain what punitive damages *are*, not to establish whether arbitrators have the authority to award them: "The issue of punitive damages may arise with great frequency in arbitrations. Parties to arbitration are informed that arbitrators can consider punitive damages as a remedy. Generally, in court proceedings, punitive damages consist of compensation in excess of actual damages and are awarded as a form of punishment against the wrongdoer. If punitive damages are awarded, the decision of the arbitrators should clearly specify what portion of the award is intended as punitive damages, and the arbitrators should consider referring to the authority on which they relied." Id., at 26–27. A glance at neighboring passages, which explain the purpose of "Compensatory/Actual Damages," "Injunctive Relief," "Interest," "Attorneys' Fees," and "Forum Fees," see id., at 26–29, confirms that the SICA manual does not even attempt to provide a standardized set of procedural rules.

. . . My examination of the Client Agreement, the choice-of-law provision, the NASD Code of Procedure, and the SICA manual demonstrates that the parties made their intent clear, but not in the way divined by the majority. New York law specifically precludes arbitrators from awarding punitive damages, and it should be clear that there is no "conflict," as the majority puts it, between the New York law and the NASD rules. The choice-of-law provision speaks directly to the issue, while the NASD Code is silent. Giving effect to every provision of the contract requires us to honor the parties' intent, as indicated in the text of the agreement, to preclude the award of punitive damages by arbitrators . . .

* * *

Questions

1. Should arbitrators have the power to award punitive damages? What are the arguments for and against such a result?

2. How convincingly does the majority in *Mastrobuono* distinguish *Volt*? What weight should a court give to a choice of law clause? Can a court limit the application of a choice of law clause to the chosen forum's "substantive

principles'' and not include ''special rules limiting the authority of arbitrators?'' How can it know which is which? Or, should the court presume that the parties have chosen every aspect of the law of the selected forum?

3. Suppose parties have a contract that includes a choice of law clause naming a state that permits punitive damages in arbitration, and the contract also incorporates by reference a trade association arbitration procedure that specifies that there shall be no punitive damages in arbitration. If an arbitrator then awards punitive damages in a dispute arising from the contract, should a federal court vacate or affirm the award?

4. To what extent does the Supreme Court's reasoning in *Mastrobuono* turn on the contracting parties' lack of foresight and knowledge? Is this approach consistent with the Court's approach in *First Options*? Is it consistent with the approach in *Allied-Bruce Terminex*? Would such an approach change the result in the cases concerning the presence or absence of consent to arbitration clauses?

* * *

13.   ARBITRAL AWARDS AND CLAIM PRECLUSION

Vazquez v. Aetna Casualty & Surety Company

112 Misc.2d 125, 446 N.Y.S.2d 176 (N.Y.City Civ. Ct. 1982).

■ BENJAMIN F. NOLAN, JUDGE.

On February 16, 1979, plaintiff brought this action pursuant to Article 18 of the Insurance Law to recover No Fault benefits plus statutory interest and reasonable attorney fees because after a timely application had been made and appropriate proofs furnished defendant insurance carrier (Aetna) failed to pay him $3,422.50 in hospital and doctor expenses incurred when he sustained personal injuries in an accident on October 23, 1977, resulting from the use and operation of a motor vehicle covered for liability by a policy of insurance issued by Aetna.

Aetna's Answer alleged as a first affirmative defense that at the time this action was commenced there was another suit pending for a portion of the claim underlying this action. That suit was for $1,271.50 in hospital expenses incurred by plaintiff when he was a patient at the Whitestone General Hospital after the accident. The suit was brought against Aetna by the Whitestone General Hospital in a No Fault arbitration proceeding (AAA Case No. 13–6–21150–780) under an assignment executed by plaintiff while he was a patient at the Whitestone General Hospital.

In a second affirmative defense, Aetna denied coverage, alleging that the motor vehicle involved in the accident was a replacement for the insured vehicle and had not as yet been lawfully registered with the Department of Motor Vehicles at the time of the accident.

On May 25, 1979, an award was rendered in the no-fault arbitration proceeding in favor of the Whitestone General Hospital against Aetna. Thereafter, Aetna brought a proceeding in the New York County Supreme Court (Aetna Casualty & Surety Company v. Whitestone General Hospital, Index No. 16424/79) to vacate the arbitration award. In an order entered on October 2, 1979, the Supreme Court dismissed the Petition and confirmed the award.

Thereafter, plaintiff moved in this court to dismiss both of the affirmative defenses. By order, dated January 10, 1980, another Civil Court Judge struck the first affirmative defense holding that the "hospital form which was signed by plaintiff.... does not constitute an assignment to the hospital" and that since "plaintiff is not a party to the arbitration proceeding.... the outcome thereof is not binding on the plaintiff and does not compromise his claim against the Aetna policy." The Civil Court Judge refused to strike the second affirmative defense, saying that "a factual issue is posed as to whether the language of (Aetna's) disclaimer of coverage.... is consistent with the language of its second affirmative defense." On appeal, Appellate Term, First Department, in Vazquez v. Aetna Casualty & Surety Company, New York Law Journal, January 27, 1981, upheld the assignment, saying: "We construe the hospital insurance form executed by plaintiff, authorizing payment directly to the hospital of group insurance benefits 'otherwise payable' to him, as an assignment of first party benefits due plaintiff as a covered person under the subject policy and the Comprehensive Auto Insurance Reparations Act (Insurance Law, Sec. 671, subds. 2, 10). It is a routine practice for hospitals and other health care providers to take assignments to protect their bills for services rendered, and this is manifestly what was intended here; in fact, the regulations of the Department of Insurance authorize insurers to pay no-fault benefits directly to the providers of services 'upon assignment' (11 NYCRR 65.6(i)(1), 65.15(i)(1). Generally, the assignee of a claim is the real party in interest; and he alone can bring suit; the assignor loses control over the chose when he makes the assignment (6 N.Y.Jur.2d, Assignments, Sec. 71). And it has been expressly held that assignees of claims for first party benefits under the no-fault law may avail themselves of the right their assignors had to arbitrate disputed claims (Matter of Rosenblum, 41 N.Y.2d 966, 394 N.Y.S.2d 879, 363 N.E.2d 585). Under certain circumstances, an insured who has given assignments to various health care providers has been permitted to arbitrate liability questions himself because his own interest outweighed that of any single assignee (Central General Hospital v. American Arbitration Association, 91 Misc.2d 516, 398 N.Y.S.2d 198). But where the assignee has proceeded to arbitration first, and that proceeding is not stayed, and an award is thereafter made and confirmed, it is too late for the insured to relitigate the same claim in his own action. Moreover, only one claim exists for the hospital bill, and we are informed that the claim has been satisfied in full. If plaintiff's assignee has already recovered the full amount of its bill, justice dictates that no recovery be allowed."

Plaintiff now moves for summary judgment, seeking judgment for $2,151.00, which is the balance of the original claim for $3,422.50 after reduction by the $1,271.50 in hospital expenses which Appellate Term held to have been validly assigned by plaintiff to the Whitestone General Hospital and which was the subject of the award in arbitration. Plaintiff contends that he is entitled to summary judgment because all of the facts are either admitted or documented in the moving papers and not contradicted in the opposing affirmation. He further claims that he is also entitled to summary judgment on the theory of collateral estoppel because the no-fault arbitration award and the confirmation thereof in the Supreme Court conclusively determined the issues in this case in his favor.

The issues of liability and coverage are identical in both lawsuits. Aetna is the defendant in each. The claims in both are part of plaintiff's claim for all of the hospital and medical expenses he incurred in the same motor vehicle accident. In the arbitration proceeding, plaintiff's assignee sued for payment of a portion of plaintiff's claim. In the case at bar, plaintiff now seeks summary judgment for the balance of his claim. If plaintiff had not assigned a portion of his claim to the Whitestone General Hospital, there would have been no arbitration proceeding, since the entirety of plaintiff's claim would have been disposed of in the case at bar.

In opposing this motion, Aetna relies upon the recent Court of Appeals decision in Gilberg v. Barbieri, 53 N.Y.2d 285, 441 N.Y.S.2d 49, 423 N.E.2d 807 where collateral estoppel effect was denied. But, Gilberg has to be distinguished from the case at bar because the earlier case in Gilberg was a criminal action.... Equally unavailing is Aetna's contention that collateral estoppel must be denied when the parties in both proceedings are not identical. That theory, known as mutuality of estoppel, used to be the law in this State, but the Court of Appeals eventually did away with it (Schwartz v. Public Administrator of County of Bronx, 24 N.Y.2d 65 ...) Now, the party asserting the applicability of collateral estoppel must show that there is an identity of issues between the two actions "despite the apparent difference in parties" (Gerson–Ogden, Inc. v. Tempo Communications, Inc., Appellate Division, First Department, New York Law Journal, December 17, 1981), but it must nevertheless be shown that "the non-party against whom the finding would be used has such a relationship ... in the proceeding that it can be said that the two are in privity" (Baldwin v. Brooks, 83 A.D.2d 85, 87, 443 N.Y.S.2d 906 ...). Here, the defendant (Aetna) is the identical party against which the award was rendered in the arbitration, and, in fact, even the plaintiff in this action is in privity with his assignee who sued and won the award in the earlier No–Fault arbitration proceeding....

Collateral estoppel is applicable to issues resolved by arbitration ... A No Fault arbitrator's award is entitled to the same collateral estoppel effect as other arbitration awards.... Moreover, they need not be confirmed or reduced to judgment before they will be accorded such respect.... Of course, where the award has been confirmed in a Supreme Court challenge, (as was done herein) it is entitled to even greater respect. A judgment entered upon an arbitration is a judgment upon the merits ... although, in determining whether to give that determination conclusive (collateral estoppel) effect, the court has the power to say whether Schwartz standards have been violated....

Collateral estoppel may be applied offensively as well as defensively ... although there is a line of personal injury negligence cases in which collateral estoppel effect has been denied to *favorable* awards in earlier no-fault arbitration proceedings due to the complexities of parties and subtle differences in issues ... The case at bar is not a personal injury negligence action; it is, instead, an action by an insured to recover no-fault first party benefits from an insurer as an indemnitor under contract provisions mandated by the insurance law. There is no obstacle to the application of collateral effect to the earlier favorable arbitration award, since the defendant and the issue in both are identical, as long as defendant Aetna had a full and fair opportunity to litigate the issue in the arbitration proceeding.

On this motion, defendant argues that it did not have a full and fair opportunity to litigate the determination in the prior arbitration proceeding because it concluded that the arbitration proceeding was a minor matter, that it did not have any statutory or constitutional right to insist upon a rigid application of the rules of evidence, and that this court could reasonably expect that it did not defend in arbitration as vigorously as it should have. This assertion is made in conclusory fashion, unsupported by any evidentiary proofs. In fact, the precise words used by Aetna have been extracted verbatim from the opinion of the Court of Appeals in Gilberg v. Barbieri, supra, 53 N.Y.2d at p. 293, 441 N.Y.S.2d 49, 423 N.E.2d 807. The conclusions embodied in those words were justified in that case because of the existence of factors very much different from those in the case at bar. In Gilberg, the earlier case was a criminal action, the parties and issues were not identical, and the tests of Schwartz v. Public Administrator, supra, were not met. But where, as here, the parties are identical or in privity and the issues are identical in both proceedings, this court has a right to regard Aetna's argument herein with the same disdain that the Court of Appeals did in American Ins. Co. v. Messinger, supra, 43 N.Y.2d p. 192, 401 N.Y.S.2d 36, 371 N.E.2d 798, where it said: "The suggestion is that because Aetna may not have really tried in the first arbitration, it should not be bound by the resulting award. This ... is an unpersuasive and unattractive argument in a situation of issue preclusion between the same parties. We cannot visualize acceptance, for instance, of the conceptually parallel argument that a party against whom partial summary judgment has been granted in one action should be relieved of its consequences in a second action between the same parties because, lacking incentive in the first action, that party put up only a halfhearted defense and submitted nothing but its file and an incomplete or even sloppy affidavit in opposition to the motion. *The consequences of issue preclusion between the same parties are not to be vitiated by lack of enthusiasm or effort on the part of the loser.*" (Emphasis supplied). Basically, collateral estoppel applies to all issues litigated or which *might have been litigated* so long as the party in the prior proceeding had a full opportunity to establish his position.... In opposing plaintiff's motion, it is defendant Aetna's burden to submit evidentiary proof that it did not have a full and fair opportunity to litigate in the earlier arbitration proceeding the issue sought to be given collateral estoppel effect in this case. (Zuckerman v. City of New York, 49 N.Y.2d 557, 427 N.Y.S.2d 595, 404 N.E.2d 718), just as it is plaintiff's burden to show that the issue in both proceedings is identical and was necessarily decided in the arbitration proceeding (DeWitt v. Hall, supra).

Aetna's policy of insurance, as originally written, covered a Chevrolet motor vehicle owned by one, Sonia Vazquez. On October 21, 1977, the owner sold the Chevrolet and purchased a Cadillac as a replacement vehicle. On the same day, the owner submitted to her broker a policy change request for the replacement vehicle, and the broker gave her a temporary insurance identification card which specifically indicated that coverage of the replacement vehicle was "effective in accordance with the provision of (Aetna's) policy." Also, on that same day, the owner obtained a temporary registration for the replacement vehicle from the Department of Motor Vehicles. Two days later, on October 23, 1977, plaintiff was involved in a motor vehicle accident while operating the replacement vehicle. At the time of the accident, a permanent registration had not as yet been issued for the replacement vehicle. Plaintiff's suit herein is for reimbursement for the hospital and medical expenses he incurred as a result of that motor vehicle accident.

Aetna refused to pay plaintiff's claim, arguing that the broker had no right to bind it and was not its agent; and further, that the New York Automobile Insurance Plan for assigned risks, which was operative at the time of the accident, provides that coverage is not effective until the issuance of a permanent registration for the replacement vehicle.

The No–Fault arbitrator found that Aetna was responsible for bearing the burden of plaintiff's claim. In his written opinion, the arbitrator stated that, "at the time of the accident the owner had an insurance card with Aetna listed as insurer"; that, there was "no production of the broker or owner by Aetna"; that, "the New York Automobile Plan states that coverage shall be effective in accordance with the provisions of the policy or upon the issuance of a *legal* registration. . . . whichever is earlier"; that, "the policy provisions were *not* put in evidence"; and that, "although respondent Aetna argued that coverage is effective upon issuance of a 'permanent registration' the plan says 'legal registration' and nothing has been submitted to support the view that a temporary registration is not a legal registration." When Aetna thereafter appealed the arbitrator's determination, the Supreme Court rejected Aetna's challenge and confirmed the arbitration award, saying: "The arbitrator's opinion sets forth many grounds for his conclusion, and has shown a rational basis for his determination." Aetna did not appeal further.

Aetna also contends that it did not have a full opportunity to litigate in arbitration because the rules of evidence there were extremely liberal. In other words, having had a greater than usual opportunity to present evidence, Aetna now argues that it should not be conclusively bound by its failure to offer in evidence its own insurance policy which was under its control and which it could have presented but saw fit not to present. Besides being incredible on its face, this contention gives rise to the suspicion that had the policy been placed in evidence it would not have aided Aetna—a suspicion which becomes fact upon examination of the copy of Aetna's insurance policy which is attached to plaintiff's moving affirmation as Exhibit "H", and was supplied to plaintiff by Aetna under earlier discovery proceedings in this lawsuit.

[The court finds that Aetna's New York Automobile Insurance Plan, Section 11, subsection 3, relating to the coverage of replacement vehicles, states that "coverage shall be effective in accordance with the provisions of the policy or upon the issuance of a legal registration by a New York Motor Vehicle issuing office *whichever is earlier*." (emphasis supplied). The court concludes from this provision that "the replacement vehicle involved in the accident was covered pursuant to the terms of the policy upon its acquisition by the insured, and was thus insured under the Aetna policy at the time of plaintiff's accident."]

In Schwartz v. Public Administrator, supra, 24 N.Y.2d p. 72, 298 N.Y.S.2d 955, 246 N.E.2d 725, the Court of Appeals said: "A comprehensive list of the various factors which should enter into a determination whether a party has had his day in court would include such considerations as the size of the claim, the forum of the prior litigation, the use of initiative, the extent of the litigation, the competence and experience of counsel, the availability of new evidence, indications of a compromise verdict, differences in the applicable law and foreseeability of future litigation."

There is a reasonable relationship between the size of the claim ($1271.50) in arbitration and the claim of $2151.00 in this action. From the precedents cited, supra, it is clear that No Fault arbitration was an appropriate forum to produce an award capable of being given collateral effect in this action. Initiative was satisfactorily demonstrated, and the issues sufficiently litigated in the arbitration, as noted in the arbitrator's opinion and the Supreme Court confirmation. Aetna's counsel in the arbitration is the same counsel who prosecuted the Supreme Court challenge and is the same counsel who defends for Aetna in the case at bar. He is competent and experienced in this special area of the law. New evidence is not raised as an issue, and since there was no jury, a compromise verdict was not a possibility. The applicable law is identical in both proceedings. Finally, future litigation was foreseeable because this action had already been commenced against Aetna when plaintiff's assignee brought suit against Aetna in the No–Fault arbitration. Clearly, Schwartz standards were not violated.

Accordingly, the award in arbitration is entitled to collateral estoppel effect and shall be applied conclusively to this action; so that, plaintiff's motion for summary judgment is granted. But, apart from collateral estoppel, plaintiff is entitled to summary judgment because the proofs which defendant submitted were not sufficient to defeat this motion. The record reflects that all issues of fact have been admitted, are documented, or are uncontradicted, and all issues of law are resolved in favor of plaintiff, so that, there is no longer any defense to this action and no need for a trial. . . .

* * *

Note on *McDonald v. City of West Branch*

In MCDONALD V. CITY OF WEST BRANCH, MICHIGAN, 466 U.S. 284 (1984), the Supreme Court considered whether a federal court may accord preclusive effect to an arbitration award that was not appealed. The question was posed in the case brought under Title 42 U.S.C. § 1983, which provides:

> "Every person who, under color of any statute, ordinance, regulation, custom, or usage, of any State ... subjects, or causes to be subjected, any citizen of the United States or other person within the jurisdiction thereof to the deprivation of any rights, privileges, or immunities secured by the Constitution and laws, shall be liable to the party injured in an action at law, suit in equity, or other proper proceeding for redress."

The Court of Appeals for the Sixth Circuit held that arbitration awards preclude subsequent lawsuits. The Supreme Court, in an opinion by Justice Brennan, reversed.

The plaintiff, a police officer, was discharged. He filed a grievance pursuant to the collective-bargaining agreement then in force between West Branch and the United Steelworkers of America (the Union), contending that there was "no proper cause" for his discharge, and that, as a result, the discharge violated the collective-bargaining agreement. After the preliminary steps in the contractual grievance procedure had been exhausted, the grievance was taken to arbitration. The arbitrator ruled against McDonald, however, finding that there was just cause for his discharge.

McDonald did not appeal the arbitrator's decision. Instead, he filed a § 1983 action against the city of West Branch and certain of its officials, alleging he had been discharged for exercising his First Amendment rights of freedom of speech, freedom of association, and freedom to petition the government for redress of grievances. The case was tried before a jury which returned a verdict in favor of all but one of the defendants, Chief of Police Longstreet.

On appeal, the Court of Appeals for the Sixth Circuit reversed the judgment against Longstreet, the one remaining defendant,. 709 F.2d 1505 (6th Cir.1983). The court reasoned that the parties had agreed to settle their disputes through the arbitration process and that the arbitrator had considered the reasons for McDonald's discharge. Finding that the arbitration process had not been abused, the Court of Appeals concluded that McDonald's First Amendment claims were barred by res judicata and collateral estoppel.

The Supreme Court accepted certiorari and reversed. It stated:

"At the outset, we must consider whether federal courts are obligated by statute to accord res judicata or collateral-estoppel effect to the arbitrator's decision. Respondents contend that the Federal Full Faith and Credit Statute, 28 U.S.C. § 1738, requires that we give preclusive effect to the arbitration award.

"Our cases establish that § 1738 obliges federal courts to give the same preclusive effect to a state-court judgment as would the courts of the State rendering the judgment.... As we explained in Kremer, however, '[a]rbitration decisions ... are not subject to the mandate of § 1738.' Id., at 477, 102 S.Ct., at 1894. This conclusion follows from the plain language of § 1738 which provides in pertinent part that the '*judicial proceedings* [of any court of any State] shall have the same full faith and credit in every court within the United States and its Territories and Possessions as they have by law or usage in the courts of such State ... from which they are taken.' (Emphasis added.) Arbitration is not a 'judicial proceeding' and, therefore, § 1738 does not apply to arbitration awards.

"Because federal courts are not required by statute to give res judicata or collateral-estoppel effect to an unappealed arbitration award, any rule of preclusion would necessarily be judicially fashioned. We therefore consider the question whether it was appropriate for the Court of Appeals to fashion such a rule.

"On two previous occasions this Court has considered the contention that an award in an arbitration proceeding brought pursuant to a collective-bargaining agreement should preclude a subsequent suit in federal court. In both instances we rejected the claim.

"*Alexander v. Gardner–Denver Co.*, 415 U.S. 36, 94 S.Ct. 1011, 39 L.Ed.2d 147 (1974), was an action under Title VII of the Civil Rights Act of 1964 brought by an employee who had unsuccessfully claimed in an arbitration proceeding that his discharge was racially motivated. Although Alexander protested the same discharge in the Title VII action, we held that his Title VII claim was not foreclosed by the arbitral decision against him. In addition, we declined to adopt a rule that would have required federal courts to defer to an arbitrator's decision on a discrimination claim when '(i) the claim was before the arbitrator; (ii) the collective-bargaining agreement prohibited the form of discrimination charged in the suit under Title VII; and (iii) the arbitrator has authority to rule on the claim and to fashion a remedy.' Id., at 55–56, 94 S.Ct., at 1023.

"Similarly, in *Barrentine v. Arkansas–Best Freight System, Inc.*, 450 U.S. 728, 101 S.Ct. 1437, 67 L.Ed.2d 641 (1981), Barrentine and a fellow employee had unsuccessfully submitted wage claims to arbitration. Nevertheless, we rejected the contention that the arbitration award precluded a subsequent suit based on the same underlying facts alleging a violation of the minimum wage provisions of the Fair Labor Standards Act. Id., at 745–746, 101 S.Ct., at 1447.

"Our rejection of a rule of preclusion in *Barrentine* and our rejection of a rule of deferral in *Gardner–Denver* were based in large part on our conclusion that Congress intended the statutes at issue in those cases to be judicially enforceable and that arbitration could not provide an adequate substitute for judicial proceedings in adjudicating claims under those statutes. 450 U.S., at 740–746, 101 S.Ct., at 1444–1447; 415 U.S., at 56–60, 94 S.Ct., at 1023–25. These considerations similarly require that we find the doctrines of res judicata and collateral estoppel inapplicable in this § 1983 action.

"[A]lthough arbitration is well suited to resolving contractual disputes, our decisions in *Barrentine* and *Gardner–Denver* compel the conclusion that it cannot provide an adequate substitute for a judicial proceeding in protecting the federal statutory and constitutional rights that § 1983 is designed to safeguard. As a result, according preclusive effect to an arbitration award in a subsequent § 1983 action would undermine that statute's efficacy in protecting federal rights."

* * *

Questions

1. Under what circumstances will an arbitral award be given collateral estoppel effect? How can we distinguish *Vasquez* and *McDonald*? Can the difference in outcomes be explained by the fact that the arbitration award in *Vasquez* was appealed and affirmed by a court whereas the award in *McDonald* was not? Or do you think a New York court would have accorded preclusive effect to the award in *Vasquez* even if it had not been appealed? Can the cases be distinguished on the basis of the underlying right involved—that arbitral awards in civil rights cases are not preclusive but those in ordinary insurance cases are? What would be the principled basis for such a distinction?

2. Can *McDonald* and *Vasquez* be distinguished on the grounds that *McDonald* involved a federal cause of action but *Vasquez* involved a state cause of action? Would such a distinction be consistent with *Southland* and *Perry's* admonition that state arbitration-specific doctrines are preempted by the FAA?

* * *

CHAPTER EIGHT

ALTERNATIVE DISPUTE RESOLUTION WITHIN THE STATE AND FEDERAL COURTS

1. INTRODUCTION

In recent decades, many state legislatures and some federal courts have introduced alternative dispute resolution programs into their judicial systems. Some of these programs began as experimental efforts to reduce court congestion. Others were efforts to provide a mechanism for resolving small stakes disputes between neighbors or between landlords and tenants—disputes for which litigation had become too expensive, too time-consuming, and too rigid in its remedies.

Court-connected ADR programs take a variety of forms. They include mandatory pre-trial conferences to explore settlement options in the presence of a judge, and systems of early neutral evaluation, in which a neutral is assigned to evaluate the merits of a dispute prior to the commencement of discovery or motion practice. Some states have gone even further in the direction of incorporating ADR techniques developed in the private sector. In 1958, Pennsylvania became the first state to require parties in cases involving small sums to submit their disputes to a court-appointed arbitrator before permitting the case to be heard at trial. In 1970, New York and Ohio enacted legislation to the same effect. By 1995, twenty-five states had adopted court-ordered arbitration programs.[1] In the 1990s, several federal district courts followed suit, and since then the practice has spread in both state and federal courts.

Today court-ordered arbitration has became a prominent feature of the civil litigation system. In addition to court-ordered arbitration, some state courts have begun requiring parties in certain types of cases to meet with a court-appointed mediator prior to coming to trial. And recently some state and federal courts have experimented with other forms of alternative dispute resolution, such as summary jury trials, private judging, and other such techniques.

The use of court-ordered ADR is usually justified on the basis of efficiency. Supporters claim that it promotes settlement of pending cases, and thus it relieves over-crowded dockets and conserves judicial resources

---

[1]. For an overview of the growth of court-annexed arbitration in state courts, see John P. McIver & Susan Keilitz, *Court-Annexed Arbitration: An Introduction*, 14 THE JUSTICE SYSTEM JOURNAL 123 (1991).

for the cases where they are needed most. Some also claim that parties themselves are more satisfied with results obtained with ADR than with a conventional trial.[2] However, these empirical claims have not yet been validated. Some scholars have challenged the implicit assumption that court-ordered ADR leads to more settlements, or better settlements, than the normal civil justice system. Kim Dayton analyzed empirical data comparing federal districts that used mandatory arbitration with those that did not, and found that "ADR districts are not more efficient or effective in addressing their caseloads as a result of using ADR when compared with peer districts."[3] Lisa Bernstein used a simulated model of litigation processes with and without court-ordered arbitration and concluded that "when both parties are overly optimistic, the most common cause of failure to settle, court-annexed arbitration programs may actually reduce the likelihood of pre-trial settlement."[4] Despite questions about the efficiency and other alleged benefits of court-annexed ADR, the programs have expanded at a great pace. By 1991 it was reported that "40 percent of federal district courts and nearly half the circuits have enacted formal ADR rules."[5]

As court-ordered ADR programs have expanded, courts have been called upon to balance the systemic efficiency-enhancing goals against the rights of parties to receive a fair hearing for their legitimate legal claims. The cases and materials that follow discuss many of the legal issues that have arisen in relation to the use of compulsory, or court-connected, alternative dispute resolution.

2. SMALL CLAIMS COURTS

While the recent development of court-annexed mediation, court-ordered arbitration and other forms of court-connected ADR represent an innovation in civil litigation, alternative dispute resolution first entered the U.S. judicial system almost one hundred years ago in the form of small claims courts. Small claims courts were set up in the early years of the twentieth century in response to concerns expressed by legal reformers and leaders of the bar that the legal system ill-served the poor.[1] For example,

2. See, e.g., Wayne D. Brazil, *A Close Look at Three Court–Sponsored ADR Programs: Why They Exist, How They Operate, What They Deliver, and Whether They Threaten Important Values*, 1990 U. CHI. LEGAL F. 303; John L. Barkai & Gene Kassebaum, *Using Court–Annexed Arbitration to Reduce Litigant Costs and to Increase the Pace of Litigation*, 16 PEPP. L. REV. S43 (1989).

3. Kim Dayton, *The Myth of Alternative Dispute Resolution in the Federal Courts*, 76 IOWA L. REV. 889, 924 (1991).

4. Lisa Bernstein, *Understanding the Limits of Court–Connected ADR: A Critique of Federal Court–Annexed Arbitration Programs*, 141 PENN. L. REV. 2169, 2176 (1993).

5. James F. Henry, *No Longer a Rarity, Judicial ADR is Preparing for Great Growth—But Much Care is Needed*, 9 ALTERNATIVES 95, 95 (1991).

1. For an excellent, concise history of the small claims movement, see Barbara Yngvesson & Patricia Hennessey, *Small Claims, Complex Disputes: A Review of the Small Claims Literature*, 9 LAW & SOC. REV. 219, 221–228 (1975).

Elihu Root, President of the American Bar Association, noted in his 1916 Presidential Address that "There is no country in the world in which the doing of justice is burdened by such heavy overhead charges or in which so great a force is maintained for a given amount of litigation." Echoing this theme, Austin Scott of Harvard Law School wrote in 1923 that:

> There are two classes of controversies in particular in which the ordinary legal procedure has broken down to such an extent that it may fairly be that the result has been a denial of justice: First, those cases in which the amount in controversy is small; and second, those in which one of the parties is so poor that he cannot afford to wage a legal battle. The ordinary procedure has proved too cumbersome as a method of enforcing small claims."[2]

Such sentiments fueled a movement to establish simplified tribunals to handle the disputes of the average person. The first small claims court was established in Kansas in 1912. By 1923 five states—Massachusetts, South Dakota, California, Nevada, and Idaho—had instituted small claims systems. In addition, there were small claims courts operating in twelve major cities. The movement spread rapidly so that by 1939, nine more states set up small claims courts, and by 1972, all but nine states had done so.

The small claims courts were initially developed to assist "wage-earners and small business men who had wages or accounts to collect that were too small to justify the expense and delay of a formal legal proceeding."[3] The aim was to establish a tribunal that enabled such "average citizens" to collect their debts by a process that was fast and informal. They were intended to handle small, simple claims. The small claim court systems differed somewhat from state to state, but according to Barbara Yngvesson and Patricia Hennessey, they shared the following features:

> "1) In most courts, the adversary model for litigation was the norm, but the judge was described as an investigator, not an umpire. This meant that even in cases which deviated from the average 'simple' claim brought to the courts, lawyers should be unnecessary, and they were in fact excluded from many courts. This served to reduce procedural formalities and costs. The clerk replaced the lawyer as an aid in case preparation.
>
> 2) In most courts, only the general outlines of procedure were specified, and the details were left to the discretion of the judge. In particular, judges were not to be bound by formal rules of evidence, although decisions were to be reached on the basis of substantive law.
>
> 3) Other procedural reforms included simplified pleadings, elimination of pre-trial procedures, waiver of a jury trial by the plaintiff and the curtailment of appeal rights.

2. Austin Scott, *Small Causes and Poor Litigants*, 9 AM. BAR. ASS'N J. 457, 457 (1923).

3. Steven Weller, John C. Ruhnka and John A. Martin, *American Small Claims Courts*, in Christopher J. Whelan, ed. SMALL CLAIMS COURTS: A COMPARATIVE STUDY 5,5 (1990).

4) Court costs were reduced to a minimum.

5) The judge was empowered to stay the entry of judgment or the issue of execution. This enabled him to decide how a claim should be paid, and made it possible for him to take into consideration the defendant's economic circumstances and ability to pay.

6) In a few small claims courts, conciliation of claims was an alternative to adjudication. This required that both parties agree upon a settlement of the claim, and actively consent to a judgment, if one were entered.''[4]

In the 1960s and 1970s, social reformers again looked to small claims courts to be mechanisms to address serious social problems. In particular, consumer advocates saw small claims courts as potential tools for consumers to use against large businesses in disputes over inferior quality goods and exploitative prices. However, these reformers found that the ideal of the small claims court had become perverted. Instead of offering wage-earners redress in disputes with large employers, they found that large corporations and debt-collection agencies were utilizing the courts to expeditiously and unfairly exploit the disadvantaged. They found that the average working person was more likely to be a defendant than a plaintiff in the small claims courts. Most cases were brought by large businesses and collection agencies, usually represented by attorneys against unrepresented defendants. Studies confirmed that in small claims courts, these business plaintiffs had an extraordinarily high success rate—as high as eighty-five percent—in cases against individual, usually underprivileged, defendants.[5]

As a result of these studies, many state legislatures reformed their small claims courts. Typical reforms included measures to bar attorneys from representing parties and to bar collection agencies from utilizing the small claims courts altogether. The reforms in the small claims courts attempted to restore them to their original goal as the "people's courts." And, as a result, the use of small claims courts has increased dramatically. By the 1990s, it is reported that approximately more than twenty-five percent of all civil case filings in state courts are in small claims courts.[6]

The original reformers believed that by designing specialized courts for small claims, ordinary citizens could have their disputes resolved without the delay, expense, and formality involved in full-blown civil litigation. These small claims tribunals thus offered an alternative dispute resolution within the judicial system itself. But the relaxed procedures in these courts also gave rise to a number of due process concerns and other legal challenges, as demonstrated in the cases that follow.

* * *

4. Yngvesson & Hennessey, supra. n. 1 at 223–224 (citations omitted). Reprinted with permission.

5. See, Arthur Best, et. al, Peace, *Wealth, Happiness, and Small Claims Courts: A Case Study*, 21 FORDHAM URB. L.J.

343, 346–49 (1994); Susan E. Raitt, et. al., *The Use of Mediation in Small Claims Courts*, 9 OHIO ST. J. OF DISP. RESOL. 55, 58–59 (1993).

6. Raitt, supra n.5 at 56.

City and County of San Francisco v. Small Claims Court

141 Cal.App.3d 470, 190 Cal.Rptr. 340 (1st Dist., 3d Div., 1983).

■ WHITE, PRESIDING JUSTICE

Statement of the Case

In September 1981 Gretchen Eisenberg, et al., real parties in interest in the instant case (hereafter real parties) filed over 170 individual claims in small claims court against the City and County of San Francisco (hereafter appellant or San Francisco) as the owner and operator of San Francisco International Airport (hereafter airport or S.F.I.A.), alleging that noise from the airport constituted a continuing nuisance causing damages of $750 to each claimant in the 100 days preceding the filing of the claims.[1] These cases were consolidated at the hearing on January 18, 1982. Judgment was entered in favor of 116 plaintiffs and San Francisco has appealed from the judgment to the superior court.

Real parties filed another 183 claims against San Francisco in accordance with Government Code section 911.2 which governs the timing of filing tort claims, and a hearing was set for May 1982. That hearing was postponed because San Francisco filed a petition for a "writ of prohibition and/or mandamus" in the superior court on April 14, 1982 seeking to restrain the Small Claims Division, Municipal Court, Northern Judicial District, County of San Mateo (hereafter referred to as respondent small claims court) from proceeding to hear and determine the pending airport nuisance actions or any similar cases filed by the real parties against San Francisco arising from the same subject matter. An alternative writ of prohibition was filed on April 19, 1982 ordering respondent small claims court to show cause why a writ should not issue. Real party Gretchen Eisenberg filed a demurrer to San Francisco's petition on May 7, 1982. After an extraordinary writ proceeding the superior court issued an order on May 27, 1982, denying the writ and sustaining the demurrer without leave to amend of real party Gretchen Eisenberg. It is from this order that San Francisco appeals to this court.

Discussion

This appeal by San Francisco challenges the power of the respondent small claims court to hear a large number of individuals' claims alleging that noise from the San Francisco International Airport constitutes a continuing nuisance causing damages in the amount of $750 to each claimant. It arises in the context of the consolidation of these claims by the small claims court.

---

1. The jurisdictional limit for small claims actions at the time these claims were filed was $750. Code of Civil Procedure section 116.2 has since been amended to raise the monetary jurisdiction of all small claims to $1,500. (Stats. 1981, ch. 957, § 1.)

Appellant San Francisco argues on a number of grounds that these airport nuisance claims should be taken out of small claims court. As we explain in the following discussion of each of the issues raised, we disagree.

1. Does the small claims court have jurisdiction to hear the airport nuisance cases even though they involve "complex" issues and have been filed in "waves" of "mass claims" against a public entity?

San Francisco argues vigorously that in spite of the fact that each of the claims filed by real parties in this case alleges damages within the jurisdictional amount set out in the statute in effect at the time they were filed, they are nevertheless outside the jurisdiction of the small claims court because the Legislature never intended "complex" cases to be heard in small claims courts.

Appellant directs our attention to the words "minor civil disputes" in Code of Civil Procedure section 116.1. It is useful to consider this phrase in the context of the whole section, which reads: "The Legislature hereby finds and declares that individual minor civil disputes are especially important to the parties involved and of significant social and economic consequence collectively. The Legislature further finds and declares that in order to resolve such disputes in an expeditious, inexpensive, and fair manner, it is essential to provide a judicial forum accessible to all parties directly involved in resolving such disputes. The small claims divisions of municipal and justice courts have been established to provide such a forum and thereby comprise a fundamental element in the administration of justice and the protection of the rights and property of individuals. To help fulfill this purpose, it is the intent of the Legislature that the small claims divisions of municipal and justice courts and all rules of the Judicial Council regarding small claims actions shall operate to ensure that the convenience of parties and witnesses who are individuals shall prevail, to the extent possible, over the convenience of any other parties or witnesses."

The language of this section makes it clear that the word "minor" in the first sentence refers to the financial value of the claim to the individual plaintiff. Although this is a recently added section to the statutes governing small claims courts (Stats.1981, ch. 958, § 1), it is consistent with the view of many courts about the purpose of the small claims courts. From their inception, small claims courts have been held to exist to make it possible for plaintiffs with meritorious claims for small amounts of money, to bring these claims to court without spending more money on attorney's fees and court expenses than the claims were worth. (E.g., see Brooks v. Small Claims Court (1973) 8 Cal.3d 661, 668–670, 105 Cal.Rptr. 785, 504 P.2d 1249; Leuschen v. Small Claims Court (1923) 191 Cal. 133, 137, 215 P. 391.)

In a 1926 decision which affirmed the importance and ensured the continuance of small claims courts the Supreme Court said, "The small claims court was created primarily to avoid wasteful litigation and to reduce to a minimum *costs of trial* in cases where the *demands* are small." (Hughes v. Municipal Court (1926) 200 Cal. 215, 218, 252 P. 575, emphasis added.) More recently the Court of Appeal in the Second District took substantially the same view when it said: "A small claims process was established to provide an inexpensive and expeditious means to settle disputes over *small amounts*. The theory behind its organization was that ordinary litigation 'fails to bring practical justice' when the disputed *claim is small*, because the *time and expense required by the ordinary litigation process is so disproportionate to the amount involved* that it discourages legal resolution of the dispute." (Pace v. Hillcrest Motor Co. (1980) 101 Cal.App.3d 476, 478, 161 Cal.Rptr. 662, emphasis added.)

Moreover it appears from the record in the instant case that it was precisely because the cost of litigating a suit in superior court was prohibitive that real parties decided to use the small claims court. We note that had plaintiffs failed to establish the existence of a nuisance at the outset, there would have been an end to the whole matter. The plaintiff has no right to appeal from a small claims court decision, while the defendant may appeal to the superior court for a trial de novo (Code Civ.Proc., § 117.8), and if still unsuccessful may be granted a rehearing (Adamson v. Superior Court (1980) 113 Cal.App.3d 505, 509, 169 Cal.Rptr. 866) or other relief by extraordinary writ. (Davis v. Superior Court (1980) 102 Cal.App.3d 164, 168, 162 Cal.Rptr. 167.) This is a system which balances the poor litigant's right to a day in court, with the constitutional right of defendants not to be deprived of property without due process of law. It has been refined over hundreds of years with recurring attention from the courts, legal commentators, and the Legislature. . . . We believe it is constitutionally sound and indispensable to our system of justice.

We simply find no authority for appellant's argument that the airport nuisance cases, which are indeed relatively complex compared to many matters heard in small claims court, should be thrown out for that reason. Indeed appellant cites no case which supports this proposition.

[I]n the instant case real parties brought their actions alleging nuisance. It is beyond dispute that a small claims court may hear an action in nuisance. And it has recently been established that airport noise may give rise to a nuisance action. . . .

While . . . many procedural devices and protections available in superior court are not available in small claims court, [that fact] does not persuade us that the airport cases may not be heard first in the less formal setting. On the contrary Sanderson v. Niemann, 17 Cal. 2d 563 (1941), (holding that small claims judgment has no estoppel effect on the issues of negligence in a subsequent lawsuit growing out of the same incident) is a good illustration of the balancing of interests which has characterized the development of small claims courts. . . . Sanderson recognizes that small claims courts' decisions have inherent limitations. Both sides must put their cases before the court without an attorney advocate, accept relaxed rules of evidence, and do without the usual discovery process. The plaintiff who chooses this forum has elected to accept these limitations and must accept the court's decision as final. (Code Civ.Proc., § 117.8.) Yet the defendant has the right to appeal to the superior court for a trial de novo.

(Ibid.) And under Sanderson, if there is no appeal from the small claims court's judgment, the parties are protected from any inappropriate extension of that decision, since issues resolved in that court may not operate as an estoppel in a later action.

San Francisco also argues, though it cites no supporting authority, that "broad social policy impact" of the airport nuisance cases also makes them inappropriate for an initial resolution in small claims court. In view of the Legislature's explicit recognition that small claims cases have "significant social and economic consequence collectively" (Code Civ.Proc., § 116.1) this cannot be the basis for a jurisdictional challenge. Indeed the Supreme Court in City of Long Beach v. Bozek (1982) 31 Cal.3d 527, 532, 183 Cal.Rptr. 86, 645 P.2d 137, judgment vacated and case remanded (Jan. 10, 1983) 459 U.S. 1095, 103 S.Ct. 712, 74 L.Ed.2d 943, proceedings on remand pending (holding that municipalities may not sue for malicious prosecution) said that filing suit against a governmental entity is an aspect of the constitutional right to petition for the redress of grievances. In addition "the right encompasses the act of filing a lawsuit solely to obtain monetary compensation for individualized wrongs, as well as filing suit *to draw attention to issues of broader public interest or political significance.*" (Id., at p. 534, 183 Cal.Rptr. 86, 645 P.2d 137, emphasis added.) The right to access to the courts which the Supreme Court emphatically defends in Bozek (id., at p. 533) includes the right of access to small claims courts.

San Francisco also cites City of San Jose v. Superior Court (1974) 12 Cal.3d 447, 115 Cal.Rptr. 797, 525 P.2d 701, to support the argument that the complexity of the issues should take these cases out of small claims court. In the San Jose case, the Supreme Court affirmed the denial of class certification of plaintiffs suing the city alleging nuisance and inverse condemnation because of airport noise. The court reasoned "that a class action cannot be maintained where each member's right to recover depends on facts peculiar to his case" (id., at p. 459), and held that the class failed for lack of community of interest and failure of the named plaintiffs to adequately represent the class. (id. at p. 461).

The concerns of the San Jose court are significantly different from those raised by the instant appeal. The plaintiffs there, once certified as a class, would remain a class through all levels of appellate review. Any unfairness to defendant resulting from the certification could not be cured on appeal. In the instant case, however, as we have discussed ante at page 342, appellant's right to a trial de novo in superior court is a cure for the informal procedures of small claims court which appellant decries.[3]

San Francisco objects further to the "mass filing" of these claims, complaining that its ultimate liability may exceed $135,000. It is well settled that the jurisdictional amount limitations apply to each plaintiff's individual claim, so that in a consolidated action the fact that the aggregate

---

3. We note that San Francisco does not challenge the consolidation of real parties' claims, a position which would be more anal-ogous to that of the City of San Jose in the case cited.

amount of the claims is greater does not create a jurisdictional defect. (1 Witkin, Cal. Procedure (2d ed. 1970) pp. 559–560.)

As to San Francisco's complaint that real parties continue to file "waves" of claims, the Supreme Court has said: "If the defendant is not privileged to continue the nuisance and is able to abate it, he cannot complain if the plaintiff elects to bring successive actions as damages accrue until abatement takes place." (Spaulding v. Cameron (1952) 38 Cal.2d 265, 268, 239 P.2d 625.) It is not for this court to determine whether a nuisance exists, nor whether it is permanent or abatable. These are issues for the trial court. Their relevance for the jurisdictional issue before this court is this: unless and until there is a determination that the allegedly excess airport noise is a permanent nuisance which the airport is privileged to continue, the laws of this state allow real parties to file successive actions based on nuisance.

2. Has San Francisco been denied equal protection of the law?

Appellant argues that because it must defend claims worth over $135,000 in the aggregate without the full panoply of procedural devices and protections available in municipal or superior court, it has been denied equal protection of the law. The assertion that it is "similarly situated" to a defendant in a different type of court, where one plaintiff alone could sue to recover that amount, and where plaintiffs as well as defendants would have more procedural rights, is spurious. There is no "particular burden" imposed on a municipality or municipal public utility by requiring it to defend actions in small claims courts. San Francisco is subject to the same rules as other defendants in small claims courts, including the provisions for consolidation and the method of determining jurisdictional amount.

3. Have real parties violated Code of Civil Procedure section 117.4?

By their own admission real parties have consulted attorneys and other legal advisors and have met together numerous times to discuss what to do about the noise from San Francisco International Airport. They contend that all of this activity was constitutionally protected as collective activity undertaken to petition for the redress of grievances. We agree.

Real parties rely on the decision of the United States Supreme Court in United Transportation Union v. Michigan Bar (1971) 401 U.S. 576, 91 S.Ct. 1076, 28 L.Ed.2d 339, identifying it as one of a long line of cases protecting the right of groups to act collectively to seek legal redress....

In the United Transportation case a labor union had set limits on the fees which recommended attorneys could charge union members pressing claims against their employers. The court said this practice must be allowed because "collective activity undertaken to obtain meaningful access to the courts is a fundamental right within the protection of the First Amendment." (Id., 401 U.S. at p. 585, 91 S.Ct. at p. 1082.) It also said, "However, that right would be a hollow promise if courts could deny associations of workers *or others* the means of enabling their members to meet the costs of legal representation." (Id. at pp. 585–586, 91 S.Ct. at p. 1082, emphasis added.)

Appellant points to the language of Code of Civil Procedure section 117.4: "No attorney at law or other person than the plaintiff and the defendant shall take any part in the filing or the prosecution or defense of such litigation in small claims court...." San Francisco maintains that certain activities in which real parties have engaged are a violation of this section and change the nature of the claims so that they are not "individual" and thus cannot be heard in small claims court.

Under existing law real parties could not be certified as a class essentially *because* of the individuality of their claims.... The fact that they have exercised their constitutional right to meet together "to assist and advise each other" (Railroad Trainmen v. Virginia Bar, supra, 377 U.S. 1, 6, 84 S.Ct. 1113, 1116, 12 L.Ed.2d 89) in organizing and filing their claims does not change the fundamental reality that each petitioner had a valid individual claim. Appellant does not challenge the testimony given by one of the admitted "organizers" to the effect that each claimant individually signed a claim, paid a filing fee, and alleged damages for personal injury arising from airport noise.

We cannot read the small claims statutes as denying these plaintiffs access to the court on the basis of who handed the papers to the filing clerk. The United States Supreme Court has said, "We start with the premise that the rights to assemble peaceably and to petition for a redress of grievances are among the most precious of the liberties safeguarded by the Bill of Rights. These rights, moreover, are intimately connected, both in origin and in purpose, with the other First Amendment rights of free speech and free press.... The First Amendment would, however, be a hollow promise if it left government free to destroy or erode its guarantees by indirect restraints so long as no law is passed that prohibits free speech, press, petition, or assembly as such." (Mine Workers v. Illinois Bar Assn., supra, 389 U.S. 217, 222, 88 S.Ct. 353, 356, 19 L.Ed.2d 426.)

San Francisco's reading of Code of Civil Procedure section 117.4 requires an interpretation which would conflict with the fundamental right of citizens to act collectively when seeking access to the courts. Following the principle that the Legislature is presumed to write laws which are constitutional, we cannot agree with San Francisco's reading of this statute.[5]

We are further persuaded that real parties have in no way abused the small claims process since the Legislature itself has recently made manda-

---

5. The activities of certain "coordinators" to which appellant objects but which are constitutionally protected and are not precluded by the statute include: (1) reviewing records of the Noise Abatement Center at the airport to discover the names of potential plaintiffs; (2) preparing, circulating and filing (in the sense of carrying the papers to the courthouse after individuals had signed and attached filing fees) "master" small claims complaints; (3) hiring and consulting attorneys before and after filing claims; (4) holding "workshops" and other meetings at which participants discussed and attorneys offered advice on the presentation of testimony; (5) filing a brief written by or with the assistance of a nonattorney legal advisor, and (6) hiring expert witnesses to testify on behalf of all plaintiffs.

tory the establishment of advisory services for small claims litigants. (Code Civ.Proc., § 117.18.)

The new law provides: "In each county, individual assistance shall be made available to advise small claims court litigants and potential litigants at no additional charge. Except as otherwise provided in this section, each county may determine the characteristics of the advisory service in accordance with local needs and conditions. The advisory service may be provided in person, by telephone, or by any other means reasonably calculated to provide timely and appropriate assistance. Adjacent counties may provide advisory services jointly. The service shall operate in conjunction and cooperation with the small claims division of the courts, but shall be administered in such a manner as to be independent of control of the court. Persons providing assistance may be volunteers and shall be members of the State Bar, law students, paralegals, or persons experienced in resolving minor disputes and familiar with small claims court rules and procedures. Persons providing assistance shall not appear in court as an advocate for any party...."

This provision is consistent with other language in the statute, found in the very section which appellant argues that real parties have violated, i.e., "Nothing herein shall prevent an attorney from rendering advice to a party to such [small claims] litigation, either before or after the commencement of such an action, ..." (Code Civ.Proc., § 117.4.)

Thus, it appears that all the activities of the "coordinators" of real parties to which San Francisco objects are allowed under the small claims statute and are constitutionally protected.

Since we find no violation of the statute we do not reach the issue of whether an extraordinary writ may issue to restrain its violation.

Conclusion

Real parties have engaged in concerted action to assist each other in preparing and filing claims alleging damages of $750 each arising from noise connected with the operation of the airport. We hold that the respondent small claims court has jurisdiction to hear these cases. The judgment of the superior court denying San Francisco's petition for a writ of prohibition and/or mandate and sustaining real party's demurrer is affirmed.

* * *

Questions

1. Why do you think the plaintiffs in the preceding case chose to sue in small claims court? What risks does the procedure pose to the plaintiffs? Should the defendants have challenged consolidation of the claims in order to regain a tactical advantage?

2. Why does the California Small Claims Court statute provide for asymmetric rights of appeal for the plaintiff and the defendant? Would the

statute be constitutional if it did not permit defendants to appeal? Why is it appropriate to deny plaintiffs the right to appeal?

3. Would an appeal of a small claims court judgment under the California procedure be similar to an appeal of an arbitration award? How would it differ?

4. In order to be constitutional, must a small claims court procedure guarantee the defendant a trial de novo in the Superior Court? Would it satisfy due process requirements for an appellate court to review the result in the Court of Claims for clear error or abuse of discretion?

5. Do small claims courts represent a form of poor man's justice within the legal system? Do they accomplish the same goals as private forms of ADR?

6. Some scholars who have studied the operation of small claims courts have found that they favor repeat players. Thus, for example, some small claims courts have become little more than debt collection agencies for lending institutions that extend credit to the poor. Are there features of the California Small Claims statute that limit the ability of corporations or other large entities to use the small claims courts against the less advantaged?

7. Under the New York Small Claims Court legislation, corporations are not permitted to sue as plaintiffs in small claims courts, but they can be defendants. Also, either side may have an attorney represent them, but if both are represented, the court may transfer the action to the civil court. Does this procedure solve the repeat player problem often found in small claims courts?

* * *

Bruno v. Superior Court of the City and County of San Francisco; Gridley, Real Party in Interest

219 Cal.App.3d 1359, 269 Cal.Rptr. 142 (Ct. of Appl., 1st Dist., 1990).

■ CHANNELL, ASSOCIATE JUSTICE.

This petition presents the question of whether the superior court may permit discovery in a small claims appeal. We conclude that discovery is not available. However, we conclude that respondent court abused its discretion in sanctioning petitioner's attorney for his attempt to obtain discovery.

I. FACTS

On August 24, 1989, real party in interest, Arnold S. Gridley, filed an unlawful detainer action in small claims court against petitioner Diana Lynn Bruno. The complaint asked for back rent commencing in March 1989 and for the possession of the property in which petitioner had resided since 1976. On September 20, 1989, judgment was entered in real party's favor for $2,000 and real party was awarded possession of the apartment at

600 Stanyan Street in San Francisco. On October 3, 1989, petitioner filed a notice of appeal with respondent court.

On October 4, 1989, petitioner, who was now represented by counsel, noticed the deposition of real party and Ms. Lilly Daily, real party's bookkeeper, who had appeared as a witness in small claims court to present bookkeeping evidence of overdue rent. Also on October 4, 1989, petitioner propounded to real party a set of Judicial Council form interrogatories for unlawful detainer actions. Real party refused the discovery requests and on November 22, 1989, petitioner filed a motion to compel and requested discovery sanctions.

Real party through his attorney filed opposition to the motion and requested sanctions pursuant to section 128.5 of the Code of Civil Procedure. Real party contended that discovery was not available in small claims appeals and that the conduct of petitioner's attorney in requesting discovery of "two unschooled laypersons" was "not authorized and constitutes an abuse of process and outrageous conduct." After an oral argument on December 7, 1989, which was unreported, respondent court denied the motion to compel and awarded real party $1,100 in sanctions against petitioner's counsel. As to the sanctions, the order states: "Specifically, the brining [sic] of a motion for discovery and sanctions in a small claims matter is not authorized by law, and in this instance has resulted in legal expenses being incurred by responding parties."

II. ANALYSIS

A. Discovery.

The Legislature provided for the establishment of the small claims division of municipal and justice courts in order to create an expeditious and inexpensive method of resolving disputes. (§ 116.) "The theory behind its organization is that only by escaping from the complexity and delay of the normal course of litigation could anything be gained in a legal proceeding which may involve a small sum. Consequently, the small claims court functions informally and expeditiously. The chief characteristics of its proceedings are that there are no attorneys, no pleadings and no legal rules of evidence; there are no juries, and no formal findings are made on the issues presented." (Sanderson v. Niemann (1941) 17 Cal.2d 563, 573, 110 P.2d 1025.) Ordinarily the judgment of the small claims court is conclusive upon the plaintiff but the defendant can appeal and obtain a trial de novo in superior court. (§§ 117.8, 117.10.) This trial in superior court must be conducted informally in the same manner as is the small claims action itself except that attorneys may participate. (Cal. Rules of Court, rule 155.)

Neither the statutes providing for the small claims system nor the rules of court covering small claims actions address the question of whether discovery is permitted in the small claims action itself. (§ 116 et seq.; Cal. Rules of Court, rule 1701 et seq.) However, it has generally been assumed that there is no discovery in connection with the proceeding in small claims court. . . . [citations omitted] This assumption has been supported by the express exclusion of small claims actions from the legislation enacted in

1982 to expedite litigation of civil actions where the amount in controversy is $25,000 or less. (§ 90 et seq.) This legislation permits, but limits, discovery. (§ 94.) Yet the legislation expressly excludes small claims actions and does so by excluding "*any* action under Chapter 5A (commencing with Section 116)." (§ 90 subd. (b); emphasis added.)

We are convinced that the Legislature did not intend that formal discovery procedures should be permitted in either the small claims action itself or the de novo proceeding on appeal. Obviously, formal discovery procedures in the original small claims actions would be completely inconsistent with the goals and procedures of the small claims court and would impose an unacceptable burden on unrepresented litigants. Discovery at the appeal level would also defeat the object of speedy and inexpensive settlement of disputes, the object of the entire small claims process. (§ 116.1.)

Although no case has decided whether discovery is permitted in the trial de novo in superior court, the court in Burley v. Stein (1974) 40 Cal.App.3d 752, 115 Cal.Rptr. 279, expressed in dictum a view consistent with that we reach here. In Burley, the court had before it the question of whether a defendant who had suffered a default judgment in a small claims action had standing to appeal to the superior court without first moving to set aside the default in the small claims court. The superior court in affirming the small claims judgment had commented on the " 'cynical practices' " of some defendants who in their de novo appeals of small claims judgments to the superior court had " 'begun to resort to a number of intricate and, to the small litigant, the baffling devices of interrogatories, requests for admissions, law and motion proceedings, and the like.' " (Id. at p. 755, fn. 3, 115 Cal.Rptr. 279.) The reviewing court added its own comment that discovery should not be permitted, explaining: "It would appear that the trial de novo in the superior court, except for the addition of counsel, should be tried as it was in the small claims court. To do otherwise would appear to defeat the general intent of the Legislature in providing for the efficient disposition of voluminous small claims." (Id. at pp. 758–759, fn. 6, 115 Cal.Rptr. 279.) Subsequently, rule 155 of the California Rules of Court was amended to provide: "Trial shall be conducted informally as provided in Code of Civil Procedure section 117 . . ." At least one court has read this rule as applying to pretrial discovery as well as to the trial itself. (Cooper v. Pirelli Cable Corp. (1984) 160 Cal.App.3d 294, 299, 206 Cal.Rptr. 581.)

Petitioner stresses the fact that the defendant in a lawful detainer proceeding stands in a different position than the defendant in any other small claims proceeding. He or she is in danger of losing, not just a modest amount of money, but a home. To protect this fundamental interest, the tenant has the right to raise affirmative defenses despite the summary nature of an unlawful detainer action [citations] and petitioner contends the right to raise these affirmative defenses is meaningless unless discovery essential to establish the defenses is allowed. We cannot agree. Evidence to support the defenses can be obtained by means other than formal discovery. Witnesses may be called and examined at the trial itself. Subpoenas and subpoenas duces tecum are available for the asking. (§ 1985.)

Furthermore, the superior court judge hearing the matter has power to "investigate the controversy." Section 117, subdivision (a), provides that at the hearing of a small claims action "[t]he judge may consult witnesses informally and otherwise investigate the controversy." This section applies to the small claims appeal. (Cal. Rules of Court, rule 155.) Thus if questions of fact remain insufficiently explored through the lack of pretrial discovery or cooperation between the parties, the court during trial can order the parties to disclose and/or produce anything it deems necessary for resolution of the case. This may be cumbersome and may cause delay in the few cases in which the trial court deems it necessary to use its power of investigation, but the delay and inconvenience pales to insignificance in view of the damage that would be done to the small claims process should the parties themselves have the right to pretrial discovery. . . .

B.   Sanctions.

Although we agree with respondent court that discovery is not available in a small claims appeal, we find that the court abused its discretion in sanctioning petitioner's attorney for raising this issue of first impression. . . .

* * *

Houghtaling v. Superior Court for the County of San Bernardino; Rossi, Real Party in Interest

17 Cal.App.4th 1128, 21 Cal.Rptr.2d 855 (Ct. of Appl., 4th Dist. 1993)

■ DABNEY, ACTING PRESIDING JUSTICE.

In this case we decide an issue which has been the subject of considerable uncertainty in the courts of this state, but which, by its nature, has until now escaped review. We hold that in a proceeding conducted under the Small Claims Act (Code Civ.Proc., §§ 116.110 et seq.), relevant hearsay evidence is admissible subject only to those limitations contained in Evidence Code section 352 [which allows exclusion of evidence if its probative value is substantially outweighed by danger of prejudicial effect] and the law of testimonial privileges. The trial court then exercises its sound discretion in determining the weight to which the evidence is entitled. Accordingly, in this case we hold that the trial court erred, and grant the relief requested by petitioner.

STATEMENT OF THE CASE

Petitioner's claim against defendants involved Rossi's allegedly negligent repair of a vehicle owned by Houghtaling. It appears that after the work was done by Rossi, the vehicle developed further problems while located in the state of Nebraska, and was there presented to a mechanic for repair. (It was eventually sold, allegedly for far less than its value had it been in proper condition.)

In the original small claims proceeding, the docket indicates that petitioner was permitted to introduce a notarized statement from the mechanic who worked on the vehicle in Nebraska, separately signed by the owner of the repair facility. This statement included the opinion that the vehicle's later malfunctioning was due to improper work done by Rossi.

In the superior court, at the hearing de novo, the trial court refused to accept this evidence. According to the petition, the court stated that it operated "under Superior Court rules of procedure" and that no evidence could be presented from a witness who was not subject to cross-examination.

DISCUSSION

[T]he nature of small claims proceedings results in a paucity of published authority on any issues relating to such proceedings. The texts and bench aids tend to list customary practices and variations without setting forth a great deal of substantive authority for such practices. For example, in the California Judges' Benchbook for Small Claims Court and Consumer Law (2d ed. 1989), the writers could provide nothing more helpful with respect to our issue than to say that some courts allow all hearsay, and some allow some of it, while citing no authority for either approach.[4] However, we do not write on a clean slate; the courts of appeal and our Supreme Court have on several occasions addressed themselves to specific issues of small claims proceedings.... [T]he current trend of the law is to defer to the intent of the Legislature, as grounded in historical perspective, to create an informal and flexible forum in which disputes over modest sums of money may be resolved without the necessity for incurring disproportionate expenses or consuming undue amounts of time. (See also City and County of San Francisco v. Small Claims Court (1983) 141 Cal.App.3d 470, 474, 190 Cal.Rptr. 340.) The small claims system is a response to that quandary described by Dean Pound: "For ordinary causes, our contentious system has great merit as a means of getting the truth. But it is a denial of justice in small causes to drive a litigant to employ lawyers, and it is a shame to drive them to legal aid societies to get as a charity what the state should give as a right." (Pound, The Administration of Justice in the Modern City (1913) 26 Harv.L.Rev. 302, 318.) We approach the question from this starting point.

Recognizing the goal of providing justice in small matters at a reasonable cost, the courts of this state have upheld provisions in the statutes governing small claims actions which restrict what are recognized otherwise as substantial, even constitutional, rights. Thus, the denial of any right to appeal for a plaintiff has been sustained (Superior Wheeler Cake

---

4. As the primary objection to hearsay is that such evidence is not subject to cross-examination, it is worth noting that courts have routinely restricted or forbidden cross examination in small claims matters. (See Comment, The California Small Claims Court (1964) 52 Cal.L.Rev. 876 at 881, fn. 58.)

Corp. v. Superior Court (1928) 203 Cal. 384, 387, 264 P. 488), as has the prohibition against representation by counsel. (Prudential Ins. Co. v. Small Claims Court (1946) 76 Cal.App.2d 379, 383–384, 173 P.2d 38.) And while these cases sometimes stressed that the restrictions were justified either by the plaintiff's election to submit to the small claims procedures, or the availability of expanded rights in a trial de novo, in Crouchman v. Superior Court, supra, the court relied on history and the purpose of the small claims court in its holding that the Legislature could validly provide that no jury trial should be had even at the de novo level.

In the context of hearsay, it cannot be gainsaid that the right to require the witnesses against one to appear in court, and that they be subject to cross-examination, is of major importance in our system of jurisprudence. (See Englebretson v. Industrial Acc. Com. (1915) 170 Cal. 793, 798, 151 P. 421.) The opportunity for cross-examination has been called " 'the greatest legal engine ever invented for the discovery of truth.' " (People v. Reynolds (1984) 152 Cal.App.3d 42, 46, 199 Cal.Rptr. 379, quoting 5 Wigmore, Evidence (3d ed. 1940) The Hearsay Rule Satisfied: By Cross-Examination, § 1367, p. 29.) However, the prohibition of hearsay evidence is far from all-encompassing even in litigation pursuant to the usual rules of evidence (see exceptions, e.g., Evid.Code, §§ 1220 et seq.), and the nature of small claims proceedings makes an even looser rule appropriate. . . .

[T]he law permits the introduction of hearsay evidence in a large number of situations, despite the fact that cross-examination is, by definition, not available.

It is true that in most cases the exceptions are justified, expressly or impliedly, by the underlying theory that the nature of the hearsay statement carries some indicia of reliability. Thus, Evidence Code section 1230 defines a "declaration against interest" as a statement which, due to the likely deleterious personal consequences, "a reasonable man . . . would not have made . . . unless he believed it to be true." (See Estate of Huntington (1976) 58 Cal.App.3d 197, 210, 129 Cal.Rptr. 787.) A dying declaration is admitted (Evid.Code, § 1242) on the theory that a declarant is likely to tell the truth when faced with the immediate prospect of eternity. (People v. Adams (1990) 216 Cal.App.3d 1431, 1440, 265 Cal.Rptr. 568; see also Mattox v. United States (1895) 156 U.S. 237, 244, 15 S.Ct. 337, 340, 39 L.Ed. 409.) However, some hearsay is made admissible simply as a matter of convenience or practical necessity, where no other means of proof is available; an example are the "family history" exceptions of Evidence Code sections 1310 et seq. (Estate of Hartman (1910) 157 Cal. 206, 213, 107 P. 105.) These examples strengthen the position that hearsay is not always to be considered the pariah of the world of evidence, and this is further recognized by the rule that hearsay evidence is competent to support a judgment, if admitted in the absence of any objection. (Flood v. Simpson (1975) 45 Cal.App.3d 644, 649, 119 Cal.Rptr. 675.)

None of the above objections to hearsay requires that it be excluded from small claims actions, while the exceptions support a rule recognizing its propriety in such proceedings.... After all, there is no need for concern over the danger that the jury will overestimate the value of such evidence; the trial judge is routinely called upon to evaluate proffered evidence by balancing its probative worth against the danger that it will mislead the jury. (Ibid.) Thus, there is significant precedent for permitting the judge, in a small claims matter, to receive all relevant evidence and then determine its probative value.

A second point is more practical. It is repeatedly stated that small claims courts are designed for the unsophisticated petty litigant. (See e.g., Brooks v. Small Claims Court (1973) 8 Cal.3d 661, 669, 105 Cal.Rptr. 785, 504 P.2d 1249—"inexperienced individual.") Volumes have been written on the hearsay rule, and the shelves are filled with judicial constructions and explanations. It is simply unrealistic to expect lay litigants to understand and abide by the formal rules of evidence. How is a lay plaintiff to be made to understand that the bill for services which he presents to show the repair costs for his damaged property must be authenticated as a business record? Or that the police report of an accident proves nothing in the eyes of the law? Nor would a strict enforcement of the hearsay rule serve the policies of speed and economy, if the result were to compel the parties to bring in numerous additional witnesses to testify in person. The parties might incur subpoena and witness fees; on the other hand, in neighborhood matters, a party might be unwilling to antagonize a reluctant witness by compelling his appearance. In a case such as the one at bar, of course, the practical difficulties facing a party with out-of-state witnesses would often make an effective case or defense impossible, if hearsay testimony could not be presented. If the small claims court is to be the "People's Court," it must not be encumbered with rules and restrictions which can only frustrate and hinder the litigant who resorts to that court in response to its promise of speedy and economical justice. In the case of inexperienced pro se litigants, it is better to err on the side of admitting an ore-heap of evidence in the belief that nuggets of truth may be found amidst the dross, rather than to confine the parties to presenting assayed and refined matter which qualifies as pure gold under the rules of evidence.

[M]ore importantly, the [small claims court] system is designed to depend upon the common sense ability of the judges to sort out relatively minor disputes. As mentioned above, the rules of evidence are commonly relaxed in court trials, a practice which reflects a recognition that judges are—and must be—trusted to treat questionable evidence in a fair and rational manner. We need not admonish judges not to rely on evidence to which no reasonable person could give any credence; this duty, and the ability to perform it, is inherent in the job. Our holding places no restrictions upon the type or amount of relevant hearsay evidence which shall be received, subject to the court's power under Evidence Code section 352 and its duty to respect and enforce the law of privileges.

In summary, we hold that the trial court here erred in refusing to consider the affidavit by the Nebraska witnesses presented by petitioner....

■ TIMLIN, ASSOCIATE JUSTICE, concurring and dissenting.

I concur with the majority that the trial court erred in refusing to consider the Nebraska mechanic's affidavit for admission into evidence because it was hearsay, and that a writ should issue remanding the case for a new de novo hearing. . . .

However, I disagree with the majority's holding and would remand for a new de novo hearing with the direction that the trial court determine the admissibility of the affidavit based on a consideration of the applicability of any statutory or common law hearsay exceptions (exceptions) or, if none are applicable, a determination whether the content of the affidavit and the circumstances surrounding its preparation reflect sufficient indicia of reliability and trustworthiness to justify the court's consideration of the affidavit as evidence. If so, the affidavit is admissible and should be given whatever weight the court gives to it in evaluating all the evidence.

[T]he majority's holding constitutes the adoption of a blanket and sweeping rule that all relevant hearsay evidence is admissible in small claims proceedings without regard to whether such evidence is reliable. Although the majority does retain two evidentiary rules as qualifiers to the admissibility of all hearsay, i.e., section 352 and testimonial privileges, neither relates to the reliability and trustworthiness of such evidence. In its eager efforts to buttress its stated holding, the majority, in reliance on excised snippets of general statements from cases and commentators regarding the nature of hearsay and its exceptions, ventures beyond its holding and in effect states that all rules of evidence are inapplicable in small claims proceedings. It makes the extraordinary statement on page 9 of its opinion that: "Thus, there is significant precedent for permitting the judge, in a small claims matter, to receive all relevant evidence and then determine its probative value."

On page 860 of its opinion, it urges the concept that all evidence is admissible in small claims proceedings with the comment: "In the case of inexperienced pro se litigants, it is better to err on the side of admitting an ore-heap of evidence in the belief that nuggets of truth may be found amidst the dross, rather than to confine the parties to presenting assayed and refined matter which qualifies as pure gold under the rules of evidence." (Emphasis added.) This is a picturesque and enticing analogy, but the majority's suggestion that all proffered evidence (not just relevant hearsay) be admitted into evidence should have referred more appropriately to a "slag-heap" rather than an "ore-heap." In keeping with this metaphor, I extend my personal condolences to the assayer (judge) looking for trustworthy and competent evidence in the tonnage of documents and testimony deposited with her or him. . . .

As to the majority's two assumptions: (1) the goal of small claims proceedings is to provide justice in small matters at a reasonable cost and (2) this is best served by totally abolishing the rule:

First, the litigants' opinion of whether true justice has been dispensed obviously depends in large measure on whether they believe the court's decision was "rational," which in turn will depend in large part upon whether they perceive the decision to have been based upon reliable evidence. Across-the-board acceptance by the small claims court of hearsay evidence, such as the affidavit of an out-of-state "expert," who cannot be cross-examined as to his actual expertise, relationship to the parties, or personal knowledge, will tend to decrease the appearance of fairness which is necessary to encourage public use and acceptance of the small claims court system as a method of resolving disputes which, though involving relatively small monetary amounts, are often of serious concern to the parties involved.

Second, the majority fails to explain how abolishing the rule furthers the goal of providing justice "at a reasonable cost." The Legislature has already provided that neither party may be represented by counsel in the small claims court, thus removing a major cost of litigation, i.e., attorney's fees. (Code Civ.Proc., § 116.530, subd. (a).) It has also empowered the trial court to permit "evidence by witnesses" to be offered outside the hearing. (Code Civ.Proc, § 116.520, subd. (a).) This provides litigants with flexibility in presenting testimonial evidence and presumably will further reduce costs by allowing witnesses to testify at times which will not interrupt their work, or by allowing them to testify telephonically, rather than in person, thus saving the time and cost involved in traveling to the hearing. These cost savings are equally available to plaintiffs and defendants in small claims actions.

In contrast, disallowing any and all hearsay objections will cut down on costs only for the proponent of such evidence, who need not make arrangements for the declarant to be available for cross-examination, or go to the effort of providing evidence to establish a proper foundation for an exception to the rule. However, the burden of such costs does not disappear, but instead is shifted to the opponent of such evidence, who, in the event he or she decides to attack the declarant's credibility or to show lack of trustworthiness of hearsay documentation in order to reduce its weight as evidence, will have to go to the time and expense to arrange for the declarant's availability as a witness for the opponent or to discover and obtain other such credibility-weakening evidence. The opponent's ability to investigate such hearsay evidence, so as to make arrangements beforehand to present information related to its credibility, is extremely limited because of the lack of formal discovery in small claims actions. (Code Civ.Proc. § 116.310, subd. (b).) This is a practical reason that the burden of establishing that hearsay statements have some indicia of reliability should remain on the proponent of such evidence.

For the foregoing reasons, I would not hold, as does the majority, that hearsay evidence is unconditionally admissible in small claims proceedings, subject only to the applicability of section 352 and the law of testimonial privileges, which limitations, in my opinion, are not pertinent to the purpose of the rule. Instead, I would hold that the rule applies in small claims proceedings subject to existing exceptions, but that if no exception does apply to particular hearsay evidence, as proffered, the court should then follow, as described above, a more liberal application of the rule to determine its admissibility.

* * *

Questions

1.   The two preceding cases address the appropriate procedural rules for small claims courts. Note the similarity between the concerns raised here and those discussed in chapter 6, about the need to find a balance between informality and due process. In the small claims courts, as with arbitration, an important issue is how far procedural rules can be relaxed to further the goal of informality without sacrificing important rights and protections of the parties. Does the majority in *Houghtaling* go too far by dispensing with the evidentiary exclusion for hearsay? Which approach, the majority or dissent, is the better view?

2.   In *Bruno,* the court did not permit the small claims court defendant to engage in discovery in the trial de novo. Given that the defendant did not select the informal forum in the first place, is this really fair? Might this ruling create incentives for plaintiffs to select a small claims forum in cases in which the defense must rely on discovery in order to prevail?

3.   COURT-ANNEXED ARBITRATION

A.   DESCRIPTION OF COURT-ANNEXED ARBITRATION

Understanding the Limits of Court–Connected ADR: A Critique of Federal Court–Annexed Arbitration Programs by Lisa Bernstein[1]

"In recent years the availability of private dispute resolution providers, ranging from expert mediators to rent-a-judge programs complete with black robes and model courtrooms, has increased dramatically. The alternative dispute resolution ('ADR') movement has received extensive press attention and has been hailed as a solution to crowded dockets and an inexpensive panacea for the ills of an overly litigious society. Pointing to the rapid growth of private ADR providers and studies purporting to show a high level of lawyer and client satisfaction with these alternative processes, states, joined recently by the federal government, began passing laws requiring parties to participate in an ADR process as a precondition to judicial resolution of their dispute.

"In 1978, Congress authorized the creation of the first three federal district court-annexed arbitration programs. The programs required parties to participate in a mandatory non-binding court-annexed arbitration ('CAA') hearing as a precondition to obtaining a trial. The programs

---

1. Lisa Bernstein, *Understanding the Limits of Court–Connected ADR: A Critique of Federal Court–Annexed Arbitration Pro-* *grams*, 141 PENN. L. REV. 2169, 2172–73, 2177–2185 (footnotes omitted). Reprinted with permission.

received strong support from then Attorney General Griffin Bell, who believed that compulsory court-annexed arbitration programs would 'broaden access for the American people to their justice system and ... provide mechanisms that will permit the expeditious resolution of disputes at a reasonable cost.' In 1985, Congress funded eight additional CAA pilot programs. In 1988, it authorized continued experimentation with mandatory CAA and provided funding for ten voluntary CAA pilot programs.

"The trend towards publicly sponsored or mandated ADR shows no signs of abating. One of the six 'cornerstone principles' of the Civil Justice Reform Act of 1990 was 'expanding and enhancing the use of alternative dispute resolution.' " The Act directed each federal district court to complete a cost and delay reduction plan and to specifically consider the possibility of instituting court-connected ADR programs. As of February 1992, thirty-two of the thirty-four federal courts that had completed these plans either endorsed or adopted some type of court-connected ADR....

I. THE BASIC FEATURES OF COURT–ANNEXED ARBITRATION PROGRAMS

"The Judicial Improvements and Access to Justice Act sets out the basic structure of federal CAA programs, but gives each district the authority to adopt local rules specifying important program features.

"Suits for predominantly money damages that fall below a particular amount in controversy, which, depending on the district, ranges from $50,000 to $150,000 and do not involve federal constitutional claims or conspiracies to interfere with civil rights, must be submitted to non-binding arbitration before a trial can be requested. In some districts, the parties or the trial judge may make a motion to exempt the case from arbitration where 'the objectives of arbitration would not be realized (1) because the case involves complex or novel legal issues, (2) because legal issues predominate over factual issues, or (3) for other good cause.' " In most districts the maximum amount in controversy is a jurisdictional limit, not a cap on the damages an arbitrator can award.

"Hearings are conducted by either a single arbitrator or a panel of three arbitrators chosen from a volunteer pool of lawyers. Hearings take place 80 to 180 days after the filing of the answer and decisions are rendered shortly thereafter. In some districts, hearings are open to the public, in others, they are closed. The amount of pre-arbitration discovery permitted and the types of pre-trial motions decided prior to the hearing are governed by local rule, subject to certain constraints imposed by Congress.

"At the arbitration hearing, the Federal Rules of Evidence do not apply. Arbitrators may permit the introduction of any credible non-privileged evidence, including hearsay. The arbitrators are not required to issue written or oral findings of fact or conclusions of law, and at least one district prohibits them from doing so. A few districts encourage live testimony, while others discourage it, providing by local rule that 'the presentation of testimony shall be kept to a minimum, and that cases shall be presented to the arbitrators primarily through the statements and arguments of Counsel.' One district bans live testimony altogether and requires that '[a]ll evidence shall be presented through counsel who may incorporate argument on such evidence in his or her presentation.' Some programs limit the length of the hearing.

"Good faith participation in the arbitration hearing is required of both the parties and their counsel. Most districts require parties to be present at the hearing, and some districts require the presence of a person with full settlement authority. Although the authority of the court to order a person with settlement authority to be present at an arbitration hearing has yet to be definitively established, an en banc panel of the Seventh Circuit has upheld a district judge's authority to order a person with full settlement authority to be present at a settlement conference. In some districts, if either the nonattendance of a party or the preparation and presentation of counsel is deemed not to constitute 'participation in a meaningful way' in the arbitration process, the court can impose monetary sanctions and/or strike a party's demand for a trial de novo ('trial'). The court's authority to strike a party's demand for a trial has been upheld by several district courts, but has not yet been considered by any court of appeals.

"After the arbitrator has rendered an award, which may, depending on the local rule, include costs, each party has thirty days to request a trial. When a party requests a trial, the case is restored to its original place on the docket and treated as if it had never been arbitrated; neither the record of the hearing, if made, nor the arbitrators' decision are admissible at trial. In the pilot districts, trial de novo request rates range from forty-six to seventy-four percent of arbitrated cases.

"Some districts have disincentives to requesting a trial. Most districts require the party requesting a trial to post a bond with the court in the amount of the arbitrators' fees and costs which, depending on the district and the number of arbitrators, can range from $125 to $450 for the typical case. Although complex cases often cost substantially more to arbitrate, most districts put a cap on the amount of the bond a party can be required to post in order to obtain a trial. If the party requesting the trial improves his position at trial, this bond is returned to him; if he fails to do so, it is retained by the court.

"In the past, some districts had a rule requiring the party requesting a trial to pay his opponent's post-arbitration attorneys' fees and/or costs if he failed to improve his position at trial. The authority of courts to enact such local rules absent congressional authorization was a question of some dispute. In 1988, Congress decided that pending further study by the Federal Courts Study Committee, such provisions should not be part of the pilot programs. However, in its 1990 report, the Committee recommended that Congress authorize the pilot districts to experiment with fee and cost-shifting provisions, common features of many state CAA programs.

"If a trial is not requested within thirty days of the arbitration decision, the decision is entered as the judgment of the court and has the same force and effect as a trial judgment. It cannot, however, be appealed."

* * *

B.   CONSTITUTIONALITY

Firelock, Inc. v. District Court in the State of Colorado

776 P.2d 1090 (Colo. 1989).

■ ROVIRA, JUSTICE.

This case requires us to determine whether the Colorado Mandatory Arbitration Act (Act), §§ 13–22–401 to 13–22–409, 6A C.R.S. (1987), violates the Colorado Constitution and the due process and equal protection clauses of the fourteenth amendment to the United States Constitution.

The Boulder County District Court held that the Act was constitutional and denied the petitioner's request to refrain from assigning the case for arbitration. We issued a rule to show cause pursuant to C.A.R. 21, and we now discharge the rule.

I.

In 1988, McGhee Communications, Inc. (McGhee) commenced an action in the Boulder County District Court, which is located in the Twentieth Judicial District, against the petitioner, Firelock Incorporated (Firelock). McGhee claimed that it rendered advertising services to Firelock for which Firelock did not pay. In its complaint, McGhee certified that the probable recovery would not exceed $50,000, exclusive of interest and costs, and that the case was not exempt from mandatory arbitration. See C.R.C.P. 109.1.

Firelock filed an answer denying that the requested amount was owed, asserted several affirmative defenses, and demanded a jury trial. Firelock also filed a motion to refrain from assignment for mandatory arbitration under the Act. In support of its motion, Firelock claimed that the Act violated article II, sections 3, 6, 23, and 25; article III; article VI, sections 1 and 9; and article XVIII, section 3, of the Colorado Constitution; the fourteenth amendment to the United States Constitution; and C.R.C.P. 38. McGhee resisted the motion and requested that the trial court find the Act constitutional and order arbitration to be commenced promptly.

The trial court denied the motion, and Firelock then filed a petition pursuant to C.A.R. 21. In its petition, Firelock requested that this court issue an order to show cause why the respondent district court should not be restrained from referring the case for arbitration. Firelock also requested that we make the rule absolute and declare the Act unconstitutional.

II.

The Act was approved on May 28, 1987, and became effective on January 1, 1988. The Act is scheduled to terminate on July 1, 1990. See § 13–22–402(1), 6A C.R.S. (1987). Beginning on January 1, 1989, and on each January 1 thereafter, the judicial department must submit to the General Assembly an annual report evaluating the mandatory arbitration pilot project. See § 13–22–408, 6A C.R.S. (1987).

The Act provides a framework of mandatory arbitration in eight pilot judicial districts of which the twentieth, where the Boulder District Court is located, is one. See § 13–22–402(1), 6A C.R.S. (1987). In these eight pilot districts, any civil action filed in any court of record except the county court and small claims court after January 1, 1988, and before July 1, 1990, seeking money damages in the sum of $50,000 or less, excluding costs and interest, is to be assigned to mandatory arbitration once the action is at issue. See § 13–22–402(2), 6A C.R.S. (1987).

Pursuant to the Act, the complaint and any applicable counterclaim or cross-claim governed by the Act must contain a certification that the probable amount of recovery exceeds or does not exceed $50,000, the limit imposed for mandatory arbitration. The Act establishes procedures for the selection and compensation of arbitrators, see § 13–22–403, and sets forth an outline of procedures for the arbitration hearing, see § 13–22–404. Arbitrators must be "qualified" and must file a consent to act as an arbitrator in the district in which the court is located, but an arbitrator need not be an attorney. See § 13–22–403(3). Section 13–22–405 provides for a trial de novo for any party dissatisfied with the decision of the arbitrators. The demand for a trial de novo must be filed with the court within thirty days after the filing of the arbitrators' decision. See § 13–22–405(1). The Act also provides that, unless the trial de novo results in "an improvement of the position of the demanding party by more than ten percent," the demanding party must pay the costs of the arbitration proceeding including arbitrator fees, but not exceeding $1,000. See § 13–22–405(3).

Section 13–22–406 provides that the supreme court, pursuant to its authority under article VI, section 21, of the Colorado Constitution, is empowered to promulgate rules governing the arbitration proceedings established in the Act. Pursuant to this authority, we adopted C.R.C.P. 109.1. C.R.C.P. 109.1 establishes the procedure for certification of the probable amount of recovery and the basis for any exemption from the Act, see C.R.C.P. 109.1(b), sets forth sanctions for failure to comply with the certification procedures, see C.R.C.P. 109.1(c), and provides for a detailed procedure for the selection of arbitrators, see C.R.C.P. 109.1(d). C.R.C.P. 109.1 also provides for the filing of a pre-arbitration "Disclosure Statement," see C.R.C.P. 109.1(h), sets forth limited rules for discovery, see C.R.C.P. 109.1(i), and establishes the details of the arbitration hearing and the powers of the arbitrators, see C.R.C.P. 109.1(1). C.R.C.P. 109.1(q) provides that if neither party demands a trial de novo within thirty days after the filing of the arbitrators' award, then the award becomes final and the trial court must enter judgment on the award in accordance with C.R.C.P. 58(a).

III.

On appeal, Firelock presents several reasons for finding that the Act is unconstitutional. Firelock argues that the Act violates article III and article VI, sections 1 and 9, of the Colorado Constitution, which provide for the separation of powers; article II, sections 3 and 6, of the Colorado Constitution, which provide for the right of access to courts; article II, section 23, of the Colorado Constitution and C.R.C.P. 38, which provide for the right to trial by jury; article II, section 25, of the Colorado Constitution and the equal protection and due process clauses of the United States Constitution; and article XVIII, section 3, of the Colorado Constitution, which provides the General Assembly with authority over consensual arbitration. We will address each of these arguments in turn.

A.

Firelock asserts that the Act violates the separation of powers provision of the Colorado Constitution because section 13–22–402(2) requires "that the pilot district courts must refrain from exercising their general jurisdiction pending arbitration." Firelock also asserts that the Act "is an unconstitutional delegation of judicial power to unqualified private citizens" because it allows arbitration to be "conducted by persons who are not only not members of the judiciary, but indeed who do not even have to be licensed attorneys."

Article III of the Colorado Constitution provides:

> The powers of the government of this state are divided into three distinct departments,—the legislative, executive and judicial; and no person or collection of persons charged with the exercise of powers properly belonging to one of these departments shall exercise any power properly belonging to either of the others, except as in this constitution expressly directed or permitted.

"The fundamental meaning of the separation of powers doctrine is that the three branches of government are separate, coordinate, and equal." Pena v. District Court, 681 P.2d 953, 955–56 (Colo.1984). The purpose of article III is to prevent one branch of government from exercising any power that is constitutionally vested in another branch of government. Van Kleeck v. Ramer, 62 Colo. 4, 156 P. 1108 (1916).

According to article VI, section 1, the judicial power of the state is vested

> in a supreme court, district courts, a probate court in the city and county of Denver, a juvenile court in the city and county of Denver, county courts, and such other courts or judicial officers with jurisdiction inferior to the supreme court, as the general assembly may, from time to time establish.

With respect to the authority vested in district courts, article VI, section 9, states that "[t]he district courts shall be trial courts of record with general jurisdiction, and shall have original jurisdiction in all civil, probate, and criminal cases, except as otherwise provided herein."

We must decide, therefore, whether the General Assembly can constitutionally require a district court to refrain from exercising its original jurisdiction in some civil cases while arbitration is proceeding. To answer this question, we must examine the nature of the judicial function and determine whether the arbitration panels provided in the Act exercise judicial authority.

In Mizar v. Jones, 157 Colo. 535, 537, 403 P.2d 767, 769 (1965), we noted "that courts do exist primarily to afford a forum to settle litigable matters between disputing parties." A "court" consists of " 'persons officially assembled, under authority of law, at the appropriate time and place, for the administration of justice.' " In re Allison, 13 Colo. 525, 528, 22 P. 820, 821 (1889). In Union Colony v. Elliott, 5 Colo. 371, 381 (1880), we quoted Blackstone's definition of a court:

> A court is defined to be a place where justice is judicially administered.... In every court there must be at least three constituent parts; the *actor, reus* and *judex*; the *actor* or plaintiff who complains of an injury done; the *reus* or defendant, who is called upon to make satisfaction for it; and the *judex* or judicial power which is to examine the truth of the fact, to determine the law arising upon that fact, and if any injury appears to be done, to ascertain, and by its officers to apply the remedy.

It is significant that, in Blackstone's definition of a court, a court must have the authority to apply the remedy.

Many courts have said that the essence of judicial power is the final authority to render and enforce a judgment or remedy. E.g., Cedar Rapids Human Rights Comm'n v. Cedar Rapids Community School Dist., 222 N.W.2d 391, 396 (Iowa 1974); Attorney General v. Johnson, 282 Md. 274, 385 A.2d 57, 64 (1978); Breimhorst v. Beckman, 35 N.W.2d 719, 733 (Minn.1949). " 'It is not enough to make a function judicial that it requires discretion, deliberation, thought, and judgment. It must be the exercise of discretion and judgment within the subdivision of the sovereign power which belongs to the judiciary....' " Solvuca v. Ryan & Reilly Co., 101 A. 710, 715 (Md.1917).

It is clear that, under the Act, the arbitrators' decision is not an exercise of the sovereign power of the state because the decision is nonbinding, and the arbitrators do not perform a judicial function because they do not possess the final authority to render and enforce a judgment. See Attorney General v. Johnson, 385 A.2d at 65 (because either party can reject the decision of the arbitration panel and because the panel cannot enforce its decision even if the parties accept it, the panels do not exercise the judicial power of the state in the constitutional sense).

According to the Act, the arbitration panel must file its decision with the district court, and if neither party demands a trial de novo within thirty days after the filing, only then will the decision be enforceable. Thus, neither party need be bound by the arbitrators' decision because either party can demand a full and complete trial on the facts and the law by the district court with no effect given to the arbitrators' decision. Furthermore, the district court, not the arbitration panel, enters the judgment in accordance with C.R.C.P. 58(a). See C.R.C.P. 109.1(q).

Therefore, we conclude that the arbitration process created by the Act does not vest judicial authority in another branch of government in violation of article III of the Colorado Constitution because the arbitration panels do not perform "a judicial function."

Firelock relies on Wright v. Central Du Page Hospital Association, 63 Ill.2d 313, 347 N.E.2d 736 (Ill.1976), where the Illinois Supreme Court struck down provisions relating to the establishment of medical review panels in medical malpractice cases. The Illinois statute provided for a three member arbitration panel consisting of one circuit judge, one practicing physician, and one practicing attorney. The circuit judge was to preside over the proceeding and decide procedural and evidentiary issues, but as to other issues, both legal and factual, the power and function of the lawyer and physician member of the panel were the same as that of the judge. The determinations of the panel were to be made in a written opinion stating its conclusions of fact and conclusions of law with a dissenting member filing a separate opinion. Either party could reject the panel's decision and proceed to trial as in any other civil case. The expenses of the panel were to be apportioned among the parties equally, except that a party who rejected a unanimous decision of the panel and who failed to prevail at trial could be taxed with the reasonable attorney's fees of the prevailing party, the costs of the panel, and the costs of the trial.

The Illinois Supreme Court held the statute to be unconstitutional because, among other things,

> the physician and lawyer member of the medical review panel are empowered to make conclusions of law and fact "according to the applicable substantive law" over the dissent of the circuit judge. This, we hold, empowers the nonjudicial members of the medical review panel to exercise a judicial function in violation of [the Illinois] Constitution.

Id. 347 N.E.2d at 739–40 (citation omitted).

We find this case to be inapposite because, here, the Act does not provide for a member of the judiciary in the arbitration panel with equal authority in the decision. Thus, there is no provision allowing two nonjudicial members of the panel to make conclusions of law and fact over the dissent of a member of the judiciary. Because the Act does not provide a mixed panel of judicial and nonjudicial members whereby the authority of the judiciary is diluted by the presence of laymen, we find Wright to be inapposite.

B.

Firelock claims that the Act unconstitutionally impedes the right of access to courts guaranteed by article II, sections 3 and 6, by forcing litigants to arbitrate their claims before access is given to the district court and by requiring a party who requests a trial de novo to pay the arbitration costs up to $1,000 if he does not improve his position by at least 10%.

Article II of the Colorado Constitution is entitled "Bill of Rights." Article II, section 3, provides that "[a]ll persons have certain natural, essential and inalienable rights," including, among others, the right of "enjoying and defending their lives and liberties." Section 6 of article II provides that: "Courts of justice shall be open to every person, and a speedy remedy afforded for every injury to person, property or character; and right and justice should be administered without sale, denial or delay."

Generally, a burden on a party's right of access to the courts will be upheld as long as it is reasonable. "In a proper case ... the right of free access to our courts must yield to the rights of others and the efficient administration of justice." People v. Spencer, 185 Colo. 377, 381–82, 524 P.2d 1084, 1086 (1974) (enjoining a *pro se* plaintiff who filed numerous unfounded lawsuits from proceeding *pro se* as plaintiff in the courts of this state).... (citations)

Many other reasonable burdens similar to the one imposed by the Act are present within our system of justice. For example, section 13–32–101, 6A C.R.S. (1987), requires the payment of a docket fee at the time of first appearance in all civil actions and special proceedings in all courts of record. C.R.C.P. 54(d) provides that "[e]xcept when express provision therefor is made either in a statute of this state or in these rules, costs shall be allowed as of course to the prevailing party unless the court otherwise directs." In disputes between landlords and tenants over the return of a security deposit, the willful retention of a security deposit renders the landlord liable for, among other things, reasonable attorney fees and court costs. See § 38–12–103(3)(a), 16A C.R.S. (1982). Finally, C.R.C.P. 68 requires a prevailing party to pay costs incurred after the receipt of an offer of settlement when the judgment obtained by the prevailing party is not more favorable than the offer. Although this list is not all inclusive, it is demonstrative of the extent of a permissible burden on the right of access to the courts.

We conclude that the litigants are not denied their right of access to the courts because the Act provides for de novo review of the decision of the arbitration panel. Furthermore, the requirement that a prevailing party pay the costs of arbitration up to $1,000 if the party does not increase his position by at least 10% at trial does not place an unreasonable burden on the right of access to the courts. Therefore, we hold that the Act does not violate article II, section 6, of the Colorado Constitution.

C.

Firelock next asserts that article II, section 23, of the Colorado Constitution establishes a constitutional right to a jury trial in civil actions and the Act impermissibly infringes on this right. Firestone also argues that this court created the right to a jury trial in civil cases when we adopted C.R.C.P. 38 and that the Act violates that right.

The United States Constitution's guarantee of a civil jury trial provided for in the seventh amendment does not apply to the states. Edwards v. Elliott, 88 U.S. 532, 557, 22 L.Ed. 487 (1874). Article II, section 23, provides that "[t]he right of trial by jury shall remain inviolate in criminal cases; but a jury in civil cases in all courts, or in criminal cases in courts not of record, may consist of less than twelve persons, as may be prescribed by law." ... Although we have held that trial by a jury in a civil action is not a matter of right under the Colorado Constitution, see Setchell v. Dellacroce, 169 Colo. 212, 215, 454 P.2d 804, 806 (1969), this action falls within a category of cases for which C.R.C.P. 38 allows a jury trial as of right because the action is for "money claimed as due on contract." The Act, however, does not deprive a party of the right to a jury trial.

The Act provides for de novo review by the district court thereby giving either party the opportunity for a jury trial, and the provision for the payment of the costs of arbitration if the party does not increase its position by 10% is not an unreasonable burden on the availability of a jury trial. Reasonable prerequisites to the availability of a jury trial are not unusual. For example, section 13–70–103, 6A C.R.S. (1987), requires the payment of a jury fee "in each cause tried by jury."

We hold that the Act does not violate article II, section 23, of the Colorado Constitution because there is no constitutional right to a jury trial in civil cases and the Act does not violate C.R.C.P. 38 because it does not preclude either party from rejecting the result of the arbitration and proceeding to the district court for a de novo jury trial.

D.

Firelock next argues that the Act violates article II, section 25, of the Colorado Constitution and the equal protection clause of the United States Constitution. According to Firelock, the Act creates two classifications which violate the right to equal protection. First, the Act treats litigants in the pilot districts differently than litigants outside the pilot districts. Second, within the pilot districts, the Act treats litigants differently based on the monetary amount of the claim.

The fourteenth amendment to the United States Constitution provides that no state shall "deprive any person of life, liberty or property without due process of law, nor deny to any person within its jurisdiction the equal protection of the laws." U.S. Const. amend. XIV, § 1. The due process clause of article II, section 25, of the Colorado Constitution guarantees the right of equal protection to the citizens of Colorado. See, e.g., Heninger v. Charnes, 200 Colo. 194, 197 n. 3, 613 P.2d 884, 886 n. 3 (1980). In interpreting the equal protection guarantee under the Colorado Constitution, we have followed the analytical mode developed by the United States Supreme Court in construing the equal protection clause of the fourteenth amendment. Tassian v. People, 731 P.2d 672, 674 (Colo.1987). The equal protection clause guarantees that all persons who are similarly situated will receive like treatment by the law. See J.T. v. O'Rourke, 651 P.2d 407, 413 (Colo.1982).

Statutes facing a constitutional challenge are presumed to be constitutional, and the party challenging the statute bears the burden of proving it to be unconstitutional beyond a reasonable doubt. High Gear and Toke Shop v. Beacom, 689 P.2d 624, 630 (Colo.1984). We must first decide which standard of review applies to a challenge to the Act, and then we must apply that standard.

Firelock argues that a standard of strict judicial scrutiny must be applied in resolving its equal protection challenge because the Act infringes on Firelock's fundamental rights, namely, the right of access to court and the right to a trial by jury. To pass strict scrutiny, the government must establish that the statutory classification is necessarily related to a compelling governmental interest. See Parrish v. Lamm, 758 P.2d 1356, 1370 (Colo.1988). "In the absence of a statutory infringement on a fundamental right or the creation of a suspect class, ... equal protection of the laws is satisfied if the statutory classification has a reasonable basis in fact and bears a reasonable relationship to a legitimate governmental interest." Lee v. Colorado Dep't of Health, 718 P.2d 221, 227 (Colo.1986). "When a statutory classification significantly interferes with the exercise of a fundamental right, it cannot be upheld unless it is supported by sufficiently important state interests and is closely tailored to effectuate only those interests." Zablocki v. Redhail, 434 U.S. 374, 388, 98 S.Ct. 673, 682, 54 L.Ed.2d 618 (1978); see also MacGuire v. Houston, 717 P.2d 948, 952–53 (Colo.1986) (Although a restriction on eligibility to serve as an election judge affects the fundamental right of association for political purposes, the injury to the right "is not of such character and magnitude to require strict scrutiny.").

As discussed in part III.B. regarding the right of access to courts and part III.C. regarding the right to trial by jury, the Act does not unreasonably infringe upon or "significantly interfere with" any fundamental right. Furthermore, neither of the classifications creates a suspect class, such as one based on race or national origin. Therefore, the strict scrutiny standard is not the correct standard to apply. Because the strict scrutiny standard is not appropriate and because there is no classification triggering an intermediate standard of review, see, e.g., Kadrmas v. Dickinson Public Schools, 487 U.S. 450, 461, 108 S.Ct. 2481, 2487, 101 L.Ed.2d 399 (1988); Tassian, 731 P.2d at 675, the rational basis standard is the applicable standard of review.

We next examine the classifications advanced by Firelock to determine whether they are rationally related to a legitimate governmental interest. First, the General Assembly's decision to examine the success or failure of the Act in eight pilot districts is not a violation of equal protection.

> "The Fourteenth Amendment does not prohibit legislation merely because it is special, or limited in its application to a particular geographical or political subdivision of the state." Rather, the Equal

Protection Clause is offended only if the statute's classification "rests on grounds wholly irrelevant to the achievement of the State's objective."

Holt Civic Club v. City of Tuscaloosa, 439 U.S. 60, 70–71, 99 S.Ct. 383, 389–90, 58 L.Ed.2d 292 (1978) (citations omitted); accord Kadrmas v. Dickinson Public Schools, 487 U.S. 450, 461, 108 S.Ct. 2481, 2489, 101 L.Ed.2d 399 (1988).

Here, the General Assembly chose to examine the success or failure of the Act by implementing its provisions in several judicial districts for a limited period of time during which evidence could be gathered to determine whether the Act would be beneficial on a statewide basis. The purpose of the General Assembly is evident from the Act's provision for an annual report from the judicial department to the General Assembly evaluating the management of the pilot project, the training of arbitrators, and the availability of arbitrators. See § 13–22–408, 6A C.R.S. (1987).

Second, it is not unreasonable for the General Assembly to determine that claims below $50,000 should be subject to arbitration while claims above $50,000 are not. In Bushnell v. Sapp, 194 Colo. 273, 571 P.2d 1100 (1977), we addressed a similar argument with respect to the Colorado Auto Accident Reparations Act or "No-fault statute," sections 10–4–701 to 10–4–723, 4A C.R.S. (1987). In that case, the appellant argued that the $500 medical expense threshold created an arbitrary classification and thereby denied him equal protection of the laws. We rejected this argument, stating:

> Where and how to draw the line between major and minor claims of this nature is for the legislature to determine, and not the courts. . . . We do not find those criteria here to be unreasonable. Nor do we find the resulting classifications to be arbitrary or irrational. Perfection in classifications has never been constitutionally required and the fact that some inequity may result is not enough to invalidate a legislative classification based on rational distinctions.

Id. at 1106 (citations omitted). Here, the General Assembly's choice that the Act apply to claims of $50,000 and below is not irrational. Other examples of reasonable monetary classifications include a $5,000 limitation in county court, § 13–6–104(1), 6A C.R.S. (1987), a $2,000 limitation in the small claims division of county court, § 13–6–403, 6A C.R.S. (1988 Supp.), and a $50,000 limitation for diversity jurisdiction in federal court, 28 U.S.C.A. § 1332 (West Supp.1989).

Arbitration is favored by the law in Colorado. . . . Arbitration promotes quicker resolution of disputes by providing an expedited opportunity for the parties to present their cases before an unbiased third party. See Norris, National Trends in Mandatory Arbitration, 17 Colo.Law. 1313 (1988); Littlefield, Court–Annexed Arbitration Comes to Colorado, 16 Colo.Law. 1941 (1987). By expediting the adversary process, arbitration promotes quicker settlement of cases thereby speeding up access to the courts and decreasing the costs to the parties. . . .

Although administrative convenience is not a legitimate governmental purpose, see Tassian, 731 P.2d at 676, we believe that the governmental interest advanced by arbitration is more than mere administrative convenience. When the governmental interest served by arbitration is considered in light of the burden placed on the parties, we have no trouble concluding that the Act promotes a legitimate governmental interest and the procedures created by the Act are reasonably related to that interest.

Accordingly, we hold that the Act does not violate the equal protection guarantee of the United States and Colorado Constitutions.

E.

[W]e conclude that the Mandatory Arbitration Act, §§ 13–22–401 to 13–22–409, 6A C.R.S. (1987), does not violate the Colorado Constitution or the United States Constitution. Therefore, we discharge the rule to show cause and direct the district court to proceed with the assignment of the case to arbitration. . . .

■ ERICKSON, JUSTICE, specially concurring:

While I acknowledge that the right of access to the courts is an important one, Colo. Const. art. II, § 6, the burgeoning case load in our courts has itself caused delay and increased costs. Access to the courts for all litigants may be improved by different alternatives for dispute resolution, such as arbitration and mediation. See McKay, The Many Uses of Alternative Dispute Resolution, 40 Arb.J. 12 (Sept.1985).

In my view, the mandatory arbitration pilot project in issue was a legislative method of reducing delay and providing access to the courts by winnowing out those cases that can be resolved by simpler and less costly methods. It is certainly not obvious to me that the method selected by the legislature will prevent some litigants from obtaining access to the courts. Since a number of cases may be satisfactorily resolved before trial, it would appear that arbitration will actually improve access to the courts. See Levin, Court Annexed Arbitration, 16 J.Law Reform 542 (Spring 1983). Accordingly, I concur in the majority's decision to discharge the rule.

■ LOHR, JUSTICE, dissenting:

I respectfully dissent. The majority holds that the Mandatory Arbitration Act, §§ 13–22–401 to 13–22–409, 6A C.R.S. (1987), violates neither the Colorado Constitution nor the due process or equal protection clauses of the fourteenth amendment to the United States Constitution. Unlike the majority, I am persuaded that the Mandatory Arbitration Act violates the right of every person to obtain access to the courts as guaranteed by article II, section 6, of the Colorado Constitution. I would therefore make the rule issued in this case absolute. Because I would resolve the case on right of access grounds, I would not reach the other constitutional arguments raised by the defendant, Firelock Incorporated.

Article II, section 6, of the Colorado Constitution states:

Courts of justice shall be open to every person, and a speedy remedy afforded for every injury to person, property or character; and right and justice should be administered without sale, denial or delay.

We have previously recognized that this provision "guarantees to every person the right of access to courts of justice in this state." Board of County Comm'rs v. Barday, 197 Colo. 519, 522, 594 P.2d 1057, 1059 (1979) ... The constitutional right of access to the courts means "that for any act of another *which constitutes an injurious invasion of any right of the individual which is recognized by or founded upon any applicable principle of law*, statutory or common, the courts shall be open to him and he 'shall have remedy, by due course of law.'" Goldberg v. Musim, 162 Colo. 461, 469, 427 P.2d 698, 702 (1967) (quoting Cason v. Baskin, 20 So.2d 243, 250 (Fla.1944)) (emphasis in original). Article II, section 6, "limits very stringently the power to exclude resident plaintiffs from our court system where jurisdiction has otherwise been properly established." McDonnell–Douglas v. Lohn, 192 Colo. 200, 201, 557 P.2d 373, 374 (1976) (because of article II, section 6, the doctrine of forum non conveniens has only the most limited application in Colorado courts).... The lesson of McDonnell–Douglas is that we must carefully scrutinize any innovative procedure, however well intended, that interferes with the fundamental right of every person to obtain access to the courts to obtain redress for their legally cognizable grievances.

[T]he procedure by which a litigant must submit his claim for mandatory arbitration as a condition precedent to trying his case in a court restricts access to the courts in two important ways. First, the litigant may not present his claim to a court until he has undergone the delay[2] and expense attendant to an arbitration proceeding. § 13–22–402(2). Second, in order to obtain access to a court after arbitration has been completed, the litigant must accept the consequence that he will be required to pay the costs of the arbitration proceeding, including arbitrator fees, up to a maximum of $1,000 should he fail to improve his position by more than ten percent. § 13–22–405(3). These burdens of time and expense are considerable and will likely have the practical effect of preventing litigants with smaller claims from ever obtaining access to the courts to assert them. In short, for some litigants these barriers to access to the courts will not simply burden such access but as a practical matter will bar entry into a judicial forum. The majority does not explain why these obviously important limitations on a litigant's fundamental right of access to the courts are permissible except to analogize them to the collection of docket fees, the award of costs to a prevailing party, and the imposition of certain other incidental costs of litigation applicable in special situations. See maj. op. at 1096. The majority simply offers the conclusion that the burdens are

---

2. The arbitration proceeding "shall be held within ninety days of the date on which the case is at issue between the parties." § 13–22–404(1). "The arbitrators shall file their decision with the court within ten days of the hearing...." § 13–22–404(7). Each party has thirty days after the arbitrators' decision is filed to demand a trial de novo. §§ 13–22–404(8), 13–22–405(1). Thus, the arbitration process is designed to defer resort to the courts for up to 130 days, exclusive of the time required for the hearing itself.

reasonable. I cannot agree that it is constitutionally permissible to burden the fundamental right of access to the courts in these significant ways.

In sum, I regard the mandatory arbitration process at issue in this case as limiting access to the courts in a manner that conflicts with both the spirit and the letter of article II, section 6, of the Colorado Constitution. See Aldana v. Holub, 381 So.2d 231, 238 (Fla.1980) (medical mediation statute violated due process because application of its rigid jurisdictional periods proved arbitrary and capricious, and enlargement of these periods would effectively deprive claimants of access to the courts); People ex rel. Christiansen v. Connell, 2 Ill.2d 332, 118 N.E.2d 262, 265–69 (1954) (statute that imposed mandatory waiting period before divorce action could be filed held to obstruct litigants' constitutional right of access to the courts without delay); State ex rel. Cardinal Glennon Memorial Hosp. v. Gaertner, 583 S.W.2d 107, 110 (Mo.1979) (statute requiring that medical malpractice claims be referred to medical malpractice review panel before being filed in court held unconstitutional based on fact that it "imposes a procedure" as a precondition to constitutionally established right of access to the courts); Jiron v. Mahlab, 99 N.M. 425, 659 P.2d 311, 313 (1983) (statute requiring medical malpractice claimant to appear before a review commission prior to filing suit deprives plaintiffs of their constitutional right of access to the courts if the review requirement "causes undue delay prejudicing a plaintiff by the loss of witnesses or parties"); cf. Mattos v. Thompson, 491 Pa. 385, 421 A.2d 190, 195–96 (1980) (striking as unconstitutional a statute giving arbitration panel original jurisdiction over medical malpractice claims where delays involved in statutory procedures oppressively burdened the right to a jury trial so as to "make the right practically unavailable").

In reaching the conclusion that the Mandatory Arbitration Act cannot be squared with the constitutional right of access to the courts, I do not mean to imply that all efforts and methods to resolve disputes outside of the judicial forum violate that constitutional right. I would hold only that the particular mandatory procedure involved in this case imposes constitutionally impermissible burdens on that right. I would therefore make the rule absolute.

* * *

Questions

1. The *Firelock* court distinguished the *Wright* case in which the Illinois Supreme Court found that the medical review procedure empowered non-judicial members to "exercise a judicial function." Yet under the Illinois procedure at issue in the *Wright* case, the losing party was entitled to a trial de novo, just as they are under the Colorado procedure. Under the Colorado procedure, do not the arbitrators also exercise "judicial functions"? Are there other differences between the Illinois and Colorado procedure that could explain the different results in the two cases?

2. Courts in many states have held that compulsory court-annexed arbitration is only constitutional where the procedures permit a party who had a right to a jury trial to reject the arbitral award and proceed to a de novo trial. See, e.g., *Valler v. Lee and Hensley*, 190 Ariz. 391, 949 P.2d 51 (Ct. Of Appls., Div. 2, 1997); *Barazzotto v. Intelligent Systems, Inc.* 40 Ohio App.3d 117, 532 N.E.2d 148 (1987). Does this mean that parties have an absolute right to a jury trial notwithstanding the existence of a compulsory court-ordered arbitration system, or are there circumstances in which a party can lose that right? For example, would it be constitutional for a court-ordered arbitration procedure to provide that a party who failed to appear in an arbitration forfeited its right to a trial de novo? See, *Williams v. Dorsey*, 273 Ill.App.3d 893, 652 N.E.2d 1286 (Ct. Of Appls., 1st Dist., 1995). Would it be constitutional for a court-ordered arbitration procedure to deny a trial de novo to a party who refused to cooperate in discovery? See, *Casino Properties, Inc. v. Andrews*, 112 Nev. 132, 911 P.2d 1181 (S. Ct. Nev. 1996).

3. Most state compulsory arbitration procedures specify that the parties must participate in the arbitration in "good faith" or participate in a "meaningful fashion." See, e.g., Illinois Supreme Court Rule 91(b), 145 Ill. 2d R. 91(b) (requiring parties to participate in court-ordered arbitration "in good faith and in a meaningful manner"); Nevada Appellate Rule 22(a) (requiring party to participate in court-ordered arbitration "in good faith."). And most state courts have held that a party who fails to engage in good faith or meaningful participation can be barred from rejecting an award and thereby precluded from a trial de novo. See, *Middleton v. Baskin*, 618 A.2d 1263 (Sup. Ct. R.I., 1992). Does the possibility of a party being barred from a trial de novo weaken the constitutional basis for such systems?

4. Who decides whether a party participates in "good faith"? Can an arbitrator make that determination? The Illinois statute requires arbitrators to make a finding as to lack of good faith in the first instance, and requires courts to accord that finding presumptive validity. For example, in *Allstate Insurance Co. v. Avelares*, 295 Ill.App.3d 950, 693 N.E.2d 1233 (Ct. Of Appls., 1st Dist. 1998), the court denied the defendant's motion for de novo review of an adverse arbitral award because the arbitrators had found that defendant did not appear at the arbitration hearing, and that the appearance by defendant's attorney did not constitute participation in a meaningful manner. Does such a procedure delegate excessive authority to an arbitrator, who can not only decide a case on its merits, but also prevent judicial review by finding the defendant's participation to fall short of good faith?

5. If the issue of good faith participation is determined by a court, on what can the a court base its determination? How could a court determine, after the fact, whether a party participated in good faith? Must there be a transcript for a court to find lack of good faith? What kinds of evidence would it need to make such a determination? Can the arbitrator be required to testify about the conduct of the parties? Similarly, if the arbitrator makes the lack of good faith determination in the first instance,

how can a court review it if there is no record made of the arbitration proceedings? See *West Bend Mutual Insurance Co. v. Herrera,* 292 Ill. App.3d 669, 686 N.E.2d 645 (Ct. of App., 1st Dist. 1997).

6.   Both the Illinois and the Colorado court-annexed arbitration statutes involve some degree of fee-shifting for parties who lose at arbitration, request a trial de novo, and then fail to improve their position significantly at trial. Does the additional burden on a party that fee-shifting imposes act as a serious impediment to their right to a judicial resolution of their dispute? Are there other features of the mandatory arbitration procedure that might impede a party's access to the courts?

7.   Can a party who lost at court-ordered arbitration obtain a trial de novo on some counts of a complaint but not others? Can the court sever the issues in dispute? Does the grant of a trial de novo vacate the arbitral decision in its entirety, or does it constitute an appeal of the specific issues on which the losing party seeks review? See *Action Orthopedics Inc. v. Techmedica, Inc.* 775 F.Supp. 390 (M.D.Fla.1991); *Bridges v. City of Troy,* 112 Misc.2d 384 (Sup. Ct. Rensselaer Co. 1982). Would a rule that permits partial appeals operate to undermine the effectiveness of a court-ordered arbitration system? See *Watkins v. K–Mart Corp.,* 1997 WL 597913 (E.D.Pa.1997).

8.   Consider the following hypothetical: As a result of a three-party automobile accident, an injured passenger sued both the driver of the vehicle she was riding in (the "host vehicle") and the driver of the other vehicle (the "stranger vehicle") for negligence. Under a state mandatory court-annexed arbitration procedure, the case was sent to arbitration and the arbitrator found that the driver of the stranger vehicle was negligent and the driver of the host vehicle was not. If the driver of the stranger vehicle rejected the arbitral award and sought a trial de novo, can the driver of the host vehicle, who was exonerated by the arbitration award, move to have the arbitral award in her favor declared final? Stated differently, does the de novo trial have the effect of eliminating the host vehicle's favorable ruling and make her once again potentially liable to the plaintiff? See *Valler v. Lee and Hensley,* 190 Ariz. 391, 949 P.2d 51 (Ct. App., Div. 2, 1997).

* * *

C.   GOOD FAITH PARTICIPATION

Employer's Consortium, Inc. v. Aaron

298 Ill.App.3d 187, 698 N.E.2d 189 (Ill.App., 2 Dist. 1998).

■ DOYLE, JUSTICE

Plaintiffs, Employer's Consortium, Inc., and Cory & Associates, Inc., sued to recover on promissory notes made by defendant, Carrie A. Aaron. The case was referred to mandatory arbitration. The arbitrators found the plaintiffs had not participated in good faith and in a meaningful way pursuant to Supreme Court Rule 91(b) (145 Ill.2d R. 91(b)). Based on this finding, the trial court debarred the plaintiffs from rejecting the arbitrator's award. Plaintiffs appealed the trial court's ruling. We affirm.

Plaintiffs' amended complaint alleged defendant owed approximately $33,000 on 11 separate promissory notes. Defendant's answer admitted making the notes but denied defaulting and asserted several affirmative defenses. Defendant was present with her attorney at the arbitration hearing on January 14, 1997. Plaintiffs were represented by counsel.

Plaintiffs' attorney made an opening statement but did not call any witnesses. The chairperson for the arbitrators offered plaintiffs' attorney the opportunity to contact any potential witnesses. Plaintiffs' attorney declined to call any witnesses and did not request a continuance. Plaintiffs' attorney then rested the case and submitted the unverified complaint along with the attached copies of the promissory notes to the arbitration panel. The arbitration panel made an award in favor of defendant. The arbitration panel also entered a unanimous Rule 91(b) finding that plaintiffs failed to participate in good faith and in a meaningful manner and listed as the factual basis therefor "failure to present any evidence."

On January 31, 1997, defendant filed a motion to bar rejection of arbitration. Defendant attached the affidavit of her attorney in support of the motion. Plaintiffs filed a written response including affidavits from plaintiffs' counsel and Andrew Cory. Plaintiffs' first affidavit stated inter alia that their counsel was informed the night before the arbitration hearing that Andrew Cory, president of the plaintiff corporations, would be unable to attend. The affidavit of Andrew Cory stated that he "was outside the State of Illinois and was unable to attend the arbitration." Defendant's motion to bar rejection was granted on March 11, 1997. Following denial of their motion for reconsideration, plaintiffs appealed.

Plaintiffs present a single issue for review, namely, whether the trial court properly debarred plaintiffs from rejecting the arbitration award based on the panel's finding that the plaintiffs failed to participate in good faith and in a meaningful manner as is required by Rule 91(b).

This issue requires a two-part analysis. First, we must consider whether the trial court's finding that plaintiffs failed to participate in good faith and in a meaningful manner was against the manifest weight of the evidence. Martinez v. Gaimari, 271 Ill.App.3d 879, 883, 208 Ill.Dec. 262, 649 N.E.2d 94 (1995). Second, we must consider whether debarring plaintiffs from rejecting the award was an abuse of discretion. Williams v. Dorsey, 273 Ill.App.3d 893, 901, 210 Ill.Dec. 310, 652 N.E.2d 1286 (1995).

The supreme court adopted Rule 91(b), requiring good-faith participation at mandatory arbitration hearings. That rule provides in pertinent part:

> "(b) Good–Faith Participation. All parties to the arbitration hearing must participate in the hearing in good faith and in a meaningful manner. If a panel of arbitrators unanimously finds that a party has failed to participate in the hearing in good faith and in a meaningful manner, the panel's finding and factual basis therefor shall be stated

on the award. Such award shall be prima facie evidence that the party failed to participate in the arbitration hearing in good faith and in a meaningful manner and a court, when presented with a petition for sanctions or remedy therefor, may order sanctions as provided in Rule 219(c), including, but not limited to, an order debarring that party from rejecting the award, and costs and attorney fees incurred for the arbitration hearing and in the prosecution of the petition for sanctions, against that party." 145 Ill.2d R. 91(b).

The committee comments to this rule indicate the intent of the rule was to prevent parties and lawyers from abusing the arbitration process by refusing to participate. 145 Ill.2d R. 91, Committee Comments. Arbitration is not to be considered simply a hurdle to cross on the way to trial. 145 Ill.2d R. 91, Committee Comments. The purpose of mandatory arbitration is to subject a case to the type of adversarial testing that would be expected at trial. Martinez, 271 Ill.App.3d at 883–84, 208 Ill.Dec. 262, 649 N.E.2d 94.

Supreme Court Rule 91(b) provides that the finding of an arbitration panel that a party did not participate in good faith is prima facie evidence of that fact. 145 Ill.2d R. 91(b). The party subject to sanctions of Rule 91(b) has the burden of presenting evidence sufficient to rebut the prima facie evidence. Martinez, 271 Ill.App.3d at 883, 208 Ill.Dec. 262, 649 N.E.2d 94....

Here, the record does not provide sufficient evidence to rebut this prima facie finding. On the date of the hearing, plaintiffs' counsel appeared before the arbitration panel. She made a brief opening statement and submitted a copy of the unverified complaint along with the attached exhibits to the arbitrators. The chairperson of the arbitrators then offered plaintiffs' counsel the opportunity to contact any witnesses. Plaintiffs' counsel did not call any witnesses, nor did she request a continuance. The panel then entered an award in favor of defendant and made the unanimous finding that the plaintiffs had failed to participate in good faith and in a meaningful manner as required by Rule 91(b).

Plaintiffs concede that their counsel's performance before the panel was ineffective. Plaintiffs admit in their brief that "[p]laintiffs' counsel may have been unprepared or even inept" and that plaintiffs' presentation "may have been considered sloppy and unprepared participation." Plaintiffs' counsel had several options. For example, she could have requested a continuance to allow witnesses to appear. She could also have examined the defendant, who was present, regarding the notes. Plaintiffs' counsel, however, did nothing and rested her case solely on the complaint.

Plaintiffs did not present evidence to provide the arbitrators with the basis for an award. Even if the unverified complaint and attached exhibits had been accepted by the arbitration panel as evidence, plaintiffs would not have presented a prima facie case. The making of the notes was undisputed. The issues in dispute centered around payment and other affirmative defenses raised by defendant. Plaintiffs presented no evidence regarding payment of the notes and did not address the affirmative defenses. It is highly unlikely that plaintiffs would have proceeded in this manner at trial.

This was not the adversarial testing necessary to maintain the integrity of the arbitration process. Martinez, 271 Ill.App.3d at 883–84, 208 Ill.Dec. 262, 649 N.E.2d 94.

Plaintiffs also argue that their participation in the arbitration process was in good faith regardless of its quality. To prevent imposition of a sanction, plaintiffs have the burden of demonstrating that their actions were reasonable or justified by extenuating circumstances. Kubian v. Labinsky, 178 Ill.App.3d 191, 197, 127 Ill.Dec. 404, 533 N.E.2d 22 (1988). The only evidence of extenuating circumstances presented to the trial court was the affidavit of Andrew Cory. The affidavit stated simply that Cory could not attend the arbitration hearing because he was outside the state. Plaintiffs presented no evidence that this was reasonable or the result of extenuating circumstances. Plaintiffs also provided no explanation for counsel's failure to request a continuance when confronted with the absence of plaintiffs' primary witness. Plaintiffs argue that a sanction under Rule 91(b) was inappropriate because although "counsel may have been unprepared or even inept" she did not refuse to participate. We disagree. Rule 91(b) requires parties to participate "in good faith and in a meaningful manner." (Emphasis added.) 145 Ill.2d R. 91(b). A trial court need not find intentional obstruction of the arbitration proceeding. The purposes of Rule 91(b) are defeated whether a party's conduct is the result of inept preparation or intentional disregard for the process. See Martinez, 271 Ill.App.3d at 883, 208 Ill.Dec. 262, 649 N.E.2d 94 (validity of excuse held less important than failure to present evidence).

Finally, plaintiffs argue that the Rule 91(b) finding was deficient because the panel stated as a basis for its findings only the "failure to present any evidence." Without citation to authority plaintiffs argue that the panel's finding failed to provide a sufficient explanation and reasoning. We disagree. Given these facts, the panel's explanation is sufficiently clear to inform plaintiffs of the basis for its finding.

Therefore, after a thorough review of the record, we cannot conclude that the trial court's finding that plaintiffs did not participate in good faith was against the manifest weight of the evidence.

[The court next considered whether the trial court had abused its discretion in debarring plaintiffs from rejecting the award. The court found that it did not, stating:]

It is essential to the integrity of the mandatory arbitration process that the parties proceed at the arbitration hearing in good faith and subject their claims to the sort of adversarial testing that would be expected at trial. Martinez, 271 Ill.App.3d at 883–84, 208 Ill.Dec. 262, 649 N.E.2d 94. A trial court has discretion to enforce supreme court rules and impose sanctions on the parties as appropriate and necessary to promote the unimpeded flow of litigation and maintain the integrity of our court system. Sander v. Dow Chemical Co., 166 Ill.2d 48, 68, 209 Ill.Dec. 623, 651 N.E.2d 1071 (1995). More importantly, Rule 91 specifically allows for an order debarring a party from rejecting the award as a sanction for failure to participate in good faith and in a meaningful manner. Here, having presented no evidence, the plaintiffs failed to participate in the hearing in good faith and in a meaningful manner. It is immaterial whether plaintiffs' failure to participate was the result of lack of preparation or an intentional disregard for the process. The trial court concluded that plaintiffs' actions warranted debarment from rejecting the award as a sanction. We cannot conclude that this was an abuse of the trial court's discretion.

For the foregoing reasons, the judgment of the circuit court of Du Page County is affirmed.

* * *

Questions

1. Does the court in *Employer's Consortium* impose the same test for determining good faith participation in arbitration as it would use for determining whether there was attorney malpractice? Or, does it impose a more demanding test for good faith participation? If it is more demanding, how demanding is it? Does the requirement that parties participate in arbitration in a "meaningful manner" mean that an attorney for a party must be prepared for the hearing? Must she be *well* prepared? How is a court to determine whether there was adequate preparation? How is an arbitrator to make such a determination?

2. Is attorney negligence a reason to deny a party a right to a trial de novo after an arbitral award? If so, what redress would the party have against the attorney? Could an arbitral finding of lack of meaningful participation constitute evidence of attorney malpractice?

3. Must a party's attorney be an expert in the subject matter of the dispute in order to satisfy the criteria for good faith presentation of the case? Must she be a specialist in the substantive area of law? What if the arbitrator is not an attorney himself, and thus incorrectly adjudges the attorney to be inept? Would such a finding be amenable to judicial review?

4. Suppose it is well established under the law of a state that a plaintiff in an action to collect on a promissory note need only to produce the note itself and allege nonpayment in order to make out a prima facie case. If such a dispute were sent to a court-ordered arbitration and the plaintiff, through its attorney, makes out a legally sufficient prima facie case in this fashion, can the arbitrator find that the plaintiff did not participate in good faith? Must the party attempt to rebut the defendant's affirmative defense in order to be in good faith? What if the affirmative defense is so lacking in credibility that the plaintiff's attorney decides not to offer a rebuttal? If the arbitrator finds that the attorney failed to participate in a meaningful manner, should a court use the arbitral finding as a basis for barring that party from obtaining a trial de novo? How do the facts of *Employer's Consortium* differ from this hypothetical?

* * *

State Farm Insurance Co. v. Kazakova

299 Ill.App.3d 1028, 702 N.E.2d 254 (Ct. App., 2d Dist. 1998).

■ JUSTICE CERDA delivered the opinion of the court:

The issue on appeal is whether a non-English-speaking defendant failed to participate in good faith and in a meaningful manner at a mandatory-arbitration hearing and violated the notice to appear by failing to provide a foreign-language interpreter so she could testify. Defendant, Stella Kazakova, appeals from the orders of the circuit court of Cook County (1) finding that she did not participate in good faith and in a meaningful manner at the mandatory-arbitration hearing and that she violated the notice to appear by not appearing with a foreign-language interpreter; (2) sanctioning her by debarring her from rejecting the arbitration award in favor of plaintiff, State Farm Insurance Company, as subrogee of Robin Depender; and (3) denying her motion to vacate the sanction. We reverse.

FACTS

In 1995, plaintiff filed a negligence complaint arising out an automobile collision between the vehicles of Depender and defendant. Defendant filed an answer, denying the allegations of negligence. Defendant also filed a jury demand.

The case was assigned to mandatory arbitration. The hearing was held on September 4, 1996, but the proceedings were not transcribed. The arbitrators entered an award finding in favor of plaintiff and awarding damages. The award stated in part:

"We note for the record that defendant personally appeared pursuant to a proper Rule 237 request but was unable to testify due to her inability to speak and understand English. In addition, we unanimously find that defendant failed to participate in the arbitration hearing in good faith for the following reasons: 1) Failed to produce a witness who was competent to testify; 2) Failed to present any evidence to counter the evidence presented by plaintiff on the issues of liability and damages; 3) Failed to present any evidence whatsoever in defense of the claim."

Defendant filed a notice of rejection of the arbitration award. Plaintiff moved the court to debar defendant from rejecting the mandatory-arbitration award and to enter judgment on the award. The motion was based in part on defendant's failure to testify at the arbitration hearing due to her inability to speak English, her failure to bring an interpreter, and her failure to introduce any evidence in defense. Plaintiff also sought sanctions under Supreme Court Rule 137 (155 Ill.2d R. 137) for filing an answer in bad faith. Defendant opposed the motion, arguing in part that she was not required to bring an interpreter.

On December 30, 1996, the trial court made a finding that, because defendant "fail[ed] to appear" at the arbitration hearing "prepared to testify," she failed to participate in good faith and in a meaningful manner and violated plaintiff's notice to appear. The trial court barred defendant from rejecting the arbitration award, entered judgment on the award in favor of plaintiff, struck defendant's rejection of the arbitration award, and denied plaintiff's motion for Supreme Court Rule 137 sanctions.

Defendant filed a motion to vacate judgment, which was denied.

Defendant appealed.

DISCUSSION

Defendant argues that (1) defendant's failure to speak English was not a failure to participate in good faith and in a meaningful manner and was not a violation of the notice to appear at the arbitration; (2) it was an excessive sanction to debar defendant from rejecting the arbitration award; (3) the actions of the trial court and the arbitration panel violated equal protection; and (4) Supreme Court Rule 91(b) (145 Ill.2d R. 91(b)) is unconstitutional. We find that it is not necessary for us to decide the constitutional issues....

The arbitration in this case was scheduled pursuant to supreme court rules establishing a nonbinding, court-annexed arbitration system to resolve certain civil actions. 134 Ill.2d Rs. 86 through 95; Introductory Comments, at 86. Applicable to mandatory-arbitration hearings is Supreme Court Rule 237, which provides that the appearance at the trial of a party may be required by serving her with a notice. 166 Ill.2d Rs. 90(g), 237.

Supreme Court Rule 90(g) provides as follows:

"The provisions of Rule 237, herein, shall be equally applicable to arbitration hearings as they are to trials. * * * Remedies upon a party's failure to comply with notice pursuant to Rule 237(b) may include an order debarring that party from rejecting the award." 166 Ill.2d R. 90(g).

Supreme Court Rule 91(b) provides a standard for parties' conduct at the arbitration hearings:

"All parties to the arbitration hearing must participate in the hearing in good faith and in a meaningful manner. If a panel of arbitrators unanimously finds that a party has failed to participate in the hearing in good faith and in a meaningful manner, the panel's finding and factual basis therefor shall be stated on the award. Such award shall be prima facie evidence that the party failed to participate in the arbitration hearing in good faith and in a meaningful manner and a court, when presented with a petition for sanctions or remedy therefor, may order sanctions as provided in Rule 219(c), including, but not limited to, an order debarring that party from rejecting the award, and costs and attorney fees incurred for the arbitration hearing and in the prosecution of the petition for sanctions, against that party." 145 Ill.2d R. 91(b).

A party can reject the arbitration award and proceed to trial. 174 Ill.2d R. 93(a)....

The express concerns behind Supreme Court Rule 91(b) are to prevent the abuse of the arbitration process and to uphold the integrity of the arbitration process. 145 Ill.2d R. 91(b), Committee Comments, at lxx. Defendant did not choose not to participate; she was not able to participate without an interpreter. In order to meet the standard of good-faith and meaningful participation, a defendant does not have to hire an interpreter to assist plaintiff's efforts to prove its case. If a defendant does not provide an interpreter and a plaintiff desires to examine defendant as an adverse witness, plaintiff should bear the cost of an interpreter. We hold that defendant did not violate Supreme Court Rule 91(b) by not providing an interpreter....

If a defendant does not notify plaintiff that defendant will not be able to testify in English and that defendant will not provide an interpreter at the arbitration hearing, plaintiff would not be made aware of the need to arrange its own interpreter to be present, if desired. Certainly that lack of notification would be a breach of civility; it might be successfully argued in a future case that such conduct also could form the basis for Supreme Court Rule 91(b) sanctions. We do not know on this record if plaintiff was aware prior to the hearing of defendant's inability to testify in English. We do not decide today whether the failure to notify would violate Supreme Court Rule 91(b).

Even if we held that defendant should have provided an interpreter as part of her good-faith and meaningful participation in arbitration, we would reverse on the basis that debarring defendant from rejecting the arbitration award was harsh and unjustified. The arbitration proceedings could have been stayed until defendant provided an interpreter, and plaintiff could have been awarded attorney fees and costs incurred for the arbitration hearing. 145 Ill.2d R. 91(b); see 166 Ill.2d R. 219(c)(i) (one possible remedy is to stay further proceedings until the party complies with the supreme court rule).

In addition, we believe that the standard to be applied in deciding whether to bar defendant from rejecting the award is whether her conduct was characterized by a deliberate and pronounced disregard for rules and the court. Walton v. Throgmorton, 273 Ill.App.3d 353, 359, 210 Ill.Dec. 1, 652 N.E.2d 803 (1995); Valdivia v. Chicago & North Western Transportation Co., 87 Ill.App.3d 1123, 1125, 42 Ill.Dec. 842, 409 N.E.2d 457 (1980). Defendant was present and available to testify at the arbitration hearing. She could have been examined by plaintiff if a Russian-language interpreter had been present....

As defendant did not violate Supreme Court Rule 91(b) or 237, the trial court erred in barring her from rejecting the arbitration award.

The judgment of the trial court is reversed, and the cause is remanded with directions to permit defendant to reject the arbitration award.

Reversed with directions.

* * *

Questions

1.   In *Employer's Consortium*, the mere presence of a party or its attorney at a court-ordered arbitration hearing was not sufficient to constitute good faith. Rather, the court held that the party or its attorney must actually participate "in a meaningful way." Why then is the mere presence of the defendant sufficient to satisfy the requirement of good faith in *State Farm Insurance?*

2.   In *State Farm Insurance,* the court found that it was not incumbent upon the non-English-speaking defendant to provide an interpreter, even though an interpreter was necessary to permit her to participate in the hearing. Without an interpreter, such a party can neither present her own case, nor be subject to cross-examination. If the plaintiff in *State Farm Insurance* had appeared alone and had not had a English-speaking lawyer to present her case on her behalf, would the arbitrators have been justified in finding a lack of meaningful participation? Should it be grounds to debar her from seeking a trial de novo? What other problems might follow from such a result?

3.   The court in *State Farm Insurance* stated that the standard to be applied in deciding whether to bar defendant from rejecting the award is "whether her conduct was characterized by a deliberate and pronounced disregard for rules and the court." Is this standard consistent with the standard that the court applied in *Employer's Consortium?*

* * *

D.   FINALITY OF AWARDS

Flynn v. Gorton

207 Cal.App.3d 1550, 255 Cal.Rptr. 768 (Ct. App., 4th Dist., Div. 3 1989).

◼ SCOVILLE, PRESIDING JUSTICE.

The trial court sustained a demurrer to John Flynn's cross-complaint without leave to amend after determining that a prior judicial arbitration award against Flynn was res judicata. Because we hold a judicial arbitration award has no conclusive effect on issues raised in a subsequent proceeding on a different cause of action, we reverse the judgment. As we shall explain, Flynn's action was not barred by res judicata because his cross-complaint stated a different cause of action than that involved in the judicial arbitration proceeding. Nor was Flynn barred under the doctrine of collateral estoppel from relitigating issues already resolved in the arbitration. Since we believe the monetary limits on judicial arbitration, along with the option of trial de novo, combine to dampen a defendant's incentive to litigate the issues, application of collateral estoppel to such a proceeding would be unfair and unexpected by the parties. More importantly, it could impair the efficiency and impede the purpose of the judicial arbitration system.

FACTS

John Flynn and Achilda Gorton were involved in an automobile accident in 1983. Flynn was turning left and Gorton was entering the intersection when their cars collided. Kim Blackburn was a passenger in Gorton's car.

Gorton brought a personal injury suit against Flynn, alleging his negligence caused the collision. Flynn generally denied the allegation and claimed Gorton's negligence contributed to the accident.

Gorton elected to submit the case to arbitration and agreed that any award would not exceed $25,000. The arbitrator awarded her $20,281.08 in full settlement of her claims. The award became a final judgment which Flynn satisfied in full.

Blackburn then filed a personal injury complaint against Flynn and Gorton, alleging both were negligent. Flynn cross-complained against Gorton for implied indemnity, contribution and declaratory relief. He alleged Blackburn's injuries resulted from Gorton's negligence in causing the accident and he was entitled to a determination of each party's comparative negligence and an apportionment of damages.

Gorton demurred to Flynn's cross-complaint, arguing it was barred under the doctrine of res judicata because it presented the same claim decided in the judicial arbitration action. She asked the court to take judicial notice of the court files, the arbitrator's award, and his cover letter explaining the award. The award was silent as to the arbitrator's reasons for the decision. However, in the arbitrator's cover letter, he stated: "[O]nce I had completed the application of very basic accident reconstruction principals [sic] . . ., it became very clear that the issue of liability was no issue at all, and very clearly in favor of the plaintiff."

Flynn opposed the demurrer, arguing his cross-complaint for indemnity raised a new issue. The trial court sustained Gorton's demurrer without leave to amend.

On appeal Flynn argues the issue raised in his cross-complaint, i.e. whether Gorton was partially responsible for her passenger's injuries, was not addressed in the arbitration action. He contends the arbitration award did not resolve whether: (1) under comparative fault principles, Gorton was responsible in part for the collision and thus for Blackburn's injuries; and (2) whether Gorton otherwise contributed to her passenger's injuries, e.g. by failing to have seat belts or by somehow aggravating Blackburn's injuries after the collision. Flynn asserts the arbitration award and court file are silent on the issue of the parties' comparative fault in causing the collision, and it may be that the approximately $20,000 award to Gorton reflected an offset for her contributory negligence. He argues under these circumstances his action was not barred by res judicata.

DISCUSSION

The doctrine of res judicata is composed of two parts: claim preclusion and issue preclusion. Claim preclusion prohibits a party from relitigating a previously adjudicated cause of action; thus, a new lawsuit on the same cause of action is entirely barred. (Frommhagen v. Board of Supervisors (1987) 197 Cal.App.3d 1292, 1299–1300, 243 Cal.Rptr. 390.) Issue preclusion, or collateral estoppel, applies to a subsequent suit between the parties on a different cause of action. Collateral estoppel prevents the parties from relitigating any *issue* which was actually litigated and finally decided in the earlier action. (Carroll v. Puritan Leasing Co. (1978) 77 Cal.App.3d 481, 490, 143 Cal.Rptr. 772.) The issue decided in the earlier proceeding must be identical to the one presented in the subsequent action. If there is any doubt, collateral estoppel will not apply. (Southwell v. Mallery, Stern & Warford (1987) 194 Cal.App.3d 140, 144, 239 Cal.Rptr. 371.)

Res judicata and collateral estoppel share common goals. Both prevent inconsistent results and promote finality and judicial economy by bringing an end to litigation.

Judicial arbitration was enacted by the Legislature in 1978 to serve similar ends. Due to the cost, complexity and delay involved in court adjudication, the Legislature declared that arbitration should be encouraged or required as "an efficient and equitable method for resolving small claims." (Code Civ.Proc., § 1141.10, subd. (a).) Under the statute, court-ordered arbitration is mandatory in certain courts for civil actions in which the amount in controversy does not exceed a specified amount. (Code Civ.Proc., § 1141.11.) Such arbitration can also be elected by stipulation of the parties or by the unilateral decision of the plaintiff if he or she agrees that any award will not exceed the statutory amount. (Code Civ.Proc., § 1141.12.)

Unlike commercial or true arbitration, judicial arbitration is not binding, since any party dissatisfied with an award may elect trial de novo.[2] (Code Civ.Proc., § 1141.20.) The Legislature, however, seeking to encourage finality of judicial arbitration awards, enacted disincentives to trial de novo. (See Demirgian v. Superior Court (1986) 187 Cal.App.3d 372, 376, 231 Cal.Rptr. 698.) For example, if a party requesting trial de novo does not obtain a more favorable judgment, he or she is liable for significant costs and fees. (Code Civ.Proc., § 1141.21.)

Discouraging trial de novo is essential to the proper functioning of the judicial arbitration system. Along with its goal of resolving small claims efficiently and affordably, judicial arbitration is intended to ease court caseloads. (Kanowitz, Alternative Dispute Resolution and the Public Interest: The Arbitration Experience (1987) 38 Hastings L.J. 239, 292.) The success of judicial arbitration in achieving these goals is dependent on a small incidence of trial de novo election. (Id. at p. 293.)

---

2. As was said by this court in Dodd v. Ford (1984) 153 Cal.App.3d 426, 432, fn. 7, 200 Cal.Rptr. 256, " 'Judicial Arbitration' is obviously an inapt term, for the system it describes is neither judicial nor arbitration. The hearing is not [necessarily] conducted by a judge, and the right to a trial de novo removes the finality of true arbitration. 'Extrajudicial mediation' would be closer to correct.''

If trial de novo is not requested within the statutory period, a judicial arbitration award becomes final and is not subject to appeal. (Code Civ. Proc., § 1141.23.) There is no question the Legislature intended the award, once final, to be a binding resolution of the particular cause of action. Code of Civil Procedure section 1141.23 provides that a final award shall have "the same force and effect as a judgment in any civil action or proceeding," except that it shall not be subject to appeal and generally may not be attacked or set aside. Accordingly, a final judicial arbitration award, if clear and unambiguous, is res judicata in any subsequent proceeding on the same cause of action.

In the instant case, Flynn's indemnity action would have been barred if it had stated the same cause of action as Gorton's arbitrated negligence claim. The two proceedings, however, did not involve the same cause of action. Gorton's negligence claim involved her primary right to be free of personal injury, whereas this action concerns Flynn's right to equitable indemnity against third party damages. (See Slater v. Blackwood (1975) 15 Cal.3d 791, 795, 126 Cal.Rptr. 225, 543 P.2d 593; Busick v. Workmen's Comp. Appeals Bd. (1972) 7 Cal.3d 967, 975, 104 Cal.Rptr. 42, 500 P.2d 1386.) Thus, Flynn's action was not barred under the cause preclusion aspect of res judicata.

Collateral estoppel is equally inapplicable here, but for different reasons. It would be unfair and unwise to give collateral estoppel effect to judicially arbitrated resolutions of issues. To begin with, as this case well illustrates, there are practical difficulties. No record is made of arbitration proceedings and generally no findings of fact or conclusions of law are required. (Cal.Rules of Court, rules 1614, 1615.) Thus, it is difficult to determine from the award alone what issues were actually litigated and how they were resolved.

Even if this difficulty could be surmounted, it is unfair to bind the parties to judicially arbitrated resolutions of issues. The doctrine of collateral estoppel is based on the premise that a thorough fact-finding process was completed in the first proceeding. (Shell, Res Judicata and Collateral Estoppel Effects of Commercial Arbitration (1988) 35 UCLA L.Rev. 623, 648.) However, in judicial arbitration, the low monetary amount in controversy and the option of trial de novo can leave parties without a serious incentive to litigate. Because the stakes involved are low, the parties may be willing to accept a compromise position without much of a fight. (See Mahon v. Safeco Title Ins. Co. (1988) 199 Cal.App.3d 616, 622, 245 Cal.Rptr. 103.)

Moreover, it is unlikely parties would expect a judicial arbitration award to have collateral estoppel effect in other proceedings where the stakes may be higher than they were in the arbitration proceeding. If they did, the result might be intensified litigation, delays and costs, as well as an increased rate of trial de novo election. Such a development would be directly contrary to the purposes underlying judicial arbitration legislation.

In summary, we hold that judicial arbitration awards should be accorded claim preclusion, but not issue preclusion, effect.

Accordingly, we reverse the trial court's judgment and remand this matter for further proceedings in light of the views expressed herein.

* * *

Question

Why does the court say there is a different standard for collateral estoppel in court-ordered arbitration than in private arbitration? To what extent does the court rely on alleged deficiencies in the arbitration process to reach its conclusion? To what extent does it rely on the expectations of the parties? How could these concerns be answered?

* * *

Habick v. Liberty Mutual Fire Insurance Co.

320 N.J.Super. 244, 727 A.2d 51 (N.J. Super. A.D. 1999).

■ WECKER, J.A.D.

Plaintiff, Rosemarie Habick, appeals from Law Division orders denying her application to vacate or modify a PIP arbitrator's determination that certain medical treatment was not required as a result of accident-related injuries, see N.J.S.A. 39:6A–4, and declaring that plaintiff would be bound by that ruling in her pending UM [Uninsured Motorist] arbitration arising out of the same accident. We conclude that the Law Division Judge erred only in denying modification of the award to exclude issues not before the arbitrator, and we otherwise affirm the orders appealed from.

After plaintiff's 1992 automobile accident, her PIP carrier, Liberty Mutual Fire Insurance Company, paid for treatment of a knee injury and a TMJ condition through 1995 and approved arthroscopic surgery on her right knee. When plaintiff's treating physician later recommended knee replacement in lieu of the arthroscopic procedure, Liberty denied payment on the basis of its own medical examiner's report. Plaintiff then filed for arbitration of her PIP claim, as permitted by N.J.S.A. 39:6A–5h. Because the other driver was uninsured, plaintiff also filed for uninsured motorist coverage, and her UM arbitration was pending at the time she sought relief from the PIP arbitrator's decision. The UM arbitrators adjourned any hearing pending the final outcome of the PIP arbitration.

The PIP arbitrator denied plaintiff's claim for further TMJ treatment as well as the knee replacement surgery, finding that neither treatment was warranted by a condition caused by the accident. . . .

[T]he PIP arbitrator's award does not refer to the pending UM arbitration.

Habick, obviously recognizing the potentially binding effect of the PIP arbitration upon her UM claim, filed a verified complaint in the Law Division seeking a judgment either vacating the award or, in the alternative, modifying the award to limit its scope to the issues submitted, and "to reflect that it be without prejudice to any claim plaintiff may have outside the scope of the PIP arbitration proceedings."

There is no dispute that plaintiff suffered from osteoarthritis of both knees prior to the accident. Two factual issues were submitted to and decided by the PIP arbitrator, each of which is potentially before the UM arbitrators. The first is whether the accident aggravated the condition of plaintiff's right knee, thereby necessitating knee replacement surgery, or whether the deterioration of plaintiff's osteoarthritic knee instead reflected the natural progression of the disease and was unrelated to the accident. The second factual issue decided by the PIP arbitrator that is potentially before the UM arbitrator(s) is whether this accident was a proximate cause of Habick's continuing TMJ symptoms. The PIP arbitrator ruled that it was not.

In denying relief to Habick from the PIP arbitration award, the Law Division Judge wrote:

> the arbitrator found that Liberty was not responsible for any *additional* treatment.... [T]he arbitrator gave a factual basis for reaching his conclusion. It is based on those findings that the plaintiff seeks to overturn the arbitrator's award.The court has reviewed the submissions of counsel and the findings of the arbitrator and can find no evidence that this arbitrator in the instant case exceeded his power. There is nothing in the record before the court to reflect that [the arbitrator], who had the benefit of the testimony of the plaintiff and her witnesses as well as all relevant medical evidence, made a finding that was with a gross, unmistakable or manifest disregard to the applicable law of this state.

The judge also denied plaintiff's motion for reconsideration, writing with respect to the binding effect of the PIP arbitration:

> As to whether the findings of [the PIP arbitrator] are binding on the U.M. arbitrator, the court finds in the affirmative. The plaintiff in her P.I.P. arbitration submitted all facets of her case most favorable to her position for the arbitrator's consideration. A finding was made by the arbitrator and since there are no new facts to be considered by the U.M. arbitrator, the decision of [the arbitrator] is binding on all issues he ruled on in presenting his findings.

I.

There are two separate questions before us. The first question is whether the judge erred in refusing to vacate or modify the arbitration award. We are aware of no reported case addressing the standard of review applicable to a motion to vacate a PIP arbitration award (or opposition to confirming that award).

There can be little doubt that arbitration is a favored means of dispute resolution. See, e.g., United Services Auto. Ass'n v. Turck, 156 N.J. 480, 486, 721 A.2d 1 (1998). The Arbitration Act, N.J.S.A. 2A:24–1 et seq., enacted in 1923, provides narrow grounds for vacating an arbitration award:

The court shall vacate the award in any of the following cases:

a. Where the award was procured by corruption, fraud or undue means;

b. Where there was either evident partiality or corruption in the arbitrators, or any thereof;

c. Where the arbitrators were guilty of misconduct in refusing to postpone the hearing, upon sufficient cause being shown therefor, or in refusing to hear evidence, pertinent and material to the controversy, or of any other misbehaviors prejudicial to the rights of any party;

d. Where the arbitrators exceeded or so imperfectly executed their powers that a mutual, final and definite award upon the subject matter submitted was not made.

[N.J.S.A. 2A:24–8]

Neither party to this appeal suggests that the Act is inapplicable to PIP arbitration, which was enacted as part of the 1983 amendments to the New Jersey Automobile Reparation Reform Act, N.J.S.A. 39:6A–1 et seq.

Permissible grounds for modifying an arbitration award are set forth in N.J.S.A. 2A:24–9. They include circumstances "Where the arbitrators awarded upon a matter not submitted to them unless it affects the merit of the decision upon the matter submitted; . . . ." Id., § b. In that event, "The court shall modify and correct the award, to effect the intent thereof and promote justice between the parties." Id.

A majority of the Supreme Court further narrowed the scope of review under the Arbitration Act with respect to an award reached by voluntary contractual arbitration among private parties. Tretina Printing, Inc. v. Fitzpatrick and Assoc., Inc., 135 N.J. 349, 358, 640 A.2d 788 (1994) (4–3 decision) (quoting Perini Corp. v. Greate Bay Hotel & Casino Inc., 129 N.J. 479, 548–49, 610 A.2d 364 (1992) (Wilentz, J. concurring)):

Basically, arbitration awards may be vacated only for fraud, corruption, or similar wrongdoing on the part of the arbitrators. [They] can be corrected or modified only for very specifically defined mistakes as set forth in [N.J.S.A. 2A:24–9]. *If the arbitrators decide a matter not even submitted to them, that matter can be excluded from the award.* [emphasis added.]

There is no allegation of "fraud, corruption, or similar wrongdoing on the part of" this arbitrator. Later in this opinion we will address the matter not submitted to the arbitrator.

The Tretina majority carefully circumscribed the exceptions on policy grounds that would permit a broader review of private, voluntary arbitration:

Finally, . . . we add our recognition that in rare circumstances a court may vacate an arbitration award for public-policy reasons. For example, in Faherty v. Faherty, 97 N.J. 99, 477 A.2d 1257 (1984), we held that "whenever the validity of an arbitration award affecting child support is questioned on the grounds that it does not provide adequate protection for the child, the trial court should conduct a special review of the award." Id. at 109, 477 A.2d 1257. That heightened judicial scrutiny is required because of the courts' traditional role as *parens patria*. Id. at 111, 477 A.2d 1257.

[135 N.J. at 364, 640 A.2d at 788.]

PIP arbitration justifies neither a public policy exception nor one based on the courts' *parens patria* responsibility. . . .

[P]laintiff seeks a review standard comparable to the substantial-credible-evidence test applicable to judicial or to administrative agency fact findings. . . .

Plaintiff's reliance upon a comparison between PIP arbitration and public sector arbitration of any kind is misplaced. Parties may be subject to mandatory public-sector arbitration either to reach a collective bargaining agreement involving a public entity—so-called "interest arbitration," e.g., Division 540, supra, 76 N.J. 245, 386 A.2d 1290—or to resolve certain labor disputes arising under such a collective bargaining agreement—"grievance arbitration," e.g., Scotch Plains–Fanwood Bd. of Educ. v. Scotch Plains-Fanwood Educ. Ass'n, 139 N.J. 141, 651 A.2d 1018 (1995)[4]. The substantial-credible-evidence standard of review, applicable only to interest arbitration, has its rationale in entirely different circumstances than those underlying PIP arbitration. See Division 540 supra, 76 N.J. at 253–54, 386 A.2d 1290:

> The statute subjects the development Authority to compulsory and binding arbitration. Because it is compulsory, principles of fairness, perhaps even due process, require that judicial review be available to ensure that the award is not arbitrary or capricious and that the arbitrator has not abused the power and authority delegated to him. . . .

> We conclude that when, as here, the arbitration process is compulsory, the judicial review should extend to consideration of whether the award is supported by substantial credible evidence present in the record. . . .

The rationale for the broader public sector standards of review is essentially bottomed on fairness to the parties, for whom arbitration of collective bargaining agreements is compulsory, e.g., New Jersey State P.B.A., Local 29, 80 N.J. at 294, 403 A.2d 473; the public's interest in

---

4. "Interest" arbitration . . . involves the submission of a dispute concerning the terms of a new contract to an arbitrator, who selects those terms and thus in effect writes the parties' collective agreement. It is to be distinguished from "grievance" arbitration, which is a method of resolving differences concerning the interpretation, application, or violation of an already existing contract. [New Jersey State P.B.A., Local 29, 80 N.J. at 284, 403 A.2d 473 (citations omitted) (explaining history and scope of public sector interest arbitration).]

avoiding violations of law or public policy; and protection of the public welfare.... [citations]. Plaintiff would have us conclude that the same rationale requires a broader standard of review when an insuror seeks to vacate or modify a PIP arbitration award.

Plaintiff reasons that because only the insured, and not the insuror, can choose to arbitrate a PIP claim, the insuror should not be limited by the Tretina standard. From that proposition, plaintiff argues that it would be unfair and contrary to the policy of encouraging PIP arbitration to apply a stricter standard of review to the insured than to the insuror; therefore a broader standard of review should apply to all PIP arbitration.

We assume that the same standard of review should apply irrespective of which party is dissatisfied with a PIP arbitration's outcome, cf. Division 540, supra, 76 N.J. at 253 n. 4, 386 A.2d 1290. Because PIP arbitration elected by the insured becomes mandatory for the carrier, plaintiff would have us view the carrier's challenge to an arbitration award as if it were the result of mandatory public sector arbitration. While that contention may have some facial validity, closer examination leads us to a different view. We reject plaintiff's premise that it would be unfair to subject the insuror to the limited Tretina standard of review.

Although the terms of PIP coverage, including the insured's right to elect arbitration, are mandated by statute, the carrier's participation in this market, circumscribed as it is by state law, is nevertheless voluntary. The PIP carrier has entered into a contract with its insured. Moreover, unlike the insured, whose interest lies in the outcome of a single PIP arbitration, the carrier's interest lies more in a predictable, consistent procedure and scope of review applicable across the board to all of the PIP arbitrations it faces. While a broader standard might allow the carrier to prevail in vacating certain arbitration awards it deems erroneous, such a standard would also jeopardize the finality of those awards the carrier deems favorable.

Additionally, to allow a substantial-credible-evidence test of a PIP award would require a verbatim record, with the attendant expense and delay that PIP arbitration is intended to avoid. The net result would be to defeat the overall purpose of, and public policy behind, PIP arbitration: to provide a prompt, efficient, and inexpensive means of dispute resolution that will minimize and not maximize resort to the courts. We therefore see no fundamental unfairness in holding both sides to the limited scope of review mandated by Tretina. We are satisfied that PIP arbitration warrants no different standard. Thus to the extent that plaintiff's contention is that the arbitrator was wrong because he believed the wrong expert, her appeal from the confirmed award is without merit.

However, we agree with plaintiff that the Law Division Judge erred in failing to recognize that the arbitrator's award went beyond the scope of his authority and therefore warrants modification.... [The court concluded that the arbitrators decided certain medical issues that had not been presented.]

Therefore, to the extent the arbitrator's award purported to make findings with respect to issues other than the total knee replacement procedure and continued TMJ treatment after the cut-off date, the award must be modified to exclude those findings as beyond the scope of the arbitrator's authority.

II.

Because we affirm the order effectively confirming the arbitration award as modified, we address the second issue raised by this appeal: whether the PIP award bars relitigation of medical causation in plaintiff's anticipated UM arbitration. Had plaintiff sought a determination of PIP benefits in a non-jury proceeding before the court, as permitted by N.J.S.A. 39:6A–5(c), rather than opting for PIP arbitration, she would be bound in a subsequent suit against a third-party tortfeasor by a final judgment dismissing her claim for failure to prove that injuries caused by the accident warranted the treatment requested. See Kozlowski v. Smith, 193 N.J.Super. 672, 674–75, 475 A.2d 663 (App.Div.1984) (prior PIP litigation denying benefits after finding no medical causation bars relitigation of causation in subsequent personal injury action.) We see no reason why prior PIP litigation should be any less binding in a subsequent UM arbitration than it would be in a subsequent personal injury lawsuit....

We look to the underlying principles of collateral estoppel, which the motion judge invoked to declare that the PIP arbitrator's determination with respect to causation would bind plaintiff in her anticipated UM arbitration. As Habick correctly contends, New Jersey follows the Restatement (Second) of Judgments respecting collateral estoppel....

Section 27 of the Restatement sets forth the basic rule of collateral estoppel:

> When an issue of fact or law is actually litigated and determined by a valid and final judgment, and the determination is essential to the judgment, the determination is conclusive in a subsequent action between the parties, whether on the same or a different claim.

The guiding principle is that the party to be bound had a "full and fair opportunity to litigate the issue" in the earlier proceeding. There can be no question that plaintiff had the opportunity in a PIP arbitration to present all of the evidence respecting causation that she could bring in a UM arbitration. Moreover, plaintiff chose to resolve her PIP claim in the arbitration forum and not in court. Although plaintiff's PIP and UM claims seek different remedies, the parties are identical, and several issues of medical causation that will arise in the UM arbitration were decided in the PIP arbitration. In considering the preclusive effect of an arbitration, we are guided largely by fairness and by the Restatement. Nogue, supra, 224 N.J.Super. at 386, 540 A.2d 889. There is nothing inherently unfair in giving that arbitration decision, once final, preclusive effect.

In other contexts, an arbitration award has been given preclusive effect in a subsequent judicial proceeding, so long as the party to be bound had the opportunity to make its case in the arbitration. See, e.g., Konieczny v. Micciche, 305 N.J.Super. 375, 384–87, 702 A.2d 831 (App.Div.1997) (new home purchaser suing home inspector in negligence is bound by facts previously found in arbitration against the builder under New Home Warranty & Builders' Registration Act, N.J.S.A. 46:3B–1 et seq.)....

Section 84 of the Restatement specifically addresses the preclusive effect of an arbitration award:

(1) Except as stated in Subsection (2), (3), and (4), a valid and final award by arbitration has the same effects under the rules of res judicata, subject to the same exceptions and qualifications, as a judgment of a court.

(2) An award by arbitration with respect to a claim does not preclude relitigation of the same or a related claim based on the same transaction if a scheme of remedies permits assertion of the second claim notwithstanding the award regarding the first claim.

(3) A determination of an issue in arbitration does not preclude relitigation of that issue if:

(a) According preclusive effect to determination of the issue would be incompatible with a legal policy or contractual provision that the tribunal in which the issue subsequently arises be free to make an independent determination of the issue in question, or with a purpose of the arbitration agreement that the arbitration be specially expeditious; or

(b) The procedure leading to the award lacked the elements of adjudicatory procedure prescribed in § 83(2).

(4) If the terms of an agreement to arbitrate limit the binding effect of the award in another adjudication or arbitration proceeding, the extent to which the award has conclusive effect is determined in accordance with that limitation.

Habick does not suggest that "a scheme of [auto insurance] remedies" permits her to relitigate causation. The questions raised by her arguments are whether "a legal policy or contractual provision" specific to the UM arbitration, or the "purpose ... that the [PIP] arbitration be especially expeditious," or an absence of procedural safeguards in the PIP arbitration warrant an exception to the general rule of preclusion.

Plaintiff cites the legislative intent to provide speedy resolution of medical claims for injured parties as a public interest policy basis for excepting PIP awards from the preclusive effect of collateral estoppel, apparently relying on Restatement § 84(3)(a). Habick also contends that the PIP and UM arbitration procedures are significantly different, and that PIP arbitration therefore does not warrant preclusive effect under § 84(3)(b). The procedures in each case are governed by a set of rules promulgated by the American Arbitration Association. Whereas § 8 of the PIP rules provides for a single arbitrator in all cases, § 8 of the UM rules permits either party to request a panel of three arbitrators if both "the amount claimed and available coverage limits exceed" the statutory minimum. Whereas review of a PIP arbitration award is limited by statute and case law, as discussed in Part I of this opinion, UM arbitration review, governed by the insurance generally provides for de novo proceedings in the Law Division when the award exceeds the statutory minimum and either partly rejects the award. See Craig and Pomeroy, New Jersey Auto Insurance Law, § 23:3–3 (1998).

We are not persuaded that these differences are material. We find no legal policies implicated by UM arbitration that would be infringed or hindered by giving the PIP arbitration preclusive effect. Nor does plaintiff provide us with any basis in the UM provision of plaintiff's insurance contract to warrant an exception. . . .

The PIP arbitration challenged here reasonably met the standards set forth in the Restatement, §§ 27, 28, and 84 to warrant preclusion. The policies behind the doctrine of collateral estoppel—fairness, finality, and judicial economy—are all served by giving preclusive effect to the confirmed PIP arbitrator's decision (as modified) that neither Habick's claimed need for knee replacement nor her TMJ syndrome were a proximate result of this automobile accident.

III.

In light of our conclusion that Habick is bound by the judgment confirming the PIP arbitrator's decision, the scope of that decision must be clear. Habick is barred in the UM arbitration (or any personal injury litigation arising out of this accident) from alleging future pain and suffering, or loss of enjoyment or earnings, due to projected knee replacement surgery. She is not, however, foreclosed from offering evidence of aggravation of the preexisting arthritic condition of her right knee, and pain and suffering related to treatment for that aggravation, short of total knee replacement surgery. . . .

As modified, we affirm the orders appealed from.

* * *

Questions

1. Does the *Habick* court disagree with the *Flynn v. Gorton* court about the relevant factors to use in determining whether to give an arbitral award collateral estoppel effect? Or, is the difference in the two approaches a result of the two courts' different assessments of the values and due process protections available in arbitration?

2. Why does the *Habick* court reject the plaintiff's argument that there should be a higher level of judicial review for court-ordered arbitration than for private arbitration? What other arguments might the plaintiff have made to support her position?

* * *

4. COURT-ORDERED MEDIATION

Decker v. Lindsay

824 S.W.2d 247 (Tx.Ct.App. 1992).

■ SAM H. BASS, JUSTICE.

We are faced with two questions today: (1) Can a party be compelled to participate in an alternative dispute resolution (ADR) procedure despite its objections?, and (2) Have relators established their right to mandamus relief?

John and Mary Decker, relators, seek mandamus relief against respondent, Judge Tony Lindsay, who signed an order on October 18, 1991 referring their suit against Jordan Mintz, the real party in interest, to mediation under TEX.CIV.PRAC. & REM.CODE ANN. § 154.021(a) (Vernon Supp. 1992).

Judge Lindsay's mediation order was made on her own motion, without any hearing. She consulted with neither party before entering her order. See TEX.CIV.PRAC. & REM.CODE ANN. § 154.021(b) (Vernon Supp.1992). However, only relators objected to the referral (timely, on November 1, 1991), and they submitted their objections for a ruling without oral argument. TEX.CIV.PRAC. & REM.CODE ANN. § 154.022(b) (Vernon Supp.1992). Judge Lindsay overruled their objections on November 22, 1991. See TEX.CIV.PRAC. & REM.CODE ANN. § 154.022(c) (Vernon Supp.1992). Relators filed this proceeding on December 3, 1991.

The October 18, 1991, order requires the parties to agree on a mediation date "within the next 30 days," or by November 18, 1991. If no agreed date is scheduled, the order provides that the mediator will select a date within the next 60 days, or by December 18, 1991. The order also reads, "TO BE MEDIATED PRIOR TO TRIAL SETTING OF 1–20–92."

We are concerned primarily with the following provisions of Judge Lindsay's order:

Mediation is a *mandatory but non-binding settlement conference*, conducted with the assistance of the Mediator. . . . Fees for the mediation are to be divided and borne equally by the parties unless agreed otherwise, shall be paid by the parties directly to the Mediator, and shall be taxed as costs. *Each party and counsel will be bound by the Rules for Mediation printed on the back of this Order* . . . .

Named parties shall be present during the entire mediation process. . . . *Counsel and parties shall proceed in a good faith effort to try to resolve this case* . . . . Referral to mediation is not a substitute for trial, and the case will be tried if not settled. (Emphasis added.)

Two of the Rules for Mediation, affixed to the order, are relevant to our discussion:

2. Agreement of the Parties. Whenever the parties have agreed to mediation they shall be deemed to have made these rules, as amended and in effect as of the date of the submission of the dispute, a part of their agreement to mediate....

6. Commitment to Participate in Good Faith. While no one is asked to commit to settle their dispute in advance of mediation, all parties commit to participate in the proceedings in good faith with the intention to settle, if at all possible.

Mandamus issues only to correct a clear abuse of discretion or the violation of a duty imposed by law when there is no other adequate remedy by law.... Mandamus relief may be afforded where the trial court's order is void.... However, the order of the trial court must be one beyond the power of the court to enter; it is not enough that the order is merely erroneous.... The relator bears the burden of establishing his entitlement to mandamus relief....

Relators assert Judge Lindsay's order is void and constitutes a clear abuse of discretion for the following reasons, which they also stated in their objection to mediation filed with the trial court: (1) the lawsuit arises out of a simple rear-end car collision, where the only issues are negligence, proximate cause, and damages; (2) trial is likely to last for only two days; (3) it is relators' opinion that mediation will not resolve the lawsuit, and they have not agreed to pay fees to the mediator; (4) mediation may cause relators to compromise their potential cause of action under the Stowers doctrine; (5) the law does not favor alternative dispute resolution where one of the litigants objects to it and when the litigants have been ordered to pay for it; and (6) court-ordered mediation, over the relators' objection and at their cost, violates their right to due process under the fifth and fourteenth amendments to the United States Constitution and article I, section 13 of the Texas Constitution and their right to open courts under article I, section 13 of the Texas Constitution.

The real party in interest disputes relators' contention that the lawsuit and its issues are simple. The real party in interest has raised the defense of unavoidable accident and asserts that the parties have wide-ranging disagreement over Mr. Decker's claimed economic and medical damages.

Relators contend that trial will last for only two days. Consequently, it will take only slightly more time than the mediation ordered. However, the proposed joint pretrial order, signed by counsel for the relators and counsel for the real party in interest, provides an estimated trial time of three to four days.

While relators assert that mediation will not resolve the lawsuit, the real party in interest suggests that in a day invested in mediation, where communication between the parties is facilitated, relators may change their evaluation of the lawsuit.

Under Tex.Civ.Prac. & Rem.Code Ann. § 154.054(a) (Vernon Supp.1992), the court may set a reasonable fee for the services of an impartial third party appointed to facilitate an ADR procedure. Unless otherwise agreed by the parties, the court must tax the fee as other costs of the suit. Tex.Civ. Prac. & Rem.Code Ann. § 154.054(b) (Vernon Supp.1992). No fee was ever set for the mediation in this case. On December 6, 1991, after this proceeding was filed, the mediator advised the parties that she waived her fee in the case.

We cannot say that Judge Lindsay abused her discretion in impliedly finding the first three reasons advanced by relators were not reasonable objections to court-ordered mediation. Mediation may be beneficial even if relators believe it will not resolve the lawsuit. The statute certainly allows a reasonable fee to be charged, and relators never challenged the reasonableness of the fee, but now the fee issue is moot. ...

Relators rely on Simpson v. Canales, 806 S.W.2d 802 (Tex.1991), for their contention that the law does not favor alternative dispute resolution procedures where one of the parties objects to it and when the parties are compelled to pay for it. Relators' reliance on Simpson is misplaced. In Simpson, the supreme court found that the trial court abused its discretion in appointing a master to supervise all discovery because the "exceptional cases/good cause" criteria of Tex.R.Civ.P. 171 had not been met and the blanket reference of all discovery was unjustified. 806 S.W.2d at 811–12. Although the supreme court commented that the parties had been ordered to pay for resolution of discovery issues by a master that other litigants obtained from the court without such expense, the matter of expense was not a basis for the court's decision. See 806 S.W.2d at 812.

Relators also argue that chapter 154 of the Texas Civil Practice and Remedies Code presents a "voluntary" procedure, and that mandatory referral to a paid mediator is not within its scope.

Section 154.002 expresses the general policy that "peaceable resolution of disputes" is to be encouraged through "voluntary settlement procedures." Tex.Civ.Prac. & Rem.Code Ann. § 154.002 (Vernon Supp.1992). Courts are admonished to carry out this policy. Tex.Civ.Prac. & Rem.Code Ann. § 154.003 (Vernon Supp.1992). A court cannot force the disputants to peaceably resolve their differences, but it can compel them to sit down with each other.

Section 154.021(a) authorizes a trial court *on its motion* to refer a dispute to an ADR procedure. However, if a party objects, *and there is a reasonable basis* for the objection, the court may not refer the dispute to an ADR procedure. Tex.Civ.Prac. & Rem.Code Ann. § 154.022(c). The corollary of this provision is that a court may refer the dispute to an ADR procedure if it finds there is no reasonable basis for the objection. A person appointed to facilitate an ADR procedure may not compel the parties to mediate (negotiate) or coerce the parties to enter into a settlement agreement. Tex.Civ.Prac. & Rem.Code Ann. § 154.053(b) (Vernon Supp.1992). A mediator may not impose his or her own judgment on the issues for that of the parties. Tex.Civ.Prac. & Rem.Code Ann. § 154.023(b) (Vernon Supp.1992).

Therefore, the policy of section 154.002 is consistent with a scheme where a court refers a dispute to an ADR procedure, requiring the parties to come together in court-ordered ADR procedures, but no one can compel the parties to negotiate or settle a dispute unless they voluntarily and mutually agree to do so. Any inconsistencies in chapter 154 can be resolved to give effect to a dominant legislative intent to compel referral, but not resolution. See, e.g., Southern Canal Co. v. State Bd. of Water Eng'rs, 159 Tex. 227, 318 S.W.2d 619, 624 (1958).

However, Judge Lindsay's order does not comport with the scheme set forth in chapter 154. Her order, and the mediation rules that are a part of it, do more than require the parties to come together; they require them to "negotiate" in good faith and attempt to reach a settlement.

Finally, relators object to Judge Lindsay's order on the constitutional grounds of due process and open courts.

Relators' brief does not contain any argument or authorities supporting their contention that their due process rights under the fifth and fourteenth amendments to the United States Constitution and article I, section 13 of the Texas Constitution have been violated. Therefore, they have not demonstrated their entitlement to mandamus relief on this ground. See Wood v. Wood, 159 Tex. 350, 320 S.W.2d 807, 813 (1959). They have not brought forth contentions that chapter 154 is in and of itself unconstitutional. . . .

However, in one very important respect, Judge Lindsay's order violates the open courts provision. It requires relators attempt to negotiate a settlement of the dispute with the real party in interest in good faith, when they have clearly indicated they do not wish to do so, but prefer to go to trial. As we noted above, the order does more than refer the dispute to an ADR procedure; it requires negotiation. Chapter 154 contemplates mandatory referral only, not mandatory negotiation.

Having reviewed the arguments of relators, which do not attack the statute, but only the order of referral, and those of the real party in interest and the documents submitted to us, we conclude that Judge Lindsay's order is void insofar as it directs relators to negotiate in good faith a resolution of their dispute with the real party in interest through mediation, despite relators' objections.

We conditionally grant the petition for writ of mandamus, and order Judge Lindsay to vacate those portions of her order of October 18, 1991, that require the parties to participate in mediation proceedings in good faith with the intention of settling. We are confident that Judge Lindsay will act in accordance with this opinion. The writ will issue only in the event she fails to comply.

* * *

Questions

1. Why did the court in *Decker v. Lindsay* vacate that portion of the order that required the parties to attempt to negotiate a settlement of the dispute

in good faith? Is not good faith participation by the parties a necessary precondition for a successful mediation? Without some obligation of good faith, could the parties simply show up at the mediation but otherwise refuse to participate? Would such conduct constitute compliance with the court's order to mediate? If the court does not require good faith, is the court's order to mediate simply ordering the parties to engage in a futile act?

2. Is it possible for a court to order a party to mediate in good faith? How would it determine whether there was good faith? Can the court require that the mediator attest to each side's good faith? What would be the pitfalls of such an approach?

3. Several states, including Texas, Florida, and California, require parties to engage in mandatory mediation before they can obtain a trial in certain types of civil cases. Does this innovation signify a major shift in the civil justice system away from a system in which the trial is used to identify fault and impose sanctions toward a system which promotes compromise and conciliation instead? Is this innovation a good thing? Who wins and who loses when disputes are resolved rather than decided? Is there a virtue in identifying fault that might be lost?

* * *

Raad v. Wal–Mart Stores, Inc.

1998 WL 272879 (U.S.D.C., D. Neb. 1998).

[Plaintiff-buyer sued defendant-seller about delivery of non-conforming goods. The district court found the defendant's conduct egregious and in violation of the state's Consumer Protection Act. It then considered the defendant's appeal of the magistrate's order regarding sanctions against the defendant for failure to mediate the dispute in good faith. The court affirmed the magistrate's order, which appears below.]

■ PIESTER, MAGISTRATE J.

Pending is the plaintiff's motion for sanctions stemming from the defendant's failure to have its representative present at the court-ordered mediation session held in this case. The issue arose as a result of the Mediation Closure Notice's statement that "Wal–Mart representative was not present." Upon being apprised of the notation, I entered an order requiring counsel to file affidavits as to the facts and the appropriateness of sanctions. Plaintiff thereafter filed the pending motion, and affidavits supporting and opposing the motion have been filed under seal. Letter briefs have also been submitted. Based on the information contained in the affidavits, I conclude that the defendant did not comply with this court's Mediation Reference Order, and that sanctions are appropriate.

The Mediation Reference Order

The mediation reference order (filing 19) was entered on October 28, 1997 following the receipt of correspondence from counsel indicating that mediation may well serve to expedite settlement of this case. The mediation reference order makes clear that each party must attend the mediation session or be represented by a person who, himself or herself, has "full settlement authority" to consummate a settlement without conferring with anyone else. After including explicit instructions on such authority, the order includes the following language:

> The purpose of this provision is to have at least one person present for each party who has both the *authority to exercise his or her own discretion, and the realistic freedom to exercise such discretion without negative consequences*, in order to settle the case during the mediation without consulting someone else who is not present.

Filing 19, para. 3, n.1. (Emphasis in original). In addition, the order contains the following instructions:

> 3.   * * * Such persons are further ordered to prepare for and partici-pate in the mediation in objective good faith.
>
> 4.   In preparing for the mediation, counsel shall:
>
> a.   Confer with their clients to assure compliance with paragraph 3, above.
>
> b.   Confer with opposing counsel to:
>
> i.   Attempt to resolve any problematic circumstances that might give rise to a contention of lack of full settlement authority or a lack of objective good faith.
>
> 5.   * * * If, as a result of [counsel's preliminary, pre-mediation] discussions, counsel for any party is of the view that the parties' positions and interests are so divergent that resolution of the dispute is not possible, counsel shall seek a telephone conference with the under-signed magistrate judge and opposing counsel to determine whether this order should be withdrawn. Such telephone conference shall be arranged in sufficient time to avoid the incurring of expenses by the mediation center, and by parties, representatives, and counsel in attending the mediation session, ordinarily at least three working days before it.
>
> 6.   The parties and counsel are warned that the court may impose sanctions, including, but not limited to, dismissal of a claim or defense, monetary sanctions, or such other sanctions as may be appropriate, in the same manner that a party or a lawyer might be sanctioned under Fed.R.Civ.P. 16(f) should such persons or entities fail to comply with this order in objective good faith.

Id. It is with these provisions in mind that I consider the parties' affidavits.

Facts

After the mediation reference order was entered Mr. Eske, counsel for plaintiff, telephoned Mr. Colleran, counsel for defendant, to schedule the mediation session. In Mr. Colleran's absence, his secretary provided Mr. Eske with "a list of dates in December that both Mr. Colleran and a Wal–Mart representative would be available." (Filing 27). Mr. Eske's affidavit continues, "When the mediation session was rescheduled to January 1998 at Mr. Colleran's request, I was not informed that only he would be attending." Id.

The mediation session was held on January 16, 1998. Plaintiff attended with his two attorneys, Mr. Eske and Mr. Marolf. The only person attending on behalf of defendant was Mr. Colleran. Mr. Colleran immediately informed those present that the Wal–Mart representative would not be personally attending but would be available by telephone. No prior arrangements had been made for such telephone participation, however. This was the first notice to the plaintiff or his attorneys that no representative from Wal–Mart would be present. Rather than object to proceeding without the defendant's representative personally present, Mr. Eske decided to remain at the mediation session and attempt to go forward.

The defendant's representative, Mr. Blake Clardy, is corporate counsel for Wal–Mart Stores, Inc. and is stationed at the corporate headquarters in Bentonville, Arkansas. At the commencement of the mediation session Mr. Colleran telephoned Mr. Clardy. Both Mr. Clardy's and Mr. Colleran's affidavits state, "Through this arrangement, I [or, 'Mr. Clardy'] was able to actively participate in the mediation without being physically present." Filings 28, 29. There is no further description of what is meant by "actively participate." None of the attorneys' affidavits mentions any involvement, comments, offers, or other proposals put forth by Mr. Clardy, nor the use of a speaker telephone to facilitate his participation. I infer that his "active participation" was in the form of, at most, periodic telephone conversations with Mr. Colleran, and little, if any, conversation with either plaintiff or his attorneys.

The mediation ended without a settlement, and counsel differ as to why. Noting that Mr. Colleran had previously deposed plaintiff without a Wal–Mart representative present, Mr. Eske opines that "I considered [before agreeing to mediation] the primary benefit of mediation in this case to be providing Mr. Raad with the opportunity to present his case directly to Wal–Mart, and providing Wal–Mart with the opportunity to respond directly to Mr. Raad." "[T]he failure of a Wal–Mart representative to attend the mediation session was detrimental to the success of the mediation, and it precluded the parties from engaging in constructive dialogue or meaningful settlement negotiations." Filing 27. Mr. Clardy states, "The inability to mediate the underlying dispute was not the result of my not being physically present." Filing 29. This conclusion is echoed by Mr. Colleran: "The inability to mediate the present case was not the result of Mr. Clardy's physical absence, [sic] instead, it was the result of the parties

[sic] difference of opinions as to the merits of the underlying dispute." Filing 28.

Discussion

This court's mediation program operates in accordance with a "Mediation Plan" that was adopted by General Order of the court ("Plan"). Mediation is not mandatory. To the contrary, if any party objects to the entry or any provision of a mediation order, the judge entering it must confer with counsel in an attempt to resolve the objection, and in the absence of resolution, must withdraw the order. Plan, para. 3(d).

The Plan offers participants the option of mediating their dispute through the auspices of private mediators or mediation services or in accordance with the court's Plan. (Plan, para.3(b)). In the absence of the indication of a preference, cases are referred to "mediation centers" established under the Nebraska Dispute Resolution Act, for scheduling with mediators who, because of their training and experience, have been approved to mediate cases referred from this court.

The Plan specifically provides that "Failure of a party, an attorney, or a fully authorized representative of a party to attend the mediation session shall be cause for the imposition of sanctions against the offending party and/or counsel." Plan. para. 3(c). Of note is the omission from the Plan of any prerequisite for the awarding of sanctions requiring either that the opposing party object or refuse to participate in the face of a failure to attend, or that the failure to attend be shown to have had any detrimental effect on the outcome of the mediation.

The omissions are reasonable. If a party were required—at the commencement of a mediation session its opponent chose, without notice, not to attend—to object or waive any right to sanctions emanating from its opponent's failure to abide by the mediation reference order, such a requirement might well destroy any hope for eventually settling the dispute. I think most people faced with such a circumstance, would find themselves faced with the dilemma of either proceeding and thereby perhaps disclosing some of their strategies and evidence, to their risk and possible detriment, or to stalk out of the meeting, thereby risking their investment in the process of their preparation time and expense. Faced with such a dilemma, it is reasonable that some would prefer to proceed if possible, in order to salvage whatever "good will" might be produced by negotiating, even with the limitations caused by the absence. Such a course would be cloaked with reluctance, in all probability, but represents the most viable means to make useful the time, effort, and expense—at that point, already spent—in preparing to negotiate a settlement, gathering the client and counsel and paying for the mediation session. While, as the discussion below will illustrate, such settlement negotiations are already at that point fraught with difficulty, it is not inconceivable that they could succeed, and in fact, some do. If, however, a party is forced to object, it will object, thereby nearly ensuring an unsuccessful result to the process. I therefore conclude that the plaintiff's proceeding here, in an attempt to make the mediation session productive, despite the absence of defendant's authorized representative, should not disqualify the plaintiff from receiving an award of sanctions.

Nor should the court proceed to a factual inquiry regarding the effects "in fact" of the defendant's failure. First, such an inquiry would almost certainly be inconclusive. The interplay of human dynamics and privilege precludes any firm finding either identifying "the" specific reason or reasons the mediation was not successful or, even if identified, the relative role of each. In addition, a court could not find "what might have happened if" the failure had not occurred. The end result is most probably caused by many forces, and it could probably never be attributed solely or even principally to one party's failure to attend.

Second, such an inquiry may invade the substance of the parties' private negotiations, thereby "poisoning the well" from which productive negotiations might yet emanate. Negotiation is a delicate art. Parties and their lawyers do things in negotiations for multitudes of tactical reasons, some of which they are not even able to articulate, if they are conscious of them at all. To delve into these strategic choices in an attempt to lay bare the underlying motivation behind various offers and counteroffers would defeat whatever of those strategies may yet bear fruit. Simply put, such reasons are none of the court's business.

Third, the "evil" to be deterred by the attendance rule is not the failed result of the negotiations, although that certainly is an interest at stake; indeed, mediations and settlement negotiations can fall short for multitudes of reasons. Rather, the rule seeks to deter the affront to the process and the abuse of the opponent that can and does occur when one side does not participate in good faith.

When a party agrees to participate in a mediation process in good faith, the court is entitled to rely on that representation and the implicit assurance that accompanies it that the participation will in fact be in accordance with the court's order-Mediation requires the disclosure of parties' interests and candid sharing of ideas and proposals for resolving the parties' dispute. It requires preparation and forthright discussion. As is discussed infra, to fail to so participate sabotages the process. In addition, it enables the offending party to gain by subterfuge information about the opponent's case, strategy, and settlement posture without sharing any of its own information. Instead of a negotiation session, the meeting becomes a discovery session, to the unfair benefit of the offending, absent party; to the extent that happens, the court's auspices have been callously misused. Meanwhile, the opposing side has spent money and time preparing for a good-faith, candid discussion toward settlement. If the absent party does not reciprocate, most or all of that money and time spent has been wasted. All of these "evils" occur regardless of what the ultimate outcome of the mediation session was or might have been.

I have no doubt that, as stated in Mr. Clardy's affidavit, the defendant is involved in thousands of pending lawsuits across the nation, and it is physically impossible to have personal control by corporate counsel in each case. I also have no doubt that practicality dictates that corporate counsel seek to be excused from court orders requiring his attendance at such mediations. That is one reason the mediation reference order allows a party to delegate authority to a person who can attend personally, including counsel. That is why the order also invites a telephone conference with me for the purpose of seeking a modification or withdrawal of the order BEFORE the scheduled mediation, and why it encourages conferences among counsel to ensure that such problems as this do not arise, or if they are expected, to allow for them to be resolved BEFORE the mediation session. Having failed to take advantage of those opportunities, however, defendant cannot now, after the mediation session ends in failure, fairly be excused for failing to abide by the terms of the order.

[D]efendant and its counsel unilaterally decided to circumvent the court's order, and now, being challenged by the motion for sanctions, argue only that "Mr. Clardy was present at the mediation via telephone." Defendant's brief in opposition, p.2. I do not believe any reasonable interpretation of the order's provisions could include such a stretched use of the term "present," but even if the order could be said to be ambiguous, counsel could easily have sought clarification.

Sanctions will be awarded. Although the Plan allows imposition of such punitive measures as dismissing claims or defenses, the record before me is much too sparse to consider such drastic measures. The expenses caused by defendant's violation of the order is a sufficient measure in this in-stance.... I shall award sums in recognition of those expenses, as follows:

(a) (i) Five hours of attorney time @ $150 = $750.00 (ii) Four hours @ $75.00 = $300.00

(b) (i) Four hours of corporate counsel's time @ $150 = $600.00;

(ii) Four hours of corporate counsel's travel time @ $150 = $600 .00, plus estimated travel and lodging expense in the amount of $300.00;

(c), (d), and (e) combined, $1,000.00.

* * *

Questions

1. Was the mediation in the *Raad* case mandatory or voluntary in a practical sense?

2. On what basis did the magistrate find the defendant's conduct to be in bad faith? Did the defendant in fact refuse to participate in the mediation? Is it possible that the magistrate's view reflected his view of the conduct of the defendant in the underlying motion? Is this an appropriate consider-ation?

* * *

5.   PERSPECTIVES ON COURT-ORDERED MEDIATION

The Mediation Alternative: Process Dangers for Women by Trino Grillo.[1]

California enacted a statute in 1981 that provided that all cases of child custody and visitation were to be submitted to mandatory mediation before they could be heard by a judge. Under the statute, the court appoints a mediator who has a master's degree in psychology or social work and some experience in counseling or psychotherapy. After the law had been in effect for eight years, Professor Trina Grillo studied the impact of mediation on the resolution of family disputes and concluded that the results were extremely problematic. Excerpts from her critique of mandatory mediation appear below.

"The introduction of mediation into family court processes was another part of the effort to make the adversary system fit the realities of divorce more closely. Mediators stepped into the increasingly uncertain legal world of dissolution with a new process which minimized the role of principles and fault. Mediation appeared to provide the opportunity to bring the lessons of context and subjective experience to dissolution proceedings. In mediation, the parties' legal rights would not be central. Instead of relying solely on abstract principles and rules, parties and mediators could attend to the reality of complex relationships. Precedent, legal rules and a legalized formulation of the facts might be seen as irrelevant to the mediation process and an unnecessary constraint on the mediator. Individuals could be seen in relation to one another, and morality treated as 'a question of responsibilities to particular people in particular contexts.'

"The informal law of the mediation setting requires that discussion of principles, blame, and rights, as these terms are used in the adversarial context, be de-emphasized or avoided. Mediators use informal sanctions to encourage the parties to replace the rhetoric of fault, principles, and values with the rhetoric of compromise and relationship. For example, mediators typically suggest that the parties 'eschew[] the language of individual rights in favor of the language of interdependent relationships.' They orient the parties toward reasonableness and compromise, rather than moral vindication. The conflict may be styled as a personal quarrel, in which there is no right and wrong, but simply two different, and equally true or untrue, views of the world.

(1) *Are All Agreements Equal?*

"The reason for the lack of focus on values and principles in many models of mediation is, in part, simply practical. If the essence of mediation entails trading off interests and compromising, each person's interests are

---

1.   Trino Grillo, *The Mediation Alternative: Process Dangers for Women*, 100 YALE   L.J. 1545, 1559–1564, 1607–1610 (1991). Reprinted with permission.

important, but which person violated societal values and why he did so, is not. To the extent that principles and faultfinding based on those principles enter into the discussion, reaching an agreement might be delayed or disrupted. De-emphasizing principles also might appear to be the sensible approach in a society that is increasingly pluralistic in terms of cultures, religions, and varieties of family structures. Where there are conflicting moral codes, as there often are when couples divorce, making the only standard for agreement be that it is accepted by both parties means that it will not be necessary for a third party to decide which moral code is superior.

"Sometimes, however, all agreements are not equal. It may be important, from both a societal and an individual standpoint, to have an agreement that reflects cultural notions of justice and not merely one to which there has been mutual assent. Many see the courts as a place where they can obtain vindication and a ruling by a higher authority. It is also important in some situations for society to send a clear message as to how children are to be treated, what the obligations of ex-spouses are to each other and to their children, and what sort of behavior will not be tolerated. Because the mediation movement tends to regard negotiated settlements as morally superior to adjudication, these functions of adjudication may easily be overlooked.

(2) *Conceptual Underpinnings: Family Systems and Circular Causality*

"On a more theoretical level, the reluctance to discuss principles is based on the view, held by most mediators, that the family is a self-contained system. Under this view, all parts of the family are equally implicated in whatever happens within it. Each part of this system is simultaneously a cause for, and an effect of, all the other parts. Relationship problems represent 'a mutually regulated dance between oppressor and oppressed.' Causality is circular; that is, '[n]o specific situation or person is considered the antecedent, cause, or effect of [the] problem.' Under this approach, 'the mediator can view the interactional system between the husband and wife in such a way that each spouse's behavior appears perfectly complementary to that of the other spouse and the concepts of reasonable and unreasonable no longer apply.'

"Although this systems approach can be a useful one in understanding how families and other social organizations work, it has some serious shortcomings. Most critically, it obscures issues of unequal social power and sex role socialization. Structures within the nuclear family are viewed in isolation from outside social attitudes and forces. Thus, a person who has been a victim of violence can be seen as deserving her fate because of her self-defeating patterns of behavior and participation in cyclical negative interactions with her spouse. In this manner, the family systems approach imposes a value-free universe. It does not leave room for the situation in which one parent is complying with the legitimate expectations of society and the other is not. Yet the family systems approach would suggest that both parents, as well as the children, are all somehow responsible for a family's ills.

"In sum, the notion that people are jointly responsible for their interactions is only partly true. Moreover, an unrefined family systems perspective can deprive a divorcing spouse of the opportunity to appear virtuous in society's eyes and her own. No matter how much she struggles, her good works are for naught so long as she is connected to someone who is acting irresponsibly. To the extent mediation incorporates such a family systems perspective, the spouse who is doing 'good work' must bear the burden of the other spouse's noncompliance.

The Destroyers of Context: Prospectivity and Formal Equality

a.   *Prospectivity*

"Kenny had spent ten days with his father Jerry and was scheduled to return to his mother on a flight arriving on Thanksgiving afternoon. That morning, Jerry called Linda and told her that flying was expensive, and that he was returning to his ex-wife's area at Christmas anyway. He said he intended to keep Kenny with him until then; Kenny's stepmother would care for Kenny at their home. Linda, her Thanksgiving dinner in the oven and relatives scheduled to arrive, thought of going herself to pick up Kenny or going to court, but decided that the worst thing for Kenny would be a custody battle.

"When Kenny returned at Christmas, his behavior was odd; for the first time in his life he was violent and aggressive toward other children. Upon questioning Kenny, Linda discovered that he had not been cared for by his stepmother during the day as promised, but had instead been sent to unlicensed day care where the teacher had regularly used corporal punishment, to which Linda was passionately opposed and to which Kenny had never before been subjected.

"In mediation, Linda asks that she be given primary custody of Kenny. She says that Jerry has been untruthful, unreliable, and has risked Kenny's emotional and physical well-being. She tries to argue that such a young child needs one home base, and that should be her home since she was effectively his sole parent for most of his first three years of life. The mediator does not allow her to make these points. Instead, she says that the past is not to be discussed; rather, they must plan together about the future. She says that whether Jerry participated in Kenny's life for his early years is irrelevant; he is here now. The Thanksgiving situation is past history, and she is sure that they both have complaints about the past. Blaming one another is counterproductive. The mediator tells Linda that she must recognize that the parent who has the child is responsible for choosing day care. Linda must learn to give up control.

"The chief means by which mediators eliminate the discussion of principles and fault is by making certain types of discussion 'off-limits' in the mediation. Mediation experts Jay Folberg and Alison Taylor propose the following as one of the 'shared propositions' upon which nearly all mediators agree:

> "*Proposition 5*. In mediation the past history of the participants is only important in relation to the present or as a basis for predicting future needs, intentions, abilities, and reactions to decisions."

"It is typical for mediators to insist that parties waste no time complaining about past conduct of their spouse, eschew blaming each other, and focus only on the future. For example, one of the two essential ground rules mediator Donald Saposnek suggests a mediator give to the parties is the following:

> "There is little value in talking about the past, since it only leads to fighting and arguing, as I'm sure you both know.... Our focus will be on your children's needs for the future and on how you two can satisfy those needs.... [U]nless I specifically request it, we will talk about plans for the future.

"Thus, while one of the principal justifications for introducing mediation into the divorce process is that context will be substituted for abstract principles, in fact, by eliminating discussion of the past, context—in the sense of the relationship's history—is removed. The result is that we are left with neither principles nor context as a basis for decisionmaking.

"In Linda's case, the questions of whether Jerry had been remiss in not returning Kenny or in secretly placing Kenny in an inadequate child care situation were ruled irrelevant by the mediator. The mediator did not permit discussion of these issues because reaching an agreement was paramount, and because, under family systems theory as interpreted by the mediator, Jerry could not be at fault—Linda and Jerry were equally responsible for everything. That Jerry had virtually disappeared, leaving Linda to struggle to raise her son alone, and that Jerry had not kept his word about returning Kenny after his visit were simply not proper subjects of discussion. There was nothing Linda could say to introduce these concerns into the dialogue. Further, she could not refer to the past to demonstrate she was a responsible and loving parent. Her attempts to protect her son were labeled as controlling.

* * *

IV. ALTERNATIVES TO MANDATORY MEDIATION

"It has been said that '[d]isputes are cultural events, evolving within a framework of rules about what is worth fighting for, what is the normal or moral way to fight, what kinds of wrongs warrant action, and what kinds of remedies are acceptable.' The process by which a society resolves conflict is closely related to its social structure. Implicit in this choice is a message about what is respectable to do or want or say, what the obligations are of being a member of the society or of a particular group within it, and what it takes to be thought of as a good person leading a virtuous life. In the adversary system, it is acceptable to want to win. It is not only acceptable, but expected, that one will rely on a lawyer and advocate for oneself without looking out for the adversary. The judge, a third party obligated to be neutral and bound by certain formalities, bears the ultimate responsibility for deciding the outcome. To the extent that women are more likely than men to believe in communication as a mode of conflict resolution and to appreciate the importance of an adversary's interests, this system does not always suit their needs.

"On the other hand, under a scheme of mediation, the standards of acceptable behavior and desires change fundamentally. Parties are to meet with each other, generally without their lawyers. They are encouraged to look at each other's needs and to reach a cooperative resolution based on compromise. Although there are few restrictions on her role in the process, the mediator bears no ultimate, formal responsibility for the outcome of the mediation. In sum, when mediation is the prototype for dispute resolution, the societal message is that a good person—a person following the rules—cooperates, communicates, and compromises.

"The glories of cooperation, however, are easily exaggerated. If one party appreciates cooperation more than the other, the parties might compromise unequally. Moreover, the self-disclosure that cooperation requires, when imposed and not sought by the parties, may feel and be invasive. Thus, rather than representing a change in the system to accommodate the 'feminine voice,' in actuality, mandatory mediation overrides real women's voices saying that cooperation might, at least for the time being, be detrimental to their lives and the lives of their children. Under a system of forced mediation, women are made to feel selfish for wanting to assert their own interests based on their need to survive.

"There are, then, many good reasons why a party might choose not to mediate. While some argue that mediation should be required because potential participants lack the information about the process which would convince them to engage in it voluntarily, this is not a sufficient justification for requiring mediation. If the state were committed only to making sure that disputants become familiar with mediation, something less than mandatory mediation—such as viewing a videotaped mediation or attending an orientation program—could be required, and mediators would certainly not be permitted to make recommendations to the court. That more than the simple receipt of information is required under a statutory mediation scheme demonstrates a profound disrespect for the parties' ability to determine the course of their own lives. Perhaps intrusion on the parties' lives might be justified if, in fact, children were demonstrably better off as a result of the process. There is no credible evidence, however, that this is so. The legislative choice to make mediation mandatory has been a mistake.

"The choice presented today in California and in some other states is between an adversary process with totally powerful legal actors, in which clients never speak for themselves (and often do not know what is going on), and a mediation process in which they are entirely on their own and unprotected. The adversary system admittedly works poorly for child custody cases in many respects. There are, however, some ways to avoid damaging custody battles under an adversary system, such as enacting presumptions that make outcomes reasonably clear in advance, court-sponsored lectures on settlement, and joint negotiation sessions with lawyers and clients present. When in court, lawyers could be held to higher standards with respect to communicating with their clients, and judges could refrain from speaking to lawyers when their clients are not present. (It is difficult to imagine how a client can know whether to trust his lawyer when significant parts of the proceedings take place out of earshot).

"The only reason to prefer mediation to other, more obvious alternatives is that the parties may, through the mediation process, ultimately benefit themselves and their children by learning how to communicate and work together. Whether this will happen in the context of a particular mediation is something only the parties can judge.

"Any reform proposals, of the adversarial system or of a mediation alternative, should be rejected if they result in further disempowerment of the disempowered. Reform must operate on two simultaneous levels: first, by changing the institutions and rules that govern custody mediation, and second, by encouraging the respect of each mediator for the struggles and lives of the individuals involved in mediation. Any reforms should evince a concern for the personhood of the mediation clients, a concern that is lacking under current mediation practices.

"With respect to institutional changes, an adequate mediation scheme should not only be voluntary rather than mandatory, but should also allow people's emotions to be part of the process, allow their values and principles to matter in the discussion, allow parties' attorneys to participate if requested by the parties, allow parties to choose a mediator and the location for the mediation, allow parties to choose the issues to mediate, and require that divorcing couples be educated about the availability and logistics of mediation so as to enable them to make an intelligent choice as to whether to engage in it.

"The second aspect of reform represents more of a personal dynamic, one which is harder to institutionalize or to regulate. But the mediator must learn to respect each client's struggles, including her timing, anger, and resistance to having certain issues mediated, and also must learn to refrain, to the extent he is capable, form imposing his own substantive agenda on the mediation.

CONCLUSION

"Although mediation can be useful and empowering, it presents some serious process dangers that need to be addressed, rather than ignored. When mediation is imposed rather than voluntarily engaged in, its virtues are lost. More than lost: mediation becomes a wolf in sheep's clothing. It relies on force and disregards the context of the dispute, while masquerading as a gentler, more empowering alternative to adversarial litigation. Sadly, when mediation is mandatory it becomes like the patriarchal paradigm of law it is supposed to supplant. Seen in this light, mandatory mediation is especially harmful: its messages disproportionately affect those who are already subordinated in our society, those to whom society has already given the message, in far too many ways, that they are not leading proper lives.

"Of course, subordinated people can go to court and lose; in fact, they usually do. But if mediation is to be introduced into the court system, it should provide a better alternative. It is not enough to say that the adversary system is so flawed that even a misguided, intrusive, and disempowering system of mediation should be embraced. If mediation as currently instituted constitutes a fundamentally flawed process in the way I have described, it is more, not less, disempowering than the adversary system—for it is then a process in which people are told they are being empowered, but in fact are being forced to acquiesce in their own oppression."

Question

Does Grillo's critique of the use of mandatory mediation apply to areas other than family law disputes? Or is her critique unique to the family law context? Is it possible that even accepting her critique, mandatory mediation can be a positive innovation in landlord-tenant disputes, debtor-creditor disputes, or simple consumer complaints?

---

6.   COURT-INDUCED SETTLEMENT

G. Heileman Brewing Co., Inc. v. Joseph Oat Corporation

871 F.2d 648 (7th Cir.1989).

Before BAUER, CHIEF JUDGE, CUMMINGS, WOOD, JR., CUDAHY, POSNER, COFFEY, FLAUM, EASTERBROOK, RIPPLE, MANION AND KANNE, CIRCUIT JUDGES.

■ KANNE, CIRCUIT JUDGE.

May a federal district court order litigants—even those represented by counsel—to appear before it in person at a pretrial conference for the purpose of discussing the posture and settlement of the litigants' case? After reviewing the Federal Rules of Civil Procedure and federal district courts' inherent authority to manage and control the litigation before them, we answer this question in the affirmative and conclude that a district court may sanction a litigant for failing to comply with such an order.

I.   BACKGROUND

A federal magistrate ordered Joseph Oat Corporation to send a "corporate representative with authority to settle" to a pretrial conference to discuss disputed factual and legal issues and the possibility of settlement. Although counsel for Oat Corporation appeared, accompanied by another attorney who was authorized to speak on behalf of the principals of the corporation, no principal or corporate representative personally attended the conference. The court determined that the failure of Oat Corporation to send a principal of the corporation to the pretrial conference violated its order. Consequently, the district court imposed a sanction of $5,860.01 upon Oat Corporation pursuant to Federal Rule of Civil Procedure 16(f). This amount represented the costs and attorneys' fees of the opposing parties attending the conference.

II.   THE APPEAL

Oat Corporation appeals, claiming that the district court did not have the authority to order litigants represented by counsel to appear at the pretrial settlement conference. Specifically, Oat Corporation contends that, by negative implication, the language of Rule 16(a)(5) prohibits a district court from directing represented litigants to attend pretrial conferences.[1] That is, because Rule 16 expressly refers to "attorneys for the parties and any unrepresented parties" in introductory paragraph (a), a district court may not go beyond that language to devise procedures which direct the pretrial appearance of parties represented by counsel. Consequently, Oat Corporation concludes that the court lacked the authority to order the pretrial attendance of its corporate representatives and, even if the court possessed such authority, the court abused its discretion to exercise that power in this case. Finally, Oat Corporation argues that the court abused its discretion to enter sanctions.

A.   Authority to Order Attendance

First, we must address Oat Corporation's contention that a federal district court lacks the authority to order litigants who are represented by counsel to appear at a pretrial conference. Our analysis requires us to review the Federal Rules of Civil Procedure and district courts' inherent authority to manage the progress of litigation.

Rule 16 addresses the use of pretrial conferences to formulate and narrow issues for trial as well as to discuss means for dispensing with the need for costly and unnecessary litigation. As we stated in Link v. Wabash R.R., 291 F.2d 542, 547 (7th Cir.1961), aff'd, 370 U.S. 626, 82 S.Ct. 1386, 8 L.Ed.2d 734 (1962):

Pre-trial procedure has become an integrated part of the judicial process on the trial level. Courts must be free to use it and to control and enforce its operation. Otherwise, the orderly administration of justice will be removed from control of the trial court and placed in the hands of counsel. We do not believe such a course is within the contemplation of the law.

---

1. Rule 16(a)(5) provides: (a) Pretrial Conferences; Objectives. In any action, the court may in its discretion direct the attorneys for the parties and any unrepresented parties to appear before it for a conference or conferences before trial for such purposes as.... (5) facilitating the settlement of the case. Fed.R.Civ.P. 16(a)(5).

The pretrial settlement of litigation has been advocated and used as a means to alleviate overcrowded dockets, and courts have practiced numerous and varied types of pretrial settlement techniques for many years. See, e.g., Manual for Complex Litigation 2d, §§ 21.1–21.4 (1985); Federal Judicial Center, Settlement Strategies for Federal District Judges (1988); Federal Judicial Center, The Judge's Role in the Settlement of Civil Suits (1977) (presented at a seminar for newly-appointed judges); Federal Judicial Center, The Role of the Judge in the Settlement Process (1977). Since 1983, Rule 16 has expressly provided that settlement of a case is one of several subjects which should be pursued and discussed vigorously during pretrial conferences.[2]

The language of Rule 16 does not give any direction to the district court upon the issue of a court's authority to order litigants who are represented by counsel to appear for pretrial proceedings. Instead, Rule 16 merely refers to the participation of trial advocates—attorneys of record and pro se litigants. However, the Federal Rules of Civil Procedure do not completely describe and limit the power of the federal courts. HMG Property Investors, Inc. v. Parque Indus. Rio Canas, Inc., 847 F.2d 908, 915 (1st Cir.1988) (citations omitted).

The concept that district courts exercise procedural authority outside the explicit language of the rules of civil procedure is not frequently documented, but valid nevertheless. Brockton Sav. Bank v. Peat, Marwick, Mitchell & Co., 771 F.2d 5, 11 (1st Cir.1985), cert. denied, 475 U.S. 1018, 106 S.Ct. 1204, 89 L.Ed.2d 317 (1986). The Supreme Court has acknowledged that the provisions of the Federal Rules of Civil Procedure are not intended to be the exclusive authority for actions to be taken by district courts. Link v. Wabash R.R., 370 U.S. 626, 82 S.Ct. 1386, 8 L.Ed.2d 734 (1962).

In Link, the Supreme Court noted that a district court's ability to take action in a procedural context may be grounded in " 'inherent power,' governed not by rule or statute but by the control necessarily vested in courts to manage their own affairs so as to achieve the orderly and expeditious disposition of cases." 370 U.S. at 630–31, 82 S.Ct. at 1389 (footnotes omitted). This authority likewise forms the basis for continued development of procedural techniques designed to make the operation of the court more efficient, to preserve the integrity of the judicial process, and to control courts' dockets. Because the rules form and shape certain aspects of a court's inherent powers, yet allow the continued exercise of that power where discretion should be available, the mere absence of language in the federal rules specifically authorizing or describing a particular judicial procedure should not, and does not, give rise to a negative implication of prohibition. See Link, 370 U.S. at 629–30, 82 S.Ct. at 1388;[5]

---

2. Rule 16(c)(7) states: (c) Subjects to be Discussed at Pretrial Conferences. The participants at any conference under this rule may consider and take action with respect to.... (7) the possibility of settlement or the use of extrajudicial procedures to resolve the dispute;.... Fed.R.Civ.P. 16(c)(7).

5. In Link, plaintiff's counsel, who was aware of a pretrial conference, deliberately failed to attend the conference. The district

see also Fed.R.Civ.P. 83 ("In all cases not provided for by rule, the district judges and magistrates may regulate their practice in any manner not inconsistent with these rules or those of the district in which they act.").

Obviously, the district court, in devising means to control cases before it, may not exercise its inherent authority in a manner inconsistent with rule or statute. As we stated in Strandell v. Jackson County, 838 F.2d 884, 886 (7th Cir.1987), such power should "be exercised in a manner that is in harmony with the Federal Rules of Civil Procedure." This means that "where the rules directly mandate a specific procedure *to the exclusion of others*, inherent authority is proscribed." Landau & Cleary, Ltd. v. Hribar Trucking, Inc., 867 F.2d 996, 1002 (7th Cir.1989) (emphasis added).

In this case, we are required to determine whether a court's power to order the pretrial appearance of litigants who are represented by counsel is inconsistent with, or in derogation of, Rule 16. We must remember that Rule 1 states, with unmistakable clarity, that the Federal Rules of Civil Procedure "shall be construed to secure the just, speedy, and inexpensive determination of every action." This language explicitly indicates that the federal rules are to be liberally construed. Cf. Hickman v. Taylor, 329 U.S. 495, 507, 67 S.Ct. 385, 392, 91 L.Ed. 451 (1947). There is no place in the federal civil procedural system for the proposition that rules having the force of statute, though in derogation of the common law, are to be strictly construed. C. Wright & A. Miller, Federal Practice and Procedure: Civil 2d § 1029 (1987).

"[The] spirit, intent, and purpose [of Rule 16] is ... broadly remedial, allowing courts to actively manage the preparation of cases for trial." In re Baker, 744 F.2d 1438, 1440 (10th Cir.1984) (en banc), cert. denied, 471 U.S. 1014, 105 S.Ct. 2016, 85 L.Ed.2d 299 (1985). Rule 16 is not designed as a device to restrict or limit the authority of the district judge in the conduct of pretrial conferences. As the Tenth Circuit Court of Appeals sitting en banc stated in Baker, "the spirit and purpose of the amendments to Rule 16 always have been within the inherent power of the courts to manage their affairs as an independent constitutional branch of government." Id. at 1441 (citations omitted).

We agree with this interpretation of Rule 16. The wording of the rule and the accompanying commentary make plain that the entire thrust of the amendment to Rule 16 was to urge judges to make wider use of their powers and to manage actively their dockets from an early stage. We therefore conclude that our interpretation of Rule 16 to allow district courts to order represented parties to appear at pretrial settlement conferences merely represents another application of a district judge's inherent authority to preserve the efficiency, and more importantly the integrity, of the judicial process.

court dismissed the suit even though the Federal Rules of Civil Procedure did not ex-   pressly provide for it. . . .

To summarize, we simply hold that the action taken by the district court in this case constituted the proper use of inherent authority to aid in accomplishing the purpose and intent of Rule 16. We reaffirm the notion that the inherent power of a district judge—derived from the very nature and existence of his judicial office—is the broad field over which the Federal Rules of Civil Procedure are applied. Inherent authority remains the means by which district judges deal with circumstances not proscribed or specifically addressed by rule or statute, but which must be addressed to promote the just, speedy, and inexpensive determination of every action.

B.   Exercise of Authority to Order Attendance

Having determined that the district court possessed the power and authority to order the represented litigants to appear at the pretrial settlement conference, we now must examine whether the court abused its discretion to issue such an order.

At the outset, it is important to note that a district court cannot coerce settlement. Kothe v. Smith, 771 F.2d 667, 669 (2d Cir.1985).[8] In this case, considerable concern has been generated because the court ordered "corporate representatives with authority to settle" to attend the conference. In our view, "authority to settle," when used in the context of this case, means that the "corporate representative" attending the pretrial conference was required to hold a position within the corporate entity allowing him to speak definitively and to commit the corporation to a particular position in the litigation. We do not view "authority to settle" as a requirement that corporate representatives must come to court willing to settle on someone else's terms, but only that they come to court in order to consider the possibility of settlement.

As Chief Judge Crabb set forth in her decision which we now review:

> There is no indication ... that the magistrate's order contemplated requiring Joseph Oat ... to agree to any particular form of settlement or even to agree to settlement at all. The only requirement imposed by the magistrate was that the representative [of Oat Corporation] be present with full authority to settle, should terms for settlement be proposed that were acceptable to [Oat Corporation].

G. Heileman Brewing Co., Inc. v. Joseph Oat Corporation, 107 F.R.D. 275, 276–77 (1985).

If this case represented a situation where Oat Corporation had sent a corporate representative and was sanctioned because that person refused to make an offer to pay money—that is, refused to submit to settlement

---

8. Likewise, a court cannot compel parties to stipulate to facts. J.F. Edwards Constr. Co. v. Anderson Safeway Guard Rail Corp., 542 F.2d 1318 (7th Cir.1976) (per curiam). Nor can a court compel litigants to participate in a nonbinding summary jury trial. Strandell, 838 F.2d at 887. In the same vein, a court cannot force a party to engage in discovery. Identiseal Corp. v. Positive Identification Sys., Inc., 560 F.2d 298 (7th Cir.1977).

coercion—we would be faced with a decidedly different issue—a situation we would not countenance.

The Advisory Committee Notes to Rule 16 state that "[a]lthough it is not the purpose of Rule 16(b)(7) to impose settlement negotiations on unwilling litigants, it is believed that providing a neutral forum for discussing [settlement] might foster it." Fed.R.Civ.P. 16 advisory committee's note, subdivision (c) (1983). These Notes clearly draw a distinction between being required to attend a settlement conference and being required to participate in settlement negotiations. Thus, under the scheme of pretrial settlement conferences, the corporate representative remains free, on behalf of the corporate entity, to propose terms of settlement independently—but he may be required to state those terms in a pretrial conference before a judge or magistrate.

As an alternative position, Oat Corporation argues that the court abused its discretion to order corporate representatives of the litigants to attend the pretrial settlement conference. Oat Corporation determined that because its business was a "going concern":

> It would be unreasonable for the magistrate to require the president of that corporation to leave his business [in Camden, New Jersey] to travel to Madison, Wisconsin, to participate in a settlement conference. The expense and burden on the part of Joseph Oat to comply with this order was clearly unreasonable.

Consequently, Oat Corporation believes that the district court abused its authority.

We recognize, as did the district court, that circumstances could arise in which requiring a corporate representative (or any litigant) to appear at a pretrial settlement conference would be so onerous, so clearly unproductive, or so expensive in relation to the size, value, and complexity of the case that it might be an abuse of discretion. Moreover, "[b]ecause inherent powers are shielded from direct democratic controls, they must be exercised with restraint and discretion." Roadway Express, Inc. v. Piper, 447 U.S. 752, 764, 100 S.Ct. 2455, 2463, 65 L.Ed.2d 488 (1980) (citation omitted). However, the facts and circumstances of this case clearly support the court's actions to require the corporate representatives of the litigants to attend the pretrial conference personally.

This litigation involved a claim for $4 million—a claim which turned upon the resolution of complex factual and legal issues.[9] The litigants expected the trial to last from one to three months and all parties stood to incur substantial legal fees and trial expenses. This trial also would have

---

9. G. Heileman Brewing Company hired RME Associates, Inc., a consulting firm, to build a waste water treatment plant at Heileman's brewery in LaCrosse, Wisconsin. Subsequently, RME entered into a contract with Joseph Oat Corporation whereby Oat Corporation agreed to design, engineer, construct and test the system. Oat Corpora-

tion was the exclusive licensee in the United States for the system's developer, N.V. Centrale Suicker Maatschappij (CSM), a Dutch corporation. A contract dispute arose between Oat Corporation, Heileman, and RME involving the malfunctioning of the waste water treatment system. . . .

preempted a large segment of judicial time—not an insignificant factor. Thus, because the stakes were high, we do not believe that the burden of requiring a corporate representative to attend a pretrial settlement conference was out of proportion to the benefits to be gained, not only by the litigants but also by the court.

Additionally, the corporation did send an attorney, Mr. Fitzpatrick, from Philadelphia, Pennsylvania to Madison, Wisconsin to "speak for" the principals of the corporation. It is difficult to see how the expenses involved in sending Mr. Fitzpatrick from Philadelphia to Madison would have greatly exceeded the expenses involved in sending a corporate representative from Camden to Madison. Consequently, we do not think the expenses and distance to be traveled are unreasonable in this case.

Furthermore, no objection to the magistrate's order was made prior to the date the pretrial conference resumed. Oat Corporation contacted the magistrate's office concerning the order's requirements and was advised of the requirements now at issue. However, Oat Corporation never objected to its terms, either when it was issued or when Oat Corporation sought clarification. Consequently, Oat Corporation was left with only one course of action: it had to comply fully with the letter *and* intent of the order and argue about its reasonableness later.

We thus conclude that the court did not abuse its authority and discretion to order a representative of the Oat Corporation to appear for the pretrial settlement conference on December 19.

C. Sanctions

Finally, we must determine whether the court abused its discretion by sanctioning Oat Corporation for failing to comply with the order to appear at the pretrial settlement conference. Oat Corporation argues that the instructions directing the appearance of corporate representatives were unclear and ambiguous. Consequently, it concludes that the sanctions were improper.

Absent an abuse of discretion, we may not disturb a district court's imposition of sanctions for failure of a party to comply with a pretrial order. The issue on review is not whether we would have imposed these costs upon Oat Corporation, but whether the district court abused its discretion in doing so. National Hockey League v. Metropolitan Hockey Club, Inc., 427 U.S. 639, 642, 96 S.Ct. 2778, 2780, 49 L.Ed.2d 747 (1976) (citations omitted).

Oat Corporation contends that the presence of Mr. Fitzpatrick, as an attorney authorized to speak on behalf of the principals of Oat Corporation, satisfied the requirement that its "corporate representative" attend the December 19 settlement conference. Oat Corporation argues that nothing in either the November 19, 1984 order or the December 14, 1984 order would lead a reasonable person to conclude that a representative or principal from the Joseph Oat Corporation was required to attend the conference personally—in effect arguing that sanctions cannot be imposed because the order failed to require a particular person to attend the conference.

We believe that Oat Corporation was well aware of what the court expected. While the November order may have been somewhat ambiguous, any ambiguity was eliminated by the magistrate's remarks from the bench on December 14, the written order of December 18,[11] and the direction obtained by counsel from the magistrate's clerk.

On December 14, in the presence of Oat Corporation's attorney of record and all those in the courtroom, the magistrate announced that the pretrial conference had been impaired because Oat Corporation had not complied with Paragraph 5(c) of the November order requiring it to send to the conference a corporate representative. The magistrate clearly stated that the order's purpose was to insure the presence of the parties personally at the conference. From that moment on, Oat Corporation had notice that it was ordered to send a corporate representative to the resumed conference. Moreover, prior to the December 19 conference, Oat Corporation's counsel contacted the magistrate's office to determine if the magistrate really intended for corporate representatives to be in Madison, Wisconsin, for the settlement conference. Counsel was assured that such was the case.

When the conference resumed on December 19, Mr. Possi was present acting in his capacity as Oat Corporation's attorney of record. Mr. Fitzpatrick, who was not an attorney of record in the case, asserted that he was directed to attend the conference and speak on behalf of Oat Corporation's principals.[14] Mr. Fitzpatrick also stated that he interpreted the November

---

11. On December 18, 1984, the oral order was reduced to writing. It stated: The progress of the conference was impaired by the fact that neither plaintiff Joseph Oat Corporation, or its carrier National Union, was represented, in addition to counsel, by a representative having full authority to settle the case. . . . It appearing that a substantial possibility exists that a number of the claims and issues in these cases may be susceptible of settlement, and that other related matters might be considered (including the avoidance of unnecessary proof, cumulative evidence, and redundant litigation; the possibility of adopting amendments to the pleadings, the restructuring of the parties; and the adoption of special procedures for managing this complex and protracted litigation) so as to secure the just and speedy determination of this litigation as the least expense to the parties, IT IS HEREBY ORDERED: . . . . 2. In addition to counsel, each party and the insurance carriers of plaintiff Oat and defendant RME, shall be represented at the conference in person by a representative having full *authority*

to settle the case or to make decisions and grant authority to counsel with respect to all matters that may be reasonably anticipated to come before the conference; . . . . (Order of Dec. 18, 1984) (emphasis supplied).

14. On December 19, the following dialogue took place between the magistrate and Mr. Fitzpatrick:

THE COURT: I made it clear on December 14th, that for purposes of this conference . . . that each party in addition to be represented by counsel would have present the party itself for purposes of authorizing or discussing settlement in this case, speaking specifically about the order which is dated December 18th but was entered I think clearly enough on the 14th. That in addition to counsel, each party . . . shall be represented at the conference in person by a representative having full authority to settle the case or make decisions relevant to all matters reasonably anticipated to come before the conference. . . . As a matter of fact, Mr. Possi called yesterday to find out from my secretary if that is what I really meant . . . he was

order not as requiring the presence of a principal of Oat Corporation at the conference scheduled for December 14, but as requiring the presence of the insurance carriers with authority to discuss settlement.

The distinction is clearly drawn between an attorney representing a corporation and a corporate representative. As we define in this opinion—consistent with the meaning given by the magistrate—a corporate representative is a person holding "a position with the corporate entity." Although Mr. Fitzpatrick was representing the corporate principals and Mr. Possi the corporation, no corporate representative attended as required by the magistrate's order. We therefore conclude that the court properly sanctioned Oat Corporation pursuant to Rule 16(f) for failing to send a corporate representative to the settlement conference.

III. CONCLUSION

We hold that Rule 16 does not limit, but rather is enhanced by, the inherent authority of federal courts to order litigants represented by counsel to attend pretrial conferences for the purpose of discussing settlement. Oat Corporation violated the district court's order requiring it to have a corporate representative attend the pretrial settlement conference on December 19, 1984. Under these circumstances, the district court did not abuse its discretion by imposing sanctions for Oat Corporation's failure to comply with the pretrial order. The judgment of the district court is hereby AFFIRMED.

POSNER, CIRCUIT JUDGE, dissenting.

Rule 16(a) of the Federal Rules of Civil Procedure authorizes a district court to "direct the attorneys for the parties and any *unrepresented* parties to appear before it for a [pretrial] conference." The word I have italicized could be thought to carry the negative implication that no *represented* party may be directed to appear—that was the panel's conclusion—but I hesitate to so conclude in a case that can be decided on a narrower ground.

The main purpose of the pretrial conference is to get ready for trial. For that purpose, only the attorneys need be present, unless a party is acting as his own attorney. The only possible reason for wanting a represented party to be present is to enable the judge or magistrate to explore settlement with the principals rather than with just their agents. Some district judges and magistrates distrust the willingness or ability of attorneys to convey to their clients adequate information bearing on the desirability and terms of settling a case in lieu of pressing forward to trial.

informed that it is what I really meant; and I would like to have your explanation as to why no one from Joseph Oat is here from [sic] that authority.

MR. FITZPATRICK: I am here as a representative of Joseph Oat which I understood your order to be. I have discussed this thing thoroughly with the principals of Joseph Oat. They directed me to come to the conference.

They directed me that I could speak for them, with authority to speak for them. Their direction was I should make no offer to settle the case. That is their position. That is the position they choose to take and they designated me as the representative to communicate that to the Court. (Transcript of Dec. 19, 1984).

The distrust is warranted in some cases, I am sure; but warranted or not, it is what lies behind the concern that the panel opinion had stripped the district courts of a valuable settlement tool—and this at a time of heavy, and growing, federal judicial caseloads. The concern may well be exaggerated, however. The panel opinion may have had little practical significance; it is the rare attorney who will invite a district judge's displeasure by defying a request to produce the client for a pretrial conference. . . .

The narrowly "legal" considerations bearing on the question whether district courts have the power asserted by the magistrate in this case are sufficiently equivocal to authorize—indeed compel—us to consider the practical consequences for settlement before deciding what the answer should be. Unfortunately we have insufficient information about those consequences to be able to give a confident answer, but fortunately we need not answer the question in *this* case—so clear is it that the magistrate abused his discretion, which is to say, acted unreasonably, in demanding that Oat Corporation send an executive having "full settlement authority" to the pretrial conference. This demand, which is different from a demand that a party who has not closed the door to settlement send an executive to discuss possible terms, would be defensible only if litigants had a duty to bargain in good faith over settlement before resorting to trial, and neither Rule 16 nor any other rule, statute, or doctrine imposes such a duty on federal litigants. See Strandell v. Jackson County, 838 F.2d 884, 887 (7th Cir.1987) . . . There is no federal judicial power to coerce settlement. Oat had made clear that it was not prepared to settle the case on any terms that required it to pay money. That was its prerogative, which once exercised made the magistrate's continued insistence on Oat's sending an executive to Madison arbitrary, unreasonable, willful, and indeed petulant. This is apart from the fact that since no one officer of Oat may have had authority to settle the case, compliance with the demand might have required Oat to ship its entire board of directors to Madison. Ultimately Oat did make a money settlement, but there is no indication that it would have settled sooner if only it had complied with the magistrate's demand for the dispatch of an executive possessing "full settlement authority."

Sufficient unto the day is the evil thereof: We should reverse the district court without reaching the question whether there are any circumstances in which a district court may compel a party represented by counsel to attend a pretrial conference.

■ COFFEY, CIRCUIT JUDGE, with whom EASTERBROOK, RIPPLE and MANION, CIRCUIT JUDGES, join, dissenting.

Because Rule 16 of the Federal Rules of Civil Procedure, amended by the Supreme Court and Congress as recently as 1983, specifically designates who may be ordered to appear at a pretrial conference, I disagree with the majority's determination "that the action taken by the district court in this case constituted the proper use of inherent authority to aid in accomplishing the purpose and intent of Rule 16." Majority Opinion at 652. Rule 16 of the Federal Rules of Civil Procedure states in relevant part:

"(a) Pretrial Conferences; Objectives. In any action, the court may in its discretion direct the attorneys for the parties and any unrepresented parties to appear before it for a conference or conferences before trial for such purposes as (1) expediting the disposition of the action; (2) establishing early and continuing control so that the case will not be protracted because of lack of management; (3) discouraging wasteful pretrial activity; (4) improving the quality of the trial through more thorough preparation; and (5) facilitating the settlement of the case."

Unlike the majority, I am convinced that Rule 16 does not authorize a trial judge to require a represented party litigant to attend a pretrial conference together with his or her attorney because the rule *mandates in clear and unambiguous terms that only an unrepresented party litigant and attorneys may be ordered to appear.*

Although I recognize that all courts, including those of federal jurisdiction, possess certain inherent authority, such as the contempt power and the power to determine whether the court has jurisdiction, this authority is limited. We recently warned that:

"'Inherent authority' is not a substitute for good reason.... 'Inherent authority' like its cousin in criminal law the 'supervisory power', is just another name for the power of courts to make common law when statutes and rules do not address a particular topic. Cf. United States v. Widgery, 778 F.2d 325, 328–29 (7th Cir.1985)." ... (citations).

[P]rior to 1983, Rule 16 only provided district court judges with the discretion to require the attendance of attorneys for parties at such proceedings. As pointed out earlier in this opinion, the Supreme Court and Congress took a good hard look at Rule 16 in hopes of improving judicial efficiency and only increased the power of district court judges to the extent of authorizing them to compel the attendance of "unrepresented parties" at pretrial conferences.

However, it is very clear that the amendment explicitly stopped short of providing trial judges with the broad and sweeping authority to compel the presence of "represented parties" at pretrial conferences that the majority now seeks to achieve by judicial fiat. "[T]he Supreme Court and Congress, acting together, ... addressed the appropriate balance between the needs for judicial efficiency and the rights of the individual litigant,"[1] when they chose to amend Rule 16 in a limited manner. The majority upsets this careful balance and acts contrary to the Supreme Court's mandate in the Bank of Nova Scotia case when it relies upon an alleged "inherent authority" to permit district court judges to exercise a power which the drafters of Rule 16 explicitly denied them.... The obvious intent of the Supreme Court and Congress that only attorneys and unrepresented parties be required to participate in pretrial conferences is clearly supported by the specific references to "attorneys" and "unrepresented parties" throughout Rule 16. Rule 16(a), as noted previously, allows for the

---

1. Strandell, 838 F.2d at 886–87.

court to "direct the attorneys for the parties and any unrepresented parties to appear before it." Rule 16(b), concerning scheduling, requires a judge to "consult[ ] with the attorneys for the parties and any unrepresented parties." Rule 16(c), regarding subjects to be discussed at a pretrial conference, states that "[a]t least one of the attorneys for each party participating in any conference before trial shall have authority to enter into stipulations and to make admissions regarding all matters that the participants may reasonably anticipate may be discussed." Similarly, Rule 16(d), concerning final pretrial conferences, provides that "[t]he conference shall be attended by at least one of the attorneys who will conduct the trial for each of the parties and by any unrepresented parties." . . .

The newly created "inherent authority" to require represented litigants to appear at a pretrial conference is based upon a legal foundation of quicksand. Exercise of this power has posed and will continue to pose a substantial invitation for judicial abuse. The purpose of a pretrial conference is to set the parameters of litigation, clarify the issues and organize its presentation with the aid of the respective attorneys, and now, unrepresented party litigants in the hope of improving judicial efficiency at trial.

[I]n our judicial system all party litigants are entitled to their day in court to present their claims or defenses before an impartial judge or jury. Our trial judges must never fall prey to becoming part of a process that even subliminally suggests a pressure to forego the essential right of trial.

. . . Creation of an "inherent authority" to require the presence of a party litigant at a pretrial conference presents a host of problems. Certainly, the court has the power to command the attendance of attorneys at the conference under the provisions of Rule 16 and as "officers of the court." However, I am convinced that if the attorney does not wish to have the litigant personally appear before the court at the pretrial conference, he is not bound to do so, lest, among other problems, the litigant make an admission of some type which would be damaging to the case and which had not previously been elicited in discovery proceedings. I believe we are all aware of the fact that the appearance of fairness, impartiality and justice is all imperative, and based upon logic I fail to understand how a litigant sitting at a *command appearance before a judge* who injects himself into an adversarial role for either of the parties' positions during settlement negotiations can feel that he or she (the litigant) will have a fair trial before the judge if he or she fails to agree with the judge's reasoning or direction regarding a recommended settlement. We may express in grandiose terms all sorts of theory and postulation about being careful not to influence, intimidate and/or coerce a settlement, but under the pressure that our trial judges experience today from their ever-burgeoning caseloads, we would be foolhardy not to anticipate an undesirable and unnecessary psychological impact upon the litigant in circumstances of this nature. The difficulties associated with active judicial participation in settlement negotiations is expressly exacerbated when the trial is scheduled before the court rather than a jury of one's peers. The appearance of partiality and impropriety must be avoided at all lengths if our nation is to continue to show respect for its judicial judgments. Since litigants are neither trained in the law nor have the basic understanding of the nuances of legal proceedings that we as lawyers have gained through years of education, professional training and experience, they could well be confused and dismayed with judicial participation in settlement negotiations.

My conclusion that judges lack the inherent authority to require the presence of a represented party litigant at a pretrial conference does not deprive trial judges of the ability to effectively handle their caseloads. Judges remain free to require the attendance of attorneys and unrepresented parties at pretrial conferences. However, if further measures are taken to coercively require the presence and active participation of a represented party at a pretrial conference, it is my considered belief that judges will be no longer worthy of the aura of impartiality for "the guiding consideration is that the administration of justice should reasonably appear to be disinterested as well as be so in fact." Public Utilities Commission v. Pollak, 343 U.S. 451, 466–67, 72 S.Ct. 813, 822–23, 96 L.Ed. 1068 (1952) (Frankfurter, J., in chambers)....

■ EASTERBROOK, CIRCUIT JUDGE, with whom POSNER, COFFEY and MANION, CIRCUIT JUDGES, join, dissenting.

Our case has three logically separate issues. First, whether a district court may demand the attendance of someone other than the party's counsel of record. Second, whether the court may insist that this additional person be an employee rather than an agent selected for the occasion. Third, whether the court may insist that the representative have "full settlement authority"—meaning the authority to agree to pay cash in settlement (maybe authority without cap, although that was not clear). Even if one resolves the first issue as the majority does, it does not follow that district courts have the second or third powers, or that their exercise here was prudent.

The proposition that a magistrate may require a firm to send an employee rather than a representative is puzzling. Corporate "employees" are simply agents of the firm. Corporations choose their agents and decide what powers to give them. Which agents have which powers is a matter of internal corporate affairs. Joseph Oat Corp. sent to the conference not only its counsel of record but also John Fitzpatrick, who had authority to speak for Oat. Now Mr. Fitzpatrick is an attorney, which raised the magistrate's hackles, but why should this count against him? Because Fitzpatrick is a part-time rather than a full-time agent of the corporation? Why can't the corporation make its own decision about how much of the agent's time to hire? Is Oat being held in contempt because it is too small to have a cadre of legal employees—because its general counsel practices with a law firm rather than being "in house"?

At all events, the use of outside attorneys as negotiators is common. Many a firm sends its labor lawyer to the bargaining table when a collective bargaining agreement is about to expire, there to dicker with the union (or with labor's lawyer). Each side has a statutory right to choose its representatives. 29 U.S.C. § 158(b)(1)(B). Many a firm sends its corporate counsel to the bargaining table when a merger is under discussion. See Ronald J. Gilson, Value Creation by Business Lawyers: Legal Skills and Asset Pricing, 94 Yale L.J. 239 (1984). Oat did the same thing to explore settlement of litigation. A lawyer is no less suited to this task than to negotiating the terms of collective bargaining or merger agreements. Firms prefer to send skilled negotiators to negotiating sessions (lawyers are especially useful when the value of a claim depends on the resolution of legal questions) while reserving the time of executives for business. Oat understandably wanted its management team to conduct its construction business.

As for the third subject, whether the representative must have "settlement authority": the magistrate's only reason for ordering a corporate representative to come was to facilitate settlement then and there. As I understand Magistrate Groh's opinion, and Judge Crabb's, the directive was to send a person with "full settlement authority". Fitzpatrick was deemed inadequate only because he was under instructions not to pay money. E.g.: "While Mr. Fitzpatrick claimed authority to speak for Oat, he stated that he had no authority to make a [monetary] offer. *Thus*, no representative of Oat or National having authority to settle the case was present at the conference as the order directed" (magistrate's opinion, emphasis added). On learning that Fitzpatrick did not command Oat's treasury, the magistrate ejected him from the conference and never listened to what he had to say on Oat's behalf, never learned whether Fitzpatrick might be receptive to others' proposals. (We know that Oat ultimately did settle the case for money, after it took part in and "prevailed" at a summary jury trial—participation and payment each demonstrating Oat's willingness to consider settlement.) The magistrate's approach implies that if the Chairman and CEO of Oat had arrived with instructions from the Board to settle the case without paying cash, and to negotiate and bring back for the Board's consideration any financial proposals, Oat still would have been in contempt.

Both magistrate and judge demanded the presence not of a "corporate representative" in the sense of a full-time employee but of a representative with "full authority to settle". Most corporations reserve power to *agree* (as opposed to power to discuss) to senior managers or to their boards of directors—the difference depending on the amounts involved. Heileman wanted $4 million, a sum within the province of the board rather than a single executive even for firms much larger than Oat. Fitzpatrick came with power to *discuss* and *recommend*; he could settle the case on terms other than cash; he lacked only power to sign a check. The magistrate's order therefore must have required either (a) changing the allocation of responsibility within the corporation, or (b) sending a quorum of Oat's Board.

Magistrate Groh exercised a power unknown even in labor law, where there is a duty to bargain in good faith. 29 U.S.C. § 158(d). Labor and management commonly negotiate through persons with the authority to discuss but not agree. The negotiators report back to management and the union, each of which reserves power to reject or approve the position of its agent. We know from Fed.R.Civ.P. 16—and especially from the Advisory Committee's comment to Rule 16(c) that the Rule's "reference to 'authority' is not intended to insist upon the ability to settle the litigation"—that the parties cannot be compelled to negotiate "in good faith". A defendant convinced it did no wrong may insist on total vindication. See Hess v. New Jersey Transit Rail Operations, Inc., 846 F.2d 114 (2d Cir.1988), and Kothe v. Smith, 771 F.2d 667 (2d Cir.1985), holding that a judge may not compel a party to make a settlement offer, let alone to accept one. Rule 68, which requires a party who turns down a settlement proposal to bear costs only if that party does worse at trial, implies the same thing. Yet if parties are not obliged to negotiate in good faith, on what ground can they be obliged to come with authority to settle on the spot—an authority agents need not carry even when the law requires negotiation? The order we affirm today compels persons who have committed no wrong, who pass every requirement of Rules 11 and 68, who want only the opportunity to receive a decision on the merits, to come to court with open checkbooks on pain of being held in contempt.

Settling litigation is valuable, and courts should promote it. Is settlement of litigation more valuable than settlement of labor disputes, so that courts may do what the NLRB may not? The statutory framework—bona fide negotiations required in labor law but not in litigation—suggests the opposite. Does the desirability of settlement imply that rules of state law allocating authority within a corporation must yield? We have held in other cases that settlements must be negotiated within the framework of existing rules; the desire to get a case over and done with does not justify modifying generally applicable norms. . . .

The majority does not discuss these problems. Its approach implies, however, that trial courts may insist that representatives have greater authority than labor negotiators bring to the table. And to create this greater authority, Oat Corp. might have to rearrange its internal structure—perhaps delegating to an agent a power state law reserves to the board of directors. Problems concerning the reallocation of authority are ubiquitous. . . .

These issues will not go away. The magistrate's order was to send a representative *with the authority to bind Oat to pay money*. What is the point of insisting on such authority if not to require the making of offers and the acceptance of "reasonable" counteroffers—that is, to require good faith negotiations and agreements on the spot? Fitzpatrick had the authority to report back to Oat on any suggestions; he had the authority to participate in negotiations. The only thing he lacked—the *only* reason Oat was held in contempt of court—was the ability to sign Oat Corp.'s check in the magistrate's presence. What the magistrate found unacceptable was that Fitzpatrick might say something like "I'll relay that suggestion to the Board of Directors", which might say no. Oat's CEO could have done no more. We close our eyes to reality in pretending that Oat was required only to be present while others "voluntarily" discussed settlement.

[The dissenting opinion of RIPPLE, CIRCUIT JUDGE, with whom COFFEY, CIRCUIT JUDGE, joins, is omitted.].

■ MANION, CIRCUIT JUDGE, joined by COFFEY, EASTERBROOK and RIPPLE, CIRCUIT JUDGES, dissenting.

Federal Rule of Civil Procedure 16 states that district courts may order "the attorneys for the parties and any unrepresented parties" to appear at pretrial settlement conferences. Despite this seemingly clear language, the majority holds that district courts have "inherent power" to compel parties represented by counsel to appear in court to discuss settlement. Because Rule 16 leaves no room for any such use of inherent power, I respectfully dissent.

Inherent power is not a license for federal courts to do whatever seems necessary to move a case along. Inherent power is simply "another name for the power of courts to make common law when statutes and rules do not address a particular area." Soo Line R. Co. v. Escanaba & Lake Superior R. Co., 840 F.2d 546, 551 (7th Cir.1988). Since inherent power's purpose is to fill gaps left by statute or rule, it necessarily follows that where a statute or rule specifically addresses a particular area, it is inappropriate to invoke inherent power to exceed the bounds the statute or rule sets. Cf. Bank of Nova Scotia v. United States, 487 U.S. 250, 108 S.Ct. 2369, 2373–74, 101 L.Ed.2d 228 (1988) (a federal court may not invoke its supervisory—i.e. inherent—power over criminal proceedings to circumvent Fed.R.Crim.P. 52(a)'s harmless error inquiry).

We recently applied this principle in Strandell v. Jackson County, 838 F.2d 884 (7th Cir.1987). In Strandell, we recognized that district courts must exercise their inherent power "in harmony with the Federal Rules of Civil Procedure." After carefully examining Rule 16 and its accompanying advisory committee note, we held in Strandell that a district court may not order an unwilling litigant to participate in a summary jury trial because Rule 16, which addresses the district courts' power to insist on pretrial settlement proceedings, did not authorize district courts to conduct mandatory summary jury trials. See id. at 186–88. Implicit in this holding is that no inherent power exists to conduct mandatory summary jury trials; Rule 16 shut the door on such proceedings.

The issue here—whether a district court may order a represented party to appear at a settlement conference—is slightly different from the issue in Strandell. But the proper analysis is the same. Since Rule 16 specifically addresses the use of settlement conferences in the federal courts, we must determine whether Rule 16 limits a district court's power over who the court may order to appear at those conferences. . . .

As originally enacted, Rule 16 provided that district courts could "direct the attorneys for the parties" to appear for pretrial conferences. In 1983, Rule 16 was amended to provide, among other things, that the possibility of settlement is an appropriate subject to consider at pretrial conferences. Fed.R.Civ.P. 16(c)(7); see also Fed.R.Civ.P. 16(a)(5) ("facilitating" settlement). But Rule 16(c) states only that "the *participants* at any conference under this rule" may consider settlement (emphasis added); Rule 16(c) does not say who those "participants" may be. Rule 16(a), on the other hand, provides that a district court may "direct the *attorneys for the parties and any unrepresented parties*" to appear for a pretrial conference. Rule 16(a) thus defines who the "participants" at a pretrial conference are: attorneys and unrepresented parties....

The language of Rule 16's sanctions provision, Rule 16(f), reinforces Rule 16's distinction between represented and unrepresented parties. The only language in Rule 16(f) specifically addressing appearance does not authorize sanctions if "a party fails to appear;" instead, sanctions are appropriate if "no appearance is made *on behalf of a party....*" (Emphasis added.) This choice of language is significant. In the normal course, an attorney appears "on behalf of" a represented client at a pretrial conference. An unrepresented party has nobody to appear on his behalf except himself.

Congress has provided that litigants may "conduct their own cases personally *or by counsel....*" 28 U.S.C. § 1654 (emphasis added). Rule 16's distinction between represented and unrepresented parties is consistent with a litigant's statutory right to representation by an attorney. It is also consistent with the attorney's traditional role in litigation. Litigants hire attorneys to take advantage of the attorneys' training and skill and, as Judge Posner notes, "to economize on their own investment of time in resolving disputes." Dissenting opinion at 657, Part of an attorney's expertise includes evaluating cases, advising litigants whether or not to settle, and conducting negotiations. I realize that attorneys may sometimes convey inadequate information to their clients regarding settlement. But an attorney has a strong self interest in realistically conveying to the client relevant information necessary for the client to make an informed settlement decision, and in accurately conveying the client's settlement position to the court and opposing litigants. The attorney also has an ethical duty to convey that information. The threat of malpractice suits and disciplinary proceedings should be sufficient to make any attorney think twice before trying to mislead his client or the court. Attorneys play an important role in our adversary system, and we should not denigrate that role by presuming that attorneys will be incompetent to perform one of the most important functions for which their clients hire them. Nor should we presume that Rule 16's drafters meant to encroach on a litigant's right to conduct his case through counsel. Rule 16's clear language shows that the rule's drafters presumed otherwise....

One may ask why the majority strains to get around Rule 16's clear language and the advisory committee's admonition against coercive settlement practices. Implicit in the majority's opinion—and explicit in the dissent to the panel opinion—is the notion that to effectively manage their case loads, district courts need the power to order represented parties to appear at settlement conferences. See majority opinion at 650–51; G. Heileman Brewing Co. v. Joseph Oat Corp., 848 F.2d 1415, 1427 (7th Cir.1988) (dissenting opinion); see also Judge Posner's dissenting opinion

at 657. Even if this is so (and I do not think it is), it does not justify expansively interpreting the district courts' inherent power to exceed the bounds Rule 16 sets. Moreover, as Judge Coffey and Judge Posner demonstrate, if any benefits do result from allowing district courts to order represented parties to attend settlement conferences, those benefits do not come without substantial costs. One of those costs is that expansively construing inherent power encourages judicial high-handedness. This case (in which Judge Posner has accurately labeled the magistrate's actions as "arbitrary, unreasonable, willful, and indeed petulant," dissenting opinion at 658) and the case uninvolving the Secretary of Labor, Will, cited by Judge Coffey, dissenting opinion at 661–62, aptly demonstrate that danger. Another cost is the expense and imposition on litigants that litigants try to avoid by hiring attorneys. A third cost is the denigration of the attorney's role in litigation. Perhaps the greatest cost, as Judge Coffey explains in detail, dissenting opinion at 662, is the damage to the appearance of fairness and the federal court's image as a neutral forum, factors that are essential to the court's proper functioning. Say what we will about the difference between coercing settlement and coercing attendance, it is difficult to believe that a litigant who has been forced to appear against his will, and possibly to listen to the opposing party or a judicial officer berate his litigation position, is going to walk away from that experience feeling he will get a fair shake from the court at trial if he resists the pressure to capitulate.

Obdurate litigants who unreasonably refuse to settle may cause headaches for the courts and opposing litigants. But litigants have no duty to settle, or even negotiate, and Rule 16 makes clear that federal courts have no business trying to force litigants to negotiate. If a litigant's position is legally or factually unsound, procedures such as judgment on the pleadings, Rule 12(b) dismissal, and summary judgment exist to dispose of the case at an early stage. District courts also have substantial power—of which they should take full advantage—to deter and punish frivolous litigation and undue delay. See 848 F.2d at 1421–22 (mentioning, among other things, the district courts' scheduling power under Rule 16 and the courts' sanctioning powers under Rule 16, Rule 11, and 28 U.S.C. § 1927). And district courts still have other methods—without forcing unwilling litigants to appear in court under threat of contempt—to facilitate settlements, including the time-honored method of pushing cases to early trials. See id; see also Strandell, 838 F.2d at 887. Where these methods do not produce settlements, it is unlikely that coercion will. And where coercion does succeed in producing a settlement, it is unlikely that success will advance the cause of justice or the federal court's image as a neutral forum....

"Federal judges spend lots of time telling other officials to stay within constitutional and statutory bounds, however those bounds may chafe in particular circumstances." Newman–Green, Inc. v. Alfonzo–Larrain R., 854 F.2d 916, 926 (7th Cir.1988). However much federal courts may desire the power to address unwilling parties directly in endeavoring to induce settlements, Rule 16 commands that the courts work through the parties' attorneys if that is what the parties desire. Rather than straining to circumvent Rule 16's clear command, we should demand that those of us in the federal judiciary practice what we preach so much to others, and work within the entirely reasonable limits that Rule 16 sets. Because the magistrate did not have the power to order Oat to send a corporate representative to the settlement conference, I would reverse the district court's judgment.

* * *

Questions

1. Some of the *Heileman* dissenters accuse the majority of imposing an obligation on the parties to negotiate a settlement in good faith. If this were so, how would such a requirement be operative? For a court to determine whether the parties approached the settlement conference in good faith, can it rely on the parties' overt behavior in the conference, or must it examine the reasonableness of the positions taken by each side? And if it examines the parties' positions, how can a court determine their reasonableness without forming some views about the merits of the under-lying dispute? Where might those views come from? Without benefit of an orderly presentation of evidence, can a judge know whether a party's position in settlement negotiations is reasonable or whether it is asserted in bad faith? Is there a danger that a pretrial conference in which the parties had a good faith obligation to attempt to settle might lead a judge form a premature view of the merits of the dispute?

2. Rule 16 was amended in 1993, in part in reaction to the *Heileman* opinions. Currently Rule 16 provides:

> **(c) Subjects for Consideration at Pretrial Conferences:**
>
> At any conference under this rule consideration may be given, and the court may take appropriate action, with respect to. . . .
>
> (9) settlement and the use of special procedures to assist in resolving the dispute when authorized by statute or local rule; . . .
>
> . . . If appropriate, the court may require that a party or its representa-tive be present or reasonably available by telephone in order to consider possible settlement of the dispute.

The Committee Notes to the proposed change in Rule 16 state:

> "Paragraph (9) is revised to describe more accurately the various procedures that, in addition to traditional settlement conferences, may be helpful in settling litigation. . . . [T]he judge and attorneys can explore possible use of alternative procedures such as mini-trials, summary jury trials, mediation, neutral evaluation, and nonbinding arbitration that can lead to consensual resolution of the dispute without a full trial on the merits. . . . The rule does not attempt to resolve questions as to the extent a court would be authorized to require such proceedings as an exercise of its inherent powers.

"The amendment of paragraph (9) should be read in conjunction with the sentence added to the end of subdivision (c), authorizing the court to direct that, in appropriate cases, a responsible representative of the parties be present or available by telephone during a conference.... This sentence refers to participation by a party or its representative. Whether this would be the individual party, an officer of a corporate party, a representative from an insurance carrier, or someone else would depend on the circumstances.... [I]t should be noted that the unwillingness of a party to be available, even by telephone, for a settlement conference may be a clear signal that the time and expense involved in pursuing settlement is unlikely to be productive and that personal participation by the parties should not be required.

"The explicit authorization in the rule to require personal participation in the manner stated is not intended to limit the reasonable exercise of the court's inherent powers, e.g. *G. Heileman Brewing Co. v. Joseph Oat Corp*...."

If a fact pattern similar to *Heileman* arose today, how should the court rule? What would be the best arguments for both sides?

* * *

7. PERSPECTIVES ON SETTLEMENT CONFERENCES

Managerial Judges by Judith Resnik[1]

Prior to the 1983 amendments to Rule 16 which established the practice of mandatory settlement conferences, Judith Resnik wrote the following article, warning of the dangers that such practices entail:

"The role of judges before adjudication is undergoing a change as substantial as has been recognized in the posttrial phase of public law cases. Today, federal district judges are assigned a case at the time of its filing and assume responsibility for shepherding the case to completion. Judges have described their new tasks as 'case management'—hence my term 'managerial judges.' As managers, judges learn more about cases much earlier than they did in the past. They negotiate with parties about the course, timing, and scope of both pretrial and posttrial litigation. These managerial responsibilities give judges greater power. Yet the restraints that formerly circumscribed judicial authority are conspicuously absent. Managerial judges frequently work beyond the public view, off the record, with no obligation to provide written, reasoned opinions, and out of reach of appellate review....

"Partly because of their new oversight role and partly because of increasing case loads, many judges have become concerned with the volume

---

1. Judith Resnik, *Managerial Judges,* 96 HARV. L. REV. 374, (1982) (footnotes omitted). Reprinted with permission.

of their work. To reduce the pressure, judges have turned to efficiency experts who promise 'calendar control.' Under the experts' guidance, judges have begun to experiment with schemes for speeding the resolution of cases and for persuading litigants to settle rather than try cases whenever possible. During the past decade, enthusiasm for the 'managerial movement' has become widespread; what began as an experiment is likely soon to become obligatory. Unless the Supreme Court and Congress reject proposed amendments to the Federal Rules, pretrial judicial management will be required in virtually all cases.

"In the rush to conquer the mountain of work, no one–neither judges, court administrators, nor legal commentators–has assessed whether relying on trial judges for informal dispute resolution and for case management, either before or after trial, is good, bad, or neutral. Little empirical evidence supports the claim that judicial management 'works' either to settle cases or to provide cheaper, quicker, or fairer dispositions. Proponents of judicial management have also failed to consider the systemic effects of the shift in judicial role. Management is a new form of 'judicial activism,' a behavior that usually attracts substantial criticism. Moreover, judicial management may be teaching judges to value their statistics, such as the number of case dispositions, more than they value the quality of their dispositions. Finally, because managerial judging is less visible and usually unreviewable, it gives trial courts more authority and at the same time provides litigants with fewer procedural safeguards to protect them from abuse of that authority. In short, managerial judging may be redefining *sub silentio* our standards of what constitutes rational, fair, and impartial adjudication. . . .

"Under this new regime of judicial management, discovery disputes and efforts to promote settlement would not be the only occasions upon which [a judge] would become acquainted with the parties' attorneys and the details of lawsuits. Rather, by virtue of rule 16, he would be obliged to issue pretrial orders within 120 days of filing of a complaint. To do so with any intelligence, he would need to learn a good deal about the lawsuits to which he was assigned.

"Informal judge-litigant contact provides judges with information beyond that traditionally within their ken. Conference topics are more wide ranging and the judges' concerns are broader than either are when proceedings are conducted in court. The supposedly rigid structure of evidentiary rules, designed to insulate decision-makers from extraneous and impermissible information, is irrelevant in case management. Managerial judges are not silent auditors of retrospective events retold by first-person storytellers. Instead, judges remove their blindfolds and become part of the sagas themselves.

"The extensive information that judges receive during pretrial conferences has not been filtered by the rules of evidence. Some of this information is received ex parte, a process that deprives the opposing party of the opportunity to contest the validity of information received. Moreover, judges are in close contact with attorneys during the course of management. Such interactions may become occasions for the development of intense feelings—admiration, friendship, or antipathy. Therefore, management becomes a fertile field for the growth of personal bias.

"Further, judges with supervisory obligations may gain stakes in the cases they manage. Their prestige may ride on 'efficient' management, as calculated by the speed and number of dispositions. Competition and peer pressure may tempt judges to rush litigants because of reasons unrelated to the merits of disputes. . . .

"In the past, such exposure to parties and issues and such a comparable interest in the proceedings might have resulted in recusal or disqualification. Despite a flexible approach to the procedural safeguards required to ensure due process, the Supreme Court has consistently required an 'impartial' judge—an individual with no prior involvement or interest in the dispute. Interest is broadly defined; indirect as well as direct benefits suffice to require disqualification. Statutory disqualification rules, recently amended and made more stringent, impose similar limits that disqualify judges with only a minute financial interest in the controversies before them. Nevertheless, neither the Supreme Court, the lower federal courts, nor Congress has considered the effect of judicial management on impartiality.

"I recognize that case management is not the only anomaly in the rules governing judicial disqualification and recusal. Many current practices assume that trial judges can compartmentalize their minds, disregard inappropriate evidence, and reconsider past decisions in light of new information. Motions to reconsider, reduce sentences, and vacate convictions, as well as most appellate remands, are decided by the very judges whose prior decisions are being challenged. I find these practices inconsistent with common perceptions of impartial adjudication. Yet reconsideration by the same judge who first heard a case is far less worrisome than factfinding by the judge who *managed* the case. As 'repeat adjudicators,' judges are generally confined to the record. They rely upon traditional adversarial exchanges, publicly explain their decisions, and know that their work may be reviewed on appeal. In contrast, as pretrial case managers, judges operate in the freewheeling arena of informal dispute resolution. Having supervised case preparation and pressed for settlement, judges can hardly be considered untainted if they are ultimately asked to find the facts and adjudicate the merits of a dispute. . . .

"Proponents of management may be forgetting the quintessential judicial obligations of conducting a reasoned inquiry, articulating the reasons for decision, and subjecting those reasons to appellate review—characteristics that have long defined judging and distinguished it from other tasks. Although the sword remains in place, the blindfold and scales have all but disappeared."

* * *

For and Against Settlement: Uses and Abuses of the Mandatory Settlement Conference by Carrie Menkel–Meadow[2]

In the following article, Carrie Menkel–Meadow addressed Resnik's position, as well as that of Owen Fiss in *Against Settlement*, Chapter 4, supra., by attempting to describe a broad and positive role for the judicial settlement conference:

"Those who criticize the role of the judge in settlement functions assume the judge's proper role is purely adjudicative. Owen Fiss has stated starkly: 'Courts exist to give meaning to public values, not to resolve disputes.' Judith Resnik has argued that judges are required to provide reasoned explanations for their decisions, are supposed to rule without concern for the interests of particular constituencies, are required to act with deliberation, and are to be disinterested and disengaged from the dispute and disputants. Those who criticize the settlement function, I fear, have enshrined the adjudicative function based on an unproven, undemonstrated record of successful performance, just as the efficiency experts have exalted settlement conferences relying on unconvincing statistics. For me, the more fruitful inquiry is to ask under what circumstances adjudication is more appropriate than settlement, or vice-versa. In short, when settlement?
. . .

"I will not repeat the often stated assertion that settlement is a 'docket-clearing' device. We have examined the efficiency argument and found it wanting. What settlement offers is a substantive justice that may be more responsive to the parties' needs than adjudication. Settlement can be particularized to the needs of the parties, it can avoid win/lose, binary results, provide richer remedies than the commodification or monetarization of all claims, and achieve legitimacy through consent. In addition, settlement offers a different substantive process by allowing participation by the parties as well as the lawyers. Settlement fosters a communication process that can be more direct and less stylized than litigation, and affords greater flexibility of procedure and remedy.

"But settlement is not all things to all people. Settlements can be coerced, either by the power of the parties, by a strong judge in a settlement conference, or by inexorable trial dates. Settlements can be economically wasteful if the participants fail to consider all of the information bearing on the dispute and prevent thorough investigation and airing of all issues. They can be achieved in illegitimate and private ways. For example, several parties may gang up on another, parties may distort facts, or make incorrect predictions about the probable trial outcome. They can be unfair and unprincipled, based on factors extraneous to the merits. As discussed above, private settlements also can be problematic when there is a need for a clear or authoritative ruling. Significantly, settlements may be

---

2. Carrie Menkel–Meadow, *For and Against Settlement: Uses and Abuses of the Mandatory Settlement Conference*, 33 UCLA L. Rev. 485 (1985). Reprinted with permission.

disturbing on a systemic or societal level if separate classes of disputants are allocated routinely or by paid choice to one form of dispute resolution.

"For me, the central question in this dispute about dispute resolution should not be whether cases should always be settled or always be adjudicated, but rather when and how settlements are most appropriately achieved. I remain agnostic on the issue of whether we can specify in advance which types of disputes are best settled and which are best adjudicated. . . .

"As greater numbers of judges and courts use settlement conferences, our information about particular practices increases. Our current sources of data include reports and articles written by judges and settlement officers, training materials written for new judges, some survey data collected by social scientists and court administrators, and descriptive and critical reports by academics. As we review this data, it is useful to think about how the manager of the settlement conference, whether judge or magistrate, views his or her role. What emerges from the data is a variety of role conceptions that parallel the various conceptions of the goals of settlement. For some, efficient case management is the primary role; for others, the primary role is the facilitation of substantive or procedural justice. For others still, the primary role is simple brokering of what would occur anyway in bilateral negotiations. Some judges avoid active settlement activity because they view adjudication as their primary role. . . .

A.   *The Dangers of Efficiency-Seeking Settlement Techniques*

"For those who seek to use the settlement conference as a docket-clearing device, the conference becomes most problematic in terms of the substantive and process values (i.e., *quality* of solution) previously discussed. Judges see their role as simplifying the issues until the major issue separating the parties (usually described as money) is identified and the judge can attempt to 'narrow the gap.' In one study judges and lawyers were asked to report on judicial settlement activity. Seventy-two percent of the lawyers reported that they participated at least once in settlement conferences in which the judge requested the parties to 'split the difference.' The same study noted that when local rules require settlement conferences judges tend to be more assertive in their settlement techniques (using several techniques that some of the lawyers considered to be unethical). According to the study, jurisdictions with mandatory settlement conferences took more time in moving cases toward trial. This confirms the findings of earlier studies.

"A much touted settlement technique is the use of the 'Lloyds of London' formula: The settlement judge asks the parties to assess the probabilities of liability and damages and, if the figures are within reasonable range, to split the difference. The difficulty with such settlement techniques is that they tend to monetarize and compromise all the issues in the case. Although some cases are reducible to monetary issues, an approach to case evaluation on purely monetary grounds may decrease the likelihood of settlement by making fewer issues available for trade-offs.

Furthermore, a wider definition of options may make compromise unnecessary. As the recent outpouring of popular and scholarly literature on negotiation illustrates, the greater the number of issues in controversy between the parties, the greater the likelihood of achieving a variety of solutions. Parties may place complementary values on different items. The irony is that settlement managers, who think they are making settlement easier by reducing the issues, may in fact be increasing the likelihood of deadlock by reducing the issues to one. Furthermore, as I have argued at length elsewhere, using money as a proxy for other interests the parties may have, may thwart the possibilities for using party interests for mutual gain.

"In addition to foreclosing a number of possible settlements, the efficiency-minded settlement officer seems prone to use coercive techniques such as suggesting a particular result, making threats about taking the case off the docket, directing meetings with clients or parties. Lawyers find these techniques problematic. Thus, the quest for efficiency may in fact be counterproductive.

B. The Search for Quality Solutions

"Some recent data seem to indicate that greater satisfaction can be achieved with a different settlement management role–the facilitator of good settlements. Brazil's survey of lawyers practicing in four federal districts reveals that lawyers favored intervention techniques that sought to produce the 'best result.' Lawyers favored such techniques because judges who analyzed the particular facts of the case (as opposed to those who used formulas like 'Lloyds of London'), offered explicit suggestions and assessments of the parties' positions, occasionally spoke directly to recalcitrant clients, and expressed views about the unfairness of particular results. . . .

"[I]f judges (or magistrates) will serve as Howard Raiffa's 'analytic mediators' (i.e., asking questions to explore the parties' interests and attempting to fashion tailor-made solutions from an 'objective' outside-of-the-problem position, but with additional information), then judicial and magistrate settlement managers may be providing both better and more efficient (in the Pareto optimal sense) solutions to litigation problems. . . .

"To the extent that settlement procedures are used to achieve substantive outcomes that are better than court-defined remedies, they have implications for how the settlement conference should be conducted and who should conduct it. First, those with knowledge about the larger implications of the litigation–the parties–should be present (this is the principle behind the mini-trial concept with business personnel in attendance) to offer or accept solutions that involve more than simple money settlements. Second, such conferences should be managed by someone other than the trial judge so that interests and considerations that might effect a settlement but would be inadmissible in court will not prejudice a later trial. Some argue for a separate 'settlement officer' because the skills required for guiding negotiations are different from those required for trying cases. Third, some cases in which issues should not be traded off should not be subjected to the settlement process at all. For example, in employment discrimination cases, parties should not be asked to accept monetary settlements in lieu of a job for which they are qualified. Finally, a more traditional mediator's role may be more appropriate when the substantive process (i.e., direct communication between the parties) may be more important than the substantive outcome (i.e., employer-employee disputes, some civil rights cases). . . .

Conclusion

"My own view is that settlement is now the norm. The pertinent question is how can it be used most effectively (for the parties and for other users of the system) when traditional adjudicators are brought into the process. Can judges, who are historically neutral rule declarers, fact finders, and expeditors, perform this new function without a new socialization process? As settlement conferences become mandatory, socialization of settlement officers and research and evaluation of the settlement process must be conducted simultaneously. If many judges use the sorts of 'Lloyds of London' formulas described above, additional training will be necessary to expose settlement officers to the problematic aspects of these practices. Settlement officers will have to learn not how to commodify and monetarize all issues, but rather how to identify alternative issues that the parties may value differently, in the hope of reaching settlements that are fair, perhaps norm-based, and that take account of the parties' needs. To the extent that I have criticized the limited remedial imagination of courts, the settlement conference provides an opportunity to temper the rigidity of win/loss trials with flexible solutions."

* * *

Questions

1. Judith Resnik, in the excerpt from *Managerial Judges*, claims that pretrial conferences "remove the judges' blindfolds and make the judge part of the saga." How might that occur? Does the risk of such a change in the judicial role outweigh the benefit of pretrial conferences?

2. To what extent do Carrie Menkel–Meadow's proposals to reshape judicial settlement conferences respond to the concerns raised by Resnik and Fiss about the change in the judicial role that a mandatory settlement conference can provoke? To what extent did the drafters of the Federal Rules adopt Menkel–Meadow's proposals in the 1993 amendments?

* * *

Note on *Conolly v. National School Bus Service*

The Seventh Circuit recently considered whether a party can be compelled to explore settlement possibilities with a judge's law clerk. In CONNOLLY V. NATIONAL SCHOOL BUS SERVICE, INC., 177 F.3d 593 (7th Cir.1999), the plaintiff sued her former employer for sexual harassment, seeking compensatory and punitive damages of $40,000. The suit was settled on the even of trial for $10,000. Subsequently, her attorney, Rossiello, sought attorney fees of $97,000 under the attorney fee provision of Title VII, 42 U.S.C. Section 2000e–5(k). The district court used the lodestar approach, applied a several factor test, and as a result, reduced the fee award to $23,000. The attorney appealed. On appeal, the Seventh Circuit reversed the award on the ground that the district court reduced the fee award, in part, because the attorney had refused to participate in a court-ordered settlement effort before the judge's law clerk. The Court of Appeals stated:

"Contrary to Rossiello's contentions, Judge Lindberg had ample evidence before him of Rossiello's dilatory tactics. Given the deference we show to a district court judge's determination of reasonable attorneys' fees, we would ordinarily affirm Judge Lindberg's reduction from the lodestar amount based on the record before us. Rossiello, however, legitimately complains of one factor Judge Lindberg relied on in reaching his decision.

"Shortly before the scheduled trial date, Judge Lindberg ordered the parties to meet with his law clerk in order to mediate the dispute. Rossiello refused to allow his client to meet with the law clerk. In reducing Rossiello's award, Judge Lindberg cited Rossiello's refusal to mediate as one of the reasons he believed Rossiello to have unreasonably delayed the disposition of the case. We believe Rossiello had no obligation to mediate before the judge's law clerk and that reduction of his attorney's fee award on this basis was therefore an abuse of discretion. . . .

"Rossiello makes much of the fact that at the time the law clerk had only recently been admitted to the bar and did not have sufficient familiarity with the facts of the case. We do not find either factor particularly significant. One could be a quite effective mediator without being versed in the minutiae of a case. For this same reason, we do not find the law clerk's recent admission to the bar particularly significant. We see no necessary correlation between a person's skill in facilitating settlement and the amount of time which has passed since their admission to the bar.

"However, we do not believe that Fed.R.Civ.P. 16(a), which gives district court judges the power to conduct pretrial settlement conferences, allows a district court judge to delegate this power to a law clerk. Law clerks serve as judicial adjuncts. Their duties and responsibilities are to assist the judge in his work, not to be the judge. A judge's law clerk may therefore properly assist the judge in the judge's settlement efforts, but to allow the clerk rather than the judge to conduct a settlement conference is to confuse the adjunct with the judge. . . .

"Since the suggestion that the parties mediate before Judge Lindberg's law clerk was improper, Rossiello was well within his rights to refuse the invitation. He therefore cannot be punished for this refusal through a reduction in the award of statutory attorneys' fees. We conclude that it was an abuse of discretion to reduce the attorneys' fee award based on Rossiello's refusal to have the district court's law clerk mediate the case.''

* * *

Question

If it is not permissible for a judge to order parties to mediate or explore settlement prospects with her law clerk, is it permissible for a judge to order the parties to mediate their dispute before a mediator? Good faith mediation, by its very nature, requires the parties to explore settlement prospects with an independent mediator. The Seventh Circuit's opinion states that it was not basing its objection on the lack of training of the law clerk, so what is the basis of the court's objection to the District Court's procedures? Would the same objections apply to any form of court-ordered mediation?

8. SUMMARY JURY TRIALS

A summary jury trial is a settlement enhancing technique in which the parties present a summary of their cases to a jury. As described by the Sixth Circuit in *In Re NLO, Inc.*, 3 F.3d 153 (6th Cir. 1993):

"A summary jury trial is a nonbinding mini-trial designed to give the attorneys and their clients an indication of what they may expect at a full-blown trial on the merits. The parties exchange evidence before the summary jury trial has commenced, and are limited to the evidence thus disclosed. A jury is selected from the regular jury pool. The parties then present opening statements, summarize the evidence which would be presented at a full trial (no live testimony is permitted), and present closing statements. The jury is then charged with the law and asked to respond to a series of interrogatories concerning liability and damages. See S. Arthur Spiegel, *Summary Jury Trials*, 54 U. CINN. L. REV. 829 (1986)."

The following cases explore whether courts have the power, either under Rule 16 or under their inherent power to control their dockets and encourage parties to settle, to compel parties to participate in a summary jury trial.

Strandell v. Jackson County, Illinois

838 F.2d 884 (7th Cir.1987).

■ RIPPLE, CIRCUIT JUDGE.

In this appeal, we must decide whether a federal district court can *require* litigants to participate in a nonbinding summary jury trial. In a nonbinding summary jury trial, attorneys summarize their case before a jury, which then renders a nonbinding verdict. The purpose of this device is to motivate litigants toward settlement by allowing them to estimate how an actual jury may respond to their evidence. Thomas Tobin, Esquire, appeals from a judgment of criminal contempt for refusing to participate in such a procedure. We vacated the judgment by an order dated September 10, 1987, 830 F.2d 195; we now issue a full opinion.

I

Facts

Mr. Tobin represents the parents of Michael Strandell in a civil rights action against Jackson County, Illinois. The case involves the arrest, strip search, imprisonment, and suicidal death of Michael Strandell. In anticipation of a pretrial conference on September 3, 1986, the plaintiffs filed a written report concerning settlement prospects. The plaintiffs reported that they were requesting $500,000, but that the defendants refused to discuss the issue. At the pretrial conference, the district court suggested that the parties consent to a summary jury trial. A summary jury trial generally lasts one day, and consists of the selection of six jurors to hear approximations by counsel of the expected evidence. After receiving an abbreviated charge, the jury retires with directions to render a consensus verdict. After a verdict is reached, the jury is informed that its verdict is advisory in nature and nonbinding. The objective of this procedure is to induce the parties to negotiate a settlement.[1] Mr. Tobin informed the district court that the plaintiffs would not consent to a summary jury trial, and filed a motion to advance the case for trial. The district court ordered that discovery be closed on January 15, 1987, and set the case for trial.

During discovery, the plaintiffs had obtained statements from 21 witnesses. The plaintiffs learned the identity of many of these witnesses from information provided by the defendants. After discovery closed, the defendants filed a motion to compel production of the witnesses' statements. The plaintiffs responded that these statements constituted privileged work-product; they argued that the defendants could have obtained the information contained in them through ordinary discovery. The district court denied the motion to compel production; it concluded that the defendants had failed to establish "substantial need" and "undue hardship," as required by Rule 26(b)(3) of the Federal Rules of Civil Procedure.

On March 23, 1987, the district court again discussed settlement prospects with counsel. The court expressed its view that a trial could not be accommodated easily on its crowded docket and again suggested that the parties consent to a summary jury trial. On March 26, 1987, Mr. Tobin advised the district court that he would not be willing to submit his client's case to a summary jury trial, but that he was ready to proceed to trial immediately. He claimed that a summary jury trial would require disclosure of the privileged statements. The district court rejected this argument, and ordered the parties to participate in a summary jury trial.

---

1. The guidelines for a summary jury trial are set forth in Lambros, Report to The Judicial Conference of the United States, reprinted at 103 F.R.D. 461–98 (1984).

On March 31, 1987, the parties and counsel appeared, as ordered, for selection of a jury for the summary jury trial. Mr. Tobin again objected to the district court's order compelling the summary jury trial. The district court denied this motion. Mr. Tobin then respectfully declined to proceed with the selection of the jury. The district court informed Mr. Tobin that it did not have time available to try this case, nor would it have time for a trial "in the foreseeable months ahead." Tr. of March 31, 1987 at 5. The court then held Mr. Tobin in criminal contempt for refusing to proceed with the summary jury trial.

The district court postponed disposition of the criminal contempt judgment until April 6, 1987. On that date, the district court asked Mr. Tobin to reconsider his position on proceeding with the summary jury trial. Mr. Tobin reiterated his view that the court lacked the power to compel a summary jury trial, and maintained that such a proceeding would violate his client's rights. The district court entered a criminal contempt judgment of $500 against Mr. Tobin. Mr. Tobin filed a notice of appeal that same day.

II

The District Court Opinion

The district court filed a memorandum opinion setting forth its reasons for ordering a summary jury trial. Strandell v. Jackson County, 115 F.R.D. 333 (S.D.Ill.1987) [hereinafter Mem. op.]; R.144. The district court noted that trial in this case was expected to last five to six weeks, and that the parties were "poles apart in terms of settlement." Id. at 334. It further noted that summary jury trials had been used with great success in such situations.

In determining that it had the power to compel a summary jury trial, the court relied on a resolution adopted in 1984 by the Judicial Conference of the United States. The original draft of the resolution endorsed summary jury trials "with the voluntary consent of the parties." Id. at 335 (quoting Report of the Judicial Conference Committee on the Operation of the Jury System Agenda G-13, at 4 (Sept.1984)). The final draft of the resolution, however, omitted this phrase. Id. (quoting Report of the Proceedings of the Judicial Conference of the United States, at 88 (Sept.1984)).

The court then determined that Rule 16 of the Federal Rules of Civil Procedure permits a mandatory summary jury trial. The court pointed out that Rule 16(a) authorizes a court in its discretion to require attorneys "to appear before it for a conference or conferences before trial for such purposes as (1) expediting the disposition of the action ... and ... (5) facilitating the settlement of the case." Furthermore, Rule 16(c) provides that "[t]he participants at any conference under this rule may consider and take action with respect to ... (7) the possibility of settlement or the use of extrajudicial procedures to resolve the dispute ... and ... (11) such other matters as may aid in the disposition of the action." The court admitted that "its discretion in this context is not unbridled." Mem. op. at 335. However, the court held that Rule 16 grants district courts "the power to order the litigants to engage in a process which will enhance the possibility of fruitful negotiations." Id....

III

Analysis

We begin by noting that we are presented with a narrow question: Whether a trial judge may *require* a litigant to participate in a summary jury trial to promote settlement of the case. We are *not* asked to determine the manner in which summary jury trials may be used with the consent of the parties. Nor are we asked to express a view on the effectiveness of this technique in settlement negotiations.

A.

In turning to the narrow question before us—the legality of *compelled* participation in a summary jury trial—we must also acknowledge, at the very onset, that a district court no doubt has substantial inherent power to control and to manage its docket.... That power must, of course, be exercised in a manner that is in harmony with the Federal Rules of Civil Procedure. Those rules are the product of a careful process of study and reflection designed to take "due cognizance both of the need for expedition of cases and the protection of individual rights." S.Rep. No. 1744, 85th Cong., 2d Sess., reprinted in 1958 U.S.Code Cong. & Admin.News 3023, 3026. That process, set forth in the Rules Enabling Act, 28 U.S.C. § 2072, also reflects the joint responsibility of the legislative and judicial branches of government in striking the delicate balance between these competing concerns. See generally Hanna v. Plumer, 380 U.S. 460, 471, 85 S.Ct. 1136, 1144, 14 L.Ed.2d 8 (1965). Therefore, in those areas of trial practice where the Supreme Court and the Congress, acting together, have addressed the appropriate balance between the needs for judicial efficiency and the rights of the individual litigant, innovation by the individual judicial officer must conform to that balance.

In this case, the district court quite properly acknowledged, at least as a theoretical matter, this limitation on its power to devise a new method to encourage settlement. Consequently, the court turned to Rule 16 of the Federal Rules of Civil Procedure in search of authority for the use of a mandatory summary jury trial. In the district court's view, two subsections of Rule 16(c) authorized such a procedure. As amended in 1983, those subsections read: The participants at any conference under this rule may consider and take action with respect to.... (7) the possibility of settlement or the use of extrajudicial procedures to resolve the dispute;.... (11) such other matters as may aid in the disposition of the action. Fed.R.Civ.P. 16(c)(7), (11).

Here, we must respectfully disagree with the district court. We do not believe that these provisions can be read as authorizing a *mandatory* summary jury trial. In our view, while the pretrial conference of Rule 16 was intended to foster settlement through the use of extrajudicial procedures, it was not intended to require that an unwilling litigant be side-tracked from the normal course of litigation. The drafters of Rule 16 certainly intended to provide, in the pretrial conference, "a neutral forum" for discussing the matter of settlement. Fed.R.Civ.P. 16 advisory committee's note. However, it is also clear that they did not foresee that the conference would be used "to impose settlement negotiations on unwilling litigants...." Id.; see also 6 C. Wright, A. Miller & M. Kane, Federal Practice and Procedure § 1525 (Supp.1987) ("As the Advisory Committee Note indicates, this new subdivision does not force unwilling parties into settlement negotiations."). While the drafters intended that the trial judge "*explor[e]* the use of procedures other than litigation to resolve the dispute,"—including "*urging* the litigants to employ adjudicatory techniques outside the courthouse,"—they clearly did not intend *to require* the parties to take part in such activities. Fed.R.Civ.P. 16 advisory committee's note (emphasis supplied). As the Second Circuit, commenting on the 1983 version of Rule 16, wrote: "Rule 16 ... was not designed as a means for clubbing the parties—or one of them—into an involuntary compromise." Kothe v. Smith, 771 F.2d 667, 669 (2d Cir.1985).

Our interpretation of how Rule 16 was intended to be used with respect to settlement procedures is substantially reinforced by the drafters' commentary with respect to other parts of the rule. For instance, the last sentence of Rule 16(c), added in 1983, reads as follows: "At least one of the attorneys for each party participating in any conference before trial shall have authority to enter into stipulations and to make admissions regarding all matters that the participants may reasonably anticipate may be discussed." Fed.R.Civ.P. 16(c). The drafters' notes describe it in the following terms:

> The last sentence of subdivision (c) is new. It has been added to meet one of the criticisms of the present practice described earlier and insure proper preconference preparation so that the meeting is more than a ceremonial or ritualistic event. The reference to "authority" is not intended to insist upon the ability to settle the litigation. Nor should the rule be read to encourage the judge conducting the conference to compel attorneys to enter into stipulations or to make admissions that they consider to be unreasonable, that touch on matters that could not normally have been anticipated to arise at the conference, or on subjects of a dimension that normally require prior consultation with and approval from the client. Fed.R.Civ.P. 16 advisory committee's note (citation omitted).

Our decision is consistent with two decisions issued by this court prior to the 1983 amendments to Rule 16. In J.F. Edwards Constr. Co. v. Anderson Safeway Guard Rail Corp., 542 F.2d 1318 (7th Cir.1976), the court ruled that a district court could not use Rule 16 to compel parties to stipulate facts to which they could not voluntarily agree. One year later, in Identiseal Corp. v. Positive Identification Sys., 560 F.2d 298 (7th Cir.1977), this court reiterated that Rule 16 was noncoercive when it determined that district courts lacked the power to order that a party undertake further discovery.... Although J.F. Edwards and Identiseal antedate the amendments to Rule 16, nothing in the amended rule or in the Advisory Committee Notes suggests that the amendments were intended to make the rule coercive.

The use of a mandatory summary jury trial as a pretrial settlement device would also affect seriously the well-established rules concerning discovery and work-product privilege. See Fed.R.Civ.P. 26(b)(3); see also Hickman v. Taylor, 329 U.S. 495, 67 S.Ct. 385, 91 L.Ed. 451 (1947). These rules reflect a carefully-crafted balance between the needs for pretrial disclosure and party confidentiality. Yet, a compelled summary jury trial could easily upset that balance by requiring disclosure of information obtainable, if at all, through the mandated discovery process. We do not believe it is reasonable to assume that the Supreme Court and the Congress would undertake, in such an oblique fashion, such a radical alteration of the considered judgments contained in Rule 26 and in the case law. If such radical surgery is to be performed, we can expect that the national rule-making process outlined in the Rules Enabling Act will undertake it in quite an explicit fashion.

B.

The district court, in explaining its decision to compel the use of the summary jury trial, noted that the Southern District of Illinois faces crushing caseloads. The court suggested that handling that caseload, including compliance with the Speedy Trial Act, required resort to such devices as compulsory summary jury trials. We certainly cannot take issue with the district court's conclusion that its caseload places great stress on its capacity to fulfill its responsibilities. However, a crowded docket does not permit the court to avoid the adjudication of cases properly within its congressionally-mandated jurisdiction.... As this court said in Taylor v. Oxford, 575 F.2d 152 (7th Cir.1978): "Innovative experiments may be admirable, and considering the heavy case loads in the district courts, understandable, but experiments must stay within the limitations of the statute." Id. at 154.

Conclusion

Because we conclude that the parameters of Rule 16 do not permit courts to compel parties to participate in summary jury trials, the contempt judgment of the district court is vacated.

* * *

Federal Reserve Bank of Minneapolis v. Carey–Canada, Inc.

123 F.R.D. 603 (D. Minn. 1988).

■ JANICE M. SYMCHYCH, UNITED STATES MAGISTRATE.

I. BACKGROUND

This is an asbestos case, involving claims of property damage to a commercial building. Plaintiff claims its property was allegedly damaged and the health of its employees endangered by defendants' fireproofing of the Federal Reserve Bank with asbestos-containing products. Plaintiff argues that because the product threatens serious health risks, it requires immediate removal. This entails relocating the operation of the bank, and tearing it apart beam by beam. Plaintiff seeks compensatory and punitive damages, in the amount of $48 million dollars, attributable to this process. It claims defendants are liable under negligence, strict liability, fraud, and conspiracy theories.

Defendants deny liability and argue that there is no actual harm to plaintiff's property, and no proven health risk for low-level asbestos exposure. They allege that plaintiff has overreacted by ripping up its premises and relocating only on a "potential" health risk. They further dispute the abatement process used by the plaintiff, arguing the same result could have been accomplished for less than $8 million dollars. W.R. Grace also claims that the majority of asbestos in the facility is attributable to Carey-Canada and Celotex, and that removal of the codefendants' asbestos necessarily involves removal of its asbestos. It argues then, that none of the costs of abatement are chargeable to it.

The case is set for jury trial commencing January 16, 1989, if settlement efforts are not fruitful. The summary jury trial is set to run for three days, December 12–14, 1988, and to be followed by settlement conference.

At the pretrial conference, each party voiced objections to the SJT, and ultimately objected to required participation in it. They argue that the process is too expensive, as it would cost each party approximately $50,000. Further, they cited the fact that the SJT would not be an accurate synopsis of a jury trial because several major evidentiary rulings would not be made by Judge Devitt until the last week in December, whereas the SJT was to take place December 12–14. Finally, they argue that the parties are truly at loggerheads and possibility of settlement is extremely remote, and advancement to trial definite. They view the SJT process as using valuable trial preparation time without contributing significantly to clarification of issues or attorney preparation for trial.

II. DISCUSSION

This court is called upon to decide whether the court may compel attendance and participation in a non-binding summary jury trial absent consent of the parties. This is an issue of first impression in Federal District Court in Minnesota and in the Eighth Circuit Court of Appeals. The undersigned finds that in light of the court's inherent power to manage and control its docket, and in light of Rules 1 and 16 of the Federal Rules of Civil Procedure, and Local Rule 3 of this court, that the court possesses the authority to compel participation and attendance in a summary jury trial.

The Supreme Court has long acknowledged the power of the court to control and manage its docket. In Link v. Wabash, 370 U.S. 626, 82 S.Ct. 1386, 8 L.Ed.2d 734 (1962), the Court made clear that this power is inherent, and not dependent upon any express statute or rule conferring such power. The ability of a court to use its discretion to manage its crowded docket must be protected. "The exigencies of modern dockets demand the adoption of novel and imaginative means lest the courts, inundated by a tidal wave of cases fail in their duty to provide a just and speedy disposition of every case." Lockhart v. Patel, 115 F.R.D. 44 (E.D.Ky. 1987). Parties and attorneys are often and understandably reluctant to accept and participate in procedures outside the traditional norm. It is often difficult to focus the attention of counsel and litigants on settlement as an alternative means of resolving a case. The need to compel the parties to address settlement, is an integral aspect of the docket management function of the court in this era of complex, protracted litigation.

Since the introduction of the summary jury trial in 1984 by United States District Judge Thomas Lambros, from the Northern District of Ohio, it has gained widespread use and acceptance as a valuable settlement tool. Moreover, it is clear that settlement of cases prior to litigation provides a major cost saving for the parties as well as conservation of judicial resources. There may be a variety of reasons why cases do not settle. Parties may refuse to accept settlement as they feel that they are entitled to and need their day in court. Parties may believe that the only way to prevail on a weak case is to get the case before a jury. Parties may be unable to objectively recognize or assess the strengths and weaknesses of their position without submission of the issues to a finder of fact. These reasons, among others, act as impediments to settlement of cases which should otherwise be resolved without trial.

The SJT provides a means by which to eliminate these barriers to settlement. SJT is the only dispute resolution technique which uses the input of a jury of laymen as fact finders. It is this facet of SJT which permits the parties, not the attorneys, to believe that their story has been told, and a decision reached by an objective body. The decision resulting from the SJT inevitably results in both sides re-examining and reevaluating their positions and demands.

SJT is a flexible pretrial procedure which adds appreciably to the analysis of trial bound cases. Generally, it is used in cases where settlement seems unlikely and settlement negotiations are at or near impasse. Even in cases where SJT does not result in settlement, it provides clarification of the issues, and results in superior preparation for trial. The SJT does not abolish any substantive rights of the parties; they are still entitled to a binding trial, if the summary proceedings do not lead to settlement of the case. The SJT represents one alternative which courts are employing in an effort to secure to civil litigants just, speedy, and inexpensive determination of their claims of which litigants may be otherwise deprived because of the overwhelming and overburdening caseloads in many federal courts.

As stated above neither the Federal District Court in Minnesota nor the Eighth Circuit Court of Appeals has addressed the question presented here. Several recent district court opinions in other jurisdictions have held that the court is authorized to order mandatory summary jury trials. McKay v. Ashland Oil Co., Inc., 120 F.R.D. 43 (E.D.Ky.1988); Arabian American Oil Company v. Scarfone, 119 F.R.D. 448 (M.D.Fla.1988); cf. Rhea v. Massey–Ferguson, Inc., 767 F.2d 266 (6th Cir.1985). As in this matter, each of these cases involved complex issues, parties who were poles apart in terms of settlement and cases which promised to consume a good deal of trial time. . . .

In Arabian American Oil, a case expected to consume seven courtroom weeks, the district court cited Fed.R.Civ.P. 16(a)(1), (5) and (c)(11), along with its inherent power to control its own docket, as a basis for compelling SJT participation. No local rule existed which expressly authorized its use. In its decision, the court articulated that under Article Three of the United States Constitution, its mission was to promptly administer justice in matters before it. Arabian American Oil, 119 F.R.D. at 449. The SJT represents one alternative dispute resolution process which allows the courts to secure civil litigants a just, speedy, inexpensive determination of their claims. The court also continued on that, even if settlement does not result, a clarification of issues results, which is invaluable in the later trial. Similarly, the undersigned finds the SJT to be a legitimate device to implement this court's policy to provide litigants with an expeditious resolution of their case.

The only contrary authority is in the Seventh Circuit, where it set forth both directly and indirectly, in the cases of Strandell v. Jackson County, Illinois, and G. Heileman Brewing Company v. Joseph Oat Corp., 848 F.2d 1415, reh'g granted (7th Cir.1988). In Strandell, a case in which one trial was to last five to six weeks, the Seventh Circuit, in reversing the district court, concluded that the district court did not have the authority to order a mandatory summary jury trial. While the Court noted that the Advisory Committee Notes to Fed.R.Civ.P. 16 intended that the courts "explor[e] the use of procedures other than litigation to resolve the dispute,—including the use of adjudicatory techniques outside the courthouse," it found that the litigants' participation could not be required. Strandell v. Jackson County, Ill., 838 F.2d 884 at 887 (7th Cir.1987); Fed.R.Civ.P. 16 Advisory Committee Notes.

The Seventh Circuit reasoned that compelled participation would result in litigants' loss of their right to proceed to trial, and forced courthouse settlements. Id. at 888. The Strandell district court decision, did not, however, even indirectly suggest that the parties would be denied their trial right, if no settlement was achieved. Although the district court informed the litigants that no court time was available until the distant future, they were not denied their right to trial altogether or informed that a summary jury trial was the only allowable mechanism of adjudication for resolution of their dispute. It goes without saying that the court's discretion is not so unbridled as to permit the forced settlement of lawsuits. Kothe v. Smith, 771 F.2d 667 (2d Cir.1985); Lockhart v. Patel, 115 F.R.D. 44 (E.D.Ky.1987);

Furthermore, the Seventh Circuit was concerned in Strandell, at 888, that the violation of privilege or protection of work product issues might come into play. This concern is misplaced. Because of the extensive pretrial procedures involved in preparing litigation in federal courts and because a SJT is based on facts disclosed by discovery and is to be a synopsis of the actual trial, it is difficult to believe that anything would be disclosed at a SJT that would not ultimately be disclosed at the actual trial. If the Seventh Circuit implication is that a SJT prevents the litigant from saving some surprise for the trial, the Federal Rules of Civil Procedure are designed to avoid that eventuality. Trial by ambush is no longer an accepted method of practice. . . .

For these reasons, the view of the Seventh Circuit is rejected, and the rationale of the above-cited District Court opinions accepted here as the better approach on the question at hand. In addition to the case precedent, an analysis of the applicable rules and comments confirms the view that the parties may be compelled to participate in settlement efforts, such as the SJT.

Rule 1, Fed.R.Civ.P., states that the rules "shall be construed to secure the just, speedy, and inexpensive determination of every action." Rule 16(a), concerning pretrial activities, states, "in any action, the court may in its discretion direct the attorneys for the parties and any unrepresented parties to appear before it for a conference or conferences before trial for such purposes as (1) expediting the disposition of the action . . . and (5) facilitating settlement of the case." Rule 16(c)(7) and (11) provide that "the participants at any conference under this rule may consider and take action with respect to . . . (7) the possibility of settlement or the use of extrajudicial procedures to resolve the dispute . . . and (11) such other matters as may aid in the disposition of the action." Fed.R.Civ.P. 16(c)(7) and (11); See Strandell v. Jackson County, Ill., 115 F.R.D. 333 (S.D.Ill.1987). Local Rule 3, further provides that "Each judge may prescribe such pre-trial and discovery procedures as the judge may determine appropriate . . . each judge on their own initiative, on motion of any party to an action, or by stipulation of the parties may order the attorneys and the parties to appear for a pre-trial conference to consider the subject specified in Fed.R.Civ.P. 16, or other matters determined by the judge." Local Rule 3(C). . . .

The Federal Rules of Civil Procedure were amended in 1983. The Advisory Committee Notes articulate that the obvious goal of the amendments was the promotion of case management of which settlement is a valuable tool. Fed.R.Civ.P. 16 Advisory Committee Note to 1983 Amendments. Therefore, it is difficult to reconcile the argument that Rule 16 does not permit courts to order the parties to participate in summary jury trials with the goals of that rule. It is hard to imagine that the drafters of the 1983 amendments actually intended to strengthen courts' ability to manage their caseloads while at the same time intended to deny the court the power to compel participation by the parties to the litigation.

Moreover, the Judicial Conference of the United States has passed a formal resolution endorsing the use of SJT as a potentially effective means of promoting settlement. Report of Judicial Conference Committee on the Operation of the Jury System, Agenda G–13, Page 4, September 1984. The Judicial Conference was aware that SJT were not specifically or expressly provided for or authorized by the Federal Rules of Civil Procedure, and language which would have limited the use of SJT "only with the voluntary consent of the parties" was purposely deleted from a previous draft of the report. Therefore, it appears that compelled attendance and participation in summary jury trials is consistent with the Federal Rules of Civil Procedure.

This court believes that, in a case such as this, it is reasonable to require the parties to engage in settlement efforts with some degree of intensity. The parties argue that the investment of attorney time and money would be wasted on the SJT proceeding. However, an investment of three days for the SJT when compared to a potential real jury trial lasting four-to-six courtroom weeks is reasonably proportionate. The court further believes that the SJT procedure, even if it does not lead to settlement, will be of substantial benefit in this case by clarifying issues for trial, both for the parties and the court.

The parties complain also that the SJT procedure would not be a representative synopsis of the actual trial as contemplated by the purpose underlying the procedure due to the pending evidentiary motions before Judge Devitt. This court finds the complaint to be without merit. Because of the nonbinding nature of the SJT procedure, evidentiary rules are more flexible than in an actual jury trial. Furthermore, in order to more adequately reflect the outcome of an actual trial, this court can decide crucial evidentiary issues for the purpose of the SJT proceeding.

The parties have voiced a concern over the potential for premature publicity and public disclosure as a result of the SJT. This concern was alleviated by this court's agreement to close the SJT to the public. The closing of the SJT is within the discretion and power of the court. See Cincinnati Gas & Electric Company v. General Electric, 117 F.R.D. 597 (S.D.Ohio 1987), aff'd 854 F.2d 900 (6th Cir.1988).

For the foregoing reasons, this matter is deemed appropriate for SJT, as a step in consideration of settlement in this case. The court finds it likely that the procedure will be of benefit to both the parties and the court both in the event of settlement or nonsettlement. Having carefully considered the parties' objection to participation in the procedure, it is the court's view that the objection must be overruled. Resort to a totally voluntary system of the use of SJT, where the attorneys are aware of the court's inability to compel their attendance and participation would undercut the potential efficacy of the procedure.

Therefore, based upon the arguments of counsel, and all the files and proceedings herein,

IT IS HEREBY ORDERED that:

1.   The parties' objections to participation in a court-ordered summary jury trial are OVERRULED, and their requests that the order for SJT be vacated are DENIED; and

2.   The attached pre-SJT order shall supplement and modify the earlier order herein, and shall govern the SJT proceedings.

* * *

Questions

1.   The *Strandell* case was decided prior to the 1993 amendments to Rule 16, which expanded the authority of federal district court judges to explore settlement possibilities. Would *Strandell* come out the same way under the new Rule 16?

2.   Does the *Federal Reserve Bank* decision give the courts the discretion to impose high costs on the parties simply to get to trial. Might the requirement of a summary jury trial so raise the costs of trial that some parties would be priced out of the civil justice system altogether? Or are there principles emerging to determine which types of cases are appropriate for a mandatory summary jury trial and which are not?

3.   Does a mandatory summary jury trial pose problems of a change in the judicial role akin to those that were raised in relation to mandatory settlement conferences? Which type of settlement device poses fewer risks to the parties' due process rights at trial?

* * *

9.   PERSPECTIVES ON THE ROLE OF COURT-CONNECTED ADR IN CIVIL LITIGATION

Mark Galanter, in an path-breaking essay, *Why the "Haves" Come Out Ahead: Speculations on the Limits of Legal Change*, 1974 LAW & SOC. REV. 95 (1974), attempts to explain why the civil justice system is rarely effective at achieving redistributive goals. Galanter portrayed the world of civil litigation as involving two types of players, "those claimants who have only occasion recourse to the courts," which he calls one-shotters (OS), and "repeat players (RP) who are engaged in many similar litigations over time." He says examples of OSs are spouses in a divorce case, the auto-injury claimant, and the criminal accused. Examples of RPs are insurance companies, prosecutors, and finance companies. With this admittedly simplified and stylized characterization of the parties, Galanter posits that the two will "play the litigation game differently." Thus he speculates as to some of the systematic advantages of the RPs:[1]

---

   1. Mark Galanter, *Why the "Haves" Come Out Ahead: Speculations on the Limits* of *Legal Change*, 1974 LAW & SOC. REV. 95 (1974). Reprinted with permission.

''(1) RPs, having done it before, have advance intelligence; they are able to structure the next transaction and build a record. It is the RP who writes the form contract, requires the security deposit, and the like.

(2) RPs develop expertise and have ready access to specialists. They enjoy economies of scale and have low startup costs for any case.

(3) RPs have opportunities to develop facilitative informal relations with institutional incumbents.

(4) The RP must establish and maintain credibility as a combatant. His interest in his ''bargaining reputation'' serves as a resource to establish ''commitment'' to his bargaining positions. With no bargaining reputation to maintain, the OS has more difficulty in convincingly committing himself in bargaining.

(5) RPs can play the odds. The larger the matter at issue looms for OS, the more likely he is to adopt a minimax strategy (minimize the probability of maximum loss). Assuming that the stakes are relatively smaller for RPs, they can adopt strategies calculated to maximize gain over a long series of cases, even where this involves the risk of maximum loss in some cases.

(6) RPs can play for rules as well as immediate gains. First, it pays an RP to expend resources in influencing the making of the relevant rules by such methods as lobbying. (And his accumulated expertise enables him to do this persuasively.)

(7) RPs can also play for rules in litigation itself, whereas an OS is unlikely to. That is, there is a difference in what they regard as a favorable outcome. Because his stakes in the immediate outcome are high and because by definition OS is unconcerned with the outcome of similar litigation in the future, OS will have little interest in that element of the outcome which might influence the disposition of the decision-maker next time around. For the RP, on the other hand, anything that will favorably influence the outcomes of future cases is a worthwhile result. The larger the stake for any player and the lower the probability of repeat play, the less likely that he will be concerned with the rules which govern future cases of the same kind. Consider two parents contesting the custody of their only child, the prizefighter vs. the IRS for tax arrears, the convict facing the death penalty. On the other hand, the player with small stakes in the present case and the prospect of a series of similar cases (the IRS, the adoption agency, the prosecutor) may be more interested in the state of the law. * * *

(8) RPs, by virtue of experience and expertise, are more likely to be able to discern which rules are likely to ''penetrate'' and which are likely to remain merely symbolic commitments. RPs may be able to concentrate their resources on rule-changes that are likely to make a tangible difference. they can trade off symbolic defeats for tangible gains.

(9) Since penetration depends in part on the resources of the parties (knowledge, attentiveness, expert services, money), RPs are more likely to be able to invest the matching resources necessary to secure the penetration of rules favorable to them.

"It is not suggested that RPs are to be equated with 'haves' (in terms of power, wealth and status) or OSs with 'have-nots.' In the American setting most RPs are larger, richer and more powerful than are most OSs, so these categories overlap, but there are obvious exceptions. RPs may be 'have-nots' (alcoholic derelicts) or may act as champions of 'have-nots' (as government does from time to time); OSs such as criminal defendants may be wealthy. What this analysis does is to define a position of advantage in the configuration of contending parties and indicate how those with other advantages tend to occupy this position of advantage and to have their other advantages reinforced and augmented thereby. This position of advantage is one of the ways in which a legal system formally neutral as between 'haves' and 'have-nots' may perpetuate and augment the advantages of the former."

Professor Galanter then analyzes the impact of lawyers and legal institutions on the advantages of RPs. He concludes that each of those features of the legal system exacerbates the RP advantage. For example, he claims, RPs have a greater ability to buy more and better quality legal services. "Not only would the RP get more talent to begin with, but he would on the whole get greater continuity, better record-keeping, more anticipatory or preventive work, more experience and specialized skill in pertinent areas, and more control over counsel." Lawyers who serve OS's, on the other hand, "tend to make up the 'lower echelons' of the legal profession." In addition, lawyers who serve OSs are often more beholden to the intermediate institutions who provide them business, institutions such as criminal court assigned counsel offices or other business suppliers, than they are to the client. Galanter concludes that the "haves" have systemic advantages in the civil justice system that "interlock, reinforce and shield one another."

Question

Does the introduction of mandatory alternative dispute resolution mechanisms within the civil justice system alter the systematic advantages of Repeat Players over One-Shotters? Which types of mandatory ADR are best adapted to alter the distributive biases of the civil justice system?

*

Appendix A

The Federal Arbitration Act

9 U.S.C. Title 9, 61 Stat. 669, 9 USC § 1 et. seq.

Sec. 1. "Maritime transactions" and "commerce" defined; exceptions to operation of title

"Maritime transactions", as herein defined, means charter parties, bills of lading of water carriers, agreements relating to wharfage, supplies furnished vessels or repairs to vessels, collisions, or any other matters in foreign commerce which, if the subject of controversy, would be embraced within admiralty jurisdiction; "commerce", as herein defined, means commerce among the several States or with foreign nations, or in any Territory of the United States or in the District of Columbia, or between any such Territory and another, or between any such Territory and any State or foreign nation, or between the District of Columbia and any State or Territory or foreign nation, but nothing herein contained shall apply to contracts of employment of seamen, railroad employees, or any other class of workers engaged in foreign or interstate commerce.

Sec. 2. Validity, irrevocability, and enforcement of agreements to arbitrate

A written provision in any maritime transaction or a contract evidencing a transaction involving commerce to settle by arbitration a controversy thereafter arising out of such contract or transaction, or the refusal to perform the whole or any part thereof, or an agreement in writing to submit to arbitration an existing controversy arising out of such a contract, transaction, or refusal, shall be valid, irrevocable, and enforceable, save upon such grounds as exist at law or in equity for the revocation of any contract.

Sec. 3. Stay of proceedings where issue therein referable to arbitration

If any suit or proceeding be brought in any of the courts of the United States upon any issue referable to arbitration under an agreement in writing for such arbitration, the court in which such suit is pending, upon being satisfied that the issue involved in such suit or proceeding is referable to arbitration under such an agreement, shall on application of one of the parties stay the trial of the action until such arbitration has been had in accordance with the terms of the agreement, providing the applicant for the stay is not in default in proceeding with such arbitration.

Sec. 4. Failure to arbitrate under agreement; petition to United States court having jurisdiction for order to compel arbitration; notice and service thereof; hearing and determination

A party aggrieved by the alleged failure, neglect, or refusal of another to arbitrate under a written agreement for arbitration may petition any United States district court which, save for such agreement, would have jurisdiction under title 28, in a civil action or in admiralty of the subject matter of a suit arising out of the controversy between the parties, for an order directing that such arbitration proceed in the manner provided for in such agreement. Five days' notice in writing of such application shall be served upon the party in default. Service thereof shall be made in the manner provided by the Federal Rules of Civil Procedure. The court shall hear the parties, and upon being satisfied that the making of the agreement for arbitration or the failure to comply therewith is not in issue, the court shall make an order directing the parties to proceed to arbitration in accordance with the terms of the agreement. The hearing and proceedings, under such agreement, shall be within the district in which the petition for an order directing such arbitration is filed. If the making of the arbitration agreement or the failure, neglect, or refusal to perform the same be in issue, the court shall proceed summarily to the trial thereof. If no jury trial be demanded by the party alleged to be in default, or if the matter in dispute is within admiralty jurisdiction, the court shall hear and determine such issue. Where such an issue is raised, the party alleged to be in default may, except in cases of admiralty, on or before the return day of the notice of application, demand a jury trial of such issue, and upon such demand the court shall make an order referring the issue or issues to a jury in the manner provided by the Federal Rules of Civil Procedure, or may specially call a jury for that purpose. If the jury find that no agreement in writing for arbitration was made or that there is no default in proceeding thereunder, the proceeding shall be dismissed. If the jury find that an agreement for arbitration was made in writing and that there is a default in proceeding thereunder, the court shall make an order summarily directing the parties to proceed with the arbitration in accordance with the terms thereof.

Sec. 5. Appointment of arbitrators or umpire

If in the agreement provision be made for a method of naming or appointing an arbitrator or arbitrators or an umpire, such method shall be followed; but if no method be provided therein, or if a method be provided and any party thereto shall fail to avail himself of such method, or if for any other reason there shall be a lapse in the naming of an arbitrator or arbitrators or umpire, or in filling a vacancy, then upon the application of either party to the controversy the court shall designate and appoint an arbitrator or arbitrators or umpire, as the case may require, who shall act under the said agreement with the same force and effect as if he or they had been specifically named therein; and unless otherwise provided in the agreement the arbitration shall be by a single arbitrator.

Sec. 6.   **Application heard as motion**

Any application to the court hereunder shall be made and heard in the manner provided by law for the making and hearing of motions, except as otherwise herein expressly provided.

Sec. 7.   **Witnesses before arbitrators; fees; compelling attendance**

The arbitrators selected either as prescribed in this title or otherwise, or a majority of them, may summon in writing any person to attend before them or any of them as a witness and in a proper case to bring with him or them any book, record, document, or paper which may be deemed material as evidence in the case. The fees for such attendance shall be the same as the fees of witnesses before masters of the United States courts. Said summons shall issue in the name of the arbitrator or arbitrators, or a majority of them, and shall be signed by the arbitrators, or a majority of them, and shall be directed to the said person and shall be served in the same manner as subpoenas to appear and testify before the court; if any person or persons so summoned to testify shall refuse or neglect to obey said summons, upon petition the United States district court for the district in which such arbitrators, or a majority of them, are sitting may compel the attendance of such person or persons before said arbitrator or arbitrators, or punish said person or persons for contempt in the same manner provided by law for securing the attendance of witnesses or their punishment for neglect or refusal to attend in the courts of the United States.

Sec. 8.   **Proceedings begun by libel in admiralty and seizure of vessel or property**

If the basis of jurisdiction be a cause of action otherwise justiciable in admiralty, then, notwithstanding anything herein to the contrary, the party claiming to be aggrieved may begin his proceeding hereunder by libel and seizure of the vessel or other property of the other party according to the usual course of admiralty proceedings, and the court shall then have jurisdiction to direct the parties to proceed with the arbitration and shall retain jurisdiction to enter its decree upon the award.

Sec. 9.   **Award of arbitrators; confirmation; jurisdiction; procedure**

If the parties in their agreement have agreed that a judgment of the court shall be entered upon the award made pursuant to the arbitration, and shall specify the court, then at any time within one year after the award is made any party to the arbitration may apply to the court so specified for an order confirming the award, and thereupon the court must grant such an order unless the award is vacated, modified, or corrected as prescribed in sections 10 and 11 of this title. If no court is specified in the agreement of the parties, then such application may be made to the United States court in and for the district within which such award was made. Notice of the application shall be served upon the adverse party, and thereupon the court shall have jurisdiction of such party as though he had appeared generally in the proceeding. If the adverse party is a resident of the district within which the award was made, such service shall be made upon the adverse party or his attorney as prescribed by law for service of notice of motion in an action in the same court. If the adverse party shall be a nonresident, then the notice of the application shall be served by the marshal of any district within which the adverse party may be found in like manner as other process of the court.

Sec. 10.   Same; vacation; grounds; rehearing

(a) In any of the following cases the United States court in and for the district wherein the award was made may make an order vacating the award upon the application of any party to the arbitration—

(1) Where the award was procured by corruption, fraud, or undue means.

(2) Where there was evident partiality or corruption in the arbitrators, or either of them.

(3) Where the arbitrators were guilty of misconduct in refusing to postpone the hearing, upon sufficient cause shown, or in refusing to hear evidence pertinent and material to the controversy; or of any other misbehavior by which the rights of any party have been prejudiced.

(4) Where the arbitrators exceeded their powers, or so imperfectly executed them that a mutual, final, and definite award upon the subject matter submitted was not made.

(5) Where an award is vacated and the time within which the agreement required the award to be made has not expired the court may, in its discretion, direct a rehearing by the arbitrators.

(b) The United States district court for the district wherein an award was made that was issued pursuant to section 580 of title 5 may make an order vacating the award upon the application of a person, other than a party to the arbitration, who is adversely affected or aggrieved by the award, if the use of arbitration or the award is clearly inconsistent with the factors set forth in section 572 of title 5.

Sec. 11.   Same; modification or correction; grounds; order

In either of the following cases the United States court in and for the district wherein the award was made may make an order modifying or correcting the award upon the application of any party to the arbitration—

(a) Where there was an evident material miscalculation of figures or an evident material mistake in the description of any person, thing, or property referred to in the award.

(b) Where the arbitrators have awarded upon a matter not submitted to them, unless it is a matter not affecting the merits of the decision upon the matter submitted.

(c) Where the award is imperfect in matter of form not affecting the merits of the controversy.

The order may modify and correct the award, so as to effect the intent thereof and promote justice between the parties.

Sec. 12. Notice of motions to vacate or modify; service; stay of proceedings

Notice of a motion to vacate, modify, or correct an award must be served upon the adverse party or his attorney within three months after the award is filed or delivered. If the adverse party is a resident of the district within which the award was made, such service shall be made upon the adverse party or his attorney as prescribed by law for service of notice of motion in an action in the same court. If the adverse party shall be a nonresident then the notice of the application shall be served by the marshal of any district within which the adverse party may be found in like manner as other process of the court. For the purposes of the motion any judge who might make an order to stay the proceedings in an action brought in the same court may make an order, to be served with the notice of motion, staying the proceedings of the adverse party to enforce the award.

Sec. 13. Papers filed with order on motions; judgment; docketing; force and effect; enforcement

The party moving for an order confirming, modifying, or correcting an award shall, at the time such order is filed with the clerk for the entry of judgment thereon, also file the following papers with the clerk:

(a) The agreement; the selection or appointment, if any, of an additional arbitrator or umpire; and each written extension of the time, if any, within which to make the award.

(b) The award.

(c) Each notice, affidavit, or other paper used upon an application to confirm, modify, or correct the award, and a copy of each order of the court upon such an application.

The judgment shall be docketed as if it was rendered in an action. The judgment so entered shall have the same force and effect, in all respects, as, and be subject to all the provisions of law relating to, a judgment in an action; and it may be enforced as if it had been rendered in an action in the court in which it is entered.

Sec. 14. Contracts not affected

This title shall not apply to contracts made prior to January 1, 1926.

Sec. 15. Inapplicability of the Act of State doctrine

Enforcement of arbitral agreements, confirmation of arbitral awards, and execution upon judgments based on orders confirming such awards shall not be refused on the basis of the Act of State doctrine.

Sec. 16. Appeals

(a) An appeal may be taken from—

(1) an order—

(A) refusing a stay of any action under section 3 of this title,

(B) denying a petition under section 4 of this title to order arbitration to proceed,

(C) denying an application under section 206 of this title to compel arbitration,

(D) confirming or denying confirmation of an award or partial award, or

(E) modifying, correcting, or vacating an award;

(2) an interlocutory order granting, continuing, or modifying an injunction against an arbitration that is subject to this title; or

(3) a final decision with respect to an arbitration that is subject to this title.

(b) Except as otherwise provided in section 1292(b) of title 28, an appeal may not be taken from an interlocutory order—

(1) granting a stay of any action under section 3 of this title;

(2) directing arbitration to proceed under section 4 of this title;

(3) compelling arbitration under section 206 of this title; or

(4) refusing to enjoin an arbitration that is subject to this title.

Appendix B

Labor Management Relations Act, § 301(a)

61 Stat. 136 (1947), as amended; 29 U.S.C.A. § 185(a) (1988).

Suits for violation of contracts between an employer and a labor organization representing employees in an industry affecting commerce as defined in this chapter, or between any such labor organizations, may be brought in any district court of the United States having jurisdiction of the parties, without respect to the amount in controversy or without regard to the citizenship of the parties.

Appendix C

American Arbitration Association Commercial Arbitration Rules*

R-1. Agreement of Parties**

The parties shall be deemed to have made these rules a part of their arbitration agreement whenever they have provided for arbitration by the American Arbitration Association (hereinafter AAA) under its Commercial Arbitration Rules or for arbitration by the AAA of a domestic commercial dispute without specifying particular rules. These rules and any amendment of them shall apply in the form in effect at the time the demand for arbitration or submission agreement is received by the AAA. The parties, by written agreement, may vary the procedures set forth in these rules.

R-2. AAA and Delegation of Duties

When parties agree to arbitrate under these rules, or when they provide for arbitration by the AAA and an arbitration is initiated under these rules, they thereby authorize the AAA to administer the arbitration. The authority and duties of the AAA are prescribed in the agreement of the parties and in these rules, and may be carried out through such of the AAA's representatives as it may direct. The AAA may, in its discretion, assign the administration of an arbitration to any of its offices.

R-3. National Panel of Arbitrators

The AAA shall establish and maintain a National Panel of Commercial Arbitrators and shall appoint arbitrators as provided in these rules. The term "arbitrator" in these rules refers to the arbitration panel, whether composed of one or more arbitrators and whether the arbitrators are neutral or party-appointed.

R-4. Initiation under an Arbitration Provision in a Contract

(a) Arbitration under an arbitration provision in a contract shall be initiated in the following manner:

i. The initiating party (the "claimant") shall, within the time period, if any, specified in the contract(s), give to the other party (the "respondent") written notice of its intention to arbitrate (the "demand"), which demand shall contain a statement setting forth the nature of the dispute, the names and addresses of all other parties, the amount involved, if any, the remedy sought, and the hearing locale requested.

* © 1999 American Arbitration Association. Reprinted with permission.

** A dispute arising out of an employment relationship will be administered under the AAA's National Rules for the Resolution of Employment Disputes, unless all parties agree otherwise after the commencement of AAA administration.

920

ii. The claimant shall file at any office of the AAA two copies of the demand and two copies of the arbitration provisions of the contract, together with the appropriate filing fee as provided in the schedule included with these rules.

iii. The AAA shall confirm notice of such filing to the parties.

(b) A respondent may file an answering statement in duplicate with the AAA within 15 days after confirmation of notice of filing of the demand is sent by the AAA. The respondent shall, at the time of any such filing, send a copy of the answering statement to the claimant. If a counterclaim is asserted, it shall contain a statement setting forth the nature of the counterclaim, the amount involved, if any, and the remedy sought. If a counterclaim is made, the party making the counterclaim shall forward to the AAA with the answering statement the appropriate fee provided in the schedule included with these rules.

(c) If no answering statement is filed within the stated time, respondent will be deemed to deny the claim. Failure to file an answering statement shall not operate to delay the arbitration.

(d) When filing any statement pursuant to this section, the parties are encouraged to provide descriptions of their claims in sufficient detail to make the circumstances of the dispute clear to the arbitrator.

R–5. Initiation under a Submission

Parties to any existing dispute may commence an arbitration under these rules by filing at any office of the AAA two copies of a written submission to arbitrate under these rules, signed by the parties. It shall contain a statement of the nature of the dispute, the names and addresses of all parties, any claims and counterclaims, the amount involved, if any, the remedy sought, and the hearing locale requested, together with the appropriate filing fee as provided in the schedule included with these rules. Unless the parties state otherwise in the submission, all claims and counterclaims will be deemed to be denied by the other party.

R–6. Changes of Claim

After filing of a claim, if either party desires to make any new or different claim or counterclaim, it shall be made in writing and filed with the AAA. The party asserting such a claim or counterclaim shall provide a copy to the other party, who shall have 15 days from the date of such transmission within which to file an answering statement with the AAA. After the arbitrator is appointed, however, no new or different claim may be submitted except with the arbitrator's consent.

R–7. Applicable Procedures

Unless the parties or the AAA in its discretion determines otherwise, the Expedited Procedures shall be applied in any case where no disclosed claim or counterclaim exceeds $75,000, exclusive of interest and arbitration costs. Parties may also agree to use the Expedited Procedures in cases involving claims in excess of $75,000. The Expedited Procedures shall be applied as described in Sections E–1 through E–10 of these rules, in addition to any other portion of these rules that is not in conflict with the Expedited Procedures. All other cases shall be administered in accordance with Sections R–1 through R–56 of these rules.

R–8. Jurisdiction

(a) The arbitrator shall have the power to rule on his or her own jurisdiction, including any objections with respect to the existence, scope or validity of the arbitration agreement.

(b) The arbitrator shall have the power to determine the existence or validity of a contract of which an arbitration clause forms a part. Such an arbitration clause shall be treated as an agreement independent of the other terms of the contract. A decision by the arbitrator that the contract is null and void shall not for that reason alone render invalid the arbitration clause.

(c) A party must object to the jurisdiction of the arbitrator or to the arbitrability of a claim or counterclaim no later than the filing of the answering statement to the claim or counterclaim that gives rise to the objection. The arbitrator may rule on such objections as a preliminary matter or as part of the final award.

R–9. Mediation

At any stage of the proceedings, the parties may agree to conduct a mediation conference under the Commercial Mediation Rules in order to facilitate settlement. The mediator shall not be an arbitrator appointed to the case. Where the parties to a pending arbitration agree to mediate under the AAA's rules, no additional administrative fee is required to initiate the mediation.

R–10. Administrative Conference

At the request of any party or upon the AAA's own initiative, the AAA may conduct an administrative conference, in person or by telephone, with the parties and/or their representatives. The conference may address such issues as arbitrator selection, potential mediation of the dispute, potential exchange of information, a timetable for hearings and any other administrative matters. There is no administrative fee for this service.

R–11. Fixing of Locale

The parties may mutually agree on the locale where the arbitration is to be held. If any party requests that the hearing be held in a specific locale and the other party files no objection thereto within 15 days after notice of the request has been sent to it by the AAA, the locale shall be the one requested. If a party objects to the locale requested by the other party, the AAA shall have the power to determine the locale, and its decision shall be final and binding.

R–12. Qualifications of an Arbitrator

(a) Any neutral arbitrator appointed pursuant to Section R–13, R–14, R–15, or E–5, or selected by mutual choice of the parties or their appointees, shall be subject to disqualification for the reasons specified in Section R–19. If the parties specifically so agree in writing, the arbitrator shall not be subject to disqualification for those reasons.

(b) Unless the parties agree otherwise, an arbitrator selected unilaterally by one party is a party-appointed arbitrator and is not subject to disqualification pursuant to Section R–19.

R–13. Appointment from Panel

If the parties have not appointed an arbitrator and have not provided any other method of appointment, the arbitrator shall be appointed in the following manner:

(a) Immediately after the filing of the submission or the answering statement or the expiration of the time within which the answering statement is to be filed, the AAA shall send simultaneously to each party to the dispute an identical list of names of persons chosen from the panel. The parties are encouraged to agree to an arbitrator from the submitted list and to advise the AAA of their agreement.

(b) If the parties are unable to agree upon an arbitrator, each party to the dispute shall have 15 days from the transmittal date in which to strike names objected to, number the remaining names in order of preference, and return the list to the AAA. If a party does not return the list within the time specified, all persons named therein shall be deemed acceptable. From among the persons who have been approved on both lists, and in accordance with the designated order of mutual preference, the AAA shall invite the acceptance of an arbitrator to serve. If the parties fail to agree on any of the persons named, or if acceptable arbitrators are unable to act, or if for any other reason the appointment cannot be made from the submitted lists, the AAA shall have the power to make the appointment from among other members of the panel without the submission of additional lists.

(c) Unless the parties have agreed otherwise no later than 15 days after the commencement of an arbitration, if the notice of arbitration names two or more claimants or two or more respondents, the AAA shall appoint all the arbitrators.

R–14. Direct Appointment by a Party

(a) If the agreement of the parties names an arbitrator or specifies a method of appointing an arbitrator, that designation or method shall be followed. The notice of appointment, with the name and address of the arbitrator, shall be filed with the AAA by the appointing party. Upon the request of any appointing party, the AAA shall submit a list of members of the panel from which the party may, if it so desires, make the appointment.

(b) If the agreement specifies a period of time within which an arbitrator shall be appointed and any party fails to make the appointment within that period, the AAA shall make the appointment.

(c) If no period of time is specified in the agreement, the AAA shall notify the party to make the appointment. If within 15 days after such notice has been sent, an arbitrator has not been appointed by a party, the AAA shall make the appointment.

R–15. Appointment of Neutral Arbitrator by Party–Appointed Arbitrators or Parties

(a) If the parties have selected party-appointed arbitrators, or if such arbitrators have been appointed as provided in Section R–14, and the parties have authorized them to appoint a neutral arbitrator within a specified time and no appointment is made within that time or any agreed extension, the AAA may appoint a neutral arbitrator, who shall act as chairperson.

(b) If no period of time is specified for appointment of the neutral arbitrator and the party-appointed arbitrators or the parties do not make the appointment within 15 days from the date of the appointment of the last party-appointed arbitrator, the AAA may appoint the neutral arbitrator, who shall act as chairperson.

(c) If the parties have agreed that their party-appointed arbitrators shall appoint the neutral arbitrator from the panel, the AAA shall furnish to the party-appointed arbitrators, in the manner provided in Section R–13, a list selected from the panel, and the appointment of the neutral arbitrator shall be made as provided in that section.

R–16. Nationality of Arbitrator

Where the parties are nationals or residents of different countries, the AAA, at the request of any party or on its own initiative, may appoint as a neutral arbitrator a national of a country other than that of any of the parties. The request must be made prior to the time set for the appointment of the arbitrator as agreed by the parties or set by these rules.

R–17. Number of Arbitrators

If the arbitration agreement does not specify the number of arbitrators, the dispute shall be heard and determined by one arbitrator, unless the AAA, in its discretion, directs that three arbitrators be appointed. The parties may request three arbitrators in their demand or answer, which request the AAA will consider in exercising its discretion regarding the number of arbitrators appointed to the dispute.

R–18. Notice to Arbitrator of Appointment

Notice of the appointment of the neutral arbitrator, whether appointed mutually by the parties or by the AAA, shall be sent to the arbitrator by the AAA, together with a copy of these rules, and the signed acceptance of the arbitrator shall be filed with the AAA prior to the opening of the first hearing.

R–19.   Disclosure and Challenge Procedure

(a) Any person appointed as a neutral arbitrator shall disclose to the AAA any circumstance likely to affect impartiality or independence, including any bias or any financial or personal interest in the result of the arbitration or any past or present relationship with the parties or their representatives. Upon receipt of such information from the arbitrator or another source, the AAA shall communicate the information to the parties and, if it deems it appropriate to do so, to the arbitrator and others.

(b) Upon objection of a party to the continued service of a neutral arbitrator, the AAA shall determine whether the arbitrator should be disqualified and shall inform the parties of its decision, which shall be conclusive.

R–20.   Communication with Arbitrator

(a) No party and no one acting on behalf of any party shall communicate unilaterally concerning the arbitration with a neutral arbitrator or a candidate for neutral arbitrator. Unless the parties agree otherwise or the arbitrator so directs, any communication from the parties to a neutral arbitrator shall be sent to the AAA for transmittal to the arbitrator.

(b) The parties or the arbitrators may also agree that once the panel has been constituted, no party and no one acting on behalf of any party shall communicate unilaterally concerning the arbitration with any party-appointed arbitrator.

R–21.   Vacancies

(a) If for any reason an arbitrator is unable to perform the duties of the office, the AAA may, on proof satisfactory to it, declare the office vacant. Vacancies shall be filled in accordance with the applicable provisions of these rules.

(b) In the event of a vacancy in a panel of neutral arbitrators after the hearings have commenced, the remaining arbitrator or arbitrators may continue with the hearing and determination of the controversy, unless the parties agree otherwise.

(c) In the event of the appointment of a substitute arbitrator, the panel of arbitrators shall determine in its sole discretion whether it is necessary to repeat all or part of any prior hearings.

R–22.   Preliminary Hearing

(a) At the request of any party or at the discretion of the arbitrator or the AAA, the arbitrator may schedule as soon as practicable a preliminary hearing with the parties and/or their representatives. The preliminary hearing may be conducted by telephone at the arbitrator's discretion. There is no administrative fee for the first preliminary hearing.

(b) During the preliminary hearing, the parties and the arbitrator should discuss the future conduct of the case, including clarification of the issues and claims, a schedule for the hearings and any other preliminary matters.

R–23.   Exchange of Information

(a) At the request of any party or at the discretion of the arbitrator, consistent with the expedited nature of arbitration, the arbitrator may direct (i) the production of documents and other information, and (ii) the identification of any witnesses to be called.

(b) At least five (5) business days prior to the hearing, the parties shall exchange copies of all exhibits they intend to submit at the hearing.

(c) The arbitrator is authorized to resolve any disputes concerning the exchange of information.

R–24.   Date, Time, and Place of Hearing

The arbitrator shall set the date, time, and place for each hearing. The parties shall respond to requests for hearing dates in a timely manner, be cooperative in scheduling the earliest practicable date, and adhere to the established hearing schedule. The AAA shall send a notice of hearing to the parties at least 10 days in advance of the hearing date, unless otherwise agreed by the parties.

R–25.   Attendance at Hearings

The arbitrator and the AAA shall maintain the privacy of the hearings unless the law provides to the contrary. Any person having a direct interest in the arbitration is entitled to attend hearings. The arbitrator shall otherwise have the power to require the exclusion of any witness, other than a party or other essential person, during the testimony of any other witness. It shall be discretionary with the arbitrator to determine the propriety of the attendance of any other person other than a party and its representatives.

R–26.   Representation

Any party may be represented by counsel or other authorized representative. A party intending to be so represented shall notify the other party and the AAA of the name and address of the representative at least three days prior to the date set for the hearing at which that person is first to appear. When such a representative initiates an arbitration or responds for a party, notice is deemed to have been given.

R–27.   Oaths

Before proceeding with the first hearing, each arbitrator may take an oath of office and, if required by law, shall do so. The arbitrator may require witnesses to testify under oath administered by any duly qualified person and, if it is required by law or requested by any party, shall do so.

R–28. Stenographic Record

Any party desiring a stenographic record shall make arrangements directly with a stenographer and shall notify the other parties of these arrangements at least three days in advance of the hearing. The requesting party or parties shall pay the cost of the record. If the transcript is agreed by the parties, or determined by the arbitrator to be the official record of the proceeding, it must be provided to the arbitrator and made available to the other parties for inspection, at a date, time, and place determined by the arbitrator.

R–29. Interpreters

Any party wishing an interpreter shall make all arrangements directly with the interpreter and shall assume the costs of the service.

R–30. Postponements

The arbitrator may postpone any hearing upon agreement of the parties, upon request of a party for good cause shown, or upon the arbitrator's own initiative. A party or parties causing a postponement of a hearing will be charged a postponement fee, as set forth in the administrative fee schedule.

R–31. Arbitration in the Absence of a Party or Representative

Unless the law provides to the contrary, the arbitration may proceed in the absence of any party or representative who, after due notice, fails to be present or fails to obtain a postponement. An award shall not be made solely on the default of a party. The arbitrator shall require the party who is present to submit such evidence as the arbitrator may require for the making of an award.

R–32. Conduct of Proceedings

(a) The claimant shall present evidence to support its claim. The respondent shall then present evidence to support its defense. Witnesses for each party shall also submit to questions from the arbitrator and the adverse party. The arbitrator has the discretion to vary this procedure, provided that the parties are treated with equality and that each party has the right to be heard and is given a fair opportunity to present its case.

(b) The arbitrator, exercising his or her discretion, shall conduct the proceedings with a view to expediting the resolution of the dispute and may direct the order of proof, bifurcate proceedings and direct the parties to focus their presentations on issues the decision of which could dispose of all or part of the case.

(c) The parties may agree to waive oral hearings in any case.

R–33. Evidence

(a) The parties may offer such evidence as is relevant and material to the dispute and shall produce such evidence as the arbitrator may deem necessary to an understanding and determination of the dispute. Conformity to legal rules of evidence shall not be necessary. All evidence shall be taken in the presence of all of the arbitrators and all of the parties, except where any of the parties is absent, in default or has waived the right to be present.

(b) The arbitrator shall determine the admissibility, relevance, and materiality of the evidence offered and may exclude evidence deemed by the arbitrator to be cumulative or irrelevant.

(c) The arbitrator shall take into account applicable principles of legal privilege, such as those involving the confidentiality of communications between a lawyer and client.

(d) An arbitrator or other person authorized by law to subpoena witnesses or documents may do so upon the request of any party or independently.

R–34. Evidence by Affidavit and Posthearing Filing of Documents or Other Evidence

(a) The arbitrator may receive and consider the evidence of witnesses by declaration or affidavit, but shall give it only such weight as the arbitrator deems it entitled to after consideration of any objection made to its admission.

(b) If the parties agree or the arbitrator directs that documents or other evidence be submitted to the arbitrator after the hearing, the documents or other evidence shall be filed with the AAA for transmission to the arbitrator.

All parties shall be afforded an opportunity to examine and respond to such documents or other evidence.

R–35. Inspection or Investigation

An arbitrator finding it necessary to make an inspection or investigation in connection with the arbitration shall direct the AAA to so advise the parties. The arbitrator shall set the date and time and the AAA shall notify the parties. Any party who so desires may be present at such an inspection or investigation. In the event that one or all parties are not present at the inspection or investigation, the arbitrator shall make an oral or written report to the parties and afford them an opportunity to comment.

R–36. Interim Measures

(a) The arbitrator may take whatever interim measures he or she deems necessary, including injunctive relief and measures for the protection or conservation of property and disposition of perishable goods.

(b) Such interim measures may take the form of an interim award, and the arbitrator may require security for the costs of such measures.

(c) A request for interim measures addressed by a party to a judicial authority shall not be deemed incompatible with the agreement to arbitrate or a waiver of the right to arbitrate.

R–37. Closing of Hearing

The arbitrator shall specifically inquire of all parties whether they have any further proofs to offer or witnesses to be heard. Upon receiving negative replies or if satisfied that the record is complete, the arbitrator shall declare the hearing closed. If briefs are to be filed, the hearing shall be declared closed as of the final date set by the arbitrator for the receipt of briefs. If documents are to be filed as provided in Section R–34 and the date set for their receipt is later than that set for the receipt of briefs, the later date shall be the closing date of the hearing. The time limit within which the arbitrator is required to make the award shall commence, in the absence of other agreements by the parties, upon the closing of the hearing.

R–38. Reopening of Hearing

The hearing may be reopened on the arbitrator's initiative, or upon application of a party, at any time before the award is made. If reopening the hearing would prevent the making of the award within the specific time agreed on by the parties in the contract(s) out of which the controversy has arisen, the matter may not be reopened unless the parties agree on an extension of time. When no specific date is fixed in the contract, the arbitrator may reopen the hearing and shall have 30 days from the closing of the reopened hearing within which to make an award.

R–39. Waiver of Rules

Any party who proceeds with the arbitration after knowledge that any provision or requirement of these rules has not been complied with and who fails to state an objection in writing shall be deemed to have waived the right to object.

R–40. Extensions of Time

The parties may modify any period of time by mutual agreement. The AAA or the arbitrator may for good cause extend any period of time established by these rules, except the time for making the award. The AAA shall notify the parties of any extension.

R–41. Serving of Notice

(a) Any papers, notices, or process necessary or proper for the initiation or continuation of an arbitration under these rules, for any court action in connection therewith, or for the entry of judgment on any award made under these rules may be served on a party by mail addressed to the party, or its representative at the last known address or by personal service, in or outside the state where the arbitration is to be held, provided that reasonable opportunity to be heard with regard to the dispute is or has been granted to the party.

(b) The AAA, the arbitrator and the parties may also use overnight delivery or electronic facsimile transmission (fax), to give the notices required by these rules. Where all parties and the arbitrator agree, notices may be transmitted by electronic mail (E-mail), or other methods of communication.

(c) Unless otherwise instructed by the AAA or by the arbitrator, any documents submitted by any party to the AAA or to the arbitrator shall simultaneously be provided to the other party or parties to the arbitration.

R–42.   Majority Decision

When the panel consists of more than one arbitrator, unless required by law or by the arbitration agreement, a majority of the arbitrators must make all decisions.

R–43.   Time of Award

The award shall be made promptly by the arbitrator and, unless otherwise agreed by the parties or specified by law, no later than 30 days from the date of closing the hearing, or, if oral hearings have been waived, from the date of the AAA's transmittal of the final statements and proofs to the arbitrator.

R–44.   Form of Award

(a) Any award shall be in writing and signed by a majority of the arbitrators. It shall be executed in the manner required by law.

(b) The arbitrator need not render a reasoned award unless the parties request such an award in writing prior to appointment of the arbitrator or unless the arbitrator determines that a reasoned award is appropriate.

R–45.   Scope of Award

(a) The arbitrator may grant any remedy or relief that the arbitrator deems just and equitable and within the scope of the agreement of the parties, including, but not limited to, specific performance of a contract.

(b) In addition to a final award, the arbitrator may make other decisions, including interim, interlocutory, or partial rulings, orders, and awards. In any interim, interlocutory, or partial award, the arbitrator may assess and apportion the fees, expenses, and compensation related to such award as the arbitrator determines is appropriate.

(c) In the final award, the arbitrator shall assess the fees, expenses, and compensation provided in Sections R–51, R–52, and R–53. The arbitrator may apportion such fees, expenses, and compensation among the parties in such amounts as the arbitrator determines is appropriate.

(d) The award of the arbitrator(s) may include: (a) interest at such rate and from such date as the arbitrator(s) may deem appropriate; and (b) an award of attorneys' fees if all parties have requested such an award or it is authorized by law or their arbitration agreement.

R–46.   Award upon Settlement

If the parties settle their dispute during the course of the arbitration and if the parties so request, the arbitrator may set forth the terms of the settlement in a "consent award."

R–47.   Delivery of Award to Parties

Parties shall accept as notice and delivery of the award the placing of the award or a true copy thereof in the mail addressed to the parties or their representatives at the last known addresses, personal or electronic service of the award, or the filing of the award in any other manner that is permitted by law.

R–48.   Modification of Award

Within 20 days after the transmittal of an award, any party, upon notice to the other parties, may request the arbitrator, through the AAA, to correct any clerical, typographical, or computational errors in the award. The arbitrator is not empowered to redetermine the merits of any claim already decided. The other parties shall be given 10 days to respond to the request. The arbitrator shall dispose of the request within 20 days after transmittal by the AAA to the arbitrator of the request and any response thereto.

R–49.   Release of Documents for Judicial Proceedings

The AAA shall, upon the written request of a party, furnish to the party, at the party's expense, certified copies of any papers in the AAA's possession that may be required in judicial proceedings relating to the arbitration.

R–50.   Applications to Court and Exclusion of Liability

(a) No judicial proceeding by a party relating to the subject matter of the arbitration shall be deemed a waiver of the party's right to arbitrate.

(b) Neither the AAA nor any arbitrator in a proceeding under these rules is a necessary party in judicial proceedings relating to the arbitration.

(c) Parties to an arbitration under these rules shall be deemed to have consented that judgment upon the arbitration award may be entered in any federal or state court having jurisdiction thereof.

(d) Neither the AAA nor any arbitrator shall be liable to any party for any act or omission in connection with any arbitration conducted under these rules.

R–51.   Administrative Fees

As a not-for-profit organization, the AAA shall prescribe filing and other administrative fees and service charges to compensate it for the cost of providing administrative services. The fees in effect when the fee or charge is incurred shall be applicable.

The filing fee shall be advanced by the party or parties making a claim or counterclaim, subject to final apportionment by the arbitrator in the award.

The AAA may, in the event of extreme hardship on the part of any party, defer or reduce the administrative fees.

R–52. Expenses

The expenses of witnesses for either side shall be paid by the party producing such witnesses. All other expenses of the arbitration, including required travel and other expenses of the arbitrator, AAA representatives, and any witness and the cost of any proof produced at the direct request of the arbitrator, shall be borne equally by the parties, unless they agree otherwise or unless the arbitrator in the award assesses such expenses or any part thereof against any specified party or parties.

R–53. Neutral Arbitrator's Compensation

(a) Unless the parties agree otherwise, members of the National Panel of Commercial Arbitrators appointed as neutrals on cases administered under the Expedited Procedures with claims not exceeding $10,000, will customarily serve without compensation for the first day of service. There-after, arbitrators shall receive compensation as set forth herein.

(b) Arbitrators shall be compensated at a rate consistent with the arbitrator's stated rate of compensation, beginning with the first day of hearing in all cases with claims exceeding $10,000.

(c) If there is disagreement concerning the terms of compensation, an appropriate rate shall be established with the arbitrator by the AAA and confirmed to the parties.

(d) Any arrangement for the compensation of a neutral arbitrator shall be made through the AAA and not directly between the parties and the arbitrator.

R–54. Deposits

The AAA may require the parties to deposit in advance of any hearings such sums of money as it deems necessary to cover the expense of the arbitration, including the arbitrator's fee, if any, and shall render an accounting to the parties and return any unexpended balance at the conclusion of the case.

R–55. Interpretation and Application of Rules

The arbitrator shall interpret and apply these rules insofar as they relate to the arbitrator's powers and duties. When there is more than one arbitrator and a difference arises among them concerning the meaning or application of these rules, it shall be decided by a majority vote. If that is not possible, either an arbitrator or a party may refer the question to the AAA for final decision. All other rules shall be interpreted and applied by the AAA.

R–56. Suspension for Nonpayment

If arbitrator compensation or administrative charges have not been paid in full, the AAA may so inform the parties in order that one of them may advance the required payment. If such payments are not made, the arbitrator may order the suspension or termination of the proceedings. If no arbitrator has yet been appointed, the AAA may suspend the proceedings.

Expedited Procedures

E–1. Applicability

Unless the parties or the AAA determines otherwise, these procedures shall apply in any case in which no disclosed claim or counterclaim exceeds $75,000, exclusive of interest and arbitration fees and costs. Parties may also agree to use these procedures in larger cases.

Unless the parties agree otherwise, these procedures will not apply in cases in which there is no disclosed monetary claim or in cases involving more than two parties.

E–2. Limitation on Extensions

Except in extraordinary circumstances, the AAA or the arbitrator may grant a party no more than one seven-day extension of time to respond to the demand for arbitration or counterclaim as provided in Section R–4.

E–3. Changes of Claim or Counterclaim

A claim or counterclaim may be increased in amount, or a new or different claim or counterclaim added, upon the agreement of the other party, or the consent of the arbitrator.

After the arbitrator is appointed, however, no new or different claim or counterclaim may be submitted except with the arbitrator's consent.

If an increased claim or counterclaim exceeds $75,000, the case will be administered under the regular procedures unless all parties and the arbitrator agree that the case may continue to be processed under the Expedited Procedures.

E–4. Serving of Notices

In addition to notice provided by Section R–41(b), the parties shall also accept notice by telephone. Telephonic notices by the AAA shall subsequently be confirmed in writing to the parties. Should there be a failure to confirm in writing any such oral notice, the proceeding shall nevertheless be valid if notice has, in fact, been given by telephone.

E–5. Appointment and Qualifications of Arbitrator

(a) The AAA shall simultaneously submit to each party an identical list of five proposed arbitrators drawn from its panel from which one arbitrator shall be appointed.

(b) The parties are encouraged to agree to an arbitrator from this list and to advise the AAA of their agreement. If the parties are unable to agree upon an arbitrator, each party may strike two names from the list and return it to the AAA within seven days from the date of the AAA's mailing to the parties. If for any reason the appointment of an arbitrator cannot be made from the list, the AAA may make the appointment from other members of the panel without the submission of additional lists.

(c) The parties will be given notice by the AAA of the appointment of the arbitrator, who shall be subject to disqualification for the reasons specified in Section R–19. The parties shall notify the AAA within seven days of any objection to the arbitrator appointed. Any such objection shall be for cause and shall be confirmed in writing to the AAA with a copy to the other party or parties.

E–6. Exchange of Exhibits

At least two business days prior to the hearing, the parties shall exchange copies of all exhibits they intend to submit at the hearing. The arbitrator shall resolve disputes concerning the exchange of exhibits.

E–7. Proceedings on Documents

Where no party's claim exceeds $10,000, exclusive of interest and arbitration costs, and other cases in which the parties agree, the dispute shall be resolved by submission of documents, unless any party requests an oral hearing, or the arbitrator determines that an oral hearing is necessary. The arbitrator shall establish a fair and equitable procedure for the submission of documents.

E–8. Date, Time, and Place of Hearing

There shall not be an administrative conference. In cases in which a hearing is to be held, the arbitrator shall set the date, time, and place of the hearing, to be scheduled to take place within 30 days of confirmation of the arbitrator's appointment. The AAA will notify the parties in advance of the hearing date.

E–9. The Hearing

(a) Generally, the hearing shall not exceed one day. Each party shall have equal opportunity to submit its proofs and complete its case. The arbitrator shall determine the order of the hearing, and may require further submission of documents within two days after the hearing. For good cause shown, the arbitrator may schedule additional hearings within seven business days after the initial day of hearings.

(b) Generally, there will be no stenographic record. Any party desiring a stenographic record may arrange for one pursuant to the provisions of Section R–28.

E–10. Time of Award

Unless otherwise agreed by the parties, the award shall be rendered not later than fourteen days from the date of the closing of the hearing or, if oral hearings have been waived, from the date of the AAA's transmittal of the final statements and proofs to the arbitrator.

Appendix D
Model Standards of Conduct For Mediators[1]

Introductory Note

The initiative for these standards came from three professional groups: The American Arbitration Association, the American Bar Association, and the Society of Professionals in Dispute Resolution.

The purpose of this initiative was to develop a set of standards to serve as a general framework for the practice of mediation. The effort is a step in the development of the field and a tool to assist practitioners in it—a beginning, not an end. The model standards are intended to apply to all types of mediation. It is recognized, however, that in some cases the application of these standards may be affected by laws or contractual agreements.

Preface

The model standards of conduct for mediators are intended to perform three major functions: to serve as a guide for the conduct of mediators; to inform the mediating parties; and to promote public confidence in mediation as a process for resolving disputes. The standards draw on existing codes of conduct for mediators and take into account issues and problems that have surfaced in mediation practice. They are offered in the hope that they will serve an educational function and provide assistance to individuals, organizations, and institutions involved in mediation.

I. Self–Determination: A Mediator shall Recognize that Mediation is Based on the Principle of Self–Determination by the Parties.

Self-determination is the fundamental principle of mediation. It requires that the mediation process rely upon the ability of the parties to reach a voluntary, un-coerced agreement. Any party may withdraw from mediation at any time.

COMMENTS:

• The mediator may provide information about the process, raise issues, and help parties explore options. The primary role of the mediator is to facilitate a voluntary resolution of a dispute. Parties shall be given the opportunity to consider all proposed options.

---

1. The Model Standards of Conduct for Mediators were prepared from 1992 through 1994 by a joint committee composed of two delegates from the American Arbitration Association, John D. Feerick, Chair, and David Botwinik, two from the American Bar Association, James Alfini and Nancy Rogers, and two from the Society of Professionals in Dispute Resolution, Susan Dearborn and Lemoine Pierce.

The Model Standards have been approved by the American Arbitration Association, the Litigation Section and the Dispute Resolution Section of the American Bar Association, and the Society of Professionals in Dispute Resolution. The views set out in this publication have not been considered by the American Bar Association House of Delegates and do not constitute the policy of the American Bar Association.

• A mediator cannot personally ensure that each party has made a fully informed choice to reach a particular agreement, but is a good practice for the mediator to make the parties aware of the importance of consulting other professionals, where appropriate, to help them make informed decisions.

II. Impartiality: A Mediator shall Conduct the Mediation in an Impartial Manner.

The concept of mediator impartiality is central to the mediation process. A mediator shall mediate only those matters in which she or he can remain impartial and evenhanded. If at any time the mediator is unable to conduct the process in an impartial manner, the mediator is obligated to withdraw.

COMMENTS:

• A mediator shall avoid conduct that gives the appearance of partiality toward one of the parties. The quality of the mediation process is enhanced when the parties have confidence in the impartiality of the mediator.

• When mediators are appointed by a court or institution, the appointing agency shall make reasonable efforts to ensure that mediators serve impartially.

• A mediator should guard against partiality or prejudice based on the parties' personal characteristics, background or performance at the mediation.

III. Conflicts of Interest: A Mediator shall Disclose all Actual and Potential Conflicts of Interest Reasonably Known to the Mediator. After Disclosure, the Mediator shall Decline to Mediate unless all Parties Choose to Retain the Mediator. The Need to Protect Against Conflicts of Interest also Governs Conduct that Occurs During and After the Mediation.

A conflict of interest is a dealing or relationship that might create an impression of possible bias. The basic approach to questions of conflict of interest is consistent with the concept of self-determination. The mediator has a responsibility to disclose all actual and potential conflicts that are reasonably known to the mediator and could reasonably be seen as raising a question about impartiality. If all parties agree to mediate after being informed of conflicts, the mediator may proceed with the mediation. If, however, the conflict of interest casts serious doubt on the integrity of the process, the mediator shall decline to proceed.

A mediator must avoid the appearance of conflict of interest both during and after the mediation. Without the consent of all parties, a mediator shall not subsequently establish a professional relationship with one of the parties in a related matter, or in an unrelated matter under circumstances which would raise legitimate questions about the integrity of the mediation process.

COMMENTS:

- A mediator shall avoid conflicts of interest in recommending the services of other professionals. A mediator may make reference to professional referral services or associations which maintain rosters of qualified professionals.

- Potential conflicts of interest may arise between administrators of mediation programs and mediators and there may be strong pressures on the mediator to settle a particular case or cases. The mediator's commitment must be to the parties and the process. Pressure from outside of the mediation process should never influence the mediator to coerce parties to settle.

IV. Competence: A Mediator shall Mediate Only When the Mediator has the Necessary Qualifications to Satisfy the Reasonable Expectations of the Parties.

Any person may be selected as a mediator, provided that the parties are satisfied with the mediator's qualifications. Training and experience in mediation, however, are often necessary for effective mediation. A person who offers herself or himself as available to serve as a mediator gives parties and the public the expectation that she or he has the competency to mediate effectively. In court-connected or other forms of mandated mediation, it is essential that mediators assigned to the parties have the requisite training and experience.

COMMENTS:

- Mediators should have information available for the parties regarding their relevant training, education and experience.

- The requirements for appearing on the list of mediators must be made public and available to interested persons.

- When mediators are appointed by a court or institution, the appointing agency shall make reasonable efforts to ensure that each mediator is qualified for the particular mediation.

V. Confidentiality: A Mediator shall Maintain the Reasonable Expectations of the Parties with Regard to Confidentiality.

The reasonable expectations of the parties with regard to confidentiality shall be met by the mediator. The parties' expectations of confidentiality depend on the circumstances of the mediation and any agreements they may make. The mediator shall not disclose any matter that a party expects to be confidential unless given permission by all parties or unless required by law or other public policy.

COMMENTS:

• The parties may make their own rules with respect to confidentiality, or other accepted practice of an individual mediator or institution may dictate a particular set of expectations. Since the parties' expectations regarding confidentiality are important, the mediator should discuss these expectations with the parties.

• If the mediator holds private sessions with a party, the nature of these sessions with regard to confidentiality should be discussed prior to undertaking such sessions.

• In order to protect the integrity of the mediation, a mediator should avoid communicating information about how the parties acted in the mediation process, the merits of the case, or settlement offers. The mediator may report, if required, whether parties appeared at a scheduled mediation.

• Where the parties have agreed that all or a portion of the information disclosed during a mediation is confidential, the parties' agreement should be respected by the mediator.

• Confidentiality should not be construed to limit or prohibit the effective monitoring, research, or evaluation of mediation programs by responsible persons. Under appropriate circumstances, researchers may be permitted to obtain access to the statistical data and, with the permission of the parties, to individual case files, observations of live mediations, and interviews with participants.

VI. Quality of the Process: A Mediator shall Conduct the Mediation Fairly, Diligently, and in a Manner Consistent with the Principle of Self–Determination by the Parties.

A mediator shall work to ensure a quality process and to encourage mutual respect among the parties. A quality process requires a commitment by the mediator to diligence and procedural fairness. There should be adequate opportunity for each party in the mediation to participate in the discussions. The parties decide when and under what conditions they will reach an agreement or terminate a mediation.

COMMENTS:

• A mediator may agree to mediate only when he or she is prepared to commit the attention essential to an effective mediation.

• Mediators should only accept cases when they can satisfy the reasonable expectations of the parties concerning the timing of the process. A mediator should not allow a mediation to be unduly delayed by the parties or their representatives.

• The presence or absence of persons at a mediation depends on the agreement of the parties and the mediator. The parties and mediator may agree that others may be excluded from particular sessions or from the entire mediation process.

• The primary purpose of a mediator is to facilitate the parties' voluntary agreement. This role differs substantially from other professional-client relationships. Mixing the role of a mediator and the role of a professional advising a client is problematic, and mediators must strive to distinguish between the roles. A mediator should, therefore, refrain from providing professional advice. Where appropriate, a mediator should recommend that parties seek outside professional advice, or consider resolving their dispute through arbitration, counseling, neutral evaluation, or other processes. A mediator who undertakes, at the request of the parties, an additional dispute resolution role in the same matter assumes increased responsibilities and obligations that may be governed by the standards of other processes.

• A mediator shall withdraw from a mediation when incapable of serving or when unable to remain impartial.

• A mediator shall withdraw from a mediation or postpone a session if the mediation is being used to further illegal conduct, or if a party is unable to participate due to drug, alcohol, or other physical or mental incapacity.

• Mediators should not permit their behavior in the mediation process to be guided by a desire for a high settlement rate.

VII. Advertising and Solicitation: A Mediator shall be Truthful in Advertising and Solicitation for Mediation

Advertising or any other communication with the public concerning services offered or regarding the education, training, and expertise of the mediator shall be truthful. Mediators shall refrain from promises and guarantees of results.

COMMENTS:

• It is imperative that communication with the public educate and instill confidence in the process.

• In an advertisement or other communication to the public, a mediator may make reference to meeting state, national, or private organization qualifications only if the entity referred to has a procedure for qualifying mediators and the mediator has been duly granted the requisite status.

VIII. Fees: A Mediator shall fully Disclose and Explain the Basis of Compensation, Fees, and Charges to the Parties.

The parties should be provided sufficient information about fees at the outset of a mediation to determine if they wish to retain the services of a mediator. If a mediator charges fees, the fees shall be reasonable, considering among other things, the mediation service, the type and complexity of the matter, the expertise of the mediator, the time required, and the rates customary in the community. The better practice in reaching an understanding about fees is to set down the arrangements in a written agreement.

COMMENTS:

- A mediator who withdraws from a mediation should return any unearned fee to the parties.

- A mediator should not enter into a fee agreement which is contingent upon the result of the mediation or amount of the settlement.

- Co-mediators who share a fee should hold to standards of reasonableness in determining the allocation of fees.

- A mediator should not accept a fee for referral of a matter to another mediator or to any other person.

IX. Obligations to the Mediation Process: Mediators have a Duty to Improve the Practice of Mediation.

COMMENT:

- Mediators are regarded as knowledgeable in the process of mediation. They have an obligation to use their knowledge to help educate the public about mediation; to make mediation accessible to those who would like to use it; to correct abuses; and to improve their professional skills and abilities.

(American Bar Association, 1984).

Appendix E

Standards of Practice for Lawyer Mediators in Family Disputes

Preamble

For the purposes of these standards, family mediation is defined as a process in which a lawyer helps family members resolve their disputes in an informative and consensual manner. This process requires that the mediator be qualified by training, experience, and temperament; that the mediator be impartial; that the participants reach decisions voluntarily; that their decisions be based on sufficient factual data; and that each participant understands the information upon which decisions are reached. While family mediation may be viewed as an alternative means of conflict resolution, it is not a substitute for the benefit of independent legal advice.

I. The Mediator Has a Duty to Define and Describe the Process of Mediation and Its Cost Before the Parties Reach an Agreement to Mediate

Specific Considerations

Before the actual mediation sessions begin, the mediator shall conduct an orientation session to give an overview of the process and to assess the appropriateness of mediation for the participants. Among the topics covered, the mediator shall discuss the following:

A. The mediator shall define the process in context so that the participants understand the differences between mediation and other means of conflict resolution available to them. In defining the process, the mediator shall also distinguish it from therapy or marriage counseling.

B. The mediator shall obtain sufficient information from the participants so they can mutually define the issues to be resolved in mediation.

C. It should be emphasized that the mediator may make suggestions for the participants to consider, such as alternative ways of resolving problems and may draft proposals for the participants' consideration, but that all decisions are to be made voluntarily by the participants themselves, and the mediator's views are to be given no independent weight or credence.

D. The duties and responsibilities that the mediator and the participants accept in the mediation process shall be agreed upon. The mediator shall instruct the participants that either of them or the mediator has the right to suspend or terminate the process at any time.

E. The mediator shall assess the ability and willingness of the participants to mediate. The mediator has a continuing duty to assess his or her own ability and willingness to undertake mediation with the particular

941

participants and the issues to be mediated. The mediator shall not continue and shall terminate the process, if in his or her judgment, one of the parties is not able or willing to participate in good faith.

F. The mediator shall explain the fees for mediation. It is inappropriate for a mediator to charge a contingency fee or to base the fee on the outcome of the mediation process.

G. The mediator shall inform the participants of the need to employ independent legal counsel for advice throughout the mediation process. The mediator shall inform the participants that the mediator cannot represent either or both of them in a marital dissolution or in any legal action.

H. The mediator shall discuss the issue of separate sessions. The mediator shall reach an understanding with the participants as to whether and under what circumstances the mediator may meet alone with either of them or with any third party. *Commentary*: The mediator cannot act as lawyer for either party or for them jointly and should make that clear to both parties.

I. It should be brought to the participants' attention that emotions play a part in the decision-making process. The mediator shall attempt to elicit from each of the participants a confirmation that each understands the connection between one's own emotions and the bargaining process.

II. The Mediator Shall Not Voluntary Disclose Information Obtained Through the Mediation Process Without the Prior Consent of Both Participants

Specific Considerations

A. At the outset of mediation, the parties should agree in writing not to require the mediator to disclose to any third party any statements made in the course of mediation. The mediator shall inform the participants that the mediator will not voluntarily disclose to any third party any of the information obtained through the mediation process, unless such disclosure is required by law, without the prior consent of the participants. The mediator also shall inform the parties of the limitations of confidentiality such as statutory or judicially mandated reporting.

B. If subpoenaed or otherwise noticed to testify, the mediator shall inform the participants immediately so as to afford them an opportunity to quash the process.

C. The mediator shall inform the participants of the mediator's inability to bind third parties to an agreement not to disclose information furnished during the mediation in the absence of any absolute privilege.

III. The Mediator Has a Duty to Be Impartial

Specific Considerations

A. The mediator shall not represent either party during or after the mediation process in any legal matters. In the event the mediator has represented one of the parties beforehand, the mediator shall not undertake the mediation.

B.   The mediator shall disclose to the participants any biases or strong views relating to the issues to be mediated, both in the orientation session, and also before these issues are discussed in mediation.

C.   The mediator must be impartial as between the mediation participants. The mediator's task is to facilitate the ability of the participants to negotiate their own agreement, while raising questions as to the fairness, equity and feasibility of proposed options for settlement.

D.   The mediator has a duty to ensure that the participants consider fully the best interests of the children, that they understand the consequences of any decision they reach concerning the children. The mediator also has a duty to assist parents to examine the separate and individual needs of their children and to consider those needs apart from their own desires for any particular parenting formula. If the mediator believes that any proposed agreement of the parents does not protect the bests interests of the children, the mediator has a duty to inform them of this belief and its basis.

E.   The mediator shall not communicate with either party alone or with any third party to discuss mediation issues without the prior consent of the mediation participants. The mediator shall obtain an agreement from the participants during the orientation session as to whether and under what circumstances the mediator may speak directly and separately with each of their lawyers during the mediation process.

IV.   The Mediator Has a Duty to Assure That the Mediation Participants Make Decisions Based Upon Sufficient Information and Knowledge

Specific Considerations

A.   The mediator shall assure that there is full financial disclosure, evaluation and development of relevant factual information in the mediation process, such as each would reasonably receive in the discovery process, or that the parties have sufficient information to intelligently waive the right to such disclosure.

B.   In addition to requiring this disclosure, evaluation and development of information, the mediator shall promote the equal understanding of such information before any agreement is reached. This consideration may require the mediator to recommend that either or both obtain expert consultation in the event that it appears that additional knowledge or understanding is necessary for balanced negotiations.

C.   The mediator may define the legal issues, but shall not direct the decision of the mediation participants based upon the mediator's interpretation of the law as applied to the facts of the situation. The mediator shall endeavor to assure that the participants have a sufficient understanding of appropriate statutory and case law as well as local judicial tradition, before reaching an agreement by recommending to the participants that they obtain independent legal representation during the process.

V. The Mediator Has a Duty to Suspend or Terminate Mediation Whenever Continuation of the Process Would Harm One or More of the Participants

Specific Considerations

A.   If the mediator believes that the participants are unable or unwilling to meaningfully participate in the process or that reasonable agreement is unlikely the mediator may suspend or terminate mediation and should encourage the parties to seek appropriate professional help. The mediator shall recognize that the decisions are to be made by the parties on the basis of adequate information. The mediator shall not, however, participate in a process that the mediator believes will result in harm to a participant.

B.   The mediator shall assure that each person has had the opportunity to understand fully the implications and ramifications of all options available.

C.   The mediator has a duty to assure a balanced dialogue and must attempt to diffuse any manipulative or intimidating negotiation techniques utilized by either of the participants.

D.   If the mediator has suspended or terminated the process, the mediator should suggest that the participants obtain additional professional services as may be appropriate.

VI. The Mediator Has a Continuing Duty to Advise Each of the Mediation Participants to Obtain Legal Review Prior to Reaching Any Agreement

Specific Considerations

A.   Each of the mediation participants should have independent legal counsel before reaching final agreement. At the beginning of the mediation process, the mediator should inform the participants that each should employ independent legal counsel for advice at the beginning of the process and that the independent legal counsel should be utilized throughout the process and before the participants have reached any accord to which they have made an emotional commitment. In order to promote the integrity of the process, the mediator shall not refer either of the participants to any particular lawyers. When an attorney referral is requested, the parties should be referred to a Bar Association list if available. In the absence of such a list, the mediator may only provide a list of qualified family law attorneys in the community.

B.   The mediator shall inform the participants that the mediator cannot represent either or both of them in a marital dissolution.

C.   The mediator shall obtain an agreement from the husband and the wife that each lawyer, upon request, shall be entitled to review all the factual documentation provided by the participants in the mediation process.

D. Any memo of understanding or proposed agreement which is prepared in the mediation process should be separately reviewed by independent counsel for each participant before it is signed. While a mediator cannot insist that each participant have separate counsel, they should be discouraged from signing any agreement which has not been so reviewed. If the participants, or either of them, choose to proceed without independent counsel, the mediator shall warn them of any risk involved in not being represented, including where appropriate, the possibility that the agreement they submit to a court may be rejected as unreasonable in light of both parties' legal rights or may not be binding on them.

Appendix F

Proposed Standards for Lawyers Who Conduct Divorce and Family Mediation

Prepared by American Bar Association Family Law Section Task Force July, 1997.

Preamble

These model Standards of Conduct for lawyers who serve as divorce and family mediators are intended to perform three major functions: (1) to serve as a guide for the conduct of family mediators; (2) to inform the mediating parties; and (3) to promote public confidence in mediation as a process for resolving disputes.

The Standards draw on existing codes of conduct for mediators and take into account issues and problems that have surfaced in divorce and family mediation practice. They are offered in the hope that they will serve an educational function and provide assistance to individuals, organizations, and institutions involved in divorce and family mediation.

Divorce and family mediation (family mediation or mediation) is a process in which an impartial third party—a mediator—facilitates the resolution of a dispute between family members by promoting their voluntary agreement (or "self-determination"). The family mediator facilitates communications, promotes understanding, focuses the family members on their interests, and seeks creative solutions to problems that enable the family members to reach their own agreements.

Family mediation is not a substitute for the need for family members to obtain independent legal advice or counseling or therapy. Nor is it appropriate for all families. Experience has, however, established that, as a component of a multifaceted dispute resolution system, family mediation is a valuable option for many families because it can: (1) increase the self-determination of family members; (2) promote the best interests of children; and (3) reduce the economic and emotional costs involved in resolution of family disputes.

Experience has also established that lawyers with knowledge of family law and the necessary special training and aptitudes can effectively perform the mediator's role. It is to such lawyers that these Standards are addressed. These Standards can also provide helpful guidance to non-lawyers who are engaged in family mediation, as many of the problems they address are common to all family mediators, regardless of professional background.

Effective mediation requires that the family mediator be qualified by training, experience and temperament; that he or she be impartial; that the participants reach their decisions voluntarily; that their decisions be based on sufficient factual data; that the best interests of children be taken into

946

account and that the mediator be prepared to identify families whose history includes domestic violence or child abuse and take appropriate measures.

Standard I

A family mediator should recognize that mediation is based on the principle of self-determination by the parties.

A. Self-determination is the fundamental principle of family mediation. It requires that the mediation process rely upon the ability of the parties to reach a voluntary, uncoerced agreement.

B. The primary role of a family mediator is to facilitate a voluntary resolution of a dispute. A family mediator should facilitate the development, full disclosure, and evaluation of relevant factual information for parties to explore and negotiate. The mediator can provide information about the process, raise issues, and help parties explore and evaluate options.

C. A family mediator should encourage the parties to seek information and advice from their attorneys during the mediation process and to seek information and advice from other professionals, where appropriate.

D. A party may withdraw from family mediation at any time.

Standard II

A family mediator should be qualified by education, training and temperament to undertake the mediation and satisfy the reasonable expectations of the parties.

A. To effectively perform the role of family mediator, a lawyer should:

1. be knowledgeable about family law;

2. be aware of the psychological impact of divorce and separation on parents and children;

3. have special education and training in the process of mediation;

4. have special education and training in domestic violence and child abuse and neglect.

B. Family mediators should have information available for parties regarding their relevant training, education and expertise.

C. Family mediators should accept cases only when they can satisfy the reasonable expectations of the parties concerning the timing of the process.

D. Individual states should set standards and qualifications for family mediators including procedures for performance-based evaluations and for grievances against mediators. In developing these standards and qualifications, state regulators should consult with appropriate professional groups, including professional associations of family mediators.

E. The requirements for appearing on a list of family mediators appointed or recommended by a court should be made public and available to all interested persons.

F.   When family mediators are appointed by a court or other institution, the appointing agency should make reasonable efforts to insure that each mediator is qualified for the appointment.

Standard III

A family mediator should define and describe the process of mediation and assess the capacity of the parties to mediate before the parties reach an agreement to mediate.

A.   Before family mediation begins a mediator should provide the parties with an overview of the process and its purposes, including:

1.   informing the parties that family mediation is consensual in nature, that a mediator is an impartial facilitator, and that a mediator may not impose or force any settlement on the parties;

2.   distinguishing family mediation from therapy, marriage counseling, the provision of legal advice, or other forms of dispute resolution such as arbitration or litigation;

3.   advising the parties that mediation is one of several alternative processes potentially available to resolve their dispute and describing the advantages and disadvantages of the alternatives to mediation;

4.   informing the parties about the need to employ independent legal counsel throughout the mediation process;

5.   discussing the issue of separate sessions with the parties, including a description of the circumstances in which the mediator may meet alone with either of them or with any third party and the conditions of confidentiality concerning these separate sessions;

6.   informing the parties that the presence or absence of other persons at a mediation depends on the agreement of the parties and the mediator, unless the mediator believes that the presence of another person is required because of a history or threat of violence or other serious coercive activity by a party.

7.   describing the obligations of confidentiality on the mediator and the parties;

8.   advising the parties of the circumstances under which the mediator may terminate the mediation process and that a party has a right to terminate mediation at any time.

B.   The parties should sign a written agreement to mediate their dispute and the terms and conditions thereof within a reasonable time after first consulting the family mediator.

C.   The family mediator should assess the capacity and willingness of the parties to mediate before proceeding with the mediation. A mediator should not agree to conduct the mediation if the mediator believes one or more of the parties is not able to participate or is unwilling to participate in good faith.

Standard IV

A family mediator should disclose all actual and potential conflicts of interest reasonably known to the mediator. After disclosure, the mediator should decline to mediate unless the parties choose to retain the mediator. The need to protect against conflicts of interest also governs the conduct that occurs during and after the mediation.

A. A conflict of interest is a dealing or relationship that might create an impression of possible bias.

B. A family mediator should disclose any biases or strong views relating to the issues to be mediated before the mediation begins.

C. In the event that the family mediator has represented one of the participants before, the mediator should not undertake the mediation.

D. A family mediator should avoid the appearance of conflict of interest both during and after the mediation:

1. the mediator should not represent either party or the parties jointly during or after the mediation process in any matter;

2. the mediator should avoid conflicts of interest in recommending the services of other professionals.

E. Potential conflicts of interest may arise between administrators of mediation programs and mediators and there may be strong pressures on the mediator to settle a particular case or cases. The mediator's commitment must be to the parties and the process. Pressure from outside of the mediation process should never influence the mediator to coerce parties to settle.

Standard V

A family mediator should fully disclose and explain the basis of compensation, fees and charges to the parties.

A. The parties should be provided with sufficient information about fees at the outset of mediation to determine if they wish to retain the services of the mediator.

B. The mediator's fees shall be reasonable, considering among other things the mediation service, the type and complexity of the matter, the expertise of the mediator, the time required, and the rates customary in the community for mediation services and rates charged by the mediator for other professional services that the mediator is qualified to provide.

C. The parties written agreement to mediate their dispute should include a description of their fee arrangement with the mediator.

D. A mediator should not enter into a fee agreement which is contingent upon the results of the mediation or the amount of the settlement.

E. Mediators who share a fee should disclose the nature of their relationship to the participants and hold to standards of reasonableness of effort in determining the allocation of fees.

F.   A mediator should not accept a fee for referral of a matter to another mediator or to any other person.

G.   A mediator who withdraws from a mediation should return any unearned fee to the participants.

Standard VI

A family mediator should conduct the mediation in an impartial manner.

A.   A mediator should avoid conduct that gives the appearance of partiality towards one of the parties.

B.   A mediator should guard against partiality or prejudice based on the parties personal characteristics, background or performance at the mediation.

C.   A mediator should not allow a mediation to be unduly delayed by the parties or their representatives.

Standard VII

A family mediator should insure that the parties make decisions based on sufficient information and knowledge.

A.   The mediator should facilitate adequate disclosure so that the parties can make informed financial and other decisions.

B.   The mediator should facilitate the parties acquisition and development of information about the needs of the children so that the parties can make informed parenting decisions.

C.   The mediator should facilitate the parties understanding of the significance of all information disclosed during the mediation process.

D.   The mediator may recommend to the parties that either or both obtain expert consultations in the event that the mediator believes that additional knowledge or understanding is necessary for balanced negotiations.

E.   The mediator should facilitate the parties understanding of the applicable doctrines and practices of family law before reaching an agreement. The mediator may define the legal issues that may influence the parties resolution of their dispute, but should refrain from giving the parties legal advice based upon the mediator's interpretation of the law as applied to the facts of their situation.

F.   The mediator should recommend to the parties that they obtain independent legal representation before concluding an agreement.

G The mediator should allow counsel for the parties to be present at the mediation sessions. If only one party is represented, the mediator may exclude counsel from participation in the mediation session.

H.   With the agreement of the parties and their counsel, the mediator may elect to draft the agreements and ancillary papers that document the parties resolution of their dispute to be filed with the court. The mediator should recommend to the parties that any binding agreement drafted by the mediator be reviewed by independent counsel for the parties before it is signed and filed with the court.

Standard VIII

A family mediator should maintain the reasonable expectations of the parties with regard to confidentiality.

A.   A mediator should not disclose any matter that a party expects to remain confidential unless given permission by all parties or unless required by law, other public policy or other provision of these Standards.

B.   The mediator should discuss the parties expectations of confidentiality with them prior to undertaking the mediation.

C.   The mediator should inform the parties of the limitations of confidentiality such as statutory, judicially or ethically mandated reporting prior to undertaking the mediation.

D.   The mediator shall disclose a party's threat of violence against another party likely to result in imminent death or substantial bodily harm to the threatened party and the appropriate authorities.

E.   If the mediator holds private sessions with a party, the obligations of confidentiality with regard to those sessions should be discussed and agreed upon prior to their being undertaken.

F.   If subpoenaed or otherwise noticed to testify or to produce documents the mediator should inform the parties immediately to afford any of them an opportunity to quash the process. The mediator should not testify or provide documents in response to a subpoena which the mediator reasonably believes would violate an obligation of confidentiality to the parties without an order of the court.

G.   Confidentiality should not be construed to limit or prohibit the effective monitoring, research, or evaluation of mediation programs by responsible individuals. Under appropriate circumstances, researchers may be permitted to obtain access to statistical data and, with the permission of the parties, to individual case files, observations of live mediations, and interviews with participants.

Standard IX

A family mediator should effectively assist parents in determining how to promote the best interests of their children.

A.   The mediator should emphasize that the parents are, in most instances, in the best position to fashion a parenting arrangement that serves the child's best interests.

B.   The mediator should inform parents about the range of options available for post-divorce or separation parenting arrangements and the costs and benefits thereof.

C.   The mediator should provide parents with information about community resources and programs that can help them and the children cope with the consequences of family reorganization and make appropriate referrals if necessary.

D.   The mediator should inform parents about the problems that continuing conflict creates for children's development and discuss with them what steps might be taken to ameliorate the effects of conflict on the children.

E.   The mediator should help the parents develop a parenting plan which covers the child's physical residence and parental decision-making responsibilities for the child with appropriate levels of detail as agreed to by the parties.

F.   The mediator should advise parents that parenting plans may need to be revised as the developmental needs of the child evolve over time and help the parents develop appropriate dispute resolution mechanisms to facilitate future revisions.

G.   The mediator should be sensitive to the impact of culture and religion on parenting philosophy and other decisions.

H.   The mediator should advise a lawyer for the child or guardian ad litem of their ability to participate in the mediation sessions. The lawyer for the child or guardian ad litem should participate in the mediation sessions at their option and review resulting agreements insofar as they relate to the children.

I.   Except in extraordinary circumstances, the child should not participate in the mediation process without the consent of both parents and the child's guardian ad litem or lawyer.

J.   Prior to including the child in the mediation process, the mediator should consult with the parents and the lawyer or guardian ad litem for the child about whether a child should participate in the mediation process and the form of that participation.

K.   The mediator should inform all concerned about the available options for the child's participation (which may include personal participation, an interview with a mental health professional or mediator reported to the parents or a videotape statement) and discuss the costs and benefits of each with the participants.

Standard X

A family mediator should be trained to recognize a family situation involving child abuse or neglect and should take appropriate steps to shape the mediation process accordingly.

A.   As used in these Standards, child abuse or neglect is defined by applicable state law.

B.   The mediator should be knowledgeable about the symptoms and dynamics of child abuse and neglect and the governing laws and procedures and attend appropriate training programs on the subject. A mediator should not undertake a mediation in which the family situation has been assessed to involve child abuse or neglect without adequate training.

C. If the mediator has reasonable ground to believe that the child is abused or neglected within the meaning of the jurisdiction's child abuse and neglect laws, the mediator shall report the suspected abuse to the appropriate authorities.

1. The mediator should consider making appropriate referrals for the parents and children for therapy and assessment.

2. The mediator should consider suspending the mediation process until the allegations are resolved.

Standard XI

A family mediator should be trained to recognize a family situation involving domestic violence and take appropriate steps to shape the mediation process accordingly.

A. As used in these Standards, domestic violence is defined by applicable state law.

B. A mediator should be knowledgeable about the symptoms and dynamics of domestic violence and other forms of domestic abuse and the governing laws and procedures and attend appropriate training programs on these subjects. A mediator should not undertake a mediation in which the family situation has been assessed to involve domestic violence without adequate training.

C. A mediator should make a reasonable effort to screen for the existence of domestic violence prior to entering into an agreement to mediate with the parties. The mediator should continue to be alert to the possible need for further screening for domestic violence throughout the mediation process.

D. If domestic violence appears to be present the mediator should consider taking the following measures:

1. holding separate sessions with the parties even without the agreement of all parties;

2. strongly encouraging the parties to be represented by counsel throughout the mediation process if they are not already;

3. establishing appropriate security arrangements;

4. allowing a friend, representative or attorney to attend the mediation sessions to support the victim of domestic violence;

5. referring the parties to appropriate community resources;

6. suspension or termination of the mediation sessions, with appropriate steps to protect the safety of victims.

D. The mediator should understand the impact of witnessing violence between parents on children and make appropriate referrals, if necessary, for therapy and assistance to both parents and children.

E. The mediator should ensure that victims of domestic violence consider whether parenting plans resulting from mediation protect the physical safety and psychological well-being of themselves and their children.

Standard XII

A family mediator should withdraw from further participation in the mediation process when the mediator reasonably believes that further participation will not further the parties self-determination.

A. Circumstances under which the mediator should consider withdrawing include, but are not limited to:

1. If a party has committed or is threatening to commit acts constituting domestic violence or child abuse or neglect against the other or the child;

2. if a party is unable to participate further in the mediation due to drug, alcohol, or other physical or mental incapacity;

3. if the parties are about to enter into an agreement that the mediator reasonably believes to be unconscionable;

4. if a party or parties is using the mediation to further illegal conduct;

5. if a party's conduct indicates that the party is not participating in the mediation in good faith.

B. If the mediator does withdraw, the mediator should take all reasonable steps to minimize prejudice to the parties which may result from withdrawal.

Standard XIII

A family mediator should be truthful in the advertisement and solicitation for mediation.

A. Mediators should refrain from promises and guarantees of results.

B. In an advertisement or other communication, a mediator may make reference to meeting state, national, or private organizational qualifications only if the entity referred to has a procedure for qualifying mediators and the mediator has been duly granted the requisite status.

Standard XIV

A family mediator should improve the practice of mediation.

A. Mediators should use their knowledge about mediation to help educate the public about the process.

B. Mediators should help make mediation services widely available to the general public.

C. Mediators should mentor less experienced mediators.

D. Mediators should correct abuses in and generally improve the practice of mediation.

E. Mediators should continuously improve their professional skills and abilities by participating in relevant continuing education programs.

INDEX

References are to pages

ADHESION CONTRACTS
Defenses to arbitration. See Arbitration and Arbitrators, this index

AFFIRMATIVE ACTION
Class action consent decree and claims of non-parties, 220 et seq.

AGE DISCRIMINATION IN EMPLOYMENT ACT (ADEA)
See Employment Disputes, this index

AGREEMENTS TO ARBITRATE
See Arbitration and Arbitrators, this index

AGREEMENTS TO MEDIATE
See Mediation and Mediators, this index

AMERICAN ARBITRATION ASSOCIATION (AAA)
See Arbitration and Arbitrators, this index

ANTITRUST DISPUTES
American Safety doctrine, 403, 419
International disputes, 401 et seq.
Public interest arguments, 415
Treble damages provisions, 416

APPRAISAL
See also Evaluators and Fact–Finders, this index
Arbitration and appraisal hearings distinguished, 619 et seq.

ARBITRATION AND ARBITRATORS
Generally, 303 et seq., 672 et seq.
Adhesion contracts
Generally, 516 et seq.
Bias of arbitrators, 522, 705
Challenges to, 350
Choice of arbitrator, 523
Consent, 542
Constructive fraud, 705
Definition, 535
Due process, 525
Duty to read, 542
Employment contracts, 528 et seq.
Fraud, 705
Hidden arbitration provisions, 543
Illiterate signatories, 539n
Medical malpractice claim, 533 et seq.
Mutuality challenge, 553 et seq.

ARBITRATION AND ARBITRATORS
—Cont'd
Adhesion contracts—Cont'd
Negotiability of provision, 535
Neutrality of arbitrator, 523
Reasonable expectations requirement, 522, 535
Unconscionability, 522
Affidavits, 675n
Agreements to arbitrate
Pre-dispute agreements to arbitrate, infra
Submission agreements, infra
American Arbitration Association, 304
Ancillary disputes, application of arbitration provisions to, 378 et seq.
Appeal. Judicial review, infra
Appointment of arbitrators
Generally, 611 et seq.
New York Arbitration Act, 311
Peremptory challenges, 530
Appraisal vs arbitration hearing, 619 et seq.
Arbitrability, who determines
Generally, 484 et seq.
Clear and unmistakable evidence standard, 502
Invalid contract arguments, 514
Law and fact questions, 484 et seq.
Policy favoring arbitration as factor, 509
Standard of review, 499 et seq.
Void contract arguments, 514
Waiver questions, 512
Assigns, binding effect of arbitration provisions on, 597
Award
Claim preclusion, infra
Clarification
Generally, 735 et seq.
Functus officio doctrine, 771 et seq.
Collateral attack on award, arbitral immunity and, 715 et seq.
Collateral estoppel, 790 et seq.
De facto preclusive effect, 391
Ex parte awards, 607 et seq.
Facial error, 759
Finality, 755
Functus officio doctrine, 771 et seq.
Impeachment of award, 723 et seq.
Modification and functus officio doctrine, 771 et seq.

ARBITRATION AND ARBITRATORS
—Cont'd
Award—Cont'd
  Opinion, inclusion of, 304
  Preclusive effect, 391
  Provisional Remedies, infra
  Punitive damages, infra
  Remedies, infra
  Scope of award, 672 et seq.
  Timely issuance, 721 et seq.
  Vacation of award, infra
Bias
    Generally, 689 et seq.
  Adhesion contract analysis, bias as factor,
    522
  Consumer arbitration, 705 et seq.
  Disclosure obligations, 691
  Disclosure of interest in matter, 689 et
    seq.
  Due process rights, 705 et seq.
  Party association, 689 et seq.
  Per se rule, 693
  Presumption of bias, 532
  Subliminal systemic bias, threat of, 714
Choice of arbitrator, 523
Choice of law
    Generally, 325
  Punitive damages, 780 et seq.
Choice of law clauses and federal preemption,
  351 et seq., 360
Civil liability of arbitrators. Immunity, arbi-
  tral, infra
Claim preclusion
    Generally, 790 et seq.
  Collateral estoppel, 790 et seq.
  Court-annexed arbitration, 843 et seq.
  Failure to appeal, 796 et seq.
  Judicial review and, 796 et seq.
Collateral attack on award, arbitral immunity
  and, 715 et seq.
Collateral estoppel
    Generally, 790 et seq.
  Court-annexed arbitration, 843 et seq.
Commerce, relation of dispute to
    Generally, 325 et seq., 362 et seq.
  Lopez case and, 376
Commercial arbitration generally, 309 et seq.
Confidentiality
    Generally, 687 et seq.
  Discovery of prior arbitration records, 687
    et seq.
  Testimony of arbitrators on judicial re-
    view of award, 723 et seq.
Consumer protection laws
    Generally, 545 et seq.
  Federal preemption, 551
  Notice requirements, 549, 558 et seq.
Continuance to obtain evidence, 676 et seq.
Convention on recognition and enforcement
  of foreign arbitral awards, 401
Court-annexed arbitration
    Generally, 819 et seq.
  Collateral estoppel, 843 et seq.
  Costs, 834

ARBITRATION AND ARBITRATORS
—Cont'd
Court-annexed arbitration—Cont'd
  De novo trial, right to, 834
  Definition, 6
  Due process, 822 et seq.
  Finality, 843 et seq.
  Good faith participation, 834, 835 et seq.
  Interpreter, right to, 840 et seq.
  Res judicata, 843 et seq.
  Standard of review, 847 et seq.
Damages
  Costs, 751
  Punitive damages, 681 et seq., 774 et seq.
  Requests for, 672 et seq.
  Sanctions, 751
  Scope of award, 672 et seq.
  Treble damages, statutory provisions, 416
De facto preclusive effect of award, 391
De novo trial, court-annexed arbitration and,
  834
Default, 603 et seq., 607 et seq.
Defenses to arbitration
    Generally, 482 et seq.
  Adhesion contracts, 516 et seq.
  Arbitrability, who determines, 484 et seq.,
    499 et seq.
  Arbitrability standard, 493 et seq.
  Burden of proof, 483
  Consumer protection laws, 545 et seq.
  Duress, 516 et seq.
  Employment disputes, 570 et seq.
  Fraud, arbitration agreement secured by,
    infra
  Notice requirements, 549, 558 et seq.
  Public interests, 563 et seq.
  Stay motion, raising by, 483
  Unconscionability, 516 et seq.
Definitions, 5 et seq.
Disclosure obligations of arbitrators, 689 et
  seq.
Discovery
    Generally, 651 et seq.
  Confidentiality of arbitration proceedings
    and, 687 et seq.
  FAA requirements, 658
  Nonparties, authority of arbitrator re, 660
    et seq.
  Power to order, 653
  Protective orders, 660 et seq.
  Sanctions, 668 et seq.
  Stay for purposes of, 651 et seq.
  Supervision of, 660
  Third-party production, 660 et seq.
Distinctions among ADR processes generally,
  9 et seq.
Documentary evidence, 675n
Due process
  Bias as impairing rights of, 689 et seq.,
    705 et seq.
  Contractual vs statutory rights disputes,
    602
  Court-annexed arbitration, 822 et seq.
  Employment arbitration, 585

ARBITRATION AND ARBITRATORS
—Cont'd
Due process—Cont'd
Employment discrimination claims, arbitration of, 456
Ex parte awards, 607 et seq.
Ex parte evidence, 675
Full and fair hearing rights, 676 et seq.
Right to counsel, 625 et seq.
Statutory vs contractual rights disputes, 602
Waiver of rights to, 602
Duress, 516 et seq.
Employment disputes
Generally, 570 et seq.
Defenses to arbitration, 570 et seq.
Discrimination claims, 585 et seq.
Discrimination laws, conflicts with FAA
Generally, 443 et seq.
ADEA claims, 443 et seq.
Title VII claims, 455
Due process concerns, 585
Seamen, special treatment of, 571
Unconscionability, 590 et seq.
Voluntariness, 590
Enforceability of agreements to arbitrate
Generally, 378 et seq.
See also Pre-dispute agreements to arbitrate, infra
English arbitration law of 1898, 311
Evaluators and Fact–Finders, this index
Evidence
Generally, 672 et seq.
Affidavits, 675n
Continuance to obtain, 676 et seq.
Documentary evidence, 675n
Ex parte evidence, 675
Expert testimony, 668 et seq.
Generally, 676 et seq.
Qualifications of witness, 681 et seq.
Perjury, 683
Privileges, 680
Relevancy determinations, 676 et seq.
Scope of damages requested, 672 et seq.
Self-incrimination privilege, 680
Testimony of arbitrators on judicial review of award, 723 et seq.
Ex parte communications
Awards, 607 et seq.
Evidence, 675
Ex parte hearings, 603 et seq.
Expert testimony
Generally, 668 et seq., 676 et seq.
Qualifications, 681 et seq.
Federal Arbitration Act
Generally, 312 et seq.
Authority to enact, 315
Burden of proof on defenses to, 483
Commerce, relation of dispute to
Generally, 325 et seq., 362 et seq.
Lopez decision and, 376
Constitutionality, 320, 332
Discovery, 658
Employment discrimination claims

ARBITRATION AND ARBITRATORS
—Cont'd
Federal Arbitration Act—Cont'd
Employment discrimination claims —Cont'd
Generally, 443 et seq.
ADEA claims, 443 et seq.
Title VII claims, 455
Employment disputes, application to, 570 et seq.
Express preemption, 355
Federal preemption, infra
Federal question jurisdiction, 348, 496n
Forum shopping, 347
Fraud, arbitration agreement secured by, 507
Fraud claims, 413, 420 et seq.
Goals of, 385 et seq.
Immunity, arbitral, 720
Intent of Congress, 320, 348
Interstate commerce, employees engaged in, 570 et seq.
Labor agreements, application to, 456n
Maritime disputes, 325 et seq.
Motion to compel, 483
New York Arbitration Act compared, 312
Nonparties, authority of arbitrator re, 663 et seq.
Notice requirements, 558 et seq.
RICO claims, 420 et seq.
Securities Acts, conflicts with
Generally, 378 et seq.
International disputes, 392 et seq.
10(b) claims, 420 et seq.
12(2) claims, 438 et seq.
Waiver of statutory claims, 423, 443
Securities law disputes, application to, 385 et seq.
Standard of review of award, 735 et seq.
State notice requirements, 558 et seq.
Uniformity of law, intent to create, 347
United States Arbitration Act (USAA), 312
Federal preemption
Generally, 325 et seq.
Consumer protection laws, 551
Finality, arbitral, 755
Fraud, arbitration agreement secured by
Generally, 505 et seq.
Factum vs inducement, fraud in, 516
Severability analysis, 505 et seq.
Fraud claims, application of FAA to, 413, 420 et seq.
Full and fair hearing requirement, 619 et seq.
Functus officio doctrine, 771 et seq.
Hearing
Generally, 616 et seq.
Appraisal vs arbitration hearing, 619 et seq.
Default, 607 et seq.
Ex parte awards, 607 et seq.
Ex parte evidence, 675
Ex parte hearings, 603 et seq.
Expert testimony, 668 et seq.

ARBITRATION AND ARBITRATORS
—Cont'd
Hearing—Cont'd
Oral hearings, 619 et seq.
Presence of parties, 619 et seq.
Right to, 616 et seq.
Right to counsel at, 625 et seq.
Submission, 721 et seq.
Immunity, arbitral, 715 et seq.
Impeachment of award, 723 et seq.
Injunctions. Provisional remedies, infra
International disputes
Comity considerations, 418
Convention on recognition and enforcement, 401
FAA application to
Antitrust disputes, 401 et seq.
Securities Acts disputes, 392 et seq.
Interpretation of arbitration provision. Scope of arbitration, infra
Judicial review
See also Vacation of award, infra
Collateral attack on award, arbitral immunity and, 715 et seq.
Facial error, 759
Finality, arbitral, 755
Fraud, 683
Functus officio doctrine, 771 et seq.
Perjury, 683
Record on motion to vacate, 687
Scope of judicial review, 741 et seq.
Standard of review, infra
Testimony of arbitrators, 723 et seq.
Labor arbitration
Generally, 456 et seq.
See also Labor Arbitration, this index
Labor Management Relations Act
Standard of review of award, 727 et seq.
Substantive vs procedural characterization of Acts, 499
Med-arb, 6
Misconduct, 689 et seq.
Modification of award and functus officio doctrine, 771 et seq.
New York Arbitration Act
Generally, 308 et seq.
Federal Arbitration Act compared, 312
Revocability doctrine, challenged, 308 et seq.
Nonparties, authority of arbitrator re, 660 et seq.
Notice
Generally, 549, 558 et seq.
Actual notice, 605
Ex parte awards, 607 et seq.
Ex parte evidence, 675
Formal requirements, 605
Parties to arbitration agreement, 611 et seq.
Preclusive effect of award, 391
Preemption. Federal preemption, supra
Presumption of arbitrability
FAA, 498
Labor arbitration, 481
Provisional remedies

ARBITRATION AND ARBITRATORS
—Cont'd
Provisional remedies—Cont'd
Generally, 627 et seq.
Criteria for, 639
Four factors for preliminary injunction, 638
Injunctions, 627 et seq.
Irreparable harm, 638, 640 et seq.
Jurisdiction to issue injunction, 640 et seq.
Success on merits as factor, 649
Public interests in opposition to arbitration, 563 et seq.
Public law claims, application of arbitration provisions to
Generally, 378 et seq.
Antitrust laws, 415
Employment discrimination laws, 443 et seq.
Punitive damages, 774 et seq.
Punitive damages
Generally, 681 et seq., 774 et seq.
Choice of law, 780 et seq.
Public policy, 774 et seq.
Securities law arbitrations, 780 et seq.
Quasi judicial privilege, 104
Remedies
Generally, 774 et seq.
Bond, 741 et seq.
Damages, supra
Provisional remedies, 627 et seq.
Res judicata, court-annexed arbitration and, 843 et seq.
Revocability doctrine
Challenge to, 308 et seq.
Justifications for, 305
RICO claims, 420 et seq.
Right to counsel, 625 et seq.
Rule 11 sanctions, 751
Rules, AAA, 304
Scope of arbitration
Generally, 378 et seq.
See also Arbitrability, who determines, supra; Defenses to arbitration, supra
Clear and unmistakable evidence standard, 502
Labor arbitration provisions, 469 et seq.
Separation agreement, arbitration provision in, 486 et seq.
Securities Acts, conflicts with FAA
Generally, 378 et seq.
International disputes, 392 et seq.
SEC supervision of arbitration, 425
Waiver of statutory claims, 423, 443
Severability of arbitration clause, 508
Sources of law available to arbitrators, 475
Specific performance, 311
Standard, arbitrability, 493 et seq.
Standard of review
Generally, 727 et seq.
See also Judicial review, supra
Clarification of award, 735 et seq.

ARBITRATION AND ARBITRATORS
—Cont'd
Standard of review—Cont'd
   Court-annexed arbitration, 847 et seq.
   Excess of authority, arbitrators acting in, 749 et seq.
   Facial error, 759
   Federal Arbitration Act, 735 et seq.
   Finality, arbitral, 755
   Functus officio doctrine, 771 et seq.
   Fundamental rationality, 741 et seq.
   Labor Management Relations Act, 727 et seq.
   Law, errors of, 753 et seq.
   Manifest disregard of law, 735 et seq.
   Public policy considerations, 770
   Reasoning in support of award, 735 et seq.
   Scope of judicial review, 741 et seq.
Stay
   Generally, 493 et seq.
   Burden of proof, 483
   Defenses, raising by motion for, 483
   Discovery, stay for purposes of, 651 et seq.
   Federal preemption of state laws re, 351 et seq.
Submission agreements
   FAA and, 412
   Form, 304
   Signing of formal submission, 736
   Waivers, 602
Successors, binding effect of provisions on, 597
Tort claims, application of arbitration provisions to, 378 et seq.
Tort liability of arbitrators. Immunity, arbitral, supra
Transcripts, confidentiality, 687 et seq.
Unconscionability
   Adhesion contracts, 522, 528 et seq.
   Employment contract provisions, 590 et seq.
Uninsured motorist coverage, 484 et seq.
United States Arbitration Act (USAA)
   Generally, 312
   Federal Arbitration Act, supra
Vacation of award
   Generally, 602 et seq., 683
   See also Judicial review, supra
   FAA grounds for, 602
   New York Arbitration Act, 312
Void contract arguments, 514

ASBESTOS LITIGATION
ADR resolution proposal, 256
Class Action Settlement, this index

AWARDS
See Arbitration and Arbitrators, this index

BIAS
See Arbitration and Arbitrators, this index

CHILD CUSTODY AND SUPPORT
See Family Law Disputes, this index

CLAIM PRECLUSION
Arbitration and Arbitrators, this index
Class Action Settlement, this index

CLASS ACTION SETTLEMENT
Generally, 204 et seq.
See also Settlement, this index
Absentee vs representative class members
   Claim preclusion, 220 et seq.
   Conflicting interests, 261
   Fairness determinations, 210
   Inventory plaintiffs, 257
   Partial settlements, 228 et seq.
   Steering committees, 228
Affirmative action decree, 220 et seq.
Asbestos litigation, 255 et seq.
Attorneys, role in
   Collusive settlements, 285 et seq.
   Conflicts of interest, 286
   Fee awards and conflicts of interest, 286
Attorneys, role of
   Client, determination of in class action, 211, 215
   Conditional classes, 228
   Fairness of representation, 210
   Fees award, fairness and, 213
   Tentative classes, 228
Certification for settlement
   Asbestos litigation, 255 et seq.
   Breast implant litigation, 238 et seq.
   Collusion by defendants, 285 et seq.
   Conditional class, 228 et seq.
   Discovery opportunities and fairness requirements, 235
   Discretion of District Courts, 295
   Future plaintiffs, creation of class of, 258, 287
   Inventory settlements, 286
   Justiciability, 295 et seq.
   Limited fund rule certification, 291 et seq.
   Notice requirements, 233
   Objections by class members, 242
   Opt-out rights, 233
   Overlapping class actions, 295 et seq.
   Product liability actions, 238 et seq.
   Provisional certification, 238
   Standing, 295 et seq.
   Support of class members as factor, 241
   Tentative class, 228 et seq.
Claim preclusion
   Generally, 220 et seq.
   Bar orders, 247
   Consent judgment, effect of, 227
   Defendants, collusion by, 285 et seq.
   Future plaintiffs, creation of class of, 258, 287
   Indemnification liability, 247
Collusive settlements, 230
Complex litigation manual, 280 et seq.
Conflicts of interest
   Absentee vs representative class members, 210, 261
   Asbestos cases settlement plan, 289
Court approval. Fairness, infra

CLASS ACTION SETTLEMENT—Cont'd
Employment disputes
    Generally, 206 et seq.
  Claim preclusion and, 220 et seq.
Fairness
    Generally, 206 et seq.
  Appellate review of determination of, 209
  Asbestos litigation, 255 et seq.
  Attorneys' fees award and, 213
  Attorneys' opinions as to, 234
  Damages, distribution of, 215 et seq.
  Discovery opportunities and, 235
  Employment discrimination class, 206 et seq.
  Hearing, 208
  Modification of agreement by court, 219, 245
  Notice requirements, 233
  Objections by class members, 242
  Objectors class, 207
  Partial settlements, 228 et seq.
  Representation, 210
  Scope of judicial inquiry, 208
  Success on merits, determination of possibility of, 209, 214
  Support of class members as factor, 241
  Toxic torts, 215 et seq.
Fee awards and conflicts of interest, 286
Justiciability and certification for settlement, 295 et seq.
Limited fund restrictions, 288
Manual for complex litigation, 280 et seq.
Modification of agreement by court, 219, 245
Notice requirements, 233
Objectors class, 207
Opt-out rights
  Certification for settlement and, 233
  Denial of opt-out rights, 288
  Encompassing opt-out class, creation of, 260
  Limited fund restrictions, 288
  Objectors and, 253
  Second opt-out rights, 244
Partial settlement, 228 et seq.
Reasonableness. Fairness, supra
Standing and certification for settlement, 295 et seq.
Tentative class certification for settlement, 228 et seq.
Toxic torts, 215 et seq.

COLLECTIVE BARGAINING
See Labor Arbitration, this index

CONCILIATION
See Mediation and Mediators, this index

CONFIDENTIALITY
Arbitration and Arbitrators, this index
Mediation and Mediators, this index

CONFLICTS OF INTEREST
Arbitration and Arbitrators, this index
Class Action Settlement, this index
Mediation and Mediators, this index

CONSUMER DISPUTES
Adhesion contracts
    Generally, 533 et seq.
  Consent, 542
  Duty to read, 542
  Illiterate signatories, 539n
State consumer protection laws, arbitration provisions and, 545 et seq.

COURT–ANNEXED ARBITRATION
See Arbitration and Arbitrators, this index

COURT–INDUCED SETTLEMENT
See Settlement, this index

COURT–ORDERED MEDIATION
See Mediation and Mediators, this index

DEFINITIONS
    Generally, 5 et seq., 9 et seq.
Appraisal, 619 et seq.
Arbitration, 5
Conciliation, 6
Court-annexed arbitration, 6
Distinctions among ADR processes generally, 9 et seq.
Evaluative mediation, 33
Facilitative mediation, 33
Fact-finding, 6
Med-arb, 6
Mediation, 33
Mini-trial, 7
Multi-door courthouse, 7
Negotiated investment strategy, 7
Ombudsman, 7, 145
Rent-a-judge, 8

DISCOVERY
Arbitration and Arbitrators, this index
Small claims procedures, 810 et seq.

EMPLOYMENT DISPUTES
    See also Labor Arbitration, this index
ADEA claims, 443 et seq.
Adhesion contracts, arbitration provision as, 528 et seq.
Affirmative action consent decree, 220 et seq.
Arbitration
    Generally, 570 et seq.
  Discrimination claims, 585 et seq.
  Due process concerns, 585
  FAA and, 349 et seq.
  Seamen, special treatment of, 571
  Unconscionability, 590 et seq.
  Voluntariness, 590
Class action settlements
    Generally, 206 et seq.
  Affirmative action decree, 220 et seq.
  Claim preclusion, 220 et seq.
Discrimination claims of employee subject to collective bargaining arbitration, 577 et seq.
Federal Arbitration Act, application to, 570 et seq.
Mediation, 73

EMPLOYMENT DISPUTES—Cont'd
Ombudsmen
 See also Ombudsmen, this index
 Privilege, 165 et seq., 172 et seq.
Sexual harassment claims, 585 et seq.
Title VII claims
 Generally, 455, 585 et seq.
 Union employees, 577 et seq.

ENVIRONMENTAL DISPUTES
Class action settlements
 Generally, 215 et seq.

EVALUATORS AND FACT–FINDERS
 Generally, 144 et seq., 165
 See also Ombudsmen, this index
Agreement to utilize
 Generally, 147 et seq.
 Legal effect of, 152
Arbitration and appraisal hearings distinguished, 619 et seq.
Cross-examination of, 159 et seq.
Decisions, legal status of, 152 et seq.
Definitions, 6
Evaluation and fact-finding distinguished, 165
Hybrid mediation and fact-finding, 145
Labor factfinding boards, 145
Mediator and fact-finder distinguished, 144
Ombudsmen, 145
Reports, legal status of, 152 et seq.
Settlement
 Evaluation and, 176
 Evaluative services, settlement calling for, 147

FACT–FINDERS
See Evaluators and Fact–Finders, this index

FAMILY LAW DISPUTES
Arbitration provisions in property settlement agreements, 563 et seq.
Best interest of child standard, arbitration and, 569
Child custody mediation, 133 et seq.
Confidentiality requirements in mediation, 61 et seq.
Court-ordered mediation, 865 et seq.
Custody disputes, arbitration of, 568
Divorce mediation, 129 et seq.
Evaluators' recommendations, right to challenge, 159 et seq.
Liabilities of mediators, 97 et seq.
Mandatory mediation, 133 et seq.
Mediation, confidentiality requirements, 61 et seq.
Mediation, divorce, 129 et seq.
Mediators
 Recommendations, right to challenge, 159 et seq.
 Unauthorized practice charges against, 112 et seq.
Tort liability of evaluative mediators, 101
Visitation disputes, arbitration of, 568

FEDERAL ARBITRATION ACT (FAA)
See Arbitration and Arbitrators, this index

FEDERAL PREEMPTION
See Arbitration and Arbitrators, this index

FRAUD CLAIMS
Federal Arbitration Act, 413, 420 et seq.

FUNCTUS OFFICIO DOCTRINE
Generally, 771 et seq.

GRIEVANCE ARBITRATION
See Labor Arbitration, this index

INJUNCTIONS
See Arbitration and Arbitrators, this index

INSURANCE DISPUTES
Claims preclusion, 790 et seq.
Court-annexed arbitration, 840 et seq.
Coverage disputes, 484 et seq.
Damages evidence, 676 et seq.
Uninsured motorist coverage, 484 et seq.

INTERNATIONAL DISPUTES
Comity considerations, 418
Convention on recognition and enforcement of foreign arbitral awards,

401
FAA application to, 392 et seq., 401 et seq.

LABOR ARBITRATION
 Generally, 456 et seq.
 See also Arbitration and Arbitrators, this index
Collective bargaining agreements, generally, 474
Discrimination claims, arbitration of, 577 et seq.
Factfinding boards, 145
Federal Arbitration Act, application to, 456n, 570 et seq.
Federal common law of, 456 et seq.
Federal court jurisdiction, 458
Federal preemption
 Labor Management Relations Act, 466
Grievance arbitration
 Generally, 456 et seq.
Judicial review, 727 et seq.
Labor Management Relations Act
 Generally, 456
 State law, applicability of, 466
Norris–LaGuardia Act, 466
No-strike clauses and arbitration provisions
 Generally, 466 et seq.
 Implied no-strike clauses, 469
Presumption of arbitrability, 481
Sources of law available to arbitrators, 475
Standard of review, 727 et seq.
Wagner Act, intent of, 459

LANDLORD–TENANT DISPUTES
Fraud, arbitration provision secured by, 505 et seq.

LIABILITY OF ARBITRATORS
See Arbitration and Arbitrators, this index

LIABILITY OF MEDIATORS
See Mediation and Mediators, this index

MANDATORY ARBITRATION
See Arbitration and Arbitrators, this index

MANDATORY MEDIATION
See Mediation and Mediators, this index

MARRIAGE COUNSELING
Confidentiality, 61

MASS TORTS
See Toxic Torts, this index

MED–ARB
Definition, 6

MEDIATION AND MEDIATORS
Generally, 33 et seq.
Agreements to mediate
Generally, 50 et seq.
Compulsory participation, 57 et seq.
Performance of, 54
Waiver, 55
Attorney acting as mediator
Conflicts of interest, 121 et seq.
Liabilities, 97 et seq.
Professional responsibilities, 112 et seq.
Quasi-judicial privilege, 104
Child custody mediation, 133 et seq.
Civil liability. Liabilities of mediators, infra
Compelled testimony of mediators, 83
Conciliation
Definition, 6
Limitations of, 48
Confidentiality
Generally, 59 et seq.
Agreements, 60
Privileges, evidentiary, 63 et seq.
Protective orders, 87 et seq.
Waiver of mediation privilege, 73
Court-ordered ADR programs generally, 799
Court-ordered mediation
Generally, 34, 855 et seq.
Child custody disputes, 865 et seq.
Good-faith requirements, 855 et seq.
Sanctions, 859 et seq.
Validity, 855 et seq.
Definitions, 5 et seq., 33
Discovery master, mediator acting as, 34
Disqualification of mediator with conflict of interest, 121 et seq.
Divorce mediation, 129 et seq.
Ethical standards in mediation, 20 et seq.
Evaluative mediation, 33
Evidentiary privileges, 63 et seq.
Facilitative mediation
Generally, 33
Definition, 6
Fact-finder and mediator distinguished, 144
Hybrid mediation and fact-finding, 145
Immunity. Liabilities of mediators, infra

MEDIATION AND MEDIATORS—Cont'd
Liabilities of mediators
Generally, 97 et seq.
Conflicts of interest, 119, 121 et seq.
Immunity, 101 et seq.
Judicial functions, 111
Litigation privilege, 101 et seq.
Negligent mediation, 112
Quasi judicial privilege, 101 et seq.
Licensing of mediators, 101
Mandatory mediation
Generally, 34
Court-ordered mediation, supra
Divorce and child custody, 133 et seq.
Med-arb, 6
Mutual gains bargaining, 45
Negligent mediation, 112
Negotiation by mediator, 40
Neutrality
Generally, 41
Attorney mediators, 100
Divorce mediation, 129 et seq.
Ombudsmen compared, 175
Privileges
Generally, 63 et seq.
Litigation privilege, 101 et seq.
Ombudsmen, statements made in presence of, 165
Protective orders, 87 et seq.
Quasi judicial privilege, 104
Professional responsibilities of mediators, 112 et seq.
Protective orders, 87 et seq.
Quasi judicial privilege, 104
Revocation of consent to mediation, 59
Role of the mediator, 20 et seq.
Settlement in
See also Settlement, this index
Confidentiality and enforcement of, 75 et seq.
Mandated and negotiated settlements, 6
Mediation and settlement, 176
Memorialization of, 43
Repudiation of settlement agreement, 73
Testimony of mediators, 83
Tort liability. Liabilities of mediators, supra
Unauthorized practice of law restrictions, 112 et seq.
Witnesses, mediators as, 83

MEDICAL MALPRACTICE CLAIMS
Adhesion contract, arbitration provision as, 533 et seq.
Arbitration procedure, 668 et seq.
Bias of arbitrators, 705 et seq.

MINI–TRIAL
Definition, 7

NEGOTIATION
Dispute Analysis, this index
Mediation and Mediators, this index
Settlement, this index

NEIGHBORHOOD JUSTICE CENTERS (NJC)
Defined, 7

NEW YORK ARBITRATION ACT
See Arbitration and Arbitrators, this index

OMBUDSMEN
Generally, 145
See also Evaluators and Fact–Finders, this index
Confidentiality of communications with, 146
Definition, 7
Independence of, 175
Neutrality of, 175
Privilege, 165 et seq., 172 et seq.

PREEMPTION
See Arbitration and Arbitrators, this index

PRELIMINARY INJUNCTIONS
See Arbitration and Arbitrators, this index

PRETRIAL CONFERENCES
See Settlement, this index

PRIVILEGES
Arbitration and Arbitrators, this index
Mediation privilege, 64
Ombudsmen, 165 et seq., 172 et seq.

PROFESSIONAL RESPONSIBILITIES
See Attorneys at Law, this index

PROVISIONAL REMEDIES
See Arbitration and Arbitrators, this index

QUASI–JUDICIAL IMMUNITY
Arbitrators, 721
Mediators, 104

RACKETEER INFLUENCED AND CORRUPT ORGANIZATIONS ACT (RICO)
Arbitrability of claims based on, 420 et seq.

SECURITIES LAW DISPUTES
Arbitrability, who determines, 499 et seq.
Federal Arbitration Act, application to
Generally, 378 et seq., 385 et seq.
International disputes, 392 et seq.
RICO claims, 420 et seq.
10(b) claims, 420 et seq.
12(2) claims, 438 et seq.
Fraud claims
Generally, 420 et seq.
Waiver of, 423, 443
Punitive damages, 681 et seq., 780 et seq.
Sanctions in arbitration proceedings, 749 et seq.
SEC supervision of arbitration, 425
Self-incrimination privilege, 680
Standard of review of arbitration awards, 749 et seq.
Waiver of fraud claims, 423, 443

SETTLEMENT
Generally, 176 et seq.

SETTLEMENT—Cont'd
See also Mediation and Mediators, this index
Agreements
Consideration for, 196
Doubtful claims, 196
Interpreting, 191 et seq.
Public stake in, 197 et seq.
Validity of settlement, attacking, 195
Voluntariness, tests of, 204
Antitrust settlements, 197 et seq.
Authority to settle, 75 et seq.
Bargaining and mutual gains, 45
Class Action Settlement, this index
Conflicts of interest among multiple parties to, 178
Consent judgments, 199
Court-induced settlement
Generally, 871 et seq.
Good faith obligation, 889
Judges' roles in, 890 et seq.
Law clerks role in, 896 et seq.
Pretrial conference rule, 889
Repeat and one-shot players, 909 et seq.
Court-ordered ADR programs generally, 799
Court-ordered mediation. See Mediation and Mediators, this index
Divorce settlement, legal rules and, 188 et seq.
Evaluators and Fact–Finders, this index
Evidentiary privileges, 63
Government settlements, 197 et seq.
Mediation and settlement, 176
Mediation confidentiality and enforcement of, 75 et seq.
Memorialization of settlement reached during mediation, 43
Mutual gains bargaining, 45
Oral agreement, enforceability of, 75 et seq.
Pretrial conferences
Generally, 889
See also Court-induced settlement, supra
Privileges, evidentiary, 63
Public interest, settlements, affecting
Generally, 197 et seq.
Defining public interest, 204
Public law requirements and, 187
Rejection, actions constituting, 676 et seq.
Stipulated judgments, 199
Summary jury trials, 898 et seq.

SMALL CLAIMS COURTS
Generally, 800 et seq.
Discovery, 810 et seq.
Evidentiary standards, 813 et seq.
History, 801
Mass claims by group, 803 et seq.
Right of appeal, 805

SUBMISSION AGREEMENTS
See Arbitration and Arbitrators, this index

SUMMARY JURY TRIALS
Generally, 898 et seq.

TORT LIABILITY OF ARBITRATORS
See Arbitration and Arbitrators, this index

TORT LIABILITY OF MEDIATORS
See Mediation and Mediators, this index

TOXIC TORTS
Asbestos litigation, 255 et seq.
Class action settlements, 215 et seq.
Complex litigation manual, 282 et seq.
Future plaintiffs, creation of class of
    Generally, 258
     Collusion problems, 287

UNCONSCIONABILITY
Defenses to arbitration. See Arbitration and
    Arbitrators, this index

**UNITED STATES ARBITRATION ACT
  (USAA)**
See Arbitration and Arbitrators, this index

VACATION OF AWARD
See Arbitration and Arbitrators, this index